YOU CAN *Change* YOUR LIFE

To Pat and Vere who changed my career in 1978 and Jonathan whose kindness has changed many lives since.

YOU CAN *Change* YOUR LIFE

Russell Grant

EBURY
PRESS

First published in Great Britain in 2006

1 3 5 7 9 10 8 6 4 2

First published by Ebury Publishing
Random House UK Ltd, Random House, Vauxhall Bridge Road,
London SW1V 2SA

Random House Australia (Pty) Limited
20 Alfred Street, Milsons Point, Sydney, New South Wales 2061, Australia

Random House New Zealand Limited
18 Poland Road, Glenfield, Auckland 10, New Zealand

Random House South Africa (Pty) Limited
Isle of Houghton, Corner Boundary Road & Carse O'Gowrie,
Houghton, 2198, South Africa

Random House UK Limited Reg. No. 954009
www.randomhouse.co.uk

A CIP catalogue record for this book is available from the British Library

Edited by Fantasma Partnership
Copy Edited by Clare Wallis
Designed and typeset by seagulls

ISBN: 0091908485

Papers used by Ebury are natural, recyclable products
made from wood grown in sustainable forests.

Printed and bound in the UK by Clays Lts, St Ives Plc.

Copies are available at special rates for bulk orders. Contact the sales development team on 020 7840 8487 or visit www.booksforpromotions.co.uk for more information.

All the celebrity placings and analyses included in this book
are based on the best and most up-to-date information available.
Please notify me of any inaccuracies and I will amend them in future editions.

Contents

Preface

Do you long to change your life? Are you looking for a greater sense of self-fulfilment and happiness, something to breathe new life into your day-to-day existence? Are you struggling in a relationship perhaps? Or are you unhappy in your job? Do you yearn for a new challenge, a new romance, more money – or simply a brand new you?

The good news is that change is possible, whoever you are. We can all transform our lives by tapping into the potential locked away within each and every one of us. There are limits to what each of us can achieve, of course, but within those limits, we can all change our lives for the better.

The key to real self-fulfilment is self-knowledge. In other words, you can only achieve the goals you set yourself by first knowing and understanding the person you really are. One of the most powerful keys to that understanding, I believe, lies in astrology and the planets that exert a powerful influence over our lives and personalities.

Once you understand the way they affect and mould you, you will be ready to achieve whatever realistic goals you set yourself.

Astrology has been around for 3,000 years and dates back to the ancient civilizations of Mesopotamia, Egypt, India and Greece. The people of Babylon and Athens were convinced that the skies encircling them exercised a huge influence over their lives. It was their mathematicians and astronomers who first divided the 360 degrees of that sky up into 12 distinct sectors, each of 30 degrees, and each containing the fixed constellations of the night sky. It was their wise men who gave them the distinct names and properties we still call the signs of the zodiac, and they who connected each of those signs with the planets – literally 'the wandering stars' that moved around them. These sophisticated civilizations believed in the power of astrology absolutely. To them it was a simple science.

Here in the 21st century, however, astrology no longer holds such a grip over society as a whole. Millions of people do believe in its power, of course, but when they leave the safety of popular horoscopes and enter the realms of 'proper' astrology, too many see it as a confusing and complicated affair, steeped in semi-mysticism and mystery.

Yet to me, at least, astrology seems as simple and straightforward as it must have been to the ancients. The main reason for this is that the forces at the heart of it, the planets, are far from mysterious. As far as I'm concerned, Mars and Jupiter, Venus and Saturn are not remote objects, affecting us as they orbit the Sun in outer space, but a collection of tangible personalities that fill the inner space that is our selves. Think of them, if you like, as a collection of friends or confidantes, on hand at any time to help you deal with a problem, think something through or simply provide the kind of company you need at a particular moment in your life. Seen this way, for instance, Mars is our source of energy and motivation, Jupiter, the joy-bringing optimist within us all. Venus is the part of us that allows us to tap into love and affection, while Saturn is the voice of reason and restraint. Between them they influence everything within our personality, from our energy and romantic feelings to our creativity and self-control. Understand how they work – or don't work – within yourself and you are on your way to self-fulfilment and happiness.

Sounds great, but how do I take advantage of this, you are probably asking yourself? Well, each of us has, if you like, our own personal solar system. The planets are arranged differently within that solar system according to the positions they stood in relation to where and when we were born. And as a result of this, the planets act in very different way to guide and misguide, motivate and inspire us. Only when you know how they are arranged within you will you be able to appreciate what makes you tick; only then will you come to see how and why you face certain problems and frustrations, and how you can overcome them.

By purchasing this book, you are entitled to a 'natal' birth chart, drawn up by me via a specially-designed website. (For details of how this works, turn to page 505.) Your chart or horoscope, literally a map of the sky when you were born, will help you shine a light on the real you. It might be, for instance, that you are failing to tap into the talents that are lying there within you. It might be that you don't even know what these talents are. On the other hand, it might be that you are a square peg trying to fit into a round hole, someone who is doing things that are simply not natural or favourable to your planetary make-up. Or it might be that you aren't aware of negative traits in your personality and aren't controlling them as a result. Whatever it is you are doing wrong, it is preventing you from reaching your potential, and it is acting as a barrier to the grail that is real self-fulfilment and the happiness that comes with it. Your chart will help you overcome that barrier, opening a new chapter in your life. It is a journey of self-discovery, a look inside yourself that will in all probability surprise and inspire you. Hopefully it will change your life as well…

Russell Grant

Introduction

Going For Gold – Understanding And Harnessing Your Potential

In the 40 years or so that I've been involved in teaching and studying astrology, people seem to have become more and more confused about what it actually is. The problem lies, I think, with the incredible growth of the Internet and the modern media, and the mixed messages they have spread. Today, people have access to so many newspaper columns and online websites dedicated to 'predicting the future' that there is a widespread misconception that this is astrology's sole purpose. (It is also based on an oversimplified version of astrology revolving entirely around people's birth or Sun signs, just one of the many, many elements that make up our complex astrological personalities.) But to me this is not what astrology is about.

I believe that astrology is a key, a tool, a passport that unlocks a door to a detailed understanding of who we are, what forces are at work within us and how we can capitalize on them. Essentially, astrology tells us what we as individuals can do and what we are capable of. It shows us our potential. Once we have understood this, we are free to fulfil that potential to the absolute maximum.

Of course, everyone's potential is going to be different. While some people are suited to becoming ballet dancers or athletes, opera singers or brain surgeons, some are more suited to being computer programmers or engineers, soldiers or even astrologers. It is vital you understand this. There is no point in seeing yourself as Picasso when you are more geared to being Michelangelo, no use in seeing yourself as a marathon runner when you are a sprinter. The good news is that by realizing what you cannot do, you are free to devote yourself to achieving the things you *can* do. From being the person who sits in front of the television saying, 'Oh, if only I could do that!' you can transform yourself into the person who does it in reality.

As an example of what I'm talking about here, I'll recount the memory of a conversation I had with the athlete Kelly Holmes in 2001. (Kelly and I had become friends through our charitable work.) She was in Edmonton, Canada, preparing for that year's World Athletics Championships, and was wrestling with the direction she was going in and generally struggling with herself. She wanted to know whether she really had it in her to fulfil her ambitions of becoming an Olympic champion. 'What does my chart say, Russell?' she asked me, ending the sentence with one of her trademark giggles.

One of the things people don't understand about astrology is that the idea of destiny isn't always about a fate that can't be avoided. Free will plays a huge part in it. So the first thing I replied to Kelly was, 'The only way you'll find out is by trying, giving it a go.' But the other thing I told her related to something I saw in her chart.

Kelly was born on 19 April 1970, which means her Sun sign is Aries and her Sun sign's ruler is the planet Mars. (Don't worry if you don't understand what this means yet.) What you need to know about Aries is that those who are born with their Sun in this sign have a strong desire for things, whether it is sex or personal success. People with a strong Mars are also inclined to be successful at sports. The more degrees Mars is in relation to the Sun when they are born, the greater this desire. Kelly was born with her Sun at 28 degrees of Aries in her chart, almost at the end of the 30 degrees that make up each sign. (The 12 zodiac signs divide up a circle of 360 degrees.) This, along with her strong Mars, indicated to me that she had a huge desire, a fanaticism almost, to reach her goals, at any cost. I could see that this was driving her on.

I sensed that Kelly was going to get to her goal, but that this was going to happen at the end of her career. In 2001 the time wasn't quite right, but I told her that if she persisted it would happen. 'Things don't look bad at the moment, but they are going to get a lot, lot better,' I said.

Of course, persistence and resilience could be Kelly Holmes's middle names. She ran well at the World Championships that year, but it was in 2004 that she reached her heights. In Athens, she won two Olympic gold medals, an achievement unequalled by any female athlete in modern athletics history. She is now, of course, Dame Kelly.

Kelly scaled the heights, fulfilling the potential that was in her. But if she had asked me back then whether she could succeed by switching careers to become a singer or a scientist, a painter or a politician, I would have given her a different answer. Her astrological chart did not indicate the potential to succeed in that sphere. Even if she had said she wanted to be a marathon runner, the answer would probably have been the same. In the same way, you must understand what you are and are not capable of achieving before setting off in search of your own goals.

Of course, very few of us will set the bar as high as Kelly did. Olympic champions are a rare breed indeed, but we can all emulate what she did. Kelly analyzed her strengths and weaknesses, she homed in on the areas in which she knew she was more likely to succeed, accepted her limitations, then she got down to the job of achieving her dream.

This book is a step-by-step guide to exploring, understanding and then capitalizing on this inner universe. It will show you how to understand and manage the planetary forces that are at work within Planet You. Whether your goal is getting a better job, finding happiness in your relationship or simply understanding yourself better, this new-found knowledge cannot fail to reap you rewards. By understanding your potential and by dealing in reality, you can fulfil your dreams. You, too, can go for gold.

ONE

DIVINITIES AND *Demons*

The Planets Within Us

The Personal Solar System

When I was seven or eight years old, the highlight of my week was dashing to the shops to pick up my favourite comic book, *The Beezer*. The strip I turned to first every Friday was the adventures of the Numskulls, a group of characters that lived inside a man, controlling his every movement. There were five Numskulls in all. Brainy, naturally enough, controlled the brain, Blinky the eyes, Luggy the ears, Snitch the nose and Cruncher the mouth.

I was fascinated by the way they worked together. If Blinky was reading, he would call down to Brainy, 'I'm reading and I need to know the capital of Paraguay.' Brainy would run along to a giant library that existed somewhere inside the head and look it up. He'd pass on the message to Cruncher, who would get the mouth to say it out loud. 'Asunción.' It was all great fun. In the way the simplest, childhood ideas sometimes do, it embedded itself deep in my imagination.

It was when I was 15 or so that the memory of the Numskulls came back to the forefront of my mind. By then I was becoming increasingly interested in mythology and astrology. At this point in my life I had a passion for storytelling and devoured everything I could lay my hands on. I read the Brothers Grimm and Hans Christian Andersen, the fabulous myths and legends of ancient Greece, and stories of gods and monsters battling for control of the world. These myths loomed large when I began studying the basics of classical astrology, learning about the influence of the planets on our personality.

During this process, I was struck by how certain stereotypes occurred repeatedly. Time and again, whether in the gods and myths of the Egyptians and Phoenicians, the Greeks or Romans, I saw masculine figures like Mars and Zeus, feminine figures like Aphrodite and Isis. I also saw figures that represented all the traditional virtues and vices that we associate with mankind: power and greed, courage and cowardice, beauty and tragedy, sorrow and joy. Then, when I began studying the planets in astrological terms, I saw the different qualities attached to the Sun and the Moon, Venus and Mars and the rest of the solar system echoed these archetypes. They were there in our everyday language: a person with a Saturnine personality tended towards gloominess, while on the other hand a more joyous person affected by Jupiter was referred to as jovial. Similarly, words like mercurial, martial and lunatic referred to the typical qualities of Mercury, Mars and the Moon. It was a slow process, but as I absorbed all these influences, a different approach to astrology began to take root, and it was here that my memory of the Numskulls suddenly returned to me.

Part of the problem with astrology for many people is that it seems too abstract, too ephemeral. The planets are gaseous objects in space. People ask themselves how they can have any relation to our lives. But I saw that these planets were, in fact, different facets of human personality. We all know we have different sides to our personality – the good and the bad, the outgoing and the introverted, the creative and the crafty. The planets were nothing more or less than the distinctive parts that make up the whole of a human being. 'They're no different to the Numskulls,' I suddenly thought to myself.

Silly as it sounds, it was a breakthrough moment. For the first time, I realized that there was another way of looking at astrology. What if, just like Brainy and the rest of the Numskulls, we looked at the planets as personalities, tangible characters that reflect and control different aspects of each of us. As I thought about this, I began to see the planets not as anonymous dots in outer space, but as distinct personalities, alter egos, helping and hindering us and ready to be tapped into at a moment's notice. When I began to look at it in this way, I saw Saturn not as a giant planet with rings around it but as an autocratic teacher, able to instil some much-needed discipline when we need it but also inhibiting and constraining us at times. I saw Mercury not as the planet closest to the Sun, but as a source of mental inspiration and stimulation, an intellectual adventurer always ready to take us under his cerebral wings. In short, I began to see the planets as forming an inner solar system.

In the years that have followed, I have thought about this more and more. I have come to see the planets less as remote objects in outer space, but as powerful influences within the inner space that is our personalities. I have come to see that all of the planets have a role to play in life. Each of them, whether it is the Moon or Pluto, Jupiter or Mars, is there, ready, willing and able to bring out the best aspects of our personality, and help us fulfil our potential. All we have to do is get in touch with whatever gift they have to offer and we can all gain success.

Introducing the Planets

In the past few decades, science has finally, if slightly grudgingly, begun to concede there is some connection between human personality and the position of the planets at birth. Even the most sceptical minds have been amazed to find strong correlations between people's personalities and professions and the positions of planets like Mars, Saturn, the Moon and Jupiter at birth.

Having looked at the detailed birth charts of thousands upon thousands of people around the world, for instance, the French husband and wife team, Michel and Françoise Gauquelin, saw that there was a statistically inexplicable tendency for successful sportsmen and women to be born with Mars rising or culminating in their chart. (The previous example of Kelly Holmes only strengthens the argument, of course.) In the same way, actors tended to have Jupiter in these positions, while scientists and writers had Saturn and the Moon respectively in these positions in the sky.

Their work confirmed what astrologers have known for millennia – that we are all moulded by the solar system and the planets that move around it. Man has been fascinated by the planets since ancient times. Early civilizations noticed that while most of the stars in the night sky remained in the same fixed position, five of them moved around the sky throughout the year, in much the same way as the Moon and the Sun did. They called them 'wandering stars', which, when the Greeks came to study the skies, were translated into planets, after one of their words for 'wanderer'.

The Egyptians and Babylonians were the first civilization known to have studied astrology. They produced detailed almanacs charting the positions of the Moon, the Sun and the planets in relation to each other over years. It was these ancient astrologers who first came up with the idea of the zodiac as well. Each of them divided the 360 degrees of the sky that encircled them. The number of sections varied, but eventually the Greeks settled on the 12 sections that we still use today.

The names of the planets varied according to each civilization. The Babylonians, the first real astrologers, called the planets after their Gods. The Greeks chose guardians to watch over each of the seven 'planets'. It was when the Romans replaced the Greek names with their own equivalents that the modern names were born, however.

The oldest surviving 'horoscope', derived from the Greek *hora* for time and *skopos* for observer, dates from 410 BC and is of a boy born when 'the Moon was below the Horn of the Scorpion, Jupiter in the Fish, Venus in the Bull, Saturn in the Crab, Mars in the Twins…' Since those ancient days, the planets have remained a cornerstone of human civilization. The calendar is based around the planetary movements: it takes Earth 365 days to orbit the Sun. Even the days of the week are named after these heavenly objects: Saturday (after Saturn), Sunday (after the Sun), Monday (the Moon), Tuesday (after the German god Tiw, their equivalent of the god of war Mars), Wednesday (after Woden, the Norse version of Mercury), Thursday is linked to Jupiter (after Thor) and Friday, (Freyja's or Venus's Day).

Yet for all the progress science has made in the past centuries, no-one has come close to explaining why the planets exert such an influence over us. Some have argued that their influence is physical, that they subject us to forces whether they are electromagnetic, gravitational or have a form beyond our understanding. The Moon is, I suppose, the most obvious example of how this works. As we know, the waxing and waning of the Moon influences the oceans of Earth, creating the tides. Given that we humans are 70 per cent water, what kind of influence is it having on us? A respected scientist, Percy Seymour, formerly a principal lecturer in astronomy and astrophysics at Plymouth University and a researcher at the Royal Observatory, Greenwich, has argued quite persuasively that we should keep an open mind on the science behind astrology.

To others, the influence of the planets is subtler and more abstract than that. The Greeks and Romans were more interested in the planets as psychological entities, reflecting the human condition in all its colours. Plato, for instance, thought the heavens above him represented all that existed on Earth on a higher plane. This then reflected on each of us below like an image in a mirror, each one of these images unique to us as individuals. A fascinating thought.

What is in no doubt, however, is that astrology has an amazing power to explain, chart and map the bewildering range of personalities that exist in the human world. Five minutes spent looking at your horoscope (literally a map of the heavens at the moment you were born) can tell you as much about yourself as five years of expensive therapy.

So let's find out more about the astronomy, mythology, astrology and personality of the objects at the centre of this subject, the ten, oh-so-powerful forces in our lives.

The Sun: The Creator

ASTRONOMY: The Sun is the heart and soul of our solar system, a burning ball of gas, one million kilometres wide, with temperatures on its surface averaging 5,500°C. It is so large you could fit over one million Earths inside it.

The Earth, and indeed the entire solar system, depends on the Sun to provide its energy. In order to do this, the Sun consumes four million tons of hydrogen every second, converting it into helium. In 15 minutes our Sun radiates as much energy as mankind consumes in all forms during an entire year. Yet there is no fear of it burning out in the near future. It has enough fuel to continue burning for another five billion years.

For much of his early history, mankind rather presumptuously assumed our Earth was the centre of the universe and the Sun orbited us. (A Greek philosopher Aristarchus was the sole dissenting voice.) It wasn't until the 16th century that Copernicus successfully argued that it was in fact the other way around. And even then his view was only accepted when Newton formulated his laws of motion.

MYTHOLOGY: The Egyptians were the first to worship the Sun god. The pharaoh Akhenaten began the cult of the god, Amon Ra. The Babylonians too had a Sun god, Shamash. The Greek god of the Sun was Helios, who drove the chariot of the Sun across the sky every day. To the Romans, the Sun was the king of the Planets; indeed, they built temples to *Sol Invicta*, 'the Unconquerable Sun'. (It is no surprise that the Sun rules the sign of Leo, whose symbol is the Lion, the king of the animal kingdom.)

Many of the astrological characteristics associated with the Sun have their roots in mythology. Helios's headstrong son Phaethon came to grief when he demanded his father let him ride his chariot across the sky, destroying Earth in the process. In astrology, a negative Sun is associated with arrogance and self-absorption. Similarly, the story of Icarus, who flew too close to the Sun, is symbolic astrologically of having 'too much Sun' in your horoscope.

ASTROLOGY: Just as the Sun dominates the solar system, so it casts a giant shadow over astrology and the astrological planets. This is no surprise, of course; it is, after all, the source of all our light, energy and heat. All the planets revolve around it. Without it, life would cease. In the same way, when it comes to astrology, the Sun represents your heart and soul. The Sun indicates your ego, your individual behaviour, and also points to your potential, your creativity and the way you express yourself. You wouldn't be you without it.

Given all this, it makes sense that your Sun sign, the sign of the zodiac in which the Sun rested when you were born, is hugely important. In general, people with a powerful, positive Sun influence in their chart are very creative and beautiful. On the other hand, the negative side of the Sun is conceited, self-centred and connected to that phrase, 'They think the Sun revolves around them' or 'They think they are the centre of the universe.' This can show itself in narcissism. Finally, someone lacking the power of the Sun in their lives lacks a sense of personal direction and of purpose in life. They are not quite whole.

PERSONALITY/GENDER: As a personality, the Sun is the core of you, the true self, the part of yourself that represents your real purpose in life. He is a masculine planet.

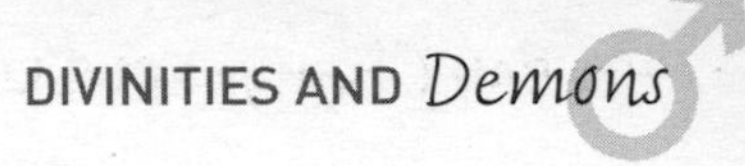

KEY WORDS: Creative, true self, heart and soul, arrogant.

FAMOUS SUN: I always think a very positive Sun sign is Bette Midler. She has this wonderful power to draw you in to what she is doing. Like the Sun itself, you know she could easily drive you mad, but there is something about her that is so fabulous.

The Moon: The Matriarch

ASTRONOMY: The Moon is Earth's only satellite. Current thinking is that it was formed long, long ago when Earth was in collision with a Mars-sized planet.

Only half the Moon is visible from Earth. This is because the time the Moon takes to spin on its axis is exactly the same as the time it takes to orbit the Earth. This is no coincidence. Because the Moon is not completely round and bulges slightly, its gravitational force became unbalanced. This forced the Moon's rotation to slow down, until its bulge was aligned with Earth.

Astronomers have worked out that the force exerted by the Moon on Earth is having a similar effect on Earth's rotation. Gradually the Earth is slowing down. One day, the length of time Earth takes to spin round its axis will be the same as the Moon takes to orbit us. When that happens, we will only be able to see the Moon from one side of Earth. (This, incidentally, has already happened on Pluto, where you can only see its moon, Charon, from one side of the planet.)

The physical influence of the Moon on Earth is well known.

During the month the Moon appears to grow ('wax') and shrink ('wane'). This has been used as the basis for calendars and time measurement since prehistoric times. This is how we get the length of our month – the time that passes from one full Moon to the next.

MYTHOLOGY: Throughout human history, the Moon has had more symbolic significance than any of the planets, including the Sun. Yet its qualities have always been feminine. In Neolithic times she was the great goddess of life and death. She was Selene to the Greeks, Diana, Artemis and sometimes the goddess of the hearth, Vesta, to the Romans.

In terms of astrology, the Moon has always represented the nurturing of life, but she is always associated too with her phases, the 28-day cycle that is mirrored on Earth in the menstrual cycle, and the waxing and waning impact on the tides. Because she shines no light of her own, merely reflecting that of the Sun, the Moon is also associated with feelings and emotions. The phases of the Moon have often been associated with madness, giving rise to the English word 'lunatic'.

ASTROLOGY: While the Sun provides the warmth and light, the Moon doesn't have a light of her own. She merely reflects what the Sun shines onto her; hence the planet was seen as passive and therefore feminine. So the Moon represents sensitivity, moodiness and reflectiveness. A person with a strong Moon influence in their birth chart will have a strong sensitivity to what is happening around them so that they cannot sometimes create emotion and feelings for themselves. They are always reflecting the feelings of others. The Moon governs our emotional responses and behaviour, our desire for domestic and emotional security, our links with the family and the past. It also is a key to our instincts, in particular our maternal instincts.

PERSONALITY/GENDER: For this reason, the Moon's personality is feminine, that of the matriarch, the caring soul who protects. She is the mother, the nurturer, the caring soul within you. Believe me, you have one.

KEY WORDS: Instinctive, emotional, fluctuating, tenacious.

FAMOUS MOON: The surrealist artist Salvador Dali was born with the Moon at the high point in the sky for the day. A wild and unpredictable personality, he said he painted as much with emotions as with the artistic side of his nature. His strange, dream-like paintings have a hint of madness about them.

Mercury: The Teenager

ASTRONOMY: Mercury is the nearest planet to the Sun and the second smallest in the solar system. He experiences the widest range of temperatures of any planet in the system, from -170°C at night to 350°C during the day. He has no moons.

Because it is the closest planet to the Sun and is often masked by the light of its vast neighbour, it is difficult to see Mercury from Earth. Even at night it is hard to see because when the Sun sets, so does Mercury. The best time to spot him is near sunrise or sunset, when it is out of the light, or on the rare occasions that Mercury passes directly between the Sun and the Earth. When this occurs, he can be seen as a small spot on the Sun's surface.

MYTHOLOGY: The Egyptians saw Mercury as Thoth, the transporter of souls, while the Greeks and the Romans saw him as Hermes and Mercury, respectively. (The Greeks also called it Apollo when it appeared in the morning sky.) His position as the 'Messenger of the Gods' means that in astrology, he is always associated with communication, movement and travel, but he is also the symbol of the rational mind.

The fact that Mercury has such a short orbit of the Sun – just 88 days – also lies at the root of its reputation for being unreliable, a 'here today, gone tomorrow' personality, as summed up by the word 'mercurial'.

ASTROLOGY: With his orbit never more than 28 degrees away from that of the Sun, Mercury will always be either in the same sign as the Sun or next to it. How close Mercury is to the Sun within its narrow 28-degree corridor indicates how closely the mind (Mercury) is in tune with the core of a person, as represented by the Sun.

Because one half of him is always bathed in darkness while another is always in light, Mercury is also seen as being 'two-faced'. If planets like Mars, Saturn and Jupiter are very masculine, and the Moon and Venus feminine, then Mercury is a planet that can go either way. He has a foot in both camps, the planet of bisexuality and hermaphrodites.

Due to his speed, Mercury is also associated with communications, short journeys, our mental ability and expression. The essence of Mercury is a mischievous and clever mind. On the positive side, this results in a curious and inquisitive person who is not put off by the search for knowledge. People with a positive Mercury will enjoy anything that involves gaining information, whether it be reading books or, on a more superficial level, being constantly on the mobile phone exchanging bits of gossip.

As we have seen, while there is a side that always faces the Sun, there is also one that is constantly swathed in darkness. So there is a darker side to Mercury as well. It can lead to people cutting themselves off. They will be no less interested in searching for knowledge; it's just that they will strive to do this in different ways, depending on their mood.

PERSONALITY/GENDER: Mercury as a personality is represented by the messenger, the communicator. A masculine planet, he represents the part of ourselves that stimulates and excites us mentally. Mercury can be very Puckish, fun, so Mercury is the live wire, the eternal teenager within you.

KEY WORDS: Communication, the mind, ingenious, fickle.

FAMOUS MERCURY: Michael Jackson was born with Gemini rising, so has Mercury as a ruler. The youthful energy and power to communicate is strong within him, even if it perhaps has a darker side to it.

Venus: The Lover

ASTRONOMY: The second planet from the Sun and Earth's nearest planetary neighbour, Venus experiences the longest days of any planet in the solar system, the equivalent of an amazing 243 Earth days. It is the only planet where the Sun rises in the west and sets in the east. She has no moons. Besides the Sun and the Moon, Venus is the brightest object in the sky. She cannot be seen in the middle of the night but you can try and spot her near the horizon at sunrise or sunset.

Because she is closer to the Sun than the Earth, Venus shows phases, like the Moon. Sometimes these can be seen with the naked eye. However, even through a telescope, Venus reveals few secrets. A thick blanket of cloud surrounds the whole planet.

MYTHOLOGY: One of the most recurring archetypes in mythology is the goddess of love and beauty. To the Babylonians this was Ishtar, the love goddess, but for the Greeks she was Aphrodite.

Her creation is one of the great stories of Greek mythology. When the original ruler of the earth, Uranus, was overthrown by his son, Cronus, he was castrated and his creative seeds scattered through heaven and earth. Some fell into the seas, from where the goddess Aphrodite rose up, carried by waves and riding a giant seashell. Aphrodite meant 'borne by the sea foam'. (She is, of course, the subject of Botticelli's great painting *The Birth of Venus.*) Venus, as she was renamed by the Romans, remained one of the most popular European goddesses, even into the Middle Ages, and has always represented the most powerful human need for love, sex and relationships.

ASTROLOGY: Venus is the planet of love and relationships. But unlike her neighbour Mars, which represents desire, Venus is passive and represents the need to attract and be loved or appreciated. This can apply not just to romance but to business too. Venus is about two people coming together in a financial partnership that enhances or enriches one's individual need to be loved or appreciated.

On a positive front, people with a strong Venus influence are kind, gentle, compassionate, generous, beautiful people to know-all the things one would wish to be. However, because she is the goddess of the things one wants to have lots of, negative Venus can be indulgent, hedonistic, vain and decadent. The 'heavy duty' Venus is also the harlot, whore or prostitute who makes money out of sex or out of exploiting her looks.

Venus rules in two signs, Libra (the marriage sign, naturally) and Taurus, resulting in two distinct sides to her. In Taurus she represents self-worth, the idea of loving oneself. In Libra she is more concerned with being loved by others.

PERSONALITY/GENDER: Venus is the lover, that side of your personality that you turn to for love and affection. She is very much a feminine planet.

KEY WORDS: Love, unity, harmony, vanity.

FAMOUS VENUS: Elizabeth Taylor and Catherine Zeta Jones represent the ultimate, exquisite beauty of Venus, women who demand adoration both on and off the screen – and get it.

♂

Mars: The Dynamo

ASTRONOMY: The fourth planet from the Sun, just past Earth, Mars is known as the Red Planet because of his vivid colour. Mars can often be spotted from Earth and his red colouring, though more pronounced when seen through a telescope, is even noticeable with the naked eye. Usually he travels across the sky from east to west. However, for 70 days of his two-year orbit, he reverses direction across the sky. This is the best time to observe Mars because he's at the closest point to Earth. Mars is closer in temperature to Earth than any of the other planets in the solar system, hence our long fascination with the idea of perhaps one day colonizing him.

MYTHOLOGY: The Greek god of war was Ares, one of the few legitimate children the promiscuous king of the Greek gods, Zeus, had with his wife Hera. Like the red planet itself, Ares was a violent and bloodstained character. The Romans renamed him Mars. Throughout history he has come to characterize not just force in a violent sense, but in a dynamic and motivational sense as well. Early on in the Roman Empire, Mars was worshipped as a god of growth and fertility. In medieval times Mars was a portent of terrible things to come, a precursor to war, famine and plague. The two moons of Mars are named after the two sons of Ares, Phobos and Deimos.

ASTROLOGY: Mars represents the absolute opposite of Venus. While Venus represents beauty and serenity, Mars is dynamism and aggression. And while Venus represents the need to attract and be loved, Mars represents pure, naked desire. Your sexual drives and desires will be defined by the position of Mars within your chart.

Positive Mars is irresistible. He represents desire and animal magnetism. If he were personified he would be an Indiana Jones-type character. As Mars is also the planet of control, he needs to be in charge of events, having the reins of power in his hands. And because power is nothing without control, so the negative aspect of Mars can reflect itself in dominance, bossiness and even cruelty. For this reason, Mars should be used in a way that channels his energy in a good way, towards a positive goal or ambition.

PERSONALITY/GENDER: The Mars part of your personality is the dynamo, the assertive go-getter who energizes and motivates you. This may be an aspect of your personality that needs to be nurtured and encouraged to show itself. In some people, however, it will need to be kept under control. Given these properties, it is no surprise that he is a masculine planet.

KEY WORDS: Energy, driving force, initiative, aggression.

FAMOUS MARS: When Pablo Picasso was born in Malaga, Spain, at 11.15 p.m. on 25 October 1881, Mars had just crossed the eastern horizon. Throughout his life Picasso personified Mars's relentless drive and dynamism, continuing to paint and live life to the full well into his nineties.

♃

Jupiter: The Optimist

ASTRONOMY: The fifth planet from the Sun and the biggest in the solar system, Jupiter is larger than all the other eight planets put together. Given its vast size, it is not surprising that Jupiter is one of the easiest planets to spot from the Earth. Other than the Moon, it is the brightest object you can see in the middle of the night and though Venus is brighter, Jupiter is further from the Sun, so it's visible long after the Sun and Venus have set. In all, Jupiter has at least 39 moons; four of which – Io, Europa, Ganymede and Callisto – are easily visible with binoculars. It was Galileo's discovery of these moons in 1610 that provided the first, hard scientific evidence that not all heavenly bodies revolved around the Earth.

Jupiter is one of the four 'gas giant' planets. Unlike rocky worlds such as Earth, Jupiter is composed almost entirely of gas. Inside this swirling ball of gas lies a small core of solid rock. The bright colours in Jupiter's clouds are caused by complex interactions of gases such as hydrogen, helium, carbon dioxide, water and methane, mixed with clouds of ammonia ice.

Jupiter's most prominent feature, the Great Red Spot, a thunderstorm that has raged for more than 300 years, is visible even from Earth. Jupiter has a gigantic magnetic field, which explains its multitude of moons. Many of the smaller ones are asteroids that have been drawn in by Jupiter's immense gravity.

MYTHOLOGY: To the Babylonians Jupiter represented the king of the gods, Marduk, a fortunate coincidence since they couldn't possibly have known that Jupiter was the largest planet in the solar system. The Greeks, too, named it after the king of the gods, Zeus, ruler of Olympus.

To the Greeks, Zeus was a father figure, someone who cared for and protected the people. So if the Sun is the 'king' of the planets in terms of its central importance, Jupiter is the king in the sense of abundance and generosity, greatness and majesty. The legend of Zeus illustrates how too much abundance can be damaging, however. Zeus had frequent affairs, including one with Leto that produced the twins Apollo and Artemis, much to the anger of his wife Hera.

Of all the gifts Zeus could bestow, the most important was joy. The belief that people born under the influence of Jupiter were inclined to be more joyous, fun-loving people gave birth to the word 'jovial'.

ASTROLOGY: As you would expect of the largest planet in the known solar system, everything about Jupiter in the archetypal sense is big. A person with a strong Jupiter likes to do things in a big way. Whether it is food, sex, entertaining, they do so on a grand scale. Jupiter, like the benevolent Zeus, is the avuncular figure guiding everybody. In contrast to Saturn who makes you work for everything, Jupiter is also a gift-bringer, with happiness and laughter his primary blessing. (It is no surprise that everyone's favourite suite in Holst's *Planets* suite is Jupiter, the joy-bringer.) As a planet he is lovable, representative of a generosity of spirit, so where you find Jupiter in your chart is where you are at your happiest, where you find your laughter and pleasure.

You want Jupiter not just in yourself but in the people around you, because they uplift you and make you laugh. They are also eternal optimists. If this becomes a negative, however, it can become blind optimism. And again, because of the grandiose nature of Jupiter, this then leads to the great expectations that come with biting off more than you can chew. Similarly, people with a strong Jupiter have to guard against overabundance and excessiveness.

PERSONALITY/GENDER: Another masculine planet, Jupiter is the optimist within you, the part of your personality that lifts you out of the doldrums and lightens your life, sprinkling joy as it does so.

KEY WORDS: Mental and physical expansion, travel, big money.

FAMOUS JUPITER: Elvis Presley was born on 8 January 1935 at 4.35 a.m. in Tupelo, Mississippi, with Jupiter as his ruling and rising planet. Few artists of the 20th century represented such a perfect Jupiter personality, bringing joy to millions and leading an abundant life that ultimately proved his undoing.

♄

Saturn: The Autocrat

ASTRONOMY: The second-largest planet in the solar system, sixth in line from the Sun, Saturn is distinctive for its spectacular rings. Another 'gas giant', the planet's density is so small it would float on water – if there was an ocean large enough to drop it in.

Saturn has the most spectacular ring system in the solar system. These rings aren't solid, but made up of billions of separate chunks. They range from microscopic particles to rocks that are a few metres in diameter. It's thought that the rings are made mainly of water ice, although some chunks may have rocky centres. No-one is sure how they formed, but we do know that they change over time. Some particles are lost into space and these are replaced by debris released by Saturn's moons. Upon closer inspection, Saturn's rings are composed of many hundreds of smaller bands, with gaps in-between. The largest break, the Cassini Gap, is visible from Earth. Saturn's moons may create some of these gaps as they sail through, clearing debris from their paths.

Saturn is the furthest planet that can be seen with the naked eye, but without the aid of a telescope, it can be tricky to spot against the background of stars. The giveaway sign of any planet is that it doesn't 'twinkle' like stars do.

MYTHOLOGY: The Greeks called Saturn Cronus, after one of the great Titans of mythology. Cronus fought a ten-year war with Zeus, but was eventually beaten and imprisoned in Tartarus, a dark and gloomy place at the far ends of the Earth. The Romans renamed the planet Saturn, but it retained qualities that reflected Cronus, representing our limitations and constraints, our own personal versions of Tartarus. He is also associated with darkness and depression, hence the word 'saturnine'. Yet Saturn is also a mentor, a wise head ready to guide any willing apprentice. The 18 moons surrounding Saturn are named after various Titans, gods, goddesses and other important figures in Greek mythology.

ASTROLOGY: In astrological terms, Saturn balances the influence of Jupiter. If Jupiter is expansion, growth and things that are big, then Saturn is restriction and limitation. He is very cautious and small. If Jupiter is Mr Micawber, Saturn is Scrooge. Saturn is often an autocrat; he has to have things in place. He will not take a risk unless it is a calculated one. Saturn people tend to only do things when they know they can win or know they have powerful allies who can help them succeed.

Within you Saturn is your ambition. He is the career planet. Within you he is the planet constantly goading you on to the next thing; once you've had one success, he is goading you on to the next. The positive Saturn within you can't stand the idea of failure, despises rejection and waste, whether a wasted opportunity or idea or even a pea on the plate. It is making use of everything you are given. Because he is the planet of duty, responsibility and accountability, Saturn can't abide fools or wastrels and needs everything to be absolutely accounted for.

Where Saturn is placed in your chart is where you normally find sorrow or the area of your life that you have to work at the most. There's a sense of personal imprisonment to him, yet his controlling nature can be a lifesaver. When you go beyond your limits, it is Saturn that makes you take stock. He prioritizes, tells you what you want to do and where you will find your greatest sense of achievement and success.

PERSONALITY/GENDER: The autocrat within you, the part of you that exercises self-control and offers down-to-earth advice. He is masculine.

KEY WORDS: Restriction, limitation, self-control, crystallizing.

FAMOUS SATURN: Margaret Thatcher was a very Saturn person. Saturn is conservative with a small 'c' and Thatcher had Saturn rising in her chart in the sign of Scorpio when she was born. You don't get more stern than Maggie – it was little surprise she became known as the Iron Lady.

The ancient civilizations knew of only five of the planets. It has only been in the last few hundred years that we have learned of the existence of further planets. Saturn is the last of the 'I' planets, the ones we use for everyday matters in our lives. The next three planets are concerned with more complex and subtle aspects of our lives.

Uranus: The Anarchist

ASTRONOMY: The third-largest planet in the solar system, and the seventh planet from the Sun, Uranus is another giant ball of gas. Four times bigger than Earth, it is the only planet to spin on its side. It has at least 21 moons. The atmosphere is mostly hydrogen and helium, with small quantities of methane. It is the methane that absorbs the red light from the Sun's ray, giving the planet its distinct blue colour.

To the naked eye, Uranus is hard to spot. Even through a telescope he is a fairly featureless planet. It appears as a greenish disc, without any distinguishing marks. However, it is possible to spot seasonal changes in the planet's atmosphere during the year.

Other planets spin around an axis that is perpendicular to their direction of travel, but Uranus is tipped on its side and spins in the same direction as he travels, so he rolls around his orbit. No-one knows for certain what happened to Uranus to make it like this. It means that each of Uranus's poles faces away from the Sun for half of the planet's orbit, so each pole alternates between nights and days that last for 42 years.

MYTHOLOGY: Uranus was not known in the ancient world. It was the first planet to be discovered with the aid of a telescope. When Wilhelm Herschel spotted it in 1781, he named it 'the Georgium Sidus' (the Georgian Planet). So as to continue the tradition of naming planets after classical gods, it was later given the name Uranus after the father of the ancient world.

Due to the fact he was discovered during the American and French revolutions, Uranus has become associated with freedom, independence, rebelliousness and a revolutionary nature. Uranus also orbits on his belly, at an angle 90 degrees off from every other planet in the solar system. He is, in this sense too, at odds with the rest of the planets.

ASTROLOGY: The new planets are very much linked to what was going on in the world when they were discovered by man, so Uranus is associated with a time of colossal change in the world. This is reinforced by the fact that it marks the end of Saturn's conservative and traditional power. So everything Saturn stands for, Uranus is very often dead against. If Saturn is order, Uranus is chaos, including the chaos within us all. This can show itself in not being able to bear tidiness, but it is also excitement and surprise, an exhilaration that takes us out of the treadmill of life.

In this sense Uranus is where we rebel. It's where we aim and want to be different. Uranus is the anarchist within us. He is also where we need to accept who we are. He is the place where you keep what you might call your fetishes, your idiosyncrasies, and what other people might call your perversions. In other words, he is everything in us that makes us different. He is the planet that says don't hang around in the closet so if you are gay, you are gay.

Positively, Uranus is the sign of the genius, the unusual, the individual – anything that makes us different from the next person. Negatively, he is the person who needs to be shocking and outrageous, eccentric and bizarre, over the top, using a sledgehammer to crack a nut.

PERSONALITY/GENDER: Uranus represents the anarchist within us all. Masculine in nature, he is the fierce, rebellious spirit that helps you shake off your chains.

KEY WORDS: Change, shock, freedom, disruption, friendliness.

FAMOUS URANUS: Bill Clinton has a strong Uranus influence in his chart. Elsewhere in his chart, the former president of the United States has very powerful strengths, both in terms of intellect and personality. He is a brilliant man who could charm the birds out of the trees. Yet Uranus represents his Achilles heel, a flaw in his personality that almost seems to want him to create chaos in his life; for example, by conducting affairs under Hillary's nose.

Neptune: The Fantasist

ASTRONOMY: The fourth-largest planet in the solar system, at some points in its orbit Neptune drifts out past Pluto to become the furthest planet from the Sun. It has at least 11 moons. On the planet surface, winds blow at more than 2,000 kilometres per hour, the fastest in the solar system.

Another 'gas giant', Neptune's deep blue colour is a mystery. Neptune cannot be seen from Earth with the naked eye. Even through powerful telescopes, the planet can be hard to spot. Indeed, when Galileo saw it, he thought it was just another star.

MYTHOLOGY: When Zeus took over Mount Olympus, he divided the world between his two brothers, Poseidon and Hades. Hades was given the underworld while Poseidon (renamed Neptune by the Romans) received the oceans. As a result, the planet is heavily associated with water and its properties.

Neptune is unique in that he was the first planet to have been 'discovered' before it was actually seen by human eye. Neptune's gravitational field affects the orbit of Uranus, so its existence was deduced using Newton's laws of motion. Then it was spotted by Johann Gottfried Galle in September 1846. Neptune's largest moon is named after Poseidon's son, Triton. The rest are named after sea nymphs and others associated with the water.

ASTROLOGY: In astrological terms, Neptune is defined by water, so the sense of seeing the world as if underwater permeates the astrological side of the planet. It is as if things are being seen distorted. When Neptune is 'in transit' passing through someone's charts, they often feel as if they can't see where they are going, as if they are in a dream. This is what Neptune is about within us. It is the side we don't understand because it is not necessarily tangible. It is our psychic and spiritual side.

People with a powerful Neptune are drawn towards total fantasy and glamour, often living in a fantasy world. But image is a veneer; you can make yourself look beautiful, but like Dorian Gray, there is something else going on in your attic. With Neptune what you see is very often not what you get. People with a strong Neptune can be liars, deceivers and cheats. With this negative Neptune, the fantasy can translate into worry, anxiety, grief and guilt. If you think too much about Neptune in your chart, you try to create a reason for him being there, but the thing about Neptune is that he is not reasonable or rational. Yet if we harness Neptune and understand our fantasies, we are all capable of great things.

PERSONALITY/GENDER: Neptune is the fantasist within us, the source of our romantic and spiritual dreams. In keeping with the nebulous, confused energy of the planet, the gender of Neptune has changed through history. In early civilizations, Neptune was feminine, but in the classical Greco–Roman worlds, where Poseidon and Neptune represented him, he became masculine. It is the male Neptune we use today, although many of his facets, such as romance and glamour, are feminine.

KEY WORDS: Nebulous, confusion, blurred, self-deceiving.

FAMOUS NEPTUNE: Neptune is the mystique within us and Marilyn Monroe represented that perfectly. On screen she represented a dream version of femininity: she was sexy, funny and vulnerable. Off screen, she lived in a fantasy world. She wanted the perfect dream union but she married completely the wrong men. Even her death, perhaps of a drugs overdose, had an air of mystery about it. Neptune is all about us that we don't understand. Did we ever understand Monroe?

Pluto: The Enigma

ASTRONOMY: Pluto is the smallest planet in the solar system, around half the size of Earth's Moon. For most of its orbit, Pluto is the furthest planet from the Sun (except for 20 years during its 248-year orbit, when it comes closer to the Sun than Neptune). It is the coldest planet in the solar system, with temperatures as low as

-220°C. From the surface of Pluto, the Sun looks so small that it appears to be just a bright star in the sky.

This remote ball of ice remains a bit of a mystery. No probes have visited Pluto and so no maps have been made of the surface. Due to his small size and distant location, some astronomers argue that Pluto isn't a planet at all, but a giant asteroid.

Pluto is the only planet that spins at the same rate as its moon orbits. You can only see Pluto's moon from one side of the planet. Pluto can't be seen from Earth with the naked eye. It's possible (though tricky) to spot the planet through a telescope if you know exactly where to look. Even powerful Earth-based telescopes aren't strong enough to see Pluto's dark surface in detail.

MYTHOLOGY: Pluto was discovered by accident in 1930. Astronomers had begun to search for a new planet beyond Neptune after calculations of his orbit suggested there might be a large mass beyond it. The sums proved wrong, but by then Pluto had been found.

The new planet quickly took on the qualities of the underworld with which Pluto, Hades in Greek, was associated. He was seen as the world of the dead. The 1930s were also a dark period for the world, defined by the Depression and Mob rule in the United States, the birth of the atomic bomb and the rise of fascism in Europe.

Pluto is also symbolic of the unknown, what is hidden from us. He sits at the far end of the solar system where the Sun can't shine on him. His one moon is named after the ferryman of the dead, Charon.

ASTROLOGY: Pluto is perhaps the most fascinating planet of them all because he is so complex and absolutely psychologically-based.

In myth, Hades was able to move between worlds by wearing an invisible cloak. Pluto is our invisibility; he is where we can hide our true selves. He is where we can hide from others what we are really after, and where we can hide our true plans and motives. He is the planet of psychology, total utter control. This is not control in the Mars sense of being in control of one's physical energy. Here it is the sense of psychological control of others, of being in control of situations by manipulating and manoeuvring, perhaps in a Machiavellian style, until one gains control over others. You don't get the word 'plutocrat' for nothing. They are bigger than tycoons; they don't just want success and money, they want to change the world in the likeness of themselves, whether it is a Rupert Murdoch who wants to take control of the world's media or Charles Manson who had a very powerful Scorpio–Pluto energy and took power to the degree of death.

Pluto is also the death within ourselves; he is where we transform ourselves. Therefore, you often find Pluto is where you will cut things off. He is also the avenging angel. Pluto is where you seek revenge, where you are unforgiving, relentless and ruthless, and where you can be most cruel. But it is also where you can transform yourself from a snake to a dove and show a side of you that transcends all that is horrible, nasty and evil. In this sense Pluto is the most powerful placement.

PERSONALITY/GENDER: Pluto represents the enigma within us, the mysterious part of our personality where our deepest secrets lie. He is, once more, a masculine planet.

KEY WORDS: Elimination, transformation, power, control, obsessive, craving.

FAMOUS PLUTO: Pluto people are very powerfully equipped psychologically. Influencing people and winning them over by using their cloak of invisibility is second nature to them. Tony Blair, one of our most skilled contemporary politicians, has a very powerful and emphatic Pluto.

TWO

PLANET *You*

Understanding the Horoscope

You've now met the ten different planets and been introduced to their ten very different personalities. Each of us needs to be in touch with all of the planets within ourselves. Each of them has a part to play in our lives, but the way in which they interact will be unique to each of us.

So the next step on your journey to self-awareness and self-fulfilment is to discover how these diverse characters are arranged within you: which ones are dominant, which ones are spaced and placed positively, which ones have the capacity to be negative, which ones are working together in harmony, and which ones are in conflict with each other. You also need to know which planets are void of any contact in your chart, which one's qualities you may need to conjure up to achieve the change you are looking for.

You will find all this in your personal horoscope or natal chart. But before we begin to look at that chart, you'll need to understand its fundamental structure. You will also need to understand the key pieces of information within it and how to extract them for your own reading. It may not sound very dramatic or exciting, but read on...

The Stage Play of Your Life

Back in the 1970s, I wrote a stage play called *Olympian Rhapsody*. It featured a cast of characters based on astrological and mythological figures, each of them pursuing a particular goal and tripping up over each other along the way. I don't think it caused Harold Pinter any sleepless nights, but it was well received. I mention it here because the play was based on an idea that took root around that time and remains powerful – that the planets within our birth chart are like people all waiting to play their part in our lives.

Many people find it hard to get their head around the concepts that form the basics of astrology and the horoscope, and in particular the relationship between the key elements: the planets, the signs of the zodiac and the houses. What struck me as I penned *Olympian Rhapsody* 30 years ago was that the play summed up the whole astrology thing rather well. A horoscope is, to all intents and purposes, a stage play too. And the subject of that play is none other than the person whose birth chart it describes. In this case, that's you.

This is exactly how you should think about the personal horoscope you are about to discover. Your birth chart is a play based entirely on the subject of your life, inspired by the things that inspire you, reflecting the person you are inside, and ready to go into production immediately.

It is going to need four components to make it a successful production: actors, a stage, costumes, lighting and a script. In the case of this particular production, however, all these components are in the hands of one person – you. You are not only the writer of this play, you are also its costume designer, set designer and make-up artist; in fact, you are the star of the show.

So let's look at these four components, and see how they fit into the horoscope that is the inspiration for this play.

THE CAST

The players are, as you've probably guessed, the planets themselves the ten different personalities we've already met. Who takes the leading and supporting roles depends on the way your inner solar system is set up. It might be, for instance, that Mercury is strong within you, making him the leading man – or woman. (In Shakespeare's day the female parts – yes, even Juliet – were played by young boys.) Venus, too, might be prominent, making her the leading lady. Pluto, on the other hand, might be a distant, shadowy figure, very melodramatic. If his influence is a negative one, this might make him the perfect villain.

THE SCENERY

The different scenes and the sets against which the play will take place are in each of the segments of your horoscope, known as the houses of the zodiac. There are 12 of them in all, each corresponding to different areas of your life. The second house, for instance, is where the financial aspects of your life take place. So if one of your planetary stars is featured in this scene, for instance, the backdrop might be a bank. Equally it might be where you have to raise funds to put the play on.

THE COSTUMES

The costumes are the signs of the zodiac that your planets occupy. If in your chart, for instance, the Sun is in Gemini or aspected to

Mercury, it might be dressed as a teenage skateboarder. Or if the Moon is neatly linked to Jupiter, it might be a Victorian schoolmaster, rather like Mr Chips or Professor Dumbledore in *Harry Potter*. (Again, don't worry if you don't get the connection yet. Concentrate on understanding the analogy.)

THE SCRIPT

Finally, the words through which the actors interact with each other represent what we astrologers call the aspect of the planets. The aspects are basically the positions that the Sun and the Moon, Neptune, Saturn and the rest occupy in relation to each other within the birth chart. Depending on how they are set up, they react with each other in different ways, sometimes harmoniously, sometimes contentiously. It is this interaction that makes up the dialogue of your play. So, for example, if Mercury is in conflict, or 'square', with Mars, the two strong qualities of these characters (Mercury's mental agility and Mars's energy) might lead to a quarrelsome, argumentative, spiteful pair. The dialogue here might involve the two of them running around full of ideas but never concentrating long enough to bring any of them to fruition as they are too Tweedledum and Tweedledee, more interested in a row than exploring the brilliant, spontaneous ideas that you would get with a positive Mercury–Mars aspect.

In the pages that follow, you will be introduced to each of these elements of the horoscope. They are easy concepts to understand, but if they ever begin to seem abstract or unreal, think of them in terms of the characters in the stage play of your life. It might also help here and there if you personalize the planets; perhaps see Venus played by Elizabeth Taylor or Mars by Richard Burton. By doing so they will soon loom more clearly into view…

WHAT IS THE ZODIAC?

The solar system is in a state of constant motion. As Earth rotates and moves around the Sun, so the other planets are also travelling through space at differing speeds and trajectories. While it takes Earth 365 days to orbit the Sun (366 in a leap year), it takes the closest planet Mercury 88 days to complete one circuit, and Pluto, the farthest from the Sun, a staggering 248 years. All this means that the relative positions of the planets as viewed from Earth change, moving in a band across the sky. This 360-degree band, best thought of as a wide belt looped around Earth across the constellations, is known as the ecliptic and has been divided up by astrologers throughout the ages.

Contrary to recent so-called 'revelations' that there are 13 signs, this band is fixed and is what we call in western astrology, the tropical zodiac. It is made up of 12 signs – 12 it is and 12 it will remain.

The Babylonians were the first to section off the sky, into three strips named after three of their gods, Anu, Enlil and Ea. It was the middle strip, through which the planets moved, that corresponded with our modern ecliptic. Today we segment 12 different sections of 30 degrees. These are what everyone knows as the signs of the zodiac, from Aries to Pisces. The name 'zodiac' is Greek and probably means 'circle of animals', a reference to the crab, ram, goat, scorpion, bull and other symbols that have, since the golden age of Athens, been associated with the signs of the zodiac.

The roots of the zodiac are tied in closely with the Sun's progress through the sky during the course of the year, and the cycle of life, death and rebirth associated with it since the dawn of man. For this reason, for instance, the signs of the first quadrant – Aries, Taurus and Gemini – have traditionally related to individual and personal development. And the zodiac has also been divided up into sub-groups: the elements, qualities, the feminine and the masculine and the polar signs.

Before we get into that, let's take a look at the 12 signs, their qualities and properties. If you're a Southern Hemisphere birth, fear not, we'll address you in a jiffy – the principles are exactly the same, so don't be put off.

ZODIAC SIGNS

It took many thousands of years for the modern signs of the zodiac to take the shape we all now recognize from the daily horoscopes or sun sign forecasts in the newspapers and magazines. The most powerful influence in shaping the 12 phases was the solar year, the movement of the Sun through the sky and the seasons that accompany it. Each of the signs coincides with the Sun's position at that time of the year.

This, in turn, gave birth to powerful mythologies associated with both the seasons and the constellations that filled that section of the sky at that time of the year. In turn, each of these mythologies has given rise to particular qualities associated with each sign of the zodiac. It is these qualities that reflect on the planets as they pass through them. It is these – to go back to our stage play analogy – that will be the costume and make-up in which our planets will be dressed.

Note: You will notice that the dates here might not match those you are familiar with from your favourite newspaper or magazine (unless, of course, you follow my horoscopes!) This is because, contrary to popular belief, the signs do not change at midnight on a given day – it is not that cut and dried. If you take into account the various other factors at play, the Sun might enter Aries a day earlier or later each year. They can also change morning, noon or night. (Now you can see why time is so crucial.) So the newspaper horoscopes are, in general, only ever approximate.

Aries
Around 21 March – around 20 April

Symbol: The Ram | *Quality:* Cardinal
Element: Fire | *Ruler:* Mars

Since Greek times Aries has been linked with the vernal equinox or first day of spring (autumn down in the Southern Hemisphere), when the days and nights are of equal length once more, but the Sun is ready to dominate the sky again. So for thousands of years it has been associated with the emergence of the ego, and the individual's breaking away from the collective human world where he has lived until now. (To understand the background to the signs better, think of the collective nature of humanity as the darkness and the individual nature as the light.) For this reason, Aries is associated with the assertiveness and initiative needed to establish itself on its own. Its association with Mars, its ruling planet, can lend this energy an aggressive and impetuous edge as well. As the sign of the emerging ego, Aries is also associated with immaturity and naivety.

As a result, planets placed in Aries show their qualities by leading rather than following. They show themselves as individuals first and foremost, remaining true to their emerging selves. However, the Ram can sometimes be a ewe or lamb and follow the flock that depends on the position of the other planets to the Aries placements.

KEY WORDS: Dynamic, energetic, impulsive, passionate, egotistical.

Taurus
Around 21 April – around 20 May

Symbol: The Bull
Element: Earth
Quality: Fixed
Ruler: Venus

Taurus once represented the beginning of the zodiac. In Egypt it was during the period of Taurus that the cattle and oxen ploughed the fields. As a result, it has always been associated with earthiness and practicality. It has also been a byword for steadfastness, something that was underlined by the star Aldebaran, 'the bull's eye', which sat fixed in the middle of the section of the sky that was Taurus. The bull has also been long been associated with fertility, both in terms of agriculture and sex.

Its links with Venus and the goddesses of love go back to Babylon and the battle of Gilgamesh, when Ishtar, the goddess of love, sent a bull into battle on her behalf. It's no mistake that when Jupiter wanted to ravish the nymph Europa he transformed himself into a bull. Venus remains Taurus's ruler in modern astrology. Again, today it is the most fertile and fruitful of signs. Planets in Taurus reflect its nature by behaving in a way that is linked to the bull's traditional qualities of stability and abundance.

KEY WORDS: Practical, possessive, stoic, faithful, artistic.

♊

Gemini

Around 21 May – around 21 June

Symbol: The Twins | *Quality:* Mutable
Element: Air | *Ruler:* Mercury

The constellation of Gemini is dominated by two stars of seemingly similar sizes. In mythology these were representative of Castor and Pollux, the inseparable twin sons of Zeus. While Pollux was immortal, Castor was not. When his brother died, Pollux insisted on being placed in the heavens alongside him. Together, Zeus decreed they should spend half their time in heaven and half in the underworld.

This notion of the divine twins repeats itself throughout mythology, from the Indian Ashvins, a pair of healers born to the Sun god, Surya, to Nissyen and Evnissyen, the very different siblings in the Cymraeg (Welsh) epic, the Mabinogion. While Nissyen is a peacemaker, Evnissyen provokes war. So it is no surprise that duality, 'two sides', is the element most commonly associated with the sign of Gemini. Gemini is symbolic of the struggle between the positive and the negative aspect of a personality, between the light and the dark, perhaps the ying and the yang. The intellectual side of Gemini is drawn from Mercury, its ruling planet.

Planets in Gemini tend to reflect the duality of the sign. For instance, the Sun in Gemini can reflect itself in a need for adventure and travel that betrays a restlessness to find the real self.

KEY WORDS: Clever, cerebral, versatile, volatile, mercurial.

Cancer

Around 22 June – around 23 July

Symbol: The Crab *Quality:* Cardinal
Element: Water *Ruler:* Moon

The Egyptians symbolized Cancer with a scarab beetle, while the Greeks denoted it with a turtle or tortoise. Later, however, it became the sign of the crab – like its predecessors, a creature with a hard exterior and a soft interior.

In the annual cycle of the Sun, Cancer marks the summer solstice (winter in the Southern Hemisphere), the time of the year when the longest day (and therefore the shortest night) occurs. It is, if you like, a moment of maturity, much like an adolescent reaching adulthood. Just as Aries marks the beginning of the journey away from collective humankind towards the individual, so Cancer represents the moment when the Sun turns back. The ego has essentially reached its high-point and is ready to be merged into society once more. For this reason, Cancer represents home and family, and their protection.

Cancer is also ruled by the Moon, which means it is also strongly feminine and in touch with its emotions, something that is underlined by its position as the first of the Water signs, of which we will see more later. The powerful, lunar influence also lends this sector of the zodiac a moodiness and insecurity. Planets placed in Cancer reflect themselves by nurturing relationships, and bringing out instinctive and intuitive aspects of the personality.

KEY WORDS: Habit-forming, tenacious, sensitive, moody, emotional.

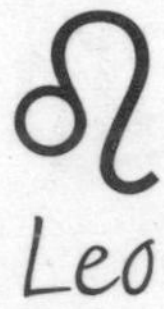

Leo

Around 24 July – around 23 August

Symbol: The Lion
Element: Fire
Quality: Fixed
Ruler: Sun

Leo's lion symbol was probably derived from an Egyptian goddess, Sekhmet, a lion-headed deity who represented the Sun at its height in the sky at mid-day. This time of the year also coincided with the Sun at its brightest in the sky. Since then, the king of the planets, the Sun, and the king of the animals have been strongly linked. Leo is associated with so-called regal qualities such as fearlessness, courage and wisdom. As we saw while looking at the planets, the power of the Sun can be a force for creativity and dignity, but, if left to run amok, can lead to a need to conquer, rule and dominate as well.

The planets reflect different aspects of these qualities when they reside in Leo. For instance, Mercury can display his creative abilities through thoughts and ideas.

KEY WORDS: Proud, noble, generous, creative, warm-hearted.

♍
Virgo
Around 24 August – around 23 September

Symbol: The Virgin
Quality: Mutable
Element: Earth
Ruler: Mercury

Virgo is associated with the harvest season. Indeed, the allegory or symbol for the sign represents the harvest goddess holding grain. It is during this season that summer gives way to mellow autumn. In a personal sense, this marks the transformation from a virginal or childlike state into a more mature, fully grown personality. With the transition from the individual now complete, this is also the phase when devotion to the collective needs of others is at its most heightened. For this reason, Virgo has long been seen as the sign of service, associated with carers and healers.

Virgo is ruled by Mercury, the planet of the mind, but because Virgo is an Earth sign, this results in a more analytical and precise kind of intellect than in Gemini. Planets in Virgo reflect these qualities; for instance, the Sun in Virgo focuses on creating a world that is perfect in every fine detail, while the Moon in Virgo will concentrate on caring for the feelings of others.

KEY WORDS: Systematic, discerning, critical, conscientious, helpful.

♎

Libra

Around 24 September – around 23 October

Symbol: The Scales
Quality: Cardinal
Element: Air
Ruler: Venus

Libra represents the period of the autumn equinox (spring in the Southern Hemisphere), another important transitional moment in the year. Once more, the days and nights are of the same length. Unlike Aries – when the forces of daylight are growing stronger – during Libra, night is beginning to dominate once more. As with Virgo, this reflects itself in the needs of the collective whole taking precedence over the individual. Indeed it is the opposite of Aries – the sign of the self – and is associated with partnerships and marriage in particular. This period is therefore all about balance, hence the symbolism of Libra, the scales, constantly weighing up situations.

In general, Libra brings out the least self-centred aspects of the planets. For instance, Mars's energy can be turned to fighting for equality, while Mercury's flair for communication can be used for diplomatic purposes.

KEY WORDS: Harmonious, tactful, refined, fair, indecisive.

♏

Scorpio

Around 24 October – around 22 November

Symbol: The Scorpion
Quality: Fixed
Element: Water
Ruler: Mars & Pluto

It is during this period that autumn takes hold and Earth begins to close down for the winter once more. So it is no surprise that to the ancients, this was a period when the gods were assumed to return to the underworld until the winter solstice summoned them back in readiness for the regeneration of the spring. It was during this period that the Celts celebrated Samhain, the night when it was said the worlds of the living and the dead were open to each other. (The forerunner of the modern Halloween.) In Latin America, this is known as the Day of the Dead.

Scorpio is therefore heavily associated with a journey to the deepest, most private and intimate aspects of our inner personalities. It is a place where we face up to the demons that lie within us. Naturally, it is ruled by Pluto, the planet of secrets and the hidden.

The planets reflect these qualities in their own ways. Venus in Scorpio can show itself as a sexual explorer, and Mercury may turn its intellectual powers to studying the psychological aspects of its personality. But the planets also reflect the resurrection that occurs at the end of this period of self-examination. For the Moon, for instance, this period of self-reflection can revitalize and reinvigorate its personality.

KEY WORDS: Intense, secretive, resolute, jealous, obsessive.

Sagittarius
Around 23 November – around 21 December

Symbol: The Centaur
Element: Fire
Quality: Mutable
Ruler: Jupiter

With the darkest days of the year, the period of Sagittarius has long been associated with reflection and an interest in philosophy and higher-minded subject matter. With the Sun's presence at a minimum, the interest of the collective good is at its height and individuality is at its lowest ebb. So in Native American culture, for instance, it was the time to sit around the campfire and pass on the tribal legends in the form of storytelling.

Yet it is a time for optimism too, with the knowledge that the new solar year is soon to come. It is no surprise that the Sagittarius symbol, the centaur, is pointing its arrow upwards at the stars. The planets reflect these aspects of Sagittarius in different ways. Mars, for instance, may tend to put all its energies into personal development or therapy during this phase, and Jupiter has an abiding interest in travel or the metaphysical.

KEY WORDS: Excessive, expansive, candid, optimistic, extravagant.

Capricorn

Around 22 December – around 20 January

Symbol: The Goat *Quality:* Cardinal
Element: Earth *Ruler:* Saturn

The winter solstice (summer in the Southern Hemisphere), which falls during this phase, marks the final phase in the Sun's journey away from the light. As the days slowly begin to lengthen once more, the Sun turns back once more towards the light. The return from the underworld towards humanity, from the collective to the individual, is beginning once more. In mythology, this period marked the time when humanity showed its mastery of Earth and all its temptations. It is a time of morality and responsibility, a time when we demonstrate we have overcome the weaknesses associated with youth.

Because Capricorn is ruled by Saturn, these qualities are exaggerated still further so that the sign is associated with extreme control, in the form of stiffness, reserve and total discipline. And, because Capricorn is an Earth sign, they are associated with the world and society. These aspects show themselves in the planets when they are placed in Capricorn. Venus in Capricorn is extremely loyal but demands a successful or ambitious partner, while Saturn in its own sign displays the kind of conservative respect for society that is connected with politics, leadership and authority in general.

KEY WORDS: Cautious, reserved, prudent, responsible, constructive, disciplined.

♒

Aquarius

Around 21 January – around 19 February

Symbol: The Water Bearer *Quality:* Fixed
Element: Air *Ruler:* Saturn & Uranus

Aquarius has always been associated with water, hence its symbol, the water carrier. The Egyptians associated it with the flooding of the Nile and the spiritual forces of renewal and fertility. The Babylonians connected it with their god Utnapishtim, who had heeded divine warnings of the end of the world and built a boat that saved him from a giant flood. (This story is the model for that of Noah in the Biblical book of Genesis, of course.)

More modern astrologers, however, have connected Aquarius with Prometheus, who had been freed from imprisonment and torment by Chiron. It is these qualities of independence and intellectual freedom, with which Aquarius is most associated. This reflects itself differently in the planets that sit within the sign. When it is in Aquarius, the Moon is free to be emotional, quirky and answerable to no-one, while Mercury tends to display some of his most brilliant facets here.

KEY WORDS: Individual, detached, cold, ingenious, rebellious.

Pisces

Around 20 February – around 20 March

Symbol: The Fishes
Element: Water
Quality: Mutable
Ruler: Neptune & Jupiter

The symbol of the two fishes is again linked to the flooding of the Nile, which was at its height when the Moon was full in Pisces. Its association with water was only deepened when the planet Neptune was discovered and made her ruler.

As with the planet Neptune, Pisces is associated with the dreamy and mystic aspects of the diffuse oceans. However, because it is in the period when the collective whole is still stronger than the individual ego, Pisces can produce confusion and changeability. The weak, still insecure ego isn't sure whether to believe what it sees.

Planets react differently to a placement here. While Venus, who emerged from the sea after all, is in seventh heaven being able to work her love magic in romantic Pisces, logical Mercury becomes waterlogged amidst all the confusion and unreality.

KEY WORDS: Soft, compassionate, nebulous, unreal, imaginative.

Traditional Factors

HOW THE SIGNS OF THE ZODIAC ARE GROUPED TOGETHER

The 12 signs of the zodiac can be subdivided into four different groups – elements, qualities, polar signs, and masculine and feminine – all of which allow a deeper interpretation of the chart.

The Elements

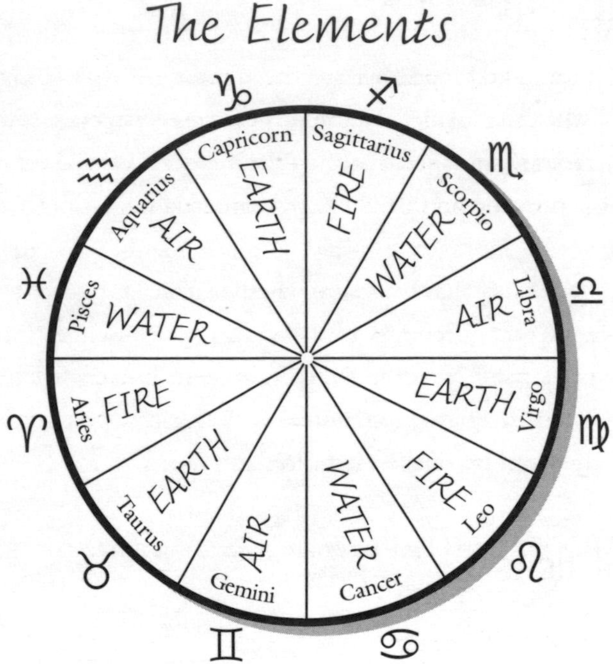

The zodiac can be divided up into the four essential elements of life: Fire, Earth, Air and Water. None of us can survive without each of them – we need fire for warmth, the earth to feed ourselves, the air to breathe and water to drink. The number of planets that fall into each of these categories can tell us much about a person's fundamental personality.

FIRE SIGNS

Aries, Leo and Sagittarius are the three Fire signs. They are each energetic and enthusiastic signs; they represent a burning desire to be creative and expressive.

EARTH SIGNS

Taurus, Virgo and Capricorn are the three signs that fall into this category. As their name suggests, they represent more down-to-earth qualities such as steadiness and stability. They also represent a practical nature and an instinct to gain materially.

AIR SIGNS

This group is made up of Gemini, Libra and Aquarius. They each indicate a nature that thirsts for knowledge and communication. They also show a rational and intellectual quality.

WATER SIGNS

Cancer, Scorpio and Pisces are the Water signs. They represent sensitivity and an artistic nature. Water signs also suggest an eagerness to experience their true feelings. They are also a signal of psychic qualities.

The way the planets are divided into these four categories offers some telling insights into people's personalities. If someone's chart indicates they have more planets in Air and Fire signs, for instance, this suggests an ability to express and communicate well. At the same time, a lack of Earth and Water signs suggest an inability to tune into other people emotionally as well as a lack of practicality.

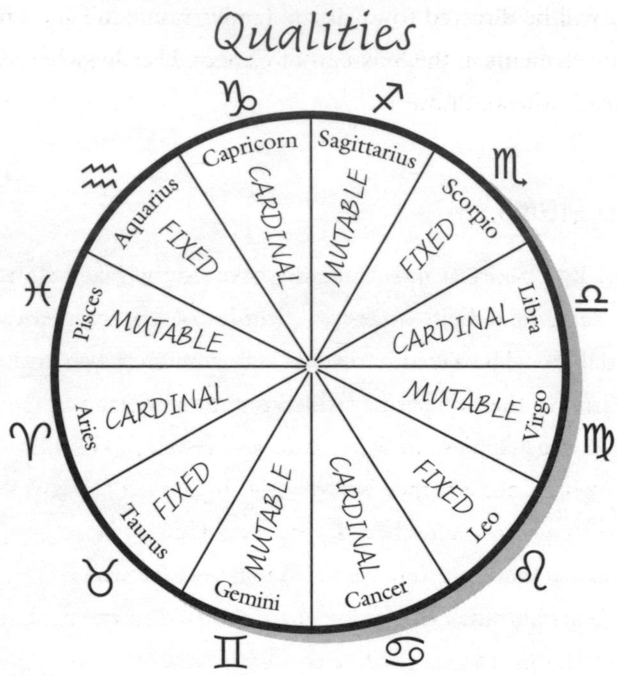

The zodiac can also be divided into three 'qualities', which describe the way people respond to their environment and those around them. Four signs fall into each of the three categories: Cardinal, Fixed and Mutable.

CARDINAL SIGNS

Aries, Cancer, Libra and Capricorn make up the quartet of signs that are known as Cardinal signs. In general people with Cardinal signs are active, enterprising and high achievers, although this can spill over into pushiness and overambition. Precisely how these Cardinal characteristics are expressed varies between the signs. For instance, in Capricorn, the Cardinal instincts will direct that person towards their career or public prestige. In Cancer, on the other hand, this energy will be directed towards the family, home life and emotional security, elements in the Sun sign of Cancer. Usually, where Cardinal signs lead others follow.

FIXED SIGNS

Taurus, Leo, Scorpio and Aquarius make up the Fixed signs. As the name suggests, their qualities include consistency, loyalty and dependability. The Fixed nature usually denies change and can play King Cnut in their ability to challenge fundamental and natural law. Taureans are happiest in a predictable lifestyle, Leos like to know where they stand, whether in a relationship or a job, Scorpios prefer to keep things to themselves having examined and explored a situation – fixity therefore represents the status quo which they happily know. The contradiction to the rule is Aquarius, who adores change and new things. However, they are often loath to let go of what they already have.

MUTABLE SIGNS

Gemini, Virgo, Sagittarius and Pisces make up this group. In stark contrast to the Fixed signs, this group indicates flexibility, adaptability and an ability to move on and be mentally on the ball at all times. Very often this quartet enjoy having two or more things on the go at once. Geminis are notorious for getting bored – by having a second string to their bow they can work out their angst by moving onto something different when the time comes.

Here again the way the planets divide themselves between the qualities tells us much about a person's personality. A large number of planets in Fixed signs, for instance, indicates someone who can be rigid in their views, perhaps even dogmatic. On the other hand, a preponderance of planets in Mutable signs suggests someone who is constantly changing and is unable to stick to anything for any length of time.

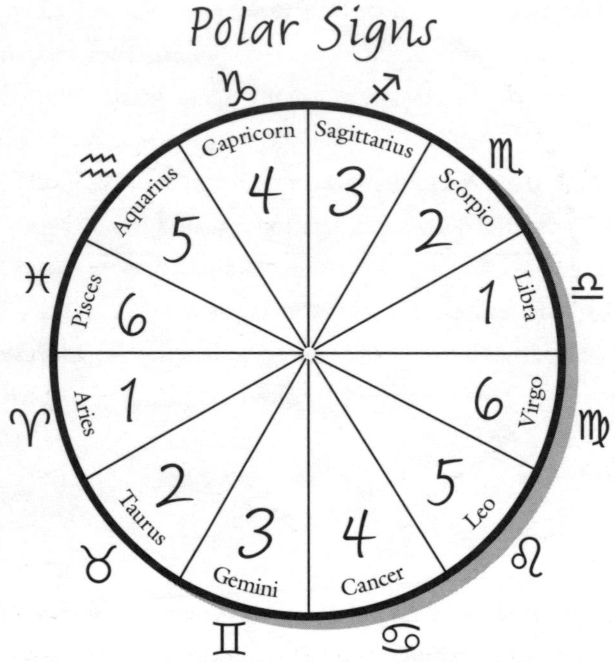

Opposites attract, or so the old saying goes, and in the same way signs that are opposite each other often complement each other. The qualities present in one sign often make up for deficiencies in the other.

For instance, Aries, a sign that indicates someone who is wrapped up in themselves, is opposite Libra, a sign that is indicative of an interest in other people. The result is the two balance each other:

Aries–Libra
Taurus–Scorpio
Cancer–Capricorn
Virgo–Pisces
Gemini–Sagittarius
Leo–Aquarius

Masculine and Feminine

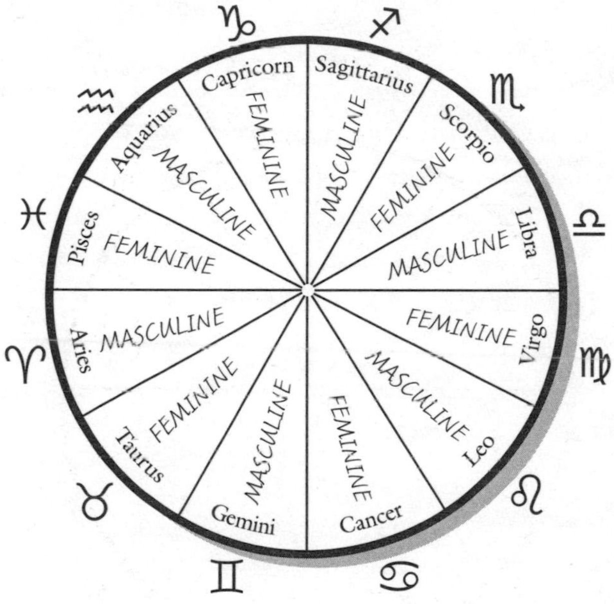

The zodiac is also divided into symbolic masculine and feminine signs. The masculine signs represent assertive, more extrovert tendencies, while the feminine signs suggest qualities that are more sensitive and receptive to others. Don't assume that a man with the majority of his planets in feminine signs is automatically gay – on the contrary, he may be at ease with his feminine side or comfortable in the company of arty, sensitive people. The same goes for a woman with a majority of her planets in masculine signs. She won't automatically be butch and wear a lumberjack's shirt, but she may attract men and be more assertive than passive. The 12 signs are divided up as follows:

MASCULINE: Aries, Gemini, Leo, Libra, Sagittarius, Aquarius
FEMININE: Taurus, Cancer, Virgo, Scorpio, Capricorn, Pisces

Ruling Planets

Since the beginning of astrology, civilizations have assigned different planets as guardians or rulers of each section of the zodiac. The mythological links between the two are often strong. Aries, for instance, has long been associated with personal growth and has as its ruler, Mars, the planet most strongly associated with drive and energy. In other instances, two planets have been assigned as rulers. The more powerful, personal planets – Mercury, Venus, Mars, Saturn and Jupiter – have rulership of two signs each. The complete list is as follows:

Aries – MARS
Taurus – VENUS
Gemini – MERCURY
Cancer – MOON
Leo – SUN
Virgo – MERCURY
Libra – VENUS
Scorpio – MARS and PLUTO

Sagittarius – JUPITER
Capricorn – SATURN
Aquarius – SATURN and URANUS
Pisces – NEPTUNE and JUPITER

Astrologers summarize the traditional factors in a table that illustrates how the 12 zodiac signs are divided between the elements, qualities, polar signs and masculine/feminine signs. Looking at the table, you can see that no two signs have the same combination. Each has a unique combination of factors at work in the sign. The table also shows the ruling planet for each sign.

SIGN	SYMBOL	RULER	SYMBOL	ELEMENT	QUALITY	TYPE
Aries	♈	Mars	♂	Fire	Cardinal	Masculine
Taurus	♉	Venus	♀	Earth	Fixed	Feminine
Gemini	♊	Mercury	☿	Air	Mutable	Masculine
Cancer	♋	Moon	☽	Water	Cardinal	Feminine
Leo	♌	Sun	☉	Fire	Fixed	Masculine
Virgo	♍	Mercury	☿	Earth	Mutable	Feminine
Libra	♎	Venus	♀	Air	Cardinal	Masculine
Scorpio	♏	Mars & Pluto	♂♇	Water	Fixed	Feminine
Sagittarius	♐	Jupiter	♃	Fire	Mutable	Masculine
Capricorn	♑	Saturn	♄	Earth	Cardinal	Feminine
Aquarius	♒	Saturn & Uranus	♄♅	Air	Fixed	Masculine
Pisces	♓	Neptune & Jupiter	♆♃	Water	Mutable	Feminine

The Houses

As well as the 12 signs of the zodiac, the birth chart is also divided up into 12 sections called the houses. Each of the 12 houses represents different aspects of everyday life – from money and materialistic matters to love and romantic affairs – and offers another powerful clue to your overall personality and potential.

By looking at the house each planet occupies and the sign ruling it, you will see where that planet's energies will be concentrated more strongly in your life. For instance, if the Moon (associated with your emotions and instincts) was placed in your 2nd house (which you'll see is to do with, amongst other things, possessions and money), this would indicate that money is very important to your sense of emotional well-being and security. If, on the other hand, the Moon was placed in your 4th house (which you'll see is to do with home, the family and the past), it is likely your relationship with your parents and siblings would loom large in your emotional inner life. And most importantly, a double-whammy as the 4th house is the Moon's natural celestial home.

The areas of life represented in each house are simply summed up as follows:

1st House: The personality, health, physical appearance, outward behaviour and personal image as projected to others; self-interests. How others see and perceive you.

2nd House: Possessions, money, spiritual and materialistic values, ownership, sensuality and acquisition. Self-worth as in how much you're worth materially.

3rd House: Communications, speech and mental attitude, ideas, short journeys, school days, everyday affairs, siblings, the kind of neighbourhood and community you attract.

4th House: Home, the past, parents (mothers, in particular), childhood, family, emotions and feelings, roots. History, grandparents, security.

5th House: Creativity, love, leisure, pleasure, children, pets, speculation, sports, enterprise, live entertainment, enjoyment and your heart's desire.

6th House: Work, service to others, health, employment conditions, duty, organizational talents, rational mind. Your job, being useful.

7th House: Love and marital relationships. Business and personal partnerships, long-term commitments and relationships on all levels. The kind of person you are attracted to and feel most at ease with.

8th House: Shared money matters, official financial affairs such as tax, attitudes to life and death, shared emotions, sex, desire and passion, psychological make-up and private life. What screws you up – obstacles and obsessions, repression and intimate, private fears.

9th House: Further education, global travel, mental and physical explorations, principles, philosophy and religious views, in-laws, intellectual horizons, law. International connections, opportunity and the luck factor. Your life vision.

10th House: Ambitions, achievements, social status, public image and standing, career, success and failure, parents (fathers, in particular). Where you want to be recognized, your reason for being, your mission and purpose in life. Destiny.

11th House: Friendships, hobbies, aims and aspirations, clubs and groups, humanitarian ideals, intellectual capacity, future hopes and wishes. What you do for the greater good and where or how you can change the world.

12th House: Imagination, dream world, secrets and sorrows, hidden artistic powers, need for seclusion, the imagination and subconscious, worries and phobias, where you escape to, charity and voluntary work, psychic and spiritual abilities, irrational fears and inhibitions. Guilt and grief carried to extraordinary extremes. The victim or the martyr, the saint or the crusader.

The Angles

THE IMPORTANCE OF THE ASCENDANT (RISING SIGN), DESCENDANT, MIDHEAVEN (ALSO KNOWN AS THE MC) AND NADIR (ALSO KNOWN AS THE IC)

When scientists discovered to their amazement that there were indeed facts that underpinned the basic principles of astrology, it was no surprise that the strongest evidence related to the most powerful positions the planets occupy in our birth charts. When the previously sceptical French scientist analyzed thousands of birth charts of prominent sportsmen and women, artists, politicians, scientists and celebrities, he found a strong link between their area of expertise and the position of certain planets at the moment of their birth.

In the charts of hundreds of successful sportsmen, for instance, he discovered that the planet Mars was a strong presence in a statistically high number of cases. More specifically, he saw that the influential planets tended to be in one of four positions: when it was rising in the east, setting in the west or at the high and low points in the sky. Gauquelin called these 'periods of intense activity'. Astrologers have another name for these areas. They are the Ascendant, Midheaven, Nadir and Descendant – or the angles of the chart.

THE ASCENDANT

This is the sign of the zodiac that was rising in the eastern horizon at the moment of your birth. This gives powerful information about our outer personality, the way we project ourselves to others on a personal, one-to-one level.

THE DESCENDANT

This where the sun sets, the western horizon. It indicates what we seek in others through our relationships, often what we don't possess within our own persona. It can also decree the kind of enemies, competitors and rivals we attract too – summed up in a love–hate relationship.

THE MIDHEAVEN

This marks the point in the sky directly overhead at the time of your birth (noon in the chart). This symbolizes our ambitions and how we want to be known and regarded as a success, the image we project – how the public sees us, accepts us or reviles us. It also symbolizes our role in public life and the kind of career we are drawn to.

THE NADIR

This is the polar opposite point of the Midheaven and marks the point in the sky directly below you when you were born. It's midnight time. The Nadir represents your roots and the formative part of your life. It can tell the kind of growing-up pains you had and whether you felt loved or rejected. The kind of roots you have reveal the kind of person you are under fire – comfortable with yourself or a flake.

THE MOON'S NODES ☊

Another very important angle that astrologers take into account is the nodes of the Moon. These are the two points in the Moon's orbit where it moves out of the band of sky occupied by the zodiac, cutting the plane of the ecliptic. The ancients called the ascending, or north node, the Dragon's Head. It is generally taken as the point where the Moon crosses the ecliptic from south to north. The descending or south node, or Dragon's Tail, is where the ecliptic is crossed from north to south. The nodes are marked by a symbol rather like a bracelet or a pair of headphones! The north node is marked on the charts we use here. (It will also be on the chart you receive via the dedicated website.) The nodes are in perpetual retrograde motion and have, I believe, powerful karmic and spiritual influences. However, this is not the book in which to analyze this powerful force in detail, so I will not be going into how to interpret them within the birth chart.

THE ASPECTS

Much of our personality can be explained by the way the different planetary personalities interact with each other. Some will complement and stimulate each other; some will clash and contradict each other. These relationships will reveal themselves in what we refer to as the aspects, that is, the relative positions of the planets to each other. This is one of the major key areas that a birth chart will show. The signal aspects to be interpreted in a birth chart are these:

Conjunctions: A conjunction occurs when two planets are placed either exactly or almost exactly at the same point on a birth chart. (The variance astrologers allow is nine degrees.) The wider the gap between the two planets, the weaker the influence. If there is no difference at all in degrees or separation between the two planets, then obviously the influence is at its strongest but if too close, especially if the Sun is involved in the conjunction, it can be said to be combust. (For instance, if the Sun is at 15 Aquarius and Mercury is at 16, the Sun overpowers Mercury so much he cannot function at his best. He is blinded by the Sun as you would be if you looked directly at this heavenly body.) More reasonable would be, say, two or three degrees between the planets because with that degree of distance, Mercury can work his own planetary magic with much more clarity and be less influenced by the Sun.

The Sextile: This aspect occurs when two planets are 60 degrees apart in a chart. Again there is some leeway, this time up to six degrees either side. The closer the two planets are in degrees to an exact sextile, the stronger their influence on each other. A golden rule here is that a sextile often occurs when a planet in one sign aspects another with a compatible element, for instance, an Air sign and a Fire sign, a Water sign and an Earth sign, for instance.

The Square: As the name suggests, this aspect occurs when two planets are 90 degrees apart in the birth chart. The leeway here is nine degrees either side. A simple rule is often, but not always, that a square occurs when planets within the SAME quality – Cardinal, Fixed or Mutable – aspect one another.

The Trine: This occurs when two planets are 120 degrees apart, again with a leeway of nine degrees either side. Two planets linking in a trine with each other indicate a harmonious relationship. A trine often occurs when planets in the SAME element – Fire, Earth, Air and Water – aspect each other.

The Opposition: Again, as the name suggests, this occurs when two planets are directly opposite each other on a birth chart, that is, 180 degrees apart. This indicates that the two planets will have a challenging relationship with each other. Think back to polar opposites.

Aspects can work in positive and negative ways. They can be harmonious, meaning the two planets work easily together. Both the trine and the sextile aspects are regarded as harmonious and easy to live with. On the other hand, aspects can be challenging, meaning the relationship between the planets is tense and stressful to live with. As their names indicate, the square and the opposition represent challenging aspects, although an opposition is easier to deal with and overcome than a square. However, too many trines and not enough squares equally isn't good as a person can become lazy and think the world owes them a living. As with all things, a good balance is essential to a positive outcome.

The most subtle of the aspects is the conjunction, which can work in both a negative and positive way.

TABLE OF ASPECTS

This table shows the glyph representing each of the major aspects, their exact distances, orb and nature.

NAME OF ASPECT	GLYPH	EXACT DISTANCE	ORB	NATURE
Conjunction	☌	0°	9°	Variable
Sextile	⚹	60°	6°	Harmonious
Square	□	90°	9°	Challenging
Trine	△	120°	9°	Harmonious
Opposition	☍	180°	9°	Challenging

THREE

EXPLORING PLANET *You*

Getting and Understanding Your Own 'Natal' Birth Chart

Your Personal Natal Birth Chart

So, finally, we have laid the foundations. It is now time to start exploring Planet You.

To begin analyzing the way the planets are arranged within your own personal solar system, the first thing you will need is to have a birth chart drawn up. Drawing up a 'natal' birth chart (a horoscope showing the precise positions of the planets at the moment of your birth) can be a complicated business. Ordinarily it requires a mass of astronomical information and a lot of expertise. The good news, however, is that by visiting the dedicated website specially constructed to complement this book (see page 505), you can download your own personal birth chart with a few simple clicks of your mouse. There are a few simple pointers you need to bear in mind, however.

TIME AND PLACE OF BIRTH

To obtain the most accurate picture of your planetary personality, it is a huge advantage to know the precise time of your birth, or at least within 30 minutes. Regardless of where you were born, this needs to be in Greenwich Mean Time (GMT), the standard time measurement used by astrologers worldwide. If you were born in the UK, you must be careful not to use a time of birth based on British Summer Time, which since 1972 has been in operation between March and October. If you were born during this period you should deduct one hour from your birth time to arrive at the time in GMT. For the precise dates, and for details on how BST and GMT worked prior to 1972, please refer to the detailed table on converting Summer Time.

If you were born outside the UK, you also need to convert the time of your birth to GMT. If, for instance, you were born in New York, you need to add five hours. (Unless you were on an American Summer Time or Daylight Saving Time, in which case you need to check carefully the precise difference in times between GMT.) To help you do this, there is a table below showing the world's time

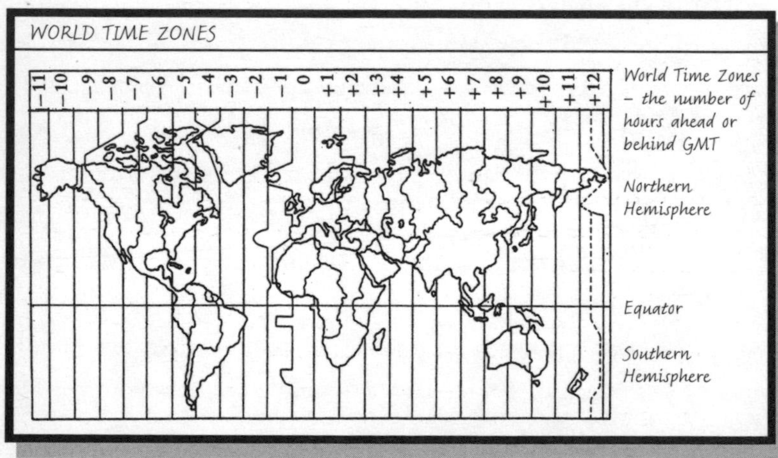

BRITISH SUMMER TIME					
1916	21 May to 1 Oct	1947	*1 Jan to 13 Apr	1982	28 Mar to 24 Oct
1917	8 Apr to 17 Sep	1947	*10 Aug to 2 Nov	1983	27 Mar to 23 Oct
1918	24 Mar to 30 Sep	1948	14 Mar to 31 Oct	1984	25 Mar to 28 Oct
1919	30 Mar to 29 Sep	1949	3 Apr to 30 Oct	1985	31 Mar to 27 Oct
1920	28 Mar to 25 Oct	1950	16 Apr to 22 Oct	1986	30 Mar to 26 Oct
1921	3 Apr to 3 Oct	1951	15 Apr to 21 Oct	1987	39 Mar to 25 Oct
1922	26 Mar to 8 Oct	1952	20 Apr to 26 Oct	1988	27 Mar to 23 Oct
1923	22 Apr to 16 Sep	1953	19 Apr to 4 Oct	1989	26 Mar to 29 Oct
1924	13 Apr to 21 Sep	1954	11 Apr to 3 Oct	1990	25 Mar to 29 Oct
1925	19 Apr to 4 Oct	1955	17 Apr to 2 Oct	1991	25 Mar to 28 Oct
1926	18 Apr to 3 Oct	1956	22 Apr to 7 Oct	1992	29 Mar to 25 Oct
1927	10 Apr to 2 Oct	1957	14 Apr to 6 Oct	1993	28 Mar to 24 Oct
1928	22 Apr to 7 Oct	1958	20 Apr to 5 Oct	1994	27 Mar to 23 Oct
1929	21 Apr to 6 Oct	1959	19 Apr to 4 Oct	1995	26 Mar to 29 Oct
1930	13 Apr to 5 Oct	1960	10 Apr to 2 Oct	1996	31 Mar to 27 Oct
1931	19 Apr to 4 Oct	1961	26 Mar to 29 Oct	1997	30 Mar to 26 Oct
1932	17 Apr to 2 Oct	1962	25 Mar to 28 Oct	1998	29 Mar to 25 Oct
1933	9 Apr to 8 Oct	1963	31 Mar to 27 Oct	1999	28 Mar to 24 Oct
1934	22 Apr to 7 Oct	1964	22 Mar to 25 Oct	2000	26 Mar to 29 Oct
1935	14 Apr to 6 Oct	1965	21 Mar to 24 Oct	2001	25 Mar to 28 Oct
1936	19 Apr to 4 Oct	1966	20 Mar to 23 Oct	2002	31 Mar to 27 Oct
1937	18 Apr to 3 Oct	1967	19 Mar to 29 Oct	2003	30 Mar to 26 Oct
1938	10 Apr to 2 Oct	1968	18 Feb to 31 Dec	2004	28 Mar to 31 Oct
1939	16 Apr to 19 Nov	1969	1 Jan to 31 Dec	2005	27 Mar to 30 Oct
1940	25 Feb to 31 Dec	1970	1 Jan to 31 Dec	2006	26 Mar to 29 Oct
1941	*1 Jan to 4 May	1971	1 Jan to 31 Oct	2007	25 Mar to 28 Oct
1941	*10 Aug to 31 Dec	1972	19 Mar to 29 Oct	2008	30 Mar to 26 Oct
1942	*1 Jan to 5 Apr	1973	18 Mar to 28 Oct	2009	29 Mar to 25 Oct
1942	*9 Aug to 31 Dec	1974	17 Mar to 27 Oct	2010	28 Mar to 31 Oct
1943	*1 Jan to 4 Apr	1975	16 Mar to 26 Oct	2011	27 Mar to 30 Oct
1943	*15 Aug to 31 Dec	1976	21 Mar to 24 Oct	2012	25 Mar to 28 Oct
1944	*1 Jan to 2 Apr	1977	20 Mar to 23 Oct	2013	31 Mar to 27 Oct
1944	*17 Dep to 31 Dec	1978	19 Mar to 29 Oct	2014	30 Mar to 26 Oct
1945	*1 Jan to 2 Apr	1979	18 Mar to 28 Oct	2015	29 Mar to 25 Oct
1945	*15 July to 7 Oct	1980	16 Mar to 26 Oct	2016	27 Mar to 30 Oct
1946	14 Apr to 6 Oct	1981	29 Mar to 25 Oct		

* see Double Summer Time table

DOUBLE SUMMER TIME IN THE UK					
1941	4 May to 10 Aug	1943	4 Apr to 15 Aug	1945	2 Apr to 15 July
1942	5 Apr to 9 Aug	1944	2 Apr to 17 Sep	1947	13 Apr to 10 Aug

Between 1941–45 and in 1947 between the following dates, Double Summer Time operated; this meant that the time was 2 hours ahead of GMT. So for births during these periods, deduct 2 hours from the birth time to convert it to GMT.

zones and the number of hours you need to add or subtract if you were born in a particular area.

Why do I need to know my precise birth time?

As I explained earlier, a horoscope is comparable to a stage play, in which your life is the subject. We need three elements to stage this production: the planets, the zodiac and the houses. It is the latter that is affected by the lack of a precise birth time. Without it, we will not be able to calculate the Ascendant, and without the Ascendant we cannot accurately mark out the houses. (As an example, a rising sign can change one degree every four minutes. If your birth time is an hour out, that means your Ascendant could be as much as 15 degrees out – a huge discrepancy.)

The bottom line is that in the absence of an accurate birth time, you will get a very different horoscope. It will still be a very insightful one: we will be able to interpret the positions of the planets in the signs and their aspects, which is still an advance on just the Sun sign, but we will not be able to analyze the positions of the planets in the houses. Nor will we be able to look at the Angles or the aspects of the fast-moving Moon.

We will have a performance, and a very good one, but we will be missing much of our background scenery and some of our most important players too (or some players might have to appear in the buff!). So it is important you do all you can to get your birth time.

What if I don't know my time of birth?

Almost everyone knows their date and place of birth. Not all of us know the precise time of our birth, however. Fortunately for people born in certain parts of the UK, such as Scotland and Northern Ireland, your birth certificate should record the information. This is the case in many other countries, including the United States. If you were born in England or Wales, however, the time of birth is not generally recorded. If you were born here and are unsure of your precise birth time, your first step should be to ring your parents. Your mother, in particular, is likely to know the time you arrived in the world. (She was the one doing all the hard work, remember!) If she is not around or cannot remember, try looking at clippings books for announcements in newspapers, which often name the precise time of birth.

If this fails, your next port of call should be the hospital or maternity home where you were born. It is a statutory obligation for medical authorities to record every detail of a birth. Even if the hospital no longer exists, approach the health authority, which should be the custodians of the old hospital records. I know many people who, having convinced themselves they would never ever find their true birth time, were surprised when a letter with the exact details popped through the letterbox, courtesy of their local health authority. One tip they've passed on to me is that a small contribution to the hospital or the authority's charity seems to help the process move along more quickly somehow!

If, however, even this fails to turn up your birth time, there is one other possibility. There are a number of specialist astrologers who are experts in the art of 'rectification'. They conduct a detailed interview with their clients in which they reconstruct a map of the major events in their lives. They then use this map to work backwards to arrive at the most accurate assessment they can give of a birth time. There are some exceptionally good professionals around these days, many of them contactable through the Internet, via astrological magazines or the British Astrological Psychic Society. They may, in the end, be your answer.

INTERPRETING YOUR CHART

You are probably now staring at your own personalized birth chart with a mixture of excitement and mild panic. It looks like a collection of hieroglyphics and squiggles. Utterly meaningless. The first

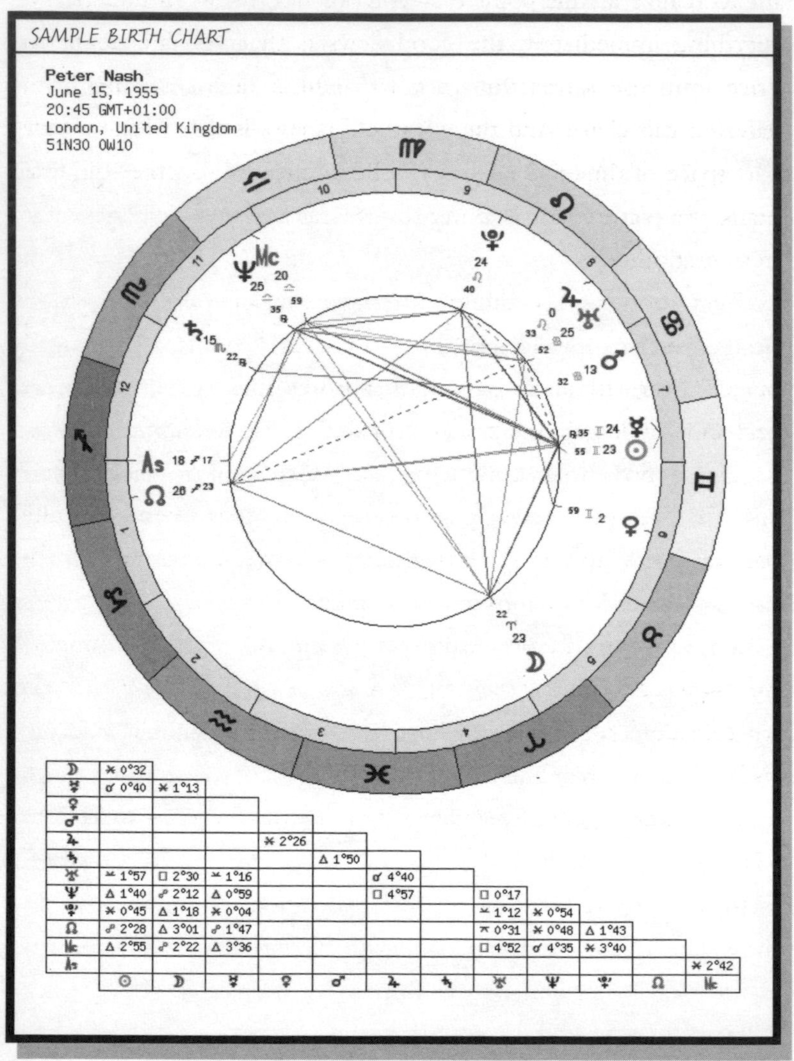

thing to say is DON'T BE PUT OFF. I know it all looks very confusing and complicated, but it really isn't. Astrology is an endlessly interesting science, with an infinite number of possibilities. I've spent the past 40-plus years immersing myself in its study, and I am still learning something new every day. So although it's important to realize at this point that you are not going to understand everything immediately, the good news is that you are going to derive immense satisfaction, not to mention a lot of fun, from analyzing this chart. And the even better news is that within a very short space of time indeed you will begin piecing together the first details of a picture that is going to grow clearer and clearer as your interpretation goes on.

Very soon this seemingly meaningless collection of waves and lines is going to transform itself into an easy-to-read road map of yourself. Bear with me as I guide you through the basics of the birth chart and you'll soon see it is all very logical and straightforward.

Please note that the birth charts used in this book (and provided via the dedicated website that has been specially constructed to go with this book) include slightly more detailed information than is covered in this book. Specifically, the wheels include a marking for the Moon's north node, whilst the table of aspects includes other, minor aspects. They do not need to be taken into consideration for the purpose of following and understanding this book.

So now let's get down to the nitty-gritty of exploring Planet You.

Finding Your Way Around the Birth Chart – A Guide

OUTER RIM

The Ascendant

You will see that the outer rim of the wheel is divided into 12 sections, much like a clock. Each of the dozen, 30-degree sections corresponds to a sign of the zodiac. The signs are arranged according to which of them was in the Ascendant at the time of birth. They always travel ANTI-clockwise (or widdershins) from the Ascending sign. For instance, Libra rising will put Scorpio as ruler of the 2nd house. The exact position of the sign rising in the east at this point (expressed by the letters Asc. and a number of degrees) marks 9 o'clock precisely on the clock. So, for instance, if this was Aries, the next sign moving anti-clockwise would be Taurus, then Gemini and so on, ending with Pisces at 10 o'clock.

The Descendant

Directly opposite the Ascendant is the Descendant. This is easy to work out: if you are Taurus rising, then your Descendant is Scorpio. It is indicative of the kind of person you are drawn or attracted to.

The Midheaven

As you'll remember, the Midheaven is the symbolic point in the sky that was directly overhead at the time of birth – your High Noon sign. It is a powerful guide to your aspirations and the image you project to the world at large. This is marked with the letters MC (from the Latin *medium coeli*), along with the number of degrees it stands within its sign of the zodiac.

The Nadir

The symbol of our roots and formative years, this is exactly opposite the Midheaven. So you will see it 180 degrees away from the MC, marked IC (from the Latin *immum coeli*), again with the number of degrees marked alongside it.

The Houses

On the inner edge of the outer rim you will see the chart has also been subdivided into 12 sections, numbered from 1 to 12. These sections represent the houses, each one representing a different area of your life. The houses can be complicated due to the many house systems in use among astrologers worldwide. I am using the Equal House system, on which I learned astrology as a young man. The Equal House system is dead easy for beginners to understand.

INSIDE THE OUTER RIM

The Planetary Positions

In compiling your personal chart, I have used detailed astronomical tables of planetary positions to mark the exact placements of the ten heavenly bodies at the time of birth. These have been marked inside the wheel. You will see all ten planets (in the form of their, almost!, familiar glyphs) sitting in their positions within the outer rim. Again, each one will be marked with the number of degrees they are within their sign of the zodiac (always counting anti-clockwise, remember).

TABLE OF ASPECTS

The second component of your chart is the triangular box at the bottom left corner. This represents the aspects your planets make with each other. Again it all looks rather daunting at first, but by taking time to look at it carefully you will soon see it is straightforward to read.

The symbols for each of the five aspects are:

Conjunction	☌
Sextile	⚹
Square	□
Trine	△
Opposition	☍

The aspects in colour: positive, negative and variable planets

As you look at the chart you will see each aspect is coloured according to whether it is positive (harmonious or GREEN), negative (challenging or RED), or variable (neutral or PURPLE). By taking each of the planetary symbols lined along the bottom of the triangle and running your finger upward along the column you can work out which are well aspected and which are not. Start with the Sun – as is normal, at the left of the bottom row – then work your way along through the Moon and Mercury until you reach Neptune and Pluto, making a note of each aspect. Note, too, the overall dominant colours of each column. This is going to tell you whether overall you have a positive, negative or unaspected planet.

Note: The aspects are also marked within the wheel itself by lines joining the aspected planets. These lines too are in the positive, negative and variable colours, green, red and purple. The lines help illustrate deeper relationships and meanings to the chart as well. For instance, if there is a relationship between three planets so that the first is trine to the second, the second is trine to the third and the third is trine to the first, this will form a large equilateral triangle. This aspect is known as a grand trine and infers that the planets involved have an even deeper influence.

Okay, that's the basic set up of the chart you have in front of you. It's now time for you to start analyzing it. Now, again, don't worry (not even if you're Cancerian!), we will be going through everything step-by-step. By the time you've taken the last of those steps you will be ready to create a brand new you, ready to take on the world.

FOUR

YOU CAN *Change* YOUR LIFE

Interpreting Your Chart

Six Steps to Self-Knowledge:

THE STEP-BY-STEP GUIDE TO INTERPRETING YOUR BIRTH CHART

Okay, you've had a good introductory look at your chart. You understand what's what. It's time to interpret the information it contains. The pages that follow lay out the hundreds of possible permutations your chart may contain. There is a section on each of the planetary placements, each of the Ascendants and Midheavens and all of the potential major aspects you may have in your chart.

As you will see, the pages that follow are crammed with information. But when you extract the information that is relevant to you and put it together, it will give you a clear picture of a complete astrological personality. Picking your way through this will take some time. And it is best to do this in a simple, straightforward manner. Astrologically, the Sun and Moon are known as 'the lights', which is why, along with the Ascendant, they are usually the first areas you take into account. From there you follow through the rest of the planets and the aspects. As you go through each, make a note of each piece of information you extract along the way. By the time you've worked your way through the list, a whole fresh, new insight into your inner self will have begun to take shape.

1. Place your Sun

Look where the Sun falls in your natal chart. Make a note of the sign and the house it is situated in. Now look at the table of aspects. Run your finger along the column for the Sun and make a note of its aspects. See which colour dominates. If it is green you have a positive Sun. If it is red you have a negative one. If purple dominates it is neutral, so you have a mix of positive and negative qualities. Having done this, turn to the section on Sun placings (pages 84–118). Read the introduction, then look up the section relevant to your Sun placing. If you have a negative Sun, read the advice on how to overcome this.

2. Place your Moon

Look where the Moon falls in your natal chart. Make a note of the sign and the house it falls in. Look at the table of aspects. Run your finger along the column for the Moon and make a note of its aspects. Look at which colour dominates. If it is green you have a positive Moon. If it is red you have a negative one. If purple dominates it is neutral, so you have a mix of positive and negative qualities. Having done this, turn to the section on the Moon's placings (pages 118–150). Read the introduction, then look up the section relevant to your placings. If you have a negative Moon, read the advice on how to overcome this.

3. Look at your Ascendant and Midheaven

Look at where your Ascendant and Midheaven are placed in your chart. Then turn to the section on interpreting them and read the introduction (page 150). Then turn to the relevant section on your placing.

4. Place your planets, from Mercury to Pluto

Look where the each of the remaining eight planets are placed in your chart. Make a note of the sign and the house each one falls in. Then, once again, use the table of aspects to see which colour dominates with each planet. Remember reds indicate a negative planet, green a positive one. Then, one by one, read each of the sections on placing the planets (pages 165–321). Make sure to read the introduction before reading the relevant section on your placement.

5. Read your aspects

Look at the table of aspects and make a note of each conjunction, sextile, square, trine and opposition that is marked there. (If you can't remember the symbols, turn back to the section introducing the aspects earlier in the book on page 66.). Then turn to the section on how to use the good and bad elements of the aspects. From there, go on to read the relevant section on each of your personal aspects (pages 321–459).

6. Look at your 'missing' planet

Your chart may indicate a lack of the influence of one particular planet. To check this, look once more at the table of aspects. You may find that one, or perhaps more, planets don't have any aspects in your chart. This is significant and you should read the sections on the relevant planet or planets. Read also the case studies at the back of the book to give you an idea of how the different planets play a role in different people's lives. As you do so, think about its role in moulding a personality and think about how that role might be applied in your own life.

Placing Your Planets: the Sun

The Sun is one of the most important components of Planet You. He is the very core of you, your true self. By looking at the placement of the Sun in your personal solar system, you gain a real insight into your essential nature. He looks at the heart of you and tells you how creative you are, how you express yourself and your ego. Because the Sun rules Leo, it is particularly powerful if you have the Sun or Ascendant in this sign. Equally he burns with a radiance in Leo's house, the 5th.

POSITIVE AND NEGATIVE SUN

As with all the planets, it is possible to have a positive, negative or neutral quality to your placement. If, looking at your aspects chart, you see more green, yours is a positive Sun. If, on the other hand, you have more red aspects, this means you have a more dangerous Sun. Purple aspects or an equal amount of red and green gives a more neutral solar energy – in which case you need to be aware of both the positive and negative sides of the Sun.

SUN IN ARIES OR 1ST HOUSE

The first sign in the zodiac, Aries represents the emerging ego, the child within you. So it should be no real surprise for you to discover that there are many childlike aspects to someone who has their Sun placed here.

Firstly, you have an assertive, impulsive and sometimes impetuous energy. Like a child let loose in a playground, you are usually overflowing with enthusiasm and get-up-and-go. You are also so busy charging at life that you sometimes forget to look after yourself and can be accident-prone. Your childlike innocence can get you into trouble too as it makes you too trusting and liable to be at the mercy of more manipulative people. And your devil-may-care ego also means that you can be self-centred.

On the more positive side, you are highly competitive, sporty and have a strong need to show the entire world what you are capable of doing. You can get extremely frustrated and impatient if you are denied this opportunity. It is then that you show the typical Arian anger, blowing your short fuse spectacularly. Fortunately, your explosions don't last long and tend to be quickly forgotten.

If you have a positive Sun in Aries or the 1st house

You understand your vitality can light up a room but you use that asset sensibly and wisely. Unlike someone with a negative Sun in Aries, you have the inbuilt discipline and self-control to go after one thing at a time, which is the secret of success. You know that other people's support is important if you are going to achieve your ambitions, so you use your sexy charm to win allies. You will aim and fire at the right time. Your health is usually strong and robust and creatively you are full of confidence and enterprise.

If you have a negative Sun in Aries or the 1st house

You have a real tendency to want to be centre-stage. Like the Sun itself, you want everyone to bask in your undoubted brilliance and energy. You will do all you can to take the leading role, even if you are the last to arrive on stage. Whether it is entering a room, a bar or restaurant, starting a job, whatever it is, you want to make an impact, you want to be noticed. Now some may enjoy this, they may find you sexy, vital and dynamic. However, after a while it will wear off and people will begin to ask themselves, 'My god, who does this person think they are? Do they think they're god's gift?' If you are denied the attention you seek, things can turn nasty. If you are a woman, you can be seen as loud, raucous and gauche, but whoever you are, you can behave like that archetypal, wayward teenager, Harry Enfield's Kevin, living up to that phrase, 'Throwing the toys out of the pram'. You always want your way and if you don't get it, heaven help everyone around you.

Your sometimes overactive nature also means that you tend to want to do several things at the same time and end up failing to do any of them properly. You become a Jack-of-all-trades and a master of none of them. You can wear yourself to a frazzle running out of energy – you are good for a sprint but rarely a marathon. Healthwise, look after your blood count and watch out for wear and tear on your muscles.

How to overcome a negative Sun in Aries or the 1st house

You must remember that Aries is the least evolved of the solar placings. It is the emerging ego, after all. A good way to approach a negative side in any sign within your birth chart is to look at the polar sign, the one directly opposite on the horoscope. In this case it is Libra. One way for you to overcome your negative Sun in Aries is to draw on the even-handed, diplomatic nature of the person who has their Sun in Libra. The key is self-control and realizing that you are not the only person on the stage. You need to realize there has to be give and take, compromise, sharing and caring.

Famous Sun in Aries: Mariah Carey, Russell Crowe, Charlie Chaplin, Ewan McGregor, Reese Witherspoon, Sarah Jessica Parker, Alec Guinness, Andrew Lloyd Webber, Elton John, Diana Ross, Steve McQueen, Leonard Nimoy, Eric Clapton, Al Gore, Maya Angelou, Colin Powell, Marlon Brando, Emma Thompson, Bette Davis, Victoria 'Posh Spice' Beckham, Eddie Murphy.

SUN IN TAURUS OR 2ND HOUSE

If you have your Sun in Taurus, you are one of the world's solid citizens. You are a safe pair of hands, a reliable person with a straight-forward, down-to-earth attitude to life. This makes you popular because there's nothing more appealing in a friend than reliability. People see that you are someone who will always be there for them. They also know where they stand with you, which makes you even more popular. Because of this secure, safe side of your nature, you regard financial security as hugely important. You like to keep money saved away for rainy days and are careful about the way you spend your money. With Venus as your ruling planet, however, you do like spending that money on life's luxuries. You enjoy nothing more than pampering yourself and can pay the price for that in terms of weight and general fitness as you are one of the less sporty Sun signs. Never forget self-worth. Valuing your own talents, skills and abilities is very important as not everything can be counted in cash or currency. Wealth-creation comes from using your creative self.

If you have a positive Sun in Taurus or the 2nd house

You love having beautiful things (and people) around you, but you are not so materialistic that you can't see that happiness is worth more than just possessions. You are concerned with what you can offer to people who are worse off than you. I once knew a lady who had an extreme example of this placing. She was a healer and she lived in near-poverty because she spent so much time looking after others. She wouldn't take money for anything but she was as happy as could be. Her self-worth was more important to her than anything. Of course, what happened was that people she'd helped would find out that she didn't have much and would give her wonderful gifts. She wasn't rich in the conventional sense of that word, but in terms of respect and friendship and self-worth, she was one of the wealthiest people I know. So a positive Sun in Taurus can start off as poor as a church mouse financially, but end up rich in many other ways.

If you have a negative Sun in Taurus or the 2nd house

Taurus is the sign of money and it rules your life. You are totally dependant on how much you own or how much you are worth. And you never think you have enough on a material level. As a result of this, you don't take enough account of the feelings of other people. You don't even take into account your own feelings because all you are wondering is how you can make more money! You can be covetous and envious if someone has more than you.

You have little concept or interest in self-worth. Instead you put a price tag on everything. This may cause you problems in your personal life because you may marry for money or convenience rather than love. You can be very possessive as well because, again, everything is about ownership. You are like the spoilt child who runs around saying, 'That's mine.'

How to overcome a negative Sun in Taurus or the 2nd house

You have to realize that, as the ancient wisdom says, it is sometimes better to give than receive. You need to appreciate that giving to others rather than grabbing everything for yourself can be rewarding too. You also have to learn that self-worth isn't actually measured in monetary or material terms. Okay, so you may have a fabulous job, house and lifestyle, the newest car and smartest clothes, but the fact is the person down the road with the ordinary job, the beaten-up car and the rundown house may just well be a happier, more fulfilled person than you. Money really isn't everything.

Famous Sun in Taurus: Queen Elizabeth II, George Clooney, Fred Astaire, Barbra Streisand, Jack Nicholson, Uma Thurman, Stevie Wonder, Renee Zellweger, Al Pacino, Shirley MacLaine, Daniel Day Lewis, Liberace, Saddam Hussein, Adolf Hitler, Andre Agassi, Audrey Hepburn, Katharine Hepburn, James Brown, Tony Blair, George Lucas, Cher, Pierce Brosnan, David Beckham.

SUN IN GEMINI OR 3RD HOUSE

If you have your Sun placed in Gemini, then like Mercury, the ruler of this sign of the zodiac, you are a quicksilver soul. Your mind works at an amazing speed, leaping around impatiently from place to place. You have a real fear of being bored, which means you are constantly flitting from one subject to the next or juggling more than one thing at a time. You might read a book and watch TV at the same time, or chat on the phone while surfing the Internet simultaneously. Your butterfly brain can cope with this quite easily. In fact, it's a safe bet that you've skipped straight to this section of the book rather than reading what you think was the boring introductory bit! Because of this need for stimulation, you are not really suited to an office-based job, stuck behind the same desk, day in, day out. To you this would seem like a prison sentence. For you it is better to work when you feel like it, to be your own boss.

If you have a positive Sun in Gemini or the 3rd house

You understand the scattergun nature of your mind, aware that you are someone who needs to be doing lots of different things, switching from one thing to another when duty calls. As Mercury is the planet of communications, you are highly articulate, with a real gift for words. This makes you a natural for jobs like journalism, PR or sales. With your Sun in Gemini, you could sell sand to the Arabs!

Community matters interest you and the more involved you can become locally, the better, as you can come up with great ideas for crusades or fundraising with a neighbourhood thrust. You love to learn, are curious and inquisitive and often find that once you start, you can't stop. Travel of any kind, but particularly short trips, are great for mental inspiration and you take to the high road (or the low) as often as you can. Not only is it educational, but it also keeps you out of mischief.

If you have a negative Sun in Gemini or the 3rd house

You will suffer from the worst aspects of this sign's flibbertigibbet personality. For instance, your impatient, ever-busy nature means you are all over the place. You just can't sit still. You are brilliant but your boredom threshold is zero with the result that you are constantly going off at a tangent. Your surroundings can be a total mess and if they're not, your mind is! (This is why negative Geminis are constantly on the phone or the move. They can't concentrate their minds, they're bored so they ring someone up and bother them.) Your most annoying trait, certainly to others, is that you are incapable of finishing anything, and after making arrangements, you let people down.

You can also be intolerant of people whose mind doesn't work as quickly as yours. You can be gobby, trite and shallow, leading a transient lifestyle. You also have a tendency to get so wrapped up in things that you fail to eat. People with Sun in Gemini tend to be highly strung, living off their nerves – another reason they sometimes don't eat properly.

Ideas come naturally to you. But sticking with them when the initial excitement has waned is another matter. You will also refuse to be held accountable and use your gift for talking Blarney to get out of a fix. Because your ruling planet has one side permanently dark and the other light, a negative Gemini is in the dark and keeps everybody else in the dark. This means you are prone to lying, deceiving, withholding information and cheating so as to cover your tracks.

How to overcome a negative Sun in Gemini or the 3rd house

The problem with a negative Sun here is that you try to do too much. You need to tap into the cleverness of a positive Gemini Sun who understands priorities. Because you are constantly thinking, you need a career that will consistently stimulate your mind. Choose something that has to do with writing, researching or communication. Travel, too, is great because you keep yourself on your toes. To complement this, you should have a second string that capitalizes on these learning experiences. If you travel a lot, teaching might be a fine second job, allowing you to broadcast your experiences whilst keeping you on the cerebral straight and narrow at the same time. Whatever it is you do, it needs to be conversational. You must be able to reach out and communicate at all times. You must never be put in solitary confinement, for that would be a fate worse than death!

The other key thing is being honest. When you know you have done something wrong, don't cover up your errors or blame them on others. Hold your hand up and declare *mea culpa*. That way you will win the respect and support of people who will be mighty impressed by your honesty.

Famous Sun in Gemini: Johnny Depp, Elizabeth Hurley, Angelina Jolie, Nicole Kidman, Morgan Freeman, Annette Bening, Judy Garland, Bob Dylan, Mike Myers, Kylie Minogue, John F. Kennedy, Rupert Everett, Clint Eastwood, Marilyn Monroe, Joan Rivers, Tom Jones, Paul McCartney, Errol Flynn, Venus Williams, Steffi Graf, Prince, Melanie 'Scary Spice' Brown.

SUN IN CANCER OR 4TH HOUSE

I am sure it won't come as a shock to learn that if you have your Sun in Cancer, you are ruled by your feelings and emotions. Your ruling planet is, after all, the Moon, the planet that reflects the mood of a person or situation around her rather than creating them for herself. Therefore you're very sensitive. You can easily be hurt by what, to others, might seem like the smallest barbed comment. Just as the Moon governs the ebbs and flows of the oceans, so she affects the highs and lows of your emotional tides.

Like the crab that is the symbol of Cancer, your home is of huge importance to you. You need to know you have somewhere safe and secure to return to each time you leave. Take great care to make sure that home is as comfortable and relaxing an environment as possible.

Because emotional security is so vital to you, you surround yourself with the familiar – and the familial. This emotional, family-oriented nature makes you a very maternal or nurturing person. There's nothing you enjoy more than entertaining your nearest and dearest. You love connections with the past, whether it is memories or other mementoes of nostalgia. You can be fervently patriotic for your home town or country. All of this adds to your sense of belonging.

If you have a positive Sun in Cancer or the 4th house

You are a great fun person with a hearty belly laugh and an ability to lift others. You are a protective, caring, compassionate and considerate soul. You have a great gift for listening to others and their troubles as well. You are a real homemaker, and enjoy nothing more than improving your domestic scene to make it as cosy and comfortable as you like it. The same applies in a work situation. If you are a positive Cancerian you will turn the office into a family, bringing in home-baked goodies or organizing social get-togethers back at your place. And always in these situations it is how much others enjoy themselves that governs how happy you are. Like the Moon, your pleasure is reflected in the pleasure of others. You have an innate interest in your family tree, links with the past, history and the days of yore. You find it difficult to either forgive or forget. Yes, even though you're positive, we all have some faults!

If you have a negative Sun in Cancer or the 4th house

You can be moody, cranky and sulky, taking offence from remarks where no offence was intended. People will be able to spot you instantly because you will look as though you're about to cry with shyness. You are painfully timid and, like the crab, walk sideways around contentious situations because you so hate confrontation.

Despite this, you will carp, complain and moan about someone rather than tell them to their face what you really think. At other times you will tell them but they will return your fire and you will spend the rest of your life remembering the slight – conveniently forgetting you started it.

You are very clannish; you cling onto the family like a child clutching its mother's apron strings. Men, especially, tend to remain living with their mothers well into adulthood or even worse, compare the love of their life with their mother! Imagine what that does for happy adult families!

Because you place such weight on relationships, when you fall for someone you really fall for them. This makes it really difficult for you to end relationships. You would rather cling on in an unhappy relationship than face the prospect of breaking up the domestic set-up, no matter how bad for you it might be in emotional terms. You can be a drudge and a doormat, never really getting a life of your own.

How to overcome a negative Sun in Cancer or the 4th house

You have to break away from the familial ties. Your parents or minders aren't going to be around forever. If you don't become independent, you are going to be totally lost when they do leave. This does not mean never seeing relatives or those you know again, it simply means you need to broaden out your social circle, make new friends, perhaps by taking up a hobby or joining a club of some kind. This is, in the end, only an extension of the family, but it is an extended community in which you are going to expand and spread your wings. Get involved with research into where you live, the house, your name, anything that allows you to strengthen those ties that give you a continuity with history. Also, stop being so defensive. Unless you do, people will be afraid to say anything in case you bite their head off, and if you want to be part of 'the gang' then you've got to take the rough with the smooth and stop taking everything so personally. It isn't always about you, you know!

Famous Sun in Cancer: Tom Hanks, Meryl Streep, Princess Diana, George W. Bush, George Michael, Pamela Anderson, Tom Cruise, Tom Stoppard, the Dalai Lama, Sylvester Stallone, Ringo Starr, Giorgio Armani, Harrison Ford, Bill Cosby, David Hasselhoff, Carlos Santana, Robin Williams, Anna Friel, Liv Tyler, Nelson Mandela, Tobey Maguire, Camilla Parker Bowles.

SUN IN LEO OR 5TH HOUSE

Leo is a royal sign – the symbol is the lion and the ruling planet is the Sun himself. So it is no surprise that if you have your Sun in Leo, you are someone who loves to be noticed. Your rather regal demeanour helps you achieve this; in fact, it is hard not to notice you, even in the largest of crowds. You are someone who wants to lead rather than follow. Because you are a Fire sign, you can get pretty hoity-toity if you are not allowed to do this. You can also get extremely frustrated if you can't express your supreme creative energy in the way you want. The strength of the Sun in your planetary life means that you are capable of great performances in music, dancing, acting and general entertainment. You exude the 'X' factor.

You are in an eternal search for your heart's desire. When it comes to matters of the heart, you thrive on being in love. If you haven't got anyone in your amorous life, you are like a pussy with a poorly paw. You have a very strong parental instinct and are highly attuned to caring for your children, or indeed anyone you take under your big-hearted wing.

As the monarch of the zodiac, you pride yourself on your good taste and are very picky about quality and standing. Similarly, when it comes to your career, you need a job that will deliver the status, kudos and rewards that you expect. You definitely prefer being a big fish in a small pond rather than a minnow indistinguishable from the masses in a big pond.

If you have a positive Sun in Leo or the 5th house

You are highly creative, enterprising and know precisely what you want in life. You will be a person who makes others feel good and special. But you will look at all enterprising avenues to secure your heart's desire. Anywhere where the limelight blazes down on you is right up your street, but you also appreciate the talents and abilities of other people as well as your own. This means that as a positive Sun in Leo, you make loyal, lifelong friends, which in turn means you will always have the audience that appreciates you. When it comes to your affairs of the heart you know how to treat your beloved. You are the epitome of the saying 'do as you would be done by'. Nothing is too much trouble.

You are a flirt and enjoy the thrill of the chase but you still prefer to choose a mate for life. You hope your children will be a chip off the old block but if you can't have any of your own, you'll adopt or foster, and treat them as though they were. And if that's not possible, you'll become a surrogate mum or dad to a friend or relative's child.

If you have a negative Sun in Leo or the 5th house

Does a fur coat and no knickers ring a bell?! You like to be the centre of attention and will do it in an outrageous way, just like your polar sign of Aquarius. Like the Sun, you want to be noticed and made a fuss of. This egocentric streak means you don't give a tinker's cuss about other people. It's that classic line comedians come out with. 'Anyhow that's enough of me talking about myself, what do you think about me.' It's about you, you, you. It is the sign of the massive ego, after all.

This is not to say that a negative Leo isn't a lot of fun, or that you can't be extremely talented and entertaining. It's just that after a while the 'look at me' act does begin to turn sour. You can become something of a one-trick pony, and you don't see that for a show to work you need other people providing support acts. You also need a rapturous audience.

You can spoil yourself in love with a myriad of wee trysts and affairs, expecting your partner to turn a blind eye. What's sauce for the goose! As for your children, you end up in competition with them; the minute they are born they are grabbing a piece of the attention action. Let's face it – when it comes to attention-seeking, nobody does it better than you.

How to overcome a negative Sun in Leo or the 5th house

The first thing you must do is accept that sometimes taking a back seat can be illuminating and rewarding. If it's in a love affair, a friendship or a business relationship, eradicate the idea that you have to steal centre-stage all the time. You will learn more and have perhaps just as much, even greater, influence by looking and taking everything in.

Stand still for a moment every now and again and realize that even though you have your talents, so, too, do other people. Appreciate that others are good at what they do as well, even if they aren't as entertaining or effective as you. To avoid becoming the star that folks tire of, spread yourself around a bit, diversify with your talents and your undoubted radiance will be seen by a bigger and wider public. Try fresh creative initiatives and be interested in other people. You will feel so much better for it, and people will appreciate that you are multi-talented and faceted – it is this what makes you such a class act.

Famous Sun in Leo: Napoleon Bonaparte, Madonna, Jennifer Lopez, Ben Affleck, Jacqueline Kennedy Onassis, Matt LeBlanc, Monica Lewinsky, Bill Clinton, Kevin Spacey, Mick Jagger, Arnold Schwarzenegger, Sandra Bullock, Magic Johnson, Dustin Hoffman, Lucille Ball, Whitney Houston, Robert De Niro, Sean Penn, Robert Redford, Pete Sampras, Halle Berry, Geri Halliwell, Martin Sheen.

SUN IN VIRGO OR 6TH HOUSE

Your Sun is in the sign of health and service, so your greatest talent is organizing. You might well make a brilliant secretary or PA. Whatever you do you seem to have a brain with a capacity to file things away and bring them out when you need them. If working in a group, whether it be at home or in the office, you will be at the very heart of the operation, always there to help things tick over.

Your added gift for service might show itself in the medical professions in particular because Virgos have a great interest in the human body, especially their own. You are a walking medical encyclopaedia and aren't above inventing an ailment for yourself when you need a little tea and sympathy.

Tidiness is something that is important to you at home and at work, and also when it comes to the body and matters of hygiene. You like everything and everyone to be ship-shape and Bristol fashion, at least in your terms. Even if your place looks like a tip, you will argue that *you* still know where everything is.

You are ruled by Mercury, the planet of communication and the mind, the planet you share with Gemini, but being an Earth sign, you tend to focus your intellect on the practical and the precise, the more methodical, matter-of-fact, even mundane, aspects of life.

However, despite having so much going for you, you are not someone to brag about your abilities – quite the opposite, in fact. You are modest and unassuming, quite content in the knowledge that everyone knows you are the lynchpin of things and without you things will rarely flow or function.

If you have a positive Sun in Virgo or the 6th house

Take another look at what you've just read and you should see yourself mirrored there in so many ways. The key thing here is that you can highlight the positive parts as they will undoubtedly be you to a 'T'.

To you, the most important thing is that you feel of use, that whatever you do in life should be worthwhile. With your itchy fingers, you hate to be a spare part or just hanging around. You aren't averse to hard work; in fact, you are as keen as mustard to throw yourself in the middle of a muddle and sort it out. You are a perfectionist and a dealer in detail. You are fastidious, ethical and full of good advice and patience. Travel and business link together nicely for you. If you play your part at the local education centre or university, whether as a lecturer or student, you are happy lurking around libraries, gaining more knowledge. Hygiene is number one on your list of credentials and that goes for everyone else, too; you like people to be as clean as a whistle outside and in and won't hesitate in speaking your mind frankly and honestly.

If you have a negative Sun in Virgo or the 6th house

Your greatest failing is that you are so critical of people. You are a real pedant, capable of driving others crazy with your constant nitpicking and analytical approach. This stems from your need for precision and tidiness, for everything to be organized and in its place. You, unfortunately, see yourself as being perfect, and the fact that not everyone is like you is hard to handle. You can be extremely intolerant of other people's peccadilloes and foibles. And because you have Mercury's gift of the gab, when you let people know this, as you far too often do, you can do so in language that can cut to the quick. You can be very sarcastic and caustic, sending out a sting like a wasp.

This narrow-mindedness can appear in other ways. You can be puritanical and bigoted because you are so concerned with your own tiny little bit of space that you can't see the big picture. You can also get so wrapped up in detail that you don't see the wood for the trees. For instance, if you have a letter to write, you will spend ages getting it just right, doing draft after draft until it is perfect. But by the time you have got it just the way you want it, word-perfect with every colon and semi-colon in the right place, you've missed the deadline. You lose track of time and priority.

How to overcome a negative Sun in Virgo or the 6th house

Your fixation with having everything in apple pie order has to be confronted. You must realize this is bordering on an obsessive compulsive disorder, which given this is the sign of hygiene, can lead to all sorts of strange and peculiar behaviour. Learn to chill out, be less anal about things and let life be slightly less than perfect every now and again. Psychologically, you have to be very organized about things. Making lists is a very Virgo trait, and should be used in a positive way. Once you learn to focus on the broad canvas, you can go back and touch up the detail. If you have a task to fulfil, give yourself a time limit and do it within that frame, regardless of what happens. You must learn to distinguish between the petty things and the important things. Once you do then you are halfway to delegating your work to people who may not be as good as you. (Or perhaps they are and that's the problem?) Either way, so what? It will give you more time to play.

Famous Sun in Virgo: Hugh Grant, Peter Sellers, Lance Armstrong, Freddie Mercury, Cameron Diaz, Sean Connery, Claudia Schiffer, Van Morrison, Keanu Reeves, Adam Sandler, Tommy Lee Jones, River Phoenix, Lauren Bacall, Chrissie Hynde, Raquel Welch, Sophia Loren, Stephen King, Bill Murray, Jeremy Irons, Macaulay Culkin, Charlie Sheen.

SUN IN LIBRA OR 7TH HOUSE

Your sign is the sign of the scales and balance is everything to you. You could work for the diplomatic service, so good are you at being even-handed and seeing both sides of every situation. This quality provides a great sense of justice and fair play. You can't abide selfishness or unfairness in people and will go to great lengths to find the truth.

Because partnerships are life-blood to you, you will do whatever is necessary to preserve the status quo and keep everyone happy. Conflict is something you hate – you would rather carry the can and take the blame for something that isn't your fault than have an argument. Confrontations aren't your scene, unless you have a negative Sun in Libra, then watch you go!

With Venus as your planetary ruler, beauty in all its forms is a feast for your eyes and heart. You enjoy life's luxuries and are drawn to people and places whose outward appearance, courtesy and charm are music to your ears.

If you have a positive Sun in Libra or the 7th house

A positive Sun in Libra takes a leaf out of their polar sign, Aries. You are someone who is decisive about what you want in life. And, because you are a Venusian, what you want in general is anything that brings you the best on offer. Of course, nothing brings you more enjoyment than those you love and if you have a partner who is also a buddy, what could be better. You are great at supporting friends, enjoying an active social life or being there for them when they need you. You are aware one of your most irresistible assets is your grace and charm, and you know exactly how to use it. You are a master at getting what you want by stealth, a mistress of using the iron fist in the velvet glove. A permanent partnership is what you seek more than anything and because you are brilliant at finding equilibrium in everything, you get the same with your relationships. If you don't, you're not afraid to speak up.

If you have a negative Sun in Libra or the 7th house

If you have this placing, your theme song might be that old classic from the musical *Oklahoma*: 'I'm just a girl (or boy) who can't say No'. You are incapable of making a decision, let alone sticking to it. And you want to please everyone so much you can't say 'No' to what they ask, so then they take liberties with you. Prevarication and vacillation are your middle names. The positive Libran Sun means you weigh things up carefully before making a decision but strike once that decision has been made, but the negative side means you can't stop juggling the pros and cons. You want everything to be 50–50, but of course life isn't like that and your mind is in a constant state of flux as a result. You can be infuriating in this respect. Getting you to make a decision can take days, weeks, months, even years. And, as we all know, he or she who hesitates is usually lost.

Your need to be in a relationship can eclipse everything else in your life. So great is your fear of being alone that you would rather stay in a relationship that is seriously flawed than make the break you know is needed. You place such great store in having a partner, you tend to idealize the one you are with, placing them on a pedestal from which, ultimately, they are bound to fall.

You bother much too much about what other people think. You can be in a room of 100 people, 99 of whom think you are wonderful, but one of whom doesn't. You will spend the entire evening trying to persuade that one individual to like you rather than enjoying the company of the other 99 who think you are gorgeous.

How to overcome a negative Sun in Libra or the 7th house

Remember you can only please some of the people some of the time. Your inability to say 'No' and to make a decision has got to be dealt with. Start by listening to your inner self, the you that knows deep down what will bring you the most pleasure. So if you are faced with a choice, once you've made your decision, let everyone know that's what you think in the most forthright but polite way you can. And if you think something or someone is being unfair, tell them. Don't bury away your resentment and allow them to do the same thing to you again and again. Familiarity breeds contempt but you will get what you deserve unless you confront the reason for your anger or annoyance. Learn to understand what true friendship is. Don't go pursuing the affection and advice of those who want you to trip up or look a fool. Learn to cherish those that are closest to you rather than obsessing about those glamorous or influential people you'd like to befriend but who, in the long term, won't be there for you when it really matters. If a relationship isn't working out, don't mutter 'better the devil you know' – this is an issue about self-respect and what you really deserve in life. The longer you beat about the bush, the more you will be used.

Famous Sun in Libra: John Lennon, Margaret Thatcher, Catherine Zeta Jones, Michael Douglas, Matt Damon, Gwyneth Paltrow, Olivia Newton-John, Will Smith, Roger Moore, Brigitte Bardot, Julie Andrews, Sting, Kate Winslet, Sarah Ferguson, Carrie Fisher, Jean-Claude Van Damme, Hugh Jackman, Sigourney Weaver, Luciano Pavarotti, Susan Sarandon, Alicia Silverstone, Paul Simon.

SUN IN SCORPIO OR 8TH HOUSE

If your Sun is placed in Scorpio then you are someone whose personality runs very deep indeed. You are like an iceberg, showing only a third of the real you and keeping the other two-thirds under the surface. Actually, we can carry the ice analogy on a bit further. Scorpio is a Water sign, it is also fixed, and what is fixed water? Ice, of course. Scorpios often appear to be ice-cool on the outside. People make the mistake of thinking that the calm, collected exterior represents the real you. They think you are emotionally cold too, but this isn't strictly true, as your sign is also ruled by fiery Mars, who governs your kingdom jointly with the god of the underworld. The truth is that no matter how relaxed you may look on the outside, your passions and desires plum the depths on the inside. So even when Mars gets hold of you with fiery relish, Pluto can repress the volcano. This means you are good at keeping your head when all around you others are losing theirs. However, many Scorpio problems are connected to the fact that you do keep your feelings submerged and out of sight (though never out of mind).

You are an ace at detective work, psychology, carrying out investigations, even spying, for you have a penetrating gaze that can cut right through to the heart of any matter. Control is a big issue with you. Pluto people have an intense desire to control; they are dab hands at using psychology for all kinds of reasons. Like the god of the underworld himself, you will use a cloak of invisibility to do this, exuding Machiavellian charm. However, this can also manifest itself in a destructive, even tyrannical, side to your personality. You want to be in charge. Strip away your complex character and you will find sex and money tattooed somewhere on your psyche. You are a secretive, enigmatic, even mysterious, person. You are the smile on the Mona Lisa because you don't want to give too much away. (Read Sun in Aries and mix 'n' match with this more Plutonian account to give you an idea of how Mars works.)

If you have a positive Sun in Scorpio or the 8th house

You know what you want and will get it by hook or by crook. You are still obsessive, jealous and envious but don't display these tendencies in a frightening way. You know there is no point in pursuing things in life unless you have the respect of other people. Even if what you are driving towards is world domination, you will tend to do so in a way that is for the greater good of others. Scorpio is also the sign of empowerment and transformation. So you have an ability to regenerate and reinvent yourself whenever the need arises. You can suffer the most dreadful or traumatic setbacks and bounce back quickly.

There are three levels to Scorpio, the dove, the eagle and the snake. You are able to shed the skin of one and become another easily. This also means you can be a fantastic helper. You can persevere against all the odds, having a grim determination not to let go. In a positive person like you, this means you know how to rally troops to bring out the best in others. Mars gives you qualities of leadership and Pluto enables you to be the clever spy, with enough cunning and connivance to beat everyone at their own game.

Sexually, you have a voracious appetite but, and it's a big but, only if you meet the right person. You don't display your libido for everyone; in fact, you have great control and willpower and will only reveal your innermost self for someone who triggers your hot passions. You have a supreme psychic power that can be used for the good of all but is especially good for self-examination and analysis.

If you have a negative Sun in Scorpio or the 8th house

If you have a negative Sun in Scorpio then you might well be a character from a B horror movie. You want to convince people that you're really scary, but your bark is very much worse than your bite because it is all an act. You pretend to be a nasty piece of work so as to warn people off. The truth is that at the first sign of a challenge you will collapse and fall apart. You only come across as a ghoul because you want to control.

Control is the big issue for you but you want it for all the wrong reasons. You not only want to control your life and your destiny, but you want to control the lives and destinies of everyone around you as well. This desire can seep into your relationships, workplace, sex life, health, you name it. Somewhere along the line you're up to your sinister machinations. Basically, you're a control freak, mad for power, and will use psychology and below-the-belt tactics to gain the upper hand.

Another big weakness is your inability to move on. This can make you resentful, ruthless and full of rage. There are masses of people taken in by the crocodile smile who will then get their head chewed off. You are drawn to relationships with people you will never see again. This will attract you to sexual liaisons that are sometimes dangerous and very often clandestine – this can move you towards the twilight world, something you love.

The positive Scorpio digs deep to find the vein of gold to help others, but with you the reverse is true. You want to find gold in the belief it will bring you power.

How to overcome a negative Sun in Scorpio or the 8th house

This is not going to be easy and it may be wise to enlist a helper along the way. It doesn't have to be someone you know; in fact, someone who doesn't know you would be best. The key thing to remember is that control can come in different forms. You can get the same results from playing Robin Hood as the Sheriff of Nottingham. You can turn from a snake to a dove if you can understand the benefits of the whole.

As we saw in the iceberg analogy, yours is a Water sign and it is fixed. By overcoming your fixed ideas, obsessions and psychological defects you can easily transform. However, old habits die hard and you are too fixed: this where you need most help. Your problems can border on a compulsive obsessive disorder and this isn't easily shifted. It's a psychological blockage, a kind of mental constipation that requires an intellectual laxative. This is where counselling or outside help comes in. In the end, however, you need to want to do something yourself. No-one can ever make you do what you don't want to do.

Famous Sun in Scorpio: Hillary Clinton, Prince Charles, Grace Kelly, Richard Burton, David Schwimmer, Whoopi Goldberg, Julia Roberts, Winona Ryder, Simon Le Bon, Bill Gates, Leonardo DiCaprio, Martin Scorsese, Bjork, Jodie Foster, Calvin Klein, Danny DeVito, Johnny Lee Miller, Joni Mitchell, Demi Moore.

SUN IN SAGITTARIUS OR 9TH HOUSE

To understand someone with the Sun in Sagittarius, you only have to look at the symbol, the archer aiming an arrow at the skies above. If you have your Sun here you have a spirit of adventure, dislike having limits imposed upon you and are a thoroughly independent, freedom-loving soul. For you, the sky really is the limit. You are imbued with a hankering for discovery, adventure, expansiveness and growth. This gives you a deep-seated need to go wherever you want to go, when you want to go, with no restrictions on your thought and actions.

On a more personal level, this restless, questing nature also means you are going to be uncomfortable in relationships that make you feel too tied down. You won't be happy in a situation where your partner needs to know exactly where you are and what you are up to at any time of day or night. Given your forthrightness, you will let your partner know your displeasure in no uncertain terms.

You have a cavalier attitude to many things, which can make you unreliable. Again you hate to be tied down and any kind of strict regimen will be given short shrift. Travel is an absolute love, be it intellectual through learning or study or physical via the seven seas.

If you have a positive Sun in Sagittarius or the 9th house

You have an insatiable hunger for knowledge and intellectual stimulation. If your opposite sign Gemini is the eternal student, then

Sagittarius is the sign of the philosopher who has soaked up every piece of knowledge around. Use the luck that comes with your sign by doing something with your life that demands opportunity or good fortune. You have a great ability to be in the right place at the right time.

Your warm and positive personality is your invitation to meet many people who will be good for you to know. You are a great communicator, networker and 'ideas' person, enough to have an address book of contacts that you can call on at any time. Don't be surprised if you end up with a lover or part of a business syndicate that has its roots in another country. International as well as intellectual openings will frequently occur and what you must be sure to do is not look a gift horse in the mouth.

If you have a negative Sun in Sagittarius or the 9th house

Your natural expansiveness will sometimes get the better of you. You will shoot your arrows higher than you should and completely miss the target. You can exaggerate and indulge in one-upmanship. Whatever someone else has done, you will have to make out that you have done something even more impressive, even if you've never been there or tried it.

Your words can hurt. You are straightforward to the point of bluntness, even rudeness. You wound people and are then insensitive about why others feel hurt by you. In matters of the heart, in particular, your honesty can be brutal and heartbreaking.

It is your unfaithfulness and inability to commit that is the biggest problem. Once you stray you will lose the love, trust and respect you once had and will never get it back again. Be warned against inventing a tissue of lies as one will lead to another and you will compromise yourself ethically and morally. Strangely, you can be very blinkered, leading to intolerance and prejudice – this is unforgivable for a sign like yours.

How to cope with a negative Sun in Sagittarius or the 9th house

Think before you open your mouth. Remember that words are powerful weapons and that as a Sagittarian you are gifted with a great deal of power in the linguistic and cerebral departments. So if you find yourself in a situation where someone else's feelings might be in danger of getting hurt, try to temper your language and weigh up the consequences of what you are about to say before the words come out and it is too late to take them back again. Don't make promises you have no intention of keeping, and if you tend to exaggerate, then again, think about what you are saying. Put your brain into gear!

Be aware that in the end, whether you say something that is an out and out lie or make a commitment you don't follow through, you are letting yourself as well as other people down. You're a fascinating and interesting person in your own right so you don't have to make up tales as you go along to appear more so as you will only set people sniggering behind your back. Don't shoot your arrows so high. A lower goal that is achievable and reachable will please everyone, so why not try it?

Famous Sun in Sagittarius: Kenneth Branagh, Brad Pitt, Billy Connolly, Tina Turner, Maria Callas, Jimi Hendrix, Christina Aguilera, Britney Spears, Ben Stiller, Woody Allen, Gianni Versace, Sinead O'Connor, Judi Dench, Keith Richards, Teri Hatcher, Steven Spielberg, Samuel L. Jackson, Kiefer Sutherland, Jane Fonda, Bette Midler.

SUN IN CAPRICORN OR 10TH HOUSE

If you have your Sun in Capricorn, imagine yourself as a version of your ruling planet, Saturn. Like Saturn, you are constrained and held in by a set of concentric rings. Like a corset, it limits and restricts you in many ways. As a result of this your attitude to life is summed up by a seriousness and a dedication to duty. Punctuality is up there on your list of what maketh a man. You cannot abide lateness, unreliability, waste, lies, cutting corners, laziness – and that's just for starters.

The good news is that because you are known for your sense of responsibility, the people around you regard you as a pillar of strength. Your steady nerves and careful, cautious nature means people turn to you in times of crisis. So it is quite likely that you will hold a position of authority at some stage of your life, perhaps at a very high level indeed. At home too, you are the lynchpin of family life. You enjoy the sense of satisfaction you get from looking after your kith and kin. However, you are highly ambitious, a careerist who can be self-critical, calculating and conniving.

The restrictions on you mean you are, despite outward appearances, shy, modest and retiring. This is largely because you have gone through difficulties in your early years where you constantly had to gain the appreciation and support of your elders. To you, your reputation and standing within your profession and peer group is everything. This doesn't mean you are boring, far from it. You are also the owner of the driest, drollest sense of humour of all the Sun signs.

If you have a positive Sun in Capricorn or the 10th house

You have all of the good facets outlined above. You are punctilious and prudent, but not to the extent that your material wealth is more important than everything else in life. You work beyond the call of duty and it is this dedication and diligence that will be the difference between you and the might-have-beens.

You are keen to be recognized more for your achievements and what you have accomplished than for what you earn. It is how you are perceived that is important to you because you know some of the decisions you make can affect the world around you or even the world at large. Your best years may not be until you reach a certain, shall we say, mature age. But they *will* come and the more you put into things, the more rewards you will eventually collect.

You have an important relationship with your father, who may be the reason for your success (or negatively for your failure), even if he provided the spur by making you think, 'I'll show you'.

You have a fabulous turn of phrase and comic patter that is all about timing. Heritage and tradition make you feel safe and secure but you can also appreciate change – time moves on and you understand this.

If you have a negative Sun in Capricorn or the 10th house

If you have a negative Sun in Capricorn, you only have to read two books to understand yourself properly. They are *A Christmas Carol* and *Silas Marner*. Like the lead characters in both, you have an avaricious, materialistic outlook. Money is everything to you and you will do whatever you can to grab it or save it. This can mean that the sense of duty and responsibility for which you are so admired can get the better of you, so you end up overworking, even to the point of being a workaholic. As a result the rest of your life can become pointless. Saturnine, the word invented to describe this dark, depressive side of the planet, suits you down to the ground at times. Ask you how you are feeling and you'll doubtless say, 'Oh, not so good,' in a voice that suggests it was a miracle you lasted the night. You are also the last person someone will come to for a compliment. You see sex as being the same as feelings, but as we all know, this just ain't the case.

How to overcome a negative Sun in Capricorn or the 10th house

Not everything should be based on life's material things. It's time to learn that you have capabilities and talents that need exploring. Get yourself on a learning curve and see just how many things you can do with your skills. When it comes to a pat on the back, your own will suffice. You don't have to go round asking people if you are good.

One key to change is to stop limiting and restricting yourself by ring-fencing your talents or experiences. Be spontaneous – do something without asking why. You must get over the fear of the unknown and the only way to do it is by behaving badly – in other words against your preset grain. There is much, much more to life than work and routine – you need to have some fun and when you do then you will begin to see the light. Stop being so mean with your money too. If you've earned it, spend some of it too. Yes, we all want to save but not every penny we make. You can't take it with you.

Famous Sun in Capricorn: Jude Law, Rowan Atkinson, Jim Carrey, Mel Gibson, Michael Stipe, Nicholas Cage, David Bowie, Elvis Presley, Tiger Woods, Anthony Hopkins, Dr Martin Luther King, Denzel Washington, Kevin Costner, Dolly Parton, Annie Lennox, Muhammad Ali, Melanie 'Sporty Spice' Chisholm, Jimmy Page, Chris Evert, Rod Stewart, Diane Keaton, Cary Grant.

SUN IN AQUARIUS OR 11TH HOUSE

The eccentric Sun in Aquarius is ruled by two very different planets: the chaotic Uranus and the stringent Saturn. So it is not surprising that if you have your Sun placed here, you are someone who swings from unpredictability to stern seriousness, attracted to the avant-garde, risqué and off-the-wall. Dull, dreary or 'normal' personalities need not apply for membership of your circle of friends. You prefer your pals to be wacky, rollercoaster people – a bit like you. The only thing that is predictable about you is that you are unpredictable. You can be contrary and perverse when you want to, and shocking and outrageous behaviour is part of your celestial CV. You are extreme when it comes to opinions too; indeed, whatever you do has an air of excitement or the unexpected about it.

If you have a positive Sun in Aquarius or the 11th house

Your greatest strength is your quickness of thought. Like Oscar Wilde, you should declare your genius because you undoubtedly are blessed with it. In terms of ideas and intuition, you are way ahead of most people in the way you think and act. And because you were born in an Air sign, you are a natural communicator. You may excel in science or the computer world, or do something that will change the world and be good for everyone. You aren't selfish but are incredibly impatient. You will fight against bigotry and narrow-mindedness but need to take care as you may have a little of this in yourself. If you get a bee in your bonnet, you won't be moved.

You are the best of club members and if you can't find an organization that you can put your original mark on, then you should form your own. You swear fealty to your friends – in fact, you have more best friends than anyone. If you have this placement, you are someone willing to try anything once, and if you like it, once again!

If you have negative Sun in Aquarius or the 11th house

With negative Sun in Aquarius one word sums you up best: wilful. You cannot wait for anything, you want everything yesterday and if you don't get it then you will explode. You have bouts of hysteria and tantrums that any diva would be proud of. But where does it get you?

You also love change. Sometimes you will make changes just for the sake of it. The old saying 'If it ain't broke, don't fix it' holds no meaning for you. You have an opinion on everything and everyone, regardless of whether you know what you are talking about. You are inclined to say you have been there, done that and got the T-shirt, when in fact you haven't been remotely near there, done it or even seen the T-shirt. You have a habit of assuming far too much, and can be presumptuous and contemptuous of people. You need to take a leaf out of your polar sign and look at negative Leo. This will show you that you have to stop behaving as if you are superior.

How to overcome a negative Sun in Aquarius or the 11th house

If you are going to be accepted by others, you have to accept people. You have to see that everyone isn't going to be like you or how you have decided they should be. You have to live and let live, understand others are who they are, say *vive la difference.*

If you feel someone is queering your pitch or cramping your style, you must watch against becoming overly protective, or insanely irrational and unreasonable. You have a brilliant mind and by channelling this intellect into creative avenues, humanitarian ideals or social activities, people will soon see that your heart is in the right place and you're not all bad. Never give yourself too much time to think; by keeping occupied you will surprise yourself as much as anyone.

Famous Sun in Aquarius: Abraham Lincoln, James Dean, Jennifer Aniston, John Travolta, Peter Gabriel, John McEnroe, Michael Jordan, Justin Timberlake, Phil Collins, Vanessa Redgrave, Emma 'Baby Spice' Bunton, Oprah Winfrey, Paul Newman, Princess Caroline of Monaco, Christina Ricci, Jane Seymour, Cybill Shepherd.

SUN IN PISCES OR THE 12TH HOUSE

If your Sun is placed in Pisces, Water has a strong influence on your personality. Pisces is a Water sign and its rulers are Jupiter and Neptune. Water has the effect of diffusing and distorting things, and with your Piscean Sun you are someone who carries a cloud of confusion around with you. The main consequence of this is that you may live in a constant muddle or be absent-minded and dizzy. The fact that you have a tendency to live in your own dream world at times only exacerbates this, and if things aren't going the way you want, you retreat into your fantasy realm even more.

This behaviour can spill over into your love life. You will idolize your partners, seeing them through rose-tinted spectacles and, as a result, be blind to their glaring faults. When, inevitably, things go wrong, the reality check is such a shock it leaves you reeling. You can be very sensitive even though you come across as a cold fish. Given the pain that real life causes when it comes crashing in on you, this can make life hard to deal with. You are romantic, and gifted psychically and artistically. You should pursue the sophisticated and glamorous areas of life as you are able to put your own enchanting or bewitching spell on things you touch. You are susceptible to atmospheres and your clairvoyant antennae can beep into action when danger lurks. (Read Sun in Sagittarius to see how a Jupiter Pisces is likely to be.)

If you have a positive Sun in Pisces or the 12th house

You are willing to face up to the reality of a situation. Indeed, you use this realism to help others, whether working as a doctor, vet, nurse or just a Good Samaritan. Perhaps, in the wake of a visit to the dark side of the Piscean psyche, you use your own personal experience to help others in drug or drink rehab.

You buck the trend of the inefficient, overly sentimental Pisces label. Instead you take a leaf from the book of your polar sign Virgo and take the view that there is a place for everything and everything in its place. You are a born romantic and make not only a wonderful lover but are easily and quite happily seduced. (You can always blame the magic of the moment, and usually do!)

All round, you're a jolly good egg to whom nothing is too much trouble. There's an army of people who would like to canonize you. You've usually been through traumas and grief and it is this that has strengthened your spirituality or religious faith. You should use your psychic powers through mediumship or healing.

If you have a negative Sun in Pisces or the 12th house

You can become dependent on anything that takes the pain of real life away from you. This means you are drawn to drink, drugs, false prophets and gurus – anything that offers you an escape. You live in a world of denial and refuse to confront whatever or whoever is causing you hurt or pain. Like Lord Nelson (a Scorpio) you turn a blind eye.

You can also live in a world that swings between paranoia and suspicion because you suffer from delusions and illusions that have no rationale whatsoever. You need an emotional crutch and cry wolf so often that when something really is wrong people have run out of patience and sympathy.

How to overcome a negative Sun in Pisces or the 12th house
More than almost any other placement, you are someone who must learn to help yourself. If you don't, you will slide down the slippery slope to oblivion and very few people will care. You want them to care, don't you? Understand that you're not the only person in the world who has gone through a terrible time, or suffered loss or unhappiness. Yours are only some of the long string of disasters that are occurring everywhere every day. There are people who are far worse off than you, and who deal with their troubles in a positive way. They live to fight another day, and so must you.

Famous Sun in Pisces: Drew Barrymore, Sharon Stone, Bruce Willis, Kurt Cobain, George Harrison, Elizabeth Taylor, Patsy Kensit, Rupert Murdoch, Liza Minnelli, Michael Caine, Spike Lee, Prince Albert of Monaco, Prince Andrew, Juliette Binoche, Chelsea Clinton, Glenn Close.

Placing Your Planets: the Moon

The most important thing to remember about the Moon is that she does not have any energy or power of her own. Whereas the Sun is omnipotent and can create and generate his own heat and light, the Moon is in the dark and astrologically her energy comes from the reflected moods of other people. In this sense, she is unique. She is the only planet (in astronomical terms, of course, she is not even a planet!) whose properties in terms of your personality are moulded by the emotions and feelings of people around you. As a result of this, the emotions of a lunar-type person (someone who has the Moon as their ruling planet, or has the Moon in her own house, the 4th house, or Moon in her own sign, Cancer, or was born under a full Moon or a new Moon or has dominant Moon aspects in their horoscope) are going to depend a lot on who shares their immediate environment at work, play and at home.

In general as a lunar type, you're going to feel so much more comfortable with familiar faces and places. Because you are so highly sensitized, you will avoid people or situations you do not feel comfortable with. Think of the crab, your wee animal. It is totally defensive. With its shell on the outside it can deflect so much of what it doesn't want to feel and will walk sideways round a problem. And with those pincers going eight to the dozen, it will appear alarming, even though so much of it is just show. If you are strongly Lunar or Cancerian, defence is the best form of attack.

MOON IN ARIES OR THE 1ST HOUSE

While the Moon is fundamentally to do with the emotions, Aries is, remember, the sign of the emerging ego, so there is a tremendous need for action and excitement if you have this placing. You can also be impulsive and quick-tempered. At the same time you can be passionate and caring, with a strong maternal streak. An ardent nature manifests itself big-time.

If you have a positive Moon in Aries or the 1st house

You are protective, caring and kind. You also have the ability to brush off difficulties by shrugging your shoulders, removing yourself from the problem and dealing with it. If defence is the best form of attack, in Aries it is second nature. You fight for your life or principles or if anyone you love is under attack. In fact you are even better at giving your all for others than yourself. However, your feelings can be rather fragile as you are fierce in the defence of your emotions, too.

If you have a negative Moon in Aries or the 1st house

With the Moon in Aries or the 1st house, there is a tendency for you to be far too self-aware and self-absorbed. You may be totally dependent on your own moods and feelings, possibly not taking into account how others feel. You may tend to whine on about the troubles you have and completely ignore the fact that somebody close has not only gone through worse but was the one who came to you for sympathy. You know the scenario: someone comes for help and says, 'I don't know what to do. We're going to have the house taken away from us if we don't pay this month's mortgage.' You, as a Moon in Aries, says, 'Oh dear, I remember when we had our solarium built we were lucky to have an insurance maturing. Another cup of tea, Earl Grey wasn't it?'

How to overcome a negative Moon in Aries or the 1st house

You shouldn't wallow in your feelings and you certainly shouldn't make others wallow in them with you. No matter how aware you are of your trials and tribulations, there are times when you need to deal with them on your own. Be conscious of the need to be sympathetic. You will naturally refuse to be a pushover for hard luck stories but learn to be a little more compassionate. Go off in search of somewhere secluded. Once you've done that, have a good hard look at why it is you feel the way you do. You are bright enough to get to the root of it, and once you have done that you are ready to deal with it.

Famous Moon in Aries: Marlon Brando, Alan Bates, Kiefer Sutherland, Dennis Hopper, Al Capone, Patrick Swayze, James Cagney, Kevin Spacey, Stevie Wonder, Rex Harrison, Jennifer Lopez, Doris Day, Jamie Lee Curtis, Janet Jackson, Salma Hayek, Tyra Banks, Pamela Anderson, Sally Field, Jerry Hall, Jacqueline Kennedy Onassis, Grace Jones, Angelina Jolie, Eva Longoria.

MOON IN TAURUS OR THE 2ND HOUSE

You have a deep-seated need for emotional and material security. You tend to find this in the things you own and possess. You need to know you can afford to do what you want, so you fret continuously about your bank balance and have a real tendency to become acquisitive, hoarding things. You can also be defensive of anything that threatens the security and ownership of anything you call your own.

If you have a positive Moon in Taurus or the 2nd house

You have an ability to create wealth, to spin straw into gold. You do so by being yourself and relying on your strong financial instincts. You also tend to hold on to what you have got, thereby securing yourself in monetary terms. Having the Moon in the 2nd can mean fluctuating finances. This is because the ebb and flow of the material tides means you can concentrate more on the emotional rather than the economic.

If you have a negative Moon in Taurus or the 2nd house

Your need to be secure financially can override everything, and it reflects itself in a way that is locked in the past. You are the sort of person who may save money in a shoebox or a cookie jar. You have a real hunger to collect things, whether it is postage stamps or antiques, anything that you believe will accumulate value and come to your rescue 'in your old age'. Strangely, for someone who wants to protect their monetary gains, you can suddenly blow it all on *la dolce vita*, as when your emotional defences are breached, you need retail or gourmet therapy to deal with it.

How to overcome a negative Moon in Taurus or the 2nd house

Your need for financial and physical security is part of you. But you can nurture it by taking on the traits of the positive Moon. You need to open your eyes to today's world. Look at the financial pages of the newspapers, read reports on stocks and shares, whatever it takes to tap into the here and now rather than living in the past. Don't make your mind up by taking on board what others say, experience things for yourself instead. That way you will free yourself up and can enjoy the fruits of what you earn as a reward for speculating. Maybe you will accumulate and maybe you won't. If it's the latter don't worry. After all, it's ONLY MONEY.

Famous Moon in Taurus: Prince Charles, Hugh Grant, Bill Clinton, William Shatner, Vincent Price, Yul Brynner, Peter Sellers, Ronald Reagan, Elton John, Walter Matthau, Bob Dylan, Christina Aguilera, Halle Berry, Tina Turner, Meryl Streep, Lauren Bacall, Joan Collins, Katharine Hepburn, Diana Ross, Dionne Warwick, Cameron Diaz.

MOON IN GEMINI OR THE 3RD HOUSE

Here we have a meeting of the head and the heart, the cerebral Mercury, ruler of Gemini, and the emotional Moon. It is a great placing to have, provided, that is, you can handle it. If you can, then you are someone who can see both the logical and the emotional sides of situations. But this is a very tight balancing act, and if one side dominates the other there will be a tendency either to make decisions based purely on the rational or purely on the emotional. If it is the latter, whenever you face trouble you instinctively tend to hide or run away completely, rather than facing the problem. You let the heart rule the head. You can have an instinctive need to communicate and to be near those you know, friends or relatives. One way you release anxiety is to talk, and talk, and talk. You need to be reassured, which is why this can be the placement of a real worry guts.

If you have a positive Moon in Gemini or the 3rd house

You have an ability to think around a problem. You understand the importance of putting yourself in other people's shoes when weighing up a situation. You can balance the rational and the emotional well. You are a wonderful agony aunt or uncle, you are able to see the problem, pinpoint the answer and put a person who is 'out of their mind' with worry at ease. This placement is excellent for having supportive siblings or relatives who come to your aid. Community and neighbourhood ventures can fulfil your need to belong and be part of a wider local family.

If you have a negative Moon in Gemini or the 3rd house

You are constantly veering between the rational and the emotional side of your feelings. One moment you are weighing things up with an ice-cold logic, the next you are letting your emotions run riot. The result is at best chaos and confusion, with an inability to make decisions. At worst, it can result in acute anxiety and stress that may lead to more serious health problems. You shut yourself off from people who mean you no harm. This is part of your need to protect yourself from the slings and arrows of the world. You can listen to too much gossip and make decisions based on rumour rather than reality. Thereby, you end up accusing people of being bad when in fact they are merely the subject of others' hang-ups.

How to overcome a negative Moon in Gemini or the 3rd house

If you need a theme song to guide you through the difficult decisions in life it should be Joni Mitchell's 'From Both Sides Now'. You need to learn to look at things from both points of view. Use your intuition and instinct, and marry them with your common sense. When you do, you will avoid some of the pitfalls and errors you have made in the past. In doing this, you may also benefit from drawing on the advice of advisers and counsellors. But you have to be careful they are independent people, individuals without an axe to grind. They may be strangers or people one step removed from your day-to-day life. The important thing is that they stimulate you to have the internal debate you need.

Most importantly, speak as you find, avoid chatterboxes and superficial friends who want you as part of their gang for a reason. Detach yourself and make decisions based on what you know and what you see. Keep yourself occupied by getting involved in local events so that you can use your ingenuity for specific issues concerning you, yours and those you know. This way you will be able to spread a little happiness more easily.

Famous Moon in Gemini: Rowan Atkinson, Alec Guinness, Art Garfunkel, David Hasselhoff, Gene Hackman, Jim Carrey, Pierce Brosnan, Kirk Douglas, Roger Moore, Fred Astaire, Paula Abdul, Claudia Schiffer, Brigitte Bardot, Bette Davis, Goldie Hawn, Gwyneth Paltrow, Jennifer Conelly, Heidi Klum, Kylie Minogue, Roseanne Barr.

MOON IN CANCER OR THE 4TH HOUSE

As the ruler of this sign, the Moon is doubly powerful here in her home zone, where she feels comfortable and at ease. As a result, you are very emotional, caring and sensitive. In fact, you are so sensitive you must be careful not to go over the top by taking offence where none was ever intended. Your own home is your haven. The lunar in you loves to come home but that doesn't always mean a property, by the way. It can mean that wonderful and very descriptive saying: home is where the heart is. In other words, where you feel most happy, comfortable and more importantly, contented and protected.

If you have a positive Moon in Cancer or the 4th house

You have a powerful store of memories. In your case, however, you don't let it get in the way of your future. If, let's say, you had a hard time at school or at home with your parents, perhaps being bullied or abused, you can use that memory to ensure it never happens to you again. You may even set up a charity to ensure people don't have to go through what you have or get involved with a safe house.

You don't idealize your past with your family. You know that life is about creating your own history and you know you have to get on with that. You are also one of the most kind, compassionate people walking this earth. You would give your help and support to anyone.

Again, very often you do so because you have been there yourself. You know how people are feeling and you empathize with them.

If you have a negative Moon in Cancer or the 4th house

You are someone who finds it very difficult to move on. Indeed you have a fear of letting go of the past. This is all rooted in your need for the emotional security the past provides. Change terrifies you, so you are surrounded by emotional and physical baggage. You hoard things too. This also makes you someone who hangs on in a relationship, even when it is long past its sell-by date. You are a real Miss Haversham, sitting there in your wedding dress years after you've been left at the altar. (This is something that is even more pronounced when you have Venus in Cancer.)

You are something of a 'Mini Me' in relation to your mother or father. You recreate your room to look like theirs, filling it with heirlooms that remind you of your childhood. As an example of this placing at its most extreme, I'll tell the story of a close friend. She had both the Sun and Moon in Cancer and the Moon was under a new Moon too! She had a house that was overrun with clutter. The place was turning into a museum. One day we finally persuaded her to have a life-laundry and give it all to a jumble sale. When the sale went ahead she was first in the queue and bought back every item. It was classic behaviour of a negative Moon in Cancer.

Even more typical is the inability to forgive. No Moon in Cancer or in the 4th can ever forget. This harbouring of slights and hurts can really hold you back when you should be moving on.

How to overcome a negative Moon in Cancer or 4th house

The solution to your problems lies in two very simple but very profound words: LET GO. You are never going to reach the goals you set yourself in life unless you move on and divest yourself of the emotional and physical baggage that you are dragging around with you and is dragging you down at the same time. Say goodbye to the past and look forward to the future. It's a simplistic message I know, but you'd be amazed how many people are incapable of seeing it. Don't allow sentimentality to prevent you from making progress. Just because you've been in the same place, same home, same marriage, same whatever for an eternity, doesn't make it right if it's very wrong and causing you hurt or harm. By cutting the apron strings you can liberate yourself in an instant. On a lesser level, getting into car boot sales or genealogy will also enable you to enjoy the past without having to cling to it!

Famous Moon in Cancer: Olivia Newton-John, Harrison Ford, Benny Hill, Bob Hope, Anthony Quinn, Elvis Costello, Dennis Quaid, Keanu Reeves, Errol Flynn, Mike Myers, Leonard Nimoy, Paul Simon, Tim Allen, Robert Duvall, Walter Cronkite, Janis Joplin, Drew Barrymore, Linda Blair, Liza Minelli, Mira Sorvino, Nancy Sinatra, Shakira, Camilla Parker Bowles.

MOON IN LEO OR THE 5TH HOUSE

With this placing in your chart you have the powerful emotions of the Moon working in the area to do with the creative you and affairs of the heart. Even more profoundly she is working in the part of your life to do with children. As a result, you have a very strong need not just to be loved and to love, but also to do the things in life that you love doing best. You want children to carry on your name, so your offspring become not just a part of your maternal needs (even if you're a man) but also that continuity with history that is so important to your sense of personal immortality. You need to have the feeling that long after you've gone, a little part of you will still be alive and well in the world.

You are someone who takes pleasure in life, who relishes in following your heart's desires, in doing the things that you love. There is nothing you enjoy more than enjoying yourself socially with friends to whom you are loyally devoted. You also have a strong creative urge that may have come from something you did as a child or was inherited from your parents.

If you have a positive Moon in Leo or the 5th house

You are fiercely loyal and loving. Romantically you are totally in tune with what love is all about and have an instinctive ability to turn on the charm and create a rapport. It also makes you a most ferocious and protective parent. If anyone, but anyone, does anything to one of your offspring, you will have their guts for garters. If it isn't children, your pets will stimulate your parental streak just as much. Remember that brilliant Cat Stevens song 'I Love my Dog as much as I Love You'? That's the kind of pet owner you are.

You have the ability to make someone feel very special. Creatively you have an ability to do things that you can really 'feel', what comes naturally and straight from the heart. This never fails to bring love, enjoyment or pleasure, so always follow your heart.

If you have a negative Moon in Leo or the 5th house

You need to experience the thrill of being loved because the falling in love part can be your undoing. Too often relationships are all about the initial excitement, the giddy sensation of tumbling head over heels in love. Once that first flush has passed, you have a real tendency to drop people like a ton of bricks, and move on to the next conquest.

An inner emotional fury or frustration can build against anyone or anything that prevents you from enjoying your life. Even your children can be a source of anger or competition to you. You can see them as queering your pitch, getting in the way of your own personal desires and needs. If this happens, resentment might build up and you may need to seek help or counselling.

How to overcome a negative Moon in Leo or the 5th house

You need to learn that love isn't all about that frisson of excitement that comes when you first fall for someone. It is deeper and more profound than that. Join a club or society where you know you can meet people who share your interests or desires. That way you can kill two birds with one stone. On one hand, you will be in the comfortable situation of being with people who share what you enjoy. If that leads to romance, then you know you are going to be with someone who shares something important in common with you as you shoot off into the wide blue yonder doing your thing together.

If you find that your children are becoming a burden because they are stopping you from living your life, don't let it get out of hand. Any issues connected with children should be dealt with immediately and that includes seeking the advice of experts who can prevent things from getting seriously out of hand.

Famous Moon in Leo: Queen Elizabeth II, Tom Cruise, Tom Hanks, George Michael, Ted Danson, Oliver Reed, Peter Ustinov, Ringo Starr, Mikael Gorbachev, Paul McCartney, Martin Sheen, David Bowie, Renee Zellweger, Nancy Reagan, Paris Hilton, Margaret Thatcher, Marlene Dietrich, Kirsten Dunst, Jane Fonda, Dolly Parton, Famke Janssen, Barbra Streisand, Charlize Theron, Catherine Deneuve.

MOON IN VIRGO OR THE 6TH HOUSE

With this pedantic placing in your chart, you are tuned into your emotional tides, but have difficulty in expressing your emotions without analyzing them.

You are acutely aware of things that are going on around and inside you. Your antennae are highly tuned to things that aren't quite right. It may be something physical that can lead you to become totally fixated on medical matters (put down that medical dictionary!). Or it may be something that makes you feel uncomfortable, unsafe or unsure, perhaps a situation at work. The downside to this is that it can result in health issues, especially with your habit of worrying over things that affect your well-being. Be watchful for hypochondria or psychosomatic ailments that stem from becoming self-obsessed about everything from your bowels to your business.

If you have a positive Moon in Virgo or the 6th house

If I hold a party I will always invite someone with a strong Virgo connection, one to the Moon especially. I know they will be there at the end: clearing up, washing up, emptying the ashtrays and getting the Hoover out!

If you have this placing, you have a deep-seated need to feel worthwhile and emotionally involved in whatever it is you are doing. If you don't feel this way, you don't feel whole as a person. You may throw your lot in with voluntary or charity work, where you can see something useful coming out of your time and efforts. Anything connected with research or detail will appeal as you are content with doing the most boring stuff – it appeals to your routine and keeps your mind occupied.

If you have a negative Moon in Virgo or the 6th house

You have a strong sense of when something is wrong and can be obsessive. When it comes to illness, you are either a hypochondriac or someone who gets ill psychosomatically. You are also prone to illnesses like bulimia and anorexia. You may also be a comfort eater. In short, you are prey to all those things that can send your health whizzing off skewiff.

You are too pedantic and pernickety by half and are prone to making yourself ill by worrying about things you can never change or simply aren't your fault. You spend more time look at the minutiae rather than the fuller picture and accordingly miss the point. You worry over everything and nothing. When there's nothing to worry about, you'll invent something. Emotionally, you can severely restrict your feelings from flowing, possibly because you spend too much time rehearsing someone's reaction rather than getting on with it.

How to overcome a negative Moon in Virgo or the 6th house

Get to the core of yourself and start being totally honest about it. If you have become totally obsessed with something, say, keeping your house neat and tidy, ask yourself, what if I don't bother today? The world isn't going to end; you aren't going to bring some terrible problem into everyone's life. At the same time, if your home is one big mess, then do the reverse of this: throw stuff away, rationalize your world and get rid of some of the emotional baggage. Once you get shot of it, you won't suffer a calamity or die!

You have to become what I call Virgo-rational. That is, you have to make lists and prioritize things. You have to tell yourself, 'I can only do this if this happens. If it doesn't I can't do that.' You have to get past all the lunar guilt that will accompany this decision by being practical and rational. (I once knew a woman who had to look after her mother while also suffering from ME. She had a stressful job, too. Rather than calling for help, she tried to do everything and ended up having a physical and nervous breakdown.)

Dealing with this isn't easy. Your need to be of service is so great that it has to be a balancing act. If you act too selfishly in solving a problem you are going to slip into that uncomfortable zone where you feel you are no use. Emotionally learn to give a little more spontaneously, live for the emotional moment and see what the reaction is. It may surprise or even shock you. Even if nothing happens, at least you will get an answer rather than trying to predict the result in your head.

Famous Moon in Virgo: Jack Nicholson, John Travolta, Kenneth Branagh, Richard Burton, Sean Connery, Lance Armstrong, Bill Cosby, Robert Redford, Dustin Hoffman, Maria Callas, Madonna, Shirley MacLaine, Jodie Foster, Courtney Cox.

MOON IN LIBRA OR THE 7TH HOUSE

This placement is everything to do with one-on-one relationships, not just of the marital and romantic kind but of the business type too. If you have your Moon in Libra you have a deep-seated need to be in a harmonious twosome or partnership. You have to be comfortable with the partner you share your life with and are caring, devoted and protective of them. If a relationship is unhappy, however, your emotions can fluctuate wildly, leading to real problems. You become emotionally unbalanced, not being able to see the woods for the trees as everything you do is clouded by your feelings.

If you have a positive Moon in Libra or the 7th house

You will have a partnership in which you and your other half can understand each other without even speaking. A telepathic ESP energy links you together. You are, in the real sense of that overused phrase, soul mates. In a work situation, you might be a PA who is so attuned to your boss that you send his wife flowers on her birthday and make all his travel arrangements without even consulting him or her. Or you might be part of a creative partnership in which you complement each other and make sweet harmony. In this respect, think of partnerships like Rodgers and Hammerstein, and Torvill and Dean. (If there are more difficult aspects in the charts, of course, relationships like this can be of the 'Can't live with them, can't live without them' kind). In a domestic relationship, you and your partner are comfortable in each other's emotional company and understand and accept each other's differences. Each of you just knows you are with the right person.

If you have a negative Moon in Libra or the 7th house

So profound is your need to be one part of a couple, you find it impossible to do anything without your other half. Even if your partner is driving you crazy, you feel alone and isolated, and although you know you are in the wrong relationship, you tell yourself, 'Better the devil you know.' You are basically too insecure and afraid to believe there's anyone else out there who will want you.

On a more everyday level, you need to share every experience in your life and find it hard to do things on your own. You ring up friends or family to join you, even if it's just a trip to the shops. If you want to go and visit an exhibition or join a club, you want someone else as company. You are indecisive and procrastinating, usually because you are desperate to ask, 'What do you think?' This is a cop-out, of course, because if things then go wrong you can defend yourself by saying, 'Well I wasn't sure and it was *you* who told me what to do.'

How to overcome a negative Moon in Libra or the 7th house

You need to tap into the intellectual side of Libra. You need to strip away the emotional influences of Venus and the Moon and look at things logically. If you are in a relationship, for instance, you have to consider whether you really love the person you're with. If not, ask yourself, 'Is it worth the emotional torment and imbalance of clinging onto to someone who does all the taking while you do all the giving?'

If you find it hard to do things on your own, think about it logically. By experiencing a holiday, nightclub or social gathering there is much more of a chance of you meeting someone who is right for you. By turning up with someone else, people are going to assume that you are a couple, which will stymie your chances of romance. Go on your own and mingle with people who share similar interests. Because you have gone along as a free spirit, the prospect of a fresh, exciting relationship springing to life is all the greater.

This applies, of course, as much to business situations. Rather than going to a conference or a meeting with colleagues you know, head off on your own. A new world of possibilities will open itself up to you. Take responsibility for your decisions and actions. If you make a choice and it fails, so what? Pick yourself up and start all over again. The sense of accomplishment you will feel one day will be as good as falling in love. You've got it all so start believing in yourself.

Famous Moon in Libra: Sting, George W. Bush, Don Johnson, Sylvester Stallone, Leonardo DiCaprio, Jude Law, Shania Twain, Bruce Springsteen, Nicole and Natalie Appleton.

MOON IN SCORPIO OR THE 8TH HOUSE

If you have this insightful placement, you are someone who lives life with an absolute intensity, a person through whom the emotional forces of life flow like a raging torrent. You are like a vast underground cavern, full of still, dark waters that run very deep indeed. You allow only a chosen few into these subterranean emotional depths. Most folks will see you as unfeeling, distant and cold instead, which of course you are not.

This is a powerful, psychologically-based lunar position. You will often be motivated by compulsions, obsessions and desires, fixations that seem to have no rhyme or reason. Your feelings can be blocked by a barrier erected by an incident years back, perhaps sexual or emotional abuse. As a result you build a barrier that you may need therapy or counselling to overcome. Equally you may have accepted the sexual desires within you but learned to control them as you know they can destroy. This placement is about learning to have control over your feelings.

If you have a positive Moon in Scorpio or the 8th house

You have learnt emotional self-control. You know the potential of your feelings but rather than letting them control you, you manage them, perhaps by using periods of celibacy. There does not always have to be intimate one-to-one sexual desire for you to feel deeply gratified or satisfied. You may instead be drawn to the kind of relationship that a student would have with a guru or mentor, or a gay person might have with a straight one. It is a relationship on a more transcendental level, which less sensitive or controlled people wouldn't understand. It is one between people who are simpatico with each other's needs and feelings. You will have a very strong understanding of your partner's drives and emotions without it having to be consummated with a physical affair of any kind. Your desires are assuaged by just being with one another.

Issues affecting life–death matters are also relevant to this configuration. You may derive emotional pleasure and well-being from spiritual activities.

If you have a negative Moon in Scorpio or the 8th house

This is a very hard and heavy placing to deal with. It indicates someone whose feelings are not only complex in the extreme but also someone who deals with them in a way that can be hard to fathom.

You are someone controlled by their deepest desires. You give in to all forms of temptation and are totally disempowered by your needs and feelings, especially sexually. Another problem is an inability to see the difference between tender feelings and pure lust. You have a capacity not only to trifle with a person's emotions but to manipulate them in all kinds of ways in the name of love, when actually it is pure, loaded lust. There can be a difficult mother fixation to overcome too. Perhaps a mother who smothered or who is the reason for complicated psychological difficulties that you now have to live with. Ultimately this aspect may require therapy or counselling to ensure you don't beat yourself up with guilt or avoid close intimate relationships. You believe in fate so much that you take away the option of choice from your life vocabulary.

How to overcome a negative Moon in Scorpio or the 8th house

The key to dealing with this difficult placing is understanding your own psychological make-up. The only way you are going to learn to control the destructive side of your nature is by confronting your demons. Stop telling yourself that it is natural to have these urges and to act on them, especially if they hurt or involve other people who have no choice in the matter. Total and utter consent must be requisite for a healthy, private relationship. Be conscious of the fact that some things you do are for the wrong reason.

Turn the tables from being controlled to being the controller. If you don't, you may do something that you'll not only regret but could mess up your whole life. If you cannot do this by yourself then help is out there to comfort and guide you. Hypnotherapy or spiritual guidance can be helpful in gaining control of your feelings. Then you will be able to stop doing what you know you mustn't and shouldn't.

Famous Moon in Scorpio: Charlie Chaplin, Barry Gibb, Bruce Lee, Eddie Murphy, George Harrison, James Dean, Prince Andrew, Uri Geller, Jimmy Carter, Patrick Stewart, Warren Beatty, Julie Andrews, Alanis Morissette, Bette Midler, Elizabeth Hurley, Elizabeth Taylor, Marcia Cross, Kate Moss, Sharon Stone, Kim Wilde.

MOON IN SAGITTARIUS OR THE 9TH HOUSE

With this placing you need to feel comfortable in your mind and spirit. You need the upliftment demanded by philosophical Sagittarius, so you are drawn emotionally to ritual, ceremony and the habits of religious worship. Being an agnostic or atheist is not necessarily an option with this placement, unless you are so high-minded that it gives you a chance to question. Even then, you will be attracted to a faith that might not be orthodox but could be, for instance, ancestor worship. The bottom line is you need a spiritual home. You need to know what happens after life, where Valhalla or paradise is. Home for you can be a church, mosque, synagogue or any place of worship.

The 9th house is also about expansion and growth. So with this placement it is very likely you are also interested in other countries, cultures and creeds. You may have a relationship or marry someone from a completely different race or background to you and emigrate to another country.

If you have a positive Moon in Sagittarius or the 9th house

You have an infectious optimism and help people who feel down or depressed. You are someone who has a strong faith and who feels comfortable with it. You may also be drawn to countries and cultures where you feel comfortable spiritually, perhaps places where you may have a sense of déjà vu, as though you lived there in a previous life.

You are emotionally drawn to subjects that involve research into ancient civilizations from Egypt to the Aztecs, and are intrigued by metaphysical subjects: history or geography. Saving Planet Earth will appeal, as will matters of ecology and environment, whether it be swimming with dolphins or saving the whale. You have an acute vision of what you want to reach in your lifetime. Living abroad is very likely – or at least a long way from where you call home – as you become emotionally involved with a person or place that makes you feel good.

If you have a negative Moon in Sagittarius or the 9th house

You roam the seven seas but you never feel at home. You are on an eternal search for life's Holy Grail but you don't know what it looks like or where it is; so you forget your commitments and just go off at a moment's notice.

Your feelings can be superficial. This is because you are afraid to settle down in case it rules you out from what is happening elsewhere in the world. Spiritually, you are always thinking you have found the elixir to life and end up entangled in too many different disciplines. You are drawn into cults or religions that appear to be family-orientated but which are centres where false prophets control your minds. When it comes to brainwashing, you are a sucker.

How to overcome a negative Moon in Sagittarius or the 9th house

The mistake that many people with a negative Moon in Sagittarius make is that they move on impulse, perhaps to a place they have visited on holiday once, or to where a friend or relative has moved. But when they move, they discover it's not the right place at all. A holiday destination can look completely different if you know you're not going home in two weeks' time. The key is to go back to a place, several times. If you go back again and again and you still feel the same way about the place, there is a good chance this is where you should settle. So the key to overcoming the negative is exploring. You need somewhere where you feel you are there for a purpose, a reason; a place that in a practical sense brings out the creative side of you.

You need to feel strong ties with the culture and history of the location. You should beware, however, of getting hooked on the exotic accent or background of someone. Once the novelty wears off you will be back to basics, so spend some time with any person from another country before you commit yourself. Even if you don't commit to a person, at least commit to a place and then emotionally everything else will follow.

Finally, with this placement it is imperative you dig deep and look into the past, so involvement in archaeology or ancient civilizations is a must to give you the sense of continuity with your long-gone ancestors that you need.

Famous Moon in Sagittarius: Al Pacino, Billy Graham, Charlton Heston, Charlie Sheen, Freddie Mercury, Liberace, Richard Gere,

Neil Armstrong, Nicole Kidman, Judy Garland, Oprah Winfrey, Yoko Ono, Gloria Estefan, Mary Tyler Moore.

MOON IN CAPRICORN OR THE 10TH HOUSE

Note this is the Moon, the planet of motherhood, in the sign ruled by Saturn, which I think of as the father figure. This denotes a relationship that is comfortable in the extreme, the Darby and Joan couple in their dotage, completely at ease with each other. Sex has long gone, finished. They had their moments in the past but now it is about comfort and security, and simply being together offers them this.

This placement is also symbolic of a balance between your feelings and the boundaries placed upon your expression of them. With this in your chart, you are someone who needs to be in a relationship in which you feel you have a defence against the world about you. Your partner needs to be used to your habits and idiosyncrasies, not placing boundaries on you, and vice versa. Your funny little ways, instead of being a problem, actually end up becoming a habit that makes you feel content. Your emotions will be centred on ambitions either for the man or woman of your life or your family. You will be there to nurture and support, to catch them if they fall. Every fibre of your feelings is devoted to helping your kith and kin succeed where perhaps you have failed or have experiences that can help.

If you have a positive Moon in Capricorn or the 10th house

You may be someone who has a career that requires you to deal with the family or women. This may be a family in the literal sense or in the broader sense of the community or even the nation as a whole (which is a family in its own right too, of course). This might also be in politics or business, where you are the head of a large corporate or constitutional family.

This placement can bring great acclaim or even fame. It will also help you achieve great emotional involvement and satisfaction. You should have a sound relationship with your father or a figure to whom you can turn for wisdom. You have ambitions that are based upon what you wanted to be when you were growing up or are linked to your family's vocation in some way. Alternatively, you will have some kind of calling, viewing your work more as a vocation than a career. Whatever you do, you have an emotional dependency upon having a mission and purpose in life. If it happens to fall into the same area as your home, family, father or upbringing, then even better.

If you have a negative Moon in Capricorn or the 10th house

This is not an easy aspect to deal with as the younger you are, the harder it is to come to terms with your feelings. One setback, one rejection, one tiny failure and it could haunt you for the rest of your life. What's worse is that rather than helping you, you may find your father, or someone you rely on, castigates and blames you, making you feel even more wretched. This feeling can stay with you for a very long time, until you have the experience to work things out and yell, 'I told you so.' A disciplinarian upbringing or autocratic father who didn't give you the love or feelings when you needed it means you are now detached from your own feelings. You didn't ever really understand or know a happy home life.

You could end up notorious for being someone who will do *anything* to become famous, or be taken advantage of by others who can see your desperate need to be a success and appeal to your base side. If you can cut corners and get what you want more quickly you don't care. The trouble is other people do and that means your career collapses like a house of cards.

You may be someone who wants to be ordinary; spending time with your family and next of kin, but who, outside of home, wants to be recognized and wants to be famous and successful. Juggling these two disparate needs within you can cause problems.

How to overcome a negative Moon in Capricorn or the 10th house

The problem of balancing private and public life is a tricky one. I have dealt with quite a few people with this placement, including a prime minister and the head of a giant corporation. Yet in essence it is a relatively simple thing to work out, but maybe not so easy to enact. It requires you to draw the line between the two sides of your life. You need to say to staff or colleagues: 'Okay, from 5 p.m. on Friday until Monday morning, you do not interrupt me with work matters unless it is a matter of incredible importance.' The first thing you should do every New Year is to block out all your holidays and let everyone know that you're out of contact then, too.

This aspect is about setting boundaries. The negative side of this placement is about being self-restricting. The positive side is about balancing your life out. Understand, too, that happiness can be achieved, but you need to work at it. Don't spend your life feeling emotionally repressed and then take it out on your own children by believing, 'I suffered, so will you too.' That is meaningless and worthless; it means you have neither evolved nor understood why you went through what you did. Instead, take a different route, learn to outwardly express your appreciation and adoration for people, places or situations that you genuinely feel something for. The more you give out, the more you will get back. Don't be afraid to ask for help when you need it. Ask for the universe to support you and it will, either in the guise of those you love or through more mystical measures. Be Mr Pickwick and you won't fail to find eventual emotional happiness.

Famous Moon in Capricorn: Napoleon Bonaparte, Adolf Hitler, Abraham Lincoln, Arnold Schwarzenegger, George Clooney, Johnny Depp, Gene Kelly, Michael Douglas, Cher, Annie Lennox, Christina Ricci, Christina Aguilera, Liv Tyler, Lucille Ball, Kim Basinger.

MOON IN AQUARIUS OR THE 11TH HOUSE

With this quirky placement in your birth chart you are someone who waxes and wanes like the Moon itself. Your emotions and feelings can switch on and off in a second. One moment you are effusive, extremely 'full on', the next you are imitating Greta Garbo, telling the world to go away and let you be alone. At the same time you are someone who thrives on friendship. You love your friends and the emotional rapport and connection they bring. When it comes to friends, you also practise fidelity and faithfulness.

Emotionally, you hate people getting too close, filling your immediate and intimate space. If someone suffocates you, you make a dash for dear life itself.

You excel at working for a collecting cause where you and others share the same ambitions for a better world. Your idea of emotional excellence is being able to swap feelings whilst still maintaining independence within a group. You are very hard to live with, as very few signs can gauge how you are going to behave from one minute to the next. In truth, half the time you're not even sure what you want emotionally. Nonetheless you are at your best with friends and in a platonic situation, rather than one that doesn't give you a means of escape.

If you have a positive Moon in Aquarius or the 11th house

That line 'You can choose your friends, you can't choose your family' must have been written by someone with an Aquarian Moon. You need friends who become family. You want your individuality to shine whether at home, work or in a social setting. If your style is cramped then so are you, becoming cranky and moody – and remember this is *positive* Moon in Aquarius.

Although you can have a tendency to keep a distance and sometimes come across as aloof, you are unbeatable as a genuine bosom buddy. Your humanitarian nature stems from your knowledge that what you do for others will reflect on you. Cool, calm and collected sums you and your feelings up. You don't express your feelings easily, just in case someone reciprocates in a way that bowls you over too much.

A great club person, you are at the centre of anything at which you can come and go as you please and no-one holds you to account. You hate to be restricted by time, rules or regulations, as you are not just a free spirit but also a wild wind that blows in all directions. Your intuition is incredible as you can assess and judge a complete stranger's character with ominous accuracy.

If you have a negative Moon in Aquarius or the 11th house

This is a placement that could be summed up by Freddie Mercury singing 'I Want to be Free', but in a totally selfish way. You may have made an emotional mistake in the past and now don't want the responsibility that is attached to it. You will go through hell and high water to shake off anyone or anything that has become a pain in your butt. Your tolerance level is at zero and if anything attaches themselves to you without your say-so, you are determined to shake off the offending person or issue.

Due to the influence of Aquarius's ruling planet Uranus, you are a rebel and an anarchist. This can cause even more trouble as it makes you so attractive to people who want to get to know you. This makes matters even worse as you can be damned rude in your efforts to make sure they don't get near you.

You are also someone who runs away from the norm. You may even want to detach yourself from your actual family. If you are expected to go to a family 'do' then you just won't go; whether you can't be bothered or because it is expected of you, it is a tie you'd prefer not to have.

You are odd to the point of eccentricity, your behaviour unpredictable. People won't know how you are going to feel from one moment to the next. Typically, you may also have an unusual relationship with your mother in that emotionally you find it hard to deal with any kind of feelings, especially the mothering kind. This again may be connected to your childhood, which is so unbelievable that if you wrote it for a TV soap opera people would find it too far-fetched. Indeed, your childhood may be the key to your independence and aversion to emotional attachments.

How to overcome a negative Moon in Aquarius or the 11th house

Because freedom is so important to you, the environment in which you live is vital. As your idea of family is very different to everybody else's, you need to decide precisely what you want from people around you. You must learn to be patient and tolerant with relatives or family duties that demand your time and feelings because let's face it, you're the one out of step, not them! Therefore, it is vital that you live in an environment where you have your own space, somewhere where you can switch off and on as your personality dictates. If you are stuck in a situation where you don't have this, get out before you make everybody's life a misery. You thrive on friendships and the fact that you can see your pals whenever you want, so joining or even starting a club or organization in which you can be part of a family of friends will be good for you.

Your emotional world may stutter every so often but if you realize that a friend could grow into a lover, kindred spirit or someone special, hang on in there because this is the kind of affair that you should foster. But think carefully before forging any kind of legal partnership. The mere mention of the L word may be anathema to you. You will be more honest and faithful in a relationship where there are no ties, where you can leave whenever you want.

Famous Moon in Aquarius: Woody Allen, Russell Crowe, Bruce Willis, Denzel Washington, Kevin Kline, Ashton Kutcher, Cary Grant, Larry Hagman, Pierce Brosnan, Muhammad Ali, Britney Spears, Marilyn Monroe, Uma Thurman, Teri Hatcher, Princess Diana, Sophia Loren, Joan Crawford, Calista Flockhart.

MOON IN PISCES OR THE 12TH HOUSE

This is a very effective placement because there's a natural relationship between the Moon and Neptune, one of the ruling planets of Pisces. After Neptune, the Moon is the most 'watery' of all the planets in astrological terms, so this creates a highly charged emotional placement indeed. The most positive way this manifests itself is that it makes a person gifted in the psychic or spiritual. They are exceedingly altruistic, more willing to put others before themselves. What they do in life is always unconditional, whether they are your friend, relative or lover, they have a wonderful quality about them that can often be saintly.

I've known two or three people who have had this placement and they were all blessed with compassion, sympathy, a softness and gentleness beyond compare. People with this configuration are tuned into a higher vibration; they have an understanding of the intangible and are able to feel the agony or ecstasy of life with graphic sensitivity. They spurn people who are violent or vulgar – anyone or anything base or prosaic disturbs their refined feelings.

If you have a positive Moon in Pisces or the 12th house

You are the sort of selfless person who simply turns up unannounced when you know a friend of family member has a need for help or assistance. You know what it takes to dish out tea and sympathy. In dealing with your own troubles you are philosophical. You realize it is a spiritual learning curve and the more you suffer, the more wonderful and beautiful you believe everything will turn out. Similarly, you are able to turn the other cheek when people upset or betray you, as you believe it is part of their karma to go through the experience of acting or behaving in a way that is hateful or hurtful. You put it down to experience and are willing to forgive and forget.

In matters of the heart, romance is what you yearn for. Sex, lust, even love can sometimes not be all it is cracked up to be, whereas romance is a thing filled with fantasies and aspirations. Even if things don't work out with a fairy-tale ending, at least you can live the dream. Always refusing to blame or shame, you are the epitome of an old soul who is here to help others go through the ups and down of life. You have the wisdom to know this is your last emotional turn on the life cycle, which is why you are able to help those who can't help themselves.

If you have a negative Moon in Pisces or the 12th house

On the surface you may appear to be doing good deeds for altruistic reasons, but in reality you are doing what you do because you want people to give you credit for it. This is because your emotions and feelings are geared more towards selfishness rather than selflessness. You do these things because you want people to like you and love you.

Your problems may have manifested themselves from a very early age when you always had to do something to win affection. Love was never given freely and unconditionally. Even in your adult life, unless you break out of this vicious emotional circle, you will end up with a partner who can toss you to one side and make you cry out more and more! Masochism is your strongest suit, followed by drowning your sorrows in drink or drugs. It might alleviate pain for a short while but when you wake or sober up, you are back where you started in the same boat.

This can be a very difficult placement for anyone to live with. You are insecure and emotionally flaky, with a very fertile imagination, believing what you want to believe rather than in reality. This can lead to dark feelings such as identity crises, persecution complexes and plain old paranoia. But the blame rests entirely with you. If you keep coming back for more like a dog with its master then you will be an eternal Aunt Sally crying out 'I am Not Worthy.' Of course you are. You must believe it.

This lunar placement can make you prone to unrequited love or a desire for a person or situation that is simply unobtainable. This might take the form of a fixation with a screen god or goddess, or on a more mundane level a fantasy about the girl or boy next door. You will tend to keep these heartfelt yens secret because not only do you have a fear of being rebuffed but you are also afraid of waking up to reality. The basest part of all this is lying to yourself and then having to lie to others because you so fear the truth. You'd rather live a lie.

How to overcome a negative Moon in Pisces or the 12th house

There is nothing wrong with living in a fantasy or idealized world if you know it is just the land of make-believe. The key to dealing with this placement is to grit your teeth, stiffen your upper lip and be honest, if only with yourself. It is a start. You are then free to enjoy your fantasies through theatre, music, dance, drama, or whatever artistic form of escape makes your toes tingle. Indulge yourself in glamorous pursuits or pastimes and allow yourself to enjoy the finer things of life – always keeping an eye on your budget in the process, of course.

Start doing things, not for the approval of others, but simply in order to help them without any thought of reward. Perform an act of charity that no one else will ever know about, apart from you. You will feel not only good about yourself, but what's more you will begin to see the power doing charitable things without taking any credit for them whatsoever.

Romantically, the key to dealing with your tendency to pursue the unobtainable is simple. There is love out there for you – check out of your fantasy world and step into the real one. There are people just like you out there so advertise yourself. You can do this in the nicest possible way, via the Internet and magazines that cater for you. Some divine man or woman will shower you with all the love in the world.

On a psychic level, instead of believing yourself to be 'gifted' when you're not, visit your local spiritualist church and sit in a developing circle. Stop kidding yourself or others you are some kind of Nostradamus or Doris Stokes and admit it's just your way of appearing more exciting. Accept, too, that it is far more exciting to extract your psychic gifts genuinely and honestly. Then you really can help others as much as yourself.

Famous Moon in Pisces: Elvis Presley, Jerry Seinfeld, O.J. Simpson, Paul Newman, Prince, Alicia Silverstone, Audrey Hepburn, Cybill Shepherd, Gillian Anderson, Ginger Rogers, Catherine Zeta Jones, Grace Kelly, Hillary Clinton.

Your Ascendant – How Other People See You

Each element of your birth chart provides an important piece in the cosmic jigsaw that is your overall personality. Your Sun sign, for instance, reveals your heart and soul, the real you. On the other hand, your Ascendant, the sign that was rising in the east at the moment you were born, reflects the way others see you, their first impressions on meeting you. It provides a picture of the personality you project to others. It is, if you like, your image. The Ascendant is also the indicator of your ruling planet and marks the starting point from where the houses fall into line as well as indicating what sign rules them. The strength of the Ascending sign's influence will vary according to its exact position. It will also be influenced by its relationship to the rest of the chart, in particular, aspects to the planets.

IF YOU HAVE ARIES RISING

To friends and co-workers there will be no mistaking your energy and enterprise. You are a real dynamo, drop-dead sexy, someone who wants to make it to the top and enjoys the competition that comes with the territory. All this will be evident in your outward personality. To your nearest and dearest, however, you will show a different, more tender and loving side. (This is because, with Aries in your first house, the sign at the other side of the zodiac, your Descendant, in this case Libra, with its ruling planet Venus, rules the seventh house of relationships.) So to them you are a compassionate and caring soul, unless you are a negative Aries rising, in which case you will be inclined to be selfish and hot-headed, impatient to get on with ploughing your own furrow in life.

Famous Aries Ascendant: Alec Guinness, Errol Flynn, Barbra Streisand, John Lennon, Shakira, Bill Cosby, Heather Locklear, Ariel Sharon, Che Guevara.

IF YOU HAVE TAURUS RISING

Just like someone with their Sun in Taurus, you have a strong need to lay down roots and get into a life groove. Emotional, material and physical security are high on your list of priorities and, with Scorpio/Mars and Pluto ruling your Descendant, you have a very loyal and loving nature. This may, however, make you seem possessive and jealous within relationships if you are inclined towards the negative.

People also recognize that you have an obstinate nature; in fact, you can be more like a mule than a bull. They will see that you are someone who won't be steamrollered into doing things unless you approve of them. 'True, tried and tested' might be your motto and those who love you should understand this.

Famous Taurus Ascendant: Carlos Santana, Zinedine Zidane, Michael Schumacher, Serena Williams, Sigourney Weaver, Charles Manson.

IF YOU HAVE GEMINI RISING

Your intelligent, highly communicative nature will be obvious to all who cross your path. People will recognize that you are versatile and open to new experiences. On the other hand, people will also recognize a somewhat scatterbrained aspect to your personality, seeing that you are full of great ideas with either no foundation or no conclusion. You can seem disorganized and dissipate your energy going off in all directions.

With your Descendant ruled by Sagittarius/Jupiter, you are someone who hates being tied down, often a real commitment-phobe. Therefore you will be a free spirit romantically and if negatively disposed, inclined towards more than one affair at a time!

In appearance, you will be something of a Peter Pan, eternally youthful with a perpetual twinkle in your eyes and a grin on your lips. This childlike exterior is underlined by your quick, chatty nature and taste for casual yet fashionable clothes, not to mention dashing off at the last minute to see a man about a dog!

Famous Gemini Ascendant: Bruce Springsteen, Drew Barrymore, Steffi Graf, Ricky Martin, Prince Albert of Monaco, Pamela Anderson, Mick Jagger, Hillary Clinton, Saddam Hussein, Tony Blair, Kelly Osbourne.

IF YOU HAVE CANCER RISING

You will be thin-skinned in the extreme and can be oh so easily hurt. You are also apt to take things the wrong way, taking offence where none was ever intended. You have a tendency to worry about nothing and churn over anything people say to you, making a crisis out of a drama, if indeed there was a drama in the first place.

Your strong need for peace and quiet means you can come across as cool, calm and collected first-off. You will present a stoic, stiff-upper-lip exterior rather than showing your real emotions. This can affect your relationships too, making you sometimes seem very cool and detached emotionally. This is in contrast with your inner personality which, as your Descendant is ruled by Capricorn and its very paternal governing planet, Saturn, means you are actually highly protective and intensely devoted. The good news, however, is that this astute side of your personality makes you very well equipped when it comes to business and financial affairs. People around you will see this and like what they see.

Famous Cancer Ascendant: Cher, Judy Garland, Julia Roberts, Steven Spielberg, Albert Einstein, Bill Gates, Arnold Schwarzenegger, John Travolta, Mariah Carey, Robert de Niro.

IF YOU HAVE LEO RISING

You are so keen to make an impression that you might be seen as something of a show-off, determined to hog the limelight at every possible opportunity. Others may see you as being arrogant, self-absorbed or a prima donna.

In relationships you will tend to seek out someone who stands out in the crowd like you. This is down to the influence of Aquarius/Saturn and Uranus on your Descendant, which demands emotional freedom and a partner who is an equal as a friend as much as a lover.

You will also be someone who takes great pride in your appearance, especially your hair. You like to be noticed and don't scrimp when it comes to buying the most fashionable wardrobe. Designer clothes and even carrier bags (even if you've never shopped at Harrods or Saks) are most definitely your scene because you're a Knightsbridge/5th Avenue kind of sign.

Famous Leo Ascendant: Sting, George W. Bush, Bruce Willis, Marilyn Monroe, Johnny Depp, Lucille Ball, Roger Moore, George Michael, Prince Andrew, Prince Charles, Camilla Parker Bowles, Elton John, Lauren Bacall, Jack Nicholson.

IF YOU HAVE VIRGO RISING

You have a gift for communication and getting your ideas across in a crisp, concise and clear manner. You are excellent at analyzing your own actions and project a real sense of control and self-confidence about you. Nothing gets past your incisive brain.

In your one-to-one affairs, however, your Descendant is ruled by Pisces and its governing planets Neptune and Jupiter. So while you have an infuriating habit of idealizing partners, you also have a very romantic nature that can often get lost in your nitpicking ways. Your dress, too, reflects the key elements of your nature. You are neatly turned out, and opt for simple, understated clothes that complement your looks. Think of rag-bag and that can be you, too, as a hippy-type wardrobe appeals to your non-fussy needs.

Famous Virgo Ascendant: Peter Sellers, Tiger Woods, Kurt Cobain, Nicole Kidman, Kevin Costner, Tom Hanks, J.R.R. Tolkien, Pele, Dolly Parton.

IF YOU HAVE LIBRA RISING

Being involved in a partnership of any kind is hugely important to you. Being without somebody else to share life's up and downs can make you down and depressed, so it is no surprise that you put a great deal of effort into forging romantic, professional and platonic friendships. You are *the* zodiac's diplomat and a great ambassador for yourself. You are highly skilled at keeping everyone around you on an even keel.

A patently 'together' exterior masks someone with a hugely sexual side to them. With Aries and its ruler Mars in charge of your Descendant, you not only know what or who you want, but will put a lot of energy into getting it.

This chic, sophisticated Venusian side of your personality is something you try to project in the way you dress. For instance everything has to match – even those garments not obvious to the naked eye. ***Note***: watch out for the giveaway dimple – most Librans have one or two somewhere!

Famous Libra Ascendant: Bill Clinton, Jennifer Lopez, Leonardo DiCaprio, Cary Grant, Britney Spears, Keanu Reeves, Olivia Newton-John, Harrison Ford, Brigitte Bardot, Jim Carrey, David Bowie, Jane Fonda, Grace Kelly, James Dean.

IF YOU HAVE SCORPIO RISING

How can folks not fail to recognize the burning intensity of your personality. It is there in your penetrating eyes and in your amazing powers of concentration. You are totally mesmeric.

Due to your deep-rooted need to be emotionally and psychologically involved in everything you do, your emotions and energies aren't very far from the surface. People may well see the hidden frustration bubbling over when things don't go as well as you'd planned or you meet an obstacle you have to overcome.

When it comes to relationships, you have Taurus on the Descendant. You demand loyalty and can sometimes become totally obsessive about your other half. Your partners will see someone who is passionate about them. Unfortunately, they may also see someone who can take this to extremes and be unreasonably jealous, with envy and revenge boiling away inside.

Your appearance is in keeping with the rest of your personality. You may favour dark and dramatic clothing in rich colours that reflects your intensity. Oh and don't forget the shades. You invented power dressing.

Famous Scorpio Ascendant: Jacqueline Kennedy Onassis, Catherine Zeta Jones, Burt Reynolds, Adolf Hitler, Sylvester Stallone, Marlon Brando, Leonard Nimoy, Michael Douglas, Napoleon Bonaparte, Bette Davis, Margaret Thatcher, Al Pacino, Charlie Chaplin, Diana Ross, Katharine Hepburn, Maria Callas.

IF YOU HAVE SAGITTARIUS RISING

You are a warm and expansive character, laid-back and easy-going, yet with a sense of adventure and positivity that is hard to hide. Indeed, such is your enthusiasm, sagacity and optimism, people will see you as someone who is prone to biting off more than they can chew.

This questing, pioneering need within your personality has to be satisfied before you commit yourself to settling down into a relationship. Otherwise, the presence of Gemini and Mercury ruling your Descendant may make you crave for emotional freedom and that can be a problem. It's always important to reserve some space for yourself in any one-to-one affair.

Your appearance complements your inner self. You have warm and open features with a zest for life and living. There's something about you that appeals to everyone from the minute you walk in a room with your smile and casual approach in appearance.

Famous Sagittarius Ascendant: Princess Diana, Angelina Jolie, Christina Aguilera, Liv Tyler, Fred Astaire, Tom Cruise, Elvis Presley, Freddie Mercury, Elizabeth Taylor, Elizabeth Hurley, Sean Connery, Oprah Winfrey.

IF YOU HAVE CAPRICORN RISING

You are blessed with a plentiful supply of common sense, down-to-earth pragmatism and a wry, dry sense of humour. However, this is often hidden behind your chronic shyness and lack of self-confidence. This reserve can come across as aloofness at times. One rejection can affect you all your life – get over it. Those who are close to you will see the real you, a dutiful, reliable partner, thanks to Cancer and the Moon on your Descendant. You may not say 'I love you' as often as you should, but there will be no doubting your devotion.

The ruling influence of Saturn may lend you the typical Saturnine look. You will tend to wear more formal, smart clothes in keeping with your desire not to stand out from the crowd, although you dress to impress.

Famous Capricorn Ascendant: Abraham Lincoln, Paul Newman, Liberace, Bono, Gisele Bundchen, Naomi Campbell, Meg Ryan, Anthony Hopkins.

IF YOU HAVE AQUARIUS RISING

Your stubborn, dogmatic and occasionally outrageous personality is hard to miss. You have a habit of telling everyone within earshot that you're right and they're wrong. You are extreme in everything you do, from your crazy hair colour to your ill-fitting clothes. You certainly have a distinctive look and avoid the fashion of the times. There's something about you that is dead shocking but that's you, love you or loathe you – and make no mistake people will. However, don't judge this book by its cover as you make a wonderful friend as your myriad of buddies will testify. When the chips are down you are someone others will see as a real pillar of strength. When others leave their friend in the lurch, you coming running to the rescue. In relationships too, with Leo and the Sun ruling your Descendant, you are someone whose big-hearted, faithful nature warms up your partner's life.

Famous Aquarius Ascendant: Teri Hatcher, Matt Damon, Michael J. Fox, Orlando Bloom, Jim Morrison, Condoleeza Rice, Eric Cantona, Steve Jobs.

IF YOU HAVE PISCES RISING

You are blessed with a philosophical and wise nature. You also have a very spiritual approach to life with a great gift for taking setbacks in your stride and putting it down to Providence. People notice this and are impressed by your ability to deal with fate.

In romantic terms, however, the presence of Virgo/Mercury on your Descendant means that while you are a warm and loving person, you can cut your partner to the quick with an acid tongue. People will see you as someone who wants the perfect partnership, but of course the danger is that perfection in anything doesn't exist.

Your outward appearance is eye-catching. You can look divine in something most folks will throw away but you also like to be comfortable and let your hair down, literally.

Famous Pisces Ascendant: Ringo Starr, George Clooney, Gwyneth Paltrow, Pope Benedict, Robert Redford, Demi Moore.

The Midheaven – The Targets You Set Yourself

The Midheaven, the point in the sky immediately above your head when you were born, reflects the objectives and goals you will set yourself in life. For this reason it has an acute bearing on your ego, career, ambitions and professional prospects. It will come into play more and more the older you get as you develop and evolve your need to achieve and be recognized for doing your own 'thing'.

IF YOU HAVE ARIES MIDHEAVEN

You are someone who thrives on competition and have a strong desire to blaze your own trail, so you need a career that brings out this gutsy side of you, testing your initiative at every turn and allowing you to be your own person at the same time. Your mission and purpose in life is to go where no other man or woman has gone before.

Famous Aries Midheaven: George W. Bush, Prince Andrew, Prince Charles, Jack Nicholson, Bill Gates.

IF YOU HAVE TAURUS MIDHEAVEN

You have a deep-rooted need for security on all conceivable levels. You are drawn to a career that brings considerable material rewards as well as a sense of stability. You also enjoy showing others that you are reliable and trustworthy too. Any vocation that is nine-to-five suits your nature.

Famous Taurus Midheaven: Marilyn Monroe, Johnny Depp, Roger Moore, Elton John, Lauren Bacall.

IF YOU HAVE GEMINI MIDHEAVEN

Freedom of speech, in the literal sense, is central to your very being, so you need a profession that allows you to travel or communicate without any limitations. You are suited to coming up with ideas, talking and being as mobile as possible. However, this flexibility may also manifest itself in regular bouts of boredom and frequent changes of career but equally you are happy having two ambitions running parallel to each other.

Famous Gemini Midheaven: Peter Sellers.

IF YOU HAVE CANCER MIDHEAVEN

To bring out the best in yourself, you feel you have to belong to a 'family' structure, so your strengths will lie in working with the public or society in general as they are an extended family. Being in a profession for life can suit you as it gives you the security you need.

Famous Cancer Midheaven: Keanu Reeves, Jennifer Lopez, Leonardo DiCaprio, Britney Spears, Harrison Ford, Brigitte Bardot, Jim Carrey, David Bowie, Jane Fonda, James Dean, Bill Clinton.

IF YOU HAVE LEO MIDHEAVEN

Image is of huge importance to you, so it is vital that you not only succeed but are seen to succeed. You want to be recognized and, if possible, famous for what you do. Power is something you desire too, so ideally your career should enable you to climb to the top with you in charge. Your organizational skills and creative aptitudes are the key to you achieving these things.

Famous Leo Midheaven: Cary Grant, Jacqueline Kennedy Onassis, Michael Douglas, Adolf Hitler, Napoleon Bonaparte, Grace Kelly, Charlie Chaplin, Katharine Hepburn.

IF YOU HAVE VIRGO MIDHEAVEN

In your career, two sides of your personality need to be satisfied. Your ability to communicate and use your agile mind may give you ambitions to sort out problems for other people, but your need to be of service will play a pivotal role in defining your direction. You have the ability to tidy up other people's lives even when yours is in a mess.

Famous Virgo Midheaven: Burt Reynolds, Marlon Brando, Leonard Nimoy, Bette Davis, Margaret Thatcher, Elvis Presley, Diana Ross.

IF YOU HAVE LIBRA MIDHEAVEN

Your ambitions are at their strongest when they are for other people. You are the original supporter of the down and outs, but watch out as they could bite the hand that feeds them by taking away your own professional opportunities. Harmony must prevail, whether it be working in a close-knit team or helping others to cooperate with each other. A career in which an attractive personality, a considerate nature and an immaculate appearance are required will fit you like a glove.

Famous Libra Midheaven: Princess Diana, Angelina Jolie, Christina Aguilera, Fred Astaire, Elizabeth Taylor, Elizabeth Hurley, Catherine Zeta Jones, Oprah Winfrey.

IF YOU HAVE SCORPIO MIDHEAVEN

You keep your ambitions to yourself and your ultimate aim is a position of power, so that you can exercise complete control. Your mission and purpose in life is often grandiose, you want to rule the world and that's just for starters. Your nature makes you an excellent prospect for a career that demands a degree of cloak and dagger, and you can be dramatic and enigmatic, leaving rivals gasping with curiosity.

Famous Scorpio Midheaven: Paul Newman, Liberace, Sean Connery, Prince William.

IF YOU HAVE SAGITTARIUS MIDHEAVEN

Variety is the spice of your life so travel and anything of an international flavour is the key to your career. You will work best in a cosmopolitan environment that provides you with constant intellectual challenges, perhaps learning languages or just gathering knowledge about far-flung places. Whatever your mission and purpose in life at the start, little acorns lead to your personal empire expanding.

Famous Sagittarius Midheaven: Ringo Starr, Audrey Hepburn.

IF YOU HAVE CAPRICORN MIDHEAVEN

Capricorn is the natural ruler of the Midheaven angle. As a result, you set yourself goals and ambitions that are much harder to achieve than for most other people. You are totally geared towards everything this part of the chart stands for. You have an acute sense of your own destiny and won't allow anything to stand in your way unless you are negative in your approach and curry favour to get other people's approval. If you do, remember this: the only approval you need is your own. Success may come late in your career but whenever it comes, you have the ability to lay a foundation stone that can never be toppled. Whatever you do may be a long haul but the slog will be worth it.

Famous Capricorn Midheaven: Alec Guinness, Barbra Streisand.

IF YOU HAVE AQUARIUS MIDHEAVEN

Your need to be an individual shines through in your career. You hate anything regular and rigid so are perfect for freelancing or self-employment. You are never happier than when being your independent and inventive self, so you are suited to doing things in your own time. Do it for anyone else and you'll clock-watch. You find it hard to accept authority because your natural inclination is to rebel and break as many rules as possible. You have an urge to make the world a better place but make sure the subject of your desire for change shares your ambitions – some folks prefer the devil they know.

Famous Aquarius Midheaven: Errol Flynn.

IF YOU HAVE PISCES MIDHEAVEN

You have a selfless streak running right through you. Your ambition is to look after others before looking after yourself. This compassionate, kind-hearted nature will be best rewarded in a career where you feel you are doing good. Anything where image, glamour and beauty is part and parcel of your profession is undeniably going to attract you, but improving your own lot is secondary to helping those worse off than yourself. Your approach to life and living is unconditional.

Famous Pisces Midheaven: Cher, Judy Garland, Hillary Clinton.

Placing Your Planets – Mercury to Pluto

Mercury

Within Planet You, Mercury is the part of your personality that reflects and influences your mental abilities and powers of communication. If you like, Mercury is a version of Brainy, the Numskull who controlled the thinking processes inside the man's head in my favourite cartoon strip. In astrology, he is also linked traditionally with short distances, news and views, your neighbourhood and community, as well as education, learning, networking, daily travel and the nervous system. Mercury rules the signs of Gemini and Virgo, so is particularly significant for people with a strong placement such as the Sun, Moon or Ascendant in either of these signs. Mercury is also very strong when he is placed in the Gemini and Virgo signs or houses, that is the 3rd and 6th.

MERCURY IN ARIES OR THE 1ST HOUSE

If you have this placement, you have a quick and decisive mind that makes you a strong advocate (devil's or otherwise) in arguments. You are very confident and determined, too, and this can show itself in controversial statements, designed to provoke and made purely for your own enjoyment. You may sometimes struggle to marshal your ever-lively mind and lack concentration as a result. You have a circuitful of nervous energy that needs to be channelled or used positively if you are not to suffer from tension, breakdown or hypochondria.

If you have a positive Mercury in Aries or the 1st house

You are intelligent and articulate. There's a daredevil mind waiting to strike. You are great at initiating intellectual or cerebral ventures and projects but woe betide if you get bored or the novelty wears off.

The excitement of travel never fails to bring out the spring lamb in you. Whether it is a trip out to the funfair or just visiting a new place, it is all part and parcel of the adventure you crave to blow away the cobwebs of monotony. Take one project at a time, as you can learn more easily and educate yourself far more copiously if you surround yourself with one subject and one alone. Take only one hobby, too; whether you play sport or administer at your local club, you will do a good job so long as you aren't distracted by what seem like more interesting diversions. The trouble is they might appear interesting at first but eventually they will go the way of everything else – monotony.

If you have a negative Mercury in Aries or the 1st house

Unfocused, provocative, hyperactive and very self-centred, you should take care not to put your own thoughts and desires ahead of everyone else's. Otherwise, not only will you be seen as selfish, but you will also lose out on the experiences and lessons other people can regale you with. Be careful to finish what you begin. Realize your initial enthusiasm can be a boon to everyone around you but unless you pace yourself, you will be left with a zillion loose ends around you, all waiting to be tied up. You need more prosaic and fixed aspects in your horoscope to see something through to a conclusion, successful or otherwise. Talking about conclusions, there is more than a tendency for this Mercury to jump to them, to be premature in his actions and react to one side of a story rather than waiting to hear both. Watch out for this too.

How to overcome a negative Mercury in Aries or the 1st house

Improve concentration, show more compassion in expressing opinions, find an outlet for nervous energy. All these things will lead to being more single-minded: if you are offered too many choices then you will want to try them all. Instead, take one thing at a time. Look at what is spread out in front of you and go for what picks your brains, gives you a mental appetite and adds to your intellect. By going on a learning curve, you can stimulate your brain and you will find that one thing will lead to another quite naturally but reserve your next move for when you are quite certain you have concluded what led you there in the first place. Be willing to trade ideas with other people and don't always assume your opinion is the be all and end all. It isn't, but by taking a little bit of your thinking and merging it with someone else's considered opinion, you will have learned simply by listening rather than hogging the airwaves.

Famous Mercury in Aries: Queen Elizabeth II, Marlon Brando, Leonard Nimoy, Fred Astaire, Al Pacino, Charlie Chaplin, Diana Ross.

MERCURY IN TAURUS OR THE 2ND HOUSE

There is a solid, steady side to your Mercurial intelligence. It makes you cautious and practical on the one hand, but reliable and highly methodical on the other. You can also be as stubborn as a mule with opinions that are unshakeable, regardless of the arguments against them. You have a real interest in money matters and are good at wheeler-dealing and driving a hard bargain. You may also be clever at investing. Figures that add up to profit seem to glide into your mind like cash into a till.

Because agile Mercury is in fixed Taurus, he is able to stand still and concentrate on what he is doing. He has the ability to deal with routine and even acute boredom because this winged warrior knows what has to be done if success and riches are going to come your way. Concentrate your mind on special activities such as accountancy on the computer, figures and currency or gardening and horticultural activities so you can think whilst you are doing something practical.

If you have a positive Mercury in Taurus or the 2nd house

You are steady and astute, and have financial acumen that may come naturally, or else picked up through experience, a setback perhaps, or another financial life lesson. Make no bones about it, Mercury in this position gives you an ability to add up profits and losses very quickly, although the more positive your attitude, the more profits you will make. You also place a lot of value on self-worth; in other words, you are happy to invest in yourself whether it be your image, equipment or education, because in the long run you know you must speculate to accumulate. By doing so early on, you will be rewarded with a reputation that is worth its weight in gold.

If you have a negative Mercury in Taurus or the 2nd house

You will choose to learn the hard way about almost everything but especially money. You will get your fingers burned because money will burn a hole in your pocket. You may have to live your early/teenage years having next to nothing and watching the rest of your peer group splashing out when you can't. You try to join them and as a result end up poorer than before. You must learn about the value of things. You must understand that worth isn't always about the price tag; it is about finding out how what you learn, save or discover can be good for you in the future. Your natural obstinacy won't let you take advice lightly if it rails against what you have chosen to believe – and it is then you will cost yourself time, effort and energy, all of it wasted because of your too-rigid mind.

How to overcome a negative Mercury in Taurus or the 2nd house

Weighing things up is always important to Venus, and here Mercury is in a Venus sign. You have to weigh up the difference between what something is worth and what something costs. Learn, too, that the best things in life are often free. So if you get the opportunity to do something or are invited to share with others, see it as a chance to increase your self-worth. And just because you haven't paid the earth for something doesn't mean it has no value. Because you are apt to be possessive, you need to learn to let go of things. You will profit far more by sharing what you own and seeing the pleasure it brings to others. By being generous with your spirit, your goods and your self, you will get back much more than you ever thought possible. Although we live in a secular world, it doesn't mean you have to follow a secular theme.

Famous Mercury in Taurus: Renee Zellweger, Barbra Streisand, Uma Thurman, Johnny Depp, Cher, Liberace, Katharine Hepburn, Jack Nicholson.

MERCURY IN GEMINI OR THE 3RD HOUSE

With this double-dose of Mercury power, you are blessed with an extremely quick and clever mind. There are pros and cons to this, however. Yes, on the one hand, you are witty and a great communicator, but you can hog the conversation and your opinions change with the wind. Perseverance isn't a strong suit either. You are great at starting projects but less good at finishing them. You need to keep busy for the sake of your nervous energy, which may cause you health problems otherwise. You are very inquisitive and want to know the whys and wherefores of everything and if you can't find out, you'll just make it up!

If you have a positive Mercury in Gemini or the 3rd house

There is something so cute and adorable about you and it isn't just your face! It's you, your attitude, approach and general demeanour that gives you a puckish and youthful glow. At 80 you still have the mind of an eight-year-old, with an eternal thirst for knowledge that needs consistently quenching. You have a real interest in what's going on around you, whether it is through being community spirited, or having a lively relationship with a sibling or cousin, aunt or uncle, that kind of relative.

Travel is very important to you as for you, variety is the spice of life. You want to experience all that the world has to offer, whether it's visiting easy-to-reach distances or places that have a tale to tell. Ideas spring from you like the fountain of youth springs from your personality. There is never a dull moment with you around as you always find something interesting and adventurous to do, and give the pessimists and doom-mongers a splash of happiness and optimism to wipe away their gloom.

If you have a negative Mercury in Gemini or the 3rd house

The main problem with this Mercury placement is never really feeling settled. You are always wanting to be upwardly mobile, all gung-ho to move onwards and upwards when in fact you don't know what you're aiming at, have no realizable goal and are totally harebrained about where to go and what to do. It's time to concentrate your mind or you will be forever chasing your tail.

You still have the same capacity as any positive Mercury in Gemini but somehow you just can't embrace it. You are impressionable, thinking that just over the hill there is something more interesting going on, but trust me, it isn't. Life is what *you* make it, you have Mercury in Gemini and as such you are an eternal student with an inquiring mind. So use that mind, but use it in tandem with something else. This is one placement where Mercury can work on two things at once but not 22! Theory and practice can work well together so long as you don't waste your ingenuity and ideas by chasing after something that looks better on paper than in reality.

How to overcome a negative Mercury in Gemini or the 3rd house

Because you have the potential to be a very clever and ingenious person, you must understand the dangers of a butterfly mind. If not, you will come up with splendid ideas but never receive the rich rewards that should go with them. You will gossip and tell everyone else your thoughts, not believing or realizing their worth and before you know it, they will have capitalized on your brilliance to make a mint. You need to learn when to shut up and keep your own counsel. Learn that you don't have to fill thin air with small talk just for the sake of it. Silence is golden and this is no metaphorical statement. You can have thoughts and brainwaves that are sensationally ahead of their time. When you do, don't tell anyone, write them down, copyright them, do whatever you have to do, but don't tell a soul!

Mercury is also in need of stimulation, which is why you must read, learn, travel or work. In fact, you must do anything, just don't do nothing. The devil will literally make work for idle hands. You will end up following the flock when you are too brainy to do so. Concentrate on something that fascinates you. When you do, don't let it go, get really into it, research the facts and make yourself a doyen of a particular subject. A hobby on the side is good for you, as is networking and socializing. You are no good without people to interact with, but make sure they encourage and promote you. Avoid anyone superficial, untrustworthy or brainless, as it's too easy to go down to their level when they should be reaching up to yours. Have belief and faith in your ideas. They really are out of this world.

Famous Mercury in Gemini: Marilyn Monroe, Angelina Jolie, Errol Flynn, Kylie Minogue, George Michael, Tom Cruise, Audrey Hepburn, Elizabeth Hurley.

MERCURY IN CANCER OR THE 4TH HOUSE

If you have this placement in your chart, you are the owner of a great imagination. Your psychic potential is in the zodiac top three. Unless your Mercury is afflicted, you can also possess a fine memory, but this affinity for the past can keep you rooted in events that are long gone. More positively, your fascination with family history deepens your sense of belonging. A home of your own, a sanctuary or place where you feel safe is central to your life; you may even work there too.

You are a compassionate person, but your emotions may rule your head at times. You are also prone to dramatizing things, sometimes making mountains out of molehills. This can express itself in worrying about your family as well. Your mother can often have a more powerful effect on you than other relatives. You often yearn to make sentimental journeys to destinations that played a part in your personal history, perhaps where you lived, the school you went to, where you were born – any place that makes you feel proud and patriotic.

If you have a positive Mercury in Cancer or the 4th house

Mercury is the god of the mind and occupies a very sensitive watery sign – this means you have the ability to express your feelings in a fulsome way. You can put thoughts and words behind your emotions, meaning you can open up rather than clam up. There will be a fascination with history, ancestry, perhaps even the street where you live, and you will want to beaver away mentally to find out more about where you belong. Visits to local places of interest or resorts are good for you because although Cancer is the sign of the home, you don't want to become homebound. Following the trail of the family tree will get you out and about. Working from your home space is good, as you will have the mental discipline to do what you want from a safe and secure environment. Feeling at home is everything you do and making people feel part of your family makes you popular with those you know.

If you have a negative Mercury in Cancer or the 4th house

You are a real worry guts, tending to overanalyze your feelings, your thoughts and everything people say to you, whether in jest or not. You are constantly on the lookout for deeper meanings to situations that, in truth, are simple. This pessimistic and overanalytical attitude can get on people's nerves because you will build up something out of all proportion and get into funny, peculiar, weird habits that not only rule your life but everyone else's too. This placement can also make you a wanderer, finding it hard to settle down and plant roots. You are perpetually in search of a location that reminds you of your happiest childhood years, but it doesn't exist. You need to admit this was another time, when you had totally different people around you. In the same vein, you clutter your life with remnants of things from the past. Your home is a car boot sale just waiting to happen. For goodness sake, learn to let go – what's gone is gone, forgive and forget. Understand that and you will unburden yourself in a thrice.

How to overcome a negative Mercury in Cancer or the 4th house

Put things in perspective and do something with your mind that will take it off whatever worry you might have. Be logical, but not analytical to such a degree that you become paranoid. By weighing up the common-sensical pros with the emotional cons, you will see that the balance between the two can give you the peace of mind you crave. Can I suggest you join a local history group or genealogy society, or simply get into something that is connected with your own personal past so you strengthen your sense of belonging. Find a space in the place you live that you can call your own, stack it full with a comfy armchair, photos of loved ones, mementoes, whatever you like to create your sacred space. Work from here, contemplate from here and call it your own. If you haven't enough room then try a small potting shed, greenhouse or tent! But you need a place to call your own. Learn to develop your wonderful intuition, join a psychic group or get involved with spiritual activities. Serve in a charity shop (if you can resist all the cast-offs!). Do something that occupies your kind but hypersensitive self. Finally, don't brood or dwell. And rather than build something or someone up into a hell or devil, learn to forgive even if you can't forget. If you think about it, all that negative energy is doing you more harm than good. And the object of your obsession probably hasn't thought of you once.

Famous Mercury in Cancer: Harrison Ford, Princess Diana, Liv Tyler, Judy Garland, Camilla Parker Bowles.

MERCURY IN LEO OR THE 5TH HOUSE

You put the D into Diva and the P into Prima Donna. Nothing wrong with that, so long as it is seen as being over the top, theatrical and a part of your personality. Anything connected with the performing arts is right up your street, whether actor, director or writer! Your gift for communication is wonderful to see in full flood. You may come across as knowing everything about everything, which will annoy some folks who see you as a chancer, someone who comes in and takes their glory. You are a great organizer but want everything done your way. You should take time to relax and realize that no-one, not even you, is indispensable. Sports are good for you, especially the dextrous kind like tennis. You also have a knack for flattery and are great at wooing potential lovers. You plan romantic moments well in advance but prefer the chase. You have a vital and dynamic creative streak and should use your mind and hands to create something that is unique to you.

If you have a positive Mercury in Leo or the 5th house

There is something very special about you. Each and every individual Mercury in Leo will produce and express a talent totally different from anyone else. Your first job is to specialize in something. It might be creative writing, sports, an artistic project or enterprising venture; it doesn't matter what, just so long as you recognize you have something in you that needs bringing to the surface.

You are generous to a fault and can have an almost uncanny knack of understanding children or teenagers when everyone has given up on them. Your own offspring will grab your complete attention, and you will want to supervise and teach them so that you can bring out their best. If you can't have children, then pets will make a most admirable substitute because your goal in life is to love and care for others.

If you have a negative Mercury in Leo or the 5th house

Fluid Mercury is in fixed Leo and/or the 5th house, which means you can be a right handful. More immature than your own children, even! In fact, your own family may well find you a source of embarrassment mainly because you simply demand things. Watch what you say and how you say it, or you will upset people with your overbearing, domineering, dogmatic way. You don't mean to but you can come across as if you are the queen (or king) of Sheba and everyone else are peasants. Where humility, sincerity or graciousness is concerned, you haven't a clue. You can also expect far too much from your children and may even try to live your own life through them.

How to overcome a negative Mercury in Leo or the 5th house

It's more than likely you read the section above on a negative Mercury and said, 'Well that's certainly not me.' But all the heads around you were nodding as if to signal 'Oh, yes it is.' But that's the problem – no-one dare tell you! Remember the fabulous Bette Davis in *Whatever Happened to Baby Jane?* She played the huge ex-movie star, dressed in a party frock in full make-up. She thought everyone was looking at her because they recognized her but in fact she simply looked ridiculous. Be aware of this because Mercury is making you say or do things that can have the same effect. Instead take him and use him to your advantage. Specialize in something that doesn't steal all the limelight. Learn to accept that sometimes the chorus or a cameo role can be more rewarding. You have a part to play in life that may not always be headline news, but so what? Often a supporting role will give you much more than you ever realized.

Do things for people unconditionally and don't always assume that when people say nice things they actually mean them. Your ego is so easily massaged and like most pussy cats, you will roll over for your tummy to be tickled. If you are turned down romantically, professionally or for any other reason, don't be slighted. Get over it.

Famous Mercury in Leo: Jacqueline Kennedy Onassis, Sylvester Stallone, Bill Clinton, George W. Bush, Napoleon Bonaparte, Ringo Starr, Peter Sellers.

MERCURY IN VIRGO OR THE 6TH HOUSE

With this placement, you have a powerful, logical mind. The downside of this, however, is that you can get lost in the details and fail to see the woods for the trees. This can make you a very pernickety, pedantic person and, unless you learn to loosen up a little, you'll have problems with your nerves. A preoccupation with health matters means you can be a walking medical dictionary. That's fine just so long as you don't believe that with every ache and pain you have a severe symptom. Workwise, too, if you cry wolf too often, one day someone will turn round and bite you. Travel and learning really interests you because you are after knowledge in all shapes and forms.

If you have a positive Mercury in Virgo or the 6th house

Nothing escapes you. You are intelligent, thorough and tidy – well, to the extent that you know where everything is. You are the archetypal list-maker and are great at rationalizing and filing. This means you are the perfect PA and life-laundry organizer, perfect for those who are in a total confused muddle about their lives.

You say what you mean and mean what you say, and enjoy doing it. Ethically and morally, you believe in total sincerity and may be far too modest. Workshops, retreats and study courses are right up your street and the more you can master the art of communications with all the clever gadgets at your disposal, the happier you will be. You hate to miss a trick; if there is something new and inventive to be mastered, you're the person to do it. You will be popular with co-workers because you are ready with sane and sage advice, offering stacks of common sense and sympathy that enables people to sort their own lives out. You have a wicked sense of humour, often seeing humour that others miss.

If you have a negative Mercury in Virgo or the 6th house

This isn't so bad for you as it is for everyone else. You can get so uptight about silly, petty details that not only do you miss the overall picture but you can't even see what's going on in front of your nose. A born pedant, you can fuss and interfere so much that it gets hard for anyone to get on with their job of work. Your sticky fingers are in there mucking everything up, but the truth is you are 100 years too late. Because you have spent so much time boning up on something, you don't know there have been other inventions and newer models made.

Children and young people can feel threatened intellectually by you. In a starchy, Victorian way you teach them about your elders but fail to help with the basics like writing, reading or maths. It's time to chill out and realize that a puritanical approach will alienate and harm rather than support and help. Finally, watch out for your psychosomatic illnesses or otherwise hypochondria may set in when you feel up against it, again, hiding the true cause of the problem.

How to overcome a negative Mercury in Virgo or the 6th house

The art of relaxation is more important than you realize. There is a simple message you need to learn and that is *there is no such thing as perfection.* You must allow some leeway, as no-one will ever, or at least rarely, be able to come up to your level of quality. In fact, be honest, not even you can reach what you would class as passable – so let it go. So long as you and others do their best, that's all that matters.

You are a superb communicator if you drop your airs and graces and learn to take advantage of some of the puckish, Mercury fun that is lying deep down within you. A chuckle, a giggle and a night letting your hair down isn't bad or ungodly. In fact, it is very good for you and those around you. Get busy arranging and organizing the lives of a person, club, group or organization that is crying out for an administrator like you. You are wanted, so head for those who would welcome your kind of tidy, together talents.

Famous Mercury in Virgo: Prince Charles, Keanu Reeves, Sting, Lance Armstrong, Madonna, Michael Douglas, Lucille Ball, Freddie Mercury, Lauren Bacall, Sean Connery.

MERCURY IN LIBRA OR THE 7TH HOUSE

A natural for a job in the diplomatic service, you use your communication skills to promote harmony and peace. However, your ability to see both sides of every argument can be a disadvantage at times. You can spend an eternity weighing up the pros and cons when a quick decision is what's needed. This indecision can also leave you open to others who can sway you into thinking their way. You are a great tactician and know how to say the right thing at the right time. In fact, you watch your p's and q's so that you can win someone round to your way of thinking. You can be a verbal smoothie, going out of your way to avoid an argument (unless your Mercury is afflicted, then watch out).

If you have a positive Mercury in Libra or the 7th house

You are a natural peacemaker and it is in your intellectual nature to see everyone getting on with everyone else. Nothing gives you greater happiness than to see the people you love enjoying each other. Music and beautiful things move you; even a Disney movie can reduce you to tears, such is the extent to which you want to see harmony working. But lest we forget, this is an airy planet in an airy sign so you aren't a sentimentalist. On the contrary, your mind is leaps and bounds ahead of the rest. Woe betide anyone who belittles you, undermines you or is discourteous. You will not only show them the door but you will do so with a well-balanced argument as to why they shouldn't darken your doorstep again. You fight for rights, fairness and truth, despising injustice of any kind. You will go to the ends of the earth to ensure you clear your name or that of anyone else who has been sullied by lies or nastiness.

You would make a great QC or barrister, simply because you have a natural affinity with balance – the ability to see both sides of the question and to be totally unbiased when necessary. You can calm the savage breast of people who are going through inner anger or outer conflict. You are great to have around when someone needs to talk something through as you can help them get a balanced view. Travel to beautiful places soothes your soul.

If you have a negative Mercury in Libra or the 7th house

This next statement might not seem negative but it is: you are someone who spends so much time thinking of others and what they think that you completely forget yourself. By doing this, you overlook your own needs and that's a crime. You can be argumentative, mainly because you're not sure what it is you want. You can't make choices for fear of missing out on something better. Your indecision leads to frustration that builds until you are making accusations or casting ultimatums. The upshot of this is that you play for time when time has run out and accordingly miss out on every opportunity. You can be a manipulator, and can become jealous if you introduce friends who then run off together.

How to overcome a negative Mercury in Libra or the 7th house

You have got to stop worrying about what people think of you and how you live your life. The golden rule is you can do whatever you like so long as it doesn't hurt anyone. Even if what you are doing is risqué or 'different', so long as it's between consenting adults – who cares? Learn to go with your judgement, which in reality is well tuned when it comes to decisions. When the clock is ticking, there is no point in going all round the houses with your prophecies of what might happen if you do this or that. You will miss the boat. Plump for your first choice or your instinct. Even if it doesn't work out, you will have lost nothing. In fact, you will have gained the knowledge that you can make quick choices!

When people are rude, tell them why you are angry. That is

their lesson to learn. Don't get screwed up and say nothing. You must follow your own convictions. This life is about cause and effect, so if you hate the cause, have an effect on the situation by speaking your mind honestly and fairly. After all, that is what you are best at.

Famous Mercury in Libra: Catherine Zeta Jones, Leonardo DiCaprio, Brigitte Bardot, Olivia Newton-John, Margaret Thatcher, Bill Gates, Kate Winslet, Beyonce Knowles, Gwyneth Paltrow.

MERCURY IN SCORPIO OR THE 8TH HOUSE

Your intuition and instinct is highly tuned and is a big influence on the way you approach life. You are good at rooting out the truth in any given situation, but you can become obsessive in this regard. At times, so much is going on inside your head that you can become lost in your own complex world. You have an interest in psychology and business but also a fascination with life and death that can turn into a fixation with the occult and other supernatural subjects. You are a deep thinker and could never be described as shallow. You never judge a book by its cover and once someone opens you up, they will find a person who has a mind like a JCB – you dig away until you find answers. And not just to the original question; issues concerning joint finances and other documentation will play a greater role in your life than they would in others.

If you have a positive Mercury in Scorpio or the 8th house

You are perspicacious, insightful, instinctive and extremely deep. No-one can ever lie to you. They wouldn't know it, but you can see right through their untruths. While you remain poker-faced, you can be opening up Aladdin's Cave without anyone knowing.

You are secretive and sure of yourself – and what you are not sure about, you will find out. You have the mind of Miss Marple or Sherlock Holmes, brilliant at mysteries and the macabre. Your psychic powers combined with your astute mind not only make you a great detective and researcher but additionally you have a sixth sense, which makes a formidable weapon in your personal armoury. Loyal and faithful, you despise anyone who does not return these qualities. You will benefit through inheritance or the misfortune of others as fate will often give you the assistance you need with business, finance or red tape.

If you have a negative Mercury in Scorpio or the 8th house

Obsessive and compulsive, jealous and wracked with thoughts of revenge, this placement gives you the melodramatic and grand operatic traits one should expect when the innocence of Mercury finds his way into Hades. You don't do anything by halves, but take care when you set out to destroy others with what you know or find out. You may do the classic Scorpionic thing of stinging yourself. You are secretive but in an almost psychotic way: you play mind games to hurt others and follow the teachings of Machiavelli in an effort to win power and control over others. All in all, an afflicted Mercury in Scorpio harbours so many complex and complicated thoughts that there needs to be a release, an escape. Counselling or therapy would be most helpful. You must remember one thing, however: you can't fight fate so it's not even worth trying.

How to overcome a negative Mercury in Scorpio or the 8th house

It can be a lonely and sometimes chilling existence living with a negative Mercury. The most important thing to learn is trust – starting with yourself. Suspicion can lead to manias and neuroses so you must nip things in the bud before they even begin. There is nothing, absolutely nothing, wrong in taking advice from an expert who can help you.

You have a mind that is best put to positive use in, for example, forensics or detective work with the police or other uniformed areas, or as an investigator for an insurance company. If you don't, you might resort to criminal activities yourself, mainly because you are totally fascinated with the underworld. Being a member of a secret organization will indulge your passion for the unknown and occult. Equally, you might enjoy creative writing, giving John le Carré or Agatha Christie a run for their money. If your offspring become remote or distant, take them under your compassionate and loving wing or you will drive them away.

Famous Mercury in Scorpio: Hillary Clinton, Roger Moore, Grace Kelly, Eminem, Ioan Gruffudd, Demi Moore, Julia Roberts, Jodie Foster, Condoleeza Rice, Diego Maradona, Prince Charles, Jacqueline Stallone.

MERCURY IN SAGITTARIUS OR THE 9TH HOUSE

Your supercharged mind needs constant stimulation. You are always on the lookout for a mental challenge. Your concentration may let you down, however. You are good at seeing the big picture, but not so good at the smaller, more detailed one. You can be guilty of playing Pollyanna or Walter Mitty, being overoptimistic and not thinking things through fully.

You love travelling, learning new languages and discovering foreign cultures. You want to know how others live and if you can go there and see for yourself, ever better. You find learning and knowledge dead sexy, giving you a head start in the local quiz league or making you an entertaining raconteur or teacher.

If you have a positive Mercury in Sagittarius or the 9th house

Broad-minded and optimistic, they should just call you Mr Micawber. You are seriously into 'knowing' that everything will be all right. You are a happy, hopeful friend who gives the kind of support we all need sometimes. However, be sure you've someone to call on when you need advice, as sometimes you do all the giving. Intellectually, you are a pioneering soul going where most Mercury placings have never been before. You may be a tiny bit faddish but that is only because sometimes you want to find out more about umpteen things and you don't have enough hours in a day. This can make you a Jack of all trades, master of none, so instead choose two things that are poles apart and go for them both.

You see the good in people, sometimes to your detriment – you can be overly trusting when a little bit of suspicion wouldn't go amiss. Generous with both words and deeds you are the kind of happy go lucky fellow that everyone adores. Travel is not so much a desire but a necessity for you as boredom is your greatest enemy. Along with the package breaks to Spain, you will be drawn to faraway places with strange-sounding names, the more exotic the better. Your energy and *joie de vivre* belies your true age as you are a teenager, 14 going on 40! For good mental health, you must always have a book on the go, and if you can get involved with any kind of higher education, do so. You have a positive outlook and an attitude that attracts opportunity and good luck, simply because you are a magnet for it. Your judgement is well tuned, and wisdom is imbued in you at birth. You are an honourable person and abhor all kinds of hypocrisy, bigotry and prejudice.

If you have a negative Mercury in Sagittarius or the 9th house

You are unfocused and all over the place. You can't choose what to do for the best and as a result try everything or nothing. Either way, you lose opportunities as you rapaciously try to grab everything that's going. You do things to see what you can get out of a situation or person, and have the gall to persuade the people involved to believe you are doing it for the best of reasons.

You can be totally prejudiced and narrow-minded when it comes to your religious beliefs, education or indeed anything. You believe you know best, your opinions being far, far superior to what other folk believe. Your judgement is weighted to what suits you, and you have no compunction in lying, exaggerating or going against common sense if it means you will miss out on something. You are quick to point the finger of blame against others when it is obviously your fault, and forgiveness isn't your scene either, given your meanness of spirit. You are far too judgemental and critical when people do not come up to your expectations of them.

How to overcome a negative Mercury in Sagittarius or the 9th house

Start off thinking you will get nothing out of a situation or venture and just do it for the fun or thrill factor. That way if it works out well, it will be an extra bonus. How much nicer is that than having great expectations that come to nothing?

Don't judge everyone by your own standards. How would you feel if you were always called to account because of what somebody else thinks you should be like? Do things out of a genuine kindness and desire to help, and do them unconditionally. Perhaps spend some time at a youth or community centre, or use some of your experience or knowledge to help those who cannot afford to help themselves but who are eager to learn.

Enjoy time on your own; don't always flood your life with people and when you meet someone who knows a wee bit more than you, don't make them feel a fool or take the mickey out of them – it will backfire on you. Being generous with your mind and spirit will win the gratitude of the universe. Understand that there doesn't have to be a motive in everything and you don't always have to win or gain. Enjoy a laugh and enjoy the craic.

Famous Mercury in Sagittarius: Britney Spears, Christina Aguilera, Maria Callas, Bjork, Jude Law, Ricky Martin, Calista Flockhart, Scarlett Johansson, Woody Allen, Steven Spielberg.

MERCURY IN CAPRICORN OR THE 10TH HOUSE

Your logical and practical mind makes you good with figures and money matters. You approach tasks rationally, taking one thing at a time. You have big ambitions but can be prone to negativity and pessimism. You may have a powerful mental connection with your father or grandfather or a man who doubles as a father but is a relative, friend, lover or boss.

Shrewd and cunning with amazing business acumen, it takes a hell of a clever person to get one over you. You are the opposite of gullible and don't suffer fools gladly. You prefer to use few words and some days would prefer not to talk at all! Taciturn you might be, but your mind is always tossing over thoughts and listing the good versus bad points of an idea or enterprise. By sleeping on a choice or decision you come up with a solution to the most complicated and mysterious problem.

You travel for a purpose. You may well be working even on your holiday. This is because you hate wasting time and if you can take a break *and* make a contact or two whilst you're there, you will be completely satisfied, even if your partner isn't! Ambitious to a degree from a young age, you will not lose your appetite for success until the day you die. If you do suffer failure or disappointment, you will retreat for a while, think things over and come back fighting.

If you have a positive Mercury in Capricorn or the 10th house

You are a stickler for protocol and form. Tradition is very important as it gives you continuity, something to go on when making choices or decisions. You are full of sensible advice and enjoy being asked to come up with a solution to what is bugging someone. You are an assiduous worker. You may even take some perverse delight in form filling or market research: lists, research and filing away information is second nature to you. You are a total perfectionist but may drive yourself too hard sometimes. In fact, not knowing when to switch off is your biggest fault.

Diligent, dedicated and determined once you've made up your mind, nothing on earth will shift you from attaining your ambition. You like to have a clear mission and purpose in life and enjoy anyone who is befuddled, dizzy and ditzy, although you couldn't stand working with them where imperatives are concerned. You aren't averse to a few machinations and cunning plans, but use them not just for yourself, but for the benefit of all.

The owner of a wry, dry sense of humour, you will have them rolling in the aisles with your acid lines and immaculate timing. Conscientious and fastidious, you do things by the book – not following the rules and regulations could cause too much hassle later.

If you have a negative Mercury in Capricorn or the 10th house

You are always up to something. You can't stand to be doing nothing when you could be competing with a person who annoys you or is out to frustrate your ambition. You are more than a careerist; you want to be the one and only when it comes to success and recognition, and will be happy to sabotage and undermine anyone who gets in your way. You will play every trick in the book to ensure no-one gets the better of you, cutting any corner to reach the dizzy heights of success. You don't care how you get to the top so long as you get there. However, you can be the architect of your own downfall, creating self-made rules to justify why you should or shouldn't do something. In doing this, you restrict and limit your options by being small- or narrow-minded, too self-critical and always thinking you could have done better.

You may have a very difficult relationship with your father or father figure, including your boss. You don't care what they think, yet you always want their approval. You can go on guilt trips that take you far away from your original destination. You can be cruel, sarcastic and caustic, not just cutting people to the quick but dead! Cool, calm and collected, you are always assuming the worst in people, and are so suspicious. You can pretend that something doesn't matter when in truth it is eating away at you, leading to depression, persecution complexes and a wallowing in self-pity.

How to overcome a negative Mercury in Capricorn or the 10th house

Get a life! That's my first advice. Stop beating yourself up and see what you are missing in life. Okay, you are a duty-bound creature, but sometimes you use responsibilities as an excuse for you *not* to do something. There's a wonderful world out there and yet you limit yourself to known people, known places and what you know. The true, tried and tested is safe – but wouldn't it be good to throw caution to the wind and do something wild and spontaneous every now and again? That's precisely what you should do. Instead of marching past the travel agents, go and see what's on offer.

Don't see everyone as a potential threat to your ambitions – they are not trying to get one over you. Perhaps by sitting down and discussing a situation, you will not only find you were barking up the wrong tree but you have a friend for life as well.

Understand that you need to take time to make choices but that doesn't mean forever. A good overnight sleep is enough for you to solve and resolve anything then get on with it. If you recognize a nasty habit of wanting to hurt or undermine people when they are celebrating a happy time, then either avoid them or preferably do something nice even if it kills you! Congratulations is a word you don't often use and mean. It's time to turn the tables on the negative, pessimistic you.

Famous Mercury in Capricorn: Rowan Atkinson, Teri Hatcher, Annie Lennox, Cary Grant, David Bowie, Jane Fonda, Elvis Presley, Paul Newman, James Dean, Brad Pitt, Orlando Bloom, Princess Caroline and Princess Stephanie of Monaco, Mel Gibson, Anthony Hopkins, Michael Schumacher.

MERCURY IN AQUARIUS OR THE 11TH HOUSE

I have no hesitation in proclaiming this placement as the mark of a genius. You are so ahead of your time you are a creature of the future. You have a flash of brilliance within you and have a quick, highly original mind. However, you can get stuck on particular ideas, failing to move on when necessary. Concentration can be a problem, too.

You are highly sociable and have many friends, but not many are close to you. You have an interest in humanitarian issues but need to form a club or group so that you can attract others of a similar ilk – it is worth realizing that no man (or woman, for that matter) is an island.

You'd make a great astrologer, or student of the metaphysical or New Age subjects as you are intrigued by the supernatural or abnormal. The more unconventional someone or something is, the more it gets your vote as you are completely drawn to the zany, quirky and extraordinary. Most other people will find it hard to get on your wavelength and you may need to know them for a while before you can sustain good communications. In fact, someone might think you are joking when you are dead serious and serious when you are just joking!

If you have a positive Mercury in Aquarius or the 11th house

You are always one step ahead of everyone else. Your foresight and vision has to be seen to be believed. You can prophesy lucidly, due to an intuition that is totally uncanny. Put your mind to something and you're immediately on a lateral wavelength and come at things from an entirely different angle. Soon, hey presto, you have sorted out a difficult situation.

You are so friendly that some people might think you want something but this placing is just totally friendly – there really is no hidden agenda. You are best in a social setting or putting your mind behind ideas and ventures that are for the greater good. Platonic friendships with no strings attached are right up your street, once things get heavy with emotion or possessiveness then you run a mile. You harbour hopes and wishes from an early age and aspire to them. You realize that time moves on and things change; you are willing to sacrifice the past for something more apt for a modern age. You should get involved with anything connected with modern inventions, especially during this Age of Aquarius. If something has been created so that communications can flow then you should get your gizmo or gadget immediately. Being at the cutting edge is what makes you who you are – a child of the future.

If you have a negative Mercury in Aquarius or the 11th house

You can be intolerant to a degree, tarring people with the same brush and making generalized sweeping statements about everyone when you have only had one bad experience. These are traits that reflect the worst of this afflicted position. Aquarius is the sign of live and let live – if you don't follow this rule, you will be labelled an extremist and find the wrath of the gods will be unleashed upon you by those you accuse or issue ultimatums to. You need proof or evidence before you say or do anything you'll live to regret. Not that my warning will stop you, once you're on a roll you are always right, never wrong. If someone has done something wonderful, you've always done something better. Humility is not your strong suit.

You go all designer with anything from clothes to equipment but haven't a clue as to why – you want to create an impression of someone who is state-of-the-art but your mind is state-of-the-arK! You want to disrupt and cause chaos when you find things are running smoothly and take great pleasure in this. You can be shocking, totally destructive and bring change where none is necessary. The upshot is you might win admiration from the odd bod around you but your community and humanity won't thank you for behaving like an anarchist. All you will succeed in doing is creating an unholy alliance to stop you and your ridiculously eccentric ideas in their tracks.

How overcome a negative Mercury in Aquarius or the 11th house

The last thing I would ever ask you to do is follow the flock but I do want you to be more sensitive to other people's needs and not to automatically condemn what they suggest or say as stupid. Be their friend, help them to understand that perhaps what they are doing will be bad for everyone, including themselves. Put your clever mind to good use, adopt a hobby, join a club or get involved with a global campaign that shows you care. Communicate your concerns to the wider world and you will soon have your own band of disciples who realize you have the solution to age-old problems.

If people criticize or shoot your ideas down see this in the right way, realizing that that they will only do this if they don't understand, that fear is often at the bottom of any attack. If your ideas are radical, accept that some folks find change alarming. Disarm them by taking the trouble to explain your position and before long you will have converted more to your cause. Those that still don't agree are either on another planet or you can agree to disagree. Get your Mercury on a positive track by realizing not everyone is as clever, fast or progressive as you. But it doesn't mean they are dolts; it just emphasizes the fact you are light years in front. Be your usual warm and curious self and don't allow impatience or rudeness to scar what could be a beautiful friendship.

Famous Mercury in Aquarius: Muhammad Ali, Jim Carrey, Oprah Winfrey, Jennifer Aniston, Kate Moss, David Jason, Neil Diamond, LL Cool J, Bob Marley, Wolfgang Amadeus Mozart, Kevin Costner, Alicia Keys.

MERCURY IN PISCES OR THE 12TH HOUSE

Yours is a mind that works on a higher plane, giving you a flair for psychic and mystical thought. You have a very vivid imagination, with a strong artistic bent as well. On the other hand, your flair for the instinctive and aesthetic can keep your feet off the ground and you may become confused and forgetful. This in turn means you can develop irrational fears that have no obvious roots. Yours is a romantic Mercury who is intrigued and motivated by fine words and delicate prose. You may be a poet and not yet know it. You are intrigued by religion and faith, especially if it is oriental in its basis – Buddhism to Chinese astrology, for example.

You are a wonderful charity or volunteer worker and know how to uplift those who are down. You are drawn to a different vibration than most other Mercury placements. Investigating your dreams is something you should do, as by contacting your subconscious mind you will learn much about yourself. Inclined to believe your own fantasies and, at times, likely to live in La-La Land, you should avoid any substances or liquids that add to your escapist nature. Otherwise, you might go off at a tangent and ruin what is a beautiful mind.

If you have a positive Mercury in Pisces or the 12th house

You can empathize with so many people that you seem to have a psychic link with them. Your powers of telepathy and ESP draw you close to folks who are as sensitive, genuine and sincere as you. You will do anything to help the downtrodden and underprivileged, coming up with ideas and plans that are almost saintly as you. However, take care not to go too over the top. There is no point in you caring for others if you end up the victim, so be practical. Help those who want to help themselves.

Your intellectual Mercury works in a very emotional and sensitive way so you can actually 'feel' words. You take what you express and what is said to you seriously. You have a love of the stage, dance, movement, or anything that brings the mobility of Mercury in touch with the class act of Pisces.

You communicate on a wavelength that only the most beautiful people understand, and for you that's just fine – the vulgar, blasphemous and uncultured have no place in your world. You can understand the language of love and romance through flowers, cards and pretty things. These kind of poetic gestures are often your way of getting through to people.

If you have a negative Mercury in Pisces or the 12th house

This placement is a real turn up for the books as almost everything you read in the positive segment is reversed. Instead of being a helper, you are a victim and believe everyone owes you a living. You can say and do things for completely unscrupulous and corrupt reasons. You lie through your teeth and what's worse, actually believe that it's the truth. That's what makes this afflicted Mercury so dangerous as you can live a fantasy life so vivid that you would swear blind that someone has done something they haven't or that you are in the right when you are absolutely wrong. This is because Mercury has the power to think and believe and Pisces has the power to distort and confuse, and you can fall straight into the trap.

Be warned too of being impressionable and gullible, for as much as you can come across as though butter wouldn't melt in your mouth, it's ironic that you can be completely taken for a ride too. You must be very careful of drugs, drink or even prescribed pills that react against you, causing you ailments or allergies that add to your nebulous state. If this goes too far, you will need to be helped either by a therapist or counsellor as it may be too hard for you to sort out reality from fantasy on your own.

How overcome a negative Mercury in Pisces or the 12th house

This is no easy task for you – if your Mercury is afflicted, you need to admit it first. You can go into such denial that even if your best friend or family tell you that your behaviour is odd and peculiar, you won't believe it. But unless you do, you'll be on the slippery slope to all kinds of perversions and problems. It will be worth talking to an expert who can help you escape from your imprisoned mind.

Getting real and accepting that you are prone to living lies is half the battle. The other half is giving yourself to people like you who can also help you reform yourself. Once you have come to terms with this side of your nature, then you can do something about it. Getting involved in the arts or in spiritual activities will help you channel what is fundamentally a very creative and colourful mind into something more real. That is the second step. The first is, as I've said, admitting the problem.

Mix with people from a different world to the one that got you in this mess. The point is, like anything you have got to want to save yourself, and once you have psyched yourself up, you can do anything. It is not easy to get over or even understand a paranoid or neurotic mind. But it started somewhere, maybe with a worry, trauma or despair. Once you can get to the cause then you can cure the symptom. All is not lost but remember, it's time to Get Real.

Famous Mercury in Pisces: Pope Benedict, Elizabeth Taylor, Prince Andrew, Elton John, Bruce Willis, Sharon Stone, Robbie Williams, Celine Dion, Cindy Crawford, John Travolta, Osama Bin Laden.

♀

Venus

The planet Venus, as we have seen, is the part of Planet You most closely associated with love and partnerships. She is also the planet of the arts and beauty, and is connected to possessions and money. All these facets of your personality are reflected by Venus's position within your birth chart.

Because Venus rules the signs of Taurus and Libra, she is especially potent for people with strong placements such as their Sun or Ascendant in these signs. It is also very strong in Taurus and Libra and her natural houses, that is, the 2nd and 7th.

VENUS IN ARIES OR IN THE 1ST HOUSE

Your passion can get the better of you at times. You have a strong sexual desire and can fall in love quickly, but you can also throw yourself into relationships in a reckless, all-or-nothing manner. You can be just as impulsive with money, although this doesn't mean you haven't got an eye for business. Ardent in your feelings, you also send out positive signals to anyone you fancy. Whether physically beautiful or not, and you probably are with Venus in the 1st, you possess a sexy charm that is irresistible.

If you have a positive Venus in Aries or the 1st house

Alluring and sexy, you know what you want in a relationship and aim to get it. You know that a partnership works by a balance of give and take and will measure your feelings enough to excite your partner while keeping something in reserve. You adore the flirting and wooing when it comes to love but even a positive Venus needs someone who will keep the passion flowing long after the first flush of love has worn off. Financially, you know the power that money brings and will spend it making yourself look good enough to eat for someone who has captured your fancy.

If you have a negative Venus in Aries or the 1st house

You think of only yourself and very little else. You're not bothered if a man or woman you fancy is already attached – as far as you're concerned, they're fair game and you'll aim your well-honed Cupidic arrows at them, smiting them. Once you're finished with them, you'll dump them as quickly as you picked them up. You are a luxury lover but aren't bothered if your credit runs out. You will still spend and then expect your amorous charms to get you out of financial bother. You will stop at nothing to get your way as the only person who matters is you and whatever you want you must have.

How to overcome a negative Venus in Aries or the 1st house

The diagnosis is easy but is the application? Like most planets in Aries or the 1st house, you must understand pretty quickly that you share a relationship with someone else – otherwise it's not a relationship. It's a matter of turning your heart 180 degrees and meeting your partner halfway. By compromise, kindness and playing servant every so often to your lover's master or mistress needs – and always keeping a little bit of love in reserve – you will have something to crow about in the future. On the money front, learn to buy for a reason. If it's a personal investment into your appearance and the way you look, then go for it. But if you have absolutely no idea why you're buying then don't buy!

Famous Venus in Aries: Renee Zellweger, Audrey Hepburn, Marilyn Monroe, Abraham Lincoln, Alec Guinness, Fred Astaire, Elizabeth Taylor, Katharine Hepburn, Jack Nicholson.

VENUS IN TAURUS OR IN THE 2ND HOUSE

You are a sensual and tactile lover but can take this too far and become very possessive. You invented *la dolce vita* so much so that it borders on the sybaritic. You spend too much on pretty but totally useless things. Food and drink is another weakness that may lead to health problems. In your desire for material security, you attract people, situations and issues that sit well in your comfort zone. Loyal and faithful in love, your devotion knows no ends for someone who returns these virtues.

If you have a positive Venus in Taurus or the 2nd house

You completely understand that what you sow in life, you will reap later. No cash flow problems for you because you cut your cloth according to what you need. You're a wee bit of a good time guy or girl, enjoying life to the absolute full. But you're no fool when it comes to love. You will give your heart completely to someone who is prepared to match your feelings. You adore being possessed, so much so that you see your partner's jealousy when you talk to someone else as a compliment. You understand that moderation in all things is a wise idea so know when and how to stop. Investing for the long term, either financially or in your appearance, is something you do readily.

If you have a negative Venus in Taurus or the 2nd house

There's a touch of the femme fatale about you but you lack the subtlety and sophistication to really pull it off. If you like someone, you can be promiscuous to a degree because you find it hard to control your earthy feelings, happily jumping into bed with them. Sensual pleasures accompanied by perfumes and oils are right up your street. But danger lurks as once forbidden fruits have been scoffed you then think you own the person by rights. The result can be all kinds of sexual shenanigans based on obsession, jealousy and envy. If this happens, self-worth goes out the window and you feel cheap. You then can't understand it when your lover runs off with someone who appears frigid to you. Everyday money matters mean little to you, as you're only interested in big bucks. Unfortunately, this is a position you will probably never enjoy.

How to overcome a negative Venus in Taurus or the 2nd house

The first lesson to learn is value *yourself* more. Don't worry about money or lovers; start thinking that you are worth more than the price you put on your head. Okay, you may go after love to prove to yourself that you are worth something but it's coming across as desperation or padding for your lack of security. You are a good soul but you mustn't let relationships that only satisfy on a superficial level bring you down. For you, to win the respect and love of someone super-cool, you must let them take time to prove themselves and if they can't wait then it is *they* that aren't worth it, not you. Before long you will attract Mr or Ms Right. As for money, be more prudent and only put into a situation or investment what you know you can afford, and be sure of financial return.

Famous Venus in Taurus: Princess Diana, Marlon Brando, Adolf Hitler, Johnny Depp, Liv Tyler, Charlie Chaplin.

VENUS IN GEMINI OR IN THE 3RD HOUSE

Your approach to romance is superficial and intellectual. If someone is handsome and beautiful *and* has a mind to go with it, then you will meet your match! You are very flirtatious and flighty. Once in a relationship, you can be fickle, blowing hot and cold so your partner doesn't know what they've done right or wrong. This is, in part, because you need a strong mental bond with people. You find commitment very hard to make but once you do it's a battle you can win. You may draw money from more than one source because part of your nature is to always have two things on the go, be it lovers or jobs!

If you have a positive Venus in Gemini or the 3rd house

Amiable and very friendly, you have social charms and graces that will knock people dead. You may not come across as flirty but you know the right things to say and how to act, and it's this that makes you the most attractive sign in the room. You put plenty of thought into each and every move. Whether you are acting or just doing your social thing, it has the desired effect and most folks will swoon in your presence. On the money front, take it easy. You have an easy-come, easy-go attitude, believing you can always meet someone to bail you out if necessary.

If you have a negative Venus in Gemini or the 3rd house

Straight and to the point, you say things you should really keep in reserve. You need to learn the art of diplomacy and seduction because you give away your intentions far too easily, coming across as someone who is so light and airy that all you're good for is a night of love. You chitter-chatter about the silly things that no lover would be at all interested in. You can cling onto your 'friend' for safety, sending out signals that you're not available when you *so* are. When it comes to cash, you are totally reckless and buy everything you don't want, clothes that don't suit for instance. You have such an appalling dress sense that you overlook your very beautiful assets.

How to overcome a negative Venus in Gemini or the 3rd house

Substance is the first thing you need. So when on a date, add an air of the enigmatic, and always keep something fantastically mysterious in reserve. For goodness sake, don't give your game away, but don't be a freeloader or tease, as it will hurt someone who is sincere about you. Dress to impress; don't buy what everyone else is wearing, but go for something chic and cheap (in cash terms!) because you can put on a bin liner and look a zillion dollars. Remember what sets you apart is your mind and body; so bring the two together in a relationship and you'll have your partner hot to trot for many years to come. You are exciting and stimulating. Make this your mantra but don't forget, it's also about the 'X' Factor – whatever it is, keep it safe! When it comes to spending, if you ain't got it, don't spend it!

Famous Venus in Gemini: Harrison Ford, Uma Thurman, Jacqueline Kennedy Onassis, Kylie Minogue, Cher, Bette Davis, George Michael, Ringo Starr, Al Pacino.

VENUS IN CANCER OR IN THE 4TH HOUSE

Home is where the heart is for you, and yours is likely to be extremely comfortable with a lived-in feel. Security is important to you, so you are a devoted, almost maternal partner. However, this compassionate streak may develop and become claustrophobic. On the positive side, the need for security means you are also a fine homemaker. You are close to your family, and have strong relationships with children and female relatives. You give of yourself completely in love but sometimes too quickly and without reserve when the other person isn't quite ready.

If you have a positive Venus in Cancer or the 4th house

You would be like a tiger or tigress if called upon to defend the one you love. You might appear soft and gentle, which of course you are to those you care for, but if anyone should come between you and your beloved then you will fight tooth and claw to save a relationship. Sometimes even when it's finished you will hang on in there. However, once the penny has dropped that it is over, you have the ability to move on after retreating to lick your wounds first. Those who fall for your protective charms adore you; one particular person will become hopelessly devoted to you. Money is invested wisely and you are more than happy to secure it in a nice fiscal pot that will mature when you do.

If you have a negative Venus in Cancer or the 4th house

Not knowing when to give up or let go is a problem you will have to face sometime. Your love persona is easily hurt and can go into denial because you are so sensitive. You take offence at the slightest criticism – this can drive a wedge through your relationships as your other half never knows what to say or is always walking on eggshells. Eventually the affair will crack because your partner cannot go on having to cope with your inability to be rational or laugh something off. Rejection is something you can carry in your heart to the grave, thereby ruining every affair you have in your life because you hark back to a failure years back that has no place in your current world.

On the cash front, you're a hoarder, which is okay if you invest it properly. But sticking it in a jar behind the cookies – well, I ask you!

How to overcome a negative Venus in Cancer or the 4th house

An afflicted Venus in Cancer or the 4th requires a lot of ameliorating. You need to be stroked and cared for and told that everything will be all right. So finding a partner or loved one who is going to give you oodles of compassion, sympathy and open displays of affection is so very important. You must get out of the habit of always looking back, comparing a present partner with one from the past, or worse still your mother or father. You need to be an independent man or woman and not someone who uses familiar faces as a crutch. Stand on your own two feet; accept that once something is gone it is finished. Shrug it off and get on with your life. Be as tough with others as you would be with yourself. Financially, find yourself a great savings account and keep it topped up for a rainy day. Make sure it's one that gives you revenue for doing absolutely nothing.

Famous Venus in Cancer: Angelina Jolie, Errol Flynn, Keanu Reeves, Napoleon Bonaparte, Judy Garland, Liberace, Elizabeth Hurley, Camilla Parker Bowles.

VENUS IN LEO OR IN THE 5TH HOUSE

With this placement you are guaranteed to live life to the hilt. You are affectionate but demanding, and are capable of being vain and seeing yourself as the centre of the universe. This may lead to flings and flirtations. You are faithful to your other half but cannot resist being flattered by others. You may take it too far, conveniently forgetting you are already spoken for. Your children or pets are the apple of your eye. Heaven forbid if you ever fall *out* of love as you function best when you are *in* love. Adoration is at the heart of your loving persona. You love luxury and extravagance and don't consider the cost, financial or otherwise, of acquiring it.

If you have a positive Venus in Leo or the 5th house

There is no doubt you are gifted with special talents of love. You are giving and caring, exuding a warm heart as big as Olympus itself and draw people to you with powers of attraction that know no bounds. You bowl folks over with your affection. Everybody in your circle really does love you, although some folks will think you are putting on the style artificially as there is a bit of the actor in you. You are so generous with your time and cash that some folk may take advantage of you. If you see this happening, you will give them short shrift because although you love to love and be loved, you won't be taken for a fool.

If you have a negative Venus in Leo or the 5th house

Your behaviour is false and phoney. You refuse to mix with the hoi polloi – only the upper crust will do. You can turn on a sixpence if you find someone doesn't have power, money or ambition, even if you've been dating them. You put on the swank and will carry a Harrods or Saks shopping bag to show off and let people know you are top-notch. (Unfortunately the bag was given to you by someone else with your Christmas or birthday gift in it.) You like to be seen at the right places clutching your trophy hubby or wife. Whether you like them or not is irrelevant – they are a means to an end. It's who you know that matters and if ever asked to choose between being poor and true love to a nobody or no love but a champagne lifestyle to a hideous somebody, you'd choose the somebody.

How to overcome a negative Venus in Leo or the 5th house

You must learn to love for the right reasons, to see someone as they really are and accept them for that. Allow true love to win on all levels, otherwise you might miss out on something wonderful. For instance, you might choose the golden lifestyle but then find that the person you turned down ends up more successful and honoured than the one you chose over them. What are you going to do then? Lose your dignity and run to their side, saying it was all some dreadful mistake? You might treat someone like it was all just a soap or movie but Hollywood isn't real and the sooner you get real, the better. That way you will realize that getting behind your heart's desire, even uniting with someone who might be on the bottom rung, is the right way to hit the headlines and be totally happy.

Famous Venus in Leo: Madonna, George W. Bush, Sylvester Stallone, Tom Cruise, Olivia Newton-John, Lauren Bacall.

VENUS IN VIRGO OR IN THE 6TH HOUSE

You lack confidence and can be very shy. You yearn for the perfect partner, but your reserve is a barrier. You can be prudish about sex. Business, on the other hand, is something that comes more naturally to you. You enjoy routine but need to work in a pleasant environment. Working with the one you love is by far and away your best option as loving Venus is tied by earthy Virgo and you could end up a vestal virgin (or eunuch!) unless you find a partner who complements your need to achieve something as a couple.

If you have a positive Venus in Virgo or the 6th house

You go out of your way to be helpful and useful because this is your way of showing affection. However, sometimes you can be too servile to your other half and they might take advantage of this. You feel more comfortable expressing your heart through letters, cards or gifts – less humiliating if you get a negative response! Your modesty is what makes you so attractive, which is why you are the Cinderella or Prince Charming of the stars. You are understated and gentle, appreciating that love expressed in a simple way can be endearing and enduring. Financially, you put cash to good use and would never be extravagant or a spendthrift. What you buy has to fulfil a purpose.

If you have a negative Venus in Virgo or the 6th house

Your unresponsive nature makes it hard for anyone to get through to your heart. There is a barrier, something you have gotten into your head about love and affection that means you find it hard to cope with. (You know that love leads to sex and that is distasteful to you. After all, sex can be unhygienic and messy, something you abhor.) Even if you are in a relationship, you are cold and clinical in your love life. What's worse, if you fancy someone you are as distant and chilly as Siberia and that's with someone you like. You strive for the perfect partner but nag and nitpick until you drive away the one person who does love you. Money-wise, prudence leads to parsimony, another unattractive quality. All this means you end up having very little fun or enjoyment because you're too intent on your own way of doing things.

How to overcome a negative Venus in Virgo or the 6th house

If you aren't content with your love life or the way your behave when confronted by affection, you need to get to the root of the problem and deal with it. It might stem from your parents or a previous encounter, however long or brief. It's possible you may need the help of a marriage guidance counsellor or other professional adviser to help sort out your heart. This is neither a weakness or failure. I firmly believe that half your problems are down to your inability to let yourself go a little more. That doesn't mean sexually, and that's where you get it all wrong. You need romance rather than lust, but because you think someone wants to bed you immediately (maybe due to a past situation or a Puritanical parent), you assume everyone is the same. It's time to take things little by little and allow love to grow slowly. By doing so you will soon meet someone you trust and respect, and the chilly winds will turn to warm breezes of affection.

Famous Venus in Virgo: Catherine Zeta Jones, Sting, Jennifer Lopez, Lucille Ball, Brigitte Bardot, Roger Moore.

VENUS IN LIBRA OR IN THE 7TH HOUSE

With twice the normal helping of Venus at work in this placement, it is no surprise you are very romantic. But sometimes it is love itself that you are infatuated with and you can be undermined by your overwhelming need to be in a relationship. You can be overshadowed by partners and even lose your real personality. You have a very Venusian love of luxury, which can hit your bank balance hard!

If you have a positive Venus in Libra or the 7th house

You have a wonderful way of making people feel special. No matter what their position or place in life's pecking order, you put them at their ease and you are totally adored by those who cross your rose-strewn path. Your love life might not be quite as rosy, but only because you may expect too much from your other half. Once you have learned that it's not about you doing all the giving, everything will settle down and you will enjoy a successful marriage or partnership. This is because your powers of attraction are at their peak, and Venus in Libra and/or the 7th house knows instinctively the magic formula to adopt when it comes to keeping your beloved. Cash-wise, you are prone to giving gifts and tokens of your love, esteem and affection for the slightest reason. They are always appreciated, as indeed you are.

If you have a negative Venus in Libra or the 7th house

Because you are never satisfied and always looking for someone better in love you are never entirely happy. In fact, you can be a downright misery, not just in yourself but also for those you scoop up and then toss to one side because they aren't ideal. So who are you to assume that you deserve someone who is perfect? If you keep attracting people who don't come up to your expectations or fall short of your idea of a lover, then isn't it time to ask yourself why? Do you always manipulate a situation to suit you? Are you constantly trying to change them? You can't make a silk purse out of a pig's ear. In the end, there is an old saying that we get the partner we deserve in life. Financially, remember you can't make things right with just money. In this case it really cannot buy you love.

How to overcome a negative Venus in Libra or the 7th house

You've got to learn, and fast, that you must accept someone warts and all. I know you might find it distasteful that someone has a physical disorder or blemish, but if that's how you feel then don't lead them on in the first place. There is no such thing as the perfect partner. Besides, if you continue deluding yourself that you are such a catch, one day you will meet someone who will give you a taste of your own medicine. Give a relationship time to blossom and very soon you will see that it doesn't matter if someone has three heads, so long as they are kind, faithful, cherishing and devoted. Accept someone as they are and you might be lucky enough to find someone who does the same with you.

Famous Venus in Libra: Lance Armstrong, Bill Clinton, Michael Douglas, Grace Kelly, Freddie Mercury, Prince Charles, Peter Sellers, Sean Connery.

VENUS IN SCORPIO OR THE 8TH HOUSE

A highly desirable and loving placement. You are a very sensual and passionate person to whom a good, satisfying sex life is of vital importance. You are prone to jealousy and possessiveness. When it comes to playing psychological love games you are the past master or mistress and woe betide your other half if he or she does you down. Revenge is second nature to you. You have a real talent when it comes to business and money matters.

If you have a positive Venus in Scorpio or the 8th house

You glide into relationships like a swan ready to mate for life. You will stand by your man or woman through thick and thin. Nothing or no-one will stop you offering your support, love and devotion to the person you love. Your affair will go through many stages; where one chapter ends so another will begin. With each transition your partnership will move onto a new level. The knack is knowing that things won't ever remain the same and that by maturing together you will stay together until your swansong is sung. When it comes to money, it brings power and control but you know it can never compete with genuine love.

If you have a negative Venus in Scorpio or the 8th house

You are totally, utterly and outrageously controlling. Half the trouble is you don't even know you're doing it. You will use all kinds of psychological tactics combined with manipulative machinations that would make even Machiavelli blush. You can't fathom the difference between love and lust, and make the mistake of muddling up the two. That means you and your other half are often on a different sexual wavelength as you give them what they *don't* want. You are envious, covetous and avenging, using cloak and dagger tactics to catch someone out when they are involved in something innocent. Money is another weapon in your game of control and it can even be united with sexual blackmail so that you get your way, such is your overwhelming need to be on top.

How to overcome a negative Venus in Scorpio or the 8th house

Your highly charged nature won't make this easy. Talking to someone you've never met might help, but be sure to choose an expert in their field, a therapist or counsellor who will recognize the symptoms. Then you can open up and pour out your heart. The way you are behaving is so destructive that you are intent on wrecking anything that's good and you need to find out why. It could stem from any experience or encounter that has made you feel unworthy or insecure. Whatever it is, you must learn to trust your other half and allow them to lead their own life. That way you can chill out and understand that you don't need to snoop or pry because there is nothing going on. Once you trust, you will find happiness.

Famous Venus in Scorpio: Hillary Clinton, Teri Hatcher, Annie Lennox, Leonardo DiCaprio, Christina Aguilera.

VENUS IN SAGITTARIUS OR THE 9TH HOUSE

Your need for independence and autonomy rules everything. You can't stand being tied down in a relationship and prefer partners who are friends as well as lovers. You are cultured and philosophical, and have a love of travel that may result in becoming involved with someone from another country, maybe even emigrating there. Your free-living philosophy doesn't help you when it comes to money matters, where you can display a reckless streak.

If you have a positive Venus in Sagittarius or the 9th house

You know how to make someone happy because you allow them their own space. This desire for individuality within a relationship is what keeps you both in tune. You never lose your identity, which is so important. You know you can go your separate ways and come back stronger and happier than ever. The trick is to find someone who is as trusting and respectful of you as you are of them. Moneywise, you certainly have no problem spending, but you do so as part of the loving experience, sharing journeys, lectures or the creative arts with your partner.

If you have a negative Venus in Sagittarius or the 9th house

You take things a step too far when it comes to loving freedom, using it as a justification for doing whatever you want without any explanations. After a while, it is obvious you are incompatible with your partner because you don't share the same interests, friends or outlook and your relationship is simply a façade. This means there is no depth, intensity or passion there. Before long, the whole arrangement falls apart at the seams as you go your way and your so-called beloved goes theirs, with little love lost. On the cash front, it's all for one and one for you. You know no bounds – if you want something then you must have it, whatever the cost.

How to overcome a negative Venus in Sagittarius or the 9th house

You must decide straight away whether you are the marrying kind or just want a bit of fun. If you are going for a permanent partnership, you have got to get over your biggest problem – commitment. You are a commitment-phobe, like it or not. Can I suggest that when you start a relationship that you get to know the person first as a friend? If you can meet a mate with whom you share interests or hobbies, then love may grow from that firm foundation. To presume that you are going to live happily ever after with someone you jumped into bed with for 24 hours makes you very shallow, which you are not. So give your relationships and heart a chance by laying the foundations of mutual understanding via hobbies or social outings and then watch what develops. Nurture and cultivate things, then a love will blossom – one that allows you both to be friends as well as lovers.

Famous Venus in Sagittarius: Rowan Atkinson, Cary Grant, David Bowie, Margaret Thatcher, Jane Fonda.

VENUS IN CAPRICORN OR THE 10TH HOUSE

Venus is far from happy in Capricorn because the restrictions of this sign are anathema to a planet where love knows no bounds. Deep down you are a loyal and loving person, but you have a hard time showing it. You are ambitious in love and may view your choice of partner as something more than a romantic decision. You are equally shrewd when it comes to money and need a profession that is profitable and creatively satisfying at the same time. You find responsibility hard to carry at times and have to battle between duty and laissez-faire. With Venus in the 10th you are supreme in jobs devoted to women.

If you have a positive Venus in Capricorn or the 10th house

You aren't interested in an affair based purely on love and are attracted to a person who will make something of themselves. You are very ambitious for your other half in life and will be a driving force behind his or her life career or purpose.

The chances are you will have met your amour through your job or some form of vocational event or mission. You enjoy being with a person who other people love and respect. You are a power behind the throne and enjoy sharing in the limelight of recognition that your man or woman accomplishes. You are duty-bound to help your other half but often show you care in ways that other signs would find alarming and not terribly loving – but that's you. When it comes to money you are the arch-accountant, putting your cash to good use and knowing where every penny goes. You believe that cash should be used as a means to an end and will ensure that your appearance and that of your partner is smart and cool, cutting a dash to creating the right professional impression.

If you have a negative Venus in Capricorn or the 10th house

As cold as ice, you make no bones that you are intent on marrying for money. As for love, well if it can be bought then how much is it? Other people perceive you are being honest, responsible and hard-working, but actually you fly on the coattails of what other people have achieved, taking credit where it's far from due. You dismiss failure as something that's not even in your vocabulary, whereas if we work on the adage that we attract the partnership we deserve, then your other half should be a layabout and the world's worst husband or wife. If you can get something for nothing, you will, and if you have to scheme, plot and use cunning to achieve your ends, nothing is so low that you won't stoop to conquer. All in all, an afflicted Venus here is acquisitive, avaricious, money-grabbing and willing to use others as their scapegoat or excuse.

How to overcome a negative Venus in Capricorn or the 10th house

First and foremost, you need to recognize what kind of person you believe you want, and then look at the one you appear to be attracting. Once you've ascertained that you are only going with someone to see what you can get, then you know that you are stacking up bad love karma by the truckload. Venus is about love – you must follow your heart, not your head or bank balance. When you learn to give, you will be assuming the right stance to receive affection back: as you sow, so shall you reap. The minute you yield to romance for your heart's sake is the moment you find happiness. Regrets? Well, there will be a few but the loyalty, love and devotion will be worth it.

Famous Venus in Capricorn: Jim Carrey, Britney Spears, Burt Reynolds, Elvis Presley, Paul Newman, James Dean, Prince Andrew, Maria Callas.

VENUS IN AQUARIUS OR THE 11TH HOUSE

Your individualistic, avant-garde approach to romance is very attractive. However, it takes a very special person to understand you and that's why you may go through more relationships than I have had hot dinners. You can be distant emotionally and shy away from commitment because of your dread of having your wings clipped. You have a knack of making money in original ways too. You may draw a lot of pleasure from a hobby or pastime.

If you have a positive Venus in Aquarius or the 11th house

The perfect partner for you is someone who is prepared to go with your eccentric whims and outrageous desires. Once you find that person, you are the most committed and caring of signs, even rivalling Cancerians on that front! You are a wonderful friend and lover; you know what your partner wants and aim to provide it – you will travel over heaven and earth to make them happy. You are loyal and faithful without reproach because you know when you've found somebody who can put up with you that you've met one in a million. Your natural charisma and unpredictability will forever keep an affair on its toes and you have the knack of playing different roles to please your partner. There is nothing boring about you, which is the biggest turn-on in love. Money, what's that? Well, it's nice if you've got it but if you haven't then you've got love to keep you warm.

If you have a negative Venus in Aquarius or the 11th house

You are so totally into yourself that you haven't got time for anyone else. Your natural magnetism still attracts people, of course, but you keep anyone who wants commitment at arm's length and if someone tries to get too close, you're out the door. You fall for those who don't take you seriously and ignore those who do. Even if the right person appears, you send out the wrong signals, coming across as passionate and delectable one moment, cold and detached the next. So is it any wonder people and partners don't know where they stand with you? You are reckless with cash and can't quite work out what it's there for. Apart, that is, from buying you exactly what *you* want.

How to overcome a negative Venus in Aquarius or the 11th house

Dealing with this negative placing should be fairly easy because you have all the personality weapons at your disposal: an electrifying charm and fascinating aloofness, in particular. What you need to do is concentrate on what part you should play in life. If you do, before long you will find that fulfilment and happiness come to you very naturally. One area to consider is your sexuality. Maybe you're on the wrong bus and denying your true proclivities, but don't experiment with other people just so you can find out. People have feelings as well as you, and to break someone's heart so you can discover your true self is not on and will add to your bad karma. Start off with someone you like as a friend and persevere with the relationship. In the end you will realize that what's important is finding a soul mate, a kindred spirit you can share your mind, body *and* spirit with.

Famous Venus in Aquarius: Muhammad Ali, Bruce Willis, Leonard Nimoy, Oprah Winfrey, Elton John, Ricky Martin, Kate Moss, Mel Gibson, Sharon Stone.

VENUS IN PISCES OR THE 12TH HOUSE

Venus is probably at her happiest and most content in this position. You are a beautiful soul but are highly strung emotionally, and prepared to make huge sacrifices for love. Your sentimental nature makes you gullible and often guilty of self-deception, playing the victim when things don't go your way. You are artistic and enjoy working on projects alone. You can be very spiritual and have an interest in the occult. If you believe you can find love through magical means, you will try everything and anything to attract the love of your life to your heart.

If you have a positive Venus in Pisces or the 12th house

You are well versed in the art of seduction. Enjoying the sensual aspects of love suits you more than anything else. Candlelight, romantic poetry, prose ... you have the gift of setting the scene for a wonderful evening. Yet you can also delude yourself, reading signals into the smallest things – what you *think* someone means. But do they really? When it comes to love, you need to embrace reality, as often with Venus here, you will go through the agony of unrequited love. But when you do meet the right person, you will fall hook, line and sinker and do everything you can for him or her. Nothing is too much trouble, but take care or you could end up a doormat.

Fantasy is always at your amorous beck and call because your pleasure can come from the sheer imagination of what love is. And the fantasy is very often so much more to your liking than the real thing. With your cash, you love to buy intoxicating smellies, pretty accoutrements and clothes fit for a prince or princess. When it comes to these things, money is no object.

If you have a negative Venus in Pisces or the 12th house

When in love, you are so completely and utterly in another world that you can lose touch with reality a little. You can drink yourself stupid if you feel your heart is broken and sometimes that can be for seven days a week. You will also try other substances to take away the pain. You will play games with people's minds and feelings, using the worst of all possible tactics to win their love and all you succeed in doing is alienating the very person you want to love you.

The minute you walk into a room and see someone smiling at you (out of politeness), you are ready to elope with them. You live in such a world of your own that you try blackmail, manipulating your way into a person's life, not caring who you hurt until you get them, even if they are already attached. But what does that matter – you *must* have what you want. Then, of course, when you get them you drop them like a ton of hot bricks, as the reality doesn't measure up to the fantasy. You spend as much as you can trying to bewitch your beloved but in the end it boils down to time and money wasted. Cash to you is a plaything and you kid yourself as to how much you're worth. You never face up to the truth – you are so good at sweeping things under the carpet.

How to overcome a negative Venus in Pisces or the 12th house

There is only one way to deal with afflicted Venus here and that is to pull yourself together. You will continue to make your life (and everyone else's) a misery until you understand that not everyone fancies you. Think about it, you don't fancy everyone you meet. What you need is someone kind, caring and wonderful to be with, someone who is beautiful from the outside in. Only then will you get over the fact they may look like the back of a bus, only then will you see that in the long run it is the fact they adore you and will do anything for you that really matters. So don't judge a book by its cover. On the financial front, use what riches you have to make your surroundings more comfortable and to enhance your image. It will be money well spent.

Famous Venus in Pisces: Drew Barrymore, Orlando Bloom, Kurt Cobain, Michael Jackson, Barbra Streisand, Diana Ross, Vincent van Gogh.

Mars

At the heart of Planet You is Mars, the planet of energy and impetus, where your drive and determination lives. He is associated with aggression and competitiveness, including in sexual matters. The position of Mars within your chart tells you a great deal about these facets of your personality. Because Mars rules Aries and Scorpio, he is particularly potent if people have strong placements in those two signs. If you have a Sun or an Ascendant in Aries or Scorpio, Mars is extra powerful. The same applies if it is the Aries and Scorpio houses, that is, the 1st and 8th.

MARS IN ARIES OR THE 1ST HOUSE

With a double helping of Martian machismo, you are someone with a great deal of energy, drive and self-confidence. You are very competitive and highly sexed. However, you have to be careful to channel all this in a positive direction. You put yourself first and can be conceited and egocentric. You can also act on impulse or out of a lack of patience. You may be prone to accidents and need to exercise regularly to maintain your health. You are audacious by nature. Hot-headed and headstrong, you have a combustible temper that can become an infernal rage that needs defusing as soon as possible. Otherwise you might have an accident and do yourself – and others – damage.

If you have a positive Mars in Aries or the 1st house

You are a go-ahead person with the right amount of caution and patience to be able to reach your goal. You might not get there in double-quick time but you will get there. You are pioneering and enterprising. You don't let the grass grow beneath your feet before you are off on another great adventure. Your ability to single-mindedly focus on one goal and then put all your vigour and vitality into achieving it brings you success. Your sexuality is never in question. You know what you want and have no hang-ups. Indeed, you enjoy sex so much that you need a partner who is as mean a sex machine as you.

If you have a negative Mars in Aries or the 1st house

You think you are God's gift. Selfish, impatient, impetuous, impulsive and impolite, you won't let anyone stand in your way. You throw people aside with an attitude that is cruel and rash. Your recklessness will be your downfall; despite warnings from people, your hot-headed approach and frustrated rage will eventually give you plenty of opportunity to repent at your leisure. Sexually, you are out simply to satisfy your urges and desires. You don't give a toss about satisfying anyone else's.

How to overcome a negative Mars in Aries or the 1st house

It's all about learning what other people want. Listen to their opinions and don't dismiss them as fuddy-duddies just because their time scales don't match yours. Just because you want everything yesterday doesn't mean you can have it. Even if you can, you'll probably find you don't want it any way, whether it is a job or sex. Patience is a virtue and learning to satisfy those who adore you will make you a winner in the end.

Famous Mars in Aries: Angelina Jolie, Paul Newman, Princess Caroline of Monaco, Clint Eastwood, Russell Crowe, Monica Lewinsky, Keira Knightley.

MARS IN TAURUS OR THE 2ND HOUSE

Your energy is of the down-to-earth, nose-to-the-grindstone variety. You believe in hard work and determination and won't stop until you've finished or run out of time or energy. You have a slow fuse emotionally but when you lose your temper you can do so in a big way. One of my closest Taurean friends refuses to lose his temper. He prefers to leave the room, as he knows that once his fuse is lit it cannot be doused and the result could be Vesuvius. You are a sexually driven person but can be possessive in relationships. You are driven to make money and achieve material success, but will also be generous with your hard-earned cash to those you love.

If you have a positive Mars in Taurus or the 2nd house

You are impervious to shallow people or born losers. This is because you believe you can be a self-made success if you believe in yourself and allow your vitality and stamina to be slowly applied to the job in hand. You keep energy in reserve just in case. You are steadfastly loyal and faithful to the one you love. Sexually, you might take a while to get going, but once you let rip then the earth really does move.

If you have a negative Mars in Taurus or the 2nd house

You spend too much time considering your own motivations and needs, and not enough on the desires of the one you love, whom you can take for granted. You tend to assume what is good for you is good for them, or worse still, is what they actually want. It saves you a guilt trip and allows you to be in control. Sexually, you need gratification when you want it – if your other half doesn't then tough luck, they're going to have it thrust upon them anyway. You view your partner in much the same way as you would inanimate objects; in other words, you own them.

How to overcome a negative Mars in Taurus or the 2nd house

You need to see that the person around you has feelings. They are not the dining-room table or the television set, they need to be reassured, shown open love and their sexual feelings taken into account. You have to start respecting their desires and passions as much as your own. Don't assume so much, but instead learn to be tender and romantic rather than behaving like a bull in an Ann Summers shop.

Famous Mars in Taurus: Muhammad Ali, Bette Davis, Madonna, Bruce Willis, Adolf Hitler, Lucille Ball, Liv Tyler, Tom Cruise, Liberace, Charlie Chaplin, John F. Kennedy, Mick Jagger, Mariah Carey, Kate Moss.

MARS IN GEMINI OR THE 3RD HOUSE

You need to combine your energy and excellent mental abilities in the right way. Otherwise, you will be in danger of frittering away your talents. Your sex life is characterized by versatility. You have a great love of debate, but have a habit of being less than diplomatic at times. You can have rows with authorities and perhaps neighbours. Sibling rivalry is evident with this placing and it can last all your life. You are full of great ideas that appear as if from nowhere. The sensible thing is to use them and not allow them to evaporate over the day. Your volatile temper is over and done with in a jiffy. You are so variable you can have bad days when you are all over the place, and good days when you can cope and deal with whatever the world throws at you.

If you have a positive Mars in Gemini or the 3rd house

You are the perfect match for those who want great sex and witty conversation to follow. You are great at talking about what you intend to do in an intimate situation, then delivering with aplomb. You have a gift for PR, marketing and talking yourself up. In fact, your powers of self-publicity can't be matched. This frank, honest and forthright approach appeals to many people.

If you have a negative Mars in Gemini or the 3rd house

You are intellectually vapid. It's not that you don't have the skills and the aptitudes, but things have a habit of going in one ear and out the other. You don't pay any attention to what others have to say as you believe what you spout is far more interesting. (Ever heard the expression empty vessels make the most noise?) You are argumentative for no reason, sometimes declaring black is white just to get a reaction. Sexually, you are promiscuous as you can't be bothered to delve into the real person and probably get bored halfway through foreplay.

How to overcome a negative Mars in Gemini or the 3rd house

Take a good look in the mirror. The reflection you see may have more than one side to it because what you perceive yourself to be and how others see you are totally different. You may think you have to put up with so much, that you are long-suffering and patient, but actually patience is a virtue that you don't understand. And as for long-suffering, ask the people who have spent time with you socially, sexually or professionally. What will emerge is that you are a self-centred flake who has good ideas but does nothing with them. Now you know, you can do something about it. For instance, you can listen. You can also take time to give pleasure to someone else intellectually (or intimately). You can even do yourself a favour by following a brainwave through from concept to conclusion. Application and dedication should be your new buzzwords. Who knows, it might be the making of you.

Famous Mars in Gemini: Barbra Streisand, Uma Thurman, Kylie Minogue, Al Pacino, Diana Ross, Sean Connery, Camilla Parker Bowles.

MARS IN CANCER OR THE 4TH HOUSE

If you have this placement, you have a tendency to let your passionate, emotional nature boil over. Home and family are high on your list of priorities and you like to be in charge there. This may reflect the influence of your mother, who may have been a formidable woman in this respect. Sexually, you have potent desires but need kisses and cuddles as much as the act itself as it is the close proximity of bodies that is your real turn-on. Your temper is based on your moods, so an outburst is likely to be followed by grudges and sulks. Forgiving or forgetting isn't easy.

If you have a positive Mars in Cancer or the 4th house

Your family, past or present, means the world to you and you spend much of life creating families on all levels. You use them as your protection against the world because you need someone or somewhere nice to come home to. You will defend your loved ones to the hilt and your happiest times will be spent when you can be the breadwinner. This gives you all you need to get by. Sexually, you are all for the sensual and tactile side of passion and if your partner is the same you will never stray, but to feel loved and desired increases your need for security.

If you have a negative Mars in Cancer or the 4th house

Your tendancy to compare one person with another can lead to emotional imbalance and down right resentment. Whether male or female, you will still put the memories of someone you were very close to ahead of those who share your life now. Such comparisons can be a problem for them and a big one for you, too. You see, your memory will be selective. You will only remember the good times and forget the times that were, to be brutally honest, horrid. The same goes with sex – you convince yourself that someone you once knew was the perfect lover when they were nothing of the sort. This then creates more hang-ups in you and your partner.

How to overcome a negative Mars in Cancer or the 4th house

Stop searching in everyone for the someone that doesn't exist. Treat each sexual partner as a new challenge, and when you find someone you adore, enjoy them for what they are. The same goes for friendships or co-workers; they are all individuals, they are not your father, brother, lover, boss or anyone else. You must treat everyone you meet on merit. It really doesn't become you to blame people for you being born or for your early struggles. Instead of getting angry, use this self-same energy for moving onwards and upwards.

Famous Mars in Cancer: Leonard Nimoy, Keanu Reeves, Alec Guinness, Audrey Hepburn, John F. Kennedy, Richard Gere.

MARS IN LEO OR THE 5TH HOUSE

You are filled with vitality, passion and a real lust for life. You find danger dead sexy. This makes you a born leader. However, you have a stubborn streak that can reveal itself in pushiness and an attitude that says you are always in the right. You also crave quick results when they are not possible. Your positive side shines through in your love life, where you are a virile and lusty lover. Here too you want things to happen fast and can fall in love easily and often. Others are intrigued by your temper, which is more a dramatically rehearsed outburst than a normal tantrum.

If you have a positive Mars in Leo or the 5th house

You are so creative in everything you do that it is a lucky person indeed who finds themselves being your lover. Ardent, confident and cocksure, you can make erogenous zones tingle with delight as you have a certain tender but tactile touch that means there's no going back once you've worked your supple charms. Follow your heart in all things and you won't go far wrong as you have a flair and style that is given oomph by your strength and stamina. Whatever you decide to do, it will end with you crowned champion.

If you have a negative Mars in Leo or the 5th house

You think you're the last of the red-hot lovers. What rot! You may not know it but your ego and your self-love is enough to drive people crazy. Have you ever wondered why no-one wants to stay for coffee, let alone a cigarette? It's because you idolize yourself to such a degree you believe your own publicity. You also have the potential to be a creative success but never get further than the starting blocks. Instead you are distracted by sex or rivals who use psychological bait to flatter you. They succeed; so while you think that everything is over bar the shouting, in truth nothing's happened at all. You're still stuck in the starting blocks.

How to overcome a negative Mars in Leo or the 5th house

Be very, very wary of anyone who flatters you because they are masking their own intention – to get you out of the picture. You are a force to be reckoned with, but because you never actually get motivated, you can be stopped in your tracks by those who see you as a threat with just a few well-chosen words. Finish what you have started and you'll see why they wanted you out of the race. Sexually, you live off past glories. Each person is a new conquest and you must prove to them you are a red-hot lover by seeing to their personal needs first and your own second.

Famous Mars in Leo: Fred Astaire, Harrison Ford, Sting, Jennifer Lopez, Hillary Clinton, Cher, Brigitte Bardot, Ringo Starr, James Dean.

MARS IN VIRGO OR THE 6TH HOUSE

Hard-working and practical with a good eye for detail, your weakness is that you don't take the initiative. You can handle boring routine but don't like it if you can't slip out of it every so often. You get particularly annoyed at colleagues who don't share the workload or who get you to do their dirty work. Your lack of self-confidence affects your sex life too, where you are timid and mechanical, and may even have a blockage about sex in general. Your health may suffer because of the stress that builds up, so regular exercise is important for you. You can internalize your anger as you don't want to make a show of yourself. If you take too long over completing something perfectly or as you idealized it, the frustration can erupt out of you.

If you have a positive Mars in Virgo or the 6th house

You like everything in its place and if you are going to take a risk, will take a calculated gamble. You are compliant enough to be able to swing with the roundabouts and eventually come out with a success. Any work that demands detail, perfect measurements and organized files brings out the best in you. Health and hygiene are very important to you indeed, which is why intimate relationships can be a problem. You need to meet someone whose sexual desires revolve around inner and outer cleanliness. You may prefer to be a virgin until you meet the right person – celibacy is an easy option for you.

If you have a negative Mars in Virgo or the 6th house

You totally lack the spontaneity needed to enjoy life. You become so fearful of doing something that breaks rules – whether official or your own self-imposed ones – that you do nothing. Then gradually you wonder why you feel like the drudge when people only invite you out because they have some job or task for you to do, one that no-one else likes. (That's not popularity, that's you being taken in.) Sexually you can be stiff and frigid, filled with all kinds of obsessions or neuroses acquired from old wives' tales.

How to deal with a negative Mars in Virgo or the 6th house

It's time to get a life. Do something off the cuff, and hang the consequences. No, I am not saying you should put your health at risk sexually. There is such a thing as safe sex, after all. But unless you go for broke in your lifestyle and allow someone to romance, wine and dine you, you will never know what you've been missing. You could discover a side of you that is full of courage and not only that, you might enjoy the thrill of it all. All it takes is for you to say 'yes'.

Famous Mars in Virgo: Princess Diana, Sylvester Stallone, Britney Spears, George W. Bush, Teri Hatcher, Johnny Depp, Jacqueline Kennedy Onassis, Napoleon Bonaparte, George Michael, Elizabeth Hurley, Peter Sellers.

MARS IN LIBRA OR THE 7TH HOUSE

Your drive is often directed towards bringing harmony to situations around you. Sexually, it's in your nature to be driven by your libido, and before you know it, you've fallen for the wrong person completely. Sex is important but you must be careful not to let it dominate the relationship, but allow your silky charm to come shining through out of the bedroom, too. Your temper is based on Air sign logic, which often means it is illogical, allowing little things to get to you and yet taking big hassles in your stride.

If you have a positive Mars in Libra or the 7th house

Caring and sharing, you combine the feminine traits of protectiveness with the masculine energy of attack. Put the two together and you have the smooth approach that proves irresistible to the many whom you desire. It's unlikely you will be on your own for too long, in fact, there's probably a clamour for your company that leads to an abundance of riches when it comes to relationships. You are honest about your feelings and you're so sexy you're like a walking aphrodisiac. The planet Mars in the sign of Venus couldn't be anything else, of course!

If you have a negative Mars in Libra or the 7th house

It's weird thing but for a sign that is a peacemaker by nature, you display dictatorial elements in your make-up that bring out the worst in Mars. You are argumentative, a bully and totally selfish. This is because the balance of Libra is completely out of kilter. So instead of thinking of others, you are interested only in yourself, your needs, your desires, your passions and that's that. Hang the rest. You are totally hot-headed, probably out of the frustration of not being able to come to decisions without a lot of hand-wringing. And even when you do make a choice, it is usually the wrong one.

How to overcome a negative Mars in Libra or the 7th house

Time to take your other half into your confidence. Don't go it alone and don't assume that what you want is what they want. It simply isn't so. Instead of riding roughshod over your partner, your motto should be half a dozen of one and six of the other. That way you can end up with a decent dozen where everybody is happy. Be aware that your anger stems from things such as injustice and unfairness. Those are the things to get on your high horse about. When you've done something wrong, sort it out with some Air sign common sense, not by brooding negatively on something that can be resolved by practical action.

Famous Mars in Libra: Bill Clinton, Abraham Lincoln, Michael Douglas, Roger Moore, Margaret Thatcher, Elvis Presley, Freddie Mercury, Maria Callas.

MARS IN SCORPIO OR THE 8TH HOUSE

You have a rugged, determined nature and are prepared to fight for everything in life. You relish research and investigation, and would be suited to a career in MI5 or exploring the supernatural or occult. Your sex drive is fast and furious but you can be obsessive, jealous and avenging in intimate relationships. Your temper can erupt into a destructive rage if allowed to develop, so it is probably best not to let it. You are a creature of psychology, and are much deeper and craftier than people realize. You are controlling, too.

If you have a positive Mars in Scorpio or the 8th house

Nothing, and I mean nothing, will deflect you from doing what you have decided to do. You are like a knight in shining armour or an Amazon warrior riding to the rescue against tyranny, despair and injustice. You will not put up with bullying, abuse or any other kind of unfair behaviour from anyone. Sexually, you are dynamite – once you have weaved your seductive and sensual charms, your partner will be putty in your gorgeous hands. You are a remarkable person. But still waters run deep, and others should be wary of your devious side.

If you have a negative Mars in Scorpio or the 8th house

If you can't win someone over, you will use every trick you've ever learned: manipulation, plotting, scheming, you name it. Your ultimate goal is control, getting someone to do your bidding, probably sexually first and financially second. And if the two are involved at the same time, then even better. Sexually you are rampant but lack the tenderness required to keep your other half on their erogenous toes. In fact, in the end they might just lie back and think of England. You can be obsessive, compulsive and abusive. All in all, you are a right piece of work.

How to overcome a negative Mars in Scorpio or the 8th house

Ramming something down a person's throat will not make them like it, and as soon as you get that into your head the better. You can only control someone up to a point and even if you achieve that, where is the respect, trust and love that you really want? It's time to stand back and look back at the mess you have made of your intimate, private life. It's time now to turn over a new leaf. And that means realizing that it's not about self-satisfaction, but about keeping the love of your life happy. If you have sexual desires they cannot cope with, you need to find a consenting adult who shares them or seek help via counselling to sort it out. What is for sure is that by continuing as you are, you will never be happy – and you will make others unhappy as a result.

Famous Mars in Scorpio: Leonardo DiCaprio, Olivia Newton-John, Grace Kelly, Oprah Winfrey, Jude Law, Jimi Hendrix, Joseph Stalin.

MARS IN SAGITTARIUS OR THE 9TH HOUSE

You hate to feel life falling flat and have a constant need for adventure and excitement. Your boundless supply of energy and enthusiasm needs to be channelled positively, perhaps through sport or competitive activities. You are always ready to face a challenge and relish travel. You can be too forceful with your opinions and blow your top if people disagree with you. Indeed, you pontificate to such a degree you always end up believing that the right way is your way. Your temper is fiery but it is the safety valve you need when the going gets tough. It saves on the blood pressure.

If you have a positive Mars in Sagittarius or the 9th house

You are just like Tigger in *Winnie-the-Pooh*, a total handful and an amazement to us all. It is this jolly, bright and infectious nature of yours that makes so many people want to be part of your life. You are the kind of person that everyone wants around when they are feeling down. Your sexual effervescence, too, brings admirers flocking to you, all of them keen on a piece of your action. You grasp opportunity quickly. You see life as a voyage of discovery and you want to sample every type of culture, creed and country while you can. You want to be a winner in all you do and will do everything in a just, honest and forthright way. Therefore, if you make a commitment to someone, that person will be very, very special.

If you have a negative Mars in Sagittarius or the 9th house

The thought of settling down and committing yourself to one person for the rest of your life is anathema, but have you told your partner that? Probably not. You are likely to string them along with a lot of maybes and could bes, which is okay if your other half feels the same way. However, you may well be having an affair with someone who is already attached and unobtainable as that presents the kind of obstacle you like. Until they leave their partner for you! That really sends you shimmying down the drainpipe. Worse still, perhaps *you* are already hitched and having an affair, and coming up with the lines, 'My wife or husband doesn't understand me' and 'Yes, I will leave them when the time is right.' Trouble is, if you have kids who you adore and you can't face life without them or the dog! So as you can see, this placement is all about you having your cake and eating it.

How to overcome a negative Mars in Sagittarius or the 9th house

We know that the path of true sex never runs smooth, but don't let your libido rule common sense. You could get yourself into intimate entanglements that get totally out of hand. You must lay your cards on the table from the first. If you want a bit of fun then say that's what you want. You don't have to make a song and dance about it, but don't cover your tracks or true intentions just to get into someone's bed. You have the kind of drive and vigour that is adorable, and by knowing what you want and not lying through your teeth, you can make yourself and a lot of other people happy in the process.

Famous Mars in Sagittarius: Renee Zellweger, Judy Garland, Prince Charles, Jack Nicholson, Jennifer Lopez, Luciano Pavarotti, Robert Redford.

MARS IN CAPRICORN OR THE 10TH HOUSE

You are so driven by your ambitions that you devote all your energy and drive to achieving your goals. This may be at the expense of your family and your love life, where you need to develop sensitivity to go with your unquestionable lust. You tend to bottle up your tensions, which can lead to eruptions of temper. You can make enemies easily as even when you don't mean to, you come across as a threat.

If you have a positive Mars in Capricorn or the 10th house

When you find something sexy, you go for it. And finding your mission and purpose, and succeeding in areas of prestige and kudos, satisfies you just as much as good old romp. Because you are ultra-ambitious, you want to attract someone who is equally turned on by this. Together, you hope, you will straddle the world like a couple of career Colussi. That might be easier said than done but it is not entirely impossible. A marriage of convenience may be a likely outcome. But so long as it serves a purpose for you both, so what?

If you have a negative Mars in Capricorn or the 10th house

You need to differentiate between what you want to achieve when it comes to your career and vocation, and what you desire in a person. If you don't, your other half will become a professional widow or widower waiting for you to satisfy your ambitious urges – and that might never happen.

You will use someone to get yourself to the top and have no

remorse or repentance about doing so because you are so determined to succeed, you aren't bothered about silly things such as your partner's sensibilities. They knew what they were getting into, you say, but did they really? You can use people more than you realize, only calling them up when you want something, leading them to think there is more to your affair than there is. Although it might not prick your conscience, trust me, you are lighting the fuse to a time bomb in the other person and it will only be a matter of time before it explodes right in your face.

How to overcome a negative Mars in Capricorn or the 10th house

There is absolutely nothing stopping you from arranging a square deal in your life so that you can have what you want and others can have what they want. You are a sexy beast and that is part of your animal magnetism and charm. Although even the most refined folks sometimes like a wee bit of rough, that doesn't mean you shouldn't be aware of the feelings of others. Passions and desires can come in different guises and sizes and you can satisfy those urges in yourself and others. Just be open about your ambitions, that you do want help to succeed in your career and make something of yourself – there is bound to be someone out there who thinks just like you. However, don't make someone a victim to your ambitions just because they have contacts that you want to get at – what comes around, goes around. Besides, it's all so unnecessary when there are plenty more pebbles on the beach who are just as influential.

Famous Mars in Capricorn: Jim Carrey, Christina Aguilera, Marlon Brando, David Bowie, Prince Andrew, Katharine Hepburn.

MARS IN AQUARIUS OR THE 11TH HOUSE

Your need for emotional and personal independence makes you an unconventional and unpredictable personality with an erratic energy and an air of nervous tension. You make friends quickly but can lose them just as fast because of your aggression and need to compete. You are as inventive in your sex life as you are elsewhere, which is to say very inventive and experimental. Your temper is hard to control as once it gives, it just has to burst, sometimes at the most incredible times.

If you have a positive Mars in Aquarius or the 11th house

You have no problems with your sexuality. You have nothing to hide in the closet and are happy to do your own physical thing. Indeed, the more you do, the merrier. You will go from one extreme to another with an insatiable sexual appetite one minute and on the verge of celibacy the next. You need a friend as well as a lover and aren't turned on by idiots, not even pretty ones, whom you will be content to love and leave. But once you find your soul mate, that is, someone who thinks, emotes and is driven by the same sexual drum beat as you, then you will find happiness. For a satisfying and happy intimate life, you need a very understanding partner, as even a positive placed Mars in Aquarius/11th is prone to fits of restlessness and avoiding commitment. You are a great club person, but although you have a well-developed esprit de corps, you still like to be top dog, as you hate taking orders. You are selective about your friendships but those you love, you love for life. You are wonderfully inspirational and totally aspirational.

If you have a negative Mars in Aquarius or the 11th house

Commitments, promises, guarantees – call them what you want, but they are anathema to you. You can make the mistake of acting in sexual haste and repenting at leisure. You may go into denial about your true sexuality and spread misery all over the place because you don't know what you want. You aren't content in sorting your problems out yourself; you have to bring other people in. You are contrary and changeable, and expect folks to cope after you have dumped them and gone your own way.

How to overcome a negative Mars in Aquarius or the 11th house

Do everyone a favour and stay single for as long as possible – well at least until you have sorted out whether you are Arthur or Martha. (Even if you are bisexual, at least you have made that decision.) But whatever you are, accept this is how nature intended you to be. You don't have to go around feeling shame or apportioning blame. Instead, quietly get on with your life. There are people out there in the same boat – this isn't some kind of cosmic conspiracy to test you.

Live and let live must be your motto. Avoid getting into heated arguments over issues of prejudice or intolerance or it won't be long before people realize that you protest a little bit too much. You can make a great friend, so throw yourself into any relationship and if it leads to something more then that's the way it should be. Don't obstruct your sexual flow, just follow it. And remember there is no such thing as 'normal'.

Famous Mars in Aquarius: Lance Armstrong, Cary Grant, Scarlett Johansson, Ian McKellen, Jane Fonda, Lauren Bacall, Leonardo da Vinci, Will Young, Tony Hancock, Julie Christie, Vivienne Westwood, La Toyah Jackson, Stella McCartney, Isadora Duncan.

MARS IN PISCES OR THE 12TH HOUSE

At heart you have a strong drive to help and serve others, but your strong fantasy life means that you can be unrealistic and foolhardy about how you do this and are easily taken in or mistake signals of friendship for something much more than was ever intended. You are not only ultra-sensitive but also very emotional indeed, combining this with a sensual and passionate sexual nature. You may be sexually indiscreet as there is something exciting about menace and danger, but you must take care not to get involved with people who are bad for you. You can keep feelings to yourself for fear of ridicule or rejection, but don't be labelled by what society decrees as right or wrong. Inner anger can often lead to outbursts of temper that fizz and erupt just as quickly as they are gone and forgotten.

If you have a positive Mars in Pisces or the 12th house

You are a wonderful friend, lover and partner to the right person. It's very likely you are going to meet someone who will share everything you have to offer and will not take advantage of you. Fantasies, whether sexual or romantic, will be fulfilled. However you achieve this, it will be a part of your secret side. Even if everyone knows this secret, you still like to keep it under wraps as it adds to the mystery of it all. Seduction is something that oozes from every pore. Once someone has spent time with you, they want to be with you forever. You are as sensitive to their desires and passions as you are to your own, you are a selfless lover and whatever you give to a person is done totally unconditionally. You are charitable to the core and will do whatever you can to make a person or animal's life comfortable and complete.

If you have a negative Mars in Pisces or the 12th house

There is more than a little perversion in your sexual desires or passions, so self-control is very necessary indeed. You could inflict yourself on someone and cause them all kinds of psychological pain or upset. It's possible you had problems coming out sexually or admitting to certain proclivities, but it is nothing to be ashamed of. You may have been made to feel that you were behaving unnaturally and that is the problem at the root of your lifestyle now. The cause may have been an uncompromising parent who didn't understand you or condemned how you felt as being weird or queer. It might have been bullying at school, where you were sensitive to the pressure to be a butch boy or a girlie girl. You may have felt that you couldn't win – but you can.

How to overcome a negative Mars in Pisces or the 12th house

As time goes by, you may realize that your psychosomatic illnesses or problems stem from your sexuality. You can deal with this with the help of complete strangers, close friends or just by being you. Be confident in your actions. You might think you're on your own and there is no-one else like you, but that is ridiculous and, of course, totally self-centred. There are more self-help groups than you realize. Just look, go on the net, pop into the library or call your Citizen's Advice Bureau. The minute you take to drink or drugs to drown your sorrows is the moment you take the first step on the road to self-destruction. You need to get to the heart of the matter and if your sexual needs, desires and passions are fragile and flaky, then one tender lover of whatever your preferred persuasion will soon put that right. Have faith in yourself and faith in the knowledge that you are different but wonderfully so. You can be an inspiration and role model for us all.

Famous Mars in Pisces: Marilyn Monroe, Annie Lennox, Burt Reynolds, Errol Flynn, Rowan Atkinson, Elizabeth Taylor, Elton John.

♃

Jupiter

As we have seen, Jupiter is the planet of expansion, both physical and mental. Happy Zeus defines these aspects of ourselves, as well as our self-confidence, sense of optimism and luck. He is also linked with justice, travel and high finance. Because Jupiter rules Sagittarius and Pisces, he is even more influential in the charts of people who have a powerful Sun or Ascendant placement in these two signs. Similarly he is strong when placed in the 9th and 12th houses.

JUPITER IN ARIES OR THE 1ST HOUSE

Your powerful sense of adventure and enterprise is so driven that it inspires others to feel the same way. You have an infectious sense of humour. However, you can be self-interested and your sense of your own importance can be overblown.

If you have a positive Jupiter in Aries or the 1st house

Your personality is all and everything. With this god of happiness and optimism in Aries or the 1st, you have an in-built capacity to be loved, liked and enjoyed by all.

If you have a negative Jupiter in Aries or the 1st house

You have a tendency to interfere, pontificate and be arrogant. The minute you open your mouth you are off and never know when to stop. Despite this annoying trait, folk tolerate you because you are fun.

How to overcome a negative Jupiter in Aries or the 1st house

A slice of humble pie well chewed and swallowed will help you deal with all your negative traits. Be aware that other people have a right to free speech; just because they hold different opinions to yours doesn't make them wrong.

Famous Jupiter in Aries: Sting, Angelina Jolie, Johnny Depp, George Michael, Al Pacino, Brad Pitt, Russell Crowe, David Beckham, Whitney Houston, Nicolas Cage.

JUPITER IN TAURUS OR THE 2ND HOUSE

You are blessed with enormous joie de vivre and an earthy, slapstick sense of humour. You appreciate the finer things in life and use your plentiful supply of common sense to make money, sometimes by the astute picking up of bargains. You place great importance on material possessions, especially property, which you see as a status symbol. Your home will tend to be luxurious, comfortable and as big as you can afford.

If you have a positive Jupiter in Taurus or the 2nd house

You have the capacity, luck and opportunity to make a lot of money in your lifetime. This comes from using your shrewd business acumen and financial judgement.

If you have a negative Jupiter in Taurus or the 2nd house

Your spending can take over so that it can't be stopped and you exceed your income. You run yourself into debt, and despite fines or interest fees, you continue to lead a lifestyle you are neither accustomed to or can afford.

How to overcome a negative Jupiter in Taurus or the 2nd house

Being a shopper is fine but you are a shopaholic, and like any other disease, you need to realize this is nearly as bad as over-reliance on drink or drugs. You need to tailor your budgets to suit your needs and you need to learn that if you see something you don't *have* to have it. If you can't do it, professional help needs to be enlisted. You need someone who can aid and advise you financially. A money manager, prudent partner or strong Saturn in your chart will help counteract your out of control extravagance.

Famous Jupiter in Taurus: Keanu Reeves, Teri Hatcher, Ringo Starr, Audrey Hepburn, John Lennon, Bob Dylan, Tony Blair, Robert Downey Jr, Winston Churchill.

JUPITER IN GEMINI OR THE 3RD HOUSE

You have a broad mind that is interested in all aspects of life, yet you are also prone to losing concentration and changing your mind at the last minute. You are guilty sometimes of over-exaggeration and tall tales, and make too many promises you will never keep. Despite this, you are popular in your neck of the woods and may even hold a position of some status there.

If you have a positive Jupiter in Gemini or the 3rd house

No party, event or occasion is complete without your popular presence. You keep folk enthralled with your stories, so much so that you easily make friends who are well-connected and who can help you turn your ideas into reality.

If you have a negative Jupiter in Gemini or the 3rd house

You can turn people against you by promising them the earth and delivering nothing. You want to feel important and out of the ordinary; even being a big fish in a small pond means something to you. However, this can lead you to 'keep up with the Joneses' in an effort to impress, even telling tall tales of who you know and what you know.

How to overcome a negative Jupiter in Gemini or the 3rd house

One day the penny will drop, and all those folks who thought you were honourable and honest will realize you are just a façade. So if you invent or promise anything, make sure you have the wherewithal to supply or deliver. If you do, you will win respect. But if you don't, and let a person down, this could lead to your being condemned as a chancer.

Famous Jupiter in Gemini: Grace Kelly, Jacqueline Kennedy Onassis, Muhammad Ali, Liv Tyler, Barbra Streisand, Oprah Winfrey, Elizabeth Hurley.

JUPITER IN CANCER OR THE 4TH HOUSE

You are a wonderful person, a good-natured soul, and full of sympathy, generosity and consideration for others. This makes you a lovely family person, who enjoys nothing more than having fun with and being surrounded by your kith and kin. You have an astute business sense and may well put money into real estate or bricks and mortar, which gives you additional security.

If you have a positive Jupiter in Cancer or the 4th house

You are a joy to behold. Your fabulous sense of humour has everyone rocking in the aisles and you are wonderful when dealing with people who have gone through a terrible time. You've the kind of shoulder that everyone wants to cry on. Your home life is the be all and end all of your happiness because feeling comfortable and snug as a bug in a rug is all you really desire.

If you have a negative Jupiter in Cancer or the 4th house

You are inclined to be so protective and defensive of your relatives that your children or partner can feel suffocated by your big-hearted warmth. You mean well but every so often you forget that everyone has their limits and you need to learn theirs. Investing in property or land is fine just so long as you don't end up robbing Peter to pay Paul.

How to overcome a negative Jupiter in Cancer or the 4th house

Allowing your loved ones and family space to do their own thing is so important. Not everyone wants a domestic party every day. Sometimes we all need to retreat. Respect this and find some quality time for yourself along the way.

Famous Jupiter in Cancer: Annie Lennox, Harrison Ford, Bruce Willis, Leonard Nimoy, Rowan Atkinson, Liberace, James Dean, Katharine Hepburn, Sean Connery.

JUPITER IN LEO OR THE 5TH HOUSE

You are full of star quality. Dramatic, flamboyant and full of theatrical flair, you are someone who lives life to the absolute full, and you are great at getting those around you to do the same. You are a huge optimist but can come over as pompous when you are in full flow. You attract lovers with your generosity and humour.

If you have a positive Jupiter in Leo or the 5th house

You have a love of children, especially your own, and kiddies generally make you feel good. Your avuncular attitudes give you the wisdom and kindness that young people love. Your affairs of the heart are well placed and you are lucky in love. An absolute sucker for fun, pleasure and enjoyment, very little gets you down.

If you have a negative Jupiter in Leo or the 5th house

You can be far too judgemental of loved ones and your children. You always think that what you have to say is sage and worth listening to, but it's not really; you just like the sound of your own voice. You hate people enjoying themselves without you. You want to be the life and soul of everyone's world and can't believe it when people want to arrange events or occasions without you.

How to overcome a negative Jupiter in Leo or the 5th house

No-one is indispensable, not even you, and the sooner you realize that generosity of spirit is just as important as any other kind of generosity, the better. Take heed of the old theatrical adage, leave 'em wanting more. Do that and your popularity will never wane; indeed, folks will seek your company out.

Famous Jupiter in Leo: Kylie Minogue, Bette Davis, Elizabeth Taylor, Diana Ross, Nicole Kidman, Pope John Paul II, Julio Iglesias, Mick Jagger, Bill Gates, Vin Diesel.

JUPITER IN VIRGO OR THE 6TH HOUSE

Jupiter hates being trapped in the trammelled sign of Virgo. It makes you a detail person at heart with lots of common sense, but can leave you confused about whether to look at the small picture or the broader one. You have a lively, sceptical mind and are good at helping others at work. Exercise and a healthy diet, perhaps vegetarian, should be a key part of daily life. Your working world benefits from your warm personality, and medical matters play a more than average part in your life.

If you have a positive Jupiter in Virgo or the 6th house

Charitable to a fault, you are a philanthropist and champion those causes or charities that mean something to you. You just want to better the world in general, helping those who are suffering or are unprivileged in particular. You will be very lucky in your business or work, mainly because your spirit and humour bonds well with your co-workers.

If you have a negative Jupiter in Virgo or the 6th house

Thinking you know best and assuming you are the sole discoverer of something brings out the bombastic and arrogant side of you. Don't think you have total rights to anything or anyone, and don't believe for one minute you are immune to health hassles and fail to defend yourself against bugs, germs or viruses.

How to overcome a negative Jupiter in Virgo or the 6th house

You are only human, and the sooner you realize that the better, especially in matters of health. You must learn to take care of yourself more than you do. You sincerely believe that some healing angel will dash in and look after you when your body goes wrong, but the truth is you have to administer to your own sickness and protect yourself whenever you can. In your business world, be prepared to learn something new every day. No-one will think badly of you if you don't have immediate answers to problems; in fact, they will love and respect you more if you admit your faults or intellectual gaps.

Famous Jupiter in Virgo: Renee Zellweger, Errol Flynn, Michael Douglas, Julia Roberts, Mel Gibson, Lisa Marie Presley.

JUPITER IN LIBRA OR THE 7TH HOUSE

Your love of life makes you popular, but you can be prone to laziness. Money is a strong motivating force and you have the ability to make business partnerships profitable ones. This may mean you marry for money or position or gain it on the way, but you also need an intellectual rapport with your partner. The key to a successful and happy affair is having the tolerance and acceptance of each other's funny little ways. By following this maxim you will be destined for a wonderful relationship.

If you have a positive Jupiter in Libra or the 7th house

There is nothing mercenary about you in your close relationships. Even though you might be accused of elevating your life through your marriage or partner, you and I know you are led by genuine love. Because of this, you will have the sort of happy partnership that means all you need is to make each other laugh to get by.

If you have a negative Jupiter in Libra or the 7th house

You can be a gold-digger. You might try to arrange your marriage so you end up with someone you don't love but who can keep you comfortable and in luxury. If it's not money, you may marry for status or what you can get out of the affair.

How to overcome a negative Jupiter in Libra or the 7th house

Love is more important than anything in a relationship. If you don't love someone then don't hurt them or demean yourself by getting involved with someone purely for material reasons. In the end, Jupiter is about happiness and if that happiness doesn't spring from the heart then it will result in a broken heart.

Famous Jupiter in Libra: Jennifer Lopez, Catherine Zeta Jones, Madonna, Sting, Bill Clinton, Sylvester Stallone, George W. Bush, Cher, Christina Aguilera, Brigitte Bardot, Freddie Mercury, Judy Garland.

JUPITER IN SCORPIO OR THE 8TH HOUSE

You have a lust for life that you pursue with great energy, although whether it's sex or wine, you can overindulge. Your libido is extremely active so you need an energetic and satisfying sex life but you can be too demanding for your partner. In life, fortune smiles on you, as somebody's loss is your gain. Your tendency to be suspicious and financially controlling must be tempered.

If you have a positive Jupiter in Scorpio or the 8th house

Well-honed psychologically, you know how far you can go with others. By knowing your own strength, you can reap the rewards in sticky and awkward situations. People trust you and this results in friendships with people from all classes and tendencies.

If you have a negative Jupiter in Scorpio or the 8th house

Both money and sex represent power to you. You are very happy to compromise yourself sexually to get what you want in other ways. You use your mystique to create a person who isn't really you. You are dishonest with other people's money and may try to make people dependent on you in order to control them.

How to overcome a negative Jupiter in Scorpio or the 8th house

It's easy to give in to criminal tendencies but in the end the law or the tax office will catch up with you. Honesty is the best policy for no other reason than it is better to have people love and adore you because you are a genuinely nice guy or girl than because they fear you. Because you can mix with all sorts, you have every chance of achieving this.

Famous Jupiter in Scorpio: Uma Thurman, Britney Spears, Napoleon Bonaparte, Lucille Ball, Fred Astaire, David Bowie, Elvis Presley, Elton John.

JUPITER IN SAGITTARIUS OR THE 9TH HOUSE

With a double helping of Jupiter imbued into your chart, you have a particular yen to expand your horizons both mentally and physically through travel or education. You are good at tuning into local cultures. Your optimistic, happy-go-lucky persona helps you to broaden your circles and meet the people you need to grow, develop and evolve. You have a strong belief in justice, which may provide links to the law, politics and religion. You have a strong faith and desire to worship a supreme and higher being.

If you have a positive Jupiter in Sagittarius or the 9th house

There is so much about you that epitomizes the essence of Jupiter. You enjoy people, other countries, and learning, and enjoy helping those who find it hard to help themselves. On top of it all, you attract good fortune through your good works and your jovial, optimistic personality makes you the best company.

If you have a negative Jupiter in Sagittarius or the 9th house

You might think you're immortal and have some kind of divine right to whatever you want but how wrong you are. You expect far too much from others and want to do as little as possible to get it. You live on your smooth charm and ability to make people laugh, but when the mask falls and the myth dies, you are left friendless and a laughing stock.

How to overcome a negative Jupiter in Sagittarius or the 9th house

Having faith in yourself and your abilities is a good start. That means you don't have to lie or create a myth about yourself to make it seem that you are more interesting than you really are. You have a great intellect so use it to the full, don't take the easy way out – you can also create opportunity by using your personality positively. Don't take people for fools or project an annoying self-importance; otherwise you will merely build up a posse of enemies who will want to bring you down a peg or three.

Famous Jupiter in Sagittarius: Prince Charles, Marlon Brando, Lance Armstrong, Burt Reynolds, Prince Andrew, Olivia Newton-John, Hillary Clinton, Lauren Bacall, Maria Callas.

JUPITER IN CAPRICORN OR THE 10TH HOUSE

You have a gargantuan need to achieve but do so steadily rather than spectacularly, largely because of your sensible and dutiful approach to life. Your fixation with success and recognition may be to the detriment of other aspects of your life. However, your workaholic side is lightened by your ability to mix business with pleasure and 'do a deal' when you're also enjoying yourself.

If you have a positive Jupiter in Capricorn or the 10th house

You have judgement, wisdom and a crafty sense of humour that all combine to make you seem less ambitious than you really are. You flatter to deceive and it's this that can disarm your rivals and competitors into assuming you're not really serious about your life mission and purpose. Oh, how wrong can they be? You will win recognition and reach the pinnacle of your profession or career simply because people trust and respect you. You have a dignified air of authority and you know what you're talking about.

If you have a negative Jupiter in Capricorn or the 10th house

You are solely motivated by fame and fortune but want to do as little hard work as you can to achieve it. You mix with low life or can be tempted by get-rich-quick schemes to jump the queue or save time. In the end, either the law, your conscience or plain greed will catch up with you, or the recognition you wanted will take the form of a notoriety you will deserve.

How to overcome a negative Jupiter in Capricorn or the 10th house

If you want longevity and prestigious success, you must do everything lawfully and abide by the rules of the game. You have a weapon at your command that few people have: good fortune and a fine personality. So why spoil your chance of happiness by cutting corners or dealing with deadbeats who will betray your honour as soon as look at you? Rise above such temptations now and what you achieve will be long-lasting and well-deserved.

Famous Jupiter in Capricorn: Peter Sellers, Charlie Chaplin, Adolf Hitler, Margaret Thatcher, Paul Newman, Jack Nicholson.

JUPITER IN AQUARIUS OR THE 11TH HOUSE

Your blend of invention, intellect and originality make you a natural leader. You have a deep-rooted need for friends and a lively social life. Your ability to inspire others will make you an ideal founder or member of an organization or club, especially one with a community or social conscience. You have a futuristic outlook and take the long-term view.

If you have a positive Jupiter in Aquarius or the 11th house

Your humanitarian qualities are what make you stand out. You are determined to help when you can and are ready to forgive someone's difficulties or problems caused by circumstances and events conspiring against them in life. Your kindness attracts good people to you, including movers and shakers from all aspects of business and the world who end up becoming influential friends. These people can help you attain your aims and aspirations. You are a truly beneficient soul.

If you have a negative Jupiter in Aquarius or the 11th house

Rather than doing things for the greater good, you do them to see what you can get out of the situation. You don't do anything without filthy lucre or some aggrandizement being offered to you. You want to crystallize your hopes and wishes by mixing with the great and the good, but in the end you will be declared a fake and phoney, someone who puts on airs and graces to mask their true intentions.

How to overcome a negative Jupiter in Aquarius or the 11th house

You think your cocky Jack the Lad or Jill the Lady personality is enough to win people over. To a point you're right, at least for the first few meetings, and then folk get wise to you. So rather than pull the wool over their eyes, let all those who cross your path know your true intentions. Then let them judge whether you or what you are doing is worthy. Better that than be cavalier in your actions and find yourself barracked and barred wherever you go. Keep your dignity intact.

Famous Jupiter in Aquarius: Queen Elizabeth II, Marilyn Monroe, Princess Diana, Alec Guinness, Jim Carrey, Jane Fonda.

JUPITER IN PISCES OR THE 12TH HOUSE

You have a very well-developed philosophical and compassionate streak, with strongly held beliefs, especially where the tenets are spiritual or psychically-based. These two elements combine to make you a natural for the caring professions or the voluntary sector, where your kindness and sympathy can be spread far and wide. You have spells when you need some solitude, however.

If you have a positive Jupiter in Pisces or the 12th house

You might not be a saint but you are as near as most people will get. This angelic side of you is motivated by a desire to help in whatever charitable area you can. Whether you run a rescue home for animals or serve in a shop much of the week, you have a knack of raising money for those causes that you care about. You raise their profile too. The chances are you've suffered in the past, but the more you give unconditionally of time, money and effort, the more you will receive as your own life goes on.

If you have a negative Jupiter in Pisces or the 12th house

Why do you really do the things you do? On the surface you seem to be as good and godly as most other people with this aspect. But although you are likely to appear generous and charitable, you must be getting something out of it or you wouldn't do it. You can be very secretive and hide your true intentions, or go after the sympathy vote by making up tales about the awful life you've led.

How to overcome a negative Jupiter in Pisces or the 12th house

If you don't prick your own conscience then it will be done for you. When it happens you will be left shame-faced and very few people (probably only those with the positive Jupiter in Pisces or 12th) will ever give you a second chance. Transcend your negativity by working on the sublime spiritual plane that can be yours if you renounce greed and self-interest and devote yourself to those who really need help. Before long you will become devout at doing good, perhaps even becoming a leader. And you will be doing it all for the right reasons.

Famous Jupiter in Pisces: Leonardo DiCaprio, Cary Grant, Abraham Lincoln, Roger Moore, Tom Cruise, Penelope Cruz, Pope Benedict, Anastacia, Sigmund Freud.

♄

Saturn

Saturn, as its constraining rings symbolically remind us, is the planet of limitation and inhibition. He also represents your fears, weaknesses and your sense of failure or loss of meaning in your life. He also stands for what you need to do to strengthen your vulnerable areas. As you piece together the components of Planet You, it is Saturn that shows you how these facets are reflected in you.

Because Saturn rules both Capricorn and (with Uranus) Aquarius, he is especially strong in these two signs. Aspects to the Sun and Ascendant also strengthen or weaken his powers. He is powerful too in the Capricorn and Aquarius houses, the 10th and 11th.

SATURN IN ARIES OR IN THE 1ST HOUSE

You swing wildly between being strong and assertive one moment and brittle and inhibited the next. You need to resolve this ongoing struggle within you and become more self-sufficient and less self-pitying. If you do, you will gain confidence, particularly as you get older. If you don't, you may suffer from depression, which may affect your physical health.

If you have a positive Saturn in Aries or the 1st house

You show strength in adversity and have the ability to take your time and be patient even though inside you want immediate results. You are serious and committed but this doesn't prevent you from taking off and throwing caution to the wind in a responsible way. You are a fine administrator and competitor all in one.

If you have a negative Saturn in Aries or the 1st house

Depression, ill-health and cowardice are just some of the symptoms of a negative Saturn here. Basically your self-esteem is at rock bottom and one slight or setback can be enough to make you give up for good. You have little or no staying power and want to dodge duty or responsibility in case things go wrong or you are not up to the challenge.

How to overcome a negative Saturn in Aries or the 1st house

The chances are you were ridiculed or put under the cosh by a father or father figure. The result is a total lack of confidence and belief in yourself. This may manifest itself through illness or an inherent weakness that you can and will overcome. Concentrate for a while and pinpoint what it is that interests you in life. Whether it is a hobby, pastime or job, once you come up with the answer then you can, in your own time, build up a niche for yourself in that area. It might not be an overnight success but before you know it, you will become a leader in your particular field. Don't allow other people to get to you – you may be their patsy because of their weaknesses.

Famous Saturn in Aries: Errol Flynn, Kylie Minogue, Bette Davis, Julia Roberts, Celine Dion, Lisa Marie Presley, Michael Schumacher, Vin Diesel, Lucy Liu, Tina Turner.

SATURN IN TAURUS OR THE 2ND HOUSE

Your emotions are kept under a tight lid. You are conservative with a small 'c', and practical, patient and very cautious. Your strict routines may be too constraining for you, however. You are also materialistic and have an undeveloped spiritual side. Money will not come easily to you, but hard work will pay off. For this reason, you will guard what money you make carefully.

If you have a positive Saturn in Taurus or the 2nd house

You are a classic 'doer'. You won't give up on anything. Instead, with a cool, calm and collected attitude, you will commit yourself doggedly to achieving whatever you set out to do and do it. You are almost obsessed with savings and investments, not because you want to own lots of money but to give you a cushion for your later years. It is not having to worry about financial security in the future that motivates you more than anything else.

If you have a negative Saturn in Taurus or the 2nd house

A fear of not having enough money or possessions that you can call your own makes you acquisitive and avaricious. You can also be parsimonious and just dead tight. Your lack of charity to others and even yourself can make you a figure of fun. Your nickname? Scrooge. You make do with very little but your inability to speculate and be enterprising means you will never own more than a tiny amount. What money you do have may be to hold on to as a result of taxes, mortgages, officialdom and the like. Money really is the root of all evil for you.

How to overcome a negative Saturn in Taurus or the 2nd house

You need to learn very quickly that to have more than you start off with in this life you have to take a chance. It doesn't have to be high risk. It can be small safe investments that you can afford. Every little bit helps. But if you cling in Silas Marner fashion to the idea that a hole in the ground is the ideal way to multiply your money then you are going to be in trouble if someone discovers your hoard and runs off with it.

Famous Saturn in Taurus: Jennifer Lopez, Catherine Zeta Jones, Lucille Ball, Muhammad Ali, Uma Thurman, Ringo Starr, Barbra Streisand, Al Pacino.

SATURN IN GEMINI OR THE 3RD HOUSE

You have a mind that will be suited to science and highly academic study. You may appear cold and cynical, and prone to bouts of ill health or depression. This may be linked to traumas in your childhood; your schooldays in particular may have been the cause of tears. You may also have had a hard time dealing with siblings. Your sense of humour is wickedly dry and sarcastic.

If you have a positive Saturn in Gemini or the 3rd house

You will not flinch until you have mastered a mental puzzle, mystery or subject that you've set out to accomplish. You will be a workaholic and burn the midnight oil, reading up and investigating all the facts and figures you need in order to achieve. Your conscientious mentality is what will bring you long and hard-earned success.

If you have a negative Saturn in Gemini or the 3rd house

You lack the confidence and self-esteem to overcome literal difficulties; you may suffer from dyslexia or other disorders. They can be cured but you build hurdles and reasons why you can't do something before you've even tried. You give up before you've even started, then you spend the rest of your life complaining that you never got the chances and opportunities everyone else seems to get.

How to overcome a negative Saturn in Gemini or the 3rd house

If nothing comes easily to you then you must understand that wherever Saturn lies, it is about self-will, self-assurance and self-reliance. So if you want to be self-made, you must take more of the rough with the smooth to achieve your cerebral and mental goal. You can be top of the class if you learn from experience and realize from the start that you must toil and labour over words, sentences and grammar. When you acquire the know-how, the sense of achievement you will feel and the plaudits you will receive will make it all worthwhile. And you can cock a snook at the teacher, relative or employer who told you you'd never succeed.

Famous Saturn in Gemini: Lance Armstrong, Harrison Ford, Alec Guinness, Diana Ross, Robbie Williams, Eminem, Mick Jagger, Cameron Diaz.

SATURN IN CANCER OR THE 4TH HOUSE

Your intense need for emotional and physical security means you have a very strong belief in your family and roots. This may reflect a remote set of parents or difficult and deprived circumstances during childhood. Unfortunately, you have a habit of internalizing your worries and this inhibited side of you can harm those domestic ties that are so important to you. You should use your practical intuition much more, rather than being sceptical of it.

If you have a positive Saturn in Cancer or the 4th house

Although you reflect the hard-done-by face of Saturn in Cancer or the 4th, you have used your remarkable staying power to bounce back against all the odds. It's as though the responsibility thrust upon you, most probably at an early age when others were out enjoying their youth, has helped you come through against all the odds. You are sensible and serious about all domestic, property and family matters and, as a result, cherish and treasure anything that you achieve when you could have gone under.

If you have a negative Saturn in Cancer or the 4th house

You will use your unloving childhood or disciplinarian parents as an excuse for why you don't deserve to be secure and happy. This results in you forever accepting that the slough of despond you have chosen to live in is all you will ever have. If you think pessimistically then you will never, ever have anything. It's time to snap out of feeling sorry for yourself or you will be a victim for the rest of your life.

How to overcome a negative Saturn in Cancer or the 4th house

Here's a clue on how to snap out of it: consider the heavy experiences you have gone through and realize that you are still standing and still around. If you can withstand the agony, despair and disappointment of a lost youth, no roots and a lack of love, then you can do anything. Start to build and erect your own world, a family of your own and allow hope and a philosophical approach to colour your attitude. Before long that cheeky grin and smile will have people adoring you because you are a fighter and everyone loves a fighter.

Famous Saturn in Cancer: Leonardo DiCaprio, Sylvester Stallone, George W. Bush, Angelina Jolie, Michael Douglas, Napoleon Bonaparte, Cher.

SATURN IN LEO OR THE 5TH HOUSE

You are bound by a strong ethical code and have a dignified and noble sense of honour to go with it. It may have been inherited from a father figure who laid down the law when you were growing up. This means you can take life a little too seriously and forget that it's important to have fun sometimes. The same thing goes for your love life, where again you need to loosen up a little. You have a great ability to organize and this may help you reach the position of respect and authority you crave.

If you have a positive Saturn in Leo or the 5th house

You have a talent, or let's call it a gift. Once you discover what it is then you must go for it. It won't be easy because people will talk you out of it and tell you it's not worth the hassle, but this is precisely the time to go hell for leather and do your creative thing. You have a fine enterprising and ambitious character and can build towards success over a period of time. You are drawn to lovers who are older or wiser, and when you fall in love it will usually be forever. But again, beware of critics who may tell you what's wrong with your affair. Quite frankly, who cares? Certainly not you!

If you have a negative Saturn in Leo or the 5th house

You are too swung by the criticism of others and almost want to be talked out of doing what is very natural to you. Come on, get a grip. You have potential in you that is just waiting to be tapped. If you are forever being held back by your lack of confidence or what people say, you will never get anywhere. You will always be a wannabee or might have been. Is that what you want? I don't think so. Your love can suffer because you don't believe you deserve to have anyone love you.

How to overcome a negative Saturn in Leo or the 5th house

You are in such a parlous state it's no wonder you give up on yourself – but *I* won't. You see I know you have a genuine capability, aptitude, special talent, call it what you will. Not getting things right at the beginning doesn't mean you should give up completely. What you need to do is come back with a new vigour, putting your talent into something bigger and better. With this placement you will soon find a friend or ally who believes in you. You will probably meet them at an event, club or occasion where you mix with folks of a mutual interest.

Famous Saturn in Leo: Bill Clinton, Hillary Clinton, Adolf Hitler, Liv Tyler, Freddie Mercury, Liberace, Charlie Chaplin, Elton John.

SATURN IN VIRGO OR THE 6TH HOUSE

You have a most meticulous and methodical approach to life. You also have a very evolved sense of duty and discipline. On the negative side, you may be so unwilling to change you get stuck in a rut. You are also prone to complaining and criticism of others, including yourself. You may be a hypochondriac and are a poor patient.

If you have a positive Saturn in Virgo or the 6th house

You will work every hour that God sends to perfect something that is important to you. You may prefer to work alone in a solitary office or environment that enables you to get on with what you want to do. You will hate people peering over your shoulder before you've finished. You are also happy to sacrifice some of your time and effort to help those who deserve it. You won't give charitably to every collecting box but will help those who help themselves. If anyone lets you down, you will drop them forever more.

If you have a negative Saturn in Virgo or the 6th house

You have a fear of delegating, so much so you end up dealing with life's minutiae and never, ever moving on. You get stuck in a time warp and forget that change is happening all around, computers have been invented, as have any number of other labour-saving devices. But you are suspicious of them all, and will rant and rave when things go wrong. The state of your health often reflects the state of your life. To avoid those nasty jobs it's so very convenient to fall ill.

How to overcome a negative Saturn in Virgo or the 6th house

You must realize immediately that there is perfection and there is pedantry. If you are a pedant you will spend too much time, in fact most of your life, trying to attain the impossible. But despite your obvious talents for management and organization, you never achieve your goal because you end up doing what a clerk or secretary could do. Either you won't fork out the money, or you live with the adage that if a job's worth doing, then do it yourself. You must loosen up, give up control and trust other people to do those petty, futile little jobs, otherwise you will never achieve success.

Famous Saturn in Virgo: Olivia Newton-John, Prince Charles, Pope John Paul II, Valentino Rossi, Chelsea Clinton, Twiggy, Princess Anne.

SATURN IN LIBRA OR THE 7TH HOUSE

You have a very warm, polite and pleasant nature. Underneath this you have a well-developed sense of fair play and justice. If you feel someone is being ill-treated or is somehow downtrodden, you will fight their corner for them. You take relationships seriously and may wait to settle down. There may also be an age or intellectual difference between you and your eventual partner.

If you have a positive Saturn in Libra or the 7th house

You are well balanced and people seek you out for your opinion as they know it will be unbiased, with no hidden agenda. You are a great 'people person' and can inspire folks to do your bidding. You adopt a serious but laconic tone that brings out the best in friends and your partner. Your relationships are so good that people envy your ability to balance so much in your life, keeping all your balls in the air and never dropping one!

If you have a negative Saturn in Libra or the 7th house

You send out such wrong signals and vibrations that people give you a wide berth. You can't help but foist your life experiences on the top of others, thereby putting them off from expanding, growing or trying something new. You quite wrongly tell them it will never work out. 'Look what happened to me,' you'll say. Your relationships are governed by how you fared in the past. You may feel guilty about a lost love or feel you are not worthy of affection.

How to overcome a negative Saturn in Libra or the 7th house

Before you can win anyone's love or affection, you have to forge a relationship with yourself. That means learning to trust, respect and support your own actions. How would you feel if someone constantly sniped at you (perhaps they have) with criticism, complaints, telling you you're useless and will never achieve anything? Not very good. And that is precisely what you are telling yourself. Give yourself some encouragement. Take little steps to begin with, and you'll grow in confidence, realizing that people are seeking out your company. And not only that, they are coaxing out your pearls of wisdom, because you, at last, have learned to give yourself some credit where it's due.

Famous Saturn in Libra: Sting, Britney Spears, Christina Aguilera, Judy Garland, Maria Callas, George Bush Sr, Justin Timberlake, Beyonce Knowles, Alicia Keys.

SATURN IN SCORPIO OR THE 8TH HOUSE

You are imbued with deep reserves of stamina and concentration, and have a clear sense of where you are going in life. You do have a bad habit of storing up your feelings, however. You are also drawn to the dark side of life and have a morbid interest in death. In intimate relationships you find it hard to give of yourself completely. You find financial matters complex, leading you into tiresome delays or questioning involving government and officialdom, or even less savoury characters. You can be as cold as ice, even cruel, definitely repressive and possess a ferociously jealous and envious nature.

If you have a positive Saturn in Scorpio or the 8th house

You can make your mark on the world by doing those jobs other people find a bit too deep, intense or even taboo. By getting involved with activities that are mysterious, investigative or demanding secrecy you can rise to the top. Sexually, you might find the whole area of passion and emotion tedious, which can lead to difficulties in matters of intimacy. That's because whatever you do in life is done with such psychological depth you question and dwell on everything. You are a leader in an area that demands expert skills and forensic knowledge.

If you have a negative Saturn in Scorpio or the 8th house

You can't help it, you are just so attracted to people or situations that most people abhor. On a sexual or financial level, if you can satisfy all your primeval desires and needs then you will do so. But it is important that whatever you get involved in, you know the risks. There can be a fear of any intimate involvement on any level, be it economic or emotional as the thought of any kind of dependency is anathema. The result is you end up feeling quite alone and isolated, and morbid to a terrifying degree. You have a calculating and cruel streak.

How to overcome a negative Saturn in Scorpio or the 8th house

Psychologically, you are as keen to know what makes you tick as anyone else. And it is by finding this out that you can find the escape from the loneliness and isolation you feel. Your obsessive fear may stem from something that happened to you and has become embedded deep down in your psyche. Dealing with this may not be a task you can achieve on your own, so if you have to accept counselling, therapy or advice, then do so. Better to be safe than sorry. With a little bit of assistance you will then be able to take back control of your life.

Famous Saturn in Scorpio: Queen Elizabeth II, Annie Lennox, Bruce Willis, Rowan Atkinson, Marilyn Monroe, Marlon Brando, Margaret Thatcher, Paul Newman, Oprah Winfrey, Lauren Bacall, Peter Sellers.

SATURN IN SAGITTARIUS OR THE 9TH HOUSE

You have dignity and are honourable and honest with it, although you can sometimes be rather indiscreet. Your worthy character makes you popular but you can feel intellectually hemmed in and need to escape occasionally. You have talent as an academic and intellectual, although you may be erratic. You can lack the courage to take on challenges and need verbal encouragement and praise.

If you have a positive Saturn in Sagittarius or the 9th house

You don't underestimate your power to learn, for you know that knowledge is power and will do your utmost to learn something that will stand you in good stead. Anything that requires working on your own, in different climates or countries, or that demands complete dedication and intellectual graft, suits you. However, you do need to stop and have fun as all work and no play makes you deadly dull. You take your beliefs very seriously and are intrigued by other religions, civilizations and subjects that are linked to history, geography, science or metaphysics.

If you have a negative Saturn in Sagittarius or the 9th house

You lack the mental control and concentration to follow things through. You want the easy way to a solution and aren't bothered whether it is accurate; so long as you come up with an answer, any old answer will do, especially as you can easily blind those who question you with science. You can be seriously intolerant and bigoted, and the word 'hypocrite' might stick in your craw but it is a label you may have to get used to. You don't have the courage of your convictions, lack vision and imagination, and are unscrupulous and unethical if it saves time, effort or hassle.

How to overcome a negative Saturn in Sagittarius or the 9th house

You will be found out unless you back up your all-too-easy words with hard facts. So yes, you can buy a degree or a doctorate off the

Internet, but one day you will meet someone who will be your nemesis and that will be that. Why not save all the angst and legal problems that will ensue, not to mention the permanent damage to your name and reputation, and use your capable mind to do something that will enhance your reputation and enrich your future? You'll amaze everyone, including yourself, if you take a workshop, get into a teach-yourself book or sign on for higher education. It will give you your degree with absolute dignity – just think what you will accomplish in intellectual terms. You've the intelligence and the brainpower now, so use your judgement and common sense.

Famous Saturn in Sagittarius: Madonna, Jacqueline Kennedy Onassis, Abraham Lincoln, Fred Astaire, Roger Moore, Grace Kelly, Michael Jackson, Prince Albert of Monaco, Sharon Stone, Pope Benedict, Osama Bin Laden.

SATURN IN CAPRICORN OR THE 10TH HOUSE

With a double helping of Saturn in your chart, you are extremely solid and reliable. You have both patience and persistence and are driven by a fundamental, psychological dislike of failure or rejection. You are highly materialistic and this can make you miserly and greedy. In this sense, and in others, you are never quite satisfied, always reaching for more and more. Your family life and emotional relationships can suffer because of all this, although you may be prepared to make that sacrifice if you meet someone who backs you to the hilt.

If you have a positive Saturn in Capricorn or the 10th house

When they say it's lonely at the top, they must have meant you. You are perfectly comfortable with your life position, however. You are a loner and very happy to be so. You are ultra-ambitious and won't entertain anything other than total success. You are a careerist and follow your ambitions in your diligent fashion. Whatever you do you are committed and responsible; like the mountain goat you are happy to go ever higher until you reach the summit of recognition and distinction. Because of this, your later years will be your best years. You are a very political animal and, as such, can survive all the intrigue.

If you have a negative Saturn in Capricorn or the 10th house

You are so out in the cold that you have very few, if any, friends. This stems from the fact you are suspicious and untrusting of everyone. According to you, everyone and everything is out to get you, take away your money or learn your secrets. They aren't, but that's how you are and all because of things that happened with your father, your teacher or a boss. You feel you constantly have to prove yourself, but rather than fail and be seen as weak, you cut yourself off and avoid the angst and hassle by being autocratic, overbearing and an emotional desert. Yes, you will achieve and even find success, but it won't add up to much, and it won't lead you to happiness.

How to overcome a negative Saturn in Capricorn or the 10th house

You need to be more accessible and put your trust in someone. If your past relationships were bad, whether familial or emotional, that doesn't mean *every* person you meet will criticize, treat you badly or make you the butt of their cruel jokes. You can actually be a very supportive and loving person if you clamber out of your ivory tower and learn to give and live a little. You're like a wee dog that needs to be shown affection and respect. Once you receive it, each and every day a little more of the good things in life will be yours. So, reach out to someone, whoever it is. If you sense mutual cooperation and respect, then grab your chance of happiness. The chances are it will be someone you used to look down on. Drop the caste system – we are all brothers and sisters under the sun.

Famous Saturn in Capricorn: Princess Diana, Prince Andrew, Leonard Nimoy, Audrey Hepburn, James Dean, Sean Connery, George Clooney, Hugh Grant, Meg Ryan, Val Kilmer, Steve McQueen, Neil Armstrong.

SATURN IN AQUARIUS OR THE 11TH HOUSE

You have the vitality and dynamism to do the right thing for the world around you. You are imbued with a genuine humanitarian streak and are conscientious in all you do. However, your independent nature might render you liable to loneliness and a need for seclusion. This may be self-inflicted, given your love of solitary pastimes. Your few friends will be loyal and may be older either in years or experience. You can also find it hard to decide between tradition and more futuristic ideas, although with evidence and proof you can merge the two.

If you have a positive Saturn in Aquarius or the 11th house

You make a marvellous, dedicated, dogged and faithful friend. You appreciate more than anyone how important true friendship is, so when you find someone you can tell everything to, you will be theirs for life. You are keen on creating strong foundations for future enterprises or aspirations and will work till the cows come home, going through the right course of action, gaining the permits or blueprints required. You do nothing by halves. This results in an ability to crystallize your ideas and dreams and make something of them – with a little help from your dear friends, of course.

If you have a negative Saturn in Aquarius or the 11th house

You make a rod for your own back by not moving from the place you were at the very beginning. It's as though you're afraid of the past and you're fearful of what the future might bring. Does it matter? So what if you reveal your Achilles heel or have a failure? You are clearly the kind of person everybody loves to love if only because you love a moan and yet underneath it all, you are an optimist and happy to have a go. So what's gone wrong? Did somebody steal your candy when you were a kid or a parent not recognize your true talents and set you tasks that weren't part of your character or nature? Probably, but that doesn't mean everyone you meet is keen to show you up or bring you down. You are a shrinking violet who needs to get a bit of sunshine.

How to overcome a negative Saturn in Aquarius or the 11th house

Give yourself the chance to socialize, or join a group or society for serious political reasons or simply to chill out. Suck it and see. Joining a club or organization would also give you the opportunity to administrate or show your committee or management skills. Before long you'll see there was nothing to be afraid of – and you'll have everyone in stitches to boot.

Famous Saturn in Aquarius: Teri Hatcher, Cary Grant, Johnny Depp, Brigitte Bardot, Jim Carrey, George Michael, Tom Cruise, Elvis Presley, Elizabeth Taylor.

SATURN IN PISCES OR THE 12TH HOUSE

You have an ingrained compassionate and sympathetic side to your nature and this may lead to spiritual or emotional suffering, but there is a touch of the masochist in you too. You have a habit of dealing yourself self-inflicted wounds, sometimes just by being defeatist. This may make you melancholic at times, something that is exacerbated by self-pity and a habit of seeing the worst in everything and everyone. You may also prefer to spend time alone, persuading yourself you need a safe refuge. All this can lead to clinical depression or neuroses, however, so you must build the inner strength necessary to overcome this. Draw on the encouragement of others to overcome your feelings of inadequacy.

If you have a positive Saturn in Pisces or the 12th house

You do so much for others that sometimes you don't think enough of yourself. You too need spiritual comforting and a chance to recharge your emotional batteries so don't sell yourself short as a person or leave yourself short of time to do what you need to do. You have a dedication and devotion to those you love that goes way beyond the call of love or duty. You appreciate the faith and support those people give you, if only because you've done without so much from people you thought cared and should have cared, but didn't really.

If you have a negative Saturn in Pisces or the 12th house

Beating yourself up and imprisoning yourself in guilt, a persecution complex or a fear of the unknown will only make you suffer more than is necessary. This masochistic tendency of yours probably comes from way back when you were made to feel totally and utterly useless and worthless by those who should've known better. Don't hit the bottle or take to drugs or anything else, as self-deception is self-destructive.

How to overcome a negative Saturn in Pisces or the 12th house

It won't be easy, but you must now see the error of your ways in allowing those people who were responsible for your upbringing or employment to bring you down. Enlist the support of people who are experts in medical, financial or emotional matters. Get out and see what true suffering is. Join a charity or volunteer to help others. Become political if you believe an institution hasn't had its just desserts. You will always find it easier to confront situations that don't directly affect you, but that's fine. An unconditional and noble approach is even better and whatever you achieve, it will make you feel as wonderful as someone who has won the lottery. When you see how much goodness and kindness you bring to others you can begin building the new you, transforming yourself from a victim to a little angel.

Famous Saturn in Pisces: Burt Reynolds, Keanu Reeves, Jane Fonda, Elizabeth Hurley, Katharine Hepburn, Jack Nicholson, Bjork, Halle Berry, Russell Crowe.

Uranus

Uranus is associated with change and upheaval. He is the planet of chaos. He is also about what is futuristic, unexpected and original within Planet You. Because Uranus spends seven years in each sign, his influence varies almost from generation to generation. As co-ruler of

Aquarius, he is especially influential in that sign and his house, the 11th. Otherwise, however, his house position has far more significance.

URANUS IN ARIES OR THE 1ST HOUSE

You have a unique and magnetic personality, and are extremely independent. You relish risk-taking but can be wilful and perverse in this, making you a disruptive influence. You have a need for almost constant stimulation and excitement.

If you have a positive Uranus in Aries or the 1st house

You are very individual and attract people turned on by your genius and outlandishness. You are spontaneous to a degree and are able to solve complex matters with an amazing inventiveness. You offer food for thought to others and their fuddy-duddy ways, and have the ability to make things happen.

If you have a negative Uranus in Aries or the 1st house

Unreliable and rebellious, you are a force for change but not a good one. You draw people into your anarchy and through the chaos, create personal problems for yourself and others as your reputation is one of a born troublemaker.

How to overcome a negative Uranus in Aries or the 1st house

Making a drama out of crisis or doing something for a laugh will get you nowhere. Concentrate your mind on a subject, sport or hobby and before you know it you can change the world in a positive way.

Famous Uranus in Aries: Jacqueline Kennedy Onassis, Leonard

Nimoy, Brigitte Bardot, Roger Moore, Audrey Hepburn, James Dean, Grace Kelly, Elvis Presley, Elizabeth Taylor, Sean Connery.

URANUS IN TAURUS OR THE 2ND HOUSE

You have an erratic relationship with money and material things. You are just as likely to make millions as you are to lose every penny you own on a wild gamble. Your personality contains a mix of originality and common sense, but you can also be stubborn and selfish. You may have problems displaying your affections.

If you have a positive Uranus in Taurus or the 2nd house

You could make a mint by following your ideas and brainwaves. You might not know it, but you are so far ahead of your time in your thoughts and downright brilliance, you could put yourself in the top earning bracket.

If you have a negative Uranus in Taurus or the 2nd house

The trouble is, you don't realize just how much you could be worth. You allow people to put a dampener on your dreams and schemes, when by following them you could be worth a small fortune.

How to overcome a negative Uranus in Taurus or the 2nd house

Why listen to others? They may have a vested interest in bringing your ideas down. By investing in your brilliant brainwaves you will be laughing all the way to the bank. Join a course or get a job that allows you to cut your teeth on the thing you loving doing the best, then watch the bounty flood in.

Famous Uranus in Taurus: Muhammad Ali, Burt Reynolds,

Napoleon Bonaparte, Ringo Starr, Barbra Streisand, Jane Fonda, Al Pacino, Jack Nicholson.

URANUS IN GEMINI OR THE 3RD HOUSE

You possess a highly inventive and original mind. You may come up with ideas capable of changing everyday life. As a young person, you found authority and discipline at school extremely hard to swallow and needed plenty of room to be by yourself. This is something that has continued into adulthood, as you find it hard to relax. Although you have a logical mind, you can also be contrary. Last-minute travel, especially by air, can provide you with stimulation and opportunity at journey's end.

If you have a positive Uranus in Gemini or the 3rd house

You are in a class of your own, and if you have the encouragement from a friend, relative or teacher, you can achieve whatever you choose as your destiny. Yes, *whatever* it is, you can make it your own and become a hero or heroine in your field.

If you have a negative Uranus in Gemini or the 3rd house

The problem is, you simply don't realize or understand that you are a genius. Because it is said that genius and madness aren't far apart, you may decide to listen to folks who say you are bonkers or crazy. You're not, unless you allow other people to stop you.

How to overcome a negative Uranus in Gemini or the 3rd house

Those folks who tell you not to bother because you haven't the makings of anyone special are just jealous, don't know what they are talking about or shouldn't be in their job. Let me assure you, anything based on your ideas is sure to be a success. Don't give up before you have started. Begin with creative writing or the arts and then let nature take its course.

Famous Uranus in Gemini: Bill Clinton, Hillary Clinton, George W. Bush, Harrison Ford, Sylvester Stallone, Michael Douglas, Cher, David Bowie, Freddie Mercury, Prince Charles, Elton John, Diana Ross.

URANUS IN CANCER OR THE 4TH HOUSE

You are eccentric, moody and highly unpredictable. You yearn for the security of home one moment, then itch to run away into the wild open spaces the next. Your childhood may have been disrupted in some way, perhaps via an unusual mother.

If you have a positive Uranus in Cancer or the 4th house

You need a home that is unusual. Your attitude to the family is seen as odd. This is because you want to be free of constraints and ties so you can benefit emotionally. You would like to be a free agent and your family to be friends more than relatives. There are very few tight, strong bonds with your kin who will see you as aloof and probably uncaring.

If you have a negative Uranus in Cancer or the 4th house

Nervous tension can build if you find your home environment suffocating. You cannot bear being held onto or told what to do. The reaction will be screaming tantrums and rebellious, anarchic behaviour. Discipline will break down and you will be seen as dysfunctional. The cause is perhaps due to the loss of someone you really loved at home. You were bereft, and found yourself without security and support, so you took it out on everyone around you.

How to overcome a negative Uranus in Cancer or the 4th house

You must become more self-assured and self-reliant. Look to yourself to find the answers to happiness, and start by ensuring that even if you are in a conventional family set-up you need an unconventional solution. This could mean having a home of your own. Even if it's the garden shed, it will serve its purpose.

Famous Uranus in Cancer: Annie Lennox, Sting, Olivia Newton-John, Bruce Willis, Rowan Atkinson, Oprah Winfrey.

URANUS IN LEO OR THE 5TH HOUSE

You have original and incredible creative potential that puts you ahead of your time. Success may come completely out of the blue. As a child you were very bright and original, and may have been adopted, fostered or had some other unusual upbringing. You can be domineering, stubborn and bossy, and won't tolerate lesser talented people telling you what to do. When it comes to affairs of the heart, you are attracted to those whom others find bizarre or even outrageous.

If you have a positive Uranus in Leo or the 5th house

Variety is the spice of your life and you should start by having a go at everything and anything to test your creative capabilities. Once you discover your forte, it won't be long before you find success. But zip your lip when others help you – that is all they are trying to do. An unconventional relationship with your children or a lover adds to your reputation of being 'different'.

If you have a negative Uranus in Leo or the 5th house

If you are too dishevelled and wayward, you will get nowhere. You have a budding genius within you but power is nothing without control and that's what you must do, control yourself. You have a rampant sexuality but must take care not to involve people who cannot consent for themselves.

How to overcome a negative Uranus in Leo or the 5th house

You are so headstrong, and even violent, that you need to take classes in disciplines such as yoga, meditation or the like. You need to find an inner peace. Solitude is needed for you to concentrate your clever mind. Then, by joining a group that is creative or artistic, you can begin to allow your genius to surface. You will be misunderstood at times but put it down to the fact that you're way ahead of the game.

Famous Uranus in Leo: Princess Diana, Hugh Grant, Madonna, Jim Carrey, Tom Cruise, Prince Andrew, Sharon Stone, Michael Jackson.

URANUS IN VIRGO OR THE 6TH HOUSE

You are inventive, with an eye for detail and a knack for working problems out. You find it difficult to relax and may suffer from tension and stress. You need to be freelance or self-employed, or in any job that allows you to pull the strings, as a nine-to-five routine might drive you crazy. Healthwise, you are given to trying alternative and unorthodox medicines, which for you can be more efficacious than the norm. Working with modern communications, electronics or aviation will give you a thrill.

If you have a positive Uranus in Virgo or the 6th house

Self-made and ready to try anything new, you will be first in the queue when it comes to unusual inventions or devices that can save you time and put you ahead of the rest. You can be a successful practitioner in any business or lifestyle that reveals your skills as a pioneer or initiator. If you're the first to do anything, you'll be happy.

If you have a negative Uranus in Virgo or the 6th house

You may not know what to do in your career and could get trapped in a job that is so safe and reliable you lose your individual flair and know-how. You gradually lose all interest and do something very silly as you react against the imprisonment you find yourself in. It can lead to stress, tension and some kind of breakdown.

How to overcome a negative Uranus in Virgo or the 6th house

A visit to a careers advisor is very important because you must explore all the options. You mustn't plump for an ordinary existence to keep other people happy. You have a natural brilliance that requires careful handing, perhaps via a special school or course that allows your freedom of speech, artistry and creativity to blossom. Only by coaxing forth your talents will you find happiness. You may be toasted as the talk of your particular field or vocation too.

Famous Uranus in Virgo: Teri Hatcher, Keanu Reeves, Johnny Depp, Kylie Minogue, George Michael, Elizabeth Hurley.

URANUS IN LIBRA OR THE 7TH HOUSE

Your desire for harmony can conflict with your need for freedom, so a relationship that is open or platonic is ideal for you. You are an interesting and original person, and a good friend to those to whom you get close. If you get wed or committed too early, you will suffer separation and/or divorce. You are a free spirit and need a spouse or lover who complements that.

If you have a positive Uranus in Libra or the 7th house

You are clever enough to know that if you tie yourself down with an ordinary partner and live an ordinary family existence, it won't be long before you are off. Therefore, you cleverly enjoy the fruits of it all without getting hitched. And because you can go when you want, you probably never will – unless it is for a very, very good reason.

If you have a negative Uranus in Libra or the 7th house

An unconventional 'open' relationship that allows you to be permissive and do what you want, when you want, is fine. So why do you trap yourself in an affair that is the complete opposite? It will end in tears. Don't listen to others any more – what's good for them would never be good for you, and now you are living with the consequences of their advice.

How to overcome a negative Uranus in Libra or the 7th house

If you haven't yet committed to one person through a legal ritual or ceremony then don't before you have gone through precisely what it entails. If you decide to go ahead, then I presume you know what you're doing. But if not, steer clear of making your life and everyone else's a misery by remaining officially single.

Famous Uranus in Libra: Angelina Jolie, Jennifer Lopez, Uma Thurman, Catherine Zeta Jones, Lance Armstrong, Adolf Hitler, Charlie Chaplin.

URANUS IN SCORPIO OR THE 8TH HOUSE

Sex and/or cash is an Achilles heel, due to your irresponsible or obsessive attitude to it. You may gain money through unusual circumstances but will argue with your partners over financial affairs if you do. You have plenty of energy and stamina but are intransigent once you've made your mind up. Sexually, you can have unusual, even perverse, desires. The occult and psychology fascinate you, as does anything that most people find morbid or macabre.

If you have a positive Uranus in Scorpio or the 8th house

You realize that to be dependent on someone is anathema to you, so you have steered clear of such restrictions by keeping your options open sexually and financially. The result is a peculiar but fruitful pact with yourself and others. You will come into money by unusual methods.

If you have a negative Uranus in Scorpio or the 8th house

You are extremely wild and effusive physically, but not quite sure where to direct this energy. It can lead to sexual problems as you find others cannot relate to your idea of passion or desire. This can lead to friction in or out of bed, as you are an enigma with funny little habits that others find odd or unbelievable. You aim to shock sexually and don't care who you hurt or involve.

How to overcome a negative Uranus in Scorpio or the 8th house

The easiest solution is to join a club or group that caters for your kind of sexuality. That way you will meet people of a mutual mind. However, it is very important not to fuel your fetishes with money or allow your fantasies to run riot by involving someone who doesn't feel the same way as you. It isn't easy to have an afflicted Uranus here and it may mean counselling so that you can find it easier to live with yourself and certainly to live with others.

Famous Uranus in Scorpio: Christina Aguilera, Liv Tyler, Orlando Bloom, Jessica Alba, Gisele Bundchen, Beyonce Knowles, Venus Williams, Tiger Woods, Ellen MacArthur.

URANUS IN SAGITTARIUS OR THE 9TH HOUSE

You are original with a flair for entertaining. Your search for constant mental stimulation means you seek out new horizons and exciting experiences. Attracted to foreign places and people, you are an adventurous traveller who relishes surprising experiences and loves to expect the unexpected. Your religious beliefs may be unusual.

If you have a positive Uranus in Sagittarius or the 9th house

Your life is a voyage of discovery and each day can bring a rich, enlightening experience. You have a flair for languages and find joy in any form of travel, culture or international connection. You have the wild rover coursing through your veins, and always want to be where you aren't. You are attracted to magic, New Age activities and any subject matter that isn't mainstream.

If you have a negative Uranus in Sagittarius or the 9th house

You will either be the leader or follower of a cult. Either way, you are misguided and off the planet with your schemes and ideas. You have foresight and vision but don't use it as a force for good. Travel can throw up all kinds of bad vibes and you will miss out on opportunity because you are too extreme or outlandish in your views. Totally bigoted and prejudiced, when you get something into your head it is very hard to shift it. You end up hating people or groups, which is rich coming from someone who has spent their life trying to be 'different'. Is it the case that you despise what you are most like? Think about it.

How to overcome a negative Uranus in Sagittarius or the 9th house

It's not a matter of being normal but rather just using your judgement and common sense more. You are highly intellectual and by putting your brilliant brain to good use, not only will you see the light but also you will raise the consciousness of yourself and others to good effect. One reason you behave unusually or are attracted to harebrained ideas is because you hate the thought of conforming. Well, you will never do that but at least your ideas and vision can be acceptable and perhaps make the planet a better place.

Famous Uranus in Sagittarius: Cary Grant, Britney Spears, Fred Astaire, Scarlett Johansson, Walt Disney, Keira Knightley, Salvador Dali, William Shakespeare.

URANUS IN CAPRICORN OR THE 10TH HOUSE

You are torn between the need to be unconventional and to conform. You are an inspiring leader but resent authority in others. You will therefore tend to have an unpredictable career that reflects your need for independence and autonomy. You are blessed with plenty of initiative. You are cool but prone to emotional outbursts.

If you have a positive Uranus in Capricorn or the 10th house

You are a stickler for taking the best of the old and transforming it to something that is more modern. This brilliant regime means coming at life from a different angle, but never chucking the baby out with the bathwater – it will win you prizes and plaudits galore. People will see that although you are radical, you are sensible with it and know how far you can go.

If you have a negative Uranus in Capricorn or the 10th house

You want a place at life's top table and yet you do nothing to make yourself more acceptable to others. Whether it's your behaviour, appearance or ideas that don't go down well, you cannot find anyone to vouch for you. There is no doubt you are clever but you are wilful and perverse too. Although your approach is a novelty to begin with, pretty soon people tire of your boorish, even loutish and vulgar, ways and drop you.

How to overcome a negative Uranus in Capricorn or the 10th house

There are times in life when you have to play the game of etiquette. If you are going to rise to the top, and you can do it in sparkling style, you have to put people at their ease first. If you are going to win supporters, and we all need them if we are to succeed, you will need to pay lip service and cross your fingers when you say certain things. Then when you have achieved your ambition, you can do what the hell you like.

Famous Uranus in Capricorn: Errol Flynn, Lucille Ball, Bette Davis, Katharine Hepburn, Howard Hughes, Mother Teresa.

URANUS IN AQUARIUS OR THE 11TH HOUSE

You are popular but will always maintain a distance that allows you to remain an individual. This will mean you are a member of a wide social circle, but are never fully integrated. Inventive and original, you have an interest in astrology or New Age subjects. You are a faithful friend who believes in fidelity in all things (although you do tend to bob around seeing only the people who suit your particular mood that day). As for subject matter, you are fascinated by anything that can become a *cause célèbre* or lost cause – you'll soon breathe life into it. Long-term planning is fun but things never turn out as you predicted.

If you have a positive Uranus in Aquarius or the 11th house

You are a leader rather than a follower; if you can start your own crusade, group or organization, then you will. From it will come all kinds of opportunities you'd never have imagined. Your future destiny takes twists and turns that are totally unpredictable. By keeping fluid and flexible you will aspire to the kind of great things that were once just a dream in the back of your mind.

If you have a negative Uranus in Aquarius or the 11th house

You isolate yourself from the social circuit, losing out on the interaction you would actually enjoy. Your future has become out of your control, as you don't know what you want and where you want to go. Because you have no real friends and can't take advice, you end up as a disparate traveller on the road to nowhere.

How to overcome a negative Uranus in Aquarius or the 11th house

You believe that you are an individual first and foremost and don't want to be tainted by conformists or traditionalists. But to other people like you, you are normal. Instead of trying too hard to be different, concentrate on aspiring to do your bit to change the world through humanitarian actions or getting involved in campaigns against monopolies or globalization. Before you know it, a collective cause with people who have the same ecological conscience will have made a difference.

Famous Uranus in Aquarius: Alec Guinness, John F. Kennedy, Nelson Mandela, Indira Gandhi, Spike Milligan, Frank Sinatra, Vivien Leigh, Richard Nixon.

URANUS IN PISCES OR THE 12TH HOUSE

You are fascinated by the occult and the supernatural and have an intuition that flashes into operation readily. You can see pictures, hear voices and have all kinds of other psychic experiences that can help you understand everything from your reason for being here to life after death. Unusual events may leave you in seclusion or living a secret existence. You will find romance with someone who has to remain clandestine because it would raise too many eyebrows and demand far too many explanations.

If you have a positive Uranus in Pisces or the 12th house

You find that by joining a spiritual or astrological club or society you hold the key to a deeper meaning of life. You are quite sure that by delving into the arcane and unknown in a measured and inquisitive way, you can find the secret to so many elixirs of life. Curiosity as well as necessity is the mother of invention and you are its child.

If you have a negative Uranus in Pisces or the 12th house

You can come up with so many crackpot ideas and belief forms that people find you hard to believe or, worse still, think you're crazy. You will go out to shock others with your romantic or emotional involvements, and you may find yourself involved with scandal or outrage. But none of it really bothers you until one day it gets you into such deep water that you realize that you've done nothing memorable in your sad life at all.

How to overcome a negative Uranus in Pisces or the 12th house

Before you can reach the point of making amends, realize here and now that not everyone is going to understand or commend you. You are a child of the future. Sometimes your extreme views and actions won't win an argument and merely turn people more against you. So if you want to win approval and allies you need to do so in a way that doesn't scare people or make them afraid. If you can come up with a formula for putting people at their ease then everybody, including you, will be happy, and you will achieve your goal.

Famous Uranus in Pisces: Marilyn Monroe, Queen Elizabeth II, Marlon Brando, Margaret Thatcher, Paul Newman, Judy Garland, Liberace, Lauren Bacall, Peter Sellers, Maria Callas.

Neptune

Neptune, as we have seen, is the part of Planet You most associated with the spiritual and the psychic. He is also closely linked with the refined aspects of your personality, the artistic and aesthetic, and the glamour too. He also reflects the areas in which you make sacrifices.

Because of his great distance from the Sun, Neptune's journey through the zodiac takes 168 years, remaining in each sign for 14 years. Neptune moved from Capricorn into Aquarius in 1998, and will remain there until the year 2012. This means there is no-one alive with Neptune in Aries, Taurus or Pisces, so I have not analyzed these planetary positions.

Neptune is co-ruler of Pisces so his influence is strongest if you have a strong placing – Ascendant, Sun, Moon or Midheaven in Pisces or the 1st house. Otherwise the house position is more significant than the sign one.

NEPTUNE IN THE 1ST HOUSE

A highly sensitive placement indicating a talent for the arts, music, dance and drama. You have a love of beautiful things, and enjoy peace and tranquility. You are, however, prone to self-deception and walk around with your head in the clouds. This can make you confused and unable to see your way ahead. You are genteel and hate anyone who is vulgar or uncouth. Image is important to you in yourself and others; if you can mask anything you don't like about yourself you will do so. You hate confrontation of any kind and will wriggle out of anything distasteful.

If you have a positive Neptune in the 1st house

You have great integrity and you work on the highest spiritual vibration. You are born with such a sensitive nature you can detect an atmosphere for good or bad. You despise people who are ugly in looks or behaviour and find it hard to accept or deal with the grotesque in the world, preferring to look away. But you are compassionate, charitable and long to do what you can to ease the suffering of others. You have a mesmerizing mystique and look at life with a romantic gloss.

If you have a negative Neptune in the 1st house

Your nefarious activities undermine all that is good. You are in total denial about yourself and life in general. You aren't averse to getting involved with people who are bad for you; in fact, you may be drawn to the criminal element, seeing it as just play-acting, like in the movies. You hide away from stark reality and prefer to take to intoxicants or opiates rather than admit what is wrong. Self-deception is rife.

How to overcome a negative Neptune in the 1st house

It's time to wake up and smell the roses. Really, if you carry on as you are, you will waste your life and your many wonderful, glorious talents. You can just as easily escape into a world of creativity and then at least you will have something to show for your dreams and fantasies. Go on, get involved with colour, fashion, photography or whatever turns you on. Find your niche and never look back.

NEPTUNE IN THE 2ND HOUSE

You are generous to a fault, sometimes giving away more than you can afford. Your dreamy nature may also make you ideal material for con artists. Avoid get-rich-quick salesmen. However, you have an innate understanding of beautiful things and should become an expert in anything from antiques to products specifically for women, glamour or image. You aren't a material being so need to take care you don't lose track of your finances as a result.

If you have a positive Neptune in the 2nd house

You are consistently at the centre of all things bright and beautiful. You reveal your social skills by making everyone welcome and have an almost telepathic sense for being able to make folks feel comfortable and at ease. By using this in business or financial matters, you will never go hungry. Turn your own hand, head and heart to products or merchandise that fuel people's fantasies or sexual needs and you could really live it up financially.

If you have a negative Neptune in the 2nd house

Your finances ebb and flow like the tides, but there is more ebb than flow. You must learn not only the value of money but also your own self-worth. Undermining your talents and becoming disillusioned with the secular is no reason to secrete yourself away from the madding crowd. Like it or not, you need cash to eat, to live and to survive, so don't deny yourself what you need due to paranoid or compulsive behaviour.

How to overcome a negative Neptune in the 2nd house

Even if you have to go to an accountant, money manager or just a sensible friend, you must learn about the true meaning of money. It's not bad or evil if you earn enough to do what you want. You also need to get to the root of your low self-esteem – you do not value yourself anywhere as much as you should. Don't you understand that by realizing and releasing your formidable talents and abilities, you can earn enough for yourself. And if you still hate filthy lucre, be philanthropic and give it away to the most deserving cause. For now, though, invest in yourself by developing your gifts for beauty and fine things.

NEPTUNE IN GEMINI OR THE 3RD HOUSE

You are imaginative if lacking in focus sometimes. You may have suffered with dyslexia or some other problem with reading or writing, but have learned to use it to your advantage. You have a talent to amuse and to hypnotize people with your stories and ideas. You would be successful in the movie industry, coming up with arty ideas for glamour, fashion or anything connected with communications. However, be warned of scandals or indiscretions. Don't join in the throng but speak as you find.

If you have a positive Neptune in Gemini or the 3rd house

Your mental capacity is like a walking fairy tale and yes, it does have a happy ending. But you must channel your technicolour mind into areas where you are best suited, where a vivid imagination is required. You are at your most caring and sensitive in your local community and have a spiritual connection with a friend or family member that will stay with you all your life. A romance will blossom with the boy or girl next door, so to speak.

If you have a negative Neptune in Gemini or the 3rd house

You dwell on far too much, putting two and two together and coming up with five. You distort the facts and live too much on fiction. What's worse, to get yourself out of a hole you lie and deceive and soon start believing what is baseless tripe. You need a good dose of reality.

How to overcome a negative Neptune in Gemini or the 3rd house

You are gullible and impressionable where others are concerned. Even if you're as good as gold, you are attracted to folks who aren't. If you're not careful, you could end up their fall guy or girl. One way to deal with this is not to get involved with anything or anyone until you have run it past a lawyer, honest friend or loved one. You are too nice and need trustworthy advisors at every stage of your life. There's one born every minute, but don't let it be you.

NEPTUNE IN CANCER OR THE 4TH HOUSE

Your imagination can run away with you, such is your need to escape from the realities of life. Your childhood may have been special, and your family affairs could have been mysterious or confused. This may have moulded you into someone with little organization in your life. There's a skeleton in your cupboard that you may not know about – or maybe you do. This aspect can often mean leading a double life: one public, one secret. You are filled with a longing for a bygone age, full of sloppy sentimentality and nostalgia.

If you have a positive Neptune in Cancer or the 4th house

You are caring, kind and totally devoted in an almost sacrificial way to your kith and kin. Those you love are more important to you than anything. You need a place that is comfortable, serene and romantic – anyone or anything that ruffles your sensitive feathers has to go. Living near water would be good for you – if this isn't possible, there's always a goldfish bowl. You need to establish a tranquil haven that's good to come home to.

If you have a negative Neptune in Cancer or the 4th house

How you wish you could have an ordinary family or domestic existence, and yet it seems to slip through your fingers, either because you never knew many of your relatives, or where you lived was a figment of your imagination. Very often everything seems fine but as life goes on you begin to realize that perhaps your parents or even you were living a lie. It's hard to take and can make you feel very insecure and you are left worried, anxious and always searching for solid roots.

How to overcome a negative Neptune in Cancer or the 4th house

You need substance to your life and there's absolutely no reason why you shouldn't have it. Somewhere along the line you will be able to work for a home of your own, no matter how bijou (in fact, the more bijou the better). You will also be able to meet someone who cares for you. You cannot feel guilty about your parents or other familial mistakes. You just happened to be around at the time. Divorce yourself from the domestic negatives of the past and stand on your own two feet with a clean slate. You'll soon find yourself a refuge, a home that is built on solid ground.

NEPTUNE IN LEO OR THE 5TH HOUSE

The artistic side of your personality rules the more practical side, leaving you prone to being overly idealistic and gullible. You may also be weak when it comes to addictions like gambling and general decadence. You are easily flattered as your ego is so fragile and flaky. This may cause you much pain in the romantic area of your life, where you suffer from never knowing if someone loves you for who you are. But it may also lead you to a life in the creative public arena where you exude oodles of star quality. To me, Neptune in Leo is the Hollywood position.

If you have a positive Neptune in Leo or the 5th house

You have an inborn gift to please and delight people. It is something so natural to you that you've only got to open the refrigerator door to go into a huge routine when the light flickers on. You love the glories of the past and have a nostalgic view of romance and love. You and your partner idealize each other. You may receive the odd knock en route but the path of true love never ran smooth.

Remember, gather ye rosebuds while you may. Your offspring are very arty and sensitive, and should be encouraged to bring out their talent, whatever it maybe.

If you have a negative Neptune in Leo or the 5th house

You are prone to envy. If anyone gets what you wanted or were hankering after, you won't be happy. You will resort to underhand methods to undermine their relationship, life and anything else rather than allow them to get away with happiness. It's time you woke up to reality and saw someone as they really are and not as you would like them to be. Children or a pet are a source of great joy to you but don't live your life through them.

How to overcome a negative Neptune in Leo or the 5th house

Instead of living on past glories and achievements, realize that you still have the gifts and talents that you once had. Perhaps now is the time to use to them to teach, help or support others. Or if you've never known 'stardom', what's to stop you finding it now? It's never too late and so long as you don't live in a perpetual La-La Land, with drive, ambition and application (look for where Mars and Saturn are in your chart), you could be hailed as one of the best in your field. You can dream like the best of 'em but play to your strengths, be pragmatic, know what you can do well and go for it.

NEPTUNE IN VIRGO OR THE 6TH HOUSE

Non-conformist and questioning, you don't take easily to conventional ideas. This may mean discipline at work is hard to achieve and you may be frustrated by routine in general. You fixate on imagined problems, losing all sense of proportion in the process. Hypochondria or psychosomatic ailments are one example of this. Drugs and alcohol should be approached with care.

If you have a positive Neptune in Virgo or the 6th house

You are the archetypal charity or social worker. Whether you do it professionally or it's just your natural bent, you put people at their ease and give them hope. Scrupulously moral and ethical, you fight corruption and dishonesty with a crusader-like zeal. You prefer a working or business environment with beautiful surroundings, where there is a spirit of harmony between colleagues.

If you have a negative Neptune in Virgo or the 6th house

You don't give yourself enough credit. You always believe you can do better. Your search for perfection is never complete, as you look to become a paragon at whatever you do. This can lead to a fractured emotional life as you can carp and criticize the smallest fault in others. Your health issues are based on psychosomatic problems that stem from neuroses and paranoia.

How to overcome a negative Neptune in Virgo or the 6th house

You have to learn that you can only ever do your best – nothing more, nothing less. And if you are absolutely sure that you are giving your all, then who's complaining? Only you, and that's the point. Everyone else is satisfied, so why aren't you? Come on, stop being so fussy or you'll make yourself ill. Even your worst is as good as others' best. You would benefit from spiritual or faith healing.

NEPTUNE IN LIBRA OR THE 7TH HOUSE

Neptune was in Libra during the era of late 1960s' 'flower power' and this is reflected in your personality. You are drawn to the aesthetic and the artistic, and in love will look for a person who is highly romantic. Emotional commitment is rarely handled at the right speed, however, with you either jumping in too soon or waiting too long.

If you have a positive Neptune in Libra or the 7th house

You spread a lot of happiness. In relationships you give of yourself completely, in fact you devote or even sacrifice your own time and needs to make someone happy. You are romantic, seductive and loving. Who could ask for anything more? Nothing is too much trouble when you find the person of your dreams, but don't put them on too high a pedestal as we all have feet of clay.

If you have a negative Neptune in Libra or the 7th house

A relationship or partnership will be at the heart of any distress. At some stage you will feel betrayed, let down or stabbed in the back by someone you cared for and trusted – or vice versa. The problem is rooted in an affair not having enough practical management or down-to-earth appeal. You both evade the truth for fear of upsetting one another and the result is lies, fabrications and denial.

How to overcome a negative Neptune in Libra or the 7th house

No-one is perfect – not you, your other half, your business partner, no-one. The sooner you get that into your head, the better. It's good to have a challenge or two in any relationship – it helps it grow and evolve – but if you act like a doormat, you'll be treated like one and that's where you've gone wrong. You must retain your individuality and take someone as you find them, for real. What you see is what you get, and if you don't like what you see, then don't go there in the first place.

NEPTUNE IN SCORPIO OR THE 8TH HOUSE

Your intuition and imagination are drawn to mysterious subjects. You need a tangible set of goals on which to focus your energies. You have a desire to act out sexual fantasies. Your sex life can be linked to money too. Infatuations fill your thoughts for if you like someone you see, you immediately think of ways to seduce them, whoever they are. You are fascinated by life after death beliefs and are into anything from psychotherapy to hypnotism.

If you have a positive Neptune in Scorpio or the 8th house

You are so sexually sophisticated that you can massage and tinker with parts of the body other heavenly bodies cannot reach. You can fulfil fantasies of a romantic or intimate nature and are a dab hand at manipulating people. You have an irresistible charm and are seductive to the nth degree. Money matters can be a source of pain or agony, but only if you are dependent on others or they on you. Then emotional blackmail can enter into any negotiations or transactions.

If you have a negative Neptune in Scorpio or the 8th house

This placement is linked with deep psychological problems, and demands growth in all areas if you are to raise yourself above your deep-seated fears and hang-ups that come with this afflicted aspect. You are a victim of your own obsessions and paranoia, based on groundless worries that more negative folks have sown in your mind. Your imagination has been allowed to run riot – now you must rein it in.

How to overcome a negative Neptune in Scorpio or the 8th house

First of all, you need to reason with yourself. Question your anxieties and if you can't get to the root cause then you should visit your GP or a counsellor, who can set you on the road to a healthy mind. It's not easy, but every so often we all need to regenerate and even transform our lives. Your problem is a psychological blockage that needs to be shifted so you can move on. It can be done, but the first step is wanting to do it. The second step is seeking advice or support from strangers who are bona fide in their area of expertise. Soon you will be reborn.

NEPTUNE IN SAGITTARIUS OR THE 9TH HOUSE

You have a sage-like wisdom and may be interested in mystical and spiritual subjects. You also have strong ideals and a great interest in global affairs. This may draw you to campaigns or movements aimed at ecology or protecting the environment. You trust people or situations without question, buy you must keep your feet on terra firma and be realistic about your goals and opinions. A faith or belief in a higher being is crucial to your psychological welfare. You are a visionary.

If you have a positive Neptune in Sagittarius or the 9th house

You are philosophical to the point of seeing only good in everyone. You must therefore guard against cheapskates or shysters who take advantage of your good nature. You inspire people with your thoughts and ideas, and are in a class of your own in areas of culture, the arts and subjects that demand a high level of sensitivity to understand them fully. You take on intellectual challenges to raise your consciousness and you are totally fascinated by and nostalgic for people or places that hold sentimental memories.

If you have a negative Neptune in Sagittarius or the 9th house

Take great care about false prophets and religious sects that are so wacky they represent complete madness. You can fall victim to shallow and dishonest types as you trust everyone you meet, especially if they are simpatico with you – or so you think. They have probably used sharp practice and Machiavellian tactics to find out all they can to entrap you. It's not that you're stupid, just far too good for this world. Be warned if you aren't the one being caught, you could easily be the catcher…

How to overcome a negative Neptune in Sagittarius or the 9th house

You need to be more questioning and suspicious of people who are too good to be true – because this is precisely what they are. You can't put everything down to coincidence or some kind of spiritual reasoning or happening; it doesn't work like that. To avoid the charlatans and quacks, get yourself a second opinion from someone who has no axe to grind or vested interest and the fakes will run a mile.

NEPTUNE IN CAPRICORN OR THE 10TH HOUSE

You possess drive and determination aplenty, but can be conservative and overly careful about using it. You tend to want an ideal job and may end up wandering aimlessly through a succession of careers in pursuit of it. Blending business and pleasure, perhaps in an artistic or glamorous vocation, may provide the answer. Your vivid imagination can run riot. A vocation or calling of a spiritual type, to do with water – from naval to aquatic sports or oil – suits you.

If you have a positive Neptune in Capricorn or the 10th house

You realize that your image plays an important part in getting you where you want. There is no point in turning up scruffy or looking like a round peg in a square hole because you will be judged by the first impression you give. By fitting the role from head to toe, being perceived as smart, chic and elegant, you will rise to the top of your profession. You will receive a bonus or help from someone in power because you are so likeable and are a Good Samaritan.

If you have a negative Neptune in Capricorn or the 10th house

You are fooled into thinking that you can get something for nothing. Then when you realize that a person's motives are entirely dishonourable, it's too late. Hopping onto the casting couch or doing immoral favours might get you a moment's recognition but not perhaps in the way you want. You are very ambitious but your destiny should be reached with dignity. You should not do anything you would ever be ashamed of or it could be used against you later.

How to overcome a negative Neptune in Capricorn or the 10th house

Because this afflicted placement can lead to scandals or notoriety, you must keep your nose clean at all times. No matter how much you try to keep things hidden, they have a habit of popping out when you least expect it. So from the word go, don't do anything you or your parents would be ashamed of later on. By using that rule as your yardstick you will be fine. You are a very talented person in fields relating to beauty, glamour and where image matters. You can get where you want on your own merits so you certainly don't need anyone giving you a leg-up. Do I mean that in the literal sense? Well, that's another matter, as long as it's done in the best possible taste!

NEPTUNE IN AQUARIUS OR THE 11TH HOUSE

You possess a strong humanitarian streak. You want to help others and have a desire to 'save the world', but only according to your gospel. This need to care may clash with your desire for emotional freedom. You may choose friends based on a false premise or idealize them, ending up in the wrong company in the process. You have a powerful vision and only want to do things for the greater good of everyone. You will achieve your life's hopes and wishes via a collective.

If you have a positive Neptune in Aquarius or the 11th house

Being a member or leader of a group or organization with a social or global conscience is good for you and your soul. You cannot bear to be with people who are shallow, hypocritical, glib or trite. Everything you do has to be for the right reasons and the thought of allowing ugliness or untruths to litter the world when you can do something about it fills you with dread. You aspire to altruism – with you it comes from the heart.

If you have a negative Neptune in Aquarius or the 11th house

You are apt to follow a hope or wish, but solely for selfish reasons. You do nothing unless there's something in it for you and if that means using downtrodden people, you have no worries about taking advantage of them. You feign selflessness when actually you are a double-crossing double dealer who is disingenuous to a degree. If that's not you, then be warned of someone who it is.

How to overcome a negative Neptune in Aquarius or the 11th house

As the universe looks after its own, then everything you say or do that is negative, bad or plain unjustifiable will be clocked up and come back to haunt you sometime in the future. You won't get away with it. You might play the atheist or agnostic and say you don't believe in such rubbish, in which case carry on as you are. But is it worth taking the chance when, with just a little bit of kindness, you can book your place in heaven? And that especially means the one here on Earth.

NEPTUNE IN THE 12TH HOUSE

You have a vivid imagination that makes you highly impressionable and susceptible to delusions. You indulge in self-deception and have a need to escape from reality and society, withdrawing from people and preferring to be on your own. You are caring and have a richly evolved psychic ability. You are a born romantic and adore anyone or anything that adheres to your fantasy of perfection. Your dreams are a source of creative inspiration and your altruism towards those who are suffering knows no bounds. You are, however, a mystery to all you meet, always giving the impression you are keeping something back – and you probably are.

If you have a positive Neptune in the 12th house

If you devote your life towards helping others then you will derive happiness and satisfaction. However, you are human and although you do things unconditionally, you must take more care of your own health. You should take time out by going on retreats or into seclusion in beautiful places where you can find a sacred space to sort out your own mind. You are highly artistic and will channel your mystical and unworldly brilliance into crafts or dreams that give real meaning to your life and help others too.

If you have a negative Neptune in the 12th house

You are totally misunderstood – or so you say. The trouble is you do little to warrant support or assistance from others, as you don't do enough to help yourself. If you have gone through bad times and are racked with guilt or anxieties, then do something practical about it. By wallowing in self-pity you will only make matters worse. You fantasize too much, resorting to escapism and finding refuge in drink or drugs.

How to overcome a negative Neptune in the 12th house

Join a movement for dance, music, drama, spiritualist pursuits – anything that will give voice to the Neptune that has been distracted and disparaged by past unhappiness. By masking your despair, by doing things that bring you joy and happiness, you will soon transcend your earthly woes and tears. Hope is all you need, plus the belief that by starting a new cycle built on real creativity you can unlock the door to the future and throw away the key to your miserable past.

Pluto

Pluto, as we have seen, is the planet most associated with elimination and transformation, particularly death, destruction, regeneration and rebirth. He is also the planet of that which can't be seen. So within Planet You, he is the secret part of you, the facets of your personality that are hidden from the rest of the world.

As the co-ruler of Scorpio, traditionally ruled by Mars, Pluto is especially strong in people who have their Sun or Ascendant in Scorpio. He is also strong in the 8th house.

As the most remote planet in the solar system, Pluto's orbit of the Sun takes longer than any other – 248 years. He moved into Sagittarius in 1995 and will remain there until late 2008. Given this, and the rate he passes through the signs, the sign position affects whole generations of people. He is, however, a subtle force, working in the background, unless your Ascendant, Sun, Moon, or Midheaven is in Scorpio, or Pluto is in the 1st House. Because there is no-one alive with Pluto in Aries, Taurus, Capricorn, Aquarius or Pisces, I have only listed Pluto's position in seven of the signs.

PLUTO IN THE 1ST HOUSE

Pluto's influence is strong here and you are an enigmatic personality as a result. You have a great deal of potential, but may struggle to bring it out because of psychological difficulties. You are also someone who likes to dig deep so as to get under the skin of subjects.

If you have a positive Pluto in the 1st house

You enjoy the trappings of power and like to control every situation you find yourself in. Your life is governed by fate, destiny, kismet or whatever you want to call it, and you should listen when it calls. You are very secretive and often have a hidden agenda, but usually for the good. Healthwise, you suffer from illnesses that are shrouded in mysterious symptoms. But you have the ability to regenerate yourself with amazing powers of recovery.

If you have a negative Pluto in the 1st house

You try to fight the inevitable and, as a result, find yourself at the bottom of the pile just when you'd dragged yourself up by your stocking tops. You mix with the wrong types and try underhand tactics to get your way. Remember this: power corrupts and absolute power corrupts absolutely.

How to overcome a negative Pluto in the 1st house

Que sera sera. What will be, will be. Make that your motto and you will be fine. Know your strengths and don't take on anyone or anything more powerful than you. If you do, you will be the loser, but by following fate you will be the ultimate winner.

PLUTO IN THE 2ND HOUSE

You are emotional and passionate but are jealous and possessive with it. You can gain great power in business where your need for material success is satisfied. You have to tread carefully, however, as you find money a means of control and are just as likely to make big losses as you are to make big gains. You have the potential to be a plutocrat.

If you have a positive Pluto in the 2nd house

You are an inspiration to us all. You can take the tiniest acorn and from it create an oak of success and gain. You are very aware of your strengths and have the psychological ability to reshape your life to cope with the changes in your business world. You are never down for long. You are soon up and at 'em again. You are very empowering.

If you have a negative Pluto in the 2nd house

Money is at the root of your troubles. It presents psychological barriers that aren't easily overcome. You can be obsessed with material gain and are envious and covetous of those who have what you think should be yours by some kind of divine right. You will stoop to anything to get what you want and aren't averse to dealing with undesirable types.

How to overcome a negative Pluto in the 2nd house

By converting your negative energy into a more positive flow, you can find success and wealth in many varied ways. Of course, it may be that it is your karma to go through loss and disappointment first, and nothing will prevent that from happening. However, by adopting a positive attitude, you should see this as your lowest moment, as something that is happening for a reason. If you take the easy way out, you will never rise to great affluent heights. But if you are empowered by the experience, you will find yourself gaining control, power and wealth because fate decreed you deserve it.

PLUTO IN GEMINI OR THE 3RD HOUSE

You are torn over whether to follow your baser instincts to communicate, or satisfy your need to keep your deeper thoughts to yourself. You hate small talk, and demand depth and intensity. You can use this skill to be a researcher or a detective. You may be unsure of yourself sexually as you know you need a partner who will be intimate with you intellectually, sharing your innermost feelings. There is sibling rivalry where you either love or loathe your brother or sister, with no in-between.

If you have a positive Pluto in Gemini or the 3rd house

A psychological reason for every deed, action or word underpins your everyday life. You look for a deeper meaning to even the most normal occurrences. Nothing escapes your eagle eye, and if anyone lies to you or takes you for a fool you can see right through them. You can transform your community by getting involved with its running or activities, with the result that you are seen as a controlling and empowering force. People come to you when they are in trouble as you are able to see a solution and resolve any struggles that may manifest themselves.

If you have a negative Pluto in Gemini or the 3rd house

Someone close to home will be jealous or envious of you to such a degree that they may play dark tricks or indulge in mischievous deeds, making you feel intimidated or threatened. Take care of vendettas or feuds that get out of hand. The least said, soonest mended. Be warned of people who hit below the belt by spreading lies or attempting a character assassination.

How to overcome a negative Pluto in Gemini or the 3rd house

Know who your friends are and always be aware that things can change abruptly. Someone you trust and believe in one minute could suddenly turn and become sinister and evil towards you the next. With that in mind, always keep something in reserve and keep those very important and sensitive matters locked away. Be secretive, keep your own counsel and don't get involved in slanging matches. Just one word out of place could result in libel or slander.

PLUTO IN CANCER OR THE 4TH HOUSE

You face a struggle to come to terms with issues from your childhood. You have highly charged feelings and worry to an almost psychotic degree. Sexually, you are repressed by aspects of your parents' experience or early family life. You are a determined, gritty fighter but can cling to those you are involved with emotionally much too tightly. You must choose where you live carefully, as your surroundings colour you psychologically. You constantly have to challenge feelings of insecurity.

If you have a positive Pluto in Cancer or the 4th house

Nothing you feel or sense should be taken lightly. You have instincts and habits that are born from a deep, psychic source. You pick up vibrations that should be heeded, as they will be the difference between sadness and happiness. Your home is a profound part of your being – you must have a base where you can feel secure and unthreatened. You will rise from the ashes of despair the minute you find the courage to break free of any guilt, grief or emotional ties from the past.

If you have a negative Pluto in Cancer or the 4th house

You are seen as a bag of nerves but you're not really. It's just that you're so highly sensitive that you come across as jittery and full of neuroses. You need to find a home away from it all where you can be yourself and live incognito without being judged or held responsible for your family's misdemeanours. You want to be invisible and let the world pass you by. However, you always create a psychological obstacle to prevent you from being inwardly content and secure.

How to overcome a negative Pluto in Cancer or the 4th house

You cannot be held answerable for your family's wrongs – you are not your mother, father or anyone's keeper. What happened to them has nothing to do with you. Don't let your past, or relations with your parents, disempower you or make you feel helpless. Stand on your own two feet and seek the help of people who can make you realize that you *are* in control of your feelings and emotions and do not have to reap the whirlwind of those who have gone before you.

PLUTO IN LEO OR THE 5TH HOUSE

Sex and the need to procreate are powerful factors in your life. This is especially the case if your Sun, Moon or Ascendant is in Leo. Sex can also be a way of providing you with the control you crave. You are potentially a great leader with excellent organizational skills. If Pluto is positively disposed, it means that you can work for the good of others as well as yourself. If it is negative, it means you are obsessed with power. A fatal attraction will play a prominent part in your love life.

If you have a positive Pluto in Leo or the 5th house

You have creative gifts that can bring fame and fortune. You are in the hands of fate – when it comes to the time and place it will happen, but if you prepare for the big day, whenever it arrives, you will take the world by storm. You are like a Hollywood film mogul in that what you say goes and no-one will argue with it. A child or pet will become an intense part of your life. If anyone hurts them, you will seek revenge. Your affairs of the heart are passionate but can end as quickly as they began, as they become too hot to survive. You are a powerhouse and a real force to be reckoned with.

If you have a negative Pluto in Leo or the 5th house

You want to control everything and everyone around you. You take it personally if someone turns down your work or ideas – you will hate them forever more. You have an almost pathological dislike of people who use or abuse you, and you will get even. You have a torrid relationship with children or loved ones, and a breakdown usually occurs because you are an irresistible force meeting an immovable object.

How to overcome a negative Pluto in Leo or the 5th house

The reason why you don't get anywhere in love, sex or business is because people see your dark side. You must lighten up, chill out and not be so intense. Yes, your ideas are good but are they better than anyone else's? Don't take slights so seriously that you become fixated, obsessed even. You must learn to move on, as for every enemy you make, there are two powerful friends or allies to be made. Get things into proportion or one day you will blow a gasket and self-destruct.

PLUTO IN VIRGO OR THE 6TH HOUSE

Serious and intense, you have enviable powers of concentration and discipline, but you are also a born worrier and may fret about small things over which you have no control. You can be critical of others, too, and have a tendency to undermine others in order to achieve power. You can become obsessed with health, work or hygiene to the point of despair.

If you have a positive Pluto in Virgo or the 6th house

You are a wonderful transformer and can take anything that is out of date or broken and regenerate it. The same can be said for your own physical well-being, where your powers of recovery enable you to quickly come back fighting. Sexually you are inhibited, but all it takes is a meeting with the right person and you will blossom like a lotus.

If you have a negative Pluto in Virgo or the 6th house

You can suffer all kinds of physical and psychological illnesses but they remain undiagnosed as there appears to be no reason for them. They are probably a symptom of a fundamental unhappiness in your working or business life. You have a feeling of inadequacy or worthlessness.

How to overcome a negative Pluto in Virgo or the 6th house

Ultimately you must realize that we all have a part to play in life and you are no different. It's a matter of finding the right job or business role for you. It doesn't matter if you have to trawl here, there and everywhere, or whether you have to undergo retraining to learn a new skill, the important thing is that you find something you enjoy. You put every fibre of your being into what you do and if it's not appreciated, your happiness suffers. Being useful to someone will be good for you but not half as good as finding employment that you can put your heart and soul into and make your own.

PLUTO IN LIBRA OR THE 7TH HOUSE

Your need to dominate in relationships can lead to break-ups because of the psychological battles in which control or sex is at the heart of the conflict. You may have secret enemies who hide their true motives and work against you. You pick arguments with those close to you to test their loyalties. Achieving fairness is important to you but you can become insanely jealous if a loved one does you wrong.

If you have a positive Pluto in Libra or the 7th house

You are controlling, but do it in the nicest possible way. You are naughty but ever so nice about how you do things. You make your point, and like all those with Pluto aspects, lay it on thick with a trowel. You have ample sex appeal and with your deep, dark, brooding personality you attract lovers to you like moths to a flame. When you fall in love, it is forever and completely. If you do separate or divorce, it is hard for you to let go.

If you have a negative Pluto in Libra or the 7th house

Like Svengali, you have an invisible power that completely takes over someone's life in a most unhealthy way. You play psychological games with your partner, threatening or cajoling them if they try to get away or react against you. You can be cruel and vindictive, and yet your persona is so laid-back or softly spoken no-one would believe you could hurt a fly. Sexually you have hang-ups that need sorting out before they ruin a relationship.

How to overcome a negative Pluto in Libra or the 7th house

If you try to take over someone's life, then where love once roosted hate will begin to take over. Once this occurs you will never win back the trust and respect you once had. A leopard cannot change its spots but if you are going to have a wonderful partnership or marriage, you must deal with your inner problems, which probably narrow down to control and sex. If you need to seek help then do so; it is better to deal with what is wrong at source than let it destroy the good thing that you have.

PLUTO IN SCORPIO OR THE 8TH HOUSE

This is the most prominent placement for Pluto. Having Pluto here makes you very intense and determined, with an obsessive need to hold power. You have a lot to handle with this aspect. It may make you extremely driven to achieve your goals and a shrewd businessperson. This drive can be at the centre of psychological or sexual hang-ups. You are also attracted to situations or environments that most people would find alarming, to say the least. You are extremely inquisitive and leave no stone unturned in your search for what you set out to learn.

If you have a positive Pluto in Scorpio or the 8th house

It is second nature for you not to trust a soul, but once you do give your trust and loyalty then you would die for those whom you love. You are not content with first answers and so will trace something from its root to the top and back down again. You are a deeply reserved, secretive and sexual animal. You are adroit at psychology and use it to gain control or power. You use your gifts to incite truth and do your best to transform bad to good. You have the will to take on corporations and institutions and win. You believe in the maxim, 'Don't get mad, get even.' Yes, this is positive Pluto!

If you have a negative Pluto in Scorpio or the 8th house

You can fool some of the people some of the time, but never all of the people all of the time. If you resort to megalomanic behaviour or terrorize people, one day you will get your comeuppance. What comes around goes around and the sooner you learn this, the better. To continue on a tyrannical rampage to get your own way is control freakery gone mad. No matter how you use your power, whether it is through sex, money or threats, in the end you will press the self-destruct button and lose all you have gained.

How to overcome a negative Pluto in Scorpio or the 8th house

It's a simple message: whatever you do, follow the fickle finger of fate and let it lead you past temptation. Let the negative in you die so you can be 'reborn' again, having learned your lessons. It is better to abide by the laws of karma whilst you can. This means using your concentrated power and energy to reform and renew, not just your life but also those of people around you who deserve better. Resolve issues that are outstanding and if you harbour thoughts of revenge, let them go. You can't afford to have bad blood around when you are about to regenerate yourself and your life in a more positive form.

PLUTO IN SAGITTARIUS OR THE 9TH HOUSE

You have a strong drive to transform and improve yourself intellectually. You can become compulsive about bettering yourself and becoming the fount of all knowledge – as knowledge is power. You have strong beliefs that you try to indoctrinate into others. This may make you self-righteous and a fundamentalist or zealot. You have a secretive side that may come into conflict with Sagittarius's more open, free and liberated mindset.

If you have a positive Pluto in Sagittarius or the 9th house

You have deeply held convictions and religious values. You do nothing lightly and are in search of the holy grail of spirituality. You have an avid interest in lands where ancient civilizations and mysteries flourished. You are fascinated by the psychology of people who have found fame, power and fortune. You hate superficiality of any kind, fight for justice and despise hypocrisy and bigotry. You are fixated by learning and travel for reasons that would escape many people.

If you have a negative Pluto in Sagittarius or the 9th house

You can mix with the wrong kind of people, those who preach hate or who gain control over people's mind to hypnotize or create mass hysteria. You might follow false Messiahs or have a Jesus complex of your own. You find it hard to take orders or relax and are continually plotting and scheming in cloak and dagger style to see whose world you can take over next.

How to overcome a negative Pluto in Sagittarius or the 9th house

Being cynical and control-mad is one thing if you keep it to yourself, but the minute you try to infect others, you can create destruction on many levels, but mainly your own. You undoubtedly have an insightful and incredible mind, but you must find something that really is bad, unjust or wrong and use that brilliance to bring people over to your side and create something good. You can do it. And what's more, you needn't resort to cheap psychological shots when you can use that same firebrand mind of yours to transform the world about you in a visionary and conscious-raising way.

PLUTO IN THE 10TH HOUSE

The goals you set yourself in your career must fulfil you psychologically. You have the potential to go a long way – right to the top, in fact. You will get there, although you have to be careful not to become obsessed with power and be too ruthless in getting to your goals. You will use your gift for manipulating others to climb to the top. You won't suffer fools and will be a cruel and vengeful enemy if anybody is foolish enough to compete with you or stand on your ambitious feet. Your career will be made up of a number of interesting chapters with definite beginnings and ends. Your destiny will be reflected by whatever fate has in store for you. Of course, you still have free will but there are some things you cannot change or control. You have to accept that some things are inevitable and irrevocable.

If you have a positive Pluto in the 10th house

You want nothing less than total success in whatever you do. Once you have your goal or purpose in your sights, you move inexorably to your target. If anyone stands in your way, you will annihilate them. You are a transformer and a catalyst so whatever vocation or profession you are involved with, there is no dispute as to who is boss. Even if you're not, you will be the power behind the throne, the puppet-meister.

If you have a negative Pluto in the 10th house

You don't care who you hurt, push aside or threaten, for your ambitions know no bounds. Nothing or no-one must thwart or frustrate your success. However, your recognition comes at a price because your reputation may in the end be the reason for your downfall. So the old saying hoves into view, 'Be nice to those on your way up as you will meet them on your way down.' And you do!

How to overcome a negative Pluto in the 10th house

Fate always plays a starring role whenever Pluto is involved. Because he falls here in Saturn's domain, there is more than just an air of kismet and karma combining to dictate your fate. So it is best that whatever you do in life is always for the right reasons because if not, you will do the Scorpio thing (Pluto's sign remember) and ultimately sting yourself to death. Cruel, cold, calculating, obsessive, compulsive, jealous, vindictive, vengeful: yes, all these can be you, but they don't have to be. Turn your back on them before it's too late.

PLUTO IN THE 11TH HOUSE

You are someone for whom many things are all or nothing. You are either completely immersed in a subject or have nothing whatsoever to do with it. Equally, friendships can be love–hate affairs. You have a strong desire to be accepted and expect your goals to be taken seriously by others as well. You make very powerful and influential friendships but some of these friends may loathe you.

If you have a positive Pluto in the 11th house

You are fanatical about a hobby or pastime to the point it takes over your life. You're never sure when to call it a day and even when you do, it's not easy for you to get over it. You make the transition from part-time pursuit or activity to career or profession easily but it's hard to find an occupation that calls for the kind of interests you have. You have high humanitarian ideals and, by using an obsessive and reforming zeal, will do your best to make changes for the good of all.

If you have a negative Pluto in the 11th house

You will frequently be at odds with the authorities, especially if they obstruct what you want to do. Your aspirations will be halted by jobsworths, officials obsessed with doing things 'by the book', who bring out the worst in you. This can lead to vendettas and revenge tactics that sabotage your hopes and wishes as you are seen as a troublemaker or a ne'er do well. You try to control your friends and, as with most things you are involved with, there are periods when everything falls apart and you have to start again. Your life is a series of cycles.

How to overcome a negative Pluto in the 11th house

Getting het up (and that's an understatement) about issues that you cannot change is a waste of energy. See where you can make a difference and concentrate on that one thing. By doing so you can metamorphose into something wonderful that will win you friends in high places and put you in control of other aspirations or visions that mean something to you. Don't get fixated or stuck with petty people or projects that don't deserve your attention.

PLUTO IN THE 12TH HOUSE

You are highly secretive and hide away in seclusion. You mask your true feelings, bottling up difficulties or frustrations until they fester psychologically, rather than sharing them with others or dealing with them. This can lead to introversion and neuroses. The unknown fascinates you, and you have an interest in cults and clandestine clubs. Your world is cloaked in mystery and you carry your enigmatic label well. Sexually you are full of fantasies and fetishes that need a positive release or they could cause you emotional problems. You have sublime psychic powers and believe there is a cosmic conspiracy working for or against you.

If you have a positive Pluto in the 12th house

Nothing is simple with you. There is a complicated reason or explanation for everything, which is what makes you so hard to understand. Very often you don't want to share your feelings, opinions or attitudes. You are happy to remain in the shadows and away from it all. You love with a deep intensity and your romantic liaisons are likely to be carried out with circumspect and invisible discretion.

If you have a negative Pluto in the 12th house

Psychologically you are mysterious and far removed from your average person. You are unworldly and simmer with an obsessive intent. Getting on the wrong side of you is not a good idea. If anyone harms or hurts you then you can wait years, a lifetime even, to get revenge – to you, a dish best eaten cold. However, the truth is that despite your reputation as a destroyer, if push came to shove, you'd run away and cry.

How to overcome a negative Pluto in the 12th house

What's at stake here? That's what you have got to find out first. Your aimless, worthless lifestyle is entirely down to you. There are other people who've been through the mill, been traumatized and lost everything but they have returned to live another day. See your life as a TV mini-series with each episode leading to another. With each new episode you can be reborn, put wrongs to right and be transfigured into another character. Eventually, the reason for your existence will be made clear.

Mapping Out Planet You: The Aspects

HOW TO DRAW ON THE GOOD AND BAD ASPECTS OF YOUR CHART

In this section you are going to read through the aspects that apply to your chart. There may be quite a lot of them, but it is important that you read through each of them carefully. Each holds the key to an important part of your overall personality. You will almost certainly see that your aspects represent a mixture of the positive and negative. Again, each is important and you need to dwell on all of them.

If an aspect is POSITIVE, sit back, take a walk or do whatever helps you best to concentrate and contemplate. Then see if you can think of times when this aspect of you has manifested itself. Analyze how you behaved and how you felt on those occasions, and store those memories away. They may be a positive, uplifting and self-motivating tool in the future. Think too about how you might be able to use these elements of your personality to tackle areas in which you feel challenged or that life is lacking.

If, on the other hand, your chart contains NEGATIVE personality traits, take a good look at yourself and see if you can think of when this darker side of you has shown itself. Be brutally honest – don't hold back, but equally don't beat yourself up. To face this side of yourself is the only way you are going to avoid making the same mistakes over and over again. When you have done this, consider how you might work to transform these heavier aspects of your personality and stop your personal history repeating itself.

If your natal chart contains a good vibrant, healthy balance of aspects, think about how each of them might have helped or hindered you.

WHY BAD ASPECTS CAN BE GOOD FOR YOU, AND GOOD ASPECTS BAD...

This bit is very important. Having a list of purely positive aspects isn't necessarily going to make you a successful person, so it's not necessarily good news if that's what your chart shows. How so? Well, every person *needs* some challenging, heavier aspects to give them impetus and motivation, good old-fashioned get-up-and-go. If you have too few negative squares or oppositions, you won't gather up the steam you need to give yourself the incentive to make things happen or change. Too many positive aspects can also lead to indolence or the belief that you are immortal, exempt from life's trials and tribulations. Someone with a high percentage of positive aspects can be convinced nothing can go wrong in their world. It's as if they have some divine status, as if a higher force or being will always rush in at the last minute to protect them. It won't.

The harsh reality is that no-one is immune from life's ups and downs, and you must be aware of that. Only if you have shortcomings and know what they are and how to deal with them can you really make the most of your planetary gifts, both positive and negative. This is why some of the most successful people have aspects that would make other folks' toes curl. They have succeeded because heavy aspects often create a driven or obsessive personality. By harnessing the force within they are empowered to deal with all that life throws at them. So as you start going through your aspects, remember – don't jump to conclusions too quickly. Bad can often be good and good can sometimes be bad!

PUTTING THE ASPECTS TOGETHER: THINGS TO WATCH OUT FOR

By the end of this exercise you will have a list of aspects that you will have analyzed one by one. As you put together the complex cosmic jigsaw that is Planet You, it is important that you also look at how each of the individual aspects relate to each other. There are many, what I hesitate to describe as minor aspects, some of which are too subtle or complicated to go into here. They will have to wait until the next book! But, at this point, it is only right and proper to describe some of the most important configurations that you should look out for.

Look out for where the aspect falls in your chart

Conjunctions, for instance, will have more strength if they occur in a planet's 'home zone' – the sign or house it rules. For example, if the Moon is in conjunction with another planet in its home sign of Cancer or in the 4th house, this conjunction will have a greater significance. Naturally it follows that it is a double whammy if all the boxes are ticked: for instance, the Moon in conjunction with another planet in Cancer *and* in the 4th house.

Also look at where the aspect falls physically in the chart. A conjunction of three or more planets together in one sign or house anywhere in your horoscope is powerful. In astro jargon, this is called a stellium. So even if your Sun sign is, for example, Pisces, if you have three or more planets in Libra or three or more planets (not necessarily in one sign) in the 5th, this will overpower even your Sun sign – or at least give it a good run for its money. In this case you would be just as much Libran as a Piscean or, via the 5th House, with the essence of Leo. It may also make you a Piscean who won't change.

Look out for 'exact' aspects

The closer the aspects are to the exactitude, the more powerful their effect is going to be. For instance, if two planets are EXACTLY 120 degrees apart in the chart – say one at 25 degrees Scorpio and another at 25 degrees Cancer (remember the same element very often creates a flowing, easy-going aspect), then the trine aspect is given more positive strength and power. But if they only just make a trine – say 25 degrees Scorpio to 16 Cancer – that makes it much weaker in comparison.

You may also discover 'disassociate' aspects in your chart, that is, two planets that fall into the corridor of degrees that form an aspect, but are not in the signs, elements or qualities that traditionally make that aspect. For instance, one planet could be two degrees in one sign, say Gemini, and the other 28 degrees in Taurus. They are not in conjunction in the same sign, but they are still within the nine-degree orb that defines a conjunction. So this is a 'disassociate' conjunction. This can happen for all the aspects – a disassociate trine, disassociate square, disassociate sextile and so on...

Look out for aspects forming a network

Aspects can form aspects with each other, so that a network of planets combines powerfully throughout the chart. There are three major arrangements of this kind that you should be aware of:

1) A grand trine: This is where three or more planets form trines with each other, that is planet one is trine with planet two, which is trine with planet three, which inevitably will be trine with planet one.

The effect of this grand trine is to encourage the influence of each of the planets involved to flow freely through the chart. If we think back to our theatre analogy, it is like having three really complementary actors in a scene, each of them bringing the absolute best performance out of each other. This is a most auspicious aspect to have and can be spotted on the chart by an equilateral green triangle or pyramid within the circle. (The pyramid, of course, is said to be one of the most powerful and enduring structures in the world and spiritually it represents the trilogy evident in certain faiths and religions.)

Some astrologers do NOT include the Midheaven and Ascendant in these powerful connections but I do. My view is that we should take advantage of everything we have at our disposal. To be able to change your life you need to know about every single one of the tools, aids and gifts you are capable of drawing on.

2) A T-square: This is formed when an opposition is joined to two squares, that is, two planets in opposition are both squared by another planet at 90 degrees. This looks like a squashed triangle on the chart. It is a very challenging aspect but is often evident in the horoscopes of people who become very successful. To me, the planet that is the apex of the T-square is very important, as it is the release valve of an aspect that can be at the root of stress and tension. So if the Sun opposes Pluto and Mercury and in turn is squared by Mars, then Mars holds the key to bringing out the best in the individual. It could be through sport or other physical activities, but it is physically and mentally dynamic so it requires single-minded action to work. To draw on the power of a T-square, you really have to go for the burn.

3) The grand cross or square: This is a T-square with two oppositions and all the planets involved then square to one another. This is often said to be a 'cross to bear' for the individual who has to deal with it, but you shouldn't run away with the idea it is bad.

This aspect has a definite phoenix from the ashes quality to it. Okay, your life might not be honey and roses straight away, but if you rise to the challenge, deal with all the setbacks, take in your stride the traumas that haunt your life and learn from them, you will resurrect your life. It can be done – remember, there are those who knuckle under and those who go under. A grand cross or square is only bad if you give into it.

The Aspects of the Sun

SUN CONJUNCT MOON

This is a very positive aspect to have in your chart as it represents harmony between the two most important planetary personalities within you: the essential you that is the Sun and the emotional you that is the Moon. If you have these two planets sitting alongside each other, your overall personality and emotions are well balanced. You are someone who is, in general, happy with your life. You enjoy a good social life, but at the same time can keep an emotional distance between yourself and others. You also have the ability to make fresh starts in life when necessary. You will have been born under a new Moon with this conjunction, which means you are constantly looking to make a fresh start in the area of your life this aspect falls in.

SUN SEXTILE MOON

This is another positive aspect and means you will be able to express your emotions with ease. Again, you will have a very balanced attitude to life, something you may well have picked up from your family life, which is also stable and secure unless other more negative aspects to the Moon counteract this. You also have a strong creative force within you, which provides you with another important outlet for expressing your feelings.

SUN SQUARE MOON

This challenging aspect places the Sun and the Moon at odds with each other. As a result, you can feel emotionally insecure and generally ill at ease with yourself. You can be torn between the reality of what you need in practical terms and what your emotions tell you you want. You frequently have to fight with yourself to find a happy medium between these two conflicting parts of your personality. This conflict within will not be made any easier by the fact you are keen to prove to yourself and others that you've got what it takes:

setting yourself high standards and goals. (It's interesting to note that President George W. Bush has this aspect.)

SUN TRINE MOON

Again this indicates that you have a powerful balance for the good between your Sun and Moon, your ego and your emotions. You are someone who feels comfortable within yourself and content with the world in general. The chief danger you face is failing to acknowledge your weaknesses and flaws. This can lead to feelings of infallibility. If you succeed in developing enough self-awareness, however, you are likely to achieve whatever goals you set yourself.

SUN OPPOSITION MOON

If you have this aspect within your chart, it means you were born during a full Moon, which has both advantages and disadvantages. On the positive side, you are blessed with an acute and highly aware intuition. This helps keep you open to new ideas and openings at all times. This ability also makes you highly sensitive, however, and you can suffer from a lack of self-assurance. Your happiness will be dictated by your ability to strike a balance between these two forces. You will find your life has distinct endings – remember this: as each door shuts, another opens.

SUN CONJUNCT MERCURY

The Sun can never be more than 28 degrees from Mercury so the only prime aspect that can occur is a conjunction. If this is the case, you are blessed with plenty of brainpower and are a quick thinker and good communicator. However, you do have a tendency to be stubborn and highly opinionated. The strength of this aspect will be affected by the sign it falls in, so you should check this. If it falls in a fixed sign (Taurus, Leo, Scorpio or Aquarius), for instance, then your obstinacy is likely to be even more marked. You are someone who is prone to coming out with that favourite old phrase, 'Anything you can do I can do better!' If it falls in an air sign or Virgo, your ability to communicate will be heightened further.

Important note: If Mercury is too close to the Sun, let's say within two degrees, it is said to be 'combust', that is, the Sun smothers Mercury (a planet who loves his space). A better balance is achieved if Mercury is at least three degrees away from the Sun.

SUN CONJUNCT VENUS

The Sun is never more than 48 degrees away from Venus so the only major aspect he can make is a conjunction. If you have this in your chart it means that love, beautiful things and people are central to your very being, so much so, in fact, that they are each a powerful factor in dictating whether or not you find true, complete happiness. You need lots of love but also enjoy being seen as an affectionate and loving person. This can make you averse to any confrontational situations, which others interpret as an easy-going attitude to life. This approach means you are a great believer in compromise and making the peace, regardless of what you might be feeling deep down. Other negative aspects to either the Sun or Venus elsewhere in the chart can lead to vanity or loving yourself a bit too much. There is also a tendency to never be completely satisfied with what you've got, always wanting more or something different.

SUN CONJUNCT MARS

If you have this red-hot aspect, you are someone who leads from the front. You possess a strong will and rarely fail to exercise it. Mars's energy means you thrive on competition, but you have to tread carefully in case your impulsive nature makes you jump in before you've thought things through properly. Fools rush in and all that. You are intolerant of people who disagree with you; indeed, you find it tough to cope with criticism in general. Such is your anger at times that you can be accident-prone so be careful in this respect. Things such as road-rage, or any kind of rage, are often signs of your frustration trying to get out. Channel it into a more creative force. When you are at boiling point, don't drive or do something stupid. Instead play sports, do DIY or whatever you can to release your pent-up fury. There is a tendency to be ruthless and exercise your sexy personality to its limits, sometimes beyond. Keep a hold on your libido.

SUN SEXTILE MARS

The power of Mars is well focused if you have this aspect in your chart. You are constantly on the lookout for new, stimulating outlets for your boundless energy. You have a knack of getting on well with people and, even though your opinions are very strong, you aren't so dogmatic that you won't listen to the point of view of others. Your sex appeal is so appealing that people almost swoon when you walk into a room.

SUN SQUARE MARS

With this aspect in your chart, you are guaranteed to have masses of dynamism and get-up-and-go, but you have to be careful not to push yourself too hard in chasing your ambitions or else you will do yourself harm. Sometimes you neglect to look before you leap, ploughing into a project or new move without planning it properly. By the time you discover you've failed to anticipate a problem, it will be too late. You have a strong need for attention that can sometimes make you appear overbearing. You have the capacity to be cruel and a bully (alternatively, you can bring this on yourself from others). Relationships with men are difficult and this gender can often be your bête noire. Be warned of dissipating your energies and be single-minded in all your goals. You hate to lose.

SUN TRINE MARS

If you have this aspect in your chart you have an easy-going nature that allows you to easily win friends and influence people. You are energetic and brimming with a sexy self-confidence, but not to the extent that people find it threatening. Your ability to take people as you find them adds to your popularity and you are drawn to people who adopt this same outlook on life. Men want to be your friend as you draw the masculine gender to you like moths to a flame. There's something about that others find stimulating.

SUN OPPOSITION MARS

If you have this aspect, there's a conflict between the dynamism and drive of Mars and the ego at the heart of you, as represented by the Sun and the sign it is in. As a result you will have a hugely competitive, very assertive nature that regularly rubs people up the wrong way. In fact, so powerful is your desire to chase your ambitions at all costs that you must learn to rein it in. You have to learn that life isn't war and you don't have to view every encounter in life as a battle within that conflict. You also have to stop judging yourself by whether you win or lose in these battles, and appreciate yourself for what you are, regardless of the outcomes. You've a will to win, but need to cultivate humility.

SUN CONJUNCT JUPITER

If you have this wonderful aspect in your chart, you are an open-minded, kind-hearted soul who loves to have fun. You are generous to a fault (unless Saturn has hard aspects to either planet) and will help the underdog. If you have a fault, it is that you can't do things in moderation, whether it is working or playing. You live life to the full and may pay the price for that in terms of your long-term health. Opportunities will arise in foreign lands, and a love of travel, mental or physical, will enable you to use your love of expansion in a positive way internationally or intellectually. The one negative here is a Mr Micawber personality – blind optimism.

SUN SEXTILE JUPITER

With this happy aspect in your chart, the joy-bringing and pleasure-seeking properties of Jupiter shine through. You have an open, enthusiastic and optimistic nature that draws people in and wins you many like-minded friends. Your popularity is only increased by your gift for communication. Travel figures high on your list of priorities, as does learning.

SUN SQUARE JUPITER

If you have this aspect in your chart, you have a real tendency to bite off more than you can chew. You have tons of potential and love nothing more than a challenge. It's just that too often you don't think things through in advance, dive in, then discover you've overstepped the mark. The fact you're not very good at taking advice from others only makes matters worse. This inability to understand the old motto 'Moderation in all things' may also affect your health. The key to dealing with this side of your personality is stepping back and taking a deep breath before committing yourself to things. With a little more caution and planning, things will work out better. A tendency to excess, exaggeration and believing you are 'divine' needs caution, especially as your judgement can be way off beam with this aspect. Matters of money and law require your most practical approach.

SUN TRINE JUPITER

With this fantastic aspect in your chart, there is a danger you will fail to fulfil your true potential. You are easy-going and more than happy to watch others succeed where you could easily do well yourself. Your rounded, grounded personality also means you are more interested in people's qualities as human beings than their status or wealth. If you have this loveable aspect and are failing to achieve, you have to ask yourself the question, 'How badly do I want it?' You definitely have the potential. It may be that you need to apply yourself harder. Fame and fortune will come through Sun or Jupiter careers, and by casting your net further than your average Joe.

SUN OPPOSITION JUPITER

This aspect in your chart indicates that you have many of the qualities, particularly buckets of optimism and charm, needed to achieve great things. The problem is, however, that you are also guilty of missing the real point both with yourself and other people. You are then surprised when people let you down or you make a mistake, when if you'd thought about it, this possibility always existed. You are only going to overcome this problem by realizing your limitations and acting accordingly. People will respect you more for this, too. Financial concerns require outside advice as you may have champagne tastes with lemonade pockets. In legal matters, always err on the side of caution.

SUN CONJUNCT SATURN

This aspect indicates that you may well have suffered a tough or traumatic childhood and that you have had to fend for yourself from an early age. Life has been a serious business for you and as a result, you treat it that way. You plan projects carefully and then succeed in them. Your problem is that you find it hard to cope when you don't succeed, and you are prone to becoming bitter about such setbacks. Realize you have the scope and ambition to make something of yourself. Don't travel through life on a guilt trip. Trust me, you *do* deserve happiness, but it's up to you to earn and savour it. The only person you owe anything to is yourself.

SUN SEXTILE SATURN

With this aspect in your chart you have wisdom, perhaps well beyond your years. You have a great ability to learn from experience and as a result, project an air of wisdom and calm authority to others. All this, combined with your tendency to plan your objectives in painstaking detail, means you invariably succeed. Older people will be very helpful and supportive of you.

SUN SQUARE SATURN

If you have this aspect in your chart, you face a frequent battle with your lack of self-esteem and depression. You find it hard to push yourself forward because you have such a low opinion of yourself and your abilities. As a result, you will have to make mistakes before achieving success. However, the good news is that you will be able to draw on those negative experiences, translating them into positives. This, ultimately, will be your strength as you proceed through life. Very often your relationship with your father or boss will raise difficult issues and you may have to learn hard lessons in dealing with authority.

SUN TRINE SATURN

With this aspect in your chart, you combine many qualities necessary for success. You have potential galore and know where your strengths lie and how to use them. You are also unafraid of responsibility and have a knack for knowing when to cash in on a situation. All this should enable you to achieve your ambitions with relative ease. The people around you who respect what you have to say will hold you in high esteem.

SUN OPPOSITION SATURN

This aspect in your chart can not only mean you have a real lack of self-confidence but also a misunderstanding of your priorities. Your low self-esteem and sense of self-worth can make you feel like life is a real battlefield and that you are a victim. Breaking out of this cycle is difficult, but it can be done. The key is taking a risk or grabbing an opportunity that will turn things around. By doing so, you will begin to value yourself more. From there you can build your self-confidence and go on to surprise yourself and all around you. By wanting your father or boss's approval for everything you do, you can fail to look after your own needs. (Rupert Murdoch's son, James, has this aspect in his chart.)

SUN CONJUNCT URANUS

You can be dictatorial and dogmatic with this summer–winter aspect. You are capable of being headstrong, contrary and a law unto yourself. Despite this dislike of authority, you can often trip yourself up, due to self-made rules and regulations. A tendency to cut off your nose to spite your face also lurks in this aspect. Your outlook on life is cool and cautious; you have the Greta Garbo approach to life – wanting to be alone. Seclusion suits you, as does being creative in a silent, solitary way. You find trivial, superficial people a waste of time and that's one thing you hate – waste. Punctuality is important, as is never repeating a failure or allowing your Achilles heel to show. You can be happiest on your own and yet this can lead to ruminating on your depressions. Take up a profession or pastime that enables you to collect and contemplate in the peace and quiet of your own company. Learn to love yourself a little bit more and you'll rise to any occasion.

SUN SEXTILE URANUS

With this wayward aspect in your chart, you are someone who is extremely open and communicative. You enjoy nothing more than sitting down and discussing every aspect of your life. Your broad-minded, original outlook is made even more appealing by a philosophical nature. If there is one thing you cannot stand, however, it is deceit and dishonesty. You need freedom and can't abide being hemmed in.

SUN SQUARE URANUS

If you have this rebellious aspect to your chart, you are a really uncompromising individual. You have a real need to do things your own way, regardless of how it might upset or cause problems to those around you. You really don't mind going against the flow, and are capable of wilfully taking the opposite side in an argument. Deep down you are intuitive and sensitive but even so, you go out to shock or cause a hiatus, knowing you will hurt yourself more than others. Your life would be changed markedly if you learned the art of compromise. You are ingenious but lack the self-control and discipline to make something of yourself. You start too many things that you never finish. You are a live wire of nervous tension – watch your blood pressure!

SUN TRINE URANUS

If you see this aspect in your birth chart, it means you have a real and profound interest in other people and what makes them tick. You also have a talent for listening and are generous without appearing patronizing. It is little wonder that you attract people to you in droves. But it's your ability to make even the most drab and boring situation bright and sparkling that makes you such a hit. You sparkle like no other cosmic combination and so long as you twinkle, you'll always come across as a star. However, it is imperative that you have space.

SUN OPPOSITION URANUS

This aspect makes you a complex soul. You have a deep-seated need to constantly prove you have what it takes to succeed. As a result, you are constantly looking for people to challenge or compete with you. Actually you're not naturally competitive but you can create problems for yourself because you just want to contradict life, people, and the world, just for the sheer hell of it. You always want to be on the go and can never totally relax properly. This, unsurprisingly, makes you difficult to live with and can drive you away from even those to whom you are closest. Commitment can be a real hang-up for you.

SUN CONJUNCT NEPTUNE

With this refined aspect in your chart you have considerable creative gifts and may be highly talented in the arts – if not, then you certainly appreciate it in others. Unfortunately this unique gift is counterbalanced by an extreme sensitivity that makes it hard for you to cope with the realities of the outside world, where your lack of self-confidence is all too readily taken advantage of by other people. As a result, you have a tendency to take the line of least resistance and undersell yourself. If you continue to do this, it will lead to disillusionment later in life when you realize you haven't fulfilled your potential.

Warning! You can deceive and seduce just as easily as you can confuse and kid yourself. A tendency towards escapism can lead you to getting hooked on all kinds of substances or outlets that are a health hazard. Best to listen to life's wake-up calls for everyone's sake.

SUN SEXTILE NEPTUNE

If you have this genteel aspect, you have a strong compassionate streak within you. You are always keen to help those less fortunate than you. Your easy-going nature means you also fit in with others, so you are well suited to working with the general public in a way that brings out your sympathetic, caring nature. You are arty and creative with a good imagination. Your psychic powers are well honed, as is your interest in matters spiritual and medical. Your image is very important to your success.

SUN SQUARE NEPTUNE

As if the natural lack of self-esteem that you have as a result of this aspect isn't enough, you have a habit of making it worse for yourself. You are constantly setting yourself targets you aren't ever going to achieve, or else filling your life with people who don't appreciate you for who you are. The only way you are going to get somewhere with the undoubted potential within you is by building up your sense of self-worth. The best way to do this is via a series of small successes, setting yourself easily attainable goals that will boost your opinion of yourself each time you reach them.

Be warned of your neurotic nature, which can leave you submerged in a load of doubts and worries that when analyzed don't exist. Lies, betrayal and treachery can figure in your life, but make sure you're not the one doing the dirty or it will come back to haunt you. You hate confrontations of any kind.

SUN TRINE NEPTUNE

With this glamorous aspect in your chart you are not short of flair and creative ability. The problem is you will not be able to fulfill your potential until you learn to harness your gifts properly. To do that you have to slow down your overactive mind. You learn things quickly and constantly move from one subject to another. But this gives you a problem with working for others, meeting deadlines and schedules. Only by introducing reality and discipline to your life will you fully tap into your talents. Music, drama, performance, indeed anything that allows you to be anyone but yourself will appeal as you are drawn to the sensitive and romantic side of life. Fantasy often suits you better than reality; your dreams have powerful meanings as when you sleep your psychic energies really get going.

SUN OPPOSITION NEPTUNE

If your chart has this foggy aspect within it, you have a problem separating fact from fiction. You see crises where there aren't any and behave like an ostrich with its head in the sand when you are confronted by real difficulties. You compound all this by surrounding yourself with people with whom you don't have an honest emotional rapport – an insurance policy against getting hurt if you fall out with them. If you are going to achieve anything, you will need to perform a serious reality check. Be warned of false prophets, for with this aspect you will be attracted to people who perform tricks and give the impression of being first-class at whatever they do, but they are actually disingenuous. Also, don't live in a land of make-believe when it comes to what you can do – stick to what you *can* do and do it well. You are a very interesting person without having to make up stories about yourself.

SUN CONJUNCT PLUTO

With this awesome aspect in your chart, there is something mysterious and hidden at the very heart of you. This may mean that people find it hard to get to know you. You give the impression of holding back. This may be rooted in a problem you had with your father during childhood. If it weren't for this elusiveness to your personality, you would be much more popular. You have real presence and with your powerful ego and strong opinions can cut a charismatic figure. The most complex part of you is a desire to control others, very often you don't even know you're doing it but you are. It is a natural part of your nature to dominate in all ways, especially psychologically. Take care: what goes around, comes around.

SUN SEXTILE PLUTO

If you have this probing aspect in your chart, there is a strong psychic side to your nature. You possess a sixth sense that helps you negotiate life's trickier problems. You may even have an active interest in the mystical and spiritual side of things. You have a great deal of willpower and are capable of doing not only what you want in life but influencing others to fulfil their potential as well. You have a doggedness that means you won't give up until you've finished.

SUN SQUARE PLUTO

There is a real aura of unease and enigma around you. It is as if you are always on the lookout for trouble of some kind. As a result, people find it hard to get close to you, often because they simply can't anticipate how you are going to react. This is because you have a tendency to act with your emotions rather than your mind, and feel threatened by people you consider more powerful than you. If you are going to achieve the goals you set yourself, you need to compromise more often. Don't use your sexuality to gain control over others and be careful of attracting or giving out abuse if you fail to get your way. You can have an obsessive, compulsive nature that means you may have psychological issues that require self-help or the guidance of advisers or counsellors.

SUN TRINE PLUTO

With this transforming aspect in your chart there is no doubting your enormous personal potential. You are a potent leader, someone whose creativity and intuition commands respect. You are astute at discerning other people's strengths and weaknesses and if you can channel this skill properly, you're capable of achieving almost anything to which you aspire. You have a tremendous, hypnotic quality that is further enhanced by your sexiness. You aspire to greatness basically because you know when to let go and move on, knowing when fate has decreed that one chapter of your life has come to close and allowing it to go. This is in stark contrast to the conjunction, square or opposition aspects of Sun and Pluto.

SUN OPPOSITION PLUTO

Defensive and suspicious by nature, you often feel you are beaten even before you've faced up to the challenge. Your distrust and resentment of people who are different to you also acts as a wedge between you and potential new friends or partners. You will not achieve any of your goals until you learn to open your mind and give others the benefit of the doubt. You want your way whatever the cost; sometimes this means putting yourself on the line because you become totally fixated with one tiny thing to the cost of everything else. Prioritize in order of importance rather than your personal obsession. You have awesome creative flair and power that can be lost whilst you 'play' around with things that are superficial. You have the gifts to change the world and make something of nothing if you care to use them.

SUN CONJUNCT ASCENDANT

With your chart showing this aspect, you have a definite need for attention and recognition. Whilst you have no real problems in making friends, you are more likely to worry about those who are resistant to your charms than those who are drawn to you naturally. You need to overcome this and concentrate on those who care about you if you are going to achieve happiness. Much will depend whether the Sun is the 1st or 12th house as to how you use this aspect. Sun in the 1st will give a love of drama and showmanship – you want to be noticed. Sun in the 12th is much more reclusive, with a tendency to hide your light under a bushel.

SUN SEXTILE ASCENDANT

Your easy-going nature, lively sense of fun and ready wit make you a popular personality. You have a strong sense of honesty and deal with people accordingly. Equally, you are repelled by people who don't share this philosophy and appear deceitful or false. You radiate a lot of warmth.

SUN SQUARE ASCENDANT

With this ego-based aspect in your chart, your desperation for the approval of others comes over as a huge chip on your shoulder. This is a real turn-off for others and you may find it difficult to make friends unless you make adjustments. Try not to come on so strong and life will become a lot easier. Arrogance and coming across as though you're always right must be tempered or you'll gain a reputation for being a 'know-all'.

SUN TRINE ASCENDANT

In general, you are someone with more than enough optimism and self-confidence to fulfil your goals, yet there is a part of you that tends to dwell on your failures more than your successes. This can hold you back at times. Focus on the positives rather than the negatives and you will find it easier to live up to your real potential. You have enormous charm and are loved by all, but learn to love yourself a little more before worrying about others. Although this is a positive aspect, it can make you vulnerable to what others say or think.

SUN OPPOSITION ASCENDANT

With this challenging aspect to your chart, there is a real need for admiration. You crave the compliments that will bolster your shaky sense of self-esteem. You have a tendency to look for these ego boosts by associating with people of importance, hoping somehow that their status and power will reflect on you. The Sun on your Descendant can create relationship problems unless you operate the old maxim, give and take.

SUN CONJUNCT MIDHEAVEN

This is an auspicious aspect to have on your chart as it usually signifies someone who looks for recognition and respect in life – usually getting it. By pursuing a creative career, even if you don't succeed in a big way, you will at least be loved and very popular with your boss and co-workers.

SUN SEXTILE MIDHEAVEN

This glowing aspect indicates you are someone who is willing to work really hard for whatever goal you set yourself. For a good idea of how to pursue that goal, look at the sign on the Midheaven in your chart. From that you can deduce what sort of vocation you would excel at. One thing is almost certain: you want to be seen as the person in charge, and be recognized and given credit for all you achieve.

SUN SQUARE MIDHEAVEN

You may face a hard battle to live up to the potential shown in your chart, but with the requisite amount of hard work and self-belief, you will get there in the end. Very often you can choose the wrong career or go about getting success in the wrong way. You can be a round peg in a square hole. Be warned of employers or bosses who see you as a threat to their position.

SUN TRINE MIDHEAVEN

With this golden aspect in your chart, you can achieve what you want in life. You will also be in the fortunate position of being able to do so without being aggressive, unpleasant or rude to those with whom you associate along the way. Play to your creative strengths; by doing so you will shine like a beacon to people who matter. Your reputation will soar after one success and repeated successes will enable people to see you as synonymous with your particular trade or industry. You are not interested in being second-best and have a knack of attracting powerful or successful people into your orbit. It's who you know as much as what you know that matters.

SUN OPPOSITION MIDHEAVEN

While this edgy aspect suggests you will eventually find success in achieving your goals, it also indicates that you will do so in an inconspicuous manner. You won't win worldwide fame for your exploits, but you will find happiness at home, which is just as important in your book. The big dichotomy is career versus home. If you can gain the right balance, you can have the best of both worlds, but the competing demands of family affairs and personal ambitions will become an issue that needs working out before it causes a rift somewhere in your world.

The Aspects of the Moon

See Sun for aspects between Sun and Moon.

MOON CONJUNCT MERCURY

If you have this lively aspect in your chart, there is a good balance between the emotional part of you as represented by the Moon and the intellectual side in the form of Mercury. This means you have much common sense and are good at putting your experiences and problems in proper context. You do have a tendency to talk a lot, however, and you can become confused occasionally about your feelings. It's important not to let your heart rule your head or vice versa – keeping an equilibrium between the two is good for your well-being.

MOON SEXTILE MERCURY

With this positive aspect you have a lot going for you. You are sensitive and thoughtful but highly entertaining to talk to because of your wide range of interests and broad circle of friends. Your gift for communication helps you professionally too. You are endowed with sympathy and can easily turn your life experiences into lessons for others to learn from.

MOON SQUARE MERCURY

This aspect creates problems in discerning what is true and also what is important. You are highly sensitive and sometimes see insults and put-downs where none exist. You are also so immersed in your own world at times that you cannot see the bigger picture. Instead you talk endlessly about nothing in particular, the trivial details of your day-to-day life. You worry a lot and can make mountains out of molehills.

MOON TRINE MERCURY

With this amiable aspect you are blessed with a way about you that endears folks to you. You are a raconteur, great with kids or young people as you're on their wavelength, but you have a great emotional intelligence too. By combining these two elements of your personality, you can effectively put your past experiences into their proper context so as to learn for the future. You are also good at understanding and sympathizing with others and their foibles and failings. You have a wonderful empathy; people feel that 'you know' what troubles them and your presence is like a panacea.

MOON OPPOSITION MERCURY

This volatile aspect sets the emotions and the mind at odds with each other. As a result, you can seem cold and aloof at times, yet at other times you can't put a lid on the outpouring of feelings that flood from you. You are mercurial emotionally, often jumping down people's throats for no apparent reason. You are also prone to self-obsession, droning on and on about the intimate details of your life when no-one else is remotely interested. Your groundless problems and irrational worries can bring out the worst in others. Be warned about hypochondria, or inventing illnesses or issues to extract sympathy from people. Your main issue is insecurity.

MOON CONJUNCT VENUS

Due to this very feminine aspect in your chart, you are extremely sensitive to criticism and will do everything in your power to keep the atmosphere around you as harmonious as possible, so you are adaptable and gifted at putting people at ease. You are also someone who will try to do everything you conceivably can. You arc a born diplomat and can attract the interest of women for all kinds of reasons, whether you are male or female.

MOON SEXTILE VENUS

With this congenial aspect in your chart, you have a strong need for harmony within relationships, both personal and professional. This means you will always be open to compromise and deal-making – anything, in fact, to avoid friction. The fact that you are very sociable helps you to further achieve the good relations you crave. The feminine gender will take you under their wing as you come across as a genuinely nice person.

MOON SQUARE VENUS

This fickle aspect indicates problems with a woman, and that could include your mother. You are easily manipulated emotionally so need to watch out for undue influence from relatives in this respect. The key to growing and achieving your goals is cutting the apron strings. You need to become your own person; otherwise you will be a pale reflection of what your parents told you you must be.

MOON TRINE VENUS

Your open, optimistic nature attracts people to you. You also tend to keep friends and partners for the long term because of your live-and-let-live attitude. Sympathetic and likeable, you have a social life that can be the passport to success in other areas of your life. You will make friends aplenty. The love of your life, or certainly someone you are simpatico with emotionally, may be found through meetings or activities at which you feel comfortable and at your ease, thereby bringing the best out in you.

MOON OPPOSITION VENUS

This nagging aspect in your chart can create problems because people may doubt your motives. They think you are after something, when in fact you are simply after acceptance or friendship. You can't rush this process and need to take your time in persuading people that you are exactly what you seem. Be warned of carping on about things or even becoming a cauldron of self-pity. You don't have to throw yourself at people in a negative way. People will like you for who you are, without you wearing the word 'desperate' on your forehead.

MOON CONJUNCT MARS

You are very easily upset, yet struggle to show your feelings and so the frustration builds. When your desires do erupt, they arrive in an explosion of emotion that can often exacerbate difficult situations. You can also be aggressive towards people around you, yet find it hard to accept such behaviour when it is directed at you. For these reasons, you need to put yourself in other people's shoes sometimes. Imagine if you were dealing with you and your highly sensitive moods. How would you cope?

MOON SEXTILE MARS

Your irresistible charm means you have no difficulties in getting along with others. You are not someone to carry grudges (unless heavy aspects adorn the Moon too!) and only show your displeasure on those rare occasions when you think it is absolutely necessary. No situation is more likely to bring out this side of you than your domestic life, where you are extremely protective of your nearest and dearest. You have tremendous sex appeal but need to have feelings for someone before you can have a satisfactory intimate life.

MOON SQUARE MARS

Problems with intimacy – that's what this aspect in your chart shows. There is always something blocking the free flow of your feelings, making it difficult for you to give your all. You can't climb down from your high horse as you see it as a sign of weakness. Accordingly, you can find yourself constantly locking horns in arguments and confrontations, especially with people who don't share your point of view. The paradox is that once you've had a row, you then worry about what might happen afterwards. However, you need to learn to control this aspect of your personality because it can adversely affect your health. You must proffer the olive branch of peace every now and again.

MOON TRINE MARS

Your natural ability to see eye to eye with, and respect, other people makes you exceptionally good at dealing with the ordinary and everyday aspects of your life. You are secure in yourself and because you have little fear of rejection are comfortable expressing emotions and showing people you feel for them. With this aspect, your relationship with children can be superb as you have the ability to come down to their level and not make them feel small.

MOON OPPOSITION MARS

This see-saw aspect means you have real problems compromising or seeing someone's point of view. You can get yourself into a squabble over the most seemingly trivial of matters. To make matters worse, you have difficulty with people in authority and find it hard to cope with criticism. As a result, you scurry away to the doctor or dose yourself up with pills to gain the sympathy vote. Remember, everyone is entitled to their opinion so don't take everything so personally.

MOON CONJUNCT JUPITER

With this delicious aspect in your chart, you enjoy the best of the Moon and Jupiter parts of your personality. You are generous and optimistic, and have an eye on furthering your world. You have a strong spiritual side to your life. The only cloud on this horizon is that you tend to see the good and neglect the bad – or the other way round – and must learn that into everyone's life a little rain must fall, or alternatively live every minute as though it were your last!

MOON SEXTILE JUPITER

This heart-warming aspect indicates a strong combination of mind, body and spirit. This means that you treat life seriously, and draw useful lessons from your depth of thought. An optimist at heart, you always look for the silver lining when you face a problem. You have a philosophical approach to dealing with the downs of life and consequently can lift yourself up minutes after suffering a setback. Your physical powers of recovery are good too.

MOON SQUARE JUPITER

This hard aspect pitches the qualities of the Moon and Jupiter within you against each other. The result is that you react in a very dramatic, emotional manner. When you face problems, this results in you becoming overexcited and jumping to the wrong conclusion. When others face problems, you can react with overwhelming generosity, even putting yourself in financial difficulty in the process. The path to attaining a balance is to realize that charity often begins at home first.

The competing forces at work here mean you can veer between periods of excessive energy, when you don't know what to do with yourself, and other periods when you are overcome with lethargy.

MOON TRINE JUPITER

With this warm-hearted aspect in your chart, you are someone whose positive energy infects everyone around you. You have an optimistic nature and even when times get hard you deal with things in a matter-of-fact manner that invariably deals with the situation quickly and without drama. Your only weakness here is that you are so generous, you are occasionally guilty of biting off more than you can chew. Family affairs can be the source not only of great joy but sheer pleasure too. Home is where the heart is and laughter there is the best tonic you can ever have.

MOON OPPOSITION JUPITER

If you possess these two planets in opposition, you have a tendency to deny unpleasant truths about situations and people, even when the evidence is clear. This can mean you turn your generous nature on those who don't deserve it. Take care that you don't befriend people who then use you for their own ends. Your sensitive nature means you go to great lengths to avoid confrontations and would rather humour people than risk offending them and sparking a row. Emotionally, leave something in reserve. Give too much too quickly and you'll have nowhere to go or retreat to.

MOON CONJUNCT SATURN

This chilly aspect is a difficult one and causes you problems in forming relationships. Saturn's influence makes you cautious and pessimistic by nature. You work on the assumption that you should always expect the worse, and aren't surprised when that's normally what you get. The key to turning this around is seeing the glass half full, becoming more optimistic, and valuing who you are and what you do in life more fully. Often one of your parents can be dominated by the other and there is little love lost between them or between you and them. This can be indicative of a Victorian-type upbringing.

MOON SEXTILE SATURN

With the planets in this aspect, you have a strong desire to understand other people. You know that good communication is central to a happy life and a successful relationship in particular, and work hard to achieve this. You look for partners who share this same determination to be open and clear in relationships. Controlled emotions help you get to grips with situations that would freak others out.

MOON SQUARE SATURN

If you have this heavy aspect, you are rooted in the past and in particular with your relationship with your family, which still exerts a powerful hold over you. This can make you moody and prone to melancholy. The answer is to tap into self-reliance; you don't really need anyone to tell you who you are or who to be. You are copping out from your personal responsibilities. Too much work and not enough play can make you dull.

MOON TRINE SATURN

Ultra-caution is at work in you if you have this aspect. You will only throw yourself into a relationship if you are 100 per cent sure about it beforehand. On a more positive note, however, you know that you only get out of life what you put in. As a result of this, you treat people with the respect you expect to get in return. All this means that you may not have many close friends, but those you do have are friends for life. Your early years may not have been as comfortable, cosy or fun-loving as they were for other people. It's possible that much love came from your grandparents because your own parents had emotional issues between them that left you pushed you to one side. In the end you rose above it and through your gritty nature carved a niche for yourself.

MOON OPPOSITION SATURN

With this aspect in your chart, you can take life very seriously indeed. This may well be because you were taught duty and responsibility in your childhood. Because of this, you have a wisdom and outlook beyond your age, and you have always sought out the friendship of people older than you. Your partner may be someone who reflects the attitudes of your parents. Given all this, there is a chance, however, that you are something of a loner, even a recluse. If so, you need to learn to mix more and enjoy a richer social life. Take the good times as and when they come without analyzing them too closely. Friends are better than family as your family can often have you under their thumb. Remember you can choose your friends!

MOON CONJUNCT URANUS

With this restless aspect in your chart, you have a strong need for emotional freedom. You don't like being burdened by the expectations and preconceptions of others and tend to choose friends and partners who let you be yourself. Unsurprisingly, this means these people are similarly independent, free-spirited types. Your relationship with your mother could be described as tense as you both have differing views on behaviour.

MOON SEXTILE URANUS

You have a genius and uncanny intuition that many see as being way beyond your years; it makes people notice you. Yet you use this wisdom wisely, choosing partners who provide you with the mix of mental stimulation, love, logic and excitement you crave. Emotionally you are not someone who will go for the norm.

MOON SQUARE URANUS

This stressful aspect can make you too hot to handle at times, especially if you don't get your way. You are unpredictable and your short-fused temper regularly gets you into scrapes with friends and family. Many of your emotional problems stem from your early years. You may have been brought up too strictly or perhaps had no discipline at all, leaving you insecure and unsure of how to treat others' feelings. To win a person over, you need to honour your commitments and realize when you've overstepped the mark. You then need to apologize sincerely, with grace and humility.

MOON TRINE URANUS

Given the inquisitive intelligence indicated by this aspect, you are always open to original and novel experiences. As a result you lead a life that is full, with many friends drawn to your unusual way of embracing life and living. For true happiness choose a partner who shares this same bright intellect and passion for life. Emotionally you will be thrown into bizarre situations that would drive other people crazy, yet for you they are the oxygen you need to keep you and any relationship on its toes.

MOON OPPOSITION URANUS

With this hard aspect in your chart, you face frequent battles between the logical and emotional sides of your personality. This means you protect your emotions with a veneer of coldness and aloofness. You may also pick partners who are so ill-suited to your feelings that a relationship can never blossom. Your relationship with your mother constantly left you on your toes, so you find it hard to give of your emotions totally as you feel you don't really know where you stand. You must learn to trust, and trust can only come if you are prepared to give a person time. You must be patient and not give up the ghost.

MOON CONJUNCT NEPTUNE

You possess a very well-developed sense of romance, but it is hard for you to find amorous happiness because you concern yourself too much with how others feel. You have a tendency to daydream and can become completely lost in your fantasy world. Your biggest difficulty with this aspect is self-delusion. You see someone as you want them to be and not how they really are. This can lead to emotional disappointment when one day they fall off the pedestal you have put them on. It is hard for you to face the truth, as you hate anything that makes you face reality. Your relationship with your mother could have been confusing, or perhaps you didn't know everything that went on in her life so that she remains a mystery.

MOON SEXTILE NEPTUNE

The blend of imagination and sensitivity indicated by this warm aspect makes you a very artistic individual. You also have an altruistic impulse to help others less fortunate than you. This aspect is encouraged by your easy-going nature, which allows you to tolerate people who in the end may be out to take you for a ride. Channel your feelings at the movies, or through dance and drama, as you're better off learning quickly that your sensitivity needs protection at all times.

MOON SQUARE NEPTUNE

You can play games with yourself far too much. If you are faced with something unpleasant or unsavoury, you will reinvent the facts so that the problem looks utterly different. In fact, it isn't even a problem at all any longer. Yet if you face up to reality, rather than indulging in your fantasy world, you will find you can cope with the tough realities of life perfectly well. Your mother may have had problems such as being neurotic, with an inability to confront issues. This means your relationship with her could have become confused, as you may have ended up mothering her. Nothing wrong with that, but for your own emotional development, admit it. Life is filled with sacrifices and in this case, it's her image that must be seen honestly and truthfully.

MOON TRINE NEPTUNE

You enjoy using your artistic gifts and imagination to inspire and help others. In relationships, you can be attracted to people who share the same enlightened and open-minded outlook as you. Charitable to the end, you often worry more about the underdog than yourself. Yes, you can help those who can't help themselves but you also have a mission and purpose to love and be loved. So leave some quality time for someone to come in, scoop you up and pamper you. You may have inherited glamorous talents from your mother that bring out the best in you and others. Social graces are important: manners maketh a man.

MOON OPPOSITION NEPTUNE

The influence of Neptune conspires to make your grasp of what is true and false foggy. If you don't like what you see, you are only too willing to create an alternative reality that suits you better. This may mean you are susceptible to people who offer you this false land to live in, losing your identity in the process. To avoid this, you need to learn that life isn't all a bed of roses: there will be bad times as well as good ones. Both should be embraced in their own way. You also need to develop more self-confidence by setting yourself small, easily achievable goals. Taking to the bottle or drugs in an effort to chase away the blues will only lead to problems that spread dishonour and disillusionment. Your relationship with your mother is hard to define, as your impression of her may not be as she really is.

MOON CONJUNCT PLUTO

This highly charged aspect indicates that your emotions run very deep indeed. In fact, you have a tendency to get so intensely involved that you lose sight of everything else. This can show itself in the form of possessiveness and jealousy of your partner. It can also make you vengeful. You need to learn to lead your life with a lighter touch. This aspect neither forgives nor forgets, and remember the phrase, 'Hell hath no fury like a woman scorned'? Well, no matter what your gender, you have an attraction for women who have psychological problems. Don't let them take them out on you.

MOON SEXTILE PLUTO

You have deep-seated emotions but know how to control them. You are not a slave to them. This is not to say feelings aren't important to you – they are vitally important. However, you can keep things in perspective and also make room in your life for others, doing your best to help and understand their needs. In an intimate situation you need to have some kind of emotional involvement, otherwise sexually you will go unfulfilled.

MOON SQUARE PLUTO

Fear rules this aspect if it appears in your chart. You are so afraid of the future that you cling to the past. You are so terrified of being hurt in a close relationship that you opt for brief, fiery flings that burn out almost as soon as they have caught alight. This can make you emotionally demanding. You need to learn to embrace the future, and when you learn it isn't to be feared you will be ready to move on to happier times. Psychological turmoil could come from your relationship with your mother, which wasn't necessarily healthy. Perhaps you didn't get the nurturing or love you needed. It is very important to leave that emotional baggage behind, or you could end up emotionally bitter and twisted.

MOON TRINE PLUTO

You are someone who knows what they want and won't do anything by halves in an emotional or sexual situation. However, you are not someone who bestows their affections readily. Your emotions are heightened to such a degree that some folks will run scared, in which case don't cry over a wimp who is flakier than a chocolate bar. You crave a partner who can give you as good as you get. You are not interested in someone who is going to judge you by your money or your success in life. You will give your all, but it's all or nothing in return.

MOON OPPOSITION PLUTO

With this obsessive aspect in your life, you have an overwhelming need for affection, but if someone gets too close then you have no hesitation in backing off. You can be jealous and envious, with a need to be in total control. Such is your desire to 'own' someone that you can even resort to emotional blackmail and become vengeful when your feelings are not reciprocated. You are drawn to complex personalities who can cause you more pain than it is worth. Pitch your tent with them and you will have an episode that would get top ratings for any soap opera. Your relationship with your mother can be a battle of egos and psychological one-upmanship.

MOON CONJUNCT ASCENDANT

If you have this aspect in your chart, you are someone who is in a Catch 22 situation. On the one hand, you long for the love and affection a relationship brings, but on the other you are terrified of getting hurt by committing yourself to someone. The end result is that you are ultra-cautious in every move you make and don't take the leap of faith until you are really sure of your ground. Try not to give a false impression of yourself, otherwise when you do get involved with someone, they'll realize you're not the person they first fell for.

MOON SEXTILE ASCENDANT

You are extremely thin-skinned, easily hurt, gullible and emotional. As a result you suffer from an inferiority complex that can really hold you back. However, the good news is that you are someone who learns from experience and your skin is likely to thicken a little as you grow older and wiser and see that people think more of you than you realize. You exude a compassion that comes into its own the more you get to know someone.

MOON SQUARE ASCENDANT

With this aspect in your life, familiarity breeds contempt, plus you face the risk of being trapped in your past, especially if the Moon is rooted in the 4th house. You find it difficult to break from the established patterns of your upbringing, even when you know they are destructive. You have a tendency to indulge in self-pity, something that can make you a target for others to prey upon. You must look for ways to break this cycle and move into a world in which the promise of the future far outweighs the memories of the past. Your personality can come across as saccharine sweet or moaning and complaining, constantly making excuses for your own shortcomings. Look on the bright side.

MOON TRINE ASCENDANT

Your creative personality and laid-back approach to life make you popular. Your giving nature and willingness to help others only adds to your appeal. However, you must be wary of those who might try to exploit this, as not everyone is as selfless as you. Your personality is gilded with such easy-going feelings that you manage to make the people you meet feel very special. This gift for being able to mix with princes or paupers is what makes folks rush to you like an agony aunt; a shoulder to cry on is one thing, but don't let them take advantage of you.

MOON OPPOSITION ASCENDANT

If you have this challenging aspect in your chart, you have a deep-seated need for emotional security and tend to have intense relationships that feed this. You are never happier than when you know you are loved and needed by someone. You must be careful what such relationships do to you, however, as you have a habit of moulding yourself to fit in with your partner. You can lose sight of the real you in the process. Because the Moon habits your Descendant, emotionally you are rarely satisfied and can be too demanding on a partner's feelings. So don't chase off a prospective Romeo or Juliet by smothering the affair at birth.

MOON CONJUNCT MIDHEAVEN

You have a huge capacity for caring for others, both at home and in the wider world. The sign on the Midheaven will give you a strong clue as to how this will be directed. Careerwise you can be an enormous public success. This kind of aspect often means public approval – assuming the rest of the aspects to the MC and Moon are positive. It can also be an indicator of fame or notoriety.

MOON SEXTILE MIDHEAVEN

With this winning aspect in your chart, you will have a strong need to express the potential indicated by the sign on your Midheaven so you should pay particular attention to that section. Winning the support of the public or your family is good for your career. You will receive the back-up of those who are in a position to help secure your success.

MOON SQUARE MIDHEAVEN

If you have this hard aspect in your chart, you are likely to come up against frequent frustrations in the pursuit of your goals. The obstacles may be self-inflicted, perhaps because of a lack of effort or focus, or they may be placed there by people trying to deny you what you want. You need to develop persistence and strength to overcome these hurdles. Emotionally you may be ill-suited for a career or vocation you would love to do. Alternatively, you may be forced into ambitions by your parents or family when you'd rather be doing something else; your heart is elsewhere. It is very important that you pursue a career (look at the sign on the MC) that helps you occupy your comfort zone and to hell with other folks' expectations of you.

MOON TRINE MIDHEAVEN

This excellent aspect helps you exude all the qualities and personal characteristics of the sign on your Midheaven. Study this section closely to discover what those are and draw on them in pursuit of your goals. In the meantime, this aspect can win you supporters and admirers in the sphere of your career. They will help you get on. If you follow a vocation that is caring and compassionate, you will go straight to the top. Public recognition will surely follow as you hit the right note in your profession. This aspect is all about doing what you are naturally drawn to – any occupation that jars your senses is wrong for you.

MOON OPPOSITION MIDHEAVEN

You can feel strongly rooted in the past, both in terms of your family and your interests, which may lean towards history in all its forms. You are also someone who keeps your innermost thoughts to yourself and need an inner sanctum where you can protect and nurture this private side of you. Your biggest challenge is if you have to work away from where you feel most protected. You may give up an opportunity because you don't want to go away from home. Nostalgia is a big problem with this aspect as you cling on tenaciously and lose chances on the way. It's worth cultivating a career where you intend to settle down.

The Aspects of Mercury

Mercury's aspects to the Sun and Moon are under those planets.

MERCURY CONJUNCT VENUS

Because Mercury and Venus can never be more than 75 degrees apart, the only aspects they can form are the conjunction and sextile. If you have Mercury in conjunction with Venus, you have a highly developed sense of beauty and may even have a career that draws on this. You are a relaxed, laid-back person with a charming and diplomatic nature, but there is also a side of you that is financially astute and geared to making money. An appreciation or talent for the arts combined with mental agility enables you to create things that other people will be impressed by, whether singing, dancing, acting or going down the crafts route. You also have a talent to amuse.

MERCURY SEXTILE VENUS

With this aspect, you too have a strong appreciation of beauty, and may be gifted in the visual arts and writing. An easy-going person who doesn't find compromise difficult, you get on well with most people, although you are repelled by overly aggressive and forceful personalities. You are a natural tactician and make an excellent ambassador for yourself. You have the ability to blow your own trumpet without people realizing you're doing it. You have a love of youth and children, and need to feel alive and always doing something purposeful, whether working or playing.

MERCURY CONJUNCT MARS

You are the owner of a very bright and quick mind but have trouble keeping your opinion to yourself. No-one doubts that what you have to say is interesting and worth hearing, but you must not jump in when others are speaking. Advice should be delivered only when it is requested. More generally, you must learn to draw on your past mistakes. You can be very opinionated and must learn to curb what you see as being forthright and honest, but what other folks can see as plain rude. Learn to zip your lip – you don't have to fill every silence. Remember, sometimes it can be golden.

MERCURY SEXTILE MARS

Such is your curiosity, you will continue soaking up information like a sponge until you draw your last breath. You are a natural, entertaining communicator but you also know how to listen to others, an endearing trait that wins you many friends. You have a deep-rooted dislike of people who lie and cheat; honesty is the best policy is your undoubted life maxim. You can channel your talents through exploits that call upon both brain and brawn.

MERCURY SQUARE MARS

You are certainly not short of energy and opinions, but what you lack sometimes is the ability to marshal these qualities to your best advantage. Too often you start things without finishing them or jump into an argument without having listened properly to what others were saying. You can also pass yourself off as an expert, when you know deep down you are nothing of the sort. You are also capable of being rather too sharp with your tongue and need to watch out for this if you want to achieve your goals. People in glasshouses shouldn't throw stones and yet sometimes you have a whole armful of rocks and boulders to hurl at people. Perhaps you should give a thought to the fact you could shatter your own world by hurling them.

MERCURY TRINE MARS

With this aspect you have a choice: to use your undoubted abilities or to fritter them away. You have a sharp mind and a lot of creative ability, but too often it gets you nowhere because you simply can't be bothered to apply it. The longer you allow this to happen, the more frustrated you will be when you finally realize your mistake. By harnessing your skills you could make a great sportsman or woman, orator or a creative writer. In fact with Mercury's mind and Mars's action, there is little you cannot do by being single-minded and alert. When opportunity strikes, be sure to grab it.

MERCURY OPPOSITION MARS

You need to learn to think first, act later. You are intelligent and the owner of an agile mind, but you are too quick to fall into arguments and are poor at compromising once the insults start flying. The result is that you risk damaging friendships and your prospects of progress. You must become more measured and learn to weigh up the evidence before leaping in with judgements that may be wrong.

There may be a tendency to take on too much because your mind flits around all kinds of subjects and ideas. If you can't settle on one venture or enterprise, you may take on too much. The result will be lots of projects started but none completed. Be more committed to what you begin.

MERCURY CONJUNCT JUPITER

You have an ability to communicate your wisdom easily and in a way that involves others. You have an ongoing hunger to learn more at every turn in life. Every now and again, however, you must learn to sit back and smell the roses.

This is a splendid aspect for learning and study. You yearn for knowledge; whether it's doing a local quiz, reading travel guides to faraway and exotic places or visiting the local historic site down the road, you have a hunger for learning. If you remember that knowledge is power, you won't go far wrong. Travel is essential to this aspect, whether mental or physical. Boredom will strike unless you are doing or thinking about something. Ideas that spring to mind can be your lucky break.

MERCURY SEXTILE JUPITER

With this jolly aspect in your chart, you will have a real gift for passing on the knowledge that you are always hungry to accumulate. You may become a teacher or mentor and combine this with a love of travelling. Wherever you go, however, you have a low tolerance for those who bend and abuse the truth, and you will always be vocal about your feelings in this respect. Matters of law or information intrigue you because, for you, a little learning is far from a dangerous thing. In fact, it is essential.

MERCURY SQUARE JUPITER

Your butterfly mind is constantly looking to cut corners. You are always looking to become an instant expert, always looking for ways to avoid the hard study necessary to acquire real, deep knowledge. You also have a weakness for playing fast and loose with the truth and can be naive when dealing with others. Be careful you don't get burned by people out to exploit this innocence.

Exaggeration is a problem that can come between you and success. Talk is cheap so be careful what you say as one day someone will hold you to it. Don't make decisions based on one fact; it is important to research whatever you are intending to get involved in. Be warned about fraud and conmen (or women!) as you are easy prey.

MERCURY TRINE JUPITER

You are blessed with an extremely positive, optimistic outlook that, if channelled properly, will be the key to your success. You will not only see the best in people, you will bring it out too. This, allied to your tolerant and generous nature, will make you a popular figure. Anything international or intellectual is right up your street. It's possible you will deal with foreign places or even live in another land. If so, you'll find that alien cultures and countries will give you joy through their differences from your native land. Learning a language might be your passport to success away from home.

MERCURY OPPOSITION JUPITER

You need to learn the art of shutting up and listening. Too often you behave like the fount of all knowledge, even though you are patently not that. This is not to say you aren't full of curiosity, but you must learn to combine this with hard work and study. If you are honest with yourself about your weaknesses, your strengths will shine through. 'Ask me no questions and I will tell you no lies' is an appropriate adage as sometimes you might be a tad economic with the truth to appear more interesting. Indecision can come from having too many leads. Instead of settling on just one, you want to try them all. This can prove costly. Wasted time and effort is just as expensive as throwing money down the drain.

MERCURY CONJUNCT SATURN

This aspect in your chart indicates you are a serious-minded and studious person, with bags of common sense to draw upon. Because your mind is always hard at work, some see you as slightly standoffish and aloof, but you do work well on your own rather than as a member of a team. Be careful how you deal with setbacks, however, as you can be prone to dwelling on them and becoming depressed and disheartened. Anything connected with science, mathematics, history or geography may be a boon to you as you have a fascination for anything factual.

MERCURY SEXTILE SATURN

You have the ability to shine at one subject. You are constantly learning and are fascinated by something that could be a *cause célèbre.* You are honest and plain-speaking and are drawn to people with similar qualities. You are much better working alone rather than with masses of people. You are committed and conscientious, and when you take something on you are determined to see it through. You make a fantastic committee person and would be suited to local politics or community ventures.

MERCURY SQUARE SATURN

You have difficulty unleashing your imagination and as a result can have a very blinkered, narrow-minded view of the world. You can be myopic and closed to new experiences, partly because of your fear of the challenges they may pose. You need to overcome this if you are going to succeed, otherwise you will be continually held back in life. You may want to write but find it a painful experience as every word will be torn from your brain, then you have to constantly go back and decide whether it's the right one. The same goes for communications generally. You want to do so much but can be held back by your own lack of confidence and self-criticism. You want everything perfect but the sooner you understand that perfection is never going to be possible, the sooner you will allow yourself the odd mistake. Go easy on yourself.

MERCURY TRINE SATURN

You know how to maximize your mental abilities and are used to acknowledging and working within your limitations. This makes you someone whom others respect and confide in easily. Organized and conscientious, if you do something, you do it well. In fact, you find it easy to delegate just so long as you've been able to take your 'student' through the pattern first. Everything does have a formula with you. 'If you want a job doing well then do it yourself' is the right approach if you find you've got idiots around you – and there will be many at times. You will enjoy making lists, putting things together rationally and are fascinated by anything that is historical or from the past. A wry, dry sense of humour can tickle many folks' fancy!

MERCURY OPPOSITION SATURN

Such is your lack of self-belief that you resort to politics and scheming to get the recognition you crave. The irony is that if you concentrated on using your natural intelligence instead, you wouldn't need to play tricks on anyone. The key thing is for you to start believing in yourself; once you do, success will follow. You must be careful not to tar people with the same brush as yourself. You may be too quick to generalize and forget that we are all individuals. Don't write off ideas as rubbish, run them past people who know and even if others rain on your parade, that's no reason to give something up. Calculated risks are worth taking.

MERCURY CONJUNCT URANUS

As far as you are concerned, the worst thing in the world is boredom. You can't abide it, so busy and perpetually inquisitive is your mind. You have a particular fascination with the mechanics of the world, how things work and why they do so. You need a partner who is like-minded and has a similar low boredom threshold. A fascination for astrology, New Age subjects and the occult is your cup of tea (tasseography too, if you fancy!). Your mind is very open to new ideas and you are the opposite of a fuddy-duddy. When it comes to modern gadgets and inventions, you want to be first in the queue to try things out. Travel is good for you and the more impromptu or out of the blue, the better.

MERCURY SEXTILE URANUS

You've all the brainpower in the world at your disposal. You are switched on and clever with a wide-range of interests, a real Renaissance person. The only downside to this is that occasionally you need to impose a little discipline. Otherwise things can become chaotic and lacking in focus. Take one flash of inspiration and follow it through, as you've an intuition for knowing what people want at the time they want it. You are ahead of the pack when it comes to ideas.

MERCURY SQUARE URANUS

You are something of a controversialist. You behave as if you know it all and have a habit of alienating people with your contrary opinions. Your inability to compromise affects you in both your professional and personal life. Be warned of bigotry, hypocrisy or being vocally extreme – it can land you in hot water! You can also be drawn to people or cults who will see you as gullible and impressionable to what they preach. The trouble with this aspect is this: if what you or others theorize doesn't work out in practice, it's because there is a catch that you may find out about too late. Beware of anyone who befriends you too quickly – they are up to something.

MERCURY TRINE URANUS

You could be the model for Rodin's famous sculpture *The Thinker*. You take time to mull things over before speaking and have a love of diverse conversation. Your inquiring and curious mind is keen to get stuck into anything that stimulates and also makes you good at problem-solving. Yet you are good at sharing knowledge too and make a good teacher. You are drawn to things metaphysical, New Age or astrological. Travel is important to you if only so you can discover how other people live or what can be unearthed in faraway places. Unusual thought forms and voyages of discovery are what you need to bring out your ingenious intellect.

MERCURY OPPOSITION URANUS

You have a naughty habit of telling people all the time that you're right about absolutely everything, even when you know you are in the wrong. This utter inability to meet people halfway is a real Achilles heel because it has the effect of antagonizing almost everyone. You will not achieve the long-term happiness you crave unless you learn to give an inch or two. Your views are far too extreme and can offend and annoy people you don't even know. Rumours can be rife. Curiosity killed the cat, in which case you must be careful as you only have nine lives! When traveling, odd things may happen that can cause you to divert from your chosen course, not always for the better.

MERCURY CONJUNCT NEPTUNE

You are something of a master of self-deception. Your sensitive nature makes you want to soften or sweeten every bad situation you face. As a result, you are always idealizing partners or seeing more good in a bad situation simply so you can cope. This isn't going to help and you need to face up to reality more often if you want to fulfil your potential. Your supremely artistic nature is channelled beautifully if you take up an art or craft that brings out your hidden talents.

MERCURY SEXTILE NEPTUNE

You are blessed with psychic powers and should trust in them implicitly. You are reluctant to trust first impressions, preferring instead to delve deeper so that you can discover the real truth. Because of this, you are drawn to people with a more spiritual outlook on life. Your compassionate nature is best served by working for charities or with children, as your unconditional nature is keen to sacrifice for the cause of others. However, don't be used as a doormat.

MERCURY SQUARE NEPTUNE

So powerful is your escapist imagination, it often runs away with itself, particularly when you face harsh or ugly truths. This habit of glossing over the hard facts is a particular problem when you are dealing with affairs of the heart. You can persuade yourself that even the most fleeting flirtations are serious love affairs. Lies and liars will abound in your world, whether you have to tell the odd white lie or are a victim of other folks' false charms, you must guard against the phoney. Don't believe all you hear or what you're told. You must escape back to the real world.

MERCURY TRINE NEPTUNE

With this charming aspect in your chart, you have an artistic side that you find easy to express in the most imaginative ways. You are tolerant of other people, too. Yet you are also a self-contained soul, not reliant on other people's happiness to find it yourself. You are never happier than when living in your own mind. You should try creative writing, photography, painting or anything that allows you to use your wonderful technicolor mind to its best advantage. Anything psychic or spiritual will bring out the best in you, too. Doing things that transcend the ordinary and material appeals to your aesthetic nature.

MERCURY OPPOSITION NEPTUNE

There's an air of paranoia about you. You have great potential and a fine imagination, but unfortunately that imagination is too often used to convince yourself that you and your happiness are under threat from others. The truth is that no-one is out to get you or trip you up. Accept that and you will be halfway to achieving the breakthrough you seek. Believing you have secret enemies is your biggest problem. Remember that it's all in the mind.

MERCURY CONJUNCT PLUTO

You are gifted with a curious, driven brain that can get to the very bottom of subjects. Your determined streak can cause you problems in dealing with your nearest and dearest because you always expect to get your own way. You can become totally obsessed or fixated with one train of thought. This aspect can make you a bit of a James Bond or Agatha Christie. You are always digging deep, but sometimes the answer can be right in front of you. You are a creature of psychology, which means you come across as deep, intense and secretive – some folks may even see you as devious. Perhaps they are right as you can be controlling and certainly don't trust anyone easily. A fascination for the occult and horror can sometimes give the impression that you are more macabre than you really are, but you kind of like the label of being ghoulish!

MERCURY SEXTILE PLUTO

With this aspect to your chart you have the ability to analyze, illuminate and understand even the most hard to fathom subjects. You may have psychic abilities and be totally into belief forms that get into life–death interests, such as reincarnation or karma. You have an easy way with most people but reject anyone who practises any kind of deceit or deviousness. You take nothing lightly and will happily look into what people say just to see if there is truth in it. Study or travel that enables you to dig deep – yes, even archaeology – will be good for your brain.

MERCURY SQUARE PLUTO

You are easily distracted so tend to give up on things. You need to develop better powers of concentration and become better at sticking to a subject. You have a sharp tongue and need to be careful it doesn't cut those around you. Be wary of compulsive behaviour that doesn't allow you any leeway. If you sum up someone's character wrongly on first meeting, give yourself a break and admit it, if only to yourself. The same goes for anything where you feel driven to the negative and yet the outcome turns out to be more positive. Psychologically, you can find your mind journeying down dim and dank pathways. This can lead to problems with your sex life or make you more morbid than your average person. Getting involved with criminal people or activities must be avoided at all costs. Get into subjects that allow you to strip away the layers until you reach the truth. This will help you get over any hidden blockages you may have.

MERCURY TRINE PLUTO

You have strong powers of concentration and can stick to a task for as long as it takes. As a result, you are capable of making the very best of your creativity. You set high standards when choosing partners but reward them with a devoted and giving nature.

Subjects ranging from the occult to forensic science attract you. You could easily be involved in areas that most folks would find off-putting or hard to understand. You know that someone's got to do what other people are too sensitive or arty to do and that suits you. An easy-going approach to what the rest of the world finds morbid, or has the 'ugh' factor, brings out the best in you.

MERCURY OPPOSITION PLUTO

You may find yourself frustrated in the pursuit of your goals because you are unable to face challenges from others along the way. You are also naturally confrontational, which drives people away. You also have a habit of manufacturing crises just so you can demonstrate how to deal with them. There can be a self-destructive side to your nature. Just when things appear to be going well, you can suddenly shut off all interest. If you can't get your way, it is all too easy for you to abuse any power you have. Your occasional below-the-belt tactics will come back to haunt you, as what comes around, goes around. An interest in psychology should be used for the good.

MERCURY CONJUNCT ASCENDANT

A tendency to be wrapped up in your own world can come over to others as smugness or self-satisfaction. Others, however, are happy to listen to you rattling on about yourself because you are so lively and entertaining. You are constantly on a life-learning curve with this aspect so, whatever your age, education is very important to you. Your youthful spirit can often make it hard for others to put an age to you.

If Mercury is in the 12th house, you are more secretive and less likely to reveal your ideas or brainwaves – excellent for an interest in psychic, spiritual or New Age subjects. Mercury in the 1st is much more indicative of a live wire wanting to go here, there and everywhere, and wanting to gather knowledge and information freely.

MERCURY SEXTILE ASCENDANT

You've a natural ability to express yourself, often in a witty and highly entertaining manner that appeals to a lot of people. This means you find success in your career, although you have a habit of allowing colleagues to overshadow you. Younger people can be good for you, showing you the error of your ways or creating opportunities you wouldn't have had without them. Travel is good for you but take short breaks rather than long holidays.

MERCURY SQUARE ASCENDANT

Outwardly you appear so sure of yourself that some think you have a superiority complex. Yet inside you, it's the complete opposite. You are so lacking in self-confidence you struggle to do yourself justice, so much so that people find you suspicious. Watch out for rumours and gossip – either about you or spread by you. You might even be accused of libel and you don't want that! Speak as you find but don't be willing to believe the worst of people or a situation until you are sure. You must learn to be more committed to your ideas; a scatterbrain approach will create the wrong impression to everyone.

MERCURY TRINE ASCENDANT

You are a focused individual who knows what you want to say and how to say it. You combine this focus with an openness that welcomes and learns from the opinions of others. These two qualities combine to good effect, both in your private and professional lives.

Your travels can bring opportunity or a lucky break you weren't expecting, so feel free to start conversations with fellow travellers. Writing, reading, arithmetic – anything that enables you to use your mind will bring you success. Communication is what makes you tick and your personality comes across accordingly. You seem eager and willing to learn – this is not just endearing, but can be the making of you.

MERCURY OPPOSITION ASCENDANT

At the root of your personality is an aching to be liked. You sit around gauging what others think and say before pitching in with an opinion that fits in with what has gone before. If you only let the real you off the leash, you'd win much more of the respect and admiration you are so desperate to win.

With Mercury on the Descendant, you will meet the love of your life either on your travels or at work. The key to a successful relationship is to always discuss and talk about how you feel and what you want from life. An affair or marriage where you can go off together is so important to the development of your partnership. Otherwise you might end up so bored with your other half that you go off elsewhere to find what you're lacking at home.

MERCURY CONJUNCT MIDHEAVEN

Having this aspect in your chart indicates you are a good communicator with an ability to learn fast. You have a strong desire to be acknowledged publicly for these attributes. Any career that enables you to write, read, inform or talk will bring out the best in you. Throw in some travel too and you'll be as happy as Larry. You need to be on the go all the time. However, although you give the impression you're busy, make sure you are as you know what a great actor you can be!

MERCURY SEXTILE MIDHEAVEN

With this positive aspect to your chart, you need much mental stimulation. If you don't get it you will tend to change course on a regular basis. By doing this, you will fail to bring out the best of yourself and risk a life of eternal restlessness. Careerwise, communication, travel, learning and study should be at the heart of things. You have an eloquence and ability to do two things at once that makes you a pleasure to work with. Networking and making contacts is very important to your professional progress.

MERCURY SQUARE MIDHEAVEN

When times are tough, you struggle emotionally and your nerves get the better of you. This is a particular problem if Mercury has heavy aspects elsewhere in your chart. You must be careful of the company you keep in your career. People might steal your ideas and you will fail to get credit where it's due and your chance of success and promotion disappears. You must be careful of people who are natural-born liars and who prey on your gullible and impressionable persona. Don't speak out of turn and certainly don't try to keep up with the Joneses as they will turn round and betray you as soon as look at you. Your best bet is to find a vocation that enables you to become a master of it rather than a Jack-of-all-trades; that way people look up to you because you are the best in your field.

MERCURY TRINE MIDHEAVEN

With this positive aspect to your chart, you really need to be involved in a profession in which your intellect and ability to communicate with others is fully utilized and tested. Follow a vocation that enables you to use your mind. A boring, nine-to-five existence is your idea of hell. Whether it's writing or teaching, travelling or networking, the more people you can meet and situations you can enjoy, the better for you. You won't sit still for a minute and what's more, unlike someone with Mercury square to the Midheaven, you will also finish almost everything you start. You won't assume that what you have learned is all there is to it, either. Apply your brainpower and intellect to anything and you will come up with ingenious suggestions that bring untold fame and fortune.

MERCURY OPPOSITION MIDHEAVEN

If you have this jittery aspect, it indicates a strong fascination with your family and its history. Your relationship with your parents will be strong too, similar to one you might have with a sibling. Alternatively, you may have a brother or sister who was a father or mother figure to you when you were growing up.

You may end up with two homes or two professions with this cosmic combination. What's for sure is you find it hard to go to work and are much better carrying on a career from home. So the more you can do with loved ones in a family business, for instance, the better. If not, find a space at home from where you can run a cottage industry, using modern communications to stay in touch from your study or kitchen. By looking after your need to be where you feel happiest, you will give yourself the best chance of professional success.

The Aspects of Venus

Venus's aspects to Sun, Moon and Mercury are under those planets.

VENUS CONJUNCT MARS

With this aspect, the powers of Venus and Mars combine to make you someone who is ruled by your desires, either physically or psychologically. You pursue your goals with drive and determination, but if the passion cools you can turn your attention elsewhere in the blink of an eye. Sexual and sensual, you are hot to trot in most flirtatious directions. However, you do like your man or woman to be beautiful or there has to be some sexual chemistry. You won't jump into bed with just anyone. There has to be something there to cultivate or build upon. Using the word 'sexy' in its broadest sense, everything you do is done with a degree of passion.

VENUS SEXTILE MARS

You have a gift for seeing both sides of the story and have an optimistic, loving, tolerant nature. However, you have a weakness when it comes to money, and find it hard to rein in your spending sometimes. Sexually, you are very active but need to find someone who appeals to your heart. You enjoy the sensuality of it all, but where there's no feeling there's not enough there.

VENUS SQUARE MARS

This is a difficult aspect, resulting in a tendency to take much more than you give. You will expect much from friends and partners but reciprocate little. You also fail to take responsibility for your own actions and blame others for setbacks. Uncompromising behaviour can lead to all sorts of relationship dramas. You can easily be one half of a love–hate relationship defined by that old phrase 'Can't live with 'em, can't live without 'em.' You can be used sexually or you can do the using. This aspect makes no bones about using your powers of attraction to get what you want, but sometimes this aspect can mean you fancy those who don't fancy you and vice versa.

VENUS TRINE MARS

Your fun-loving, affectionate nature makes you highly popular. You have a particular affinity with children, who respond to your warmth and general air of jollity. Sexually you are quite a catch. Kind and sensitive to your partner's needs, you know erogenous zones as well as the road map of your town and aren't a selfish lover who satisfies your own needs only. However, if your other half is frigid or doesn't turn you on, after a while you will have no compunction in meeting your sexual needs elsewhere.

VENUS OPPOSITION MARS

You need to take lessons in the art of compromise. Even though you are highly sensitive yourself, you don't think twice about hurting other people's feelings with your hasty conclusions and caustic tongue. You need to listen to others and remember they have feelings, too. You can be very flirtatious, which can lead you into trouble, mainly because in the end someone may want to go that little bit further than you. Playing hard to get is part of your nature but you also have a reputation to think of.

VENUS CONJUNCT JUPITER

This hedonistic aspect denotes someone who is so jolly, generous and open-minded that you give everyone the benefit of the doubt, even those whose motives are plainly dubious. You will, of course, be taken for a ride every now and again but you will not hold grudges. Needless to say, this makes you very popular. Luxury-loving, you can spend money like water and hang the consequences. This cosmic combination does help you to make money as well but you would be best to invest, otherwise you will end up with little to show for your cash. This aspect indicates someone who can be lucky in love, too.

VENUS SEXTILE JUPITER

You have a sunny, outgoing disposition, and are honest and generous to a tee. But you are no pushover. You expect others to abide by the same high standards as you and will avoid sly or duplicitous types like the plague. There is a charm about you that comes from enjoyment of life. You have an active social life but prefer to mix with people you know, rather than doing things just for the sake of it. Your popularity is part of your charm, and with it comes a reputation of someone who is fair and just. Your luck comes through your dealings with people in a courteous manner.

VENUS SQUARE JUPITER

You are defensive by nature and can be an awkward customer to deal with when you are under pressure. You are inclined to expect that if you do someone a favour, they will do you a favour in return. There is nothing unconditional about this aspect; on the contrary the Latin maxim *quid pro quo* would be your motto under any coat of arms. You can attract greedy, avaricious people and you yourself can want more than you are prepared to give back. Nothing is for nothing in this world and if you want to keep someone's love, friendship or support then you need to show it. Taking liberties or using someone else to bankroll you will lead to an expensive lawsuit or settlement.

VENUS TRINE JUPITER

With this happy aspect in your chart, you have a tendency to keep your problems to yourself. You hate the idea of being a burden to others so always pretend things are fine and dandy, even when they aren't. At the same time, you have a real knack for cheering up others when they are feeling low. You are also excellent at motivating people to make more of themselves.

Money can be made through international investments and by garnering support or connections in foreign places. Your love life has the potential to be a pleasure and joy; the key to finding your soul mate is meeting someone who makes you laugh. You have expensive tastes, and usually (unless Saturn aspects are very hard in your horoscope) the wherewithal will be provided to have and enjoy them.

VENUS OPPOSITION JUPITER

At heart you are insecure and so are on a constant search for approval and get quite upset when you don't get it. Yet when it comes to romance, you avoid commitment because you can't face the responsibility or don't want to get hurt. You are a pleasure seeker and enjoy all that goes with partying and fun. However, before you go off doing your thing make sure you've enough money to do it. Be warned of trying to keep up with wasteful friends, as they will cost you a fortune. Things bought on credit have to be paid for one day so don't spend the earth for a moment's pleasure as the novelty will have worn off when it comes to pay the piper.

Your love life can be fun but that's just the problem. You could be treated (or treat someone) like a toy, and once your feelings have been trifled with, cast aside. Time to get serious about what you want in life, and sometimes the best things in life are free.

VENUS CONJUNCT SATURN

You are serious and honest, and are good at dealing with financial matters. Your straightforward nature means you often make concessions to people, although you may resent doing so. It is very important that you learn to express how you feel for someone or you could lose the love of your life. You refuse to commit to anyone unless you are totally sure of their feelings for you – and yet how can they know how you feel unless you tell them? You are a kind, loyal, devoted person who deserves someone as decent as you. They are there but don't be afraid to make the first move. You may be attracted to someone who is of an age that is very different to your own.

VENUS SEXTILE SATURN

You have a willingness to learn from older, wiser heads around you and are prepared to work hard to reach your goals. You will also endure as many setbacks as it takes to achieve them. People regard you as a safe pair of hands, which will help you along the way. Financially, you can be very clever with cash. Going for investments and non-risk savings will help you find the economic security you want when you are older. When it comes to love, you are attracted to steady, sure types (unless Uranus is aspected in your chart). In fact, the more traditional and conservative someone is, the more attractive you should find them.

VENUS SQUARE SATURN

With this dour aspect in your chart you have a fear of being exploited by others, which makes you defensive and uneasy in your dealings with people. Friendships will be difficult unless you learn to trust people more. You are suspicious of anyone who shows more than a passing interest in you. Get it into your head that you deserve happiness in love and not everyone sees you as a meal ticket. The problem is you are likely to have a wasted affair or a relationship that fails, which puts you off love or sex even more. Don't fill yourself up with guilt or grief. It is part of the Saturn test and he rewards those who pass the test well in the future. It's possible you might not find your soul mate until later on in life but don't give up on yourself.

Financial struggles are often evident with this aspect, but mainly because you don't go about earning in the right way – you miss a trick or two. So open your eyes and look around, believe in yourself and go after what you think you can't do. Sometimes a little courage and the odd risk will do you good. Otherwise, you will end up with nothing because you believe that's what you're worth. Nonsense.

VENUS TRINE SATURN

You are someone who, as the old saying goes, hides your light under a bushel. Although you are creative and highly capable, especially in money matters, you feel uncomfortable pushing yourself forward. This may hold you back unless you overcome it. You are a good judge of character and should use this to further your ambitions.

Your love life will work out wonderfully, given time. You are not likely to find your heart's desire or soul mate immediately. Like vintage wine, you get better with age and so do your financial and romantic prospects. Along the way you will learn from experience, but in the end you will find the devoted, caring and kindly partner you deserve. Money-wise, you have an instinctive knack for investments and the like.

VENUS OPPOSITION SATURN

You are forever putting yourself down at the expense of others. Yet if you only learned to appreciate your many strengths, you would see you are every bit as good as the next person. Once you have done this, you will be ready to accept any of the challenges you set yourself. It's possible your father or a father figure withheld affection from you, or they put everything into material things so that you had to earn their love or earn everything they gave you. This can make close relationships difficult, as you might suspect your partner of being calculated or cunning. 'What's in it for them,' I can hear you thinking. The one person who can get you out of this vicious circle is you, as you were the one who got yourself into it in the first place. Oh, and with a little help from your parents, too. Financially, you must be more generous with yourself. Your image can sometimes leave much to be desired so appear smart and approachable, and you'll be amazed at how far you can go in terms of love and money.

VENUS CONJUNCT URANUS

You have a vivacious and infectious personality, full of *joie de vivre*. You prefer the company of people who have a maverick, unpredictable personality and avoid dull sorts like the plague. In relationships, you may prefer to remain unattached, free to follow your love of life. Be warned of an easy-come, easy-go attitude to money and also be warned of wanting to do things always on the spur of the moment. This can prove costly and remember that novelties do wear off, whether it be in love or business. You have a fascinating charm, but it's what lies underneath that's more important. Experiment with your appearance as the more you can reinvent yourself, the more admirers you will make.

VENUS SEXTILE URANUS

With this sparkling aspect in your chart, you have a love of socializing and interacting with others. You have a lot of interesting and lively friends, partly because you are someone who prefers compromise to confrontation at any cost. Friends can be lovers, too, and it's more than likely that you will find your soul mate in someone you already know. You might even enjoy a platonic relationship, then one day Cupid will strike and then – kapow! Moneywise, you can earn a lot *and* learn a lot by being your own boss. You hate people ruling you or telling you what to do, so show them how it's done by doing what you excel at, however unusual.

VENUS SQUARE URANUS

You are someone who puts yourself first. You are quite comfortable being single and if you are ever in a relationship will be the one to break things off when the initial excitement fades. You have double standards when it comes to those who are close to you, adopting one set of rules for yourself and a completely different set for them.

Commitment is such a no-no for you and yet you may learn this the hard way. There's a saying that we get the person we deserve when it comes to relationships, so you will either attract someone who is ultra-possessive, which will drive you away OR someone just like you, who is permissive to a degree, which will annoy you too. Unless you can find someone who wants an equally 'open' affair as you, you are best off doing your own independent thing. Oh, and you will always find someone who wants to share your bed because you've a way with you that is desirable and attractive but you can also be hurtful and selfish. Financially, take care against taking risks big or small with ventures or expenditures that don't do the job you want them to.

VENUS TRINE URANUS

'You only get out from life what you put in' could be your motto. You are someone who lives life to the hilt and works hard to make sure everyone around you has a good time too. As a result, you are surrounded by a lot of happy, life-affirming friends. You have a glow about you – call it charisma, call it magnetism, but whatever it is, it is electrifying.

You can stumble upon the love of your life quite by accident, or perhaps your relationship is very unusual in some way, maybe because of how it began or how it is. A love affair will be long-lasting if you start off as buddies with an intuitive link that joins you together. It will also benefit if you give each other the freedom to do what you want (apart from sexually!). You can find success and riches by pursuing a profession that is very unusual and inventive.

VENUS OPPOSITION URANUS

You have a strong anarchist streak within you and struggle to deal with authority of any kind. You are forever doing all sorts of unwise, often unpleasant, things purely for the sake of it. You can be someone who uses people. As soon as they have served a purpose, you drop them like a hot brick. Your rebellious energy could be put to much better use by latching onto something that interests you and building it up into a mission or profession that no-one else would dare touch. You are a freewheeler in life and the minute someone tries to pigeonhole you, you hit the roof. Your love life can be interesting: a cocktail of different types of partners, as you're never quite sure what you want. Look for more temperate aspects in your horoscope to tone this down.

VENUS CONJUNCT NEPTUNE

You are a dreamer and a fantasist who withdraws into an alternative universe when confronted by aggressive or angry people. Your sensitive nature means you have great artistic flair, which you use to your advantage in your career. You biggest problem is in love. You are easily hurt in relationships; you are so keen for someone to be your Cinderella or Prince Charming that you paint this fairy-tale affair in your mind's eye and then one day you see the beast, instead of beauty. You either run for cover or batten down the hatches and pretend all is well. It is essential that in love you see someone for what they really are, otherwise your starry affair will bring you down to earth with a bump. Happiness can be found but you must accept someone warts and all.

VENUS SEXTILE NEPTUNE

You are imbued with great compassion, which makes you adept at solving other people's problems. Sometimes your romantic and emotional nature has allowed you to get carried away and you find it less easy to deal with your own pain than that of others. Involvement in the arts or a charity will bring out the very best in you. It's likely you could meet someone who will become a good friend or life-long partner by doing what you enjoy. Also open up your eyes, as you may not realize when a person has feelings for you, as you are too busy looking after others.

VENUS SQUARE NEPTUNE

You live in your own rose-tinted world and reject anything that doesn't fit into it. You are highly sensitive and prone to being taken advantage of by others, so you are best suited to working on your own. This thin-skinned nature means you can have your heart broken easily. Be warned of women in particular; you can be easily deceived by them, or maybe it's the other way round – but the fairer sex is very unfair to you.

When it comes to cash, 'A fool is easily parted from his gold' – keep this motto at the front of your mind. Artistically you can have great potential but could somehow choose the wrong channel for your talents. Look into everything in case opportunities for success and satisfaction escape you.

VENUS TRINE NEPTUNE

You have a great combination of sensitivity, honesty and creativity, which makes you highly respected and trusted. You can find the love of your life by doing good for others. If you are prepared to give of yourself unconditionally then you will be rewarded by meeting someone who is just as giving, caring and loving as you.

You have a wonderful talent for the arts and things of beauty. Women can be compassionate friends and anything you do that in some way aids or honours the feminine gender will be good for you financially. Image and looking good is one way to get where you want in life. The impression you give is chic and sophisticated and it is this that gets you noticed. So try anything once by adorning yourself in colours, fabrics or styles that are sensational.

VENUS OPPOSITION NEPTUNE

You can build other people up inside your mind to such an extent that it comes as a shock when they turn out to be a lot less wonderful in reality. On the other hand, you can be too forgiving of those you are involved with romantically. You may be drawn to beautiful people who have no substance, which is why you must question your heart. You don't want to involve yourself in a disingenuous affair that is actually totally unrequited. Don't fool yourself in love. Beware of get-rich-quick schemes or anything that could take away your hard-earned cash. If you buy anything get it valued or guaranteed or you could be fooled as to its worth.

VENUS CONJUNCT PLUTO

This compelling aspect means you have a huge desire for intense, possessive partnerships. Your need is so great, in fact, that you will ditch one lover for another if you feel they will bring you even greater passion. You are blessed with a hypnotic persona that can get you far. Any relationship you enter into will not be your average affair; it will have some kind of psychological game-playing attached. The sexual chemistry is sizzling – it has to be to gain your interest. But this, combined with the obsessiveness of this aspect, can lead to 'bunny boiler'-type affairs. If you can meet someone of a like mind, you will hit sexual heights not even the Karma Sutra could satisfy. Financially, money is power and can give you control over people or situations you crave. Be warned of the interaction between money and sex as it can lead to unhealthy, even dangerous, liaisons.

VENUS SEXTILE PLUTO

You understand that it takes two to tango. You understand too that success in a relationship or partnership relies on meeting people halfway and communicating openly and honestly. You enjoy discovering what makes other people tick and use this knowledge successfully. If someone sexy psychologically turns you on, then so is your heart. This aspect can help create an affair that brings the best out in both of you, although you would never allow someone shallow or fickle into your heart. Financially, you can gain through secret means and methods as well as via your partner or inheritance.

VENUS SQUARE PLUTO

You have trouble understanding that what you want is not necessarily what you need. This can cause you problems in matters of the heart. You also have an ability to use your charm or sex appeal to get what you want, but you also have a nasty habit of making promises you know you'll never be able to keep. You can attract someone to you who isn't easy to live with, but that's the way you like it. You want a partner who can keep you on your toes and yet when they do, you can become insanely jealous, envious or angry. You will tend to keep these feelings under wraps but it is very important you release your pent-up feelings creatively. If you don't, not only will you cause yourself psychological illnesses, but also you could destroy the very thing you love. In many ways, love that is toxic to someone else is a tonic to you. You are totally attracted by forbidden fruit. One taste and you're smitten for good or bad.

VENUS TRINE PLUTO

Love has the ability to change your life dramatically. When you find the right partner, you become a completely different person. You have a strong belief in yourself and your talents, and also have the ability to instill this confidence in your nearest and dearest. You have a psychological drive and desire for someone who is enigmatic, deeply sensual and sexual with a kind of taboo attached to them. You certainly don't want someone who is superficial. You need someone who has some 'oomph' about them in an almost intangible way. Perhaps they are into sexual rituals that turn others off but are a real turn-on for you. Whatever the situation, this is a positive aspect and so you will derive pleasure from their carnal knowledge. You can also find a suitable partnership with someone who not only wields power but has financial magnetism too.

VENUS OPPOSITION PLUTO

You are someone who feels things intensely and you deal with your relationships in one of two ways. Either you expect far too much of people with whom you are romantically involved or you steer clear of emotional attachments altogether to protect yourself from any suffering. Be careful what you wish for in love as you might get it. You could get involved with someone who is psychologically way out of your depth. The trouble is, they weave a personal and sexual magic that means you find it hard to let go and yet you must. It may even be in your destiny to get involved with a person who is then taken away from you – fate decrees it, and you can't fight fate. Financially, be wary of getting involved with anything or anyone that isn't lawful or honest.

VENUS CONJUNCT ASCENDANT

Although you like to cultivate an image of someone who is sociable and charming, people can see through you. They can spot that you are ultimately self-centred and are merely putting on an act to get the attention you crave. To make matters worse, you are capable of behaving like a spoilt child when you don't get what you want. You need to mature a little and become more attuned to what others are feeling. Venus in the 12th house gives you the capacity to be more tuned into the selfless side of this aspect, helping those in distress. You may become involved in a secret love affair or find your feelings go unrequited. This house placement leads to a beautiful soul spiritually. If you have Venus in the 1st, well, Carly Simon sang a very apt song about you: 'You're So Vain'. There is no doubt that this placement can make you a very beautiful person physically but beauty is only skin deep, remember.

VENUS SEXTILE ASCENDANT

You are one of life's natural diplomats and are frequently called upon to solve other people's disputes and problems. However, your generous nature means you can be exploited in this respect, with people frequently taking advantage of you. You are honest about what you want in life and give anything that is dishonest or deceitful a very wide berth. Things of beauty, especially your image, should be and often are to the forefront. You realize that an ability to attract the right people into your life can lead to all sorts of gains and successes.

VENUS SQUARE ASCENDANT

You are so wrapped up in other things that you can prevent yourself from capitalizing on your considerable creative potential. Your natural caution also prevents you from doing anything unless you are certain it will yield returns. You need to cut the ties that bind you to the past and take a risk or two. It is safe to come outdoors and see the world. In fact, unless you adopt a more open attitude, opportunity will pass you by. Professionally this aspect can lead to many dividends but only if you develop your capacity to be social and befriend people on their way up. There may be a tendency to use people to your own ends, both at home and in your vocation.

VENUS TRINE ASCENDANT

You ooze charm and know how to use it to your advantage. You are good at schmoozing people so that they join your side, and you are also an expert at using your gifts to deflect criticism, which you dislike intensely. You are a beautiful soul, but the less you agree with this, the better! This is because vanity is never far from your side; the more gracious and sincere you appear, the more your prospects and popularity will soar. Relationships and love mean more to you than most people, which is good, as by cultivating the right image (which you do naturally), you will have more givers than takers flocking to your side. You exude a personality that attracts the artistic, cultivated and sensitive to you.

VENUS OPPOSITION ASCENDANT

Basically insecure, you make yourself look self-assured by seeking out people whose success might reflect on you. Such is your desire to be with the sophisticated set, you tend to idealize people who don't really deserve it. Venus on your 7th house cusp can make love and having someone in your life all the more important. In fact, it means you cannot go through the day without having someone you know or care for near you – and if not, you'll soon get on the phone. Having some physical presence is essential for you, but if you don't develop your own self-reliance, you won't be able to cope if you are left alone. You must also be warned of bringing someone into your life for the sake of it. A bad relationship or love affair will use and abuse you – it isn't worth the agony or the pain you inflict on yourself. Are you a masochist? Well that depends on your own dignity and this aspect *demands* you establish a relationship with yourself before anyone else.

VENUS CONJUNCT MIDHEAVEN

You are imbued with a formidable armoury of charm and diplomacy that you use to good effect. You are drawn to a career connected with glamour and beauty, and excel at creating harmony where there has previously been discord. You like to be thought of as loving and caring. The most important thing to take on board with this aspect is how you look. Remember this is how the world perceives you. If you present yourself in a dishevelled or ungroomed way, you will be seen as someone who is intellectually and morally like that. First impressions count for far more than you can ever imagine with this cosmic combination. Your natural charm will shine through, but you need a winning frame to enclose the portrait of your personality.

VENUS SEXTILE MIDHEAVEN

You don't function well in chaotic or confrontational situations. Instead, you seek out more friendly and harmonious environments in which to bring your talents to bear. Any career that brings out your artistic or musical side, or just plain good manners, will have you heading right for the top. You can win over the public or individuals with your kindness and courtesy. You will represent the underdog compassionately and the chances of you finding the love of your life in a professional capacity are greatly increased. You are your own best publicist because you know what to say, and when and how to say it.

VENUS SQUARE MIDHEAVEN

You are frustrated in your career, mainly because you keep coming up against people at senior levels who are arrogant, rude or unpleasant. If you are a woman, the old glass ceiling will hit your head. But more than that, you aren't simpatico with the situation you find yourself in. Wearing the wrong outfits, being formal when it's casual or acting in a superior way when actually you need to be sweet and gentle – these are the types of mistakes you are making. You must take great care with your professional image or you could lose out to people less talented but more shrewd and clever. Oh, and *never* mix business with pleasure.

VENUS TRINE MIDHEAVEN

With this aspect to your chart, you have a strong need to draw enjoyment from your career. For this to happen, you need a working environment that is happy and filled with friendly, sociable colleagues. Any profession that allows you to adopt a beautiful image or puts you in the midst of the arts, money or other things that appeal to your sense of the cultured and cultivated will bring out the best in you. Your love life will blossom as your chances for meeting Mr or Ms Right are greatly enhanced by this enriching ray. You will not excel in a competitive or assertive vocation but one where all that is refined and gorgeous gives you a head start over all your rivals.

VENUS OPPOSITION MIDHEAVEN

This aspect will only cause problems if you forget your roots. Knowing where you come from is critical to career success. If you were born with a silver spoon in your mouth, for instance, you must be careful about how you are perceived. Venus in this position can represent someone who comes across as precocious and spoilt. Instead of building up friends, they can drive people way because they think they are God's gift. In an argument, 'Who do you think you are?' might be heard quite often. By acting with humility and becoming more self-made, that is, proving that you've got where you're going because of you, *not* because of nepotism, you will win more admirers and supporters than even you could imagine.

The Aspects of Mars

For aspects to the Sun, Moon, Mercury or Venus, see those planets.

MARS CONJUNCT JUPITER

You have so much energy and stamina you leave people trailing in your wake. You take risks, but always in the belief that you will prevail, which you invariably do. Even if you fail, it isn't for a lack of effort. Your natural embracing of life leaves other people breathless. You are inspirational in everything you do, a born leader. People come to you in their droves because your infectious enthusiasm is like a magnet to those who are looking for someone to follow. Fortune favours the brave. Whatever enterprise or venture you take on, you do with a zest and zeal that is hardly ever matched by others. You can be a success by pursuing your chosen goal with total conviction and commitment. Sexually, you are hungry for adventure and enjoy the thrill of the chase. The catch can be boring by comparison.

MARS SEXTILE JUPITER

Hard work and determination allied to an iron will make you someone unique. You excel in intellectual and physical areas. Spontaneity is the key to your success and happiness. The minute you grow too old or tired to go off at a moment's notice to try something, see a doctor or give your life a good shaking through. Your sexual conquests will be more than average as you have a way about you that makes you very desirable. Lots of travel is good for your mind, body and spirit.

MARS SQUARE JUPITER

Whilst you maybe blessed with short bursts of energy and stamina, you often lack the focus and perseverance to capitalize on these strengths. A major distraction is colleagues and rivals, whom you can be obsessive and bitter about. You must channel your capabilities and adrenalin into one sole venture. With your spirit of enterprise, you can either waste your chances or cash in on them. Being arrogant or opinionated will lose you points in the final summary, so say nothing and don't act in haste. If you do, you'll surely repent at leisure, as by then you'll have too much time for it. Don't take a boss or friend for granted or they will become a deadly adversary. Your sex life is hardly mundane; this aspect can lead to many conquests but few meaningful affairs. It is not conducive to settling down because you always think the other man's grass is greener.

MARS TRINE JUPITER

You are someone who can achieve goals with ease, but could accomplish even more if you didn't shy away from competition. Your ideal partner needs to attract you intellectually as well as physically. You dislike anyone who is a wet blanket or pessimist; your positive mental attitude is the winning formula in your race for the championship of life (as my friend Linford Christie used to say). Luck comes most auspiciously from men in particular, although people who are successful in all fields are attracted to your boundless, Tigger-like energy. You will attract more than average opportunities to you, which should be cashed in on without hesitation. Any involvement in travel will be good for you as pastures new are always a magnet to your buccaneering spirit. Your sex life will be exciting and with your passion you won't find it hard to lavish your desires on it. Be careful of coming across as overconfident or arrogant.

MARS OPPOSITION JUPITER

There's nothing that stimulates you more than a challenge, especially one that allows you to prove you are superior to your rivals. You will go to any lengths to prevail in a competitive situation. However, it is very important you don't count your chickens until they're hatched. Thinking you are home and dry when there is still another circuit to go can mean people will actively want to bring you down a peg or two. Take your time with things of importance – don't assume it's just a matter of a signature on a contract until you've actually signed it. Be careful when traveling, if only because last minute or badly organized trips can often mean losing an opportunity or frustrating delays. Take time to do everything properly because – and you must remember this – luck is when preparedness meets opportunity. Your private life can be full of turmoil if one of you isn't selfless or passive. Too many chiefs and not enough Indians in the bedroom can be fun but, at times, rather uncomfortable and unsettling. Your ego needs be constantly massaged and you can't live with someone who needs the same – you need a massager!

MARS CONJUNCT SATURN

You have a knack for playing to your strengths. You focus your energies towards the areas where you can succeed and away from those where you are weak and will fail. You don't like being frustrated in the pursuit of your goals and can get very angry if thwarted. You can come across as cold and unfeeling because you are ambitious to the degree of pushing everything and everyone else to one side if they get in your way. Keeping energy in reserve is important as you have a natural urge to conserve and won't give your game away until you are close to success. You are shrewd in business but need to cultivate a more gentle and sensual touch sexually.

MARS SEXTILE SATURN

You are one of those fortunate people who has just the right blend of experience and energy. As a result, you have a gift for getting things right first time, thus saving yourself the effort of having to try and try again. 'Patience is a virtue and often comes with age' is a motto you keep in your head. You know that everything doesn't happen overnight and sometimes success demands constancy and persistence. In business you make a great friend but worthy opponent, whilst sexually you have an animal magnetism but lack the tender touch.

MARS SQUARE SATURN

Your life is a stop–start affair. One moment you are overflowing with energy, the next you can't summon the strength to get out of bed in the morning. It is only by drawing on your positive experiences and putting your nose to the grindstone *all* the time that you will make the most of your talents. Frustrations can really build up in you and if it means winning by foul means rather than fair, you'll take the former. Be warned of provoking someone who makes a powerful enemy as you might bring the wrath of the gods upon you. You can be prone to cowardice when push comes to shove, so beware of bullying tactics as when the chips are down you may bring short, swift revenge upon yourself. Professionally, don't mix with people who are morally corrupt or unprincipled or you could be guilty by association. Sexually, you can have a cruel and cold streak that comes from being hurt in the past – don't take out your problems on innocent people. Your relationship with your father may have left much to be desired.

MARS TRINE SATURN

Using your energies wisely, concentrating on activities that are going to produce results rather than wasting your time on lost causes, brings success. Accordingly, you are able to succeed in your vocation, once you know your goal. An ability to delegate with management skills is what can take you to the very top of your career tree. You also exercise the right amount of self-discipline and self-control to ensure that wherever you direct your strength and stamina, you will make the very best of it. You despise waste in all forms, and punctuality is how you often judge others. You hate anyone who cuts corners and wants to take the easy way through life. Being single-minded and conscientious is your recipe for ambitious reward and recognition. Fatherly advice should be listened to, whoever gives it – older men in your life will certainly look out for you. Sexually, you are drawn to someone who is hopelessly devoted to you and no-one else.

MARS OPPOSITION SATURN

With this challenging aspect in your chart, you find it hard to choose between your sense of duty and your desires. As a result you don't manage your energies well. You also struggle with low self-esteem and will only begin to achieve success when you think more of yourself. What you want and what you get can be two very different things, so it is important to analyze yourself to the point that you know what you want so it is that that you get! Recognition is very important because you judge success by how many people recognize you for what you have done. Whatever career you choose, make sure it is something you are prepared to graft at, for if you want a quick fix or overnight success then you will be very disappointed. Everything comes to those who wait, and it's not just about waiting but about working, too. Time, effort and total commitment to your cause is what brings success – nothing less. Failure haunts you and could be your weak link but you will only fail if you don't do the right thing. *You* are master of your destiny and will be the architect of your downfall or achievements. Your sex life needs so much care and attention; your brute force is hard to take for a sensitive and caring person who loves you. Try a little tenderness instead.

MARS CONJUNCT URANUS

You are a thrill-seeker and yearn for the freedom to chase the excitement you crave. Whenever life gets boring, you'll do something outrageous to liven it up again. But this may make you unpopular with those who don't possess your rebellious nature. As if you care. You are your own person and do precisely what pleases you. Take care if you live in the fast lane because one day you might just go that little bit too far. You can be accident-prone so don't do anything risky or you might rue the day. Sexually, you yearn for the unusual, which can lead to physical experimentation as you push back the boundaries of the norm.

MARS SEXTILE URANUS

You are like a Labrador puppy that never seems to run out of steam. You are restless, hopelessly impatient and full of get up and go. You drive yourself to exhaustion in pursuit of your goals. Unsurprisingly, you need someone with similar energy levels to share your life. You're not interested in anything boring or normal, the same must go for people you seek out. To you, the eccentric and weird is wonderful. In fact anyone who is 'straight' in the conservative sense brings out a side of you that can be quite shocking. Sexually charismatic, you won't be short of a bedfellow or two or three!

MARS SQUARE URANUS

Deep down you would love to be more daring and carefree. But you also know deep down that it is your cautious approach that prevents you from getting egg on your face. You have a volcanic temper, but unless there are other aspects from Pluto, it usually disappears once you have erupted. Don't take risks with your rage; if you lose your cool steer clear from anyone or anything that can make you even more hostile or angry. Be warned of mechanical gadgets or the like that can cause accidents as there's many a slip twixt cup and lip. Your sexuality is a source of bizarre activity. You're not sure what you want or who you are but you should have fun finding out. Your energy is more suited to short bursts than long marathons; take care of physical or rough sports in which you could do yourself an injury.

MARS TRINE URANUS

You need the freedom to let your natural exuberance show itself to the world. You hate routine and are much better suited to working for yourself. Take care not to overexert yourself as you can suffer with your nerves or physical exhaustion. What makes you different from the rest is that you are ahead of your time, but like all geniuses this might not be appreciated immediately! This frustrates you, as you want instant results and immediate success. You crave excitement and doing things on the spur of the moment, so you don't have a chance to think. Being spontaneous makes you hard to live with, but then again, that's what makes you so sexy! You are easily bored and once you have conquered one thing, you are off on another great adventure. Unpredictable in an agreeable way, anything can happen when you're around and it often does. You are very gifted, highly original and lovably eccentric but some people may need some time to come around to you. Eventually they will be in awe of you, growing to love you so much they would defend you with their life. You are courageous and go where others wouldn't dare. Your sex life is dramatic and far from ordinary. If you trap yourself somewhere that society convenes is normal, you will bring unhappiness on yourself and others, so follow your vibes, and don't sit in the closet.

MARS OPPOSITION URANUS

You mask your insecurity with an arrogant and demanding façade that can rub people up the wrong way. You will do anything to get your own way and have such a strong need for excitement that you will pick an argument purely for your own entertainment. You go out to shock others, as you want to upset their apple cart. Following the adage that no-one sleeps when you're around, realize that sooner or later people will tire of you and leave you friendless. You don't have to behave so wickedly but just be your usual self and that is exciting enough. You have sexual magnetism but this can trap you into believing you are who you aren't. Maybe, just maybe, you should realize that to your own self, be true. A final thought: what does it matter if you aren't normal? And anyway, what's normal?

MARS CONJUNCT NEPTUNE

You possess a seductive personality and draw people in through your sheer glamour and charisma. Your flaw, however, is that you simply don't see the consequences of some of your actions, and this diminishes your popularity at times. Image is so important to you, and even if it's not what you're really like, being able to play act suits you just fine, so long as you know when the acting should stop and the reality begin. Be warned of being manipulative or Machiavellian in business or love. As Shakespeare put it: 'Oh, what a wicked web we weave in our efforts to deceive.'

MARS SEXTILE NEPTUNE

This is a well-balanced aspect and as a result you have a great understanding of when to put yourself first and when others must take precedence. You look for the good side in everyone you meet and have an ability to raise people's standards to meet your own. You are able to tune into the sensitive side of people's wants and needs. You can make a tender and seductive lover but must understand that fantasy is the name of your game; if you don't get it at home then you will look elsewhere. You're a wee bit of a mystery but that's what gives you the edge over more upfront people. What you see ain't what you get!

MARS SQUARE NEPTUNE

You are torn between the need to be aggressive and assert yourself, and a conflicting feeling of apathy and personal inadequacy. This may be worsened by guilt or shame over sexual issues. You can't quite fathom out what you want or even who you are. You try to put yourself in a box, care too much about social conventions and are confused about what people say you ought to be. The key is: to your own self be true. It doesn't matter what's gone before – you are unique and that's what matters. Being dishonest with yourself could result in an addiction of some kind, which won't take away the pain but merely mask it for a while. You love the twilight world with its hint of danger, which is fine just so long as you stick your toe in the water and don't take a dive. Romance and sex are two very different things; sometimes your ideal sex machine isn't tender enough or your romantic partner lacks passion. Maybe it's time to experiment a little more before committing.

MARS TRINE NEPTUNE

With this aspect you are able to balance your own needs with others' desires. You are sympathetic towards those who cannot perform this delicate tightrope act as well as you. Your attitude to love is straightforward and romantic, but sometimes you can idealize people somewhat too much. Your energy levels are best directed towards voluntary, charity or artistic work. Anything too muscular or physical will hardly motivate you unless it is to make your body more beautiful or in some way increase glamour and even sex. You love the art of seduction and do it well, but the sexual act may bore you or leave you cold.

MARS OPPOSITION NEPTUNE

You find it difficult to assert yourself because people always suspect your motives – and with good cause. You aren't always honest with people and can use passive aggression to get your way. Watch out for deceit or lies that can build out of proportion. One fib can lead to another, so nip any falsehoods in the bud. You conveniently forget what you don't want to remember as your selective memory helps you avoid what you find nasty or grotesque. You find your own sexuality a source of uncomfortable and even confusing thoughts, but if you try to mould yourself into something you are not, it will only increase the pain or hurt you might transfer onto others. Denial is not the way to handle issues. Instead, however hard it is, you must confront your demons and get to the root before you go another step further.

MARS CONJUNCT PLUTO

You have a constant need to prove your power, so when you achieve a goal you realize you were less interested in the goal than the fact that you could get it. You are demanding and possessive in love and can be just as difficult with friends. You are a person who believes that psychology is the key to most things and what you can't succeed in doing by using Machiavellian ploys, you will try to achieve with brute force. The trouble is one day you will meet someone stronger than you and, for you, defeat is harder to cope with than anything. Use your energy for the good: to improve your life and conditions, and instead of imposing your will on others, convince them of the merit and value of your ideas; that way you'll turn from sinner to saint. Sexually, you are a mean machine. However, your passion will wane if you don't meet someone who has the same desires as you.

MARS SEXTILE PLUTO

The truth is hugely important to you and you are blessed with a great ability to understand other people's motives. This allows you to be honest and straightforward with people. You may have a strong sex drive but need a relationship that stimulates you in other ways. This combination can pull victory from the jaws of defeat but the secret is to be single-minded and concentrated with your ambitions. You are empowered enough to know what you want and by psyching yourself up nothing can stand in your way. Set your goal or target and don't be diverted from it until you achieve it. Whatever your gender, men are good for you as your strength and way of doing things appeals to them.

MARS SQUARE PLUTO

You have an unenviable gift for making enemies. You have a short fuse and your habit of issuing threats or being downright abusive doesn't help your cause. If you are a woman, you can come across as oppressive, as someone who has let a position of power go to her head. If you're a man, you have to know your strengths and avoid psychological games. You have to learn to win people over by making them your friends. Remember the saying, 'Keep your friends close and your enemies even closer' – well, this counts for you, too. Be wary of macho men who are obsessive, cruel and ruthless as they may try to control or dominate you in a most unhealthy way. If you see the signs of this happening, transform yourself and your life into something completely different very quickly. Sexually, you have many issues that may be best dealt with by a therapist or counsellor. There's nothing wrong with that if it helps you sleep at night.

MARS TRINE PLUTO

You understand that power is a double-edged sword. In the right hands it is a force for good, but in the wrong hands... You are capable of great bravery and compassion and are drawn to people who share these qualities. By turning your concentrated strength towards what you are searching for in life, you can achieve your goal. You aren't a person to be taken lightly, for although you can be fair and honest, if someone treats you badly you will have no problem in picking up the sword of revenge and letting them have it. You also are very much a fatalist so that you believe that what happens in your life is a part of your destiny. Your powers of recovery are second to none, so if something happens to set you back or cause you hurt or pain, you can cut the negatives out of your life and from your memory quickly. You're never down for long and will always come up fighting. He or she who dares wins.

MARS OPPOSITION PLUTO

Your defensiveness shows itself as defiance, which can have a bad effect on people around you. You must learn to compromise more. You also have plenty of sex appeal and animal magnetism, and should learn to use it. You can be all over the place with your ambitions or goals – this means you can have a string of minor successes but little else. If you want to be known for something sensational, use the army tactics of putting all your forces together and charging into the heat of the battle with every conceivable weapon going full blazes. People will see you as a threat to their ambitions; when they do then you know you are winning. Learn the secret of empowerment: once you know you've got what it takes, then for goodness sake, take it!

You have a powerful libido but need to concentrate your passions and desires on a person who is prepared to deal with your emotional and psychological baggage too. Some things are worth waiting for.

MARS CONJUNCT ASCENDANT

There is a thin line between being assertive and aggressive. Unfortunately, you don't know where this line is, and as a result, you upset people. You need to channel your boundless energy in a more focused way, taking into account other people's feelings. If Mars is in the 1st, you might act first and think later, only to find you've broken everything from hearts to prospects. You have enormous sex appeal – use it to bide your time. Flirt, flutter your eyelashes and wiggle your butt until the time is right to strike, and not before. Mars in the 12th throws up psychological and emotional issues. It's best not to get entangled with anyone who is too secretive or isn't prepared to be honest about your relationship together.

MARS SEXTILE ASCENDANT

Your sexy energy can display itself in bouts of impulsive, even impetuous, behaviour, which is a turn-on to some folks, yet a real turn off to others. Think before you do something incorrigible. By considering the consequences of your words or actions first, you will show the positive side of your personality and win over people more easily. You project an image of someone who knows where they are going and what they want to do, even if you don't! Impetus is important to you as it motivates you, whether in your career, sex life or on the sports field. Activity and exercise is a necessity. If you don't stay active, you'll get very bored.

MARS SQUARE ASCENDANT

You feel the need to make shows of strength and are rude, aggressive and ill-mannered towards people. At the root of this behaviour is a need to mask your inferiority complex. Only by overcoming this complex will you succeed in winning friends and influencing people. The saying that the best form of defence is attack is you down to the ground. Instead of coming across as abusive or bullying, think how you'd feel if people constantly jumped down your throat. You need an outlet for your sexuality and energy, but don't assume that your needs are other people's desires – they are not. Be careful with your demands or you'll get a rude awakening when the dog turns round and bites you.

MARS TRINE ASCENDANT

You aren't afraid to take a gamble, and often this policy pays off. However, you tend to live in the present and think little about planning ahead for the future. Financially, and in many other ways, this can cause you problems. With a little more forward thinking, you have the talent to go far. You have more than your average quota of sex appeal and when it comes to taking the initiative, you are a born leader. It's worth finding out what you want from life before going after it. As with all Mars aspects, don't get drawn down side alleys or off the beaten track. If you stick to what you know and do it well, you will get to your destination more quickly. This aspect has a champion's quality to it.

MARS OPPOSITION ASCENDANT

You actively look for trouble. Often it comes to you, in the form of people reacting to your habit of speaking out or becoming angry when under pressure. But if not, you go to great lengths to find people who will challenge you. You must learn the art of compromise and how to manage your anger. With Mars on the 7th house cusp, your Descendant, the problem is quite simply you want everything your own way. You won't admit defeat and can also refuse to apologize. That's fine if you have a Venusian partner who is happy to deal with all this, but if you come up against someone who is exactly the same as you then it will lead to a lot of passion, sometimes egotistical and heated, at other times aggressive and physical. You are a person with a big sexual appetite. It is not the solution to your problems but could be the reason for them instead.

MARS CONJUNCT MIDHEAVEN

You have an innate sense of what you want in life and how to set about achieving it. Your ambition is only matched by your competitiveness and you will never stop fighting to achieve your goals. Any career that allows you to be the leader, take the initiative or be out in front brings out that victorious blend in your stars. But if you have to stay in the background or do others' bidding, it won't be long before you hit the high road and are off to something more stimulating and worthwhile. A tendency towards ego clashes with co-workers or bosses is a negative manifestation of this aspect.

MARS SEXTILE MIDHEAVEN

You are an honest, industrious person who puts everything into their work. Your example is followed by others, who respond to your infectious and inspiring leadership. You aren't content with second best; in fact, you want to be the one everyone wants. You will be, just so long as you realize you have to put some effort and time into your chosen goal. You can get where you want to in life by cultivating the right people and using some of your God-given sex appeal.

MARS SQUARE MIDHEAVEN

You are someone who will fight tooth and nail to get what you want from your career. Nothing upsets you more than people who don't share this drive and ambition, and you can clash with those who are lazy or slow-witted. Rome wasn't built in a day and neither is success, so don't take it out on others if you don't get what you want immediately. Fighting fire with fire will end up in an incendiary clash with people around you. A bad workman blames his tools. You might think you are God's gift to everyone but you aren't. Eating a little bit of humble pie will do you ever so much good. You might think you're a sexual icon too, but you may be sadly mistaken again.

MARS TRINE MIDHEAVEN

With this positive aspect to your chart, you have a blend of drive, determination and infectious enthusiasm that sparks everyone around you. You may become something of a role model to others. Where you lead, others will follow, so it is imperative to choose a career that enables you to empower yourself and get to the top in your own time. You have a very fast rhythm of life and can't abide people who plod and tread warily or carefully. Yet it's likely you will learn from experience when it comes to being too impatient. This won't prevent your success but it will make it more worth holding on to. You will excel in masculine-type professions, even if you're a woman. Sexually you're quite a catch and are happy to use your libido to get what you want professionally. You probably carry your own casting couch.

MARS OPPOSITION MIDHEAVEN

Beneath your surface is a simmering anger. You will deny it, but it is rooted in problems from the past, perhaps childhood. You try to channel this anger into physical pursuits, perhaps around the home. The battle royale probably started when your parents or teacher told you you wouldn't get anywhere in life. You believed them, even if you didn't consciously accept this. Now, instead of giving up on yourself, use this fury to spark yourself on the road to greater things. If you don't, your impotence will lead to more frustrations than you can imagine. The sooner you can strike out independently on your own, the better. And as you go, whisper these words: 'I'll show you.' I daresay you will if you keep the conviction burning.

♃

The Aspects of Jupiter

For Jupiter aspects to the Sun, Moon, Mercury, Venus and Mars, see those planets.

JUPITER CONJUNCT SATURN

Your attitude to hard work sets you apart from the rest. You combine patience with resilience and perseverance, plus a drive and motivation to succeed. You must be careful not to overdo things, however. Success will only come if you strike the right balance between work, rest and play. This aspect can be auspicious for business, giving you the potential to go to right to the top of your career ladder. The combination of these two planets is enough to make you a leader of men, big or small. Financial acumen and astuteness in all you do promises untold success and fortune if you use the conjunction well.

JUPITER SEXTILE SATURN

You understand that knowledge is power, and work hard to acquire as much of both as you can. You combine these qualities with good planning and a strong sense of self-belief. Yet for all your ambition and the focus on your goals, you are kind and caring to others, too. You have a gift of being in the right place at the right time and mustn't ever look a gift horse in the mouth. Opportunity combined with your diligence will be enough to bring you financial or career success.

JUPITER SQUARE SATURN

You have a habit of comparing yourself to others and deciding you don't measure up. It isn't true of course. In fact, it's merely an excuse not to get down to the hard work necessary to capitalize on your undoubted talents. You have got what it takes to succeed but may have gone through a bad experience with your father or someone you looked up to. Getting their approval may be at the back of all your decisions and actions but it hardly matters. Their love and guidance should have been unconditional and yet you may always believe you are a disappointment to them, whatever you do. So rather than wallowing in self-pity or personal denial, get out and prove something, if only to yourself. With age comes experience and you have enough wisdom to reach an ambition and be able to say, 'I told you so.'

JUPITER TRINE SATURN

To others you seem to lead a charmed life. Everything you touch seems to turn to gold. You know, however, that you make your own luck, and you do it by working hard and concentrating on your strengths rather than your weaknesses. You have an ability to draw people with power and influence to your attention. They like what they see – somebody with guts who is prepared to graft long and hard, perhaps even beyond the call of duty, to get where they want to go. This gift for realizing that you very often have to do a little more than it takes to get noticed is what will bring you success and ensure your destiny is fulfilled in the most fortuitous of ways.

JUPITER OPPOSITION SATURN

You are constantly wondering whether you are one of life's successes or one of its failures. When you decide it is the latter, you use this as an excuse to give up altogether. Once you rid yourself of this habit, you will be free to discover you've got all the attributes necessary to succeed. Your main problem is deciding between enterprise and consolidation, striking a happy balance between the two. With some things you should take a risk, develop and grow. By taking time out to travel or learn, for example, you can acquire new knowledge and wisdom, then lay some solid foundations to build upon what you have just gained. By doing so, you can grow a business, set yourself up in a career or just give yourself the confidence to get somewhere in life. Recognition, money, whatever it is that motivates you, can be yours, but only if you can balance the expansive powers of Jupiter with the ambitious rays of Saturn.

JUPITER CONJUNCT URANUS

This exuberant aspect in your chart indicates you have a mind that is open to all sorts of experiences and knowledge. You will educate yourself to the highest level possible and view the future with huge optimism – and with good cause. Through travel in particular, you will strike it lucky. You could find your career, love of your life, success or any number of things when you least expect to. Keep your schedule flexible, ready for new adventures and you will gain more than you lose. Be warned of gambling, as this aspect gives you a feeling that you are immune to loss. You're not, but typically with this unpredictable ray, even if you lose, somehow you learn and gain – if only through the wisdom that comes from the experience.

JUPITER SEXTILE URANUS

You love learning. To you, knowledge can be a real aphrodisiac. Yes, even the love of your life may come into your orbit through something you do connected with study or education. You simply cannot get enough of the grey stuff because you know it is the key to a bright future. Original and even eccentric, you are the kind of happy-go-lucky, take-me-as-you-find-me person who is so attractive in business. Financial windfalls are very possible and, not only that, they seem to arrive just when you need them most.

JUPITER SQUARE URANUS

You have a bad habit of taking on too much, a trait that severely restricts your ability to capitalize on your great potential. You are also impatient, and expect to jump straight to the top of the ladder rather than working your way up to the top through application and hard graft. You can be very pompous and look down at others in a patronizing way. Why? Because you assume everyone is dim or daft. Adopt a more generous and humanitarian approach. Rather than dismiss someone, see how you can help them. This way you'll make a friend who will help you through thick and thin, rather than an enemy who is looking at how they can bring you down. Travel plans can often be disrupted with this aspect, especially if you leave others to organize what is rightly your problem.

JUPITER TRINE URANUS

Lady Luck shines on you, largely because your optimistic nature draws positive people into your orbit. They then help you achieve your goals. You are honest and expect others to be the same. The more you can spread your wings through education or travel, the further you will go in life. You are excited by cultures or creeds that are different to your own. You may be totally drawn to another country as if by some intangible hold. The more you can follow through any foreign connections or opportunities, the better. The chances are you will live or work away from your country of birth. However, once the novelty wears off you want to move – is anything as good as it's cracked up to be in your mind's eye?

JUPITER OPPOSITION URANUS

You have the talent and knowledge to conquer the world. If you are going to succeed, however, you must be careful not to look down on those less gifted than you. You have the potential to get drunk on power, and that would be fatal to your chances of real fulfilment. This is not an auspicious aspect to go purely on blind faith. Your intuition or judgement could be off-beam at certain times, so when you get the green light for something, it is probably the time to go in the opposite direction. And when you get the feeling something should be avoided, then you may find that is a sure success. Unpredictable and uncanny, you are a restless soul but need to remain in one place long enough to plant some roots and settle, otherwise success or happiness will never be able to grow.

JUPITER CONJUNCT NEPTUNE

This aspect indicates there is a danger that Jupiter's expansive nature may get out of control within you. You may not be able to grasp the reality of a situation. You may leave yourself open to exploitation by others as well. Great Expectations meets Walter Mitty – that's what it can be like in literary terms! So you need to keep your feet on the ground, and deal in realities. Yet when it comes to spiritual, moral and ethical issues, no-one can touch you. You have high ideals, the only trouble is, if you try to judge others by yourself, you will be so pained and disappointed. You must accept that people are only human and do what you can to make the world a better place. Be warned of financial duplicity and legal matters where perjury is the main hurdle.

JUPITER SEXTILE NEPTUNE

You have an idealistic and imaginative streak, which despite your intelligence, makes you a target for predatory types. It also makes you prone to reading more into relationships than is actually there. In both cases, it can lead to crushing disappointment, so be wary. Following a spiritual or psychic belief is good for you, but do take on board the fact that not everyone is perfect. Wake up to the reality that you might be generous with your time and energy, but not everyone is as unconditional as you and may take advantage of your kindness.

JUPITER SQUARE NEPTUNE

If you were prepared to put in the hard work, you'd be capable of conquering the world. Instead you live in your head, daydreaming and setting yourself hopelessly ambitious targets. Your naivety leaves you vulnerable to more worldly-wise types as well. A reality check will do you the power of good. Take care of legal problems that stem from lies and deceit. You may come across people who aren't what they seem. Worse still, you will realize you knew it all along but were afraid to admit it. Financially, you should keep good people around you, those who really know what they are doing. Don't put your trust in charlatans or those whose qualifications are not just suspect, but totally phoney. Watch out, watch out, there's a quack about!

JUPITER TRINE NEPTUNE

You are a deep thinker and have a strong spiritual or religious side to your life. This makes you suited to serving others and you draw immense satisfaction from doing so. This aspect is wonderful if you want to bring out your artistic side. Whether it is foreign cultures or ancient civilizations, you adore the metaphysical and mysterious. You can be a doyen of a particular subject that most people couldn't begin to understand. You have a feeling in your bones for what you want to do and should follow to a conclusion. Your philosophical approach to everyday things makes you wonderful to know.

JUPITER OPPOSITION NEPTUNE

You need to learn a simple word: No. There is a vulnerability to you that makes you a natural target for those who want to dump all their responsibilities on you. They see you as a soft touch and know you will not be able to turn them down. In matters of the heart, you tend to idealize your partners and become bitter when, inevitably, you see them for what they really are. Never a lender nor a borrower be – if you do lend, you won't see the money again. You may have to make sacrifices in your life but for goodness sake, don't do it unless you really, really want to. Practise a *quid pro quo* – if you do something, you must get something you need in return. This will stop people stealing your time and goodwill.

JUPITER CONJUNCT PLUTO

With this aspect in your chart, you are halfway to success already. Failure isn't a word that appears in your dictionary. You have so much energy, drive and determination that you will press on until you reach your goals, no matter what obstacles are set in your way. One problem could be what I call the 'immortality fixation', by which I mean you believe you are protected from failure. Although you can make friends with the rich and famous, never forget there is always someone as ambitious and desperate for success as you coming up on the inside. Your faith can be a source of enormous comfort and joy.

JUPITER SEXTILE PLUTO

You have an innate talent for rooting out the truth. You can spot a fake a mile away. You may well use these talents in a professional sense, working to expose corruption and injustice. With this aspect, you can reach people who are in a position to make things happen. Use these individuals well if what you are seeking is not for self-gain. If you want to transform a bad or negative situation for the good, you will succeed and the credit will come to you. But misuse your power and shame will follow.

JUPITER SQUARE PLUTO

You have high expectations of life but may have to settle for something a little lower down the scale. Your ambition means you are susceptible to con artists offering you instant money-making schemes, so beware. You must also be careful with cash, which you have a habit of frittering away. Sometimes what you see as a means to an end brings more distress and upset than you realize. Whilst you think you are discreet and confidential, you have a habit of letting little things leak out and before you know it Big Brother comes down on you like a ton of bricks. It is important to aim at what you can handle. Get out of your depth and you'll have to face the consequences.

JUPITER TRINE PLUTO

You are a motivator par excellence. With this aspect you have a particular talent for bringing the best out in others. You motivate and encourage people around you to capitalize on their financial capabilities. There is something evangelistic about this aspect; like Billy Graham, you are a crusader. You have a total faith and belief in what you want to do in life, and if you can carry people along with you, even better. You can rise to a position of power and influence; when you do, make sure everything is for the greater good of others, the masses. You will then go down in history as a transformer for the good. From princes to presidents, there is something extra special about what you have to offer – you have the potential to make it happen.

JUPITER OPPOSITION PLUTO

This awesome aspect indicates you have a powerful need to develop the spiritual side of your life. This may not be plain sailing and you may encounter opposition. You must resist the urge to try to indoctrinate others and try to take control of their lives. Don't give up when the chips are down, for this is when you should be at your most courageous and stand up and fight. Put your convictions to the test. It doesn't matter if one person doesn't like something – there are plenty more fish in the sea. Besides, you have probably met a shark who is jealous and wants to steal your idea. Don't flout the law and don't take on the state, instead use government and officialdom to help and protect you.

JUPITER CONJUNCT ASCENDANT

You are blessed with a positive, optimistic outlook and approach everything convinced that success is assured. This is usually true, but you have to be careful not to overstretch yourself at times. Happy, fun-loving and a joy to behold, you have so much to give. Your gregarious personality is at its best with Jupiter in the 1st house whilst Jupiter in the 12th brings out your charitable, kind nature. Your warmth is part of your lucky charm. Do watch your weight if you have a love of luscious things – as you probably do!

JUPITER SEXTILE ASCENDANT

You have a great deal going for you. You are generous, open-minded, knowledgeable and a great communicator. If you have a weakness, it is overdoing things. You need to learn to enjoy things in moderation. Travel can prove lucky for you in more ways than one. Any desire for more learning should be encouraged as your knowledge and way with words makes you brilliant company.

JUPITER SQUARE ASCENDANT

With this aspect in your chart, you have a flair for coming up with great ideas. However, they will all come to nothing unless you can learn to manage your energies better and avoid taking on too much. Less is more should be your motto. Take care not to expand too quickly; just because you've had a brilliant idea or success, it doesn't mean you are infallible or invincible. You aren't, you are human. One swallow doesn't make a summer, remember. Be warned about exaggerating the truth, as when the true tale comes to light, you could be embarrassed or a laughing stock.

JUPITER TRINE ASCENDANT

You have the talent to succeed but you need to understand that success won't come easily. It will require hard work, something you are reluctant to put in. Self-deprecation is often your way of covering your lack of confidence, but there's no need to be this way because you have a great personality, are competent in many things and have the ability to lift people when they feel down. In fact, all in all, you are great to have around as you soon blow the blues away. You can reach people who will want to help and guide you in life – don't turn them down.

JUPITER OPPOSITION ASCENDANT

You can be a hypocrite, doling out strong opinions on the one hand, then failing to practise what you preach on the other. You may look to your partner for a boost to your self-confidence, and may be drawn to someone from a very different culture or class. With Jupiter on the 7th house cusp, you need a person in your life who is fun to be with and is an optimist. You won't be able to cope with anyone who is melancholic or doesn't give you respect or amour. You want to be king or queen in any partnership and you are looking for someone who really is your match, not your rival. You can be very lucky with this aspect and will eventually find your true love.

JUPITER CONJUNCT MIDHEAVEN

You like the idea of helping others and are drawn to a career in which you can give people the benefit of your wisdom or knowledge. You are not short of ambitions or the confidence to fulfil them. You can have the ear of people who really are very powerful and by learning the ropes from them, you will reach a position of prominence. Recognition and some kind of ennoblement is what you see as achievement. Money is also very nice, as is having people looking up to you, but far more important is the knowledge that what you have accomplished was done yourself. Your theme song? 'I Did It My Way'.

JUPITER SEXTILE MIDHEAVEN

With this ace aspect in your chart, you are full of beans and positivity, and believe you can achieve big things. You are not afraid to take the occasional calculated risk in order to get to the finishing line. If your profession takes you far and wide across the globe, you will be very happy indeed. You want a vocation that has no borders but allows you the freedom to go where you want at any time. It will do you no harm to add as many qualifications or diplomas to your name as you can. It's how people first perceive you that will give you your initial lucky break. And then you're up and running.

JUPITER SQUARE MIDHEAVEN

You have a habit of showing off a little too much, strutting around as if you are one of the world's most wonderful successes and being a pompous pain in the posterior at times. The problem is that your success isn't quite as great as you think it is. The old immortality complex is alive and kicking with this aspect – you truly believe that you can behave exactly how you like, say precisely what you want and even if it's a pack of lies, you honestly believe you can get out of it. Crossing that bridge when you come to it might be a bridge too far. If you can admit your weaknesses and show you are prepared to learn, take a cut in salary or go down the management scale a little, then such grace and humility will be repaid handsomely.

JUPITER TRINE MIDHEAVEN

You are not short of self-confidence and can achieve a good deal. Your other great asset is the pride you take in what you do. This helps you progress even further. This is one of the luckiest aspects for a professional person there is, but you tend to believe things will land in your lap without you having to work for them. Well they may, but unless you have the infrastructure and organization to capitalize on your lucky opportunities, it will be a case of here today and gone tomorrow. Don't be a flash-in-the-pan careerist – put some effort into your good fortune and you'll never want again.

JUPITER OPPOSITION MIDHEAVEN

Self-confidence isn't a problem for you. You are sure of yourself in everything you do and this allows you to make the most of your opportunities. However, having the space to breathe and recharge your batteries both physically and mentally is vital to you. You need a home that provides this. Career luck could come through a relative or an introduction from someone who either lives with you or knows you in a domestic sense. Working from a domestic set-up is good for your comfort zone, but you may find it hard to motivate yourself if you're surrounded by kids or familiar things. You're not on vacation, you are here to work – make this your mantra if you are professionally too close to home.

♄

The Aspects of Saturn

For Saturn's aspects to the Sun, Moon, Mercury, Venus, Mars and Jupiter, see those planets.

SATURN CONJUNCT URANUS

You are someone who relishes responsibility and you have the drive and self-discipline to achieve the goals you set yourself. You are capable of achieving a great deal but you must be careful not to devote yourself entirely to work. You are prone to dark moods and pessimism; if you do not spend time relaxing and enjoying life, you may suffer from depression or nervous exhaustion. You have the ability to take the past and use it to create a better future for yourself.

SATURN SEXTILE URANUS

You understand that effort pays off and use your energies efficiently to reach your goals. You are self-aware and know how to make the best of your talents, but you also know the importance of new ideas, and that tried-and-tested methods are often enhanced when married to modern inventions. This can put you ahead of the rest in business and in areas where the buck stops with you.

SATURN SQUARE URANUS

The world could be yours, if only you could overcome the fear of the unknown that is holding you back. You also hold onto the past because you're scared of the future, and yet you long for the excitement of what could be but won't let go of what you know. The stress and tension you cause yourself is untold. You must learn to step out into uncharted territory. Once you have done so, having discovered that there is nothing to fear at all, there will be no holding you back. Have the faith to realize that your experiences will save you from making any silly mistakes. Once bitten and all that. One more piece of advice, if something ain't broke, why fix it?

SATURN TRINE URANUS

You have a positive attitude to the future, which you look forward to with high expectations. You peer back to the past only for experience, to draw on the lessons you learned there to press on with life. Your example encourages others to follow. In business, you will succeed by being up-to-date with information on all that's new and modern. If you make yourself accessible with all the right gadgetry and state-of-the-art communications, you will launch yourself into a headlong rise to the top.

SATURN OPPOSITION URANUS

If you have this aspect to your chart, you are someone who is unwilling to compromise. Until you learn to do so, and to meet others halfway, you will constantly face obstacles and struggle to win friends. The problem stems from Saturn's inability to see further than the end of his nose and the Uranian dream of being totally outrageous and different. This means you have a head-on clash between what you *think* you fear and what you *think* you want.

Actually you want neither: what you actually want is to have success on a plate, but you won't get it unless you are prepared to suck it and see when it comes to your career and business dreams. Take a chance and you'll see what you fear is fear itself.

SATURN CONJUNCT NEPTUNE

You are a smart cookie. You can spot a con artist a mile away and pick out the holes in people's arguments with ease. You approach relationships in the same careful, analytical way, and won't commit yourself until you are sure a potential partner feels the same way as you. You blend materialism and spirituality in equal amounts so you can excel in any career or field of life. With this talent you can use a hard business head to make the most of artistic flair, or turn a charity into a money-making proposition and so on.

SATURN SEXTILE NEPTUNE

You have a powerful sense of what is right and wrong, and an acute social conscience to go with it. This may lead you to a career in which you fight on behalf of others, not just in your own community but worldwide. You believe that a little compassion balanced by a practical approach can get you the best of both worlds – and you're right.

SATURN SQUARE NEPTUNE

You can spend all your time worrying, while doing little to alleviate your fears. You need to begin tackling these fears by raising your self-confidence. Once you do this, you can move on to face your challenges. This is a classic aspect for paranoia and melancholia because instead of doing something about it, you dwell on it. If you feel you need help then seek it, don't just sit there. In this age of counselling and therapy, there are gifted, expert people who are there to prevent you from submerging yourself in a slough of despond. Once out of the mire, you can start to help those who were in your position. Give yourself a pat on the back and learn to love yourself a little bit more on the way.

SATURN TRINE NEPTUNE

This aspect indicates a powerful interest in the environment around you. You have a real need to improve your surroundings and may also work to change society on a more widespread level. You're no fool when it comes to charitable or altruistic appeals. You believe that people should help themselves and that sometimes the people who think they mean well are actually the ones causing more problems. You are sure that if people are given the means to help themselves they will do so and if they don't, they don't deserve your help. You take a very sensible approach to a sensitive problem.

SATURN OPPOSITION NEPTUNE

You can be so afraid of failure that you hide from the real world. The more you hide from that real world, the more you fear it. The only way you are going to face the challenges in your life is by breaking out of this vicious circle. You can only begin to do this by facing up to the reality. Because hard-headed Saturn is opposed by self deceiving Neptune, it will be hard for you to admit when things are wrong and when denial sets in you can be even more fearful. Let me put it this way – don't try to tackle your problems all at once but see them in proportion to what they really are. If you need support to do this exercise, seek it through a doctor or consultant who is expert in this field. Little by little, you will see that much of your worry was irrational and in your mind. You are too harsh on yourself; this may stem from a father or parent who withdrew affection when you most needed it.

SATURN CONJUNCT PLUTO

You are highly ambitious and will draw on every ounce of energy and experience until you fulfil your goals. You are a good judge of character and will use this ability to further your progress. However, this conjunction can also be ruthless and cruel; perhaps a man used or abused you in some way. Revenge is a dish best eaten cold, not taken out on the innocents around you. If you have issues that border on the psychological, therapy will soon root out the evil and prevent you from harbouring a hurt that prevents you from succeeding in life. Giving credit where it's due and loving thy neighbour is both empowering and transforming, and can help you transcend the bad.

SATURN SEXTILE PLUTO

You are prepared to work as hard as you need to in order to succeed. You expect others to match your energy, dedication and enthusiasm. This is a very karmic link – as all Saturn–Pluto rays are – and as a result, you are aware that what you put into something now will be rewarded later. As you sow, so shall you reap. You also realize your diligence and almost obsessive dedication means you'll leave no stone unturned in your quest for success.

SATURN SQUARE PLUTO

You are so defensive that you would rather not try something than risk failure, yet you try to mask this basic lack of confidence with anger and bitterness. Spool back to your early years. Did your father or a trusted male figure do you down or take their frustrations out on you? The more ingrained this issue has become, the harder it will be to root out. But the sooner you realize that your current distress stems from a bad experience, the sooner you can do something about it. This aspect can often coincide with a total distrust or even hatred of men. Understand that to generalize in such a sweeping way can be destructive in the extreme. You believe that the troubles of the world can't be compared with your own, which you feel are insurmountable. If you can't help yourself, ask for help from those who can.

SATURN TRINE PLUTO

You are imbued with a winning combination of determination, persistence and talent, which you combine with an ability to concentrate totally on the task in front of you. This won't go unnoticed by those in positions of power. You can reach a position of authority and influence in your life if you play to your Saturnian strengths of responsibility and hard work. You will also benefit from drawing on your Plutonian energies, in particular realizing that when something has outgrown its usefulness, it needs to be replaced by something better equipped for the job.

SATURN OPPOSITION PLUTO

You can end up as a pawn in other people's power games, so you need to be wary of people whose motives might be suspicious and instead focus on people who deal in the truth. Psychological tactics will be used but unless you are careful they could be used against you. Rather than throw in your lot with someone with whom you have a vested interest or feel some misguided loyalty to, you should sit on the fence. Otherwise, you risk getting in too deep or losing touch with your actual strengths and weaknesses. In other words, you are best off sticking to what you know and knowing your limitations. With this aspect it is imperative you stay on the right side of officialdom and make sure red tape is always neatly tied up.

SATURN CONJUNCT ASCENDANT

This aspect indicates you have had a serious sense of responsibility since an early age. You have conducted your life carefully, being sure never to make a false move, watching out for the pitfalls along the way. As a result of this, you may have achieved a position of some power professionally. Saturn in the 12th can create irrational fears and a longing for seclusion away from the hustle and bustle of life. Saturn in the 1st is more daring compared with the 12th house, and it can give you great authority and gravitas. It still takes time for you to take to someone, but for you the proof of the pudding is in the eating anyway.

SATURN SEXTILE ASCENDANT

You are respected and admired for your disciplined and conscientious approach. No-one appreciates you more than your superiors at work, who value these qualities highly. You are committed and determined to see things through. Your serious personality is balanced by a wicked sense of humour that people sometimes won't appreciate because it is so dry.

SATURN SQUARE ASCENDANT

Fear of failure roots you to the spot. You are terrified that you will not live up to people's expectations and, as a result, you daren't try things. You are seriously underestimating your abilities and should be more optimistic about what you can achieve. You can dwell on the past, leading a life filled with thoughts of lost opportunities and 'if onlys'. The thing to remember is that we have all experienced 'what might have beens'. Unless you get yourself a new existence and push the past behind you, you will get nowhere. Put down past rejections or problems to experience and vow never to let it happen again. Don't let your gloomy and pessimistic personality give you a mask of tragedy. It is unattractive and a real turn-off.

SATURN TRINE ASCENDANT

You are someone who adheres to the old saying, 'If you want a job done properly, do it yourself.' You believe in hard work and playing to your strengths. You don't waste time on things you know you won't succeed at. You may not have a lot of friends but you are very loyal to those you have. You are respected amongst your peers and exude a personality that is seen as trustworthy and reliable. If people want a job done with due diligence and an almost pedantic approach, they will ask you. Just don't get bogged down by doing everyone's dirty work. After all, they have their karma too.

SATURN OPPOSITION ASCENDANT

You are defensive about what you see as your lack of power. In a relationship you are convinced you are the junior partner and don't like it. You are drawn to people who are older, wiser and wealthier than you. With Saturn on the 7th, you are bound to want someone you can depend and rely upon, but don't be a drudge or allow anyone to see you as such. You are very ambitious for your other half and if you work with someone you love, be warned that you could end up with very little 'play' time. This in the end could tell on you both. For some cultures, this aspect represents arranged marriages, often severely limiting the romantic and creative expression of the individuals. It can also mean a marriage of convenience in any culture.

SATURN CONJUNCT MIDHEAVEN

You are limited in many ways but usually by yourself. You may feel pressure to follow in your father's footsteps or that it is incumbent on you to take on a big responsibility. As a result, you may be in a career that limits you. Actually this aspect can often give the person who has it management potential, so the sooner you can get out of any yoke you have chosen to saddle yourself with, you can get on with the business of being a self-made person, coming through against all the odds. Saturn rewards hard-working, committed, conscientious people very well.

SATURN SEXTILE MIDHEAVEN

With this aspect in your chart, you are practical and pragmatic. You approach everything in a very straightforward, matter-of-fact manner and achieve your goals by doing so. By applying yourself towards one subject or vocation, you will achieve your goal. It might not be in a spectacular way but you will accomplish more than your average person. Success is won through sheer effort and determination.

SATURN SQUARE MIDHEAVEN

You are someone who chooses to face the Seven Trials of Hercules. Every obstacle, hurdle and setback imaginable is going to be placed in your way. Yet if you take things one step at a time and persist, in the end you will fulfil your ambitions. The biggest problem you have is thinking that you owe it to someone to succeed or perhaps you are doing it for your father or a person who told you to. Pure sentimental rubbish – stand on your own two feet. The only person you owe it to is yourself and at the end of it you can stick two fingers up to your critics because you came through against the odds. This aspect demands total commitment but it also demands that you take time off and enjoy yourself in whatever way you can, otherwise you will burn so much midnight oil you end up with ill-health.

SATURN TRINE MIDHEAVEN

You are imbued with a combination of ambition and a disciplined, cautious approach to life. This will help you go far as it will be admired and appreciated by those in power. You are undoubtedly management material, going as far as becoming president or prime minister or the Captain Mainwaring of your own particular home guard. Seriously though, and Saturn *is* serious with this aspect, just stick to a dedicated work rate and you will achieve your target, winning recognition as a result.

SATURN OPPOSITION MIDHEAVEN

You may have had a parent who intimidated or struck fear into you, resulting in a deep-seated need to lay down safe and secure roots. Don't be disencouraged. If you have been carrying this emotional baggage, either seek help from someone or put your trust in fate. Whatever you were told, *you did not deserve it.* Free yourself from guilt. With a more positive outlook you will find someone who loves you for who you are. Even if you find it hard to reciprocate at first – which you will – love will grow and success will follow.

With the following three planets, the aspects are very much generational, so many people of the same age will have them. Therefore, they tend to reflect a social or collective conscience in an individual. You must look to the faster-moving planets to see how they affect you personally.

The Aspects of Uranus

Uranian aspects to all the earlier planets will be found in their sections.

URANUS CONJUNCT NEPTUNE

You have a powerful social conscience and are drawn towards helping people, whether personally or as a career. This aspect isn't strong unless Uranus or Neptune is emphasized in the birth chart.

URANUS SEXTILE NEPTUNE

If you have this aspect in your chart, you have a strong creative and intuitive side to your personality. You may find your strength in the sciences. This aspect isn't strong unless Uranus or Neptune is emphasized in the birth chart.

URANUS SQUARE NEPTUNE

You can get confused and muddled up in your thinking and become scatterbrained. Relaxing more will help you. This aspect isn't strong unless Uranus or Neptune is emphasized in the birth chart.

URANUS TRINE NEPTUNE

You have an appealing mixture of originality, ingenuity, sensitivity and compassion, which allows you to be successful in a lot of areas. This aspect isn't strong unless Uranus or Neptune is emphasized in the birth chart.

URANUS OPPOSITION NEPTUNE

You have a tendency to live on your nerves or be prone to paranoia, so make plenty of space for rest and relaxation in your life. This aspect isn't strong unless Uranus or Neptune is emphasized in the birth chart.

URANUS CONJUNCT PLUTO

You are one of life's natural leaders, although you will tend to use this talent for your own ends rather than for society as a whole. This aspect isn't strong unless Uranus or Pluto is emphasized in the birth chart.

URANUS SEXTILE PLUTO

You relish dramatic changes in your life, something that might reflect a love of exerting influence over others. This aspect isn't strong unless Uranus or Pluto is emphasized in the birth chart.

URANUS SQUARE PLUTO

You can be a disruptive influence over others. When change comes, it causes upheaval and your natural instinct is to cut anybody or anything off that is associated with it. This aspect isn't strong unless Uranus or Pluto is emphasized in the birth chart.

URANUS TRINE PLUTO

Creating the conditions for significant change or transformation at regular intervals in your life is something that you enjoy. Sometimes, however, you find it hard to get your plans to fall into place properly. This aspect isn't strong unless Uranus or Pluto is emphasized in the birth chart.

URANUS OPPOSITION PLUTO

You get a kick out of causing disruption, primarily because of the buzz of excitement it gives you. There's rarely a dull moment with people born in this period. This aspect isn't strong unless Uranus or Pluto is emphasized in the birth chart.

URANUS CONJUNCT ASCENDANT

You are something of a one-off. It may be that your appearance is out of the ordinary or that you dress in a way that sets you apart from the crowd. You have a powerful need for your own space and to be independent. This will show itself in your creative side, where you will show great originality and individuality. Uranus in the 12th can bring emotional tension but tremendous intuition in the 1st. You can startle people with your amazing ways – people love or loathe you.

URANUS SEXTILE ASCENDANT

You are a bright and lively personality who keeps everyone on their toes. You have a fiercely independent nature and will resist anything that limits you. There's something that is so different about you and it's this indefinable quality that draws people to you for all kinds of reasons. You are certainly way ahead of your time.

URANUS SQUARE ASCENDANT

You are a highly sensitive and outrageous personality, with an unpredictable streak. You seem to take a perverse pleasure in provoking a reaction from others. However, your love of shocking people can go to extremes and you end up hurting the very folks you adore the most. Sometimes you can go so over the top that you stir up a storm and the controversy you create is more destructive than you ever wanted. Remember this: it can all end in tears.

URANUS TRINE ASCENDANT

You've got an awful lot going for you. You are charismatic and magnetic with an awesome personality and are regarded as huge fun to be with. If you have an ingenious or creative side, you are blessed with an originality that people are totally wowed by. Star quality is something you have in abundance but be warned of more conservative, traditional types who see you as coming to cause consternation. They may try to block your path, but you can win over the hardest heart – if you can be bothered. You are one in a million.

URANUS OPPOSITION ASCENDANT

You are someone who really shakes things up when you are around others. You need to be independent emotionally. With Uranus on your 7th house cusp, you will want a partnership that enables you to go off and do your own thing. If you can't, it will lead to separation or divorce. You want an open affair, not one that is conventional. In fact, your sexual tastes may run the gamut of both sexes and if not, you are certainly going to experiment with more than one member of the gender you enjoy the most. Commitment is not for you – a confirmed bachelor or spinster you should remain!

URANUS CONJUNCT MIDHEAVEN

An anarchic streak runs through you. You will want to rebel against your family and your background, and will want to shock people with your job and lifestyle. Your career should be one that enables you to run your own empire. It doesn't matter whether you're freelance or self-employed, just so long as you're your own boss. You get really furious with people who don't realize what a genius you are, which I have no doubt that you are. But people who are clever often don't get credit until it's too late. Prepare to change your career many times or reinvent yourself to stay at the top of your profession. You might even choose a *nom de plume* to carry on one side of your career.

URANUS SEXTILE MIDHEAVEN

You need a career that allows you an outlet for your originality and intelligence. You revel in staying one step ahead of people. You need to have two or even three professions on the go or you'll get bored. If you can't have that, then at least choose a career that allows you to use your inventive flair and far-thinking mind.

URANUS SQUARE MIDHEAVEN

You are highly strung and don't react well to tension. When times are hard you get very emotional and tend to dramatize things so that they become worse than they actually are. You need to find a way of letting off emotional steam. Professionally, you mustn't be pushed into a career or job that doesn't suit you. If you are, you will live to fight another day but you'll be scarred or bruised by all the stress it put you through. Paddle your own canoe in life and follow a vocation that suits your unpredictable self.

URANUS TRINE MIDHEAVEN

You're full of energy and ideas, and will do well in the workplace where those in power will spot your abilities. You should be careful not to jump from job to job purely for the sake of it as this may damage your career in the long term. Any calling that allows you the breadth of vision to work your magic will give you the success and recognition you totally deserve. At times you will want to reinvent yourself and do something completely different – well, you can't keep a good Uranian down!

URANUS OPPOSITION MIDHEAVEN

An upheaval or upsetting event during your childhood may have taught you to fend for yourself. This independent and resourceful nature means you struggle to lay down roots and are restless, both personally and professionally. You need a career that allows you to do what comes naturally. The minute you become bored or are fettered by rules or regulations, you will want out. Whatever you do, have the patience at least to learn something from the experience, however short it was. Your best bet is to go for something that you can do in your time, your own way and your own place.

The Aspects of Neptune

Neptune's aspects to earlier planets will be found in their sections.

NEPTUNE SEXTILE PLUTO

These two planets are moving so slowly in relation to us that they have been in this aspect for the last century and will remain there for a long time to come, so many of you will have this placement in your chart. It will only be strong, however, if Neptune or Pluto is emphasized in your birth chart. If it is, this indicates that you have a very highly developed intuition.

NEPTUNE CONJUNCT ASCENDANT

There is an air of mystery about you – almost, at times, as if you are from another planet. You are a kind and gentle soul who often fails to make an impression on others. Your psychic sense is very well developed and you should pursue spiritual matters as much as you can. Your image is more important to you than almost any other planet. How you are seen and the first impressions you create can help you succeed or cause you to fail.

NEPTUNE SEXTILE ASCENDANT

You relish creating a sense of enigmatic mystery around yourself. People are drawn to you, often because they are fascinated to work you out. You are a born romantic and highly sensitive, too. Matters of fashion and image should concern you because the first impression you make when you meet someone will make more of an impact than you realize.

NEPTUNE SQUARE ASCENDANT

You may have a hard time keeping a grip on reality and may deceive not just yourself but those around you, too. Be wary of taking too many things that are a health hazard – you can have an addictive personality. You seem to have a downer on yourself, and beat yourself up. Why? You are kind, sensitive and adorable! Time to get another mirror and perhaps a makeover as there's nothing wrong with you that a transformation psychologically and physically wouldn't cure.

NEPTUNE TRINE ASCENDANT

You have amazing intuition and imagination, and are able to use it in a very creative way. Your artistic sense is not only highly developed but can make you more image-conscious than most. There's nothing wrong with that; in fact, it is necessary if you are going to turn heads in your direction. Once you have someone's sole attention, you can have your way with them – assuming your intentions are honourable. Who can resist you? Very few!

NEPTUNE OPPOSITION ASCENDANT

You are a born romantic, in love with the idea of either being the damsel in distress rescued from the tower or the handsome prince who comes to her aid on his charger. You have a problem seeing relationships for what they really are and have a habit of seeing only what you want to see. With Neptune on the 7th house Descendant, you must be aware that your partner may find it hard to live up to the image of them that you have created. No-one can be that perfect. Unless you realize they are human beings, you will end up disillusioned and disparaged in your relationships. Beauty is only skin deep; what you need is someone who cares for you and whose loveliness shines through from their heart.

NEPTUNE CONJUNCT MIDHEAVEN

You really can't make up your mind what you want to achieve in life.

You know you want the world to admire and respect you, but aren't realistic enough to knuckle down to something that will win you that audience. Instead you tend to daydream about a future that will never arrive unless you change. You can be confused about your career image, not really sure what shadow you are casting on the ground. Any profession that is about glamour appeals to you, as you want a career in which you can be anyone but yourself.

NEPTUNE SEXTILE MIDHEAVEN

With this aspect in your chart, you are suited to classic Neptune professions such as the arts, caring for others or drawing on your highly developed imagination. You will be in seventh heaven if you can find success doing what you do best. If you can't, follow a spiritual path, as that will eventually lead you to your calling.

NEPTUNE SQUARE MIDHEAVEN

You aren't averse to bending the truth in order to achieve your ends. You may exaggerate your work experience to win a new job, for instance. You also know how to suck up to people with influence, using them to your advantage. However, be warned of manipulating people in your career. There's no harm in getting a leg up on the professional ladder so that people can recognize your true talent, but if you hope to make it purely on the back of others then you may fall off. You are gifted but need to find a vocation that suits you – this can be the most confusing part. Strip away the kidology and you'll find your real gifts.

NEPTUNE TRINE MIDHEAVEN

You need to transcend the ordinary and normal, to do something that transcends your more material needs. You certainly don't count success in terms of earnings but more in terms of the souls you may have saved from a terrible life. You excel at working for charities at home or abroad, or practising a career that is for the good and removes the bad and ugly from this world. You have a flair for colour and design, and shine at giving yourself over to the creative and beautiful.

NEPTUNE OPPOSITION MIDHEAVEN

You have a tendency to reinvent the past to your advantage. This ability to bend the truth means you can be unreliable and untrustworthy at work. Going for the sympathy vote can have its advantages but it can also create other problems, such as beginning to believe your untruths. Knowing where reality starts and fantasy ends is important to your career prospects; otherwise your reputation could be damaged by scandal or humiliation. Be honest, if only to yourself. You may have a deep-seated need to create a home that you regard as perfect.

The Aspects of Pluto

Pluto's aspects to earlier planets will be found in their sections.

PLUTO CONJUNCT ASCENDANT

You have problems with letting people get too close to you and tend to keep relations on a social basis. Pluto in the 12th has a total fascination for the occult and anything cloak and dagger. You'd make a great spy as you can wear the invisible cloak of this planet in your day-to-day business. Pluto in the 1st is power-crazy, you want to control and rule and with your sexual magnetism you can undoubtedly do it. However, it is best to do things in a gentle and not too vulgar way as once you have been outed as someone on the make, you can never repair your image.

PLUTO SEXTILE ASCENDANT

You have a deep-rooted need to shake your life upside down every now and again. The only problem is that you sometimes overdo it and throw the baby out with the bathwater. Constant transformations in your image and your outlook are important. You know that once something has outlived its previous usefulness it is time to ditch it and wear something more with-it and eye-catching. You ooze sex appeal.

PLUTO SQUARE ASCENDANT

You will face frustrations and knockbacks in a certain part of your life. Look at which house Pluto is placed in your chart to see which area will be affected. Don't be too tenacious and cling onto hope when all is lost. Much better to cut your losses rather than assume all will be well in the end – it might not be. Once something is past its sell-by-date, hurl it into the trash can. You must be much less resistant to change as very often not only is a change as good as a rest, but it is imperative to your success and happiness. Your problem is you don't know when to let go. The answer is – as soon as it becomes an issue.

PLUTO TRINE ASCENDANT

You embrace change but have to be careful not to cut out more from your old life than is necessary. You are ready for transformation as soon as you realize your image and dress are behind the times. Of course, you look great in black and that will never alter. You've got a personality that is not only drop-dead sexy but you have the ability to control those who come into your orbit and they don't even know it. Once you have them hooked with your hypnotic eyes, you can twist someone round your little finger. It can be like taking candy from a baby. Easy now, though. Don't be too rough or tough, remember what comes around....

PLUTO OPPOSITION ASCENDANT

You have a need to control people, but often see others as wanting to control you. This leads to power struggles within relationships. You are into mind games. You want a partner who is passionate but at the same time you invite jealousy, envy and revenge into your heart. It isn't easy having this aspect because it is very complex, but if you find the going gets tough in your relationship then it may be worth seeing a complete stranger for guidance before one of you gets going. Either that or an attempt to work out the issues between you.

PLUTO CONJUNCT MIDHEAVEN

You may choose your career deliberately in order to wield some kind of power. You will throw yourself completely into your job but may change course completely and take up another job on a regular basis. You aren't content playing second fiddle and will become totally obsessed with success. Once you have achieved your aim, you will take your bandwagon elsewhere. There may be some dirty business played in your career. If you can't get your own way cleanly then you have been known to do whatever it takes to win. That can feel good for a while, until you realize you have an army of people bent on revenge. Best think again before you take on anyone who could come back and nip your professional aspirations in the bud.

PLUTO SEXTILE MIDHEAVEN

You are well equipped to cope with changes in your life and may well face many, particularly at work where upheavals may occur beyond your control. However, a transfusion of new knowledge, doing something different somewhere exotic, is just what you need. In the end you are happy to be a big fish in a small pond, just so long as you are in charge.

PLUTO SQUARE MIDHEAVEN

You will have to cope with frequent disruptions and changes at work. How well you are equipped to do this will depend on your inner strength as indicated more generally in your birth chart. Fate plays more than an average role in your career world. Like a chapter in a book, your professional journey will have abrupt beginnings and endings. Very often for no reason, you are taken away from a situation before you've had time to even think about it. The trick is to know when to let go. If you become obsessive or hellbent on revenge, you are wasting positive energy on negative issues. Move on when anything occurs that you have no control over. Accept it's nature's way of telling you a new day has just dawned.

PLUTO TRINE MIDHEAVEN

You have the ability to draw on transformation, using the experience to become stronger. You can gain a great deal through others' misfortunes. If you are meant to be somewhere or doing something, you will be in the right place at the right time. Kismet is forever looking after you and guiding you. It may be disconcerting at first but you'll soon get the hang of the fact that you have no control over your destiny. That's right, none, and don't you forget it. What's certain is that you won't do badly by it. In fact, you will owe more to fate than you realize after all is said and done.

PLUTO OPPOSITION MIDHEAVEN

You may have had a parent who exerted a great deal of power over you. It will be hard to shake off the influence of this father or father figure who played an enormous part in your life, for good or bad. Your career may involve research or detective work of some kind, perhaps in a job in which you need to don a uniform. It takes a thief to catch one and you may be a poacher turned gamekeeper, someone whose ability to read the criminal mind may have come through suffering or experience.

FIVE

Starcharts

Interpreting the Birth Charts of the Rich and Famous

I know from long experience that people getting into astrology are fascinated by the horoscopes of the rich and famous. This isn't just because they are nosy or obsessed with celebrity culture. It runs deeper than that. Looking at the detailed birth charts of well-known personalities is an excellent way for students of astrology to start pulling together all the elements of chart analysis they have learned. Reading about a Moon in Pisces or a Sun in Sagittarius can seem rather cold and abstract on paper. Seeing how those placings work for a world-famous actor or statesman brings the subject to life and makes it easier to understand. By looking at how the planets have moulded a popular personality they are familiar with, people seem better able to grasp the big picture. You know the image of the person, the character they project, but you also know it is a mask and to find out how the actual person ticks is often a revelation.

In the pages that follow I have analyzed the birth charts of a few ultra-famous individuals. Hopefully each interpretation will help show how the whole astrological cast fits together. Hopefully, too, each will help you to consolidate the principles you have learned already. But a word of caution again: don't be daunted if you fail to understand the analysis I use immediately. I am bringing to bear 40 years of study, a lifetime devoted to this ever-fascinating art and science. You are still – even after all the hard work and effort you have put into reading and understanding this book – on a celestial learning curve, a freshman. So, as you read these analyses, it is important to take your time and consider all that you have read in this book. If you do things will eventually fall into place. In the meantime, I hope these mini character studies make for interesting reading!

Prince William

BORN TO BE KING

Prince William is, without question, the world's most eligible bachelor. The elder son of Prince Charles and the late Diana, Princess of Wales, he is second in line to the throne. As he passes through his early twenties, he is beginning to look like someone who was literally born to be king, a young man who will take his accession, when it eventually comes, in his stride.

Unlike his younger brother Harry, who has had his share of public troubles, William has conducted himself with immense dignity and intelligence. He has also carried himself as well as any young man could in coping with the trauma of losing his beloved mother in such awful circumstances. At some point in the future, of course, he is going to have to make the biggest decision of his life: choose a wife fit to be his queen. How will he cope with this? And what sort of king might he make? His birth chart is very revealing in both respects.

PRINCE WILLIAM'S CHART

Prince William was born at 9.03 p.m. on 21 June 1982 in Paddington, Middlesex. I know this birth date is correct because it was given to me by his mother.

PRINCE WILLIAM'S BIRTH CHART

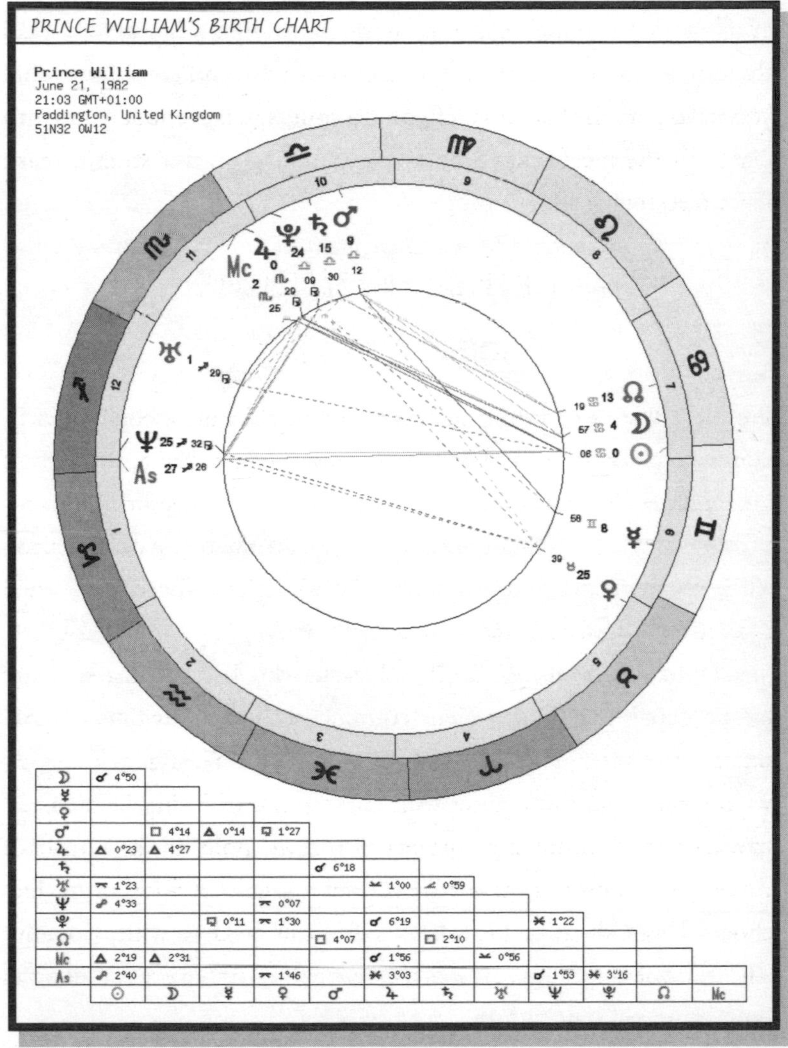

☽	☌ 4°50											
☿												
♀												
♂		□ 4°14	△ 0°14	⚼ 1°27								
♃	△ 0°23	△ 4°27										
♄					☌ 6°18							
♅	⚻ 1°23					⚺ 1°00	∠ 0°59					
♆	☍ 4°33			⚻ 0°07								
♇			⚼ 0°11	⚻ 1°30		☌ 6°19			⚹ 1°22			
☊					□ 4°07		□ 2°10					
Mc	△ 2°19	△ 2°31				☌ 1°56		⚺ 0°56				
As	☍ 2°40			⚻ 1°46		⚹ 3°03			☌ 1°53	⚹ 3°16		
	☉	☽	☿	♀	♂	♃	♄	♅	♆	♇	☊	Mc

What strikes me immediately is the extremely potent arrangement of Prince William's most important planets, the Sun and Moon. Both are placed in Cancer, the Moon at almost 5 degrees, the Sun at 0 degrees, so that they form a wonderful conjunction. To add to the potency and power, this also means that William was born on a New Moon *and* a Solar Eclipse, so this child would have an influence where he could change the world about him in a big way. This situation is given even greater dynamism, of course, by the fact that Cancer is ruled by the Moon, which makes her even more comfortable there. This set-up gets even better, though. The Moon is trine to Jupiter, which is in Scorpio *plus* the Sun forms an *exact* trine to Jupiter. This awesome astral arrangement couldn't be more appropriate for the destiny had in mind for Diana and Charles's first-born.

All this just oozes royalty. In fact, if somebody asked me to create a chart for a prince, I couldn't have done it any better. The Sun–Moon conjunction in the Moon's own sign, allied to Jupiter is wonderful enough. But with Jupiter at the top of the chart just like – if we remember our mythology – he is looking down from Mount Olympus, with Jupiter conjunct to the Midheaven, the career point of the chart. All this indicates that a Greek god is reborn!

I have had my doubts whether Prince Charles would ever be king, since the 1970s. Even if he does succeed his mother, his reign will be short-lived. I still feel that way and believe the succession might even skip a generation and go straight to William. Looking at his easy-going, free-flowing chart, I can see that he will make a marvellous monarch.

William was born under an eclipsed new Moon, which reveals a powerful yet loving mother. Diana's death would have hit him badly, and the deep feelings of loss he carries with him, as a double Cancerian, will stay with him for the rest of his life.

There is a strong link between his chart and that of Diana's, which I know very well. She was born on 1 July, which means, of course, she also had her Sun in Cancer conjunct her young son's Moon (and they both have Sagittarius rising to strengthen their bond). There is no way death can come between them. In fact with his own well-developed Neptune in his own 12th house of psychic powers, I believe he knows that she is guiding him. Therefore, when he hears people talking about her in derogatory or revealing terms, or bringing up shallow and trite news stories or even features based on fantasy or pure lies, it must crucify him. Whenever the latest peripheral figure emerges to claim their 30 pieces of silver, I am sure William is outraged – but more than that, hurt.

I am interested that he has Sagittarius rising, making the ruler of the chart, Jupiter, in his father's sign of Scorpio. Sagittarius rising and Jupiter is very royal indeed, in fact, imperial to a degree. It can gift its owner with a wonderful fun sense of humour, making him a joy to have around, and yet at the same time, Neptune rising makes him keen to play a role behind the scenes too. He will do a great deal of good we may never know about. All this underlines the fact that he is *meant* to be up there in the pantheon of sovereigns. When he takes the throne he will show the same dedication and commitment to tradition as his grandmother, Queen Elizabeth.

Looking at the chart, I am sure William has strong opinions that he is willing to share. Indeed, I believe he will have advised his father to get on with his life in recent years. Charles has Venus and Neptune conjunct in Libra, which means he is someone who tends to idealize women and but can be easily manipulated by them. William, with his outspoken Sagittarius rising (the empathy with his Dad's Jupiter in his home sign of Sagittarius!) is the type of person who would have told his father to see the reality of his situation. He would have said, 'Come on Dad, pull yourself together and get your act sorted.' His blessing of Charles's marriage to Camilla Parker Bowles would have been hugely influential. And with Neptune as the rising planet, he would have the compassion and sensitivity to understand what his father needs rather than wants.

William has another exact and highly beneficial aspect in his chart. Mercury, a couple of minutes off nine degrees in Gemini (Mercury rules Gemini) is trine to Mars at nine degrees in Libra. Mercury is also in a wider trine to Saturn, at 15 degrees Libra.

You will hopefully remember that I said an aspect is even more powerful if it is exact, in the case of a trine, 120 degrees precisely. Mars and Mercury are exactly this distance apart, which lends them an absolute empathy. If we use the stage analogy from the beginning of the book, this is like having two wonderful actors – Olivier and Burton from the older generation, or Tom Cruise and Johnny Depp from the newer generation – sharing scintillating dialogue together. Their relationship would be fantastically positive, full of opinions and sparkling wit. So this element of his chart indicates William has a quick, agile mind, can be very creative, and enjoys learning and discussion. What with Jupiter as the chart ruler and Mercury well disposed, it's clear that if he hadn't been born to royalty, then travel, learning, in fact all things international and intellectual, would have formed the basis of his vocation.

I am sure William has a tremendous affinity with his grandmother, the queen. I should think they often amuse each other, so much so that they will hoot with laughter from time to time. He trusts the queen and she adores him.

It is worth emphasizing that William does have a hidden side, due to the Water-based Sun–Moon trine to Jupiter and Neptune at home in the 12th house of secrets and sorrows. Apart from giving him great popularity with those he is in close proximity with, this indicates he also realizes discretion is the better part of valour. Some people may see a secretive trait as a negative, but that is not always the case. It can be good judgement not to tell everybody everything, particularly in a position as powerful and politically sensitive as the reigning monarch. This is why having his mother's name dragged up all the time gets to him so much. William has an unbreakable code of ethics and would wish, I am sure, that he could stamp it on everybody.

Of course, it is William's love life that in the short term at least is going to be of the most interest. Venus, naturally, holds many of the greatest clues to what is likely to happen here. She is placed at 25 degrees in Taurus, which is fantastic because as we know, Venus is the ruler of this sign. William also has his Mars, Saturn and Pluto together in Libra, which is, of course, the sign of Venus. Having these three heavy guys in this sign suggests that he will be someone who enjoys the sexual side of his life. Of course, he is not going to be short of all sorts of women throwing themselves at him.

There are less auspicious aspects in the chart, however. There is an opposition to Uranus, at one degree Sagittarius. Again it is a 'disassociated' aspect, but it is strong enough to leave Venus a bit naked. There is also a very important minor aspect here. (I have not gone into details of all the minor aspects within this book. There are so many and they are so subtle it would require another book to cover them. However, it is important to point this one out.) Neptune is rising at 25 degrees in Sagittarius. This means that his image will be very Sagittarian as watery Neptune will reflect its traits. Think of William in pictures and you see laughter, someone tall, blond, handsome and captivating, in short, Neptune–Sagittarius at its very best. However, Neptune does have an awkward aspect with Venus, who luxuriates at 25 degrees in Taurus. This is known as a quincunx. A quincunx is a very irritating aspect and when it is exact – as it is in this case – it can be prove romantically troublesome. The effect of it is to create a lack of rhythm in William's love life. William also has Neptune rising in the 12th house, which can be very idealistic. The practical impact of all this may well be that he finds it hard to find himself the right partner in life. He will seek total perfection and, dare I say it, a woman whom he would automatically compare with his wonderful mother. Who on earth is going to come up to such high standards or even want to be put in that position?

There may be other reasons why the path of true love may not run true for William. Some women simply may not fancy being a princess within the most famous and scrutinized royal family in the world. The Venus–Neptune quincunx may also create a problem with unrequited love – a situation his mother knew about only too well!

Neptune is in the 12th House, its own house, which adds to the problem. This, to me, suggests a vestige of Queen Victoria's life where, having found the love of her life, she had him taken away from her. This, of course, is what happened with her and Prince Albert. Or in this instance it can mean Diana, his beloved mum.

William's chart is absolutely fabulous in almost every other respect. But this vulnerability in Venus where she is under attack from Neptune and Uranus is something he will have to watch out for. The last thing he wants to do, I'm sure, is repeat the unhappiness his mother and father went through so publicly.

Catherine Zeta Jones

SELF-MADE SUPERSTAR

Catherine Zeta Jones has travelled a long way from her home in the lovely Welsh seaside town of the Mumbles, near Swansea. A prodigious talent as a young girl, she made her breakthrough on the West End stage as what she modestly calls 'a hoofer'. She was spotted by television bosses and jettisoned to fame in the UK in the hugely popular show *The Darling Buds of May*. Her fresh-faced, dark-haired beauty immediately turned her into Britain's Darling. But it was when she headed off to Hollywood that her life really took off. Working hard in a string of supporting roles, she eventually got spotted and made her breakthrough alongside Antonio Banderas in *The Mask of Zorro*. Bigger parts soon followed.

Her rise to the top of the Hollywood heap was completed when she met and fell in love with one of the movie industry's most powerful and successful stars, Michael Douglas. Since their marriage, she has become a mother and one of the world's most alluring actresses. Her career has gone from strength to strength, culminating with her Oscar for her role in *Chicago*.

So what was it that drove the girl from west Wales to go west to Hollywood? And what inner planetary powers helped her conquer the movie business?

CATHERINE ZETA JONES'S BIRTH CHART

This is a highly active chart for someone who, I can reveal, is a contradictory personality. In particular, there are two complex arrangements at the heart of things. Mars is square to the Sun, Uranus and Mercury. These three planets are also in a disassociate (when the signs are of the same quality) opposition to the Moon. When you have one opposition connected to any squares emanating at 90 degrees, this is a T-square. This can symbolize a tremendous challenge, a weight a person may have to carry through life either from without or within.

The powerful T-square, however, is counteracted by a fabulously positive arrangement known as a grand trine. (I mentioned this earlier, in the introduction to the Aspects.) Here, Mars is two degrees Capricorn, in an exact trine with Venus at two degrees Virgo. This trine alone is very revealing. It is no surprise it belongs to a woman regarded as one of the sexiest and most glamorous stars in the world. It is perfectly bewitching and entrancing. In turn Saturn is connected to both love planets to create a downright earthy grand trine, being exactly 120 degrees from both Mars and Venus.

A grand trine is a wonderful astrological aspect. It creates an easy, auspicious flow between the planets involved. Once they are triggered off by a passing planet in transit, there is no stopping them from blessing the person they imbue with great fortune and personal potential. So in Catherine's case she has Mars, Venus and Saturn forming her grand trine. The fact that it is rooted by Saturn in the 5th house (house of love) gives it more gravitas – often indicative of marrying a partner older or more experienced, or both! (More on this later!) This is the chart of someone who would have had to grow up quickly, bearing duty or responsibility on her shoulders. Indeed, she is entirely self-made.

This is where the heavier side of Saturn comes in. Here we have a woman who once she sets her mind on something will get it, whatever it takes. She is determined, not afraid to work and play hard if

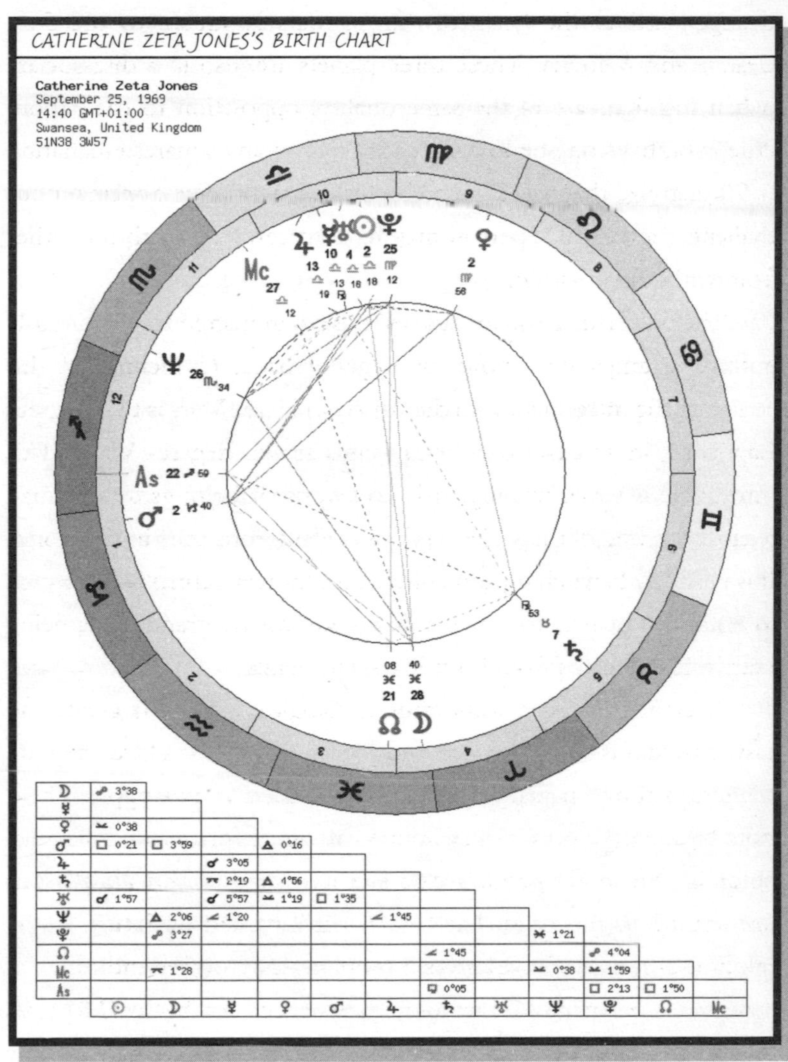

☽	☍ 3°38											
☿												
♀	⚺ 0°38											
♂	□ 0°21	□ 3°59		△ 0°16								
♃			☌ 3°05									
♄			⚻ 2°19	△ 4°56								
♅	☌ 1°57		☌ 5°57	⚺ 1°19	□ 1°35							
♆		△ 2°06	∠ 1°20			∠ 1°45						
♇		☍ 3°27							⚹ 1°21			
☊							∠ 1°45			☍ 4°04		
Mc		⚻ 1°28							⚺ 0°38	⚺ 1°59		
As							⚼ 0°05			□ 2°13	□ 1°50	
	☉	☽	☿	♀	♂	♃	♄	♅	♆	♇	☊	Mc

it means her ambitions will take root. She will also be principled, placing great store in fairness and justice. These qualities come from a stellium (three or more planets in a sign or house) in Libra and the 10th house – very cool stuff indeed.

All in all, this is someone who takes aim and fires at whatever her goal is and does so with panache, chic and sophistication. In fact, people won't even realize how ambitious she is until she's up there and they are where she left them!

What else does her chart tell us? Well, it is pretty open on the romantic front too. Some have wondered if she married Michael Douglas to further her career. However, it is not quite that simple. Catherine's chart is dominated by Libra, the relationship sign. Indeed, that is the first thing that should hit you in the eyes. She has no less than four planets plus the Midheaven in Libra, including the Sun. She also has Pluto at 25 degrees Virgo. Although the god of Hades is not in Libra, he tags on to this group because of his conjunction to the Sun and they all fall in the house of career and ambition, the 10th. Was this girl destined for mega-stardom or what? What this means is that beauty is awesomely important for Catherine; for her to be seen with someone, let alone marry them, there has to be an attraction starting with looks, charm and appearance – anything else is a welcome added extra. Librans cannot abide being intimate with partners who are unattractive in any way. There must have been a degree of desire and attraction present for the relationship to get off the ground, and there must have been a lot of that for her to marry Michael. But the fact that Michael has influence and a powerful reputation in the movie industry wouldn't have done him any harm in Catherine's eyes!

There is another clue to her choice of husband in the fact that she has Mars at two degrees Capricorn. This is very indicative of a woman who marries someone who is like her father and/or successful. Capricorn is ruled by Saturn, the sign of old age, and Mars is seen as the man you desire. So she was born to marry someone older than her (Mars in Capricorn, Saturn in the 5th linked to Venus in grand trine), and Michael ticks all the boxes and even better, he is a Sun in Libra too! It is also interesting he comes from the Douglas dynasty, which links Catherine into a domestic set-up enriched with tradition and heritage. Now that does please her Saturn!

Looking at the chart more closely, we can also see that her challenging aspects would also have helped her to make the decision to be with Michael. Because of her grand trine she can say to herself, 'I am doing this for the right reasons: I find him attractive, I love his personality, he is a Saturn-type person, older and more mature than me in a way that makes me feel comfortable with this person.' And the T-square can justify it all with: 'I worked hard for this and I deserve it.' This sets her saying to herself: 'Okay, I've got what it takes in terms of talent and sex appeal, but there has to be a means to that end. I really like this man and he could really help my career. He can help me make my name.' So we see the challenging and lively aspects of her chart working together very well. As I have said before, everyone *needs* challenging aspects and Catherine's T-square is the engine that drives the more positive forces of her grand trine onwards.

There is a dichotomy, a paradox, to her as well though. With such a lot of Libra, she is almost Aries. At times, instead of being caring and sharing, she can be 'I want, I want' – very typical of Arians, who are ambitious and driven in their pursuit of their purposes.

If there is intimacy in an affair, Catherine will always have the upper hand because of Pluto and the Moon and the sexually controlling power this brings. As a result of this, I think she is someone who gives off a degree of coolness when you first met her, but when she gets to know you and warms to you, it can make life more difficult for her as she can't be quite as detached as she would have been before. As a result, she needs to watch out for sycophants who may want to exploit or use all that she has worked so hard to achieve.

This again is where her relationship with Michael works so fundamentally well. It is a very Libran thing to delegate to someone and say, 'Go off and do what you like.' Michael would be more likely to say, 'Pull yourself together.' He is a great protecting influence.

There is another dichotomy in her, to do with the Moon in the 4th house. This suggests someone who may move away from home to find success, which she has done, but her ties to her family and her home mean she misses her roots a great deal. I suspect she goes through quite a lot of emotional turmoil because she wants to be in Hollywood *and* Wales. (Is this why she has built a new home there?) She wants to be the ordinary mother and wife to Michael but she also wants to be the international movie star.

Catherine Zeta Jones has so much going for her, but the biggest test will be to align the balance of her two different creations. But let's face it; balance is what a Libran girl is all about. It will be fascinating to watch how she resolves all this in the years to come. If anyone can do it, she can.

Oprah Winfrey

FEELING THE WORLD'S PAIN

Oprah Winfrey is without doubt the most influential and popular television personality in America. People tune into her programmes in their millions. They do so because they like and, above all, trust her. Since she broke through in the 1980s, her media empire has extended far and wide. She has even won widespread acclaim as an actress, winning an Oscar nomination for her heartbreaking performance in *The Color Purple*.

Yet given her humble and tragic beginnings on a 'dirt poor'

farm in rural Mississippi, she could never have imagined the world would become her oyster in such a way. She suffered terribly: she was raped at the age of nine, sexually abused by an uncle, falling pregnant at the age of 14 only to lose the baby in childbirth.

It is amazing that she even survived, let alone that she overcame all this to become the most rich and powerful woman in the world of entertainment. So how did she do it? And what secrets lie within her chart that might explain her Cinderella-like rise from rags to incredible riches?

OPRAH WINFREY'S BIRTH CHART

This is a good example of a chart in which having the exact time of birth is crucial. Oprah's official birth time is 4.30 a.m. (She came into the world on 29 January 1954 in Kosciusko, Mississippi.) Again, this time sounds to me like it has been rounded up or down. If we take 4.30 a.m. to be accurate, then her all-important Ascendant is 29 degrees in Sagittarius. If this figure is wrong, even by a few minutes later, then she would be in Capricorn.

Being a huge admirer of Oprah's and knowing what I know about her, I think there is a very strong chance she has Capricorn rather than Sagittarius rising. However, we will go with what we have been given, which is generally the case with birth times unless you go through the process of rectification I mentioned earlier in the book.

Even if Oprah's time given birth time is accurate, Sagittarius immediately raises its head. Oprah's Moon is placed here and it is from here that she gets her Sagittarian get-up-and-go. One of the other things that strikes me initially is that her Moon is in the 12th house, the house of secrets and sorrows. Someone with the Moon in the 12th house suffers from head to toe, spiritually, physically, emotionally, so that their pain becomes an imprisonment.

Childhood is represented by the Moon, too, so there is every chance she suffered during her childhood and kept it a secret. (It was only after looking at her chart and coming to this conclusion that I learned she was abused as a child and that she kept it a secret until quite recently.)

It is her Sagittarian side that has dealt with this. Oprah's Sagittarian zeal makes her someone who will open up and reveal all. This might be for philosophical reasons, or to help deal with her guilt or psychological upset. But it may also be for moral reasons, so that no-one should be allowed to get away with such things and that by revealing her secrets she may be able to help others in the same situation. This would be typical of a humanitarian Aquarian, someone like Oprah who wants to make the world a better place. This latter motivation also reflects her Jupiter traits; she is someone who wants justice to be done.

Because Oprah's Moon is in the depths of the 12th house, she is a deeply sensitive woman, a woman who would have had to have been very self-protective early in her life because she wasn't able to say very much. The fact that she was a black woman may have added to this. She may have thought no-one would have believed her; that the stigma of her race would have also have imprisoned her. Someone with the Moon in the 12th has to suffer at some stage in order to understand what other people go through and to enable them to crusade for what they believe is right. It is a very uneasy and uncomfortable aspect to deal with when growing up, often it is the placement of an orphaned child or one who doesn't know their family. Or it might be someone who has no ties or sense of belonging. That Moon is in a sign of someone who is always on the

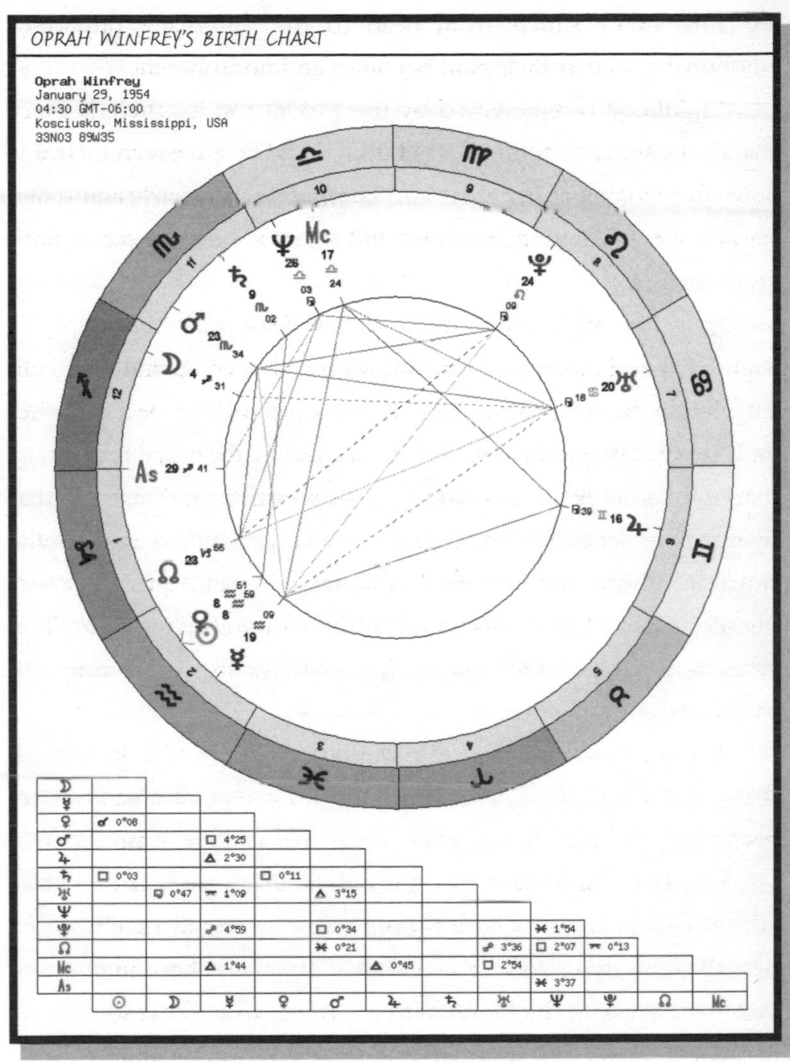

move, emotionally they have no ties or roots, they are a citizen of the world.

Her Moon also sextiles Venus and the Sun in Aquarius. This is a wonderful aspect: altruistic to a massive degree, denoting an ambassador of human kind. This means she can transcend the most base and degrading experiences she has been through. With this kind of astrological remit, Oprah is someone who would be saved from drudgery and able to make her mark in the world. She is a lesson for everyone: that if the cards you are dealt at the beginning of life are plum rotten, you can still trump them by helping yourself and making things happen against all the odds. This is why she went through what she did, in order to capitalize for herself or others. As if all this doesn't make enough sense, to complete the picture Oprah also has her Aquarian Sun conjunct Venus, the classic humanitarian and compassionate position.

Oprah's attitude to money is also explained in her chart. Someone who has not had emotional security tends to opt for the next best thing, which is material security. Having material things means Oprah has something tangible to hold on to, something that provides the roots she lacks emotionally, giving her a sense of belonging. Therefore, I would expect she is someone who has acquired a lot of property and possessions. Her ownership of these things can be exchanged, up to a point, for what she lacks, or has never really had, inside.

Jupiter is well disposed in an airy grand trine. In fact, he has a certain look in his eye as he is supported by a host of planets and he himself connects with the Midheaven. This signifies megabucks but also honour, glory and respect. It also shows a hard worker. A positive Jupiter in the 6th house person is very popular with people, so I expect colleagues love working with her although she will need to know what is going on around her. It is best no-one keeps any secrets from Oprah.

She is also extremely enterprising, thanks to her Mars–Uranus trine connection. This means she is not doing what she is doing just for herself; she is doing it to make other people's lives better. She is a social reformer and would make a great US president or head honcho of a UN department that specifically cares for those who cannot care for themselves. A goodwill ambassador of the future perhaps?

Oprah has another very interesting network within her chart. She has a T-square, an opposition with two squares either side coming off it. This, as I have explained elsewhere, is a challenging aspect that can be used to drive people on. It instils a single-mindedness and purpose. In her case, it will drive her on to fight off any voices that say 'Oprah give up'. She has the energy to get through the dramas. More importantly, she can accept psychological and physical challenges and overcome them, as I daresay she did on a sexual (Mars–Pluto) and mental (Mercury) level.

As well as this fixed T-square, as I've already mentioned, Oprah has an airy grand trine between Neptune, Jupiter and Mercury. As we know, a grand trine helps the cosmic forces of the chart flow freely together. In this case we have Neptune, representing glamour, Jupiter, luck/money, Mercury, communication, and the Midheaven, the career, all working together. So we can see that this is the chart of someone whose mission and career had to be linked to television or movies, somewhere where fantasy plays a role. This is represented by the actress at the top of the grand trine through Neptune, the image-maker. He connects to Jupiter, the planet of expansion and good fortune, someone who reaches out into the rest of the world, and they both link with Mercury, which strengthens Oprah's desire to teach. As the cornerstones of a grand trine, they are all rolled into one to create a superb outlook for self-publicity and PR in general. It's clear from this chart that Oprah would be a fantastic lecturer, or evangelist maybe, with her own college or a belief system that stems from experience.

With Mercury as kingpin in her chart, sitting in the grand trine and also in her T-square, she has a fantastic ability to tell people of her experiences. She has a gift for being a raconteur and for explaining a complex subject in the most simple of ways for everyone to understand. In other words, she is a great communicator.

Of course, no-one, not even Oprah, leads a perfect life. Her biggest problem, like a lot of Aquarians (I should know, I am one!), is intimacy. She is great at helping other people with their problems, but I am sure she finds it very difficult to solve her own. One area where she may have found life hard is in romantic relationships. The Mars square Pluto aspect indicates there must be deep-seated issues, hang-ups that may have become obsessions or blockages of a sexual nature. She would have struggled through her teenage years. This might have led to complex psychological problems within close relationships that have extended into the present. On top of this her luck with men will be a problem. I say this for two reasons. Firstly, if she has gone through the struggles and emotional traumas that I suspect she has with her fixed T-square, she may have been very suspicious of men and their motives. She might even find her judgement marred by being paranoid of someone who is out to help and guide her, then dropping her defences for a man who is a snake.

The second reason is that there are a lot of men who would find it hard to be controlled by a woman, let alone a rich and famous black woman. This is going to make a lot of men who like to control women, shy away. They might be flattered by her interest at first but they could also find it a turn-off. How do you handle a person who has had dramas in the past and who runs her own empire? It is a tough one to answer, especially as she would want someone strong herself, but not so strong that her Mars–Pluto square (part of that

T-square) would want to destroy whatever they have together. All this might make it hard for her to find true happiness with someone. The good news is there are ways through this and if anyone is equipped to find them, it is Oprah.

Hillary Clinton

FIRST LADY

Hillary Clinton is one of the most fascinating women in the world today. A brilliant, serious-minded lawyer, she met and married the similarly gifted and hugely charismatic Bill Clinton in her twenties. They joined forces to form one of the most remarkable political marriages in American – and world – history.

Yet during her husband's rise to the presidency, and throughout his two terms in the White House, Hillary was regarded less as a brilliant legal and political mind and more as the wronged woman. Her husband's affairs, in particular with Monica Lewinsky, the notorious White House intern, were a humiliating public ordeal for Hillary. It might have sunk a lesser person, but to the amazement of many, Hillary came back fighting, becoming the senator for New York and positioning herself to perhaps run for the presidency in her own right one day.

Like George W. Bush, she is a hugely polarizing figure. She is admired and reviled in equal measure. Looking at her chart, however, you see that this is something she will be able to take in her stride. And we can see that maybe, just maybe, the pain and suffering she has endured might be worth it in the long run.

HILLARY CLINTON'S CHART

As you know by now, the three most important placements when first starting to analyze and interpret the chart are the positions of the Ascendant, the Sun and the Moon. Hillary Clinton has Gemini rising. (The same as Tony Blair, incidentally.) This indicates someone who has a tremendous gift of the gab. Her Sun is in Scorpio, which suggests a brilliantly incisive person. Her Moon is in Pisces, indicating someone who can mask their true feelings, something that she has had to draw on enormously in public life.

What's interesting, however, is that each of these placements is teetering on the very edge of another sign. The Ascendant is at 29 degrees Gemini, one degree off being in Cancer rising. Her Sun is just two degrees in Scorpio, two degrees off being in Libra. Her Moon is at 29 degrees Pisces, one degree off being in Aries. What this means is that if her time of birth was just a minute or two different she would have a very different chart. (It is a distinct possibility that her published birth time of 8 p.m. on 26 October 1947 in Chicago, Illinois, suggests this time has been rounded up.) If she had arrived in the world a little earlier then her Ascendant would have been much deeper in Gemini and Moon further into Pisces, but if she had been born later she would have had an Ascendant in Cancer and even Moon in Aries.

I believe this is a chart of someone who, like the placings themselves, is very much on the edge. I don't just mean emotionally. I believe she is on the verge of doing something very significant with her life. Hillary Clinton's Moon is very powerfully placed. It is plumb on a square with the Ascendant and both are at 29 degrees in mutable signs. That Moon is at the top of the chart and its zenith. By looking at this, we know we are talking about someone who

HILLARY CLINTON'S BIRTH CHART

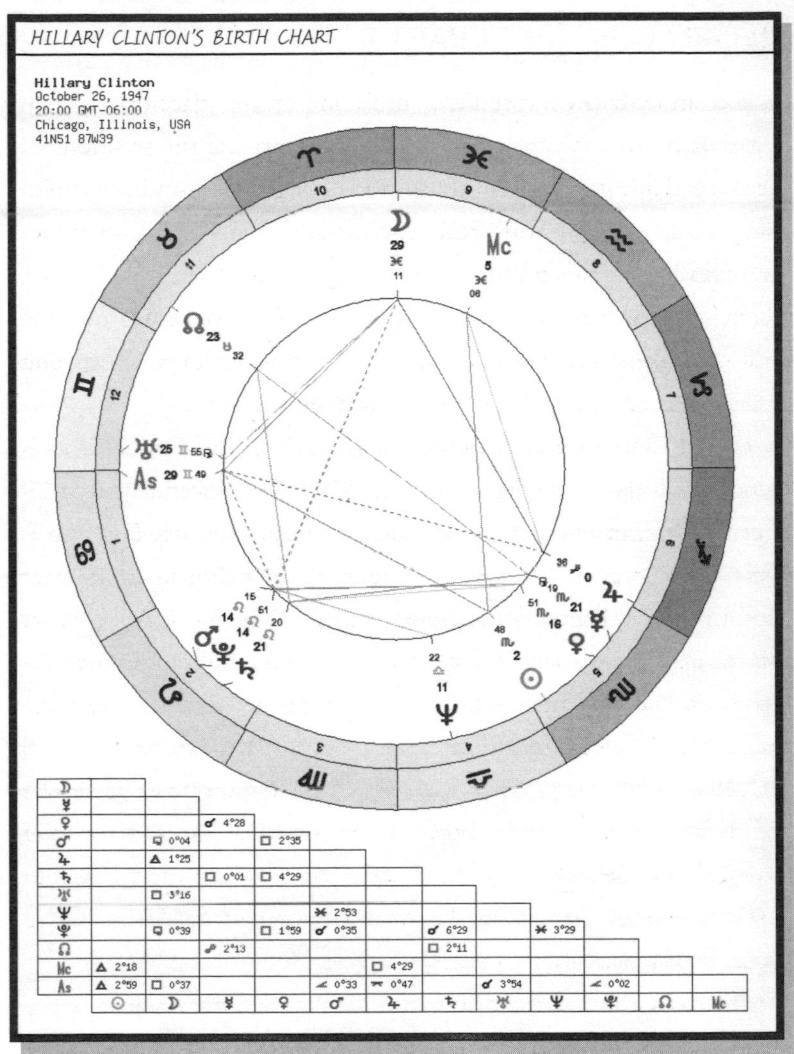

	☉	☽	☿	♀	♂	♃	♄	♅	♆	♇	☊	Mc
☽												
☿												
♀			☌ 4°28									
♂		⚻ 0°04		□ 2°35								
♃		△ 1°25										
♄			□ 0°01	□ 4°29								
♅		□ 3°16										
♆					⚹ 2°53							
♇		⚻ 0°39		□ 1°59	☌ 0°35		☌ 6°29		⚹ 3°29			
☊			☍ 2°13				□ 2°11					
Mc	△ 2°18					□ 4°29						
As	△ 2°59	□ 0°37			∠ 0°33	⚺ 0°47		☌ 3°54		∠ 0°02		

comes before the public and finds fame and or fortune, even notoriety. But we can also see that it belongs to someone for whom things are never going to be plain sailing, for whom life will never be entirely rosy. Adding to this impression is the unstable influence of

Uranus. Uranus squares the Moon. It is also the rising planet in Hillary's chart, rising in the 12th house. This can be at the centre of nervous exhaustion and hidden stress. Uranus, as we know, is the planet of genius but also of change and upheaval.

With Uranus square with the Moon, you have someone who has the potential for huge inner emotional tension. I am going to be honest here (it is a very Uranian thing to be, of course) but I suspect that one of the reasons Hillary stuck with Bill Clinton was that, although she was prepared to 'stand by her man' as she famously said alluding to the Tammy Wynette song, her Moon square Uranus placing enabled her to shrug it off. This was because she has an ambition and she could see her own star rising in time. She has a penchant for being attracted to people who will cause her emotional stress, people with 'issues'. She can paddle her own emotional canoe without being reliant on anyone for those security bolt holes the average person needs. She is not needy. Although she may be susceptible, she won't ever reveal how she truly feels with that Sun in secretive Scorpio, I mean, why should she tell you anything? That would give you something to go on and psychologically she will never leave herself vulnerable or open to attack.

The rest of the aspects to her Moon are more positive. Her Moon is in a disassociate trine to Jupiter. Because the Moon looks down on all other planets, this indicates somebody who finds the fame and fortune they desire. Jupiter's vibration from Sagittarius gives that fortuitous knack of being in the right place at the right time – and you can throw in a little of 'It's not what you know but who you know' as well.

Her Moon is also trine Mercury. This indicates someone who can emote and express their feelings, who is eloquent and empathetic when it comes to their emotions and can draw people in to her difficulties and problems, and see the ordinariness of them. Of course, with Uranus rising, there is nothing ordinary about Hillary.

Another reason this chart is exceptional is that, if you look at Mercury, not only does it court the Moon but it is also conjunct Venus in Scorpio. In this instance I suggest Mercury conjunct Venus indicates an icy hand operating within a seductive even sensual glove. Hillary comes across as soft and charming but inside there is an astute, cool, calculating mind. She loves people because of her Leo stellium, but with this lot squaring her Scorpio stellium, if you upset or cross her she will remember it and harbour a grudge. She will then live by the old saying, 'Revenge is a dish best eaten cold.' She is highly skilled at standing her ground, at saying nothing and being able to hold things back without bubbling over. She is ice-cool until she is able to let her emotions out in a torrent of feeling.

She also has the ability to put across what she wants and to put it to the public so that they lap it up. They also sympathize with her for what they see she has been through. In this respect, of course, the problems she had with her husband helped her. She turned his weaknesses into her strengths.

There are, however, some heavy aspects to this chart. She has Mars at 14 degrees Leo, Saturn at 21 degrees Leo, Pluto at 14 degrees Leo, Mercury at 21 degrees Scorpio and Venus at 16 degrees Scorpio. So you have Venus and Mercury all squaring Mars, Pluto and Saturn. I am fascinated by the fact she has these three placements in Leo because Bill Clinton is a Leo. So I suggest, again, that their relationship was one of fate and destiny. It was almost as if they somehow knew they were meant to be together and that they had something to do together. Fate led them to each other.

Pluto is the lord of kismet, Saturn is the lord of Karma – they are all connected. Also, the two love planets Venus and Mars are square to each other to put them at loggerheads. This indicates relationships on many levels will be dominated by issues and hang-ups. I believe one of the reasons Bill had to go elsewhere for affection was that as a Leo, he had a deep-rooted need for warmth, flattery and attention. He was in his element when he was flirting and falling in 'love'. He needed someone to adore him and massage his ego at all times. Yet he married a woman in Hillary who, with Venus square Mars, is only able to do that when there is something serious at stake. She could go through the motions of sex without necessarily feeling a thing, but with so much in Scorpio and Leo, when she does fall for someone it will become intense, passionate and compulsive, with more than a degree of psychological attraction and desire involved. With Hillary nothing is simple; everything is complex when love hits her heart.

Such placings create such a dramatic planetary set-up that it suggests to me that at some point in her life she may have suffered at the hands of a man, in terms of abuse of some kind. Ever since it has been her fate, goal and obsession to get even by beating men in a man's world.

Hillary has her Pluto in a wide conjunction to Saturn. Although a lot of people have this, what they probably won't have, however, is Mars involved along with the Venus–Mercury set-up that Hillary has. This is what makes her someone who constantly resurrects herself. She is on a crusading life path.

She has the ability either to go under with her problems or say 'I'll show you.' She has this atomic, ballistic, concentrated energy that seeps out until she gains dominion over her enemies. People with this usually have an axe to grind. She possesses a very complicated and hidden psyche. Hillary not only battles, but she can also command enormous inner strength and resources. The slings and arrows of the world can be shot at her and they will bounce off. Throw Mars into the vexatious mixture and it's possible to see her as a man-hater. If ever she was hurt by a man, to her all men have to answer for it, ultimately. Put that in with her square with Venus and Mercury and you get someone who has the ability to mask her intentions.

Finally when you look at the Sun in Hillary's chart, you see something else. Her Sun is in a double disassociate trine to both the Ascendant and Uranus. We can now see that the planets that come through very positively here are Uranus and the Moon, being the ruler of Cancer, therefore the ruler of the chart. So we have someone who can lead a double life. On the one hand, she leads a lunar life, whether being a mother or a senator that people will identify with and in whom people will place their trust because they identify with 'what that woman has been through'. On the other hand, she is also capable of leading a life in which she is reforming, ingenious, sparkling and ahead of her time professionally. People will look at her in awe.

Underpinning all of this is that colossal square with the Leo planets and the Scorpio planets. This is where I rest my case about people *needing* to have what seem like bad aspects in their charts to drive them on in life. This is what makes Hillary fight on. She is at the vanguard of fighting for rights, equality and justice. She is a person who is never going to give up – she is fighting so that others won't have to.

To Hillary, Bill was another lesson in life. What happened to her wasn't any different to what happens to many, many women. She was able to use that and turn it into something positive. I believe she will use it to transform herself into the first female president of the United States.

George W. Bush

BORN ON THE SIXTH OF JULY

George W. Bush is without doubt the most controversial American president in living memory. He is, of course, the son of a president, George Bush Sr, and spent the early part of his life in his father's considerable shadow. By all accounts, his early years were wild and indisciplined ones. Eventually, he turned to politics. However, even when he came to power in the disputed election of 2000, he always looked destined to be remembered as the junior of the two Bush presidents. Oh, and for his habit of making verbal gaffes.

But then America – and the world – was changed by the terrible events of 11 September 2001. The way Bush reacted to the terrorist attacks on New York and Washington, and the leadership he has shown since, has divided opinion around the world. People either love him or hate him. There seems to be no middle ground. His chart, however, indicates a person who may well be massively underestimated. One also gets a sense that his arrival on the world stage was no coincidence.

GEORGE W. BUSH'S BIRTH CHART

The first thing that strikes me is the Cancerian connection between the Suns of George W. Bush and America. America was born on 4 July 1776, with its Sun in Cancer. Bush was born at 7.26 a.m. on 6 July 1946, in New Haven, Connecticut, also with the Sun in Cancer.

This placement means the heart and soul of both dictate that they follow their solar convictions. In the sign of Cancer, nothing gives them a stronger sense of conviction than family. Family, of

GEORGE W. BUSH'S BIRTH CHART

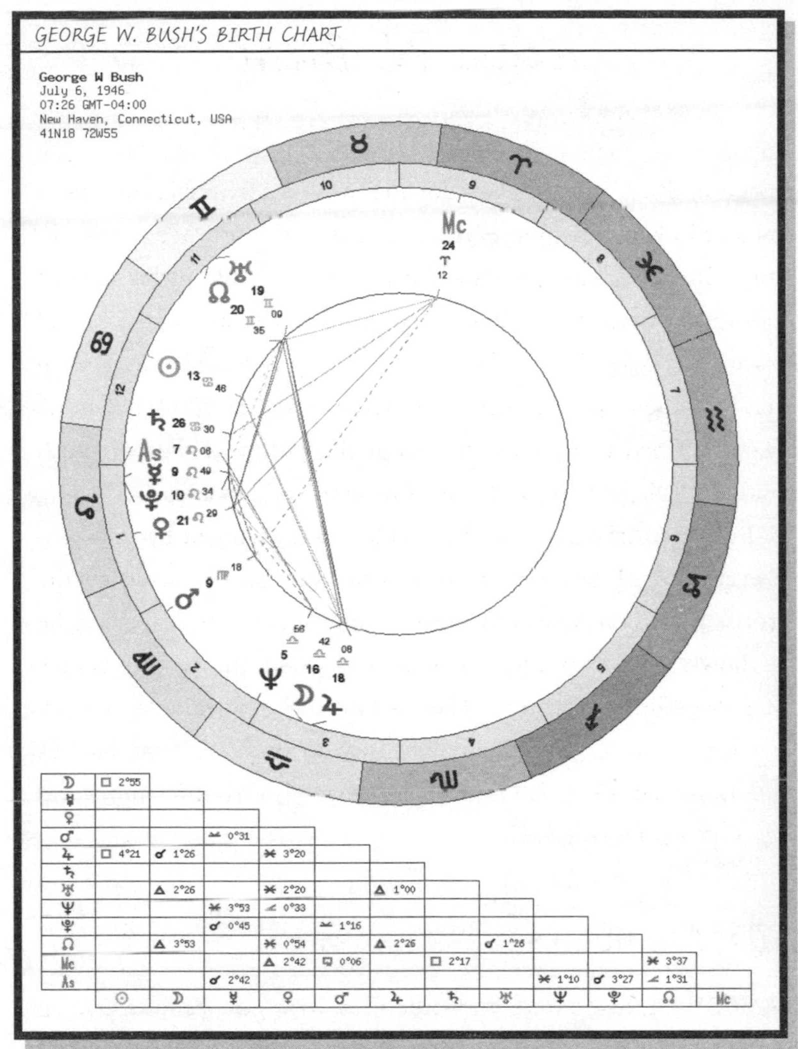

	☉	☽	☿	♀	♂	♃	♄	♅	♆	♇	☊	Mc
☽	□ 2°55											
☿												
♀												
♂			⚻ 0°31									
♃	□ 4°21	☌ 1°26		⚹ 3°20								
♄												
♅		△ 2°26		⚹ 2°20		△ 1°00						
♆			⚹ 3°53	∠ 0°33								
♇			☌ 0°45		⚻ 1°16							
☊		△ 3°53		⚹ 0°54		△ 2°26		☌ 1°26				
Mc				△ 2°42	⚼ 0°06		□ 2°17				⚹ 3°37	
As			☌ 2°42						⚹ 1°10	☌ 3°27	∠ 1°31	

course, can mean much more than the immediate kith and kin. It can also be the community or indeed the nation in which you live. (It doesn't surprise me that the home of the president, the head of the American family, is in the White House. White and silver are the colours of Cancer.)

America is a very Cancerian country that can turn in on itself and become insular, demanding seclusion with a desire to get away and lick its wounds occasionally. George W. Bush is exactly the same. In his case, his Sun in Cancer is locked away in the 12th house (along with Saturn). He is a proud patriot and I believe he sees his country as an extension of his family.

In 2004, when he won a second term in the White House, I was one of the few astrologers who predicted this would happen. I did, for several reasons, but primarily because in the same way that individuals attract the friends and partners they deserve, I believe countries attract the kind of leaders they need at certain times in their development. At that moment in time America needed someone who understood its feelings and emotions and culture. (In the same way, Tony Blair was right for the UK.)

When 9/11 happened, it was like someone knocking on the door of George W. Bush's family home and shooting dead his wife and children in the hallway. After 9/11, the actions that followed bore an element of vendetta, of revenge on behalf of the entire family. Also with his powerful Cancerian thrust, he built a great carapace around his family – his country. (The fact he called the department running it 'Homeland Security' was too classic Cancerian for words. Both words are keywords for Cancer.)

But why don't some people see that Bush and America's fates are intertwined? Well, while Republicans see the two Suns – president and nation – shining together, Democrats or liberals are blinded by the combined Suns. They see his presidency as pure ego, as Bush with his own mission and purpose. They are blinded by the ego of the man as depicted by the US Sun in Cancer and his personal Cancer Sun.

If we look more closely at his chart, we can see much more revealing information about Bush's personality. One of his most hard aspects is his Sun square Moon. This, you'll remember, is challenging and indicates someone who is torn between what they need creatively in real terms and what their inner emotions tell them they need. For Bush, this conflict isn't made any easier by the fact he is so keen to prove himself. Bush has Saturn square to his Midheaven. This indicates a person with a tremendous irrational fear of failure. Because father-figure Saturn is involved, this can involve the relationship with his own father, George Bush Sr, whom he will be desperate to please and whose approval he craves. This is a powerful motivating force within him.

Bush has Mars in Virgo sextile to the Sun. This is very sporty indeed. It indicates an energizing driving force, and very structured and organized energy. He is also someone who would be best to take one thing at a time. For success he must be single-minded in all pursuits; he will at least do something about what gets his goat. With a stellium of planets in Leo and his first house led by Mercury and Pluto, this aspect reveals that he will at times become obsessed. It also signifies someone who finds it difficult to project the right image. He does not portray his intentions well. As a result, other people tend to have to explain what he is doing. His communications can be affected by too much going on around him and in his head – hence the verbal gaffes.

Mercury and Pluto conjunct the Ascendant tells me what you see is not necessarily what you get. Pluto is the planet of secrecy, of enigma and of cloak and dagger behaviour. Bush is someone with a tendency to be wrapped up in his own secret world that can come over to others as smugness or self-satisfaction. He is also the planet that demands power and control, so with this placement just three degrees off the Ascendant, what we see is the showbizzy Leo Ascendant but what we hear is Mercury conjoined to Pluto – but they are not the same. The message here is that you should not judge a book by its cover. This represents a psychotherapist's dream…or nightmare.

Bush's Moon (the Sun and Saturn sign ruler) is in conjunction with Jupiter in Libra. The Moon, of course, is the ruler of Cancer. Jupiter is the jovial, optimistic figure. From this we can see his family and home are a huge source of happiness and comfort. Put this in the sign of Libra and we have someone who needs to be comfortable with his surroundings and feelings. With Libra being an Air sign he may intellectualize his feelings. I suspect George W. Bush is both frustrated and even offended that so many folks get the wrong end of the stick. To him, his intentions are honourable.

Elsewhere we see that Uranus, the planet of reform, is beautifully aspected to the Moon and Jupiter (both are trines). This indicates somebody who is very different, controversial or unusual in the way they do things. This is why many people misunderstand him, as he doesn't do things in an orthodox or normal way. Yet ask him and he will insist he is very normal and very orthodox, so again his self-image is very different to how it is perceived by the world.

A president with a very similar energy was Ronald Reagan. I was once asked to look at his chart. He was an Aquarian (Uranus and Saturn the ruling planets) but his background was similar to Bush's. The old saying that 'Patriotism is the last resort of the scoundrel' would have been anathema to Reagan, as it would to George W. Bush. They were both well-meaning people who needed good PR around them to present their case better than they were capable of doing themselves.

Another fascinating aspect to Bush's chart is the part Venus assumes astrologically. She is placed in Leo and well aspected to Jupiter, the Moon, Uranus and Midheaven. This indicates someone to whom women are very important. He needs a glamorous wife, someone to provide equilibrium and balance in his life. In particular, the glorious trine to the Midheaven means women around him are a source of comfort and support, and are great for his standing and global image. He has a profound relationship with the female gender, from the formidable matriarch of the family, Barbara Bush, to his admirable wife Laura and even his troublesome twin daughters Barbara and Jenna. He can be charming and make a relaxed and amiable host.

His Jupiter is very presidentially placed, with a trio of fine aspects to the Moon, Venus and Uranus – destiny had fingered him for big things. Jupiter is square to the Sun and Saturn, and in opposition to Midheaven in Aries. This gives us a clue as to why he went to the top of his profession *despite* his personal handicaps. George W. possesses a strong Jupiter, someone who sits astride of Olympus (Washington DC) being jovial but who will also have massive mood swings, times when he crashes his thunderbolts. Those bolts will be all the more destructive and when the black dog of depression (Saturn) gets him it will be all the more frightening.

Looking at the other planetary placements we see Uranus very well aspected to Venus, Jupiter, the Moon and Midheaven. This means he is someone full of surprises. He has extremes of thought too, which is what upsets his more liberal opponents, of course.

Romantic Neptune is gloriously aspected to Pluto, Mercury and the Ascendant. This indicates he is sensitive to his own feelings with a strong spiritual belief in a higher being that is sincere, genuine and true.

Finally, transforming Pluto is well placed with a range of aspects to Mercury, Neptune and the Ascendant. This is what you would expect of someone who is a plutocrat, someone controlling a large corporation or nation.

To summarize, Bush has a mass of fascinating astrologicals. If his life is a stage play, it is a psychological black comedy. The comedy comes from jovial Jupiter, the psychological depth from Pluto. In keeping with the surprising, shocking element of Uranus, the play is not a straightforward piece of entertainment either. You have to think long and hard about it. Sometimes when watching you think it's a farce and other times it makes perfect sense. It's a mixture of *film noir* and a Frank Capra movie with a happy ending. Throughout you are constantly wondering who the hero is and who the villain is! Perhaps only history will tell us which he really is.

Maria Callas

A GREEK TRAGEDY

Maria Callas was perhaps the greatest operatic talent who ever lived. On stage she had the ability to enthrall, uplift and move her audience to tears. Yet offstage her life was a mess, a saga of broken relationships and mistakes that could have come from a Greek tragedy.

Callas's first marriage was one of convenience. Her husband helped her conquer the operatic world, allowing her to bask in the worship of music fans from her native New York to Europe, but he never brought her the happiness, love and security this deeply insecure artist needed. Then, at the height of her career, Callas gave up her marriage and her career to be with the Greek tycoon Aristotle Onassis. It was a move that scandalized the world, but for a while they were happy, sharing a millionaire lifestyle together. The dream did not live long, however. After she had lost their only baby, a boy, Onassis left Callas for Jacqueline Kennedy, the widow of the assassinated president. It left Callas bitter and broken. When Onassis tried to reconcile with her after the break-up of his marriage to Jackie O, Callas was too proud to take him back. Yet she wasn't ready to move on either. Instead she became a recluse who spent her days and nights obsessing about what might have been rather than picking up her life and career. When Onassis died in 1974, Callas's life was effectively over. She died of a broken heart two years later, at the age of just 56.

On the face of it, Callas seems a victim of circumstances, someone who suffered betrayal and bad luck. Yet by looking at her birth chart, we can see that the danger signs were there for her to see. She could have lived her life differently and perhaps averted the disasters that befell her. If she had come to me for a reading, I would have told her that the key lay with the matriarchal Moon. If only she had tuned into it and listened more to *La Luna*, her life could have been very different.

MARIA CALLAS'S BIRTH CHART

There are many fascinating elements to Callas's chart. The first thing that strikes you is the influence of Jupiter. It is the ruler of the chart, being ruler of the Sagittarius Ascendant, ruler of the Sagittarian Sun Sign and conjunct the Sun too. This is real 'Wow factor' stuff. This means the influence of Jupiter, the joy-bringer, is more than just especially pronounced – it is the dominating feature through planet and sign. Here was a woman who through her huge creativity always knew she was able to marvellously uplift people and bring pleasure to their lives. Jupiter is a clue to her illustrious destiny of fame and fortune. On a personal level, her music was also the source of her greatest joy. Callas was never happier, never more alive, than when she was in the spotlight.

There was no question that Callas tuned into the Jupiter within her: she ruled opera as Jupiter/Zeus ruled Olympus. She lived through this lofty planet and that part of her astro-personality beautifully. If only that had been true of some of her other planets. Elsewhere in her chart, there were clear signs that relationships were going to be difficult for her. Firstly, her Venus is in Capricorn, a telltale pointer of someone who found love hard-going. Women with Venus in Capricorn, where the limiting influence of Saturn comes into play, are prone to placing material security above romance. They tend to find wealth and power an aphrodisiac, so it was little wonder she fell for the mega-rich Onassis, a tycoon who was going to give her all she needed materially. Romance, however, was another matter entirely. Callas's Venus is not badly placed, but it is in the first house, which has the essence of Aries. In romantic affairs, she was someone who very much demanded 'look at me' and 'put me first'. Not every man is willing to do that.

With Venus in Capricorn, it was even more obvious that Callas was someone whose experience of real emotion and love was going to come through her vocation or career. In her private life, true love was hard to find. The outlet undoubtedly came through her performances. Look at her portrayals of Tosca and Norma – they were possessed with such incredible fire and passion, lest we forget Venus is one of the planets of the voice.

With the god of sex, Mars, restricted by its conjunction with Saturn, this was possibly why she was able to live in a first marriage that was sexless. She got all the emotional satisfaction she needed from her career. That all seemed to change with Onassis, of course. Onassis was a very different kind of man and sex was definitely on the agenda – he lit her fire. She imagined it was love, but it wasn't. She mistook the Moon for Venus, a bad mistake. Why? The answers

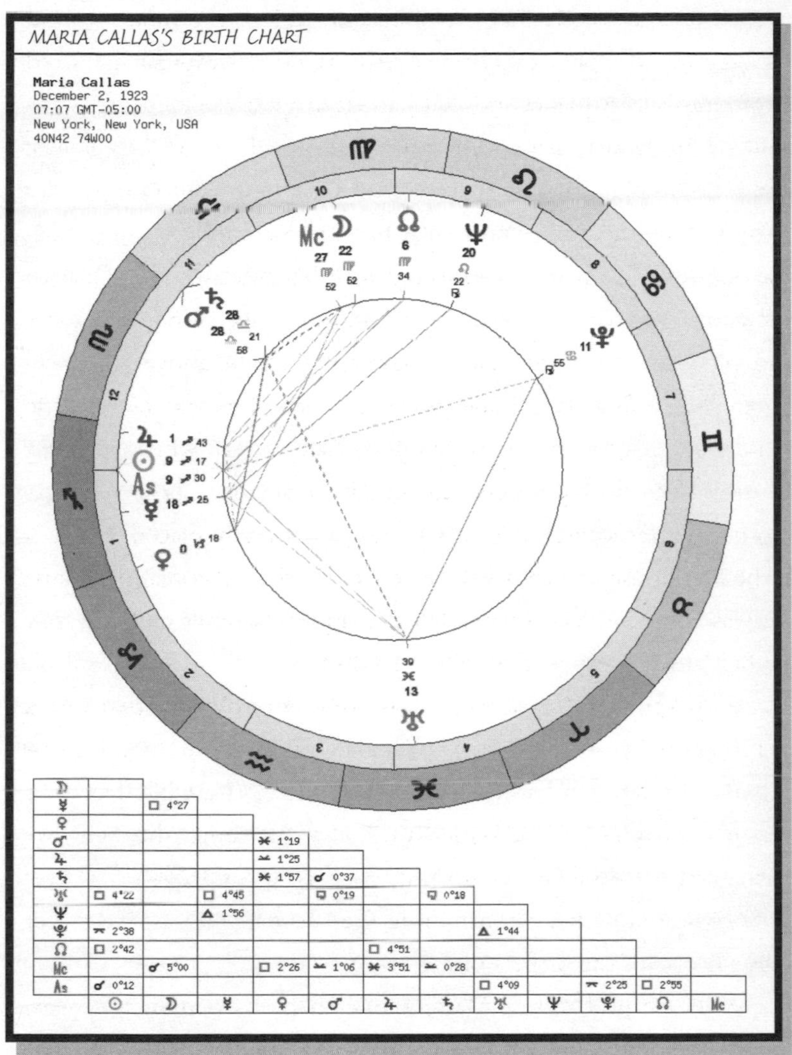

lie elsewhere in her chart. If we go back to the Mars–Saturn conjunction, we see that Mars is not just in conjunction with Saturn, it is virtually sitting on top of it. It's a powerful aspect for an astrologer to study, not such a great one to live under. It only exacerbated the situation between Onassis and Callas, in terms of the lack of romance and feelings of isolation. A woman with this aspect of Mars and Saturn can be inhibited by events early in her life. Mars represents sexual drive, while Saturn stays only if absolutely necessary. It can result in a woman fighting a war with the opposite sex or in problems with her father or a father figure, which can manifest themselves throughout her life. They can become the female version of misogynists: men-haters. For Callas this meant that she was always going to be liable to be used and abused by men. This was certainly the case with Onassis, who based their relationship on great sex and offspring rather than tender, softer feelings, where Venus would have purred. It might have been possible for him to love her, but again, other elements to Callas's chart made sure that wasn't going to happen.

As we can see, Callas has Sagittarius/Jupiter influences in abundance. Sagittarians often think of themselves as immortal, even divine, and this was something that she was sure to feel of herself. Professionally, she was the diva in every sense of the word. In this chart, Callas's most classic aspect is Sun square Uranus. This extraordinary aspect would make her difficult to live with, prone to changing her mind and striking out in the most alarming way, but it also adds charisma, magnetism and the 'what's gonna happen next' factor. It is the sign of someone who stalks the narrow line of genius and madness.

Unfortunately all this meant that she also felt Onassis was her equal. She felt that she was such a prize for him that he would never look anywhere else for love. This was a mistake. She should have realized that she couldn't control him – he wasn't a man who could be controlled. She could not be his equal in this sense, especially as he was a Greek man to whom the idea of sexual equality was complete anathema.

The most striking thing in her chart, however, is the lack of the positive influence imbued by the Moon. As a personality, the Moon is the matriarch, the part of us that provides love and stability, a sense of home and belonging. She also governs our instinctive feelings and emotional responses. Callas's Moon in Virgo conjunct the Midheaven meant she was destined to come before the public. However, that Moon was also square Mercury. This meant she couldn't help but intellectualize her feelings, control how she felt with logic or do the lunar thing of protecting herself, just in case of a brutish emotional attack. But what is just as interesting is that this aspect is the only major aspect the Moon has with another planet. It was an unnerving one for her to have as it prevented her from communicating her true feelings. Of course, she could have tried to express herself to friends and the media, but she could never express the inner Callas and this meant she was always totally misunderstood by the press, and therefore the world. It took her untimely death to make her life understandable.

The Moon is effectively on its own in Callas's chart, not interacting with any of the other planets and therefore out in the cold in terms of her psychology. Yet Callas's life could have been so different if she had brought the Moon into her life. And it was something she could easily have done. If she had listened to her Moon, she would have understood the importance of laying down roots. Callas was, by nature, a volatile person. The life she led first as a giddy, globe-trotting diva and then with Onassis, gadding around on yachts in the Med, constantly on the move among high society – only added to this sense of rootlessness. The Moon in Callas wanted to be a housewife, a homemaker, but she didn't even have a place she could really call home. So that aspect of her life was never going to be able to develop. If she had settled on a permanent base, in a villa where she could have set up a real home for her and Onassis, she could have begun to lay some foundations.

Her Moon would also have made her think about adopting a child. Onassis said that if their son had lived he would never have dreamed of leaving Callas for Jackie. If she had brought a child into their lives, it might have been very different.

Equally, if she'd listened to her Moon, she would never have given up her career for him – her Moon is conjunct her Midheaven, the career point, so the public became family. Throughout her life Callas had lived her emotions through her work. When she gave that up she had no way of living her Moon herself. It left her bereft. And she had nothing left to give anyone.

Finally, if Callas had understood the influence of her Moon, she would have realized that its negative aspect within her made it hard for her to forgive and forget. If she'd been aware of this weakness within her personality, she might have worked harder at trying to do this. She might not have felt the need to lock herself away from the world (she overcompensated by retiring into seclusion with the Sun–Jupiter conjunction locked away in the 12th house, the zodiac zone of secrets and sorrows) brooding about the pain that world had caused her. Who knows, she and Onassis might have been able to reconcile – and if they had, who knows how her life might have been revived as a result?

Afterword

So, you've made it to the end. Congratulations. You've completed your introductory journey into the fascinating world of astrology and begun exploring the endlessly absorbing subject that is Planet You.

This book is, of course, only a beginning. Astrology is a vast subject. Even after 40 years studying the subject, I learn something new almost every day. What you have discovered here is how to understand your nature, the potential outside and in, and how to see the way the planets are set up within your personality. Of course, the world – and more importantly, the solar system – around you is changing, too. Your future trends are going to be shaped by the ever-shifting energies the planets continue to radiate. This is an entirely different area of astrology, the branch where we take into account the dynamic nature of the solar system, and factors like the transits and progressions of the planets.

If you have enjoyed this first taste of astrology, perhaps this will be your next area of study. For now, however, I hope you have gained something valuable from the experience of reading this book;

perhaps some insights into yourself that will help you overcome the problems you thought were insurmountable. Now you can see that where there's knowledge and will, there's a way.

Most of all, I hope this marks the beginning of a new chapter in your life, one in which you discover a happier, wealthier, more romantic or more fulfilled you. Good luck, and enjoy your date with your new destiny...with the new you.

Glossary

Ascendant (or rising sign): sign of the zodiac that was rising on the eastern horizon at the time of birth.

Aspect: position of one planet in relation to another.

Cardinal sign: a quality of the signs of the zodiac.

Conjunction: an aspect where two planets are placed either exactly or almost exactly (up to nine degrees leeway or orb) at the same point on the birth chart.

Descendant: point setting on the western horizon at time of birth.

Disassociate aspect: an aspect when two planets are not in the signs, elements or qualities that traditionally make that aspect.

Exact aspect: an aspect where two planets are precisely the right number of degrees apart to form that aspect.

Fixed sign: a quality of the signs of the zodiac.

Grand trine: three or more planets forming trines with each other, that is, planet A trine to planet B, planet B trine to planet C, planet C trine to planet A.

Home zone: where the planet is placed in the sign or house which it rules.

House: one of the 12 sections of birth chart representing an aspect of life and living.

Midheaven or MC: the point in the sky directly overhead at the time of birth, the high noon point.

Mutable sign: a quality of the signs of the zodiac.

Nadir or IC: the point in the sky directly below at the time of birth, the midnight point. Polar opposite to Midheaven.

Opposition: an aspect where two planets are directly opposite each other on chart, that is, almost (nine degree orb) or exactly 180 degrees apart.

Polar signs: signs of the zodiac directly opposite each other on a birth chart.

Sextile: an aspect where two planets are almost (six degree orb) or exactly 60 degrees apart.

Square: an aspect where two planets are almost (nine degree orb) or exactly 90 degrees apart on the birth chart.

Stellium: a conjunction of three or more planets together in one sign or house.

Trine: an aspect where two planets are almost or exactly 120 degrees apart.

T-square: complex aspect formed when an opposition is joined to two squares, that is, two planets 180 degrees apart; both form squares with another planet at 90 degrees to each.

Zodiac: 360-degree section of sky, or ecliptic, through which planets move divided in twelve, 30-degree sections (the Equal house system) known as the signs of the zodiac.

Free Birth Chart for Every Reader

To receive your free birth chart simply log on to

www.russellgrant.com/yourbirthchart

In order to receive your birth chart, you will need to provide:

- Your date of birth
- The time of your birth (within 30 mins if possible) using a.m. or p.m. where appropriate
- The place of your birth
- A valid email address

When you get to the site, you will be asked to type in a code. This is 0091908485.

Terms & Conditions

Only one birth chart per book purchased.

Your birth chart will appear in a web window from which you can print directly on a sheet of A4 or save to your computer as a jpeg.

Your free birth chart will be available until 31/12/2009.

Should you have any problems accessing your birth chart please contact: help@russellgrant.com.

Your personal details will be retained and used by The Random House Group Ltd (TRHG) and Russell Grant only in order to send you your free birth chart and will be deleted thereafter, unless you have ticked the box indicating you would like to receive further information, in which case your personal details will be retained by TRHG and/or Russell Grant in order to send you the further information you have indicated you would like to receive from us. Your personal details will not be passed on to any third parties.

Please note your chart can only be accessed via E-mail. It cannot be sent to you in any other form of communication.

Index

Index

Index

Index

Index

ACKNOWLEDGEMENTS

The ideas outlined in this book have formed part of the teaching method I have used at my Astrological Academy and elsewhere for many, many years. They have helped a great number of people grasp the fundamentals of interpreting and analysing the birth chart. If it hadn't been for the help, support and guidance of a talented group of people they would have remained confined to the seminars and workshops. My final task in this book is to say a big thank you to those people who, between them, provided everything from Saturnine discipline and a gift for Venusian love to a Mercurial knack for turning what sounded quite complicated into something rather simple.

Firstly I must thank my dear fellow Aquarian Gail Rebuck at Random House, who first saw the potential of a book that took a new look at the ever-fascinating art of astrology. Her enthusiasm was echoed at Ebury first by the wonderful Gemini Fiona MacIntyre, then the editorial duo of the velvet-voiced Taurean Carey Smith and the indefatigable Cancerian Natalie Hunt, who were perfect partners in guiding me towards a finished manuscript.

My agent and well-balanced Libran (until she and I hit the Savoy, that is) Mary Pachnos offered a mixture of patience and sound professional advice, as well as some raucously good company during my descents into London. Thanks also to my new and dear friend from the Fantasma Partnership – another Gemini GJ.

The most important players in this particular story, however, were closest to home.

Whilst I got on with the task of producing this book, the demands on the team that help me at my website russellgrant.com were greater than ever. So I must thank Doug Beaumont, an Aries who changed my life wonderfully in 1973 and Virgo Phil McKnight who came into our professional lives in 1996. Beaumont-Knight Associates Doug and Phil have won award after award with www.russellgrant.com. They also reinvented me and I didn't feel a thing! Where would I be without you all?

Excavations at Nichoria in Southwest Greece

Volume III

Dark Age and Byzantine Occupation

EXCAVATIONS AT NICHORIA IN SOUTHWEST GREECE

VOLUME III
DARK AGE AND BYZANTINE OCCUPATION

Edited by
William A. McDonald
William D. E. Coulson
and
John Rosser

Illustrations by
Bryan Carlson, Duane Bingham,
Jennifer Moody, and others

THE UNIVERSITY OF MINNESOTA PRESS MINNEAPOLIS

Published by the University of Minnesota Press,
2037 University Avenue Southeast, Minneapolis, MN 55414
Printed in the United States of America.

Library of Congress Cataloging in Publication Data

University of Minnesota Messenia Expedition.
Excavations at Nichoria in southwest Greece.
Vol. 3 edited by William A. McDonald, William D. E. Coulson, and John Rosser.
Includes bibliographies and indexes.
CONTENTS: v. 1. Site, environs, and techniques.— v. 3. Dark Age and Byzantine occupation.
1. Nichoria site, Greece. I. Rapp, George Robert. 1931- . II. Aschenbrenner, Stanley E. III. Title.
DF221.N52U53 1978 938'.9 78-3198
ISBN 0-8166-1140-0 (v. 3) AACR2
ISBN 0-8166-0824-5 (v. 1)

The University of Minnesota
is an equal-opportunity educator
and employer.

This volume is dedicated
to the memory of

Cecil C. March

He believed in the promise
of the Nichoria project
And in the generosity of Minnesotans
to make the promise
come true.

Table of Contents

List of Figures

Because of the large number of artefacts depicted in the figures for Chapter 3, it is not possible to include pottery numbers in this listing.

List of Plates

List of Tables

List of Abbreviations

The following abbreviations are regularly used to refer to frequently cited publications (chiefly journals) with lengthy titles. The full titles of journals published in Greece are listed here in transliteration; titles of books and journal articles in chapter references are regularly cited in English translation.

AA	*Archaiologische Anzieger*
AAA	*Archaiologika Analekta ex Athēnōn*
AJA	*American Journal of Archaeology*
AM	*Athenische Mittheilungen* (Deutsche Archäologische Institut)
AR	*Archaeological Reports*
Arch Eph	*Archaiologikē Ephēmeris*
BCH	*Bulletin de Correspondance Hellénique*
BSA	*Annual of the British School of Archaeology at Athens*
Deltion	*Archaiologikon Deltion*
Ergon	*To Ergon tēs Archaiologikēs Hetaireias*
JAS	*Journal of Archaeological Science*
JDAI	*Jahrbuch des Deutsches Archäologisches Instituts*
JFA	*Journal of Field Archaeology*
JHS	*Journal of Hellenic Studies*
MME 1972	*Minnesota Messenia Expedition: Reconstructing a Bronze Age Regional Environment.* Ed. McDonald and Rapp
Nichoria I	*Excavations at Nichoria in Southwest Greece* I. *Site, Environs, and Techniques*. Ed. Rapp and Aschenbrenner
OJh	*Jahrbuch des Oesterreiches Archäologisches Instituts*
Op Ath	*Opuscula Atheniensia*
PPS	*Proceedings of the Prehistoric Society*
Praktika	*Praktika tēs en Athenais Archaiologikēs Hetaireias*

List of Authors

Stanley E. Aschenbrenner, Associate Professor, Department of Sociology-Anthropology, University of Minnesota, Duluth.

Sara C. Bisel, Collaborator in Physical Anthropology, The Smithsonian Institution, Washington, D.C.

Harriet Blitzer, Buffalo, New York.

Jill Carington Smith, Acting Director, Australian School of Archaeology, Athens, Greece.

Hector Catling, Director, British School of Archaeology, Athens, Greece.

William D. E. Coulson, Associate Professor, Department of Classics, University of Minnesota.

William P. Donovan, Professor, Department of Classics, Macalester College, St. Paul, Minnesota.

Dietmar K. Hagel, Associate Professor, Department of Classics, Queen's University, Kingston, Ontario, Canada.

Richard Hope Simpson, Professor, Department of Classics, Queen's University, Kingston, Ontario, Canada.

Helen Hughes-Brock, formerly Joanna Randall-MacIver Junior Research Fellow, Somerville College, Oxford, England.

William A. McDonald, Regents' Professor Emeritus, Department of Classics, University of Minnesota, and Director of MME.

John Rosser, Associate Professor, Department of History, Boston College, Chestnut Hill, Massachusetts.

William Wade, Professor, Department of Anthropology, University of Manitoba, Winnipeg, Manitoba, Canada.

Nancy C. Wilkie, Assistant Professor, Departments of Anthropology and Classics, Carleton College, Northfield, Minnesota.

Preface

In 1978 the Minnesota Messenia Expedition (MME) published Volume 1 of *Excavations at Nichoria in Southwest Greece* (see Rapp and Aschenbrenner 1978), which will be referred to here and in later volumes of the series as "*Nichoria* I." The title of the volume, "Site, Environs, and Techniques," reflects the major importance that MME has consistently attached to archaeological studies in which the physical environment, past and present, is treated as a necessary and fully equal partner of the cultural evidence. The attempt to understand on a regional scale the interaction of the human inhabitants with their natural surroundings was central to an earlier study, *Minnesota Messenia Expedition: Reconstructing a Bronze Age Regional Environment* (McDonald and Rapp 1972), which will be referred to as "*MME* 1972." Indeed, several authors of chapters in both books have concentrated on essentially the same problems, first at the *regional* and then at the *local* level.

During the seven seasons of excavation and study (1969-75) we gained an intimate acquaintance with the Nichoria ridge and its environs, and this experience afforded an opportunity to test at least some of the hypotheses and assumptions that were previously based on the "extensive" survey of the whole Messenian region. Earlier insights that were concerned with the physical setting—geology, physiography, vegetation, soils—have now been significantly enhanced in various respects. And we can begin to understand other aspects of the history of the local ecosystem such as the wild fauna and microfauna on which little information can be expected from a surface survey.

Most of the authors of *Nichoria* I have also explained the techniques by which they derived from certain categories of the excavated remains new insights on how the human inhabitants of the Nichoria ridge adapted their way of life to the specific micro-environment. We are now better informed, though in widely varying degrees, about such vital aspects of their activities as hunting and herding and agriculture, the use of local stones and clays, and copper, bronze, and iron metallurgy.

In Volumes II and III of the series we come to the more traditional aspects of an excavation report. At least in Greek archaeology, there is still a tendency to concentrate almost exclusively on the remains of architecture and on the pottery and other movable finds that were made or used by the people who inhabited a particular site. We hope that the Nichoria publication as a whole will contribute to the gradual realization that discarded sheep bones from which a family once ate the meat and marrow, or prills of bronze from a long-forgotten casting operation, or the debitage from the manufacture of chert scrapers may also contribute significantly, provided that the purpose of archaeological excavation is defined with proper flexibility (jargon or not) as "the recovery of the remains of fossilized human behavior."

Volumes II and III are intended in the main, however, to set out the more orthodox kinds of evidence that illuminate the history of human habitation on the Nichoria ridge (Fig. A-1; Pl. 1-1). In levels close to natural bedrock in Area V and elsewhere on and near the ridge scattered potsherds testify to the first human activity on the site during the Final Neolithic period, perhaps to be dated locally around the turn of the 4th and 3rd millennia B.C. (see Chronological Chart). Thereafter, it appears that

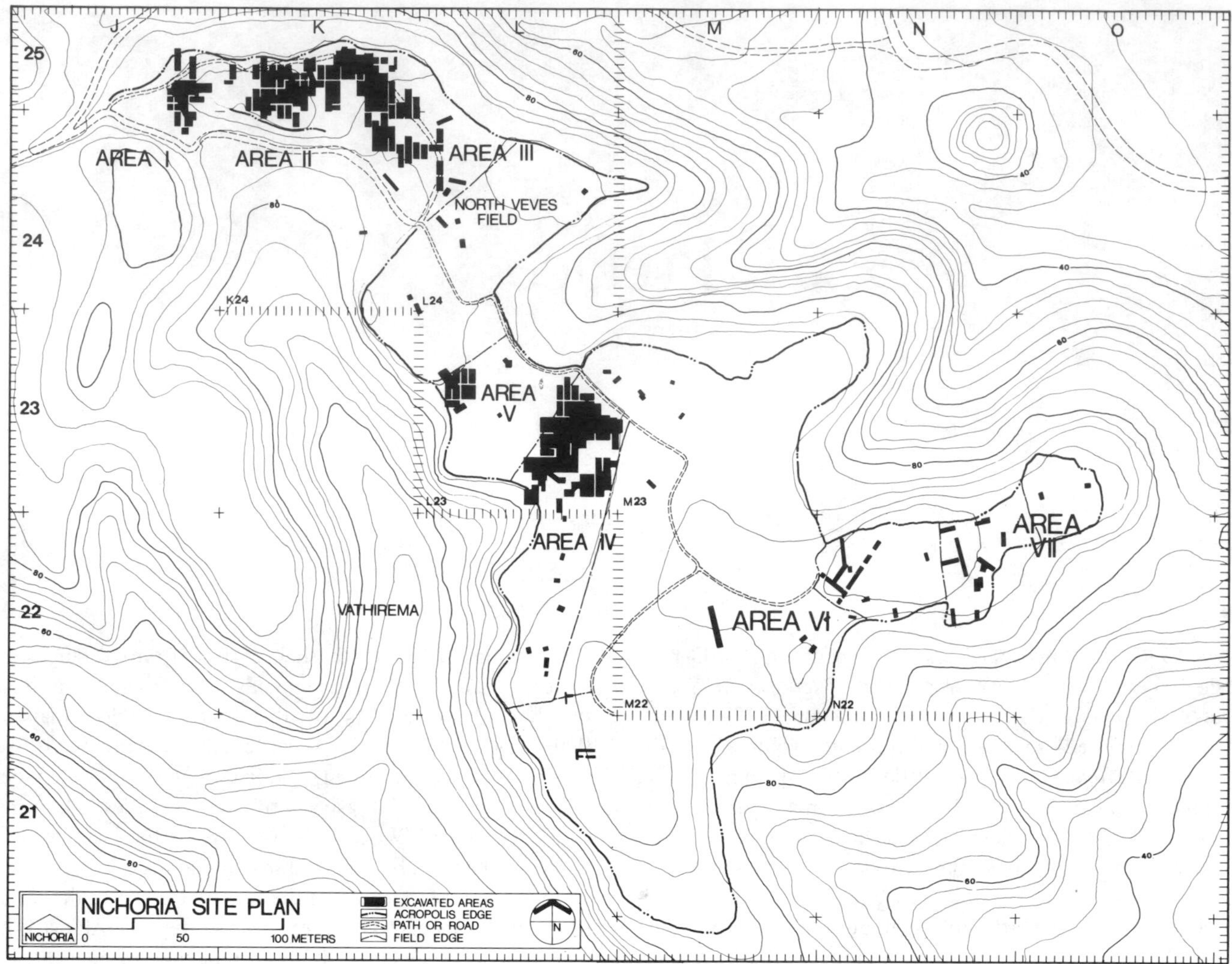

Figure A-1.

there was a considerable hiatus. A few recognizable fragments (mainly bases) of Early Helladic pots were recovered in the excavation; but later inhabitants of the Nichoria ridge had probably picked them up elsewhere because of their convenient shape (e.g., for spindle whorls). It is only from the beginning of Middle Helladic times that our excavations have produced substantial evidence of the existence of a permanent village. Thereafter, the ridgetop was occupied without documented interruption until near the end of the Late Bronze Age, i.e., Late Helladic IIIB2.

Our present information does not permit a categorical statement about the local situation during the earlier phases of the poorly documented transition from the Late Bronze to the Early Iron Age. For a century or more following the end of the 13th century, the ridge itself was either very sparsely used or (more probably) completely abandoned. But at least as early as mid-11th century a Dark Age settlement—or resettlement—can be documented; and this village persisted until the mid-8th century. From then for almost two millennia, until the 10th century A.D., Nichoria seems never to have been the site of a year-round settlement, although isolated structures (probably field houses) and a limited number of artefacts suggest that in most intervening periods the ridgetop was cultivated by farmers whose permanent homes were nearby.

In Middle Byzantine times at least one or two families lived on the northwest acropolis (Area II) and a chapel was built in the central saddle (Area IV) which had been the focus of the DA village. We found almost no evidence of habitation after the 13th century, except for an isolated building on the SE acropolis (Area VI) which was apparently constructed in relatively modern times. In addition to the MME excavations on the ridge, the record of salvage and organized excavation by the Greek Archaeological Service in the nearby cemeteries generally confirms the above sketch of the history of occupation in the Late

Chronological Chart: Nichoria Ridge and Environs
(all dates before 700 B.C. are approximate)

Final Neolithic	3500-3000 B.C.
Middle Helladic (MH) I	2100-1850
Middle Helladic II	1850-1600
Middle Helladic III	1600-1550
Late Helladic (LH) I	1550-1500
Late Helladic IIA	1500-1450
Late Helladic IIB	1450-1420
Late Helladic IIIA1	1420-1380
Late Helladic IIIA2	1380-1330
Late Helladic IIIA2/IIIB1 (transition)	1330-1250
Late Helladic IIIB2	1250-1200?
Late Helladic IIIC[a]	1200-1125?
Dark Age (DA) I	1075-975?
Dark Age II	975-850?
Dark Age II/III (transition)	850-800?
Dark Age III	800-750?
Late Geometric	750-700
Archaic[b]	700-500
Classical/Hellenistic	500-31 B.C.
Roman	31 B.C.-330 A.D.
Late Roman/Early Byzantine	330-ca. 600
Byzantine Dark Age	ca. 600-ca. 900
Middle Byzantine	ca. 900-1204
Frankish	1205-1432
Late Byzantine	1432-1460
Turkish	1460-1685
Venetian	1685-1715
Turkish	1715-1830
Modern Greece	1830-present

[a]Habitation on ridge and environs is uncertain.
[b]There is no evidence for use of ridge and immediate environs.

Bronze and Dark Ages. We are deeply obligated to our Greek colleagues for permission to study and excerpt from this material.

One of our original objectives was to gain as clear an idea as possible of the extent and plan of the villages or towns that had existed on the ridge at different periods. The 1969 tests already indicated, however, that the full realization of this goal would probably exceed our available time and staff and funds. Relatively few sections of the extensive ridgetop appear to be totally barren of cultural debris, and in at least some cases negative results may very well be the result of heavy erosion. In the following five intensive campaigns (two in 1973), trenches were dug to varying depths in only about 10% (4600m^2) of the total area, all of them in the NW half of the ridge (Fig. A-1). The area explored in detail does not constitute a scientific sample of the whole, but these results and the 1969 tests do provide useful data on which to base reasonable estimates of the growth and contraction of the inhabited areas over time. In the context of the present volume, for example, there can be no doubt that Area IV was the nucleus of settlement in DA times and Area II in the Middle Byzantine period; and we have considerable evidence as to where the DA people lived elsewhere on the ridge.

Readers of this volume are owed at least a summary of the detailed information on the site and digging methods that was presented in *Nichoria* I (see especially pp. 6-12). The modern toponym "Nichoria" serves locally to designate a high, steep-sided, and relatively clearly defined ridge located about 2 km inland from the NW corner of the Messenian Gulf (Figs. A-2, 1-2). Its crest looms to SW and directly above the village of Rizomilo. Here the Koroni highway, skirting the E side of the Messenian peninsula, forms a T with the major E-W highway connecting Kalamata and Pylos (Pl. 1-2). The Rizomilo area marks the beginning of the dissected plateau country (*kambos*) that borders the W side of the wide Pamisos valley. The modern highway engineers handled the abrupt rise in elevation by looping the road-line to Pylos around to the north of Nichoria; but the stone-paved Turkish *kalderimi* (and presumably its predecessors for millennia before it) led straight up westward from Rizomilo in the valley of the Karia River, through the Tourkokivouro (properly Smaïlakko) ravine, and directly under Nichoria's north cliffs. The long SW side of the ridge overlooks an even deeper ravine (Vathirema) through which in prehistoric times a road led up to intersect the E-W highway at Nichoria's narrow NW end (Area I). From this point the natural grade up to the northwest acropolis (Area II) is relatively easy, and the main approach to the ridgetop in most periods seems to have been here. The major prehistoric cemetery area lies just beyond (NW of) this old route intersection.

The ridge itself is formed of fine-grained, dense Pliocene marine marls (bedrock), with indurated and highly erosion-resistant horizons (caprock) particularly noticeable toward the NW end. The relatively flat top is 80 to 100 m above sea level, about 500 m long, and varies in width from about 60 m at the NW to about 150 m at the SE end. The total area available for habitation and/or cultivation is some four to five hectares.

Viewed from above (Pl. 1-1), the outline of the ridge is extremely irregular, with several gullies cutting deeply into its edges. Excavation has shown, however, that the surface was even more drastically dissected before the prehistoric inhabitants managed to check the process of erosion and at least partially fill some of the deeper gullies. If one looks at a profile view taken from the NE (Pl. 1-2), one notes near the right-hand end the above-mentioned

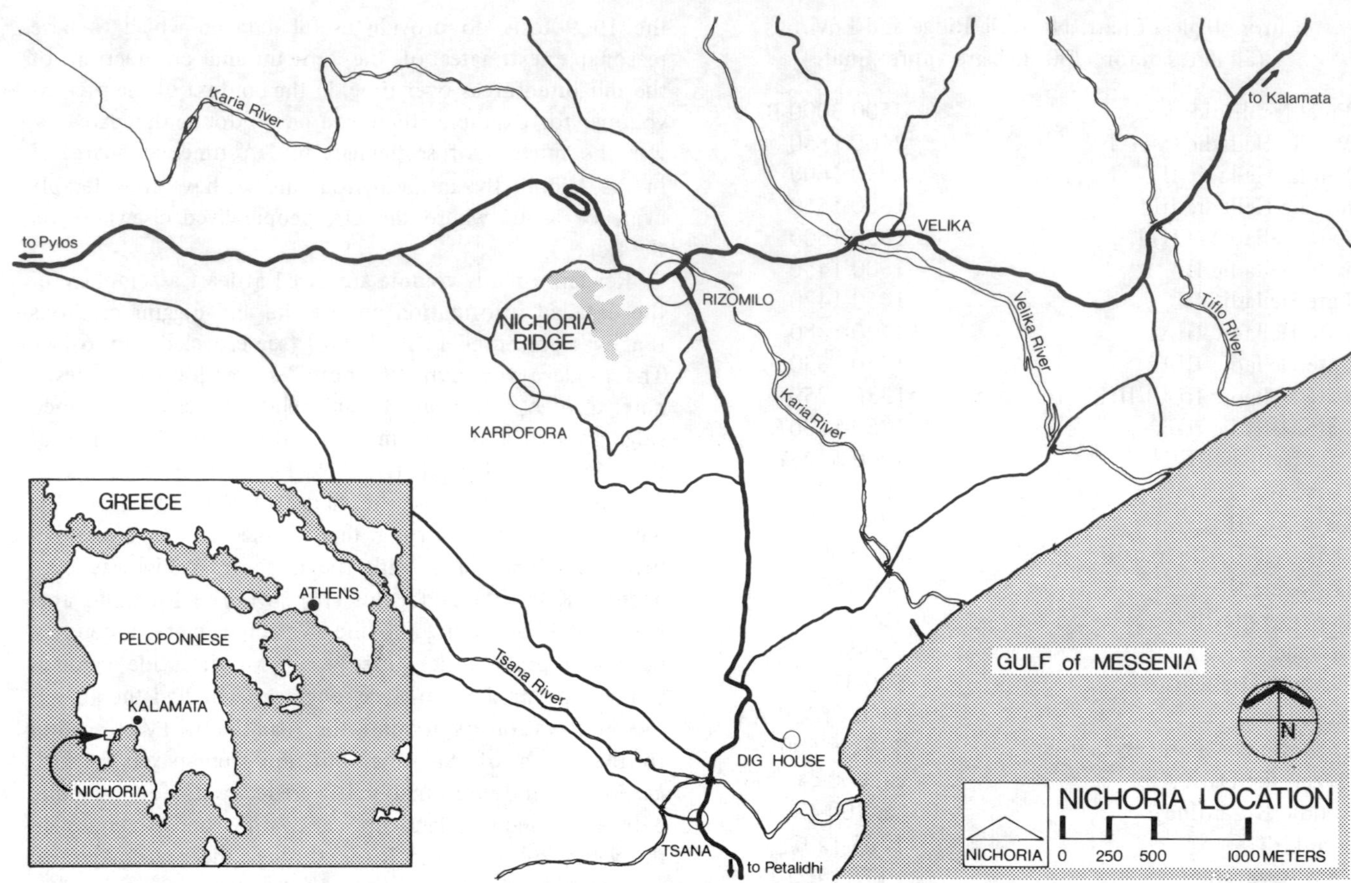

Figure A-2. Site location map

pass, then the distinctive flat-topped acropolis (Area II), and to its left (SE) a somewhat lower intervening "saddle" (Areas III, IV, V). Scanning farther left, there is a central conical hillock, and beyond it a second flat-topped eminence (Area VI) near the SE end. Also, just beyond the SE slope of Nichoria proper (Area VII) one sees on the skyline a prominent rounded hill that is locally called Trypetorachi.

The ridgetop afforded its inhabitants a magnificent panorama in all directions except due north, where the view is occluded by an even higher ridge (Sournika) that lies just across the intervening ravine. This protection from wintry north winds may have more than compensated for the obstructed view, however, and we have reason to believe that there was a lookout post on top of Sournika in Mycenaean times. From the E edge of the ridgetop one overlooks the broad valleys of the Karia and Velika Rivers, both of them perennial streams fed by great headsprings in the northern mountains. Beyond these valleys, the N rim of the Messenian Gulf and the lower Pamisos Valley appear; and in the background is the noble line of the Taygetos Mountains (Pl. 4-1). Looking down the peninsula, one sees modern Petalidhi (ancient Korone) some five km to the E-SE. Its small harbor is somewhat protected from the dangerous south winds by a spit of land that forms the very end of the E slope of massive Mount Lykodimo. From the opposite edge of the ridgetop one can see westward at least halfway across the dissected central plateau, as far as a Mycenaean lookout high up on the N slope of Lykodimo (*MME* 1972, p. 280, no. 103) from which the Pylos area on the W coast is visible.

Our system of surveying the ridgetop is best understood from a map (Fig. A-1), but a brief verbal explanation may also assist in orienting the reader. In 1969 the entire surface was permanently staked out in grids of 100 m to a side, designated from J to O (west to east) and from 21 to 25 (south to north). Thus, grid J25 designates the NW end and grid O22 the SE end of the ridge. Most of the 1969 test trenches were located to explore anomalies revealed in the geophysical survey (*MME* 1972, pp. 236-39). They are identified by the appropriate 100 m grid, followed by a numeral indicating the order of digging; so K25-III is the third test trench dug in grid K25.

For the intensive stage of excavation (1970-73) it was necessary to purchase in the name of the Greek state parcels of land that the geophysical survey and test trenches had indicated were the most promising. As the fields were acquired we designated them by "area number" rather than by grids or (as in 1969) by names of owners (Fig. A-1). Except for Area V, which was the last parcel to be purchased, area numbers follow a locational order from NW to SE. Areas VI and VII at the SE end were thoroughly tested in 1959 and 1969, but no further digging was done there in succeeding years. The accompanying chart sets out the overall scheme.

For exact positioning of trenches and location of finds in the seasons of intensive excavation, a much more precise "mini-grid" was needed. A 4 X 4 m module was adopted because it fit best our system of vertical stereo photogrammetry (*Nichoria* I, pp. 141-50). Thus, each side of the 100 m grids was subdivided into 25 units along both the N-S and E-W axis, yielding 625 squares, each 4 m on the side (Fig. A-1). The E-W subdivisions are indicated by capital letters, beginning at the SW corner, and the N-S subdivisions by small letters, beginning at the same corner. So the 4 X 4 m square in the SW corner of the L23 100 m grid is designated L23 Aa. We usually found that the most efficient digging unit was a double mini-grid, e.g., L23 ABa (oriented E-W) or L23 Aab (oriented N-S). Allowing for baulks of 1 m to be shared with contiguous trenches, the double units provided a convenient area of 7 X 3m. Precise locations within the trenches were recorded horizontally by triangulating from corner stakes, and vertically with plumb line from the nearest elevation marker.

Coming now to the organization and authorship of the present volume, Part I (Chapters 1 through 6) is concerned with the Dark Age occupation. In Chapters 2 through 5 we set out in detail the various categories of material evidence. Chapters 1 and 6 present an appraisal of the significance of the new evidence in the context of the scanty information previously available, particularly for SW Greece. William Coulson has assumed the largest share of responsibility for Part I. The assignment was a natural outcome of the way tasks were originally distributed to the trenchmasters. Coulson's digging sector was in Area IVNE, where he uncovered most of the best-preserved DA architectural remains with their associated stratified deposits. Since then he has conferred extensively with recognized specialists and has himself become thoroughly knowledgeable in handling this difficult material. He assumed sole responsibility for publishing the DA pottery (Chapter 3) which merits unusually thorough (and therefore lengthy) analysis. He was assisted by other trenchmasters, notably Richard Hope Simpson and Nancy Wilkie, in presenting the evidence for DA buildings (Chapter 2).

Chapter 4 on the DA burials includes contributions from several authors. In 1969 William Donovan discovered a Late Geometric pithos burial in the N Veves field. It was apparently made soon after DA habitation on the ridge had ceased. The excavator describes the burial proper, and William Wade and Sara Bisel provide separate reports on their studies of the skeleton. Hector Catling includes the metal grave goods with the bulk of DA metal objects in Chapter 5, and the vases are published at the end of Coulson's Chapter 3.

With generous permission from Angelos Choremis and Nicholas Yalouris, Coulson includes in Chapter 4 an overview of the evidence from the cemeteries. Without this closely connected material, our own study of the contemporary settlement would have been incomplete. The main DA cemetery appears to have been located just NW of the Nichoria ridge, overlapping slightly with that of Mycenaean times (Fig. 4-2). Before or concurrent with our work on the ridge, considerable salvage and some planned excavation was carried out by the Greek Archaeological Service in this cemetery area and elsewhere in the immediate vicinity of Nichoria. In particular, Choremis excavated several Late Bronze and DA graves in 1969 and published his discoveries along with some of the material salvaged earlier (Choremis 1973).

Locational Order of Land Parcels, NW to SE

Area I	main approach at NW end	grid J25 (overlaps S into J24)
Area II	NW acropolis	grid K25 (overlaps very slightly S into K24)
Area III	N saddle	grids K25, K24 (overlaps slightly E into L24)
(two intervening fields: N and S Veves)		
Area V	central saddle	W part of grid L23
Area IV	S saddle	E part of grid L23 (overlaps very slightly E into M23)
(several intervening fields)		
Area VI	SE acropolis	grid M22
Area VII	SE terraces	grid N22 (overlaps slightly E into O22)

Chapter 5 on the DA small finds is multiauthored. Let me record here our special debt to Dr. Catling who publishes the metal objects. He was interested and helpful during the excavation and, in spite of unusually heavy administrative and scholarly commitments, generously agreed to put at our disposal his expertise in East Mediterranean metallurgy and artefacts of metal. Jill Carington Smith discusses the evidence for a cottage textile industry and Harriet Blitzer states her reasons for deferring to *Nichoria* II the publication of all objects of chipped and ground stone. Finally, Helen Hughes-Brock and Coulson present a few miscellaneous items that have a particularly strong claim to manufacture and/or use in DA times.

In Part II (Chapter 7) Coulson, with Wilkie's assistance, publishes the sparse evidence recovered on and around the ridgetop and datable between the 8th century B.C. and the 5th century A.D.

Part III (Chapters 8 through 13) sets out the evidence for the use of the ridge in Late Roman-Early Byzantine and particularly in Middle Byzantine times. This segment of the Nichoria record assumes special significance because, except for Corinth, no comparable secular material dating from this important epoch in Greek history is published from any site in the whole of the Peloponnese. John Rosser, a specialist in Byzantine studies, participated in the later phases of the chapel excavation in Area IV and has assumed sole responsibility for the publication of all the Byzantine pottery (Chapter 10) and small finds (Chapter 12). He shares publication of the architectural remains (Chapter 9) with Donovan, who supervised the excavation of the Byzantine buildings in Area II and of most of Unit IV-2. Wade and Bisel again contribute technical sections on the human skeletal remains, to supplement Rosser's description of the Byzantine burials (Chapter 11).

In Part IV (Chapter 14), Stanley Aschenbrenner, Hope Simpson, and Rosser provide an account of the evidence for the use of the ridge and immediate environs in post-Byzantine times. The present owners of fields on the ridgetop cultivate mainly olives and figs, along with some vines and occasional annual crops. They do not regard Nichoria as prime agricultural land.

A brief explanation may be helpful here concerning the relationship of this book to the forthcoming Volumes II and IV. One natural division of the habitation sequence is at the "break" between Bronze Age and Early Iron (Dark) Age, and we have so organized the evidence to be presented in Volumes II and III. That is, Volume II will contain the record of occupation up to the end of the Bronze Age, whereas the present volume includes that of the later phases. Then, in Volume IV we shall attempt a synthesis of the results reported in Volumes I, II, and III, concentrating on the interaction of land and people, i.e., natural environment and human culture. Supplementary information from elsewhere in Messenia and the larger Aegean orbit will be incorporated when it can contribute materially to the reconstruction.

It is obvious that the writing of Volume IV must follow the completion of Volumes I, II, and III and that the natural order of Volumes II and III is the chronological one. There is no point in reviewing the reasons why the intended publication sequence of Volumes II and III had to be reversed; but anyone familiar with the complicated organization of a multiauthored series will sympathize. Actually, 18 authors accepted major tasks in the preparation of *Nichoria* I; and 20 are contributing to Volumes II and/or III. Nearly all of the latter group participated in the excavation and assumed key roles in the organization of the results for publication.

In any series of this sort, a major concern is that each volume be as independent of the others as is feasible. That is, individual volumes should be intelligible in and by themselves, but at the same time unnecessary repetition and duplication must be avoided. Plans, sections, and other illustrative material already published in *Nichoria* I are reproduced or adapted in later volumes only when they are judged essential for clarity of presentation. On the other hand, we freely cross-reference additional illustrations and information in *Nichoria* I that we believe would be particularly useful to the reader of later volumes. In spite of these efforts, however, anyone engaged in serious research concerned with the overall Nichoria record will need eventually to have the whole series easily available. We do not attempt, for instance, to summarize here or in Volume II the fairly lengthy account in the Preface of *Nichoria* I concerning the MME regional survey (1959-68) and the choice of the Nichoria site for intensive study. Those who require even more detailed information on various aspects of the MME program should consult the bibliographies in *MME* 1972 as well as the two full-scale progress reports on the excavation (McDonald 1973; McDonald et al. 1975).

In publishing their movable finds, archaeologists use a rather confusing variety of organizational devices, almost all of them with individual advantages as well as limitations. After much consultation, we have adopted a set of conventions that should facilitate access to the Nichoria material by serious scholars whose reasons for consulting our Volumes II and III will inevitably vary considerably. But our system, like most others, does require some explanation.

When individual pots or diagnostic fragments had been cleaned, mended, and preliminarily studied at the dighouse, the items that were at that stage considered to be of particular significance were assigned consecutive inventory numbers. These were divided into two categories, viz., NP1 and following for "Nichoria Pottery" (i.e., from the settlement) and TP1 and following for "Tholos Pottery." For the final publication, however, the inventory numbers are replaced by a new numbering system that corresponds to the order in which individual items are presented in the text and Catalogs. All pottery items, whether whole vases, complete or partial profiles, or specially important sherds, are now identified primarily by a number that is prefixed by **P** (for "pottery") and is always printed in **boldface**. The new numbering system is consecutive throughout this volume, beginning with **P1** and ending with **P1770**. The Catalogs also provide in parentheses the original inventory number, if such was assigned.

We use essentially the same system of new publication numbers instead of the inventory numbers originally assigned to the small finds. The N numbers (N = "Nichoria small finds") are replaced by consecutive numbers in **boldface** and without any prefixed letter. Thus, the DA small finds are numbered **1** to **243**. Delays in decisions concerning DA items to be published in Chapter 5 made it necessary to leave a safe gap before beginning the new numbering of items in Chapter 12. Consequently, the Byzantine small finds begin with **501** and continue to **581**. For the same reason, the original N numbers had to be used in the plans of individual buildings to show the exact location of DA small finds.

The Catalogs for pottery and small finds are included as integral parts of the appropriate chapters, rather than being relegated to the end of the volume. In the case of the Byzantine material (Chapters 10, 12), subsections of the Catalogs follow immediately on the relevant subsections of text; elsewhere, the full Catalog follows the text for the whole chapter. Notes and References (bibliography) conclude each chapter.

The Concordance (pp. 519-22) lists in the left-hand column the inventory designations (NP, TP, N) in strict numerical order; and opposite each item we supply the new publication number, the museum accession number (kindly provided by the Z′ ephorate at Olympia), and reference(s) to text and Catalog page(s) where the main discussion and description of the particular item occurs. Catalog entries in turn contain references to relevant Figures and Plates. We believe that the Concordance will aid readers in tracking down specific objects which are their particular concern; and the information easily accessible here should also be useful to anyone who wishes to check material stored in the Kalamata and Chora Museums or to consult MME records deposited in the archives of the American School of Classical Studies in Athens and duplicated at the University of Minnesota.

In the discussion of architectural remains, each structure whose plan was completely, substantially, or even partially recovered is referred to as a "unit"; and the units are identified by the "area" in which they occur, followed by a running number assigned in order of discovery. Thus, Unit IV-2 is the second structure whose plan became clear during the excavation of Area IV. The description of each unit is accompanied by a Table in which detailed information is supplied for every surviving wall foundation. Also, trenchmasters provide in the write-up of each unit a list of the major associated movable finds; and in the unit plans (Figures) the exact findspot of important items is shown.

I shall not duplicate here the lengthy and specific expression of our thanks that appears in the Preface to *Nichoria* I for scientific, financial, and moral support during the excavation stage from foundations, institutions, administrators, and private individuals. Nor need I reemphasize my appreciation of the loyalty and efficiency of MME staff members. The authors of the chapters to follow were invited to express in the proper context their thanks for individual help. What is called for here, however, is a brief recapitulation of our major corporate debts in connection with the preparation of the present volume. For their continued financial support in this crucial stage of the Nichoria enterprise we are especially grateful to the National Endowment for the Humanities, to the Bush Foundation of St. Paul, Minnesota, and to the Research Fund of the Graduate School of the University of Minnesota. I am personally indebted to my own department for continued access to office space and secretarial assistance which are by no means the inalienable rights of an emeritus colleague.

In addition to the authors themselves, I take the risk of singling out a few individuals who were particularly helpful in the preparation of this volume. Bryan Carlson continues his skilled association with MME cartography. He prepared the maps, plans, and sections and, in addition, spent endless hours in the organization and mock-up of the Figures in Chapters 3, 7, 10, and 12. Duane Bingham also contributed freely of his time and skill in processing the photographs that are reproduced in the Plates. Jennifer Moody drew most of the metal objects and the Byzantine pottery, and she assisted with the mock-ups of Figures in Chapter 12. Sylvia Ruud sketched the artist's reconstructions of the DA buildings. R. C. Anderson is responsible for the architectural reconstruction of the Byzantine chapel. Research assistants Julie Hansen, Vicky Walsh, and Julie Stein helped in the preparation of text and illustrations. Elizabeth McDonald gave her usual devoted and capable assistance in editing, typing, and in the preparation of the Index. Richard Hope Simpson spent several weeks in Minnesota on two occasions to help with editorial duties. Staff members of the University of Minnesota Press, in particular Beverly Kaemmer and Vicki Haire, were uniformly courteous and efficient.

Finally, I want the record to show that the authors of individual chapters in Volumes II and III have been urged to try to correlate their more traditional kinds of data with the environmental evidence already published in *Nichoria* I and elsewhere. For consistency's sake we should also have urged the reverse process, i.e., that the authors of *Nichoria* I write their chapters with due consideration for the evidence now being set out in *Nichoria* II and III. But, for us at least, the logistical problems of preparing a multivolume publication made this logical step extremely difficult. We did include in *Nichoria* I, however, a lengthy section (Chapter 8) in which the trenchmasters anticipated to some extent their fuller treatment of the excavation methods and results.

As a team, we are trying, however tentatively and inexpertly, to make in this series some progress toward an *inter*disciplinary as distinct from a *multi*disciplinary approach to all the evidence that was retrieved in the course of the Nichoria excavation. Greek archaeologists will meet the challenge of the late twentieth century only as we gradually learn, with the help of specialist colleagues, to recover, conserve, and integrate pertinent data of *all* sorts. With the broader base so provided, we should be able to achieve a more adequate reconstruction of the past, in all its complexity and diversity.

William A. McDonald
LaPointe, Wisconsin, October 1982

REFERENCES

Choremis, A. 1973. "Mycenaean and Protogeometric Graves at Karpofora, Messinias," *Arch Eph* :25-74. In Greek.

McDonald, W. A. 1970. "Nichoria-Rizomilo," *Deltion* 25:183-86.

______. 1973. "Excavations at Nichoria in Messenia: 1969-71," *Hesperia* 41:218-73.

______, and Howell, R. T. 1971. "Nichoria," *Deltion* 26:131-37.

______. 1972. "Nichoria," *Deltion* 27:266, 267.

______, and Rapp, G. 1972. *The Minnesota Messenia Expedition: Reconstructing a Bronze Age Regional Environment*. Minneapolis.

______, et al. 1975. "Excavations at Nichoria in Messenia: 1972-73," *Hesperia* 44:69-141.

MME 1972 = McDonald and Rapp 1972.

Nichoria I = Rapp and Aschenbrenner 1978.

Rapp, G., and Aschenbrenner, S. 1978. *Excavations at Nichoria in Southwest Greece. Site, Environs, and Techniques*. Minneapolis.

I. The Dark Age

1

Introduction

by

William A. McDonald and William D. E. Coulson

Nichoria is the first intensively excavated and fully published mainland site that has yielded a stratified habitation sequence extending over most of the obscure transition between the collapse of the Mycenaean civilization and the early phases of the Archaic period some 400 years later (see Chronological Chart, p. xxvii). And although Messenia was relatively isolated from the main stream of cultural development in those formative centuries, new evidence from any part of the Greek world merits the most careful attention. We follow current practice in referring to this period as the "Dark Age," in preference to "Early Iron Age" or "Protogeometric/Geometric" period.

For readers who are not thoroughly familiar with the preexisting evidence against which to gauge the Nichoria material, the authors of several recent publications provide reliable reviews of what is known or responsibly theorized about this latest prehistoric phase of Greek culture (see especially Coldstream 1968; Desborough 1964, 1972; Matz and Bucholz 1967 ff.; Snodgrass 1971). Yet, in comparison with the substantial evidence on both the preceding and following periods, our insights on this epoch are still largely a matter of "seeing through a glass, darkly." Vincent Desborough, who devoted much of his life to this study, spoke of "the haze of hesitancy and supposition" (1972, p. 321) that shields solid facts from scholarly penetration. The reasons are not difficult to establish.

In the first place, the all-important archaeological evidence is very thin and scattered. Worse still, the usefulness of the material evidence that is available is seriously lessened because "the best aid, that of well stratified habitation-sites, is almost entirely absent; its place has to be taken by graves" (Snodgrass 1971, p. 24). Then there is the problem of the dependability of the literary sources. Although the controversy is still unresolved, we are inclined to support the growing number of scholars who believe that the ancient writers, including Homer and Hesiod, offer little help in this context. Apart from a generalized and no doubt faithful folk memory of these latest preliterate times as characterized by upheaval, migration, and resettlement, the extant written records preserve no dependable framework into which the tenuous archaeological evidence can be fitted.

Still, we must not despair of eventually attaining a clearer understanding of such a crucial phase in the genesis of Greek civilization; and the remains of the DA village on the Nichoria ridge will surely play a part in the realization of that goal. In the autumn of 1958, when the ridge was first identified as a prehistoric habitation site, we noted sherds of the Middle and Late Bronze Age at a few spots on the extensive surface, but we recognized no evidence of occupation in the Dark Age. A few months later, however, a farmer uncovered a grave on a gentle hillside locally called Lakkoules, not far N of the area called Tourkokivouro where we had already tentatively located the main Mycenaean cemetery serving the settlement on the ridge (Fig. 4-2). The only item of burial furniture that was handed over to Yalouris, then ephor for W. Peloponnese, was a squat jug of diagnostic Protogeometric type; and the single, stone-lined, slab-covered, apsidal cist (Pl. 4-20) also conformed with a known DA grave type.

We therefore reasoned that the individual buried here had probably lived on the nearby Nichoria ridge and that the remains of a DA settlement might be recovered there in close proximity to those of the Mycenaean town. Three exploratory trenches dug by Yalouris and McDonald in the spring of 1959 near the SE end of the ridge (Areas VI and VII) amply confirmed Mycenaean occupation; but the only evidence of a DA presence on the ridge itself consisted of a few stray Late Geometric decorated sherds picked up on the lower S slopes.

In the following decade, before the beginning of our excavation, several additional DA graves were opened accidentally or illicitly in the Lakkoules area (Daux 1961, 1962; Papathanasopoulos 1961-62; Yalouris 1960). Their context was generally obscure, information was garbled, records were minimal, and all of the contents may not have been handed over to the authorities in Kalamata. The main fact to emerge was that the above-mentioned grave was not an isolated phenomenon, but that similar DA burials had been scattered over a considerable area of the Lakkoules hillside. Also in Lakkoules, an accidentally discovered structure, which was properly excavated by Angelos Choremis in 1968, proved to be an unpretentious but still quite recognizable example of a tholos tomb (Choremis 1973). The burial offerings, of exclusively DA type, proved that this distinctive feature of Mycenaean architecture had survived here into DA times.

Meanwhile, the MME regional survey was revealing the remarkable scarcity everywhere in SW Peloponnese of surface evidence for habitation (or even cemeteries) during and immediately following the transition from the Late Bronze to the Early Iron Age (McDonald and Hope Simpson 1969; McDonald and Rapp 1972). By 1968 the Lakkoules DA cemetery (usually named after the nearby village of Karpofora in the brief published references) had emerged as one of very few known sites where excavation might shed badly needed light on this obscure epoch in Messenian history. Indeed, if we had correctly inferred the location of the village connected with the cemetery, there was a possibility that the Nichoria ridge might provide crucial information on a habitation-based DA culture sequence. This was certainly one of the most important factors in our choice of Nichoria as the locale for an intensive excavation.

Our request for a permit was granted by the Greek Archaeological Service in 1968, with the proviso that we confine our digging to the ridge itself, leaving the cemetery areas to our Greek colleagues. For their acquiescence in this division of effort, we have to acknowledge the generosity of Messrs. Yalouris, Papathanasopoulos, and Choremis, since their established interest in the cemeteries might understandably have included the ridgetop as well.

The 1969 season confirmed our hopes that the ridge would yield evidence of a DA presence. Several of the 66 test trenches and pits that were dug over much of the ridgetop yielded DA sherds, and the diagnostic pieces appeared to be comparable with the pottery salvaged from the Lakkoules cemetery. By far the heaviest concentration came from the central saddle (Area IV) which had suffered least from erosion; but light to very light scatters were also identified on the NW acropolis (Area II), in Area III immediately to the SE, and in Area VII at the SE end of the 500 m-long ridge (Fig. A-1). Very few of the short sectors of stone-built wall foundations exposed in the tests could at that time be confidently associated with DA debris, but the stratigraphic pattern already emerging in Area IV made us reasonably confident that a DA village had succeeded the Bronze Age town. Desborough's preliminary information (1972, p. 252) that, after the Mycenaean collapse, "the inhabitants [of DA Nichoria] are found occupying another site close by" is erroneous. While diagnostic pottery from both the presumed settlement and the cemetery was certifiably "Protogeometric," that term has such indefinite chronological significance for eccentric regions like Messenia that it would have been rash to suggest absolute dating brackets (Desborough 1952, 1964, 1972; Snodgrass 1971).

Except for a Late Geometric pithos burial in Area III (pp. 260-265; Pls. 4-2 to 4-8), the test trenches yielded no evidence of DA burials on the ridge; but additional information on the DA cemetery in the Lakkoules area was produced by Choremis's continued excavation there in 1969, while he was serving as liaison between MME and the Service (Choremis 1973). A Mycenaean tholos had been reused and an apsidal grave of canonical local DA type had been set into the largest Mycenaean tumulus in the Tourkokivouro area; and a pair of similar cists was excavated on the facing hillside (see pp. 266-268 and Fig. 4-2). Thus, it became apparent that the DA cemetery had extended closer to the settlement than we had previously realized and that, in fact, it had overlapped into the main Mycenaean cemetery (Tourkokivouro) which lay immediately NW of the ridge.

Evidence on the DA settlement accumulated rapidly in the following five campaigns of intensive excavation (Fig. 1-1). Two further field seasons (1974, 1975) of study and minor probing considerably refined, and in some cases revised, earlier tentative interpretations. Where discrepancies are substantive, we have tried to set the record straight in this definitive publication. Since 1975, Coulson[1] and colleagues have devoted a great deal of further research and reflection to the DA material. In Chapters 2 through 5 they present the results, organized in standard categories, together with relevant comparative data.

The chief purpose of the summary Chapter 6 is to provide a synthesis of the traditional kinds of evidence (Chapters 2 through 5) and of local environmental data. But we have included a preliminary discussion of the information from our site that seems to bear most directly on the vexed problem of cultural continuity/discontinuity during the transition from the Late Bronze to the Early Iron Age. To anticipate fairly briefly here, we believe that the available evidence will not support a categorical conclusion. Only a fraction of the very extensive ridgetop has been intensively excavated, but we can show that the nucleus of habitation shifted considerably in other periods. It is therefore not impossible that the remains of a small settlement dating to earlier LHIIIC times may have eluded

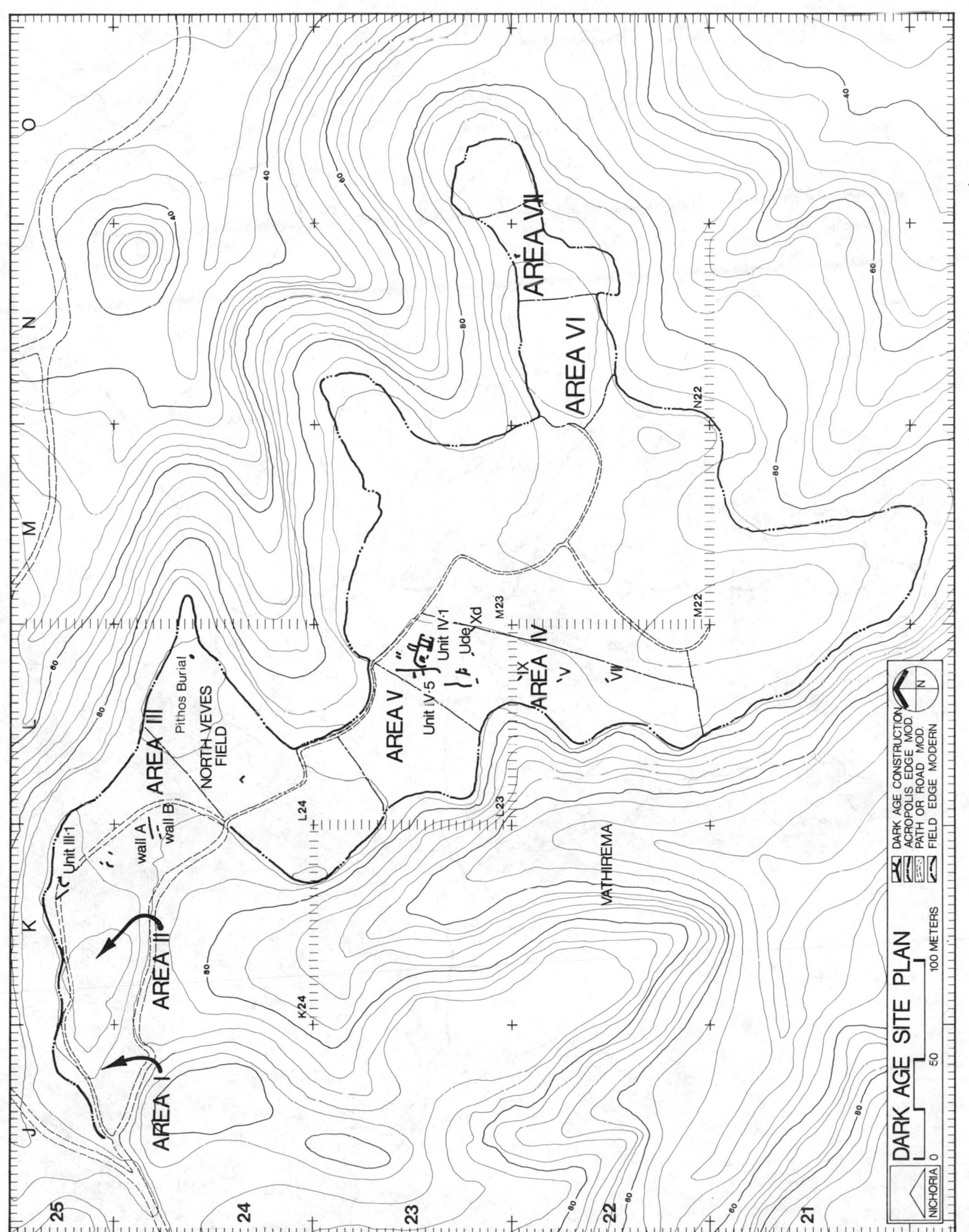

Figure 1-1. DA architectural remains

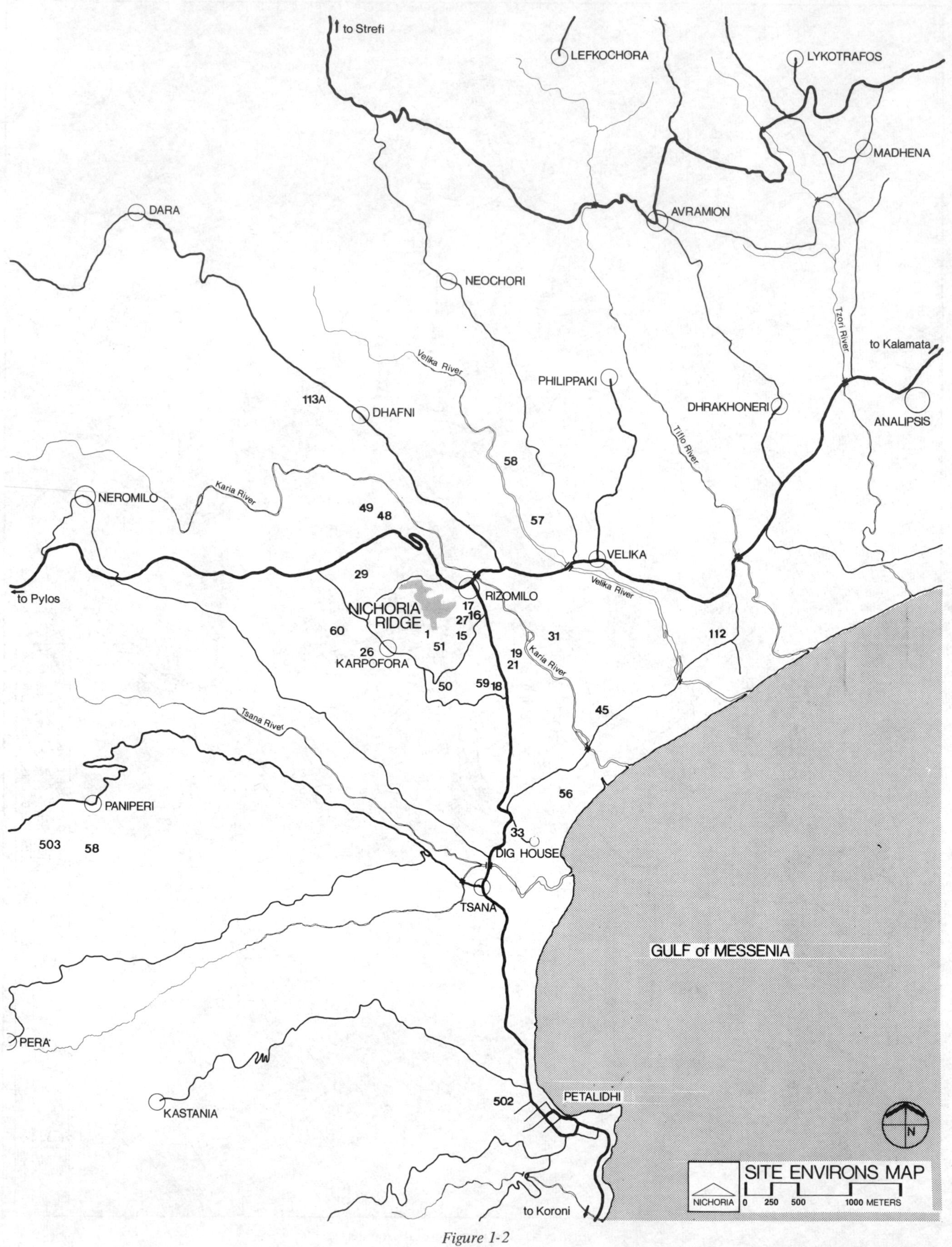

to Strefi
LEFKOCHORA
LYKOTRAFOS
MADHENA
AVRAMION
DARA
NEOCHORI
Tzori River
to Kalamata
Velika River
PHILIPPAKI
DHRAKHONERI
ANALIPSIS
113A
DHAFNI
Tiflo River
58
NEROMILO
Karia River
49
48
57
VELIKA
29
RIZOMILO
Velika River
to Pylos
NICHORIA RIDGE
17
27
16
60
1
15
31
112
26
51
19
KARPOFORA
21
Karia River
50
59
18
45
Tsana River
56
PANIPERI
33
503
58
DIG HOUSE
TSANA
GULF of MESSENIA
PERA
502
PETALIDHI
KASTANIA
N
SITE ENVIRONS MAP
NICHORIA
0
250
500
1000 METERS
to Koroni

Figure 1-2

our search. Several scattered items, both pottery and metal, could be so interpreted. Alternatively, local survivors of the Mycenaean collapse may have lived for a time in some less exposed spot nearby. Further careful excavation in the cemeteries may strengthen the case for an essentially uninterrupted sequence of burials. Desborough's judgment, based on the sparse evidence then published, was "continuity possible" (1972, p. 375).

The cultural sequence during this critical period in "provincial" regions is at present very imperfectly understood. "Abandonment" is a natural explanation for apparent gaps or "lags" in a system of relative chronology that depends mainly on data from east central Greece (Snodgrass 1971, p. 87). And, indeed, it seems often to be the correct interpretation, as in the case of Messenia generally after the breakup of the kingdom centered on the palace at Pylos (McDonald and Hope Simpson 1969). Nichoria may well reflect this overall pattern; but if it was totally abandoned for a century or so following LHIIIB2, its reoccupation appears to have occurred sooner than in Messenia generally (Fig. 1-2). The well-attested amalgam of inherited Mycenaean and novel DA traits in DA Nichoria may then have evolved in more remote Messenian "refuge" sites or even further afield.

Conversely, it is at present a tenable theory that in at least a few spots like Nichoria a remnant of the local Mycenaean population did persist. In that case, the novel DA traits would have been the result of a local merging of newcomers or new culture traits with the old stock.

NOTES

1. My contributions to the Dark Age section of this volume could not have been written without a great deal of advice and help from other scholars and financial support from various agencies. First and foremost, I am indebted to the National Endowment for the Humanities which provided me with a fellowship in 1972-73 to begin work on the DA architecture and pottery of Nichoria. I am also indebted to the American Council of Learned Societies for a fellowship in 1977-78. A portion of the ACLS funds was provided by NEH. The University of Minnesota has also been generous in its support, providing me with a Graduate School summer research grant in 1972, a salaried single-quarter leave in 1975, and a sabbatical leave in 1977-78. Financial support has also come from individual offices within the University: two travel grants from the College of Liberal Arts' Macmillan Fund; small grants from the Office of International Programs; a grant to subsidize profile-drawing from the Office of Research Development, CLA; a grant for secretarial help from the Graduate School; and secretarial help provided by my department. I owe a special debt of gratitude to my parents, Mr. and Mrs. D. A. Coulson, and to my in-laws, Dr. and Mrs. John A. King, without whose generous financial support my work on this volume could not have been completed.

Greek scholars and officials have also been generous in their help, especially with acquiring the necessary permits. I am particularly indebted to Angelos Choremis who gave me permission to study the DA material he excavated from the Nichoria cemeteries, to George Papathanasopoulos and Nicholas Yalouris for the Geometric material from the Vathirema chamber tomb, to Petros Themelis for access to the vases from Antheia, Kardamyla, and Tsoukaleïka, to the late Professor Spyridon Marinatos for the Rizes and Volimidia material (later confirmed by his successor in Messenia, Professor George Korres), to Theodora Karagiorga-Stathakopoulou for the Ramovouni-Dorion material, and to Nicholas Platon for selected vases from his excavations at Modi. In the years of study and preparation, Greek ephors have changed positions; but, over the years, the following were of help: Angelos Liangouras (Olympia), Vasilios Petrakos (Patras), Iphigenia Dekoulakou (Patras), Evi Touloupa (Ioannina), George Steinhauer (Sparta), and Ioannis Papapostolou (Chania).

Permission was also kindly granted by Sylvia Benton and the Managing Committee of the British School at Athens to study finds from Aëtos and the Polis Cave in Ithaka, by John Caskey and Lord William Taylour for the Kokevi and Pylos DA vases, and by Ulf Jantzen for the Vryses material. Lastly, I could never have completed these studies without the administrative support of the American School of Classical Studies at Athens and its fomer director, James McCredie.

I have benefited from conversations with A. J. Papadopoulos (University of Ioannina), Veronika Leon (Austrian Archaeological Institute), Hans Lauter (German Archaeological Institute), Berit Wells (Lund University), Robin Hägg (Swedish Archaeological Institute), Peter Gercke (Tiryns excavations), and, of course, the late V. R. d'A. Desborough. I am particularly indebted to Jan Bouzek, Paul Cartledge, Nicholas Coldstream, Richard Hope Simpson, and Anthony Snodgrass, all of whom took the trouble to read the pottery manuscript and to offer valuable advice. Special thanks in this respect is due to O. T. P. K. Dickinson. Vicky Walsh and Helen Hughes-Brock have been kind enough to offer comments on the DA architecture chapter. I am most indebted to Roger Howell who, over the past eight years, has provided the greatest help and encouragement.

The secretarial staff of the Department of Classics, University of Minnesota, and especially Robin Kueffer and Nancy Catalino, helped with typing the manuscript. Abigail Camp and Sylvia Ruud did the architectural reconstructions, and the pottery profiles were drawn by Jennifer Moody and, in particular, by Helen Townsend. Julie Hansen was of great help, particularly with the preparation of Chapter 3.

W.D.E.C.

REFERENCES

Choremis, A. 1973. "Mycenaean and Protogeometric Graves at Karpofora, Messinias," *Arch Eph*: 25-74. In Greek.

Coldstream, N. 1968. *Greek Geometric Pottery*. London.

Daux, G. 1961. "Chronique de Fouilles," *BCH* 85:697.

_____. 1962. "Chronique de Fouilles," *BCH* 86:725.

Desborough, V. R. d'A. 1952. *Protogeometric Pottery*. Oxford.

_____. 1964. *The Last Mycenaeans and their Successors*. Oxford.

_____. 1972. *The Greek Dark Ages*. London.

Matz, F., and Bucholz, H. G., eds. 1967ff. *Archaeologia Homerica: Die Denkmaler und das frühgriechische Epos*. Göttingen.

McDonald, W. A. 1972. "Excavations at Nichoria in Messenia: 1969-1971," *Hesperia* 41:218-73.

_____, et al. 1975. "Excavations at Nichoria in Messenia: 1972-1973," *Hesperia* 44:69-141.

_____, and Hope Simpson, R. 1969. "Further Explorations in Southwestern Peloponnese: 1964-1968," *AJA* 73:123-77.

_____, and Rapp, G., Jr., eds. 1972. *The Minnesota Messenia Expedition: Reconstructing a Bronze Age Regional Environment*. Minneapolis.

Papathanasopoulos, G. 1961-62. "Messenia," *Deltion* 17:95, 96. In Greek.

Snodgrass, A. M. 1971. *The Dark Age of Greece*. Edinburgh.

Yalouris, N. 1960. "Messenia," *Deltion* 16:108. In Greek.

2

The Architecture

by

William D. E. Coulson

with contributions by William P. Donovan, Dietmar K. Hagel, Richard Hope Simpson, William A. McDonald, and Nancy C. Wilkie

The evidence here described comes mainly from the ruins of major buildings excavated by Coulson in Area IV, which was undoubtedly the core of habitation throughout the history of DA occupation; but we have also included any information from the 1969 test trenches and from later intensive excavation that bears on DA habitation throughout the site. We report, therefore, not only remains of actual DA dwellings but also significant concentrations of habitation debris that attest to the existence of houses or work areas in the immediate vicinity. Beginning at the NW end, the sectors that produced such evidence are Areas II, III, IV, VI, and VII (Fig. 1-2). In most cases the descriptions are written by the original excavators. Thus, Area II is handled by Donovan; Area III by Hope Simpson, Wilkie, and Hagel; Area IV by Coulson with input by Wilkie, Howell, and Aschenbrenner; and Areas VI and VII by Hope Simpson. The DA material excavated by Donovan in the N Veves field is here written up by Coulson, and that recovered by Lazenby in the Tsagdis field is reported by Hope Simpson.

Vicky Walsh has also read and commented on a draft of this chapter. Some of the results of her dissertation research on prehistoric construction techniques as revealed by the Nichoria architectural remains will be published in Volume II of the series. Although including evidence from DA structures, the thesis concentrates on the Bronze Age buildings, and input from it is therefore more relevant in the earlier context.

Area II (Fig. 1-1)

In Area II no structural remains of DA houses were found; but small quantities of worn DAI and DAII sherds occurred sporadically, mainly along the N and S edges of the acropolis. The DA material was always in mixed contexts, together with far higher concentrations of LH and Byzantine pottery.

W.P.D.

Area III (Figs. 1-1, 2-1, 2-2)

DA occupation in Area III is marked not only by distinctive pottery but also in many parts by a much darker and usually more compact earth than that found in the earlier levels. The far higher concentration and better preservation of the DA material in the N trenches, especially in the levels above and beside the ruins of Unit III-4 (in K24 WXa), indicate that there must have been DA buildings along the now badly eroded N edge.

There is no distinct DAI level in Area III. DAI sherds were few and were mainly concentrated in K24 Yy and in K25 Rfg to W of Unit III-1. The DAI sherds found above Unit III-3 and in the vicinity of the DAII walls in the south central part of Area III were usually very worn and mixed with much larger quantities of DAII pottery.

The DA structures identified in Area III all belong to the DAII period. A good stratum was found in most grids, e.g., level 3 on Figs. 2-3 and 2-4, level 6 on Fig. 2-5, level 3b on Fig. 2-6, and level 7 on Section 3 of Pocket Map 4 in *Nichoria* I. By this time the Mycenaean street in the N part of Area III was covered by debris, consisting mainly of large limestone blocks which at one time were incorporated in the house walls bordering both sides of the street. The earth associated with these stones was generally dark and loose. The pottery found in the debris ranges from LHIIIA2 to DAII. Above the debris over the street

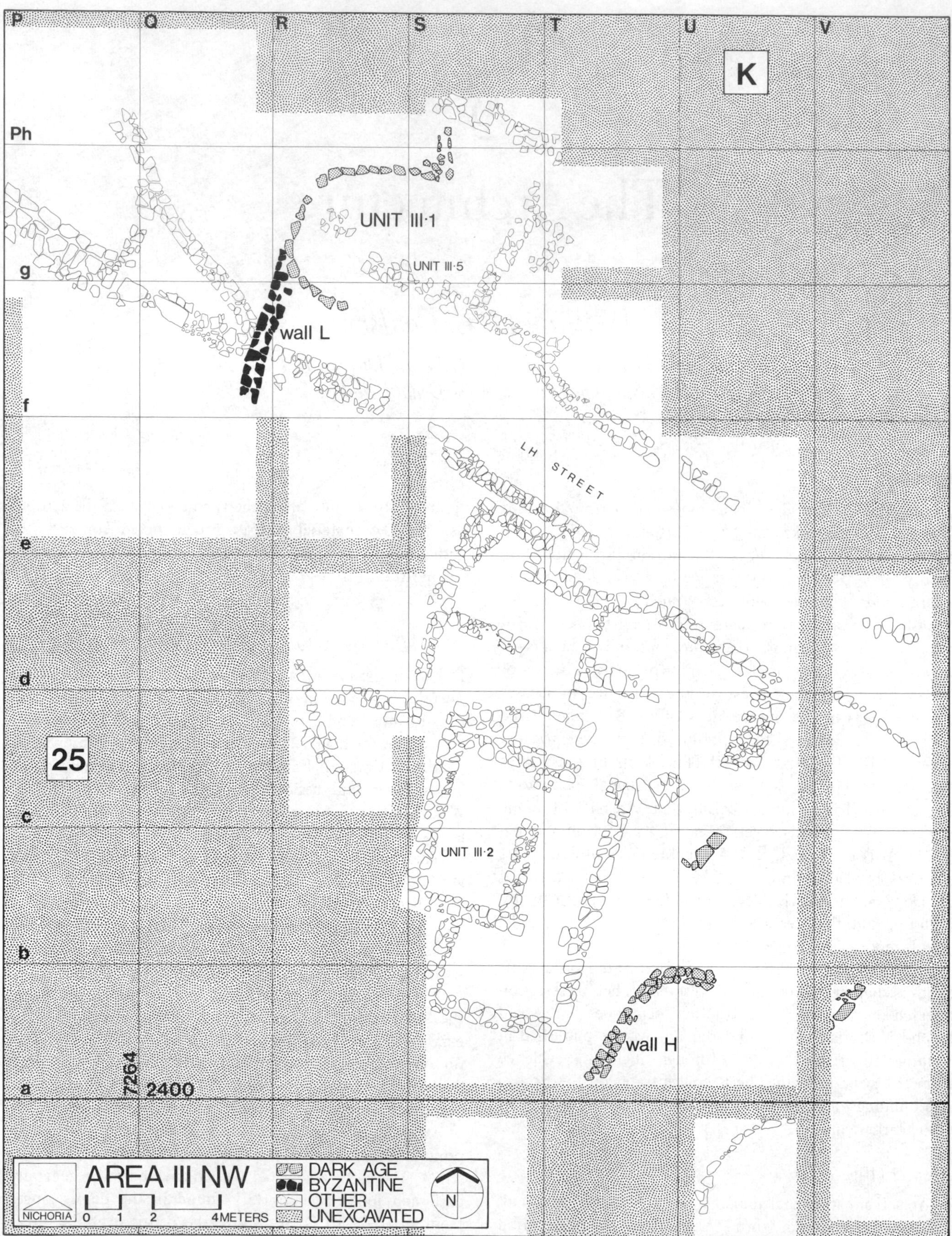
P
Q
R
S
T
U
V
K
Ph
UNIT III·1
UNIT III·5
g
wall L
f
LH STREET
e
d
25
c
UNIT III·2
b
wall H
a
7264
2400
AREA III NW
NICHORIA
0 1 2 4METERS
DARK AGE
BYZANTINE
OTHER
UNEXCAVATED
N

Figure 2-1

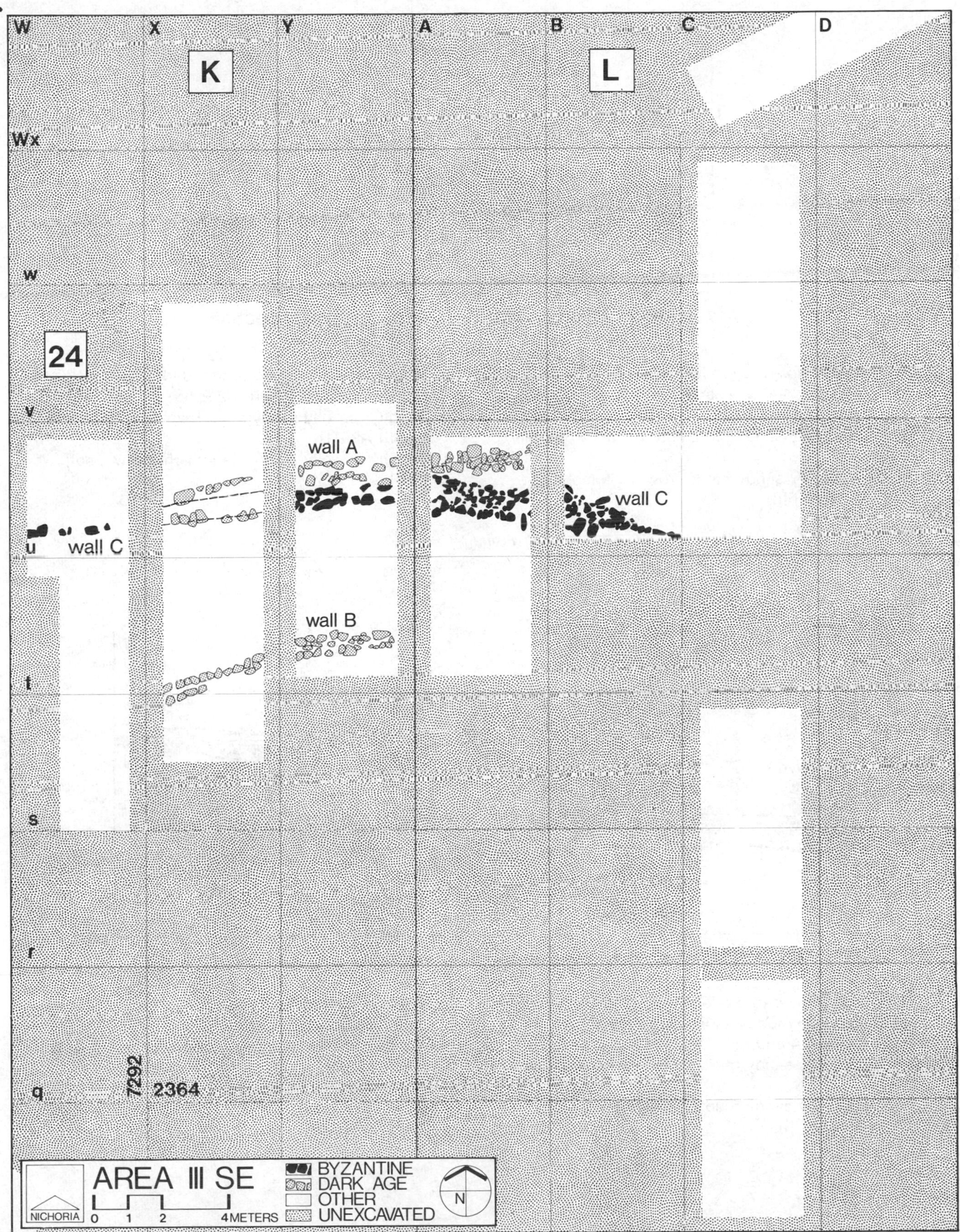
W
X
Y
A
B
C
D
K
L
Wx
w
24
v
wall A
wall C
u
wall C
wall B
t
s
r
7292
q
2364
NICHORIA
AREA III SE
0 1 2 4 METERS
BYZANTINE
DARK AGE
OTHER
UNEXCAVATED
N

Figure 2-2

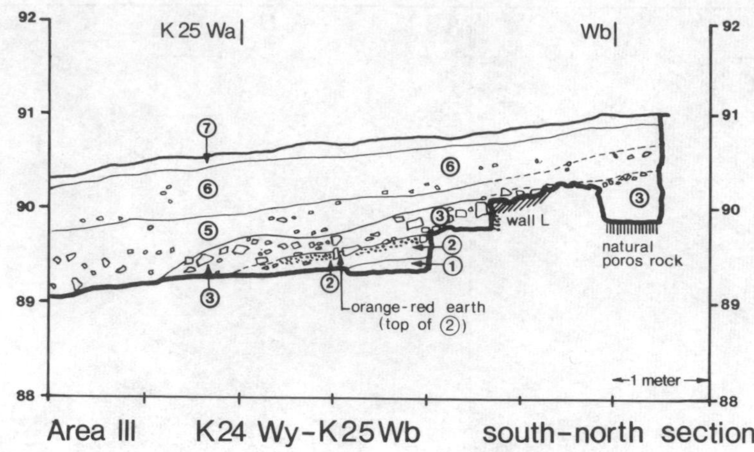

7. Plowed soil (Mixed to modern)
6. Slightly gravelly muddy sand: dark brown (Byzantine w/DA and LH)
5. Slightly gravelly sandy mud: light brown, w/tumble (DA II)
4. Slightly gravelly sandy mud: brown w/tumble (DA I - II W/LH III)
3. Slightly gravelly muddy sand: dark brown w/tumble, slightly compact (LH III A2-B2)
2. Slightly gravelly sandy mud: red w/charcoal, soft (LH III A2/B1)
1. Slightly gravelly muddy sand: light brown, soft (LH II - III A2)

Figure 2-3

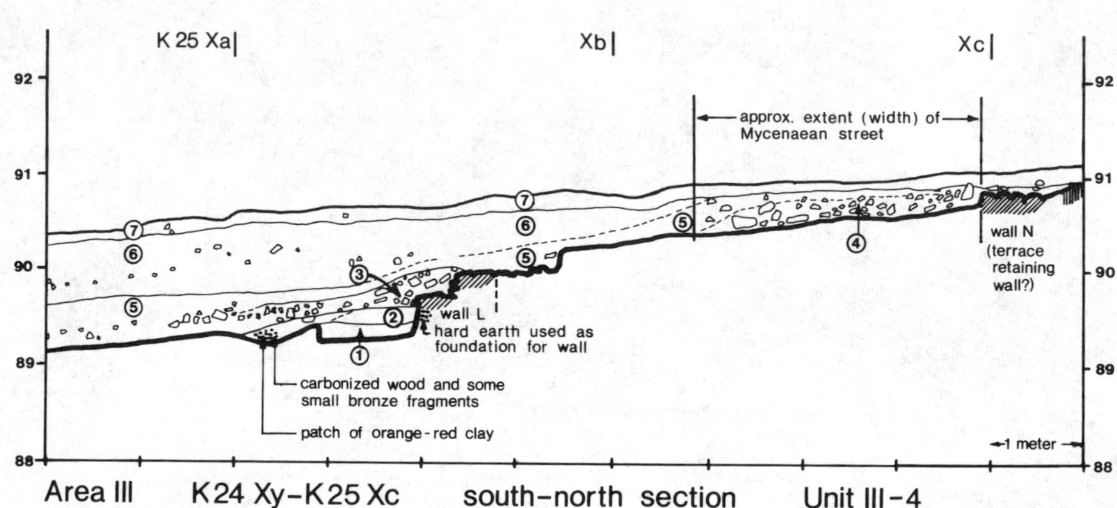

7. Plowed soil (Mixed to modern)
6. Slightly gravelly muddy sand: dark brown (Byzantine w/DA and LH)
5. Slightly gravelly sandy mud: light brown, w/tumble (DA II)
4. Slightly gravelly sandy mud: brown w/tumble (DA I - II w/LH III)
3. Slightly gravelly muddy sand: dark brown w/tumble, slightly compact (LH III A2-B2)
2. Slightly gravelly sandy mud: red w/charcoal, soft (LH III A2/B1)
1. Slightly gravelly muddy sand: light brown, soft (LH II - III A2)

Figure 2-4

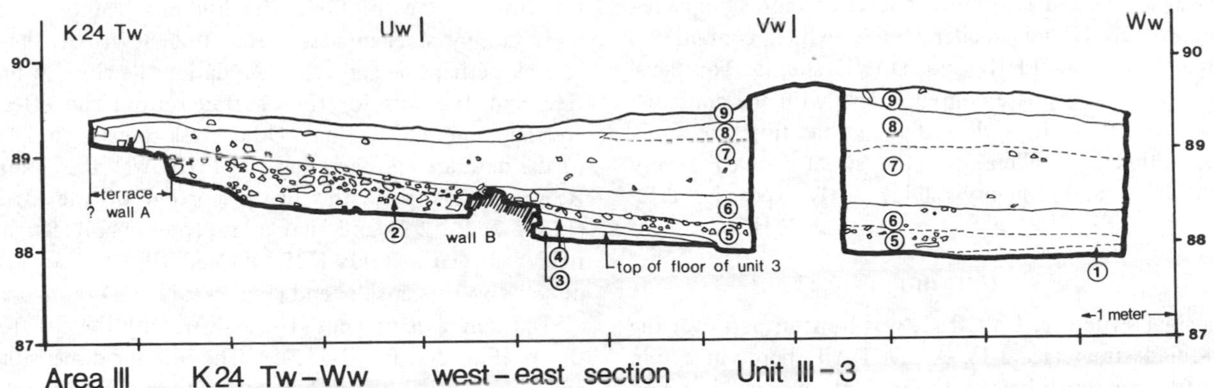

9. Plowed soil (Modern)
8. Slightly gravelly muddy sand: brown (Byzantine (w/LH and DA)
7. Slightly gravelly muddy sand: light brown (LH and DA)
6. Sandy mud: dark brown w/tumble, soft (DA II)
5. Slightly gravelly muddy sand: light brown w/tumble (30% DA II w/70% LH III A-B2)
4. Muddy sand: light brown soft w/tumble (LH III B2 w/a few DA II)
3. Sandy mud: brown, w/stone chips, very compact LH III B2 Floor of Unit III-3)
2. Slightly gravelly muddy sand: brown, w/tumble (LH III A2-B1)
1. Slightly gravelly muddy sand: yellow w/tumble (LH II-III A2)

Figure 2-5

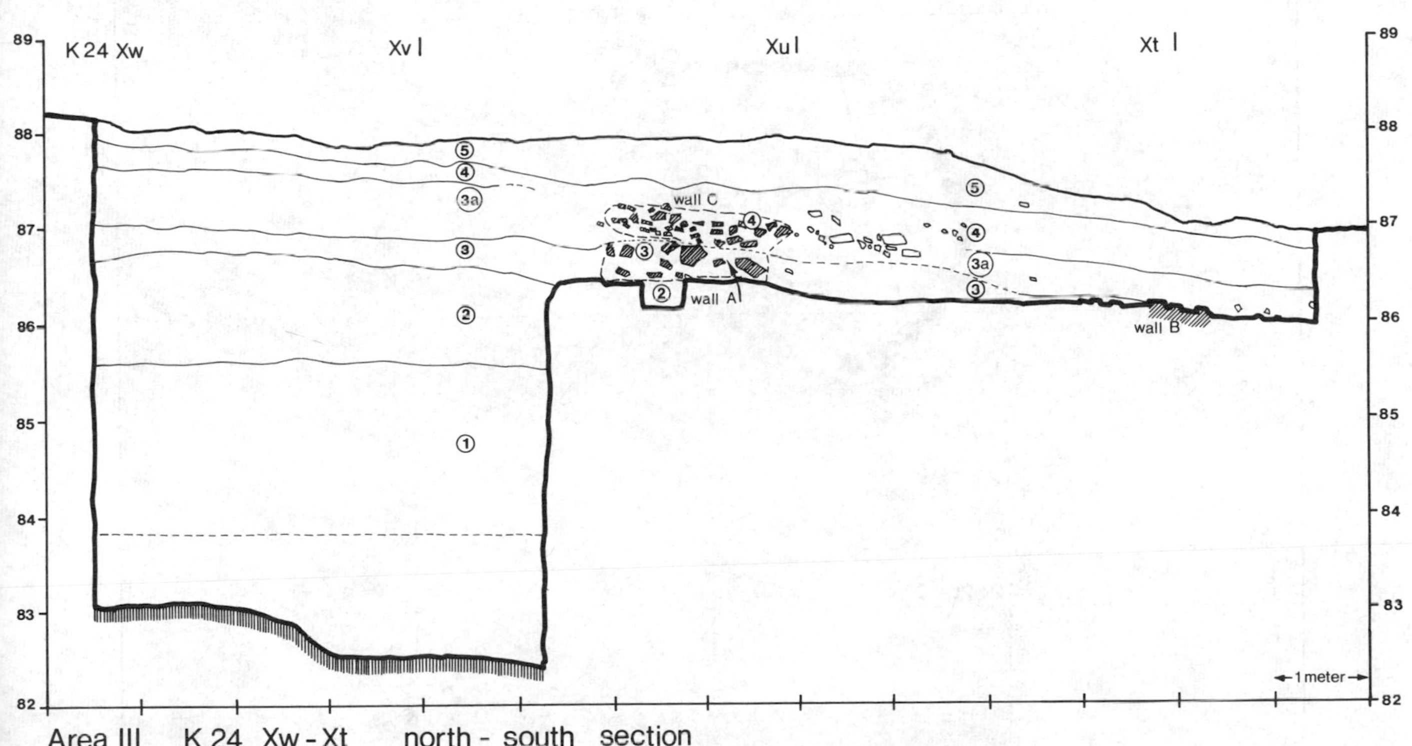

5. Plowed soil: (Mixed to modern)
4. Slightly gravelly, muddy sand: brown (Byzantine w/LH and DA II)

3a. Slightly gravelly, muddy sand: brown (DA II w/LH, but deposited after DA) (N.B. dark brown to South of Wall A: light brown to North of Wall A)

3b. Slightly gravelly, muddy sand: brown w/tumble (DA II w/LH) (N.B. light brown to South of Wall A: dark brown to North of Wall A)

2. Slightly gravelly, muddy sand: light brown (MH w/LH I - LH IIA)
1. Slightly gravelly, muddy sand: brown friable (MH II)

Figure 2-6

there was a thin and intermittent level of more compacted soft brown earth and smaller stones, which contained a similar mixture of LHIII and DAI/II sherds. This level surely represents a phase contemporary with the construction of Unit III-1. It is clear that at that time the stone tumble which had fallen onto the street formed a very uneven surface and probably still lay partly exposed.

R.H.S.

UNIT III-1

The apsidal structure, Unit III-1, was built in part over the debris-filled street (Pl. 2-1). A few DAII sherds in a thin layer of brown earth below the foundations provide a context for its construction. The building cannot be dated more closely since no associated floor levels could be discerned, perhaps because the foundations lie close to the surface and the interior thus suffered from the effects of erosion and cultivation. Other less precise indications of the date are the fact that the LHIII Wall R in grids K25 RSfg extends beneath the E portion of the structure (Fig. 2-7; Pl. 2-2) and that a late (presumably Byzantine) field wall (L) in grids K25 Qfg and Rfg was constructed directly over its apsidal end (Fig. 2-7; Pl. 2-3).

The long axis of Unit III-1 is E-W, with the apse toward the W (Fig. 2-7; Pls. 2-4, 2-5). The interior dimensions are approximately 3.75 m N-S by 4.00 m E-W. In no place

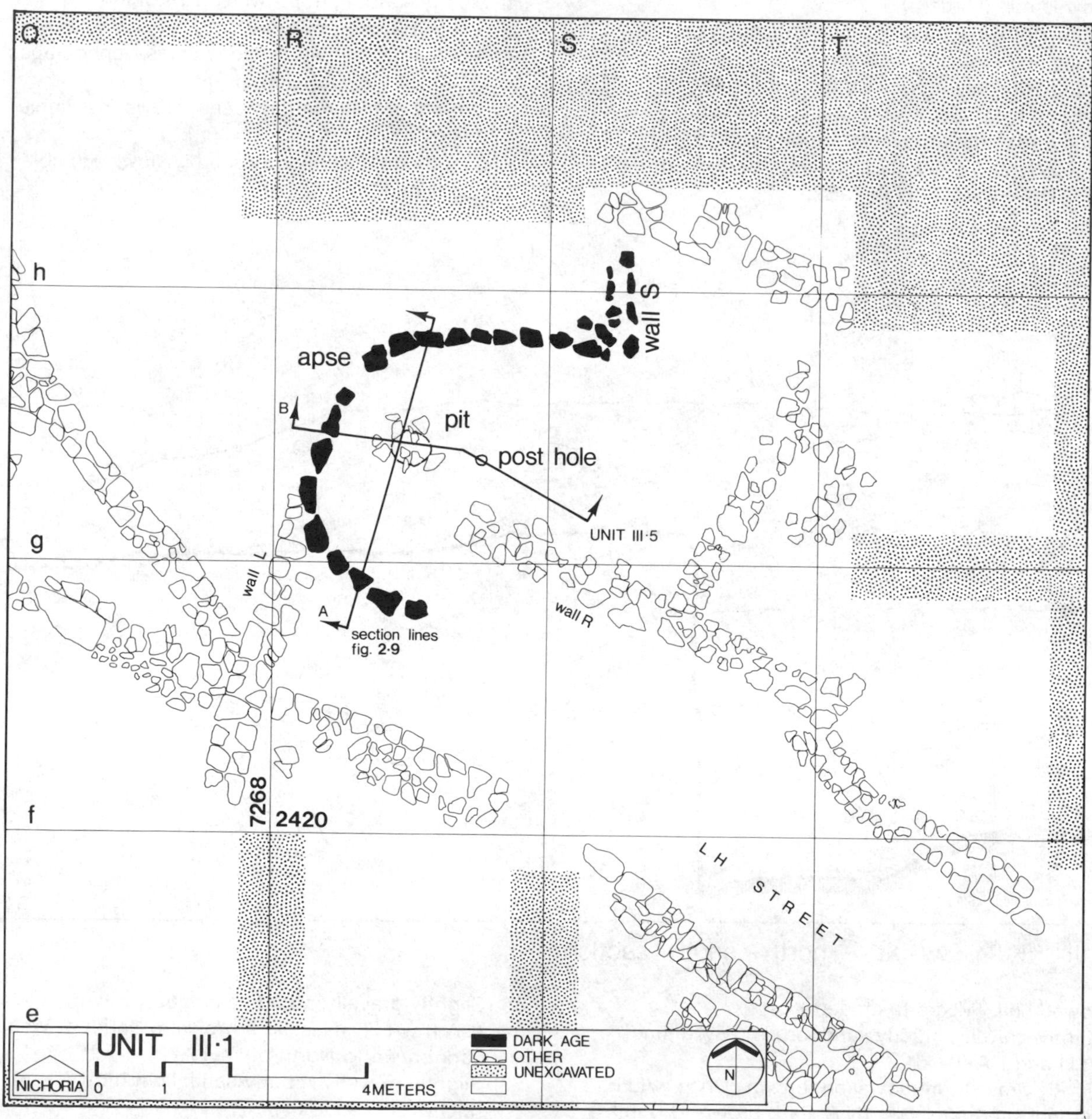

Figure 2-7

Table 2-1. Wall Specifications: Unit III-1

Wall	Grid	Length	Width	Maximum Height	Maximum Number of Courses	Bond/Butt
Apse	K25 RSfg	ca. 8.25 (pres.)	0.30	0.20	1	Butts on S
S	K25 Sgh	1.20	0.45	0.15	1	Butts on apse

is the wall more than one course high or more than a single block in thickness (Figs. 2-7, 2-9; Table 2-1). The limestone blocks are fairly large, irregularly shaped, heavily weathered, and laid without smaller stones filling the interstices. It appears, therefore, that the blocks were not intended as foundations for a solid superstructure but served simply to outline a building whose walls were of some lighter, more perishable material.

The N portion of the apsidal row of stones appears to be preserved in its entirety. At its E end the stub of Wall S (Fig. 2-7) butts against it and extends N-S for a distance of 1.20 m. Wall S, which is one course high and two rows wide, is constructed of smaller, more irregular blocks than those used in the apse. Its function is unclear. On the S side of the structure the apsidal row of stones comes to an end just as the curve of the apse begins to straighten, but it presumably continued the same distance to the E as the preserved N portion. Along the line of the S portion was found a worked piece of stone **(N699)** in a mixed LHIII/DAII context.

Associated with the structure is a pit that lies approximately on the long E-W axis (Figs. 2-7, 2-9). The diameter of the pit is ca. 1.30 m at its upper edge and 0.60 m at the bottom. Its depth is ca. 0.30 m below the base of the apsidal wall; but since no floor levels were detected, it is likely that the depth was originally slightly greater. Although the contents were carefully screened, no evidence of its intended function was recovered. The pit fill consisted of coarse to fine-grained sand and clay in which there were small weathered sherds, bone and teeth fragments of pig and small mammals (some of which showed signs of burning), a few shell fragments, and pieces of unworked chert. The cataloged finds were a bronze pin fragment **(N464)** and a chert blade fragment **(N465)**. The sherds in the fill were mainly DAII with some LHIIIA-B admixture.

Embedded in the E edge of the pit, near the bottom, was a large limestone block (Fig. 2-9). It appears to be in line with Mycenaean Wall R that once bordered the N side of the street. Additional blocks from this wall must have been removed when the pit was originally dug. The upper ca. 0.20 m of fill in the pit contained several good-sized limestone blocks which had apparently been put there during the DAII period since no later sherd material was recovered from the pit. DAII sherds occurred over the entire area of Unit III-1, and thus directly over the pit, in a thin (ca. 0.05-0.20 m) layer of compact, brown, slightly gravelly, muddy sand (Figs. 2-8, level 2; 2-9). No corresponding layer of limestone blocks such as those in the upper pit fill was revealed, however, so that the pit may have gone out of use earlier than the structure in which it is located.

Also on the long E-W axis of the building but a little E of the pit, there is a posthole ca. 0.15 m in diameter and

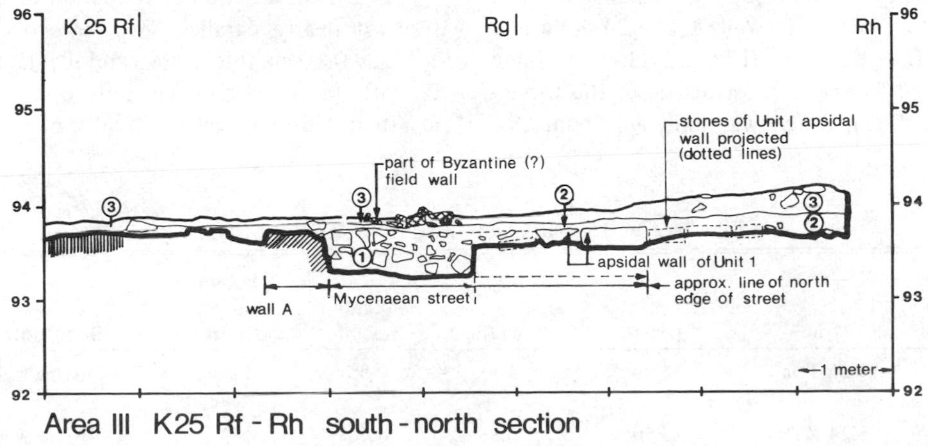

3. Plowed soil (Mixed to modern)
2. Compacted brown slightly gravelly, sandy mud: Mainly LH II and DA II w/some DA III
1. Brown, slightly gravelly, sandy mud: Mainly LH III and DA II

Figure 2-8

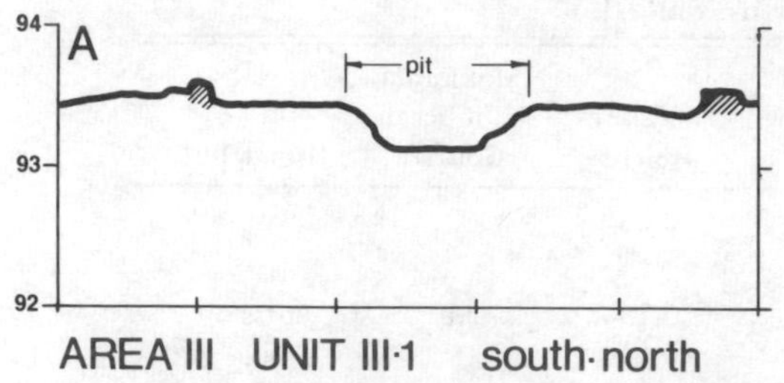

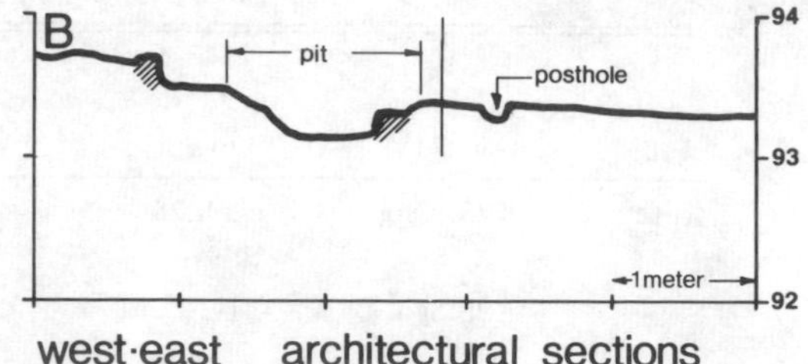

Figure 2-9

0.10 m deep (Figs. 2-7, 2-9). It probably represents the location of a wooden support for the roof. Delicate scraping and sprinkling of the earth both inside and outside the structure and various photographic methods, including infrared sensitive film, revealed no additional postholes or other indications of the nature of the superstructure.

From a DA context at Nichoria comes a trapezoidal schist plaque (**N701**) on which a number of lines are incised (Pl. 5-46). They form what appears to be a tentlike or A-frame structure with a steeply pitched roof. Perhaps this is a representation of a building such as we presume Unit III-1 to have been. Similar flimsy structures can still be seen today in the Greek countryside (Pl. 2-6).

N.W.

The curved wall (H) in K25 TUa (Pl. 2-7) may be part of another more substantial DAII apsidal house. Although no floor or other associated level was found beside the wall, DAII sherds were found near it in a level disturbed during the Byzantine period. Also, two much smaller segments of wall foundations, in K25 Ub and K25 Va respectively, appear to be DAII. They consist of only a few blocks set in line, both with faces to the SE, and not more than 0.20 m in height. Their function cannot be determined.

R.H.S.

To the DAII period also belong two parallel walls in the S central part of Area III: Wall A in K24 XYu and L24 Au, and Wall B in K24 XYt (Fig. 2-2; Pl. 2-11; Table 2-2). Wall A suffered from the construction of the Byzantine Wall C (see p. 363), which was built approximately parallel to it and slightly lower down the slope and for which Wall A probably provided building material. Only two to three courses remain. The wall is built with two rows of limestone blocks which vary in size but form a rough face on both sides, while the center is filled with rubble (Pl. 2-12). It runs fairly straight from SW to NE. Its W end, which would have come close to Mycenaean Unit III-3 (again a probable source of building material), has totally disappeared; and its E end is reduced to a tumble by erosion. To establish its date, a portion of Wall A in K24 Xu was removed (Pl. 2-13). The LHIIIA2 pottery immediately below and the mixture of Mycenaean and DA pottery in the fill shows that the structure was built in the DAII period, apparently as a terrace wall to retain the earth to the N of it. The layer of earth associated with Wall A (level 3, Fig. 2-6) consisted of slightly gravelly, muddy sand, ca. 0.25 m thick, and contained a good portion of DAII pottery mixed with some LH sherds. To the N of the wall the deposit was dark brown; to the S, where it continued to the top of Wall B, it was light brown. The layer above it (level 3a, Fig. 2-6) also contained LH and DA pottery, but in reversed stratigraphy, which proved it to be a hill-wash deposited after DA times. Within level 3a the earth N of Wall A was light brown, whereas S of the wall it was dark brown. This level continued above Wall B and to the S of it.

Wall B is of a lighter construction than Wall A, to which it is set nearly parallel. Two rows of limestone blocks, each ca. 0.10 m thick, are carefully laid and well aligned on both faces. In grid Xtu only one course is preserved, in Ytu three, at a constant width of 0.61-0.63 m. A con-

Table 2-2. Wall Specifications: Area III (except Unit III-1)

Wall	Grid	Length	Width	Maximum Height	Maximum Number of Courses	Bond/Butt
H	K25 TUa	5.00	0.55	0.35	3 small irregular	Curving wall
A	K24 XYu L24 Au	15.50 (minimum)	0.85	0.40	3	Terrace wall
B	K24 XYt	7.20	0.60	0.30	1	Terrace or house wall

tinuation of the wall could not be detected either to E or to W in K24 Ws. Although the manner of construction would indicate a dwelling, no floor was preserved. Since level 3 (Fig. 2-6) ends at this wall and level 3a continues to the S, it is probably safer to assume that this structure also served as a terrace wall that was built toward the end of the DA period.

Rather well-preserved DAI/II pottery was recovered from a deposit of eroded material (level 5, Figs. 2-3 and 2-4) which overlaid the N wall of LH Unit III-4. This deposit, which also contained fragments of iron, is further proof of DA habitation on the N edge of Area III.

D.K.H.

Very little DA pottery was found in the disturbed levels above the compacted LH debris of Mycenaean Unit III-2. But, as with Mycenaean Unit III-4, activity in the DA period had resulted in the removal of most of the walls and debris of the LHIIIB2 apsidal structure, Unit III-3. Most of this activity had evidently taken place during the DAII period, and what was left of the earlier structures had then been trampled over. This trampled surface (the top of level 6, Fig. 2-5) was similar to that observed above the debris overlying the Mycenaean street in the N part of Area III. A thin layer of the same soft brown earth had accumulated over part of the surviving walls of Unit III-3 (Pl. 2-8) and over the debris that remained (Pl. 2-9). This debris had been much disturbed and filled in with rather sticky dark brown earth (level 5, Fig. 2-5) and shapeless stones (presumably those rejected by the stone "robbers"). It is surmised that some of the blocks that had once belonged to Unit III-3 were removed during the DAII period, to be incorporated in the terrace walls discussed above. The layer of backfill (level 5, Fig. 2-5) within Unit III-3 contained about 30% DAII and nearly 70% LHIIIA-B2 pottery. The layer above (level 6, Fig. 2-5) was ca. 0.25 m thick and consisted of softer brown earth with fewer stones. It contained a slightly higher proportion of DA sherds, and both the DA and the LHIII sherds were noticeably more worn. The top of this surface was easily recognized, since it had been hardened by exposure. It had presumably formed a field surface in the DAII period, probably that contemporary with terrace Wall A (see the commentary on Nichoria I, p. 39, profile R3 and Table 4-2 on p. 35).

In the SE part of Area III some DAII sherds were found in mixed levels in trial trenches L24-IV, V, and VI and in grids L24 BCu and L24 Cpqrsvw. But the deposit was shallow in all these trenches, since here the pori rises sharply toward the E and NE. Down the slope to the S, however, trial trench K24-III struck the top of a deposit that contained sherds of DAII with a few DAI, beneath a medieval and modern fill about 2.0 m thick. This deposit seemed to represent slope-wash and was not further investigated.

It appears, therefore, that the central part of Area III was used mainly for agricultural purposes in the Dark Age. The higher concentrations of DA finds in the N trenches indicates that, in addition to Unit III-1 and to a structure presumably represented by the curved wall (H) in K25 Ta, there were at least a few other DA buildings on the N and NW edges of the ridge.

On the SE edge of Area III the existence of a group of badly eroded DAII foundations was shown in trial trenches L24-I, II and VII. Unfortunately, excavation in this sector, which probably bordered the S extension of the main street along the ridge, had to be limited to the 1969 trials (see below).

R.H.S.

UNIT N VEVES-1 (FIG. 1-1)

In the N Veves field contiguous to Area III, trial trench L24-I produced one of several examples of the apparent DA reuse of a Mycenaean structure. At a depth of 0.25 m below the modern surface Wall A runs in an E-W direction and measures 1.70 m in preserved length. Several of the blocks in its outer N face extend into the scarp, but its width appears to be approximately 0.70 m. Consisting of four courses of large, rounded white limestone blocks, the building technique recalls that of Mycenaean walls such as those in Units IV-6, IV-7, and IV-9. The W end of Wall A is partially destroyed, but enough is preserved to show that it butts on Wall B, which runs in a N-S direction. The two walls thus form the corner of a room whose preserved dimensions are ca. 1.80 m on each side (Pl. 2-14).

Wall B appears to be more carelessly constructed than A, with smaller stones in two preserved courses. Only the inner W face was excavated; the outer face still remains in the E scarp of the trench. It is clear, however, that Wall B consists of two very different sections, which suggests that there were two different periods of construction. The upper course of rounded stones is separated from the lower course of flat rectangular stones by 0.23 m of hard-packed earth. The pottery from inside the room (level 2) is predominantly DAII, but quite scrappy and mixed with some worn LHIII sherds. Thus, it appears that the foundations of a Mycenaean structure were reused in the DA period.

The partially excavated room was evidently used in DA times as a storage area, since the floor was littered with broken pithoi. Many fragments were concentrated in the angle formed by Walls A and B. In the SE of the trench and adjacent to Wall B, a stone platform measuring 0.75 m N-S × 0.60 m E-W was uncovered. It consists of two thin slabs of stone supported by smaller stones at the corners (Pl. 2-15). This platform may well have been used as the stand for a large pithos which would be partially protected by Wall B. On its E side the room was paved with thin limestone slabs. They probably belonged to the original Mycenaean building but would have provided useful support for the DA storage jars. The rest of the floor was covered with small stones. Some of them may have fallen in when the building was destroyed, but others probably served to solidify the floor.

That the reused building was destroyed by fire is evident from the signs of severe burning found within. Many of the pithos fragments show traces of burning, as do some of the small stones. There was also a layer of black ash 0.10-0.15 m thick in the W scarp of the trench, above the debris in the room; and the interior of the room was filled with bright red earth suggestive of burned mud brick. It is clear that, during or soon after the conflagration, the upper walls collapsed inward, filling the lower part of the room with mud brick and stones and smashing the jars on the floor.

The DA builders certainly reused Mycenaean foundations, and this circumstance may have dictated the apparent rectangular shape of this building. Unit N Veves-1 is the only DA building whose presence can be documented along the street that must have joined the occupied portions of Areas III and IV. Nearby test trenches K24-III, L24-II, L24-IV, L24-V, and L24-VIII produced only worn DAII sherds (probably hill-wash) with no associated architecture.

W.D.E.C.

Area IV (Fig. 1-1)

Area IV appears to have been the focus of habitation throughout the Dark Age. A discussion of its original topography and a summary of its occupation history is provided in *Nichoria* I, pp. 224-28. The sequence of habitation is especially well preserved here because of the presence of three long gullies that were being gradually filled in prehistoric times by natural and human agencies. The succession of building foundations in and near gullies, together with the deposition of fill, provides a good stratigraphic sequence.

DARK AGE I

The DAI levels produced almost no evidence for associated architecture, here or elsewhere on the ridge. Apparently, the DAI houses were few and they may have been rather flimsy. At any rate, their remains in the excavated grids seem to have been eradicated by time and later construction.

On the other hand, deposits of DAI pottery are fairly numerous in Area IV. One group was found at the E end of the later Unit IV-1, in the areas of the entranceway and courtyard, suggesting that there had been one or more dwellings here (Fig. 2-10 a, b). Other sherds occurred in mixed contexts from the nearby Mycenaean Unit IV-7. The presence of DAI sherds within this unit suggests that it may have been reused as early as DAI, but no structural remains can be associated with such a rebuilding. A similar possibility may be connected with a good group of DAI sherds that was found in Rooms 2 and 4 of Mycenaean Unit IV-6. Other sherds were recovered from the bottom of the dump to the N of Unit IV-5, indicating possible activity in or near Mycenaean Unit IV-8. Still others were found below the floor of Unit IV-5, suggesting DAI reuse of the Mycenaean building complex that extends under Units IV-1 and IV-5. Finally, a few DAI sherds are associated with Mycenaean Unit IV-9. The good group of DAI sherds from the baulk between grids L23 OPe and OPf is more than likely due to hill-wash.

This fairly sizable concentration of DAI ceramic material in the N sector of Area IV seems to suggest, then, that the DAI settlers were able to salvage portions of several ruined Mycenaean structures for their own shelter. This practice is documented more securely, however, for the later DAII period.

DARK AGE II AND II/III TRANSITIONAL
(FIG. 2-10a, b)

It appears that Area IV was the site of the main population concentration in DAII times. At the core stood Unit IV-1, probably the chieftain's dwelling but also serving important communal functions. Its E-W orientation is paralleled by a second, but very fragmentary apsidal building to the SW,

Table 2-3. Wall Specifications: Unit N Veves-1

Wall and Date	Grid	Length	Width	Maximum Height	Maximum Number of Courses	Bond/Butt
A (LHIII, reused in DAII)	L24-I	1.70	ca. 0.70	0.46	4	Butts on Wall B
B (Lower course LHIII, reused in DAII; upper course DAII)	L24-I	1.94	0.20 (E side in scarp)	0.30	2	Butts on Wall A

represented by Wall O. To the S of Wall O is the reused Unit IV-9 and the added room IV-10. And farther S in L23-IX Wall Z perhaps represents another structure. There can be little doubt that, in Area IV and elsewhere on the ridge, there were a number of DAII houses whose remains are destroyed or still undetected. Unit IV-1, the largest, most important, and the best preserved of these buildings forms a good point of departure.

UNIT IV-1 (FIGS. 2-11, 2-12, 2-13; PL. 2-16)

Unit IV-1 was discovered in 1971, and during the 1972 and 1973 campaigns it was completely excavated and most of the baulks were removed.[1] The building extends over five trenches. Running E to W, these trenches are:

L23 Xklm 9.0 m N-S × 4.0 m E-W
L23 Wklm 9.0 m N-S × 3.50 m E-W
L23 Vklm 12.0 m N-S × 4.0 E-W
L23 Uklm 12.0 m N-S × 4.0 E-W
L23 Tklm 12.0 m N-S × 4.0 m E-W

By the close of the Mycenaean period, two of the three gullies mentioned above (W and N gullies) seem to have been pretty well filled with hill-wash and cultural debris. In the NE part of Area IV, the surface sloped down gently from the E, where the Mycenaean Unit IV-3 is located (Pl 2-17). The builders of Unit IV-1 cut into this slope and leveled the tumble from earlier walls to make a usable building surface. In places, the walls of Unit IV-1 are built directly upon Mycenaean foundations. The original functions of these Mycenaean walls are discussed fully in *Nichoria* II. For present purposes we need only record that the N wall (A) of Unit IV-1 is built directly upon two Mycenaean terrace walls (α and β) which run in a NE × SW direction (Fig. 2-12); that the S wall (C) rests upon what may have been part of a Mycenaean house, i.e., on Walls C2 and C3 which bond to form a T-junction (Pls. 2-22, 2-23); and that Wall D, delimiting the W end of the first phase of our building, rests upon Mycenaean Wall K (Pl. 2-26), which may be a continuation of Wall C2 and thus part of the same earlier structure (Fig. 2-14).

Whether these Mycenaean foundations were still visible when Unit IV-1 was begun or whether they were uncovered where the slope was leveled is difficult to determine. The bottom of Wall A is at a slightly higher level than that of Wall C, indicating that there was a very gentle slope to the S across the width of the unit. Wall A rests not only upon Mycenaean terrace walls α and β but also upon tumble from them (Fig. 2-16), suggesting that in this area the DA builders did very little leveling and, further, that these foundations and tumble may have been visible on the surface. Similarly, a portion of Wall C rests directly upon the T-joint of Mycenaean Wall C3 but not upon Wall C2 where some 0.10 m of fill separates the two walls. This again suggests that at least a portion of the Mycenaean walls may have been visible on the surface.

The latest Mycenaean stratum is easy to distinguish owing to its soil color and consistency. The soil can be described as a slightly gravelly, muddy sand, soft in texture and quite yellow. It was reached both to the N and S of Walls C and Ca and is represented by stratum 5 on the N-S section (Fig. 2-12) and by no. 1 on the E-W section (Fig. 2-13).[2] In the interior of the unit (N of Wall Ca), this soft yellow soil was found at the base of Wall Ca, indicating that this inner foundation wall was set directly upon Mycenaean debris. On the exterior (S of Wall C), however, the Mycenaean stratum reaches almost to the top of the single preserved foundation course, which shows that this outer foundation wall was set down into the Mycenaean debris.

The soil of the DA occupation (stratum 6) is quite different from earlier levels and can be described as gravelly, sandy mud (Fig. 2-12). It is dark gray, brown, or black and has a high clay content. Very hard in the dry conditions of summer, it becomes soft and sticky when wet. At the base of the DA strata there is usually a great deal of limestone rubble; and throughout there is a much heavier concentration of both animal bone fragments and charcoal than in the Mycenaean levels below.

As reported above, in the E interior of Unit IV-1 and farther E, both inside and outside the courtyard, the soft yellow Mycenaean stratum was found to contain a slight admixture of DAI sherds. The fact that the NE sector of Area IV was already used in DAI times may shed some light on the question of why this important structure was built here. Not only was the location favorable in terms of relatively good drainage, but the remains of earlier buildings provided stable foundations and excellent building material.

Two major building phases of Unit IV-1 can be distinguished. In Phase 1 (Fig. 2-18) its outside dimensions were approximately 10.50 m EW × 7.0 m NS and it comprised only a large main room (Room 1) with a porch (Room 2) at its E end. Several features point to a major reconstruction that we designate as Phase 2. The apsidal Wall B at the W end (Fig. 2-22) appears to be a later addition, for it does not bond with the W end of the N side wall (Wall A). The corresponding juncture on the S side has been robbed out. Similarly, the N courtyard wall (G) does not bond with the front wall of the original building (Wall X).

Phase 1 (DAII, 10th century) (Figs. 2-11, 2-18)

It appears that in its original phase Unit IV-1 was rectangular and not apsidal. No evidence for an earlier apse was found, while there are indications that Wall D served as the original outside W wall of the building (Fig. 2-11). The building is oriented in an E-W direction, with its main entrance at the E end. The long axis is not, however, exactly E-W, but 10° S of true east.

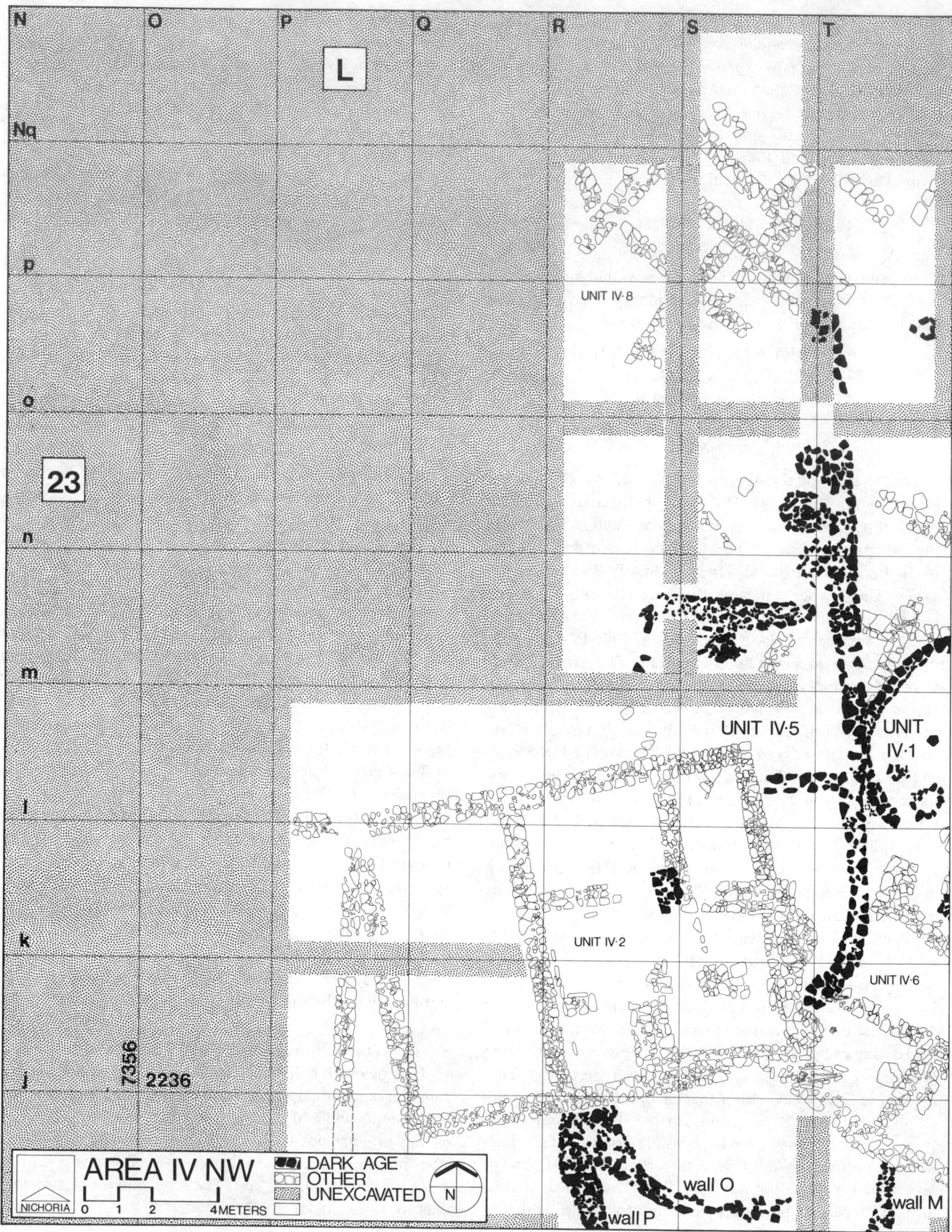
N
O
P
Q
R
S
T
L
Nq
p
o
n
m
l
k
j
23
UNIT IV·8
UNIT IV·5
UNIT IV·1
UNIT IV·2
UNIT IV·6
7356
2236
wall O
wall P
wall M
AREA IV NW
DARK AGE
OTHER
UNEXCAVATED
0 1 2 4METERS
NICHORIA
N

Figure 2-10a

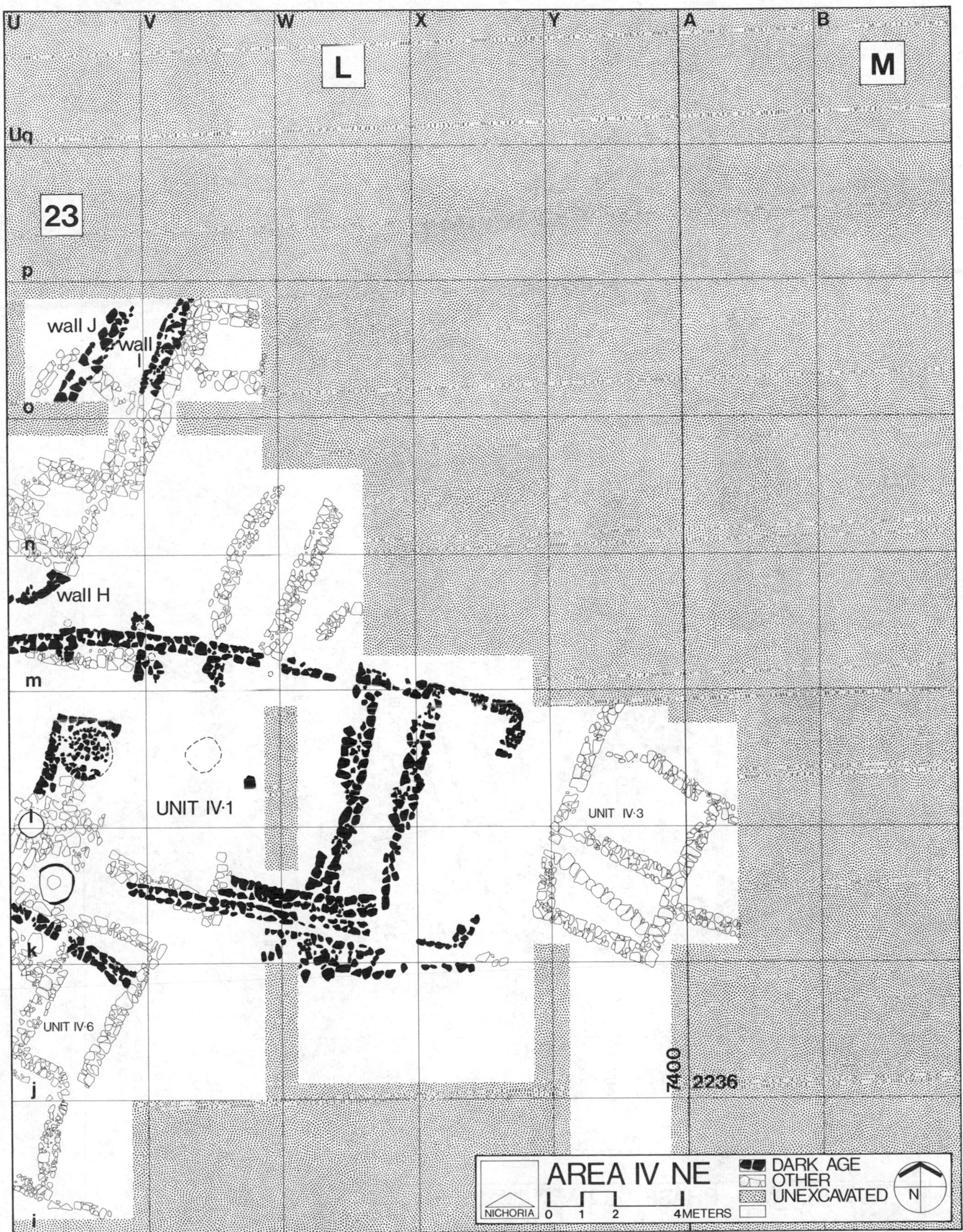
U
V
W
X
Y
A
B
L
M
Uq
23
p
wall J
wall
I
o
n
wall H
m
UNIT IV·1
UNIT IV·3
k
UNIT IV·6
j
i
7400
2236
NICHORIA
AREA IV NE
0 1 2 4 METERS
DARK AGE
OTHER
UNEXCAVATED
N

Figure 2-10b

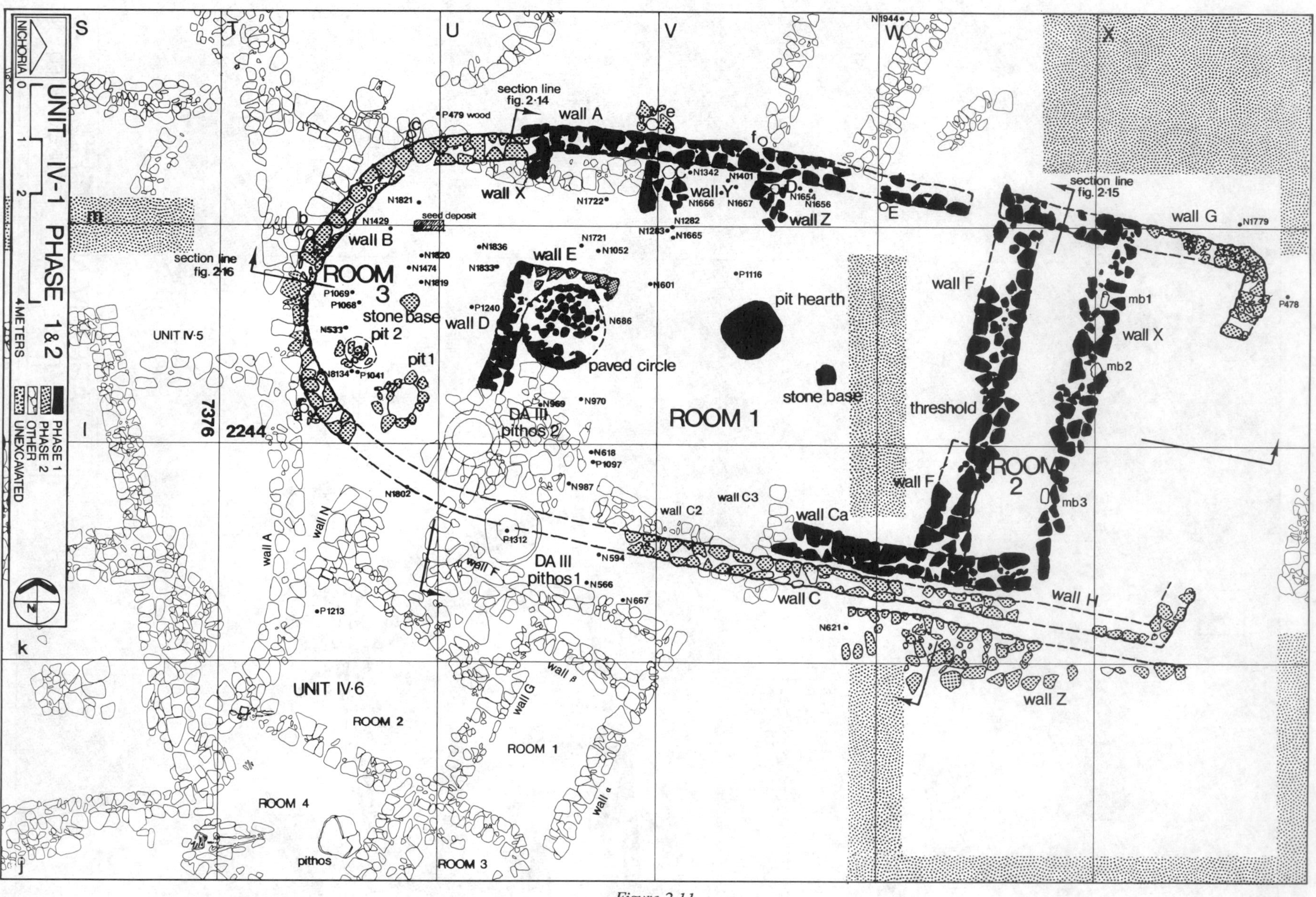

NICHORIA
UNIT IV-1 PHASE 1&2
0 1 2 4METERS
PHASE 1
PHASE 2
OTHER
UNEXCAVATED
ROOM 1
ROOM 2
ROOM 3
pit hearth
stone base
paved circle
wall A
wall B
wall C
wall Ca
wall C2
wall C3
wall D
wall E
wall F
wall G
wall H
wall X
wall Y
wall Z
threshold
pit 1
pit 2
seed deposit
section line fig. 2·14
section line fig. 2·15
section line fig. 2·16
DA III pithos 1
DA III pithos 2
UNIT IV·5
UNIT IV·6
ROOM 4
pithos
wall N
wall α
wall β
2244
7376

Figure 2-11

The main entrance is located in the cross-wall (F) which forms the E end of the main room. A little off-center to the S are the well-worn threshold blocks of the doorway itself, which has a total width of 1.36 m (Pl. 2-18). To the E and parallel with Wall F there is a lightly constructed wall (X) of only one course of stones along the entire front of the building. Wall X is clearly not a bearing wall; its width is too narrow (0.26-0.36 m), consisting of one row of irregularly shaped stones, and it is not bonded with the E ends of Walls A and Ca. It seems to have served as the foundation for a low fence or balustrade which partially enclosed the front of the porch, perhaps with solid sides formed by the E extension of Walls A and Ca (Fig. 2-19). We have restored a post in each corner to support the roof

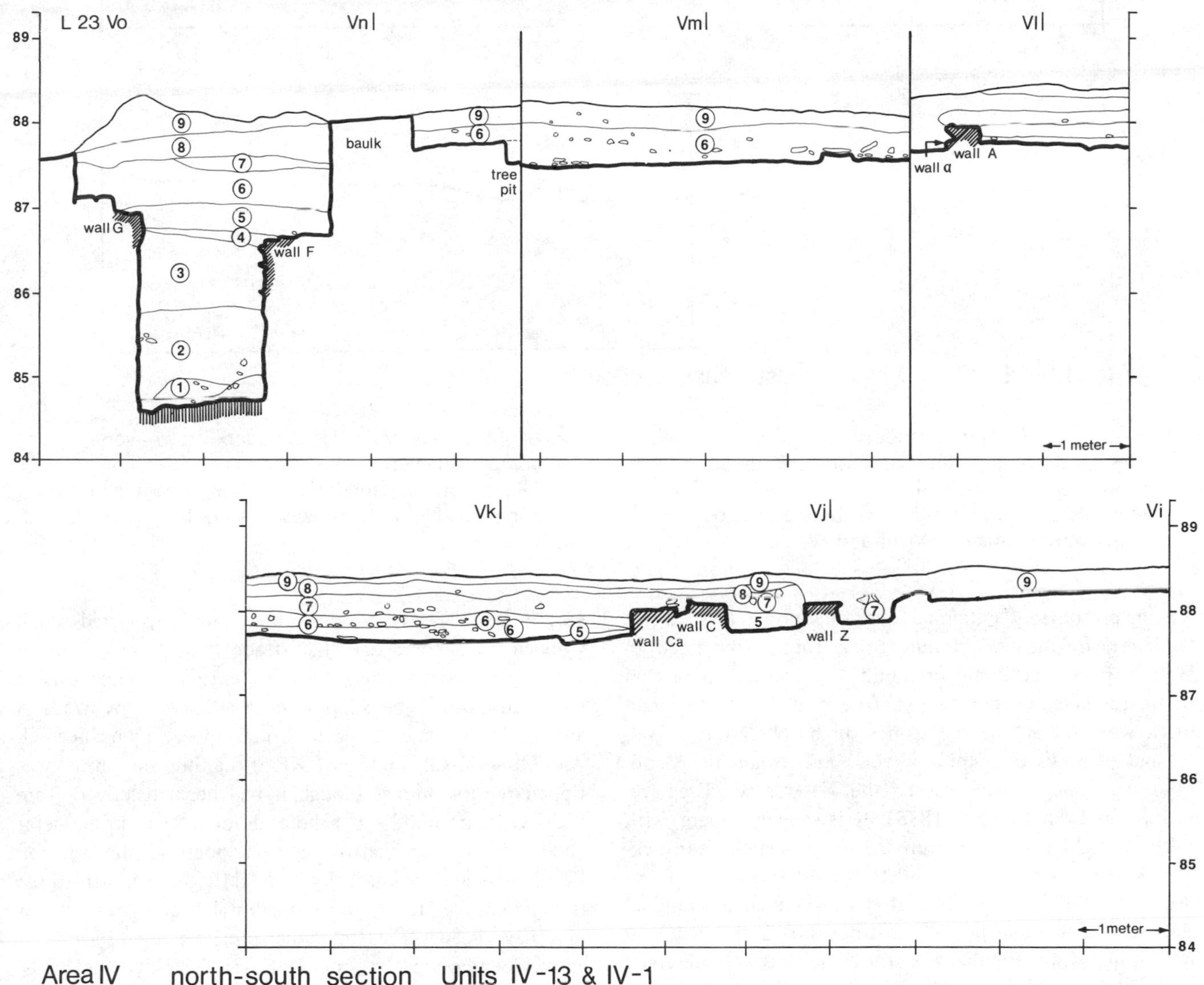

9. Plowed soil: grey, w/humus (Mixed to modern)
8. Gravelly, muddy sand: grey, w/roots, slightly compact (DA III)
7. Slightly gravelly, muddy sand: light brown, slightly compact (DA III - II)
6. Gravelly, sandy mud: black, w/tumble and rock chips, very compact (DA II)
6a. Slightly gravelly, sandy mud: red (DA II)
5. Slightly gravelly, muddy sand: yellow, soft (LH III A2-B1 w/few DA I)
4. Gravelly, muddy sand: light brown, slightly compact (LH IIIA2)
3. Gravelly, muddy sand: light brown, very compact (LH IIIA1)
2. Gravelly, muddy sand: grey, w/stone chips, slightly compact (LH IIA)
1. Muddy coarse sand: yellow, slightly compact (LH IIA)

Muddy, fine sand: yellow, soft (sterile)

Figure 2-12

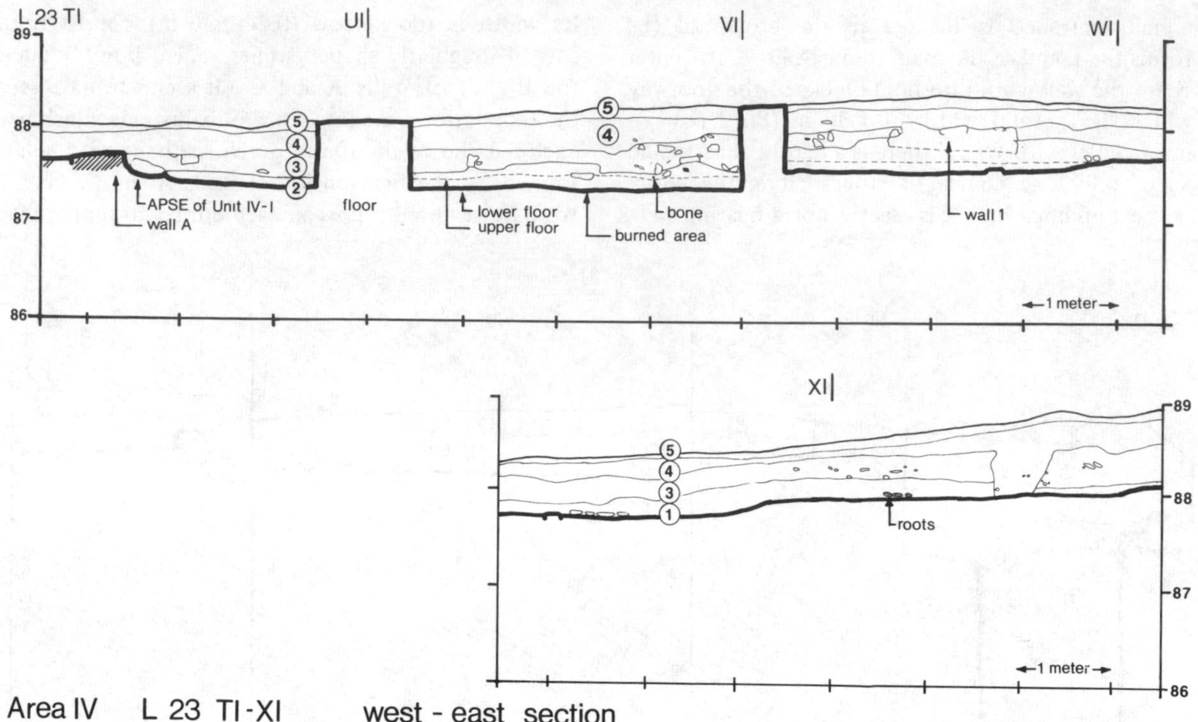

5. Plowed soil (Mixed to modern)
4. Slightly gravelly muddy sand: grey, w/humus, slightly compact (DA III)
3. Gravelly sandy mud: black, w/tumble and rock chips, very compact (DA III and IV)
2. Slightly gravelly sandy mud: dark brown, very compact (DA II)
1. Slightly gravelly muddy sand: light brown, slightly compact (LH III A2-B1 w/some DA I)

Figure 2-13

which presumably extended over the porch (Fig. 2-18).

Three fragments of mud brick found embedded in Wall X may lend some credibility to the reconstruction of a balustrade here (Fig. 2-11). Two shaped chunks of mud brick were set among the stones of the N section of Wall X, and portions of a third were found toward the S end. Mud brick no. 1 (farthest to the N) was stabilized, removed, and cataloged (**N1835**). It is roughly square, with fairly straight sides measuring 0.15 m in length and thickness (Pl. 2-19). On the top of its N edge fragments of carbonized wood may indicate that it was used in conjunction with a wooden post. Mud brick no. 2, situated 1.36 m S of no. 1, was stabilized *in situ*. It has less well-preserved edges and is slightly larger (0.24 m × 0.19 m) but with a similar thickness. The third mud brick, situated 2.52 m S of no. 2, was preserved only in fragments. It is interesting to note that these bricks were placed at regular intervals along Wall X. Nos. 2 and 3 are located symmetrically in relation to the doorway in Wall F, i.e., 0.58 m from its outer edges. Brick no. 1 is placed 1.0 m from the inner face of Wall A, and brick no. 3 is 1.10 m from the inner face of Wall Ca. Such relationships in spacing can hardly be accidental.

The function of these brick bases (if that is what they are) is unclear. We propose that they supported small wooden posts for a light balustrade that closed off the E side of the porch, except for the entrance. While such a balustrade would be supported at either end by Walls A and Ca, additional supports would appear to be needed. An oblong block found just NE of the third mud brick was tipped on its side as though it had been dislodged from Wall X. In its middle is a hole about 0.03 m in diameter and 0.05 m deep, narrowing to a point at the bottom. Considered as man-made by the MME geologist, this hole is large enough to steady a small stake; and other stakes may have been placed in similar blocks or may have been embedded among the stones of Wall X. Thus, the balustrade seems to have had three major posts, whose position is indicated by the mud bricks, with smaller stakes between. Small horizontal branches or reeds were presumably woven into a lattice, and both surfaces may have been covered in mud daub in much the same manner as fences 2-3 m high in the Middle East today.[3]

The floor of the porch was covered with tightly packed small stones (Pl. 2-20). In order to achieve a reasonably smooth walking surface, this cobble would have been partly covered with earth; but, through use and the accumulation of fill within the vestibule, the stones may eventually have

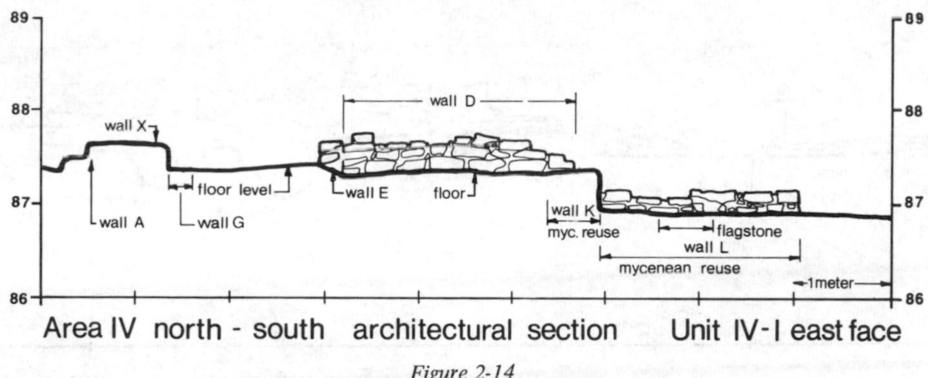

Figure 2-14

been totally covered with hard-packed earth. Indeed, the accumulation of debris may also have covered Wall X and the very bottom portion of the posts and stakes of the balustrade.

The doorway in Wall F is not exactly on the long axis of the building but is slightly off-center to the S (Pl. 2-16). The N segment of Wall F is some 1.10 m longer than the S segment. The N segment now consists of only one course of long and fairly flat stones (Fig. 2-15) resting directly on the floor and butting on Wall A. The S segment has two courses which also rest on the floor and butt on Wall Ca.

The doorway has a moderate width of 1.36 m. It was probably closed by some material like skins, since no evidence for doorjambs was found. The threshold, which shows definite signs of wear, consists of nine large flat blocks of irregular sizes, plus at least three smaller pieces (Fig. 2-15). The top of the threshold is approximately level with the floor inside the building and also with the bottom of the two segments of Wall F, indicating that the latter were set directly on ground level (Pl. 2-18).

Stratum 6a of the N-S section (Fig. 2-12) represents the floor of this first phase and stratum 6 that of the second phase; these strata are equivalent to no. 2 of the E-W section (Fig. 2-13; see n. 2). It is likely that the superstructure of the entrance complex was damaged by burning that marked the end of Phase 2. The deep red color of the mud bricks in Wall X was probably caused by intense fire; the charcoal fragments found on top of the N edge of mud brick no. 1, possibly from the post itself, indicate destruction by fire, as do other fragments of charcoal found inside the vestibule. Some of the largest charcoal fragments were found just E of the N segment of Wall F, near the threshold blocks and also near Wall A. Analysis of these fragments showed a high percentage of olive wood (*Nichoria* I, pp. 53-56), and it is likely that olive branches and twigs were used in the posts of the balustrade and perhaps for its wattle and daub superstructure.

To W of the doorway is the main room (Room 1) of the building. Further study has invalidated our original impression of interior partitions (McDonald 1972, p. 253) represented by the support walls to be discussed later. Instead, it is likely that in Phase 1 the building had only one large enclosed room with inside dimensions of approximately 8.0 m EW × 6.0 m NS. The floor immediately to W of the entrance consists of red mud that is slightly gravelly, sandy and very compact. It is pocked with small holes and with a scattering of small stones and pebbles (Pl. 2-16).[4] The builders were fairly successful in smoothing Mycenaean debris to achieve a level surface, but there is a slight downward slope E to W which is more pronounced in the later courtyard and in the porch. There is also a slight downward slope N to S which the builders failed to eliminate entirely and that resulted in a buildup of debris along the S wall (Ca).

While the doorway in the E wall was clearly the main

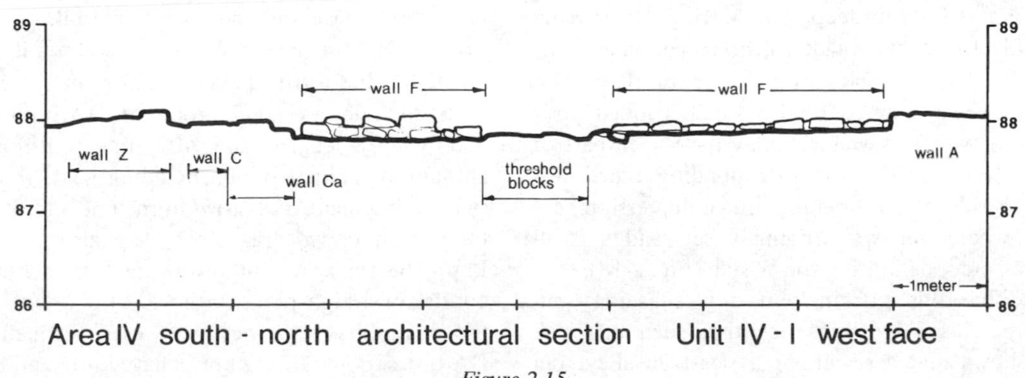

Figure 2-15

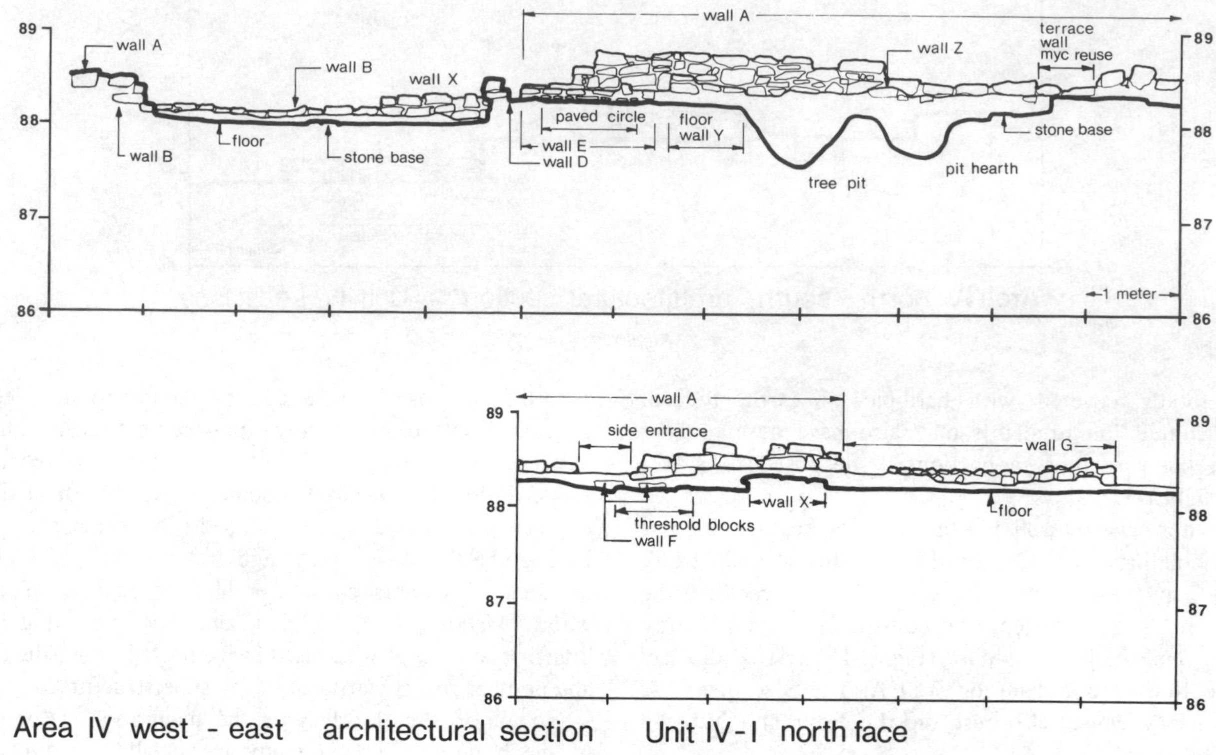

Figure 2-16

entrance, there are also traces of what must be considered a subsidiary opening in the N side (Fig. 2-16; Pl. 2-21). It is located immediately W of the point where the N segment of Wall F butts on Wall A. Here Wall A shows a definite gap. The E side of the opening was formed by placing two slabs on their sides to form a straight edge. On the W side, the outer face of Wall A has been destroyed and only a single block of the inner face remains; but it is sufficient to show that the width of the entrance was only 0.68 m.

To the NE of this opening and very near Wall A an irregular block was found, roughly oblong in shape and measuring some 0.49 m × 0.23 m (Pl. 2-21). It was tipped on its side, slanting to the N, evidently dislodged from its original position. In its middle is a roughly cut hole, ca. 0.07 m square and 0.09 m deep. The MME geologist considered the hole to be man-made, although originally the block may have had a small natural hole or flaw. This hole may have been used to hold a small wooden post, and the block in which it was set may have been part of the threshold (Fig. 2-19). No corresponding block was found on the W side of the opening; but a depression here may indicate where one was originally set, and a small post may be restored, delimiting the W side (Fig. 2-18).

It is likely that this extremely narrow subsidiary entrance was also closed by skins or other such material. Its presence shows that a street, or at least an alley, ran along the N side of the building, although no actual evidence was found. The blocks in this area were arranged in too haphazard a manner to represent paving and are probably tumble from Wall A (Pl. 2-21). The soil, however, is extremely hard packed and could well belong to an exterior walking surface. There must also have been a street giving access to the main entrance at the E end of Unit IV-1, but again excavation shed no light on its nature or direction.

The central section of Room 1 is located in L23 Vklm. As in L23 Wklm to the E, the floor is very compact, again consisting of slightly gravelly, sandy mud (stratum 6a, Fig. 2-12) but blacker than the reddish soil in the entranceway. The general N-to-S down slope is again evident, but there is also an accumulation of debris in the center where the major household activities would take place (Fig. 2-13). To the N, just inside Wall A, the floor is 0.08 m thick, but it reaches a thickness of 0.20 m in the center. Its contents included a good group of DAII pottery, approximately 60% coarse and 40% fine, with a considerable amount of animal bone, including goat, sheep, pig, *bovid* (with a fragment of a *bovid* horn cone and skull fragments). *Canid* and *cervid* fragments were also present (*Nichoria*, I, pp. 68, 69). An interesting feature is that these bones consist of a high percentage (20%) of *astragalus*, suggesting the possibility that they were used for gaming as early as DA times. Some of the bones have knife and chew marks.

As previously described, the S wall (Ca) rests in places directly upon Mycenaean foundations, especially Wall C3 (Pl. 2-22). These are the fragmentary foundations of an LHIIIB house, oriented in the same NW × SE direction as Mycenaean Units IV 3, 6 and 7, and consisting of a NW × SE wall (C2) which bonds and forms a T-junction with a NE × SW wall (C3). Wall C2 is preserved to a depth of two courses at its E end but only one course at its W end; it has a good N face, consisting of large, well-dressed flat blocks, but has an irregular S face (Pl. 2-23). The preserved portions of Wall C3 alternate between two and three courses and consist of the same well-dressed flat blocks as those of Wall C2. The S wall (Ca) of the first phase of Unit IV-1 rests directly upon Wall C3; similarly, the E portion of the S wall (C) of Phase 2 lies over Wall C2, but some 0.10 m of fill separates the W segment of Wall C from Wall C2 (Pl. 2-23).

The explanation must again take into account the slope of the surface. During late Mycenaean times there was a slight slope down to the W on which several houses were built. The Mycenaean builders in Area IV apparently made little attempt to make a level surface for their houses. Conversely, the DA builders did try to achieve a level building surface. In the process of clearing and leveling Mycenaean tumble, it is likely that they came upon the foundations of this Mycenaean house and used a portion as a support for their S wall. But since the Mycenaean foundations sloped down to the W, the DA builders had to pack fill on top of the W portion of Wall C2 (subsequently robbed out in DAIII) to achieve a level surface. It is also likely that the DA builders used blocks that had tumbled from the Mycenaean foundations as building material, since many of the stones that comprised Walls C and Ca (Fig. 2-15) have the flat, well-dressed appearance of the Mycenaean masonry at Nichoria. The presence and use of Mycenaean foundations on the S side of Unit IV-1 may also explain why the preserved portions of Walls C and Ca appear to be less sturdily constructed than their counterpart on the north (A). Walls C and Ca are nowhere preserved to a height greater than one course, whereas Wall A in places reaches a preserved height of three courses. The DA builders could utilize existing Mycenaean foundations on the S, but these were absent on the N, necessitating higher stone foundations.

Wall Ca apparently served as the original S wall of Unit IV-1. Yet its preserved length is only 4.70 m, less than half the length of the building, and it does not go beyond Mycenaean Wall C3. It is likely that its entire W part was later reused in Wall C. The question then arises why the builders left intact its E part when they built Wall C adjacent to it. Perhaps the old wall foundation served as the base of a bench or beds in Phase 2.

It is unclear what portion of the building's foundations were below ground level and what remained visible. No evidence was found of any sort of foundation trench for the exterior walls, although this might be due to the extreme hardness of the soil during excavation. Wall A is preserved up to a height of three courses in L23 Vm (Fig. 2-16); the absence of much tumble along the N side of the unit suggests that the stone foundation was not too much higher, possibly only extending to a fourth course. On the interior, the bottom of the earliest floor is at the same level as the bottom course of Wall A (Fig. 2-12), indicating that originally the foundation here was set directly upon the surface, or in places, such as adjacent to the side entrance, upon Mycenaean tumble at ground level. After construction there must have been a gradual buildup of debris against both the inner and outer faces of Wall A, thus covering up at least the lowest course of foundations. But it seems likely that at least two, and perhaps three courses remained visible above ground.

The foundations (Fig. 2-11) consist of rounded limestone blocks of irregular sizes. Most were no doubt reused from ruined Mycenaean buildings, which would explain the presence of several well-dressed blocks (Fig. 2-16; Pl. 2-16). The walls have an average width of 0.55 m and contain only a small amount of earth filler. Chinking, i.e., the use of very small pieces of stone inserted in the face of the wall to fill gaps and maximize the amount of stone in the wall, appears only in two instances in Wall A; this marks a departure from Mycenaean practice. Horizontal bonding, i.e., the tying together of the two vertical faces of a wall with a single stone which completely or largely spans the width of the wall, does occur frequently, however, especially in Wall A where it is employed at intervals of about 1.50 m. Indeed, in L23 Um there are four instances of large triangular blocks used to span the entire width of the wall, with the apex of the triangle toward the interior; small narrow stones are then placed around this apex to form an inner face. The preserved sections of Walls Ca and D are built in much the same manner.

In the middle of the building, just N of the long axis, there is a roughly circular pit with an approximate diameter of 1.08 m (Fig. 2-11). The depression just to W of it, seen in Pl. 2-16, is a modern tree pit. The ancient pit was filled with extremely soft black soil mixed with numerous carbonized fragments. The bottom slopes sharply to the W, and at its deepest point it is 0.29 m below the floor. In the N part was a scatter of stones of irregular shape and size (Pl. 2-24). The amount of small carbonized fragments recovered from the interior suggests its use as a pit hearth. The fragments themselves were identified as oak and olive (*Nichoria* I, pp. 53-57), indicating that both varieties were used for firewood. The scatter of small stones probably represents rubble that had fallen or been swept into the pit, although they might have served the purpose of retaining heat. A large flat stone in the center of this debris could have been used as a platform on which to place pots during cooking. To the E of the pit hearth is a fairly flat block which appears to have served as the base for a wooden post or column (see discussion of roofing system on pp. 30, 31, 38).

In the W portion of the building (trench L23 Uklm) were found portions of Wall D and a stone-paved circular structure (Pl. 2-25). The S portion of this grid was in a most disturbed condition, for here the pits for two DAIII storage pithoi had obliterated the SW corner of the building. Blocks from the original Wall Ca may have been reused to build Wall C, but the latter was completely destroyed by one of the above-mentioned pits. The second pit was dug into the S section of the line of Wall D (Fig. 2-17). The pits are quite deep, extending down to an area of Mycenaean flagstone paving. Wall D was built directly upon Mycenaean Wall K (Pl. 2-26), providing another instance of this practice by DA builders (Fig. 2-14). One block of Wall D rests upon the inner face of Wall K; S of this point Wall D has been destroyed. Farther N, however, it is preserved to a length of 2.70 m and reaches a height of four courses (Fig. 2-14). An argument could be made for the use of Wall D as a terrace wall to support the platform on which the stone-paved circle was built and to delimit the area of the circle. The preponderance of the evidence, however, speaks against such a use and indicates that the wall was the original outside W wall in Phase 1. This evidence may be summarized in the following points:

1. The solidarity of the construction, suitable for an outer wall.
2. Its continuation well to the S of the immediate confines of the paved circle.[5]
3. The likelihood that support Wall X of Phase 2 was simply the reused N end of the original Wall D, as indicated by their identical alignment.
4. The fact that support Wall X bonds with Wall A but that the apsidal wall (B) of Phase 2 merely butts on A.

The above points require some elaboration:

1. Wall D is a sturdy structure, as strong as either Wall A or Wall Ca. Indeed, its method of construction compares favorably with that of Wall A. Both are preserved to a height of three courses, and at its N end Wall D has four courses (Fig. 2-16); both are constructed of large flat stones carefully selected to make the best possible fit, with earth and smaller stones used as filler; and both are approximately the same width. Wall D, then, does not appear to have been designed merely to delimit the area of the circle. This latter function is exemplified by the later Wall E, which is a relatively light wall of two courses of smaller stones set in a single row (Pl. 2-25; Fig. 2-14).
2. The preserved portion of Wall D continues some 1.0 m S of the outer limits of the paved circle (Pl. 2-27). If it had been designed solely as a boundary wall, it would not have been carried so far south.
3. Support Wall X of Phase 2, some 1.03 m in length (Pl. 2-28), is aligned with the preserved section of Wall D (Fig. 2-11). It served to support and protect the base of a post which stood in the NW inner corner of the Phase 1 building. The support wall is two courses deep, has a maximum preserved width equal

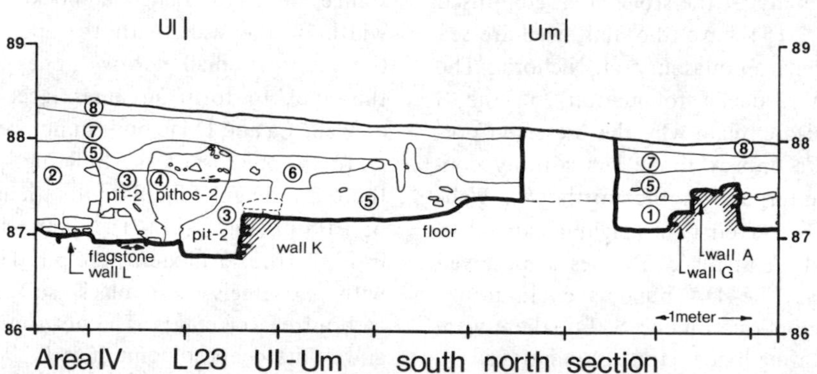

8. Plowed soil (Mixed to modern)
7. Slightly gravelly muddy coarse sand: grey w/humus, very compact (DA III)
6. Slightly gravelly muddy coarse sand: light brown, slightly compact (DA III)
5. Gravelly sandy mud: black, w/tumble and charcoal, very compact (DA II)
4. Gravelly sandy mud: dark brown (inside pithos 2) very compact (DA III)
3. Slightly gravelly sandy mud: yellow (fill for pit #2) soft (DA III)
2. Slightly gravelly sandy mud: light brown, soft (DA II - LH IIIB)
1. Slightly gravelly muddy sand: brown, slightly compact (LH III A2/B1)

Figure 2-17

to that of Wall D, and is constructed of the same flat, carefully laid stones (Fig. 2-16). Its orientation is also the same as that of Wall D, suggesting that originally Walls D and X belonged to the same wall. Subsequently, when the building was remodeled in Phase 2 and the apse added, Wall D was partially demolished to allow access between Room 1 and the new apsidal addition. Wall E was then added to delimit the N side of the circle, and the N end of Wall D was retained from the building's original back wall.

4. Perhaps the strongest single piece of evidence for the later addition of the apse is the good bond formed by Walls A and X (Pl. 2-28) compared to the mere abuttment of the apse (Wall B) on Wall A. Wall B does not even butt directly against Wall A, since there is a space of some 0.15 m of packed earth and small stones between them (Pl. 2-29). Furthermore, although a portion of the S section of the apsidal wall has been destroyed by later intrusions, the preserved curve of the apse toward the S is in line with outer (and later) Wall C rather than with the original S wall (Ca), supporting the argument that the apse is a later addition.

Thus, it appears that Wall D served as the W outside wall in Phase 1 and that the original plan was rectangular rather than apsidal. It is interesting to note, however, that the plan is not strictly rectangular, since Wall A forms a very shallow but still noticeable arc, recalling the subtly curving line of the side walls of Megaron B at Thermon (see Snodgrass 1971, p. 368).

The floor to N and E of the paved circle consists of the same hard-packed slightly gravelly, sandy mud as elsewhere in Room 1. The paved circle would have originally occupied a space against the middle of the rear wall (Fig. 2-18). It is approximately 1.60 m in diameter and is constructed of small flat stones of irregular shape (Pls. 2-25, 2-27). An attempt had been made, at least on the S side, to outline a clear outer edge by selecting stones with straight sides. Larger stones were used in the center and smaller ones at the edges. All stones are quite flat and are embedded directly in the floor. Their flatness and smoothness suggests that they might have been reused from Mycenaean tumble. A probe beneath the paving revealed no unusual substructure. Earth fill extends to a depth of 0.51 m, at which point the flagstones of a Mycenaean courtyard were encountered. The pottery from this fill rep-

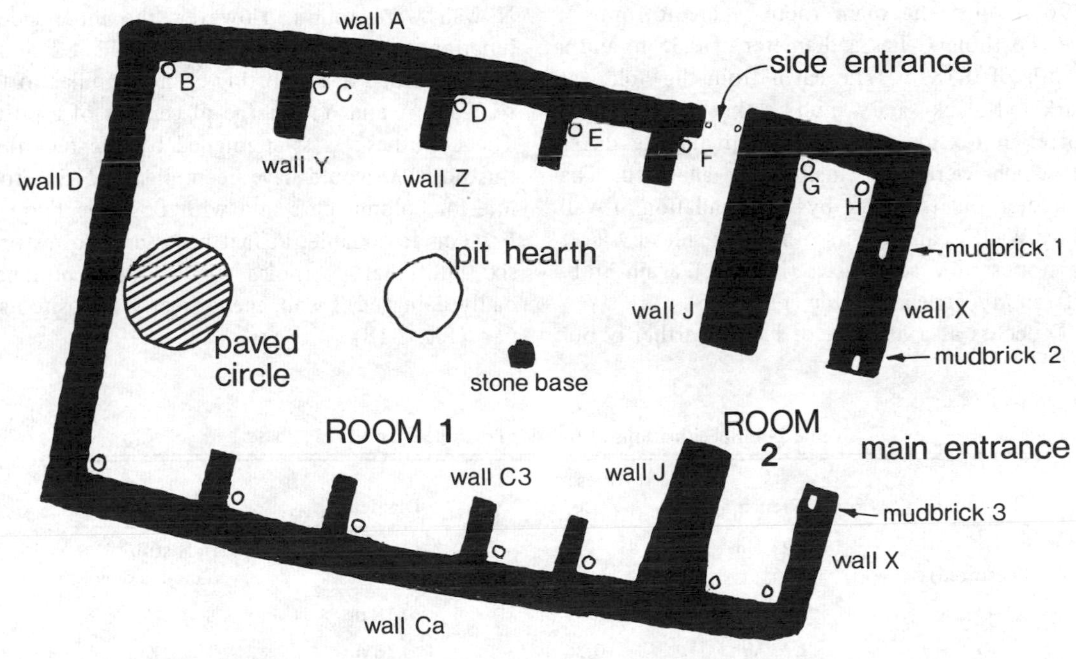

Figure 2-18

resents a transition between LHIIIA and the Dark Age. On top of the stones of the circle there was a layer of carbonized material approximately 0.05 m thick which suggests that the structure was used as an altar.[6] Snodgrass (1971, p. 408) notes that "in many early instances the sacrificial altar or hearth was located centrally, inside the temple."

Excavation in trenches L23 Uklm and Vklm produced some very intriguing evidence for the roofing system of the building. A series of three postholes (C, D, E) was discovered adjacent to the inner face of Wall A (Fig. 2-18) and regularly spaced at intervals of 1.80 m, in corners formed by support walls (Y, Z) which jut slightly into Room 1. These holes must have received the bases of wooden posts which supported the outer ends of horizontal tie-beams and sloping rafters. On the basis of the preserved evidence, we have restored a series of seven posts (B to H) regularly spaced along the N side of the building. Proceeding W to E, this arrangment is described in Table 2-4.

Posthole B was so disturbed that it was impossible to recover its measurements. At a distance of 1.80 m to the E, however, good evidence is preserved for Posthole C, in the NE corner formed by support Wall Y (Pl. 2-30). Wall Y should be considered a support for the post and not the stub of an original partition wall.[7] It butts on Wall A and juts 0.96 m into the main room where it forms a definite edge. Posthole C has a diameter of 0.35 m and a preserved depth of 0.18 m. The earth from the hole was the same dark red-black sandy mud as the floor but considerably softer in texture and mixed with minute flakes of charcoal which were too small to be analyzed. The hole was protected on its N side by the foundation of Wall A, on its W by Wall Y, and on its other two sides by large flat packing stones of varying sizes (Pl. 2-31), again probably reused from Mycenaean tumble (Fig. 2-16).

Posthole D occurs at a distance of 1.80 m farther E, but here neither support Wall Z nor the foundations of Wall A are as well preserved (Pl. 2-32). Wall A has only the lowest course, and the single course of support Wall Z appears to have been either badly disturbed or quite haphazardly constructed, now consisting of one irregularly shaped block. On its S and E sides, the posthole is also ringed with packing stones, three of which are fragments of quern stones, now irregularly placed. Posthole D has the same depth as C but has a diameter approximately 0.10 m smaller. It was filled with the same soft sandy soil containing an admixture of minute carbonized fragments.

In the case of Posthole E, no evidence for a spur wall was found and Wall A has been damaged. Two small stones on the NE side of the posthole seem to be all that is left of its packing. The diameter of the hole is the same as that of D, but it is preserved only to a depth of 0.10 m. It is likely, however, that in all cases the support walls and the packing stones originally rose to a height considerably greater than that which is now preserved, perhaps making the holes at least twice as deep (ca. 0.40 m) and ensuring more adequate support for the posts. Postholes F, G, and H (Fig. 2-18) have been restored at approximately equal intervals farther E along the N side of the building.

Because of the damaged character of the S wall (Ca), no support walls or postholes matching those along the N wall were found. However, the inner side of the T-junction formed by Mycenaean Walls C2 and C3 would have provided a supporting corner, similar to the junction of Walls A and Y, for the placement of a post (Pl. 2-22). The hypothesis is strengthened by the fact that a post in this position would have been aligned N-S with the central interior column base and with Posthole E on the N side. It seems reasonable, in fact necessary, to restore a series of six additional postholes for wooden columns along the badly damaged S wall, each directly opposite its N counterpart (Fig. 2-18).

Table 2-4. Specifications of Interior Postholes: Unit IV-1, Phase 1

Posthole	Trench	Preserved Depth	Diameter	Support Wall
B (Restored)	L23 Um	. . .	. . .	D; N stub remodeled as X
C	L23 Vm	0.35 m	0.18 m	Y
D	L23 Vm	0.25 m	0.18 m	Z
E	L23 Wm	0.25 m	0.10 m	Restored
F (Restored)	L23 Wm	. . .	. . .	Restored
G (Restored)	L23 Wl	. . .	. . .	F
H (Restored)	L23 Xl	. . .	. . .	X

Evidence for interior support of the ridge pole consists of the previously mentioned base (in L23 V1), situated in the approximate center of the building, immediately to the E of the pit hearth, and aligned N-S with Posthole E (Fig. 2-18). The stone rests directly on the floor, is roughly circular, and has a diameter of about 0.35 m (Fig. 2-16). Its flat upper surface, its similarity in diameter with Posthole C, its N-S alignment with Posthole E, and its position roughly in the center of the building all suggest that it was used as the base of a central interior post.

There is no evidence of the existence of additional interior roof supports. Indeed, this central one could have been a later precaution when the ridge pole showed signs of sagging. The stability of the roof frame would have been ensured by the horizontal tie-beams that spanned the entire width of the building and rested on the tops of the rows of posts along the side walls. Provided that they were securely fastened to the posts, the tie-beams would counteract the outward lateral thrust of the sloping rafters which in turn were fastened to them at the base and to the ridge pole at the apex of the roof (Fig. 2-20). This simple and effective structure, seen in many barns, is what architects refer to as a "pole building."

It is clear that the system of supports described above provided a fairly solid timber frame for the stability of the building and for carrying the weight of the roof, while allowing minimal interference with the view of the altar. The walls need have carried no weight and were simply needed to enclose the wooden frame. We have no solid evidence to identify the material used for the superstructure that was built above the stone foundations. The two most obvious possibilities are mud brick or wattle and daub. The fact that disintegrated mud brick was not positively identified in the debris is by no means proof that this material was not used here. We are usually unable to prove that the upper walls of most of the LH houses were of mud brick, but the balance of probability strongly suggests that this was so. If mud brick is made from onsite material and the building is not destroyed by fire, the bricks will leave no trace when the roof collapses and the walls are exposed to rain. Similarly, the organic materials used in wattle and daub will be hard to identify unless the building has been burned; and even then, burned clay fragments showing reed or twig impressions could just as well derive from roofs as from walls.

Can the stone foundations provide any evidence for the nature of the superstructure? They would, of course, have been useful in either case to prevent moisture and runoff from undermining the walls; but a wide and solid stone foundation would seem to be more essential to carry the weight of a mudbrick wall, as in the LH analogy. Walls of wattle and daub or similar organic materials were surely much thinner and lighter, yet the analogy of modern shepherds' huts such as that at Marathon (Pl. 2-33) shows that very heavy stone foundations may be used with them. In the case of our Unit IV-1 the presence of good-sized wooden posts proves that (unlike the modern examples) the walls were vertical; and one would expect to find in the stone foundations some evidence of vertical supports which were needed to stabilize walls of wattle and daub.

The presence of posts at 1.80 m intervals immediately inside the stone foundations does perhaps favor the theory that wattle and daub was the material used for the walls. If such walls were constructed above the inner edge of the stone foundations, the posts could have been utilized as major stabilization points right up to the roof; and light vertical stakes in the intervals could have been wedged between stones of the foundation without leaving obvious traces. With reasonable vertical stability, the interweaving of horizontal branches or reeds and the application of the clay daub would have been routine (Fig. 2-19).[8] And wide overhang of the roof would protect the walls from rain damage.

That the building had a pitched roof is made likely not only by the timber frame discussed above, but also by analogy with Late Geometric temple models and modern shepherds' huts at Marathon and in Boeotia (Pl. 2-34).[9] Additional support is provided by the apsidal plan of Phase 2, since it would be difficult to cover an apsidal building with a flat roof. The roofing system suggested by the preserved postholes is essentially a simple one (Fig. 2-20). Tie-beams spanning the width of the building would have rested on the posts, and the posts would also have supported the lower ends of the rafters which carried the ridge pole.[10] The rafters were probably lashed to the ridge pole and posts with pliant reeds, leather thongs, or other binding material.[11]

The spaces between the rafters would have been filled with reeds or long, straight branches. Reeds (*Arundo donax*) grow luxuriantly today along the river valleys in the Nichoria environs, and the ancient name "Kalamai" for the nearby city of Kalamata suggests that there was also a plentiful supply along this coast in antiquity. Reeds are an excellent material to support tiled roof and for partitions; in both capacities they are still used in many of the older homes in villages near Nichoria. Since no evidence for tiles was found in connection with this building and since we have argued in favor of a pitched roof, it is likely that the roof was thatched.[12] The thatch may have been laid on top of the roof frame rather haphazardly and not in tightly secured bundles, as in thatched roofs still in use in various parts of the world. It appears that small to medium-sized flat stones were placed on the thatch

Figure 2-19. Unit IV-1, artist's reconstruction, Phase 1

to keep it from blowing away, much as flattish stones are placed on the tiles of modern Greek village houses to prevent them from becoming dislodged by the wind. A scatter of such stones was found on the upper floor in L23 Vkl, i.e., on the floor associated with Phase 2 (Pl. 2-37). They could have fallen from the roof when the building was destroyed or collapsed.

The porch was probably protected by an extension of the main roof. Although no evidence of postholes was found in the line of Wall F, corner posts would be critical for the stability of the whole building. As already described, post G has been restored in the NE corner of Walls F and A. In this position, it would be located a distance of about 1.80 m from F, thus continuing the regular spacing established along Wall A (Fig. 2-18). Another post (H) would presumably be needed at the front corner of the porch.

The building probably had some sort of opening to admit light and to allow smoke to escape. A modern hut in Boeotia (Pl. 2-35) has a large opening in the center of the rear gable. In Unit IV-1, however, there was probably an opening in the gable above the E entrance. Here door and "window" would be protected from cold N winds in winter and would admit the warm SE breezes in summer. The extension of the roof over the porch would keep out winter rain and summer sun from porch and window.

The small finds associated with Phase 1 are not numerous, perhaps because the building was thoroughly cleared out when it was remodeled. Although they are discussed in detail in Chapter 5, they are grouped here by location in and around the building.

A. Trench L23 Xm, outside to NE:
   N1779. Bronze needle, frag. of
B. Trench L23 Vlm, in central portion of building:
   N1656. Clay spindle whorl
   N1665. Bronze open ring
   N1667. Clay spindle whorl
   N1777. Bronze finger ring
C. Trench L23 Tk, outside to SW:
   N1802. Iron knife, frag. of

It is interesting to note that all small finds were recovered in the N side of Room 1, close to Wall A (where it has been exceptionally well preserved) and to support Wall Y. Their position illustrates the process of buildup of debris. As the main living areas of a room are cleared, debris tends to be swept to one side and accumulates at the edges of the room.

Unit IV-1 can be dated to the DAII period on the basis of the pottery associated with it (see Chapter 3, pp. 72-90). Its function(s) can be inferred only on the basis of the architectural features discussed above, and secondarily by the character of the artifacts retrieved from its ruins. For such an early date, even Phase 1 of the building has quite a monumental character. One notes the E-W orientation, the extraordinary length and width, the shallow, partially enclosed front porch, and the

Figure 2-20. Unit IV-1, restored cross-section, Phase 1

paved circle in a prominent location against the middle of the rear wall. Few buildings of the 10th century are as large as ours. The dwellings at Karphi,[13] Kavousi,[14] and Vrokastro[15] are much smaller, with less regularly built foundations containing more earth. Horizontal bonding does not occur and chinking is used in only a few instances at Vrokastro. Even though one thinks of Cretan architecture as relatively flourishing during the Dark Age, the buildings there lack monumental character. We must look elsewhere for large buildings comparable to Unit IV-1.

The so-called Megaron B at Thermon[16] measures some 21.40 m × 7.30 m, its long walls are slightly curved, and it has a series of exterior roof supports which form an apse at the N end. The date of Megaron B is disputed, but recent opinion (Drerup 1969, pp. 14-17) places it in the 9th century, thus slightly later than the first phase of Unit IV-1. The building of period IV at Iolkos[17] is too fragmentary to attempt the reconstruction of its roofing structure, but its foundations do not contain the features of chinking or horizontal bonding seen at Nichoria. Horizontal bonding is used in only two instances in the apsidal building (10th or 9th century B.C.) at Antissa (Lesbos)[18] which measures some 17.25 m × 5.60 m.

The care in construction, the size, the E-W orientation, and the presence of what we interpret as an interior altar all suggest that Unit IV-1 was a building of paramount importance in this little DA village. Yet these combined features can scarcely be said to identify the building as a temple in the accepted sense. The domestic character of the meager small finds (e.g., finger rings and spindle whorls) and the large proportion of coarse pottery found within the building point to its use as a dwelling, probably the village chieftain's house; and the much more numerous finds in Phase 2 strengthen this impression. In such a context, Unit IV-1 may carry on the Mycenaean tradition of combining the ruler's religious, political, and domestic functions in a single large, central unit (for a more complete discussion of function, see pp. 40, 58).

Phase 2 (9th century) (Figs. 2-21, 2-22, 2-23; Pl. 2-16)

When Unit IV-1 was remodeled, the following modifications and additions were made:

a. A courtyard was added to the E of the porch.
b. The S wall (Ca) was replaced by Wall C.
c. An apse (Wall B) was added to the W of Room 1.
d. A sector of the N end of Wall D was demolished to allow easy circulation between the room formed by the apse (Room 3) and the main room (Room 1).
e. Wall E was built to the N of the paved circle, forming, with Wall D, a podium for the altar.
f. Exterior posts were added along the side walls and apse.

The addition of courtyard and apse lengthened the building from 10.50 m to an impressive 15.90 m, further emphasizing its monumentality. Most of the courtyard

Table 2-5. Wall Specifications: Unit IV-1, Phase 1

Wall and Date	Grid	Length	Width	Maximum Height	Maximum Number of Courses	Bond/Butt
A (DAII and II/III)	L23 UVWm	10.50	0.55	0.35	3	Butts on N segment of Wall F and support Wall Y. Bonds with support Wall X (continuation of Wall D).
Ca (DAII)	L23 VWk	4.70	0.65	0.16	2	Butts on S segment of Wall F.
C2 (LHIIIB, reused)	L23 Vk	3.00	0.67	0.27	2	Bonds with Wall C3 to form T-junction.
C3 (LHIIIB, reused)	L23 Vk	2.40	0.50	0.26	2-3	Bonds with Wall C2 to form T-junction.
D (DAII and II/III)	L23 U1	2.70	0.44 at S 0.25 at N	0.39	3-4	Continuation of wall to N (called support Wall X). Bonds with Wall A.
Support Wall X (DAII and II/III)	L23 Um	1.03	0.43 at S 0.18 at N	0.24	2	N end of original Wall D. Bonds with Wall A.
Support Wall Y (DAII and II/III)	L23 UVm	0.96	0.32	0.25	2	Butts on Wall A.
Support Wall Z (DAII and II/III)	L23 Vm	0.84	0.67	0.12	1	Butts on Wall A.
F (N segment) (DAII and II/III)	L23 Wlm	3.05	0.86	0.12	2	Butts on Wall A.
F (S segment) (DAII and II/III)	L23 Wk	1.95	0.83	0.22 at S 0.11 at N	2	Butts on Wall Ca.
X (DAII and II/III)	L23 WXkl	5.98	0.36 at N 0.26 at S	0.09	1	Butts on Walls A and Ca.

lies in trench L23 Xklm, with a small S section in L23 Wk. The N and S boundaries of the courtyard are formed respectively by the foundations of Walls G and H, which are very lightly built of small stones, nowhere exceeding two courses (Pl. 2-17). The space thus enclosed measures approximately 7.10 NS × 2.30 m EW. The better-preserved N wall (G) does not bond with Wall A (Pl. 2-36), suggesting that the courtyard was a later addition. In fact, the stones just to the E of Wall A have been slightly disturbed, and a small portion of the inner face is missing. These stones are quite small, but they become larger toward the E end of Wall G where they form a kind of arc which changes their alignment toward the S. Thus, Wall G seems to have had a short return to the S of about 1.20 m at its E end.

The S courtyard wall (H) is in a poor state of preservation, since a major portion has been disturbed by a modern tree pit (Pl. 2-17). Only the E portion of the outer face remains, with some 0.60 m of the short return to the N. Both sections of Wall H appear to have been constructed in the same careless manner as their N counterpart. It seems, then, that the courtyard walls were not designed to bear weight but may have acted simply as foundations for a light barrier or fence (Fig. 2-23).[19]

The courtyard was built upon the same E to W slope as existed during the earlier phase. The builders were unsuccessful in totally leveling this slope, so that the courtyard walls slope slightly down to the W. To make the courtyard, they cut into debris from the Mycenaean house (Unit IV-3) to the E (Pl. 2-17), and thus pottery lots from lower levels contained much Mycenaean admixture. In other respects the E end of the building seems to have remained unchanged from Phase 1 (Fig. 2-23).

A more important change involves the apparent replacement of the original S wall (Ca) with a new wall (C) (Pls. 2-22, 2-23). That Wall C belongs to the same period as both the courtyard and the apse is made clear by the fact that the S courtyard wall (H) is in alignment with Wall C and with apsidal Wall B (Fig. 2-11; Pl. 2-16). Despite disturbances by modern tree pits and intrusions of large storage pithoi in later DAIII times, there is a clear continuity in the S wall line from courtyard to apse, indicating that the walls all belong to the same building phase. The preserved portion of Wall C (Pl. 2-22), spanning trenches

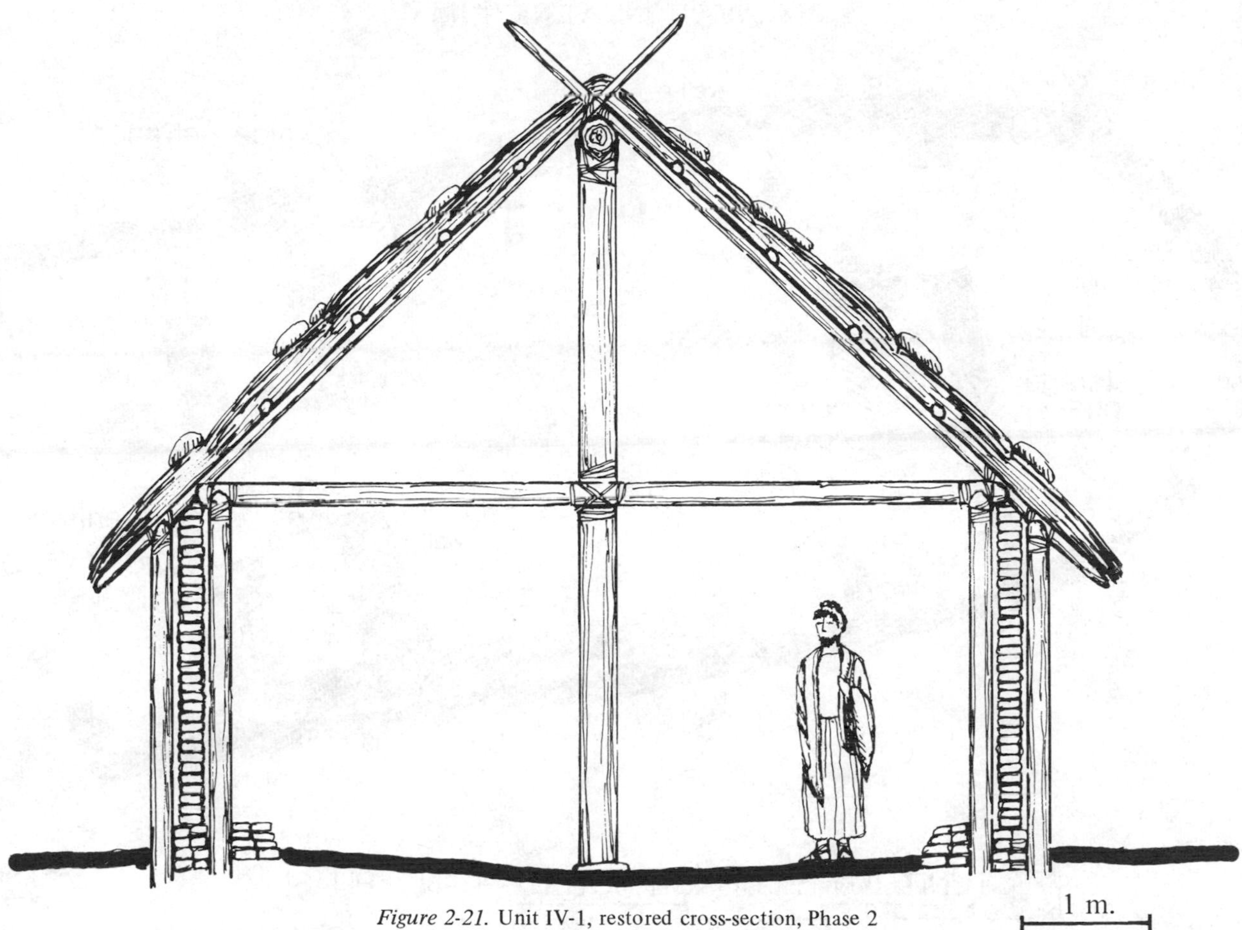

Figure 2-21. Unit IV-1, restored cross-section, Phase 2

L23 Wk and Vk and measuring some 7.50 m in length, is built like its predecessor, Ca, utilizing two parallel rows of stones with hard-packed earth fill between; but it consists of smaller stones set closer together (Fig. 2-12). Only one course remains for its entire preserved length, with a good example of horizontal bonding at its W end. There is a difference of some 0.14 m in the average width of the two walls, that of Ca being 0.60 m and of C only 0.46 m. The reason that Wall Ca was not rebuilt on its original line is unclear. It may be that the foundations along the entire S side of the building needed to be replaced, and it was possible to do so by constructing an entirely new wall before demolishing the old, thus avoiding a total rebuilding of the whole structure. As mentioned earlier, the E sector of the foundation for Wall Ca may have been preserved as the base for a bench.

The slight N to S slope on which Unit IV-1 stood has already been mentioned (pp. 19, 25, 27). Water runoff may have undermined Wall Ca, eventually necessitating its replacement with Wall C. That the builders were concerned with this problem is suggested by the presence of a loosely constructed packing wall (Z) to the S of the new Wall C (Fig. 2-15; Pl. 2-16). The preserved portion of Wall Z measures 6.30 m in length and has an average width of 0.90 m. The portion that faces Wall C has been carefully laid with a straight N edge; but the core is mostly rubble, and the S face is uneven. Its width, its loose construction, and its proximity (0.25 m) to Wall C support the idea that Wall Z was meant as a packing wall to shore up the low S side of the building.

The position of the interior posts appears to have remained the same on the N side (Fig. 2-22). What happened on the S side is unclear, since the evidence for postholes has been removed by later intrusions; but it appears that the posts restored for Phase 1 would have had to be moved slightly to the S or replaced by new posts adjacent to the new Wall C (Fig. 2-21).

The floor of Room 1 was still of rather uneven hard-packed earth, but much blacker than that of Phase 1. As debris was swept to the sides, the floor level gradually rose against Walls A and C, eventually sloping down toward the center of the building to the extent of 0.13 m (Fig. 2-16). On much of its upper surface there was a scatter of medium-sized stones (Fig. 2-23; Pl. 2-37) which were probably used to hold down the thatch (see pp. 31, 32). A considerable amount of pig and cattle bones was lying on this surface (for other finds, see pp. 37, 39, 40).

At its N end, the new apsidal Wall B butts against support Wall X and Wall A, but there is some 0.15 m of earth and rubble packing between. As argued earlier, this supports the view that the apse was a later addition (Pl. 2-29). The stone foundation of Wall B was constructed in the

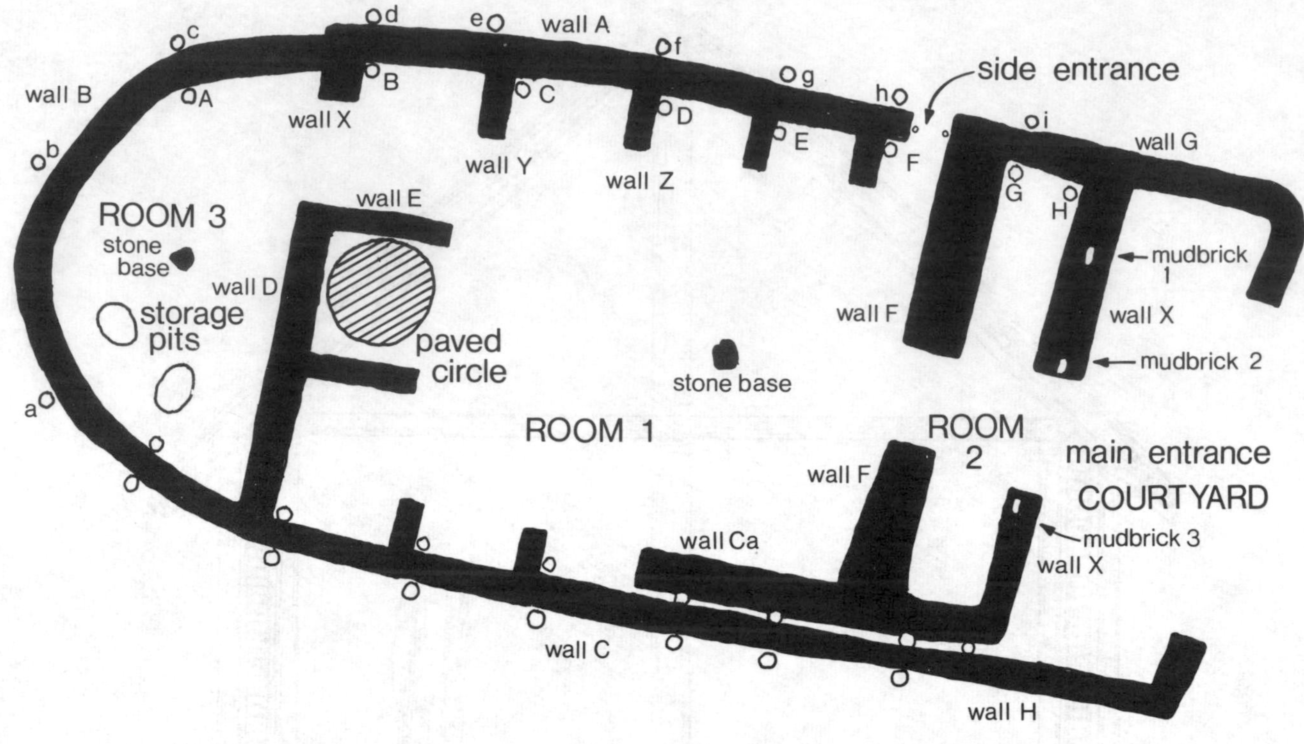

Figure 2-22

same manner as Wall A, with two rows of stones and the use of horizontal bonding, although at less regular intervals than in Wall A (Pl. 2-16). At a distance of 1.60 m from the point where Wall B butts on Wall A, a large narrow block lies across the entire width of the wall, followed by a second, rounder block some 0.70 m to the W, at the spring of the apse. At the corresponding point in the S side of the apse, there is a similar case of horizontal bonding at the point where Wall B is destroyed (Fig. 2-11). It seems, therefore, that the builders had in mind a certain symmetry in the use of horizontal bonding. Since the E wall of the later DAIII Unit IV-5 was built directly over the apex of Wall B, a small portion of the overlying wall was removed to expose the apse fully. The foundation here consists of two large, parallel, slightly rounded stones. But the construction of the apse differs from that of Wall A in its use of an outer row of large blocks and an inner row of quite small and narrow stones. The purpose was apparently to facilitate the layout of the curve and to present a relatively smooth inner face. Wall B has two preserved courses of fairly flat stones (Fig. 2-16), noticeably flatter than the somewhat rounded blocks used in Wall A and some 0.10 m less in overall width. Such distinctions in construction also suggest that Walls A and B belong to different building phases.

The floor of the apsidal addition (Room 3), which is level with the lowest wall course, consists of slightly gravelly sandy mud (Fig. 2-13), lighter in color than in Room 1 but quite hard-packed and with the same downward slope (0.13 m) toward the center. When adding Room 3, the builders again had to take into account the E to W downward slope of the terrain. Toward the W end of the building this slope evidently became steeper, so that the floor in Room 3 (L23 Tkl) was some 0.22 m lower than the floor in the center of the building (L23 Vkl). The difference in floor level was handled by making a sloping passageway, almost a ramp, between the N side of the paved circle and Wall A. Such a "split level" arrangement explains why the soil in Room 3 is lighter in color than that in the rest of the building. The builders must have cleared Mycenaean rubble to a greater depth in the apsidal addition than elsewhere and so exposed the light brown sandy soil associated with late Mycenaean levels in the area.

It is likely that Room 3 became the main storage area of the enlarged building (Pl. 2-38). Some cooking may also have been done there since the pit hearth in Room 1 appears to have been no longer in use. Evidence for the identification of Room 3 as primarily a storage area includes the presence of two pits in the SW part, deposits of charred seeds, and a considerable amount of coarse pottery,

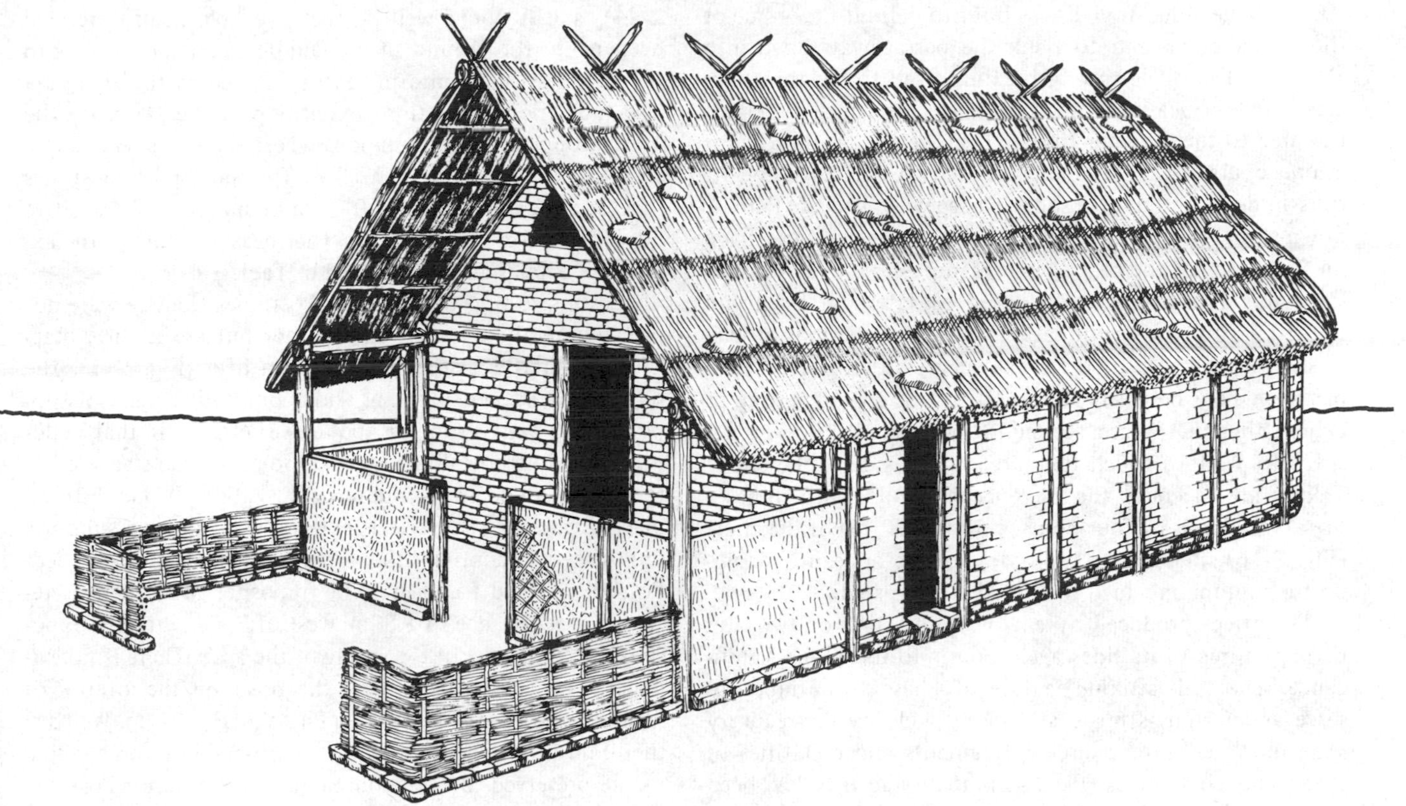

Figure 2-23. Unit IV-1, artist's reconstruction, Phase 2

including pithos fragments (Fig. 2-22). The larger pit (no. 1) has an average diameter of 0.70 m, a depth of 0.53 m, and a row of stones around its rim (Pl. 2-39). The smaller (no. 2) to the W has an average diameter of 0.60 m, a depth of 0.46 m, and is lined at the bottom with fairly flat stones (Pl. 2-40). The original stone lining of the rim has been robbed out, except for three stones on the W side. Both pits contained only earth fill and no cultural debris of any sort, so that it is unlikely that they were used for garbage and trash, as is the case with the pit in the contemporary Unit III-1 (see p. 15).

A large deposit of charred seeds, measuring some 0.50 m EW × 0.20 m NS, was found in the NW part of the room at a distance of 0.92 m from Wall B. The thickest concentration of seeds was some 0.05 m deep. A second, much smaller deposit,[20] measuring approximately 0.10-0.12 m in diameter, was found nearby. Both deposits contained mostly legume seeds (peas or beans), with a few fragments of olive wood that might be from a wooden container (*Nichoria* I, pp. 53-57). Also resting on the floor were found a skyphos **(P1041)**, a ribbed kylix stem **(P1158)**, and a coarse lid **(P1068)**, together with a considerable amount of coarse pottery, including pithos body fragments. The bones represent goat, sheep, and *bovid*, as well as *cervid* and *canid* fragments (*Nichoria* I, pp. 68, 69). The most important small finds include part of an iron knife **(N1429)**, a stone celt **(N1819)**, a lead net-sinker(?) **(N1820)**, a lead button or wheel **(N1821)**,[21] a bronze shield boss or phalaron **(N1833)**, and a fragment of an iron ax head **(N1934)**.

In L23 Tkl a round, flat stone, approximately 0.30 m in diameter, was uncovered at floor level in the center of Room 3. It lies exactly on the long axis of the building (Pl. 2-38) and is cracked right across, as though it once bore a heavy weight. This appears to have been the base for an interior post or column that supported the roof near the W apsidal end of the lengthened building (Fig. 2-21). In addition, two partially preserved and fairly symmetrically placed postholes (a and b) were found just *outside* the wall of the apse. Posthole a to the S is better preserved (Pl. 2-41). Posthole b to the N was partly obliterated by the E wall of Unit IV-5. These postholes on the outside of Wall B suggest that in Phase 2 there may have been an additional row of exterior supports (see pp. 38, 39, 41).

In order to enter Room 3 from Room 1, access was provided through the rear wall (D) of the earlier building. It appears that the N portion of its stone foundations was demolished, leaving only a stub adjacent to Wall A. The stub then became in effect a support wall (X) similar in form and function to Walls Y and Z farther E (Fig 2-22). At the same time, Wall E was built to delimit the N side of the paved circle and to flank the passageway down into Room 3. The single row of medium-sized stones that comprise Wall E clearly shows that it was designed to delimit the area to the S rather than to bear weight. At its E end it is one course high but increases to two courses at the W, thus indicating that the short passageway had an E to W down-slope. Whether or not a second passageway was made on the S side of the paved circle is impossible to determine, since this area has been disturbed by later pits for pithoi (Pl. 2-16); but the continuation of the foundations of Wall D slightly to the S of the circle suggests that it acted as a partition here between Rooms 1 and 3. It is tempting to believe that there was a second low wall, similar in every respect to Wall E, which delimited the S side of the circle. Taking into account the presence of Wall D, which has a preserved depth of four courses on the W side of the circle (Fig. 2-16), these three walls would have appeared to support a podium on which the paved circle rested.

The effect produced by enclosing the circle on two, and perhaps three of its sides again points to its special significance. That this striking feature of Phase 1 continued to serve as an altar is made still more likely by the recovery near its W edge of charcoal fragments and quantities of sheep and goat bones (Pl. 2-42), as though they had been brushed over the side after sacrifice. The presence of these remains would not by themselves distinguish the circle from a domestic hearth, but, combined with its position and elevation, they strengthen its identification as an altar.

The apparent addition of exterior posts on the long sides of the building represents the final major change that was made in the second building phase (Fig. 2-22). Our belief that the Phase 2 building had posts on the exterior as well as on the interior is based on the discovery of Postholes a and b (already discussed) outside the apse, of Posthole e opposite its interior counterpart (C), and of a possible Posthole c opposite a corresponding posthole (A) that may be restored in the interior. The presence of holes a and b is not conclusive evidence, since it could be argued that outside posts were needed for the apsidal addition only and that this innovation implies nothing about the main building. The presence of Posthole e, however, makes it appear very likely that exterior supports were not confined to the apse.

The exterior postholes lack the uniformity in dimensions of their interior counterparts, indicating that the exterior posts may have been of different sizes. For instance, Posthole e has a diameter of 0.22 m and is ringed by large, flat packing stones, evidently reused from Mycenaean tumble (Pl. 2-43). It has a depth of 0.23 m from the exterior ground level and of 0.38 m from the top of the packing stones. On the other hand, the preserved portion of Posthole c is much broader and shallower, with a diameter of some 0.33 m and a depth of 0.11 m. The circular ring of packing stones indicates that there was a posthole here (Pl. 2-44), and it could well be that the hole itself extended deeper into the ground than could be ascertained, owing to the hardness and uniform texture of the earth. There are also indications of a third exterior posthole (f) along the N side, opposite interior hole D where there appears to be a small break in the line of Wall A. Two small packing stones suggest a posthole of some 0.22 m in diameter, but positive identification was impossible. The measurements of the exterior postholes are summarized in Table 2-6.

It is interesting to note that Postholes C and e were not placed directly opposite each other but are slightly staggered; in fact, e is some 0.15 m west of C (Fig. 2-11). The only other known building with comparable pairs of supports is the early shrine of Apollo at Eretria.[22] In that building some, but not all, of the exterior posts are staggered in relation to their inner counterparts. Although our restored plan (Fig. 2-22) shows the exterior and interior supports opposite one another, the arrangement may have varied. Postholes D and f appear to be opposite, and A can be restored at a distance of 1.80 m west of B, i.e., directly opposite c, at the point of the spring of the apse. There is no evidence to suggest that any of the posts on the interior of Wall A were eliminated during Phase 2 (Fig. 2-21). We have therefore restored interior posts in Room 3 on the N-S line of the preserved interior column base and exterior Posthole c. An exterior post on the S, balancing c, should also be restored. No evidence for exterior posts exists along the disturbed S side of Room 1, but a row should almost certainly be restored here to balance those along the N wall (Fig. 2-22).

Analysis of wood charcoal[23] from just N of Posthole c showed 40% olive wood, 25% oak, and 35% unidentifiable. It would thus appear that olive and oak were the two primary wooden building materials, oak being more suitable for posts and roof timbers and olive branches for the matrix of the roof. The same combination of woods was probably used in the first phase.

The only remaining aspect in which the Phase 2 building may have differed notably from its predecessor is in the material of the walls. In the first place, we assume that the exterior posts were an innovation in Phase 2, although it must be admitted that solid evidence is lacking. On the other hand, it does seem fairly certain that the interior posts were retained in Phase 2, because otherwise there would have been no reason to retain the stub of Wall D as a support for post B. What, then, was the reason for the double row of posts? It was scarcely necessary to strengthen support for the roof, since there is no reason to believe that the weight was notably increased in Phase 2. It could be argued that, as the interior posts rotted or weakened, they were supplemented or supplanted (gradually?) by the addition of exterior posts. But we are inclined to see the double row as connected with a change in the wall material from wattle and

Table 2-6. Specifications of Exterior Postholes: Unit IV-1, Phase 2

Posthole	Trench	Preserved Depth	Diameter	Remarks
a	L23 Tl	0.20	0.14	. . .
b	L23 Tl	. . .	0.21	Partly obliterated by E wall of IV-5
c	L23 Tm	0.33	0.11	Should have had greater depth
d (Restored)	L23 Um	. . .	. . .	
e	L23 Um	0.22 (Max.)	0.38	. . .
f	L23 Vm	0.22	?	Depth unknown owing to hardness of soil
g-i (Restored)	L23 VWlm	. . .	. . .	

daub to mudbrick (or possibly some other type such as rammed earth).

In the case of the Eretria parallel, the excavators assume that walls of wattle and daub stood between the outer and inner supports. But as we have argued above, such a light wall could never occupy the full space between the posts; and, wherever it was placed on the stone foundations, the effect would be odd and the wall could have no structural connection with both rows of posts. On the other hand, we believe that the DAII builders were familiar with the use of mudbrick walls in smaller structures (see p. 46), and it would be understandable that in a building of this exceptional size and importance, they (like Mycenaean architects) believed that a timber frame would provide desirable security in the event of an earthquake or other unusual stress. The mudbrick walls may then have occupied practically the full width of the stone foundations and been steadied both by horizontal wooden members on both sides (attached to the posts) and by cross-supports of wood through the width of the wall (at least some of them also secured to the pairs of posts). A combination of wood and brick is a quite credible transitional stage in monumental architecture, i.e., (1) flimsier wall materials in a timber frame (Unit IV-1, Phase 1); (2) mudbrick walls in a timber frame (Unit IV-1, Phase 2); (3) mudbrick walls that alone supported the roof (the DAIII Unit IV-5).

Numerous small finds are associated with the second phase of Unit IV-1. The most important of these are listed below and shown on Fig. 2-11.

A. Trench Vklm, in Room 1:
- **N1401.** Bronze finger ring
- **N1283.** Bronze bar
- **N1282.** Small iron tool. Found together with **N1283** above
- **N1342** A-D. Four clay spindle whorls

B. Trench Uklm, on the exterior of the paved circle:
- **N969.** Clay whorl
- **N970.** Clay whorl
- **N987.** Clay whorl
- **N1053.** Clay whorl
- **N1721.** Clay whorl
- **N1722.** Clay whorl

C. Trench Tklm, within Room 3:
- **N1833.** Bronze shield boss or phalaron
- **N1834.** Iron ax head, frag. of
- **N1429.** Iron knife, frag. of
- **N1820.** Lead net-sinker (?)
- **N1821.** Lead button or whorl
- **N1836.** Clay whorl
- **N1819.** Stone celt

As noted in Phase 1, the small finds from Room 1 (L23 Vklm) were all in the vicinity of either Wall Z or support Wall Y. The concentration of such objects along the N side might suggest that they had been swept there when the room was cleaned.[24] On the other hand, the whole floor was strewn with a great quantity of cow and pig bones and smaller numbers of sheep and goat bones; and a decorated krater fragment **(P1116)** was found almost in the center of the room. The inhabitants appear to have cleared the room of their most precious possessions, leaving only less valuable or lost artifacts in the corners. The area N and S of the paved circle produced only clay spindle whorls, the majority of which were found to the S, together with a coarse incised lid **(P1097)**. The paucity of finds again suggests that any valuable movable objects that were originally there had been removed.

On the contrary, the finds from Room 3 were spread over the entire floor area and are much more varied in character, comprising artifacts of bronze **(N1833)**, iron **(N1429, 1834)**, lead **(N1820-21)**, stone **(N1819)**, and clay **(N1474,**

1836). A concentration of bones (already discussed) occurred just W of the paved circle and also at the W end of the room adjacent to the wall; seed deposits were found at the N end of the room; and coarse pottery covered the floor. A lid **(P1068)** and a grill fragment **(P1069)** are especially noteworthy because of their probably domestic character.

As with Phase 1, it is difficult to determine what happened to the Phase 2 building. Evidence of burning is not widespread but occurs only in certain areas. It is most noticeable in the N section, perhaps because this is better preserved than the robbed-out S side. A carbonized area, already discussed, was found just to the N of exterior Posthole c; a second[25] was found NE of the courtyard. The wood from the latter area has been analyzed as 70% oak, 5% olive, and 25% unidentifiable. The proximity of the burned deposit to the N part of the courtyard suggests that it is to be associated with Wall G and indicates that its superstructure had been constructed primarily of oak branches.

The above evidence may suggest that there was some damage by fire, most noticeable at the E end. Perhaps this accident merely hastened the decision to abandon the building. After more than a century of use and repair, the wooden posts must have been decaying and the roof timbers beginning to rot because of leaks in the thatch. The inhabitants may have decided to stop the process of constant repairs and to build a new structure with stronger materials and stouter foundations on a new site nearby.

The second phase of Unit IV-1 continues the building tradition already established for Phase 1. The building is now of even more impressive dimensions, with a total length (including the courtyard) of 15.90 m and a width of 8.0 m. Mainly because of the unusual dimensions (18 m long) of the megaron hall at Emborio, Snodgrass (1971, p. 424) says that "there can be little doubt that it is the residence of the local chieftain." A building of this size obviously required unusual measures to ensure stability. In our building, pairs of exterior and interior posts appear to have been placed along both N and S outside walls, with additional exterior posts set symmetrically at the W end of the apse (Fig. 2-22). At least two interior posts or columns along the main E-W axis appear to have helped support the roof structure. The walls were probably of mud brick, with branches or reeds over the rafters and with thatch covering the roof.

As with Phase 1, one cannot be sure that its enlarged successor served any functions beyond those of the dwelling of a prominent individual, probably the village chieftain. The character and location of the bone deposits, small finds, and pottery are compatible with purely domestic use. The storage pits, seed deposits, and fragments of pithoi and other large vessels found in Room 3 could represent simply the storage area of a single large and important family. On the other hand, the size, orientation, and plan—particularly the prominent placement of the structure we have identified as an altar—strongly suggest that this was no ordinary house. According to Snodgrass (1971, p. 408), "it is often difficult to distinguish between two classes of use [domestic and sacred]; not only was there no clear differentiation in plan but there may even, according to a recently advanced theory (Drerup 1964, pp. 199-204) have been at first no absolute distinction in use." It is worth keeping in mind that there is no conclusive evidence from contents or plan alone that would identify other DA buildings in the Aegean that are recognized as early temples. Their function is inferred solely from the fact that they underlie structures that can be so identified. It may well be that, in the Mycenaean tradition, all of these Early Iron Age buildings had both domestic and politico-religious functions. In any case, we believe that Unit IV-1 served important communal needs, certainly religious—and probably economic (i.e., collection and distribution) as well.

Unit IV-1 stands out among known DA apsidal buildings by virtue of its early date, size, and the presence of a relatively complex system of both exterior and interior supports. By way of comparison, other early apsidal buildings will be reviewed briefly below. It should be noted, however, that almost all, with the notable exception of the recently discovered buildings at Lefkandi, are later than our Unit IV-1.

a. Aegina, behind the W end of the later Temple of Aphaia. Only the apse has been uncovered, but Fiechter believes this to be part of an old terrace wall (Fiechter 1906, pp. 22, 159).
b. Aëtos. Fragments of a possible temple model similar to that from Perachora (Robertson 1948, pp. 101, 102, Pl. 45).
c. Antissa. Two apsidal buildings; an earlier structure facing W, dated to the 10th and 9th centuries B.C. and measuring some 17.25 m × 5.60 m, was succeeded in the 8th by a second structure, facing E, of approximately the same dimensions (Lamb 1931-32, pp. 41-67).
d. Eleusis, below the Telesterion. Mylonas believes that an elliptical fragment of wall beneath the Telesterion belongs to a Late Geometric apsidal temple (Kouroniotes 1930-1, p. 25; Mylonas 1961, pp. 56-59).
e. Eretria, under the Temple of Daphnepheros. This is the only published building with both exterior and interior supports. It has a N × S orientation and measures 11.50 m × 7.50 m (Auberson 1974, pp. 60-68).
f. Galataki (Solygeia). An apsidal temple of the Sub-Geometric period with an entrance in the W and an apse at the E. A small rectangular structure within the apse could have served as an altar or as the base for a wooden cult statue (see note 6) (Hood 1958, p. 5).
g. Gonnos. This temple to Athena Polias has a plan more in the shape of a horseshoe than an ellipse. Dated to the 7th century B.C., it measures some 10.0 m × 8.0 m (cf. our Phase 1) (Arvanitopoullos 1910, p. 252 and 1911a, p. 315; Helly 1973).

h. Homolion, near Gonnos. This temple is similar in plan and date to the one at Gonnos (Arvanitopoullos 1911b, pp. 284-87).

i. Lefkandi. A house with an oblong room and an apsidal end, of which only part of the arc is preserved; dated to the second half of the 8th century B.C. (Popham and Sackett 1968, p. 30). A recently discovered "Heroön" at Lefkandi measuring 45 m × 10 m and dating to the Late Protogeometric period, is similar to the second phase of Unit IV-1 at Nichoria in its use of supports along the central axis and interior and exterior posts along the side walls. It also has an exterior peripteral colonnade (Popham, Toulopa, and Sackett 1982).

j. Mycenae. This building, possibly dating at the earliest to the end of the 10th century B.C., contains three rooms and a vestibule and has a N × S orientation. It measures 9.0 m × 3.50 m (Verdelis 1962a, pp. 106, 107, and 1962b, pp. 85-87; Daux 1963, p. 746, Fig. 22).

k. Perachora. 8th century B.C. (no earlier than 800 B.C.) temple to Hera Akraia, oriented E × W and measuring some 9.0 m × 5.50 m; also Temple Model A (Payne 1940, pp. 42-51).

l. Ptoön. Probably burned in the 8th century B.C. (Weickert 1929, p. 10).

m. Samos. Terracotta model from the Heraion; contains an apse at one end, an entrance surmounted by a gable at the other; dated between 730 and 670 B.C. (Walter and Vierneisel 1959, p. 18, Pls. 29, 30).

n. Old Smyrna (Bayrakli). At least two apsidal houses can be distinguished as belonging to the first half of the 7th century B.C. The larger measures 14.0 m × 8.0 m (Akurgal 1961, pp. 12, 13, Figs. 3-5).

o. Thebes. Oldest Temple of Apollo Ismenius; dated probably to no later than the second half of the 8th century B.C. (Keramopoullos 1917, p. 66; Weickert 1929, p. 10).

p. Thermon. Megaron B below the Temple of Apollo. This building, measuring 21.40 m × 7.30 m, has a slightly curving rear wall and a hairpin peripteral colonnade. Perhaps 9th century B.C. (Rhomaios 1915, pp. 225-79; Drerup 1969, pp. 14-17).

The oval house (i.e., with an apse at each end) also occurs but seems not to be as popular as its apsidal counterpart. Examples were found at the following sites:

a. Athens, N slope of the Areopagus. This Geometric house has an elliptical plan and measures some 11.0 m × 5.0 m (Burr 1933, pp. 542-51).

b. Larissa in S Aeolis on the River Hermus. This fragmentary building measures some 8.50 m in length and possibly dates to the Archaic period (Boehlau and Schefold 1940, p. 15).

c. Melia in Caria, near the Panionium. This building, measuring 11.90 m × 8.35 m, dates to the Archaic period (Müller-Wiener 1967, pp. 116-23, Figs. 63, 64, Pl. 62:1).

d. Naxos (Grotta). Possibly an oval house but little information available (Kondoleon 1959, pp. 128, 129; 1961, p. 196; 1963, p. 149; 1965, p. 112; Sinos 1971, p. 110, Fig. 256).

e. Samos. Terracotta model from the Heraion (Sinos 1971, p. 110, Figs. 252, 253).

f. Old Smyrna. Oval houses from the Bayrakli I and III periods. Here one of the oldest of all Iron Age houses has been uncovered. Measuring some 5.0 m × 3.0 m, it belongs to the Bayrakli I (end of the 10th century B.C.) period and consists of a single room with mudbrick walls and probably a straw roof. In the Bayrakli III period (750-650 B.C.) the oval house becomes a dominant feature of the domestic architecture at Smyrna (Akurgal 1962, pp. 369-73).

Most of the above examples either are too fragmentary to be of much use as comparative material or belong to the 8th century or later. On the basis of the pottery associated with it, the second phase of Unit IV-1 can be dated to the second half of the 9th century B.C. (see pp. 90-96). Ceramically, this period forms a transition between the pottery of the DAII period and that of DAIII. It also seems that, at Nichoria, a transition occurred in this general period from rectangular to apsidal architectural forms. In Phase 1, the shape of Unit IV-1 was apparently rectangular. In Phase 2 an apse was added but otherwise the basic plan of the building did not change significantly. As we shall see, Unit IV-1 was succeeded in the DAIII period by Unit IV-5 which had an apsidal plan from the beginning.

Unit IV-1 appears to have been the major DAII building at Nichoria that made use of the apsidal plan. The only earlier local structures with an apsidal shape are a series of cist graves in the areas of Lakkoules and Tourkokivouro (see Chapter 4, pp. 266-70). Some of these graves are as early as DAI and they continue in DAII. Thus, it is evident that the apsidal shape was already known locally when Unit IV-1 was built. And it may well be that the addition of the apse in Phase 2 was influenced by the shape of the cist graves.

The two closest known parallels to the second phase of Unit IV-1 are at Thermon and Eretria.[26] The roof support system of the early temple of Apollo Daphnephoros at Eretria parallels that of our building, with its external and internal supports. It is some 4.40 m shorter than its Nichoria counterpart, whereas Megaron B at Thermon is 5.50 m longer than our bulding. The notable length of the Thermon and Nichoria buildings and the subtle curve of the long walls suggest that they may be related. The hairpin peripteral colonnade of Megaron B betrays the apsidal shape known elsewhere in the Aegean. Unit IV-1 does not have a peripteral colonnade, but the presence of exterior posts for roof support could be regarded as the source of the peripteral idea. The next step is to separate these supports from the walls so as to permit wider eaves and to form an external colonnade, a process which is beginning at Thermon.

Table 2-7 presents a synopsis of the technical details concerning the walls associated with Unit IV-1, Phase 2. It has been stressed above that most of the original foundations were reused (see Table 2-5).

NORTH ENVIRONS OF UNIT IV-1 (FIGS. 2-10a, b, 2-24; PL. 2-45)

Miscellaneous Foundations

Evidence for DA structures immediately to the N of Unit IV-1 has been largely destroyed by the plow, since these levels were quite close to the modern surface. However, there are traces in this areas of an apsidal wall (H) (Pl. 2-46) of either the DAII or the transitional period (II/III). What is preserved is a portion of the outer face with a large horizontal bonding block near what would have been the center of the apse, some 0.40 m from the point where the wall has been completely destroyed. This outer face has been carefully laid with the same rounded stones as were used in Wall A of Unit IV-1; furthermore, the horizontal bonding stone has the same character as those used in Wall A (Fig. 2-10a, b). The inner face of Wall H has been completely robbed out, with the exception of the course that butts on the S wall of Room 1 of Mycenaean Unit IV-7, where both faces are preserved. The preserved curving portion of Wall H is 1.55 m long, 0.051 m deep, and has an average height of three courses, with four at its S end. It butts on Walls D and F which form the SE corner of Room 1 in Mycenaean Unit IV-7. Some 0.10-0.15 m of fill and small packing stones comprise the butt joint (Fig. 2-24), a technique already seen in the abuttment of Walls A and B of Unit IV-1.

As with Unit IV-1, it appears that Mycenaean foundations were reused to the N of Wall H, specifically Wall D of Room 1 in Mycenaean Unit IV-7. The top of Wall D was found to lie very close to the modern surface, and hence much of this portion of the foundations of Unit IV-7 was probably still visible in DA times. The DA builders may have leveled off these Mycenaean foundations, specifically Wall D, and have placed at least one, and perhaps two stone courses on top, creating a wall in alignment with the N end of Wall H and forming part of it. The DA wall has largely disappeared because of modern plowing, and all that now remains are two stones resting on the top of Wall D but not belonging to it (Fig. 2-24). The southernmost stone is separated from Wall D by some 0.10 m of fill. This DA wall is aligned with Wall I to the NE in trench L23 Vo (Fig. 2-10a, b; Pl. 2-47).

Wall I has been built with the same type of large rounded stones as occur in Wall H and in the walls of Unit IV-1 (Fig. 2-24). It runs in a NE X SW direction with a preserved length of 3.0 m and a maximum of four courses (height 0.65 m). It butts on Wall P of Room 2 in Unit IV-7 and is aligned with Walls D and H. Its eastern face at the N has slipped slightly, and thus it is some 0.15 m wider at its N end than at the S. Its total length is unknown, for it continues into unexcavated property to the NE. The bottom course of the wall consists of extremely large stones with an average length of some 0.50-0.60 m. On top of these are piled three rough courses, all blocks more or less elliptical in shape with curved edges and earth fill between. Such wall construction contrasts markedly with that used in Mycenaean buildings, notably Wall D of Unit IV-7 (Fig. 2-24). Wall D consists of flat rectangular stones, some well dressed, laid in regular courses, rather than piled in semi-haphazard fashion on top of one another. It also contains more earth fill between the individual stones and exhibits the use of chinking. A small test cut was made beneath

Table 2-7. Wall Specifications: Unit IV-1, Phase 2

Wall and Date	Grid	Length	Width	Maximum Height	Maximum Number of Courses	Bond/Butt
B (apse) (DAII/III)	L23 Tlm	3.90 (from center of apse)	0.045	0.30 at S 0.165 at N	2	Butts on Wall A on N Side.
C (DAII/III)	L23 UVWk	7.50	0.45	0.225	1	Parallel with Wall Ca. No preserved junctures.
E (DAII/III)	L23 Ul	1.90	0.38 at E 0.19 at W	0.18	2	Butts on Wall C.
G (N courtyard wall) (DAII/III)	L23 Xlm	2.25	0.40	0.08-0.10	1	Butts on Walls A and X.
H (S courtyard wall) (DAII/III)	L23 Xk	1.40	0.20	0.11	1	Badly damaged.
Z (DAII/III)	L23 WXjk	6.30	0.25 at E 0.94 at W	0.105	1	Packing wall. No butts or bonds.

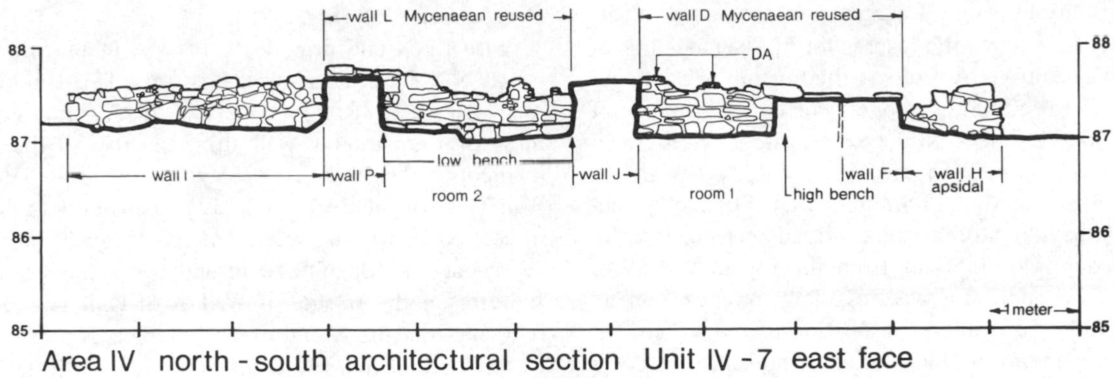

Figure 2-24

the lower course of Wall I at its N end. Here was found evidence of Mycenaean rubble on which the DA wall had been built.

Wall H, the DA portion of Wall D, and Wall I are aligned with one another, indicating that originally they may have been part of the same wall running in a NE X SW direction with an apse at the S end, giving a total length of some 9.50 m. Running parallel to Wall I at the NW is a second wall (J), measuring 3.50 m in length and consisting of a maximum of three courses at its N end (Pl. 2-48). The function of these walls is unclear. More than likely they did not belong to a building, since the inner face of Walls I and J are separated from each other by a maximum distance of only 1.50 m, providing too small a space for the interior of a building. Furthermore, Wall H is only some 0.80 m distant from Unit IV-1, thus effectively blocking the alley assumed to run along the N side of IV-1. Probably Walls H, I, and J were low terrace walls designed to protect the NW end of Unit IV-1 from erosion.

Refuse Dump

To the NE of the walls just described, in Trench L23 Top, there was a refuse dump of the DAII period. The major part is located in level 3 of L23 Top, where there is a pure DAI deposit, but it also continues into the top of level 4, where a Mycenaean admixture begins, and spills over into level 2 of L23 Sop (Fig. 2-10). The fill is quite dark, almost black, and consists of the same gravelly, sandy mud as comprised the floor of Phase 1 of Unit IV-1 (Fig. 2-12). The depression is roughly circular, but its edges are not well defined. The excavated portion has an approximated diameter of 4.30 m and a depth of some 0.80 m, i.e., 0.70 m in level 3 of L23 Top and the first 0.10 m of level 4. The presence of tumbled stones of the type used in Wall A of Unit IV-1, quantities of animal bones of goat, sheep, and pig, fragments of carbonized wood, and unworn pottery fragments all indicate that this was a refuse dump (Pl. 2-49). The most important small finds include an iron knife blade (**N853**), two fragments of bronze sheet metal (**N827, 844**), a whetstone and grinder (**N867, 871**), a bone bead (**N866**), and two clay whorls (**N852, 864**). The three best preserved vases are **P600**, **P602**, both skyphoi, and **P631**, a cup.

The pottery dates the dump to the DAII period. As has already been discussed, the earlier floor of Unit IV-1 had been cleared out when the building was remodeled, and it is likely that debris from that operation was disposed of in this refuse dump. If this is the case the pres-

Table 2-8. Wall Specifications: Miscellaneous Foundations N of Unit IV-1

Wall and Date	Grid	Length	Width	Maximum Height	Maximum Number of Courses	Bond/Butt
H(apsidal) (DAII or II/III)	L23 Um	1.55	0.31	0.51	3-4	Butts on Walls D and F of Unit IV-7
D (Unit IV-7) (Mycenaean, reused in DAII or II/III)	L23 Umn	3.29	0.55	0.66	6	Bonds with Wall F at corner
I (DAII or II/III)	L23 Vo	3.00	0.60	0.65	4	Butts on Mycenaean Wall P Unit IV-7
J (DAII or II/III)	L23 Uo	3.50	0.58	0.37	3	Runs over doorway of Unit IV-7

ence of carbonized wood fragments in the dump might support the idea that the cause for the remodeling of Unit IV-1 was damage by fire. At the bottom of the dump was found a scatter of flat stones and large fragments of pithoi. On the E side of this scatter there was a small rectangular enclosure, 0.65 m NS × 0.50 m EW in exterior dimensions and 0.24 m in depth (Pl. 2-49). Consisting of large flat stones, some placed on end, it is located at a depth of 0.58 m from the top of Wall A of Unit IV-5. The enclosure was originally bounded on all four sides but is now missing a portion of the NE corner. The enclosure seems to have been open, since no cover slabs were found; its function is unclear. It may have marked the special (sacred?) character of the intended contents, especially appropriate if the debris came from Unit IV-1.

Elsewhere in Area IV N, rather worn DAII sherds were scattered throughout trenches L23 Vmno, Wmn, and farther to the NE in trial trench M23-II. No architecture is associated with these sherds, and their deposition is probably due to hill-wash down the N to S slope. But their presence proves that the DAII settlement included some use of the higher Tsagdis field across the modern path to NE of Area IV.

SOUTH ENVIRONS OF UNIT IV-1 IN AREA IV SW FIGS. 2-10, 2-25; PL. 2-50)

A number of fragmentary walls belonging to the DAII period were uncovered to S of Unit IV-1 in Area IV SW.[27] The fragment of an apsidal wall (O) was recovered in grids L23 RSi from a great mass of closely packed stone tumble and hard, dark, gravelly sandy mud similar to that which comprises stratum 6 in Unit IV-1. The preserved portion of Wall O measures only 2.10 m in length, with an average width of 0.58 m and a height of one course. Both inner and outer faces are preserved at the W end. The stones themselves are of the same rounded shape as occur in Wall A of Unit IV-1 and consist of the same materials, i.e., white limestone, pink limestone, and coarse sandstone. Where the two faces are preserved, the fill consists of rubble and hard-packed earth, a technique also used in Wall A of Unit IV-1. To the NW of the preserved line of Wall O is a tumble of stones roughly leveled by cultivation. These disturbed blocks continue in rough fashion the arc begun by Wall O and probably represent all that is left of the original apse of the building. The pottery associated with Wall O is DAII in date; and the similarity in construction with Wall A of IV-1 confirms this dating. Thus, Wall O may once have belonged to an apsidal building oriented in the same E-W direction as Unit IV-1. Indeed, the building would have been almost parallel to Unit IV-1, although apparently much smaller.

Reused Unit IV-9 (Fig. 2-25)

With its N end directly W of Wall O and oriented in a rough N × S direction, Wall P is some 15.74 m long, spanning grids L23 Rfghi (Pl. 2-50). Also recovered from a mass of tumble, this wall turns slightly to the W where it incorporates Wall A of Mycenaean Unit IV-9. Since Wall P is irregularly built, it is perhaps best to describe it in sections. The first section at the N is 5.78 m long with an average width of 0.70 m and three courses in height. It butts on the W side of Wall A of Unit IV-9 at a point 0.30 m from the N end of Wall A. This N section appears to have been carelessly constructed with both large blocks and small stones and without a clear inner or outer face. The stones have also been less carefully selected than in other DAII foundations in Area IV and include various shapes and types of stones, including white and pink limestone, sandstone, green shale, and one red-brown chert block. Its construction suggests that this N section of Wall P may have served as a field wall or a terrace wall for the protection of the apsidal building represented by Wall O, since the E-to-W downslope which caused difficulties farther to the NE is still in evidence here.

The second section of Wall P is 1.33 m in length and stretches diagonally along the top of Wall A where it consists of one to two courses of small stones resting directly on the top of the earlier wall (Pl. 2-50). A somewhat similar use of Wall A occurs in the third section which butts on the E side of Wall A at a point 2.47 m from its N end. This section has an irregular "S" curve and is 5.89 m long, with an average width of 0.40 m and a height of three to four courses. At the point where it butts on Wall A, its base is 0.36 m below the top of Wall A and its top is level with the top of the earlier wall. Both inner and outer faces are preserved, and it is the outer (W) face that rests directly on the top of the Mycenaean wall. The inner (E) face, on the other hand, has no earlier base and extends in places to a depth of four courses paralleling Wall A. The stones at the base of Wall P on this E side are quite large, forming a sturdy foundation for the other courses, a technique noted previously with Wall I in grid L23 Vo (Fig. 2-24). White and pink limestone and sandstone have been used in this third section. The wall curves slightly to the SW so that its S end is built almost completely on top of Wall A, which is at a slightly lower level at this point. At the very S of the preserved line, Wall P appears to run in a straight N-S direction. This fourth section in grid L23 Rf has a length of 2.74 m, a width of 0.38 m, and a height of one to two courses. For most of its length, just the inner (E) face is preserved, but at the S end both faces are preserved. In this stretch, its base appears to be above the top of Wall A.

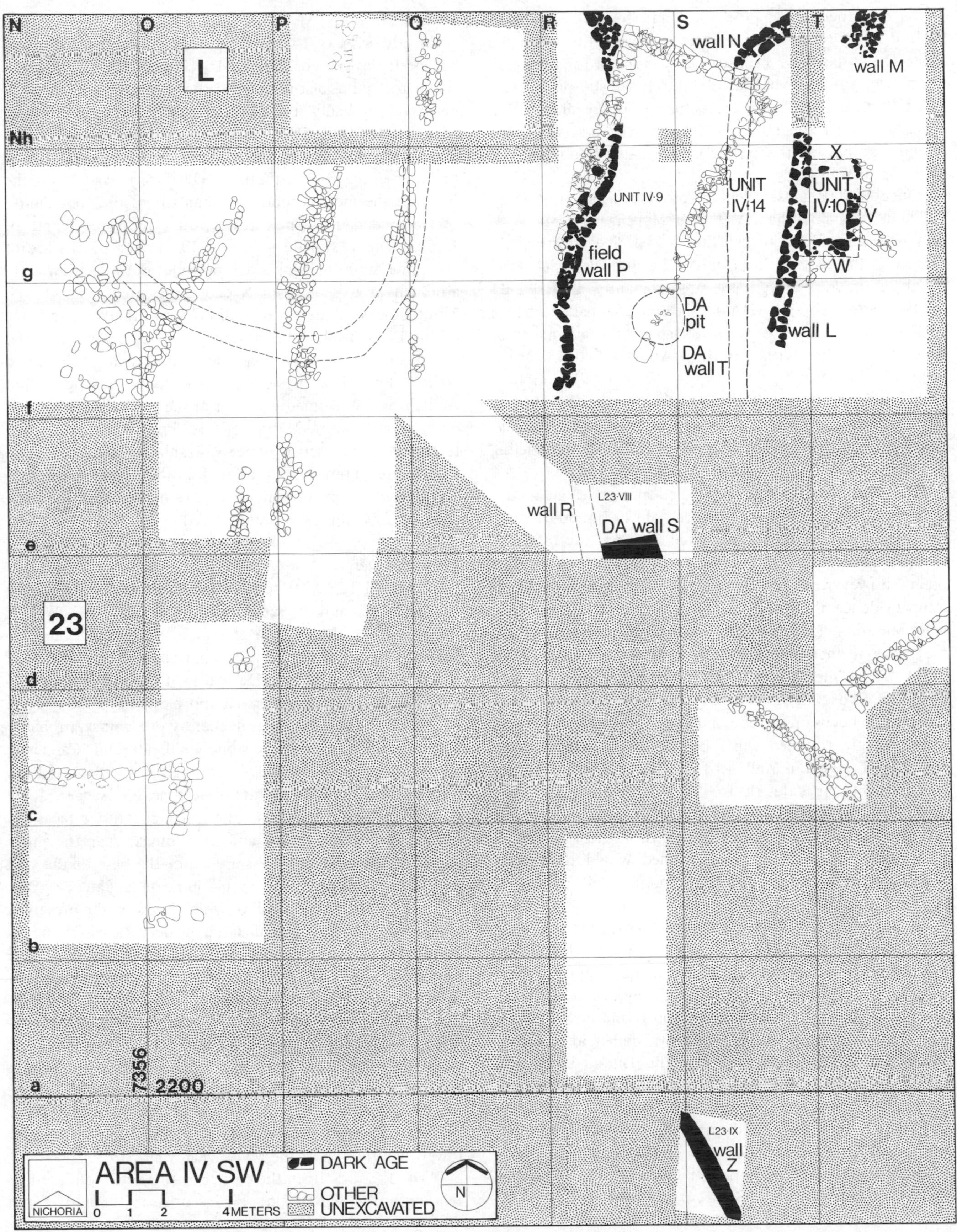
N
O
P
Q
R
S
T
L
Nh
g
f
e
d
c
b
a
23
7356
2200
wall N
wall M
X
UNIT IV·9
UNIT IV·14
UNIT IV·10
V
W
field wall P
DA pit
DA wall T
wall L
L23·VIII
wall R
DA wall S
L23·IX
wall Z
AREA IV SW
NICHORIA
0 1 2 4 METERS
DARK AGE
OTHER
UNEXCAVATED
N

Figure 2-25

As described above, the third and fourth sections of Wall P exhibit much more careful construction than the first. The stones have been carefully selected for their uniform size, and the wall has definite inner and outer faces (Figs. 2-10, 2-25). The preserved part of the second section consists of only small stones which may have served as the packing stones of the base for the continuation of Wall P on top of Wall A.

Since Wall P reuses Wall A of Mycenaean Unit IV-9, it seems probable that IV-9, like Mycenaean Unit IV-7, was reused in DAII times (Fig. 2-25). The stratified sequence is the same in both units. The floor deposits (level 3) in grids L23 RSfgh are predominantly LHIIIA2-B1 in date, although some DA admixture reflects disturbance in DAII times. Level 2, however, above the original floor is DAII in date, with a small DAIII admixture due to hill-wash. The fact that the top of the first (N) section of Wall P is 0.31 m below the top of Wall A, and that the top of the third section is level with it indicates that the Mycenaean foundation was visible when the DAII remodeling occurred.

The function of Wall P is unclear. Its irregular and curving N section suggests use as a field or boundary wall, but the more carefully constructed S part surely indicates a more substantial use for house foundations. Little remains, however, of the other walls of the building. There is no evidence that Walls B and C of the Mycenaean unit were reused. A DA wall (L), farther E in grids L23 STfgh, may have formed the E boundary of the reused unit (Pl. 2-51). Wall L measures 6.65 m in length, with a maximum height of two courses at its N end. Both inner and outer faces have been preserved, and the stones consist of the same smooth, rounded white limestone as occurs in the S end of Wall P and in Wall A of Unit IV-1. The pottery associated with it dates it to the DAII period, and it is parallel to Wall P. Its S end has been destroyed, but it may be presumed that it continued at least as far S as Wall P. The building thus formed would have been a rectangular structure measuring some 5.50 m EW × 9.50 m (minimum) NS.

In the S center of this structure an oval pit had been dug in the line of Wall C in grids L23 RSfg (Pl. 2-52). It has a maximum diameter of 2.50 m, and a depth of some 0.30 m. It was ringed on the outside by a series of small stones, presumably robbed from Wall C and now in a disturbed condition. Some had evidently fallen into the pit and were mixed with the soft dark fill. The pit apparently served as a refuse dump for the later occupants, since it produced a good series of decorated DAII pottery (**P789-91**). Small finds associated with the reuse of IV-9 are a well-preserved bronze dress pin (**N1789**) and two clay whorls (**N1699**, **1787**); pottery includes **P781**, a skyphos; **P817**, an oinochoe; and **P830**, a coarse mug.

Unit IV-10 (Pl. 2-53)

In grid L23 Tg to the E of Wall L a very small room has been designated Unit IV-10 (Fig. 2-25). The foundations are quite disturbed and lie directly over the NW corner of a badly ruined Mycenaean building that was adjacent to Unit IV-9. Fragments of three walls were uncovered, and the builders seem to have used Wall L to enclose the fourth (W) side (Pl. 2-53). Wall V on the E side is the most complete. It consists of only one course of stones laid in a single row, with a preserved length of 1.25 m and a width of only 0.30 m. The blocks are of the same smooth, rounded limestone as those in Wall L, although at its preserved N end there are smaller stones. Three blocks of the south wall (W) are preserved, and one of the north wall (X). These walls are less well preserved but seem to have been constructed in a manner similar to Wall V. Enough is preserved of the room to indicate that Walls V and W formed a corner at the SE and to show that its dimensions were 2.0 m NS × 1.25 m EW. An interesting feature is the presence of recognizable fragments of solidified (through burning?) mudbrick in the fill of the interior. The pottery from the unit was quite meager, but the diagnostic sherds indicate a general DAII date.

Trial Trenches

In trench L23-VIII to the S of Unit IV-9 (Fig. 2-25), two walls (R and S) were uncovered (Pl. 2-54). Wall R runs in a N-S direction in alignment with Wall P and appears to be a reused Mycenaean wall. It has a preserved length of 2.30 m, an average width of 0.60 m, and a maximum height of five courses. At approximately 0.70 m from its N end, the wall becomes deeper by one course, probably to neutralize the N to S slope in the terrain. Carelessly constructed with irregular faces, Wall R consists of both rounded and squarish white limestone blocks and some quite thin limestone slabs. The inner and outer faces are not always in a clear line, and some blocks span the entire width of the wall. The pottery from the base of the wall (level 3) is Mycenaean and should indicate its date.

On the other hand, Wall S, which butts on the preserved S end of Wall R, has associated pottery (level 2) that is clearly DAII. Wall S runs E-W in grid L23 Rde and has a preserved length of 1.54 m and a maximum height of three courses (Pl. 2-54). Its minimum width is 0.57 m, but its S face is hidden in the scarp. It is crudely constructed, consisting of small thin white limestone slabs, some of which appear to extend across its entire width. It butts awkwardly on Wall R at a point one course above the base of R. At the junction of the two walls, the stones of Wall S slope up against Wall R, and its top is one course lower than the top of the Mycenaean wall.

Walls R and S form the corner of some structure, but its relationship to reused Unit IV-9 is unclear. It could be part of a separate house or shed, or it could belong to the enclosing wall of a S courtyard of that unit. Wall R appears to be in alignment with Wall P, and the lightness of Wall S would suit a use such as a courtyard wall. It may well be that in front of its S entrance Unit IV-9 had a courtyard like that at the E end of Unit IV-1. A coarse, flat-based, neck-handled amphora (**P1000**) was associated with the DAII level of Wall S in a small pit at the juncture of the walls.

Farther S, trial trench L23-IX (Fig. 2-25) revealed a wall (Z) running in a NW × SE direction diagonally across the trench (Pl. 2-55). The associated pottery is DAII, and the construction is rather light. The wall has a clear inner and outer face with hard earth packing and may have been used as a terrace support against the N-S slope in this area.

Groups of DAII sherds were scattered throughout Area IV with no architectural association. Some were found under the floor levels of the Byzantine Unit IV-2 and the DAIII apsidal building IV-5 (Fig. 2-10). An especially good deposit was uncovered in level 3 of L23 Rjk, perhaps indicating that a DAII structure in this location was obliterated by the Byzantine unit. Scattered DAII sherds, including a good decorated body fragment (**P766**), were found in the predominantly Mycenaean levels associated with a large wall spanning trenches L23 OPQefg. This material is the result of hill-wash deposited against the terrace wall. DAII small finds here include fragments of a bronze spiral ring (**N1829-30**). Finally, also the result of hill-wash, a few worn DAII sherds were found at the bottom of a good DAII deposit located predominantly in grid L23 UVc and extension, but spreading into L23 Sc and Xd. Farther south, trial trench L23-V also produced worn DAII sherds with no associated architecture.

DARK AGE III

DAIII occupation was apparently confined almost exclusively to Area IV where the remains of one large apsidal building (Unit IV-5) and fragments of several others were discovered.

UNIT IV-5 (FIGS. 2-26, 2-27, 2-28; PLS. 2-45, 2-56)

Unit IV-5 is the major known DAIII building and the obvious successor to Unit IV-1. Unfortunately, it was found in an extremely incomplete state of preservation. Much of the interior and almost the entire W side were destroyed by the leveling carried out in the Late Roman/Early Byzantine period for Phase 1 of Unit IV-2 (see Ch. 9, pp. 364-68). The only part of the DAIII foundations that escaped this leveling is the E side of the unit, since it is outside the area occupied by Unit IV-2. Unit IV-5 was a very large apsidal building, oriented in a N × S direction. The best-preserved portions are its E long wall (A) in trench L23 Tklm and the E part of a joining cross-wall (Y) in L23

Table 2-9. Wall Specifications: Area IV SW (DAII)

Wall and Date	Grid	Length	Width	Maximum Height	Maximum Number of Courses	Butt/Bond
L	L23 STfg	6.65	0.60	0.25	2	. . .
O	L23 RSi	2.10	0.58	0.20	1	. . . .
P	L23 Rfghi	15.74	0.30-0.83	0.48	4	Butts against and rests on Mycenaean Wall A
Section 1	L23 Rhi	5.78	0.70	0.48	3	Butts on W side of Wall A
Section 2	L23 Rh	1.33	0.55	0.25	2	Stretches across top of Wall A
Section 3	L23 Rgh	5.89	0.40	0.40	3-4	Butts on E side of Wall A; W face rests on top of it
Section 4	L23 Rf	2.74	0.38	0.25	2	. . .
R (LHIIIA2-B1, reused in DAII)	L23 Rde	2.30	0.60	0.63	5	Butts on Wall S
S	L23 Rde	1.54	0.57	0.34	3	Butts on Wall R
V	L23 Tg	1.25	0.30	0.20	1	. . .
W (3 stones only)	L23 Tg	0.90	0.30	0.20	1	. . .
X	L23 Tg	. . .	. . .	. . .		

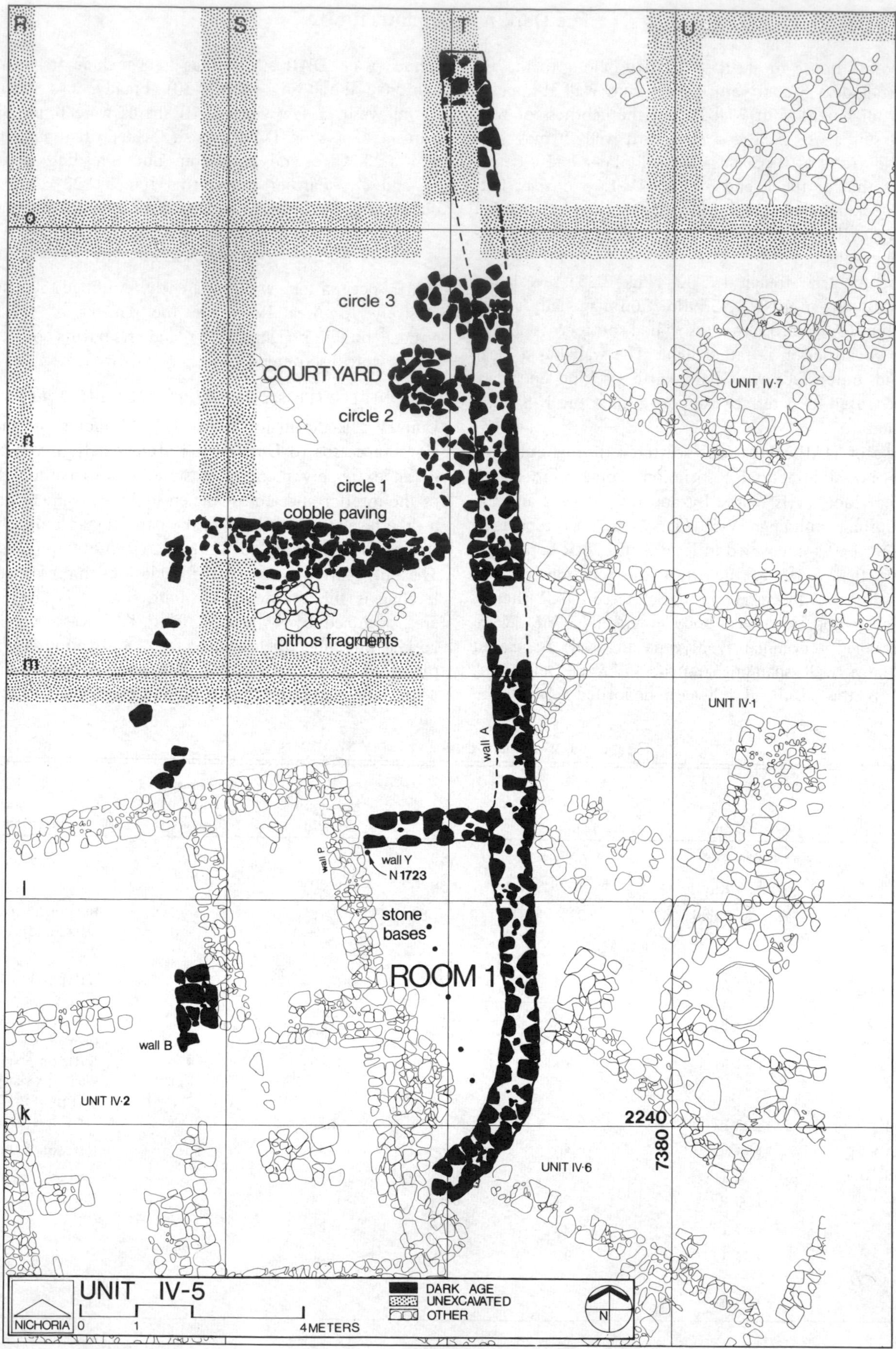
R
S
T
U
o
n
m
l
k
circle 3
COURTYARD
circle 2
circle 1
cobble paving
pithos fragments
UNIT IV·7
UNIT IV·1
wall A
wall P
wall Y
N 1723
stone
bases
ROOM 1
wall B
UNIT IV·2
UNIT IV·6
2240
7380
UNIT IV-5
NICHORIA
0
1
4 METERS
DARK AGE
UNEXCAVATED
OTHER
N

Figure 2-26

STl. A portion of Wall A was built directly over the W tip of the apse of Unit IV-1. The N end of Wall A in grids L23 Tno, although ouside the area occupied by Unit IV-2, is only partially preserved, owing to modern tree pit intrusions and the generally disturbed condition of the upper levels here (Fig. 2-26).

The description of Unit IV-5 is best begun at the relatively well-preserved SE corner where the foundation of a portion of the apse is intact. This section of Wall A consists of the spring of the apse in the S of grid L23 Tk and the beginning of its curve in L23 Tj (Pl. 2-57). It is carefully built in two lines of large, flat, rounded blocks of white and pink limestone, with some 0.15-0.20 m of hard earth fill between (Pl. 2-58). The construction is notably different from that of Wall A in Unit IV-1. The stones used in IV-1 have the same smooth appearance as those in IV-5; but they are set closer together and show less earth fill, more regular use of horizontal bonding, and occasional use of chinking. Wall A of Unit IV-5, on the other hand, shows scarcely a single example of horizontal bonding and averages 0.70 m in width, i.e., some 0.20 m wider than its counterpart in Unit IV-1.

To the W (inside) of the apsidal section of Wall A is the preserved portion of Room 1, bounded by a cross-wall (Y) on the N. Room 1 has a N-S length of 6.0 m and a restored width of 5.50 m. The floor consists of extremely hard-packed reddish brown soil on which rested numerous fragments of coarse vases. Indeed, coarse ware here is much more common than fine ware. The original floor surface was level with the top of the lowest course of stones in Wall A (Pl. 2-57), presenting definite evidence that the builders laid one course of the foundation below ground level and at least one, perhaps two courses above the floor. The second course is preserved, and a scattered tumble of stones along the edge might represent a third course. In time, the floor level undoubtedly rose and may have eventually covered the stone foundations.

The debris over the floor (level 4) was reddish brown and consisted of disintegrated mudbrick, both large and small charcoal fragments, and a large amount of coarse pottery. The red soil probably represents decayed mudbrick which had been exposed to intense heat (Pl. 2-59). Above this floor debris (level 3), the red color of the earth was more pronounced and contained more numerous charcoal fragments. The great extent of this material, which covered the entire preserved area of the apsidal room, indicates that the upper walls were of mudbrick. Similar reddened earth mixed with charcoal was found to the N of Wall Y in grids STlm. A heavy mudbrick superstructure probably explains the need for the unusually wide stone foundations.

It is likely, then, that the building was destroyed in an intense conflagration. The majority of the reddened

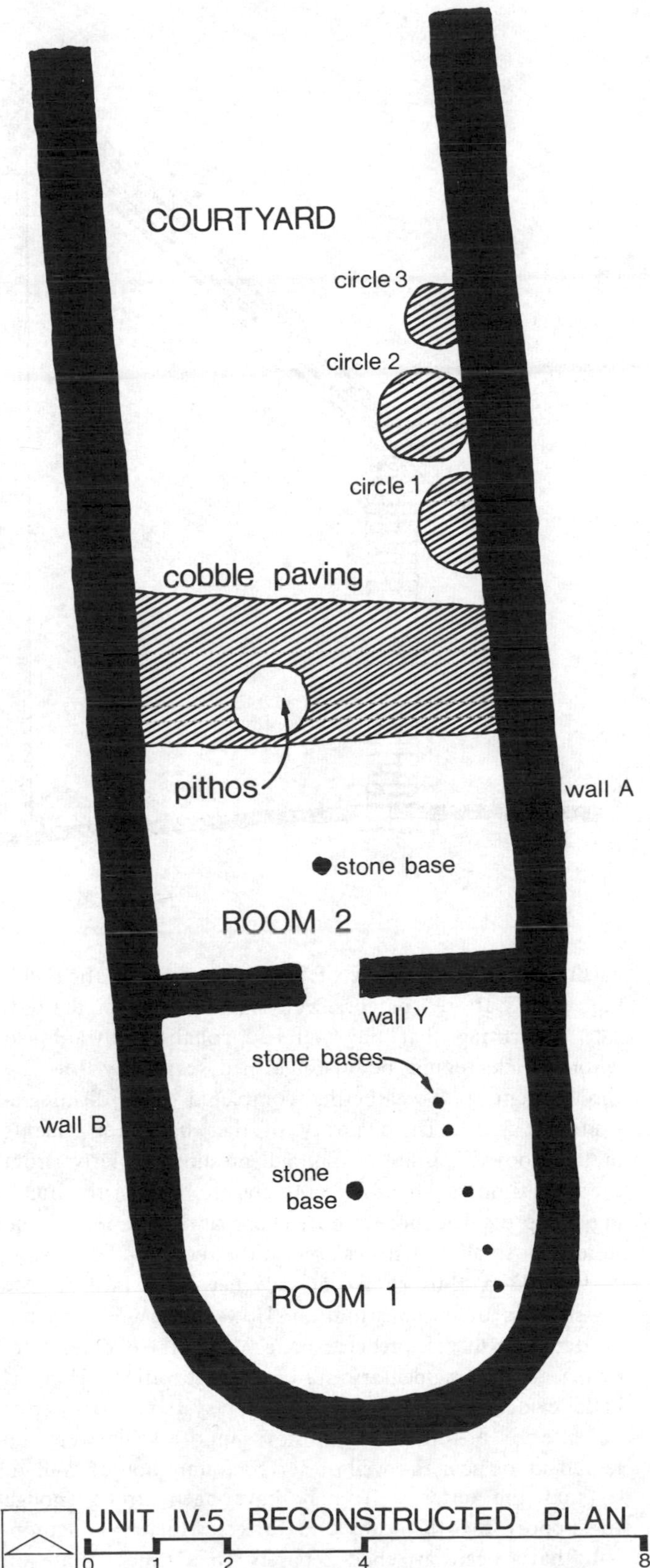

Figure 2-27

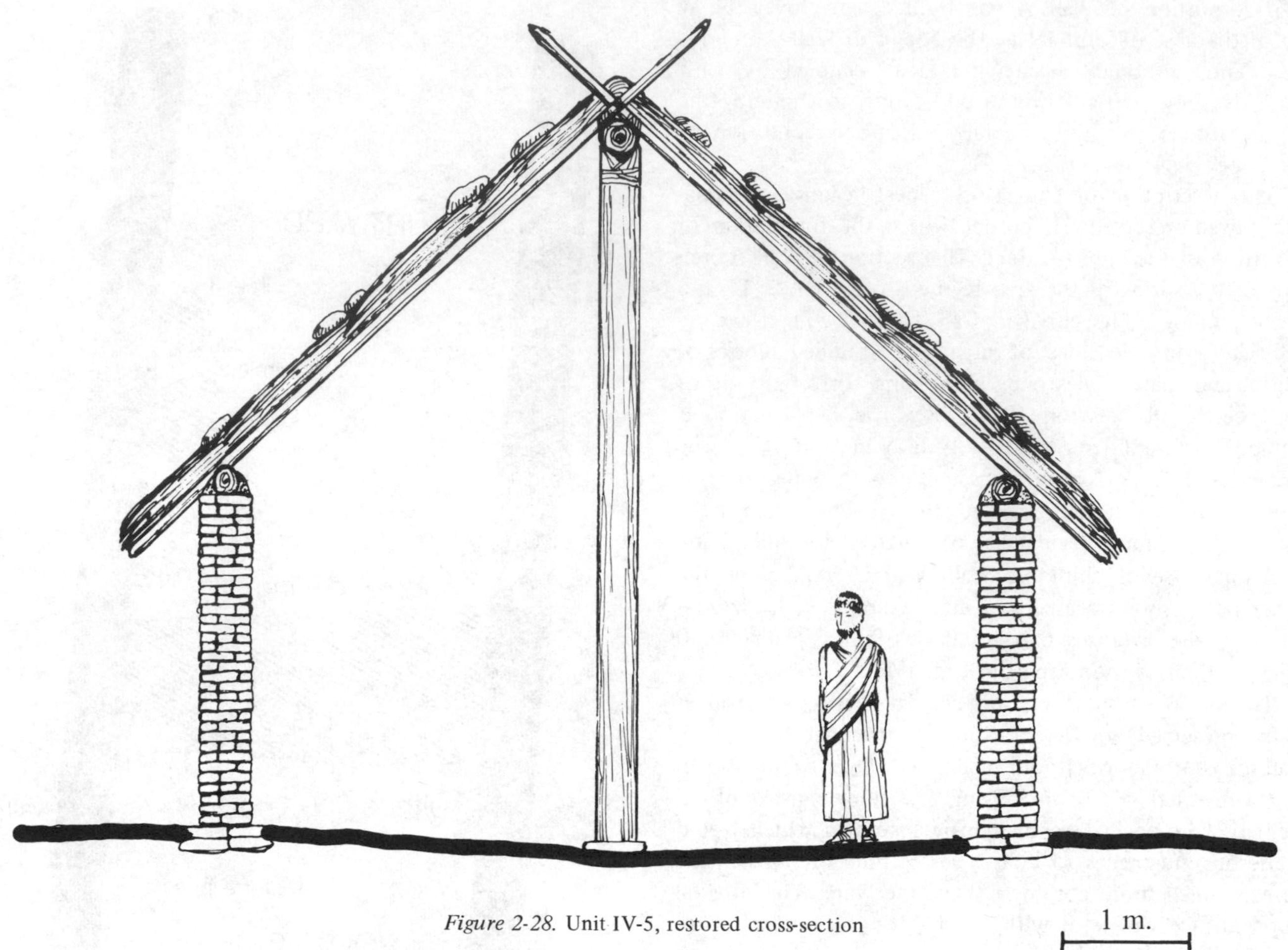

Figure 2-28. Unit IV-5, restored cross-section

earth was found to the W of Wall A, i.e., within the building; only scattered patches were encountered on the outside, indicating that the wall had collapsed inward. No whole bricks could be distinguished; evidently the fire fused them and weathering completed their disintegration (Pl. 2-59). The majority of the charcoal fragments in the floor debris are of oak and presumably derive from the roof timbers which fell onto the floor when the building collapsed. The more minute charcoal flecks could be the residue of smaller branches used in the roof.

Unit IV-5 thus shows an advance over IV-1 in the massiveness of its construction. How Unit IV-5 compared in detail with its predecessor is difficult to determine, owing to its fragmentary state of preservation. There is little evidence for the roof support system. No interior or exterior postholes or interior support walls were detected in or near the well-preserved foundation of Wall A, so that the outer walls may have been strong enough to support the tie-beams and rafters which would probably have been attached securely to a timber plate on top of the mudbrick walls (Fig. 2-28). On the other hand, although no evidence was found, a building of this size that lacked the stability of posts along the side walls would presumably need interior supports, which we have restored on the long N-S axis (Fig. 2-27). There was no scatter of stones on the preserved portion of the floor as in Unit IV-1, but it can be assumed that the roof was pitched and that thatch was regularly laid and tied down in sections.

A rather enigmatic discovery was a line of five small stones imbedded in the floor of Room 1 at intervals of approximately 0.70 m (Fig. 2-26; Pl. 2-57). The northernmost has a diameter of only 0.08 m; the other four are irregularly shaped, with an average diameter of 0.12 m. Their dimensions and oblique NNW-SSE alignment seem to rule out the possibility that they served as the bases for interior roof supports. Yet they are the only stones found imbedded in the preserved floor of the apsidal room, and their presence and relatively even spacing can hardly be accidental. They may have served as the supports for small wooden posts supporting some sort of interior canopy that divided the E side from the rest of the room, or possibly as the frame for a raised bed or shelf. The arrangement is strikingly similar to that in the main room of another large apsidal building (Unit III-3), which seems to belong to late Mycenaean times.

Room 1 is bounded on the N by cross-wall Y, which is 2.27 m in preserved length and has only one course of stones (Pl. 2-56). Its width (0.58 m) is less than that of Wall A, since it consists of smaller stones, but it still contains between 0.15 m and 0.20 m of hard-packed earth fill between the two faces and has thus been constructed in the same technique as Wall A. The floor in grid STl to the N of Wall Y consists of the same dark brown soil as was found within Room 1 and also had disintegrated mudbrick and charcoal fragments lying on it. In order to try to ascertain whether Wall Y originally extended the entire width of the building or whether it consisted of two sections separated by a doorway in the middle, a small test trench 1.0 m N-S × 1.85 m E-W was sunk below the floor level in the N end of Room 3 of the Late Roman Unit IV-2 (grid L23 Sl). The hard-packed, dark brown soil with small amorphous pieces of decayed mudbrick on its surface indicates the presence here of the undisturbed floor. Therefore, Wall Y can be identified as the E section of a cross-wall which was interrupted by a doorway in the center. It appears, then, that Wall Y is essentially preserved to its entire original length E of the doorway, with perhaps just the tip of its W end missing. The corresponding W segment of the cross-wall seems to have been totally demolished. Assuming that the length of the W section of cross-wall Y was the same as the preserved E section, the central doorway into Room 1 would be about 0.96 m wide.

There are, however, within the later Unit IV-2 several possible indications of the position of the outside W wall line of Unit IV-5 (Fig. 2-26). The first is the inner threshold to Room 2 of Unit IV-2 in grid L23 Rk. The preserved portion measures 1.78 m N-S × 0.74 m E-W and has a height of 0.32 m (two courses) at its S end and 0.115 m (one course) at the N. This threshold, in use during Phase 1 of Unit IV-2 (late 5th to early 6th centuries A.D.), consists of flat, rounded white limestone blocks of the same type as used in Wall A. It may, therefore, represent a short portion of the original W wall (B) of Unit IV-5 which was utilized in the later building. A second indication occurs outside Wall Q of the later building, in the N sector of L23 Rl, where there had been no extensive Byzantine leveling. Here there is a mass of tumbled small and large stones mixed with both fine and coarse DAIII sherds. Again, the large stones are of the rounded white limestone variety used in Wall A, and they appear to lie in a rough N × S line (Fig. 2-26). These blocks could represent a very disturbed section of Wall B, and they are in N-S alignment with the above-mentioned threshold in L23 Rk. Then, still farther N in grid L23 Rm, the DAIII level is quite close to the surface and hence badly denuded; yet several fine large blocks, two in the S of the grid and three in the N, are probably too large to have been moved far out of position. They are again in rough alignment with the two sectors farther S and could represent all that is left of the N continuation of Wall B (Fig. 2-26).

These admittedly fragile clues to the line of the W wall of Unit IV-5 do at least provide a possible basis for restoring a width of 5.50 m for Unit IV-5 (Fig. 2-27). This W wall line corresponds reasonably well with the curve of the preserved E part of the apse. Unit IV-5 would thus be considerably narrower in proportion to its length than its DAII counterpart, Unit IV-1.

The length of the DAIII building was almost certainly greater than that of its predecessor. Wall A measures some 20.20 m in length, but the nature of the N section of its foundation suggests that the entire building may not have been uniform in construction and material and, indeed, that it may not even have been roofed over its entire length. For a distance of 9.50 m from its S tip, the foundation of Wall A is carefully built, as previously described; but farther N the construction is less careful. Both large and small stones are used, and there was apparently only one original course here (Pl. 2-60). The preserved foundation increases again to two courses toward the N end, apparently to cope with the slight S-to-N downslope of the terrain. In addition to the change in Wall A toward the N, the associated floor here is less hard packed and lacked the decayed mudbrick and reddish earth. Charcoal fragments, however, continued to be found. At its N end, Wall A extends into the baulk between L23 So and To; here only a portion of its E face is visible in the scarp of the baulk which was slit (at a distance of 1.70 m from its S end) in an attempt to expose the N termination. In keeping with the careless construction of the whole N section of Wall A, its N end seems to consist of loose rubble and earth fill (Fig. 2-26). There was no evidence of a solid corner with horizontal bonding, nor for an E-W cross-wall.

It appears, then, that the N section of the building was constructed less carefully than the S section and that the two parts may have had separate functions. The S portion, which measures some 9.50 m NS × 5.50 m EW, can perhaps be considered as the main roofed part of the structure. Cross-wall Y divides it into two rooms, an apsidal room to the S and a deep vestibule (Room 2) to the N. The probability that there was a central row of supports for the ridge pole has already been mentioned. A total of two central roof supports, one in Room 1 and one in Room 2, appear in the reconstructed plan (Fig. 2-27).

The N section of Wall A with its less careful construction, irregular width, and apparent absence of mudbrick superstructure may indicate that this part of the structure was an open courtyard, some 10.70 m in length.[28] Whether or not this was a later addition, as was the case in the much smaller courtyard of Phase 2 of Unit IV-1, is impossible to determine on the present evidence. The pottery from both N and S sections appears to be uniformly of one period, although that from the courtyard is very worn and fragmentary. To add to the uncertainty, at the point where Wall A deteriorates, a modern tree pit makes it impossible to determine whether the N section simply butted on the S or whether they were bonded. Perhaps the balance of probability tilts slightly toward the view that both sections were contemporary. Whatever superstructure was borne by the N section of Wall A and its W counterpart, it would seem to have been of light materials. It need not have been more than a low fence of the type suggested for the courtyard walls of Phase 2, Unit IV-1 (Fig. 2-23). A courtyard measuring 10.70 m by 5.50 m is extraordinary and occurs in no other known building of the period. Perhaps its size should be considered as an embellishment introduced by the DAIII builders of Nichoria, and it suggests that an unusual variety and scale of activities were connected with the building.

The courtyard is divided into two sections. That to the S, adjacent to the main building, is 2.20 m in length. It appears to have been paved with small, flat cobblestones, although now destroyed on the E side and partially covered on the W side by the unexcavated baulk between grids L23 Rm and Sm (Fig. 2-26). However, a slit was made in this baulk at a distance of 1.80 m from its S side, and the cobble paving was found to extend the width of the baulk to within 0.20 m of the three large stones in the N of L23 Rm which probably represent the remains of Wall B. The paving is well preserved in the middle section on which lay the remains of a very large collapsed pithos whose diameter at mid-belly has been estimated at approximately 1.0 m. (Pl. 2-61). Fragments of other pithoi were also scattered over the cobble paving, indicating that this area was used primarily for storage. That the cobbled pavement extended only 2.20 m N of the main building is made clear by its straight N edge and by the total absence of cobbles farther N. That this section of courtyard was unroofed is made probable by the existence of the paving, plus the fact that it is bounded to the E by the irregular part of Wall A. The cobble paving, then, may represent an area of transition between the roofed building and the main courtyard.

The rest of the courtyard, 8.50 m in length, was unpaved, with a floor of hard-packed brown earth. The presence of three paved curving structures against the inner side of Wall A (Pl. 2-56) suggests that this area may also have been used primarily for storage (Figs. 2-26, 2-27). Of the three structures, only the central one (no. 2) forms a full circle; the other two are truncated by the wall. All three are paved with flat, white limestone and sandstone blocks. The southernmost structure (no. 1) is 0.50 m N of the edge of the cobble paving and has a maximum diameter of 1.50 m. A number of stones have been dislodged from its S side, but enough remain to ensure its overall shape and dimensions. Structure no. 2 is 0.24 m N of the first, with a diameter averaging 1.20 m. Its paving stones slope slightly toward the W, where a large pithos fragment was found (Pl. 2-62). A second large pithos fragment lay on its W edge. Structure no. 3, also in the form of a truncated circle, is 0.38 m N of no. 2 and is smaller than the others, with an approximate diameter of 1.10 m.

Comparable "enigmatic constructions" at Lefkandi have been interpreted as "probably foundations of olive presses or granaries, close up against the house walls" (Snodgrass 1971, p. 429). But the presence of pithos fragments in and around no. 2 and its slight slope toward the center, forming a hollow that would accommodate the base of a pithos, suggests that all three of our paved areas may have been used as stands for pithoi. Their proximity to Wall A would have protected the pithoi on the E side. Whether or not similar stands continued to the N is difficult to determine, since at this point Wall A is disturbed and then extends into the unexcavated baulk between L23 So and To. But since no evidence for additional structures was found in L23 So, it may be presumed that there were only three along the E side of the courtyard. Perhaps they were balanced by three (or more) similar stands along the opposite wall, where all traces of Unit IV-5 are lost. In addition to its function as a storage area, the courtyard would have served for the housing of animals and for various other activities for which such areas are used in modern villages.

As might be expected, the finds from Unit IV-5 are quite sparse. The only object of interest is a small bronze figurine of a quadruped (**N1723**) found in Room 1 in the protected corner formed by Wall Y and the later Wall P of Unit IV-2.

The importance of Unit IV-5 is underscored by its extraordinary length and general monumentality. Including the courtyard, it has a length of 20.20 m and a probable width of 5.50 m, although the roofed portion apparently comprised slightly less than half of this area. No other known contemporary building has a layout in which an open-air courtyard occupies more than half the unit's length. The presence of such a courtyard perhaps helps in the interpretation of the building's function. The presence of the collapsed pithos on the cobble paving, the pithos stands along the E side of the courtyard, and the large amount of coarse wares all indicate that the building served special, probably communal, functions. It is clear that Unit IV-5 is the chronological successor to IV-1, and they are located close to one another, although the orientation is different. It is likely, therefore, that Unit IV-5 had the same functions, although evidence for its sacred character is not as strong as for its predecessor. The bronze quadruped recalls the small bronze animal figures that are common to sanctuaries (e.g., Olympia and Dodona) but does not by itself prove a religious association. If the new structure contained an altar, its form and position are unknown. Perhaps it had been moved outside the building proper, to N of the supposed main entrance from the major street, where there is a magnificent view toward the bay.

The strongest argument in favor of the unit's dual private and public character must be that it obviously served as the successor to IV-1, but neither the domestic nor the religious function is as clear. On the other hand, the extensive storage capacity in and around it strengthens the impression that it may have served as a collection-distribution center for the whole village. Although we recovered no evidence to support the hypothesis, this building might have had a second story. In that case, the domestic quarters would be there, whereas the public functions of the building would be on the ground floor. It is possible, of course, that by this time the village chieftain and his family lived elsewhere.

The orientation of Unit IV-5 is also different from the EW orientation apparently preferred in DAII times. The NS orientation recalls in particular that of Arcadian buildings,[29] and the change in orientation at Nichoria in the DAIII period may have come about through Arcadian contacts. Close ties between Arcadia and Messenia are reported during the First Messenian War, when the Messenian ranks were said to have been swelled by a force of Arcadians[30] (see also the discussion on p. 326). It may be that close relations between Arcadia and Messenia had already begun before DAIII and that they culminated in the historically attested Arcadian alliance. That Unit IV-5 was destroyed by fire is made clear from the evidence of burned mudbrick and charcoal fragments within the building. Indeed, dark earth mixed with charcoal fragments characterizes the entire DAIII level in Area IV. No doubt some of the deposit represents hill-wash from the slope to the N and E of Area IV, but this only strengthens the likelihood of a widespread destruction by fire (see Table 2-9).

W END OF UNIT IV-1 (FIG. 2-11; PL. 2-16)

After the abandonment of Unit IV-1, its W end was converted into a courtyard storage area, thus continuing the original function of Room 3. The installation of two large pithoi caused great damage to the S foundations of Unit IV-1. The larger of the two pithoi (**P1336**) was placed directly in the line of Wall C (Pl. 2-16). The workmen first dug a large circular pit, roughly 1.38 m in diameter. Since the maximum diameter of the pithos is estimated to be 1.05 m, the pit was some 0.33 m wider than the pithos. They removed most of the W part of Wall C and dug through Mycenaean debris until they reached a Mycenaean flagstone paving to the N of Unit IV-6. This paving was 0.51 m below the DAII floor of Unit IV-1 and made an excellent surface on which to set the pithos. In fact, the base of the pithos was set in the ground between two flagstones and rested directly upon undisturbed soil.

Other Mycenaean structures were also utilized for support (Pl. 2-16). On the W, the pit is bounded by Wall L, which is associated with the flagstone paving, and on the S by Wall F of Unit IV-6. When the pithos was set in place, soft yellow sandy fill from the Mycenaean debris was thrown in as packing. At a point just below mid-belly, a ring of flat stones, presumably robbed from Wall C, was placed around the pithos for additional support. These stones are now preserved only on the SW side; some 0.20 m higher, at a point just above mid-belly, the pithos is completely broken. The breaks are fairly even, indicating that the upper part of the pithos projected above ground and had collapsed inward, possibly broken by tumble from the walls to the S. In fact, pithos body fragments mixed with stone tumble were found inside (Pl. 2-63). It is likely, then, that the pithos was sunk into the ground for about half its height. Its estimated original height is ca. 2.30 m.

At 0.40 m from the bottom of the pithos the fill changed to a light brown sandy consistency with no stone admixture or body fragments. This lowest fill contained the well-preserved bones of more than 200 microfauna, including dormice, mice, frogs, toads, lizards, and snakes[31] (see *Nichoria* I, pp. 75, 76). At the very bottom there were three skyphos bases and a coarse dipper (**P1312**). The dipper had probably been used to ladle liquids from the pithos. The small vertebrates, on the other hand, perhaps attracted

Table 2-10. Wall Specifications: Unit IV-5

Wall	Grid	Length	Width	Maximum Height	Maximum Number of Courses	Bond/Butt
A	L23 Tjklmno	20.20	0.70	0.28	2	. . .
Fragment of B? (reused as threshold?)	L23 Rk	1.78	0.74	0.32	2	. . .
Fragment of B?	L23 Rlm	4.75 (?)	0.65 (?)	. . .	1(?)	Possible wall line in tumble N of Unit IV-2
Y	L23 ST1	2.27	0.58	0.15	1	Butts on Wall A
Cobble paving	L23 RSm	3.50-4.35	0.17-1.08	0.11	1	. . .

by food remains or standing water, had apparently fallen into the pithos after its abandonment and been trapped there.

The second pithos (**P1337**) is smaller and less well preserved. It was placed about 1.0 m NW of the first in the line of Wall D (Pl. 2-64). It was found broken at the base and tilting slightly to the NW (Pl. 2-65). Again, while digging its pit, the DAIII workmen utilized Mycenaean foundations. On the E, the pit is bounded by Mycenaean Wall L, on the N by Mycenaean Wall K (Fig. 2-17), and on the W and S it was ringed by large flat stones which were probably robbed from Wall C (Pl. 2-66). The pit measures some 2.10 m NS × 1.08 m EW. It was filled with sterile, soft, yellow, sandy earth (Fig. 2-17). The Mycenaean flagstone paving, 0.20 m lower than that on which pithos no. 1 rests, provided support for the stemmed foot. This second pithos had been broken uniformly at mid-belly, i.e., at approximately the same level as the first. Pithos no. 2 is much smaller than its counterpart and extended only 0.60 m below ground; its total height has been calculated as 1.30 m, thus leaving some 0.70 m protruding above ground. Its interior also contained coarse body sherds mixed with flat stone fragments (the cover?), but the earth was not as tightly compressed as in the first pithos. The bottom 0.20 m contained a soft light brown fill with no stone admixture, perhaps indicating that the pithos stood empty for a time before the upper body collapsed or was smashed. No bones of microfauna were found in it.

The important small finds associated with this storage area are:

A. Trench L23 Vm, to the NE:
 N1944. Bronze pin

B. Trench L23 Vk, to the SE:
 N621. Clay whorl

C. Trench L23 Ukl, to the E and NE of the two pithoi:
 N566. Twist of gold wire
 N594. Bronze finger ring
 N601. Clay whorl
 N618. Bronze spiral ring
 N667. Iron pin, frag. of
 N686. Clay whorl, frag. of
 N1052. Clay whorl

D. Trench L23 T1, to the NW of the pithoi:
 N533. Clay whorl

W.D.E.C.

REUSE OF UNIT IV-6 FIGS. 2-10, 2-11; PL. 2-67

During the LHIIIB period the Mycenaean Unit IV-6 in grids L23 TUijk was partially destroyed by fire and subsequently abandoned. However, later inhabitants seem to have incorporated portions of its foundations in a DAIII reuse of the building (Fig. 2-11).

Following the LHIIIB destruction, human activity in the area is evidenced by a scattering of DAI sherds mixed in with the upper levels of Mycenaean material from Rooms 2 and 4 at the W end of the structure, as well as from levels outside the house to the N of Wall F. In the DAII period a deposit ca. 0.30 m thick was laid down over the top of the Mycenaean foundations that form Rooms 2 and 4. Since this was the portion of the structure that suffered the most extensive damage in the LHIIIB destruction, it would seem that the DAII activity in Unit IV-6 was not in the form of a reuse of the structure, but rather was connected in some way with the construction and use of Unit IV-1 just to the north.

DAIII material, however, was found in the upper levels of L23 Tj and Uij, i.e., over most of the Mycenaean structure. A layer of compact, gravelly, muddy sand ca. 0.25 m thick lay over the Mycenaean deposits in Room 1 at the NE corner of the structure. It contained large limestone blocks similar to those incorporated in the Mycenaean foundations along with a small number of mixed LHIII and DAIII sherds. Directly above this mixed deposit, a layer of similar material ca. 0.30 m thick, but with smaller pieces of limestone and unmixed DAIII sherds, was encountered. It is the latter stratum that should be associated with the DAIII reuse of Unit IV-6, since the lowest course of Wall β lies directly adjacent to it and immediately above the mixed LHIII and DAIII layer. A further indication of the date of Wall β is the fact that its lowest course runs directly over the foundations of Wall G which formed part of the Mycenaean structure (Pl. 2-67).

Wall β, then, seems to be associated with a modification of Unit IV-6 during the DAIII period when two large pithoi were sunk into the ground between Units IV-1 and IV-6, causing the partial destruction of walls of both structures. Excavation of the pit for the first pithos removed a portion of the N wall (Wall F) of Unit IV-6. Wall F was then replaced by Wall β which ran at a slight angle to it. As preserved, Wall β is 0.55 m wide and has a maximum height of 0.35 m in four courses at its NW end. It runs from NW to SE across Rooms 1 and 2 of the Mycenaean structure and is 4.50 m long. At its SE end it forms a butt joint with Mycenaean Wall α, and at its NW end it converges with and lies directly beside Wall F.

The extent and nature of the reuse of the Mycenaean structure in DAIII times is difficult to determine since no floor levels associated with this phase of occupation were found; nor is there any evidence for the material used to construct the upper portions of the walls.

To the south of Wall β a line of stones, a single course high, runs across Room 2 between Walls N and G of the Mycenaean structure. In the area between this line of stones and the south face of Wall β, large flat stones seem to have been placed above the tumble from the Mycenaean walls, perhaps as a level surface from which to approach the pithoi. This storage area may have been associated with the DAIII Unit IV-5 which overlies the W end of Units IV-6 and IV-1.

N.C.W.

Table 2-11. Wall Specifications: Reused Unit IV-6

Wall	Grid	Length	Average Width	Maximum Height	Maximum Number of Courses	Bond/Butt
β	TUi	4.50	0.55	0.35	4	Butts on Wall α

AREA IV SW (FIG. 2-25; PL. 2-50)

To the S of reused Unit IV-6 a fragmentary wall (M) of the DAIII period runs in a N X S direction in grid L23 Thi and slopes down to the S (Pl. 2-68). Its preserved portion is some 1.50 m in length with a maximum height of 0.15 m (one course only). It is very crudely constructed and was found in a much disturbed condition. Two rows of stones form inner and outer faces. They are quite small, with rounded edges and of white limestone. The function of the wall is unclear, although its close proximity to the S wall of Unit IV-6 perhaps suggests that it was in some way connected with that reused unit, possibily as part of an additional room.

UNIT IV-14

Farther S, Walls T and N appear to form portions of the long W wall and arc of an apsidal building, Unit IV-14 (Fig. 2-25). Like Unit IV-5, it was oriented N-S, but in this case the apse is at the N end. Wall T is preserved to a length of some 9.45 m with a maximum height of three courses (Pl. 2-69). It was not completely excavated and in some stretches only its top was exposed, but its connection with the curving Wall N is clear. Its S end continues into the unexcavated grid L23 Se, and thus the original building may have had rather monumental dimensions.

Wall T overlies Walls B and C of Mycenaean Unit IV-9. Since Wall B appears to have been reused in the DAII period, a later date is indicated for Wall T. It can be divided into three sections of varying construction and state of preservation. The first section consists of a 5.28 m stretch from the S of grid L23 Sg up to Wall C. It was carelessly constructed, like the E courtyard wall of Unit IV-5, and may have served a similar function. The W face is well preserved, but the E face is not at all clear. Also, at the S end the foundation appears to slope down to the E, indicating a slump in the terrain in that direction. The second section, measuring 2.02 m, crosses over Wall C at a point approximately 1.85 m from its N end. The third section runs between Walls C and B and measures 2.23 m in length. Only the top course was uncovered, but the inner and outer faces are clearly preserved, and the wall in this section has a width of 0.49 m. The material in Wall T consists mostly of weathered white limestone, with a few pink limestone blocks and one of caprock.

Just beyond the point where Wall T crosses over Wall B occurs the spring of the apse, represented by a small curving fragment, Wall N (Pl. 2-69). Located in grid L23 Sh, Wall N has a preserved length of 2.37 m with a maximum of two courses. It is well constructed, like the apse of Unit IV-5, and has two rows of white limestone blocks with clear inner and outer faces. The width is a uniform 0.60 m. It is fairly clear that walls T and N together form the W portion of a large apsidal building. No evidence of the material of the superstructure was found, but the width of Wall N, comparable to that of Wall A of Unit IV-5, suggests the use of mudbrick. Associated with this structure is a good group of DAIII pottery and the rim and shoulder of a bronze vessel (**N639**). DAIII pottery was also found to the W, in level 2 of grids L23 Pfg, Rfg, and Rhi, suggesting that there was a good walking surface here, to which belong a fragment of what may be a double-ax pendant (**N1893**) and the rim and neck of an oinochoe (**P1521**).

TRIAL TRENCHES

Farther S, fragmentary DAIII architectural remains were found in trenches L22-V and L22-VII. In the NE corner of L22-V there was a single light curving line of stones (Pl. 2-70), whose associated pottery, although somewhat scrappy, appears to be DAIII. This may be all that is left of the SW portion of another apsidal building, also constructed along a N X S axis.

In the SE part of trial trench L22-VII, two walls (A and B) form the corner of a room oriented in the same NW X SE direction as the other Mycenaean units in Area IV (Pl. 2-71). Built onto the preserved NW corner of this room and continuing the line of Wall B is a wall (Z) whose associated pottery dates it to the DAIII period. This N extension of Wall B consists of two irregular rows of rounded, white limestone blocks (Pl. 2-71), much like those of Wall N in grid L23 Sh. Butting on Wall A (Pl. 2-72), this extension apparently testifies to still another DAIII reuse of a Mycenaean structure.

AREA IV SE

Area IV SE produced some good DAIII pottery but little associated architecture. The debris containing these sherds represents accumulated hill-wash from higher ground to the N and E. In grid L23 Ude a single course of five large flat stones was set on a level surface. They have a NE-SW orientation and a preserved length of 2.35 m. The NW edge is straight, so it is likely that the preserved blocks represent the outer face of a DA wall (Wall A), missing its inner face (Pl. 2-73). The stones appear to be too carefully laid for a field or terrace wall and are probably all

Table 2-12. Wall Specifications: Area IV SW (DAIII)

Wall and Date	Grid	Length	Width	Maximum Height	Maximum Number of Courses	Bond/Butt
M	L23 Thi	1.50	?	0.15	1	. . .
N	L23 Sh	2.37 (1.80 on E side)	0.60	0.25	2	Rests against Wall B and may cross it
T	L23 Sfgh	9.45	0.29-0.35	0.33	3	Crosses Wall C and Wall B (?)
Section 1	L23 Sfg	5.28	0.29	0.33	3	. . .
Section 2	L23 Sh	2.02	0.35	. . .	. . .	. . .
Section 3	L23 Sh	2.23	0.49	0.33	3	. . .

that survives of some domestic structure. Associated with Wall A are a clay spindle whorl **(N1690)** and the base and lower belly of a neck-handled(?) amphora **(P1563)**. Farther S, grid L23 UVc produced an iron ring **(N1559)** and a second clay whorl **(N1534)**.

The second architectural fragment in this area is the W side of an apsidal wall (B) in grid L23 Xd (Pl. 2-74). As with Wall A, only one face is preserved, consisting of a single course of seven large flat stones, some 3.0 m in length and relatively level, with a dip of only 0.15 m to the S in the entire length. At the point of the spring of the apse (the fifth preserved block) the foundation is preserved for its total width of 0.60 m, indicating that it is the inner face of the side wall and the outer face of the apse that have been preserved. Associated with this fragmentary apsidal structure are two clay whorls **(N1553 and 1808)**, the base and lower body of a belly-handled(?) amphora **(P1564)**, and the lower profile of a round-based jug **(P1565)**. To the W of this structure, in grid L23 Wd, an interesting bronze "collar" **(N1335)**, a cup **(P1549)**, and the upper profile of a neck-handled amphora **(P1560)** were recovered. And to the SW, in grid L23 Wc, were found a fragment of what may have been a fibula **(N1620)** and a clay whorl **(N1614)**. It appears that Wall B belonged to an apsidal building that was oriented N-S, with the apse at the S end.

Although the evidence is extremely fragmentary, it appears that, except for the two reused Mycenaean structures (i.e. Unit IV-6 and Walls A and B in L22-VII), all the DAIII buildings whose segments were recovered in Area IV were apsidal and oriented along a N-S axis. Three (Unit IV-5, the apsidal wall in L22-V, and Wall B in L23 Xd) had entrances at the N, and one (Unit IV-14) had its entrance at the S. The preponderance of the apsidal shape points to this as a regular architectural feature in the DAIII period. The N-S orientation, as has already been suggested, may have been due to Arcadian influence.

W.D.E.C.

The Tsagdis Field and Area VI (Fig. 1-1)

Some DAI and DAII sherds occurred in upper levels of trial trench M23-II, and some worn DAII sherds were found in trial trenches N22-I and N22-X. In none of these cases was there any evidence of associated structures.

Area VII (Fig. 1-1)

Deposits of DA pottery mixed with Mycenaean were found in trial trenches N22-XV, XVII, and XIX. The DAII material in N22-XIX, however, occurred only in the uppermost level, which had been disturbed by the plow. The most important deposits are those from N22-XVII, on the N edge of this SE spur of the ridge. In the upper levels successive deposits of DAI and DAII sherds appeared to be associated with scant remains of wall foundations, i.e., Wall G, and Walls F and C respectively. This trench, even

Table 2-13. Wall Specifications: Area IV SE

Wall and Date	Grid	Length	Width	Maximum Height	Maximum Number of Courses
A (DAIII)	L23 Ude	2.35	0.30	0.09	1
B (DAIII)	L23 Xd	3.00	0.30	0.10 0.60 at spring of apse	1

when extended, was extremely narrow, and excavation was difficult and incomplete. The wall foundations and associated levels were above the remains of a Mycenaean terrace wall (D) which ran approximately NE to SW and was partially revealed in the W part of the trench. Wall D had only one proper face (on the NW side) and was backed against the natural stereo on the SE. It was ca. 0.60 m thick and preserved to a maximum height of 1.10 m. The area immediately outside the wall on the NW was filled with a deep deposit (down to ca. 0.10 m below the base of the wall) of dark brown earth with many stones, several of which were of large size. The top of this stratum (level 4, lots 441, 448, 452, and 472-74; and level 6, lot 471) was a little above the preserved top of Wall D. Throughout the stratum there was a mixture of DAI and LHIIIA2-B pottery. It seems reasonable to conclude that this was a deliberate deposit in the DAI period, presumably to provide a level surface for DAI structures, of which Wall G seems to have formed part.

Wall G is at a higher level and slightly N of Wall D, and on a similar alignment (Pl. 2-75). Only one course remains, ca. 0.45 m wide and 0.20 m high, preserved for about 1.0 m, apparently ending in a corner at the W end. Since the earth both beside Wall G and immediately above it contains DAI pottery, the wall is presumably to be assigned to that period. Above Wall G, but separated from it by about 0.10 m of soft dark brown earth, Walls F and C appear to form a similar corner at the W end of Wall F (Pl. 2-75). Wall F was ca. 0.50 m wide, and its one preserved course was ca. 0.30 m high. Only the outer face of Wall C remained. When Walls F and C were removed, the soft dark brown earth associated with them (level 5, lot 470) was found to contain LHIIIA2 sherds, except for two pieces that are possibly of DAI date. The stratum surrounding the walls (levels 2 and 3, lots 431, 434, 437, 440, and 457) consisted of the same soft dark brown earth and contained mainly DAII and worn LHIII sherds, with only a few DAI pieces. The stratum was ca. 0.30 m thick and extended down to the base of Wall F, immediately above the DAI stratum (levels 4 and 6). Thus, Walls F and C are presumably of DAII date, and Wall G is presumably DAI. But it should be realized that these attributions, based on so small an excavated area, are quite tentative. Of greater importance than the actual dates of the walls themselves is the clear evidence for successive DAI and DAII occupation here.

In two separate areas of trial trench N22-XV DAII sherds were found together with LHIIA material. In both cases it appears that activity in the DAII period had cut into underlying LH strata. In the NW part of the trench, in the area within the corner formed by Walls A and B (presumed to be Mycenaean), the LHIIA debris within the walls had been disturbed, probably by DAII inhabitants in search of building material. The underlying walls and a pithos (only part of whose base remained) had been badly ruined in the course of the activity. At the SE end of the trench were the remains of a small slab-built cist, presumably a grave, inserted from above into a LHIIA deposit of dumped material (*Nichoria* I, Pocket Map 4:10). The cist itself had been partially destroyed, and its sides displaced, in the course of the construction of a modern terrace wall immediately to SE. The length (ca. 0.60 m) and original height (ca. 0.30 m) could be roughly estimated, although the (presumed) cover slab and most, if not all, of the original contents were clearly missing, and no human bones were identified in its vicinity. The pottery (Level 4, lot 418) found within the confines of the base slab and the displaced, but more or less upright, slabs which had formed the sides is DAII with LHIIA, and the decorated DAII includes part of the rim of a small skyphos (**P1005**). The small size of the cist strongly suggests that it had originally contained an infant burial. Since the cist had been inserted into a LHIIA level, it is presumably either LH or DA. But the date must remain uncertain because of the extent of the modern disturbance.

R.H.S.

Summary

From the above detailed description, a reasonably clear impression can be derived about the distribution and the types of shelter constructed by the DA inhabitants of Nichoria.

In DAI times small groups of families seem to have occupied several locations scattered along the age-old traffic artery that traversed the ridge from its NW to SE end; but habitation debris is already notably concentrated in the N sector of Area IV. The only structures that can be associated with this DAI debris in Area IV are stone foundations of ruined Mycenaean houses. We therefore think it likely that flimsy superstructures of organic materials were erected over these ready-made bases that ensured stability and adequate drainage. Such reuse of earlier foundations is clearly demonstrated in the case of DAII houses. If the DAI settlers also built houses or huts "from scratch" and perhaps without stone foundations, we failed to identify such remains.

The DAII villagers were certainly more numerous and apparently more prosperous than their DAI antecedents. A good many of them continued to live in small clusters dispersed over the length of the ridge. The tiny apsidal Unit III-1 may provide an example of the typical structure that provided shelter for an ordinary family.

On the other hand, the concentration of population in the core area (IV) became more pronounced. We can document the existence of several DAII houses here, and it appears that they were somewhat more substantial than those in outlying areas. In addition to its central and more sheltered position, there is at least one further reason why Area IV may have been the preferred neighborhood. This is "where the action was," since Unit IV-1 should almost certainly be regarded as the focus of communal life. Its original construction and later remodeling reflect the people's growing ability to transcend the elemental need for simple personal shelter. The chieftain's power to conscript their labor to build his "house" may have depended in part on fear; but their need for his continued protection and the desire to honor him (or the divine force with which he was more closely associated than they) probably spurred them to take on greater architectural challenges. For it is not unreasonable to see Unit IV-1 as a modest link in form and function between the Mycenaean palace and the Archaic temple. Indeed, we view this discovery as a vindication of the belief expressed by Desborough (1972, p. 284) that "every [DA] village had its communal sanctuary" and that "there should still be something which . . . excavation will reveal in course of time."

By DAIII times the trend toward centralization in Area IV reached its culmination, and the number of villagers seems to have diminished. Almost no habitation debris of this period was recovered elsewhere on the ridge. The impression is one of a shrunken community that is tightly concentrated around its chieftain. The apparent preference in the later DAII period for apsidal ground plans and mudbrick walls on stone foundations seems now to be standard for ordinary houses. On the other hand, the tendency to lay out buildings with the long axis oriented N-S may be a DAIII innovation.

There can be no doubt that the even more monumental Unit IV-5 was planned as a worthy successor to Unit IV-1; and the ability of the little community to complete the ambitious project indicates that it was still reasonably prosperous and free from external threat. In the new building the inherited function of depot for the agricultural produce of the whole community seems actually to have intensified. It is not so clear that it also continued to be the religious center or even the residence of the chieftain and his family; but we assume that this was the case.

The increased emphasis on the storage of food in one central place, the shrinking of the village toward the center, and the strong indications that the DAIII settlement ended its life on the ridge in a conflagration suggest concern about threatened attack by outsiders who were eventually successful. This is surely a reasonable deduction, although there are, of course, other possible explanations of the archaeological data. But if we try to identify the presumed enemy, archaeological evidence fails us entirely. On the other hand, literary accounts of early Messenian history, confused and unreliable though they are (Pearson 1962), do provide an attractive connection.

Historical associations that may involve our Dark Age community will be discussed in greater detail in Chapter 6, but we can anticipate here by pointing out that both Huxley (1962, p. 31) and Coldstream (1977, p. 163) believe that Teleklos of Sparta was campaigning in Messenia in the mid-8th century B.C. Such a time frame would closely conform to the destruction and abandonment of our DAIII settlement. Another attractive historical link involves the shift in DAIII to a N-S orientation for buildings like Unit IV-5. This quite drastic change could be related to the tradition (Pausanias 4.11.1) that during the First Messenian War military assistance for the victims came from Arcadia, where N-S orientation was notably popular.

W.D.E.C.
W.A.M.

NOTES

1. For preliminary reports on this work, see McDonald (1972, pp. 251-55) and McDonald et al. (1975, pp. 85-93). Further probing and study has dictated revisions in some of those tentative statements.

2. The numbering of the various strata differs in the N-S (Fig. 2-3) and E-W (Fig. 2-4) sections through Unit IV-1. This is due to the fact that the N-S section is a complete section through Area IV NE and also includes levels from LHIIA to LHIIIB to the N of Unit IV-1, whereas the E-W section consists only of the relevant levels associated with the building, since little excavation was carried out below it. A concordance of the numbering is as follows:

	N-S section		*E-W section*	
Stratum	9	=	5	(Modern)
	8	=	4	(DAIII)
	7	=	3	(DAIII and II)
	6	=	2	(DAII/III, Phase 2, upper floor)
	6a	=	2	(DAII, Phase 1, lower floor)
	5	=	1	(LHIIIA2-B1 and DAI)

3. A good example of such a fence constructed from reeds and plastered on the exterior with mud was recently seen by the writer just outside Tod in the western Nile Delta.

4. Many of the older houses in modern Greek villages, especially in Karpofora near Nichoria, have floors pocked with holes and scattered with stones. These floors are so uneven that in some places the foundations of the walls are exposed and in others the floor surface is well above the base of the walls.

5. An argument could be made that the reason Wall D continues to the S is to delimit a second paved circle which was later destroyed by the installation of pithoi in the DAIII period. In spite of uncertainty expressed in the earlier preliminary publication (McDonald 1972, p. 253), we are now reasonably sure that the existence of a second circle should be ruled out. There is some 0.90 m of undisturbed floor between the S edge of the circle and the beginning of the disturbance caused by digging the pits for the pithoi. If there had been a second circle, one would expect to find a portion of it here, but the area is bare of stones. More important, the single preserved circle is aligned with the main E-W axis of the building, and a second circle to the S would destroy the symmetry.

6. A similar round structure at Miletus, Geometric in date, has been identified as an altar (see Kleiner 1966, p. 14 and Kleiner et al. 1967, p. 40). Three round structures (unpublished), said to be sacred, have also been found by the Swedish excavators on

Barbouna hill at Asine. An argument could be made that the Nichoria circle was used as the base for a *xoanon* and that the carbonized material found on top was from this wooden statue. But its diameter (1.60 m) is too large for a *xoanon*; the presence of charred bones immediately to the W of it would also argue for its use as an altar rather than as a statue base. Snodgrass (1971, p. 423) notes that in early temples "the central place was taken by a hearth or altar, which evidently had precedence over a cult-statue."

7. In the first published preliminary report on this building (McDonald 1972, p. 252, Fig. 9) the present writer theorized that this wall might have formed part of a partition wall. Subsequent excavation, however, showed this impression to be erroneous.

8. A similar wattle and daub system is suggested for the walls of the Geometric temple of Apollo at Eretria (see Auberson 1974, pp. 60-68, Pls. 14,15).

9. For the Argive Heraeum, see Müller 1923, pp. 52-68; Weickert 1929, pp. 65, 66; Markman 1951, pp. 259, 260; and Drerup 1969, pp. 70, 71. For Perachora, see Payne 1940, pp. 42-51. For Samos, see Buschor 1930, pp. 16-20, Fig. 6, Pl. 4; Drerup 1969, pp. 74, 75. The Danish expedition to Kalydon in 1926 recorded a modern apsidal house with a pitched roof and wattle and daub walls near the ancient city (see Clemensen 1933, pp. 146-68). The present writer has also seen and recorded modern shepherds' huts in Attica (most notably near Vrana and near the new Archaeological Museum at Marathon) and Boeotia (along the national road) with pitched roofs and wattle and daub walls.

10. The ridge pole has been equated with the *melathron* of Homer, apparently a smoke-blackened longitudinal beam that extended the length of the *megaron* and from which objects were hung (see Bagenal 1940, p. 49; cf. *Od.* 19.544).

11. Rafters are mentioned by Homer (*Il.* 23.712, 713), where the stance of two wrestlers is compared to a pair of roof rafters overlapping at the apex. This passage assumes a pitched roof and, together with the temple models, suggests a similar roof for Unit IV-1 (see Payne 1940, p. 48, Fig. 9b; also Boëthius 1919-21, pp. 161-84).

12. Thatching (*orophos*) is mentioned by Homer (*Il.* 24.450, 451) in his description of the building of Achilles' hut and is suggested for the roofing of the temple of Hera Akraia at Perachora (Payne 1940, pp. 42-51). Thatch can, of course, be of different materials and qualities. The thatch at Perachora is thought to have been of wheat straw, oat straw, or reeds. Wheat straw has been reckoned to last for about 30 years, whereas reed roofing can survive for as long as a century. Another method, although less suitable for sloping roofs and more likely to be used for the flat type, is to plaster the reeds with a coating of mud or clay and then place the protective straw above. Fragments of burned mud with reed impressions were found in Area II in association with Mycenaean houses which apparently had flat roofs. No similar fragments were found to be associated with Unit IV-1.

13. Pendlebury 1937-38, pp. 57, 58; Desborough 1952, pp. 251, 252; Drerup 1969, pp. 39, 40.

14. Boyd 1901, pp. 137-41; Desborough 1952, pp. 267, 268.

15. Hall 1914, pp. 81-85; Drerup 1969, pp. 43, 44.

16. Detailed discussion in Rhomaios 1915, pp. 225-79. See also Rhomaios 1920-21, p. 168 and 1924-25, p. 4; Drerup 1963, pp. 187-95 and 1969, pp. 14-17.

17. Theochares 1961, pp. 45, 46. Preliminary reports in Daux 1957, p. 592; 1961, p. 767; and 1962, p. 787.

18. Lamb 1931-32, pp. 41-67.

19. Similar construction is reported by Drerup (1969, Pl. 6b) in a modern hut near Teheran.

20. Field catalog no. 480.

21. This has the shape of the "conical whorls" which Iakovidis (1969-70, p. 452 and 1977, pp. 113-19) suggests may have been used as garment weights.

22. For a detailed discussion of the roofing of this building, see Auberson 1974, pp. 60-68, Pls. 14, 15. It is also discussed, but in less detail, by Bérard (1971, pp. 60, 61).

23. Field catalog no. 479.

24. Another explanation for the presence of objects along the N side is that there might have been one or more wooden shelves between the inner posts.

25. Field catalog no. 478.

26. Their identification as temples rests mainly on the fact pointed out above, i.e., that their location is on a known sacred spot on which successive temples were built. Their plan, however, and the finds from within usually provide no indication of their sacred character. If such a site were abandoned after DA times, as in the case of Nichoria, there would be no evidence for its identification as a sacred area.

27. Area IV SW was excavated by Roger Howell.

28. The courtyard has a rather abnomal length. It may well have been that Wall A doubled in use as a terrace wall. Indeed, when a long sector of the wall was first uncovered in 1971, two years before the discovery of the apse at its S end, it was identified as a terrace wall (McDonald 1972, pp. 250-52).

29. The most notable examples of N-S orientation in Arcadia are the Archaic and Classical temples of Apollo at Bassae (Kourouniotes 1910, pp. 271-332; Yalouris 1965, pp. 155-159; Cooper 1971, pp. 80-84) and one of the two small shrines in the Mt. Kotilon precinct (Kourouniotes 1903, pp. 151-88). Yalouris (1979, pp. 96-100) discusses the N-S orientation of other Arcadian temples, including the temple of Athena at Aliphera and the temple at Prasidaki near Lepreon. He attributes this orientation to the strong preservation in Arcadia of the Hyperborean cult. See also Dinsmoor 1939, pp. 115-116.

30. Pausanias 4.11.1; Coldstream 1977, p. 163. Cooper (1971, pp. 76-78) also mentions Arcadian influence in Messenia, dating to the Archaic period.

31. Because of questions regarding the identification of certain microfauna in this collection, we intend to initiate further study of it.

REFERENCES

Akurgal, E. 1961. *Die Kunst Anatoliens.* Berlin.

______. 1962. "The Early Period and the Golden Age in Ionia," *AJA* 66: 369-79.

Arvanitopoullos, A. S. 1910. "The Elliptical Temple of Athena Polias," *Praktika*: 252-56. In Greek.

______. 1911a. "The Temple of Athena at Gonnos," *Praktika*: 315-17. In Greek.

______. 1911b. "The Temple at Homolion," *Praktika*: 284-87. In Greek.

Auberson, P. 1974. "Le reconstitution du Daphnéphoréion d'Erétrie," *Die antike Kunst* 17:60-68.

Bagenal, H. 1940. In Payne 1940, pp. 49-51.

Bérard, C. 1971. "Architecture érétrienne et mythologie delphique: Le Daphnéphoréion," *Die antike Kunst* 14:60, 61.

Boehlau, J., and Schefold, K. 1940. *Larisa am Hermos* I: *Die Bauten.* Berlin.

Boëthius, C. A. 1919-21. "Mycenaean Megara and Nordic Houses," *BSA* 24:161-84.

Boyd, H. 1901. "Excavations at Kavousi, Crete, in 1900," *AJA* 5: 125-57.

Burr, D. 1933. "A Geometric House and a Proto-Attic Votive Deposit," *Hesperia* 2:542-51.

Buschor, E. 1930. "Heraion von Samos," *AM* 55:1-99.

Clemmensen, M. 1933. "Primitive hustyper i Aitolien," *Geografisk Tidskrift* 36: 146-68.

Coldstream, J. N. 1977. *Geometric Greece.* London.

Cooper, F. A. 1971. "The Temple of Apollo at Bassai." Ph.D. dissertation, University of Pennsylvania, Philadelphia.

_____. 1978. *The Temple of Apollo at Bassai: A Preliminary Study.* New York.

Coulson, W. D. E. 1975. "Area IV North." In McDonald et al. 1975, pp. 85-93.

Daux, G. 1957. "Chronique de fouilles: Iolkos," *BCH* 81:592, 593.

_____. 1961. "Chronique de fouilles: Iolkos," *BCH* 85:769-72.

_____. 1962. "Chronique de fouilles: Iolkos," *BCH* 86:785-92.

_____. 1963. "Chronique de fouilles: Mycènes," *BCH* 87:742-46.

Desborough, V. R. d'A. 1952. *Protogeometric Pottery.* Oxford.

_____. 1964. *The Last Mycenaeans and Their Successors.* Oxford.

_____. 1972. *The Greek Dark Ages.* London.

Dietz, S. 1974. "Profil af en mørk tidsalder," *Nationalmuseets arbejdsmark*: 131-42.

Dinsmoor, W. B. 1939. "Archaeology and Astronomy," *Proceedings of the American Philosophical Society* 80:115, 116.

Drerup, H. 1964. "Griechische Architektur zur Zeit Homers" *AA* 79:187-95.

———. 1969. *Griechische Baukunst in geometrischer Zeit* (= Archaeologia Homerica II, fasc. O). Göttingen.

Fiechter, E. R. 1906. In *Fürtwangler* 1906; 22, 159.

Furtwängler, A. 1906. *Aegina: Das Heiligtum der Aphaia.* Munich.

Hägg, I., and Hägg, R. 1973. *Excavations in the Barbouna Area at Asine*, fasc. 1. Uppsala.

———. 1978. *Excavations in the Barbouna Area at Asine,* fasc. 2. Uppsala.

Hall, E. H. 1914. *Excavations in Eastern Crete: Vrokastro.* Philadelphia.

Helly, B. 1973. *Gonnoi.* Amsterdam.

Hoffman, H. 1953. "Foreign Influence and Native Invention in Archaic Greek Altars," *AJA* 57:189-95.

Hood, M. S. F. 1958. "Archaeology in Greece," *AR*:3-22.

Huxley, G. L. 1962. *Early Sparta.* London.

Iakovidis, S. 1969-70. *Perati* II. Athens. In Greek.

———. 1977. "On the Use of Mycenaean 'Buttons,'" *BSA* 72: 113-19.

Keramopoullos, A. D. 1917. "The Oldest Temple of Ismenian Apollo," *Deltion* 3:66-79. In Greek.

Kleiner, G. 1966. *Alt-Milet.* Wiesbaden.

———. 1968. *Die Ruinen von Milet.* Berlin.

Kleiner, G., Hommel, P., and Müller-Wiener, W. 1967. *Panionion und Melie. 23 Erganzungschaft zum Jahrbuch des Deutschen Archäologisches Instituts.* Berlin.

Kondoleon, N. 1959. "Naxos," *Ergon:*125-29. In Greek.

———. 1961. "Naxos," *Ergon*:196-202. In Greek.

———. 1963. "Naxos," *Ergon:*149-54. In Greek.

———. 1965. "Naxos," *Ergon:*112-23. In Greek.

Kourouniotes, K. 1903. "Excavation in Kotilon," *Arch Eph:*151-88. In Greek.

———. 1910. "The Older Temple of Apollo at Bassae," *Arch Eph:* 271-332. In Greek.

———. 1930-31. "Excavations in the Telesterion at Eleusis," *Deltion* 13:17-30. In Greek.

Lamb, W. 1931-32. "Antissa," *BSA* 32:41-67.

Markman, S. D. 1951. "Building Models and the Architecture of the Geometric Period." In *Studies Presented to D. M. Robinson*, ed. G. E. Mylonas, Vol. 1, pp. 259-71. St. Louis.

McDonald, W. A. 1971. "Excavations at Nichoria in Messenia: 1969-71," *Hesperia* 41:218-73.

———. et al. 1975. "Excavations at Nichoria in Messenia: 1972-73," *Hesperia* 44:69-141.

Müller, K. 1923. "Gebaudemodelle spätgeometrischer Zeit," *AM* 48:52-68.

Müller-Wiener, W. 1967. In Kleiner et al. 1967; pp. 116-23.

Mylonas, G. E. 1961. *Eleusis and the Eleusinian Mysteries.* Princeton.

Nichoria I = Rapp and Aschenbrenner 1978.

Payne, H. 1940. *Perachora* I. Oxford.

Pearson, L. 1962. "The Pseudo-History of Messenia and its Authors," *Historia* 11:397-426.

Pendlebury, J. D. S. 1937-38. "Karphi. A City of Refuge of the Early Iron Age in Crete," *BSA* 38:57-145.

Popham, M. R., and Sackett, L. H. 1968. *Excavations at Lefkandi, Euboea.* London.

———. 1979-81. *Lefkandi I: The Iron Age Settlement and the Cemeteries.* London.

———, Toulopa, E., and Sackett, L. H. 1982. "The Hero of Lefkandi," *Antiquity* 56:169 -74.

Rapp, G., Jr., and Aschenbrenner, S. E., 1978. *Excavations at Nichoria in Southwest Greece I: Site, Environs, and Techniques.* Minneapolis.

Rhomaios, K. A. 1915. "From Prehistoric Thermon," *Deltion* 1:225-79. In Greek.

———. 1920-21. "Thermon," *Deltion* 6:118-69. In Greek.

———. 1924-25. "Thermon and Neighboring Places," *Deltion* 9: 4-7. In Greek.

———. 1933. "From the Older Temple of Phigaleia," *Arch Eph:*1-13. In Greek.

Robertson, M. 1948. "Excavations in Ithaca V," *BSA* 43:101-24.

Sinos, S. 1971. *Die vorklassischen Hausformen in der Ägäis.* Mainz am Rhein.

Snodgrass, A. M. 1971. *The Dark Age of Greece.* Edinburgh.

Theocharis, D. 1961. "Excavations at Iolkos," *Praktika:*45-54. In Greek.

Verdelis, N. 1962a. "Excavation east of the House of the Oil Merchant," *Ergon:*104-10. In Greek.

———. 1962b. "Excavations at Mycenae," *Praktika*:67-89. In Greek.

Walter, H., and Vierneisel, K. 1959. "Heraion von Samos: Die Funde der Kampagnen 1958 und 1959," *AM* 74:10-34.

Weickert, C. 1929. *Typen archaischen Architektur in Griechenland und Kleinasien.* Augsburg.

Yalouris, N. 1965. "Test Excavation at the Temple of Apollo Epikourios at Bassae," *Praktika:*155-59. In Greek.

———. 1973. "Excavation at the Temple of Apollo Epikourios in Bassae, Phigaleias," *AAA* 6, 1:39-49. In Greek.

———. 1979. "Problems Relating to the Temple of Apollo Epikourios at Bassae." In *Greece and Italy in the Classical World: Acts of the XI International Congress of Classical Archaeology*, ed. J. N. Coldstream and M. A. R. Colledge, pp. 89-104. London.

Yavis, C. 1949. *Greek Altars.* St. Louis.

3
The Pottery

by
William D. E. Coulson

Four phases of Dark Age pottery can be distinguished at Nichoria. The basis for these distinctions is primarily stratigraphic, with the majority of evidence coming from Area IV N and associated with Units IV-1 and IV-5. DAII pottery is that associated with the first building phase (see Chapter 2, pp. 19-23) of Unit IV-1, DAII/III (transitional) with the second phase, and DAIII with later Unit IV-5 and with the storage area in the upper levels of the W end of Unit IV-1. In other areas of the Nichoria ridge, such as Areas III and IV SW, where the stratigraphic distinctions are not as fine and where the transitional phase is lacking, distinctions were made partly on the architectural and stratigraphic divisions between DAII and DAIII and partly by comparisons of fabric, shape, and decoration with the clearly differentiated lots from Area IV N. Thus, in effect, the groups from Units IV-1 and IV-5 form a central body of material with which that from other areas has been compared.

The one period for which the evidence is quite sparse is DAI, owing to the lack of an identifiable stratified deposit or any architectural association. Study of the DAI material has been further hampered by a severe shortage of comparative material in Messenia or elsewhere in W Greece. The primary criterion, therefore, for distinguishing between DAI and DAII has been a physical one, with distinctions based on shapes and fabrics. Other criteria are, of course, those provided by the stratigraphy and the small amount of comparative material that does exist; but it is the physical evidence that in this case appears to be of paramount importance.

The diagnostic sherds from all phases are listed in the respective catalogs (pp. 184-259). The catalogs present detailed information on individual pieces and their stratigraphic provenience, including references to the Figure and Plate numbers of this chapter. References to comparative material, however, are not mentioned in the catalogs owing to limitations of space, but they are included in the text and in appropriate notes. For the sake of completeness, the vases discovered in the tombs in the immediate environs of the Nichoria ridge (Fig. 4-2) are included in this discussion, since they represent a body of material related to that from the settlement. In all cases, the provenience of these vases is given in the catalogs. Detailed descriptions of these graves are given in Chapter 4; here it is sufficient merely to mention that burials were found intermittently in the Nichoria environs between 1959 and 1969, culminating in an excavation by the Greek Archaeological Service under Angelos Choremis in 1969, with a publication appearing in 1973.[1]

The Nichoria DA pottery represents an extremely important body of material, since little is known about Messenia in the Dark Age (Fig. 3-1). This is partly due to the lack of finds from the period throughout Messenia and partly due to the loss of two important groups of DA material, that from Valmin's Swedish Messenia Expedition and that from Kourouniotis' excavation of the Tragana tholos. Thus, at present the Nichoria material represents the only body of vases from a settlement in Messenia and gives us a good idea of the characteristics of a local sequence of settlement pottery—hence the detailed analysis that follows.

DAI Pottery (ca. 1075-975 B.C.)

The earliest Dark Age pottery (DAI) from Nichoria is hard to identify, owing to the generally worn condition of the sherds and the lack of any identifiable stratified deposit or

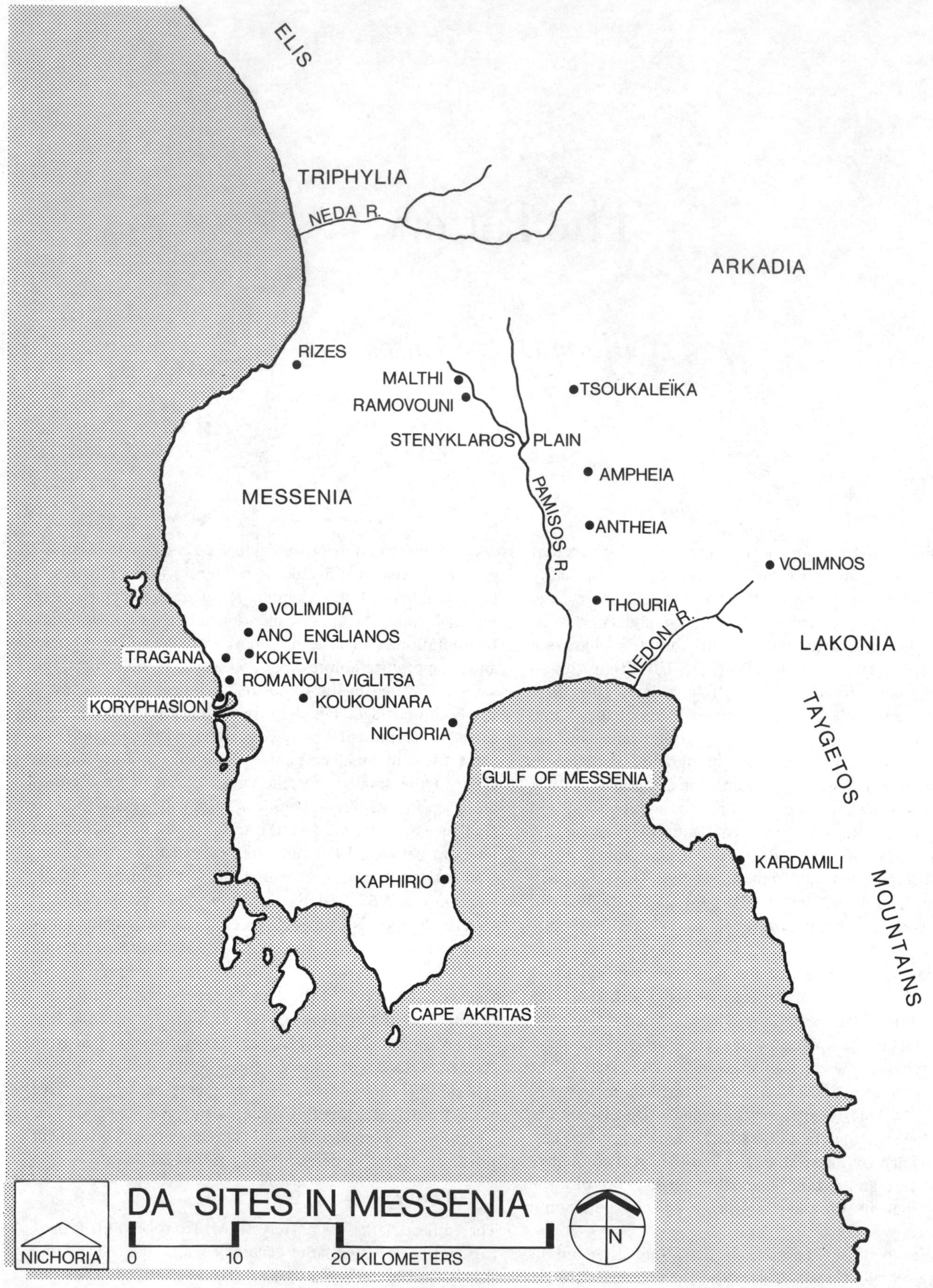
ELIS
TRIPHYLIA
NEDA R.
ARKADIA
RIZES
MALTHI
RAMOVOUNI
TSOUKALEÏKA
STENYKLAROS PLAIN
AMPHEIA
MESSENIA
PAMISOS R.
ANTHEIA
VOLIMNOS
THOURIA
VOLIMIDIA
NEDON R.
ANO ENGLIANOS
LAKONIA
TRAGANA
KOKEVI
ROMANOU-VIGLITSA
KORYPHASION
KOUKOUNARA
TAYGETOS
NICHORIA
GULF OF MESSENIA
KARDAMILI
MOUNTAINS
KAPHIRIO
CAPE AKRITAS
NICHORIA
DA SITES IN MESSENIA
0
10
20 KILOMETERS
N

Figure 3-1

any architectural association. DAI sherds are found scattered throughout the ridge, in levels that are mixed with late Mycenaean and DAII material. One group of sherds, that from level 4 of trial trench N22-XVII in Area VII, is better preserved than the rest and is associated with a wall (Wall G) that comprises the only architecture (except tombs) of the DAI period at Nichoria (see Chapter 2, pp. 56, 57). The characteristics of this group are particularly important in helping to identify other DAI sherds from the site.

Identifiable characteristics are a clay that has been fired to a dirty white color (Munsell 2.5Y 8/2 white to 10YR 8/4 very pale brown) with a rather soft and crumbly texture. In all, there are 93 examples of Munsell 2.5Y 8/2 white and 160 of 10YR 8/4 very pale brown, with six of 5Y 8/3 pale yellow, two of 7.5YR 7/4 pink, and two of 2.5YR 6/8 light red. Four pieces were misfired to 10YR 7/2 light gray. Owing to soil conditions, much of the paint has been lost (*Nichoria I,* Chapter 14), but in some cases enough is left to identify the major decorative features. The sherds themselves are quite thick, averaging 0.004-0.005 m, all with wheel ridging on the interior. Indeed, the two main characteristics of DAI sherds are the soft white texture of the fired clay and the wheel ridging, mostly on the interior but occasionally on the exterior as well.

There are only two regularly repeated types of decoration, the wavy line in a variety of shapes and sizes and the undecorated zone, both placed in the field between the handles. The paint of the wavy line and of the monochrome coating that covers the rest of the exterior and the interior (for open shapes) alternates between a washy dark reddish brown (faded) and black. The reddish brown paint is another major DAI characteristic. It occurs in DAI more frequently than in DAII and is more washy (i.e., more transparent and lighter) than in the subsequent period.

No complete vases survive from the settlement; yet there is enough evidence from profiles to be able to determine the more frequently occurring shapes of DAI. The large skyphos or deep bowl is perhaps the most common shape. It has only a slightly everted rim, high up-swung handles, and either a conical or a ringed foot. In fact, the DAI rims are all fairly straight or slightly everted; the sharply offset rims that are found in DAII do not occur in this early period. Unfortunately, there are only a few examples of cup rims and handles and krater rims. The one surprise is the occurrence of ribbed kylix stems; only one comes from the deposit in N22-XVII, but the others attributed to this phase are all of the soft white-fired clay that is so characteristic of DAI. Such stems continue into DAII, when they occur in definite stratified deposits.

Closed shapes in DAI are very poorly represented, consisting of a few oinochoe and jug rims, several "rope-handle" fragments, and a pierced amphora handle. Five whole vases, however, consisting of two skyphoi or deep bowls, a small oinochoe, an amphoriskos, and a belly-handled amphora, were found in the cemetery area. These good examples of three closed shapes usefully supplement the rather fragmentary material from the settlement.

Even more fragmentary than the closed shapes is the coarse ware, primarily because very few pieces were recognized as belonging to DAI since the lots were mixed and DAI characteristics were hard to isolate in the early stages of sorting. General characteristics of the coarse ware include straight or slightly everted rims, flat bases, rolled belly handles (probably from amphorae), ribbed and incised handle fragments, and a wall fragment with nipple decoration. Most of the coarse sherds seem to belong to amphorae that appear to represent the chief coarse ware shape.

To summarize, then, the DAI period at Nichoria is not well represented. There are only 330 cataloged pieces from the settlement. The small total of identified DAI sherds contrasts with the 828 cataloged items for the better-preserved examples for DAII, and 413 for DAIII. Although fragmentary, the DAI material is extremely important, since it represents the earliest identifiable DA material on the Nichoria ridge and possesses interesting characteristics, which are discussed below under the individual vase shapes.

OPEN SHAPES

SKYPHOI AND DEEP BOWLS (FIGS. 3-2, 3-3)

Skyphoi and their larger version, the deep bowls, form the biggest single body of vases in both the DAI and the succeeding periods. There are three broad categories of DAI skyphos and deep bowl rims which have been identified by letters A, B, C with subtypes indicated by the addition of numbers 1, 2, 3 (see Table 3-1). Type A rims (Fig. 3-2) are rather large and slightly everted, having diameters, with two notable exceptions (**P4, P5**), of 0.12 m and above. Indeed, the usual diameter of the Type A rim is over 0.15 m. Such a diameter can be considered as the dividing line between the skyphoi and the deep bowls; anything over 0.15 m may be classed as a deep bowl. Within the Type A category there are individual variations. Type A1 rims (**P2, P109**; Pl. 3-1) belong to large vases with thick sides (ca. 0.0045-0.005 m); here the tip of the rim is only slightly everted, whereas with Type A2 (**P3-5, P245**; Pl. 3-1) the rim turns outward at a much sharper angle and the sides of the vases are somewhat thinner (ca. 0.0035-0.004 m). The diameter, however, remains over 0.15 m. The two exceptions are **P4** and **P5**, whose rims turn outward at a fairly sharp angle but belong to small skyphoi with a diameter of only 0.10 m. **P5** has a slight raised band under the rim; such raised bands resemble a gentle swelling similar to the wheel ridging on the interior, but occur only below the rim. Such raised bands are to be found both on deep bowls (**P2, P11, P264**; Pls. 3-1, 3-4) and on skyphoi (**P5, P15**). On some rims, the raised band is replaced by narrow shallow incisions (**P69**, **P70**, **P239**; Pl. 3-3); and **P249** (Pl. 3-4) has a shallow incision with two flat raised bands underneath. Both raised bands and incisions are decorative features that begin in DAI and run through the whole DA sequence. Type A3 rims (**P6-12**, **P246-51**; Pls. 3-2, 3-4) are less sharply everted than A2 and have an average thickness of 0.0035 m.

Whereas the majority of the Type A rims belong to deep bowls, the Type B rims (Fig. 3-2) are about evenly divided between skyphoi and deep bowls. Again, individual characteristics run throughout the Type B category, but the common denominator is the way in which the rim turns outward from the body. In most cases, it is a gentle curve with none of the angularity exhibited throughout Type A. B1 rims belong to both skyphoi (**P13-16**, **P55**, **P56**; Pl. 3-2) and deep bowls (**P54**), whereas B2 rims (**P17**, **P18**, **P57-59**; Pl. 3-3) belong to deep bowls exclusively. There is but one exception (**P117**), which has the characteristic thickness of a deep bowl but a diameter of only 0.014 m. B3 rims contain a mixture of both elements, with the identifying feature being a rather broad and rounded top to the rim; in fact, B3 rims (**P19**, **P20**, **P62-65**, **P264**, **P266**, **P269**; Pls. 3-3, 3-4) can be considered as forming a transition to Type C. The only Type B3 rim that does not exhibit this characteristic is **P266**, which is quite worn but seems to have a rim that comes to a point at the top, with a small raised band below. Unfortunately, it is unclear to what shape this rim belongs, since it is impossible to determine its diameter. Its thickness (ca. 0.003 m) would argue for a small skyphos-type of vase.

Type C rims (Fig. 3-2) belong almost exclusively to skyphoi, with two exceptions (**P69**, **P270**) which have rim diameters of 0.20 m. The Type C category is typical of small vases with an average rim diameter of ca. 0.12-0.13 m. The common characteristic of this category is a rather thin body with an almost bulbous rim. This is especially evident in the C1 type (**P66-68**, **P270**; Pl. 3-3). When seen in profile, there seems to be a marked contrast between the rather top-heavy rim and the thin sides (ca. 0.003-0.0035 m thick). This contrast also applies to the C2 rims (**P69**, **P70**, **P272-74**; Pls. 3-3, 3-4) which have the same bulbous top. The interior of the rim, however, instead of being convex, meets the body at an oblique angle, forming a straight top to the rim. The C3 category is a rather amorphous one, consisting of rims (**P71-73**; Pl. 3-3) that are neither C1 nor C2, but which fall somewhere between the two. Table 3-1 summarizes the various idiosyncrasies of the rim types.

Type A3 rims are by far the most numerous, with a total of 74 examples. These rims belong primarily to deep bowls and have an average rim diameter of 0.15-0.16 m and an average body thickness of 0.004 m. A few examples belong to skyphoi (**P6**, **P9**; Pl. 3-2) with an average rim diameter of 0.12-0.14 m. Type B3 rims also occur frequently, with a total of 34 examples. Again, in the majority of instances, these rims belong to deep bowls with a large rim diameter of between 0.20 and 0.23 m and an average body thickness of 0.004-0.0045 m. A few rims of the B3 type, however, are quite small (**P62**, **P63**; Pl. 3-3) and belong to skyphoi with an average rim diameter of 0.12

Table 3-1. Rim Types for DAI Skyphoi and Deep Bowls

Rim Type	Number of Cataloged Examples	Average Diameter	Average Thickness of Body Below Rim
A1 (deep bowl)	3	0.20-0.22 (11)[a]	0.0045-0.005 (56)[b]
A2 (deep bowl)	14	0.16-0.18 (23)	0.004-0.0045 (70)
A3 (skyphos/ deep bowl)	74 (10 skyphoi)	0.15-0.16 (26)	0.004 (53)
B1 (skyphos)	15	0.13-0.14 (41)	0.0035-0.004 (68)
B2 (skyphos)	16	0.15 (14)	0.004 (53)
B3 (deep bowl)	29	0.23 (20)	0.004-0.0045 (70)
B3 (skyphos)	5	0.12 (5)	0.003-0.0035 (5)
C1 (skyphos)	6	0.14 (28)	0.0035-0.004 (68)
C2 (skyphos)	13	0.10-0.12 (23)	0.003-0.0035 (27)
C3 (skyphos)	5	0.13 (13)	0.003-0.0035 (27)
TOTAL	180		

[a]Numbers in parentheses denote actual number of examples, including those uncataloged, of rims with such diameter(s).

[b]Numbers in parentheses denote the total number of examples, including those uncataloged, of such body thicknesses, plus body fragments both with and without rim.

m and a body thickness of between 0.003 and 0.0035 m. The deep bowl, then, appears to be the most common open shape. Of a total of 180 rims, deep bowl rims account for 110 and those of skyphoi for only 70. Whereas the deep bowl rim is quite standard and shows relatively little variation (Types A1-A3, B3), the skyphos rims are much more varied (Types A3, B1, B2, C1-C3), and it is clearly this shape with which the potters are experimenting and which will develop more fully in the subsequent DA periods.

A total of 42 DAI skyphos and deep bowl handles were isolated on the basis of clay type and paint. These all have the same round shape, projecting diagonally from the body. The only real difference between them is their size, which becomes the criterion for their classification. Type A handles (Fig. 3-4) are all large and have a diameter of over 0.01 m. They occur in 28 examples and, on the basis of their size, can be assigned to deep bowls. Conversely, Type B handles (Fig. 3-4), of which 14 examples were isolated, have a diameter of under 0.01 m and can be assigned to the skyphoi. The fact that the Type A (deep bowl) handles are by far the more numerous supports the impression noted above of the popularity of the deep bowl shape.

Bases are less well represented than either rims or handles (see Table 3-2). It is not always possible to distinguish bases of open shapes (such as skyphoi or deep bowls) from those of closed shapes (such as oinochoai or jugs) when the interior of the base is worn and it is not possible to determine whether a monochrome coating has been applied to the interior. All DA open shapes of the three main periods appear to have had a monochrome coating on the interior. Since 40 of our bases contain traces of paint on the interior, they can be assigned with certainty to either the deep bowl or the skyphos class.

Three types of bases can be distinguished: the conical foot (Type A; Fig. 3-3), the ringed foot (Type B; Fig. 3-3), and the flat base (Type C; Fig. 3-3). The conical feet are generally small, with a diameter of 0.03 m (**P24**; Pl. 3-5), 0.035 m (**P283**), and 0.045 m (**P74**). On the basis of size, these can be assigned to skyphoi, for it is unlikely that a large deep bowl would have a small conical foot of a diameter between 0.03 and 0.035 m. There are, however, large conical feet with an average diameter of 0.055 m (**P281**, **P282**), and these probably belong to the deep bowls. Indeed, all bases with a diameter over 0.045 m probably can be assigned to deep bowls. **P281** presents an interesting feature: at the top of the conical foot on the underside is a small rectangular indentation which serves to emphasize the conical nature of the foot.

Table 3-2. Base Types for DAI Skyphoi and Deep Bowls

Base Type	Number of Examples	Average Diameter
A	22	0.03-0.045 m (15)[a] and 0.055-0.06 m (7)
B	17	0.035-0.04 m (5) and 0.06-0.08 m (12)
C	1	0.07 m (1)
TOTAL	40	

[a]Numbers in parentheses indicate actual number of bases with such a diameter.

Type B bases (Fig. 3-3) are ringed feet. Again, there are examples (**P25**, **P26**, **P79**; Pl. 3-5) with small diameters of 0.035-0.04 m. Like those of Type A, these can be assigned to skyphoi. Conversely, the large examples (**P30**, **P76**, **P78**, **P80**) with diameters ranging from 0.06 to 0.07 m probably belong to deep bowls. All have a slight hub in the center of the underside. Individual variations occur within Type B. For instance, **P30** has a rib with a small incision below on the exterior of the foot; and in **P78** the bottom of the ringed foot is not strictly horizontal (i.e., it does not lie flat on a surface) but slants diagonally toward the center of the underside, thus causing the vase to rest on the outer edges of the ringed foot. **P27** (Pl. 3-5) is an interesting example, for it is a small base (diameter 0.04 m) that is a cross between a conical and a ringed foot (a ringed conical foot), probably belonging to a skyphos.

Only one example of a flat base (Type C) was isolated (**P83**; Fig. 3-3). This type of base is more normal for closed shapes, but in the case of **P83** there appear to be fragments of black paint preserved on the interior, indicating that it belongs to an open shape. Perhaps it was a deep cup (base diameter 0.07 m), since there is no evidence for flat-based skyphoi at this early date.

Of the total of 40 DAI bases recognized, the greatest number (22) belong to Type A; of these, 15 have small diameters and probably belong to skyphoi, whereas only seven have the large diameters suitable for deep bowls. On the other hand, of the 17 Type B bases, only five have the small diameters appropriate for skyphoi, whereas 12 are the large variety appropriate for deep bowls. The general conclusion to be drawn is that conical feet (Type A) are more often found on skyphoi and that ringed bases (Type B) occur more frequently on deep bowls.

Having discussed the individual characteristics of deep bowls and skyphoi, it should be possible to put these elements together to form a more complete picture. In all, nine shapes can be distinguished among the skyphoi and deep bowls:

Shape 1: **P1**, **P167** (Fig. 3-6; Pls. 3-6, 3-7). Large deep bowls with everted rims and *bell-shaped* bodies. Rim Types A1 and A3.

Shape 2: **P235** (Fig. 3-7; Pl. 3-8). Medium-sized deep

bowl with slightly everted rim and *bell-shaped* body. Rim Type A3.

Shape 3: **P116**, **P229** (Fig. 3-7). Small skyphoi with everted rims and *bell-shaped* bodies. Rim Type B1.

Shape 4: **P101**, **P165** (Fig. 3-7; Pl. 3-9). Medium-sized deep bowls with everted rims and *ovoid* bodies. Rim Type A3.

Shape 5: **P111, P149, P171, P212, P213, P221, P230** (Fig. 3-8). Small deep bowls and skyphoi with *ovoid* bodies. Rim Types A3 and B2.

Shape 6: **P127, P222, P226, P246, P247, P263, P268, P269** (Fig. 3-9; Pl. 3-4). Small deep bowls and skyphoi with slightly everted rims and almost *straight* sides. Rim Types B2 and A3.

Shape 7: **P125, P201, P218, P223, P227, P267** (Fig. 3-10; Pls. 3-10, 3-11). Small deep bowls and skyphoi with *conical* bodies. Rim Types A2, A3, B2, and B3.

Shape 8: **P99, P1578-79** (Fig. 3-11). Skyphoi with *semiconical* body. Rim Type B1.

Shape 9: **P126** (Fig. 3-11). Skyphos with *squat* shape. Rim Type A3.

The deep bowls have exactly the shape that their name implies. They are broad and deep with large diameters and thick sides (**P1, P101, P111, P127, P167, P218, P221, P222, P235, P247, P267-69**) (for Fig. and Pl. nos. see above under shapes). They have high up-swung handles (**P154, P165, P167, P201, P218, P267**) and more often than not ringed feet. Unfortunately, no example survives complete with base, but the restored bases on **P101** and **P165** should give some idea of the total shape. **P218** is an example of a deep bowl with a restored conical foot. The skyphoi in general duplicate the shape of the deep bowls but are simply smaller in size (**P99, P116, P125, P126, P171, P212, P223, P226, P229, P230, P246, P263**). The skyphoi also have up-swung handles (**P116, P125, P171**), and, more often than not, conical feet, such as the restored example (**P223**). **P99**, however, is an example of the less frequently occurring skyphos with ringed base (here restored).

The bell shape is, of course, a direct descendant of similar LHIIIC shapes (cf. FS 285, 286; see note 5) and occurs most frequently with large and medium-sized deep bowls having the usual Type A3 deep bowl rim. The ovoid, conical, and straight shapes are variations of the bell shape using various types of rims. Owing to the lack of numerous full shapes, it is impossible to associate any one rim type (with the exception of A3) with a particular shape. Type A3 is a popular rim and is associated with all shapes, except nos. 3 and 8, where Type B1 is used. What does emerge, however, is the variety of shapes which, like the variety of rims, attests to the originality of the Nichoria potters in the DAI period.

Two complete vases (**P1578, P1579**; Fig. 3-11) of the DAI period come from the area of Tourkokivouro, just NW of the Nichoria ridge in the field of Ioannis Nikitopoulos, where a tumulus was found containing five Mycenaean built tombs and one DA apsidal cist (Fig. 4-2). Nikitopoulos no. 6, although a Mycenaean tholos tomb built in the LHIIIB period, produced two vases with striking DA characteristics. Their later date was recognized by Choremis (1973, p. 48, Pls. 18, 19), who dated them to the transitional period from LHIIIC to PG. Comparable material from the settlement can now refine his terminology and dating. **P1578** (Fig. 3-11) and its smaller version, **P1579**, present good examples of the deep bowl and skyphos shapes, respectively. **P1578** has a rim diameter of 0.15 m and therefore can be considered in the deep bowl class with a Type A1 rim, thick sides (0.0045-0.005 m), high up-swung handles, and a conical foot with a diameter of 0.05 m. **P1579** is simply a smaller version of **P1578** and has a rim diameter of 0.104 m. Both vases are similar in shape to a skyphos from Ramovouni-Dorion (Figs. 3-1, 3-11), which was found in a destruction deposit dated to the LHIIIC period,[2] and to a deep bowl from Malthi.[3] In fact, the deep shape with high up-swung handles is fairly common in late LHIIIC and Submycenaean[4] (FS 285, 286[5]), to judge from the examples from Korakou, Lefkandi, and Perati.[6] It seems, then, that the deep bowl shape which is normally associated with LHIIIC may be only slightly earlier or even contemporary with our DAI shape at Nichoria. The early DA potters at Nichoria do not simply imitate this deep bowl shape indiscriminately but experiment with variations in the smaller skyphos shape with different kinds of rims.

The deep bowl shape is also a favorite with Ithacan potters in the early Dark Age; and it is here that the closest parallels with the Nichoria vases are to be found. M20 from the Polis Cave[7] (Fig. 3-11) is a deep bowl with Type A3 rim (diameter 0.15 m) and Type B base (diameter 0.065 m) with an incision on its underside similar to that of **P1578** from Nikitopoulos no. 6. Indeed, it can be compared closely with our **P101**, **P165** (Fig. 3-7) and **P167** (Fig. 3-6). M20a[8] (Fig. 3-11) also has a Type A3 rim (diameter 0.16 m) but is broken at the lower body and its base is missing. M20b and M20c have slightly straighter rims of the B3 category and are similar in shape to **P263**, **P267**, and **P269** (Figs. 3-9, 3-10). Similarly, H12, and perhaps also H15, from the cairns of Aetos[9] have the A3 rim. Heurtley calls H12 imported LHIII, but its shape and the other vases with which it was found (H13, H15, H16-18) belong so clearly to the early Dark Age that H12 should be considered of the same period. It has been restored[10] with a flat base, but early DA is too soon for flat-based skyphoi, and more than likely it originally had a conical foot. Further parallels both to the Nichoria and to the Ithacan skyphos/deep bowl shapes are to be found in Kephallenia, specifically from Lakkithra[11] and

Mazarakata.[12] The Lakkithra examples, like the Ramovouni skyphos, are LHIIIC in date but attest to the continuing tradition of the deep bowl shape. Mazarakata nos. 68 and 77, however, are exactly parallel to M20 from the Polis Cave and to Nichoria **P101**, **P165**, **P167**, and **P1578**; hence they may be considered as belonging to the early Dark Age. It is possible, therefore, that some graves of the predominantly LHIIIC cemetery at Mazarakata are actually contemporary with our DAI.[13] The similarity in shape between the Nichoria deep bowls and, to some extent, the skyphoi and similar vases from Ithaca and Kephallenia underscores the fact that Nichoria had close ties with the Ionian islands in the early Dark Age.

The Nichoria DAI deep bowls and skyphoi exhibit a wide variety of rim types, yet they are rather conservative as far as decoration is concerned. The majority of DAI open shapes were probably slipped. The term "slip" is here taken to refer to a coating of the surface with a thin clay solution, sometimes quite different from the clay of the vase. One purpose was probably to achieve a smooth surface in order to prepare it for the painted decoration. Such a process would have been important at Nichoria, since, when fired, the clay used in the DAI period has a rather soft and porous surface. On 19 rim and body fragments, portions of a white slip have survived, and on 20 other examples fragments of a pale brown slip are preserved. Again, this total of 39 examples would probably be greater if the surfaces were in better condition. Only eight decorative motifs have been identified:

1. Solid monochrome coating (**P1, P167, P171, P201, P227, P267**; Figs. 3-6, 3-8, 3-10; Pls. 3-6, 3-7).
2. Reserved band in handle zone (**P101, P116, P125, P165, P187, P205, P221, P225, P229, P246, P247, P269, P1578**; Figs. 3-7 to 3-12; Pls. 3-4, 3-9, 3-10).

3a. Single wavy line in handle zone (**P99, P111, P126, P127, P149, P150, P152, P154-56, P176, P183, P184, P186, P194, P195, P212, P213, P218, P222, P223, P224, P226, P230, P263, P268, P280**; Figs. 3-8 to 3-12; Pls. 3-11 to 3-21).

3b. Double wavy line, probably also in handle zone (**P185**; Fig. 3-12).

4. Isolated spiral (**P235**; Fig. 3-7; Pl. 3-8).
5. Broad cross-hatching (**P193**; Fig. 3-12).
6. Piled triangles (**P50**; Pl. 3-22)
7. Accumbent concentric semi-circles (**P46, P47, P49, P106**(?), **P153, P182, P301**; Fig. 3-12; Pl. 3-22). **P106** (Fig. 3-12) could also be a spiral (cf. Motif no. 4).

All DAI open shapes have a monochrome coating on the interior. The paint on both the exterior and the interior alternates between reddish brown and black, with the former perhaps the more common. Both paints are applied in a light coating with a multiple-bristled brush. This serves to give the paint a washy and streaky appearance. Handles are completely covered in paint, and on the vases that have either a reserved band or a decorative motif in the handle zone there is a diagonal band of paint that outlines the junction between handle and body. As far as can be determined, the interior coating is the same color as that of the exterior. On 34 of the 180 DAI rims the interior paint was sufficiently well preserved to indicate a reserved band on the inside of the rim. Probably there would have been more examples of the inner reserved band had the interior decoration been in a better state of preservation. And three examples have a narrow reserved band on the exterior just under the rim.

Monochrome coating is, of course, a feature of some LHIIIC and Submycenaean deep bowls and skyphoi, for example at Athens, Lefkandi, and Perati.[14] But in these cases the paint does not have the washy character found at Nichoria. Use of reddish brown (now faded) washy paint is a common feature in Ithaca (cf. Polis M20, M20a; Fig. 3-11) and Kephallenia (cf. Mazarakata 68, 77) which reemphasizes Nichoria's connection with these Ionian islands in the DAI period. Reserved or undecorated bands are also a LHIIIC feature, but the undecorated zone tends to be a broad one, covering an area above and below the handle zone (cf. Korakou, Trench P, levels V-VI).[15] At Nichoria the undecorated band is limited strictly to the field between the handles; thus it is a rather narrow zone that is left undecorated.

The wavy line (both single and double) at Nichoria is perhaps the single most common motif and occurs in a variety of shapes and sizes: thick (**P111, P154, P222, P268, P280**), thin (**P149, P212, P213, P226**), broad (**P99, P150, P218**), angular with sharp points like a wolf's tooth (**P183, P263**), angular with rounded points (**P126**), and double (**P185**). The thick and broad types are usual for LHIIIC,[16] but the Nichoria potters have added further variations to a common theme, as it were. At Ithaca, such wavy lines do not occur on the deep bowls but are limited to the deep cups (cf. Polis M46, M49; Fig. 3-13), so the Nichoria variations can be considered a local phenomenon. A vase from one (unspecified) of the seven tholoi excavated by Marinatos (1964, p. 164) at Koukounara[17] parallels in clay type and shape **P101**, **P165** (Fig. 3-7), and **P218** (Fig. 3-10; Pl. 3-11), and it recalls **P218** in decoration, with a wavy line in faded brown paint in the handle zone. Its presence thus indicates that a late burial or sacrifice in one of the Koukounara tombs was contemporary with our DAI.

The isolated spiral is, of course, a true LHIIIC motif[18] and occurs in only one sure example at Nichoria (**P235**; Fig. 3-7; Pl. 3-8), where it is linked above to thin black bands.[19] Such spirals, although here not linked to bands above, are to be found on the Ramovouni skyphos and on both skyphoi and kraters from Lakkithra, all definitely LHIIIC in date. The presence of such decoration at Nichoria, albeit only in one example, again argues for the presence of the LHIIIC tradition at the site. The motif of piled triangles without hatching (**P50**; Pl. 3-22) is also a LHIIIC feature.[20] It occurs at Ithaca (cf. Polis M66; Fig. 3-13) and at Nichoria in DAI.

The fragment of a zone of broad cross-hatching (**P193**; Fig. 3-12) was found in a good DAI group from K24 Wy/K25 Wa in Area III. Such cross-hatching is, of course, common both at Aetos and at Polis[21] in the early Dark Age, but there it is not so broad and the lines are placed closer together. The Nichoria example, beginning as it does from the rim, is more reminiscent of the material from Amyclae and Sparta.[22] This Laconian material presents striking parallels with Nichoria in the subsequent DAII period, and thus **P193** may possibly be considered a transitional piece marking the end of DAI and the beginnning of DAII at Nichoria.

Accumbent concentric semi-circles, which occur regularly in DAII (**P46, P49, P106**?; Fig. 3-12; Pl. 3-22), may also be a transitional feature. They do occur occasionally in Ithaca (cf. Polis M24, Aetos H54), but it is the pendent semi-circles painted with broad strokes and the pendent loops that the Ithacan potters prefer (cf. Polis T2, Aetos H13, H16, H17). Thus, the heavy use of thin-stroked accumbent semi-circles as a decorative motif may be considered a Messenian trait, beginning in DAI but developing fully in DAII. **P182** (Fig. 3-12) has fragmentary concentric semi-circles in a metopal panel; again, this represents a foreshadowing of a type of decoration that will achieve full popularity in the DAII period. What difference there is lies in the verticals of the triglyph which are much thicker here than in later DAII examples.

Owing to the fragmentary nature of the DAI material, it is not possible to determine with certainty whether one type of decorative motif is used more commonly with one class of vase or another. From the evidence at hand, it would seem that the wavy line and isolated spiral are motifs especially associated with deep bowls, i.e., with vases having the Type A1, A2, and B3 rims (cf. **P111, P218, P226, P235, P268**). Also, the solid monochrome coating seems to occur most frequently on the skyphoi (cf. **P171, P227**), whereas the reserved band in the handle zone can occur with either type of vase. Of course, there are exceptions, such as **P1** and **P167** which are monochrome coated deep bowls and **P99** which is a skyphos with a wavy line in the handle zone; but the general associations just noted seem to be valid.

CUPS (FIGS. 3-3, 3-13)

Cups are very poorly represented at Nichoria in the DAI period. There are only two certain examples (**P22, P23**; Fig. 3-3) of the cup rim with attached handle (or handle fragment) and two individual handles (**P38, P290**). The rims are quite straight and the handles rather narrow with an average width of 0.01 m. What survives of the profile suggests a deep cup of the Ithacan type found at Polis (M46, M49; Fig. 3-13). rather than a squat cup with S-shaped profile like those found at Rizes[23] and Aetos.[24] Squat cups are a later development at Nichoria and belong to the DAII period. All the deep cups from Polis (except for M49 whose base is missing)[25] have ringed bases whose diameter varies from 0.04 to 0.05 m. It is likely that some of the small ringed feet (Type B) with a diameter of 0.04 m, hitherto assigned to skyphoi, might also belong to deep cups.

KRATERS (FIGS. 3-3, 3-4, 3-12)

Kraters are only slightly better represented than cups at Nichoria. Two rims (**P148, P279**; Fig. 3-3) can definitely be isolated as belonging to DAI; both have flat tops slanting inward and large diameters of 0.22 m (**P148**) and 0.30 m (**P279**). **P83** (Fig. 3-3), listed under Type C of skyphos/deep bowl bases, may in fact belong to a small krater. It is like the base of the krater from Ramovouni-Dorion, but smaller. There is, however, no evidence to associate it with the two krater rims. Two pedestal bases were also found (**P84, P208**; Fig. 3-4), but they are of a different clay color from the rims and thus cannot be linked with them. Yet, from the evidence of these few rims and bases, it seems likely that Nichoria DAI kraters had shapes similar to the Ramovouni krater and to the LHIIIC stemmed kraters from Grave A at Lakkithra,[26] with deep bodies similar to those of the deep bowls and skyphos-type handles. **P84** (Fig. 3-4) is a squat pedestal base similar to the Lakkithra examples in size and exterior shape but not in the underside of the foot. The Lakkithra kraters have almost flat bases, whereas **P84** has a high ringed foot like some of the later Geometric Ithacan kraters.[27] **P208** (Fig. 3-4), on the other hand, is a tall pedestal base, like a kylix stem but shorter. It has the same height as the pedestal of the stemmed skyphos from Derveni[28] but not the high conical foot on the underside; indeed, the Nichoria example has an almost flat foot.

Two decorated krater fragments (**P215, P330**; Fig. 3-12; Pl. 3-23) also belong to DAI. **P215** (Fig. 3-12) has in light brown paint the motif of a pair of vertical wavy lines flanked by vertical bands with a wavy line below. This is another example of a LHIIIC motif[29] in our DAI repertory, as is that of the piled triangles of **P330** (cf. also **P50**). The slight evidence presented by the Nichoria krater fragments, like that of the deep bowls and skyphoi, suggests that there is a strong LHIIIC tradition, but with considerable experimentation seen here in the unorthodox shapes of the pedestal bases.

ZOÖMORPHIC HANDLES (FIG. 3-4; Pl. 3-24)

Three fragments of zoömorphic handles (**P37, P89, P90**) were found in DAI contexts. All are fragmentary and include two horned projections that rise from the top side of the handles. The handles project straight out from the rim (**P37** is broken at the rim), and the projections occur at the point where the handle begins to turn down toward the body. **P37** preserves the rim and is broken just after the horns; conversely, the lower portions of **P89** and **P90** are preserved and are broken just beyond the horns where the handle turns in an angle toward the rim. **P89** has an interesting feature of five incisions running crosswise along the top side of the handle near the horns. Two incisions flank the horns themselves; and three others, consisting of one deep incision symmetrically flanked by two shallower ones, occur lower down the handle. **P37** has fragments of black paint preserved on top only; **P90** has traces of light brown paint all over; and on **P89** no paint is preserved.

Such horned projections recall those on the high-looped handles of angular shallow cups of Villanovan I from Tarquinia.[30] More specifically, however, similar features occur on the handles of handmade (our examples appear to be wheel-made) bowls and jugs with cutaway neck from the extensive tumulus cemetery at Vergina.[31] The bowl (almost a deep cup) numbered III Π 103 (Petsas 1961-62, Pl. 103) has a projection on the lower part of its handle exactly parallel in position to that of **P37**. The other examples (see note 31) are more like sharp angles or ribs that project outward as the handle turns toward the body. The Nichoria examples **(P89, P90)** are more pronounced but occur in the same position. Owing to their fragmentary nature, it is impossible to determine on what types of vases our handles appeared, whether on bowls or jugs with cutaway necks, as in the Vergina material, or on some other type of open or closed vase.

RIBBED STEMS (FIGS. 3-4, 3-5)

A total of 27 ribbed kylix stems belong to the DAI period. Of these, the two best preserved come from level 4 of N22-XVII **(P327)** and level 5 of L23-V **(P238**; Fig. 3-5). Eight different types can be distinguished:

Type A **(P304, P305**; Fig. 3-4; Pl. 3-25): Tall stems with height of ca. 0.06 m. The ribs are in the nature of gentle swellings of the stem. **P304** has one long swelling occupying the entire length of the stem; **P305** has perhaps two swellings. The base of both is in the form of a ringed disk foot which does not stand flat upon the surface but is balanced only on the outer edges of the disk and slopes up toward the center of the underside. The diameter of the disk foot reaches 0.05 m. White clay.

Type B **(P306-9**; Fig. 3-4; Pls. 3-26, 3-27): Tall stems with height of 0.06 m. **P306** has one rib placed at the top of the stem near the junction with the lower body; the rib has a rounded point that turns *upward.* **P307** also has one rib, but it is placed slightly lower than that of **P306.** These stems have conical feet with a diameter of ca. 0.045 m. White clay.

Type C **(P310-15**; Fig. 3-4; Pls. 3-28, 3-29): Shorter (0.05 m) than Types A or B. Small, rounded, symmetrical (i.e., does not point either upward or downward) rib placed near top of stem. Semi-conical foot with diameter of 0.05 m. White clay.

Type D1 **(P316, P317**; Figs. 3-4, 3-5; Pl. 3-30): Very small stems with total height of only 0.03-0.35 m and width of 0.15 m. Rib again placed near top of stem; rib is rounded (almost bulbous) and points *upward.* Small conical foot with diameter of 0.025 m. White clay.

Type D2 **(P318-21**; Fig. 3-5; Pl. 3-31): Small stems like Type D1, but with more than one rib pointing *downward.* No evidence for type of base, but perhaps small feet similar to Type D1. White clay.

Type E **(P322-26**; Fig. 3-5; Pls. 3-32, 3-33) Very small stems with total height of 0.04 m, but broad and flat in shape with a width of 0.025 m. Ribs consist of three gentle swellings, one of which is placed extremely high at the point where the body joins the base. High conical foot with diameter of 0.045 m. White clay.

Type F **(P327, P328**; Fig. 3-5, Pl. 3-34) Tall stems with height of 0.06 m. **P327** has one sharply pointed rib placed in the center of the stem; the rib points straight out without turning up or down. **P328** has two ribs that also point straight out in the center of the stem. High conical foot with diameter of 0.05 m. White and reddish yellow clay.

Type G **(P329**; Fig. 3-5; Pl. 3-35): Ribbed pedestal krater stem with height of 0.045 m and width of 0.03 m (i.e., fairly tall and broad). One rib, placed in the middle of the stem, extends outward horizontally, as in Type F above. Very high conical foot with diameter of ca. 0.05 m. White clay.

Types A, B, and F are tall stems with different types of ribs and feet. Types C-E, on the other hand, are small stems. The type of rib is perhaps the single most distinguishing feature. In Types A and E the ribs consist of simple swellings in the stem; the rib points upward in Types B and D1, downward in D2, and horizontally in C, F, and G. The positioning of the rib is also important. In Types F and G the rib is placed in the middle of the stem, whereas in Types B, C, and D1 it is placed near the top of the stem. Types D2 and E show a further variation with multiple ribs. An interesting feature occurs in Type E, where the rib is placed higher than the stem at the point where the body of the vase begins to flare outward, thus serving to emphasize the point where the stem joins the body. All have some form of conical foot, high, medium, or shallow, except for Type A which has a form of ringed foot.

Type A with the gentle swelling of the stem represents the more usual type of LHIIIC kylix. Examples occur at Malthi,[32] at Lakkithra[33] and Metaxata[34] in Kephallenia, and at Teichos Dymaion[35] and Lefkandi.[36] At Lakkithra, there are also examples of Types C and F.[37] The occurrence of these types at Nichoria again underscores the continuing LHIIIC tradition at the site. Such a tradition was also retained by the Ithacan potters. Indeed, Benton (1949, pp. 308-12) theorized that the ribbed stems from Aetos and Polis might belong to the early Dark Age. Polis M59 belongs to Nichoria Type A, and M60 to Type C. In the latter example the rib occurs at the bottom, whereas at Nichoria it is placed at the top of the stem. M62-65[38] (M65; Fig. 3-14) are from 0.01-0.02 m taller than the Nichoria examples but otherwise have the pointed ribs common to Type F.[39] M62-64 (M63; Fig. 3-13) have two ribs, with a third added at the point of junction between stem and body (i.e., the same principle that is applied in Nichoria Type E). M65 (Fig. 3-14) has three sharp ribs, as do three examples from Olympia,[40] and perhaps also one stem from Astakos in Aetolia.[41] These have the same sharp ribs of Type F but are slightly taller and show the addition of a third rib. M66 (Fig. 3-13) belongs to Type C, as do H4, H6, and H7 from Aetos,[42] and perhaps also a number of stems from Malthi.[43] Recently, additional parallels to the Ithaca stems have been found at Hexalophos in western Thessaly. Four ribbed kylikes were found in two cist tombs, two in Grave A and two in Grave B.[44] One from Grave A has a stem belonging to Type A (cf. Polis M59), and the stem of the other parallels that of Polis M60 (i.e., with a rib set low on the stem, almost at the bottom). The two kylikes from Grave B have what appear to be Type F stems, but the ribs do not have such sharp points as do the Nichoria and Ithaca examples.

Such detailed similarities indicate that Nichoria had a shared tradition with the rest of western Greece in the DAI period. What seems to emerge is the continuation of a common style that incorporates the LHIIIC tradition. This common style stretches from Messenia in the south through Olympia, the Ionian islands, and Aetolia (Astakos), and may even reach as far north as Epirus.[45] It is unfortunate that the Nichoria examples survive only as stems without evidence as to the kylix body. The Ithaca kylikes have straight rims, with the body beginning to turn inward immediately below the rim. The closest parallels at Nichoria are the B1 type rims (**P229**; also **P13, P14, P55, P56**; Fig. 3-2), and it may well be that some of them belong to DA kylikes. Similarly, Polis M66 (Fig. 3-13), one of the very few kylikes from Ithaca with decoration (the others, except T1, have a monochrome coating), has the motif of piled triangles. A similar motif is to be found on our **P50**, which could belong to a kylix.

The Nichoria potters, then, were in contact with this western Greek tradition. Type A, C, and F stems belong to this tradition and are found at Nichoria and elsewhere in western Greece. But Nichoria has also produced stems (Types B, D1, D2, E, and G) that as yet have not been found elsewhere; and, until contrary evidence turns up, they can be considered as local variations. Other local variations have already been seen in the numerous skyphos and deep bowl rims from Nichoria. Those in the ribbed stems may further attest to the originality of the Nichoria potters.

CLOSED SHAPES

OINOCHOAI AND JUGS (FIGS. 3-5, 3-14)

Oinochoai[46] and jugs are very poorly represented in the DAI material, and with small rim fragments it is not always possible to differentiate those belonging to oinochoai from those of jugs. Two different types of fairly angular rims occur; and, owing to their shape and size, they probably come from jugs. Type A (cf. **P39**; Fig. 3-5), represented by two examples, is a large rim with a slightly convex top and a small flute on the interior at the top of the rim. Type B (cf. **P91**; Fig. 3-5), also represented by two examples, is an angular rim with a flat top and a probable diameter of 0.075 m. The size of these rims indicates that they are from large jugs; but, unfortunately, their fragmentary nature does not indicate whether these jugs had cutaway necks.

Two definite oinochoe rims are also represented. **P303** (Fig. 3-5) is a decorated rim fragment with a black band at the rim and vertical stripes on the neck. The rim is fairly straight in profile and has a probable diameter of 0.05 m, indicating that it belonged to a small oinochoe of about the same size as **P1580** (Fig. 3-14). The latter piece is the only whole oinochoe from the DAI period at Nichoria. It was found, with **P1581** (Fig. 3-15), above two apsidal cist tombs (Tsagdis 1 and 2) some 300 m N of the Nikitopoulos tumulus (Fig. 4-2).[47] Both vases were disturbed by the plow but can be considered as belonging to these tombs, thus dating them to DAI. **P1580** has a gentle everted rim, very similar to **P16** (typed as skyphos B1), and it may well be that **P16** really belongs to a small oinochoe (Fig. 3-2).

Miscellaneous bases and handles can also be associated with the oinochoe-jug class, but here it is virtually impossible to distinguish oinochoai from jugs. Type B1 examples (cf. **P95**; Fig. 3-5) are almost flat elliptical handles that range in width from 0.009 m (**P1580**) to 0.022 m. The smaller ones (with width of 0.009-0.012 m) probably belong to small oinochoai such as **P1580** (Fig. 3-14). Those of medium size (width ca. 0.018-0.02 m) more than likely belong to average-sized oinochoai or jugs. And those having the greatest width (ca. 0.022 m and over) should belong to large oinochoai or jugs, or possibly even to neck-handled amphorae. Type B2 handles (cf. **P292**; Fig. 3-5), of which there are a total of four examples, have a flute down the center of the top and are all large, with an average width of 0.022 m. Again, these can be considered as belonging either to large oinochoai or jugs or to neck-handled amphorae. One example of a rope handle (**P94**; Pl. 3-36) certainly belongs to DAI. This is a fairly large fragment (diameter ca. 0.022 m) with loose twists to the rope, as opposed to the tighter twists found on rope handles of the subsequent DAII period. Its size again indicates a large oinochoe or neck-handled amphora.

Bases are in an even more fragmentary condition. **P1580** (Fig. 3-14) has a small ringed base (diameter 0.036 m), and it may well be that one or two of the small ringed bases typed above in category B of skyphoi actually belonged to small oinochoai. One flat base (**P93**; Fig. 3-5) of Type B closed bases has such a small diameter (0.046 m) that it too probably belonged to a small oinochoe or jug.

This fragmentary evidence from Nichoria indicates that small oinochoai or jugs had either straight or gently everted rims, flat to elliptical handles, and either ringed or flat bases. Those of medium size may have had the same features, although the evidence here is quite sparse. Those of large size had angular rims and elliptical, fluted, or rope handles (no evidence for bases), with the *caveat* that such large handles could also belong to neck-handled amphorae. **P1580** has a squat globular body shaped like the late LHIIIC jugs from Burial α in the tholos at Tragana.[48] Such a shape in DAI, then, is developed from LHIIIC jugs and false-necked jars[49] and is a forerunner of the small oinochoai found in the Lambropoulos tholos of the DAII period and the jugs from Halos in Thessaly.[50] The oinochoe does, of course, occur in LHIIIC (cf. FS 137), and rope handles are found among the Mycenaean pottery from Polis (M8a, b, d). In shape, then, the Nichoria oinochoai and jugs belong to the LHIIIC tradition, but in decoration the Nichoria potters exhibit their own idiosyncrasies. The narrow reserved band on the exterior, as seen on the skyphoi and deep bowls, seems to be a Nichoria (and also Messenian?) feature. Such a feature occurs just above mid-belly on **P1580** (Fig. 3-14). But other motifs, such as paint on the interior of the neck (**P1580, P1598**; Fig. 3-14), vertical stripes on neck (**P303**; Fig. 3-5), black bands at mid-belly (**P210**), and piled triangles on the shoulder (**P233**; Pl. 3-19) emphasize the potters' participation in the shared tradition throughout SW Greece. **P210** also has a mending hole.

AMPHORAE (FIGS. 3-5, 3-14, 3-15)

Again, few identifiable amphora fragments come from the settlement. Type A closed handles, of which there are three examples, are large rolled neck-handles. **P96** (Fig. 3-5), with a diameter of 0.0285 m, is perhaps the best preserved; and **P45** (diameter 0.022 m) is pierced (Pl. 3-36). Two types of flat bases can be associated with these neck-handled amphora fragments. Type A (two examples) is represented by **P40** (diameter 0.14 m; Fig. 3-5); in this type the exterior of the base is concave. Type B (two examples) is represented by **P41** (diameter 0.10 m; Fig. 3-5); here the exterior of the base is straight. Both types have large diameters and thus are more suited for large amphorae than for any other type of vase. A large belly-handled amphora (**P1581**; Fig. 3-15), found with **P1580** above Tsagdis 1 and 2 graves (Fig. 4-2), shows the ovoid body and Type A base of DAI amphorae. This shape is similar to forms from late LHIIIC.[51] The closest Messenian parallel comes from Ramovouni-Dorion. It has the same ovoid body and Type A base, but a straighter rim and the addition of a neck-handle. Both amphorae also have similar decorative motifs. That from Ramovouni-Dorion is dark-ground, with a wavy line flanked by a pair of thin black bands in the field just above the handle zone at mid-belly, and with coating on the interior of the neck. **P1581** is also dark-ground, with a black band flanked by two wavy lines in the handle zone and a narrow reserved band on the shoulder, with no coating on the interior of the neck. The decoration of **P161** (from the settlement; Fig. 3-14; Pl. 3-37) with a wavy line flanked by single and reserved bands echoes that from Ramovouni. The DAI amphorae from Nichoria, then, are either neck- or belly-handled, or perhaps a combination of both (hydria) as in the Ramovouni example, with the main decorative motif consisting of a wavy line in the belly-handle zone. The narrow reserved band, so favored by Nichoria potters, appears on the shoulder.

A small amphoriskos (**P1598**; Fig. 3-14) was found in the area of Lakkoules in the field of Christos Lambropoulos near the later DAII tholos and perhaps comes from one of the four cist graves found in the area (Fig. 4-3). A ribbed stem (**P1599**; Fig. 3-5) also comes from the same field. Both finds indicate the presence of DAI burials in the area. The amphoriskos parallels its larger companion (**P1581**; Fig. 3-15) in ancestry,[52] shape, and decoration but has a semi-conical foot and coating on the interior of the neck. The closest parallels to the Nichoria amphorae outside Messenia come from four pit graves at ancient Elis under the theater parodos.[53] Those from Graves 4 and 5 are more globular in shape than the Nichoria examples and can be related to the Ramovouni amphora; that from Grave 2, however, with rope neck-handles, has a more ovoid body similar to that of **P1581**.

COARSE WARE (FIG. 3-6; PL. 3-38)

Coarse handmade vases are the least well represented of all ceramic groups in DAI, mainly because their features are hard to distinguish from those of preceding or succeeding periods. One rim (**P181**), one base (**P97**), and a few miscellaneous handle fragments (**P98, P162, P163**) can be identified since they are associated with fairly good DAI groups. The rim is slightly everted, and the base is flat (like Type B of closed shapes); both fragments probably belong to coarse amphorae having the same general shape as the wheel-made examples. It is likely that the handles also belong to amphorae. Type A is a round belly-handle; Types B1 and B2 are ribbed and incised (three incisions along top) neck-handles. An interesting wall fragment (**P164**; Pl. 3-38) has a pointed nipple that projects straight out from the body of the vase.[54] Such nipples are found at Vergina[55] and also at Elaphotopos in Epirus.[56] The latter, occurring on the belly of a cup, is an especially good example and suggests a similar position for **P164**.

OVERVIEW

The DAI period, then, at Nichoria—and perhaps also in Messenia generally—is a period of considerable activity. Reuse is possible in one tholos at Koukounara and certain at Nikitopoulos tholos no. 6. Nikitopoulos no. 1 and Tsagdis nos. 1 and 2 are definite DAI cist graves, and there were additional cists near the DAII tholos in the area of Lakkoules. The Nichoria potters owed much in the shape and decoration of their vases to the LHIIIC repertory; but there is also considerable experimentation, as seen in the varied skyphos and deep bowl rims and shapes, the development of the skyphos shape and of the ribbed stem, and in the use of the narrow reserved band as a decorative motif. As has already been suggested, such a variety of local features may indicate a broad chronological range.

DAII Pottery (ca. 975-850 B.C.)

DAII is perhaps the most important phase of the Early Iron Age at Nichoria, containing the largest number (828) of inventoried pieces. Varying amounts of occupational debris occur in every excavated area of the ridge, except for Area I. The most important DA tomb, the small tholos in the area of Lakkoules (Fig. 4-2), also belongs to the same period. The best stratified pottery comes from within Unit IV-1, and the best decorated sherds were found in a dump just N of Unit IV-5.

DAII sherds are relatively easy to identify. The most consistent diagnostic feature is a clay that has been fired to a reddish yellow color which varies from Munsell 5YR 7/6 to 5YR 7/8.[57] Even though reddish yellow is the most consistent color, there are examples of other colors, probably achieved through unintentional misfiring (see Table 3-3). Munsell 2.5Y 8/2 (white) and 10YR 8/4 (very pale brown) were achieved in DAI, and the continuation into DAII of such clay colors indicates that some of the same clay beds were used in the later period. The greater number of reddish yellow sherds, however, perhaps indicates that new beds of calcareous clay were being exploited. The pinks and light reds are often the lower-fired colors in calcareous clays, especially if salt is present; gray indicates merely a difference in kiln atmosphere (Matson 1972, pp. 201-5).

As in DAI, the sherds present a soft and crumbly texture with flaky surfaces from which both slip and decoration have usually disappeared. This is due primarily to the high alkaline content of the soil. The sherds themselves, at least as far as the skyphoi and deep bowls are concerned, are approximately 0.001 m thinner than those of DAI, having an average body thickness of 0.003-0.004 m. Some sherds have wheel ridging (but not as heavy as in DAI), and others have spiral grooving on the interior. The range of shapes is the same as that in DAI, but the evidence is more abundant for cups, kraters, jugs, and oinochoai. Skyphoi and deep bowls, as before, continue to be the most popular shapes. An interesting feature, which also occurred in DAI, is the total lack of any recognizable characteristic belonging to the kantharos. This shape is found elsewhere (cf. Polis M25, M26, M44-46) but seems to be missing from the Nichoria range of shapes from DAI through DAIII.

The range of decorative motifs is much greater than in DAI, with the accumbent concentric semi-circles or cross-hatched triangles being the most popular. These decorative elements make a tentative start in DAI and come to the fore in DAII. The range of colors achieved through firing also differs from DAI, where a reddish brown or, less frequently, a washy black was the norm. In DAII, black becomes standard, either applied in a solid monochrome coating or with streaks in it. Sometimes the color varies from a streaky black to a streaky dark brown, but it is never a solid brown as in DAI. Reserved bands occur on the inner rim of 67 examples, which represents a smaller percentage than in DAI. On only six examples has a pale white slip been preserved, as compared with the 39 examples in DAI. DAII potters may have slipped their vases less frequently than in the earlier period or else they used a much finer clay solution which deteriorated more easily.

The DAII phase, then, is an extremely active period. Individual shapes and their accompanying decoration are discussed below.

OPEN SHAPES

SKYPHOI AND DEEP BOWLS (FIGS. 3-16, 3-17, 3-18)

Both skyphoi and deep bowls appear in DAII, although the

Table 3-3. Color Range of DAII Pottery

Munsell Number	Color	Number of Examples[a]
5YR 7/6 and 5YR 7/8	Reddish yellow	743
10YR 7/4, 8/3, 8/4	Very pale brown	260
2.5Y 8/2, 8/4, and 5Y 8/3	White to pale yellow	13
7.5YR 7/4, 8/4	Pink	11
2/5 YR 6/8	Light red	32
2.5YR N6/0 and 10YR 6/1, 6/2, 7/1, 7/2	Gray, light gray, and light brownish gray	65

[a]The total number of examples of clay color is 1,124. This is greater than the 828 cataloged items for two reasons: 1) because one catalog number often groups several sherds of the same type, and 2) because well-preserved body sherds, which are not inventoried, are included in the clay count.

skyphoi show a definite development whereas the deep bowls remain fairly uniform. Type A rims (Fig. 3-16), with one exception (**P842**; Fig. 3-28), all belong to small skyphoi; indeed, a class of very small skyphoi with either Type A1 or A2 rims is introduced in this period (see Table 3-4). Such small vases with a rim diameter of between 0.07 and 0.09 m and an average body thickness of 0.003 m mark a radical departure from DAI. The earlier skyphoi are large, with rim diameters no less than 0.10 m, and in only a few instances are body thicknesses as little as 0.003 m. Type A1 rims (**P331-36**; Figs. 3-16, 3-22; Pl. 3-39) are offset and almost begin to curl back around themselves; Type A2 rims (**P339-44, P762, P1005**; Figs. 3-16, 3-22, 3-25; Pl. 3-39) are also offset but have a horizontal top. The notable exception to the above classification is **P842** which has an A2 rim but a diameter of 0.164 m, putting it in the deep bowl class. Type A3 and A4 rims belong to medium-sized skyphoi that are slightly larger than the A1 and A2 class, with rim diameters between 0.09 and 0.12 m and an average body thickness between 0.003 and 0.0035 m. Type A3 (**P512, P514, P904**; Figs. 3-16, 3-24; Pl. 3-39) is everted, and Type A4 (**P596**; Fig. 3-16; Pl. 3-39) is at the halfway point between being everted and offset. The shape of **P596** and the curve of the body so close to the rim itself suggests that it

Table 3-4. Rim Types for DAII Skyphoi and Deep Bowls

Rim Type	Size of Vase	Number of Examples	Catalog Numbers of Best Examples	Average Diameter	Average Thickness of Body Below Rim
A1	Small skyphos	37	**P331-36, P792**	0.07-0.09	0.003
A2	Small skyphos	68	**P339-44, P630, P664, P1005**	0.08-0.09	0.003
A2	Large skyphos	2	**P592, P762**	0.14	0.0035
A2	Small deep bowl	1	**P842**	0.164	0.004
A3	Medium skyphos	28	**P512-14, P677, P904**	0.09-0.12	0.003-0.0035
A4	Medium skyphos	15	**P596**	0.09-0.12	0.003-0.0035
B1	Large skyphos	69	**P346-50**	0.13-0.15	0.004-0.0045
B1	Small deep bowl	1	**P597**	0.16	0.005
B2	Small skyphos	29	**P341, P916a, P1583, P1585, P1589**	0.075-0.09	0.003
B2	Medium skyphos	32	**P354, P355, P357, P359, P600, P741, P844, P925**	0.09-0.12	0.0035
B2	Large skyphos	3	**P356, P457, P993**	0.13-0.15	0.0035-0.004
B2	Large deep bowl	1	**P845**	0.24	0.005
B3	Large skyphos	2	**P603**	0.12-0.14	0.004-0.0045
B3	All sizes of deep bowl	35	**P458, P519, P520, P602, P604, P781, P782, P922, P1582, P1584**	0.152-0.24	0.004-0.005
B4	Medium skyphos	29	**P608-9**	0.10-0.12	0.003-0.0035
B4	Medium deep bowl	2	**P607, P923**	ca. 0.18	0.004
C1	Medium skyphos	8	**P363, P364, P366-67, P627, P629, P891, P892**	0.09-0.12	0.0035
C1	Large skyphos	36	**P785, P804, P987**	0.14	0.0035-0.004
C1	Small and medium deep bowl	85	**P611, P764, P800, P803, P905, P924**	0.15-0.20	0.004-0.0045
C2	All sizes of deep bowl	46	**P369, P370, P966**	0.16-0.24	0.004-0.005
C3	Medium skyphos	13	**P613-15**	0.09-0.12	0.0035-0.004
D	Large deep bowl	12	**P617, P618**	0.18-0.20	0.005
	TOTAL	554			

belongs to a rather squat skyphos. Type A rims, then, are either sharply everted or offset and belong to small and medium-sized skyphoi.

Type B rims (Fig. 3-16) are all everted, and for the most part also belong to skyphoi. The one notable exception is Type B3 (**P458**; Pl. 3-40) which belongs to the deep bowl class. Type B1 (**P346-53**; Pl. 3-41) has a long, rather angular rim with a diameter ranging from 0.13 to 0.14 m and an average body thickness of 0.004-0.0045 m, and can thus be associated with large skyphoi. Type B2 is slightly less angular than B1 and is found on both small (**P341, P916a, P1583-85, P1589**; Figs. 3-22, 3-23) and medium-sized (**P354-57, P359**; Figs. 3-16, 3-23; Pls. 3-40, 3-41) skyphoi with a diameter ranging from 0.075 to 0.12 m and an average body thickness of 0.003-0.0035 m. One exception to this classification is **P845** (Fig. 3-31) which has a B2 rim but a diameter of 0.24 m, making it a deep bowl. Type B4 rims (**P608, P609**; Fig. 3-16; Pl. 3-41) have a convex exterior lip and, with two exceptions (**P607, P923**; Fig. 3-30) that are deep bowls, belong to medium-sized skyphoi.

Type C rims (Fig. 3-16) are less sharply everted than Type B and in the case of C2 (**P369, P370**; Pl. 3-42) almost straight. Most of these rims belong to deep bowls but some are to be found on skyphoi. For instance, Type C1 occurs more commonly with deep bowls (**P611, P764, P800-803, P924**; Figs. 3-27, 3-28, 3-30, 3-31), but in some instances (**P363, P364, P366, P367**; Pl. 3-42) can be associated with medium-sized skyphoi. Conversely, Type C3 rims (**P615**; Pl. 3-42) with a small angular lip belong to small skyphoi and are not found on deep bowls.

The rim diameter and body thickness can again be used as criteria for differentiating deep bowls from skyphoi. Anything with a rim diameter between 0.15 and 0.24 m and an average body thickness of 0.004-0.005 m can be classed as a deep bowl. Deep bowls do not have the sharply offset rims of Type A, except for **P842**, which has an A2 rim with a diameter of 0.164 m (small deep bowl). Nor do they have the angular rims of Types B1, B2, and B4. There are a few minor exceptions: **P597** (Fig. 3-27) is a small deep bowl with a B1 rim; **P607** and **P923** are medium-sized deep bowls with B4 rims (diameter 0.18 m); and **P845** (Fig. 3-31) is a large deep bowl with a B2 rim (diameter 0.24 m). Deep bowl rims are mostly confined to Types B3, C1, C2, and D. Type B3 belongs to medium- and large-sized deep bowls (**P458**; Fig. 3-16), whereas Types C1 and C2 can be found on small and medium-sized deep bowls. Type C1 rims are the most numerous and can be considered as the standard rim for deep bowls in the DAII period. Type C2 (**P369**) is an almost straight rim, whereas Type D (**P617, P618**; Fig. 3-16; Pl. 3-42), of which there are only a few examples, is a large, almost rolled rim occurring on large deep bowls with an average body thickness of 0.005 m.

Of the 554 cataloged rims, Types A2, B1, B2, and C1 are the most numerous, accounting for approximately 60%. Of these, Type C1 represents the single largest group of rims with a total of 129 examples, attesting to the popularity of this type of rim for large skyphoi and deep bowls. Types A2, B1, and B2 are represented by 71, 70, and 65 examples, respectively. They constitute the next largest group of rims, underscoring the preference that Nichoria potters had for the skyphos shape. In fact, skyphoi outnumber deep bowls by a ratio of 2:1 (see Table 3-5). During the DAII period, then, the deep bowl shape begins to decline in popularity, and the attention of the potters begins to turn to smaller shapes. Using their greater technical expertise and perhaps also being stimulated by more variety in the diet, they initiate a broader range of shapes (see also Chapter 6, pp. 323, 324).

Table 3-5. Occurrence of DAII Skyphoi and Deep Bowls

Type of Vase	Number of Examples
Small skyphos	134
Medium skyphos	125
Large skyphos	112
Deep bowls of all sizes	183

The skyphoi and deep bowls have three types of handles. As with DAI handles of the same type, the basic division is one of size. Type A handles are all large, with a diameter over 0.01 m. A total of 170 individual handle fragments were found, not including those associated with preserved vases or parts of vases. On the basis of their size, Type A handles (cf. **P713**; Fig. 3-32) can be assigned to large skyphoi or deep bowls. Type B handles are rather an oddity for skyphoi and deep bowls; they are not round, but rather angular, almost rectangular. Five such handle fragments have been preserved, and, as far as can be determined from their size, they appear to belong to large skyphoi or small deep bowls. Type C handles (cf. **P916**; Fig. 3-32), of which 91 individual fragments have been preserved, are small, with a diameter under 0.01 m. Their size indicates that they belong to small and medium-sized skyphoi. All were once covered with a black or streaky black paint, now sadly worn and preserved only in patches. The entire handle was covered with such paint and not just its top and side, as is the case with many similar late Mycenaean handles. A fourth type, the double handle, occurs in one example only (**P986**; Fig. 3-31; Pl. 3-43). Instead of a monochrome coating, both handles have stripes and probably belong to a skyphos with a high conical foot, possibly of the same shape and design as that found at Alaas in Cyprus.[58]

Five different types of bases can be assigned to the skyphoi and deep bowls (see Table 3-6). All have fragments of paint preserved on the interior, indicating that they belong to an open shape. Type A bases (Fig. 3-17) have conical feet of various sizes. Type A1 have shallow conical feet with diameters of 0.035-0.045 m. Their outer edges are flattened slightly; this is barely noticeable with **P389** and **P390** (Fig. 3-17; Pl. 3-44), but fairly pronounced with **P392** and **P392a**. The latter bases also have two raised bands near the foot, whereas **P390b** has a series of incisions at the same spot. On the basis of their size, A1 bases can be considered as belonging to small and medium-sized skyphoi. Type A2 bases have high conical feet with diameters of 0.04-0.06 m. In most cases, the outer edges of the feet are pointed (**P331, P394, P396, P603, P1583**; Figs. 3-17, 3-22, 3-23, 3-25; Pl. 3-44), but in a few instances they slant inward at an oblique angle (**P395**; Fig. 3-17; Pl. 3-44). **P394** and **P396b** have incisions in the middle of the base (just below the point of transition from the body to the base), and **P396a** has a large raised band in the same position. On the basis of their diameters, A2 bases can be assigned to all sizes of skyphoi and small deep bowls. In general, Type A bases continue a form established in DAI, but with a greater variety in shape and diameter (cf. **P390, P392, P394**) and a greater height to the conical foot (cf. **P395, P1583**; Figs. 3-17, 3-23; Pl. 3-44).

Type B bases (**P400, P401**; Fig. 3-17) have shallow conical feet with rounded outer edges and occasionally with incisions (**P401**). With a few exceptions (cf. **P741**; Fig. 3-25), they have large diameters of 0.06-0.08 m and hence can be assigned to deep bowls. **P741** has a diameter of 0.05 m and belongs to a medium-sized skyphos. Such bases also occur in DAI (cf. **P281**), but again a greater variety is achieved in DAII. Type C bases (**P402-4**; Fig. 3-18) represent different kinds of ringed feet; **P402** and **P402a** have high ringed feet, **P404** a medium-sized foot, and **P403** a shallow foot. These range in diameter from 0.035 to 0.08 m and hence occur on all sizes of skyphoi and deep bowls. In shape they represent a continuation of Type B of DAI. Type D bases (**P543, P844**; Figs. 3-18, 3-26) are flat bases with diameters of 0.05-0.08 m. These belong to flat-based skyphoi which make their first appearance at Nichoria in DAII. The best-preserved example of such skyphoi is **P844** (Fig. 3-26) which has a rim diameter of 0.12 m and a base diameter of 0.08 m, putting it on the borderline between the medium and large skyphos.

Some generalities may be observed from Table 3-6. Type A bases are used more frequently with skyphoi (small and medium), whereas Type B is confined, with only a few exceptions, to deep bowls. Type C, on the other hand, is ubiquitous and can be used with either skyphoi or deep bowls. As with the rims of the same period, the majority of examples (about 60%) can be assigned to the small and medium skyphos class, again attesting to the popularity of this shape in DAII times.

If these disparate elements of rims, handles, and bases are put together to form a complete picture, 12 separate shapes of skyphoi and deep bowls can be distinguished:

Shape 1. **P331, P332, P339, P341, P630, P664, P792, P916a, P1005, P1585, P1589** (Figs. 3-22, 3-23;

Table 3-6. Base Types for DAII Skyphoi and Deep Bowls

Base Type	Size of Vase	Number of Examples	Catalog Numbers of Best Examples	Average Diameter	Remarks
A1	Small and medium skyphoi	57	**P389, P390, P390a, P390b, P392, P392a**	0.035-0.045	With raised bands and incisions. Very few examples in DAI (cf. **P27**).
A2	All sizes of skyphoi and small deep bowls	43	**P331, P394-96, P396a-b, P603, P1583**	0.04-0.06	With raised bands and incisions. Very high conical feet not found in DAI. Otherwise, continued from DAI.
B	Medium skyphoi	5	**P741**	0.05	Not found in DAI.
B	All sizes of deep bowls	32	**P400, P401**	0.06-0.08	With incisions; continued from DAI but with greater variety of shape.
C	All sizes of skyphoi and deep bowls	86	**P402, P402a, P403, P404, P627, P1584, P1585, P1589**	0.035-0.08	Continued from Type B of DAI.
D	Flat-based skyphoi	8	**P543, P697, P844**	0.05-0.08	Not found in DAI.
	TOTAL	231			

Pl. 3-39) Small *bell-shaped* skyphos. Rim Types A1, A2, B2 and base Types A1, A2, and C. Bell shape occurs in DAI (cf. Shape 3) but not small size and offset rim. Parallels at Kardamyla[59] (Fig. 3-43, left) and Kokevi.[60]

Shape 2. **P1583** (Fig. 3-23). Small skyphos with *conical* body. B2 rim and A2 base. Conical shape found in DAI (cf. Shape 7) but not small size and high conical foot. Parallels at Ano Englianos,[61] Modi (W. Crete)[62] (Fig. 3-23), and Alaas (Cyprus).[63]

Shape 3. **P354, P613, P615, P627, P629, P677, P844, P891, P892, P904, P925** (Figs. 3-23, 3-24; Pls. 3-40, 3-42). Medium-sized *bell-shaped* skyphos. Rim Types A3, A4, B2, B4, and C3 and base Types A1, A2, B, and C. Shape not found in DAI. Parallels at Kardamyla[64] (Fig. 3-43, right), Modi[65] (Fig. 3-24), and in Cyprus.[66]

Shape 4. **P600, P741** (Fig. 3-25). Medium-sized skyphos with *conical* body. Rim Type B2 and base Type B. Shape not found in DAI.

Shape 5. **P596** (Fig. 3-16; Pl. 3-39). Medium-sized skyphos with *squat* body. Rim Type A4. Squat shape found in DAI (cf. Shape 9). Parallels at Amyclae.[67]

Shape 6. **P356, P457, P592, P603, P762, P785, P804, P987, P993** (Figs. 3-25, 3-26). Large *bell-shaped* skyphos. Rim Types A2, B1-B3, C1 and base Types A2 and C. Shape found in DAI (cf. Shape 2) but common with deep bowls. Possible parallels at Tragana.[68]

Shape 7. **P844** (Fig. 3-26; Pl. 3-45). Flat-based skyphos with *conical* body. Rim Type B2 and base Type D. Shape not found in DAI.

Shape 7a. **P697** (Fig. 3-26; Pl. 3-46). Flat-based skyphos with *exaggerated conical* body. Base Type D. Shape possibly developed from Shape 9 of DAI.

Shape 8. **P520, P597, P602, P800-803, P842, P905, P924, P1584** (Figs. 3-26, 3-27, 3-28). Small *bell-shaped* deep bowl. Rim Types A2, B1, B3, C1 and base Types A2, B, C. Shape found in DAI (cf. Shape 2) but common with medium and large deep bowls. Possible parallels at Malthi,[69] Tragana,[70] and Sparta[71] (Fig. 3-29).

Shape 9. **P922, P1582** (Fig. 3-29). Small deep bowl with *conical* body. Rim Type B3 and possible base Type C. Shape found in DAI (cf. Shape 7).

Shape 10. **P519, P607, P764, P781, P782, P923** (Figs. 3-30, 3-31). Medium-sized *bell-shaped* deep bowl. Rim Types B3-B4, C1 and base Types B, C. Shape found in DAI (cf. Shape 2). Possible parallels at Tragana.[72]

Shape 11. **P604, P611, P845, P966** (Fig. 3-31). Large *bell-shaped* deep bowls. Rim Types B2-B3, C1-C2 and base Types B, C. Shape found in DAI (cf. Shape 1).

The above shapes fall basically into three categories: bell shape, conical, and squat. All three categories are to be found in DAI; in fact, DAI skyphoi and deep bowls seem to have a greater range of shapes, including ovoid bodies and those with fairly straight sides. But it is in the size of DAII vases that the difference occurs. It is the small size and, consequently, the development of the skyphos that is the important feature of shape in the DAII period.

The small bell-shaped skyphos (Shape 1) has parallels elsewhere in Messenia; this suggests a common local style in the SW Peloponnese. This does not mean, however, that Messenia became isolated in the DAII period. The shape of the small conical skyphos (Shape 2) is to be found not only at Ano Englianos (although this example probably belongs to the later DAIII period) but also, and more important, in W Crete and Cyprus. The medium-sized bell-shaped skyphos (Shape 3) has a parallel in Messenia, but also is commonly found in W Crete and Cyprus. Such similarity in shape throughout these areas of the Aegean suggests two possibilities: either that an independent and parallel development evolved in these regions from the same basic Mycenaean stock; or that, despite the assumption of a general low ebb in the seagoing trade in the Dark Age, contacts existed between Messenia and W Crete. It is quite possible for the Nichoria potters, working with the same basic skyphos shape as found elsewhere, to have developed independently variants similar to those found in Crete and Cyprus. At Alaas, such developments appear to have taken place earlier, since chronologically the pottery from the site precedes DAII at Nichoria (see n. 58). The second possibility—that contacts existed between Messenia and W Crete—should not be overlooked. If shipping routes did exist between these areas, they may have included Kythera, although as yet no pottery comparable to that of the DAII period at Nichoria has been found on that island.

The large bell-shaped skyphos (Shape 6) and small bell-shaped deep bowls (Shape 8) also have parallels elsewhere in Messenia and, more important, at Sparta (cf. also Shape 5), indicating that Messenia had ties with Sparta in the DAII period. Spartan connections would not be surprising, considering the later Spartan hegemony over Messenia. Contacts with Sparta, however, and also those with Ithaca, Achaea, and Aetolia, which continue from DAI, are better seen in the decorative elements of the Nichoria pottery.

The elements of decoration are many and varied. Twenty-two different decorative motifs are listed below with appropriate parallels:

1. Solid monochrome coating. Twenty-five good examples, of which the best are **P339, P627, P630,**

P664, P697, P713, P741, P764, P782, P785, P800, P802-4, P844, P916a, P987 (Figs. 3-22, 3-24 to 3-28, 3-30 to 3-32; Pls. 3-45, 3-46). Occurs most frequently with A1, A2, and C1 Type rims (i.e., on small skyphoi and deep bowls) and more often than not with a reserved band on the inner rim. This is by far the most common type of decoration and could occur on as many as 30% of the vases, although this is hard to determine with accuracy owing to the fragmentary nature of much of the material. Continued from DAI. **P740** has a fine pinkish buff clay and a much finer paint than the other examples. Similar monochrome coating is to be found on sherds from Amyclae[73] and on a skyphos from Agrinion.[74]

2a. Monochrome coated with reserved band in handle zone. Nineteen examples, of which the best are **P331, P354, P356, P646, P801, P892, P905, P914, P916, P1585, P1589** (Figs 3-22, 3-23, 3-24, 3-25, 3-27, 3-28, 3-32; Pls. 3-39, 3-40). Used frequently on small skyphoi with Type A rims and with reserved band on rim. A common decoration, occurring with perhaps 20% of the vases. Continued from DAI. Messenian parallels from Kokevi (no. 1657) (see n. 60) and Kardamyla (see n. 59) (Fig. 3-43, left); other parallels from Alaas;[75] also on kantharoi from Agrinion[76] and Kalydon.[77]

2b. Variations in the placement of the reserved band.

i. Reserved band extends above handle zone to neck of vase. **P904, P993** (Figs. 3-24, 3-26).

ii. Handle zone is coated[78] but neck left undecorated with thin black band at rim. **P341** (Fig. 3-22).

iii. Reserved bands in handle zone and on rim and neck with thin black band as dividing line. **P332** (Fig. 3-22).

iv. Thin reserved bands at base of feet. **P603, P1583** (Figs. 3-23, 3-25). Parallels from Modi[79] (broad band; Fig. 3-23) and Alaas.[80]

3. Black bands in handle zone(?). **P507, P521, P593, P885**. These are four small fragments of skyphoi decorated with black bands, perhaps in the handle zone, much in the same manner as on the skyphos from Derveni.[81]

4a. Wavy line in handle zone. **P346, P412, P622, P626, P690, P704, P790, P887, P891, P906** (Figs. 3-24, 3-32, 3-33; Pls. 3-41, 3-47, 3-48). Used frequently with Type B rims. Continued from DAI. Messenian parallels from Kardamyla (see n. 64) (Fig. 3-43, right), Kokevi (no. 1659) (see n. 60), and Tragana (see n. 68); also on kantharoi from Aetos,[82] Agrinion,[83] Astakos,[84] Derveni,[85] Kalydon,[86] and Kryoneri;[87] also possibly on skyphos from Modi (see n. 65), but the decoration is very worn and hard to distinguish.[88]

4b. Double wavy line in handle zone. **P377, P682** (Fig. 3-32; Pl. 3-47). One example from DAI (**P185**).

5a. Wolf's tooth in handle zone. **P602, P923, P924** (Figs. 3-27, 3-28, 3-30; Pls. 3-49, 3-50). Occurs with Type B rims and possibly Type C bases. Two examples from DAI (**P183, P263**). Messenian parallel from Tragana (see n. 68, Fig. 12, no. 5); excellent parallel from Heroön near Sparta (see n. 71) (Fig. 3-29).

5b. Double wolf's tooth in handle zone. **P1582, P1584** (Figs. 3-28, 3-29). Occurs with Type B3 rims and Type C bases. Not found in DAI.

6. Concentric circles in handle zone. **P893** (Pl. 3-51). One example only. Not found in DAI. Messenian parallels from Antheia[89] and Tragana (see n. 68; Fig. 12, no. 4). Full concentric circles as a decorative motif are rare in Messenia and may have been introduced from Attica where they are common. The shape of the Antheia skyphos with its high conical foot is also Attic, with numerous examples from the Kerameikos.[90] Other examples of concentric circles in large metopal panels with the triglyph formed by vertical lines and cross-hatching (also an Attic motif to be found in the Kerameikos[91]) come from Amyclae and Sparta.[92] It is unclear whether this motif of concentric circles was introduced into Messenia via Sparta or directly from Athens.

7a. Adjacent sets of accumbent concentric semi-circles; compass-drawn with central dot. **P673, P674, P699, P1613** (Fig. 3-32; Pl. 3-52). A very common form of decoration at Nichoria, occurring on perhaps 20% of the vases. On many sherds only fragments of arcs of one set of concentric semi-circles are preserved. Forty-six fragmentary examples; some of the best are **P525-27, P529-31, P672, P675, P686, P698, P789, P845, P913, P968** (Figs. 3-31, 3-32, 3-33; Pl. 3-52a). This motif begins in DAI (seven examples) but is developed fully in DAII. Messenian parallels from Tragana (see n. 68, Fig. 12, nos. 1-2). No examples from Laconia, but good parallels from Aetos (H35, P130). The heavy use of accumbent concentric semi-circles appears to be a Nichoria (and perhaps Messenian) characteristic.

7b. Variations in the form of the accumbent semi-circles:

i. The central dot is transformed into a spiral. **P375, P528, P620, P928, P957, P1614, P1615** (Fig. 3-32; Pls. 3-53 to 3-56). Parallels from Aetos (H54) and Kryoneri.[93]

ii. The central dot is replaced by a half-triangle. **P781** (Fig. 3-30; Pl. 3-57).

iii. Semi-circles are hand-drawn. **P781, P894** (Fig. 3-30; Pl. 3-57). Parallels from Tragana (see n. 68, Fig. 12, no. 3) and Aetos (H13,

16-17). The hand-drawn semi-circles represent a survival of the LHIIIC tradition and in DAII coexist with compass-drawn semi-circles.

8. Overlapping sets of accumbent concentric semi-circles. **P597, P607, P611, P620, P621, P700** (Figs. 3-27, 3-30, 3-31; Pl. 3-53). Seventeen examples. All have central dots except **P957** (Fig. 3-32; Pl. 3-54) which has a spiral. Those of **P611** (Fig. 3-31) are hand-drawn. Not found in DAI. No parallels from Laconia; at Aetos only overlapping pendent concentric semi-circles (H36) occur. This motif seems to be a Nichoria characteristic.
9. Alternating pendent and accumbent concentric semi-circles, compass-drawn. **P464** (Pl. 3-58). Not found in DAI. Messenian parallel from Tragana (see n. 68, Fig. 12, no. 3); also from Aetos (H16). Pendent semi-circles are rare at Nichoria (one example only), but are preferred by the Ithacan potters (cf. Aetos H13, H17). The motif may have been introduced from Ithaca.
10. Crosshatched triangles. Twenty-five examples, of which the best are **P600, P623, P677, P678, P687, P702, P766, P791, P922, P950, P971, P988, P1005** (Figs. 3-22, 3-24, 3-25, 3-29, 3-32, 3-33; Pls 3-47, 3-59 to 3-63). One example only (**P193**) from DAI; this motif is fully developed in DAII. Messenian parallels from Kokevi[94] and Kaphirio.[95] Good parallels from Amyclae[96] and Sparta;[97] other parallels from Aetos (H30, P134) and Derveni.[98]
11. Framed crosshatched triangles. **P624, P805** (Figs. 3-32, 3-33; Pl. 3-64). Not found in DAI. Messenian parallels from Kaphirio; other parallels from Amyclae and Sparta;[99] also from Asine (closed shapes only).[100]
12. Crosshatched half-triangles. **P603, P688, P689, P949** (Figs. 3-25, 3-33; Pl. 3-47). Not found in DAI. No parallels in Laconia or Ithaca, but occur on an amphora from the Kleonai territory (Kourtesa).[101]
13. Crosshatched diamonds. **P625** (Fig. 3-33). Does not occur in DAI. Rare at Nichoria, but found at Kaphirio, Amyclae (n. 97, 100) and Aetos (H18, H30, P134).
14. Hatched triangles. **P911** (two examples), **P958, P1006** (Fig. 3-32; Pl. 3-54, 3-63). Not found in DAI. Found in Ithaca (Aetos H14), Achaea,[102] and Laconia.[103]
15. Piled triangles. **P379, P466, P520, P522(?), P613, P676, P762, P926, P948** (Figs. 3-23, 3-25, 3-27, 3-33; Pl. 3-65). One example (**P50**) from DAI; this motif is fully developed in DAII. Messenian parallels from Kaphirio; other parallels from Amyclae.[104] **P762** (Fig. 3-25), with its two registers of piled triangles in metopal panels, is paralleled exactly by CVA *Cambridge* 1, Pl. 3, 92; and **P926** (Pl. 3-65), with its adjacent sets of piled triangles forming a double zigzag pattern, is similar to CVA *Heidelberg* 3, Pl. 134, 3.
16. Horizontal stripes in metopal panels. **P703** (Pl. 3-66). Not found in DAI or elsewhere in Messenia. Parallels from Aetos (H21-2), but not from Laconia. The metope-triglyph motif is common at Nichoria; **P629, P739, P947** (Figs. 3-24, 3-33; Pl. 3-67) have fragments of the vertical lines of the triglyph preserved, but unfortunately give no indication of what decoration, if any, was contained in the metope.
17. Large dots(?) in metopal panels. **P519** (Fig. 3-30). Preserved in one fragmentary example. Perhaps also **P604** (Fig. 3-31). Not found elsewhere in Messenia and Laconia. If genuine, this type of decoration seems to be an adaptation of the Aetolian sausage motif.[105]
18. Metopal panel left undecorated. **P1583** (Fig. 3-23). Not found in DAI or elsewhere in Messenia, Laconia, or W Greece.

Table 3-7 summarizes the various decorative motifs. An interesting feature is the close similarity between the decorative motifs of Nichoria (and also Kaphirio) and of Amyclae (and also Sparta), suggesting either that Messenia and Laconia had close ties in DAII or that there was a shared tradition with independent developments in both regions from a common Mycenaean stock. In every case the wolf's tooth decoration and the various types of cross-hatching and hatching are paralleled on sherds from Amyclae and Sparta. Laconian characteristics of beginning the decoration right at the rim and of incisions below the rim also appear at Nichoria. **P600, P613, P677, P678, P762, P845, P966, P971, P988,** and **P1005** (Figs. 3-22, 3-23, 3-24, 3-25; Pls. 3-47, 3-52a, 3-59, 3-62, 3-63) are examples of the major decorative motif beginning at the rim. The Laconian is a broad shallow incision below the rim; the Nichoria incisions are narrower (**P507, P520, P598, P604, P605, P614, P971**; Figs. 3-27, 3-31; Pl. 3-62), occurring often in pairs (not singly as on the Laconian examples) but still placed just below the rim.[106] A variation occurs on **P355** (Pl. 3-41), where the incisions are replaced by a raised band. Perhaps the most common arrangement of decorative motifs on Laconian examples is in the metope-triglyph form; such an arrangement also occurs frequently at Nichoria (**P600, P625, P687, P702, P703, P762, P1005, P1006**; Figs. 3-22, 3-25, 3-32; Pl. 3-59, 3-63), Kaphirio, and again in Achaea.[107] Aside from the Messenians, only the Achaeans and the Laconians use to such a great extent the motif of the metopal panel decorated with crosshatched triangles; to a less extent, similar decoration occurs at Asine.[108]

Some of the Aetos material (H20-31, 35) also has a Laconian look, and the presence of these decorative motifs in Ithaca, Messenia, and Laconia again suggests the probability of a shared ceramic traditon between these areas, and perhaps also the possibility of some sort of contact; but it is with Laconia that Messenia appears to have had the closest

Table 3-7. Occurrence of DAII Decorative Motifs

Type of Decoration	Messenia (not Nichoria)	Laconia	Ithaca	Achaea	Aetolia	Crete	Cyprus	Athens	Argolid
1. Mono coating		X			X			X	
2. Reserved bands	X	X (inner rim)			X	X	X		
3. Bands				X		X			
4. Wavy lines	X		X	X	X	X	X		X
5. Wolf's tooth	X	X							
6. Concentric circles	X	X						X	
7. Adjacent concentric semi-circles	X		X		X				
8. Overlapping semi-circles			X (pendent)						
9. Alternating pendent and accumbent semi-circles	X		X						
10. Crosshatched triangles	X	X	X	X					X
11. Framed cross-hatched triangles	X	X							X (on closed shapes)
12. Crosshatched half-triangles	X								X (on closed shapes)
13. Crosshatched diamonds	X	X	X						X (on closed shapes)
14. Hatched triangles		X	X	X					
15. Piled triangles		X							
16. Stripes			X						
17. Dots		X (?)			X (sausage)				
18. Undecorated metopal panels						X	X		

ties. Athens makes her influence felt only slightly with the idea of full concentric circles (**P893**; Pl. 3-51), which also appears again at Antheia.

As for local characteristics, the heavy use of adjacent and overlapping accumbent concentric semi-circles may be a Nichoria feature. This motif is found elsewhere, but not with the frequency with which it occurs here. The cross-hatched half-triangles may also be considered a Messenian characteristic. And if **P519** (Fig. 3-30) is restored correctly, the idea of large dots in metopal panels can also be considered a local characteristic. All this points to the great vitality of the Nichoria (and also Messenian) potters in the DAII period.

CUPS

After the skyphoi and deep bowls, cups are the most popular open shape at Nichoria. With one exception (**P768**; Fig. 3-35), the cups are uniformly small with everted rims and S-shaped profiles. There are, in fact, five distinctive cup rims that seem to conform to skyphos Types A4, B2, B4, and C3 (Table 3-8).

Of the 13 good cup profiles that are listed in Table 3-8, rims B2 and C3 are the most frequently used. There are three types of cup handles, but unfortunately the examples are too few and too fragmentary to determine whether a particular type of handle is used with a specific rim. Type A handles, of which there are 32 examples (the best are **P532**,

Table 3-8. Rim and Handle Types for DAII Cups

Rim Type	Handle Type	Number of Examples	Catalog Numbers
A4	A	1	**P631** (Fig. 3-34; Pl. 3-68)
B2	C	6	**P548, P633, P808, P847, P848, P929** (Figs. 3-34, 3-35)
B4	B	1	**P907** (Fig. 3-34)
C3	A,B	4	**P478, P532, P705, P972** (Figs. 3-34, 3-35; Pls. 3-69, 3-70)
Straight	A	1	**P768** (Fig. 3-35)

P631, P646, P768; Pl. 3-69), are quite wide (0.012-0.013 m) with a semi-circular shape and a rectangular transverse section. Those of Type B, of which 18 examples have been identified (the best are **P478, P705, P907**), are also quite wide (0.013 m) but are elliptical in shape and section. Type C handles, of which there are 14 examples (the best are **P548, P847**), are 0.013-0.014 m wide and are oval in shape and section. A moderately large number (51) of cup bases have also been preserved. All are flat, but a few exhibit individual variations: that of **P972** (Fig. 3-34; Pl. 3-70) is slightly concave, whereas those of **P532, P768, P769** (Fig. 3-35; Pl. 3-69) have concentric circular incisions on the underside similar to Rizes 2662 and 2664 (n. 108, 111), thus extending to cup bases an idea already seen in skyphos and deep bowl bases. On **P645** (Fig. 3-18) the sides are curved and are suggestive of a shape with an exaggerated S-shaped profile (Shape 2a), but on **P544** (Fig. 3-18) they extend straight from the base and perhaps indicate a broad, shallow cup (Shape 3).

There are five basic cup shapes preserved at Nichoria.

Shape 1. Shallow cups with S-shaped profile. **P478, P548, P705, P907, P972** (Fig. 3-34; Pl. 3-70). Rim diameter between 0.09 and 0.10 m. Use of rim Types B2, B4, and C3 and handle Types B and C. All monochrome coated except for **P972** which has a *thin* reserved band below rim. Not found in DAI. Good Messenian parallels from Rizes[109] and Antheia;[110] others from Aetos (H54-5 and possibly P131) and Modi[111] (Fig. 3-34). Rizes 2664 has a reserved band under the rim in the same manner as **P972**.

Shape 2a. Shallow cups with exaggerated S-shaped profile (almost conical). **P631, P645(?), P848, P929** (Fig. 3-34; Pl. 3-68). Rim diameter between 0.07 and 0.075 m. Rim Types A4, B2, and handle Type A. All monochrome coated except **P848** which has a *broad* reserved band below rim and a reserved band on inner rim. Not found in DAI. Good Messenian parallels from Rizes[112] and Antheia;[113] also from the Polis cave (PG4).

Shape 2b. Shallow cups with exaggerated S-shaped profile and carinated body. **P532, P808** (Fig. 3-35; Pl. 3-69). Rim diameter 0.09 m. Rim Type C3 and handle Type A. All monochrome coated.

Shape 3. Broad, very shallow cup. **P544(?), P633, P847** (Fig. 3-35). Rim diameter between 0.09 and 0.12 m. Rim Type B2 and handle Type C. Monochrome coated. Shape does not occur elsewhere in Messenia, but is found in Laconia (Amyclae).[114]

Shape 4. Deep cup. **P768** (Fig. 3-35). Rim diameter 0.115 m. Straight rim with Type A handle. Monochrome coated. Possible continuation of shape from DAI(?). No parallels elsewhere in Messenia, but similar shape (with flat base), although with slightly everted rim, found at Vryses in W Crete.[115]

The cups of Shapes 1 and 2a/b with S-shaped profiles appear to be the common Nichoria shapes with parallels in Messenia and Ithaca, emphasizing the fact that contacts with Ithaca continue to DAII. The Laconian (Shape 3) and W Cretan (Shapes 1 and 4) parallels again perhaps underscore the Messenian ties with these regions. As far as decoration is concerned, the Nichoria cups are all monochrome coated both on the exterior and on the interior, except for **P972** (Fig. 3-34; Pl. 3-70) which has a thin uneven reserved band under the rim and **P848** (Fig. 3-34) which has a broad reserved band under the rim on the exterior and a narrower reserved band on the interior. In this respect, the Nichoria cups differ from nos. 2662-64 from Rizes which have wavy lines on the exterior under the rim, as does H55 from Aetos. Furthermore, Rizes 2663-64 appear to be undecorated on the interior with the exception of a thin black band on the inner rim. The Antheia cups, on the other hand, are more like the Nichoria ones with their solid monochrome coating on the exterior and interior, and are paralleled by examples from Laconia and W Crete. Thus it would seem that the Rizes cups are closer to Ithacan parallels, whereas those from Antheia and Nichoria resemble more closely those from Amyclae and Vryses. An interesting feature which does not occur in the comparative material is the presence of monochrome coating and decoration on the underside of the bases of some of the Nichoria cups. **P544-46, P847** (Figs. 3-18, 3-35) are fully coated on the underside, and on **P768** (Fig. 3-35) the exterior paint spills over only to the outer edges of the underside. The most interesting of all, however, is **P815** (Pl. 3-71) which is decorated on its underside with a large cross within a circle. No parallels to such coating and decoration are to be found in Messenia or, for that matter, in W Greece or Laconia, and their presence at Nichoria may be considered a local feature.

KRATERS

Kraters are poorly represented at Nichoria; a handful of rims, a few worn decorated body fragments, and some pedestal bases represent the total evidence. Seven types of rims can be identified (Table 3-9). Type A rims (**P386**, **P635**; Fig. 3-16) belong to medium-sized kraters with a rim diameter of 0.20-0.25 m; these are everted rims with flat tops painted with stripes. Type B rims (Fig. 3-16) are offset, slightly convex, and painted with a monochrome coating on their tops. Type B1 rims (**P388**), with a rim diameter of 0.30 m and an average body thickness of 0.007 m, belong to large kraters, whereas Type B2 (**P469**) are half the size and belong to small kraters. Type C rims (**P470**, **P536**; Fig. 3-16) have the same general shape and design as those of Type B1 but have a larger body thickness (ca. 0.01 m) with a raised band decorated with diagonal slashes in imitation of rope decoration below the rim. Type D rims (**P471**; Fig. 3-16) have the same general shape as those of Type C but are everted, and not offset, with a flat diagonal top decorated with stripes. These also belong to large kraters with an average rim diameter of 0.30 m and body thickness of 0.007-0.008 m. Type E rims (**P537**; Fig. 3-16; Pl. 3-72) are similar to B2 but with a narrow lip and flat top; these have an average body thickness of 0.005 m and thus belong to small kraters. Types F (**P638**; Fig. 3-16; Pl. 3-72) and G (**P809**; Fig. 3-16) are similar in shape and are simply larger versions of the Type C1 deep bowl rim. They are distinguished from each other by the degree to which the rim is everted; those of F are slightly less everted than those of G. Both belong to large kraters with an average rim diameter of 0.28-0.30 m and a body thickness of 0.007-0.008 m.

The large krater, then, seems to be the most common size with a total of 23 examples; the medium and small kraters are represented by 13 and seven examples, respectively. It is unclear what shape these rims represent. The only good parallels come from Derveni[116] and Alaas[117] where the kraters are bell-shaped with either skyphos- or kantharos-type handles and ringed or pedestal bases. Since the skyphos is the favorite shape at Nichoria, the skyphos bell shape probably extends also to kraters, and hence some of the larger round handles (diameter 0.015 m and above) and Type C ringed bases (diameter 0.08 m and above) may belong to kraters. Six pedestal bases (Fig. 3-18) were also found and definitely belong to kraters. **P960** is a solid pedestal stem continuing a shape already known in DAI (**P208**) and probably belonging to a vase such as Alaas Pit A/8. **P816** and **P908** are broad and shallow stems with hollow, almost ringed feet and may belong to both medium- and large-sized kraters. **P897**, **P932**, and **P932a** are also broad stems with semi-conical (**P932**) and conical (**P897**, **P932a**) feet, with a single rib in the center of the foot. Such ribbing continues from DAI (**P329**) and also occurs at Alaas (J2), but there the rib is placed at the top of the pedestal and not in the center. The high foot of **P897** (Fig. 3-18) also stems from **P329** and is paralleled by the foot of a pedestaled krater with skyphos shape from Derveni (see n. 116) and by that of a krater with kylix shape from Alaas (H1); it may well be that **P897** belongs to a vase of similar design.

Table 3-9. Rim Types for DAII Kraters

Rim Type	Size of Krater	Number of Examples	Catalog Numbers of Best Examples	Average Diameter	Body Thickness	Remarks
A	Medium	13	**P386, P387, P534, P635, P973** (Fig. 3-16)	0.20-0.25	0.004-0.005	Stripes on top of rim
B1	Large	4	**P388** (Fig. 3-16)	0.30	0.007-0.008	Coating on top of rim
B2	Small	3	**P469** (Fig. 3-16)	0.15	0.005	Coating on top of rim
C	Large	4	**P470, P536** (Fig. 3-16)	0.25-0.30	0.01	Raised band with diagonal slashes. Cf. Aetos H60-1
D	Large	7	**P471, P974** (Fig. 3-16)	0.30	0.007-0.008	Stripes on top of rim
E	Small	4	**P537** (Fig. 3-16)	0.15 (?)	0.005	
F	Large	7	**P638** (Fig. 3-16)	0.28-0.30	0.007-0.008	Developed from Skyphos Type C1
G	Large	1	**P809** (Fig. 3-16)	0.28-0.30	0.007-0.008	Developed from Skyphos Type C1
	TOTAL	43				

The decoration on the krater fragments is quite fragmentary and hard to distinguish. There appear to be at least nine recognizable decorative motifs:

1. Wavy line. **P638** (Pl. 3-72). Perhaps in handle zone, similar to the pedestaled krater-skyphos from Derveni (see n. 116). Continuation of decorative motif no. 4a on skyphoi and deep bowls. Cf. Aetos P138. **P638** also has a reserved band on the inner rim.
2. Accumbent concentric semi-circles. **P639**. Continuation of skyphos motif no. 7a. Cf. Aetos H42, H46.
3. Wolf's tooth above and accumbent concentric semicircles below. **P635**. Variation of motif found on a cup from Kokevi (see n. 94) which has a wavy line above and cross-hatching below.
4. Crosshatched triangles in metopal panels. **P1617, P1618** (Pl. 3-73). Continuation of skyphos motif no. 10. Cf. Aetos H26-7, H29, P134. **P1618** has a wavy line below the metopal panels.
5. Framed hatched triangles. **P990** (Fig. 3-33). Variation of skyphos motif no. 11, which has framed cross-hatched triangles.
6. Large dots in metopal panels. **P634, P707** (Fig. 3-33; Pl. 3-74). Continuation of skyphos motif no. 14. Cf. Kalydon (see n. 105). **P707** has cross-hatching above the metopal panels.
7. Small squares in metopal panels. **P951, P975** (Figs. 3-33, 3-35; Pls. 3-75, 3-76). **P975** has small dots in the squares (cf. Aetos H26b) and fragments of accumbent concentric circles to left of metopal panel.
8. Registers (3) of half-chevrons. **P931** (Fig. 3-33). Adaptation of skyphos motif no. 15 (piled triangles). Cf. Amyclae (see n. 104).
9. Undecorated metopal panels. **P991** (Fig. 3-35; Pl. 3-77). Continuation of skyphos motif no. 18. There are, unfortunately, to date no Messenian krater parallels. The comparative evidence, however, from Ithaca and Laconia suggests conclusions similar to those proposed for the skyphos/deep bowl and cup classes.

SHALLOW BOWLS

A few fragments of shallow bowls were found. **P872** and **P1007** (Fig. 3-41) are rims, and **P417, P715, P716** (Fig. 3-17) represent handles. The shallow bowl shape with flat base is not particularly popular in W Greece; some good parallels, however, come from Alaas.[118] Yet, one difference is that the Alaas examples have inverted rims, whereas those from Nichoria are everted (**P1007**; Fig. 3-41) or straight (**P417**; Fig. 3-17). Two types of handles belong to these rims. Type A (**P417**) handle projects horizontally from the rim and is the more usual type of shallow bowl handle. The rim of **P417** is straight, with a slight groove on its interior, perhaps for the placement of some sort of lid. **P715**, on the other hand, is a large angular handle that projects slightly upward from the rim. Its size is paralleled by a shallow bowl with a conical foot from Alaas Pit A/7, and **P715** may belong to something similar.

STRAINERS OR BREAD BASKETS

Several strainer fragments were also found (**P776, P880, P918**) with well-preserved holes ranging in diameter from 0.0035 m (**P776, P918**; Pls. 3-78, 3-79) to 0.004 m (**P880**). The curve of the body on these fragments indicates a shallow rather than a deep bowl, and it may well be that such bowls were used for holding bread rather than for straining. The holes would allow air to circulate around the bread to prevent it from molding or becoming soggy. Shallow bowls of this sort are used today in Greece, and such a use may represent the continuation of an ancient tradition. One fragment (**P776**; Pl. 3-78) has a nipple decoration. Such nipples are found on DAII amphorae from the Kokevi tomb[119] and represent the continuation of a northern motif from DAI.[120] The Nichoria example, however, is the first nipple to be found on a strainer.

RIBBED STEMS

A total of 15 ribbed kylix stems belong to DAII lots. No new types are introduced, and most DAII stems fall into the same categories as those of DAI. But only Types A(?), B, C, and F are represented in the later period. These are all tall stems from high kylikes belonging to the W Greek tradition, i.e., types for which parallels can be found elsewhere in W Greece during the DAI period. The short stems (Types D and E) which appeared to be a local phenomenon in DAI do not reappear in DAII.

Type A(?) (**P1014, P1015**; Fig. 3-19; Pl. 3-80). Both examples are very worn and thus hard to classify (earlier strays?). They seem to belong to Type A with gentle swellings, perhaps two in number, in the stem. The swellings do not appear to run horizontally across the stem but are more in the nature of a spiral. No parallels elsewhere.

Type B (**P1016, P1017**; Fig. 3-19; Pl. 3-81). Ribs with rounded points, as in DAI. Good parallel from Alaas (J3) which has two rounded ribs, one at junction with lower body and the other in the middle of the stem.

Type C (**P1018-20**; Fig. 3-19; Pl. 3-82). Stems with bulbous ribs and slightly hollow feet. The Nichoria examples (especially **P1019**) appear to have only two ribs, as do similar stems from Alaas (J1, J5, H2) and from the Cesnola collection in New York.[121] Other parallels, but with three ribs, from Idalion[122] and Kourion[123] and also on stemmed animal vases from Alaas and the Cesnola collection.[124] Two fragmentary stems, with only one bulbous rib preserved, also come from Amyclae.[125]

Type F (**P1021-28**; Fig. 3-19; Pls. 3-83, 3-84). Stems with sharply pointed ribs and conical feet. **P1027** has two ribs preserved pointing *upward*; the rest point horizontally outward. Such sharp ribs (one only) are paralleled at Alaas[126] (I4, J4) but with flat, and not conical, feet and on a stemmed animal vase in the Cesnola collection.[127] Multiple sharp ribs (maximum preserved are four) appear on stems from Amyclae.[128]

The evidence presented by the Nichoria ribbed stems simply reinforces that from the other open shapes. The Amyclae stems are excellent parallels and can be classified to Types C and F, again underscoring the close ties between Messenia and Laconia in the DAII period. The Cypriot stems are as tall as the Nichoria examples but slightly broader and belong to vases of slightly larger proportions. Nevertheless, they give an idea of what the superstructure of the Nichoria stems might have been. Benton (1938-39, p. 13) supposes that the idea of ribbed stems might have arisen independently in Cyprus and W Greece. Rather, it suggests the idea of a shared ceramic tradition between these regions. The ribbed stem is part of the W Greek ceramic repertoire in DAI, lasting in Messenia through DAII and also spreading to Laconia. The idea of cross-hatched triangles in metopal panels beginning at the rim and the use of incisions below the rim may have originated in Laconia and spread to Messenia. The opposite may have happened with the ribbed stems; these are a W Greek feature which may have made its way to Laconia.

CLOSED SHAPES

OINOCHOAI AND JUGS

Oinochoai and jug rims in the DAII period are virtually indistinguishable from each other and can be used interchangeably on both types of vases. Type A rims (Fig. 3-19) are everted and belong to large and medium-sized vases. Type A1 rims can belong to both oinochoai (**P420**, **P425**; Fig. 3-19) and jugs (**P954**; Fig. 3-36) of large size with rim diameters ranging between 0.08 and 0.12 m and an average neck thickness of 0.006-0.007 m. **P721** (Fig. 3-39) is an example of an A1 rim that has been warped in firing. Type A2 rims are everted with flat tops and are found with both medium-sized jugs (rim diameter 0.06-0.07 m and neck thickness 0.004-0.005 m) and small oinochoai (rim diameter 0.04-0.05 m and neck thickness 0.003-0.004 m). When occurring with jugs, A2 rims usually have striped tops (**P426**; Fig. 3-19). Type A3 rims are pointed and appear to be limited to large oinochoai and jugs. Type B rims (Fig. 3-19), however, occur solely with large oinochoai; these rims are everted but are concave on the interior, forming a small channel, perhaps to catch excess liquid and prevent dripping. The one exception, **P773** (Fig. 3-37), is an example of a Type B rim belonging to a small oinochoe. Type C (**P553, P554**; Fig. 3-19) rims are straight and belong to medium-sized

Table 3-10. Rim Types for DAII Oinochoai and Jugs

Rim Type	Size of Vase	Number of Examples	Catalog Numbers of Best Examples	Average Diameter	Thickness of Neck	Remarks
A1	Large oinochoai and jugs	64	**P420, P425, P817, P954, P1588,** (Figs. 3-19, 3-35, 3-36, 3-37, 3-38; Pl. 3-87)	0.08-0.12	0.006-0.007	**P721** warped in firing
A2	Medium jugs	7	**P423, P426** (Figs. 3-19, 3-39)	0.06-0.07	0.004-0.005	Stripes on top of rim
A2	Small oinochoai	2	**P587, P1591** (Fig. 3-39)	0.04-0.05	0.003-0.004	No stripes on top of rim
A3	Large oinochoai and jugs	8	**P485** (Fig. 3-19)	ca. 0.10-0.12	ca. 0.005	Pointed rim
B	Large oinochoai	19	**P424, P486, P720, P772, P1586,** (Figs. 3-19, 3-36, 3-37, 3-38; Pl. 3-86)	0.08-0.10	0.004-0.005	Concave inner rim
B	Small oinochoai	1	**P773** (Fig. 3-37)	0.04 (?)	0.004	
C	Medium oinochoai and jugs	6	**P553, P554,** (Fig. 3-19)	0.07	0.004	Straight rim
D	Small jugs	8	**P555, P723** (Figs. 3-19, 3-39)	0.04-0.05	0.004	Sharply everted rim
D	Small oinochoai	2	**P1604, P1605** (Fig. 3-39)	0.04-0.05	0.003-0.004	Sharply everted rim
	TOTAL	117				

Table 3-11. Handle Types for DAII Oinochoai and Jugs

Handle Type	Shape	Number of Examples	Catalog Numbers of Best Examples	Average Width	Remarks
A1	Large elliptical	27	**P430** (Fig. 3-20)	0.02-0.026	Plain
A2	Elliptical with rib	16	**P425, P491, P954** (Figs. 3-20, 3-36)	0.025-0.03	One rib
A3	Elliptical with incisions	8	**P522** (Fig. 3-20)	0.028-0.036	Two to three incisions
A4	Elliptical with flute	17	**P658** (Fig. 3-20; Pl. 3-85)	0.02-0.026	
A5	Rope handle	15	**P730, P828, P901, P920, P1586** (Fig. 3-36; Pl. 3-85)	(diameter ca. 0.02)	Round
A6	Small elliptical	9	**P563** (Fig. 3-20)	0.01-0.015	Used with small oinochoai or jugs
	TOTAL	92			

oinochoai and jugs, whereas Type D (**P555**; Fig. 3-19) rims are sharply everted, almost offset, and belong to small oinochoai and jugs. Table 3-10 summarizes the different types of rims and sizes of vases to which they belong.

Large oinochoai and jugs with Type A1 rims are by far the most numerous and represent the common type of pouring vessel at Nichoria. Of these, the oinochoe class seems to be more popular, consisting of approximately 60% of vessels with A1 rims. As for the rest, the number of examples preserved is too few to discern with certainty the preference of the Nichoria potters. Apparently the small shape is moderately represented with 13 examples of small oinochoai or jugs, which emphasizes the potters' interest in the small shape.

The handles are quite varied and, like the rims, can occur on either oinochoai or jugs (see Table 3-11).

All handles, except the rope handle (A5), are elliptical. The rope handle is, of course, round, and represents the only occurrence of the round handle with oinochoai and jugs in DAII. The elliptical shape is the preferred one. Types A1-A5 belong to large and medium-sized vessels, whereas Type A6 is reserved for the small vase.

Bases for these pouring vessels, on the other hand, exhibit little variation in shape. The major difference is one of size which becomes the determining factor for the size of vase with which it is used (see Table 3-12). Most of the bases are used with large or medium-sized vases. Yet, all three types can be also used with the small shape; for example, **P1587** has a small conical base, **P1591, P1605** a small ringed base, and **P1604** has that peculiar combination found at Nichoria of a cross between a conical and a ringed base. **P559** (Fig. 3-20) has a large raised band, almost like a rib, on the exterior of the foot; this surely represents a transfer of the rib found on krater bases

Table 3-12. Base Types for DAII Oinochoai and Jugs

Base Type	Shape	Number of Examples	Catalog Numbers of Best Examples	Average Diameter	Remarks
A	Conical	16	**P428, P558, P1587** (Figs. 3-20, 3-39)	0.08	Conical bases with a diameter of 0.04 m also appear on small oinochoai or jugs.
B	Ringed	13	**P559, P962a, P1588, P1591, P1605** (Figs. 3-20, 3-38, 3-39)	0.10-0.16	Used with large vases but with diameter of 0.04-0.05 m. Can be used with small oinochoai and jugs.
C	Ringed-conical	14	**P824, P1586, P1604** (Figs. 3-20, 3-36, 3-39)	0.08-0.10	With diameter of 0.04-0.05 m. Can be used with small pouring vessels.
	TOTAL	43			

to those of oinochoai and jugs. **P824** has a shallower raised band, which can be considered the continuation of a decorative feature already seen on skyphos and deep bowl bases. Finally, **P558** and **P559** have incisions on their undersides, an idiosyncrasy also evident in the bases of open shapes.

What whole shapes do these disparate elements of rims, handles, and bases represent? There are five basic shapes:

Shape 1. Large (and medium) oinochoai and jugs with *circular* bodies. **P420(?)**, **P954**, **P1586** (Figs. 3-35, 3-36). Rim Types A1, B and base Types B, C. Shape not paralleled elsewhere; perhaps a local characteristic.

Shape 2. Large (and medium?) oinochoai (and jugs) with *elliptical* bodies. **P425(?)**, **P720** (Figs. 3-36, 3-37; Pl. 3-86). Rim Types A1 and B. Shape paralleled on oinochoai from Agrinion (Ioannina Museum no. 4595) and Derveni.[129]

Shape 3. Large and medium oinochoai (and jugs) with *conical* bodies. **P772, P773, P817, P1588** (Figs. 3-37, 3-38; Pl. 3-87). Rim Types A1 and B. Shape continued from LHIIIC.[130]

Shape 4. Small oinochoai and jugs with *circular* bodies. **P426(?)**, **P1587**, **P1605** (Fig. 3-39). Rim Types A2, D and base Types A, B. Messenian parallels from Antheia.[131] Not paralleled outside Messenia; perhaps a local characteristic.

Shape 5. Small oinochoai and jugs with *conical* bodies. **P723(?)**, **P1591**, **P1604** (Fig. 3-39). Rim Types A1, Á2, D and base Types B, C. Messenian parallels from Antheia (Fig. 3-43),[132] Tsoukaleïka,[133] and Kokevi;[134] other parallels from Agrinion (Ioannina Museum nos. 4589-90, 4600-1, 4603). Shape developed from LHIIIC (cf. the Tragana jugs from Burial α) and continued in Messenia and Aetolia.

The evidence presented by the oinochoai and jugs is less complete than in the case of the skyphoi and deep bowls. The elliptical (Shape 2) and conical (Shapes 3 and 5) appear to have parallels in Achaea and Aetolia, whereas the circular shape (nos. 1 and 4) is found only in Messenia and can be considered a local characteristic.

The decorative motifs on these oinochoai and jugs are not as varied as those on the skyphoi and deep bowls, and the same decorative elements are used on the pouring vessels. The major zone of decoration is on the shoulder, with neck and belly coated in monochrome black. This monochrome paint sometimes spills over to the inner rim (**P423-26, P481, P486, P487, P554, P718, P719, P723, P751, P773, P817-19**; Figs. 3-19, 3-36, 3-37, 3-39) and occasionally covers the entire inner neck (**P771, P773**; Fig. 3-37). On one example (**P428**; Fig. 3-20) the paint even covers the underside of the base. Such an extensive dark ground serves to highlight the shoulder decoration. Only on rare occasions is a second decorative motif added to the neck (**P772, P995**; Fig. 3-38). On **P772** three vertical lines of a triglyph(?) are preserved, and on **P995** fragments of arcs of accumbent concentric semi-circles. On **P1588** (Fig. 3-38) the dark ground is further emphasized by a broad reserved band on the neck with thin black bands above and below. With such pervasive monochrome coating, there needs to be some sort of device to indicate the point of transition from neck to shoulder where the decorative zone begins. This transition is indicated in four ways:

1. By two to four black bands at point of transition. **P655, P854, P898, P899, P900, P910, P952, P985, P1588** (Fig. 3-38; Pls. 3-89, 3-90, 3-94).
2. By grooving; from two to five incisions. **P420, P653, P654, P721, P725, P772, P818, P849-51, P995-97, P1009** (Figs. 3-33, 3-35, 3-38, 3-39, 3-40; Pls. 3-92, 3-93, 3-95). Cf. Ioannina Museum nos. 4592, 4598 (from Agrinion).
3. By one to three raised bands. **P773, P820, P954** (Figs. 3-36, 3-37). Cf. Derveni 493 (see n. 129) and Ioannina 4595.
4. By a row of impressed dots (made by stick). **P556.**

Grooving seems to be the most popular means of indicating this transition from neck to shoulder; occasionally such incisions also occur at mid-belly (**P557**) and on the underside of the base (**P558, P559**; Fig. 3-20; and Ioannina Museum no. 4595).

The actual decorative motifs on the shoulder continue the skyphos/deep bowl repertory:

1. Wavy line. **P817** (Fig. 3-37). In addition, this vase has a reserved band at mid-belly. It also shows an interesting feature of construction: the neck was made separately and fitted into a slot at the top of the shoulder. Cf. skyphos motif no. 4a. Parallels from Agrinion (Ioannina Museum nos. 4591, 4603).
2. Concentric circles in metopal panel with broad vertical band for triglyph. **P910** (Pl. 3-88). Cf. skyphos motif no. 6. Attic influence.
3. Adjacent sets of accumbent concentric semi-circles. Compass-drawn with central dot (not preserved in all the fragments). **P654, P934, P977, P1586, P1587, P1604, P1605** (Figs. 3-36, 3-39). In many sherds only parts of arcs of semi-circles are preserved. Cf. **P488, P724, P849, P852, P854, P898, P899, P917, P935, P952, P976, P978, P979, P996, P1010** (Fig. 3-39; Pls. 3-89, 3-90, 3-91, 3-95). In **P488**, the arcs of the semi-circles spill over to mid-belly, and in **P899, P952**, and **P1586** (Fig. 3-36; Pl. 3-90), the semi-circles are placed in metopal panels with cross-hatching and vertical lines forming the triglyph. In **P818** (Fig. 3-33) and **P933** the central dot is replaced by a spiral. Cf. skyphos motif no. 7. Messenian parallels from Antheia (II 77, 506) (see n. 131). Use of accumbent concentric semi-circles is a common motif on DA closed vases.

4. Overlapping sets of accumbent concentric semi-circles. **P653. P985** has two registers of semi-circles; on the shoulder, they are overlapping, but on mid-belly they are adjacent. **P851** (Pl. 3-92) is extremely interesting, for it represents a ghost-set of semi-circles which were painted over in antiquity. Either the artist repainted a mistake, or the original decoration had become so faded that the decoration was repainted at a later date. Cf. skyphos motif no. 8. Local style.
5. Hand-drawn concentric semi-circles. **P421, P909, P1588** (Fig. 3-38). These are interesting, for they show that both hand-drawn and compass-drawn semi-circles coexisted, although the compass-drawn kind are by far the more numerous. Good Messenian parallel from Kokevi (n. 134).[135] The same coexistence occurs on lekythoi in Attic Early PG.
6. Alternating pendent and accumbent concentric semi-circles. **P995**, which also has black bands at the lower belly. Cf. skyphos motif no. 9. Ithacan influence.
7. Crosshatched triangles in metopal panels. **P655, P720, P725, P900, P1009** (Figs. 3-37, 3-39, 3-40; Pls. 3-93, 3-94, 3-95). Cf. skyphos motif no. 10. Messenian parallels from Antheia (II 78, 203), Tsoukaleïka (see n. 131), and Kaphirio. The presence of such cross-hatching may indicate Laconian influence, but this motif is also common in Attica and the Argolid.
8. Framed crosshatched triangles in metopal panels. **P936** (Fig. 3-40; Pl. 3-96). Cf. skyphos motif no. 11. Laconian influence(?).
9. Hatched triangles. **P953, P1591** (Fig. 3-39; Pl 3-97). **P953** has the hatched triangle in a metopal panel. Cf. skyphos motif no. 14. Ithacan and Achaean influence.

Two decorated handle fragments were also found; these belong to small oinochoai or jugs. **P992** (Fig. 3-40; Pl. 3-98) is elliptical and has angular stripes, almost triangles, along its top; **P955** (Fig. 3-33), on the other hand, is flat with alternating horizontal and vertical bands. The latter decoration is one that begins in DAII at Nichoria and occurs on jug and cup handles until the end of the settlement.

As with the skyphoi and deep bowls, the common decorative motif is the accumbent concentric semi-circle. Such concentric semi-circles do appear in Attica, the Corinthia, and the Argolid. The occasional use of hand-drawn semi-circles represents the survival of LHIIIC style, such as appeared at Tragana, and it is interesting to note that both hand-drawn and compass-drawn semi-circles coexist in the DAII period. The evidence of the oinochoai and jugs, then, confirms that presented by the open shapes, namely of minimal Attic influence, but with a shared tradition and perhaps contacts with W Greece and Laconia.

AMPHORAE

Amphorae are poorly represented at Nichoria. Two good amphora rim and neck fragments are preserved from the settlement (**P821, P998**; Fig. 3-19; Pl. 3-99) and one stray find from Lakkoules (**P1606**; Fig. 3-40). These have rims similar to oinochoe/jug Types A1 and A2. **P998** and **P1606** have everted rims of the A1 Type, and **P821** has the A2 Type with flat top. The rim diameters range from 0.12 to 0.13 m, so **P821** and **P998** from the settlement probably resemble **P1606** in size and perhaps also in shape. Both neck- and belly-handled amphorae are represented. **P998** has a broad elliptical neck handle; a total of seven such handles belong to the DAII period. Conversely, **P492** (Fig. 3-20) and **P1606** have rolled belly handles (Type B); 12 such handles ranging from 0.02 to 0.028 m in diameter were found. **P1606** (Fig. 3-40) has a shallow ringed base with diameter of 0.132 m. A number of flat bases with large diameter (0.10 m and above) come from the site. As in DAI, these fall into two categories. Type A (13 examples; Fig. 3-20) has a concave exterior, whereas Type B (12 examples; Fig. 3-20) has straight sides. Such flat bases probably belong to amphorae, although the two from Kokevi[136] have shallow ringed bases. The rather squat ovoid shape of **P1606** and Kokevi 1662 is a survival from late LHIIIC and DAI and is paralleled in these earlier periods by **P1581** and by the amphorae from Ramovouni-Dorion and Elis. The elliptical shape of Kokevi 1661, however, is developed from a similar shape (no. 2) found in DAII oinochoai and jugs and is also common in Achaea and Aetolia.

A combination of old and new elements also appears in the decorative motifs of these amphorae. **P1606** has the Laconian crosshatched triangle in metopal panels in the handle zone; similar decoration in the form of a framed crosshatched triangle appears on the shoulder of a hydria found at Mavrovouni, near Gytheion.[137] Kokevi 1661 has a crosshatched diamond[138] with an adjacent isolated spiral; this latter motif constitutes a LHIIIC survival, as do the wavy lines on the belly of Kokevi 1662. The sharp wavy line on the neck of Kokevi 1662 is similar to those on the Rizes cups and also represents the survival of an earlier motif. **P1606** is coated on the inner rim, but not to such an extent as the Ramovouni and Kokevi amphorae. The amphorae, then, appear to be quite conservative in their shape and decoration and for the most part may represent the survival of an earlier tradition.

PILGRIM FLASK

One decorated body fragment of a pilgrim flask (**P752**; Fig. 3-40; Pl. 3-100) belongs to DAII. The fragment comes from the central belly of the flask and is decorated with a circle divided into four quadrants with a crosshatched triangle in each. A flask with identical decoration comes from Alaas (T.17/14), but, as yet, such flasks have not been found elsewhere in Messenia or Laconia.

ASKOS(?)

One fine wheel-made tripod foot (**P408**; Fig. 3-21; Pl. 3-101) also belongs to DAII. Several similar feet were found but belong to coarse handmade vases. **P408** is rectangular,

Table 3-13. Rim Types for DAII Coarse Bowls

Rim Type	Type of Vase	Number of Examples	Catalog Numbers of Best Examples	Average Diameter	Body Thickness	Remarks
A	Bowls or amphorae	40	**P432, P434, P494, P754, P755** (Fig. 3-20; Pl. 3-104)	0.09-0.30	0.007-0.013	Preserved decoration of raised band with finger impressions below rim.
B	Bowls or amphorae	38	**P436, P437, P495, P756** (Fig. 3-20; Pl. 3-104)	0.09-0.26	0.007-0.012	Great variation in size of these rims.
	TOTAL	78				

turning slightly outward in the same manner as the feet of Alaas T.17/11 and hence may belong to a similar bird askos.

PYXIS(?)

One possible lid fragment (**P980**; Pl. 3-102) belongs to a closed vase, possibly a pyxis. The handle of the lid is broken, and only one stump remains. The preserved portion is flat and thus belongs to the center of the lid, which is decorated on its top with black bands and oblique lines, forming a hatched pattern.

HANGING BOWL

A lug, pierced for a string (**P856a**; Fig. 3-33; Pl. 3-103), was found in a DAII lot. Below the lug, which projects horizontally from the body, are traces of cross-hatching. Such a string-holed lug probably belongs to a vase that was meant to hang from a hook in the ceiling or wall. This piece is unparalleled elsewhere in Messenia.

COARSE WARE

A great many fragments of coarse handmade vessels occur in DAII lots, but, unfortunately, very few whole shapes have been preserved. For the most part, the shapes seem to conform to those of the fine wheel made pottery. On many of the fragments the clay was fired to Munsell 2.5YR 6/8 (light red); others have been burned to Munsell 2.5YR N6/0 gray and 10YR 6/1, 6/2, 7/1, 7/2 (light gray and light brownish gray). A light red exterior with a gray core is not uncommon. The clay contains inclusions, often of small hard pieces of clay, occasionally small grits.

BOWLS

Large coarse bowls probably represent the most common open shape. There are basically two types of rims, but within these broad categories there are a number of variations (Table 3-13). Being handmade, the pottery is less standardized and more open to variation than the fine ware. The typical feature for Type A rims (Fig. 3-20) is the flat top; in addition, some rims have a concave interior (**P432, P434, P494**; Pl. 3-104), straight sides with a band of finger impressions below the rim (**P754**), or a slightly everted rim (**P755**). Since many of these rims have been unevenly made or warped in firing, it is hard to determine their diameters, which seem to range from 0.09 to 0.30 m. Type B rims (Fig. 3-20) are all everted with a rounded top (**P436, P437, P495, P756**; Pl. 3-104) and also vary in size, having the same diameter range as the A type. An almost equal number of examples exists for the two types, and thus both are widely used.

It is unclear whether all these bowls had handles; probably there were some with and some without handles. Type B (round) and Type C (grooved) handles occur in small sizes and could be used with bowls. Table 3-14 lists all the coarse handles; note especially **P448** and **P1002** which may belong to bowls. Type C (with grooves) is an extension of Type A3 of closed fine ware which has two or three incisions running down the top. With the coarse ware handles, however, the incisions are turned into deep grooves and the handle becomes wider, sometimes containing as many as five grooves. On occasion, these handles have been misfired (**P835, P836**; Fig. 3-21; Pls. 3-105, 3-106), and the depth of the grooves becomes really noticeable. The rest of the coarse ware handle types parallel those of the closed fine ware and were probably imitated from them.

Perhaps the best example of a complete bowl comes from Aetos (H105); this has a Type B rim, a Type C handle with three grooves, and a Type B flat base. Indeed, the flat base is perhaps the most commonly used with coarse ware vases at Nichoria and again may be imitated from the closed fine ware types. Type A bases (**P441, P443**; Fig. 3-21), of which eight examples have been preserved, have a concave exterior and range from 0.01 to 0.14 m in diameter. Those of Type B (**P440, P567**; Fig. 3-21), of which there are seven examples, have straight sides (like Aetos H105) and a diameter that ranges from 0.07 to 0.12 m. Those of smaller diameter probably belong to bowls, and those of larger diameter to amphorae. Three other types of coarse bases, Types C (two examples), D (one example), and E (one example) (Fig. 3-21), have also been preserved. Type C (**P444**), with a diameter of 0.08 m, is a ringed-conical base and probably belongs to a jug; Type D (**P568**), with a diameter of 0.04 m, has a rounded bottom and may belong to

Table 3-14. Handle Types for DAII Coarse Bowls

Handle Type	Shape	Type of vase	Number of Examples	Catalog Numbers of Best Examples	Average Diameter or Width	Remarks
A1	Elliptical	Neck-handled amphora or jug	9	**P445, P982, P983** (Figs. 3-20, 3-41, 3-42)	0.03	Cf. Type A1 of closed fine ware
A2	Elliptical with rib	Neck-handled amphora or jug	6	**P500** (Fig. 3-20)	0.03-0.035	One rib. Cf. Type A2 of closed fine ware
A3	Elliptical with flute	Neck-handled amphora or jug	4	**P447, P496** (Figs. 3-20, 3-43)	0.03-0.036	Cf. Type A4 of closed fine ware
B	Round	Small belly-handled amphora, jug or bowl	6	**P448** (Fig. 3-20)	0.02-0.023	
C	Elliptical with grooves	Neck-handled amphora, jug or bowl	10	**P501, P1002** (Figs. 3-20, 3-21)	0.025-0.045	2-5 grooves on top
D	Round	Large belly-handled amphora	5	**P580** (Fig. 3-21)	0.03	Cf. Type B of closed fine ware
		TOTAL	40			

a small bowl; and Type E (**P569**), with a diameter of ca. 0.07 m, is a ringed base, also belonging to a jug or oinochoe.

The coarse bowls, then, have either Type A or B rims, round or grooved handles, and flat bases. Their shape is probably conical, much like that of Aetos H105.

DIPPER

One round-based dipper (**P982**; Fig. 3-41) with Type A1 handle belongs to DAII. Its round base makes it unsuitable for anything but ladling. A similar ladle, but more conical and with a high looped handle, was found at Alaas (T.19/24).

MUG

A DAII lot produced a flat-based mug (**P830**; Fig. 3-41; Pl. 3-107) with a Type B rim and without handles. As yet, its square shape is unparalleled elsewhere in Messenia or W Greece.

DISH(?)

A rim fragment with an attached semi-circular lug (**P831**; Pl. 3-108) is similar in design to Aetos H108 and may belong to a similar flat-based dish.

TRIPOD VASES

Two tripod leg fragments (**P833, P860**; Fig. 3-21; Pl. 3-109) with pointed feet belong to coarse tripod vases. The wheel-made askos(?) foot (**P408**) is rectangular, whereas the coarse tripod feet are pointed and belong to much larger vases of the bowl variety.

STRAINER

A coarse strainer fragment (**P582**) was found with two complete holes (diameter 0.003 m) preserved and traces of four others. Its coarse nature and thick wall indicate use as a strainer rather than as a bread basket (cf. **P776, P880, P918**).

OINOCHOAI

A small coarse oinochoe (**P1590**; Fig. 3-41) is associated with burial Δ in the DA tholos in the environs of Lakkoules. It has a Type B rim with a ringed base (Type E) 0.055 m in diameter, similar to **P569** (Fig. 3-21). An oinochoe rim (**P943**) comes from the settlement, and, with **P569**, may belong to a vase similar in size and shape to **P1590**. The somewhat round shape of the latter represents a continuation of the Mycenaean tradition;[139] such a survival is seen at Asine where similar Protogeometric oinochoai have been found.[140]

JUGS

There is little evidence for coarse jugs in DAII and nothing that can be associated with large jugs. If they existed at all, they probably would have had either Type A or Type B rims and ringed bases. There was found, however, the lower profile (**P734**; Fig. 3-41) of what was once probably a small jug. Its profile is similar to that of the oinochoe (**P1590**) from the DA tholos but with a Type A flat base (diameter 0.07 m) instead of a ringed one. Although it is difficult to tell from the sparse evidence at hand, it may well be that ringed bases can be associated with coarse oinochoai, and flat bases with (small) jugs.

AMPHORAE

DAII lots produced some good neck-handled amphora fragments. The best of these is an amphora (**P1000**; Fig. 3-42; Pl. 3-110), broken at the shoulder and thus missing its rim and neck. The amphora is rather small, as far as neck-handled amphorae go, with a base diameter of between 0.082 and 0.083 m and a restored rim diameter of ca. 0.21 m. The vase has an S-shaped profile with a handle stump preserved on the shoulder and a Type B flat base. The restoration of rim and neck were made on the basis of the curve of the shoulder at the break; if correct, the amphora assumes a rather unusual shape for its size. The neck is too wide, the shoulder far too short, and the base too small; all combine to give the amphora a top-heavy appearance. Since no parallels are to be found, the shape may be considered a local one.

P983 (Fig. 3-42) is the rim, neck, and handle fragment of a neck-handled amphora of perhaps similar shape. **P496** and **P497** (Fig. 3-43) again present unusual features. Both consist of neck and rim fragments of neck-handled amphorae. With **P496** the upper part of the handle joins the vase at the rim; but with **P497** the upper handle joins the vase at the middle of the neck, so that the neck rises above the handle for a short distance. What is interesting, however, is the presence of projections from the rims of both fragments. That of **P496** is curved on its exterior and rests on top of the rim, whereas that of **P497** is oblong and is placed on the inner rim. Both projections may have served as ledges on which a lid could rest, although no lid fragments were identified in DAII lots.

A great variety of handles can be associated with these neck-handled amphorae. **P496** (Fig. 3-43) has an A3 Type (fluted) handle; but A1 (elliptical), A2 (ribbed), and C (grooved) handles also belong to such amphorae. Belly-handled amphorae, though not represented by diagnostic rim or neck fragments, are represented by Type B (small) and D (large) round handles. Those of Type B (**P448**; Fig. 3-20) range in diameter from 0.02 to 0.023 m and belong not only to small belly-handled amphorae (or amphoriskoi) but also to jugs and bowls. Those of Type D (**P580**; Fig. 3-21), however, of which five examples have been preserved, have an average diameter of 0.03 m and probably serve only as the belly handles of large amphorae. The bases of such vases are probably flat (like that of **P1000**) and of either A or B Type.

COOKING SUPPORTS (SEE ALSO CHAPTER 5, PP. 290, 291)

Four "spools" of roughly fired clay belong to the DAII period. Two are completely preserved (**P572, P737**; Fig. 3-21; Pls. 3-111, 3-112), and two approximately half preserved (**P570, P571**; Fig. 3-21; Pls. 3-111, 3-112). The complete examples range in height from 0.052 to 0.055 m with a base diameter of 0.045-0.05 m. In shape, they are broad at the ends, tapering toward the middle like a modern spool. Although similar examples have been found in Greece throughout the Bronze Age, the Nichoria pieces are the first from the Dark Age. Their use is somewhat enigmatic. For those of the Early Bronze Age found at Thermi, Lamb[141] suggests use as supports for cooking pots, whereas for similar objects from the Late Bronze Age found at Enkomi, Karageorghis[142] suggests that they may have been used for supporting or separating vases in a kiln. **P572** has been burned black on one side; but burning could support either theory. The one problem, however, is that these objects were found just N and E of Unit IV-1, in a populated area where there is no evidence for kilns. It is possible that they supported or separated the coarse handmade pots that may have been made by the women of individual households and fired over an open fire, an operation still practiced in some of the more remote areas of Greece and Cyprus today. But they could just as well act as supports for coarse cooking pots in food preparation. In any case, it seems clear that they were associated with either the making or the use of coarse pottery and not with the finer wares.

GRILL

A DAII lot also yielded a fragment of a probable grill (**P965**) of coarse clay. The fragment itself has in its center a raised knob which forms flutes on either side in which one could place a spit or cross-stick. Similar fragments were also found belonging to the transitional DAII/III period (cf. **P1069**), and a reconstruction is offered in Fig. 3-47.

PITHOI

Various pithos fragments can be assigned to DAII. The rims for the most part follow the typology of the coarse ware bowl and jug rims with either a flat (**P502, P583, P837**; Fig. 3-21) or a rounded (**P584, P759, P777**; Fig. 3-21) top. All have large diameters, with the smallest being 0.30 m (**P777**), and body thicknesses vary from 0.018 to 0.033 m. The rims with flat tops seem to belong exclusively to large pithoi, whereas those with a curved profile can be associated with smaller storage jars. **P584** has a rope band below the rim, and **P837** has an additional rope band at the rim. **P759** represents an unusual shape for a pithos rim, with a deep groove on the inner rim, perhaps to catch excess liquid and avoid dripping. Two types of bases belong with these rims: flat (**P506, P585**; Figs. 3-22, 3-41) or rounded (**P505**; Fig. 3-22) with diameters of 0.14-0.16 m. These bases are all large and probably can be associated with the larger pithos rims with flat tops, such as **P502, P583,** and **P837**. Excavation of the settlement area did not produce any pithos bases with stemmed feet, such as that which contained the burial at Rizes (see n. 108, 111), and it may be that a distinction between burial and storage pithoi can be made here, with the rather ornate stemmed foot being reserved for the burial pithoi.

On **P777** and **P903** traces of a white slip are preserved on the exterior. Such a slip would serve to mask the coarseness of the clay and hence to decorate the exterior. Incised and impressed decoration on applied raised bands are common on DAII pithoi. Some of the decorative motifs, such as finger and stick impressions and incised circles, appear on pithoi throughout the Bronze Age and represent the survival of a tradition into the Early Iron Age; but other decorative motifs, such as the hatched triangle, are copied from the fine ware of the period. The decorative motifs are listed below:

1. Undecorated raised bands (two) below rim. **P861.**
2. Raised band with flute in center. **P449, P1013.**
3. Raised band with row of finger impressions. **P838, P1003, P1607**. These raised bands are placed below the rim. **P759**, however, has a row of finger impressions along the rim.
4. Raised band with three parallel rows of incised dots (d. 0.015 m). **P662** (Pl. 3-113).
5. Raised band with decoration of incised circles. **P903, P945, P1607**. Usually placed just below the rim on the neck of the vase. **P903** (Pl. 3-114) has one circle with two circumferences (possibly a mistake was made and the circle was redrawn). With **P502** (Fig. 3-21; Pl. 3-115) and **P583** (Pl. 3-116) the incised circles are placed directly on the body of the vase *without* a raised band. On these examples, the circles are not placed in rows but are arranged haphazardly with no overall pattern; some circles intersect each other. Cf. Aetos H99 for parallel use of incised circles.
6. Raised band with row of incised triangles. **P504**. Variations on this motif occur on **P760, P839, P840. P760** has the motif of incised triangles with circles inside and a row of circles above. **P839** and **P840** (Pl. 3-117) have incised triangles with impressed dots (made with the end of a twig) inside. Cf. Aetos H98 for parallel use of incised triangles.
7. Raised band with row of incised hatched triangles. **P964, P984**. On **P984** (Pl. 3-118) the triangles alternate between angle- and side-up.
8. Raised band with three sets of piled triangles. **P778** (Pl. 3-119).
9. Raised band with incised chevrons. **P503.**
10. Raised band with diagonal slashes in imitation of rope decoration. **P584, P761, P921, P946, P1004** (Fig. 3-21). **P837** (Fig. 3-21; Pl. 3-116) has two parallel rope bands, and **P841** (Pl. 3-120) has a rope band with a row of thumb impressions above.
11. Two raised bands with diagonal slashes forming a herringbone pattern. **P586**. Cf. Aetos H102 for parallel decoration.

Of the above decorative motifs, the most common appears to be the rope band, suggesting the strong possibility that the makers of these handmade vessels were imitating baskets or other containers of organic material bound with a rope or cord.[143] Other motifs, such as the plain, hatched, or piled triangles, were influenced by the decoration of the fine wares. Still others, such as the various uses of the incised circles, probably represent the survival of a northern element.[144]

One final comment should be made: the makers of the Nichoria coarse ware seem to have preferred large shapes. **P734** (Fig. 3-41) is really the only example of a small coarse vase. Small vases, such as were found at Rizes or Agriapides,[145] are not popular at Nichoria. The coarse ware tradition with its preference for large shapes is in direct contrast to that of the fine ware which in the DAII period is basically miniature in shape. This contrast might support the hypothesis that two groups of potters were at work, those who made the kiln-fired fine ware and experimented with new shapes and decorative motifs versus those in each household who fired the coarse ware over an open fire. The coarse pottery appears to be more conservative in shape and decoration, reflecting the survival of Mycenaean characteristics and of motifs once common during the Bronze Age in N Greece.

DAII/III Transitional Pottery (ca. 850-800 B.C.)

A group of pottery, still basically DAII in character but containing features later developed in DAIII, is associated with the second building phase of Unit IV-1, i.e., with the floors in L23 Vkl and Xklm-E 2/3. This group is really transitional and is found only in association with Unit IV-1 and not with any other unit or in any other area of the Nichoria ridge. The group is quite small, consisting only of 130 inventoried pieces, as opposed to some 828 for DAII. The essentially DAII character of these transitional lots would make them hard to identify were it not for their clear stratigraphical and architectural association with the second building phase of Unit IV-1.

The clay of these transitional sherds has been fired to the same color as that of the DAII sherds, namely a reddish yellow which varies from Munsell 7.5YR 7/6 to 7/8, of which there are 198 examples.[146] The range of color variation is also the same as that of DAII (Table 3-15). Such a similar range of colors indicates that the same clay beds and the same firing techniques continued to be used. As in DAII, the texture of the sherds is soft and crumbly with flaky surfaces from which much of the slip and decoration has disappeared. The range of shapes is the same as that in DAII, with skyphoi and, to a lesser extent, deep

Table 3-15. Color Range of DAII/III Pottery

Munsell Number	Color	Number of Cataloged Examples
10YR 7/4, 8/3, 8/4	Very pale brown	51
5Y 8/3, 8/4	Pale yellow	3
7.5YR 7/4, 7/6	Pink	4
2.5YR 6/8	Light red	5
2.5YR N5/0 and 5Y 6/1	Gray and light gray	5

bowls being the most popular. An interesting development which continues into DAIII is that cup rims begin to assume more individuality and are not simply copied from the skyphos types. Thus, there begins to develop a greater range and variety of rim types for all open and closed shapes, but at the same time the range of decorative motifs begins to decline. The potters appear to become interested in form and shape rather than in decoration. The paint is still the black or streaky black/brown of DAII, used on both the exterior and the interior. There are only five examples of the reserved inner band (which also begins to decline in popularity) and one example where a slip was preserved (**P1049**). This latter is probably more an accident of preservation than intent, for it is likely that the soft porous surface of the vessels had to have been prepared with a slip before any monochrome coating or decoration could be applied. Individual types and shapes are discussed below.

Table 3-16. Development of Skyphos and Deep Bowl Rims

Rim Type in DAII	Rim Type in DAII/III	Rim Type in DAIII
	Rims with transitional phase:	
A2	A	A1
B1-B3	B1-B3	C1-C3
A1	C1	C5
A4	C2	C6
. . .	D1-D2	B
C1	E1	D1-D2
C3	E2	E1
	Rims with no documented transitional phase:	
. . .	. . .	A2
A3	. . .	. . .
B4	. . .	C4
C2	. . .	D3
D	. . .	. . .
. . .	. . .	E2
. . .	. . .	F

OPEN SHAPES

SKYPHOI AND DEEP BOWLS
(FIG. 3-44; PLS. 3-121, 3-122)

Both skyphoi and deep bowls continue into the transitional period, but, owing to the paucity of material, it is difficult to determine the ratio of one to the other. The majority of rim fragments do have smaller diameters than in DAII, an indicator that the deep bowl may be declining in popularity; such a trend certainly occurs in DAIII. Type A rims (**P1029**; Fig. 3-44; Pl. 3-121) have flat, almost square tops; these stem from Type A2 of DAII and subsequently develop into Type A1 of DAIII. And, like their DAII counterparts, they appear to belong to small skyphoi. Similarly, the everted rims of Type B (Fig. 3-44) resemble those of the same type of DAII with basically the same range in diameters and thus belong to vases of similar size. These later develop into Types C1-C3 of DAIII. Types B1 (**P1030**) and B2 (**P1032**) belong to medium skyphoi, and B3 (**P1101**) to a small deep bowl. Type C rims (Fig. 3-44) of the transitional period are not as easily categorized; basically they are offset rims belonging to small skyphoi. Type C1 (**P1033**) stems from Type A1 of DAII and later becomes Type C5 of DAIII, whereas C2 (**P1035**) stems from Type A4 of DAII and develops into Type C6 of DAIII. Type D transitional rims (Fig. 3-44), also belonging to small and medium skyphoi, have an angular inner side. This is barely noticeable in D1 (**P1036**) but quite pronounced in D2 (**P1106**); such rims subsequently reappear as Type B of DAIII. Type E transitional rims (Fig. 3-44) belong to larger vases; E1 (**P1039**) represents one of the few examples of a large deep bowl in this period, whereas E2 (**P1042**) can be associated with both medium- and large-sized skyphoi. The development of the various rim types is set forth in Table 3-16. As can be seen from this table, many of the rim types do exhibit a transitional phase between DAII and III, except for Type D1-D2 which has no antecedents in DAII but is a new type which begins in the transitional period. Other rim types seem to develop directly from the DAII to the DAIII profile. Still others either do not occur in DAII, and hence are unique to DAIII, or do not continue into DAIII.

The statistics on DAII/III rims are presented in Table 3-17 (cf. Pls. 3-121, 3-122). Except for Types B3 and E1, transitional rims belong solely to small- and medium-sized skyphoi with an average rim diameter of between 0.08 and 0.10 m and an average body thickness of 0.003 m, an indication that the Nichoria potters are gradually moving away from large to small open vases.

As opposed to the development in rim types which occur in the transitional period, handles and bases remain fairly static. Handles remain exactly the same,[147] except that the rectangular handles of Type B, seen in DAII, do not occur. The bases show little development and have the same basic features as in DAII, including incisions on the exterior of the foot (**P1051, P1122**; Fig. 3-44). On **P1122**, one incision is placed at the very bottom of the foot in the same position as the reserved band of some DAII examples. It appears, then, that the incised line begins to act as a substitute for the reserved band. The development of base types from DAII to DAIII can be seen in Table 3-18. The various types of conical bases remain essentially the same in shape throughout the three periods. The one exception is the almost flat base (Type D) of DAII which becomes slightly more concave in the transitional period but which does not continue into DAIII. There are additional shapes (Types A3, D1-D2, E1-E2) in DAIII which do not occur in the earlier periods, again indicating the interest that the later potters had in form and shape. A noticeable feature is that the popular ringed base (Type C) of DAII continues

Table 3-17. Rim Types for DAII/III Skyphoi and Deep Bowls

Rim Type	Size of Vase	Number of Examples	Catalog Numbers of Best Examples	Average Diameter	Average Thickness of Body Below Rim
A	Small skyphos	2	**P1029**	ca. 0.09	0.003
B1	Medium skyphos	9	**P1030**	ca. 0.10	0.003
B2	Medium skyphos	13	**P1032**	ca. 0.10	0.003
B3	Small deep bowl	2	**P1101**	ca. 0.16	0.0045
C1	Small skyphos	11	**P1033**	0.08	0.003
C2	Small skyphos	7	**P1035**	0.09	0.003
D1	Small skyphos	5	**P1036**	0.08	0.003
D2	Medium skyphos	6	**P1106**	0.10	0.004
E1	Large skyphos and deep bowl	14	**P1038, P1039**	0.13-0.20	0.0035-0.004
E2	Medium skyphos	10	**P1041, P1042**	ca. 0.12	0.003
	TOTAL	79			

directly into DAIII. The statistics on transitional bases are summed up in Table 3-19 (cf. Fig. 3-44).

Owing to the small amount of transitional pottery, these disparate rims and bases represent only a limited number of shapes. One of these (Shape 1), however, is important in that it foreshadows a shape that becomes popular in DAIII.

Shape 1. **P1036, P1038, P1041** (Fig. 3-46; Pl. 3-123). Skyphoi with *conical* bodies. Use of rim Types D1, E1-E2. Variation of Shape 4 (cf. **P741**) of DAII; becomes a popular shape in DAIII. Development also seen in the position of the handles, which tend to become less high-swung and more horizontal.

Shape 2. **P1039** (Fig. 3-46). Deep bowls with *conical* bodies(?). Too fragmentary to discern with accuracy. Rim Type E1. Similar to Shape 1 but with larger vases (?).

Shape 3. **P1029, P1101** (Fig. 3-46). Skyphoi with *bell-shaped* bodies. Rim Types A and B3. Shape continued from Shapes 3 and 6 of DAII (cf. **P762**).

Table 3-18. Development of Base Types

Base Type in DAII	Base Type in DAII/III	Base Type in DAIII
	Bases with transitional phase:	
A1	A1	A1
A2	A2	A2
B	B	B
D	C	. . .
	Bases with no documented transitional phase:	
C	. . .	C and D1-D2
. . .	. . .	A3
. . .	. . .	E1-E2

Evidence for the decoration on these vases is equally scant. There seems to be a continuation of DAII motifs, but what is clear is the beginning of a trend away from the use of different decorative motifs to a plain monochrome coating or a reserved band in the handle zone. The known motifs are listed below:

1. Solid monochrome coating. **P1033, P1036, P1038**(?), **P1111** (Fig. 3-46; Pls. 3-121, 3-122). Continued from Motif 1 of DAII.
2. Monochrome coated with reserved band in handle zone. **P1041, P1108** (Fig. 3-46; Pl. 3-123). Continued from Motif 2a of DAII.
3. Wavy line in handle zone. **P1029** (Fig. 3-46; Pl. 3-121). Continued from Motif 4a of DAII.
4. Wolf's tooth in handle zone. **P1039**(?), **P1101** (Fig. 3-46; Pls. 3-121, 3-122). Continued from Motif 5a of DAII.
5. Accumbent concentric semi-circles. **P1110.** Continued from Motif 7a of DAII.
6. Vertical lines of possible triglyph. **P1072.** Decoration too worn to discern what motif the metopal panel contained.
7. Cross-hatching in squares. **P1043** (Fig. 3-45). Developed from similar motifs on DAII kraters (cf. **P634, P957**).

The number and variety of decorative motifs thus seem quite limited. The great interest that the DAII potters displayed in decoration appears to be waning, and attention to shape now begins to become the paramount concern.

Table 3-19. Base Types for DAII/III Skyphoi

Base Type	Size of Skyphoi	Number of Examples	Catalog Numbers of Best Examples	Average Diameter	Remarks
A1	All sizes	16	**P1051-53**	0.04-0.06 m	Some examples have incisions
A2	Small and medium	10	**P1121**	0.035-0.045	. . .
B	All sizes	11	**P1081, P1122**	0.04-0.06 m	Some with incisions (to replace reserved band)
C	Medium	5	**P1123**	0.05 m	Developed from Type D of DAII
	TOTAL	42			

CUPS (FIG. 3-44)

Owing to the paucity of examples and complete lack of whole shapes, it is impossible to determine the status and popularity of cups in the transitional period. What is clear, however, is that cup rims begin to assume distinctive characteristics which distinguish them from their skyphos counterparts. Such a distinction could not be made with DAII cups which simply had rims of the skyphos variety. Type A cup rims (**P1077**; Fig. 3-44), which are represented by eight cataloged examples, occur most frequently. These belong to tall, deep cups similar to the single example of Shape 4 (cf. **P768**) of DAII. Such a shape subsequently develops into the standard cup of DAIII. Type B rims (**P1079**; Fig. 3-44), of which only two examples have been preserved, are representative of the popular DAII Shape 1, which declines markedly in the later period. Finally, Type C rims (**P1114**; Fig. 3-44) (two examples) are straight like those of Type A but have deep incisions (usually two) below the rim. The use of such incisions on cups is not a feature in DAII but becomes a characteristic of DAIII cups, with its first appearance in the transitional period.

KRATERS (FIGS. 3-44, 3-45)

Kraters are also poorly represented in the transitional period. The preserved fragments consist of a few rims and bases. The rims consist of two types (A and B; Fig. 3-44), both of which occur in DAII and continue with variations into DAIII. Other rims, however, develop directly from DAII into DAIII without a transitional phase; still others are unique to one period and do not occur in the other. Table 3-20 shows the development of krater rims from DAII to DAIII. Type A and B rims have a transitional phase (Table 3-20); Type B, however, has a number of variations in DAIII. It is only Type B1 which develops from an older form; B2 occurs only in DAIII. Types C and E (Table 3-20) continue directly from DAII to DAIII without a transitional phase; Type D has a different shape in each period; and Types F and G belong solely to DAII. An interesting conclusion which is apparent from Table 3-20 is that there is a greater variety of krater rim forms in DAII than in DAIII. This is in direct contrast to the developments already observed in the skyphos and cup rims between the two periods.

In DAII, owing to the presence of numerous deep bowls, it is not possible to distinguish between deep bowl and krater bases. Only the pedestal krater bases can be clearly distinguished. But because of the decline in the numbers of deep bowls which starts in the transitional period, it becomes easier to isolate semi-conical or ringed krater bases. Thus, although it might seem that there is a greater variety of krater bases in DAIII, one must remember that it was not possible to identify such bases in DAII. A ringed krater base (**P1127**; Fig. 3-45) belongs to the transitional period and is continued in Type C of DAIII. The high pedestal bases of DAII (cf. **P816**, **P897**, **P908**, **P932**) are represented in the transitional period by a single example (**P1126**; Fig 3-45). This type continues well into DAIII (**P1494**), but the ribs (cf. **P897**, **P932**), except for **P1442**, do not last beyond DAII. The solid pedestal base, however, which is

Table 3-20. Development of Krater Rims

Rim Type in DAII	Rim Type in DAII/III	Rim Type in DAIII
	Rims with transitional phase:	
A	A1	A2
A	A2	A1
B	B	B1
	Rims with no documented transitional phase:	
. . .	. . .	B2
C	. . .	C
D	. . .	. . .
. . .	. . .	D
E	. . .	E
F	. . .	. . .
G	. . .	. . .

developed from the kylix stem and which occurred in both DAI (cf. **P208**) and DAII (cf. **P960**), continues directly into DAIII (cf. **P1553**). Lastly, a new type of krater base, small in size with a high conical foot (**P1125**; Fig. 3-44), appears in the transitional period and continues into DAIII (cf. **P1493**). **P1125** also has three incisions on the exterior, much like those on some of the skyphos bases. The high conical shape of the foot and the presence of incisions would indicate that this base has been adapted from the skyphos types. The incisions, however, do not last into DAIII.

The only decorated krater fragment of note belonging to the transitional phase is part of a rim and wall (**P1116**; Fig. 3-47; Pl. 3-124) decorated with metopal panels. The best preserved of these contains a circle with a crosshatched triangle in each of its quadrants and crosshatched triangles above and a wavy line to the side. A second metopal panel to the right contains traces of stacked crosshatched triangles. The motif of the crosshatched triangle is, of course, continued from DAII, but the crowding of the decoration, the use of full circles with crosshatched triangles inside, and the stacking of the triangles are elements that are not encountered in DAII and suggest a later period. Indeed, the thickly crowded nature of the decoration, especially the cross-hatching on **P1116**, is reminiscent of that on the kantharos from pithos grave 2 at Drepanon[148] and may date this krater fragment, and hence the entire transitional phase, to the same period.

STRAINERS OR BREAD BASKETS

P1050 consists of five nonjoining fragments of a strainer or possibly, as was suggested with similar fragments from DAII lots, a bread basket. The individual holes have a diameter of 0.004 m, and a few possible traces of black paint have been preserved on the exterior. The fragments are similar to those of DAII and thus belong to a similar type of vessel.

RIBBED STEMS (FIG. 3-45)

Three ribbed kylix stems (**P1157-59**; Fig. 3-45; Pls. 3-125, 3-126) belong to transitional lots. These all have the sharp points peculiar to Type F, the most representative of DAII types. Such stems have two sets of ribs with a slightly hollow disk foot. **P1157** (Fig. 3-45; Pl. 3-125) represents an unusual development, with incisions above and below the lowest rib. The use of such incisions, like those on the conical krater base (**P1125**), has probably been adapted from the skyphos bases (cf. **P1122**). These three stems of Type F represent the tail-end of ribbed kylikes at Nichoria; such vases do not continue into DAIII.

CLOSED SHAPES (FIG. 3-45)

OINOCHOAI AND JUGS

Closed shapes are not well represented in DAII/III. This is particularly true of the oinochoai and jugs. As in DAII, it is not always possible to distinguish one from the other. Type A rims (**P1061**; Fig. 3-45), of which there are only two examples, have a flat top and a slightly concave interior. These probably belong to oinochoai and are unique to the transitional period, neither occurring in DAII nor developing in DAIII. Owing to the fragmentary nature and few examples of these rims, it has not been possible to determine the reason for their uniqueness nor to ascertain whether they belong to imports. Type B rims (**P1063**; Fig. 3-45), with five preserved examples, probably belonging to jugs, have an oblique top, and they stem from Type A2 of DAII but do not continue into DAIII. Type C (three examples), represented by **P1060** and **P1086** (Fig. 3-45), also probably belong to jugs. These first occur with Type B of DAII (cf. **P424, P488**) and have an angular bend at the top of the rim. In the transitional period the top of the rim is lengthened horizontally to form a ledge on which a lid could be placed. This type of rim does not develop in DAIII, but is shortened and adapted to fit oinochoai (cf. Type C; **P1400**). Finally, Type D (**P1133**; Fig. 3-45), preserved in one example, belongs to a large oinochoe. Such an offset rim is not found in DAII but is varied to form oinochoe Type A (cf. **P1292**) in DAIII.

Handles and bases are also poorly represented. The entire repertory of DAII closed handles is repeated in DAIII, but only three types, the round, the elliptical, and the fluted, occur in our sample of DAII/III. And as in DAII, such handles, depending on their size, can belong either to oinochoai and jugs or to amphorae. Type A (**P1064**; Fig. 3-45) handles (round), of which there are six examples, range in diameter from 0.018 to 0.025 m. Those of smaller size surely belong to oinochoai or jugs, and the larger ones to belly-handled amphorae. Similarly, Type B (**P1065**; Fig. 3-45) handles (elliptical) can be divided according to their size. Two have an average width of 0.012 m and are to be associated with pouring vessels; seven others range in width from 0.021 to 0.031 m and belong to neck-handled amphorae. Likewise, the two examples (**P1141**; Fig. 3-45) of fluted handles (Type C) range in width from 0.021 to 0.025 m and can also be identified as neck handles of amphorae.

Our sample from the transitional period does not have the same range of bases for closed vases as is found in either DAII or DAIII. The only preserved bases are flat types which remain unchanged throughout all three periods. Type A is represented by three examples, and Type B by two. The three that have smaller diameters (i.e., from 0.085 to 0.10 m) belong to pouring vessels, whereas the two with diameters between 0.16 and 0.17 m must be associated with amphorae.

Owing to the fragmentary nature of the material, it is impossible to tell what types of decoration, if any, these oinochoai and jugs had. Most of the fragments have traces of black paint, but they belong to rims and handles where one would expect such paint. Thus, it becomes impossible to determine whether the closed shapes follow the tendency of the open shapes in limiting the decoration to a simple monochrome coating.

AMPHORAE (FIG. 3-45)

The handles and bases of transitional amphorae have been discussed above. Both belly- and neck-handled amphorae appear to be represented. Two rims can be associated with these vases. **P1059** (Fig. 3-45) has an angular top and is developed from **P821** of DAII; it is appropriate for either type of amphora. **P1134** (Fig. 3-45), on the other hand, has no antecedents in DAII but begins in the transitional period and continues into DAIII. It is the rim of a squat amphora, probably belly-handled, since the rim and neck are too short to allow neck handles. Again, the preserved fragments are too few to enable one to determine what types of decorative motifs, if any, these amphorae had.

COARSE WARE

A number of coarse ware fragments belong to the transitional period, but, as with those of DAII, it is not always possible to identify with certainty the types of vases to which they belong. The color range of the fired clay is the same as that in DAII, with many fragments fired to a light red color, whereas others have been burned to light gray or light brownish gray. The larger, coarser fragments also have the same type of clay with grit inclusions as in DAII.

BOWLS (FIG. 3-45)

As in DAII, bowls probably represent the single largest group of coarse vases with the same basic rim types, i.e., Type A with a flat, angular top and Type B with a rounded top, often slightly everted (Fig. 3-45). But, within these two general types, there is a great deal more individual variation in the transitional period. These variations foreshadow the tremendous increase in variety of rims in DAIII. Type A1 (nine examples) contains a plain flat top, and A2 (seven examples) has an oblique, angular rim. All belong to bowls, except for A2 (**P1067**) which begins to turn outward at the point where it is broken at the bottom, indicating the shoulder of a large vase, probably an amphora. Similarly, Types B2 (one example) and B3 (three examples) represent bowls, whereas B1 (four examples) has the large diameter (ca. 0.17 m) and body thickness (ca. 0.01 m) requisite for amphorae.

AMPHORAE (FIG. 3-45)

Probable amphora rims have been discussed above. Handles, like those of the closed fine ware, exhibit almost no change from one period to another. In our sample from the transitional period they are limited to elliptical (Type A), round (Type B), and ribbed (Type C) forms (Fig. 3-45). The elliptical (seven examples) and ribbed (one example) shapes can again be associated with neck-handled amphorae, and the round type (six examples) with belly-handled amphorae. An addition that does occur, however, in one example is a round handle with spiral incisions (Type D) in imitation of rope decoration. This is not a rope handle in the strict sense of the term, since the cords of the rope are not rendered plastically but are simply indicated by incisions. Such a handle may be considered a coarse ware imitation of the fine ware rope handles. It does not occur in DAII but develops in the transitional period and continues into DAIII. Coarse flat bases of Types A (one example) and B (three examples) also continue unchanged from DAII and can be considered as belonging to either type of amphora.

LIDS

Two exceptionally fine coarse lids (**P1068**, **P1097**) come from transitional lots and most likely belong to bowls or amphorae. **P1068** (Pl. 3-127) has a diameter of 0.13 m and is burned dark gray on its underside. Eleven small holes, which are not pierced through the lid, are arranged at irregular intervals on the upper surface. It is not likely that these holes represent marks denoting the amount of liquid or solid substances that the container could hold; more probably they are simply elements of decoration. Similarly the impressions, probably made with the point of a finger, on **P1097** (Pl. 3-128) can also be considered a decorative feature. This second lid is missing its handle and is also burned on the underside, indicating that this side may have been closest to the heat during the firing process. No parallels in either shape or decoration have been found elsewhere in Messenia, so that these lids may be considered purely local phenomena.

TRIPOD VASE

The fragment of a tripod leg (**P1148**) belongs to the transitional phase. This leg is burned at the bottom and, unlike the coarse legs of DAII, is rectangular. It resembles in shape the DAII wheel-made askos(?) foot (**P408**) and represents a local example of a fine wheel-made shape being adapted for use with a coarse handmade vase.

COOKING STAND OR GRILL

P1069 and **P1098** belong to this rather enigmatic category. **P1069** consists of a raised rim with a knoblike projection. The inner surface is burned black, suggesting use as either a cooking stand or the support for the spit of a grill. Reconstructions of both suggestions are offered (Fig. 3-47), although the smallness of the knob would tend to indicate use as a spit support. The use of **P1098** (Pl. 3-129), however, is much clearer. It is curved, burned in the interior, and has holes pierced through the sides to allow for the movement of air. This strongly suggests that it is part of a stand that supported a cooking pot.

PITHOI

The decorated pithos body fragments of DAII/III for the

most part continue motifs already in existence in DAII:

1. Undecorated raised bands below rim. **P1154.** Continued from Motif 1 of DAII.
2. Raised band with row of finger impressions. **P1070.** Continued from Motif 3 of DAII.
3. Raised band with diagonal slashes in imitation of rope decoration. **P1155.** Continued from Motif 10 of DAII.
4. Body fragment with nipple decoration. **P1156.** In DAII, nipple decoration was found on amphorae and strainers, but now for the first time it occurs on a pithos.

DAIII Pottery (ca. 800-750 B.C.)

DAIII lots are found predominantly in Area IV, and it is evidently this portion of the ridge that was occupied almost exclusively during the latest DA phase. The best groups of sherds are associated with the debris above Unit IV-1 in the neighborhood of two large pithoi which intruded into the ruined S wall of that unit[149] and with its successor, Unit IV-5. There are 417 inventoried DAIII sherds, about half as many as those from DAII. DAIII sherds are more varied in form and color than those from DAII and thus are harder to identify. A great many continue to be fired to a reddish yellow, but the color range in the Munsell charts is greater. The other colors of DAII, such as pale brown, pink, yellow, and red, also continue but, again, in greater variation (Table 3-21). Munsell 5YR 7/6 and 7/8 were produced in DAII, but 7.5YR 7/6-8/6 are DAIII variations. Similarly, the range of browns is greater, with 10YR 6/4 not occurring in DAII. The range of grays achieved through misfiring or overfiring is also greater and suggests either that the better local clay was becoming scarce or that firing practices were becoming less precise. The range of colors would certainly indicate that the temperatures in the kilns were regulated less strictly than in DAII. Further indications of overfiring are seen in a number of sherds that have a gray-blue, light red, or orange-pink core.

Table 3-21. Color Range of DAIII Pottery

Munsell Number	Color	Number of Examples[a]
5YR 7/6 and 5YR 7/8 7.5YR 7/6, 7/8, 8/6	Reddish yellow	476
10YR 7/3, 7/4, 8/3, 8/4	Very pale brown	122
10YR 6/4	Light yellowish brown	38
10YR 6/3	Pale brown	1
5Y 8/3, 10YR 7/6	Pale yellow, yellow	3
2.5Y 8/2, 10YR 8/2	White	13
5YR 7/4, 7.5YR 7/4	Pink	22
2.5YR 6/8, 10R 6/8	Light red	28
10YR 6/2, 7/2, 5/1, 5YR 6/1, 2.5YR N4/0	Light brownish gray to dark gray	62

[a]The total number of examples of clay color is 765, which is almost twice as many as the number of inventoried pieces for DAIII. The reason for this is that well-preserved body sherds are included in the clay count but have not been cataloged.

As in previous DA phases, the sherds have a soft and crumbly texture with flaky surfaces from which slip and a great deal of the decoration have disappeared. On only two sherds are there possible traces of slip. A notable and distinctive feature is the average body thickness of the open shapes, ranging from 0.002 to 0.003 m. This is approximately 0.001 m thinner than that of similar DAII vases. Such a body thickness produces a class of skyphoi with almost paper-thin sides, a feature which later recurs with some Protocorinthian vases. The trend toward small shapes, begun in DAII, is also an important feature of DAIII. Indeed, there are only a few examples of the deep bowl, the preferred shapes being the small skyphos and the cup. Other shapes, such as the krater, oinochoe, and jug, are continued from DAII. The complete absence of the kantharos, so popular in W Greece, can again be noted at Nichoria in this period. There is also a great increase in the range and number of coarse ware shapes, particularly from Area IV SE.

The range of decorative motifs, however, declines sharply. A few examples of accumbent concentric semi-circles and cross-hatching carry over from DAII, but most vases are simply monochrome coated on both exterior and interior. The inner reserved band is dying out; only two examples (**P1259**, **P1352**) occur, and then only with the typical DAII decorative motif of accumbent concentric semi-circles. The use of black paint continues to be standard, but the paint itself takes on a different character. Instead of varying from a streaky black to a streaky dark brown, it becomes solid black with a bluish tinge and a metallic sheen. Even though most DAIII vases lack decoration, they display a great variety of rim and base forms which are discussed individually below.

OPEN SHAPES

SKYPHOI AND DEEP BOWLS

Owing to the decline of deep bowls, the skyphos becomes the most common DAIII shape. To these vases belong six basic rim types (Table 3-22). Type A rims (Fig. 3-48), stemming broadly from the same type of DAII rims (see Table 3-4), are everted with flat tops. With Type A1 the top is horizontal, but with A2 oblique or slanting, except for **P1232** which is slightly concave. All Type A rims, with one exception (**P1160**), belong to skyphoi, predominantly to medium-sized skyphoi with an average rim diameter of 0.10 m and average body thickness of 0.003 m. **P1160**, however, has a rim diameter of 0.17 m and thus belongs to a small deep bowl. Type B rims (Fig. 3-48) are somewhat like those of A2 but are much more angular and pronounced (**P1347, P1348**). **P1162** has a definite concavity in its top, forming a small channel, perhaps to catch excess liquid and prevent dripping. Type B rims also belong to medium skyphoi; the predominant rim diameter is again 0.10 m, with an average body thickness of 0.003 m.

Type C rims (Fig. 3-48) represent the most varied class, with no less than six variants. As opposed to Type A and B rims, Type C are offset, projecting almost at right angles from the body. The difference in the degree of this projection determines their classification. Again, all belong to skyphoi of various sizes. C1 rims (**P1163, P1350**) are sharply offset, i.e., they curve outward almost at right angles to the body. The curve and outward projection is less pronounced with C2 rims (**P1165, P1236, P1237**) and still less so with those of C3 (**P1166, P1170, P1179, P1239**; Pl. 3-130). Type C4 rims (**P1171**), on the other hand, are rather an oddity, existing in only four examples. They are related to Type B but without the latter's angularity. C5 rims (**P1240, P1241, P1253, P1357**; Pl. 3-131) are similar to those of C1, but the curve and outward projection are much more pronounced; indeed, the rim almost begins to

Table 3-22. Rim Types for DAIII Skyphoi and Deep Bowls

Rim Type	Size of Vase	Number of Examples	Catalog Numbers of Best Examples	Average Diameter	Average Thickness of Body Below Rim
A1	Medium skyphoi	15	**P1341, P1343**	0.10-0.12	0.003
A1	Small deep bowl	1	**P1160**	0.17	0.004
A2	Medium and large skyphoi	17	**P1161, P1232, P1346**	0.12-0.14	0.003
B	Medium skyphoi	4	**P1162, P1347, P1348**	0.10-0.12	0.003-0.004
C1	Small and medium skyphoi	28	**P1163, P1350**	0.07-0.12	0.002-0.003
C2	Medium skyphoi	35	**P1165, P1236, P1237, P1352, P1545**	0.10-0.12	0.003
C3	Small and medium skyphoi	26	**P1166, P1170, P1179, P1239**	0.07-0.13	0.003-0.004
C4	Medium skyphoi	4	**P1171**	ca. 0.10	ca. 0.004-0.0045
C5	Small and medium skyphoi	32	**P1240, P1241, P1253, P1357, P1417, P1418**	0.07-0.12	0.002-0.0035
C6	Small and large skyphoi	13	**P1243, P1254**	ca. 0.09	0.003-0.004
D1	Large skyphoi	48	**P1172, P1173, P1245, P1246, P1485, P1487**	0.12-0.14	0.003-0.004
D2	Small skyphoi	21	**P1175**	ca. 0.09	0.003
D3	All sizes of skyphoi	44	**P1177, P1178, P1361, P1488**	0.09-0.14	0.003-0.004
E1	Medium skyphos	1	**P1180**	0.10	0.003
E1	Medium and large deep bowls	18	**P1257, P1362, P1486, P1507 P1547**	0.17-0.22	0.004-0.005
E2	Medium and large deep bowls	17	**P1181, P1250**	0.17-0.21	0.004-0.005
F	Medium and large skyphoi (?)	12	**P1182**	ca. 0.10-0.14	0.003-0.004
F	Medium and large deep bowls (?)	10	**P1251, P1489**	ca. 0.17-0.20	0.004-0.005
	TOTAL	346			

curve back around itself. Those of C6 (**P1243, P1254**) are similar to C5, but the rim is elongated and projects quite far, presenting an almost top-heavy appearance. Type D rims (Fig. 3-48) also belong to skyphoi of various sizes. As opposed to Type C, Type D have only a slight eversion and, indeed, are almost straight. The angle at which the rim turns outward is quite slight with D1 rims (**P1172, P1173, P1244-46**; Pl. 3-130) and barely noticeable with those of D2 (**P1175, P1176**); D3 rims (**P1177, P1178, P1361**; Pl. 3-130) are straight.

Whereas the rims of Types A-D belong to skyphoi of various sizes, those of Type E (Fig. 3-48), except for **P1180**, belong to deep bowls on the basis of their large diameters. The progression of eversion of Type E rims is similar to that of Type D. Those of E1 (**P1257, P1362**) are slightly everted, whereas those of E2 (**P1181, P1250**) are almost straight. **P1180**, however, belongs to a medium-sized skyphos and has a rim diameter of 0.10 m. It is shaped like **P1361** (D3) but slightly more curved and thus can be classed more appropriately with the E1 than with the D3 group. Despite this exception, Type E rims can be considered as belonging to deep bowls, since their average body thickness of between 0.004 and 0.005 m would be inappropriate for the thin-walled skyphoi of DAIII. Type F rims (**P1182, P1251, P1489**; Figs. 3-48, 3-58) are quite unusual for skyphoi and deep bowls; they are everted but with a concave interior. In previous periods, such a shape has been associated with oinochoai (cf. DAII, **P424**), but it is now used with both skyphoi (**P1182**) and deep bowls (**P1251, P1489**), an interesting occurrence of the use of a predominantly closed form for an open shape.

DAIII rims exhibit other interesting features. Types A2 and C2 have incisions below the rim. The use of incisions as a decorative motif on open vases is seen only a few times in DAII (cf. **P520, P604**) where they are more commonly used on oinochoai and jugs to mark the transition from neck to shoulder. Raised bands are also used on DAIII skyphoi, specifically with C5 and D1 rims; again, this is a decorative motif hitherto associated with oinochoai and jugs. What becomes important, then, is the transfer to open shapes of forms and motifs hitherto associated only with closed vases, viz., the use of Type F rims with skyphoi and deep bowls and the use of incisions and raised bands as decorative features on skyphoi.

Of the 346 cataloged rims, Types C and D are the most numerous, accounting for approximately 65%. Of these, Type D represents the single largest group, with a total of 113 examples. The above figures and Table 3-23 also show the decline in the popularity of the deep bowl in favor of the skyphos. Skyphoi (all sizes) are represented by a total of 300 examples and deep bowls by a mere 46. Of the skyphoi, the medium size represents the largest group (120 examples); the miniature shape is represented by 99 examples, indicating the extent of the popularity of the small size in the DAIII period.

Table 3-23. Occurrence of DAIII Skyphoi and Deep Bowls

Type of Vase	Number of Examples	
Small skyphos	99	
Medium skyphos	120	300
Large skyphos	81	
Deep bowls of all sizes	46	

DAIII skyphos and deep bowl handles are not changed in shape, only in position. The same three types found in DAII occur in the later period. Type A handles, of which 203 individual fragments have been identified, are round, with diameters ranging from 0.01 to 0.016 m. These were once covered entirely in black paint and can be associated with medium-large skyphoi and deep bowls. Those of Type B (eight examples), like their counterparts in DAII, are rectangular. Type C handles (82 examples) have a diameter between 0.006 and 0.009 m and can be assigned to the class of small skyphoi.

Like DAIII rims, the bases of the period reflect a greater variety of shapes than in DAII (Table 3-24). Five basic types can be isolated, with Type A being the most popular (79 examples). Type A (Fig. 3-49) in fact represents a conical base that has three major variations. A1 is a plain conical base with rounded foot; within this type there occur minor variations, such as **P1265** which has spiral ridging on its underside with exterior incisions, and **P1188, P1190, P1375**, all of which contain two or three exterior incisions. A2 bases are also conical but with flat feet. Instead of incisions, the main decorative feature seems to be a raised band on the exterior (**P1192, P1377**). Type A3 is a cross between a conical and a ringed foot, that peculiar type of base which occurs at Nichoria in all periods. In this period its small size links it with the small skyphos.

Type B bases (Fig. 3-50) have semi-conical feet, also using the three exterior incisions as a decorative motif (**P1196**). Many Type C bases (Fig. 3-50) also have exterior incisions (**P1197, P1381**); these bases are related to those of Type B but are much flatter, with a very shallow concavity on the underside. Those of Type D (Fig. 3-50) represent the ringed foot but do not have incisions or raised bands as decorative features. Two variations occur within the D category: D1 bases (**P1198, P1274, P1383**) have shallow ringed feet with an average diameter of 0.05-0.07 m, whereas those of D2 (**P1200, P1276**) are smaller in diameter (ca. 0.04 m) but with a higher foot. Type E bases (Fig. 3-50) are similar to those of Type A but have very high conical feet. Again, there are variations in size similar to those of Type D. E1 bases (**P1277, P1278, P1387**) have the larger diameter, whereas those of E2 (**P1279, P1439**) are smaller, with an average diameter of ca. 0.03-0.04 m.

The use of incisions both as a decorative feature and as a

Table 3-24. Base Types for DAIII Skyphoi and Deep Bowls

Base Type	Size of Vase	Number of Examples	Catalog Numbers of Best Examples	Average Diameter	Remarks
A1	Medium and large skyphoi and deep bowls	29	**P1188-90, P1265, P1375**	0.045-0.08	Incisions
A2	All sizes of skyphoi	30	**P1192, P1193, P1267, P1377**	0.04-0.06	Raised bands
A3	Small skyphoi	20	**P1194, P1268, P1379**	0.03-0.04	. . .
B	Medium and large skyphoi	36	**P1195, P1196, P1270**	0.06-0.07	Incisions
C	Medium and large skyphoi	12	**P1197, P1381**	0.05, 0.07	Incisions
D1	Medium and large skyphoi	51	**P1198, P1274, P1383**	0.05-0.07	Ringed foot
D2	Small skyphoi	10	**P1200, P1276**	ca. 0.04	Small ringed foot
E1	All sizes of skyphoi	18	**P1277, P1278, P1387**	0.035-0.06	Very high conical foot
E2	Small skyphoi	6	**P1279, P1439**	0.03-0.04	Small high conical foot
	TOTAL	212			

device on shallow bases to mark the transition from foot to body (**P1197, P1381**–Type C; Fig. 3-50) is greater in DAIII than in previous periods, perhaps to compensate for the general lack of painted decoration. Raised bands also continue from DAII but now seem to be confined to A2 bases. Types A3, D2 (except for **P1276**), and E2 are bases with small diameters (ca. 0.03-0.04 m) and can be associated with the class of small skyphoi with thin sides (rim Types C1 and C5).

These disparate elements of rim, handle, and base, when put together, form seven basic shapes:

Shape 1. **P1179, P1240, P1353, P1417, P1418, P1545** (Fig. 3-55; Pls. 3-130, 3-131). Small and medium-sized skyphoi with *bell-shaped* bodies. Rim Types C2, C3, C5. Small size developed from Shapes 1 and 3 of DAII.

Shape 2. **P1488, P1245**(?), **P1352**(?) (Fig. 3-55). Medium and large skyphoi, *tall and deep*. Rim Type D3 and base Type D1. Developed from Shape 4 of DAII (cf. **P741**) via Shape 1 of DAII/III (cf. **P1038**). No other Messenian parallels.[150]

Shape 3. **P1487** (Fig. 3-56). Medium and large skyphoi, *tall with carinated body.* Rim Type D1 and base Type E2. Developed from Shape 6 of DAII (cf. **P603**). The body below the handle is definitely carinated, whereas only a hint of this occurs with DAII vases of Shape 6. Good Messenian parallel from above the court (42) at Ano Englianos.[151]

Shape 4. **P1485** (Fig. 3-56). Medium skyphos, *shallow with carinated body*. Rim Type D1 and base Type A1. Developed from Shape 9 of DAII (cf. **P922**). Again, in DAIII, there is a definite carination to the body below the handle. No other Messenian parallels.

Shape 5. **P1486, P1507, P1510**(?) (Figs. 3-56, 3-57). Large *bell-shaped* deep bowl, *shallow with rounded body*. Rim Type E1 and base Types A1 and D1. Developed from Shape 11 of DAII.

Shape 6. **P1547** (Fig. 3-57). Large *bell-shaped* deep bowl, *deep with rounded body*. Rim Type E1 and base Type B. Also developed from Shape 11 of DAII.

Shape 7. **P1489** (Fig. 3-58). Large *bell-shaped* deep bowl, *shallow with carinated body*. Rim Type F and base Type D1. No examples of carinated deep bowls in DAII.

Even though the skyphos shapes (1-4) have antecedents in DAII, they achieve their full development in DAIII. Shape 1 is that of the small skyphoi with paper-thin sides, a feature later characteristic of many Protocorinthian vases. Shape 2 is that of tall, deep skyphoi; and Shapes 3 and 4 consist of skyphoi with carinated bodies, a feature only hinted at but never fully developed in DAII. DAIII shapes, then, are interesting in their use of carination and important for their foreshadowing of devices used in later periods. The deep bowls, on the other hand, develop little in shape. The only new feature is the definite use of carination, but this is simply carried over from use with the skyphoi and really marks no radical departure from standard

DAII conventions for deep bowls.

Seven decorative motifs can be associated with DAIII skyphoi.

1. Solid monochrome coating. The best examples are **P1179, P1240, P1417, P1418, P1485-89, P1547** (Figs. 3-55, 3-56, 3-57; Pls. 3-130, 3-131). Continued from Motif 1 of DAII. Occurring on approximately 90% of both skyphoi and deep bowls, this becomes the standard decorative feature in DAIII. Similar monochrome coating is to be found on a skyphos from Ano Englianos.[152]
2. Monochrome coated with reserved band in handle zone. **P1353** (Fig. 3-55) is the only good example. Continued from Motif 2a of DAII.
3. Accumbent concentric semi-circles (compass-drawn) in handle zone. **P1259, P1352, P1518, P1546** (Fig. 3-55). Continuation of Motif 7 from DAII. **P1259, P1352** have reserved inner bands which also continue the DAII decorative tradition.
4. Crosshatched half-triangles. **P1507** (Fig. 3-57; Pl. 3-132). Continued from Motif 12 of DAII, this appears to be a local characteristic.
5. Piled triangles(?). **P1545** (Fig. 3-55). The decoration here is quite worn and by no means certain. If correctly restored, the two piled triangles would be large and would cover the entire surface of the vase. This would mark a radical departure from DAII practice (cf. Motif 15) where the triangles are confined to the upper body of the vase. No parallels found in Messenia; perhaps a local characteristic.
6. Horizontal raised bands below rim. Varying from one **(P1171, P1510)** to two **(P1253**; Fig. 3-48). **P1510** (Fig. 3-57) presents the best example and has a broad raised band placed below the rim. The vase, including band, is monochrome coated. The use of raised bands as a decorative motif occurs only on DAII skyphos and deep bowl bases. In DAIII, the band is transferred to the body of the vase and becomes quite broad.
7. Ribbing. **P1245, P1252** (Fig. 3-55; Pl. 3-130). Such ribbing consists of horizontal raised bands sweeping diagonally across the surface of the vase according to its contour. The entire surface is monochrome coated. Ribbing does not occur in the previous periods and thus can be considered an innovation in DAIII.[153]

The high percentage of monochrome coated vessels indicates that the DAIII potters are not primarily interested in the decoration of their vases but rather in form and shape. The decorative motifs that do occur are carry-overs from DAII and represent no attempt at innovation. What is new, however, is the use of raised bands and ribbing to add plastic variety to the plain monochrome coating. Little pottery of the DAIII period has been uncovered elsewhere in Messenia and thus there are few parallels to the Nichoria material. The only comparable skyphos comes from above the court (42) at Ano Englianos and is so similar in shape and decoration to DAIII skyphoi at Nichoria that it should be considered as belonging to the DAIII period and not as late as ca. 600, as the excavators suggest.[154]

CUPS

As in DAII, cups are the next most popular shape after skyphoi, and in DAIII a real development occurs in the cups. For the first time, cup rims become distinguishable from those of skyphoi; cups thus become an entity in themselves rather than an extension of the skyphos form. Two cup rim types are identifiable; those of Type A (**P1183, P1262**; Fig. 3-48) are slightly everted, whereas those of Type B (**P1184**; Fig. 3-48) are almost straight. Grooving below the rim becomes a regular feature with these cups and occurs on about 75% of the preserved examples. The number of grooves ranges from one to three, and they occur on both Type A and Type B rims. In one instance **(P1389)** the grooving extends to the underside of the base which has concentric incisions. On two examples **(P1367, P1530)**, a raised band is substituted for the grooving; and in both cases the raised band occurs with Type B rims. Such raised bands are probably adapted from those on skyphoi (cf. skyphos Motif 6). Type A rims have large diameters ranging from 0.09 to 0.12 m and belong to large, deep cups, whereas those of Type B are smaller, with an average diameter of about 0.08-0.09 m, and can be associated with small carinated cups.

As with the rims, DAIII cup handles are much more easily identified than those of DAII. There are two types of cup handles: those of Type A (**P1396, P1397**; Fig. 3-49) are elliptical and range in width from 0.01 to 0.014 m, whereas those of Type B (**P1289**; Fig. 3-49) are rectangular with a width ranging from 0.009 to 0.013 m. In general the larger Type A handles can be associated with Type A rims and the deep cups, whereas the smaller Type B handles are found with rims of the same type belonging to the smaller carinated cups. The same general distinction can be made among the flat cup bases, of which there are two basic types, both ranging in diameter from 0.04 to 0.05 m. Type A bases (Fig. 3-50) are fairly thick; those of Type A1 have straight sides, whereas those of A2 are concave at the point of transition between base and body. Type B bases (Fig. 3-50), on the other hand, are paper-thin and belong to a set of cups which, like the skyphoi with C1 and C5 rims, have paper-thin sides. Like the handles, Type A bases appear to belong to deep cups, whereas Type B bases can be associated with small carinated cups. Table 3-25 summarizes the statistics for cups.

Three distinct cup shapes can be differentiated:

Shape 1. Cups with S-shaped profile. **P1549** (Fig. 3-58; Pl. 3-133). Rim diameter 0.083-0.09 m. Rim Type A. Monochrome coated. Continued from Shape 1 of DAII.

Shape 2. Cups with exaggerated S-shaped profile and car-

Table 3-25. Rim, Handle, and Base Types for DAIII Cups

Size of Cup	Rim Type	Number of Examples	Handle Type	Number of Examples	Base Type	Number of Examples	Remarks
Large, S-shaped (D. 0.09-0.12 m)	A	21	A (elliptical)	33	A1 and A2	6 3	1-3 grooves
Small, carinated (D. 0.08-0.09 m)	B	8	B (rectangular)	9	B	28	Grooves and raised bands
TOTAL		29		42		37	

inated body. **P1490, P1509** (Fig. 3-58). Rim diameter 0.085-0.09 m. Rim Type B. Monochrome coated. Continued from Shape 2b of DAII. Two good Messenian parallels from Ano Englianos;[155] a third from the lower town, SE of the Pylos acropolis, has four grooves below the rim.[156]

Shape 3. Broad, fairly shallow cup with S-shaped profile. **P1491** (Fig. 3-58). Rim diameter ca. 0.12 m. Rim Type A. Monochrome coated. Developed from Shape 3 of DAII (which, however, is much shallower).

As in DAII, decoration on the cups is limited to monochrome coating on both exterior and interior; the use of grooving may be an attempt to compensate for this. Again, as with DAIII skyphoi, the use of carination is noteworthy. The three cups from Ano Englianos are similar in every way to those of Nichoria Shape 2 and, as with the skyphos from the same place, should be dated to the DAIII period and not later.[157]

KRATERS

A number of individual krater rim and base fragments, but no whole shapes, belong to DAIII. The rims are represented by five types. Type A (Fig. 3-48), developed from the same type in DAII, has a curved rim with a flat top. The Type A1 rim (**P1185, P1492**; Pl. 3-134) starts at an oblique angle, whereas Type A2 (**P1369**; Pl. 3-134) is horizontal. The latter rims, like their counterparts (Type A) in DAII, belong to medium-sized kraters and have striped tops. Type B rims (Fig. 3-49) are much more rounded than Type A and project outward at right angles to the body. They also show two variations. Type B1 (**P1186, P1429**; Pl. 3-134) belongs to large kraters. **P1429** has two incisions in an unusual position, namely on the underside of the exterior, just above the point of transition from rim to body. B2 rims (**P1520**; Pl. 3-134), on the other hand, belong to medium kraters and project outward at an angle slightly greater than 90°, thus giving the impression of beginning to turn down on themselves. **P1520** has three incisions on the body below the rim (influence from skyphoi?).

Type C rims (**P1187, P1430**; Fig. 3-49; Pl. 3-135), developing directly from the same type in DAII, belong to large kraters. They are almost exactly similar in shape to their DAII counterparts and have the same rope bands on the body (cf. **P536**). There are, however, individual variations. **P1187** has a small groove on the outer edge of the top, perhaps acting as a slot for the placement of a lid. **P1430** has two additional raised bands on the underside of the rim (in the same position as the incisions on **P1429**) and a third shallower band below the rope band. Type D rims (**P1263, P1372**; Fig. 3-49; Pl. 3-135), also belonging to large kraters, are offset in the same manner as those of Type C but are much more angular and omit the rope band. Those of Type E (**P1373, P1374**; Fig. 3-49; Pl. 3-135), also developing directly from the same type in DAII, are everted and can be associated with both medium and large kraters (Table 3-26).

Of the 36 krater rims, those belonging to medium-sized vessels are represented by 21 examples, and those of large by 15. No fragments of small kraters (rim diameter ca. 0.15 m) were found; this continues a trend, begun in DAII, of concentrating on the large sizes at the expense of the small.

Krater handles are of the larger skyphos type (cf. Type A), round, with an average diameter of 0.016 m. Bases, on the other hand, are quite varied and are represented by five types, ranging in diameter from 0.085 to 0.16 m. Some have traces of black paint on the interior, thus identifying them as belonging to large open vases, probably kraters. Type A bases (Fig. 3-50) are flat or almost flat; **P1207** is very slightly concave on its underside, whereas **P1281** is totally flat. Type B (Figs. 3-50, 3-51) have conical feet, and Type C (Fig. 3-51) are ringed. C1 bases (**P1284, P1392**; (Fig. 3-51) are the regular low ringed typed, comparable to skyphos Type D1, whereas **P1444** (Type C2; Fig. 3-51) is an example of an extraordinarily high ringed base, comparable to **P932** of DAII but without the exterior rib. Pedestal bases also continue from DAII, but are more varied

Table 3-26. Rim Types for DAIII Kraters

Rim Type	Size of Krater	Number of Examples	Catalog Numbers of Best Examples	Average Diameter	Body Thickness	Remarks
A1	Medium	4	**P1185, P1492**	0.20-0.25	0.007	**P1492** has concave interior
A2	Medium	13	**P1369**	0.20-0.25	0.007	Stripes on top of rim
B1	Large	5	**P1186, P1429**	0.26-0.30	0.007	Incisions on underside of rim
B2	Medium	1	**P1520**	0.24	0.005	Three incisions
C	Large	4	**P1187, P1430**	0.30 (?)	0.008-0.012	Raised bands; rope bands; lid grooves
D	Large	4	**P1263, P1372**	0.26	0.007-0.008	Angular rim
E	Medium and large	5	**P1373, P1374**	0.20-0.30	0.007	Everted
	TOTAL	36				

in shape. **P1553** (Fig. 3-51) represents a continuation (cf. **P960** of DAII) of the narrow pedestal developed from the kylix stem; however, **P1393** and **P1494** (Fig. 3-51) exhibit variations not seen in DAII. **P1393** has a small squat pedestaled stem, whereas **P1494** is broader, with a high ringed foot. One example of a small conical stem **(P1493**; Fig. 3-51) is similar to the squat shape of **P1393**, but with a conical foot (Table 3-27).

The custom of adding ribs on krater bases is continued from DAII, but in DAIII the practice spreads from pedestal bases to ordinary conical and ringed feet. On the whole, kraters exhibit little development from DAII. There is no evidence, unfortunately, as to the complete shape; the only real development seems to be the use of incisions **(P1392**; Fig. 3-51), both under the rim and on the bases. This decorative motif is no doubt inspired by its rather wide use on skyphoi of the period. There is also little evidence as to the painted decoration, since only one fragment with arcs of accumbent concentric semi-circles **(P1552)** was recovered. Traces of monochrome coating have also been preserved in a few instances, and it may well be that the kraters, like the skyphoi, were monochrome coated on both exterior and interior.

SHALLOW BOWLS

A rim **(P1368**; Fig. 3-58) and a handle fragment of a shallow bowl belong to the DAIII period. Both are very much like the restored example from DAII **(P1007)**, except that **P1368** is a little larger (rim diameter ca. 0.25 m). There seems to be little development in shape from one period to the other.

Table 3-27. Base Types for DAIII Kraters

Base Type	Size of Krater	Number of Examples	Catalog Numbers of Best Examples	Average Diameter	Remarks
A	Medium	3	**P1207, P1281**	ca. 0.10	Flat or slightly concave
B	Medium	6	**P1391, P1441, P1442**	0.085-0.10	**P1391** and **P1442** have ribs on exterior
C1	Large	8	**P1284, P1392**	0.11-0.15	**P1392** has two incisions
C2	Large	1	**P1444**	ca. 0.16	Possible rib on exterior
Pedestal	Medium (?)	3	**P1393, P1494, P1553**	0.04-0.53	. . .
Conical	Medium (?)	1	**P1493**	ca. 0.045	. . .
	TOTAL	22			

Table 3-28. Handle Types for DAIII Oinochoai

Handle Types	Shape	Number of Examples	Catalog Numbers of Best Examples	Average Width	Remarks
A1	Large elliptical	11	**P1222** (Fig. 3-52)	0.018-0.028	Cf. Type A1 of DAII
A2	Medium elliptical	8	**P1307** (Fig. 3-52)	0.01-0.017	. . .
A3	Small elliptical	4	**P1223** (Fig. 3-52)	ca. 0.01	Cf. Type A6 of DAII
B	Elliptical with rib	23	**P1464** (Fig. 3-52)	0.02-0.03	Cf. Type A2 of DAII; one rib
C	Elliptical with flute	7	**P1499** (Fig. 3-52; Pl. 3-139)	0.01-0.025	Cf. Type A4 of DAII
D	Elliptical with incisions	3	**P1465** (Fig. 3-52; Pl. 3-139)	0.02-0.03	Cf. Type A3 of DAII; 2 or 3 incisions
E	Rope handle	8	**P1466, P1513, P1523, P1559**	Diameter ca. 0.02	Cf. Type A5 of DAII
F	Double handle	2	**P1500, P1524** (Fig. 3-52; Pl. 3-139)	0.02-0.021	Used with small oinochoai and jugs
	TOTAL	66			

CLOSED SHAPES

OINOCHOAI

For the first time it becomes possible to distinguish between oinochoai and jug rims, since both assume identifiable characteristics and are thus not interchangeable as in DAII. Three types of oinochoe rims can be identified. Type A (21 examples, the best being **P1291, P1292**; Fig. 3-51) are simple everted rims very similar to Type A1 of DAII. They represent the standard oinochoe rim for DAIII. Types B and C (Fig. 3-51) are less common; Type B (seven examples) is a small everted rim belonging to a small oinochoe, whereas Type C (12 examples) is a large rim with an angular tip forming a groove on the interior, perhaps for the purpose of catching excess liquid to prevent dripping.

Handles and bases, on the other hand, are not so easily identifiable as belonging to one type of vase or the other. The handles (**P1465, P1499**; Pl. 3-139) exhibit little development over those of DAII (Table 3-28). The shape of the handles is the same as in DAII, except that it now becomes possible to distinguish between three sizes of plain elliptical handle and that the double handle (**P1500, P1524**; Fig. 3-52; Pl. 3-139) makes its first appearance on pouring vessels. Also, the DAIII handles are slightly smaller in width than their DAII counterparts.

The same ambiguity persists with the bases of closed shapes, identifiable by the absence of paint on the interior, and it is impossible to tell whether they belong to oinochoai or jugs (Table 3-29). As with handles, the same types

Table 3-29. Base Types for DAIII Oinochoai, Jugs, and Amphorae

Base Type	Type of Vase	Number of Examples	Catalog Numbers of Best Examples	Average Diameter	Remarks
A1	Oinochoe or jug	9	**P1216** (Fig. 3-52)	0.10	Some have incisions
A2	Amphora	6	**P1452** (Fig. 3-52)	0.14-0.16	. . .
B	Oinochoe or jug	7	**P1217, P1300** (Fig. 3-52)	0.08-0.11	Some have incisions
C	Oinochoe or jug	6	**P1218, P1301** (Fig. 3-52, 3-53)	0.08-0.11	**P1218** has incisions on underside
D1	Oinochoe or jug	7	**P1219** (Fig. 3-53)	0.10	Flat
D2	Amphora	8	**P1220, P1303** F (Fig. 3-53)	0.10-0.16	Flat
	TOTAL	43			

continue into DAIII with little change. These bases all have large diameters, varying from 0.075 to 0.12 m. Type A bases (Fig. 3-52) have ringed feet, Type B conical (Fig. 3-52), Type C semi-conical (Figs. 3-52, 3-53), almost flat, and Type D flat (Fig. 3-53). Type A1 (**P1216**) represents the usual ringed foot for oinochoai or jugs of the period, whereas A2 bases are larger (diameter ca. 0.15 m) and are more suited to amphorae. Similarly, D1 bases have a relatively small diameter and are suitable for pouring vessels, whereas D2 bases, with diameters of 0.10-0.16 m, can be associated with amphorae.

The use of incision makes its appearance on the bases of these pouring vessels, occurring on some bases of Types A1 and B1, probably influenced by similar use on skyphoi. On **P1218** (Type C; Fig. 3-52), this practice is carried to an extreme, and concentric incisions occur on the underside of the base itself, a feature also evident in DAII (cf. **P558**, **P559**).

DAIII oinochoai can be separated into five distinct shapes:

Shape 1. Small oinochoai with *elliptical* bodies. **P1532** (Fig. 3-59). Rim Type C. Monochrome coated on exterior; no paint on inner rim. Continuation of Shape 2 of DAII but now used with *small* oinochoai and not medium- or large-sized, as in DAII.

Shape 2. Large oinochoai with *elliptical* bodies. **P1531** (Fig. 3-59; Pl. 3-136). Rim Type C. Monochrome coated on exterior; paint on inner rim. Continuation of Shape 2 of DAII. Good Messenian parallel from Ano Englianos,[158] which is monochrome coated on the exterior with possible similar coating on the inner rim; two grooves located just under rim, and three at transition from neck to shoulder.

Shape 3. Large oinochoai with *conical* bodies. **P1213** (Fig. 3-60; Pl. 3-137). Rim Type A. Cross-hatching on neck; bands and monochrome coating on shoulder and belly; coating on inner rim. Continuation of Shape 3 of DAII, but with an abnormally squat and shortened neck.

Shape 4. Medium oinochoai with *circular* bodies. **P1511** (Fig. 3-59). Rim Type C. Concentric semi-circles and bands on shoulder and belly; no paint on inner rim. Like **P1213**, this shape has a squat neck.

Shape 5. Large oinochoai with *circular* bodies. **P1521** (Fig. 3-60). Rim Type A. Monochrome coated on exterior and inner rim. Continuation of Shape 1 of DAII.

There appears to be little development in shape from DAII to DAIII. The only really new feature is the appearance of the short neck (**P1213**, **P1511**; Figs. 3-59, 3-60; Pl. 3-137) which gives a squat appearance to the oinochoai in question. Also, medium-sized oinochoai with circular bodies (Shape 4) are now found; these do not occur frequently in DAII but become quite popular in DAIII. The elliptical shape (no. 2) continues at Nichoria and also occurs at Pylos. In fact, the similarity of **P1531** with the Pylos oinochoe in both shape and decoration would indicate that the latter should be dated (along with the Pylos cups) at least 150 years earlier than the excavators indicate.[159]

In keeping with what appears to be a DAIII tradition, these oinochoai are for the most part monochrome coated, with similar coating on the top part of the inner neck and with grooving to mark the transition from neck to shoulder. On **P1301** (Fig. 3-53), such coating even spills over to the outer third of the underside of the base. Whereas interior coating was used infrequently in DAII, it becomes a regular feature in the later period. Similarly, the use of grooving was only one device among many to mark the transition from neck to shoulder in DAII, but it becomes quite standard (cf. **P1213**, **P1521**, **P1522**, **P1531-33**, **P1556**, **P1557**, and the Pylos oinochoe; Figs. 3-59, 3-60; Pl. 3-136), although for the most part limited to two or three grooves. There is only one example (**P1557**) of a vessel with one groove, and none with as many as four or five, as occur in DAII. Painted black bands, raised bands, and impressed dots, all DAII features, do not occur in DAIII.

The known DAIII decorative motifs again simply continue those of earlier periods.

1. Solid monochrome coating on neck, shoulder, and belly. **P1521**, **P1531**, **P1532** (Figs. 3-59, 3-60; Pl. 3-136).
2. Accumbent concentric semi-circles (compass-drawn) on shoulder and upper belly. **P1511**, **P1522**, **P1533** (Fig. 3-59). Monochrome coating on neck and lower belly. Continuation of Motif 3 of DAII.
3. Cross-hatching. **P1213**, **P1557** (Fig. 3-60). **P1213** has cross-hatching on the neck and alternating black and reserved bands on the shoulder. **P1557** has cross-hatching on both neck and shoulder.
4. Metopal panels(?) on shoulder. **P1558.** The decoration here consists of traces of five vertical lines, possibly belonging to a triglyph.

The above short list exhibits nothing new in the way of decorative motifs, but does indicate that there is more flexibility in their placing. DAII motifs are mainly limited to the shoulder, but **P1557** has cross-hatching on both neck and shoulder, and **P1213** (Fig. 3-60) also has cross-hatching on the neck, with alternating black and reserved bands on the shoulder. The neck thus becomes a decorative zone and is used in conjunction with the shoulder, a feature that also appears regularly after the end of the Protogeometric period in the Attic and Atticizing sequences.

JUGS

The evidence for DAIII jugs is sparse, owing to the absence of whole shapes. The rims, however, are distinctive, lacking the twist that separates them from their oinochoe counterparts. Whereas oinochoe rims are gently everted, those belonging to jugs are rather bulbous, quite noticeable with Types A, B, and C. Type A (**P1214**; Fig. 3-51) has a slightly concave interior; Type B (**P1295**; Fig. 3-51) is almost a rolled rim; and Type C (**P1297, P1298**; Fig. 3-51) is slightly everted. Type D (**P1299**; Fig. 3-52) belongs to a small jug, whereas E (**P1496**; Fig. 3-52) has a small groove at the inner rim with two raised bands on the exterior. Incisions are also occasionally used, e.g., **P1299** with five incisions below the rim. There are only seven examples of Type A rims, six of B, 15 of C, four of D, and three of Type E. The jug rim fragments have traces of monochrome coating, suggesting that they, like the majority of the oinochoai, were once monochrome coated.

The handles and bases for jugs have already been discussed under the oinochoe heading. The only addition to note here is the presence of two small double handles (**P1500, P1524**; Fig. 3-52; Pl. 3-139) which probably belong to small jugs. A spout (**P1497**; Pl. 3-138) was also found; these occur commonly on the upper belly of small jugs.[160]

AMPHORAE

The evidence for DAIII amphorae is also quite thin, consisting of a handful of rims, handles, and bases. Both neck- and belly-handled amphorae, however, are represented. Five identifiable rims have been preserved, the best of which are **P1215**, **P1290**, and **P1495** (Fig. 3-52). **P1215** is a rather angular rim with an oblique top, probably belonging to a belly-handled amphora. **P1290** is everted with the stub of a neck handle projecting below the rim. It is likely, then, that, as in DAII, both types of neck handle are present, i.e., those that are attached directly to the rim and those that join the neck slightly below the rim. **P1495** is a rim that projects at right angles to the body, thus forming a ledge on which a lid could be placed. From its shape, it appears to belong to a belly-handled amphora with short, squat neck.

The neck handles of these amphorae simply repeat the shapes of oinochoe/jug handles, but are larger, with an average width ranging from 0.031-0.04 m (**P1403-5**; Fig. 3-52) to as much as 0.05 m (**P1498**; Fig. 3-52). Type A (three examples) is a large elliptical handle; Type B1 (two examples) is also elliptical but quite flat; Type B2 (three examples) is fluted; and Type B3 (three examples) is ribbed. Belly-handles are round and are also quite large, ranging from 0.025 to 0.03 m in diameter. Type A (nine examples) is quite round, whereas Type B (three examples) is slightly flattened and just beginning to look elliptical. The bases of these amphorae have already been mentioned in connection with those of oinochoai and jugs. Type A2 (**P1452**; Fig. 3-52) of closed shapes is a large ringed foot, whereas Type D2 (**P1220, P1303**; Fig. 3-53) is quite flat. What types of amphorae these ringed and flat bases belong to is impossible to determine. There is also scant evidence for the decoration of amphorae. The diagnostic fragments all preserve traces of monochrome coating, so that it is likely that, in accordance with DAIII practice, those vases were simply monochrome coated.

PYXIS(?)

A lid (**P1311**; Fig. 3-53; Pl. 3-138), about one-half preserved, belongs to a DAIII lot. The top is decorated by four incised concentric circles, three grouped toward the preserved edge of the lid, and one in the center. The handle itself is rectangular and was coated in black, as was the rest of the lid (both exterior and interior). The body seems too thin (0.003 m) to have belonged to an amphora and, accordingly, it must be associated with some smaller vase, perhaps a pyxis.

COARSE WARE

DAIII is an important period for coarse handmade vases; indeed, DAIII lots produced a greater variety of shapes than those of previous DA periods. Many of the best pieces come from Area IV SW. Some of the vessels had been fired to the same reddish yellow color (i.e., Munsell 5YR 7/6 and 7.5 YR 7/6) as the fine ware. They were probably fired over an open fire, and by far the greater number of pots have been burned in one form or another and vary in color from light red (2.5YR 6/8) to various shades of gray (2.5YR N3/0 very dark gray; 2.5YR N5/0 gray; 10YR 6/1 light gray; 10YR 5/2 grayish brown).

BOWLS

As in DAII, large coarse bowls probably represent the most common open shape, although on the basis of the preserved fragments it is difficult to differentiate those belonging to bowls from those of jugs or amphorae. For the sake of convenience, these disparate rim, handle, and base fragments will be discussed as a group under the "bowl" category; and, where appropriate, remarks will be made as to their possible association with jugs or amphorae.

Four basic rim types can be isolated, with variations in each category (Table 3-30). All Type A rims (Fig. 3-53) are everted in one form or another. Those of A1 have flat, angular tops and, on occasion (**P1315-17**), project almost at right angles to the body. Those of Type A2 (**P1318, P1319**) turn gently outward, without the angularity of their counterparts. Type B rims (**P1226**; Fig. 3-53) are absolutely straight with flat tops, whereas those of Type C (Fig. 3-53) are also straight but with rounded tops. C1 rims (**P1227**) are rounded, but those of C2 (**P1230, P1469**) are slightly angular. Finally, Type D (**P1320, P1525**; Fig. 3-53) are large, offset rims belonging to vases with a rim diameter of between 0.25 and 0.30 m.

Table 3-30 underscores the variety in rim types, a variety far greater than in DAII where the rims are confined to two basic types. Type A1 rims are the most numerous, accounting for approximately 50% of the total. Conversely, with handles and bases the DAII repertory is for the most part repeated (Table 3-31).

Table 3-30. Rim Types for DAIII Coarse Bowls, Jugs, and Amphorae

Rim Type	Type of Vase	Number of Examples	Catalog Numbers of Best Examples	Average Diameter	Body Thickness	Remarks
A1	Bowl, jug, or amphora	51	**P1224, P1312-17, P1321, P1322, P1502**	0.10-0.16	0.007-0.008	**P1317** probably belongs to an amphora; others to bowls or jugs.
A2	Bowl, jug, or amphora	25	**P1225, P1318, P1319, P1323, P1515**	0.15-0.20	0.007-0.01	**P1318, P1319** probably belong to amphorae; others to bowls or jugs. Some have finger impressions below rim.
B	Bowl	11	**P1226**	ca. 0.15-0.20	0.008	. . .
C1	Bowl or jug	7	**P1227**	0.10-0.20	0.007-0.009	. . .
C2	Bowl or jug	8	**P1230, P1469**	0.10-0.20	0.007-0.009	. . .
D	Amphora	5	**P1320, P1525**	0.25-0.30	0.008-0.01	Offset.
	TOTAL	107				

The basic range of elliptical, fluted, ribbed, and grooved handles of DAII fine and coarse wares and of DAIII fine wares is thus continued; but there are some innovations. For instance, Type A2 handles (**P1330**) are rectangular. Such handles are not found in DAII but begin in the transitional period and continue into DAIII. Experiments are also made with the ribbed type (A4) by increasing the number of ribs to three (**P1537**) or five (**P1475**). This is done by placing one or two ribs in the center of the handle and one at each end. But perhaps the most noticeable changes occur with the grooved type (B) which becomes much thicker and quite rectangular, with grooves not only along the top but at the sides as well (**P1334**; Pl.3-140). A further variation is to reduce the width of the handle so that it becomes almost square, with only one groove along the top (**P1335**; Pl. 3-140).

Whereas changes occur in the handles, bases remain quite static, being represented in DAIII by the two standard flat types: Type A (16 examples) with concave sides and Type B (10 examples) with straight sides. The Type A examples (**P1324, P1325**; Fig. 3-54) are rather thick, with large diameters of 0.14-0.15 m, indicating that they should be associated with amphorae. Those of Type B (**P1326**; Fig. 3-54) are smaller (diameter ca. 0.10 m) and probably belong either to bowls or to jugs. An interesting decorated base fragment consists of the outer edge of a conical foot decorated with an incised zigzag and a row of dots below (**P1566**; Fig. 3-54; Pl. 3-141). Such incised decoration recalls that on Attic pointed pyxides of Middle Geometric 1 date,[161] as does a body fragment, perhaps of a bowl, with incised dots encircling a nipple (**P1481**; Pl. 3-144). The latter is, of course, a survival from DAI, but the incised decoration may represent the continuation of Attic elements in the coarse ware tradition.

DIPPERS

Two round-based dippers belong to DAIII lots. One (**P1312**; Fig. 3-61; Pl. 3-142) is quite small, with a total height of 0.165 m, and is similar in size and shape to **P982** (DAII), indicating the continuation of this shape from the earlier period. It was found inside a large pithos (**P1336**; see Chapter 2, p. 53), which suggests that it was used for ladling liquid. The second dipper (**P1565**; Fig. 3-61) preserves only a lower profile, but a reconstruction following the curve of the belly indicates that it was at least 0.10 m taller than its counterpart, with a probable height of 0.268 m. Its round base also indicates that it was used as a ladle.

TRIPOD VASES

DAIII lots produced four tripod legs (**P1231, P1535, P1567, P1568**; Fig. 3-54; Pl. 3-143) and three fragments of a tripod vase (**P1313**; Fig. 3-62) which can be combined to indicate its profile. The vase is quite large, with an undecorated raised band below the rim. No handles were found, but it may have had neck handles. The lower portion of one tripod leg was preserved with a pointed foot. Such pointed tripod feet were found in DAII (**P833, P860**), and their use obviously continues into DAIII. **P1313** was found inside the large pithos (**P1336**) together with the smaller dipper (**P1312**; Fig. 3-61). A second pointed tripod foot (**P1535**), on the basis of its size, belongs to a much smaller vessel, perhaps shaped like **P1313**.

In DAII, a distinction can be made between pointed and rectangular tripod feet, the former belonging to coarse vases and the latter to wheel-made vessels, perhaps askoi. In DAIII, however, such a distinction becomes blurred, and rectangular feet are also used with coarse vases. The feet vary in size and thickness (**P1231, P1567, P1568**), but all have one common feature, namely, their rectangular shape.

Table 3-31. Handle Types for DAIII Coarse Bowls, Jugs, and Amphorae

Handle Type	Shape	Type of Vase	Number of Examples	Catalog Numbers of Best Examples	Average Diameter or Width	Remarks
A1	Elliptical	Bowl, jug, or neck-handled amphora	16	**P1328, P1329** (Fig. 3-53)	0.03	Cf. Type A of closed fine ware (**P1222, P1403**)
A2	Rectangular	Large jug or neck-handled amphora	19	**P1330** (Fig. 3-53)	0.03-0.04	Cf. Type A of DAII/III coarse ware (**P1149**)
A3	Elliptical with flute	Large jug or neck-handled amphora	9	**P1333** (Fig. 3-53)	0.03-0.04	Cf. Type B2 of fine ware amphorae (**P1405**)
A4	Elliptical with rib	Large jug or neck-handled amphora	12	**P1331, P1475, P1537** (Fig. 3-54)	0.03-0.045	Cf. Type B3 of fine ware amphorae (**P1498**)
B1	Large, rectangular with grooves	Neck-handled amphora	5	**P1334, P1477** (Fig. 3-54; Pl. 3-140)	0.04-0.06	Does not occur with fine ware amphorae
B2	Small, rectangular with one groove	Bowl or small amphora	3	**P1335** (Fig. 3-54; Pl. 3-140)	0.02	Does not occur with fine ware handles
C	Round	Bowl or belly-handled amphora	4	**P1479** (Fig. 3-54)	0.01-0.02	Cf. Type A of fine ware belly-handles
		TOTAL	68			

STRAINERS

Coarse strainers continue from DAII, but the DAIII examples have much larger holes. **P1505** represents two fragments of a strainer with holes of a diameter reaching 0.006 m. **P1506** (Pl. 3-144) is another strainer fragment with nipple decoration. In DAII such a vase is documented in fine ware only (**P776**), but, as with the rectangular tripod feet, the distinction between fine and coarse becomes blurred in DAIII, and nipples appear on coarse strainers.

OINOCHOAI

Two rims of coarse oinochoai (**P1501, P1526**; Fig. 3-53) are also DAIII in date. They have a definite twist that identifies them as belonging to oinochoai. **P1526** is a straight rim with a rather large diameter, probably from a big vessel. **P1501** is smaller and may belong to the type of coarse oinochoe that was found in the small DA tholos (**P1590**) in Lakkoules.

JUGS

Owing to the lack of restorable whole shapes, it is difficult to identify the rims, handles, and bases associated with jugs. Rim Types A1, A2, C1, and C2 might belong to jugs, and so might the elliptical (A1), rectangular (A2), fluted (A3), and ribbed (A4) handles and the flat bases of either Type A or B. **P1503** (Fig. 3-62) represents the upper profile of what may be a pouring vessel, but it is broken off at the point where the body begins to turn inward toward the base. Hence, it is impossible to determine whether it is from a broad-mouthed jug, or pitcher with a flat base, or a dipper with a rounded base.

AMPHORAE

Both neck-handled and belly-handled amphorae are well represented in DAIII by individual rim and handle fragments and profiles. Rim Types A1, A2, and D (Fig. 3-53) can be associated with both kinds of amphorae, as well as the two types of flat bases (Fig. 3-54). The differentiation between neck- and belly-handled amphorae is clearer in the handles; those of Types A1 through B2, either elliptical or rectangular, must belong to neck-handled amphorae, and the round kind (Type C) must be associated with belly-handled amphorae. **P1502, P1516**, and **P1561** (Fig. 3-63) represent the necks of medium-sized neck-handled amphorae (rim diameter ca. 0.18-0.20 m) with large rectangular handles (A2). **P1560** (Fig. 3-63) provides the upper profile of a much larger neck-handled amphora (rim diameter ca. 0.30 m) with a plain elliptical handle (A1). **P1563** (Fig. 3-64), on the other hand, is a lower profile with Type A flat base; the upper profile is restored with a neck similar to **P1560.** If restored correctly (and the similar body thicknesses and curve of the body indicate that it is), this neck-handled amphora has a rather unusual shape with a broad mouth and squat, almost nonexistent neck. The absence of a definite neck gives the vessel a top-heavy appearance, but the broad mouth is convenient for ladling liquids or food. The shape may be a local variation.

Profiles of belly-handled amphorae are provided by **P1515** (Fig. 3-63) and **P1564** (Fig. 3-65). **P1515** is the upper profile of a vessel with a squat neck. **P1564** is a Type A flat base; combined with **P1515** (both have similar body thicknesses), a profile of a belly-handled amphora is achieved, more canonical in shape than **P1563** (Fig. 3-64), but still with a rather squat neck. The squat necks may be a local variation in coarse amphorae. Finally, **P1514** and **P1562** are rims of large amphorae with rim diameters 0.28 m and 0.38 m respectively; they are too worn and abraded to determine to which kind of amphora they belong.

COOKING SUPPORTS (SEE CHAPTER 5, PP. 5-18, 5-19)

Two "spools," each about half preserved, belong to DAIII lots (**P1536, P1569**; Fig. 3-54). These have the same shape as the four examples from DAII and represent a continuation of this shape into the later period. The only difference from one period to the other is in size. The spools of DAIII are at least 0.01 m taller than those of DAII. **P1536** (Pl. 3-145) is 0.06 m high; **P1569** is broken at its middle but would have had a total height of 0.06 m also. Their use is enigmatic; perhaps they were employed as supports for coarse cooking pots. **P1327** (Fig. 3-54; Pl. 3-143) represents a variation on the "spool" shape not seen in DAII. The "spool" becomes thinner, slightly taller, and without a waist. It is difficult to see how an object with such a narrow base could be used for support. Furthermore, **P1327** shows no traces of burning, so it probably was not used as a support when pottery was fired or in cooking; rather, it is shaped like a pestle and may have been used to mash softer materials.

COOKING STANDS

The function of **P1504** and **P1570** as cooking stands is fairly certain. **P1504** (Pls. 3-146, 3-147) is curved, with vertical and horizontal projections at one end for the support of a pot. A similar fragment was found in DAII/III (**P1069**); one reconstruction in Fig. 3-47 shows it as part of a stand supporting a vase over a fire. **P1504** is burned on the interior, suggesting that it, too, was used as a stand to support a cooking pot. **P1570** (Fig. 3-54; Pl. 3-148), on the other hand, is in the shape of a flat oval ring, about one-half preserved. Its flat shape suggests that it was used as the stand or support for a round-based dipper (**P1312, P1565**) that could not stand by itself.

GRILL

The fragment of a grill (**P1480**; Pl. 3-149), similar in shape to those of DAII (**P965**) and DAII/III (**P1069**), indicates that this cooking form continued into DAIII. Preserved is a portion of the slot in which to place a spit.

PITHOI (SEE CHAPTER 2, PP. 53, 54)

DAIII lots contain numerous pithos fragments which show little change in shape or decoration over those of DAII. Two large pithoi, the lower sections of which were preserved *in situ*, were partially sunk into the ground just to the SE of Unit IV-5. The larger of the two (Pithos no. 1-**P1336**) was placed in the S wall line of the earlier Unit IV-1. It had a total height of ca. 2.30 m, with a maximum diameter of ca. 1.05 m. It also had a large angular rim (Fig. 3-54) with a diameter of 0.90 m and was decorated on its upper belly with a raised band containing diagonal slashes in imitation of rope decoration (Pl. 3-150). Its base has a roughly rounded bottom (Pl. 3-151) shaped like **P505** of DAII. The second (Pithos no. 2-**P1337**), placed slightly to the NW of its counterpart, is smaller, with an original height of between 1.20 and 1.30 m and a maximum diameter of ca. 0.90-0.95 m. Its rim (Fig. 3-54; Pl. 3-152) is more rounded than that of **P1336**, with a diameter of 0.75 m. The pithos was decorated, probably also on its upper belly, with a plain raised band. The base is rather unusual for storage pithoi, being stemmed with a rib in the center (Pl. 3-153). In DAII such stemmed feet appear to be associated with burial pithoi only,[162] but in DAIII this feature is found with storage pithoi as well. The rib is, of course, an extension of the use of ribs on fine ware bases, especially kraters. Both pithoi are coated with a white slip, a practice also seen in DAII (**P777, P903**).

Other miscellaneous pithos fragments also belong to DAIII. **P1571** (Fig. 3-54) is an offset rim with three ribs below the rim, belonging to a small pithos. Again, the use of ribs with pithoi (the ribs are now transferred from the base to the rim) appears to be a DAIII feature. **P1340** is a large belly handle with a diameter of 0.042 m which can be associated with a small pithos; and **P1543** (Fig. 3-64) is a flat base, similar in shape to **P506** of DAII. The clay of **P1543** is very friable and crumbly, and the technique of manufacture has been exposed. In the middle is a less well-baked core around which were placed coils (Pl. 3-154). Another interesting feature is the presence of a decorative band at the top of the base at the point where it flares into the body. This band has diagonal slashes in imitation of rope decoration, suggesting, as in DAII, that these handmade vessels were influenced by baskets bound with rope or interlaced reeds.

The decoration on these pithoi, as with DAIII vases in general, is quite conservative and simply continues motifs already known in DAII. The known motifs are listed below.

1. Undecorated raised band. **P1337**. Continuation of Motif 1 of DAII.
2. Raised band with row of finger impressions. **P1483, P1572**. Continuation of Motif 3 of DAII.
3. Raised band with row of incised circles. **P1538**. In Motif 5 of DAII the circles are placed haphazardly on the

raised band or directly on the body of the vase, but in DAIII they form a definite row.

4. Raised band with row of raised or incised triangles. **P1338, P1484, P1542. P1542** (Pl. 3-155) has a row of raised triangles; **P1338** has incised circles within an incised triangle; and **P1484** varies this with incised circles both within and outside an incised triangle. Continuation of Motif 6 of DAII, except that in the earlier period the circles are never confined within the triangles (as in **P1338**) but occur outside as well (as in **P1484**).
5. Raised band with row of incised hatched triangles. **P1539**. Continuation of Motif 7 of DAII.
6. Raised band with incised piled triangles with a rope band above. **P1527** (Pl. 3-156). Incised piled triangles occur in DAII (cf. Motif 8), but the combination of piled triangles with rope band does not.
7. Raised band with diagonal slashes in imitation of rope decoration. **P1336, P1339, P1482, P1540, P1541, P1543.** Continuation of Motif 10 of DAII.
8. Nipple decoration. **P1573** (Fig. 3-54). A pointed nipple projects straight from the body (as opposed to MH nipples which are curved) with an adjacent handle stump. Nipples do not occur on known DAII pithoi.

As in DAII, the most common decorative motif appears to be the rope band. The repertory of motifs is the same as in DAII, except for the nipple decoration. What is different, however, is the combination of piled triangles with a rope band, the confinement of circles within triangles, and the ordering of circles to form a definite row. The placing of these decorative motifs is also more varied in DAIII. In the earlier periods the motifs were mainly confined to the neck of the pithos, but in DAIII they seem to spread to the upper belly as well **(P1336, P1337)**.

Late Geometric Pottery (ca. 750-700 B.C.) (Fig. 1-2)

Late Geometric pottery has been found in three areas at Nichoria and its environs, namely, in a pithos burial on the ridge itself, in a chamber tomb at the S end of the Vathirema ravine (Feature no. 1), and in what appears to have been a cemetery (Feature no. 16) above the SE edge of the village of Rizomilo. The vases from these burials are later in style than those of the DAIII period and presumably furnish a *terminus ante quem* for DAIII.

A group of three vases comes from the pithos burial discovered in 1969 in trial trench L24-III on the Nichoria ridge.[163] The burial is that of a warrior, equipped with an iron sword and spearhead, a bronze finger-ring, two bronze bowls, and three vases. It is the three ceramic vessels that are pertinent here: a kantharos (**P1574**; Fig. 3-66; Pl. 3-157), a shallow bowl (**P1575**; Fig. 3-66; Pls. 3-158, 3-159, 3-160), and a deep cup (**P1576**; Fig. 3-66; Pl. 3-161). Both the kantharos and the bowl had been fired to Munsell 2.5YR 6/8 light red. Such a color occurs only occasionally (28 examples) in DAIII, suggesting that these vases might be imports rather than local products. The color of the cup, however, is 5YR 7/8 reddish yellow, a color achieved quite frequently in both DAII (743 examples) and DAIII (476 examples). This may suggest that there was an uninterrupted local pottery tradition in cups even after the habitation on the Nichoria acropolis had ceased. Such a possibility is strengthened by the shape and decoration of the cup. The S-shaped profile and carinated body are similar to Shape 2, perhaps the major DAIII cup shape. Also, the cup is monochrome coated on both exterior and interior, a feature on Nichoria cups of both the DAII and the DAIII periods. Its presence with vases of definitely Late Geometric character indicates that the local potters continued the cup traditions of earlier times.

The other two vases of the pithos burial reflect outside origin or influence in both shape and decoration. The kantharos shape **(P1574)** makes its appearance for the first time at Nichoria. The vase is decorated with a sharp wavy line on the neck and a panel of leaf-lozenges on the shoulder, with a reserved inner band and two registers of double crosses on the handles. Although the wavy line occurs at Nichoria as far back as DAII, the panel of leaf-lozenges[164] and the registers of double crosses on the handles[165] are Argive motifs. The shallow bowl **(P1575)** shape occurs in both DAII (cf. **P1007**) and DAIII (cf. **P1368**); it also occurs with a stray find from Romanou Viglitsa, near Koukounara in Messenia,[166] and in Laconian Late Geometric.[167] Our bowl is decorated with vertical stripes at the rim and horizontal bands below and on the interior. This motif of stripes at the rim is also reminiscent of the Argive manner.[168]

The pithos (**P1577**; Pl. 3-162) in which the warrior was buried shows local antecedents. Its rim (Fig. 3-66) is similar in shape to that of **P1337** of DAIII, and its stemmed foot also recalls that of the same pithos (but without the central rib) and that of the Rizes burial pithos.[169]

A similar mixture of local and external features is to be seen in vases of the Vathirema chamber tomb. Discovered and excavated in 1960 and 1961,[170] this tomb contained two Late Geometric inhumations on the floor and was used successively from then until Classical times. The excavators[171] assumed that the chamber was made in Late Geometric times, but it may have been a Mycenaean chamber tomb that was cleared out and reused.[172] The six Late Geometric vases (Fig. 3-67) consist of a pyxis lid (**P1597**; Pls. 3-163, 3-164) with four horses (two preserved and two missing); an imitation of a hemispherical Corinthian kotyle (**P1594**; Pl. 3-165), a high-rimmed skyphos (**P1592**; Pls. 3-166, 3-167), two deeper lakainalike skyphoi (**P1593, P1595**; Pls. 3-168, 3-169, 3-170) and a deep cup (**P1596**; Pl. 3-171).[173] All except the pyxis lid have the very pale brown, reddish yellow, and light red colors associated with Nichoria vases, indicating that they are probably local products. Especially noticeable in this category is the cup

(**P1596**) which parallels exactly the shape of **P1576** from the pithos burial. It is monochrome coated on the exterior and interior, with narrow reserved bands at the rim on both exterior and interior. Such reserved bands do not occur in our DAIII material but are used on **P848** and **P972** of DAII. A similar cup was found as a stray at Romanou Viglitsa,[174] near Koukounara; it is also monochrome coated but with a narrow reserved band at mid-belly at the point of carination and with alternating groups of horizontal and vertical stripes on the handle. A similarly decorated handle occurs on a small DAII oinochoe (**P955**) from Nichoria. Cups, then, represent a strong local tradition in Messenia (cf. also the DAIII cups from Ano Englianos) and become the one type of vase that continues virtually unchanged into Late Geometric times.

Of the other five Late Geometric vases in the tomb, the pyxis lid (**P1597**) may be an Attic import. The decoration is typically Attic, with alternating zones of vertical stripes, bands, linked lozenges, and with a quadriga at the center.[175] Two of the four horses are preserved completely, the others only in the stubs of the legs. The other vases appear to be local products but exhibit external traits. **P1592** is a high-rimmed, fairly shallow skyphos with a panel of leaf-lozenges in the handle zone and a reserved band on the inner rim. Its shape and decoration are definitely Argive.[176] Also Argive is the leaf-lozenge panel on one of the deep skyphoi (**P1593**), with interior coating and a reserved band on the inner rim. The other deep skyphos (**P1595**) is decorated with a hatched maeander pattern with leaf-lozenges above and an inner reserved band, again Argive in manner. The shape of these skyphoi (**P1593, P1595**), however, with their deep and carinated bodies, is not unlike that of the Laconian lakaina;[177] indeed, the shape of both vases appears to be a cross between a deep skyphos and a lakaina. Lastly, **P1594**, monochrome coated on both exterior and interior, is shaped like a hemispherical Corinthian kotyle.[178] The monochrome coating, however, recalls similar vases of the DAIII period at Nichoria.

The additional evidence for activity at Nichoria and its environs in Late Geometric times comes from a field on the lower S slope of the ridge (Feature no. 16).[179] Here the plow turned up a number of limestone blocks and numerous sherds. One Late Geometric sherd (**P1626**; Pl. 3-172) is decorated with the Argive leaf-lozenges which seems to be a common Late Geometric decorative motif at Nichoria. And it may well be that the stones disturbed by the plow are from a tomb of Late Geometric times, like the Vathirema chamber tomb.

In summary, the Late Geometric vases (Figs. 3-66, 3-67) exhibit both local and external influences, as can be seen in the following:

I. Local:
   A. Shape of cups (**P1576, P1596**); monochrome coating on cups; type of clay of cups.

II. Argive:
   A. Shape of high-rimmed skyphos (**P1592**).
   B. Leaf-lozenge and maeander panels (**P1574, P1592, P1593, P1595, P1626**).
   C. Registers of double crosses on handles (**P1574**).

III. Laconian:
   A. Shape of deep lakainalike skyphoi (**P1593, P1595**).

IV. Corinthian:
   A. Shape of hemispherical kotyle (**P1594**).

V. Attic:
   A. Pyxis lid (**P1597**).

Summary

The following is a brief recapitulation of the main features of the DA pottery at Nichoria. Questions of chronology will be discussed in Chapter 6. It will be sufficient here simply to review the major trends in the pottery itself.

Identifiable characteristics of sherds of the DAI period are a clay that has been fired to a dirty white color with a rather soft and crumbly texture and wheel ridging, mostly on the interior but occasionally on the exterior as well. Two decorative motifs are regularly repeated: the wavy line in a variety of shapes and sizes, and the undecorated zone, both placed in the field between the handles. Another major DAI characteristic is the use of a reddish brown washy paint.

The large skyphos or deep bowl is pehaps the most common shape. It has a slightly everted rim, high upswung handles, and either a conical or a ringed foot. Ribbed kylix stems also occur in DAI and continue into DAII. Closed shapes in DAI are poorly represented, consisting of a few oinochoe and jug rims, several rope-handle fragments, and a pierced amphora handle. Characteristics of the coarse ware include straight or slightly everted rims, flat bases, rolled belly handles, and ribbed and incised handle fragments. Most of these coarse sherds seem to belong to amphorae.

The DAI period at Nichoria is one of some activity. The potters owe much in the way of shape and decoration to the underlying LHIIIC tradition; but there is also considerable experimentation, as seen in the varied skyphos and deep bowl shapes, the development of the skyphos shape and of the ribbed stem, and the use of the narrow reserved band as a decorative motif. There is little evidence however, for the development of cups and kraters during this period.

DAII sherds are also relatively easy to identify; the most consistent feature is a clay that has been fired to a reddish yellow color. The texture of the sherds is soft and crumbly, with flaky surfaces from which both slip and decoration have been worn, owing primarily to the highly alkaline condition of the soil on the Nichoria ridge. The majority of the inventoried fragments are approximately 0.001 m thinner than those of DAI, with some wheel ridging (but not as heavy as in DAI) and spiral grooving on the interior. The range of shapes is the same as that for DAI, but the evidence is more abundant for cups, kraters, jugs, and oinochoai. Skyphoi and deep bowls, as before, continue to be the most popular shape.

The range of decorative motifs is much greater than in DAI, with the accumbent concentric semi-circle and the cross-hatched triangle occurring frequently. Features of the LHIIIC repertory appear, most notably the ribbed kylix stems and the squat, ovoid shape of some of the oinochoai and amphorae. Local developments can be seen in the preference that the potters are beginning to have for small vases and in the frequent use of the accumbent concentric semicircle as a decorative motif. An interesting development is the use of hatched and crosshatched triangles in metopal panels, features common in Laconian DA. The appearance of such motifs at Nichoria suggests that there were connections between Laconia and Messenia in DAII. Interaction between the two areas is also suggested by the close similarity in the bell shape and wolf's tooth decoration between our **P602** and Sparta (Heroön) no. 2577. Indeed, so similar are these vases that it is quite possible that they were made by the same potter. Various influences can thus be seen to be at work in DAII:

1. LHIIIC survivals, transmitted through DAI, and seen in the continuation of the ribbed kylix stems and in the squat ovoid shape of some of the oinochoai and amphorae.
2. Local variations, i.e., the popularity of small vessels and the heavy use of accumbent concentric semi-circles as a decorative motif.
3. Influence from Laconia: use of hatched and cross-hatched triangles in metopal panels and wolf's tooth.
4. Influences on cups from W Crete, specifically from Modi and Vryses.
5. Slight influence from Athens (full concentric circles) and the Argolid, particularly Asine. The high-footed skyphos from Antheia is Attic in shape and decoration, whereas the coarse oinochoe **(P1590)** from the Lakkoules tholos has certain affinities in shape with those from Asine.

The essential DAII character of the transitional DAII/III lots would make them hard to identify, were it not for the fact that they are associated with the second building phase of Unit IV-1. This pottery had been fired to the same reddish yellow color as in DAII, and it presents the same soft and crumbly texture with flaky surfaces. The range of shapes is the same as in DAII, with skyphoi and, to a lesser extent, deep bowls being the most popular. There begins to develop, however, a greater variety of rim and base types for all open and closed shapes; and at the same time the range of decorative motifs begins to decline.

The rise in the variety of types and shapes and the decline in the range of decorative motifs is the major trend in DAIII. Sherds of this period are also more varied in color than those from DAII, but have the same soft and crumbly texture. A notable feature is the development of a class of very small skyphoi with paper-thin sides varying in thickness from 0.002 to 0.003 m. The preferred shapes are now the small skyphos and the cup with an S-shaped profile. The decoration, however, is mainly limited to a monochrome coating on both exterior and interior, with no inner reserved bands. Black paint continues to be used, but instead of varying from a streaky black to a streaky dark brown, it becomes solid black with a bluish tinge and a metallic sheen. In general, DAIII appears to be a conservative period for decorative motifs but an active one in regard to variations in types of rims, handles, and bases. On the ridge DAIII pottery is practically confined to Area IV, where the major portion of the settlement of the period appears to have been located; but numerous DAIII sherds also come from Lakkoules, indicating that this continued in use as a cemetery area throughout DA habitation phases.

The Late Geometric vases from the pithos burial on the ridge and the Vathirema chamber tomb are so different in style from those of DAIII that they appear to provide a *terminus ante quem* for that period. Local characteristics are seen, however, in the deep shape and monochrome coating on the two cups **(P1576, P1596)**. The other vases exhibit Argive, Laconian, Corinthian, and Attic influences. Thus, after a relatively conservative and isolated period in DAIII, Nichoria can be linked to Late Geometric developments outside Messenia.

NOTES

1. Choremis 1973, pp. 62-74. Choremis kindly gave this writer permission to study and include in this publication the Dark Age vases from the Lakkoules tombs.

2. Karageorga 1972, p. 18, Pl. 20:2.

3. Valmin 1938, p. 325, Fig. 69. Unfortunately, the fragments of this deep bowl are now lost, so that no accurate comparisons can be made. The shape of the deep bowl appears to be similar to that of **P101.**

4. Both Styrenius (1967) and French (1969, pp. 133-36) have abandoned the term LHIIIC2 in favor of Submycenaean.

5. FS = Furumark shape. For FS 285, 286, see Furumark 1941, p. 49, Fig. 14. FM = Furumark motif.

6. Korakou: Rutter 1977, pp. 1-20, Figs. 5, 10. See also Rutter's unpublished dissertation (1974), a copy of which has been placed in the library of the American School of Classical Studies, Athens. Lefkandi, Phases 1b, 2, 3: Popham and Milburn 1971, p. 335, Fig. 1:1; p. 339, Fig. 4:1-3; p. 345, Fig. 7:1. Perati: Iakovidis 1970, pp. 219, 220, Figs. 84-85, nos. 622 (Class Γ) and 53.

7. Benton 1938-39, p. 11. The "M" designates "Mycenaean." This and several other vases were at first identified by Benton as Mycenaean and later reclassified as Protogeometric (Benton 1949, pp. 308-312). Hereafter, all vases from Polis will be listed by their original catalog numbers published in Benton 1938-39, pp. 8-17. The prefix M = Mycenaean (later changed to Protogeometric); T = Transitional; and PG = Protogeometric. K. A. Wardle in his unpublished thesis (1972, p. 106, Figs. 120, 121), a copy of which is to be found in the library of the British School at Athens, also discusses

M20, M24, M26, M49, and M66, but identifies these vases as Mycenaean.

8. After M20, Benton says "Three others similar," but gives no catalog numbers. For the sake of convenience they are here referred to as M20a, b, c.

9. Heurtley 1932-33, pp. 40, 41. Vases from Heurtley's catalog are hereafter prefaced with the letter "H."

10. Heurtley 1932-33, pp. 40, 41, Fig. 10.

11. Lakkithra no. 164 (Argostolion Museum no. 1257). See Marinatos 1932, pp. 1-47, Pl. 11. Also similar is no. 155.

12. Argostolion Museum nos. 68 and 77 (unpublished). For the published material from Mazarakata, see Kavvadias 1909, pp. 355ff. See also Desborough 1964, p. 103 and Wardle 1972, pp. 112, 113.

13. Unfortunately, from the published account it is impossible to determine with which of the 83 burials nos. 68 and 77 are to be associated.

14. For Lefkandi and Perati examples, see Popham and Milburn 1971, pp. 333-49 and Iakovidis 1970, pp. 219, 220. For Athens, see Kerameikos Grave S27, Inv. no. 444: Kraiker and Kübler 1939, Pl. 22; Styrenius 1967, pp. 11, 132. Also Furumark 1941, pp. 427, 428. For similar deep bowls from the Granary Class at Mycenae, see *BSA* 25 (1921-23) p. 33, Fig. 9; Desborough 1964, Pl. 12.

15. Rutter 1977, Fig. 5.

16. FM 53, nos. 19, 20, 23, 25.

17. Pylos Museum no. 127. It is unclear from which tholos tomb at Koukounara skyphos 127 comes. Marinatos (1964, p. 164) says that the vase was from a deposit and calls it Granary Style, but its shape and decoration are more appropriate for LHIIIC or even early DA. See also McDonald and Rapp 1972, p. 270, no. 35.

18. FM 52, nos. 7, 8.

19. Thin black bands also occur on **P205**; this is a small sherd on which only the black bands are preserved.

20. FM 61A, no. 1.

21. Aetos H18, 73; P134, 147. Polis M26; T1: PG5.

22. Desborough 1952, Pl. 38.

23. Marinatos 1965, p. 111, Pl. 121.

24. H54, 55. Also, one cup from Polis, PG1.

25. M49 has been restored with a flat base, but on the basis of its similarity with M46-48 it should be restored with a ringed base.

26. Desborough 1964, Pl. 8 and especially Marinatos 1932, Pl. 5, no. 14 (Argostolion Museum no. 990).

27. Cf. R363, 375. The prefix "R" refers to Robertson's catalog of Geometric and later pottery from Aetos. Cf. Robertson 1948, pp. 10, 68, 69.

28. Patras Museum no. 492. Cf. Vermeule 1960, p. 16, no. 53, Pl. 5, Fig. 40; Coldstream 1968, Pl. 48f.

29. FM 53, no. 38.

30. Museo Archeologico, Florence. Cf. Hencken 1968, p. 38, Pls. 37, 39.

31. Petsas 1961-62, p. 218; Andronikos 1969, Pls. 30, 32. The specific examples are: vase no. 84 from Tumulus IIIΛ (Petsas 1961-62, Pl. 103α); no. 103 from IIIΠ (Petsas 1961-62, Pl. 103ε); no. 15 from C Z (Petsas 1961-62, Pl. 119δ); nos. 7 and 10 from Tumulus A (Andronikos 1969, Pl. 30); and no. 4 from Tumulus Γ (Andronikos 1969, Pl. 32). See also Bouzek 1969, p. 73, nos. 13, 14. Other horned projections are found in Bouzek (1974, p. 52, nos. 12, 13) from Olynthus and Bohemitsa, respectively.

The horned projections and nipple decorations on a few of the coarse vases from Nichoria (pp. 68, 69) may represent direct or indirect influence from the north. Bouzek has suggested that perishable, nonceramic goods such as basketry may have been introduced into Greece by northerners and have influenced coarse ware in PG and Early Geometric times. Rutter (1975) claims to have identified a class of nonindigenous pottery in early LHIIIC contexts at sites in Attica, the Argolid, the Corinthia, and Euboea. He believes that these handmade burnished vases indicate the presence of an intrusive northern population element (see also French and Rutter 1977). The issue is still unsettled, but the possibility cannot be ignored that this phenomenon reached as far south as Messenia.

32. Valmin 1938, p. 328. These stems are unfortunately now lost, so that no accurate comparison can be made.

33. Lakkithra, Grave A: Marinatos 1932, Pl. 6, nos. 29, 29a, 43, 45, 47; Grave B: Marinatos 1932, no. 113; Grave Δ: Marinatos 1932, Pl. 12, nos. 214, 216, 219. See also Desborough 1964, Pl. 9b.

34. Metaxata, Grave A: *Arch Eph* 1933, 82, Fig. 26, no. A9. Grave Γ: *Arch Eph* 1933, Fig. 32, nos. Γ3, Γ8.

35. Teichos Dymaion nos. 790, 791. Cf. *Praktika* 1965, Pl. 175. The swelling of the stems is indistinct in the published photographs. It shows more clearly in the profiles of the kylikes published in Papadopoulos 1978-79.

36. Popham and Milburn 1971, p. 341, Fig. 5:1. See also FM 275 (examples from Mycenae, Asine, and Korakou).

37. Lakkithra Grave A: Marinatos 1932, Pl. 6, no. 44; Grave Δ: Marinatos 1932, Pl. 12, no. 225 (both Type F); Grave Δ: Marinatos 1932, Pl. 12, no. 222 (Type C).

38. Polis T1 probably also belongs to Nichoria Type F; the ribs, however, are quite worn, but originally may have been pointed. Another stem from Polis, published later, also belongs to the same type. Cf. Benton 1949, p. 309, Fig. 1:3.

39. Marinatos 1932, Pls. 6, 12.

40. 1) Furtwängler 1890, p. 199, no. 1285; 2) Benton 1949, pp. 309-11, Fig. 1:2; 3) Benton 1936, p. 81, Fig. 1; Benton 1949, pp. 309-11, Fig. 1:5. The stem in Benton 1949, p. 311, Fig. 1:5 is wrongly stated as coming from Polis.

41. The Astakos stem is merely mentioned, but not illustrated in Benton 1938-39, p. 13, n. 6. Because it is mentioned together with Olympia no. 3 (Benton 1936, p. 81, Fig. 1) which belongs to Type F, the Astakos example is assumed to belong to the same type. See also FM 276 (example from Asine).

42. Cf. *BSA* 33 (1932-33), p. 38, Fig. 8. For similar examples from Cyprus, see *BSA* 33 (1932-33) p. 63, n. 14; Benton 1938-39, p. 13, n. 6.

43. Similar ribbed stems are reported to have come from Malthi. Cf. Valmin 1938, p. 328; Desborough 1964, p. 94. These stems are now lost, but Valmin compares them to the Aetos example, so they are here assumed to belong to Type C.

44. *Deltion* 23 (1968), *Chronika* B′ 2, pp. 263-65, Pl. 201. See also *AAA* 1 (1968), pp. 289-95; Desborough 1972, pp. 98, 104, Pl. 18.

45. Coldstream (1968, p. 220) calls this a W Greek koinê, but does not include Epirus in his definition.

46. The term oinochoe is here used for the Dark Age in its usual sense, i.e., a jug with a trefoil lip.

47. Choremis 1973, pp. 71-73.

48. The history of the use of the Tragana tholos is fraught with difficulties, and much of the later material has been lost and thus cannot be checked. There appear to be three periods of use: 1) LHIIA(early)-LHIIIA2; 2) LHIIIC-DAI; 3) DAII. LHIIIC-DAI: Burial α contained three jugs, a lekythos, and a one-handled bowl (cf. *Arch Eph* 1914, p. 104, Fig. 5). Burial β contained a krater and belly-handled amphora (cf. *Arch Eph* 1914, pp. 105, 106, Figs. 7-10). The disturbed fill above the floor of the tomb produced two additional vases, indicating yet another burial on the floor (cf. *Arch Eph* 1914, p. 107, Fig. 11). *DAII:* Sherds of this period were found in the fill above the floor. Cf. *Arch Eph* 1914, p. 107, Fig. 12 (skyphos and deep bowl sherds) and p. 101, Fig. 4 (small jug). The author is indebted to O. T. P. K. Dickinson for observations concerning the first two periods. See Hope Simpson and Dickinson 1979, pp. 132, 133.

49. Cf. Deshayes 1966, pp. 50-53, DV 42, 60, Pl. 58:6-7;

Blegen 1937, Fig. 516:11, 19 – from tomb XI; *Deltion* 23 (1968) A' p. 184, Pl. 82γ (vase no. 79 from Ayios Ioannis, Monemvasias). See also FS 181.

50. Desborough 1952, pp. 150ff., Pl. 20, 6.

51. FS 58. See also Iakovidis 1970, p. 263, Fig. 114, no. 590 (from Grave 74) and list of parallels on p. 263, n. 1-9.

52. Developed from LHIIIC; cf. FS 60. For continuation into the Dark Ages, see Desborough 1972, pp. 203, 204, Pl. 47 (from Delphi). These later examples, however, have more conical bodies (i.e., less globular) than **P1598.** An amphoriskos (Argostolion Museum no. 1669) from Mavrata in Kephallenia is shaped like **P1598** with the decoration of a double wavy line in the handle zone.

53. Graves 1961:2, 4, 5, 7. Cf. Yalouris 1961, pp. 186-188; 1963, p. 120; Leon 1961-3, Beiblatt pp. 46-58; Leon 1964-65, Beiblatt pp. 52-74. Discussed in Styrenius 1967, pp. 139ff., Figs. 59, 60, 62, 63.

54. As opposed to MH nipples which are more rounded and curve outward from the body of the vase. The author is indebted to Roger Howell for this observation.

55. Andronikos 1969, Pl. 68, no. 9 and Pl. 70, 29 (from Tomb AE). See also n. 31.

56. Vokotopoulou 1969b, pp. 179ff., Pl. 25β (cup β from Grave 1). For Late Bronze Age graves at Elaphotopos, see Snodgrass 1971, p. 212. For the possibility of northern influence at Nichoria, see n. 31.

57. There is also one example of 7.5YR 8/6.

58. Alaas T.17/9. Cf. Karageorghis 1975, p. 17, Pl. 61.

59. Small skyphos, now in the Benaki Museum of Kalamata (no museum number). Cf. Themelis 1965, p. 208, Pl. 222β (vase to right).

60. Chora Museum nos. 1657, 1659. Cf. Taylour 1973, pp. 240-242, Fig. 298: 12, 13.

61. From a DA level above Court 42 at Ano Englianos. Chora Museum no. 1425. Cf. Blegen 1966, p. 185, Fig. 347, no. 617.

62. Chania Museum no. 1281 (unpublished).

63. Alaas T.17/16. Cf. Karageorghis 1975, Pl. 59.

64. Kalamata Museum no. 16 12. Cf. Themelis 1965, p. 208, Pl. 222β (vase to left).

65. Chania Museum no. 1266 (unpublished).

66. Alaas T.11/3; T.15/9; T.19/15-17, 19, 23; G2 (Hadjiprodromou Collection). Cf. Karageorghis 1975, Pls. 52, 54, 64, 75.

67. Canciane 1966, pp. 97-99, Figs. 26, 32.

68. Kourouniotis 1914, p. 107, Fig. 12, nos. 6, 7. The Tragana DA material is now lost, so it is impossible to make accurate comparisons with it.

69. Valmin 1938, p. 326, Fig. 70.

70. Kourouniotis 1914, p. 107, Fig. 12, nos. 1, 2.

71. From the Herōon. Sparta Museum, tray no. 2577. Cf. Desborough 1952, p. 289; Coldstream 1968, p. 213, Pl. 46c.

72. Kourouniotis 1914, p. 107, Fig. 12, nos. 3-5.

73. On some 20 fairly large rim fragments in tray no. 2640g in the Sparta Museum.

74. A group of some 40 Protogeometric vases from Agrinion was donated to the Ioannina Museum. The skyphos in question has a museum number of 4605. Cf. Vokotopoulou 1969a, pp. 74-94, Pls. 46-52. For no. 4605, see p. 84, no. 34. The kantharos, not the skyphos, is the common open shape in Achaea and Aetolia, and there are examples of monochrome-coated kantharoi from these regions. Cf. Ioannina Museum nos. 4582, 4586 (from Agrinion) and Patras Museum no. 487 (from Derveni: cf. Coldstream 1968, Pl. 48d). Monochrome-coated squat kantharoi also come from Kalydon (Mastrokostas 1961-62, p. 183, Pl. 212, nos. 7, 10) and Priolithos Kalavriton (Patras Museum no. 1061: cf. *Deltion* (1967) B, p. 217, Pl. 156).

75. Alaas T.19/15-19, 23.

76. Ioannina Museum nos. 4574, 4576.

77. Mastrokostas 1961-62, p. 183, Pl. 212, nos. 6, 8. Also, a possible parallel occurs on a kantharos from Liopesi (Pherae) in Achaea. Patras Museum Π 679: cf. *Deltion* 20 (1965) B, p. 223.

78. A possible variation to this decoration occurs on a small deep bowl from Malthi (see n. 3). Here the handle zone is coated but flanked by thin reserved bands; this seems to emphasize the coating in the field between the handles.

79. Chania Museum no. 1281. Also nos. 1217, 1218, 1221, 1223, 1230. In the Modi examples, however, the entire foot and lower belly are undecorated. The lower belly is also left undecorated on flat-based skyphoi. Cf. nos. 1235, 1236, 1278, 1279.

80. Alaas T.11/3.

81. Patras Museum no. 495. Cf. Vermeule 1960, p. 16, no. 53, Pl. 5, Fig. 39; Coldstream 1968, pp. 221-223, Pl. 48e. Chania Museum nos. 2095 and 2097 from Kavousi in W Crete also have similar bands as the major decorative feature in the handle zone.

82. Aetos P132. Cf. Benton 1953, pp. 269, 270, Fig. 6.

83. Ioannina Museum no. 4572.

84. Benton 1931-32, p. 239, Fig. 20, no. 3.

85. Patras Museum no. 489. Cf. Vermeule 1960, p. 16, no. 64, Pl. 5, Fig. 39; Coldstream 1968, pp. 221-223, Pl. 48c.

86. Mastrokostas 1961-62, p. 183, Pl. 212, no. 1.

87. Benton 1931-32, p. 239, Fig. 20, no. 5. Called Geometric, but probably is PG.

88. The wavy line also appears on skyphoi with high conical feet from Asine. Cf. Frödin and Persson 1938, p. 429, Fig. 277 (from Tomb PG 25); Wells 1976, p. 19, Fig. 28 (F70-30, found NW of Tomb 1970-15).

89. Kalamata Museum no. 210. Cf. Themelis 1965, p. 207, Pl. 215γ.

90. For example, no. 2032 from Tomb 48 and no. 547 from Tomb 15. Cf. Desborough 1952, Pl. 10.

91. E.g., no. 607 from Tomb T 24 and no. 1091 from Tomb 38. Cf. Desborough 1952, Pl. 10.

92. From Amyclae: von Massow 1927, pp. 46-48, Pl. 3, 17-18. From the Sanctuary of Artemis Orthia: CVA *Cambridge* 1, Pl. 3, 1; Desborough 1952, Pl. 38, 12. From the sanctuary of Athena Chalkioikos: Desborough 1952, Pl. 38, 8.

93. Benton 1931-32, p. 239, Fig. 20, no. 9. Called Geometric, but is probably PG.

94. Chora Museum no. 1658: cup with decoration of cross-hatching above and wavy line below. This combination of cross-hatching and wavy line also appears on kantharoi from Agrinion (Ioannina Museum nos. 4578-81) but in reverse order, with wavy line above and the cross-hatching below.

95. All sherds from the 1959 test trenches at Kaphirio are housed in the Kalamata Museum. Cf. McDonald and Hope Simpson 1961, p. 248, no. 75; Coldstream 1968, p. 222.

96. Fiechter 1918, p. 121, Fig. 11; von Massow 1927, Pls. 2:3, 3:3-4, 6-8, 10-12, 21-24; CVA *Heidelberg* Pl. 134:1, 3, 4, 9, 11, 14-16, 18, 21; CVA *Cambridge* 1, Pl. 3:91, 94, 95. The rendition and placing of Laconian cross-hatching is discussed by Cartledge (1975, p. 92).

97. Sanctuary of Artemis Orthia: Desborough 1952, Pl. 38:13, 15.

98. Patras Museum nos. 487, 491 (from Derveni). Cf. Coldstream 1968, Pl. 48h (487), 48g (491). Also on a kantharos from Agrinion (Ioannina Museum no. 4575).

99. Amyclae: von Massow 1927, Pl. 3:3, 11, 19; Lamb 1930, Pl. 3:91; Desborough 1952, Pl. 38:1. Sanctuary of Artemis Orthia: Desborough 1952, Pl. 38:3.

100. To date, framed crosshatched triangles have been found on oinochoai and jugs only. Cf. Frödin and Persson 1938, p. 429, Fig. 277; Wells 1976, p. 19, Fig. 29 (Jug F70-30).

101. Nauplion Museum no. 13192. Hägg 1971, p. 50, Fig. 14. There is also a Cretan PGB example in Heraklion (F 356); Cf. Coldstream 1968, Pl. 51b (left).

102. Patras Museum no. 488 (from Derveni). Cf. Coldstream 1968, Pl. 48a.

103. One example only from Amyclae, cited by Cartledge (1975, p. 94, n. 138).

104. CVA *Heidelberg* 3, Pl. 134:3, 10; CVA *Mainz* 1, Pl. 2:2; CVA *Cambridge* 1, Pl. 3:92.

105. Mastrokostas 1961-62, p. 183, Pl. 212, no. 9. These dots resemble slightly the decorative motif that Cartledge (1975) calls "half-moons." These do occur in Laconia but appear to be Archaic, derived from Argive LG/Transitional.

106. The use of incisions at Nichoria extends also to the underside of the base, where concentric incisions occur on **P394, P641**, and **P643.** On **P400, P401**, and **P403** the monochrome paint on the exterior of the base spills over onto the underside.

107. From Derveni. Cf. Coldstream 1968, Pl. 48b, g.

108. On two skyphoi with high conical feet from the recent excavations at Asine, nos. 1970-14:4 and F70-31. Cf. Wells 1976, p. 15, Fig. 17(1970-14:4) and p. 18, Fig. 27(F70-31). Single crosshatched triangles without metopal panels also appear on oinochoai and jugs from Asine. Cf. Frödin and Persson 1938, pp. 428-30, Figs. 276, 277, 279.

109. Chora Museum no. 2664. Cf. Marinatos 1965, p. 111, Pl. 121e.

110. Kalamata Museum no. 205. Cf. Themelis 1965, p. 208, Pl. 215a (vase in middle).

111. Chania Museum no. 1220 (unpublished).

112. Chora Museum nos. 2662, 2663. Cf. Marinatos 1965, Pl. 121γ-δ.

113. Kalamata Museum nos. 199, 204. Cf. Themelis 1965, Pl. 215a (vases at left and right of center cup).

114. Cup fragments in tray no. 2637 in the Sparta Museum and in the "Geometric" tray in the Museum of the British School at Athens.

115. Chania Museum nos. 826, 828, 829. Cf. Jantzen 1964, pp. 60-62, Pl. 34.

116. Patras Museum no. 492. Cf. Coldstream 1968, Pl. 48f.

117. Alaas Pit A/8, 13, J2. Cf. Karageorghis 1975, Pls. 66, 76, 77.

118. Alaas T.11/14, T.19/20.

119. Chora Museum no. 1662. Cf. Taylour 1973, Fig. 298, no. 15.

120. Handmade vases with nipple decoration occur in Epirus throughout the Bronze Age. Cf. Papadopoulos 1976, pp. 281, 282. Such nipple decoration later appears in Messenia during the Dark Age, perhaps indicating northern influence.

121. Myres 1914, p. 52, no. 458.

122. Idalion, Tomb no. 3. Cf. Gjerstad et al. 1935, Pl. 90, no. M. 65, 4.

123. Kourion, Tomb no. 25. Cf. Daniel 1937, p. 56, Pl. 4, no. 54. In general, Daniel has dated these tombs from Kourion too early. The vases look definitely Protogeometric, with parallels from Alaas suggesting a date equivalent to DAI and DAII at Nichoria.

124. Karageorghis 1975, K4, Pl. 78; Myres 1914, p. 67, no. 517.

125. Now in the sherd collection of the British School at Athens.

126. Alaas 14 and J4. Also Alaas T.1.7 and T.1.8. For these latter two vases, see Karageorghis 1977, Pls. 35, 36, nos. 40, 42. See also Pieridou 1973, p. 18, Pl. 5, 11 (from Kourion).

127. Myres 1914, p. 67, no. 518.

128. von Massow 1927, Pl. 2, nos. 20-23.

129. Patras Museum no. 493. Cf. Coldstream 1968, Pl. 48j.

130. FS137. Also, Perati vases no. 531 from Grave 46 (Iakovidis 1970, Pl. 78e, no. 531) and no. 991 from Grave 136 (Iakovidis 1970, Pl. 70b, no. 991).

131. Kalamata Museum nos. Π77-79: Themelis 1965, Pl. 215b (Π77 to left, Π78 to right).

132. Kalamata Museum nos. 200, 203.

133. Kalamata Museum no. 282: Themelis 1965, Pl. 219γ.

134. Chora Museum no. 1660: Taylour 1973, Fig. 298, no. 11.

135. Such a coexistence of hand-drawn and compass-drawn semicircles has also been noted on skyphoi and deep bowls from the DAII use of the Tragana tholos.

136. Chora Museum no. 1661 is a neck-handled amphora with decoration of isolated spiral and crosshatched diamond on the shoulder. Cf. Taylour 1973, Fig. 298, no. 15. Chora Museum no. 1662 is a belly-handled amphora with a wavy line on the neck and three wavy lines between the handles on the belly. Cf. Taylour 1973, Fig. 298, no. 14.

137. Hydria with framed crosshatched triangle on shoulder and wavy line below in handle zone. Cf. Waterhouse and Hope Simpson 1961, pp. 115-17, Fig. 2b.

138. Crosshatched diamonds in a metopal panel also occur on the shoulder of a neck-handled amphora from Mavrovouni, near Gytheion. Cf. Waterhouse and Hope Simpson 1961, p. 115, Fig. 2a.

139. Vase no. 1 from Chamber Tomb no. 11 at Berbati; cf. Säflund 1965, Fig. 39, no. 1. Also, vase no. 290 from Tomb 24 at Prosymna; cf. Blegen 1937, Fig. 173, no. 290.

140. Nos. 1970-14:3 and 1970-15:2. Cf. Wells 1976, pp. 15-17, Figs. 16, 22.

141. Lamb 1936, p. 164.

142. Karageorghis 1969, pp. 467-69, Fig. 55. Similar spools belonging to the LHIIIC period have also been found at Lefkandi; cf. Popham and Sackett 1968, p. 13, Fig. 16 (top row).

143. Bouzek 1974b, p. 48.

144. Incised circles can be found on Attic Protogeometric pyxides and bowls. Cf. Bouzek 1974b, pp. 9-13, Figs. 3-5. Such decoration may have originally been introduced into Greece from the Central Balkans via Epirus.

145. The coarse vases from the Rizes pithos burial consist of one medium-sized jug (Chora Museum no. 2265) and two very small jugs (2666, 2667). Two small coarse jugs were also found at Agriapides; cf. Kyparissis 1930, p. 87, Fig. 10 (two vases at left). Papadopoulos (1978-79) argues for a Late Bronze Age date for these two vases; but their similarity in shape to those from Rizes (especially nos. 2666, 2667) would suggest that they belong to the Dark Age (DAII?).

146. This number includes good body sherds that were not given catalog numbers.

147. Type A: 42 examples; Type B: 51 examples.

148. Especially kantharos 3-II (*Arch Eph* 1973, pp. 15-29, esp. p. 16, Fig. 1). Of the four pithos graves, the material from nos. 1 and 2 is earlier than that from nos. 3 and 4.

149. These sherds are associated with levels 1 and 2 of L23 TUVk1.

150. The shape does, however, appear in the Attic skyphoi of the Classical period; cf. *The Athenian Agora* XII, 2 (1970), Fig. 4. no. 318.

151. Chora Museum no. 1425. Cf. Blegen 1966, p. 185, Fig. 347, no. 617.

152. Blegen 1966, p. 185, no. 617.

153. Ribbing also appears later on cups of the Classical period; cf. *The Athenian Agora* XII, 2 (1970), Fig. 3, nos. 201, 203.

154. Blegen 1966, pp. 185, 186.

155. From above Court 42 at Ano Englianos. Chora Museum nos. 1423, 1424. Cf. Blegen 1966, p. 185, Fig. 347, nos. 615, 616. No. 1423 has a rim diameter of 0.075 m and no. 1424 of 0.09 m, but both have the S-shaped profile and carinated body with Type B rims.

156. Chora Museum, not numbered. Cf. Blegen 1966, p. 21, Fig.

347, no. 982. This cup has a rim diameter of 0.07 m with a Type B rim.

157. Blegen 1966, pp. 185, 186.

158. From the court of the Megaron in the black deposit. Chora Museum no. 1633. Cf. Blegen 1966, p. 64, Fig. 347, no. 827.

159. Blegen 1966, p. 10.

160. Cf. Alaas pit A/1-3, A/6. These Alaas examples have a loop handle attached to the rim. There is no evidence, unfortunately, for suggesting to what type of small jug the Nichoria example belongs.

161. Smithson 1968, pp. 103-5, Pl. 29; Bouzek 1974b, pp. 20 ff., Pl. 6.

162. For example, the Rizes pithos. Cf. Marinatos 1965, pp. 111-13, Pl. 121ς.

163. McDonald 1972, p. 228, Pl. 40c.

164. Courbin 1966, C 2464, Pl. 59; Coldstream 1968, Pl. 31c.

165. Courbin 1966, C 30, C 833, Pl. 110.

166. Pylos Museum no. 689 (unpublished) is similar in shape and decoration to the bowl from the pithos burial (**P1575**) and can also be considered Late Geometric in date.

167. Coldstream 1968, Pl. 46.

168. Courbin 1966, C 20/B, C 22/A, Pl. 58.

169. Marinatos 1965, pp. 111, 112, Pl. 121ς.

170. Daux 1961, p. 697; Daux 1962, p. 725: Yalouris 1960, p. 108; Papathanasopoulos 1961-62, p. 95.

171. Yalouris 1960, p. 108; Papathanasopoulos 1961-62, p. 95.

172. Coldstream 1977, p. 161.

173. See also Coldstream 1977, p. 162.

174. Pylos Museum no. 695 (unpublished).

175. Bohen (1980, p. 88) identifies the Vathirema lid as of "Attic workmanship" yet considers it in the context of a Boeotian tradition. In her footnote 15, however, she describes the provenience of the lid as from a tomb at "Petrolaki, Karpofora, near Rizomilo just north of the site occupied by the late eighth century fugitives from Asine." In fact, there is no local toponym Petrolaki known to us near Karpofora; the tomb is located in the Vathirema ravine immediately west of the Nichoria ridge. The late eighth century site which she mentions is presumably that of ancient Asine (modern Koroni), located over 20 km south of Karpofora.

176. Courbin 1966, C 2464, GR2, Pl. 59; Coldstream 1977, p. 162.

177. Coldstream 1968, Pl. 46m.

178. Coldstream 1968, Pl. 19j, k, l; Coldstream 1977, p. 162.

179. Feature 16 in the survey of Nichoria environs (*Nichoria* I, p. 94, Fig. 7-11).

REFERENCES

Andronikos, M. 1969. *Vergina I.* Athens. In Greek.

Benton S. 1931-32. "The Ionian Islands," *BSA* 32:3-246.

———. 1936. "Review of Alt-Olympia by W. Dörpfeld (1935)," *JHS* 56:81, 82.

———. 1938-39. "Excavations in Ithaca, III: The Cave at Polis, II," *BSA* 39:1-51.

———. 1949. "Second Thoughts on 'Mycenaean' Pottery in Ithaca," *BSA* 44:308-12.

———. 1953. "Further Excavations at Aetos (with an appendix on the Later Corinthian Pottery from Aetos by J. K. Anderson)," *BSA* 48:256-61.

Blegen, C. 1937. *Prosymna,* Vol. II. Cambridge.

———, and Rawson, M., 1966. *The Palace of Nestor at Pylos,* Vol. I. Princeton.

Bohen, B. 1976. "A New Geometric Vase from the Kerameikos," *AM* 91:15-22.

———. 1980. "A Geometric Horse Pyxis Lid from Asine." *Op Ath* 13:85-89.

Bouzek, J. 1969. *Homerisches Greichenland*. Prague.

———. 1974a. *Graeco-Macedonian Bronzes*. Prague.

———. 1974b. *The Attic Dark Age Incised Ware.* Acta Musei Nationalis, Vol. 28, no. 1. Prague.

Canciane, F. 1966. *Corpus Vasorum Antiquorum* 13:27. Heidelberg University, fasc. 3.

Cartledge, P. A. 1975. "Early Sparta c. 950-650 B.C.: An Archaeological and Historical Study." D. Phil. Thesis. Oxford.

———. 1977. *Sparta and Lakonia: A Regional History, 1300-362 B.C.* Boston.

Choremis, A. 1973. "Mycenaean and Protogeometric Tombs in Karpofora," *Arch Eph*:25-74. In Greek.

Coldstream, J. N. 1968. *Greek Geometric Pottery*. London.

———. 1977. *Geometric Greece*. London.

Coulson, W. D. E. 1975. "The Dark Age Pottery." In McDonald et al. 1975, pp. 114-16.

———. 1976. "The Protogeometric and Geometric Periods at Nichoria." In *Proceedings of the First International Congress of Peloponnesian Studies*, Vol. 2, pp. 252-54. Athens. In Greek.

———. 1979. "Dark Age Pottery from the Western Peloponnese." In *Greece and Italy in the Classical World: Acta of the XI International Congress of Classical Archaeology*, p. 186. London.

Courbin, P. 1966. *La céramique géometrique de l'Argolide.* Paris.

———. 1977. "Une pyxis géometrique argienne au Liban," *Berytus* 25:147-57.

Daniel, J. F. 1937. "Late Cypriote III Tombs from Kourion," *AJA* 41:56-85.

Daux, G. 1961. "Chronique des fouilles 1960," *BCH* 85:697.

———. 1962. "Chronique des fouilles 1961," *BCH* 86:725.

Dekoulakou, I. 1973. "Geometric Pithos Tombs from Achaia," *Arch Eph*:15-29. In Greek.

Desborough, V. R. D'A. 1952. *Protogeometric Pottery.* Oxford.

———. 1964. *The Last Mycenaeans and Their Successors*. Oxford.

———. 1972. *The Greek Dark Ages.* London.

Deshayes, J. 1966. *Argos: Les fouilles de la Deiras.* Paris.

Dietz, S. 1974. "Profil' af en Mork tidsalder," *Nationalmuseets Arkejdsmark*:131-42.

Fiechter, E. 1918. "Amyklae," *JDAI* 33:107-245.

Forrest, W. G. 1968. *A History of Sparta*. London.

French, E. 1969. "The First Phase of LHIIIC," *AA* 84:133-36.

———, and Rutter, J. 1977. "The Handmade Burnished Ware of the Late Helladic IIIC Period: Its Modern Historical Context," *AJA* 81:111, 112.

Frödin, O., and Persson, A. W. 1938. *Asine I.* Stockholm.

Furtwängler, A. 1890. *Olympia. Die Ergebnisse IV: Die Bronzen.* Berlin.

Furumark, A. 1941. *The Mycenaean Pottery: Analysis and Classification.* Stockholm. (1972 edition.)

Gjerstad, E. et al. 1935. *The Swedish Cyprus Expedition*, Vol. II. Stockholm.

Hägg, R. 1971. "Protogeometrische und Geometrische Keramik in Nauplion," *Op Ath* 10:41-52.

Hampe, R., and Simon, E. 1959. *Corpus Vasorum Antiquorum* 13: 15, Mainz University, fasc. 1.

Hencken, H. 1968. *Tarquinia and Etruscan Origins*. London.

Heurtley, W. A. 1932-33. "Excavations in Ithaca I," *BSA* 33:22-65.

Hope Simpson, R., and Dickinson, O. T. P. K. 1979. *A Gazetteer of Aegean Civilization in the Bronze Age*, Vol I: *The Mainland and the Islands.* Studies in Mediterranean Archaeology LII, Göteborg.

Huxley, G. L. 1962. *Early Sparta*. London.

Iakovidis, S. 1970. *Perati,* Vol. II. Athens. In Greek.

Jantzen, U. 1964. "Protogeometrisches aus West Kreta," *Festschrift Eugene V. Mercklin*. Waldsassen/Bayern.

Karageorga, T. 1972. "Excavations in the Region of Ancient Dorion," *Arch Eph*:12-20. In Greek.

Karageorghis, V. 1969. "Chronique des fouilles à Chypre en 1968," *BCH* 93:467-69.

———. 1975. *Alaas. A Protogeometric Necropolis in Cyprus*. Nicosia.

———. 1977. "More Material from the Protogeometric Necropolis of Alaas," *Report of the Department of Antiquities, Cyprus*. Nicosia.

Kavvadias, P. 1909. *Prehistoric Archaeology*. Athens. In Greek.

Kokkou-Viridi, K. 1977. "Four Protogeometric Graves at Argos," *Arch Eph*: 171-94. In Greek.

Kourouniotis, K. 1914. "A Tholos Tomb from Pylos, Messenia," *Arch Eph*: 99-117. In Greek.

Kraiker, W., and Kübler, K. 1939. *Keremeikos. Ergebnisse der Ausgrabungen*, Vol. I. Berlin.

Kyparissis, N. 1930. "Excavations of the Mycenaean Nekropolis in Achaia," *Praktika*:81-88. In Greek.

Lamb, W. 1930. *Corpus Vasorum Antiquorum* 4:6. Cambridge. Fitzwilliam Museum fasc. 1.

———. 1936. *Excavations at Thermi in Lesbos*. Cambridge.

Leon, V. 1961-63. "Zweiter vorlaufiger Bericht über die Ausgrabungen in Alt-Elis," *OJh* 46: Bieblatt:45-58.

———. 1964-65. "Ausgrabungen in Alt-Elis," *OJh* 47: Beiblatt:52-74.

Lukermann, F. E., and Moody, J. 1978. "Nichoria and Vicinity: Settlement and Circulation." In Rapp and Aschenbrenner 1978, pp. 78-107.

McDonald, W. A., and Hope Simpson, R. 1961. "Prehistoric Habitation in Southwest Peloponnese," *AJA* 65:221-60.

McDonald, W. A. 1972. "Excavations at Nichoria in Messenia, 1969-1971," *Hesperia* 41:218-73.

McDonald, W. A., and Rapp, G., Jr., eds. 1972. *The Minnesota Messenia Expedition: Reconstructing a Bronze Age Regional Environment*. Minneapolis.

Marinatos, S. 1932. "The Excavations Geokoop in Kephallenia," *Arch Eph*:1-47. In Greek.

———. 1933. "The Excavations Geokoop in Kephallenia, 2," *Arch Eph*:68-100. In Greek.

———. 1964. "Excavations in Pylos," *Deltion* 19:163, 164. In Greek.

———. 1965. "Excavations in Pylos," *Praktika*:102-20. In Greek.

Massow, H. von. 1927. "Von Amyklaion," *AM* 52:46-48.

Mastrokostas, E. 1961-62. "Aitolo-Acharnanian Antiquities," *Deltion* 17B:182-85. In Greek.

———. 1962. *Praktika*:127-33. In Greek.

———. 1963. *Praktika*:93-98. In Greek.

———. 1964. *Praktika*:60-67. In Greek.

———. 1965a. "Antiquities of Achaea," *Deltion* 20B:220-27. In Greek.

———. 1965b. "Excavation at Teichos Dymaion," *Praktika*: 121-36. In Greek.

———. 1967. "Antiquities of Achaea," *Deltion* 22B:213-17. In Greek.

Matson, F. R. 1972. "Ceramic Studies." In McDonald and Rapp 1972, pp. 200-224.

MME 1972 = McDonald and Rapp 1972.

Myres, J. L. 1914. *Handbook of the Cesnola Collection of Antiquities from Cyprus*. New York.

Nichoria I = Rapp and Aschenbrenner 1978.

Papadopoulos, A. J. 1976. "The Bronze Age in Epirus," *Dodoni* 5: 271-338. In Greek.

———. 1978-79. *Mycenaean Achaea. Studies in Mediterranean Archaeology* LV, 1. Göteborg.

Papathanasopoulos, G. P. 1962. "Antiquities of Messenia," *Deltion* 17B:92-99. In Greek.

Petsas, F. 1961-62. "Excavations of the Ancient Necropolis of Vergina (1960-1961)," *Deltion* 17A:218-88. In Greek.

Pieridou, A. 1973. *The Protogeometric Style in Cyprus*. Athens. In Greek.

Popham, M. R., and Sackett, L. H. 1968. *Excavations at Lefkandi, Euboea 1964-1966*. London.

———. 1979-81. *Lefkandi I: The Iron Age Settlement and the Cemeteries*. London.

Popham, M. R., and Milburn, E. 1971. "Late Helladic IIIC Pottery at Xeropolis (Lefkandi), a Summary," *BSA* 66:333-49.

Rapp, G., Jr., and Aschenbrenner, S., eds. 1978. *Excavations at Nichoria in Southwest Greece I: Site, Environs, and Techniques*. Minneapolis.

Robertson, M. 1948. "Excavations in Ithaca V," *BSA* 43:10-70.

Rutter, J. 1974, "LHIIIB and IIIC Periods at Korakou and Gonia." Ph.D. dissertation, University of Pennsylvania.

———. 1975. "Ceramic Evidence for Northern Intruders in Southern Greece at the Beginning of Late Helladic IIIC," *AJA* 79:17-32.

———. 1977. "Late Helladic IIIC Pottery and Some Historical Implications." In *Symposium on the Dark Ages in Greece*, pp. 1-20. Archaeological Institute of America, New York.

Säflund, G. 1965. *Excavations at Berbati*. Stockholm.

Smithson, E. L. 1968. "The Tomb of a Rich Athenian Lady, *ca.* 850 B.C.," *Hesperia* 37:77-116.

Snodgrass, A. 1971. *The Dark Age of Greece*. Edinburgh.

Sparkes, B., and Talcott, L. 1970. *Black and Plain Pottery of the 6th, 5th and 4th Centuries B.C. The Athenian Agora*, Vol. 12. Princeton.

Styrenius, C-G. 1967. *Submycenaean Studies*. Lund.

Taylour, W. D. 1973. In Blegen et al., *The Palace of Nestor at Pylos*, Vol. III. Princeton.

Themelis, P. G. 1965. "Antiquities of Thessaly," *Deltion* 20B:2: 207, 208. In Greek.

Theocharis, D. R. 1968a. "The Tomb of Exalophos and the Invasion of Thessaly," *AAA* I:289-95. In Greek.

———. 1968b. "Exalophos Trikalon: Antiquities of Thessaly," *Deltion* 23:263-65. In Greek.

Valmin, N. 1938. *The Swedish Messenia Expedition*. Lund.

Vermeule, E. 1960. "The Mycenaeans in Achaia," *AJA* 64: 1-21.

Vokotopoulou, I. 1969a. "Protogeometric Vases from the Region of Agrinion," *Deltion* 24A:74-94. In Greek.

———. 1969b. "New Cist Graves of the LHIIIB-Geometric Period from Epirus," *Arch Eph*:179-207. In Greek.

Wace, A. J. B. 1921-23. "Excavations at Mycenae VII – The Lion Gate and Grave Circle Area," *BSA* 25:10-38.

Wardle, K. A. 1972. "The Greek Bronze Age West of the Pindus." Ph.D. dissertation, London University.

Waterhouse, H., and Hope Simpson, R., 1961. "Prehistoric Laconia II," *BSA* 56:114-75.

Wells, B. 1976. *Asine: The Protogeometric Period*. Stockholm.

Yalouris, N. 1960. "Antiquities in Messenia," *Deltion* 16:107, 108. In Greek.

———. 1961. "Excavations in Elis," *Ergon*:177-88. In Greek.

———. 1963. "Excavations in Elis," *Ergon*:115-25. In Greek.

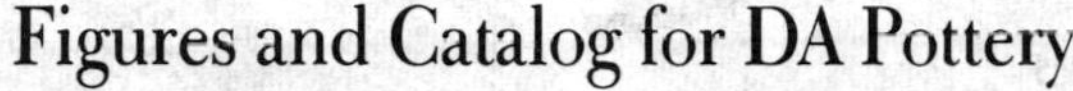

Figures and Catalog for DA Pottery

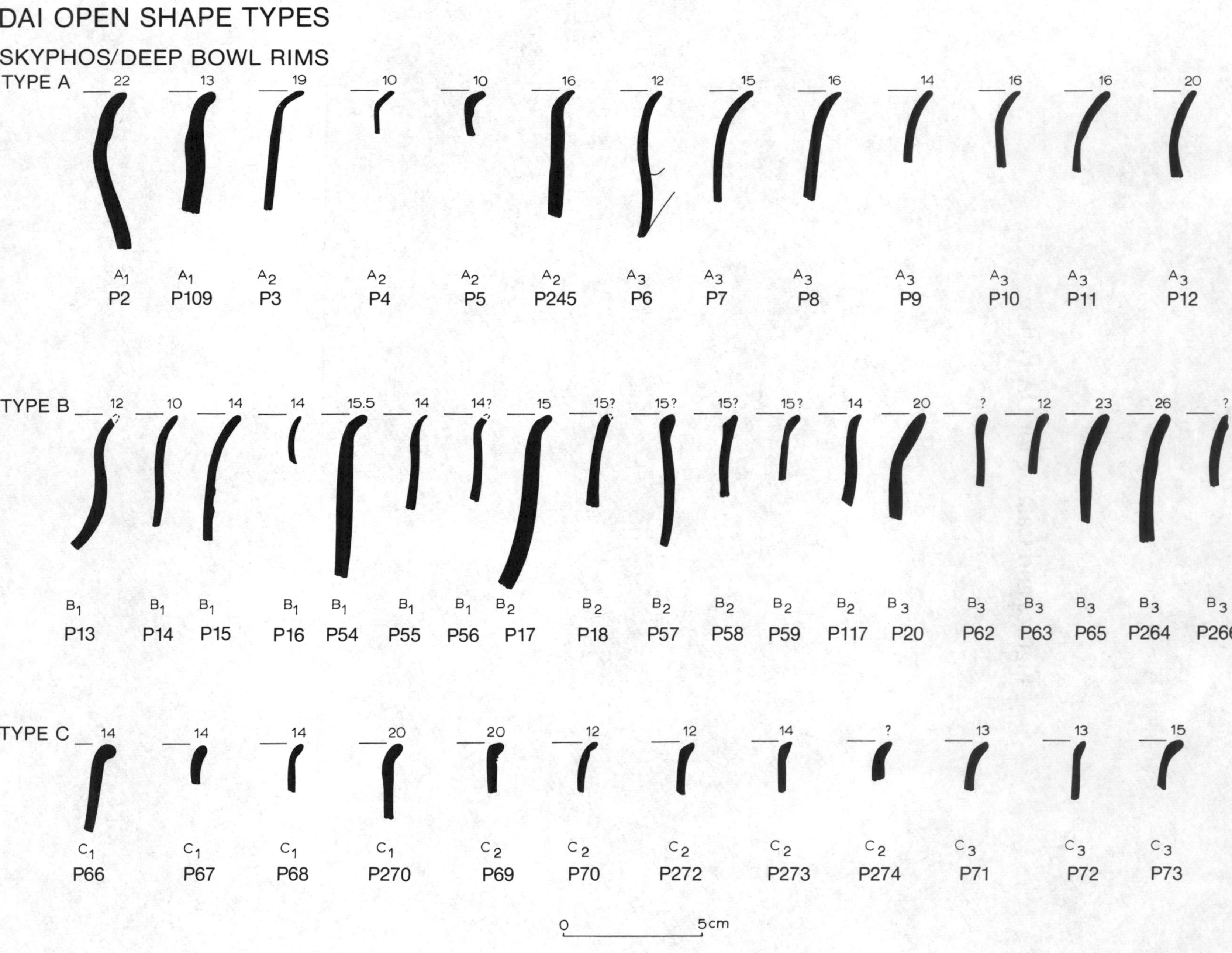
DAI OPEN SHAPE TYPES
SKYPHOS/DEEP BOWL RIMS
TYPE A
22 A_1 P2
13 A_1 P109
19 A_2 P3
10 A_2 P4
10 A_2 P5
16 A_2 P245
12 A_3 P6
15 A_3 P7
16 A_3 P8
14 A_3 P9
16 A_3 P10
16 A_3 P11
20 A_3 P12
TYPE B
12 B_1 P13
10 B_1 P14
14 B_1 P15
14 B_1 P16
15.5 B_1 P54
14 B_1 P55
14? B_1 P56
15 B_2 P17
15? B_2 P18
15? B_2 P57
15? B_2 P58
15? B_2 P59
14 B_2 P117
20 B_3 P20
? B_3 P62
12 B_3 P63
23 B_3 P65
26 B_3 P264
? B_3 P266
TYPE C
14 C_1 P66
14 C_1 P67
14 C_1 P68
20 C_1 P270
20 C_2 P69
12 C_2 P70
12 C_2 P272
14 C_2 P273
? C_2 P274
13 C_3 P71
13 C_3 P72
15 C_3 P73
0
5cm

Figure 3-2

CUP RIMS
P22
P23
KRATER RIMS
22
30
P148
P279
SKYPHOS/DEEP BOWL BASES
TYPE A
mono in
P24
mono in
P74
mono in
P281
TYPE A
mono in
P282
mono in
P283
TYPE B
mono in
P25
mono in
P26
mono in
P27
8
P76
TYPE B
mono in
P30
8
P78
6?
P79
mono in
P80
TYPE C
mono in
P83
0
5 cm

Figure 3-3

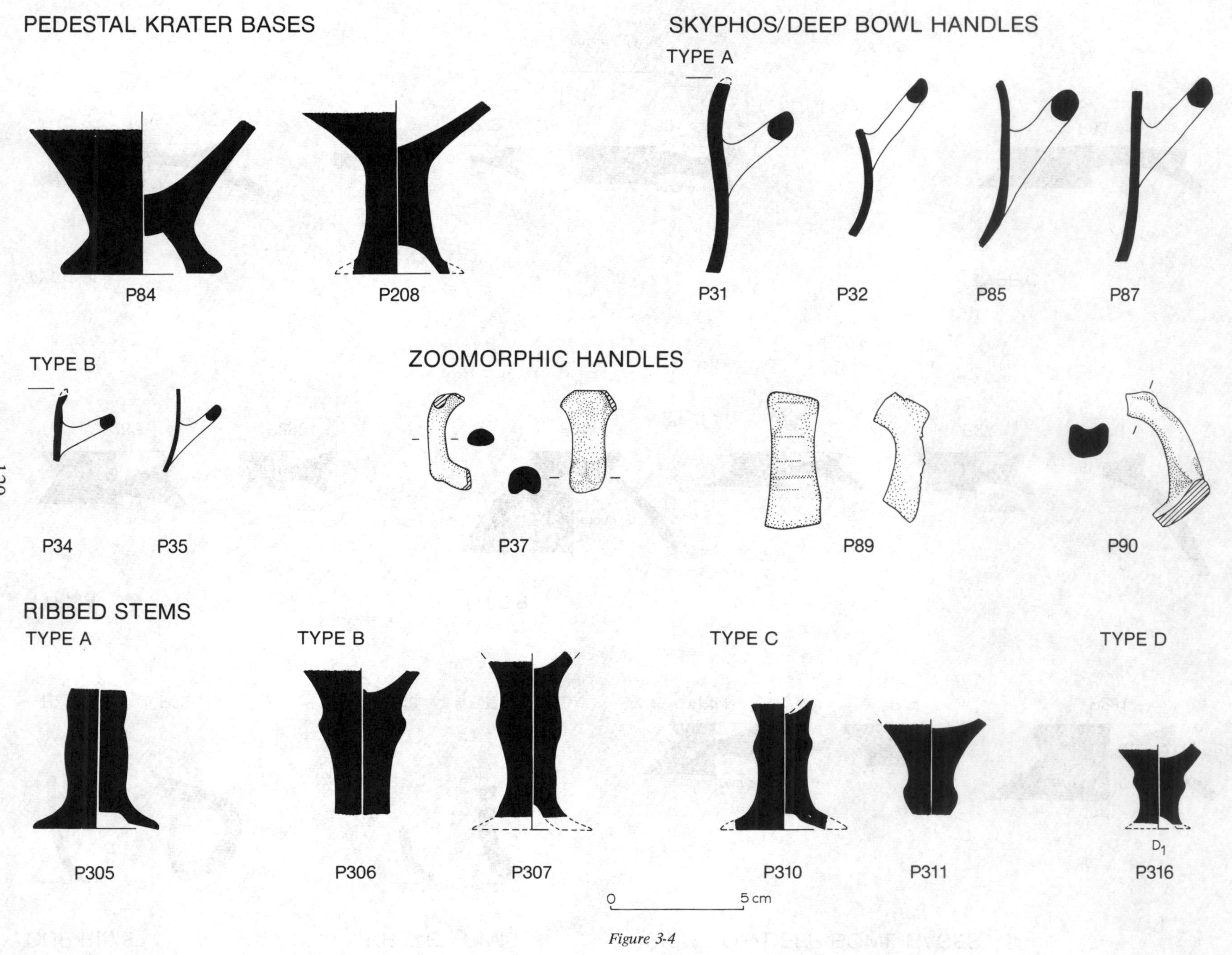
PEDESTAL KRATER BASES
P84
P208
SKYPHOS/DEEP BOWL HANDLES
TYPE A
P31
P32
P85
P87
TYPE B
P34
P35
ZOOMORPHIC HANDLES
P37
P89
P90
RIBBED STEMS
TYPE A
P305
TYPE B
P306
P307
TYPE C
P310
P311
TYPE D
D1
P316
0
5 cm

Figure 3-4

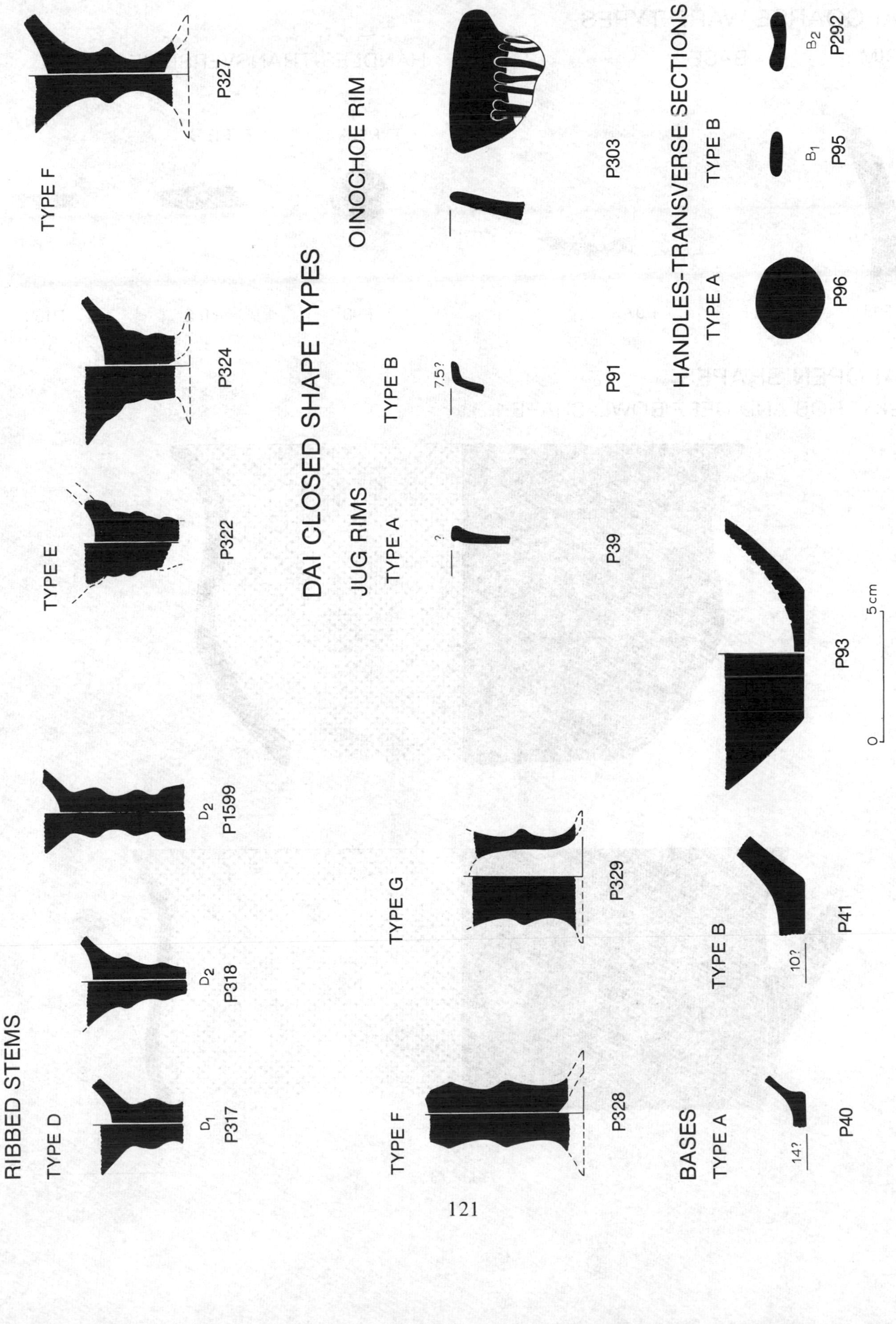

RIBBED STEMS

TYPE D

D_1 P317

D_2 P318

D_2 P1599

TYPE E

P322

P324

TYPE F

P327

TYPE F

P328

TYPE G

P329

DAI CLOSED SHAPE TYPES

JUG RIMS

TYPE A

?

P39

TYPE B

7.5?

P91

OINOCHOE RIM

P303

BASES

TYPE A

14?

P40

TYPE B

10?

P41

P93

0 5 cm

HANDLES-TRANSVERSE SECTIONS

TYPE A

P96

TYPE B

B_1 P95

B_2 P292

Figure 3-5

DAI COARSE WARE TYPES

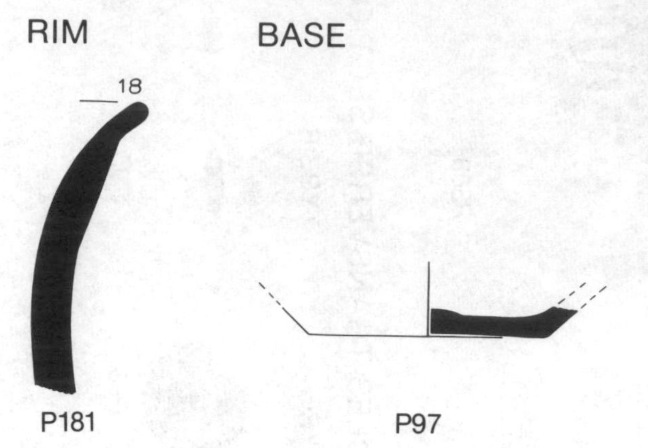

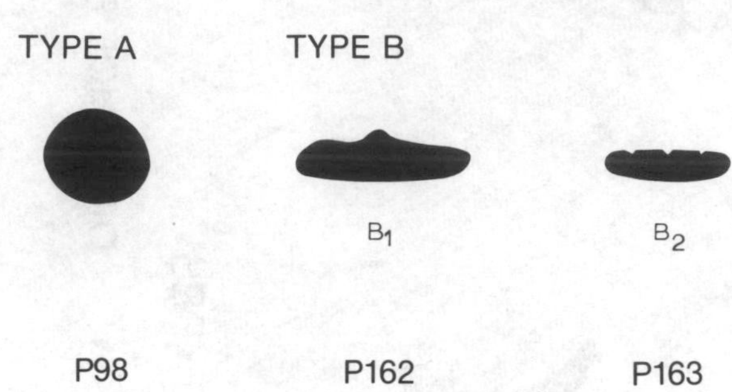

DAI OPEN SHAPES

SKYPHOS AND DEEP BOWL: SHAPE 1

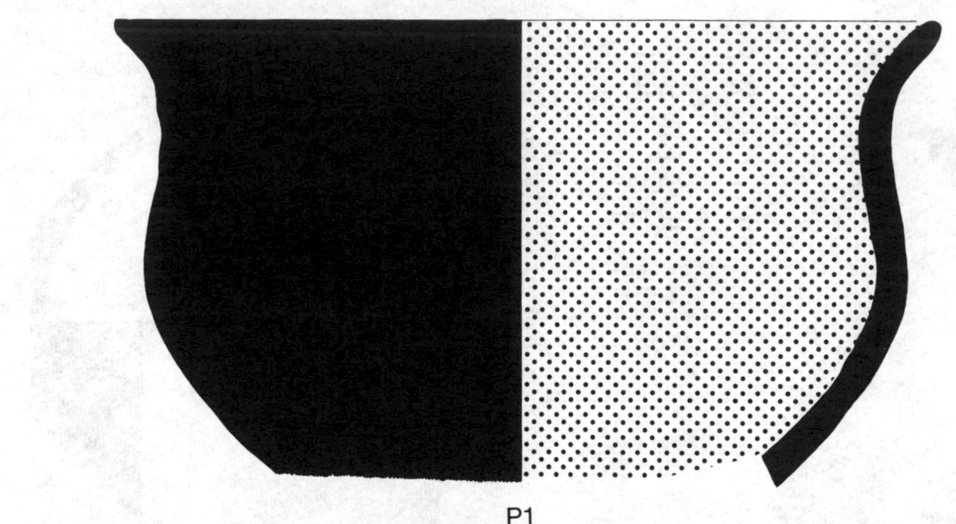

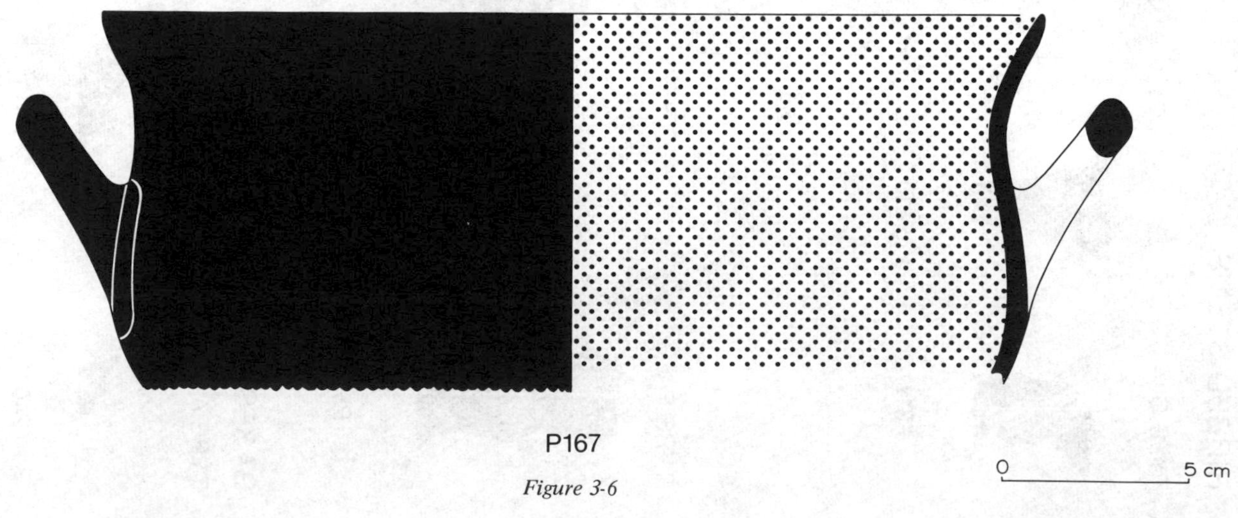

Figure 3-6

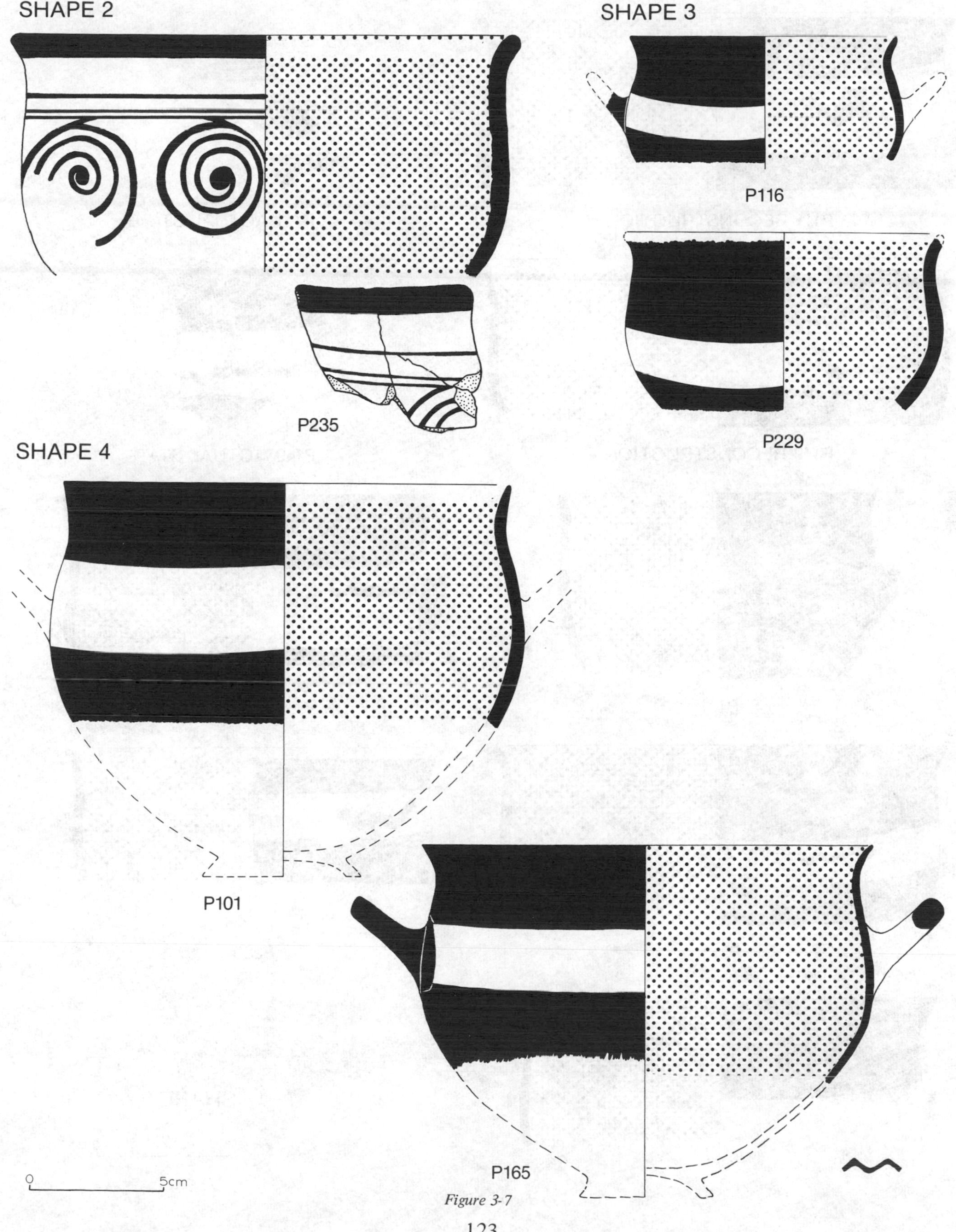

Figure 3-7

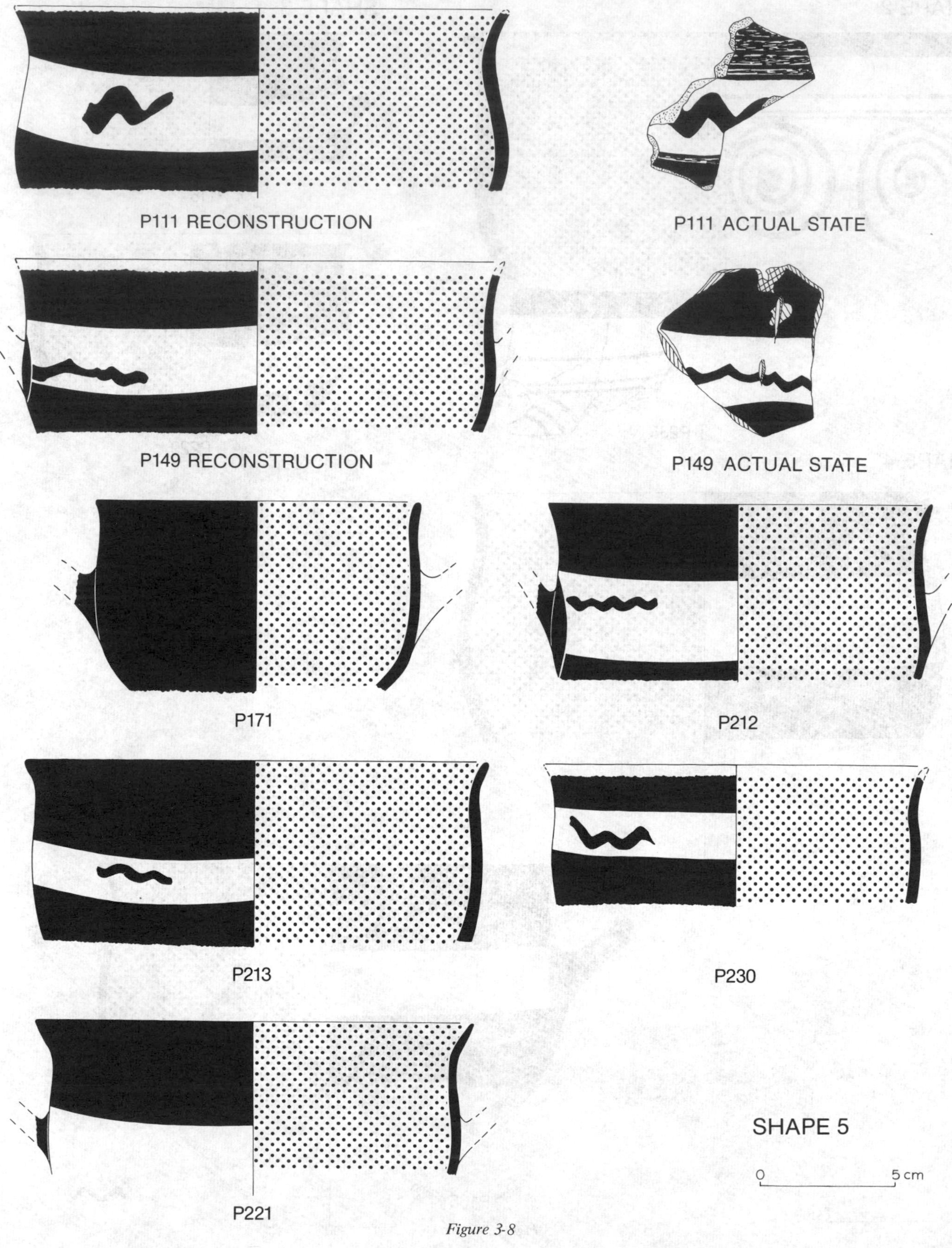
P111 RECONSTRUCTION
P111 ACTUAL STATE
P149 RECONSTRUCTION
P149 ACTUAL STATE
P171
P212
P213
P230
P221
SHAPE 5
0
5 cm

Figure 3-8

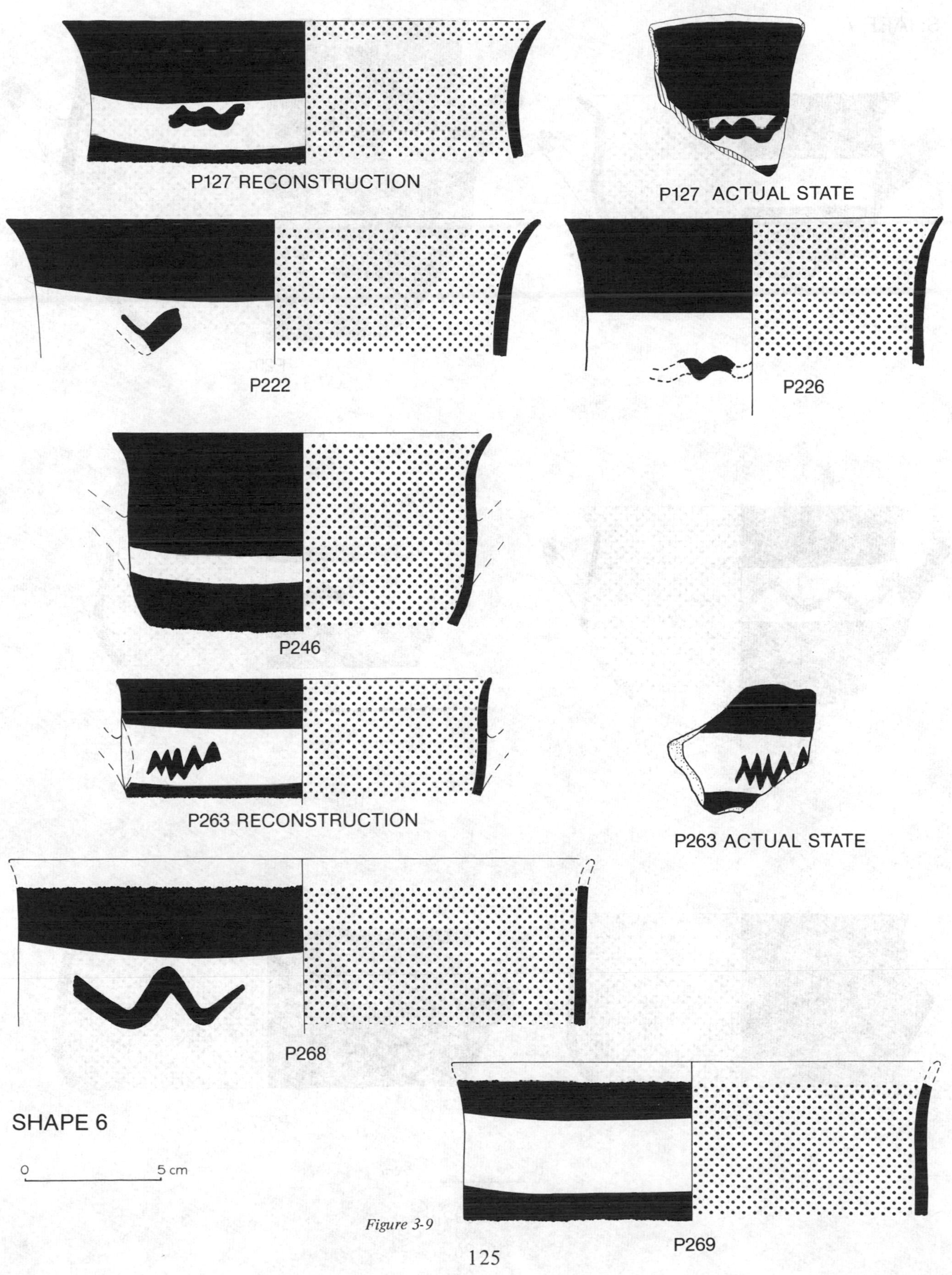
P127 RECONSTRUCTION
P127 ACTUAL STATE
P222
P226
P246
P263 RECONSTRUCTION
P263 ACTUAL STATE
P268
P269
SHAPE 6
0
5 cm

Figure 3-9

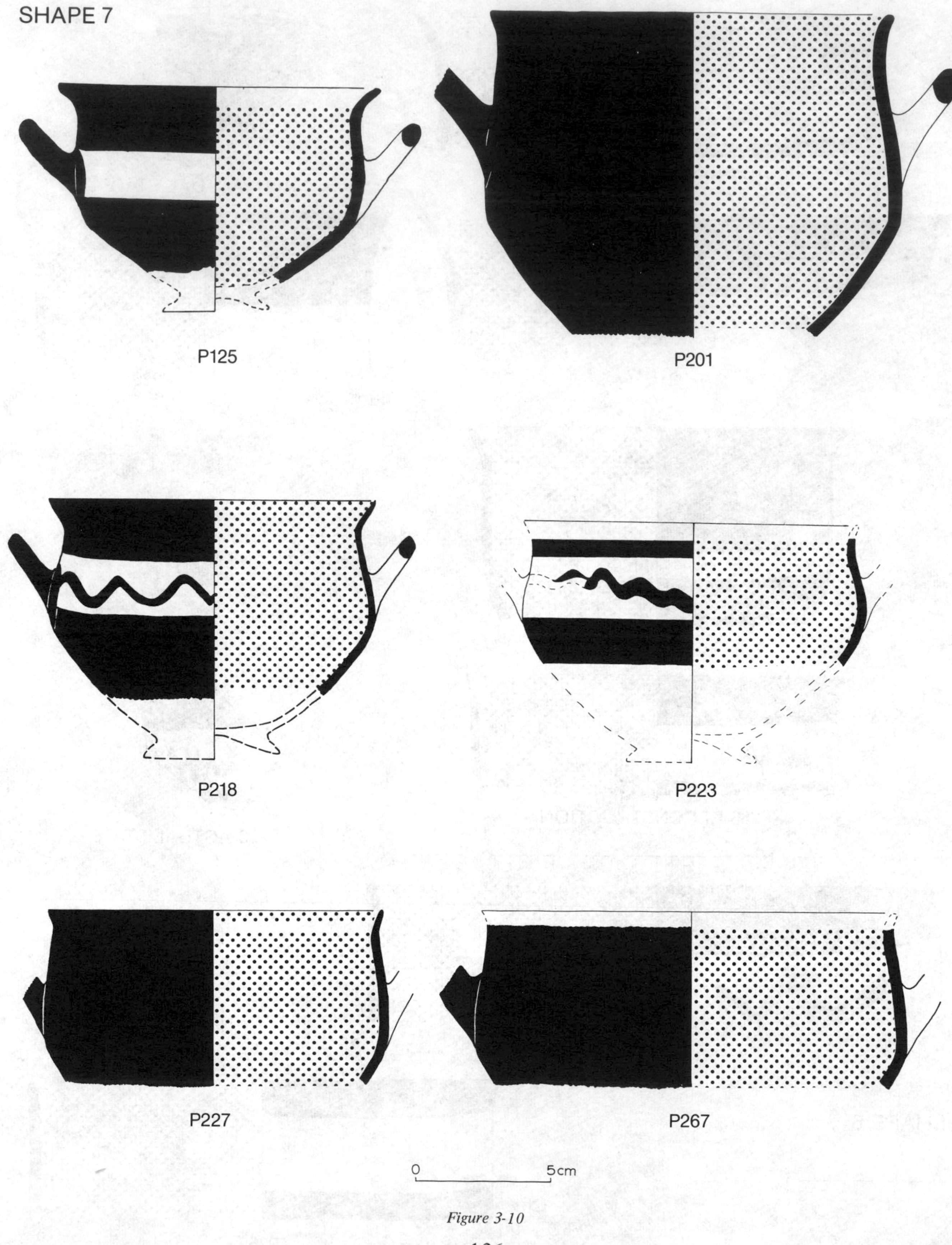

Figure 3-10

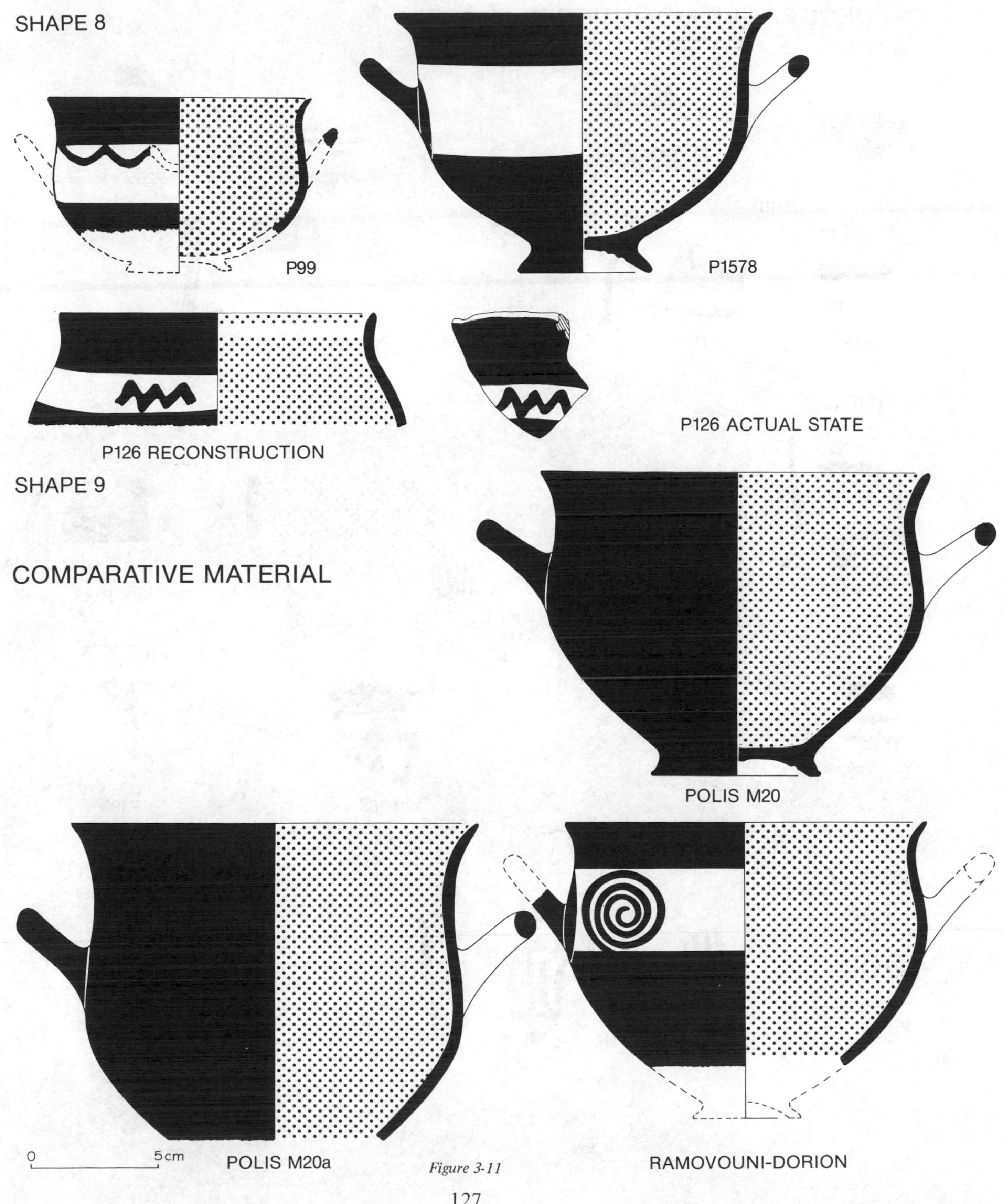
SHAPE 8
P99
P1578
P126 RECONSTRUCTION
P126 ACTUAL STATE
SHAPE 9
COMPARATIVE MATERIAL
POLIS M20
0
5cm
POLIS M20a
RAMOVOUNI-DORION

Figure 3-11

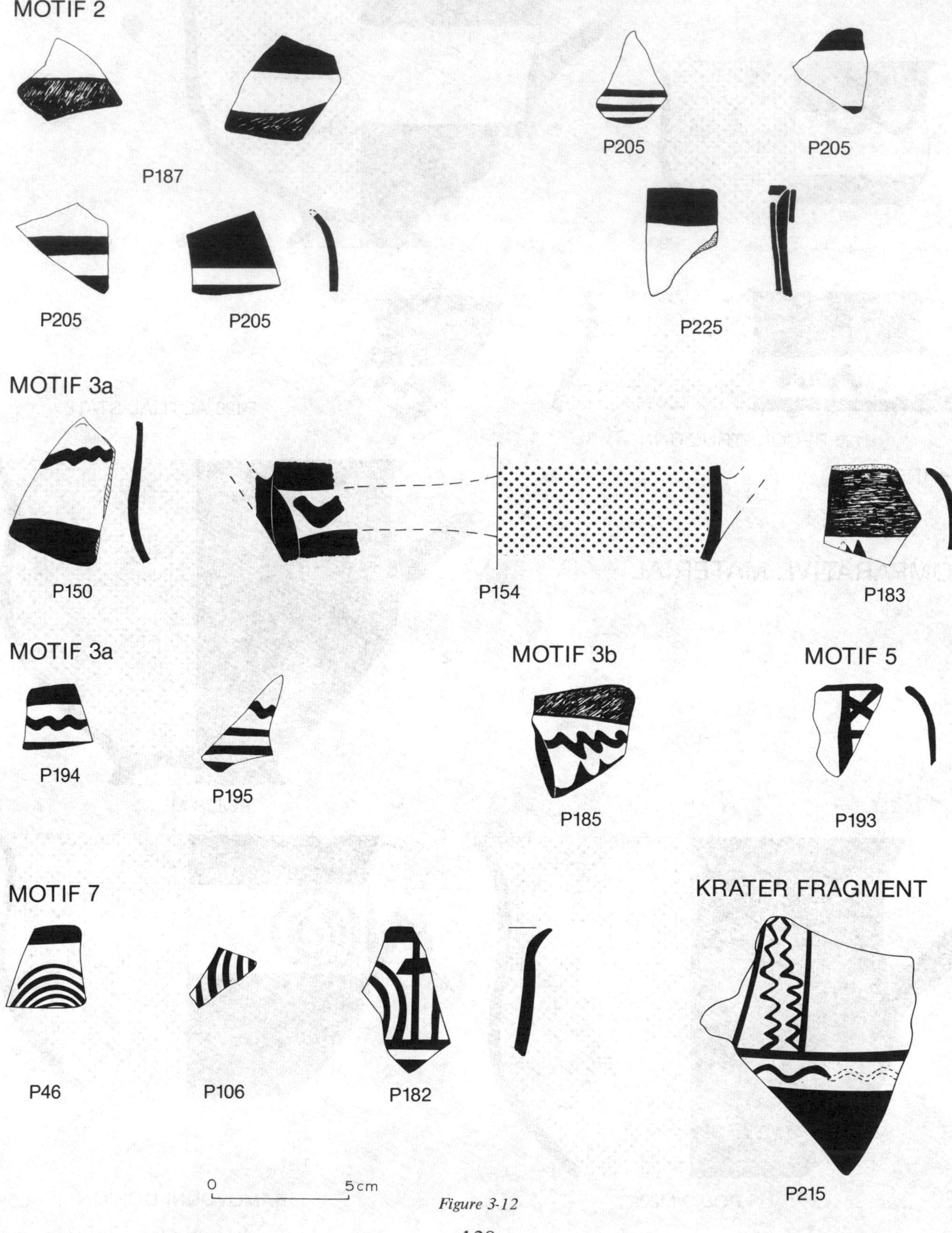
DAI DECORATIVE MOTIFS/OPEN SHAPES
MOTIF 2
P187
P205
P205
P205
P205
P225
MOTIF 3a
P150
P154
P183
MOTIF 3a
P194
P195
MOTIF 3b
P185
MOTIF 5
P193
MOTIF 7
P46
P106
P182
KRATER FRAGMENT
P215
0
5cm

Figure 3-12

ITHACAN COMPARATIVE MATERIAL

Figure 3-13

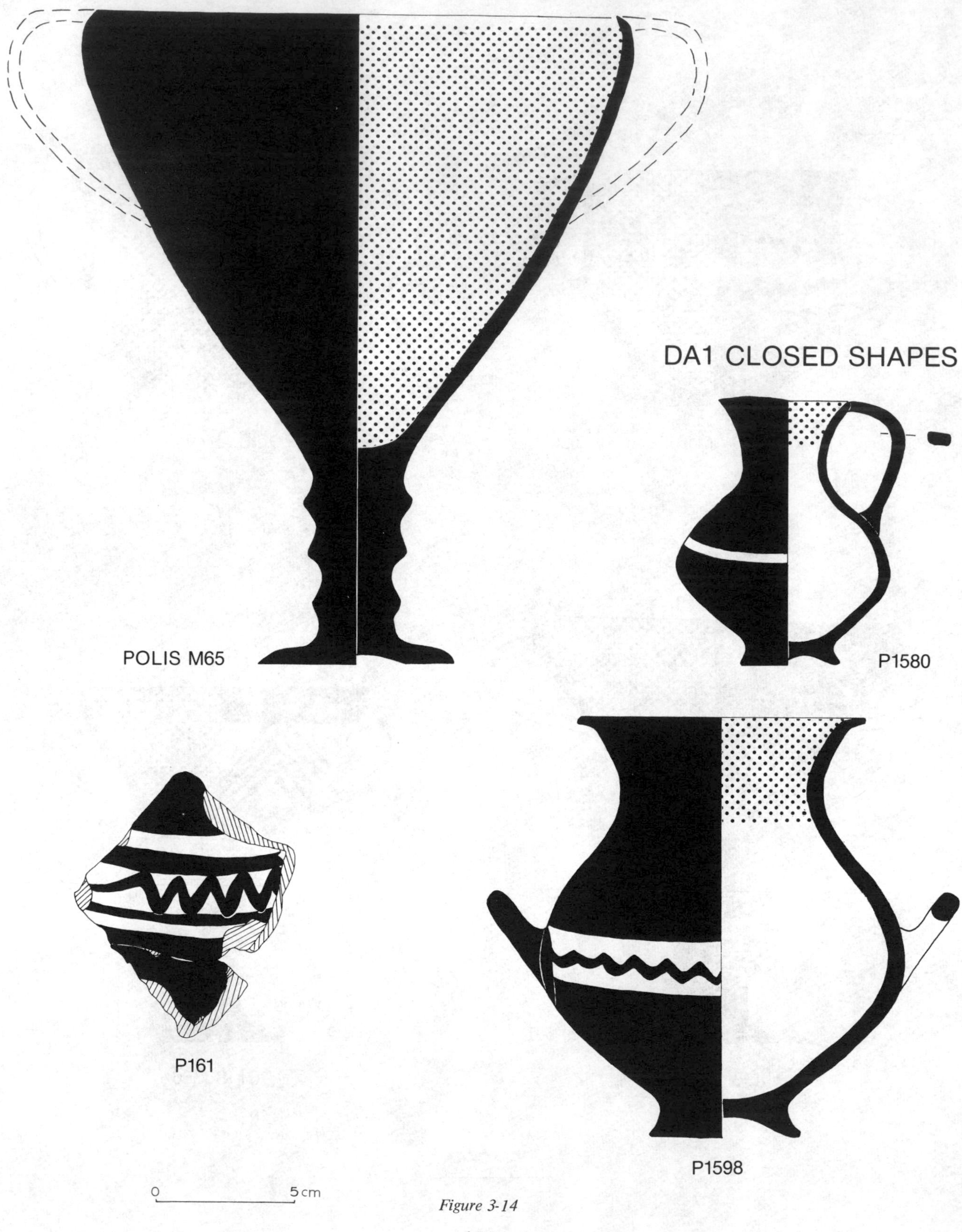
ITHACAN COMPARATIVE MATERIAL
DA1 CLOSED SHAPES
POLIS M65
P1580
P161
P1598
0
5cm

Figure 3-14

Figure 3-15

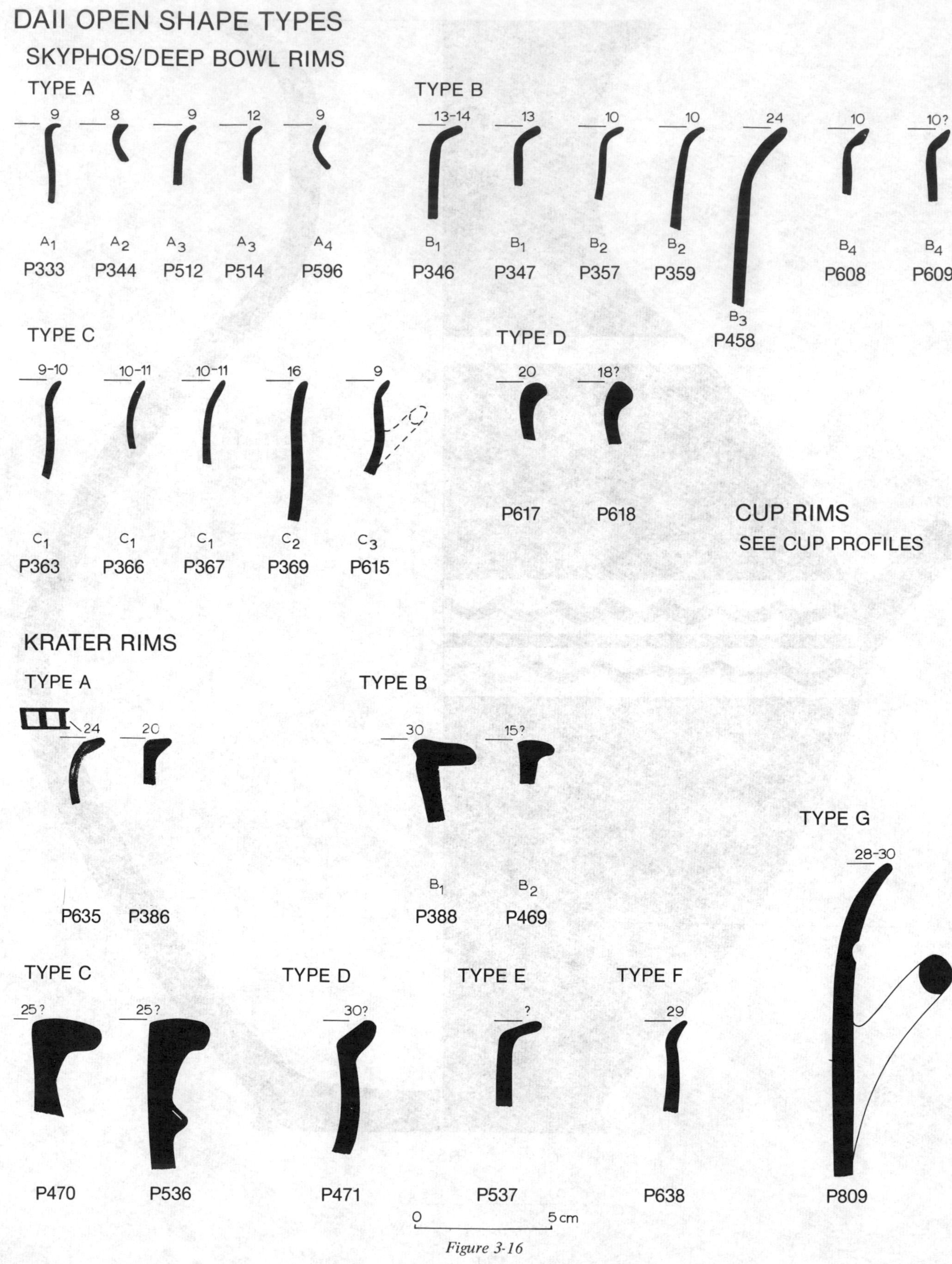
DAII OPEN SHAPE TYPES
SKYPHOS/DEEP BOWL RIMS
TYPE A
9
8
9
12
9
A1
A2
A3
A3
A4
P333
P344
P512
P514
P596
TYPE B
13-14
13
10
10
24
10
10?
B1
B1
B2
B2
B3
B4
B4
P346
P347
P357
P359
P458
P608
P609
TYPE C
9-10
10-11
10-11
16
9
C1
C1
C1
C2
C3
P363
P366
P367
P369
P615
TYPE D
20
18?
P617
P618
CUP RIMS
SEE CUP PROFILES
KRATER RIMS
TYPE A
24
20
P635
P386
TYPE B
30
15?
B1
B2
P388
P469
TYPE G
28-30
P809
TYPE C
25?
25?
P470
P536
TYPE D
30?
P471
TYPE E
?
P537
TYPE F
29
P638
0
5cm

Figure 3-16

CUP HANDLES

TYPE A
SEE P532

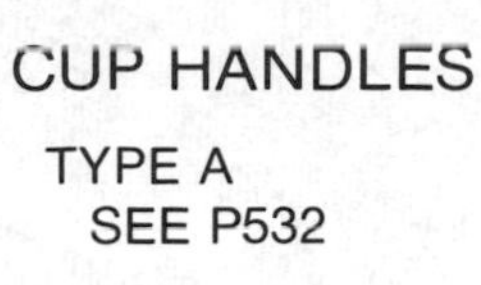

TYPE B
SEE P478

TYPE C
SEE P548

SHALLOW BOWL HANDLES

TYPE A

TYPE B

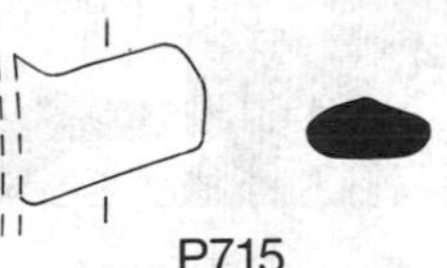

SKYPHOS/DEEP BOWL BASES

TYPE A

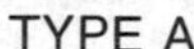

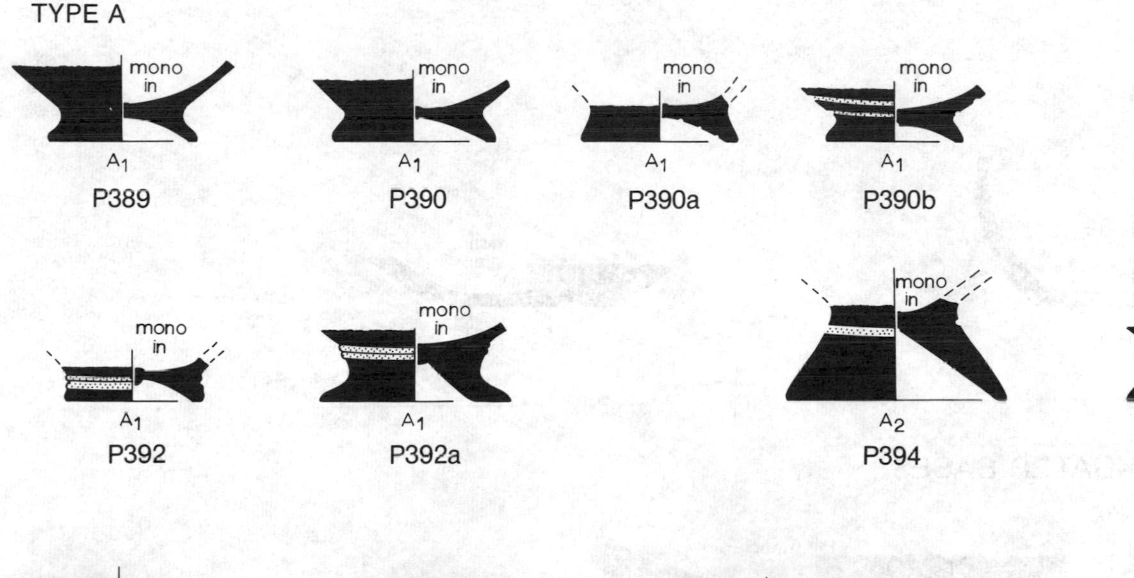

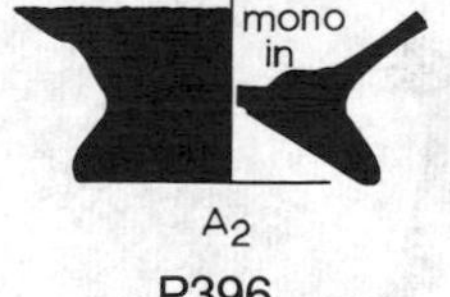

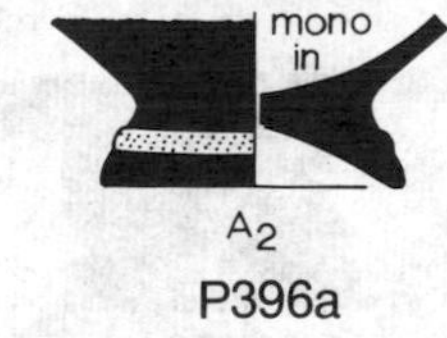

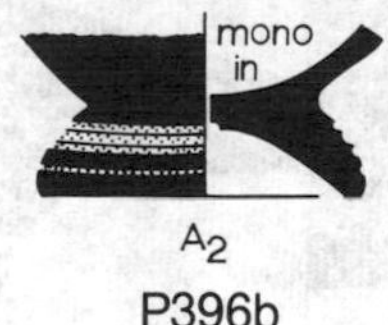

TYPE B

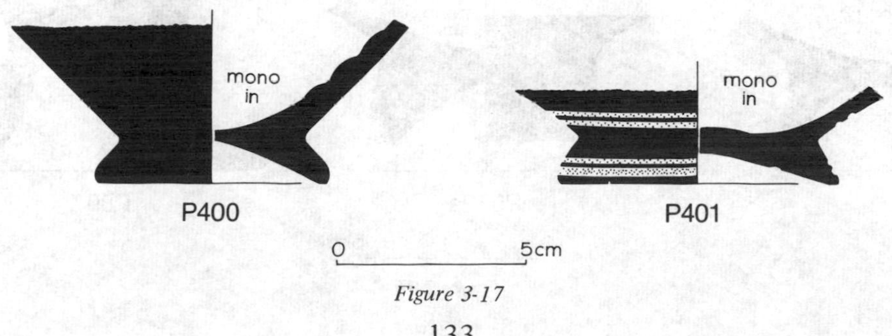

Figure 3-17

SKYPHOS/DEEP BOWL BASES

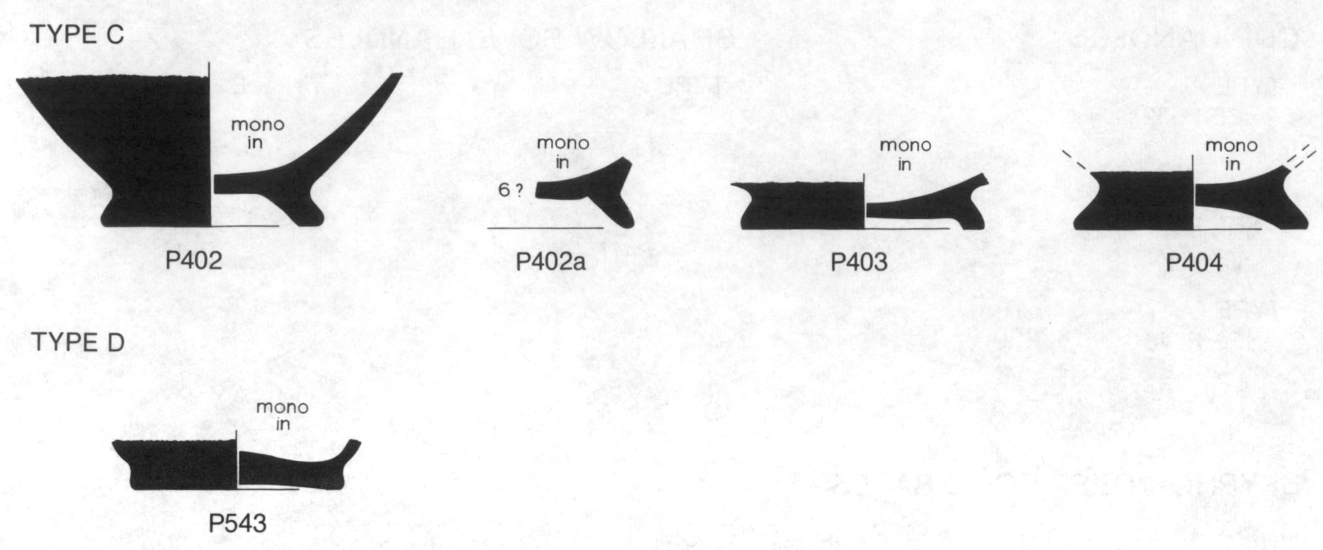

CUP BASES

PEDESTAL KRATER BASES

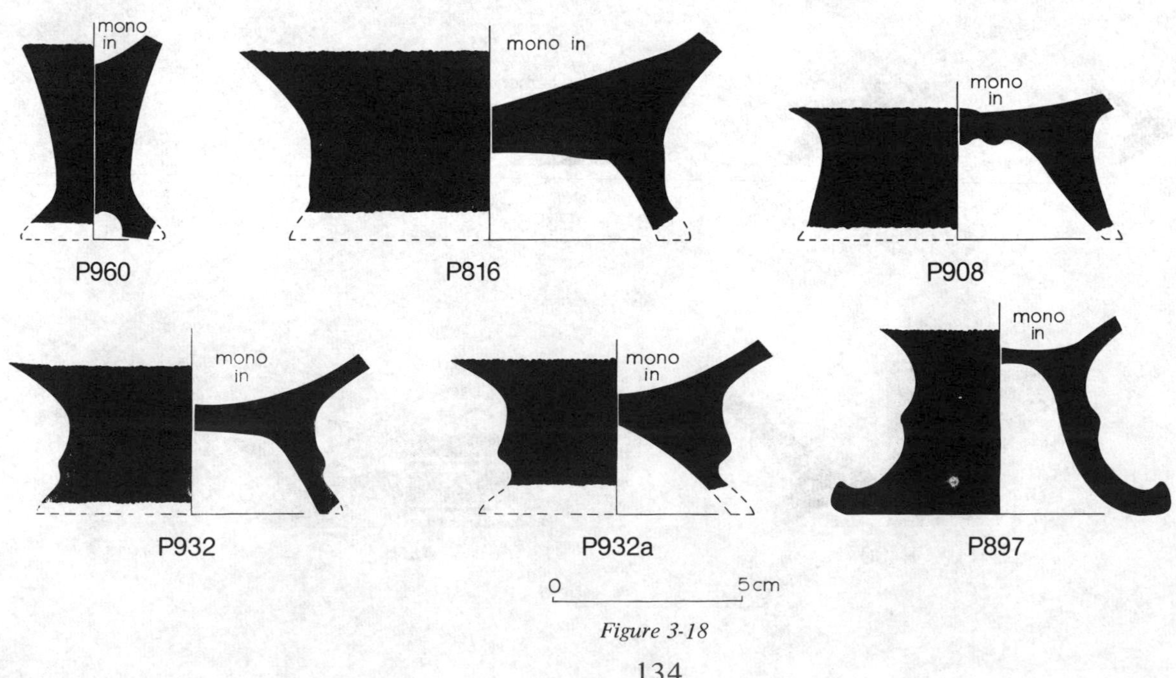

0 5cm

Figure 3-18

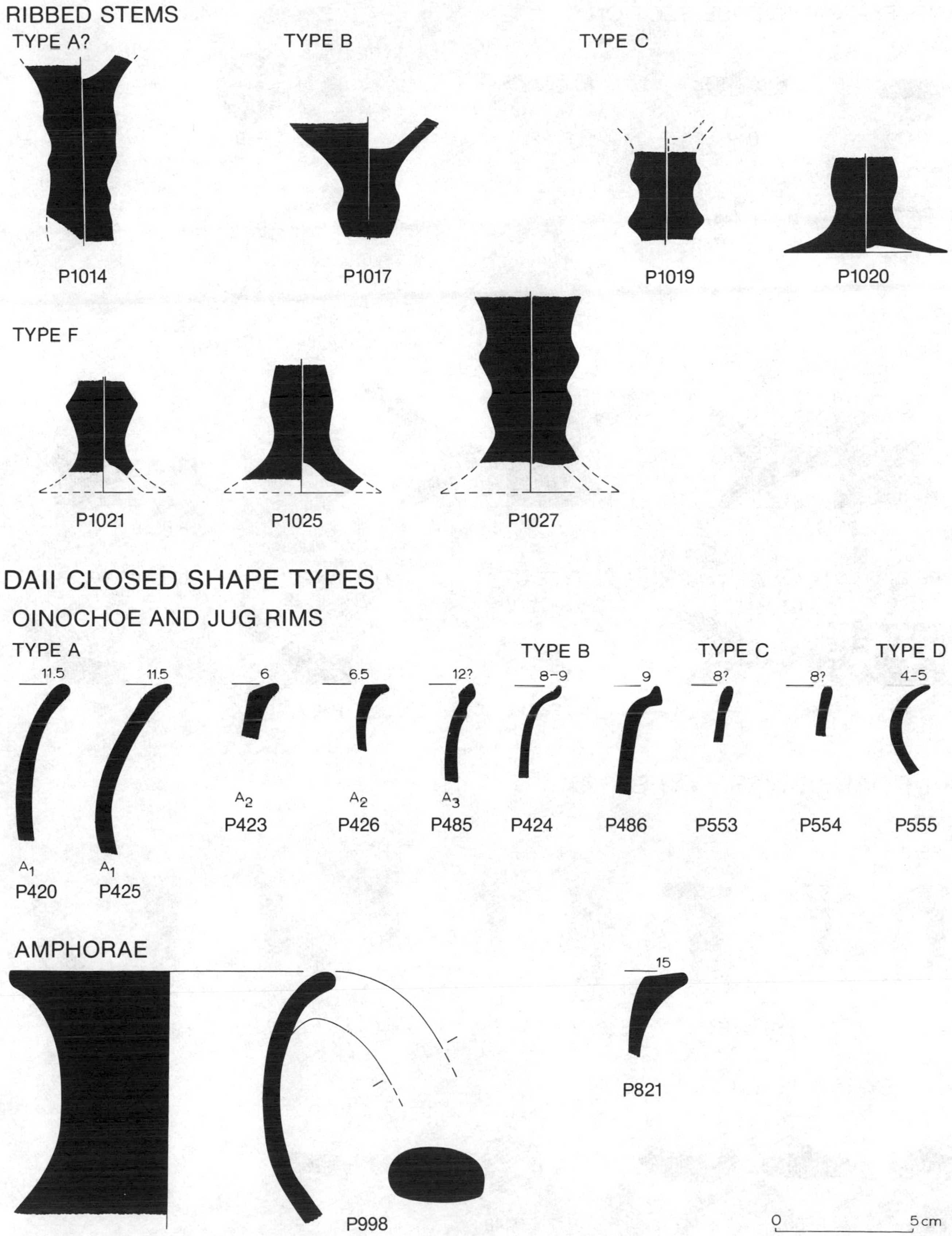

RIBBED STEMS
TYPE A?
TYPE B
TYPE C
P1014
P1017
P1019
P1020
TYPE F
P1021
P1025
P1027
DAII CLOSED SHAPE TYPES
OINOCHOE AND JUG RIMS
TYPE A
TYPE B
TYPE C
TYPE D
11.5
11.5
6
6.5
12?
8–9
9
8?
8?
4–5
A1
P420
A1
P425
A2
P423
A2
P426
A3
P485
P424
P486
P553
P554
P555
AMPHORAE
15
P998
P821
0
5 cm

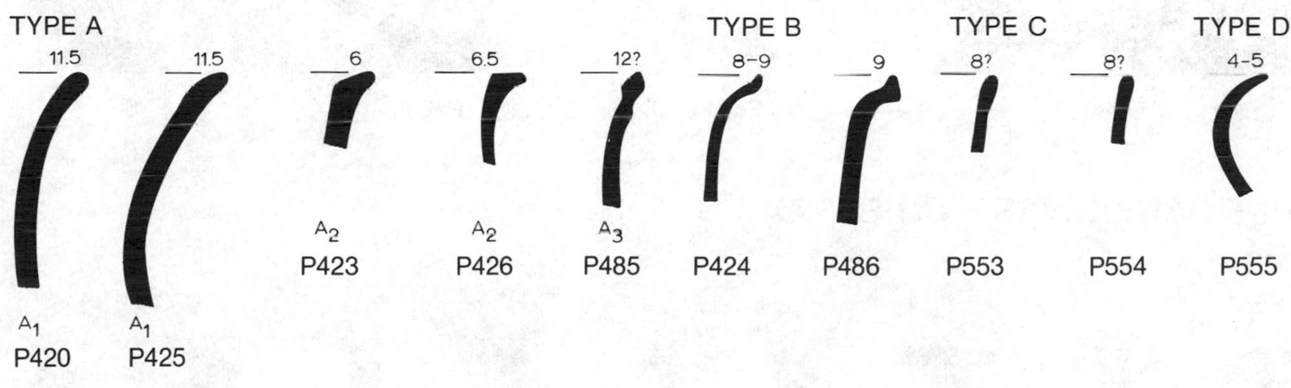

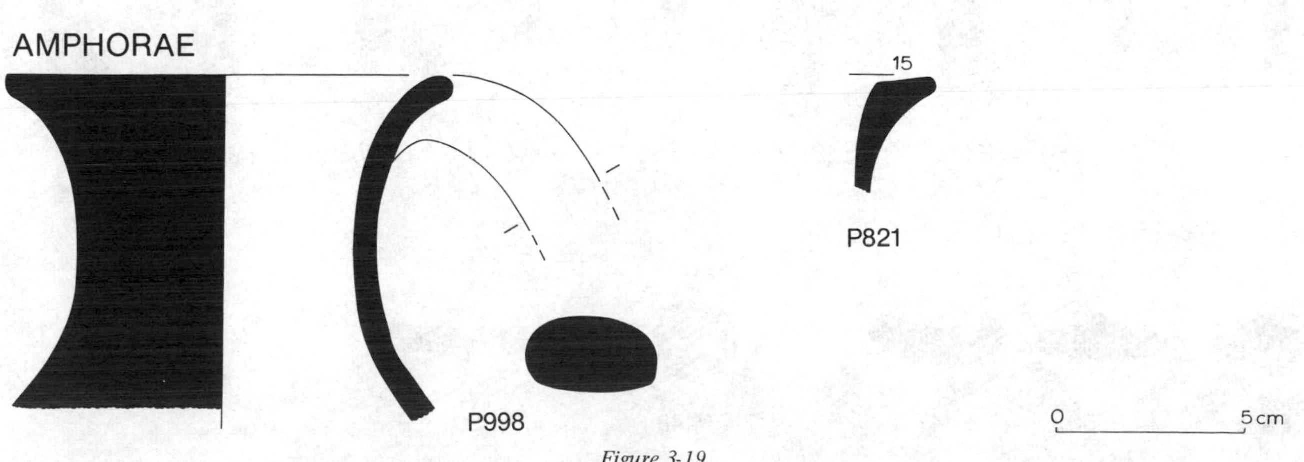

Figure 3-19

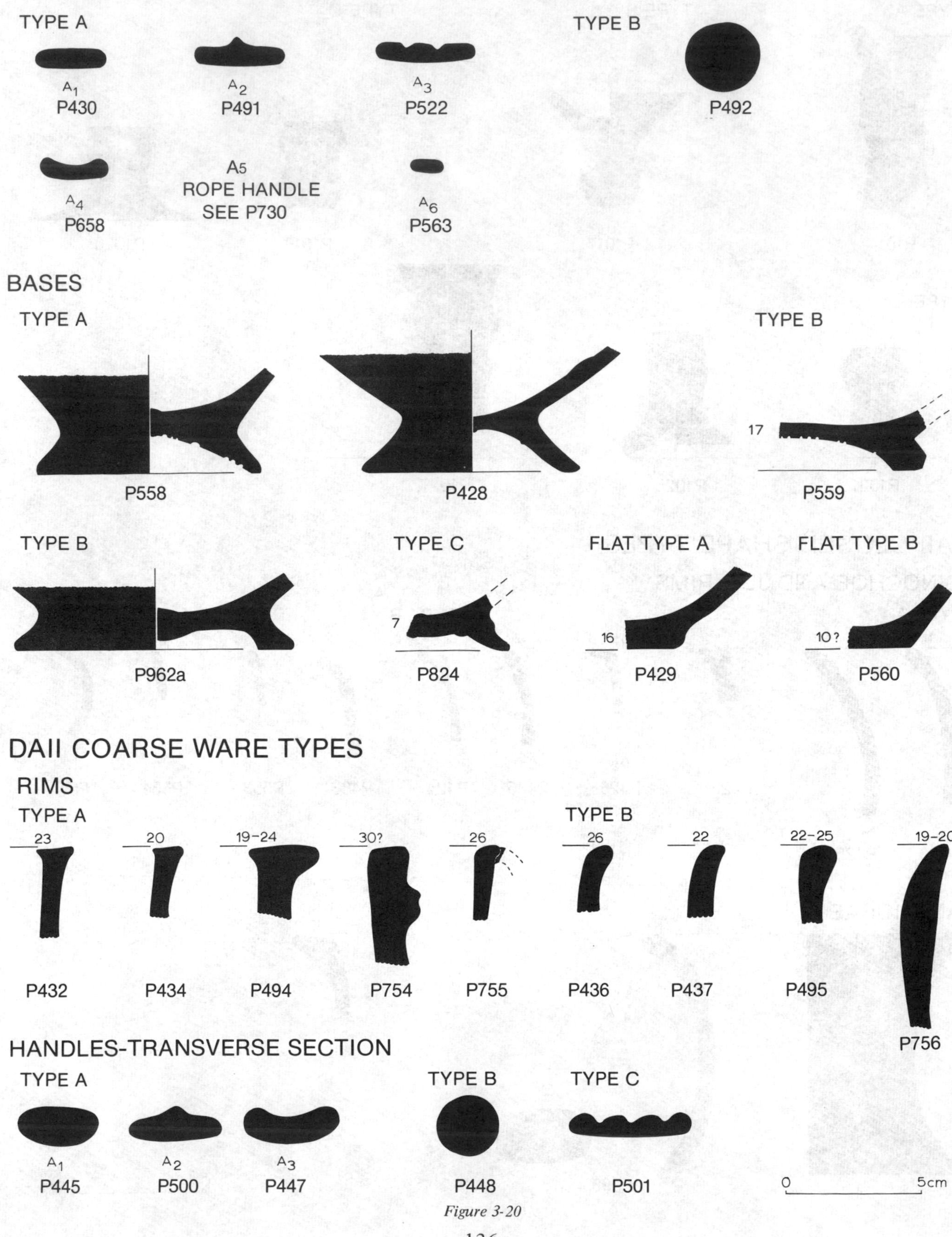
HANDLES-TRANSVERSE SECTION
TYPE A
A1
P430
A2
P491
A3
P522
TYPE B
P492
A4
P658
A5
ROPE HANDLE
SEE P730
A6
P563
BASES
TYPE A
P558
P428
TYPE B
17
P559
TYPE B
P962a
TYPE C
7
P824
FLAT TYPE A
16
P429
FLAT TYPE B
10?
P560
DAII COARSE WARE TYPES
RIMS
TYPE A
23
P432
20
P434
19-24
P494
30?
P754
26
P755
TYPE B
26
P436
22
P437
22-25
P495
19-20
P756
HANDLES-TRANSVERSE SECTION
TYPE A
A1
P445
A2
P500
A3
P447
TYPE B
P448
TYPE C
P501
0
5cm

Figure 3-20

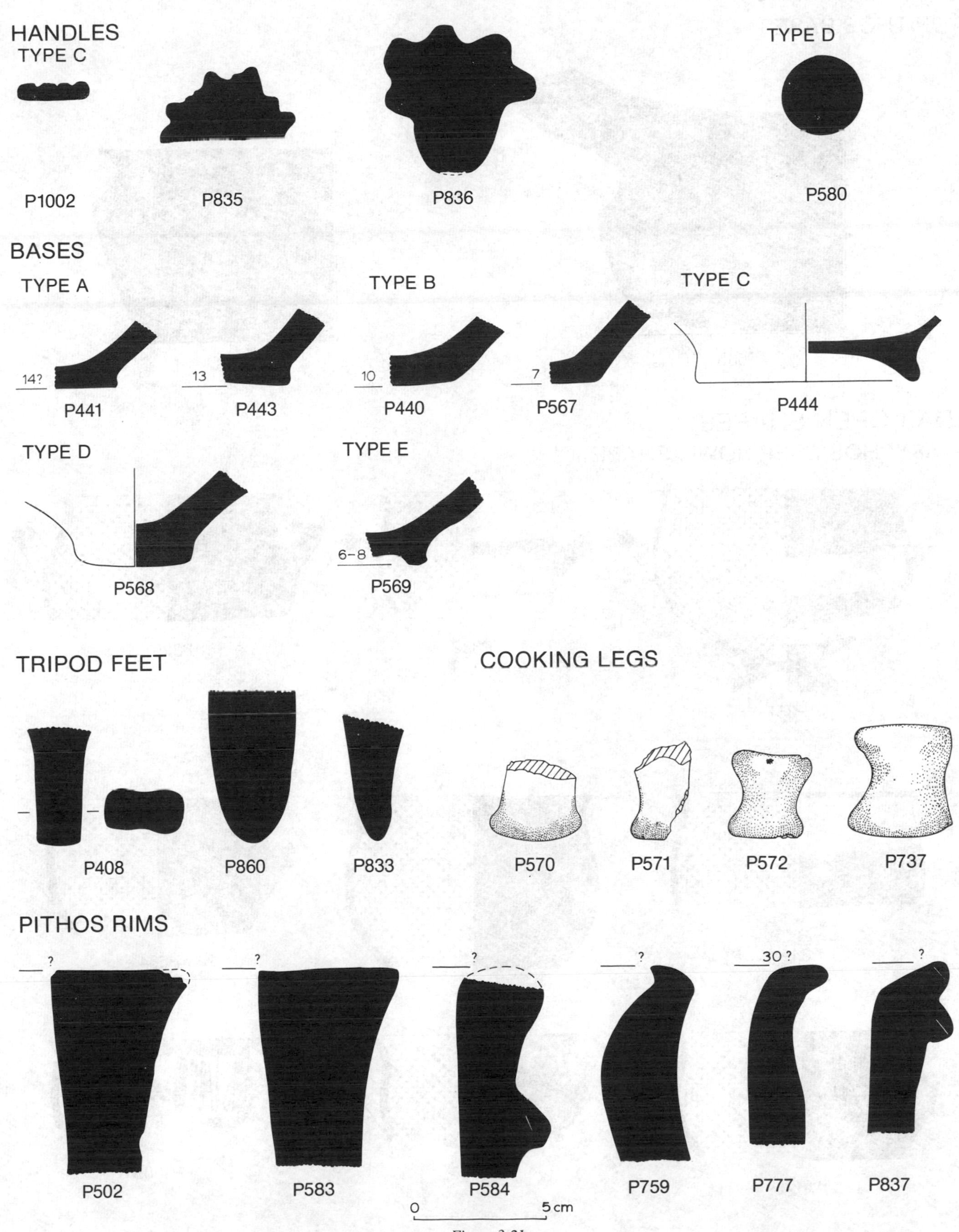
HANDLES
TYPE C
P1002
P835
P836
TYPE D
P580
BASES
TYPE A
14?
P441
13
P443
TYPE B
10
P440
7
P567
TYPE C
P444
TYPE D
P568
TYPE E
6-8
P569
TRIPOD FEET
P408
P860
P833
COOKING LEGS
P570
P571
P572
P737
PITHOS RIMS
?
P502
?
P583
?
P584
?
P759
30 ?
P777
?
P837
0
5 cm

Figure 3-21

PITHOS BASES

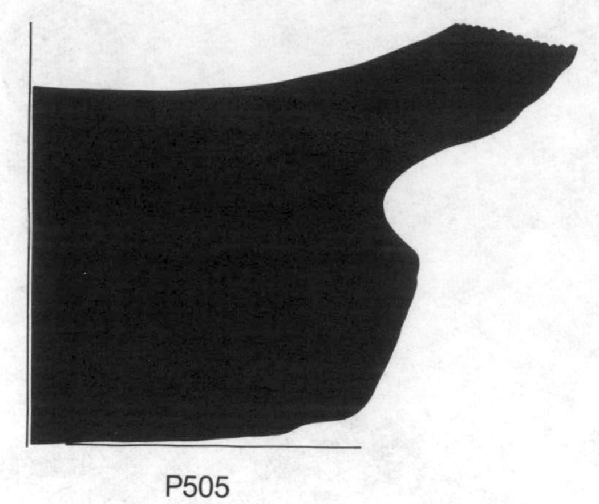

P505

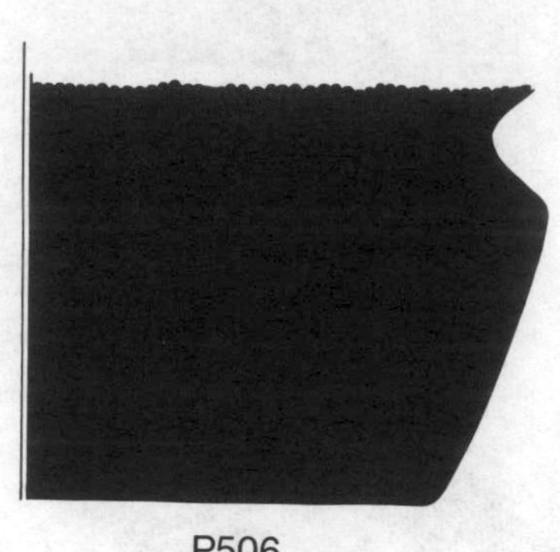

P506

DAII OPEN SHAPES

SKYPHOS/DEEP BOWL: SHAPE 1

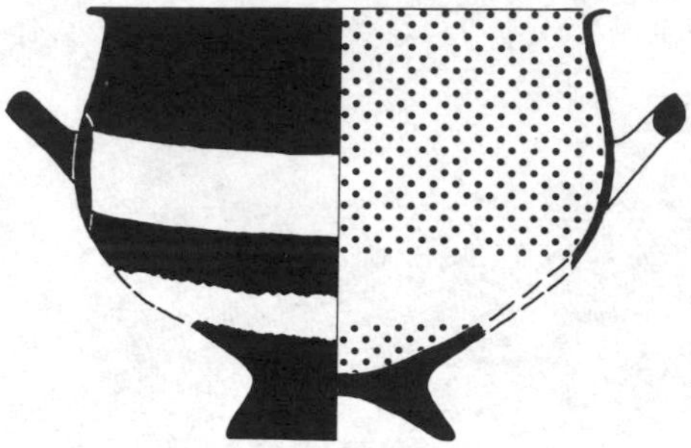

P331

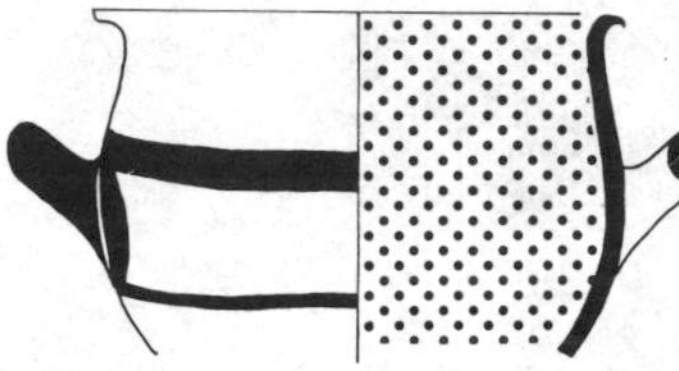

P332

P339

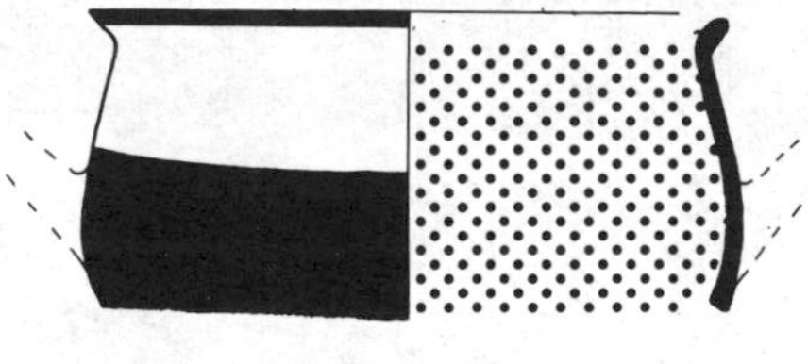

P341

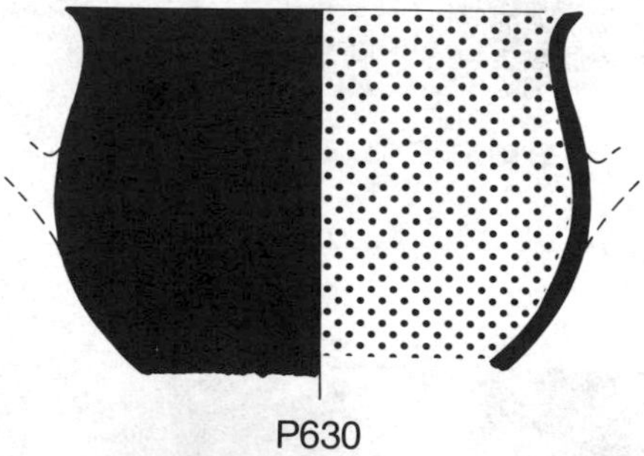

P630

P664

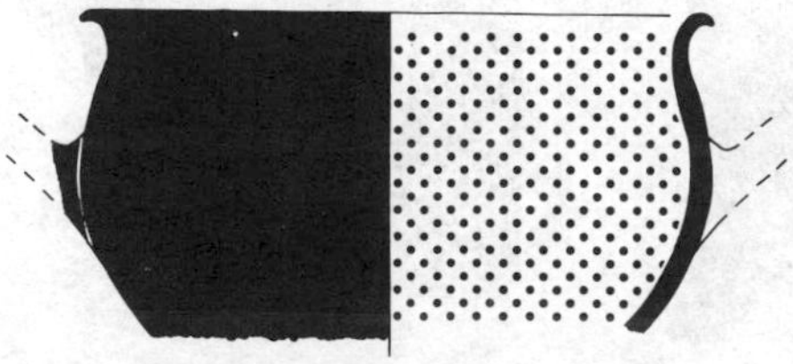

P792

P916a

P1005

0 5 cm

Figure 3-22

SHAPE 1

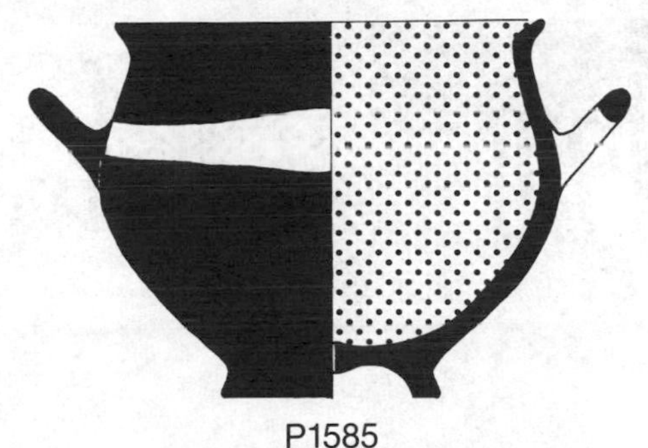

P1585

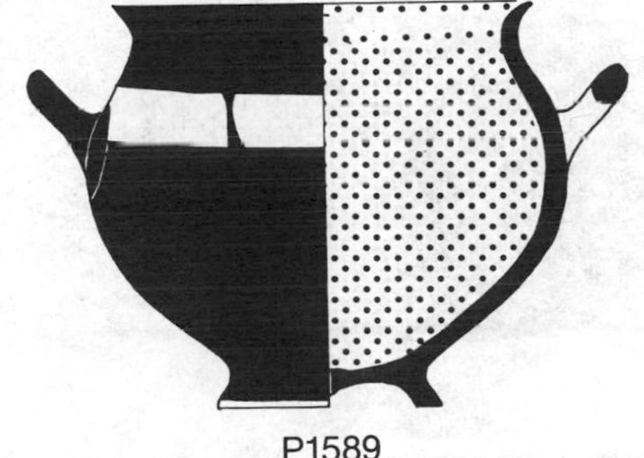

P1589

SHAPE 2

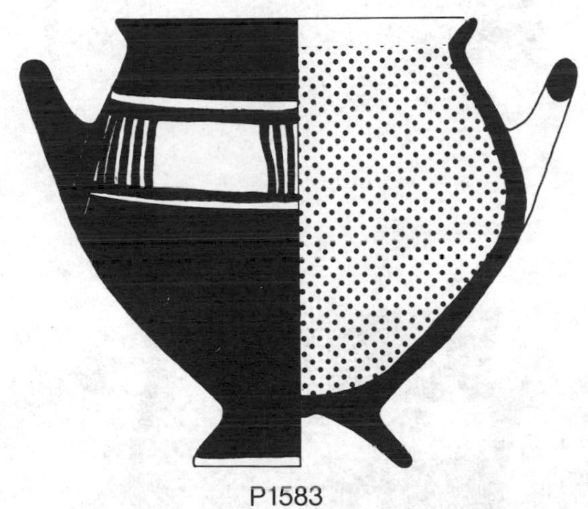

P1583

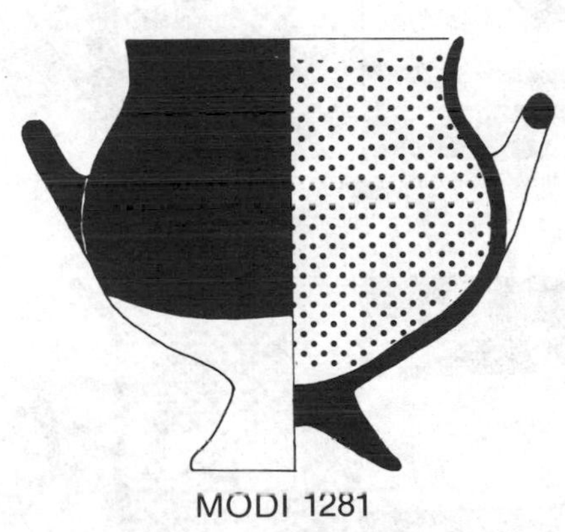

MODI 1281

SHAPE 3

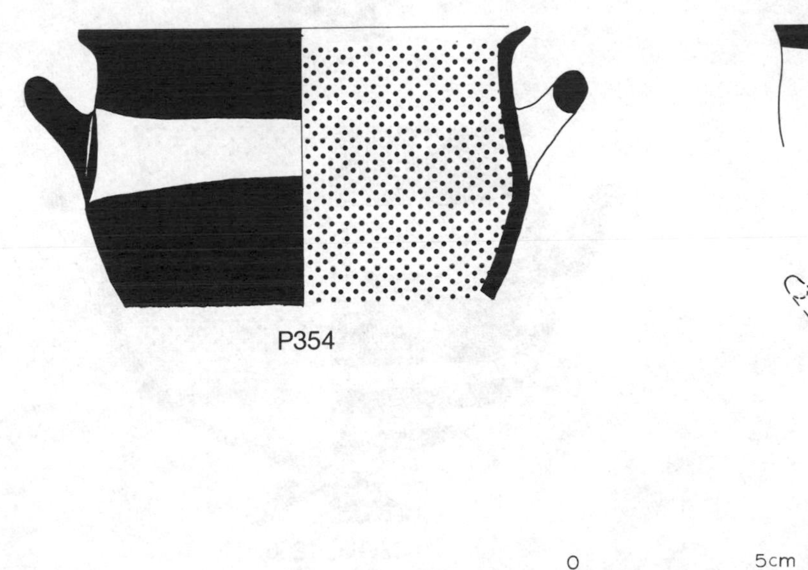

P354

P613

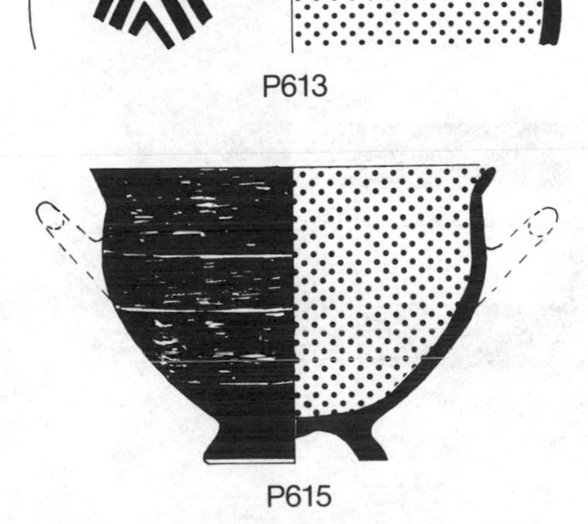

P615

Figure 3-23

SHAPE 3

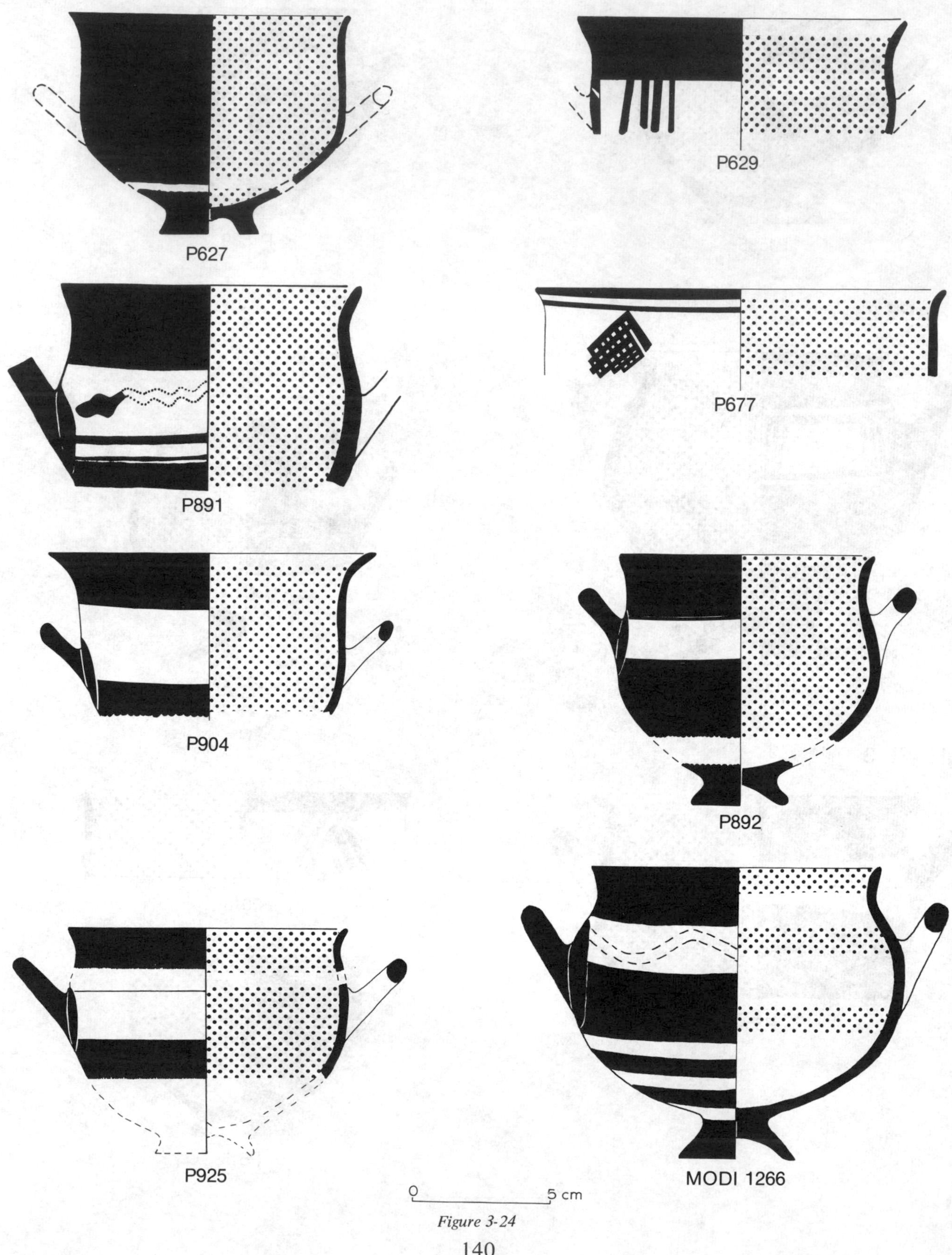

Figure 3-24

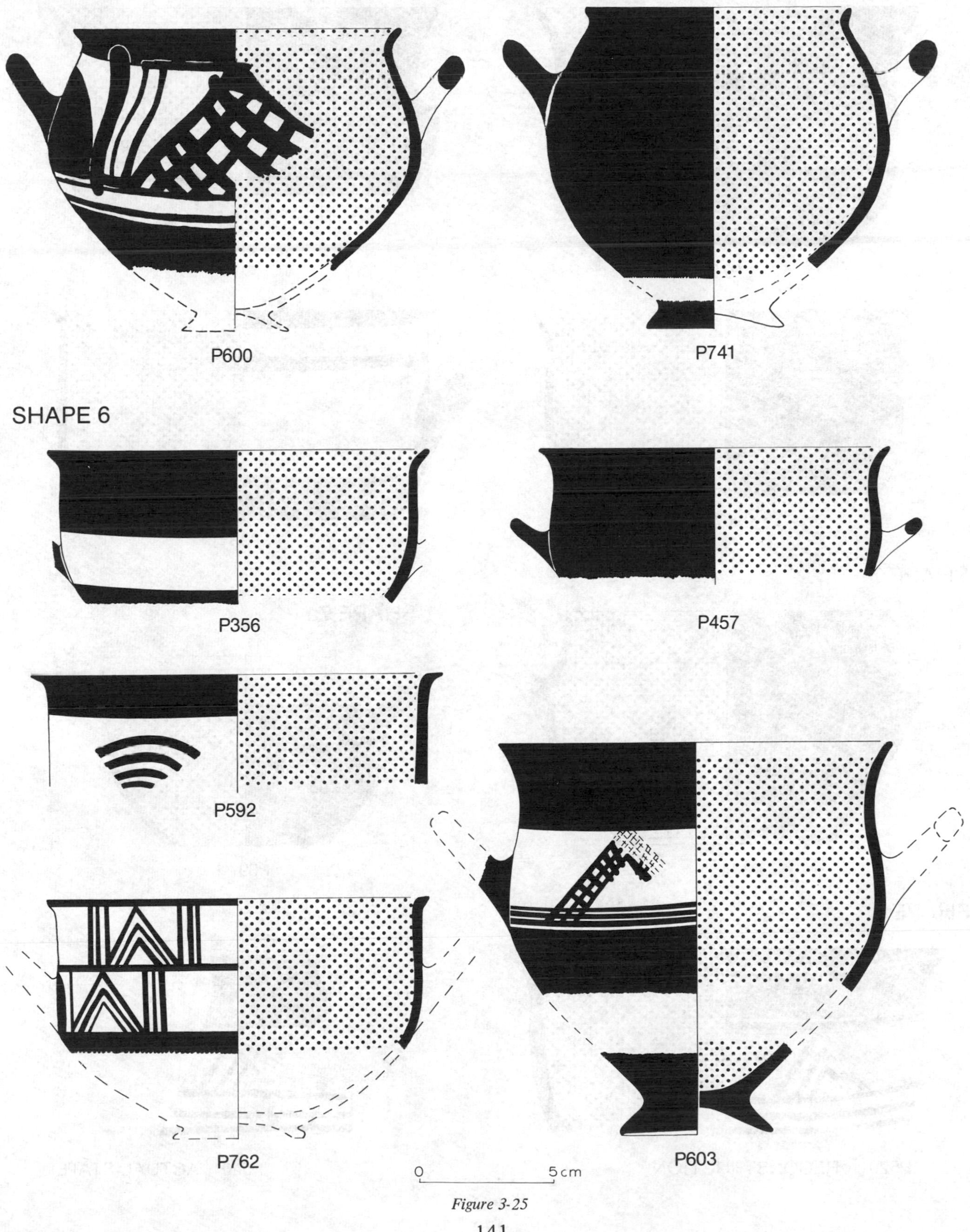

Figure 3-25

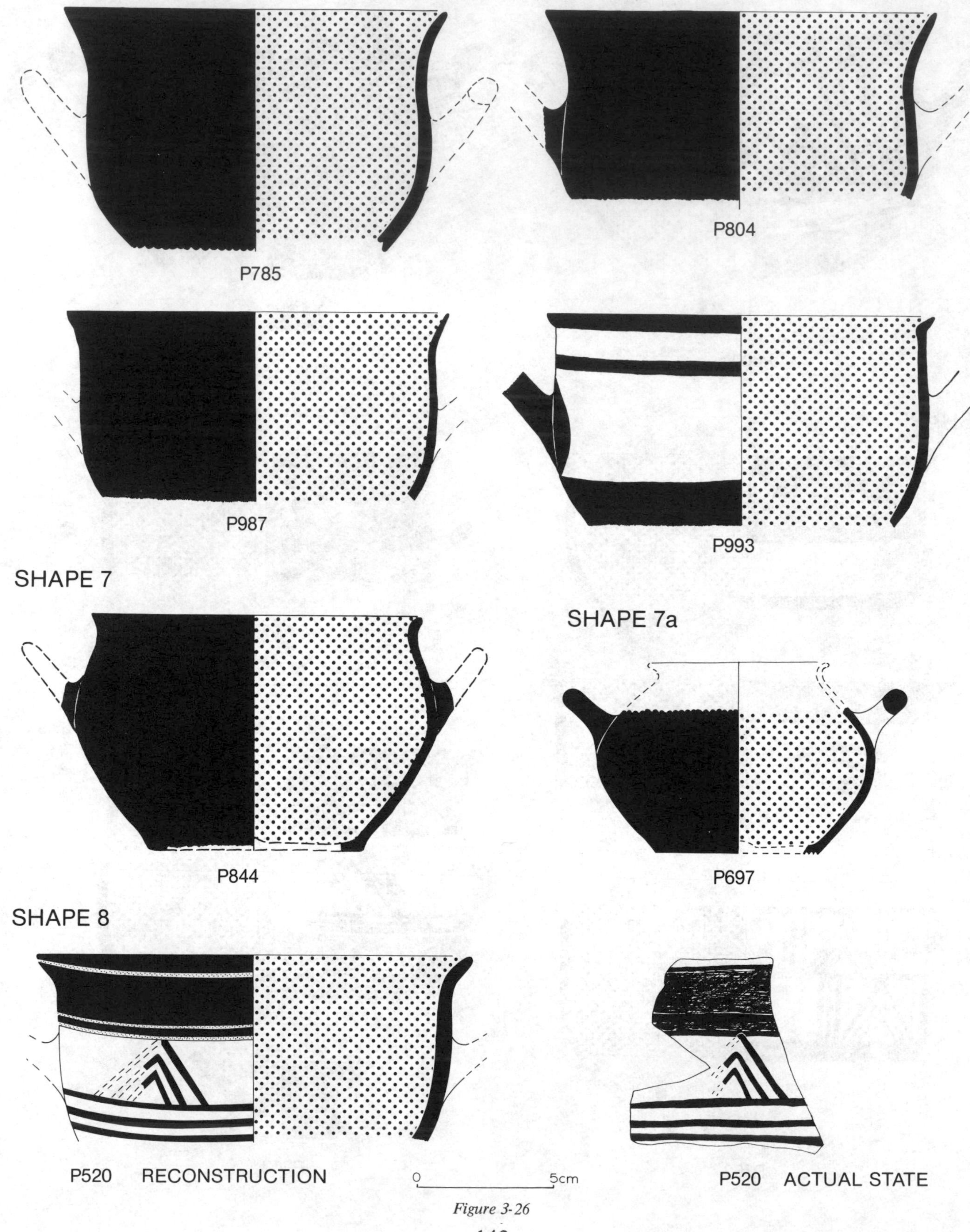
SHAPE 6
P785
P804
P987
P993
SHAPE 7
SHAPE 7a
P844
P697
SHAPE 8
P520 RECONSTRUCTION
0
5cm
P520 ACTUAL STATE

Figure 3-26

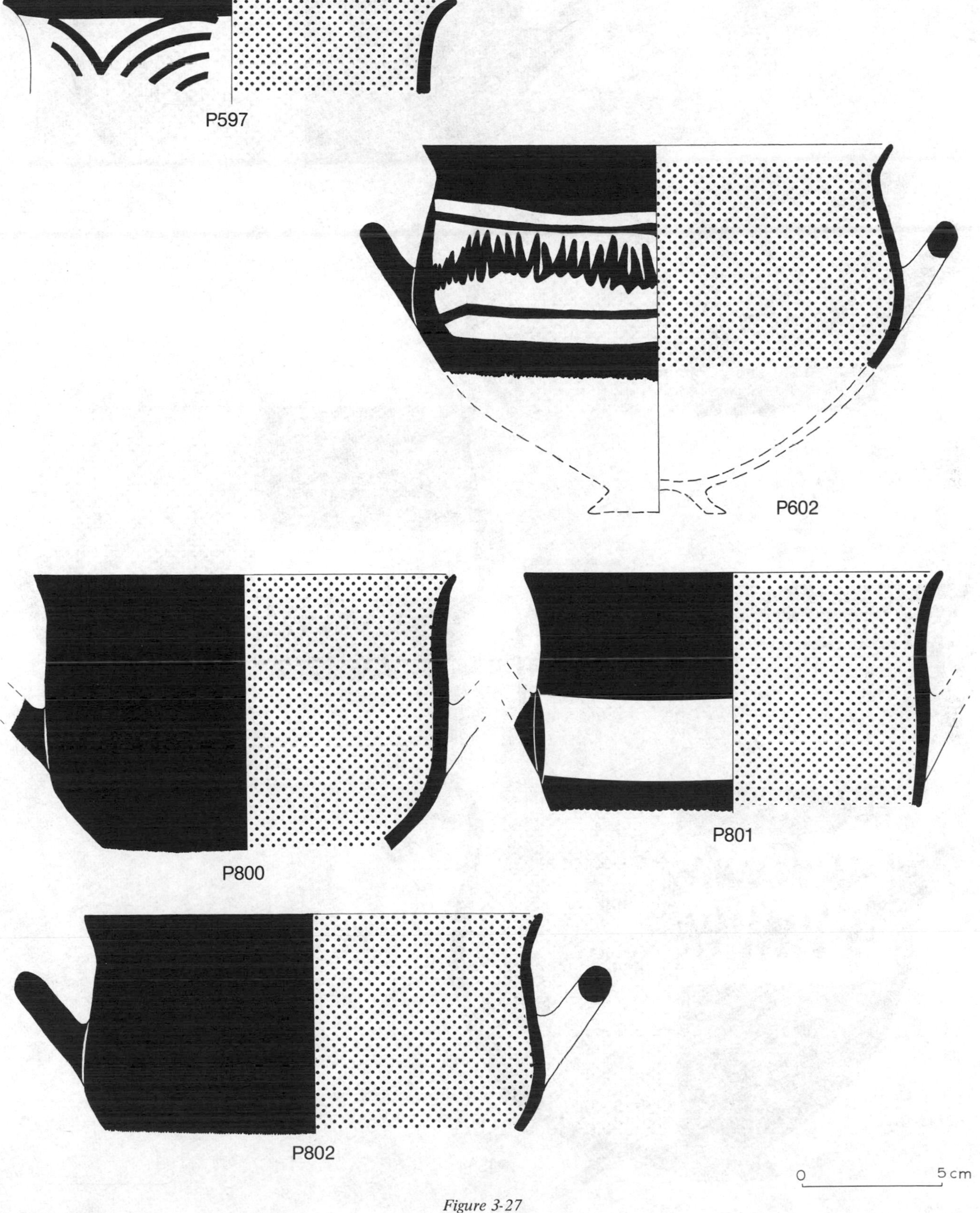

Figure 3-27

SHAPE 8

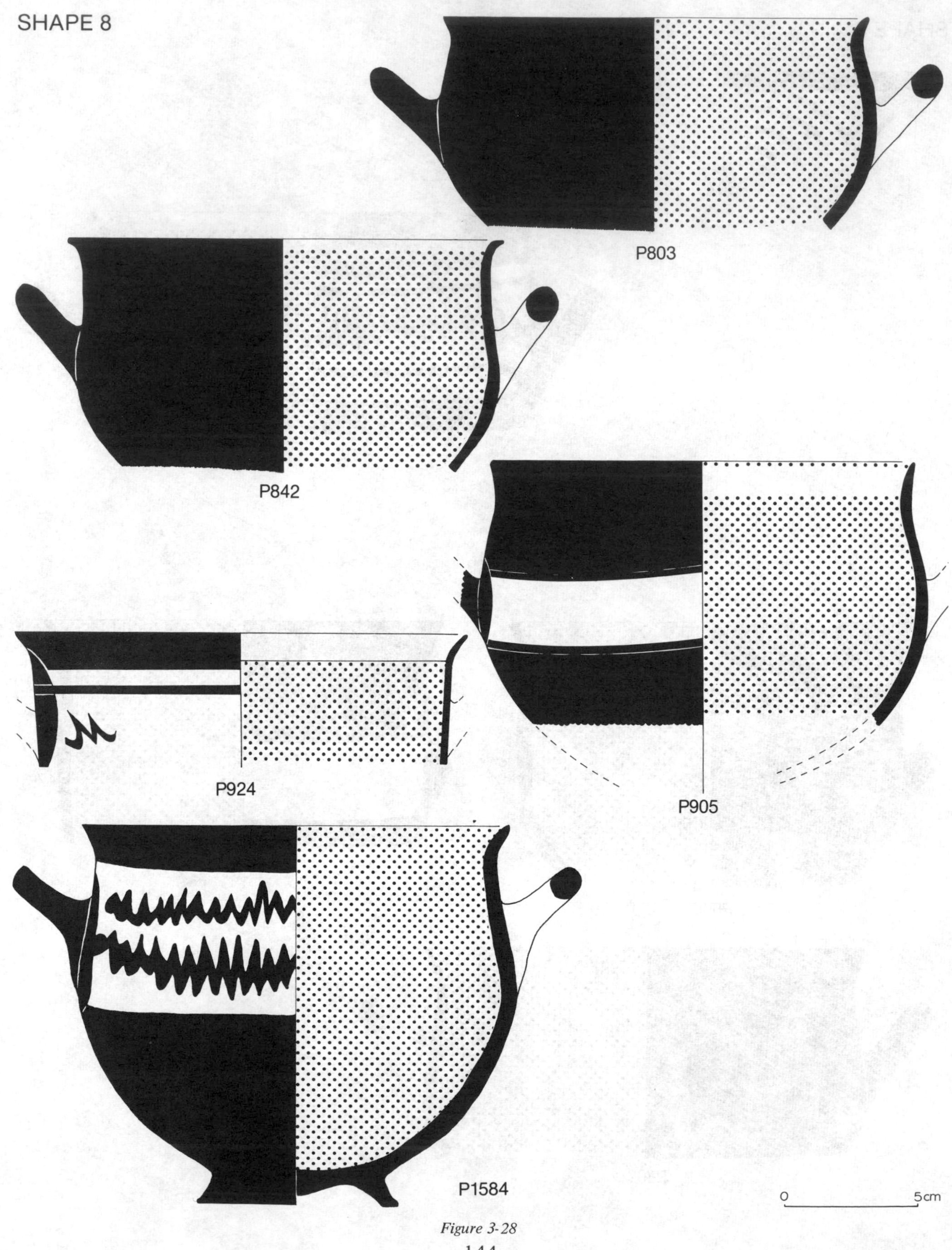

Figure 3-28

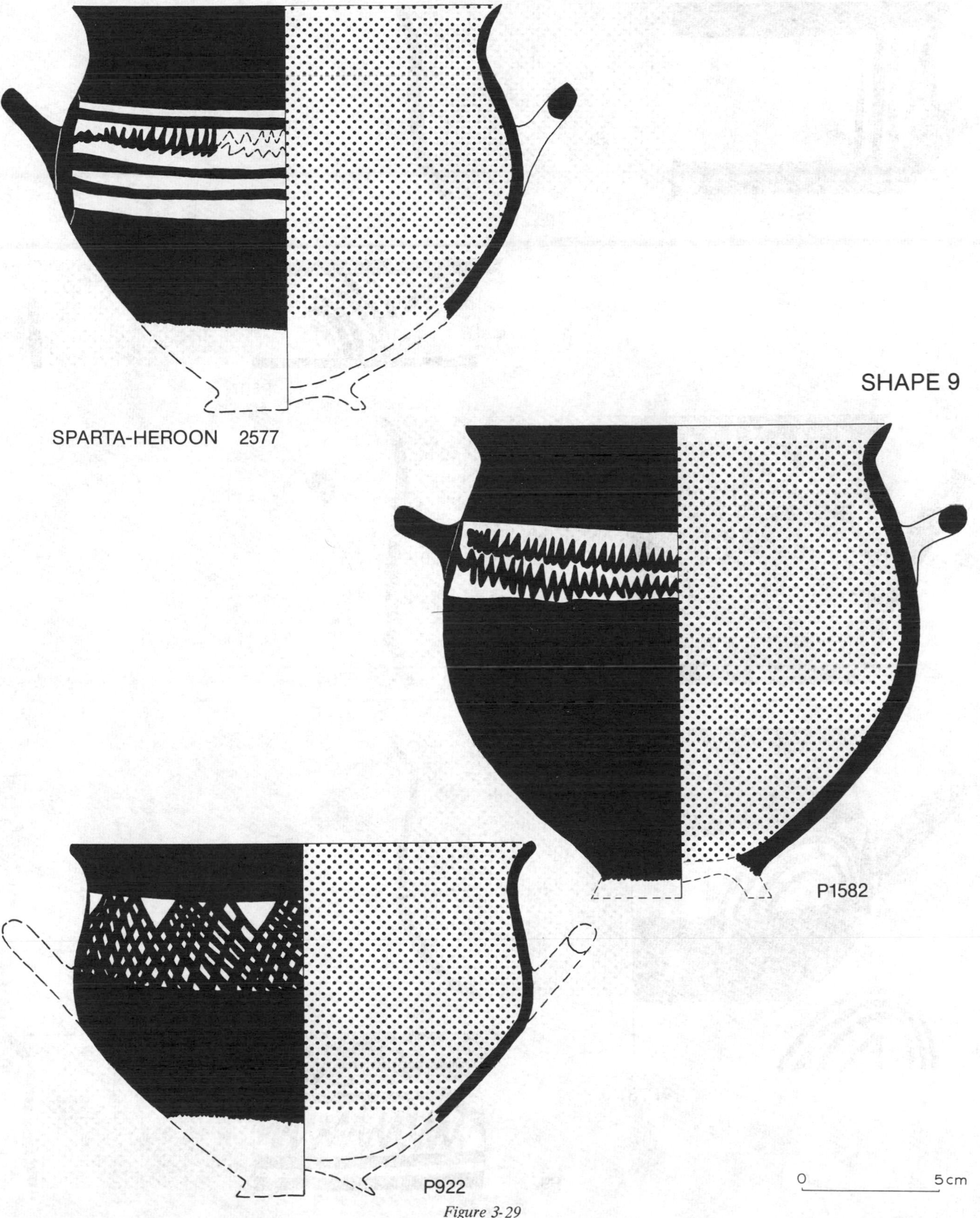

Figure 3-29

SHAPE 10

Figure 3-30

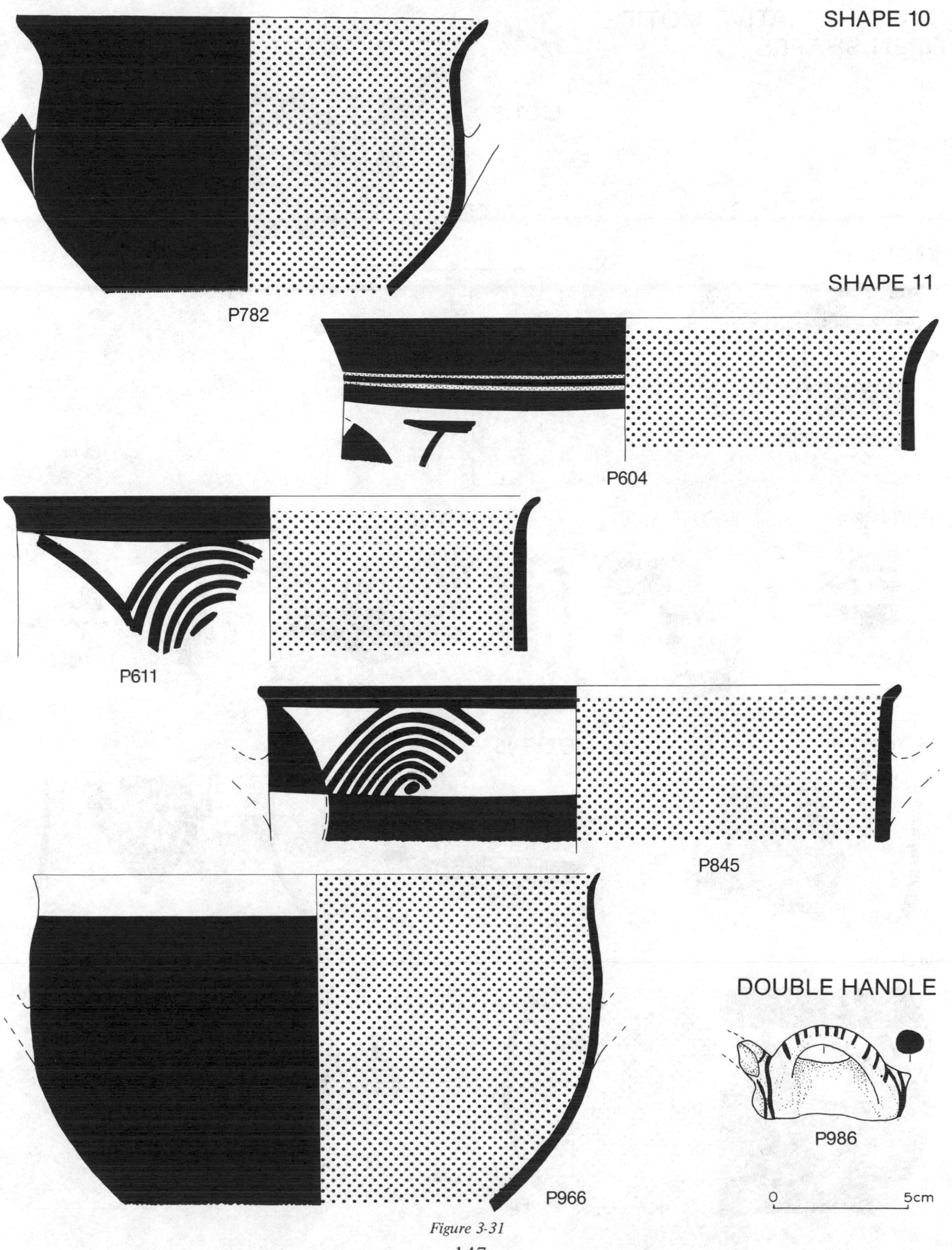
SHAPE 10
P782
SHAPE 11
P604
P611
P845
P966
DOUBLE HANDLE
P986
0
5cm

Figure 3-31

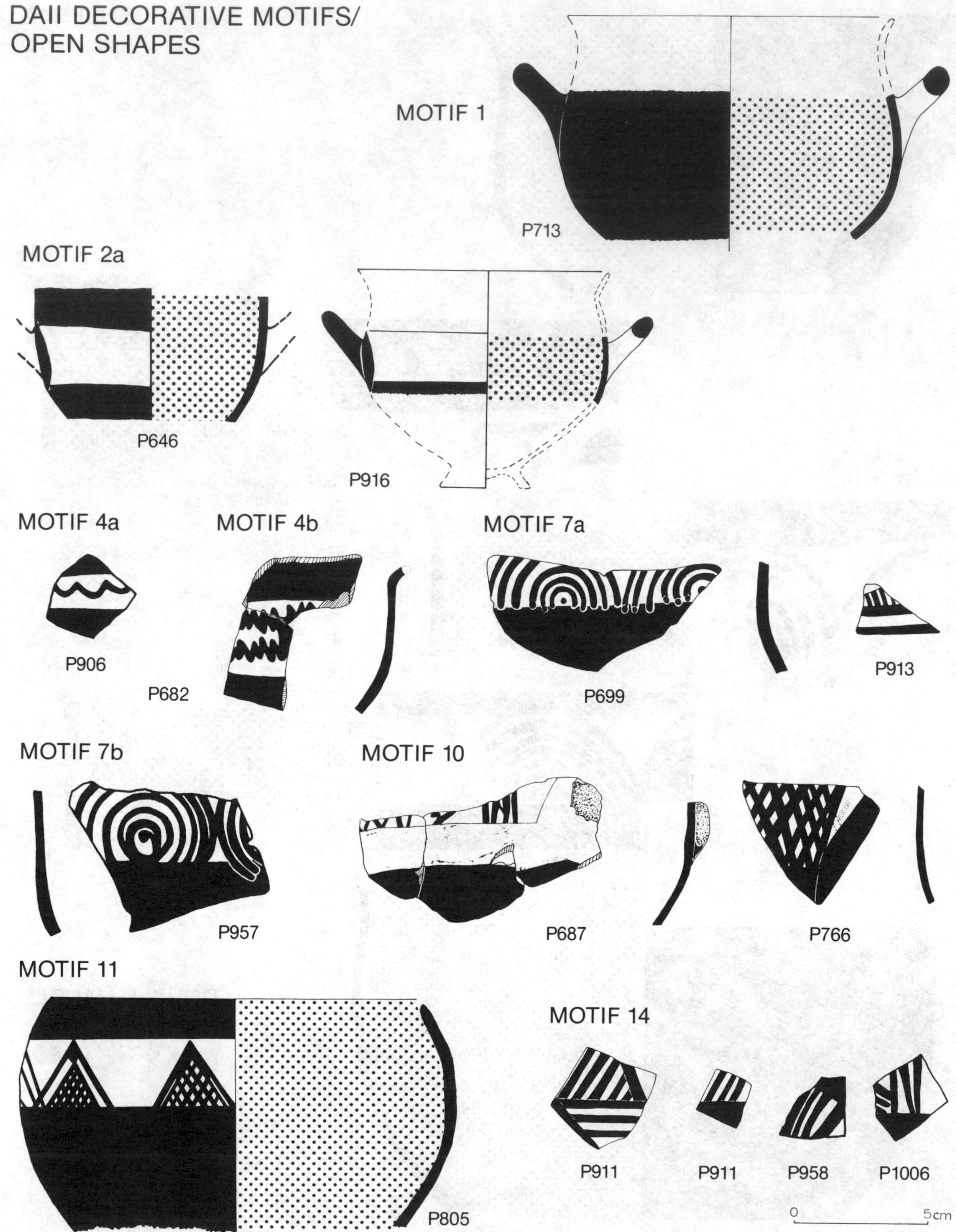
DAII DECORATIVE MOTIFS/
OPEN SHAPES
MOTIF 1
P713
MOTIF 2a
P646
P916
MOTIF 4a
P906
MOTIF 4b
P682
MOTIF 7a
P699
P913
MOTIF 7b
P957
MOTIF 10
P687
P766
MOTIF 11
P805
MOTIF 14
P911
P911
P958
P1006
0
5cm

Figure 3-32

DECORATED SHERDS
OINOCHOE
P622
P626
P790
P789
P818
P623
P791
P791
P950
P949
P624
P625
P947
P948
24
P990
28
P634
P707
P975
?
P856a
?
P931
P955
0
5cm

Figure 3-33

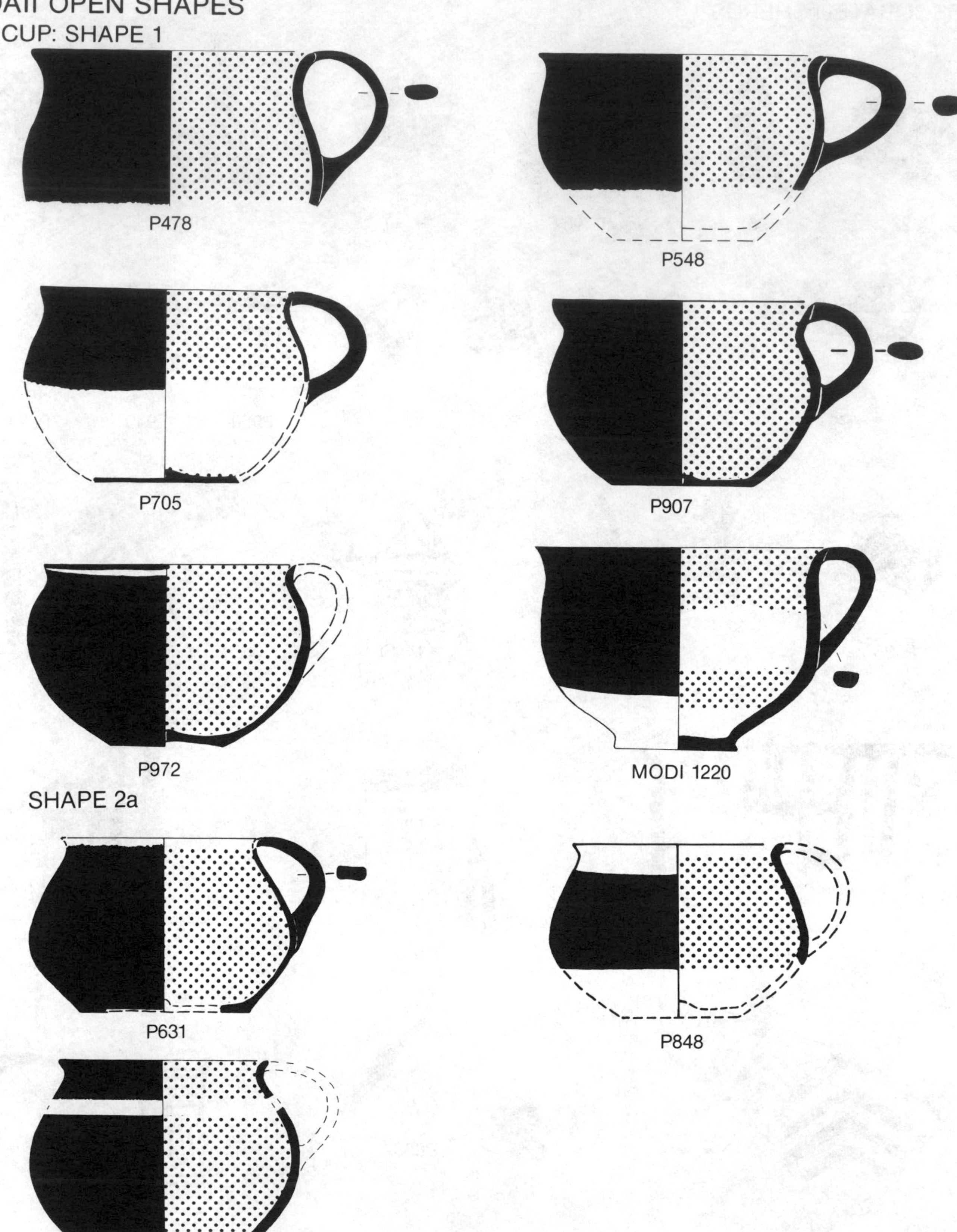
DAII OPEN SHAPES
CUP: SHAPE 1
P478
P548
P705
P907
P972
MODI 1220
SHAPE 2a
P631
P848
P929
0
5cm

Figure 3-34

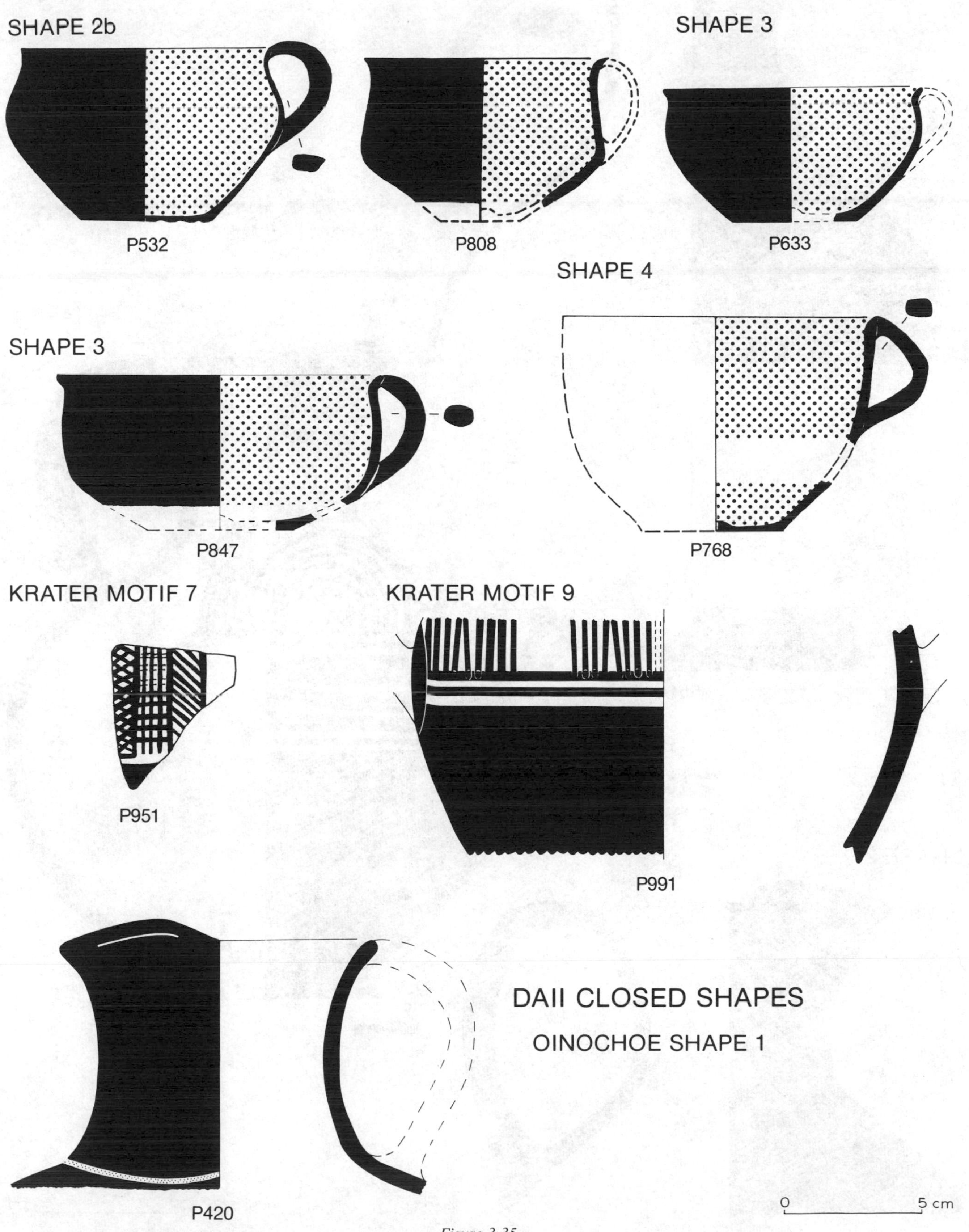
SHAPE 2b
SHAPE 3
P532
P808
P633
SHAPE 4
SHAPE 3
P847
P768
KRATER MOTIF 7
KRATER MOTIF 9
P951
P991
P420
DAII CLOSED SHAPES
OINOCHOE SHAPE 1
0
5 cm

Figure 3-35

Figure 3-36

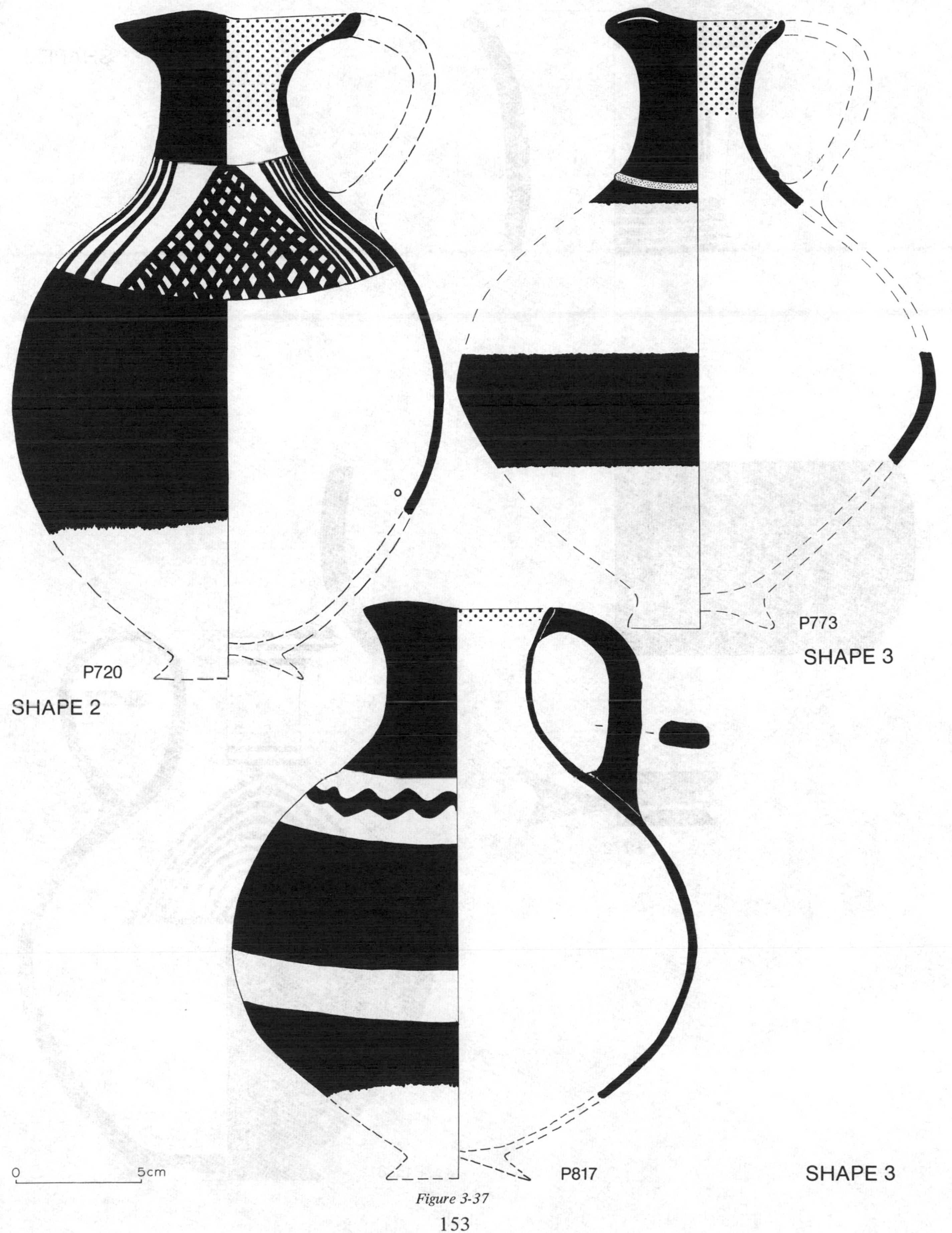

Figure 3-37

Figure 3-38

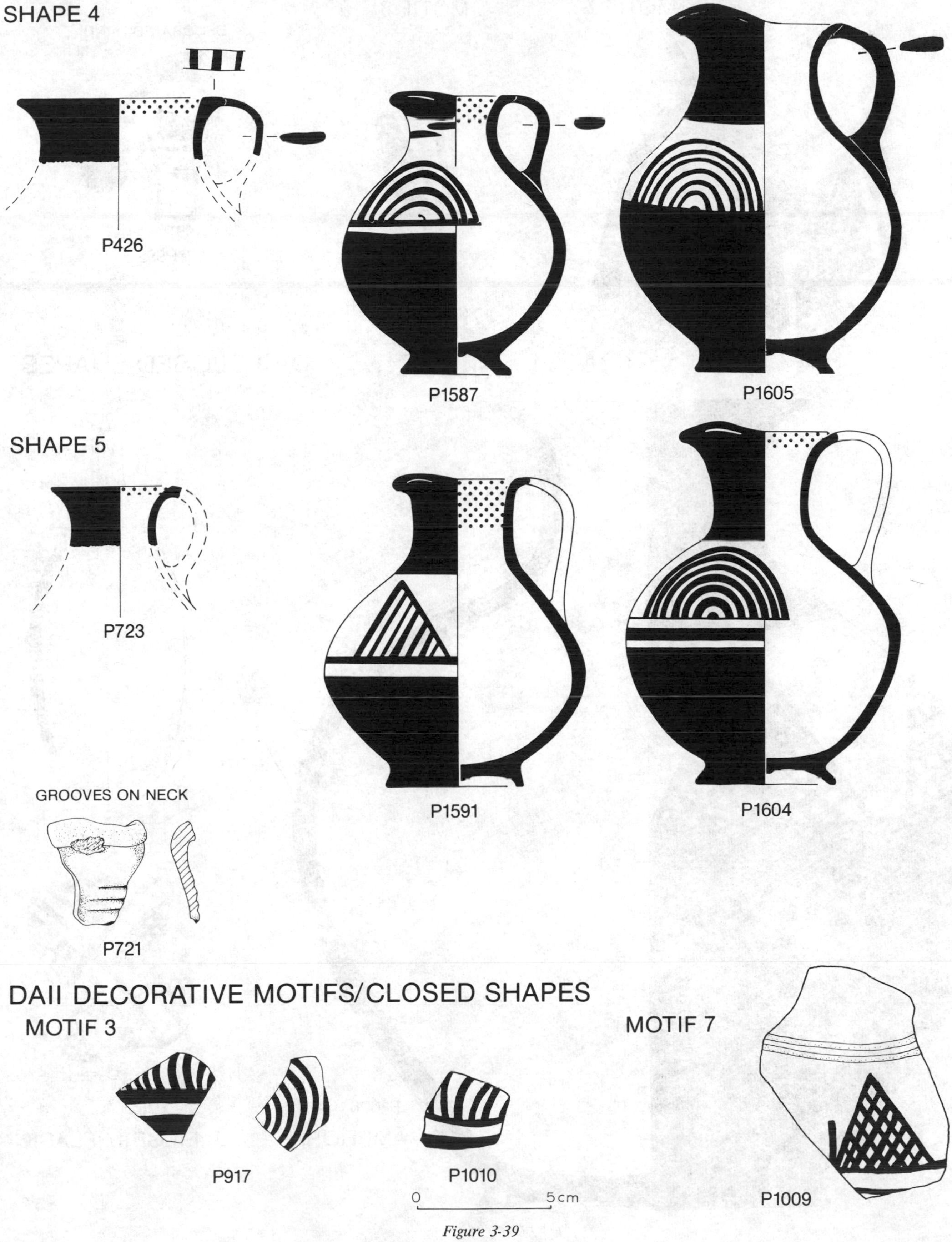

SHAPE 4

P426

P1587

P1605

SHAPE 5

P723

P1591

P1604

GROOVES ON NECK

P721

DAII DECORATIVE MOTIFS/CLOSED SHAPES

MOTIF 3

P917

P1010

0 5cm

MOTIF 7

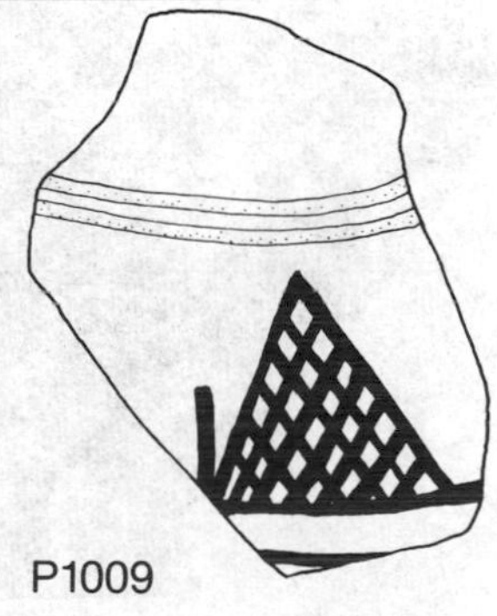

P1009

Figure 3-39

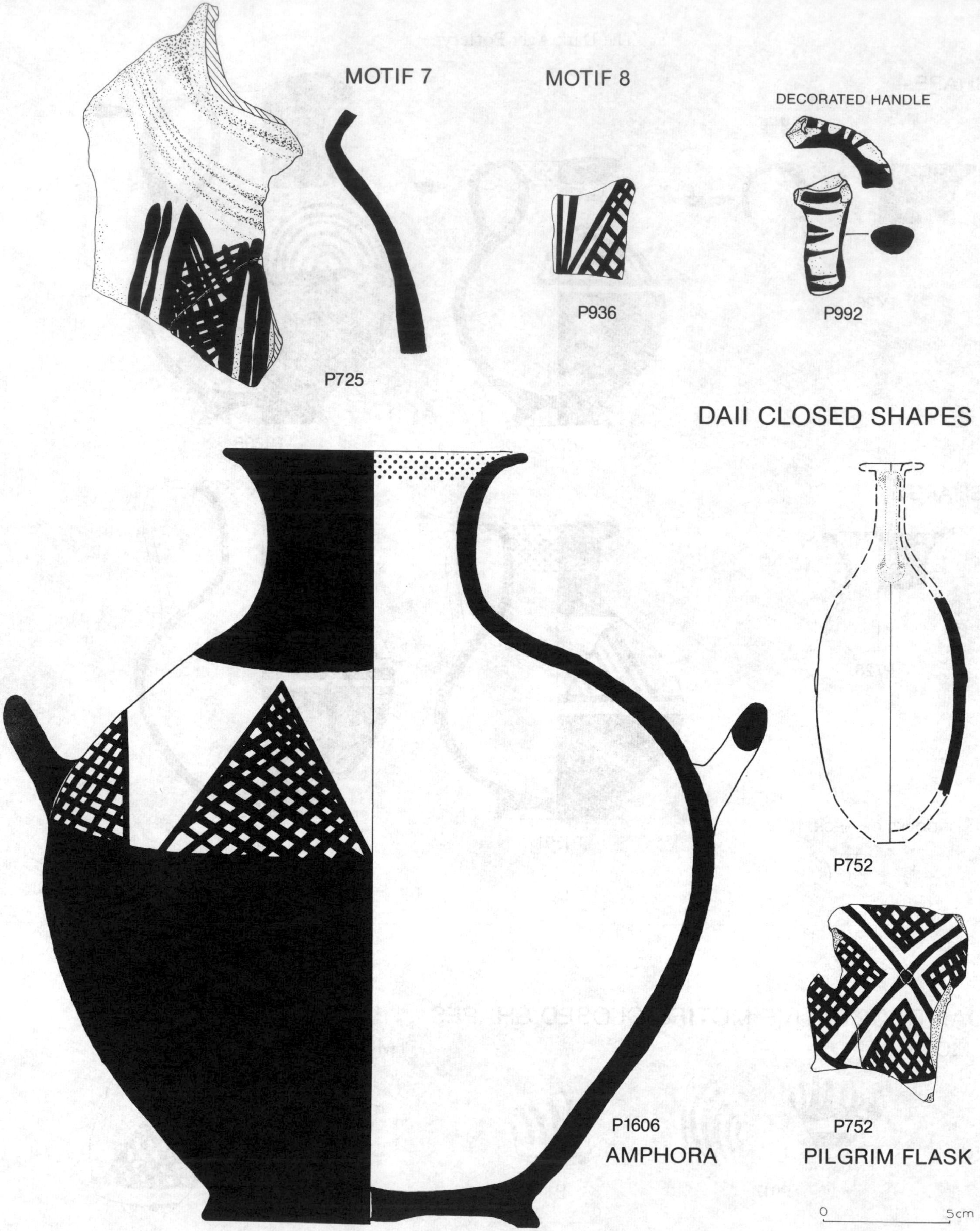

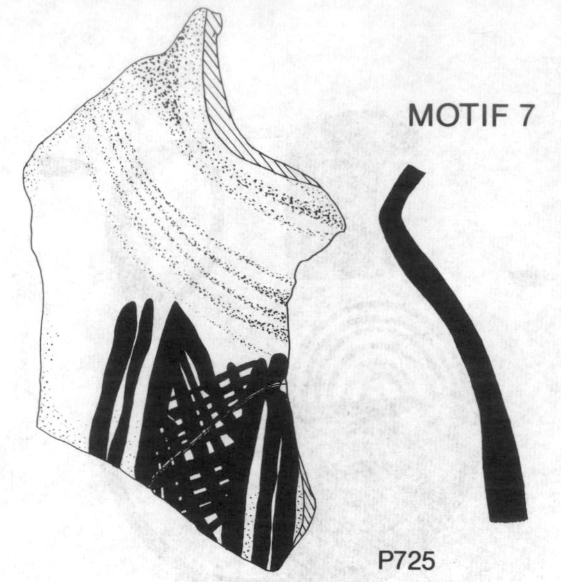

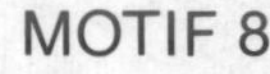

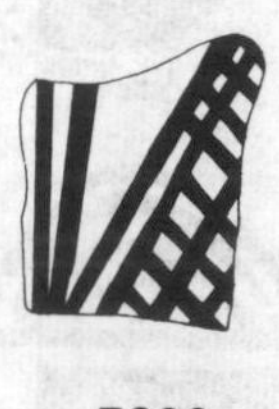

MOTIF 7
MOTIF 8
DECORATED HANDLE
P725
P936
P992
DAII CLOSED SHAPES
P752
P752
P1606
AMPHORA
PILGRIM FLASK
0
5cm

Figure 3-40

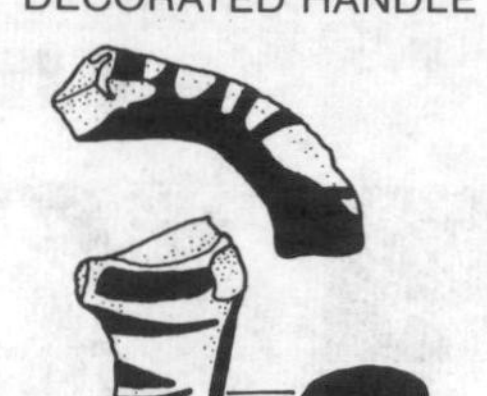

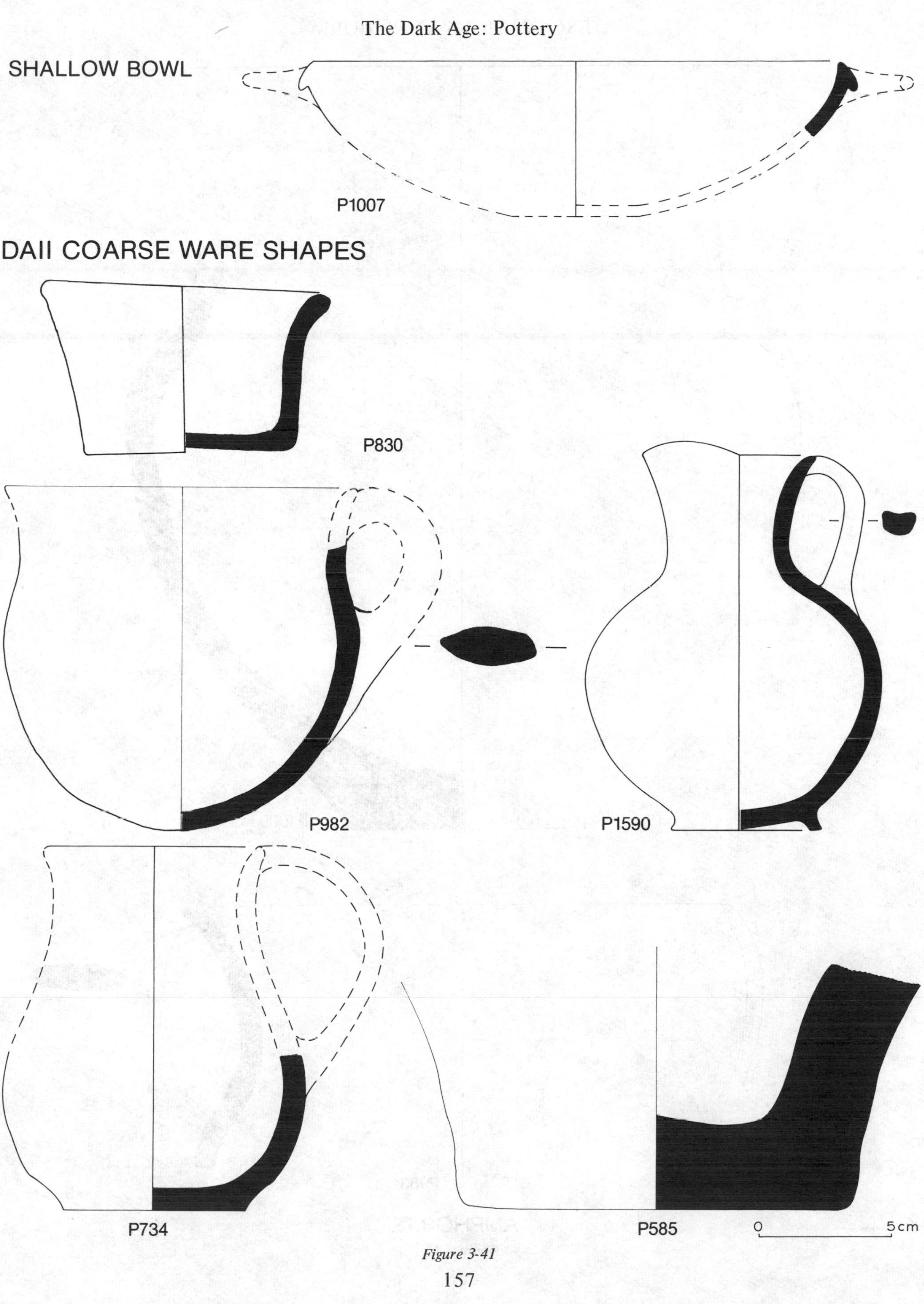
SHALLOW BOWL
P1007
DAII COARSE WARE SHAPES
P830
P982
P1590
P734
P585
0
5cm

Figure 3-41

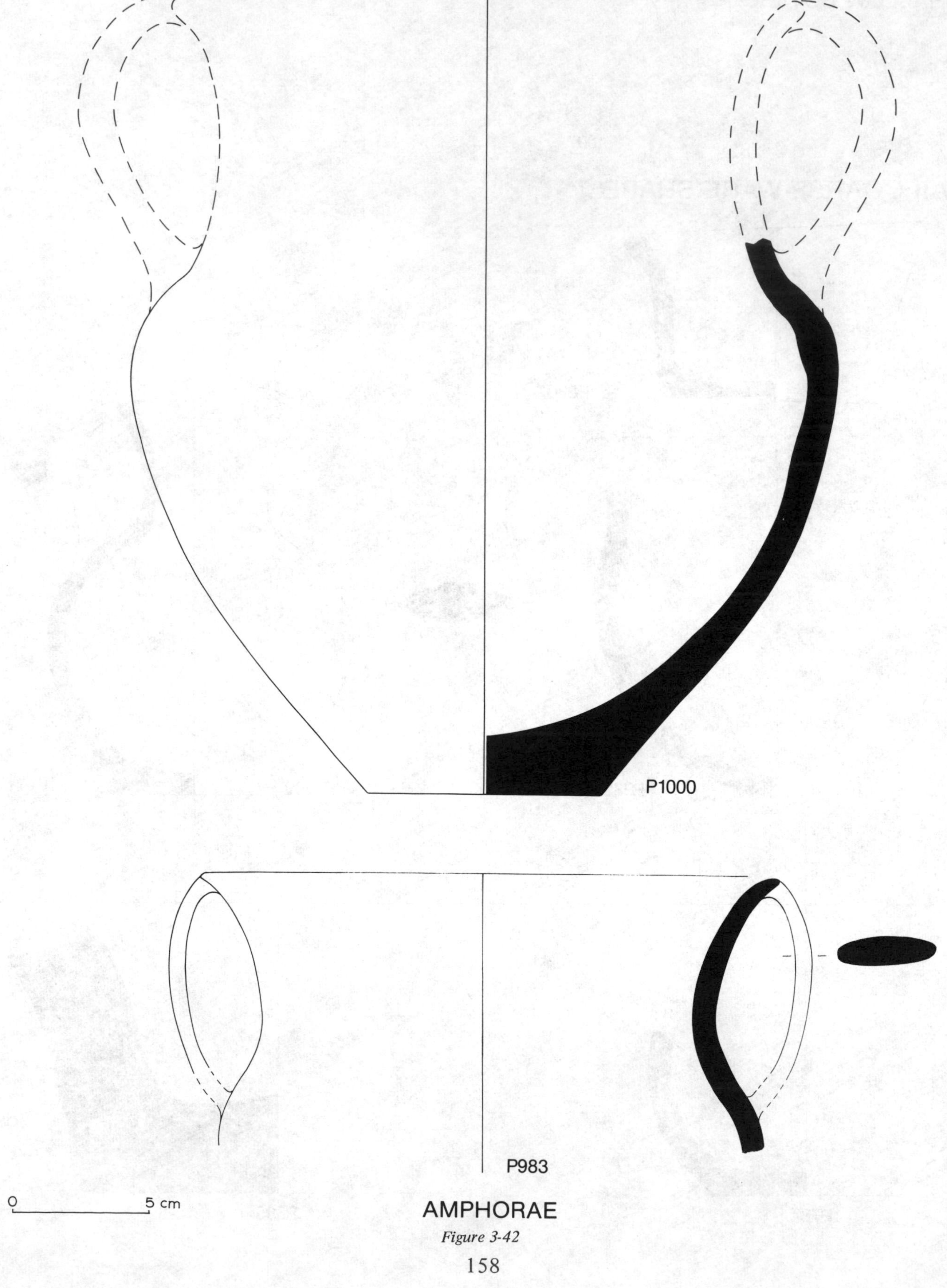

AMPHORAE

Figure 3-42

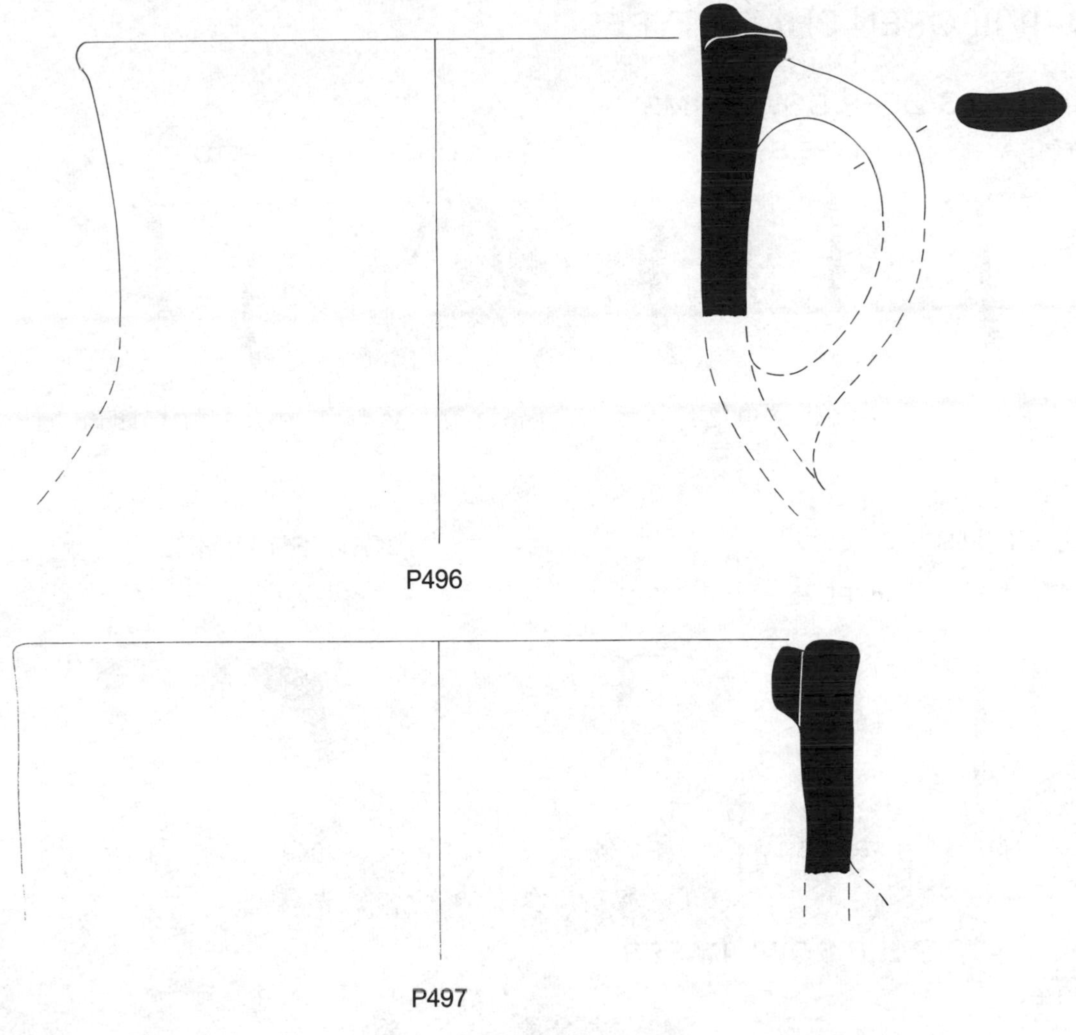
P496
P497

COMPARATIVE MATERIAL
KARDAMYLA
ANTHEIA 200
KARDAMYLA
0
5cm

Figure 3-43

DAII/III OPEN SHAPE TYPES

SKYPHOS/DEEP BOWL RIMS

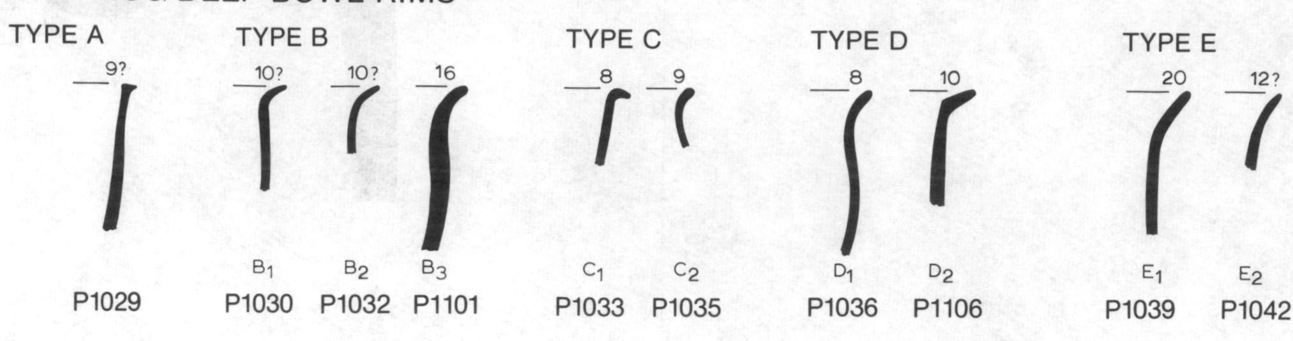

CUP RIMS

KRATER RIMS

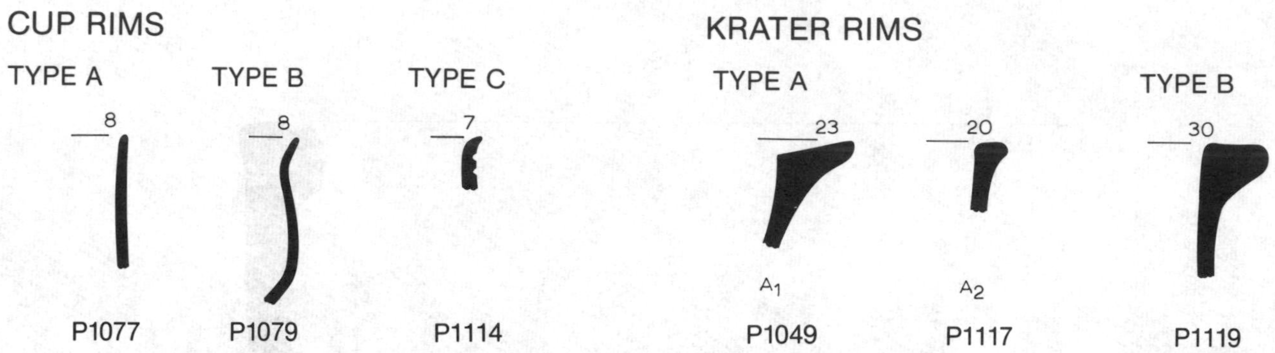

SKYPHOS/DEEP BOWL BASES

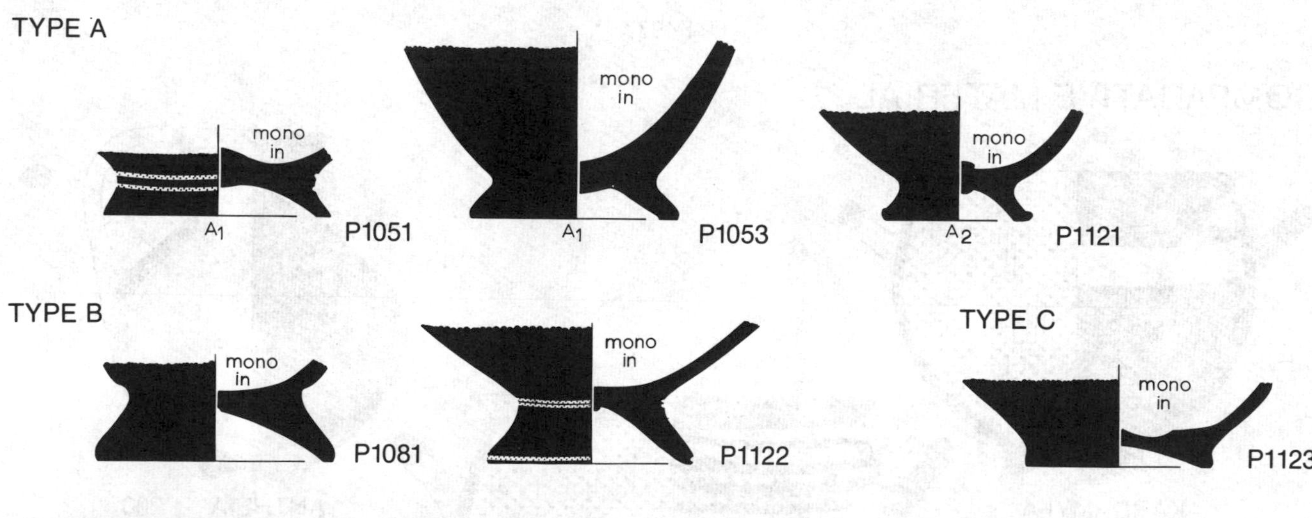

KRATER BASES

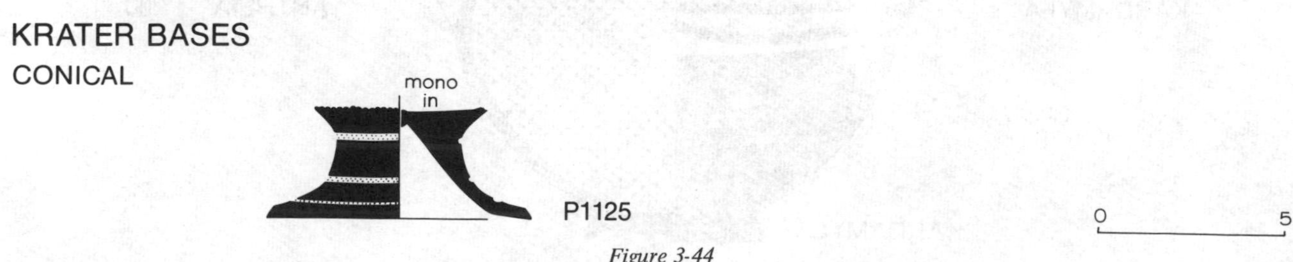

Figure 3-44

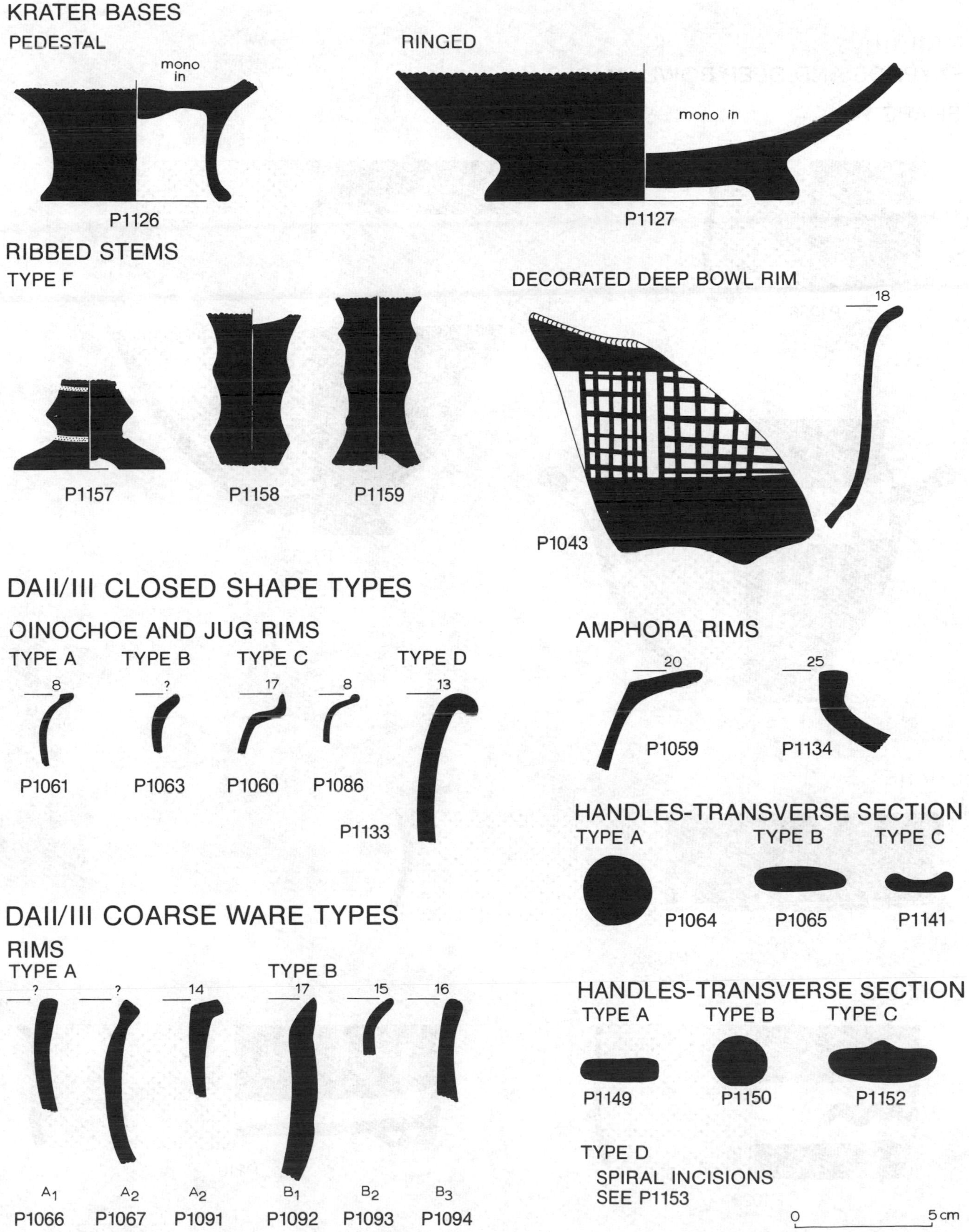

KRATER BASES

PEDESTAL

mono in

P1126

RINGED

mono in

P1127

RIBBED STEMS

TYPE F

P1157 P1158 P1159

DECORATED DEEP BOWL RIM

18

P1043

DAII/III CLOSED SHAPE TYPES

OINOCHOE AND JUG RIMS

TYPE A TYPE B TYPE C TYPE D

8 ? 17 8 13

P1061 P1063 P1060 P1086 P1133

AMPHORA RIMS

20 25

P1059 P1134

HANDLES-TRANSVERSE SECTION

TYPE A TYPE B TYPE C

P1064 P1065 P1141

DAII/III COARSE WARE TYPES

RIMS

TYPE A TYPE B

? ? 14 17 15 16

A_1 A_2 A_2 B_1 B_2 B_3

P1066 P1067 P1091 P1092 P1093 P1094

HANDLES-TRANSVERSE SECTION

TYPE A TYPE B TYPE C

P1149 P1150 P1152

TYPE D

SPIRAL INCISIONS

SEE P1153

0 5 cm

Figure 3-45

DAII/III
SKYPHOS AND DEEP BOWL SHAPES

SHAPE 1

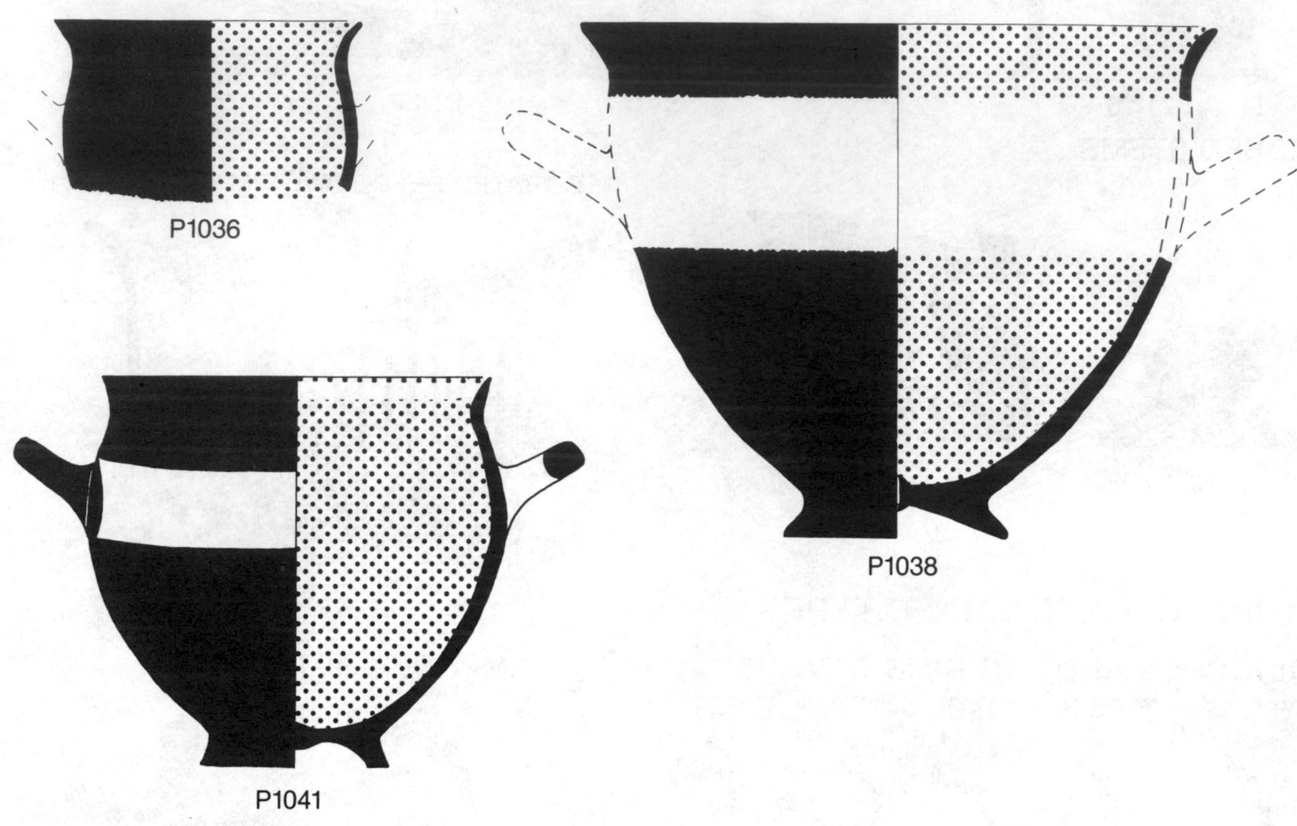

SHAPE 2

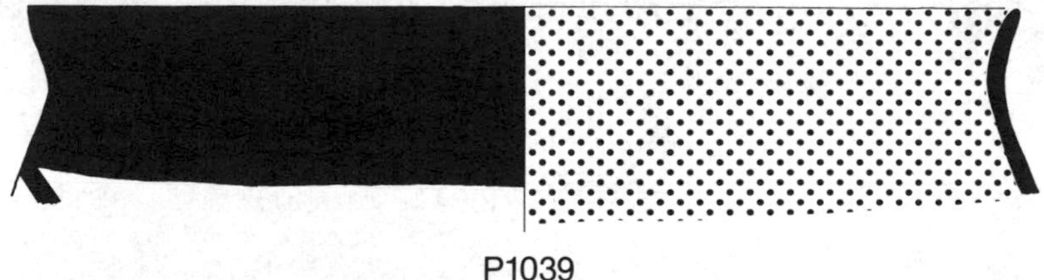

SHAPE 3

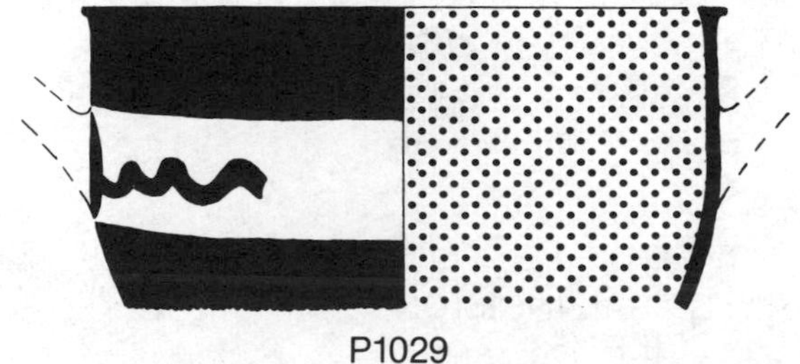

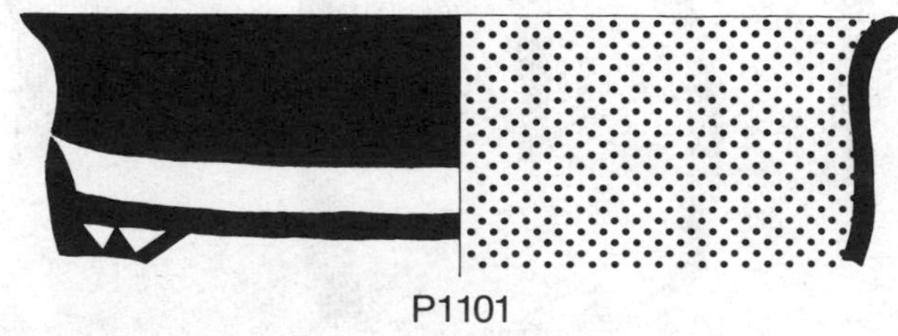

0 5cm

Figure 3-46

DECORATED KRATER FRAGMENT

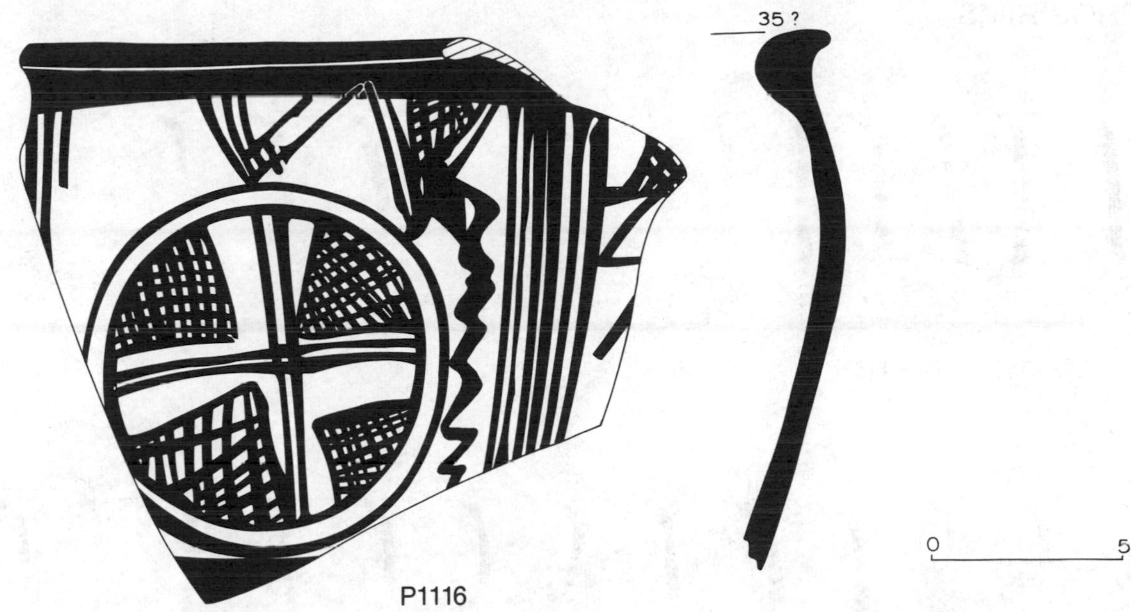

RECONSTRUCTED GRILL POSSIBILITIES

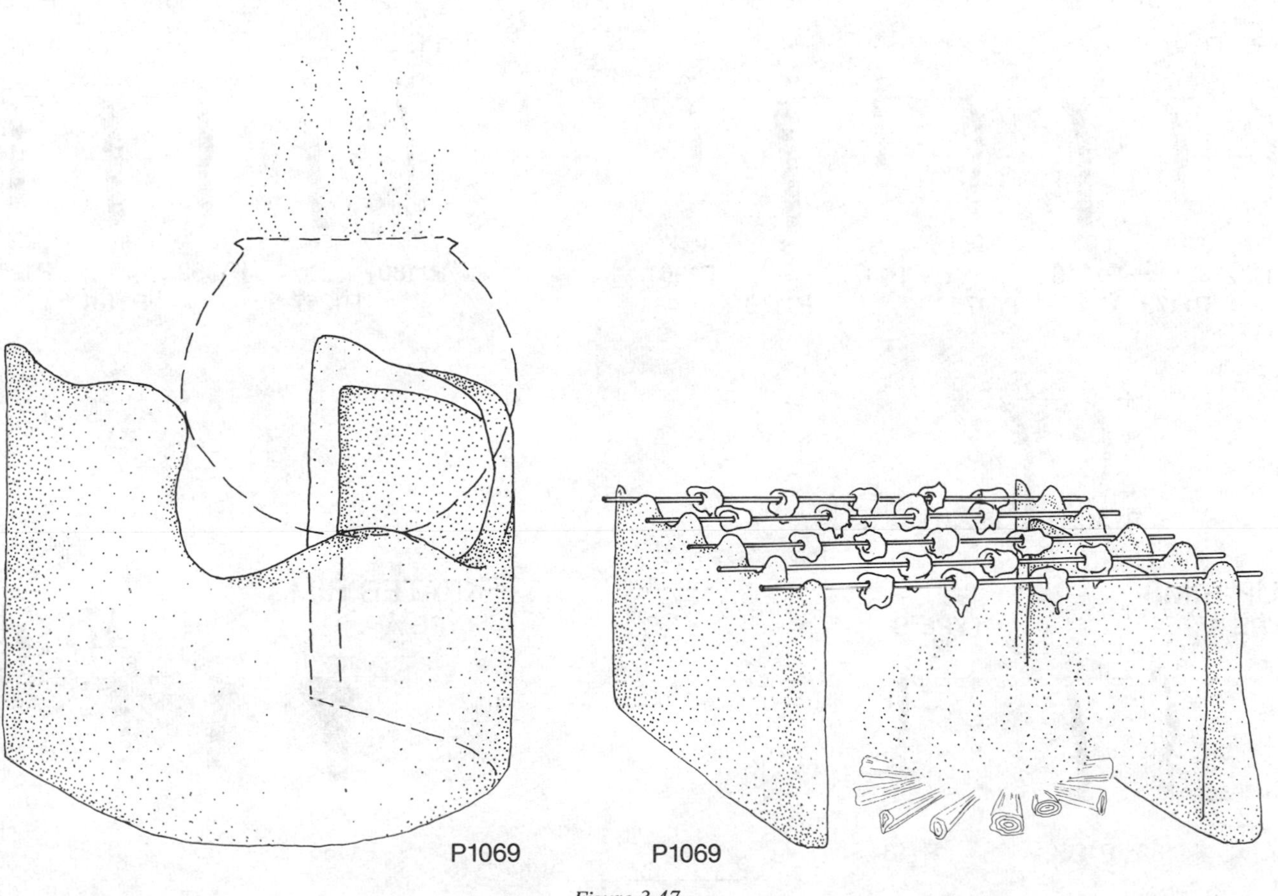

Figure 3-47

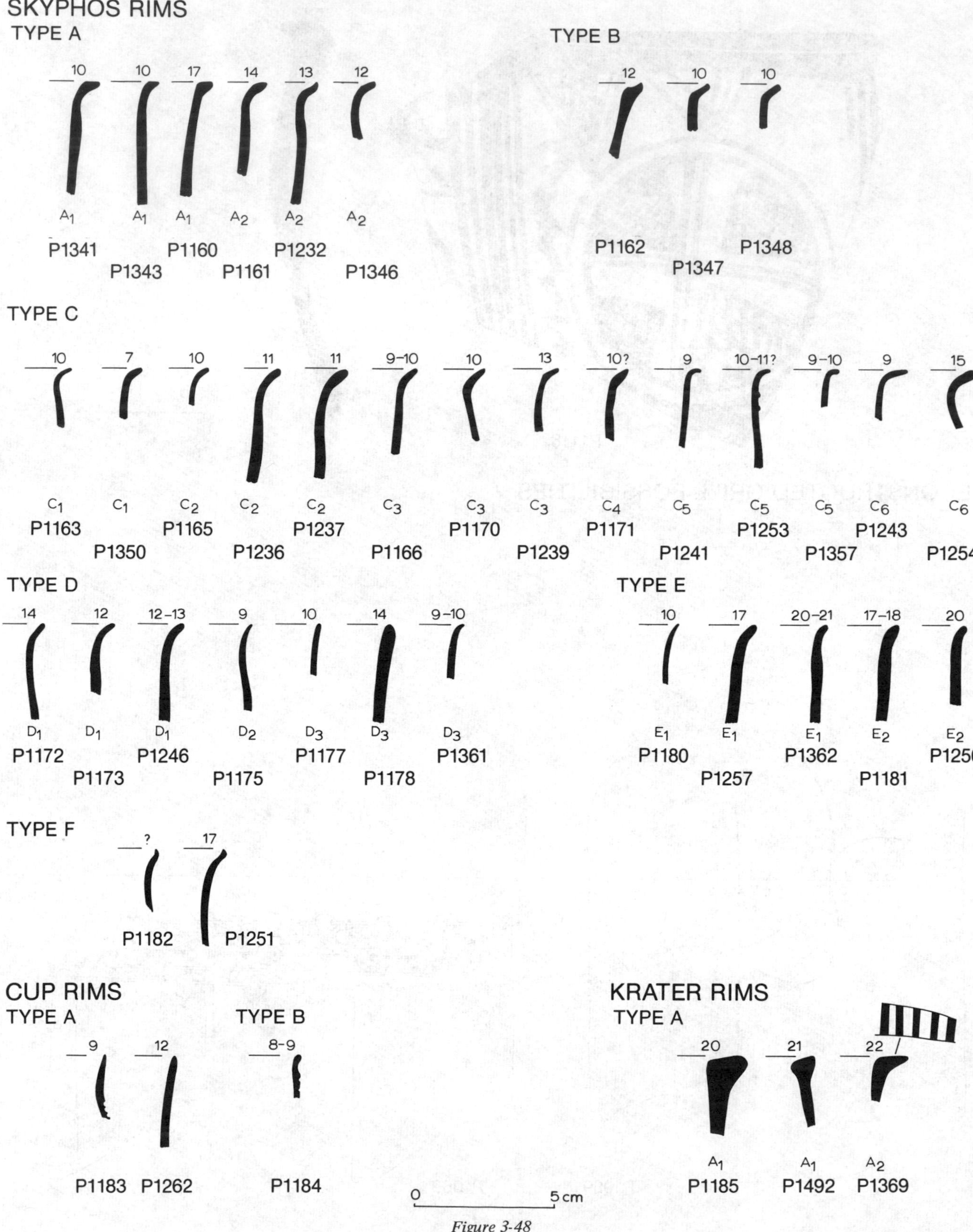
DAIII OPEN SHAPE TYPES
SKYPHOS RIMS
TYPE A
10 10 17 14 13 12
A1 A1 A1 A2 A2 A2
P1341 P1343 P1160 P1161 P1232 P1346
TYPE B
12 10 10
P1162 P1347 P1348
TYPE C
10 7 10 11 11 9–10 10 13 10? 9 10–11? 9–10 9 15
C1 C1 C2 C2 C2 C3 C3 C3 C4 C5 C5 C5 C6 C6
P1163 P1350 P1165 P1236 P1237 P1166 P1170 P1239 P1171 P1241 P1253 P1357 P1243 P1254
TYPE D
14 12 12–13 9 10 14 9–10
D1 D1 D1 D2 D3 D3 D3
P1172 P1173 P1246 P1175 P1177 P1178 P1361
TYPE E
10 17 20–21 17–18 20
E1 E1 E1 E2 E2
P1180 P1257 P1362 P1181 P1250
TYPE F
? 17
P1182 P1251
CUP RIMS
TYPE A
9 12
P1183 P1262
TYPE B
8-9
P1184
KRATER RIMS
TYPE A
20 21 22
A1 A1 A2
P1185 P1492 P1369
0 5 cm

Figure 3-48

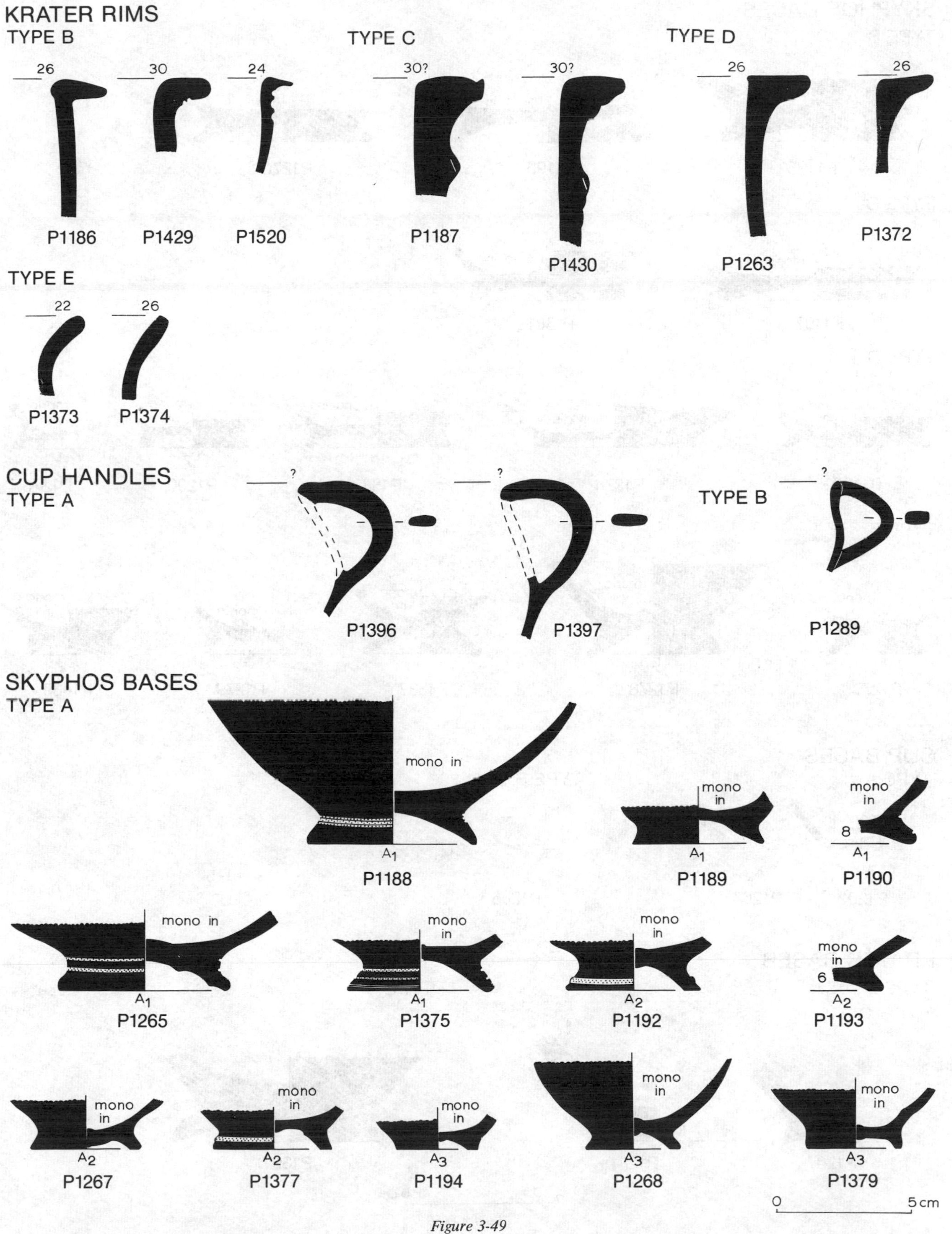

KRATER RIMS
TYPE B
TYPE C
TYPE D
26
30
24
30?
30?
26
26
P1186
P1429
P1520
P1187
P1430
P1263
P1372
TYPE E
22
26
P1373
P1374
CUP HANDLES
TYPE A
?
?
TYPE B
?
P1396
P1397
P1289
SKYPHOS BASES
TYPE A
mono in
A1
P1188
mono in
A1
P1189
mono in
8
A1
P1190
mono in
A1
P1265
mono in
A1
P1375
mono in
A2
P1192
mono in
6
A2
P1193
mono in
A2
P1267
mono in
A2
P1377
mono in
A3
P1194
mono in
A3
P1268
mono in
A3
P1379
0
5 cm

Figure 3-49

SKYPHOS BASES

TYPE B

mono in — P1195
mono in — P1196
mono in — P1270

TYPE C

mono in — P1197
mono in — P1381

TYPE D

mono in, D_1 — P1198
mono in, D_1 — P1274
mono in, D_1 — P1383
mono in, D_2 — P1200
mono in, 6, D_2 — P1276

TYPE E

mono in, E_1 — P1277
mono in, E_1 — P1278
mono in, E_1 — P1387
mono in, 4, E_2 — P1279
mono in, E_2 — P1439

CUP BASES

TYPE A

mono in, 4, A_1 — P1202
mono in, 4, A_2 — P1204

TYPE B

mono in, 5 — P1206

KRATER BASES

TYPE A

TYPE B

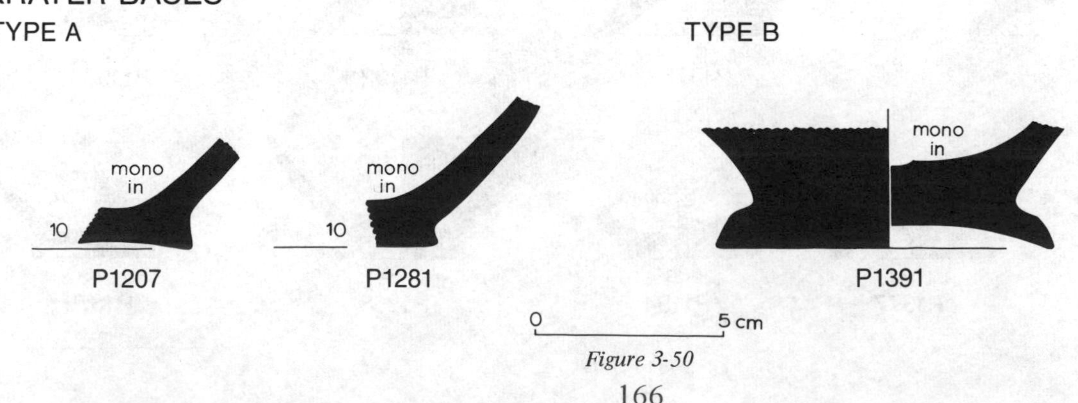

Figure 3-50

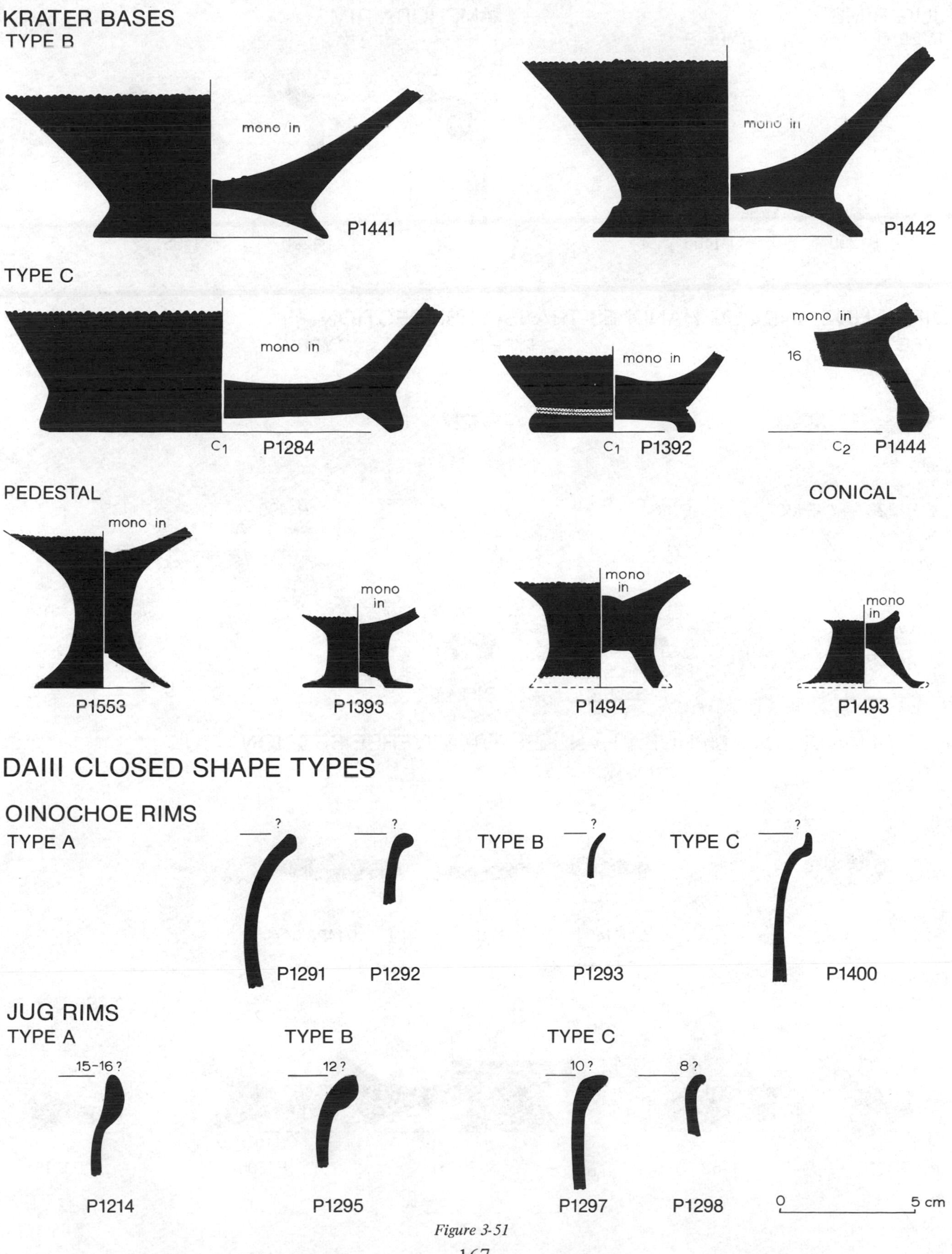
KRATER BASES
TYPE B
mono in
P1441
mono in
P1442
TYPE C
mono in
C1
P1284
mono in
C1
P1392
mono in
16
C2
P1444
PEDESTAL
CONICAL
mono in
P1553
mono in
P1393
mono in
P1494
mono in
P1493
DAIII CLOSED SHAPE TYPES
OINOCHOE RIMS
TYPE A
?
?
P1291
P1292
TYPE B
?
P1293
TYPE C
?
P1400
JUG RIMS
TYPE A
15-16 ?
P1214
TYPE B
12 ?
P1295
TYPE C
10 ?
P1297
8 ?
P1298
0
5 cm

Figure 3-51

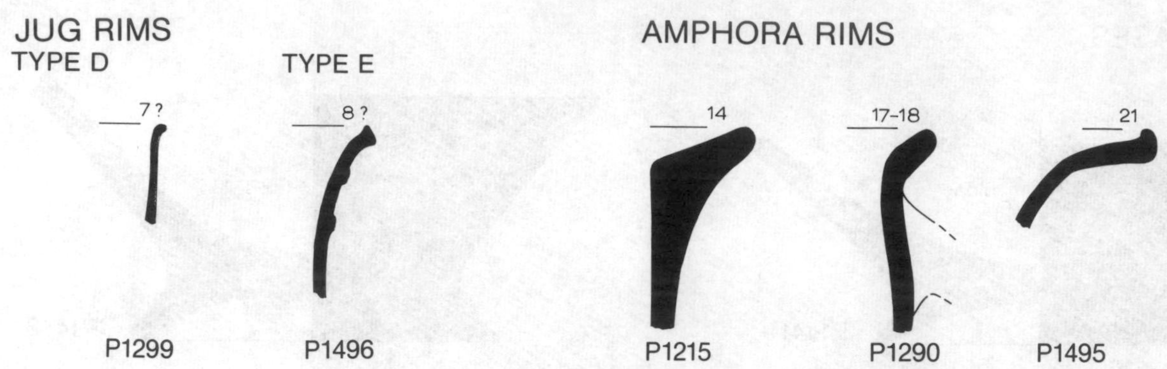
JUG RIMS
TYPE D
TYPE E
AMPHORA RIMS
7 ?
8 ?
14
17–18
21
P1299
P1496
P1215
P1290
P1495

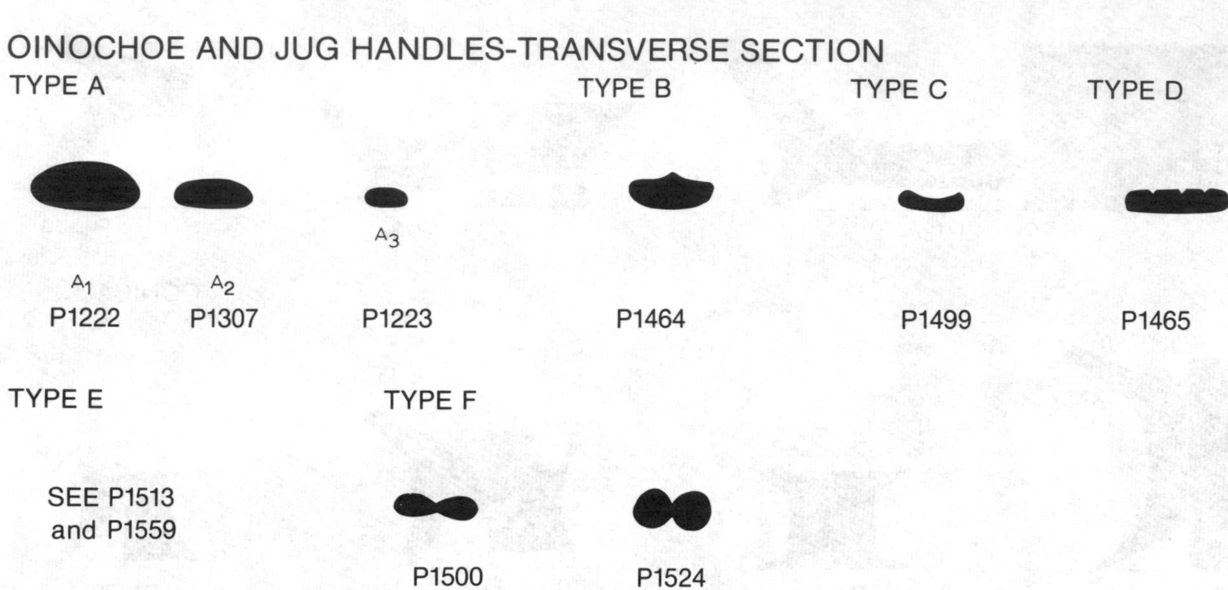
OINOCHOE AND JUG HANDLES-TRANSVERSE SECTION
TYPE A
TYPE B
TYPE C
TYPE D
A3
A1
A2
P1222
P1307
P1223
P1464
P1499
P1465
TYPE E
TYPE F
SEE P1513
and P1559
P1500
P1524

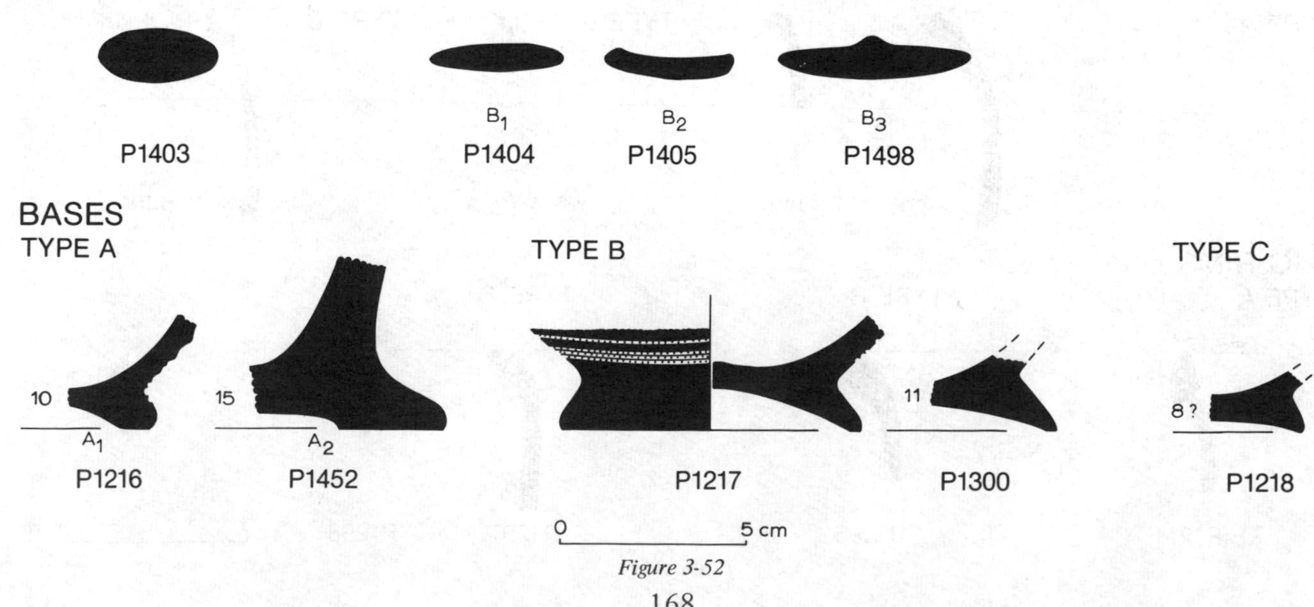
NECK-HANDLED AMPHORA HANDLES-TRANSVERSE SECTION
TYPE A
TYPE B
B1
B2
B3
P1403
P1404
P1405
P1498
BASES
TYPE A
TYPE B
TYPE C
10
15
11
8 ?
A1
A2
P1216
P1452
P1217
P1300
P1218
0
5 cm

Figure 3-52

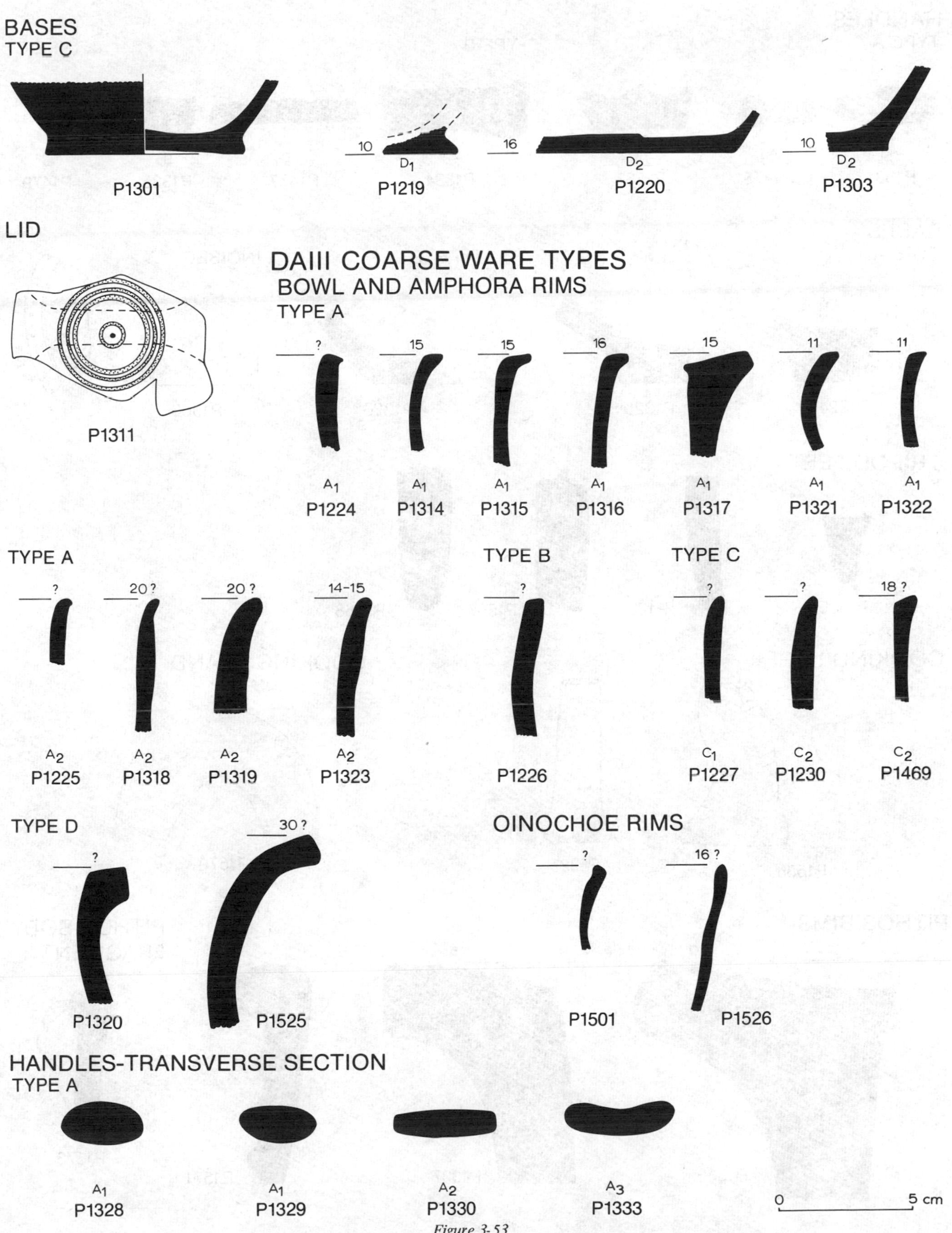
BASES
TYPE C
P1301
10
D1
P1219
16
D2
P1220
10
D2
P1303
LID
P1311
DAIII COARSE WARE TYPES
BOWL AND AMPHORA RIMS
TYPE A
?
15
15
16
15
11
11
A1
P1224
A1
P1314
A1
P1315
A1
P1316
A1
P1317
A1
P1321
A1
P1322
TYPE A
?
20 ?
20 ?
14-15
A2
P1225
A2
P1318
A2
P1319
A2
P1323
TYPE B
?
P1226
TYPE C
?
?
18 ?
C1
P1227
C2
P1230
C2
P1469
TYPE D
?
30 ?
P1320
P1525
OINOCHOE RIMS
?
16 ?
P1501
P1526
HANDLES-TRANSVERSE SECTION
TYPE A
A1
P1328
A1
P1329
A2
P1330
A3
P1333
0
5 cm

Figure 3-53

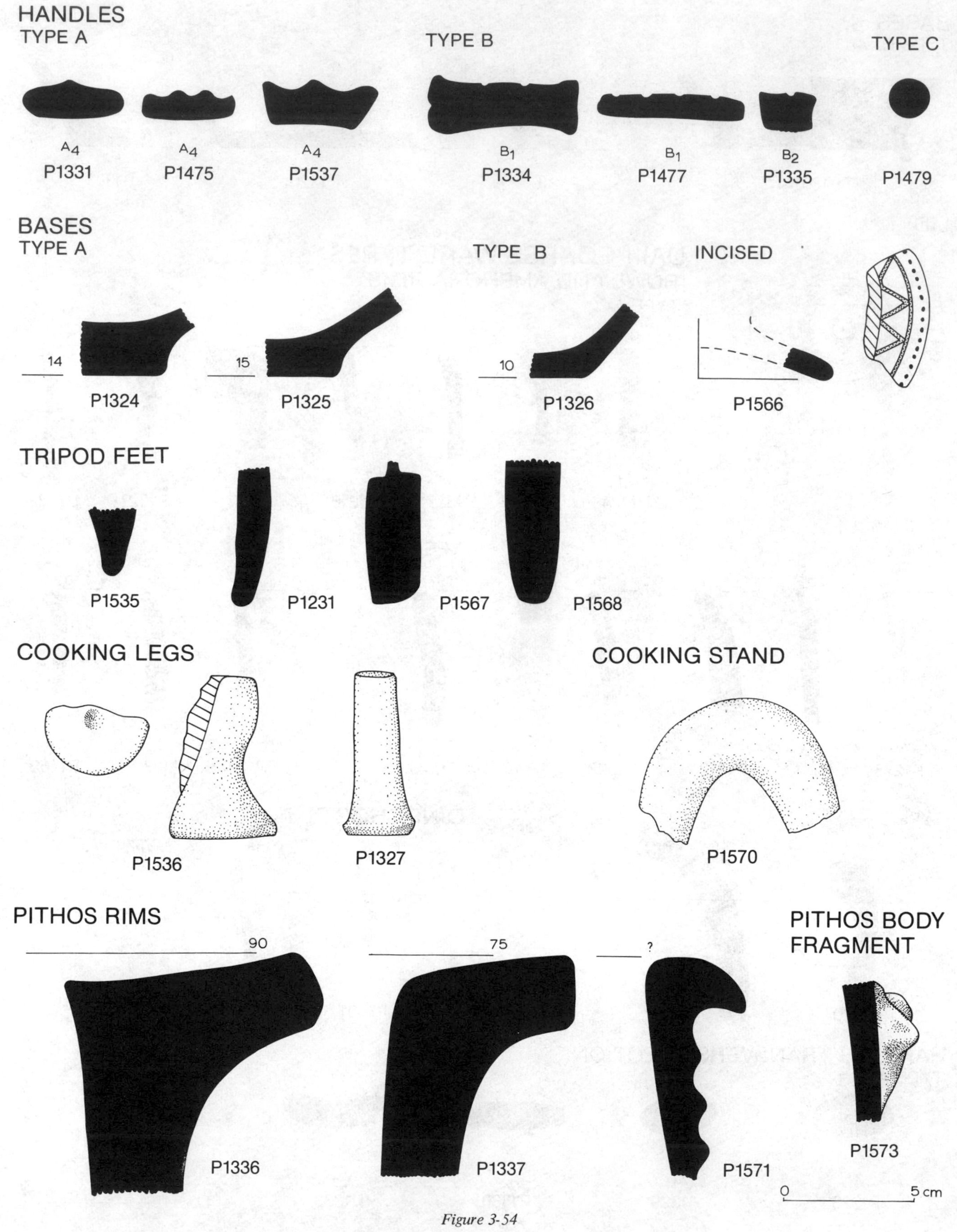
HANDLES
TYPE A
TYPE B
TYPE C
A4
P1331
A4
P1475
A4
P1537
B1
P1334
B1
P1477
B2
P1335
P1479
BASES
TYPE A
TYPE B
INCISED
14
P1324
15
P1325
10
P1326
P1566
TRIPOD FEET
P1535
P1231
P1567
P1568
COOKING LEGS
COOKING STAND
P1536
P1327
P1570
PITHOS RIMS
PITHOS BODY FRAGMENT
90
75
?
P1336
P1337
P1571
P1573
0
5 cm

Figure 3-54

DAIII OPEN SHAPES

SKYPHOS AND DEEP BOWL: SHAPE 1

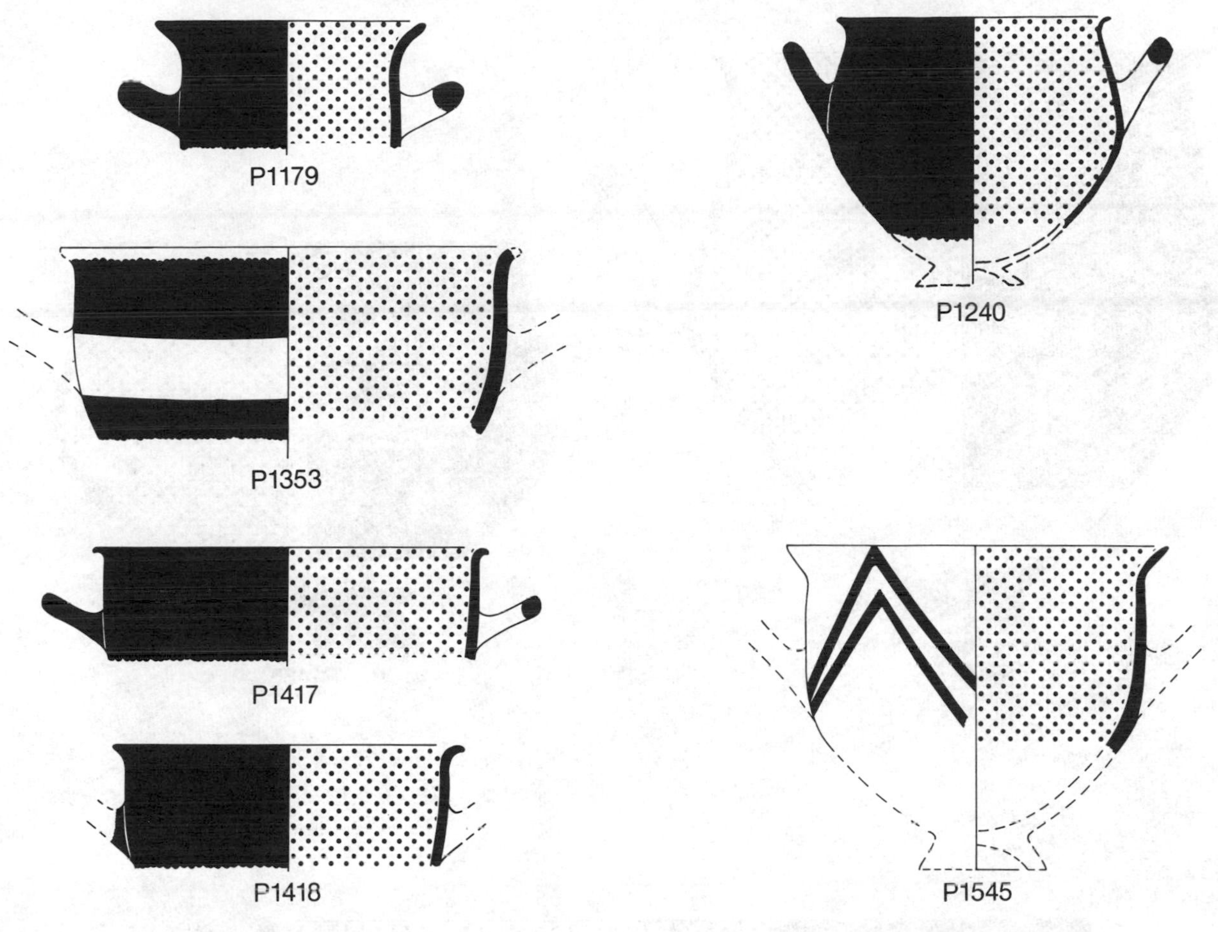

SHAPE 2

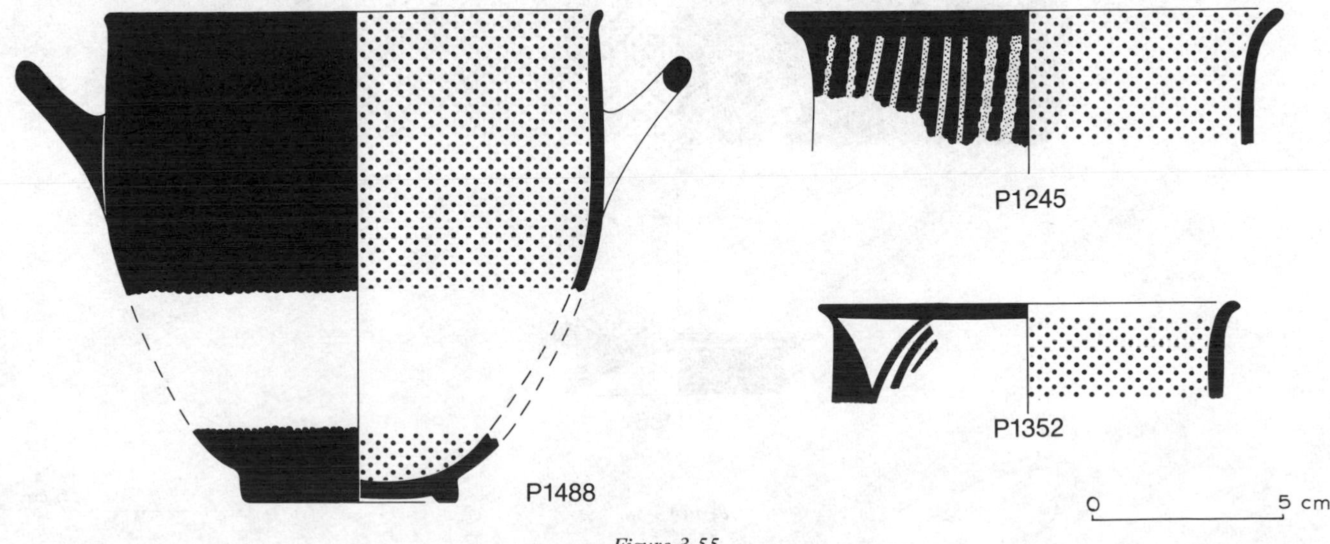

Figure 3-55

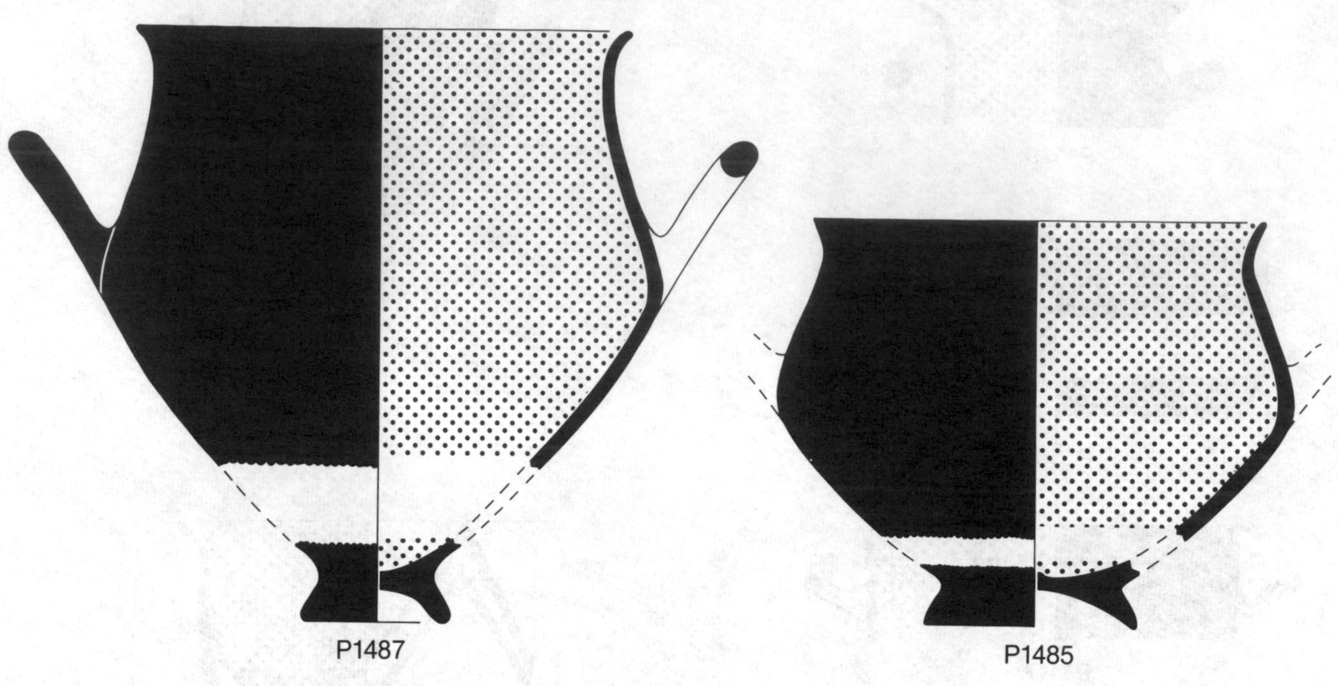

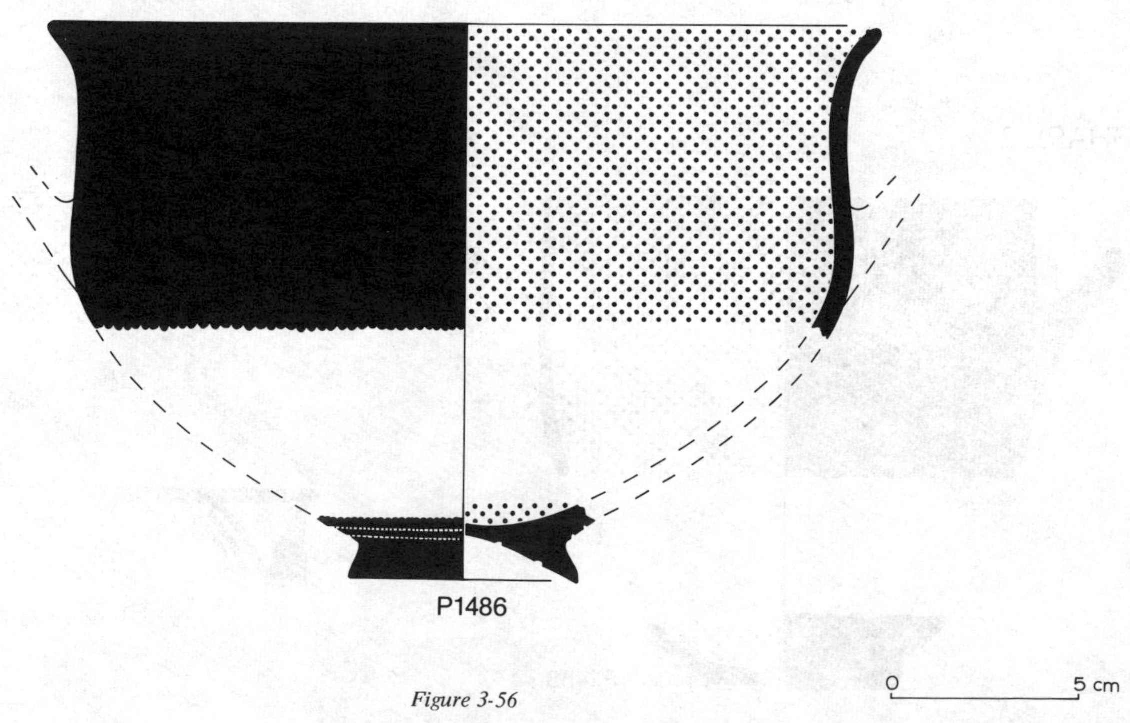

Figure 3-56

SHAPE 5

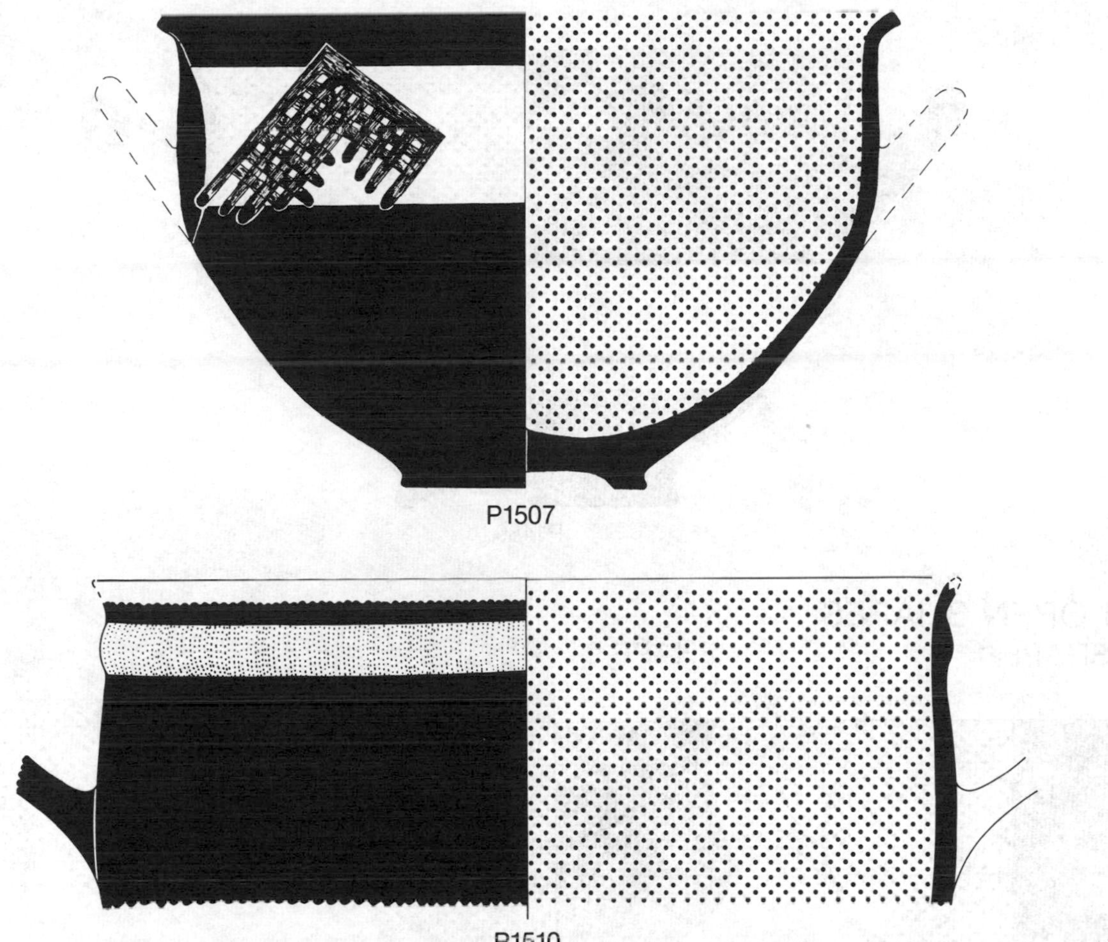

SHAPE 6

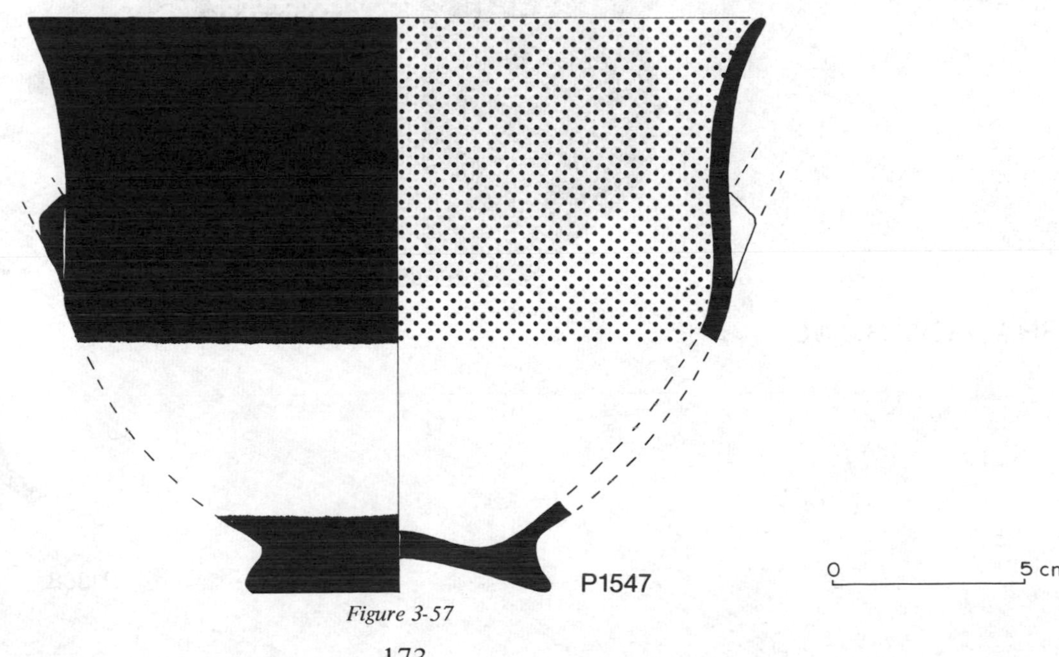

Figure 3-57

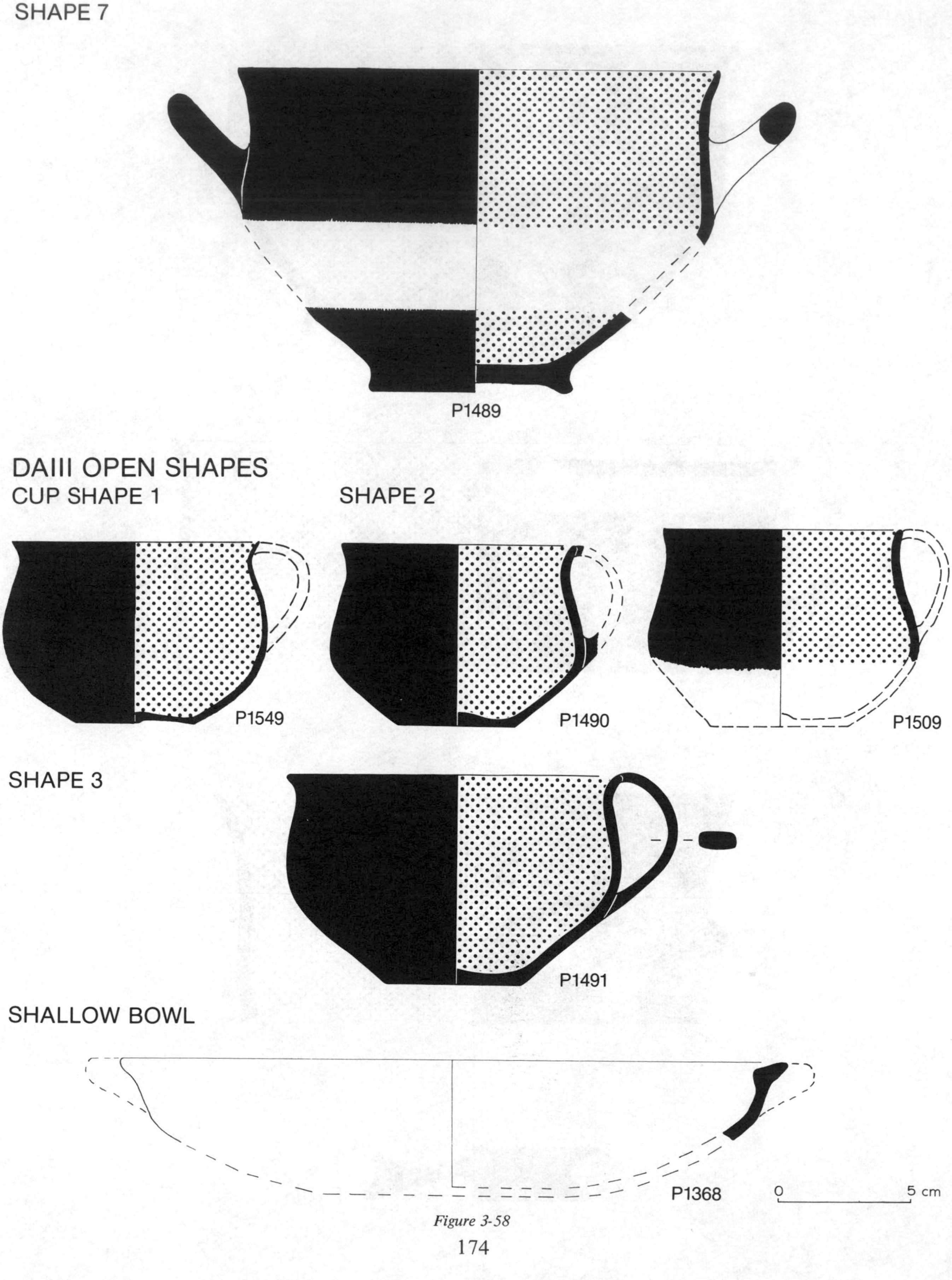

SHAPE 7

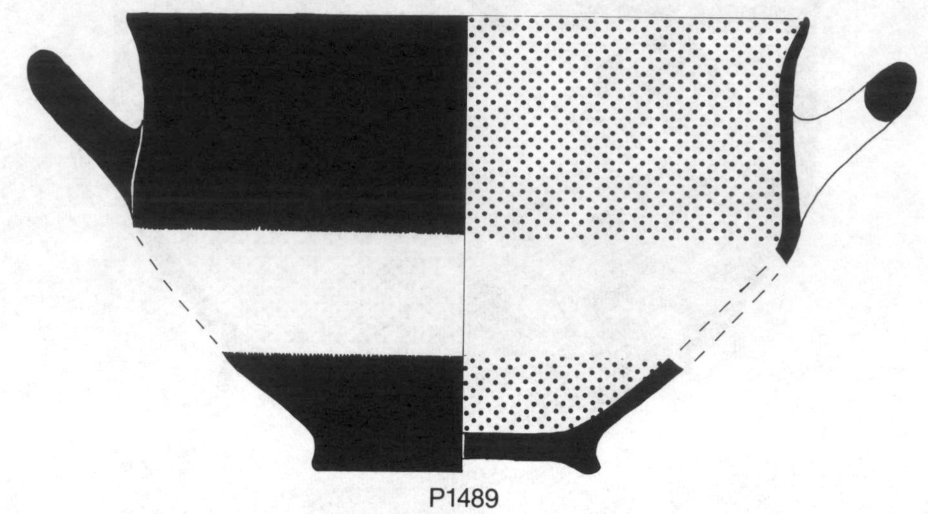

P1489

DAIII OPEN SHAPES

CUP SHAPE 1

SHAPE 2

P1549

P1490

P1509

SHAPE 3

P1491

SHALLOW BOWL

P1368

0 5 cm

Figure 3-58

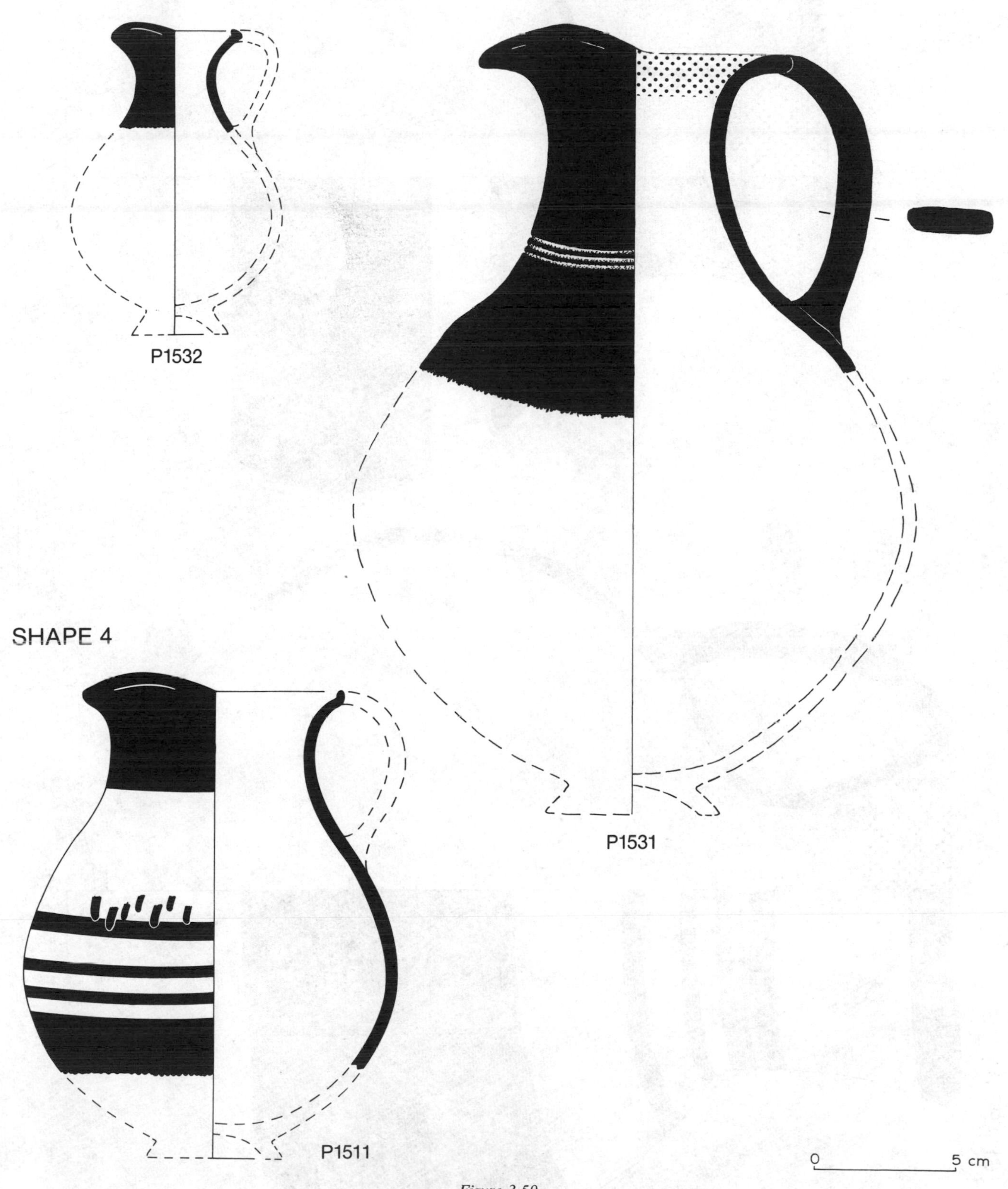
DAIII CLOSED SHAPES
OINOCHOE SHAPE 1
SHAPE 2
P1532
P1531
SHAPE 4
P1511
0
5 cm

Figure 3-59

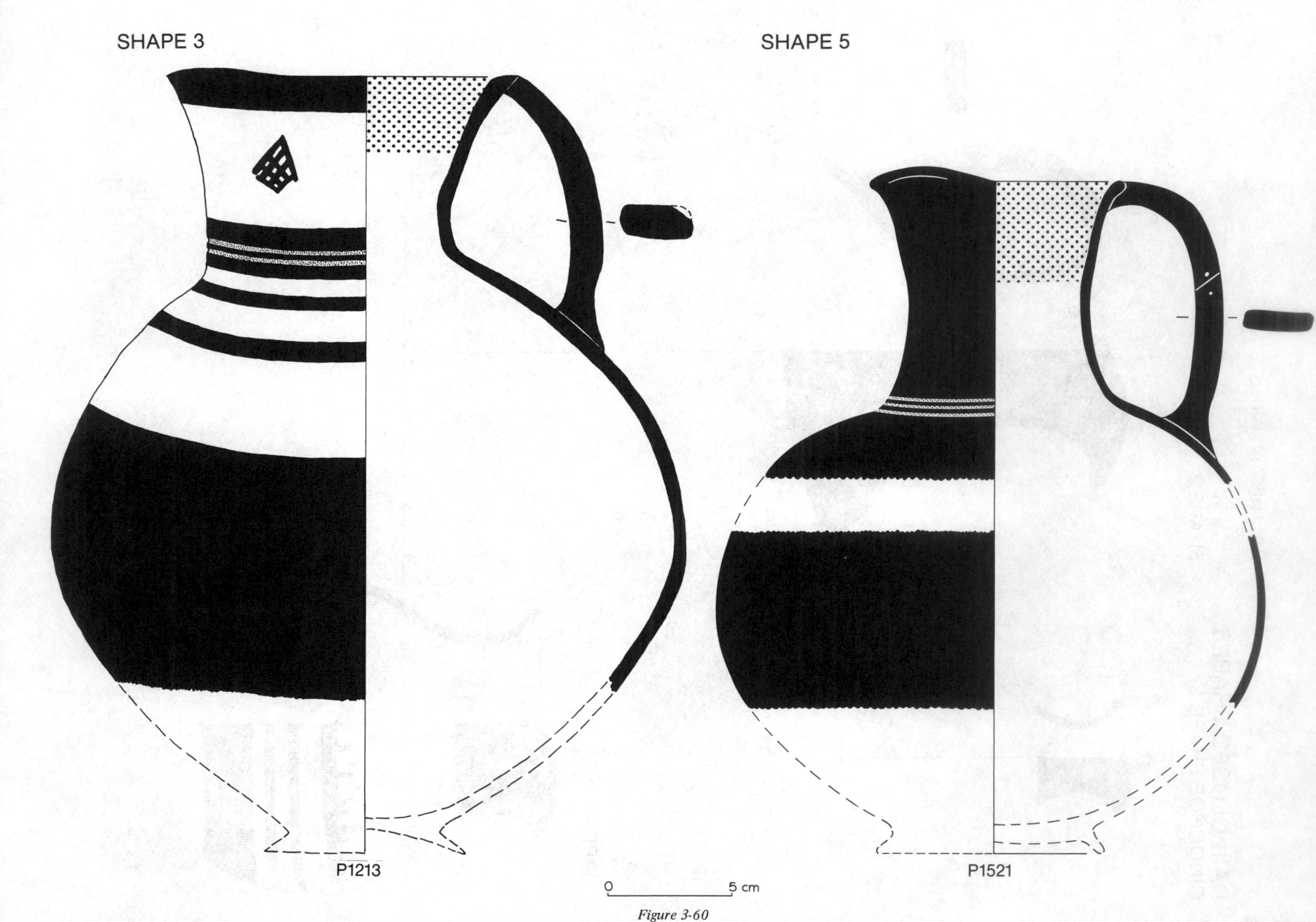

Figure 3-60

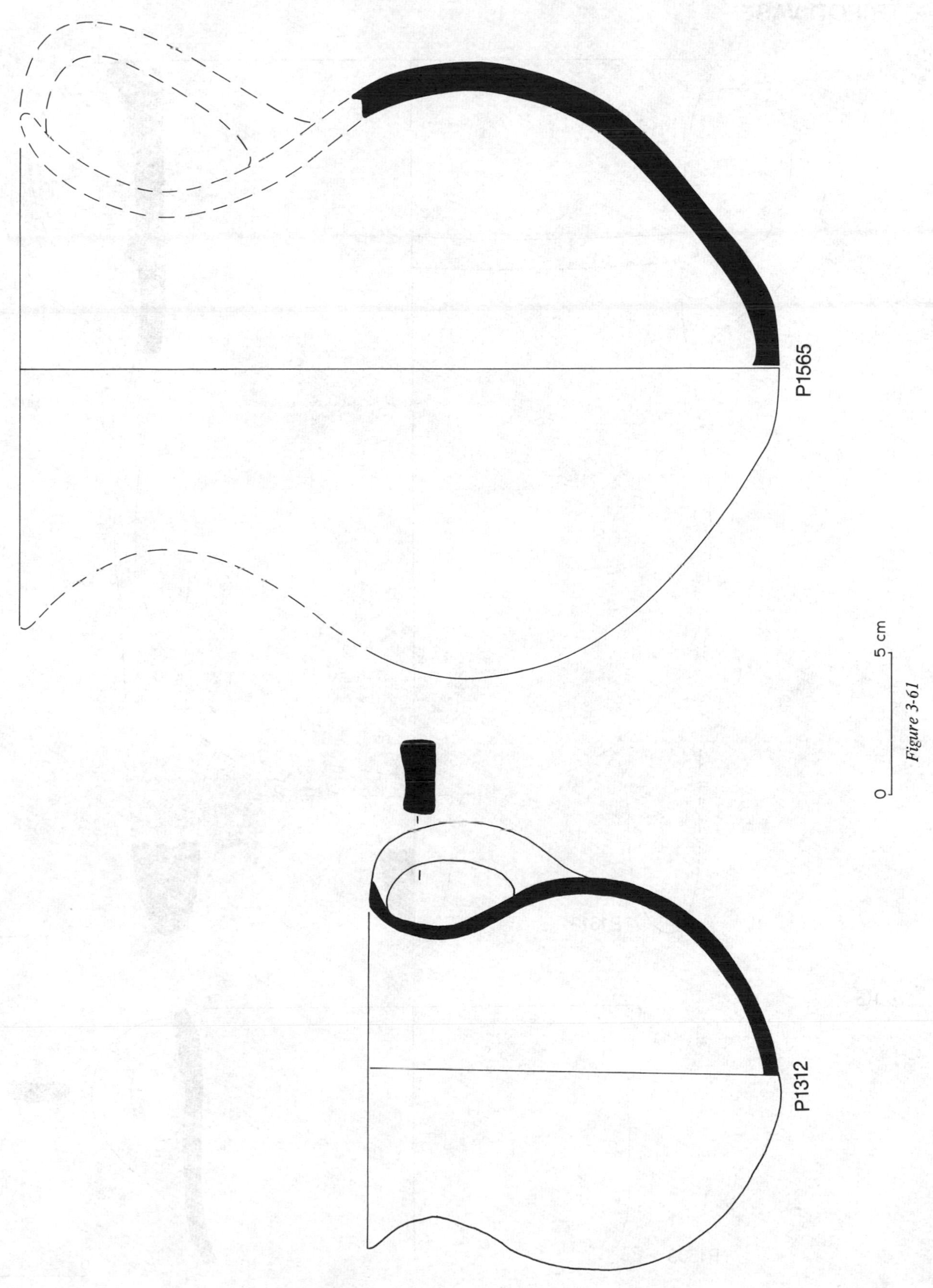

Figure 3-61

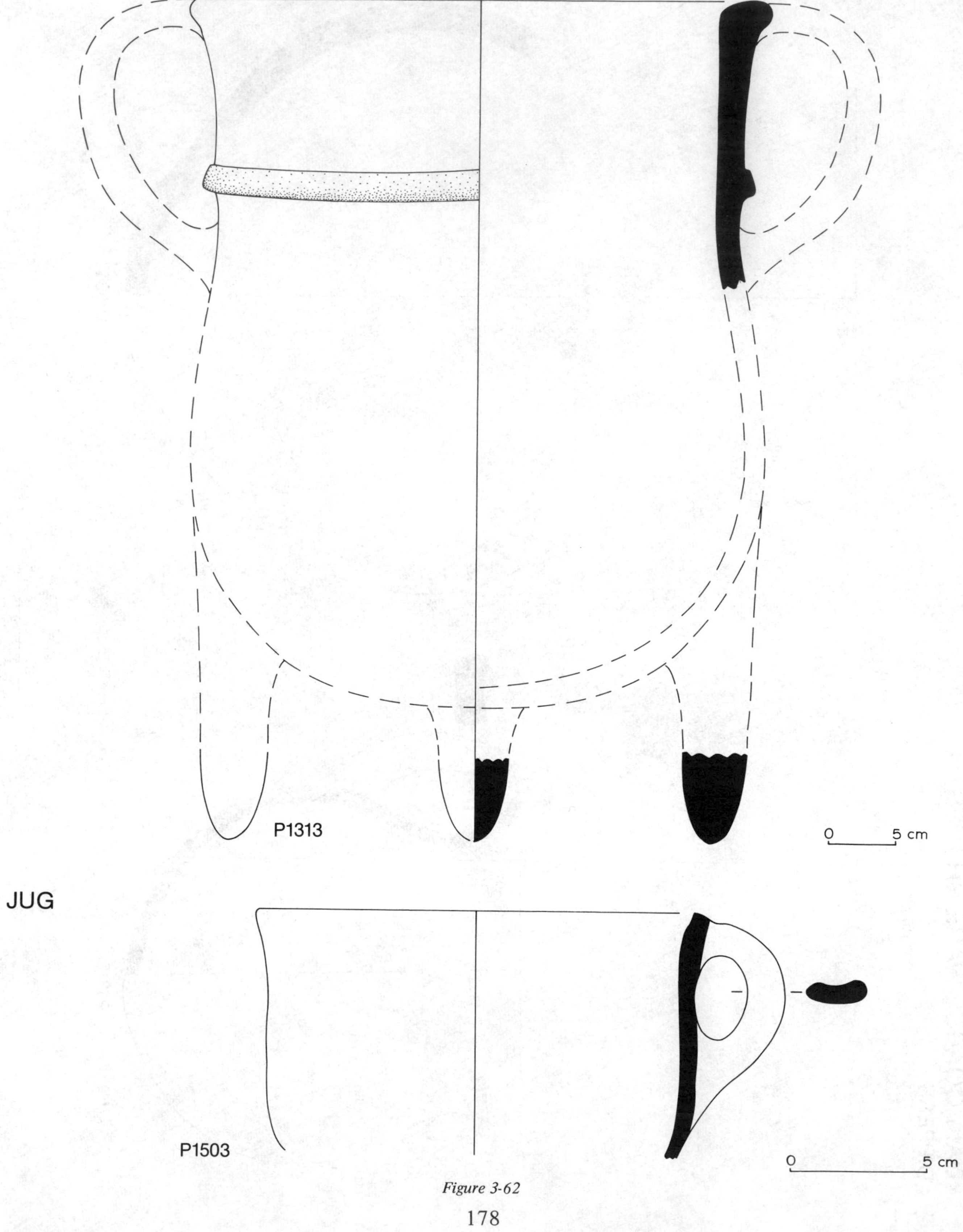

Figure 3-62

AMPHORAE

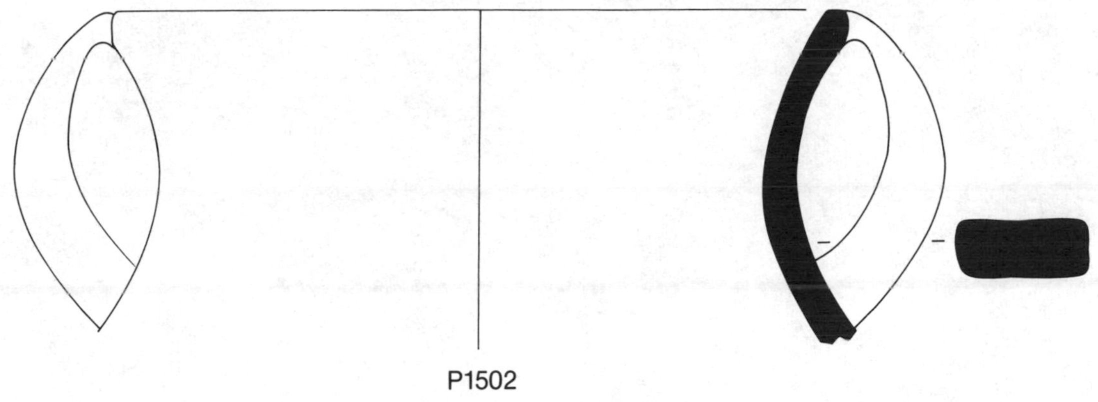

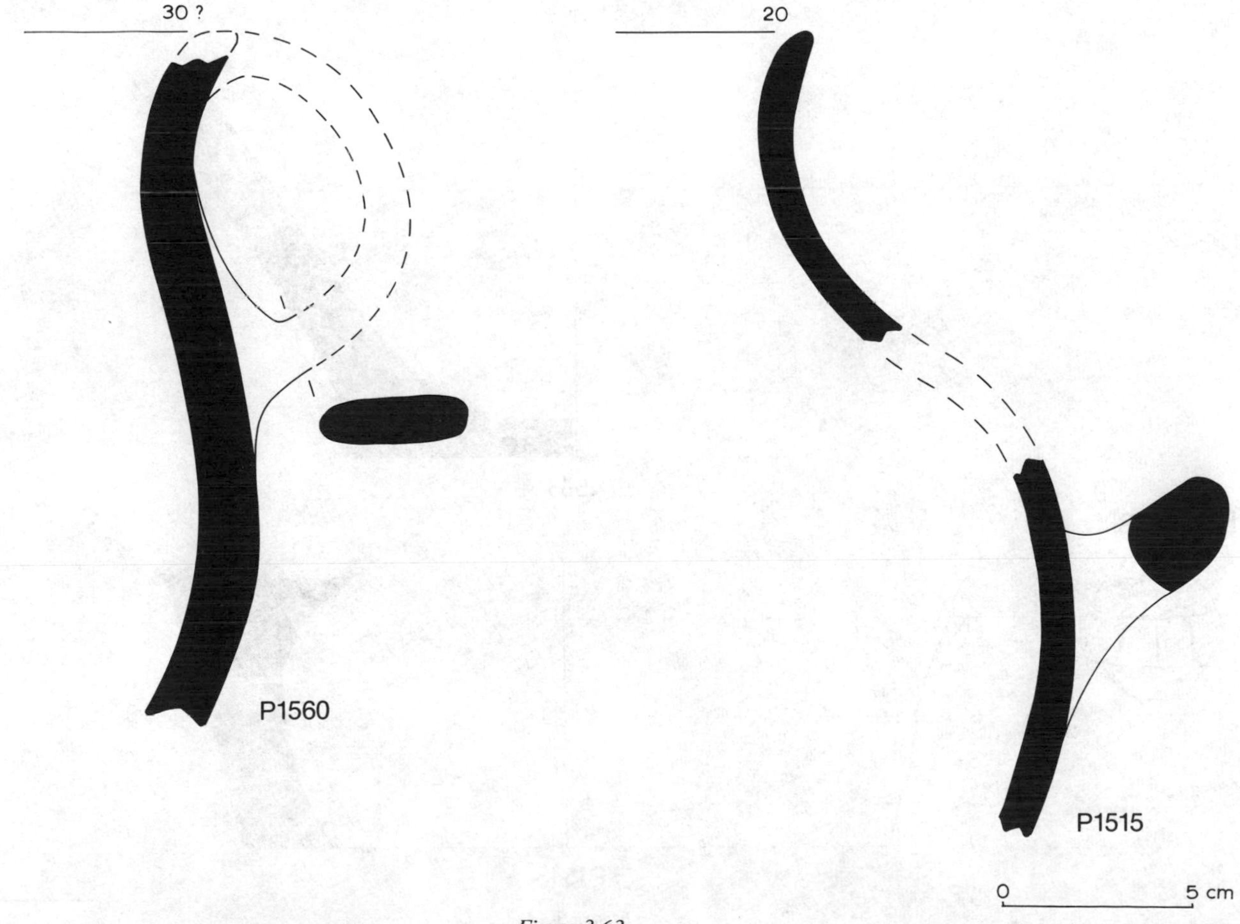

Figure 3-63

AMPHORA

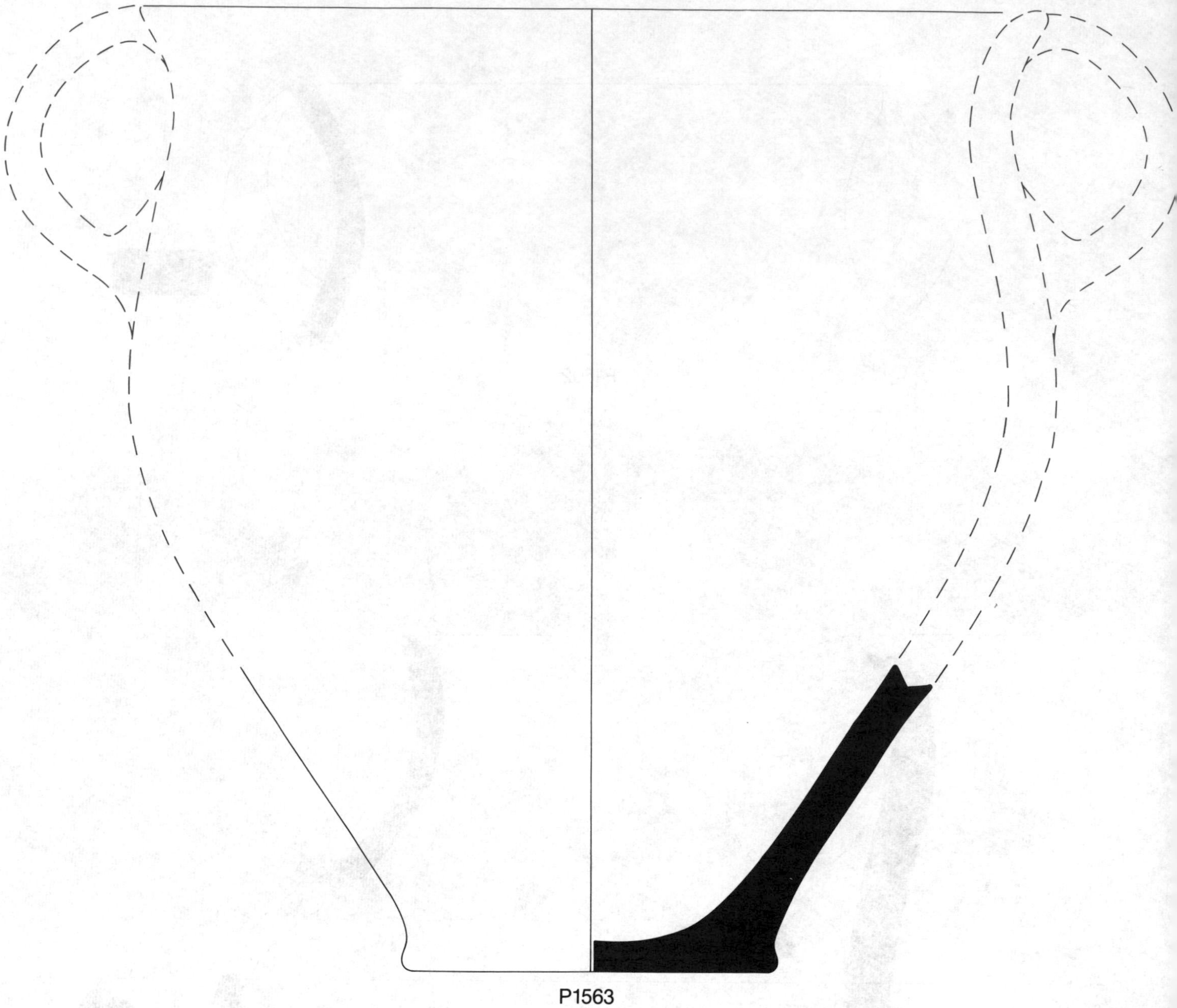

P1563

PITHOS

P1543

0 5 cm

Figure 3-64

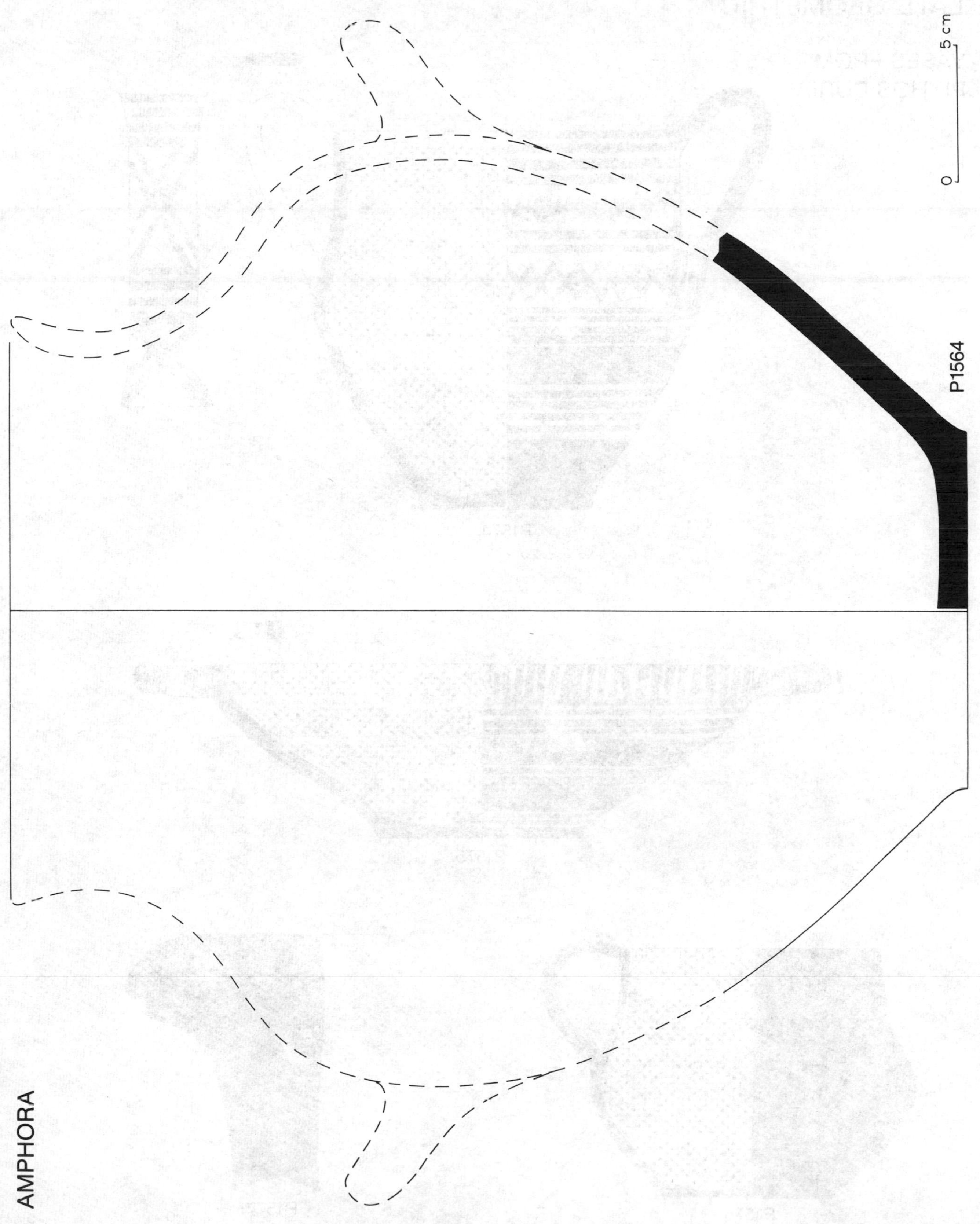

Figure 3-65

LATE GEOMETRIC

VASES FROM
PITHOS BURIAL

P1574

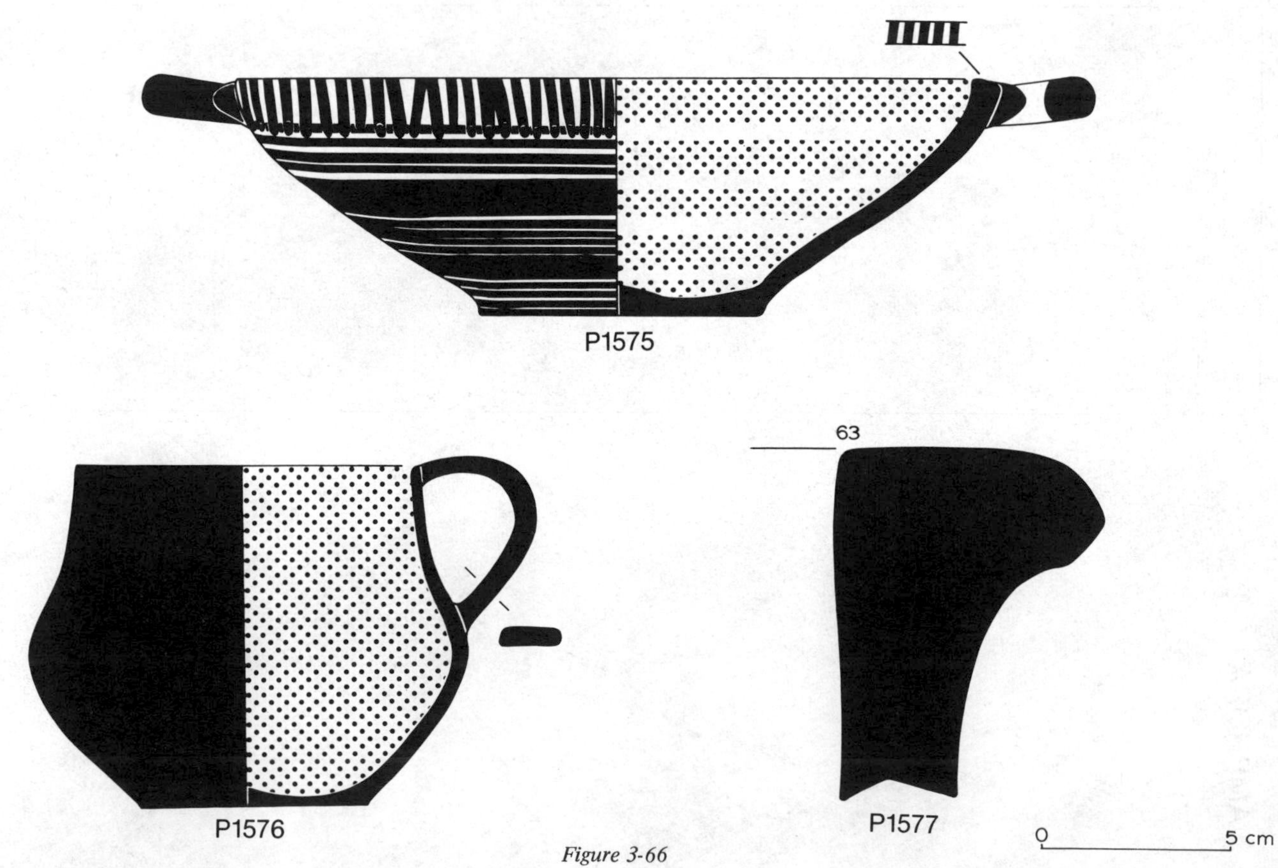

P1575

P1576

P1577

Figure 3-66

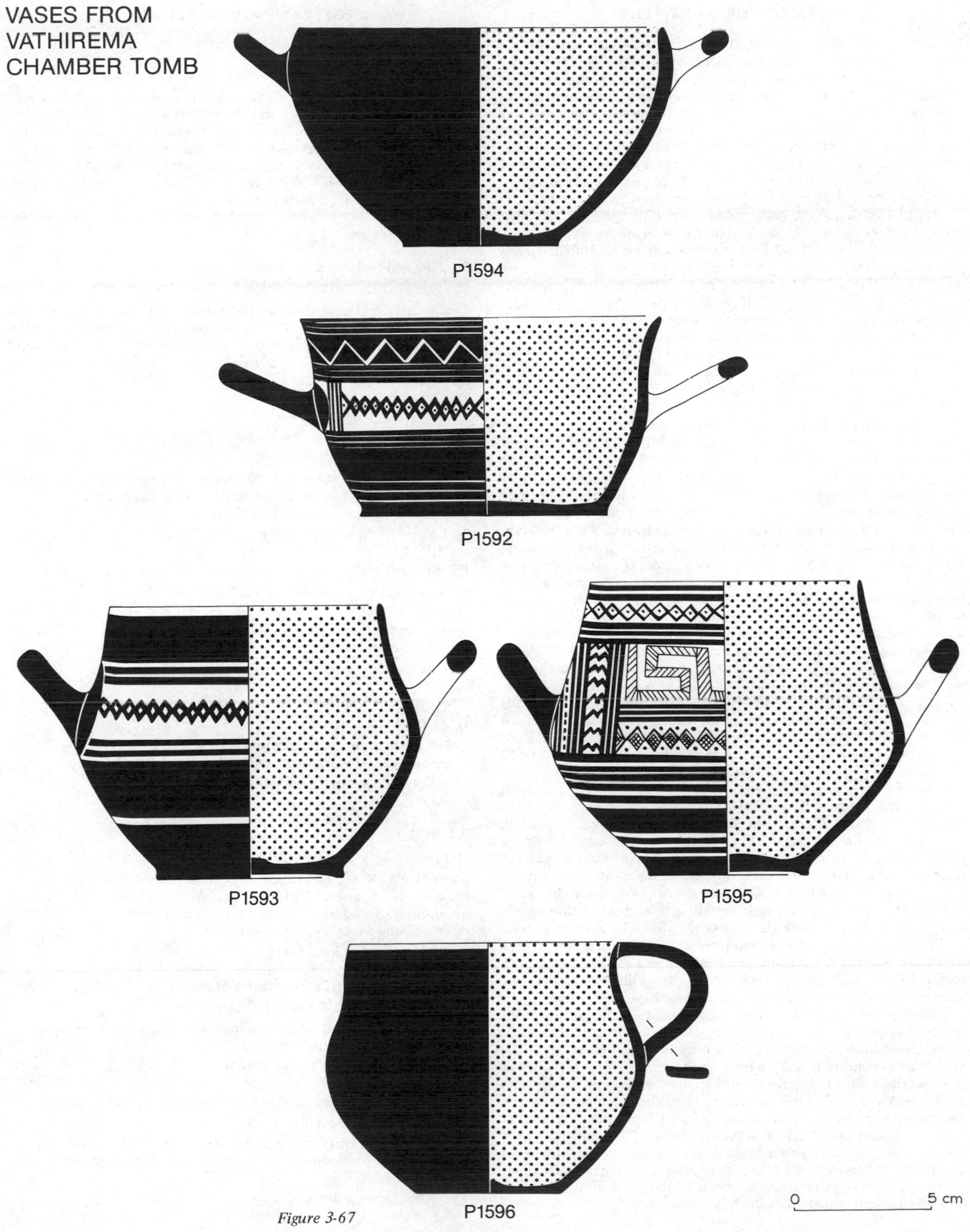
VASES FROM
VATHIREMA
CHAMBER TOMB
P1594
P1592
P1593
P1595
P1596
0
5 cm

Figure 3-67

CATALOG FOR DA POTTERY

Of the approximately 10,000 Dark Age sherds uncovered during the five seasons of excavation at Nichoria, it was possible to include in this catalog only the most representative types. Enough examples of each type of rim or base, for instance, have been included to give the reader an idea of quantity and frequency of occurrences throughout the various periods. Body sherds, unless of exceptional importance for their decoration, have been omitted. The number of rims and bases cataloged should present a general indication of the number of different types of vases for any one period. All the decorated sherds have been included, even in cases where the decoration is too worn to be identified with certainty. Detailed measurements of sherds are given, for it is often through such measurements that the shape of a vase can be identified. Unless otherwise noted, "D." stands for the diameter of the rim or base and "Th." for the thickness of the body of the vase below the rim, or in the case of a body sherd, at its center. The body of a vase usually becomes thicker near the base. Where two thickness measurements are given, the lesser measurement indicates the thickness of the body near the rim, and the larger that of the body farther down, usually at mid-belly. Sometimes an approximation of rim or base diameters is given; in such cases, the rim or base was so damaged that it was impossible to determine its diameter from the diameter chart and an estimate was made.

Identifications of color were made with the aid of the *Munsell Soil Color Charts* (Baltimore 1975), published by the Munsell Color Company, Inc. These color charts were designed primarily for the identification of soil colors, and the color of the ceramic material does not always match exactly with the charts. When this occurs, the range of Munsell colors is indicated. First the Munsell hue is given, followed by the appropriate written definition; for instance, Munsell 5YR 7/8 reddish yellow. If a great number of sherds have the same color, then for the sake of compactness the numeral designation has been omitted, leaving only the verbal description. Thus "reddish yellow clay" is the same as "Munsell 5YR 7/8 reddish yellow." Where the term "reddish yellow clay" has been used, or any other color designation with the word "clay," this refers to the color of the clay *after* firing. The texture of the clay has often been indicated, whether it has fired to a brittle, hard, or soft consistency. The surfaces of the majority of the sherds are very worn; this is indicated by the terms "flaky clay" or "worn surfaces" and designates a rather soft texture to the clay. Hard or brittle texture is so indicated. Sometimes the words "good" or "fine" or "smooth" are used to indicate exceptional preservation of the paint. This often occurs when the clay has been fired exceptionally well to a hard consistency; in such instances the paint is also well preserved and is not flaky, rough, or peeling, as is the case in the majority of examples. The term "reserved band" indicates an undecorated band which can occur on the exterior of vases at the rim, mid-belly, base, or, most frequently, at the interior of the rim. Some vases are slipped; the term "slip" represents a coating of the surface with a thin clay solution, sometimes quite different from the clay of the vase. The purpose of such a slip may be to achieve a smoother surface in order to prepare it for the painted decoration. Much of the slip has been destroyed owing to the high alkaline content of the soil at Nichoria, but where it has survived, its existence and color have been noted.

This Catalog has been divided into 3 major parts: pottery from settlement, pottery from cemeteries, and stray finds. Within these parts, the sherds are classified according to period (DAI, II, II/III, III, Late Geometric); and, within each period, they are divided into sections of homogeneous units, such as groups or deposits associated with structures or other identifiable units. While the excavation was in progress, whole pots or exceptional fragments were cataloged with NP ("Nichoria Pottery") numbers. These numbers are added in parentheses in the Catalog, so that the vases can be easily found in the Museum of Chora, Triphylias (Messenia) where the Dark Age material has been stored. The NP numbers are also listed in numerical order in the Concordance.

POTTERY FROM SETTLEMENT

DARK AGE I

Section A

From Area IVNE. No architecture is associated with this pottery, the majority of which was found in levels 3 and 4 of trenches L23 Uklm and Xklm, with a small portion from level 2 of the baulk between L23 Xkl and Ykl. This area is to the west of Unit IV-3 (LHIIIB) and comprises the courtyard and entrance to Unit IV-1. Some of the pottery comes from under the courtyard floor; the rest is part of the debris from the courtyard floor.

Open Shapes

P1. Rim and body of deep bowl. Fig. 3-6; Pl. 3-6.

H. (pres.) 0.123. Th. 0.007-0.008.

Lower body and base missing. 14 joining frags. Munsell 2.5YR 8/2 white. Brittle flaky clay; slight wheel ridging below rim on exterior, heavy wheel ridging on interior. Frags. of washy thin black paint on exterior and interior. 2 string marks at point of carination on exterior. Rim: Type A1.

L23 Xklm, level 4, lot 4321N.

P2. Rim and body frag. of deep bowl. Fig. 3-2; Pl. 3-1.

H. (pres.) 0.059. D. ca. 0.22.

White flaky clay; color like **P1.** Wheel ridging on exterior under rim and on interior; frags. of washy black paint on exterior; no paint remaining on interior. Rim: Type A1.

L23 Xklm-E2/3, level 2, lot 3356/4.

P3. Rim and body frag. of skyphos or deep bowl. Fig. 3-2; Pl. 3-1.

H. (pres.) 0.045. Th. 0.004. D. ca. 0.19.

Munsell 10YR 8/4 very pale brown. Washy black paint on exterior and interior; possible black band at bottom of body frag.; reserved band inner rim. Rim: Type A2.

L23 Xklm-E2/3, level 2, lot 3356/4.

P4-5. Skyphos rim frags. Fig. 3-2.

D. ca. 0.10.

Color varies from white (**P5**) to very pale brown (**P4**). Flaky clay, worn surfaces. Slight raised band under rim (**P5**). Rim: Type A2.

L23 Xklm-E2/3, level 2, lot 3356/4.

P6. Rim, body, and handle frag. of skyphos or deep bowl. Fig. 3-2; Pl. 3-2.

H. (pres.) 0.053. D. ca. 0.12.

Munsell 2.5YR 8/2-10YR 8/4 dirty white-very pale brown. Handle broken off at body; flaky clay, incrusted surfaces. Wheel ridging on interior. Good light black washy paint exterior and interior; reserved band inner rim. Rim: Type A3.

L23 Xklm, level 4, lot 4321N.

P7. Rim and body frag. of skyphos or deep bowl. Fig. 3-2; Pl. 3-2.

H. (pres.) 0.044. Th. 0.0045. D. ca. 0.15.

Color like **P6.** Wheel ridging on interior. Washy black paint on exterior and interior. Rim: Type A3.

L23 Xklm-E2/3, level 3a, lot 3366/1.

P8. Rim and body frag. of skyphos or deep bowl. Fig. 3-2.

H. (pres.) 0.042. Th. 0.004. D. ca. 0.16.

2 joining frags. Dirty white flaky clay. Wheel ridging on interior. Washy brown paint on exterior; light washy black frags. on interior. Rim: Type A3.

L23 Wklm, level 3, lot 4305.

P9. Skyphos rim frag. Fig. 3-2; Pl. 3-2.
H. (pres.) 0.28. Th. 0.004. D. ca. 0.14.
3 joining frags. Very pale brown flaky clay. Good smooth washy black paint on exterior and interior; reserved band inner rim. Rim: Type A3.
L23 Xklm, level 4, lot 4321N.

P10-12. Rim and body frags. of skyphos or deep bowl. Fig. 3-2.
Th. 0.004. D. ca. 0.16 (**P10-11**), 0.20 (**P12**).
Very pale brown flaky clay; worn surfaces. Frags. of washy black paint exterior and interior. Wheel ridging on interior (**P12**); string marks on exterior under rim (**P10-11**). Rim: Type A3.
L23 Xklm-E2/3, level 3, lot 3356/1-2, 3N; level 3a, lot 3361/1; and L23 Xklm, level 4, lot 4312E.

P13. Skyphos rim and body frag. Fig. 3-2; Pl. 3-2.
H. (pres.) 0.046. Th. 0.004-0.005. D. ca. 0.12.
Munsell 2.5YR 8/2 dirty white. 2 joining frags. Flaky clay; worn surfaces. Frags. of washy light black paint exterior and interior. String marks on exterior under rim. Rim: Type B1.
L23 Xkl/Ykl baulk, level 2, lot 4345.

P14. Rim and body frag. of skyphos or deep bowl. Fig. 3-2; Pl. 3-2.
H. (pres.) 0.045. Th. 0.004. D. ca. 0.10.
Very pale brown flaky clay. No traces paint remaining. Wheel ridging and string marks on exterior. Rim: Type B1.
L23 Xklm-E2/3, level 2, lot 3356/1-2, 3N.

P15-16. Skyphos/deep bowl rim frags. Fig. 3-2.
Th. 0.004 (**P16**), 0.005 (**P15**). D. ca. 0.14.
Very pale brown flaky clay; worn surfaces. Washy light brown paint frags. on exterior and interior. Reserved inner band under rim (**P16**). Wheel ridging on interior; 2 raised bands on exterior under rim (**P15**). Rim: Type B1.
L23 Xklm-E2/3, level 3a, lot 3366/1; L23 Wklm, level 3, tumble lot 4305.

P17. Rim and body frag. of skyphos or deep bowl. Fig. 3-2; Pl. 3-3.
H. (pres.) 0.067. Th. 0.007. D. ca. 0.15.
Reddish yellow exterior; light red core and interior. Very flaky clay; worn surfaces. Frags. black paint exterior. Wheel ridging interior. Rim: Type B2.
L23 Xklm-E2/3, level 2, lot 3356/3C and S.

P18. Rim frag. of skyphos or deep bowl. Fig. 3-2.
Rim mostly broken. Dirty white-very pale brown flaky clay; worn surfaces. Wheel ridging exterior and interior. Faint frags. black paint on exterior. Rim: possibly Type B2.
L23 Xklm-E2/3, level 3a, lot 3366/1.

P19. Rim frag. of skyphos. Pl. 3-3.
H. (pres.) 0.03. D. ca. 0.09.
Dirty white flaky clay with light pink core. Worn surfaces; no traces paint remaining. Rim: Type B3.
L23 Xklm-E2/3, level 2, lot 3356/1-2, 3N.

P20. Rim and body frag. of skyphos or deep bowl. Fig. 3-2; Pl. 3-3.
H. (pres.) 0.041. Th. 0.006. D. ca. 0.20.
Very pale brown flaky clay; worn surfaces. Traces black paint on exterior; no paint remaining on interior. Rim: Type B3.
L23 Xklm-E2/3, level 2, lot 3356/4.

P21. 5 possible deep bowl body frags.
Dirty white-very pale brown flaky clay; worn surfaces. Frags. of washy black paint on exterior and interior. Wheel ridging on interior.
L23 Xklm-E2/3, level 2, lot 3356/4.

P22-23. Rim, body, and handle frags. of possible cups. Fig. 3-3.
H. (pres.) 0.042-0.043. Th. 0.003-0.004. W. handle 0.01.
Munsell 2.5Y 8/2 white (with grayish tinge). Almost straight rim with flat handle. Frags. of washy black paint exterior and interior; no paint on underside of handle. Slight wheel ridging exterior, heavy wheel ridging interior. Rim: Type A.
L23 Xklm-E2/3, level 3a, lot 3366/1; L23 Wklm, level 3a, lot 3372/1-2.

P24. Base and body frag. of skyphos. Fig. 3-3; Pl. 3-5.
D. ca. 0.034. Th. body frag. 0.006.
Semi-high conical foot, about 3/4 preserved. Munsell 10YR 8/4 very pale brown. Flaky clay; worn surfaces. Frags. black paint exterior and interior. Base: Type A.
L23 Xkl/Ykl baulk, level 2, lot 4345.

P25. Skyphos base and body frag. (lower profile). Fig. 3-3; Pl. 3-5.
D. 0.035. Th. lower body 0.005.
Small ringed base. 2 joining frags. Dirty white flaky clay; worn surfaces. Washy black paint frags. on exterior; possible black bands on exterior of body, but badly preserved. Base: Type B.
L23 Xklm-W1/3, level 3, lot 2506.

P26. Base of skyphos or deep bowl. Fig. 3-3; Pl. 3-5.
D. 0.042. Th. body frag. 0.004.
Ringed base. Very pale brown-dirty white flaky clay; worn surfaces. Frags of light washy black paint exterior and possible on interior. Small hub in center of interior. Base: Type B.
L23 Xklm, level 4, lot 4311W.

P27-29. Base frags. of skyphos or deep bowl. Fig. 3-3 (**P27**); Pl. 3-5 (**P27**).
D. ca. 0.04 (**P27-28**), 0.055 (**P29**).
About ½-⅓ preserved. Dirty white flaky clay; worn surfaces. Traces of washy black paint on exterior (**P27**). Base: Type B.
L23 Xklm-E2/3, level 2, lot 3356/2; level 3, lot 3367/1.

P30. Base of skyphos or deep bowl. Fig. 3-3.
D. 0.071. Th. body frag. 0.0045.
Wide ringed base. Munsell 5Y 8/3 pale yellow on underside and 10YR 8/4 very pale brown on interior with light pink core. Flaky clay; worn surfaces. Frags. black paint on exterior; possible frags. washy black paint on interior. Base: Type B.
L23 Wklm, level 3, floor lots 2501, 2504, 2507.

P31-33. Handles of possible deep bowls. Fig. 3-4 (**P31, P32**).
D. 0.012.
Munsell 10YR 8/4 very pale brown. Flaky clay; worn surfaces. Frags. of washy black paint preserved. Handle: Type A (D. over 0.01).
L23 Xklm-E2/3, level 2, lot 3356/3; L23 Wklm, level 3, lot 4305.

P34-36. Handles of possible skyphoi. Fig. 3-4 (**P34, P35**).
D. 0.007 (**P35-36**), 0.008 (**P34**).
Very pale brown flaky clay; worn surfaces. Frags. black paint preserved (**P35**); no paint preserved (**P34, P36**). Handle: Type B (D. under 0.01).
L23 Xklm-E2/3, level 2, lot 3356/3; L23 Xklm-W1/3, level 3, lot 2506.

P37. Zoömorphic handle frag. Fig. 3-4; Pl. 3-24.

L. (pres.) 0.037. W. (pres.) 0.011.

Elliptical handle, about ½ preserved. Munsell 5YR 7/6 reddish yellow. Handle attached at right angles to rim frag. (perhaps belonging to a cup?); 2 projecting knobs (ears?) halfway along handle at point where it begins to curve downward. Frags. black paint preserved on top of handle.

L23 Xklm-E2/3, level 2, lot 3356/3C and S.

P38. Handle of possible cup.

W. 0.013. L. (pres.) 0.03.

Flat handle attached to rim. Very pale brown flaky clay; worn surfaces. No paint preserved.

L23 Xklm, level 4, lot 4311W.

Closed Shapes

P39. Rim frag. of jug. Fig. 3-5.

H. (pres.) 0.024. Th. 0.004-0.005.

Dirty white-very pale brown flaky clay; worn surfaces. No traces paint preserved. Slight hollow (small indentation) on interior of rim. Rim: Type A.

L23 Xklm-E2/3, level 2, lot 3356/1-2, 3N.

P40. Flat base of large jug or amphora. Fig. 3-5.

D. ca. 0.14.

Dirty white-very pale brown flaky clay; worn surfaces. No traces paint preserved. Base: Type A.

L23 Xklm-E2/3, level 2, lot 3356/1-2, 3N.

P41. Flat base of amphora(?) Fig. 3-5.

D. ca. 0.10.

Very pale brown flaky clay on exterior with pinkish tinge on interior; worn surfaces. No traces paint preserved. Wheel ridging on interior. Base: Type B.

L23 Xklm, level 4, lot 4311W.

P42-44. Flat handles from jug or small oinochoe.

W. 0.021 (**P42**), 0.02 (**P43**), 0.015 (**P44**).

Dirty white-very pale brown flaky clay; worn surfaces. Frags. black paint on top and small flute down center of top (**P42**). No paint preserved (**P43-44**). Handle: Type B1.

L23 Wklm, level 3a, lot 3372/1-2.

P45. Round neck handle of amphora with rim frag. Pl. 3-36.

L. (pres.) 0.095. D. ca. 0.022.

About ½ preserved. Munsell 2.5Y 8/2 white. Flaky clay; worn surfaces. No traces paint preserved (once black coated?). Handle pierced by hole near rim; W. hole 0.0035. Handle: Type A.

L23 Xklm, level 4, lot 4312E.

Section B

From Area IVNE. This pottery comes from the area of the later Dark Age reuse of Unit IV-7 (LHIIIB). No architecture can be associated with this pottery which is generally mixed with Dark Age II and some LHIIIB in levels 5, 5c, and 6 of L23 Tmn; levels 6, 7, and 8 of L23 Umn; and levels 5, 5a, and 6 of L23 UVo.

Open Shapes

P46. Decorated body frag. of skyphos or deep bowl. Fig. 3-12.

H. (pres.) 0.03. W. (pres.) 0.029. Th. 0.005.

Dirty white flaky clay. Black band at top; below, frags. of 5 (?) arcs of concentric semi-circles; washy black paint on interior.

L23 Umn, level 7, lots 1140, 1142, 1148, 1254 (combined).

P47. Skyphos body frag.

H. (pres.) 0.043. W. (pres.) 0.042. Th. 0.004.

Reddish yellow flaky clay. 2 black bands at bottom; above, faint frags. of arcs of concentric semi-circles. Good smooth black coating on interior.

L23 Umn, level 7, lots 1140, 1142, 1148, 1254 (combined).

P48. Skyphos body frag.

H. (pres.) 0.037. W. (pres.) 0.022. Th. 0.005.

Very pale brown clay. 2 black bands at bottom; above, solid black paint. No traces paint preserved on interior.

L23 Umn, level 7, lots 1140, 1142, 1148, 1254 (combined).

P49. Decorated body frag. of skyphos or deep bowl. Pl. 3-22.

H. (pres.) 0.024. W. (pres.) 0.037. Th. 0.0055-0.006.

Dirty white flaky clay; worn surfaces. On exterior 2 frags. of arcs of concentric semi-circles in black; no paint preserved on interior.

L23 UVo, level 6, lot 1852.

P50. Decorated body frag. of skyphos(?) Pl. 3-22.

H. (pres.) 0.03. W. (pres.) 0.046. Th. 0.005.

Dirty white to very pale brown flaky clay. On exterior piled triangles in black; no paint remaining on interior.

L23 UVo, level 6, lot 1852.

P51. Rim and body frag. of skyphos.

H. (pres.) 0.03. Th. 0.004. D. ca. 0.10.

Munsell 10YR 8/4 very pale brown. Possible white slip. Good frags. washy black paint on exterior and interior. Rim: Type A2.

L23 Tmn, level 5, lot 1494.

P52-53. Rim and body frags. of skyphos or deep bowl.

H. (pres.) 0.032 (**P52**), 0.035 (**P53**). Th. 0.04. D. ca. 0.20 (**P52**), 0.14 (**P53**).

Dirty white to very pale brown flaky clay. Frags. of washy black paint exterior and interior. Rim: Type A3.

L23 Tmn, level 5, lot 1494.

P54-56. Rim and body frags. of skyphos or deep bowl. Fig. 3-2.

Th. 0.006 (**P54**), 0.004 (**P55, P56**). D. ca. 0.155 (**P54**), 0.14 (**P55**).

Munsell 10YR 8/4 very pale brown. Washy black paint exterior and interior. **P55** has reserved band on exterior under rim and possible reserved band on inner rim. **P54** has wheel ridging on interior. Rim Type B1.

L23 Tmn, level 5, lot 1486; L23 Tmn, level 5c. lot 1855; L23 UVo, level 5a, lot 1499; level 6, lot 1852.

P57-61. Rim frags. of skyphos or deep bowl. Fig. 3-2 (**P57, P58, P59**).

Similar to **P17** and **P18**. Rim: Type B2.

L23 Tmn, level 5, lot 1486; level 6, lot 1874; level 5C, lots 1483, 1485 (combined); L23 UVo, level 5a, lot 1493.

P62. Skyphos rim frag. Fig. 3-2; Pl. 3-3.

H. (pres.) 0.026. Th. 0.004.

Dirty white flaky clay. On exterior black band under rim; below, reserved band; washy black paint on interior. Rim: Type B3.

L23 Tmn, level 5c, lots 1483, 1485 (combined).

P63-65. Rim frags. of skyphoi or deep bowls. Fig. 3-2 (**P63, P65**).

D. ca. 0.12 (**P63**), 0.015 (**P64**), 0.23 (**P65**).

Dirty white to very pale brown flaky clay. Frags. of washy black paint exterior and interior. Rim: Type B3.

L23 UVo, level 6, lot 1852.

P66. Rim and body frag. of skyphos or deep bowl. Fig. 3-2; Pl. 3-3.
H. (pres.) 0.035. Th. 0.005. D. ca. 0.14.
Reddish yellow flaky clay; worn surfaces. Frags. of light brown paint on exterior; good brown coating on interior. Rim: Type C1.
L23 Tmn, level 5c, lot 1855.

P67-68. Rim frags. similar to **P66**. Fig. 3-2.
Rim: Type C1.
L23 Tmn, level 5, lot 1487.

P69. Rim frag. of skyphos or deep bowl. Fig. 3-2; Pl. 3-3.
H. (pres.) 0.019. Th. 0.004. D. ca. 0.20.
Dirty white to very pale brown flaky clay; worn surfaces. No traces paint remaining. 2 incisions under rim on exterior. Rim: Type C2 (like Type C1 but with incisions under rim).
L23 Tmn, level 5, lot 1487.

P70. Rim frag. similar to **P69**. Fig. 3-2.
D. ca. 0.12.
Rim: Type C2.
L23 UVo, level 5a, lot 1493.

P71. Rim frag. of skyphos or deep bowl. Fig. 3-2; Pl. 3-3.
H. (pres.) 0.024. Th. 0.006. D. ca. 0.13.
Dirty white to very pale brown flaky clay; worn surfaces. Frags. of black paint preserved on interior only. Rim: Type C3.
L23 UVo, level 6, lot 1852.

P72. Rim frag. of skyphos or deep bowl. Fig. 3-2; Pl. 3-3.
H. (pres.) 0.023. Th. 0.004. D. ca. 0.13.
Dirty white flaky clay; worn surfaces. Frags. black paint exterior; reserved band inner rim. Rim: Type C3.
L23 UVo, level 6, lot 1852.

P73. Rim frag. of skyphos or deep bowl. Fig. 3-2.
D. ca. 0.15.
Similar to **P71** but with frags. black paint on exterior. Rim: Type C3.
L23 UVo, level 6, lot 1852.

P74-75. Skyphos base frags. Fig. 3-3 (**P74**).
D. 0.048 (**P74**), 0.08 (**P75**).
High conical feet. Dirty white to very pale brown clay. No traces paint remaining. Base: Type A.
L23 Tmn, level 6, lot 1874.

P76-79. Bases of deep bowls. Fig. 3-3 (**P76, P78, P79**).
D. ca. 0.06-0.08.
Ringed feet. Dirty white flaky clay. Traces of washy black paint on exterior. Base: Type B.
L23 Umn, level 7, lots 1140, 1142, 1148, 1254 (combined).

P80-82. Skyphos base frags. Fig. 3-3 (**P80**).
D. 0.06 (**P80**), ca. 0.075 (**P81**), ca. 0.08 (**P82**).
Ringed feet. Dirty white to very pale brown flaky clay; worn surfaces. **P81** has orange-pink core. Frags. washy black paint exterior and interior. Base: Type B.
L23 UVo, level 5, lot 1488.

P83. Skyphos base. Fig. 3-3.
D. 0.0685.
2 joining frags. Very slightly ringed foot, almost flat. Very pale brown clay. Possible frags. black paint interior. Base: Type C.
L23 UVo, level 5a, lot 1493.

P84. Large pedestal base with very high conical foot. Fig. 3-4.
D. ca. 0.062.
Base broken and only about 1/5 preserved. Reddish yellow clay. On exterior good streaky to washy black paint; traces black paint on interior; no paint on underside of base. Possibly belongs to large pedestalled krater.
L23 Umn, level 7, lots 1140, 1142, 1148, 1254 (combined).

P85. Handle and body frag. of skyphos or deep bowl. Fig. 3-4.
D. 0.011-0.012.
Reddish yellow flaky clay; worn surfaces. Frags. brown paint on handle; good brown paint on interior of body frag. Wheel ridging on interior. Body frag. carinated just below handle. Handle: Type A.
L23 Tmn, level 6, lot 1883.

P86. 6 handle frags. of skyphoi or deep bowls.
D. ca. 0.01-0.16.
Dirty white to very pale brown flaky clay; worn surfaces. Frags. black paint preserved. Handle: Type A.
L23 Tmn, level 5, lot 1494; L23 Umn, level 7, lots 1140, 1142, 1148, 1254 (combined).

P87. 2 handle frags. similar to **P86**. Fig. 3-4.
Handle: Type A.
L23 UVo, level 5a, lot 1493.

P88. Skyphos handle frag.
D. 0.006.
Dirty white flaky clay. Frags. of washy black paint preserved. Handle: Type B.
L23 Tmn, level 5, lot 1494.

P89. Zoömorphic handle frag. Fig. 3-4; Pl. 3-24.
D. ca. 0.021.
Elliptical handle, about ½ preserved. Munsell 2.5YR 6/8 light red; flaky clay. No traces paint preserved. 2 projecting ears halfway along handle. On either side of ears on top of handle are incisions (5 preserved) running crosswise.
L23 Tmn, level 5, lot 1494.

P90. Zoömorphic handle frag. (possibly from a jug) attached to rim. Fig. 3-4; Pl. 3-24.
W. (pres.) 0.015.
Elliptical handle, about ½ preserved. Dirty white flaky clay. Traces of light brown paint preserved on handle. 2 ears project from top of handle at point where handle begins to turn downward.
L23 Umn, level 8, lots 1144, 1145, 1251 (combined).

Closed Shapes

P91. Jug rim frag. Fig. 3-5.
H. (pres.) 0.018. Th. 0.004. D. ca. 0.075.
Dirty white flaky clay. Possible white slip. Frags. of washy black paint on exterior, top of rim, and interior lip of rim. Rim: Type B.
L23 Tmn, level 5c, lot 1855.

P92. Flat base (amphora?).
D. ca. 0.10-0.11.
About 1/5 preserved. Very pale brown clay. No traces paint preserved. Base: Type A.
L23 UVo, level 6, lot 1852.

P93. Flat base (jug?). Fig. 3-5.
D. 0.046.

About ½ preserved. Very pale brown flaky clay; worn surfaces. Circular incisions on interior. No traces paint preserved. Base: Type B.

L23 UVo, level 5a, lot 1493.

P94. Rope handle frag. of oniochoe or jug. Pl. 3-36.

D. ca. 022.

Round to elliptical with large twists to the rope (i.e., gives the impression of a heavy twisted cord). Lower part of hande preserved where it attaches to the shoulder of the vessel. Reddish yellow flaky clay; very worn surfaces. No traces paint remaining.

L23 Tmn, level 5, lot 1494.

P95. 10 flat handle frags. from jug or small oinochoe. Fig. 3-5.

W. (pres.) 0.012-0.018.

Dirty white to very pale brown flaky clay. Frags. of washy black paint preserved. One frag. has small flute down center of handle. Handle: Type B1.

L23 Tmn, level 5c, lot 1855; L23 UVo, level 7, lots 1140, 1142, 1148, 1254 (combined).

P96. Neck handle of amphora with rim frag. attached. Fig. 3-5.

D. 0.0285.

Round. Light gray brittle clay. Rim: Type C1; Handle: Type A.

L23 UVo, level 5a, lot 1493.

Coarse Ware

P97. Flat base (perhaps from small coarse amphora). Fig. 3-6.

D. 0.06.

Light red clay with inclusions. Partly burned. Base: Type B of closed fine ware (cf. **P41**).

L23 UVo, level 6, lot 1852.

P98. Round belly handle, possibly from amphora. Fig. 3-6.

D. 0.02-0.021.

Light red clay with inclusions. Handle: Type A.

L23 UVo, level 6, lot 1852.

Section C

From Area IVNW. A few DAI sherds were found at the bottom of the DAII dump to the north of Unit IV-5.

Open Shapes

P99. Complete upper profile of skyphos. Fig. 3-11; Pl. 3-12.

H. (pres.) 0.056. Th. 0.005. D. ca. 0.102.

Munsell 2.5Y 8/2 white. Decorated zone in field between handles; decoration consists of a wavy line in black paint; washy black paint above and below decorated zone and on interior. Carination below handles. High upswung handles found separately in same lot (D. handles ca. 0.01). Rim: Type B1.

L23 Sop, level 3, lot 3404/1.

P100. Rim, body frag., and handle frag. of skyphos.

H. (pres.) 0.03. Th. 0.005. D. ca. 0.10.

Dirty white clay. Washy black paint exterior and interior. Rim: Type A3.

L23 Sop, level 3, lot 3404/1.

P101. Upper profile of skyphos or deep bowl. Fig. 3-7.

H. (pres.) 0.091. Th. ca. 0.006-0.0075. D. ca. 0.17.

Reddish yellow clay. Possible undecorated band in field between handles; streaky black-brown paint above and below undecorated band. Good smooth streaky black-brown paint on interior. Reserved band inner rim. Wheel ridging interior. Rim: Type A3.

L23 Sop, level 3, lot 3404/5-6.

Closed Shapes

P102. Jug rim, handle, and neck frag.

H. (pres.) 0.057. Th. neck 0.004-0.005. W. Handle 0.023.

Reddish yellow clay with pinkish tinge. Flat handle with straight rim. Frags. brown paint on exterior; streaky black-brown paint on inner rim. Rim: Type A; Handle: Type B1.

L23 Sop, level 3, lot 3404/5-6.

Section D

From Area IVNW. A few DAI sherds were found below the floor of Unit IV-5 (DAIII).

Open Shapes

P103. Rim, handle, and body frag. of skyphos or deep bowl.

H. (pres.) 0.049. Th. 0.035-0.004. D. ca. 0.18-0.20.

Very pale brown to reddish yellow clay. Good smooth surfaces. Frags. washy brown-black paint exterior and interior. Possible frag. wavy line in decorated zone between handles. Rim: Type A3.

L23 Skl, level 5, lot 4521/1.

P104-5. Rim frags. of skyphoi or deep bowls.

Th. 0.005, D. ca. 0.13 (**P104**).

Dirty white to very pale brown clay. Frags. streaky brown-black paint exterior and interior. Rim: Type B3.

L23 Skl, level 5, lot 4521/1.

P106. Decorated skyphos body frag. Fig. 3-12.

H. (pres.) 0.015. Th. 0.005.

Reddish yellow clay. On exterior, 6 frags. of arcs of concentric semi-circles in brown; no paint preserved on interior.

L23 Skl, level 5, lot 4521/1.

P107. Skyphos body frag.

H. (pres.) 0.037. Th. 0.004.

Broken just short of rim. Very pale brown clay. Washy black paint exterior and interior. Slight ridging interior.

L23 Skl, level 5, lot 4521/1.

P108. Skyphos base.

D. 0.0435.

Very pale brown clay. Good washy light brown paint exterior and interior. Slight hub in center of underside of base. Base: Type B.

L23 Skl, level 5, lot 4521/1.

Section E

From Area IVNW. A good group of DAI sherds was found in levels 2 and 3 of Room 2 and level 3 of Room 4 of Unit IV-6. This house, originally belonging to the LHIIIB period, was reused in DAIII times. The majority of the pottery from the reuse of Room 2 is DAIII, but with some DAI admixture.

Open Shapes

P109. Rim and body frag. of skyphos or deep bowl. Fig. 3-2.

H. (pres.) 0.046. Th. ca. 0.008-0.009. D. ca. 0.13.

Dirty white flaky clay; worn surfaces. Frags. of washy black paint exterior; possible undecorated band in field between handles; no

paint preserved on interior. Wheel ridging interior. Rim: Type A1.
L23 Tj, level 2, lot 4417/5.

P110. Rim and body frag. of skyphos or deep bowl.
H. (pres.) 0.031. Th. 0.0045-0.005. D. ca. 0.18.
Reddish yellow clay. Good light streaky black-brown paint exterior and interior. Rim: Type A2.
L23 Tj, level 3, lot 4417/1.

P111. Upper profile of skyphos or deep bowl. Fig. 3-8; Pl. 3-13.
H. (pres.) 0.063. Th. 0.005. D. ca. 0.18.
Tip of rim missing. Reddish yellow clay. In the field between handles decoration consists of wavy line in streaky black paint; above and below decorated zone is a streaky black coating; good streaky black coating on interior. Hard clay, well fired with good smooth surfaces. Paint is fine and lustrous. Perhaps an Attic import. Rim: Type A3.
L23 Tj, level 3, lot 4419/1.

P112-15. Rim and body frags. of skyphoi or deep bowls.
Th. 0.003 (**P113-15**), 0.005 (**P112**). D. ca. 0.11 (**P115**), 0.12 (**P114**), 0.13 (**P113**), 0.19 (**P112**).
Reddish yellow clay; worn surfaces. Frags. washy black-brown paint on exterior and interior. Rim: Type A3.
L23 Tj, level 2, Room 2, lot 4417/5; L23 Tj, level 3, lot 4476/1.

P116. Upper profile of skyphos. Fig. 3-7.
H. (pres.) 0.05. Th. 0.003. D. ca. 0.10.
Very pale brown flaky clay; worn surfaces. Possible undecorated zone in field between handles; good streaky brown paint above and below; same paint on interior. Carinated body; tops of handles broken off. Rim: Type B1.
L23 Tj, level 3, lot 4476/1.

P117. Rim frag. of skyphos or deep bowl. Fig. 3-2.
H. (pres.) 0.035. Th. 0.005. D. ca. 0.14.
White flaky clay; worn surfaces. No traces paint preserved. Rim: Type B2.
L23 Tj, level 2, lot 4417/5.

P118. Rim frag. of skyphos.
H. (pres.) 0.022. Th. 0.0035.
Reddish yellow to very pale brown clay. Good light streaky brown paint on exterior and interior. Rim: Type B3.
L23 Tj, level 2, lot 4417/5.

P119. Rim frag. of skyphos.
H. (pres.) 0.019. Th. 0.006-0.0065.
Reddish yellow clay. Frags. streaky black paint exterior and interior. Rim: Type C1.
L23 Tj, level 3, lot 4476/1.

P120. Skyphos base frag.
D. 0.045.
About ½ preserved. Reddish yellow clay with pinkish tinge. Good light brown paint on exterior. Base: Type A.
L23 Tj, level 3, lot 4476/1.

P121-22. Handles of skyphoi or deep bowls.
D. 0.012.
White flaky clay. Frags. of streaky-brown paint (**P122**). Handle: Type A.
L23 Tj, level 2, lot 4417/5.

P123-24. Handles of skyphoi.
D. 0.007.
Very pale brown flaky clay. Frags. of washy black paint. Handle: Type B.
L23 Tj, level 2, lot 4417/5.

Section F

From Area IVSW. A group of DAI sherds was found in the generally mixed (LHIIIA/IIIB) levels of L23 OPe and the baulk between OPe and OPf. Farther S, on and over the edge of the hill in L23 Nc and Ocd, additional DAI sherds were found, also mixed with Mycenaean material.

Open Shapes

P125. Complete profile (with base missing) of skyphos. Fig. 3-10; Pl. 3-10.
H. (pres.) 0.089. Th. 0.004 (top)-0.005 (bottom). D. ca. 0.12.
Fine reddish yellow clay with pinkish tinge. White slip. Good fine streaky black-brown paint on exterior and interior. Undecorated zone in field between handles; reserved band inner rim. Rim: Type A2.
L23 OPe/OPf baulk, level 2, lot 4075/9-10.

P126. Upper profile (missing handles) of skyphos. Fig. 3-11; Pl. 3-14.
H. (pres.) 0.043. Th. 0.004. D. ca. 0.12.
Fine pinkish buff clay; smooth surfaces, not flaky or worn. Decorated zone (probably in field between handles) consists of a wavy line in faded black paint; above and below, streaky black-brown paint; same paint on interior. Reserved band inner rim. Possibly an Attic import. Rim: Type A3.
L23 OPe, level 3, lot 3272/3-5.

P127. Upper profile (missing handles) of skyphos or deep bowl. Fig. 3-9; Pl. 3-15.
H. (pres.) 0.056. Th. 0.005. D. ca. 0.18.
Reddish yellow clay with pinkish tinge. White slip. Decorated zone (probably in field between handles) consists of a wavy line in light brown paint; above and below, a light brown coating; on interior light streaky brown paint. Reserved band inner rim. Rim: Type A3.
L23 OPe, level 3, lot 3290/1-2.

P128-32. Skyphos rim frags.
D. ca. 0.10 (**P128, P129**), 0.14 (**P130, P132**).
Reddish yellow clay; **P130, P131** have a pinkish core. White slip (**P130**). **P130** has possible undecorated zone in field between handles. Good streaky black-brown paint on exterior and interior. **P132** has possible reserved band inner rim. Rim: Type A3.
L23 OPe, level 3, lot 3272/3-5.

P133-36. Rim frags. of skyphoi and deep bowls.
D. ca. 0.13 (**P135**), 0.14 (**P133**), 0.17 (**P136**), 0.18 (**P134**).
Very pale light brown to reddish yellow clay. Good streaky black-brown paint on exterior and interior. Wheel ridging interior (**P134, P136**). Rim: Type A3.
L23 OPe/OPf baulk, level 2, lot 4075/8, 9, 10.

P137-38. Deep bowl rim frags.
Th. 0.005. D. ca. 0.16 (**P138**), 0.20 (**P137**).
Reddish yellow fine clay; good smooth surfaces; streaky black-brown paint exterior and interior. **P137** has been fired to a light gray color on the exterior and to a dark gray on the interior; possible traces of white slip; flaky clay, worn surfaces; no traces paint remaining. Rim: Type B1.

L23 OPe, level 3 NW, lot 3290/1-2; L23 OPe/OPf baulk, level 2, lot 4075/8.

P139-44. Rim frags. of skyphoi and deep bowls.
D. 0.10 (**P142**), 0.12 (**P143**), 0.13 (**P144**), 0.15 (**P139-41**).
Dirty white to very pale brown clay. Streaky and washy black-brown paint on exterior and interior. Possible frags. white slip (**P139-41**). Reserved band inner rim (**P142**). Wheel ridging interior (**P143**). Rim: Type B3.
L23 OPe, level 3, lots 3272/3-5, 3272/1-2 NW.

P145. Deep bowl rim frag.
H. (pres.) 0.021. Th. 0.005. D. ca. 0.18.
Flaky worn clay fired to a gray color. Frags. black paint exterior and interior. Rim: Type C1.
L23 OPe, level 3, lot 3272/3-5.

P146. Skyphos rim frag.
D. ca. 0.14.
Very pale brown clay. Rim: Type C2.
L23 OPe/OPf baulk, level 2, lot 4075/8-10.

P147. Skyphos rim frag.
H. (pres.) 0.018. Th. 0.005. D. ca. 0.13.
Reddish yellow clay. Good smooth frags. black paint exterior and interior. Rim: Type C3.
L23 OPe, level 3, lot 3272/3-5.

P148. Possible krater rim frags. Fig. 3-3.
H. (pres.) 0.024. D. ca. 0.22.
Very pale brown clay. White slip. Frags. washy black paint on exterior and interior.
L23 OPe/OPf baulk, level 2, lot 4075/8-10.

P149. Upper profile of skyphos or deep bowl. Fig. 3-8; Pl. 3-15.
H. (pres.) 0.059. Th. 0.005 (top)-0.0065 (bottom). D. ca. 0.018(?)
Tip of rim and most of handles missing. Reddish yellow clay. Decorated zone in field between handles consists of a wavy line in faded black paint; above and below, streaky black-brown coating; same paint on interior. Rim: Type B2(?)
L23 OPe, level 3 NW, lot 3290/1-2.

P150. Decorated skyphos body frag. Fig. 3-12; Pl. 3-15.
H. (pres.) 0.051. Th. 0.004.
Reddish yellow clay. Decorated zone is probably in the field between the handles; decoration is wavy line in black paint; below, frags. of a washy black coating; good streaky black-brown paint on interior. Body frag. carinated below decorated zone.
L23 OPe, level 3 NW, lot 3290/1-2.

P151. Skyphos rim and body frag.
H. (pres.) 0.022. Th. 0.004. D. ca. 0.12.
Very pale brown clay. Light brown paint frags. exterior and interior; reserved band inner rim. Rim: Type A3.
L23 Nc, level 3, lot 4110/2E.

P152. Decorated skyphos body frag.
H. (pres.) 0.03. Th. 0.007.
Very pale brown clay. Decorated zone (probably between handles) consists of a wavy line in faded black paint; above and below, washy black paint; same paint on interior.
L23 Nc, level 3, lot 4110/lE.

P153. Decorated skyphos(?) body frag.
Reddish yellow clay. On exterior are frags. of 2 arcs of concentric semi-circles. Possible black paint on interior.
L23 Nc, level 3, lot 4112/1E.

P154. Decorated skyphos body frag. with handle stump. Fig. 3-12; Pl. 3-16.
H. (pres.) 0.043. Th. 0.005.
Clay fired to a gray color on exterior and interior surfaces with reddish yellow core. Decorated zone of wavy line in black-brown paint in field between handles; above and below, good streaky black-brown paint; same paint on interior.
L23 Nc, level 3, lot 4112/2E.

P155. Decorated skyphos body frag.
H. (pres.) 0.0345. Th. 0.004.
Dirty white to very pale brown clay. Decorated zone consists of a wavy line in black paint; above and below, faded black coating; possible frags. black paint on interior.
L23 Ocd, level 1, lot 4103/5C and N.

P156. Decorated skyphos body frag.
H. (pres.) 0.0385. Th. 0.004.
Very pale brown to reddish yellow clay. Decorated zone consists of a wavy line in faded black paint; above and below, frags. of black coating; frags. black paint on interior.
L23 Ocd, level 1, lot 4103/5C and N.

P157-58. Skyphos bases.
D. ca. 0.055.
Reddish yellow flaky clay. Base: Type A.
L23 OPe, level 3, lot 3272/3-5.

P159. Skyphos base.
D. 0.047.
Reddish yellow flaky clay. Base: Type B.
L23 OPe, level 3, lot 3272/3-5.

P160. Handle and body frag. of skyphos or deep bowl.
D. 0.011.
Dirty white clay. Frags. washy black paint. Yellowish white slip. Wheel ridging on interior of body frag. Handle: Type A.
L23 OPe/OPf baulk, level 2, lot 4075/9-10.

Closed Shapes

P161. Decorated wall frag. of amphora. Fig. 3-14; Pl. 3-37.
H. (pres.) 0.093. Th. 0.008-0.0085.
Reddish yellow clay. Decorated zone is probably in the middle of the belly in the field between the handles. Decoration is of a wavy line in light brown paint between 2 brown bands; above and below is a monochrome brown coating. White slip.
L23 OPe, level 3, lot 3272/1-2NW.

Coarse Ware

P162. Ribbed handle frag. Fig. 3-6; Pl. 3-38.
W. (pres.) 0.034.
Flat handle with light red clay burned to a dark gray in the core. One rib down center of handle. Handle: Type B1.
L23 OPe, level 3, lot 3272/3-5.

P163. Incised handle frag. Fig. 3-6; Pl. 3-38.
W. (pres.) 0.025.
Flat handle; burned clay. 3 shallow incisions along top of handle. Handle: Type B2.
L23 OPe, level 3, lot 3272/3-5.

P164. Wall frag. with nipple decoration. Pl. 3-38.

H. (pres.) 0.095. Th. 0.011.

Light red coarse clay with inclusions, burned slightly on exterior. Nipple projects straight out from body and is pointed (as opposed to those of Middle Helladic coarse ware which curve slightly and are more rounded).

L23 OPe, level 3, lot 3272/3-5.

Section G

From Area IVSW. A small but good group of DAI sherds was found in levels 3, 6, and 7 of L23 Shi and level 5 of L23 Thi. These levels also contained much LHIIIA-B pottery and belong to Unit IV-9 of the same period. The building was reused in DAIII times.

Open Shapes

P165. (NP73). Complete upper profile of skyphos. Fig. 3-7; Pl. 3-9.

H. (pres.) 0.091. Th. 0.004. D. 0.17.

Munsell 5YR 7/8 reddish yellow. Possible decoration of wavy line in zone between handles; above and below, streaky black-brown paint; same on interior. White slip on exterior. Rim: Type A3.

L23 Shi, level 6, lot 2407.

P166. Rim and body frag. of skyphos.

H. (pres.) 0.0365. Th. 0.0035. D. ca. 0.14.

Dirty white to very pale brown flaky clay; worn surfaces. Frags. streaky black-brown paint exterior and interior. Possible frags. of pale brown slip on exterior. Rim: Type A3.

L23 Shi, level 3, lot 2357.

P167. Upper profile of deep bowl. Fig. 3-6; Pl. 3-7.

H. (pres.) 0.11. Th. 0.005 (top)-0.007 (bottom). D. ca. 0.25.

Munsell 5YR 7/8 reddish yellow. Worn surfaces; flaky clay, burned gray in places around rim. Frags. of brown paint on exterior and interior. Wheel ridging interior. Rim: Type A3.

L23 Thi, level 5, lots 2389, 2401.

P168-69. Skyphos rim frags.

D. ca. 0.16 (**P168**), 0.12 (**P169**).

Reddish yellow flaky clay. Frags. streaky black-brown paint exterior and interior. Rim: Type A3.

L23 Thi, level 5, lots 2389, 2400.

P170. Rim and body frag. of skyphos.

H. (pres.) 0.026. Th. 0.003. D. ca. 0.10.

Reddish yellow clay. Good streaky black-brown paint on exterior and interior; reserved band inner rim. Possible undecorated band on exterior in field between handles. Rim: Type B1.

L23 Shi, level 7, lot 2408.

P171. Upper profile of skyphos. Fig. 3-8.

H. (pres.) 0.072. Th. 0.005. D. ca. 0.12.

Very pale brown flaky clay; worn surfaces. Frags. washy black paint exterior and interior. Wheel ridging interior. Rim: Type B2(?)

L23 Shi, level 3, lot 2357.

P172-73. Skyphos rim frags.

D. ca. 0.11 (**P172**), 0.16 (**P173**).

Dirty white to very pale brown flaky clay; worn surfaces. Frags. of washy black paint exterior and interior. Rim: Type B2.

L23 Shi, level 7, lot 2408; L23 Thi, level 5, lot 2411.

P174-75. Skyphos rim frags.

Th. 0.004. D. ca. 0.13.

Reddish yellow flaky and gritty clay. Frags. of streaky black paint exterior and interior. Rim: Type B3.

L23 Thi, level 5, lots 2400, 2411.

P176. Decorated skyphos body frag.

H. (pres.) 0.034. Th. 0.0045.

Very pale brown to reddish yellow clay. Decorated zone (possibly in field between handles) consists of a thick wavy line in black paint; above and below, good black coating; same coating on interior. White slip on exterior. Good smooth surfaces.

L23 Shi, level 7, lot 2408.

P177. Decorated skyphos body frag.

H. (pres.) 0.017. Th. 0.004.

Very pale brown flaky clay. Decoration consists of a wavy line in faded black paint above a black band; faded black coating on interior.

L23 Shi, level 7, lot 2408.

P178. 3 skyphos bases.

Type B.

L23 Thi, level 5, lots 2389, 2401, 2411.

P179. Handle frag. of deep bowl.

D. 0.015.

Reddish yellow flaky and gritty clay; worn surfaces. Frags. streaky black brown paint preserved. Handle: Type A.

L23 Thi, level 5, lot 1957.

Closed Shapes

P180. Rim and neck frag. of jug.

H. (pres.) 0.071. Th. 0.007-0.01. D. ca. 0.15.

Reddish yellow clay with pink core. Fine smooth streaky black-brown paint on exterior extends to inner lip of rim. Rim: Type A.

L23 Shi, level 7, lot 2408.

Coarse Ware

P181. Rim frag. Fig. 3-6.

H. (pres.) 0.075. Th. 0.009. D. ca. 0.18 (uneven).

Reddish yellow clay with grayish blue core; on exterior, fired black on one half and red on the other. Rim: Type A.

L23 Thi, level 5, lot 2389.

Section H

From Area III. A good group of DAI sherds comes from the lower hill wash and rubbish tip connected with Unit III-4 (LHIIIB). In addition, a few scattered sherds were found in the floor deposit and lowest debris of the same unit.

Open Shapes

P182. Rim and decorated body frag. of skyphos. Fig. 3-12.

Th. 0.005. D. ca. 0.12.

Very pale brown clay. Decoration quite worn but perhaps of the metope-triglyph type. Frags. of 2 black vertical lines form the triglyph, while frags. of 2 arcs of concentric semi-circles (hand drawn?) form the metope decoration. Black band under rim; washy black coating on interior. Rim: Type A2(?)

K24 Xy, level 2, lot 4369/1-2a,b.

P183. Skyphos rim frag. Fig. 3-12.

H. (pres.) 0.034. Th. 0.0035. D. ca. 0.12.

Reddish yellow clay. Decorated zone (probably in field between the handles) consists of angular wavy line (almost wolf's tooth)

in light brown paint; above, streaky brown paint; same paint on interior; reserved band inner rim. Rim: Type A3.
K24 Xy, level 2, lot 4370/1-2.

P184. Decorated skyphos body frag.
Th. 0.003.
Very pale brown clay. Decorated zone of light brown wavy line is flanked by 2 bands of the same color. Good light brown coating on interior; wheel ridging on interior.
K24 Xy, level 2, lot 4370/3-4.

P185. Decorated skyphos body frag. Fig. 3-12.
Broken just short of rim. Very pale brown clay. Possible double row of light brown wavy lines in decorated zone between handles; above, light brown coating; frags. of reddish brown paint on interior. Paint probably originally a deeper red.
K24 Xy, level 2, lot 4370/1-2.

P186. Decorated frag. of deep bowl.
Th. 0.006 (top)-0.007 (bottom).
Dirty white to very pale brown clay. Decorated zone of wavy line in faded black paint with 2 black bands above and below. Possible frags. of black paint on interior.
K24 Xy, level 2, lot 4369/1-2a,b.

P187. 6 skyphos body frags. Fig. 3-12.
Very pale brown clay. All have undecorated zones on the exterior (possibly in the field between the handles) with black coating above and below; frags. of black paint on the interior.
K24 Xy, level 2, lots 4369/1-2a,b, 4370/1-4.

P188. Rim and body frag. of skyphos.
D. ca. 0.10.
Very pale brown clay. Rim: Type A2.
K24 Xy, level 2, lot 4370/3-4.

P189. Skyphos rim frag.
Tip of rim missing. Rim: Type A2(?)
K24 Xy, level 2, lot 4369/1-2.

P190. 2 skyphos rim frags.
D. ca. 0.10.
Very pale brown clay. Rim: Type A3.
K24 Xy, level 2, lot 4370/1-4.

P191. Skyphos rim frag.
Type B3.
K24 Xy, level 2, lot 4370/1-2.

P192. Skyphos base.
Type A.
K24 Xy, level 2, lot 4370/3-4.

P193. Decorated rim and body frag. of skyphos. Fig. 3-12.
H. (pres.) 0.03. Th. ca. 0.003. D. ca. 0.12 (uneven).
Very pale brown flaky clay. Thin black band on exterior under rim with probable frag. of cross-hatching to the right. There may be a second register of decoration below, but it is too worn and broken for identification. The decoration begins right under the rim and thus is on the neck of the vase rather than in the usual position between the handles. Frags. black paint on interior; possible reserved band at inner rim.
K24 Wy/K25 Wa baulk, level 3, lot 4381/3.

P194-95. Decorated skyphos body frags. Fig. 3-12.
Decorated zone (probably in field between handles) consists of thin wavy line.
K24 Wy/K25 Wa baulk, level 3, lot 4381/3.

P196-99. Skyphos rim frags.
D. ca. 0.12-0.16.
Type A3.
K24 Wy/K25 Wa baulk, level 3, lot 4381/3; K24 Wy/Xy-K25 Wa/Xa baulk, level 3, lot 4390; K24 Yy/K25 Yab baulk, level 2, lot 4352.

P200. Skyphos rim frag.
Very worn and broken; possible Type B1.
K24 Wy/K25 Wa, level 3, lot 4381/3.

P201. Upper profile of deep bowl. Fig. 3-10.
H. (pres.) 0.116. D. ca. 0.15.
Munsell 5YR 7/8 reddish yellow. Flaky gritty clay; worn surfaces. Frags. of brown paint on exterior; no paint preserved on interior but probably also coated with brown paint. Wheel ridging on interior. Rim: Type A3.
K25 Xa, level 3, lot 4365.

P202-4. Rims of skyphoi or deep bowls.
D. ca. 0.14-0.15.
Very pale brown clay. Type B3.
K24 Wy/K25 Wa, level 3, lot 4381/3.

P205. 7 skyphos body frags. Fig. 3-12.
Very pale brown clay. All have undecorated bands, probably in zone between handles; above and below, light brown coating; frags. of same paint on interior.
K24 Wy/K25 Wa, level 3, lot 4381/3.

P206-7. 2 skyphos bases.
Type A.
K24 WyXy/K25 WaXa baulk, level 4, lot 4393/1; level 3, lot 4390.

P208. Pedestal krater base. Fig. 3-4.
H. (pres.) 0.061. D. stem 0.024.
Munsell 2.5YR 6/8 light red. Missing part of foot; hollow in underside of base. Worn surfaces; light brown slip and possible frags. of black paint on exterior.
K24 Wy/K25 Wa, level 5, lot 4383.

Closed Shapes

P209. Wall frag. of amphora.
H. (pres.) 0.076. Th. 0.01.
Very pale brown clay. Thick brown bands.
K24 WyXy/K25 WaXa, level 3, lot 4390.

P210. Belly frag. of oinochoe.
Th. 0.0045.
Reddish yellow clay with gray core. Decoration of black bands with solid black coating below. Whitish gray slip. To left, mending hole with frag. of second mending hole at upper right.
K24 Yy/K25 Yab, baulk, level 2, lot 4352.

Section I

From Area III. A small body of DAI sherds comes from the upper hill wash (i.e., levels 3, 4, and 5 of K24 Xuv) over terrace walls A-C.

Open Shapes

P211. Rim frag. of skyphos.
H. (pres.) 0.033. Th. 0.0035. D. ca. 0.10.
Dirty white to very pale brown flaky clay. On exterior, probably black coating which has now worn to the shape of an arm with a pointing finger; washy black paint on interior. Rim: Type A3.
K24 Xuv, level 3, lots 2004-2006.

P212. Upper profile of skyphos. Fig. 3-8; Pl. 3-17.
H. (pres.) 0.066. Th. 0.004. D. ca. 0.14.
Dirty white to very pale brown clay. Decoration of wavy line in light brown coating; frags. of same paint on interior. Wheel ridging on interior. Rim: Type A3.
K24 Xuv, level 4, lot 3199.

P213. Upper profile (missing handles) of deep bowl. Fig. 3-8; Pl. 3-18.
H. (pres.) 0.066. Th. 0.005. D. ca. 0.17.
Fine reddish yellow clay. Decoration of wavy line in faded black in field between handles; above and below, heavy black coating; same paint on interior. Wheel ridging on interior. Rim: Type B2.
K24 Xuv, level 4, lots 2007, 2008.

P214. Rim frag. of skyphos.
H. (pres.) 0.105. Th. 0.005-0.007. D. ca. 0.10(?)
Lip of rim missing. Possible undecorated band in handle zone; above and below, washy black-brown paint; same paint on interior. Wheel ridging on both exterior and interior. Rim: Type B2(?)
K24 Xu, level 5, lot 2208.

P215. Decorated krater wall frag. Fig. 3-12.
H. (pres.) 0.096. Th. 0.01.
Reddish yellow flaky clay; worn surfaces. Faint frags. of decoration preserved. 2 registers: above, 2 vertical bands flanking 2 vertical wavy lines in light brown; below, frag. of horizontal wavy line also in light brown. Solid brown coating below decorated zone. Wheel ridging on interior.
K24 Xuv, level 4, lot 2008.

P216. Ringed base of small skyphos. Fig. 3-13.
Base: Type A.
K24 Xuv, level 4, lots 2007, 2008.

P217. Handle and body frag. of skyphos.
H. (pres.) 0.054. D. handle ca. 0.012-0.013.
Very pale brown clay. Carinated body. Washy black coating on exterior and interior. Handle: Type A.
K24 Xuv, level 4, lot 3199.

Section J

From Area III. Miscellaneous DAI sherds were also found in various trenches of Area III. These sherds come from predominantly mixed lots (LHIIIB and DAII) with no architectural association.

Open Shapes

P218. Complete upper profile of skyphos. Fig. 3-10; Pl. 3-11.
H. (pres.) 0.0775. Th. 0.0035-0.004. D. 0.122.
Dirty white to very pale brown flaky clay; worn surfaces. Decoration of wavy line in black in handle zone; above and below, washy black coating. Same coating on interior. Wheel ridging on interior. Rim: Type A3.
K24 Uxy, level 15, lots 4460, 4461.

P219. Rim frag. of skyphos or deep bowl.
H. (pres.) 0.19. Th. 0.0035. D. ca. 0.15.
Dirty white to very pale brown clay. Frags. of washy black paint on exterior and interior. Rim: Type A2.
K24 Vy, level 2, lot 4444.

P220. Rim frag. of skyphos or deep bowl.
H. (pres.) 0.027. Th. 0.0035-0.004. D. ca. 0.15.
Very pale brown clay with pinkish core. Good streaky brown paint on exterior and interior. Reserved band inner rim. Rim: Type A3.
K24 Vy, level 4, lots 4445, 4448.

P221. Complete upper profile of deep bowl. Fig. 3-8.
H. (pres.) 0.059. Th. 0.004. D. ca. 0.16.
Tops of handles missing. Very pale brown clay. Handle zone left undecorated; above, washy black coating; same coating on interior. Rim: Type A3.
K24 Vy, level 2, lot 4444.

P222. Upper profile (missing handles) of deep bowl. Fig. 3-9.
H. (pres.) 0.063. Th. 0.0065. D. ca. 0.20.
Very pale brown clay. Frag. of thick wavy line in black in decorated zone, probably between handles; above, washy black coating; same coating on interior. Reserved band inner rim. Rim: Type A3.
K24 Vy, level 4, lots 4445, 4448.

P223. Upper profile (missing handles) of skyphos. Fig. 3-10.
H. (pres.) 0.052. Th. 0.004-0.0045. D. ca. 0.125.
Tip of rim broken off. Reddish yellow clay. Decoration of wavy line in brown paint, probably in handle zone; above and below, frags. of brown paint; same paint on interior. Wheel ridging interior. Rim: Type B3(?)
K24 Vy, level 4, lots 4445, 4448.

P224. Decorated skyphos body frag.
H. (pres.) 0.029. Th. 0.004.
Tip of rim broken off. Frag. of wavy line of black in decoration zone, probably in field between handles; above, washy black paint; same paint on interior.
K25 Vy, level 2, lot 4444.

P225. Rim of skyphos or deep bowl. Fig. 3-12.
H. (pres.) 0.039. Th. 0.004.
Munsell 7.5YR 7/4 pink. Flaky clay, worn surfaces. Possible undecorated zone in field between handles; above, light streaky black-brown paint; same paint on interior. Reserved band inner rim. Rim: Type B3.
K24 Qg, level 2, lot 1407.

P226. Upper profile (missing handles) of deep bowl. Fig. 3-9; Pl. 3-19.
H. (pres.) 0.06. Th. 0.0045-0.005. D. ca. 0.14.
Dirty white to very pale brown clay. Frag. of black wavy line in decoration zone, probably in field between handles; above, washy black coating; same coating on interior. Possible reserved band inner rim. Rim: Type A3.
K24 Vy/K25 Va, level 2, lot 4443.

P227. Upper profile of skyphos. Fig. 3-10.
H. (pres.) 0.0665. Th. 0.004. D. ca. 0.126.
Very pale brown clay. Monochrome washy black on exterior and interior. Reserved band inner rim. Carinated body. Rim: Type B2.
K25 Sc/Tc and Tb/Tc baulks, level 8, lot 1940.

P228. Rim frag. of skyphos.
H. (pres.) 0.024. Th. 0.003. D. ca. 0.12.
Reddish yellow clay; good smooth surfaces. Streaky black paint on exterior under rim with light black band below; solid black coating on interior. Reserved band inner rim. Rim: Type A3.
K25 Tab, level 3, lot 1442.

P229. Rim and body frag. of possible kylix. Fig. 3-7.
H. (pres.) 0.07. Th. 0.006-0.007. D. ca. 0.12.
Tip of rim missing. Very pale brown flaky clay. Undecorated zone, possibly at point where handles join body; above, washy black-brown coating; same coating on interior. Rim: Type B1(?)
K25 Uab, level 2, lot 3102.

P230. Upper profile of skyphos . Fig. 3-8.
H. (pres.) 0.046. Th. 0.004. D. ca. 0.14(?)
Handles and tip of rim missing. Dirty white clay. Frag. of wavy line in reddish brown paint in decoration zone, possibly in field between handles; above and below, a reddish brown coating. Good streaky black-brown paint on interior. Rim: Type A3(?)
K25 Ucd, level 4, lots 1169, 1172, 1174, 1175, 1178 (combined).

P231. Skyphos base.
Very high conical foot. Type A.
K24 Vy, level 2, lot 4444.

P232. Skyphos handle frag.
D. 0.007.
Type B.
K24 Vy, level 2, lot 4444.

Closed Shapes

P233. Decorated oinochoe shoulder frag. Pl. 3-19.
H. (pres.) 0.042. Th. 0.004.
Very pale brown clay. Decoration quite fragmentary: above, frags. of piled triangles; below, brown bands.
K24 Vy/K25 Va, level 2, lot 4443.

Section K

From Area II. Miscellaneous DAI sherds were recovered from trenches along the north and south edges of the acropolis.

Open Shapes

P234. Rim and body frag. of deep bowl.
H. (pres.) 0.065. Th. 0.005. D. ca. 0.19.
Munsell 2.5Y 8/2 white (with pale yellow tinge). Flaky clay; worn surfaces. Possible frags. of brown paint on exterior and interior. Rim: Type A3.
K25 Lfg, level 2, lot 1836.

P235. Upper profile of deep bowl. Fig. 3-7; Pl. 3-8.
H. (pres.) 0.92. Th. 0.006. D. 0.19.
5 joining frags. and 2 nonjoining handle frags. Munsell 5Y 8/3 pale yellow. Flaky clay; worn surfaces. Main decoration is worn but appears to consist of 2 sets of connected spirals set below 3 thin bands in black paint; frags. of black paint preserved on interior. Possible reserved band at inner rim. Carinated body; wheel ridging on interior. Rim: Type A3.
K25 Lfg, level 2, lot 1845.

P236. Rim frag. of skyphos.
Th. 0.003. D. ca. 0.13.
Very pale brown clay. Washy brown paint on exterior and interior. Reserved band inner rim. Pale brown slip. Rim: Type A3.
K25 Gf/Hf baulk, level 2, lot 2340.

P237. Rim and body frag. of deep bowl.
D. ca. 0.23.
Rim: Type B2.
K25 Hd/He baulk, level 1, lot 1839.

P238. Rim frag. of deep bowl.
D. ca. 0.15.
Rim: Type B3.
K25 Id/Jd and Ic/Id baulk, levels 1 and 2, lot 1807.

P239. Rim frag. of skyphos.
D. ca. 0.14.
Washy black paint on exterior and interior. 2 small grooves under rim. Rim: Type C2.
K25 Jbc/Kbc baulk, level 3, lot 2323.

P240. Rim frag. of deep bowl.
D. ca. 0.16.
Rim: Type C3.
K25 If, level 2, lot 1809.

Closed Shapes

P241-42. Rim frags. of oinochoai.
Very pale brown clay. Frags. of washy black paint on exterior and interior of rim. Rim: Type B.
K25 Hc/Ic baulk, level 2, lot 1082.

P243. Neck frag. of oinochoe.
Tip of rim missing. Very pale brown clay. Frags. of black paint preserved on exterior and on interior of upper portion of neck.
K25 Hc/Ic baulk, level 2, lot 1082.

Section L

From Area VII. A good group of DAI sherds comes from level 4 of trial trench N22-XVII. This level is associated with Wall G which is the only architectural feature of the DAI period. Levels 1, 2, 3, and 6 also contain scattered DAI sherds.

Open Shapes

P244-45. Rim frags. of skyphoi or deep bowls. Fig. 3-2 (**P245**).
D. ca. 0.16.
Very pale brown clay with pink core. Fine smooth surfaces. Glossy black-brown paint on exterior and interior. White slip exterior; wheel ridging interior. Rim: Type A2.
N22-XVII, level 4, lots 441, 448, 452, 472-74 (combined).

P246. Upper profile (missing handles) of skyphos. Fig. 3-9; Pl. 3-4.
H. (pres.) 0.07. D. ca. 0.14.
Very pale brown clay. Fine smooth surfaces. Glossy streaky black-brown coating on exterior and interior. Small undecorated band in field between handles; possible reserved band on inner rim. Rim: Type A3.
N22-XVII, level 4, lots 441, 448, 452, 472-74 (combined).

P247. Upper profile (missing handles) of deep bowl. Pl. 3-4.
H. (pres.) 0.045. D. ca. 0.16.
Very pale brown clay. Fine smooth surfaces. Glossy streaky light brown coating on exterior and interior. Frag. of undecorated zone preserved, probably in field between handles. Wheel ridging on interior. Rim: Type A3.

N22-XVII, level 4, lots 441, 448, 452, 472-74 (combined).

P248. Rim frag. of skyphos.

D. ca. 0.14.

Very pale brown clay. Wheel ridging on interior. Rim: Type A3.

N22-XVII, level 4, lots 441, 448, 452, 472-74 (combined).

P249. Rim frag. of skyphos. Pl. 3-4.

D. ca. 0.14.

Very pale brown clay. Good smooth surfaces. Glossy light brown paint on exterior and interior. Light brown slip. Under rim is a shallow incision followed by 2 flat raised bands. Wheel ridging on interior. Rim: Type A3.

N22-XVII, level 4, lots 441, 448, 452, 472-74 (combined).

P250-60. Rim frags. of skyphoi and deep bowls. Pl. 3-4 (**P250, P251**).

D. ca. 0.22 (**P256**), 0.18 (**P253**), 0.17 (**P258**), 0.16 (**P250, P257**), 0.15 (**P259**), 0.14 (**P251**), 0.11 (**P260**), 0.08 (**P255**).

Very pale brown clay. Good smooth surfaces. Glossy black-brown paint exterior and interior. Light brown slip (**P250, P253, P258**). Reserved band inner rim (**P251, P252, P254**); wheel ridging interior (**P250, P251, P253, P254**). Rim: Type A3.

N22-XVII, level 4, lots 441, 448, 452, 472-74 (combined); level 6, lot 471.

P261. Rim frag. of skyphos.

Tip of rim missing. Very pale brown flaky clay. Washy black paint exterior and interior. Wheel ridging interior. Rim: Type B1(?)

N22-XVII, level 4, lots 441, 448, 452, 472-74 (combined).

P262. Rim frag. of skyphos.

D. ca. 0.09.

Reddish yellow clay. Frags. black paint preserved on exterior and interior. Rim: Type B3.

N22-XVII, level 4, lots 441, 448, 452, 472-74 (combined).

P263. Upper profile (missing handles) of skyphos. Fig. 3-9; Pl. 3-20.

H. (pres.) 0.044. Th. 0.0035. D. ca. 0.14.

Very pale brown clay. At left, clay thickens indicating point where handle joins body. Decorated zone between handles consists of a sharp wavy line (almost wolf's tooth) in light brown paint; above, a darker brown coating; same coating on interior. Wheel ridging on interior. Rim: Type B3.

N22-XVII, level 4, lots 441, 448, 452, 472-74 (combined).

P264-66. Rim frags. of skyphoi and deep bowls. Fig. 3-2 (**P264, P266**); Pl. 3-4 (**P264**).

D. ca. 0.26 (**P264**).

Very pale brown clay. Washy black paint exterior and interior. Light brown slip (**P264**); wheel ridging exterior and interior (**P264**). Rim: Type B3.

N22-XVII, level 4, lots 441, 448, 452, 472-74 (combined); level 6, lot 471.

P267. Upper profile of skyphos. Fig. 3-10.

H. (pres.) 0.06. D. ca. 0.15.

Tip of rim missing. Very pale brown flaky clay. Monochrome black-brown coating on exterior and interior. Brown slip. Wheel ridging on interior. Rim: Type B3(?)

N22-XVII, level 1, lots 424, 428, 436, 456 (combined).

P268. Upper profile (missing handles) of deep bowl. Fig. 3-9; Pl. 3-20.

H. (pres.) 0.056. D. ca. 0.22.

Tip of rim missing. Reddish yellow clay with pinkish core. Fine smooth surfaces. Decoration, possibly in handle zone, consists of a large thick wavy line in black; above, glossy streaky black coating; same coating on interior. Wheel ridging on exterior and interior. Rim: Type B3(?)

N22-XVII, level 4, lots 441, 448, 452, 472-74 (combined).

P269. Upper profile (missing handles) of deep bowl. Fig. 3-9; Pl. 3-4.

H. (pres.) 0.056. D. ca. 0.18.

Tip of rim missing. Dirty white to very pale brown flaky clay. Undecorated zone, possibly in field between handles; above and below, frags. of glossy washy black coating; same coating on interior. Rim: Type B3(?)

N22-XVII, level 4, lots 441, 448, 452, 472-74 (combined).

P270. Rim frag. of deep bowl. Fig. 3-2.

D. ca. 0.20.

Very pale brown clay. Fine smooth surfaces. Glossy black paint exterior and interior. Reserved band inner rim. Rim: Type C1.

N22-XVII, level 6, lot 471.

P271-77. Rim frags. of skyphoi. Fig. 3-2 (**P272-74**); Pl. 3-4 (**P272**).

D. ca. 0.14 (**P273**), 0.12 (**P271, P272, P276**), 0.10 (**P277**).

Very pale brown to reddish yellow clay. Fine smooth surfaces. Glossy black-brown paint exterior and interior. Reserved band inner rim (**P274**); brown slip (**P272**). Rim: Type C2.

N22-XVII, level 4, lots 441, 448, 452, 472-74 (combined).

P278. 10 body frags. of skyphoi and deep bowls.

5 have a thickness of 0.005 and above and probably belong to deep bowls; the rest have a thickness of 0.004-0.0045 and probably belong to skyphoi. Very pale brown to reddish yellow clay. Fine smooth surfaces; glossy black-brown paint exterior and interior. 3 have wheel ridging on interior.

N22-XVII, level 4, lots 441, 448, 452, 472-74 (combined).

P279. Rim frag. of krater. Fig. 3-3.

H. (pres.) 0.036. D. ca. 0.30.

Very pale brown clay. Good streaky black paint on exterior and interior. Possible reserved band inner rim. Light brown slip frags. preserved on exterior.

N22-XVII, level 1, lot 428.

P280. Handle and body frag. of krater. Pl. 3-21.

D. handle 0.15-0.16. Th. body 0.01.

Reddish yellow clay; white slip. Good streaky black-brown coating exterior and interior. Frag. of wavy line preserved in decorated zone between the handles.

N22-XVII, level 3, lots 437, 440, 457 (combined).

P281-88. Skyphos bases. Fig. 3-3 (**P281-83**).

D. 0.035-0.055.

High conical feet. Frags. black paint exterior and interior. Light brown slip exterior (**P284, P285**). Base: Type A.

N22-XVII, level 4, lots 441, 448, 452, 472-74 (combined).

P289. Handle frag. of deep bowl.

D. 0.012.

Reddish yellow clay. Fine smooth surfaces; glossy black-brown paint. Handle: Type A.

N22-XVII, level 4, lots 441, 448, 452, 472-74 (combined).

P290. Handle frag. of cup.

W. 0.015.

Reddish yellow flaky and gritty clay. Frag. black paint preserved. Flat handle with flute down center of top.

N22-XVII, level 4, lots 441, 448, 452, 472-74 (combined).

Closed Shapes

P291. Belly frag. of oinochoe.

H. (pres.) 0.119.

Reddish yellow clay. Fine smooth surfaces. Glossy streaky black-brown paint.

N22-XVII, level 4, lots 441, 448, 452, 472-74 (combined).

P292. Handle frag. of oinochoe. Fig. 3-5.

L. (pres.) 0.0645. W. 0.022.

Reddish yellow clay. Good brown paint. Handle has large flute down center of top. Handle: Type B2.

N22-XVII, level 4, lots 441, 448, 452, 472-74 (combined).

P293-95. Handle frags. of oinochoai or jugs.

W. 0.018 (**P294**), 0.022 (**P293, P295**).

Very pale brown to reddish yellow clay. Frags. black-brown paint preserved. Simple flat handles with no flutes or incisions. Handle: Type B1.

N22-XVII, level 4, lots 441, 448, 452, 472-74 (combined).

P296. Handle and rim frag. of oinochoe.

W. handle 0.022.

Reddish yellow clay; fine smooth surfaces. Glossy streaky black paint on handle and on exterior and interior of rim. Straight rim. Handle: Type B1.

N22-XVII, level 4, lots 441, 448, 452, 472-74 (combined).

Section M

A few DAI sherds come from other 1969 trial trenches.

Open Shapes

P297. Rim frag. of skyphos.

D. ca. 0.09.

Very pale brown clay. Frags. black paint exterior and interior. Light brown slip. Reserved band inner rim. Rim: Type A2.

K24-III, level 4, lots 98, 100 (combined).

P298-99. Rim frags. of skyphoi and deep bowls.

D. ca. 0.17 (**P298**), 0.12 (**P299**).

Very pale brown clay. Frags. black paint exterior and interior. Rim: Type A3.

K24-III, level 4, lots 98, 100 (combined).

P300. Rim frag. of skyphos.

D. ca. 0.08.

Rim: Type C2.

K24-III, level 4, lots 98, 100 (combined).

P301. Rim and decorated body frag. of skyphos.

H. (pres.) 0.032. D. ca. 0.13.

Dirty white to very pale brown clay. Decorated zone (possibly in field between handles) consists of frags. of 3 arcs of concentric semi-circles in black; above, black band; frags. of black paint on interior. Light brown slip. Rim: Type C2.

L23-VIII, level 3, lot 302.

P302. Base of skyphos.

D. ca. 0.05.

About ½ preserved. Very pale brown flaky clay. Base: Type A.

L23-VIII, level 3, lot 302.

Closed Shapes

P303. Rim and neck frag. of oinochoe. Fig. 3-5.

D. neck ca. 0.04.

Dirty white to very pale brown clay. Rim coated with black paint; vertical black stripes on neck.

L23-VIII, level 3, lot 302.

Section N

Ribbed kylix stems. Ribbed kylix stems of the DAI period were found in widely scattered trenches. Some belong to good DAI groups, but others appear in a mixed context, i.e., in small DAI groups mixed with either LHIIIB or DAII pottery. For the sake of uniformity, these stems are presented here together.

P304. Kylix stem broken at top and at foot. Pl. 3-25.

H. (pres.) 0.069. D. rib 0.026. D. stem 0.023.

Munsell 2.5Y 8/2 white to 5Y 7/3 pale yellow. Flaky clay; worn surfaces. Possible frags. black paint preserved. Rib consists of one gentle swelling in center of stem. Type A.

K25 Id/Jd and Ic/Id baulk, level 2, lot 1807.

P305. Kylix stem, broken at top. Fig. 3-4; Pl. 3-25.

H. (pres.) 0.055. D. rib 0.023. D. stem 0.021. D. foot ca. 0.06.

¼ foot preserved. Munsell 7.5Y 7/4 pink. Flaky clay; worn surfaces. Foot is semi-conical. Traces black paint preserved. Type A.

K25 Sd/Se, level 1, lot 1670.

P306. Kylix stem, broken at top where body begins. Fig. 3-4; Pl. 3-26.

H. (pres.) 0.057. D. rib 0.034. D. stem 0.021.

Missing foot. Munsell 10YR 8/4 very pale brown. Flaky clay; worn surfaces. Possible frags. black paint preserved. Type B.

L23 Tj, level 2, lot 4417/5.

P307. Kylix stem, broken at top and at beginning of foot. Fig. 3-4; Pl. 3-26.

H. (pres.) 0.07. D. rib 0.028. D. stem 0.022.

Munsell 5Y 7/3 pale yellow. Flaky clay, worn surfaces. Possible frags. light brown paint preserved. Type B.

K24 TUu, level 3, lot 3132/1.

P308. Frag. of kylix stem, broken just beneath rib and at top where body begins. Pl. 3-27.

H. (pres.) 0.038. D. rib 0.031. D. stem above rib 0.028.

Dirty white to very pale brown flaky clay. Worn surfaces; no traces paint preserved. Type B.

L23 Rab, level 1.

P309. Frag. of kylix stem, broken just beneath rib. Pl. 3-27.

H. (pres.) 0.04. D. rib 0.028. D. stem above rib 0.0225.

Very pale brown clay with pinkish core. Frags. black paint preserved. Type B.

L23 Tj, level 2, lot 4417/4.

P310. Kylix stem, broken at tip of foot and at top where body begins. Fig. 3-4; Pl. 3-28.

H. (pres.) 0.05. D. rib 0.023. D. stem 0.019.

Dirty white to very pale brown clay. Frags. brown paint preserved. Small conical foot. Type C.

L23 Sop, level 3, lot 3404/1.

P311. Frag. of kylix stem. Fig. 3-4; Pl. 3-28.

H. (pres.) 0.036. D. rib 0.022. D. stem ca. 0.017.

Broken beneath rib and at top where body begins. Dirty white to very pale brown flaky clay; worn surfaces. Frags. black paint preserved; frags. of light brown coating preserved at bottom of interior. Type C.

K25 Tcd, level 2, lots 1165, 1167, 1170.

P312. Frag. of kylix stem. Pl. 3-28.

H. (pres.) 0.051, D. rib 0.021, D. stem 0.02.

Broken at foot and at top above rib. Munsell 5Y 7/3 pale yellow to dirty white. Flaky clay; worn surfaces. No traces paint preserved. Very worn; possibly Type C.

K24 Uxy, level 2, lot 1912.

P313-15. Frags. of kylix stems. Pl. 3-29.

Broken just above and below rib. Very pale brown flaky clay; very worn surfaces. Possible traces of black paint preserved. Type C.

L23 Rhi/Shi baulk, level 3, lot 4627/1-5 (**P313**); L23 Vmn, level 2, lot 1119 (**P314**); L23 OPe, level 3, lot 3272/3-5 (**P315**).

P316. Kylix stem. Fig. 3-4; Pl. 3-30.

H. (pres.) 0.032. D. rib. 0.024. D. stem 0.015.

Broken at tip of foot and at top where body begins. Dirty white flaky clay; worn surfaces. Frags. black paint preserved; light brown slip. High conical foot; one rib. Type D1.

L23 Ocd, level 2, lot 4104/3.

P317. Kylix stem. Fig. 3-5; Pl. 3-30.

H. (pres.) 0.034. D. rib 0.019. D. stem 0.015.

Broken at top where body begins and missing foot. Munsell 10YR 8/2 white (with pinkish tinge). Flaky clay; worn surfaces. Frags. black paint preserved. One rib. Type D1.

L23 Sfg, level 3, lot 2403.

P318. Kylix stem. Fig. 3-5; Pl. 3-31.

H. (pres.) 0.04. D. upper rib 0.02. D. lower rib 0.016. D. stem 0.014.

Broken at top where body begins and missing foot. Reddish yellow flaky clay; very worn surfaces. Possible frags. black paint preserved. 2 ribs. Type D2.

L23 Wklm, level 2, lots 2136, 2139.

P319-21. Frags. of kylix stems. Pl. 3-31.

Broken just above upper rib and below lower rib. Very pale brown to reddish yellow flaky clay; worn surfaces. Traces of black paint preserved. Type D2.

L23 Ukl, level 1, lot 1863 (**P319**); L23 Nc, level 1, lot 4108/2-3 (**P320**); L23-IX, level 2 (**P321**).

P322. Frag. of kylix stem. Fig. 3-5; Pl. 3-32.

H. (pres.) 0.035. D. ribs 0.027. D. stem 0.022.

Broken below lower rib and at top where body begins. Munsell 10YR 8/2 white (with pinkish tinge). Flaky clay; worn surfaces. Possible frags. black paint preserved. Small flat stem with 2 small ribs (near foot). Type E.

K25 Tcd, level 2, lots 1165, 1167, 1170.

P323. Frag. of kylix stem. Pl. 3-32.

H. (pres.) 0.027. D. rib 0.028. D. stem 0.021.

Broken below upper rib and at top where body begins. Reddish yellow clay. Flaky clay; worn surfaces. Frags. black paint preserved. Type E.

K24 Vw, level 2, lot 3650/3-4.

P324. Kylix stem, missing foot. Fig. 3-5; Pl. 3-33.

H. (pres.) 0.036. D. ribs 0.022-0.023. D. stem 0.021.

Dirty white flaky clay; worn surfaces. Traces of black paint preserved. Frag. of high conical foot at bottom. 2 ribs; third swelling (rib?) at point where body begins. Type E.

L23 Rhi, level 2, lot 2360.

P325-26. Frags. of kylix stems. Pl. 3-33.

D. rib ca. 0.023. D. stem 0.021.

Broken off below rib and at body. Dirty white to very pale brown flaky clay, worn surfaces. Faint traces black paint preserved. Type E.

L23-VIII, level 2, lot 296 (**P325**); L23 Wklm, level 1, lot 2134 (**P326**).

P327. Kylix stem, missing foot. Fig. 3-5; Pl. 3-34.

H. (pres.) 0.057. D. rib 0.025. D. stem 0.016.

Reddish yellow clay. Well-preserved surfaces. Frags. of glossy brown paint preserved on exterior, interior of body, and on underside of foot. One sharp rib; conical foot. Type F.

N22-XVII, level 4, lot 448.

P328. Kylix stem, missing foot. Fig. 3-5; Pl. 3-34.

H. (pres.) 0.057. D. upper rib 0.023. D. lower rib 0.0255. D. stem 0.018.

Reddish yellow clay; good smooth surfaces. Black coating. 2 sharp ribs, one in middle of stem, other near point where body begins. Type F.

L23-V, level 5, lot 329.

P329. Pedestal krater stem. Fig. 3-5; Pl. 3-35.

H. (pres.) 0.042. D. rib 0.036. D. stem 0.031.

About ½ preserved. Tip of foot missing. Olive gray clay with light red core. Worn surfaces. Frags. of black paint preserved. One sharp rib; very high conical foot. Type G.

N22-XVII, level 1, lots 424, 428, 436, 456 (combined).

Section O

Miscellaneous find with no stratigraphical association.

P330. Decorated krater wall frag. Pl. 3-23.

H. (pres.) 0.073. Th. 0.01.

Very pale brown clay. At top of frag. is decoration of piled triangles in light brown paint; below, light brown coating with horizontal incision in lower half. Frags. of light brown coating on interior. Wheel ridging on interior.

From dump.

DARK AGE II

Section A

From Area IVNE. A group of pure DAII sherds comes from the floor associated with the first phase of Unit IV-1.

Open Shapes

P331. Complete profile of skyphos. Fig. 3-22; Pl. 3-39.

H. 0.046. Th. 0.003. D. ca. 0.94.

Munsell 10YR 8/4 very pale brown; flaky clay; worn surfaces. Undecorated zone in field between the handles; above and below, streaky black coating; same coating on interior. Lower body missing; high conical foot. Rim: Type A1.

L23 Vkl, level 3, floor lot 4301/1-4.

P332. Upper profile of skyphos. Fig. 3-22.

H. (pres.) 0.045. Th. 0.003. D. ca. 0.007.

Very pale brown flaky clay; worn surfaces. Base missing. Undecorated zone in field between handles; above and below, frags. of monochrome black coating; frags. of black paint on interior. Rim: Type A1.

L23 Vkl, level 3, floor lot 4301/1-4.

P333. Rim and body frag. of skyphos. Fig. 3-16.

H. (pres.) 0.033. Th. 0.003. D. ca. 0.09.

Munsell 10YR 7/2 light gray; flaky clay, worn surfaces. Frags. of monochrome black on exterior and interior. Rim: Type A1.

L23 Vkl, level 3, floor lot 4301/1-4.

P334. Rim frag. of skyphos.

H. (pres.) 0.019. Th. 0.003. D. ca. 0.08.

Munsell 2.5Y 8/4 pale yellow. Flaky clay; worn surfaces. Good monochrome black paint on exterior and interior. Rim: Type A1.

L23 Vkl, level 3, floor lot 4301/1-3.

P335. Rim frag. of skyphos.

H. (pres.) 0.015. Th. 0.003. D. ca. 0.08.

Munsell 7.5YR 8/4 pink. Flaky clay, worn surfaces. Good washy black paint on exterior and interior. Rim: Type A1.

L23 Vkl, level 3, floor lot 4301/1-3.

P336. Rim and body frag. of skyphos. Pl. 3-39.

H. (pres.) 0.031. Th. 0.004. D. ca. 0.09.

Munsell 7.5YR 7/4 pink. Worn clay, flaky surfaces. Undecorated zone, probably in field between handles; above, alternating heavy black and light streaky black coating; good streaky black-brown paint on interior. Reserved band inner rim. White slip. Rim: Type A1.

L23 Vkl, level 3, floor lot 4301/1-3.

P337-38. Skyphos rim frags.

D. ca. 0.08.

Very pale brown flaky clay. Frags. washy black paint on exterior and interior. Rim: Type A1.

L23 Vkl, level 3, floor lot 4301/1-3.

P339. Upper profile of skyphos. Fig. 3-22; Pl. 3-39.

H. (pres.) 0.05. Th. 0.003. D. ca. 0.085.

Munsell 7.5YR 7/4 pink. Good streaky black coating on exterior and interior. Reserved band inner rim. Rim: Type A2.

L23 Vkl, level 3, floor lot 4301/1-4.

P340. Rim and body frag. of skyphos.

H. (pres.) 0.04. D. ca. 0.08.

Pink flaky clay, worn surfaces. Frags. monochrome black paint on exterior and interior. Reserved band inner rim. Rim: Type A2.

L23 Vkl, level 3, lot 4309.

P341. Upper profile of skyphos. Fig. 3-22; Pl. 3-39.

H. (pres.) 0.04. Th. 0.003. D. ca. 0.09.

Munsell 7.5YR 8/4 pink. Good surfaces. Undecorated zone in field between handles; above, a thin black band under rim; below handle zone is monochrome black paint; good black paint on interior. Reserved band inner rim. Type A2.

L23 Vkl, level 3, floor lot 4301/1-4.

P342-45. Rim frags. of skyphoi. Fig. 3-16 (**P344**).

Th. 0.003. D. ca. 0.08.

Munsell 10YR 6/2 light brownish gray (**P342**); 10YR 7/2 light gray (**P343**); 5YR 7/8 reddish yellow (**P344**); 7.5YR 8/4 pink (**P345**). Flaky clay; worn surfaces. Frags. black-brown paint exterior and interior. Reserved band inner rim (**P342, P344, P345**). Rim: Type A2.

L23 Vkl, level 3, floor lot 4301/1-3; level 4S, lot 4337/1-3.

P346. Rim and body frag. of skyphos. Fig. 3-16: Pl. 3-41.

H. (pres.) 0.047. Th. 0.005. D. ca. 0.13-0.14.

Munsell 7.5YR 7/4 pink. Frags. of black wavy line in decorated zone between handles; above, streaky black-brown paint; streaky black coating on interior. Rim: Type B1.

L23 Vkl, level 3, floor lot 4301/1-3.

P347. Rim and body frag. of skyphos. Fig. 3-16.

H. (pres.) 0.028. Th. 0.0045. D. ca. 0.13.

Pink flaky clay; worn surfaces. Monochrome black paint on exterior under rim; good streaky black paint on interior. Rim: Type B1.

L23 Vkl, level 3, floor lot 4301/1-3.

P348. Rim and body frag. of skyphos.

H. (pres.) 0.036. Th. 0.004. D. ca. 0.17.

Munsell 10YR 8/4 very pale brown. Streaky black-brown paint on exterior and interior. Reserved band inner rim. Rim: Type B1.

L23 Vkl, level 3, floor lot 4301/1-3.

P349-53. Skyphos rim frags. Pl. 3-41 (**P350**).

Th. 0.004 (**P349**), 0.003 (**P350-53**). D. ca. 0.16 (**P352**), 0.15 (**P349**), 0.14 (**P350, P351**).

Reddish yellow to light gray clay; worn surfaces. Frags. of washy black paint on exterior and interior. Possible reserved band inner rim (**P350**). Rim: Type B1.

L23 Vkl, level 3, floor lot 4301/1-3.

P354. Complete upper profile of skyphos. Fig. 3-23; Pl. 3-40.

H. (pres.) 0.075. Th. 0.004. D. ca. 0.115.

Munsell 5YR 7/8 reddish yellow. Flaky clay; fairly worn surfaces. On exterior, paint varies from black to brown with frags. of heavy black band under rim. Undecorated zone in field between handles. Good streaky black paint on interior; reserved band inner rim. String marks beneath rim on exterior. Rim: Type B2.

L23 Vkl, level 3, floor lot 4301/1-4.

P355. Rim and body frag. of skyphos. Pl. 3-41.

H. (pres.) 0.025. Th. 0.003. D. ca. 0.08(?)

Reddish yellow flaky clay; worn surfaces. Frags. black paint on exterior and interior. Raised band below rim on exterior. Rim: Type B2.

L23 Vkl, level 3, Wall Ca, lot 4332.

P356. Upper profile of skyphos. Fig. 3-25.

H. (pres.) 0.062. Th. 0.004. D. ca. 0.14.

Light gray flaky clay; worn surfaces. Frags. monochrome black paint preserved on exterior; possible frags. on interior. Undecorated zone in field between handles. Rim: Type B2.

L23 Vkl, level 3, floor lot 4301/1-3.

P357-62. Rim and body frags. of skyphoi. Fig. 3-16 (**P357, P359**).

Th. 0.003 (**P357, P360-62**). D. ca. 0.12 (**P360**), 0.11 (**P361**), 0.10 (**P357-59**).

Munsell 5YR 7/6 reddish yellow (**P357-60, P362**); 10YR 8/4 very pale brown (**P361**). Flaky clay, worn surfaces. Frags. washy black paint preserved on exterior and interior. **P357** has streaky heavy and light black paint on exterior. Rim: Type B2.

L23 Vkl, level 3, floor lot 4301/1-3.

P363. Rim and body frag. of skyphos. Fig. 3-16: Pl. 3-42.

H. (pres.) 0.038. Th. 0.0035. D. ca. 0.09-0.10.

Munsell 10YR 7/4 very pale brown. Flaky clay, worn surfaces. Good frags. black paint preserved on exterior and interior. Rim: Type C1.

L23 Vkl, level 3, floor lot 4301/1-3.

P364. Rim and body frag. of skyphos. Pl. 3-42.

H. (pres.) 0.023. Th. 0.003. D. ca. 0.13.

Munsell 10YR 8/3 very pale brown. Flaky clay, worn surfaces. Frags. black paint preserved on exterior and interior. Rim: Type C1.

L23 Vkl, level 3, floor lot 4301/1-3.

P365-68. Skyphos rim frags. Fig. 3-16 (**P366, P367**).

Th. 0.003-0.0035. D. ca. 0.10-0.11.

Reddish yellow flaky clay; worn surfaces. Frags. washy and streaky black-brown paint on exterior and interior. Reserved band inner rim (**P368**). Rim: Type C1.

L23 Vkl, level 3, floor lot 4301/1-3.

P369. Rim and body frag. of skyphos or deep bowl. Fig. 3-16; Pl. 3-42.

H. (pres.) 0.06. Th. 0.0045. D. ca. 0.16.

Reddish yellow clay with orange-pink core. Flaky clay; worn surfaces. Frags. black paint preserved on exterior; possible frags. also on interior. Rim: Type C2.

L23 Vkl, level 3, floor lot 4301/1-3.

P370. Rim frag. of skyphos or deep bowl. Pl. 3-42.

H. (pres.) 0.016. Th. ca. 0.004. D. ca. 0.14.

Reddish yellow clay. Frags. light brown paint preserved on exterior and interior. Possible reserved band inner rim. Rim: Type C2.

L23 Vkl, level 3, floor lot 4301/1-3.

P371-73. Skyphos rim frags.

Th. 0.004. D. ca. 0.12 (**P372**), 0.15 (**P371**).

Pale brown flaky clay. Frags. black-brown paint on exterior and interior. Reserved band inner rim (**P370, P371**). Rim: Type C2.

L23 Vkl, level 3, floor lot 4301/1-3.

P374. Decorated body frag. of skyphos.

H. (pres.) 0.035. Th. ca. 0.005.

Munsell 2.5YR N6/0 gray. Well-fired clay, good surfaces. Decoration consists of 4 frags. of arcs of concentric semi-circles (compass-drawn); above, black band. Faint traces of black paint on interior.

L23 Vkl, level 3, lot 4309.

P375. Decorated body frag. of skyphos.

H. (pres.) 0.022. Th. 0.0035.

Very pale brown clay. 4 arcs of compass-drawn semi-circles in black. Central semi-circle is in the form of a spiral connected to the central dot. Good streaky black coating on interior.

L23 Vkl, level 3, floor lots 4301/1-3, 4324, 4581 (combined).

P376. Decorated skyphos body frag.

H. (pres.) 0.033. Th. 0.0035.

Reddish yellow clay. 5 frags. of arcs of concentric compass-drawn semi-circles; above, frag. of brown band. Good black-brown coating on interior.

L23 Vkl, level 3, floor lot 4301/1-3, 4324, 4581 (combined).

P377. Decorated skyphos body frag.

H. (pres.) 0.04. Th. 0.035.

Reddish yellow clay. Frags. of 2 wavy lines in brown paint; above, brown band. Good streaky black-brown paint on interior.

L23 Vkl, level 3, lot 4309.

P378. Decorated skyphos body frag.

H. (pres.) 0.028. Th. 0.005.

Reddish yellow clay. Frags. of a crosshatched triangle; below, black band. Good black coating on interior.

L23 Vkl, level 3, floor lots 4301/1-3, 4324, 4581 (combined).

P379. Decorated skyphos body and handle frag.

H. (pres.) 0.029. Th. body 0.003-0.0035.

Light gray flaky clay. Frags. of piled triangles; above, frag. of black band. No traces of paint preserved on interior.

L23 Vkl, level 3, floor lots 4301/1-3, 4324, 4581 (combined).

P380. Rim and body frag. of skyphos.

H. (pres.) 0.066. Th. 0.004. D. ca. 0.165.

Munsell 7.5YR 7/6 reddish yellow. Flaky clay, worn surfaces. Frags. black paint preserved on exterior; good streaky black-brown coating on interior. Rim: Type B1.

L23 Vkl, level 3, Wall Ca, lot 4332.

P381. Rim and body frag. of skyphos.

H. (pres.) 0.049. Th. 0.004. D. ca. 0.18-0.19.

Reddish yellow flaky clay; worn surfaces. Faint frags. black paint on exterior and interior. Rim: Type B1.

L23 Vkl, level 3, Wall Ca, lot 4332.

P382. Skyphos rim frag.

Reddish yellow clay. Faint traces black paint exterior and interior. Rim: Type B2.

L23 Vkl, level 3, Wall Ca, lot 4332.

P383. Skyphos rim frag.

H. (pres.) 0.018. Th. .003. D. ca. 0.13.

Very pale brown flaky clay, worn surfaces. No traces paint preserved.Rim: Type C1.

L23 Vkl, level 3, Wall Ca, lot 4332.

P384-85. Skyphos rim frags.

Very pale brown to light gray clay. Flaky clay, worn surfaces. Traces of black paint preserved on exterior and interior. Rim: Type C1.

L23 Vkl, level 3, Wall Ca, lot 4332.

P386. Rim frag. of krater. Fig. 3-16.

H. (pres.) 0.019. Th. body 0.005. D. ca. 0.20.

Munsell 7.5YR 7/6 reddish yellow. Flaky clay, worn surfaces. Good frags. of streaky black-brown paint exterior and interior. Frags. of stripes on top of rim. Type A.

L23 Vkl, level 3, floor lot 4301 /1-3.

P387. Rim frag. of krater.

Like **P386** above, but no traces of paint preserved. Rim: Type A.

L23 Vkl, level 3, floor lot 4301 /1-3.

P388. Rim frag. of krater. Fig. 3-16.

H. (pres.) 0.037. Th. body 0.007. D. ca. 0.30.

Reddish yellow flaky clay, worn surfaces. Good streaky black-brown paint exterior, top of rim, and interior. Rim: Type B1.

L23 Vkl, level 3, floor lot 4301/1-3.

P389. Base and body frag. of skyphos. Fig. 3-17; Pl. 3-44.

D. 0.04.

Munsell 7.5YR 8/6 reddish yellow. Good streaky black paint preserved on exterior and on inside of base. Base: Type A1.

L23 Vkl, level 3, floor lot 4301/1-3.

P390, P390a, P390b. Skyphos bases. Fig. 3-17 (**P390, P390a, P390b**); Pl. 3-44 (**P390**).

D. 0.036 (**P390b**), 0.043 (**P390, P390a**).

⅔ preserved. Munsell 2.5YR 6/8 light red. Flaky clay, worn surfaces. Frags. of light brown paint preserved on exterior and interior. **P390a** has shallow incisions on underside; **P390b** has 2 incisions on exterior of base. Base: Type A1.

L23 Vkl, level 3, floor lot 4301/1-3.

P391, P392, P392a, P393. Skyphos bases. Fig. 3-17 (**P392, P392a**).
D. 0.035 (**P392**), 0.037 (**P391, P393**), 0.05 (**P392a**).
Incisions on exterior of base. Munsell 7.5YR 7/6 reddish yellow. Streaky black paint on exterior and on inside of base. **P392, P392a** have raised bands on base. Base: Type A1.
L23 Vkl, level 3, floor lot 4301/1-3.

P394. Skyphos base. Fig. 3-17; Pl. 3-44.
D. 0.06.
Reddish yellow flaky clay. Good smooth black paint on exterior and inside base. Large incision at point where base joins body. Base: Type A2.
L23 Vkl, level 3, floor lot 4301/1-3.

P395. Skyphos base. Fig. 3-17; Pl. 3-44.
D. 0.048.
Reddish yellow clay with orange-pink core. Good smooth black paint exterior and inside base. String marks exterior; spiral grooving on interior. Base: Type A2.
L23 Vkl, level 3, floor lot 4301/1-3.

P396, P396a, P396b. Skyphos bases. Fig. 3-17.
D. 0.038 (**P396, P396a**), 0.044 (**P396b**).
Reddish yellow clay, worn surfaces. Good monochrome black paint exterior and interior. String marks at bottom; heavy wheel ridging on interior with hub in center of interior. **P396a** has raised band on foot; **P396b** has 4 incisions. Base: Type A2.
L23 Vkl, level 3, floor lot 4301/1-3.

P397-99. Skyphos base frags.
D. ca. 0.04.
Very pale brown flaky clay. Base: Type A2.
L23 Vkl, level 3, floor lot 4301/1-3.

P400. Lower profile of skyphos. Fig. 3-17.
D. 0.064.
Munsell 7.5YR 7/6 reddish yellow. Good streaky black paint on exterior, interior, and on underside of base. Wheel ridging on interior. Base: Type B.
L23 Vkl, level 3, floor lot 4301/1-3.

P401. Skyphos base. Fig. 3-17.
D. 0.073.
½ preserved. Reddish yellow flaky clay, worn surfaces. Frags. black paint preserved on exterior, interior, and underside of base. String marks at foot. 4 incisions on foot. Base: Type B.
L23 Vkl, level 3, floor lot 4301/1-3.

P402-2a. Skyphos bases. Fig. 3-18.
D. 0.06.
⅓ preserved. Ringed foot. Reddish yellow flaky clay, worn surfaces. Good frags. black paint preserved on exterior and interior. Wheel ridging on interior. Base: Type C.
L23 Vkl, level 3, floor lot 4301/1-3.

P403. Skyphos base. Fig. 3-18.
D. 0.065.
⅔ preserved. Ringed foot. Reddish yellow clay. Good black paint preserved on exterior and on underside of base; possible frags. black paint on interior. Base: Type C.
L23 Vkl, level 3, floor lot 4301/1-3.

P404-6. Skyphos base frags. Fig. 3-18 (**P404**).
D. ca. 0.05 (**P405**), 0.06 (**P404, P406**).
Reddish yellow clay. Frags. black paint exterior and inside base. Base: Type C.
L23 Vkl, level 3, floor lot 4301/1-3.

P407. Frag. of flat base of cup (or skyphos?).
D. ca. 0.07-0.08.
Very pale brown clay with blue-gray core. Flaky clay; very worn surfaces. Faint traces of black paint preserved on exterior.
L23 Vkl, level 3, floor lot 4301/1-3.

P408. Foot of tripod vase. Fig. 3-21; Pl. 3-101.
H. (pres.) 0.045. W. 0.037. Th. 0.017.
Rectangular. Munsell 7.5YR 8/4 pink. Flaky clay, worn surfaces. Broken where foot joins body. Frags. black paint preserved. Slight flute down center of both flat sides.
L23 Vkl, level 3, floor lot 4301/1-3.

P409. Handle of skyphos.
D. 0.012.
Munsell 5YR 7/6 reddish yellow. 2 joining frags. Well-fired clay, smooth surfaces. Frags. black paint preserved. Handle: Type A (round, D. 0.01 and above).
L23 Vkl, level 3, floor lots 4301/1-3, 4324, 4581 (combined).

P410-11. 16 skyphos handle frags.
Reddish yellow (6), light gray (5), and very pale brown (5) clay. Traces black paint preserved. Handle: Type A.
L23 Vkl, level 3, floor lots 4301/1-3, 4324, 4581 (combined).

P412. Handle and body frag. of skyphos.
H. (pres.) 0.045. Th. body 0.004.
Reddish yellow clay with orange-pink core. Possible wavy line in decorative zone between handles; above and below, frags. of black coating; good streaky black paint on interior and on handle. Wheel ridging on interior. Handle: Type A.
L23 Vkl, level 3, floor lots 4301/1-3, 4324, 4581 (combined).

P413. 20 skyphos handle frags.
D. 0.01-0.014.
Munsell 5YR 7/6 reddish yellow (18) to 5Y 8/3 pale yellow (2). Frags. black paint preserved. Handle: Type A.
L23 Vkl, level 3, floor lots 4301/1-3, 4324, 4581 (combined).

P414. Handle frag. of skyphos.
W. 0.012.
Munsell 10YR 8/4 very pale brown. Flaky clay, worn surfaces. Frags. black paint preserved. Handle: Type B (almost rectangular, not round).
L23 Vkl, level 3, floor lots 4301/1-3, 4324, 4581 (combined).

P415-16. 12 skyphos handle frags.
Very pale brown clay. Frags. black paint preserved. Handle: Type C (round, D. 0.0095 and under).
L23 Vkl, level 3, floor lots 4301/1-3, 4324, 4581 (combined).

P417. Rim and handle frag. of shallow bowl or plate. Fig. 3-17.
W. handle 0.01.
Elliptical strap handle attached to rim. Rim has slight indentation on interior of lip for holding lid. Frags. black paint preserved on exterior and in indentation on inner rim. Bowl handle: Type A.
L23 Vkl, level 3, Wall Ca, lot 4332.

P418. Handle and rim frag. of cup.
W. 0.013.
Munsell 2.5Y 8/2 white. Flat to elliptical handle. Flaky clay, worn surfaces. No traces paint preserved. Cup handle: Type A.
L23 Vkl, level 3, floor lots 4301/1-3, 4324, 4581 (combined).

P419. 4 cup handle frags.
W. 0.011-0.014.
White flaky clay, like **P418**. Flat to elliptical handle. Frags. black paint preserved. Cup handle: Type A.
L23 Vkl, level 3, floor lots 4301/1-3, 4324, 4581 (combined).

Closed Shapes

P420. Rim, neck, and shoulder frag. of oinochoe. Figs. 3-19, 3-35.
H. (pres.) 0.093. Th. 0.006. D. rim ca. 0.11.
Munsell 10YR 7/1 light gray (exterior); 2.5YR 6/8 light red (interior). Clay fired to a hard, brittle texture. Frags. black paint preserved on exterior. Wheel ridging interior. Incision on exterior at transition from neck to shoulder. Rim: Type A1.
L23 Vkl, level 3, Wall Ca, lot 4332.

P421. Shoulder frag. of oinochoe.
H. (pres.) 0.035.
Light gray clay. 4 half-preserved hand-drawn concentric semicircles; above and below, black bands.
L23 Vkl, level 3, floor lot 4301/1-3.

P422. Rim frag. of jug.
H. (pres.) 0.028. Th. 0.008.
Reddish yellow flaky clay; worn surfaces. No traces paint preserved. Rim: Type A1.
L23 Vkl, level 3, floor lot 4301/1-3.

P423. Rim frag. of jug. Fig. 3-19.
H. (pres.) 0.021. Th. 0.005.
Reddish yellow flaky clay, worn surfaces. No paint preserved on exterior; frags. of brown paint on inner rim. Rim: Type A2.
L23 Vkl, level 3, lot 4338.

P424. Rim and neck frag. of jug. Fig. 3-19.
H. (pres.) 0.037. Th. 0.0035. D. ca. 0.08-0.09.
Pale brown flaky clay, worn surfaces. Good black paint on exterior and in hollow (perhaps for lid) of rim on interior. Rim: Type B.
L23 Vkl, level 3, floor lot 4301/1-3.

P425. Upper profile of oinochoe, including rim, neck, shoulder, and handle. Figs. 3-19, 3-36.
H. (pres.) 0.119. Th. neck 0.007. D. rim ca. 0.105.
About ½ preserved. Munsell 7.5YR 7/6 reddish yellow (with pinkish tinge). Flaky clay. Flat handle (W. 0.018). Frags. black paint preserved on exterior and on interior of rim. Black stripes on top of rim and on top of handle. Rim: Type A2.
L23 Vkl, level 3, Wall Ca, lot 4332.

P426. Rim, neck, and handle frag. of small jug. Figs. 3-19, 3-39.
H. (pres.) 0.028. Th. neck 0.003. D. rim ca. 0.065.
About ½ preserved. Reddish yellow flaky clay. Flat handle (W. 0.018). Frags. black paint preserved on exterior and on interior of rim. Black stripes on top of rim and on top of handle. Rim: Type A2.
L23 Vkl, level 3, Wall Ca, lot 4332.

P427. Rim frag. of jug.
H. (pres.) 0.02. Th. 0.006.
Reddish yellow flaky clay, worn surfaces. No traces paint preserved. Rim: Type A2.
L23 Vkl, level 3, Wall Ca, lot 4332.

P428. Oinochoe base. Fig. 3-20.
D. 0.08.
High conical foot. Reddish yellow flaky clay. Traces of brown paint on exterior and on underside of base. String marks on base; wheel ridging interior. Base: Type A.
L23 Vkl, level 3, floor lot 4301/1-3.

P429. Flat base, probably from amphora. Fig. 3-20.
D. 0.16.
Reddish yellow flaky clay, worn surfaces. No traces paint preserved. Base: Type A (flat).
L23 Vkl, level 4S, lot 4337/1-3.

P430. Handle frag. of oinochoe. Fig. 3-20.
W. 0.029.
Munsell 2.5Y 8/2 white. Plain flat handle (attached to body frag.). Frags. black paint preserved. Handle: Type A1.
L23 Vkl, level 3, floor lots 4301/1-3, 4324, 4581 (combined).

P431. Handle of oinochoe.
W. 0.027.
Reddish yellow clay. Frags. black paint preserved. Handle: Type A1.
L23 Vkl, level 3, floor lots 4301/1-3, 4324, 4581 (combined).

Coarse Ware

P432. Rim of bowl(?) Fig. 3-20; Pl. 3-104.
H. (pres.) 0.038. Th. 0.007. D. ca. 0.23.
Reddish yellow clay, burned black to dark gray. Coarse, gritty clay. Rim: Type A.
L23 Vkl, level 3, floor lots 4301/1-3, 4324, 3581 (combined).

P433-35. Rims of bowls(?) Fig. 3-20 (**P434**); Pl. 3-104 (**P434**).
Th. 0.007-0.0075. D. ca. 0.20 (uneven).
Reddish yellow clay, burned black to gray. Rim: Type A.
L23 Vkl, level 3, floor lots 4301/1-3, 4324, 4581 (combined).

P436. Rim frag. Fig. 3-20; Pl. 3-104.
H. (pres.) 0.03. Th. 0.008. D. ca. 0.26.
Reddish yellow clay, burned black. Rim: Type B.
L23 Vkl, level 3, floor lots 4301/1-3, 4324, 4581 (combined).

P437-39. Rim frags. Fig. 3-20 (**P437**); Pl. 3-104 (**P437**).
Th. 0.005 (**P439**), 0.007 (**P438**), 0.009 (**P437**). D. ca. 0.08-0.09 (**P439**), 0.13 (**P438**), 0.22 (**P437**).
Reddish yellow clay, burned gray in places, with dark gray core. Rim: Type B.
L23 Vkl, level 3, floor lot 4301/1-3.

P440. Flat base. Fig. 3-21.
D. ca. 0.10.
Light orange red gritty clay. Base: Type B.
L23 Vkl, level 4S, lot 4337.

P441-43. Flat bases. Fig. 3-21 (**P441, P443**).
D. ca. 0.13 (**P443**), 0.18 (**P442**).
Reddish yellow gritty clay, burned in parts to black or dark gray. Base: Type C.
L23 Vkl, level 4S, lot 4337.

P444. Ringed base. Fig. 3-21.
D. ca. 0.11.
Reddish yellow gritty clay, burned black on interior and in places on exterior. Base: Type C.
L23 Vkl, level 3, floor lot 4301/1-3.

P445-46. Handle frags. (of coarse amphorae?). Fig. 3-20 (**P445**).
W. 0.036.

Plain flat to elliptical handles. Light gray-blue clay, burned in places. Handle: Type A1.

L23 Vkl, level 3, floor lots 4301/1-3, 4324, 4581 (combined).

P447. Handle frag. Fig. 3-20.

W. 0.036.

Elliptical handle with flute down center of top. Reddish yellow clay, burned black in places. Handle: Type A3.

L23 Vkl, level 3, floor lots 4301/1-3, 4324, 4581 (combined).

P448. Handle frag. (of jug?) Fig. 3-20.

D. ca. 0.01.

Round handle. Reddish yellow clay burned black. Handle: Type B.

L23 Vkl, level 3, floor lots 4301/1-3, 4324, 4581 (combined).

P449. Pithos body frag.

H. (pres.) 0.073. Th. 0.014.

Coarse gritty reddish yellow clay, fairly smooth on exterior. Wide raised band with slight flute running down center of band.

L23 Vkl, level 3, floor lots 4301/1-3, 4324, 4581 (combined).

A second good group of DAII sherds from the first phase of Unit IV-1 comes from the entrance and courtyard area of the building. These predominantly DAII lots contain some DAI and LHIIIB admixture.

Open Shapes

P450. Rim frag. of skyphos.

H. (pres.) 0.22. Th. 0.003. D. ca. 0.06-0.07.

Reddish yellow flaky clay, worn surfaces. Frags. of light brown paint exterior; possible frags. of brown paint on interior. Rim: Type A1.

L23 Xklm-E2/3, level 3, lot 3367/1.

P451. Rim and body frag. of skyphos.

H. (pres.) 0.035. Th. ca. 0.004. D. ca. 0.07.

Reddish yellow flaky clay, worn surfaces. Good monochrome black coating on exterior and interior. Rim: Type A1.

L23 Xklm, level 4, lot 4311W.

P452. 5 rim frags. of skyphoi.

D. ca. 0.07.

Reddish yellow to very pale brown clay. Streaky black-brown coating on exterior and interior. Rim: Type A2.

L23 Xklm-W1/3, level 3, lots 2506, 2508; L23 Xklm, level 4, lot 4311W; L23 Xklm-E2/3, level 3, lots 3367/1, 3370.

P453. Rim frag. of skyphos.

H. (pres.) 0.025. Th. 0.005.

Reddish yellow with pinkish core. Good streaky black paint on exterior and frags. of black coating preserved on the interior. Rim: Type B1.

L23 Wklm, level 3, floor lots 2501, 2504, 2507.

P454-55. Rim frags. of skyphoi.

D. ca. 0.18 (**P455**), ca. 0.14 (**P455**).

Reddish yellow with pink tinge. Flaky clay, worn surfaces. Frags. of streaky black coating on exterior and interior. Rim: Type B1.

L23 WXklm, level 3a, lot 3372/1-2; L23 Xklm-E2/3, level 3, tumble lot 3370.

P456. Rim and body frag. of skyphos.

H. (pres.) 0.032. Th. 0.0045. D. ca. 0.10.

Munsell 10YR 8/4 very pale brown. Good monochrome black coating on exterior and interior. Rim: Type B2.

L23 Wklm, level 3, lots 4305, 4306, 4313.

P457. Upper profile of skyphos. Fig. 3-25.

H. (pres.) 0.054. Th. 0.004. D. ca. 0.13.

Munsell 7.5YR 7/6 reddish yellow (with pinkish core). Flaky clay, worn surfaces. Frags. of black coating preserved on exterior and interior. Shallow incisions under rim. Rim: Type B2.

L23 Xklm-W1/3, level 3, lots 2506, 2508.

P458. Rim and body frag. of skyphos or deep bowl. Fig. 3-16; Pl. 3-40.

H. (pres.) 0.066. Th. 0.004. D. ca. 0.24.

Reddish yellow clay, fired to a light gray color on the interior. Frags. of black coating on exterior and interior. Rim: Type B3.

L23 Xklm, level 4, lot 4312E.

P459. Rim frag. of skyphos or deep bowl.

H. (pres.) 0.032. Th. 0.003. D. ca. 0.18-0.20.

Reddish yellow flaky clay, worn surfaces. Frags. of streaky black paint on exterior and interior. Rim: Type B3.

L23 Xklm-E2/3, level 3, lot 3367/1.

P460-61. Rim frags. of skyphoi or deep bowls.

D. ca. 0.20 (**P460**), ca. 0.24 (**P461**).

Reddish yellow clay. Frags. streaky black paint exterior and interior. Rim: Type C1.

L23 Wklm, level 3, lots 4305, 4306, 4313; L23 Xklm-E2/3, level 3, lot 3370.

P462. 6 rim frags. of skyphoi or deep bowls.

Like **P460** and **P461**. Rim: Type C1.

L23 Xklm-W1/3, level 3, lots 2506, 2508; L23 Xklm, level 4, lots 4311W, 4312E; L23 Xklm-E2/3, level 3, lot 3367/1; level 3a, lot 3366/1.

P463. 4 rim frags. of skyphoi or deep bowls.

Reddish yellow flaky clay, worn surfaces. Frags. of black paint preserved on exterior and interior. Rim: Type C2.

L23 Xklm-W1/3, level 3, lots 2506, 2508; L23 Xklm-E2/3, level 3, lot 3367/1; L23 Xklm, level 4, lot 4321N.

P464. Decorated body frag. of skyphos. Pl. 3-58.

H. (pres.) 0.053. Th. 0.0045.

Munsell 7.5YR 7/4 pink (with grayish tinge). To right, 8 frags. of arcs of accumbent concentric semi-circles in black with heavy dots at ends of arcs; to left, 6 frags. of arcs of pendent concentric semi-circles; below decoration of concentric semi-circles is a frag. of a black band. Good streaky black paint on interior. Slight wheel ridging on interior.

L23 Xklm, level 4, lot 4312E.

P465. Decorated body frag. of skyphos.

H. (pres.) 0.032. Th. 0.0045.

Reddish yellow flaky clay, worn surfaces. 4 frags. of arcs (bottom of arcs ending in heavy black dots) of accumbent concentric semi-circles in black; below, frags. of 2 wide black bands. Faint frags. of black paint preserved on interior. Wheel ridging on interior.

L23 Xklm-E2/3, level 3, lot 3370.

P466. Decorated body frag. of skyphos.

H. (pres.) 0.033. Th. 0.005 (bottom)-0.008 (top).

Reddish yellow clay with light gray-blue core. 4 frags. of sides of piled triangles in black paint, very worn and faded.

L23 Xklm, level 4, lot 4312E.

P467-68. Small rim frags. of kraters.

H. (pres.) 0.014. D. ca. 0.15 (**P467**).
Pale clay with light gray blue core. Flaky clay, worn surfaces. No traces paint preserved. Rim: Type A.
L23 Wklm, level 3, lots 4305, 4306, 4313; L23 Xklm-W1/3, level 3, lots 2506, 2508.

P469. Rim frag. of krater. Fig. 3-16.
H. (pres.) 0.018. D. ca. 0.15(?)
Very pale brown flaky clay, worn surfaces. No paint preserved on exterior; frags. of light brown-black paint on interior. Rim: Type B2.
L23 Xklm, level 3, lot 3370.

P470. Rim and wall frag. of krater. Fig. 3-16.
H. (pres.) 0.038. Th. wall 0.01. D. ca. 0.25(?)
Reddish yellow clay. Frags. streaky black paint on interior. Beginning of raised band at point where wall frag. is broken. Rim: Type C.
L23 Wklm, level 3, lots 4305, 4306, 4313.

P471. Rim and wall frag. of krater. Fig. 3-16.
H. (pres.) 0.053. Th. wall 0.007-0.008. D. ca. 0.30(?)
Reddish yellow gritty clay with pinkish tinge; worn surfaces. Possible frags. black paint on exterior. Rim: Type D.
L23 Xklm, level 4, lot 4312E.

P472. 6 skyphos base frags.
D. ca. 0.04.
Reddish yellow flaky clay, worn surfaces. Frags. black paint preserved on exterior and inside base. Base: Type A1.
L23 Xklm-W1/3, level 3, lots 2506, 2508; L23 Xklm-E2/3, level 3, lot 3370; L23 Xklm, level 4, lots 4311W, 4312E, 4321N.

P473. Base and body frag. of skyphos.
D. 0.063.
Bright reddish yellow flaky clay, worn surfaces. No traces of paint preserved. Spiral grooving in interior. Base: Type B.
L23 Wklm, level 3, floor lots 2501, 2504, 2507.

P474. 13 skyphos base frags.
D. ca. 0.04-0.06.
Reddish yellow to very pale brown clay; flaky clay, worn surfaces. Traces of black paint exterior and interior. Base: Type C.
L23 Xklm, level 4, lots 4312E, 4321N; L23 Xklm-W1/3, level 3, lots 2506, 2508; L23 Xklm-E2/3, level 3, lot 3370.

P475. 36 skyphos handle frags.
Type A.
L23 Wklm, level 3, floor lots 2501, 2504, 2507.

P476. Handle and body frag. of skyphos.
W. handle 0.01.
Very pale brown clay. Frags. of black paint preserved. Handle: Type B.
L23 Wklm, level 3, lots 2501, 2504, 2507.

P477. 15 skyphos handle frags.
Type C.
L23 Wklm, level 3, floor lots 2501, 2504, 2507.

P478. Upper profile (including handle) of cup. Fig. 3-34.
D. ca. 0.10(?)
Reddish yellow flaky clay, worn surfaces. Traces of brown paint on handle and on interior of body. Probably monochrome black coating also on exterior. Handle: Type B.
L23 Wklm, level 3, lots 4305, 4306, 4313.

P479. 3 cup handle frags.
Type B, similar to **P478**.
L23 WXklm, level 3a, lot 3372/1-2.

Closed Shapes

P480-84. Rim frags. of oinochoai.
Reddish yellow to very pale brown clay. Traces of black paint preserved on exterior; black paint on inner rim (**P481**). Rim: Type A1.
L23 Xklm, level 4, lot 4311W; L23 Xklm-W1/3, level 3, lots 2506, 2508.

P485. Rim and neck frag. of jug. Fig. 3-19.
H. (pres.) 0.037. Th. 0.005. D. ca. 0.12.
Very pale brown flaky clay, worn surfaces. Traces of black paint preserved on exterior and on top of rim. Small incisions under rim. Rim: Type A3.
L23 Xklm, level 4, lot 4312E.

P486. Rim and neck frag. of oinochoe. Fig. 3-19.
H. (pres.) 0.045. Th. 0.005.
Reddish yellow flaky clay, worn surfaces. Frags. black paint on exterior and interior of rim. Rim: Type B.
L23 Xklm, level 4, lot 4312E.

P487. Rim and neck frag. of oinochoe.
Similar to **P486**. Rim: Type B.
L23 Xklm-E2/3, level 3, tumble lot 3370.

P488. Decorated oinochoe belly frag.
H. (pres.) 0.033. Th. 0.0035.
Reddish yellow clay with pinkish tinge. Flaky clay, worn surfaces. 7 frags. of arcs of concentric semi-circles in black. Light gray slip preserved on exterior.
L23 Xklm, level 4, lot 4311W.

P489. Flat base, probably from amphora.
D. ca. 0.15.
Similar to **P429**. Base: Type A.
L23 Xklm, level 4, lot 4311W.

P490. 2 handle frags. of oinochoai or jugs.
Flat handles, W. 0.025.
Reddish yellow to very pale brown flaky clay; worn surfaces. Handle: Type A1.
L23 Xklm-W1/3, level 3, lots 2506, 2508.

P491. Handle of oinochoe. Fig. 3-20.
W. 0.035.
Flat, but with rib down center of top. Reddish yellow clay; good frags. of black paint preserved. Handle: Type A2.
L23 Xklm, level 4, lot 4311W.

P492. Handle and belly frag. of amphora. Fig. 3-20.
H. (pres.) 0.112. Th. 0.01. D. handle 0.026.
Round handle. Very pale brown clay. Traces of black paint preserved on exterior of belly frag., but none on handle. Tip of handle frag. burned to a light gray color. Wheel ridging on interior of belly frag. Handle: Type B (round).
L23 WXklm, level 3a, lot 3372/1-2.

P493. Belly handle frag. from amphora.

Similar to **P492**. Munsell 7.5YR 6/8 light red. Handle: Type B (round).
L23 Xklm-W1/3, level 3, lots 2506, 2508.

Coarse Ware

P494. 6 coarse rims. Fig. 3-20.
Th. 0.007-0.013. D. ca. 0.19-0.24.
Reddish yellow gritty clay, burned in places. Type A.
L23 Wklm, level 3, floor lots 2501, 2504, 2507; L23 Xklm, level 4, lot 4321N; L23 Xklm-E2/3, level 3, lot 3370.

P495. 3 coarse rims. Fig. 3-20.
Th. 0.007-0.008. D. ca. 0.22-0.25.
Reddish yellow gritty clay, burned on interior. Type B.
L23 Xklm-W1/3, level 3, lots 2506, 2508; L23 Xklm, level 4, lot 4321N.

P496. Profile of rim and neck of neck-handled amphora. Fig. 3-43.
H. (pres.) 0.103. D. ca. 0.15.
Coarse gritty light red clay, burned black in places on handle. Handle joins rim just below lip. On top of rim, above point where handle joins, is a knob with a curve in its outer edge as a place to rest a lid. Simple elliptical handle, W. 0.033. Type A1.
L23 Wklm, level 3, lots 2501, 2504, 2507.

P497. Rim and neck frag. of neck-handled amphora. Fig. 3-43.
H. (pres.) 0.067. D. ca. 0.20.
Reddish yellow clay, burned black in core and on interior. On inside of rim a projecting knob, probably to rest lid.
L23 Xklm-W1/3, level 3, lots 2506, 2508.

P498. Coarse base.
D. ca. 0.09.
About ⅓ preserved. Reddish yellow clay, burned. Base: Type A.
L23 Xklm-W1/3, level 3, lots 2506, 2508.

P499. Coarse base.
D. ca. 0.10.
About ¼ preserved. Reddish yellow clay (with inclusions) with black core and burned black on interior. Base: Type C.
L23 Xklm, level 4, lot 4312E.

P500. Handle frag. Fig. 3-20.
W. ca. 0.035.
Flat handle with rib down center of top. Reddish yellow clay, burned. Handle: Type A2 (with rib).
L23 Xklm, level 4, lot 4321N.

P501. Handle and rim frag. Fig. 3-20.
W. handle 0.044.
Handle broken at rim, but frags. of 3 deep grooves are preserved on top of handle. Light red clay, burned. Handle: Type C (with grooves).
L23 Wklm, level 3, floor lots 2501, 2504, 2507.

P502. Rim and body frag. of pithos. Fig. 3-21; Pl. 3-115.
H. (pres.) 0.106. Th. 0.028-0.033.
Munsell 2.5YR 6/8 light red. Coarse gritty clay with inclusions. Decoration under rim of incised circles (D. 0.015); in places, the circles intersect. These circles form no formal pattern but are arranged in rough rows along the surface of the sherd.
L23 Wklm, level 3, lot 4306.

P503. Body frag. of pithos.
H. (pres.) 0.12. Th. body 0.025. Th. band 0.031. W. band 0.039.
Reddish yellow clay with inclusions. Body frag. has raised band decorated with incised chevrons.
L23 Xklm-W1/3, level 3, lots 2506, 2507.

P504. Body frag. of pithos.
H. (pres.) 0.07. Th. body 0.024. Th. band 0.029.
Reddish yellow clay fired to a light gray on the exterior. Body frag. has raised band decorated with incised triangle.
L23 Xklm-W1/3, level 3, lots 2506, 2507.

P505. Pithos base. Fig. 3-22.
D. 0.157 (uneven).
Munsell 2.5YR 6/8 light red. Coarse gritty clay with small inclusions. Rounded, uneven bottom.
L23 Wklm, level 3, lot 4306.

P506. Pithos base. Fig. 3-22.
D. 0.142 (uneven).
About ½ preserved. Reddish yellow clay with inclusions. Flat bottom.
L23 Xklm, level 3, lots 2506, 2508.

Section B

From Area IVNE. The LHIIIB Unit IV-7 was reused in the DAII period. Associated with this reuse are levels 5 and 6 of L23 Tmn, level 5 of L23 Umn, and level 5 of L23 UVo. The lots from these levels are not pure DAII but are mixed with much LHIIIB and some DAI and DAIII.

Open Shapes

P507. Rim and body frag. of skyphos.
H. (pres.) 0.041. Th. 0.004. D. ca. 0.09.
Munsell 10YR 8/4 very pale brown. Flaky clay, worn surfaces. Paint on exterior is preserved in the form of black bands (but very worn and could be frags. of monochrome black coating?); good black coating on interior. Shallow incisions under rim. Rim: Type A1.
L23 Tmn, level 5c, lot 1855.

P508. 8 skyphos rim frags.
D. ca. 0.09(?)
Reddish yellow to very pale brown flaky clay, worn surfaces. Frags. black paint preserved on exterior and interior. Rim: Type A1.
L23 Tmn, level 5c, lots 1483, 1485, 1855.

P509. Upper profile of skyphos.
H. (pres.) 0.036. Th. 0.003. D. ca. 0.06. D. handle 0.008.
Reddish yellow flaky clay, worn surfaces. Remains of good black coating preserved on exterior and interior. Rim: Type A2.
L23 Tmn, level 6, lot 1874.

P510. 5 skyphos rim frags.
Similar to **P509**. Rim: Type A2.
L23 Tmn, level 5, lot 1486.

P511. 3 skyphos rim frags.
Similar to **P509**. Rim: Type A2.
L23 UVo, level 5, lots 1488, 1484.

P512. Rim frag. of skyphos. Fig. 3-16; Pl. 3-39.
H. (pres.) 0.025. Th. 0.003. D. ca. 0.09.
Reddish yellow to very pale brown clay. Streaky black paint frags. on exterior and inteiior. Rim: Type A3.
L23 UVo, level 4b, lots 1467, 1472, 1473, 1477, 1479 (combined).

P513. Rim frag. of skyphos.

H. (pres.) 0.026. Th. 0.003. D. ca. 0.10.

Pale brown clay. Frags. black paint preserved on exterior only. Rim: Type A3.

L23 UVo, level 4b, lots 1467, 1472, 1473, 1477, 1479 (combined).

P514. Rim frag. of skyphos. Fig. 3-16; Pl. 3-39.

H. (pres.) 0.025. Th. 0.003. D. ca. 0.12.

Reddish yellow clay. Good frags. of streaky black paint preserved on exterior and interior. Rim: Type A3.

L23 UVo, level 4b, lots 1467, 1472, 1473, 1477, 1479 (combined).

P515. Rim frag. of skyphos or deep bowl.

H. (pres.) 0.031. Th. 0.0045. D. ca. 0.22.

Reddish yellow clay. Good streaky black-brown paint on exterior and interior. Rim: Type B1.

L23 Tmn, level 5, lots 1494, 1500.

P516. 6 rim frags. of skyphoi or deep bowls.

Similar to **P515**. Rim: Type B1.

L23 Tmn, level 5c, lots 1483, 1485, 1855.

P517. Rim and body frag. of skyphos.

H. (pres.) 0.054. Th. 0.005. D. ca. 0.14.

Reddish yellow flaky clay, worn surfaces. Traces of black coating preserved on exterior and interior. Rim: Type B2.

L23 Tmn, level 5c, lots 1483, 1485.

P518. 13 skyphos rim frags.

Similar to **P517**. Rim: Type B2.

L23 Tmn, level 5, lot 1486; level 5c, lot 1855.

P519. Complete upper profile of skyphos or deep bowl. Fig. 3-30.

H. (pres.) 0.076. Th. 0.005. D. ca. 0.20.

Reddish yellow flaky clay, worn surfaces. Frags. of metope-triglyph decoration on main body of vase above handle zone. 3 vertical lines in black for triglyph; metope decoration largely destroyed, but could consist of large black dots. One frag. of dot preserved at corner by triglyph. Above and below decorated zone are bands of dull washy black paint; good streaky black coating on interior. Rim: Type B3.

L23 Tmn, level 5c, lot 1855.

P520. Upper profile (missing handles) of skyphos. Fig. 3-26.

H. (pres.) 0.072. Th. 0.005. D. ca. 0.16.

Reddish yellow flaky clay, worn surfaces. Frags. of sides of 3 piled triangles in decorative zone, probably in field between handles; above and below are streaky brown bands. 3 incisions on exterior, one under lip of rim and others just above zone of decoration. Good streaky black-brown coating on interior. Wheel ridging on interior. Rim: Type B3.

L23 Tmn, level 5c, lot 1855.

P521. Rim and body frag. of skyphos.

H. (pres.) 0.056. Th. 0.004.

Reddish yellow flaky clay, worn surfaces. Heavy black bands under rim with lighter brown coating underneath; good streaky black coating on interior. Rim: Type B3.

L23 Tmn, level 5c, lot 1855.

P522. Rim and body frag. of skyphos. Fig. 3-20.

H. (pres.) 0.05. Th. 0.006.

Reddish yellow flaky clay, worn surfaces. In decorative zone, possibly in field between handles, is preserved the upper part of a triangle; below lip of rim are 2 streaky black bands. Good frags. of black paint on interior. Rim: Type C1.

L23 Tmn, level 5, lot 1486.

P523. 8 skyphos rim frags.

Reddish yellow flaky clay, worn surfaces. Rim: Type C1.

L23 Tmn, level 5, lot 1486; level 5c, lot 1855.

P524. 2 skyphos rim frags.

Rim: Type C.

L23 Tmn, level 5c, lot 1855; level 6, lot 1874.

P525-31. Decorated body frags. of skyphoi or deep bowls.

Reddish yellow to very pale brown clay. Frags. of arcs of compass-drawn accumbent semi-circles in black-brown paint. **P528** has innermost semi-circle connected with central compass dot, as though a spiral. Frags. of black paint preserved on interior. Wheel ridging on interior (**P530**).

L23 Tmn, level 5, lots 1486, 1494, 1500; level 6, lot 1878.

P532 (NP51). Complete cup. Fig. 3-35; Pl. 3-69.

H. 0.067. D. rim 0.09. D. base 0.047. W. handle 0.013.

Munsell 10YR 7/2 light gray. Traces of monochrome black paint preserved on exterior, interior, and on underside of base. 3 incisions in shape of concentric circles on underside of base. String marks on exterior of base. Flat base. Rim: Type C1.

L23 Tmn, level 5a, lot 1481.

P533. Rim frag. of krater.

Similar to **P386**. Rim: Type A.

L23 Tmn, level 5c, lot 1855.

P534. Rim frag. of krater.

D. ca. 0.25.

Reddish yellow clay with orange-pink core. Frags. black paint on exterior and interior; black stripes on top of rim(?) Rim: Type A.

L23 UVo, level 5, lots 1484, 1488.

P535. Rim frag. of krater.

Reddish yellow flaky clay. Frags. of streaky black paint on exterior, interior, and top of rim. Rim: Type B1.

L23 UVo, level 5a, lot 1491.

P536. Rim and wall frag. of krater. Fig. 3-16.

H. (pres.) 0.056.

Very pale brown flaky clay, worn surfaces. Frags. of streaky black paint on exterior, interior, and top of rim. Below rim is raised band decorated with diagonal slashes. Rim: Type C.

L23 UVo, level 4b, lot 1467.

P537. Rim frag. of krater. Fig. 3-16; Pl. 3-72.

H. (pres.) 0.035. Th. 0.005.

Reddish yellow flaky clay, worn surfaces. On exterior, washy black band below rim; below band are frags. of 4 vertical lines (metope from metope-triglyph decoration?) very worn and faded. Good frags. of streaky black paint on interior. Rim: Type E.

L23 Tmn, level 6, lot 1874.

P538. Rim and wall frag. of krater.

H. (pres.) 0.147. Th. ca. 0.01. D. ca. 0.30.

Reddish yellow clay with pinkish tinge. Worn surfaces; no traces paint preserved. Rim: Type F.

M23 Akl-W½ plus baulk, level 2, lot 3384/1-3; level 3, lot 3393/1-2.

P539. 7 skyphos bases.

D. 0.038-0.05.

Reddish yellow to very pale brown clay. Frags. of black paint exterior and interior. Base: Type A1.

L23 Tmn, level 5, lots 1494, 1500; level 5c, lot 1855; L23 UVo, level 4b, lot 1467; level 5, lots 1484, 1488.

P540. 4 skyphos or deep bowl base frags.
D. ca. 0.06-0.066.
Base: Type A2.
L23 Tmn, level 5, lot 1486; L23 UVo, level 4b, lot 1467; level 5, lots 1484, 1488.

P541. 4 skyphos or deep bowl bases.
D. 0.059, 0.064, 0.075, 0.085.
Reddish yellow flaky clay, worn surfaces. Frags. black paint preserved on exterior and interior. Base: Type B.
L23 Tmn, level 5, lot 1486.

P542. 6 skyphos bases.
D. ca. 0.05-0.075.
Reddish yellow clay. Frags. of streaky black-brown paint preserved. Base: Type C.
L23 Tmn, level 5, lots 1487, 1494, 1500; level 5c, lot 1855; L23 UVo, level 4b, lot 1467; level 5, lots 1484, 1488.

P543. Flat base of skyphos. Fig. 3-18.
D. 0.057.
Very pale brown flaky clay, worn surfaces. Frags. of black paint preserved on exterior and interior. Base: Type D.
L23 Tmn, level 5, lot 1498.

P544. Flat base of cup. Fig. 3-18.
D. 0.05.
Reddish yellow clay. Frags. black paint preserved on exterior and on underside of base. Concentric circular incisions on underside of base.
L23 UVo, level 4b, lot 1467.

P545-46. Flat bases of cups.
D. ca. 0.06.
Reddish yellow clay. Similar to **P544**.
L23 UVo, level 4b, lot 1467; L23 UVo, level 5, lots 1484, 1488.

P547. 2 cup handle frags.
W. 0.011-0.013.
Reddish yellow clay, worn surfaces. Traces black paint preserved. Handle: Type A.
L23 UVo, level 5, lot 1488; level 5a, lot 1491.

P548. Upper profile of cup. Fig. 3-34.
D. rim ca. 0.10. W. handle 0.014. Th. body 0.003.
Reddish yellow flaky clay, worn surfaces. Frags. of black paint preserved on exterior, interior, and on handle. Rim: Type C1(?); Handle: Type C.
L23 UVo, level 4b, lot 1467; level 5a, lot 1491; L23 Tmn, level 5C, lots 1483, 1485.

P549. 2 cup handle frags.
Similar to **P548**. Handle: Type C.
L23 UVo, level 4b, lots 1467, 1472, 1473, 1477, 1479 (combined).

Closed Shapes

P550. 2 rim frags. of oinochoai.
Type A1.
L23 Tmn, level 5c, lot 1855.

P551. 2 rim frags. of jugs.
Type A3.
L23 Tmn, level 6, lot 1874.

P552. Rim frag. of oinochoe.
Type B.
L23 Tmn, level 5c, lot 1855.

P553. Rim frag. of jug. Fig. 3-19.
Similar to **P554**. Rim: Type C.
L23 Tmn, level 6, lot 1874.

P554. Rim frag. of jug. Fig. 3-19.
H. (pres.) 0.022. Th. 0.003.
Reddish yellow clay fired gray in places. Good smooth frags. of black paint on exterior and interior of rim. Rim: Type C.
L23 Tmn, level 6, lot 1874.

P555. Rim and neck frag. of jug. Fig. 3-19.
H. (pres.) 0.034. Th. 0.005. D. ca. 0.08.
Reddish yellow to very pale brown clay. Flaky clay, worn surfaces. Good streaky black-brown paint on exterior. Rim: Type D.
L23 Tmn, level 5c, lot 1855.

P556. Neck and shoulder frag. of oinochoe.
H. (pres.) 0.057. Th. ca. 0.005-0.006.
Reddish yellow clay. Row of impressed dots (made with a stick?) at transition from neck to shoulder.
L23 Tmn, level 5c, lot 1855.

P557. Belly frag. of oinochoe.
H. (pres.) 0.03. Th. 0.005.
Very pale brown flaky clay, worn surfaces. No traces paint preserved. 4 parallel incised lines run horizontally across frag.
L23 Tmn, level 5c, lot 1855.

P558. Base of oinochoe. Fig. 3-20.
D. 0.084.
Reddish yellow clay. Frags. of streaky black paint on exterior. 4 concentric circular incisions on underside of base. Base: Type A.
L23 UVo, level 5, lot 1484.

P559. 2 base frags., probably of amphorae. Fig. 3-20.
D. ca. 0.17.
Reddish yellow flaky clay. No traces of paint preserved. Concentric circular incisions on underside of base. Base: Type B.
L23 UVo, level 4b, lot 1467.

P560. Flat base frag. (from amphoriskos?). Fig. 3-20.
D. ca. 0.10.
Light red flaky clay, worn surfaces. No traces of paint preserved. Base: Type B (flat).
L23 Tmn, level 5c, lots 1483, 1485.

P561. 2 flat handles, either from oinochoai or from neck-handled amphorae.
W. 0.034.
Reddish yellow clay. Frags. of black paint on top and sides of handles only. Handle: Type A1.
L23 Tmn, level 5, lot 1487.

P562. Handle of oinochoe or neck-handled amphora.
W. 0.035.
Flat handle. Reddish yellow flaky clay. No traces paint preserved. 2 deep incisions along top of handle. Handle: Type A3.
L23 UVo, level 4b, lot 1467.

P563. Handle frag. of small jug. Fig. 3-20.
W. 0.011.
Reddish yellow flaky clay, worn surfaces. Faint traces of black paint preserved. Handle: Type A6.
L23 Tmn, level 5, lot 1494.

Coarse Ware

P564. 6 rim frags. of coarse bowls.
D. ca. 0.15, 0.17, 0.21.
Reddish yellow clay, burned to light gray and black in places. Rim: Type A.
L23 Tmn, level 5, lot 1486; level 5c, lot 1855.

P565. 6 rim frags. of coarse bowls.
D. ca. 0.20.
Reddish yellow clay, burned gray and black in places. Rim: Type B.
L23 Tmn, level 5, lot 1486; level 5c, lot 1855.

P566. Flat base frag.
D. ca. 0.12.
Reddish yellow clay, burned gray in interior. Base: Type A.
L23 UVo, level 5a, lot 1491.

P567. 2 flat base frags. Fig. 3-21.
D. ca. 0.07.
Burned. Base: Type B.
L23 Wmn, level 2, lot 4592/2; L23 UVo, level 4b, lot 1467.

P568. Slightly rounded flat base of small bowl. Fig. 3-21.
D. 0.038.
Reddish yellow clay, burned in places. Base: Type D.
L23 Tmn, level 5, lot 1487.

P569. Ringed base frag. Fig. 3-21.
D. ca. 0.06-0.08.
Reddish yellow clay, fired to a light gray in places and with a black core. Base: Type E.
L23 UVo, level 4b, lot 1467.

P570. Leg frag. from cooking stand. Fig. 3-21; Pl. 3-112.
H. (pres.) 0.033. D. base 0.049. D. stem 0.037.
Reddish yellow clay, burned slightly at bottom and on underside of base.
L23 Tmn, level 5c, lot 1485.

P571. Leg from cooking stand. Fig. 3-21; Pl. 3-111.
H. (pres.) 0.071. D. base 0.048. D. stem 0.042.
Reddish yellow clay, burned black in places.
L23 UVo, level 4b, lot 1473.

P572. Leg from cooking stand. Fig. 3-21; Pl. 3-111.
H. (pres.) 0.052. D. base 0.045. D. stem 0.0375.
Brittle reddish yellow clay, burned on one side.
L23 UVo, level 5, lot 1484.

P573. 2 handle frags.
W. 0.03.
Handle: Type A1.
L23 Tmn, level 5c, lot 1855.

P574. Coarse handle (with wide flute down center of top).
W. 0.034.
Brittle reddish yellow clay with light gray tinges. Handle: Type A3.
L23 UVo, level 4b, lot 1467.

P575-76. Small handle frags. (from small coarse jug?).
D. ca. 0.013.
Reddish yellow clay, fired to a light gray in places. Handle: Type B (round).
L23 Tmn, level 5, lot 1494.

P577. Small round handle frag.
D. ca. 0.012-0.013.
Burned. Handle: Type B (round).
L23 UVo, level 5a, lot 1491.

P578. Handle frag. (with grooves down center of top).
W. 0.041.
2 grooves. Reddish yellow flaky clay with gray core. Handle: Type C.
L23 Tmn, level 5c, lot 1855.

P579. 2 grooved handle frags.
Burned. Handle: Type C.
L23 Tmn, level 5c, lot 1855.

P580. Large belly handle (round to elliptical in shape). Fig. 3-21.
D. 0.03 (uneven).
Reddish yellow clay, burned black at base of handle. Handle: Type D.
L23 Tmn, level 5c, lot 1855.

P581. Belly handle frag.
D. 0.026 (uneven).
Similar to **P580**. Handle: Type D.
L23 Tmn, level 5c, lot 1855.

P582. Frag. of coarse strainer.
H. (pres.) 0.045. Th. 0.008.
2 complete holes preserved; traces of 4 others. D. holes 0.003.
L23 Tmn, level 5c, lot 1855.

P583. Rim frag. of pithos. Fig. 3-21; Pl. 3-116.
H. (pres.) 0.142. Th. 0.032.
Coarse reddish yellow clay with inclusions. Decoration of incised circles on exterior (D. circles 0.014).
L23 Tmn, level 5c, lot 1855.

P584. Rim and body frag. of pithos. Fig. 3-21; Pl. 3-116.
H. (pres.) 0.115. Th. 0.022. Th. raised band 0.039.
Broken at top of rim. Below rim is raised band with rope decoration.
L23 Tmn, level 5c, lot 1855.

P585. Base of pithos. Fig. 3-41.
D. ca. 0.14. Th. body 0.034.
About ⅙ preserved. Coarse reddish yellow flaky clay with inclusions. Flat base.
L23 Tmn, level 5c, lots 1483, 1485.

P586. Body frag. of pithos.
H. (pres.) 0.077. Th. 0.024. Th. band 0.034.
Coarse light red clay with inclusions. 2 raised bands with decoration; lower band has incised slashes to right, upper band has incised slashes to left; together, decoration of both bands forms a herring bone pattern.
L23 Tmn, level 5c, lot 1855.

Section C

From Area IVNW. Apart from the stratified DAII deposit in L23 Vkl, the best group of DAII sherds comes from a dump to the north of Unit IV-5. The dump is located primarily in level 3 of L23 Top, continuing slightly into the top of level 4 and spilling over into level 2 of L23 So.

Open Shapes

P587. Rim frag. of skyphos.
H. (pres.) 0.014. Th. 0.003. D. ca. 0.08.
Munsell 7.5YR 7/6 reddish yellow. Flaky clay, worn surfaces. Good black coating on exterior and interior. Possible reserved band inner rim. Rim: Type A1.
L23 Top, level 4C and S, lot 3408/2.

P588. Rim frag. of skyphos.
H. (pres.) 0.021. Th. 0.0025. D. ca. 0.08.
Very pale brown clay. Good washy black coating on exterior and interior. Reserved band inner rim. Rim: Type A1.
L23 Top, level 3, lot 3405/6-9.

P589. 2 skyphos rim frags.
Th. 0.003. D. ca. 0.10.
Reddish yellow clay. Traces of streaky black paint on exterior and interior. Reserved band inner rim. Rim: Type A1.
L23 Top, level 4C and S, lot 3408/2.

P590. 8 skyphos rim frags.
Th. 0.003. D. ca. 0.08-0.09.
Reddish yellow clay. Frags. of streaky black-brown paint on exterior and interior. Rim: Type A2.
L23 Top, level 3, lot 3405/6-9.

P591. Rim and body frag. of skyphos.
H. (pres.) 0.027. Th. 0.0035. D. ca. 0.09.
Very pale brown clay with pinkish tinge. Black band under rim; below, undecorated zone in field between handles. Good black coating on interior. Rim: Type A2.
L23 Top, level 3, lot 3405/6-9.

P592. Rim and body frag. of skyphos or deep bowl. Fig. 3-25.
H. (pres.) 0.043. Th. 0.005. D. ca. 0.14(?)
Reddish yellow flaky clay. Black-brown band under rim; below, frags. of 4 arcs of accumbent concentric semi-circles in brown. Frags. of streaky black-brown paint on interior. Rim: Type A2.
L23 Top, level 3, lot 3405/6-9.

P593. Rim and body frag. of skyphos or deep bowl.
H. (pres.) 0.335. Th. 0.005.
Reddish yellow clay. Frags. of bands in brown paint alternate with reserved bands on both exterior and interior. Rim: Type A2.
L23 Top, level 3, lot 3405/6-9.

P594. Rim and body frag. of skyphos or deep bowl.
Similar to **P593.** Small mending hole under rim. Rim: Type A2.
L23 Top, level 4C and S, lot 3408/2.

P595. 3 skyphos rim frags.
Th. 0.003. D. ca. 0.10.
Reddish yellow clay. Frags. of streaky black-brown paint preserved on exterior and interior. Rim: Type A3.
L23 Top, level 3, lot 3405/6-9.

P596. Rim frag. of skyphos. Fig. 3-16; Pl. 3-39.
H. (pres.) 0.018. Th. 0.0035. D. ca. 0.09.
Reddish yellow clay. Frags. of black paint preserved on exterior and interior. Reserved band inner rim. Rim: Type A4.
L23 Top, level 4C and S, lot 3408/2.

P597. Rim and body frag. of skyphos or deep bowl. Fig. 3-27.
H. (pres.) 0.04. Th. 0.005. D. ca. 0.16(?)
Reddish yellow clay. Small black band below rim; below, decorated zone with two tangential sets of concentric semi-circles. Frags. of 2 arcs preserved at left; frags. of 4 arcs at right. Good streaky black coating on interior. Rim: Type B1.
L23 Top, level 3, lot 3405/6-9;

P598. Rim frag. of skyphos.
H. (pres.) 0.026. Th. 0.005. D. ca. 0.09-0.10.
Reddish yellow clay. Streaky brown-black paint on exterior and interior. Incision at base of rim. Rim: Type B1.
L23 Top, level 3, lot 3405/6-9.

P599. 7 skyphos rim and body frags.
Th. ca. 0.004. D. ca. 0.18-0.19, 0.23.
Reddish yellow clay. Frags. of streaky black paint on exterior and interior. Rim: Type B1.
L23 Top, level 3, lot 3405/1-4.

P600 (NP77). Complete upper profile of skyphos. Fig. 3-25; Pl. 3-59.
H. (pres.) 0.086. Th. 0.004. D. rim ca. 0.12. D. handle 0.011.
About ½ preserved without base. Munsell 7.5YR 8/6 reddish yellow. Thin black band under rim; below, belly motif of crosshatched triangles with metope-triglyph motif. Good black coating on interior; reserved band inner rim. Rim: Type B2.
L23 Top, level 3, lot 3405/6-9.

P601. Rim and body frags. of skyphoi or deep bowls.
Th. 0.005-0.006. D. ca. 0.16-0.18.
Reddish yellow clay. Washy black paint frags. preserved on exterior and interior. Rim: Type B2.
L23 Top, level 3, lot 3405/6-9.

P602 (NP78). Complete upper profile of skyphos. Fig. 3-27; Pl. 3-49.
H. (pres.) 0.082. D. rim ca. 0.17. D. handle 0.012.
About ½ preserved, missing foot. Munsell 7.5YR 8/6 reddish yellow (with pink core). Decorated zone of wolf's tooth in field between handles, flanked by 2 thin bands; above and below, black coating. Streaky black-brown coating on interior; reserved band inner rim. Shape uneven; possibly warped in firing. Rim: Type B3.
L23 Top, level 3, lot 3405/6-9.

P603. Profile of skyphos (missing handles). Fig. 3-25.
Th. ca. 0.0045. D. ca. 0.14.
3 nonjoining frags. Reddish yellow clay. Decoration of crosshatched triangles in handle zone; above and below, streaky black-brown paint. Small undecorated band at bottom of base. Good streaky black coating on interior; reserved band inner rim. Rim: Type B3.
L23 Top, level 4C and S, lot 3408/2.

P604. Rim and body frag. of deep bowl. Fig. 3-31.
H. (pres.) 0.054. Th. 0.006-0.008. D. ca. 0.23.
Reddish yellow flaky clay, worn surfaces. Decorated zone very worn, but perhaps concentric semi-circles below black band (1 frag. of arc preserved); to left, frag. of handle lining. Streaky black-brown paint above decorated zone. 2 shallow incisions under rim. Good streaky black coating on interior. Reserved band inner rim. Rim: Type B3.
L23 Top, level 3, lot 3405/6-9.

P605. Rim and body frag. of deep bowl.
H. (pres.) 0.042. Th. 0.005. D. ca. 0.15.
Reddish yellow clay. Good blue-black coating exterior and interior; reserved band inner rim. 2 incisions below rim on exterior. Rim: Type B3.
L23 Top, level 4C and S, lot 3408/1.

P606. 3 deep bowl rim frags.
D. ca. 0.16.
Reddish yellow flaky clay. Streaky black-brown paint on exterior and interior. Rim: Type B3.
L23 Top, level 3, lot 3405/6-9.

P607. Rim and body frag. of skyphos or deep bowl. Fig. 3-30.
H. (pres.) 0.04. Th. 0.004. D. ca. 0.18.
Very pale brown clay. Thin black band along rim; below, two sets of tangential concentric semi-circles. Set to right has central dot for compass point. Good washy black paint on interior. Rim: Type B4.
L23 Top, level 3, lot 3405/6-9.

P608. Rim and body frag. of skyphos. Fig. 3-16; Pl. 3-41.
H. (pres.) 0.029. Th. 0.003. D. ca. 0.10.
Light gray flaky clay, worn surfaces. Frags. black paint exterior and interior; reserved band inner rim. Rim: Type B4.
L23 Top, level 3, lot 3405/6-9.

P609. Rim and body frag. of skyphos. Fig. 3-16; Pl. 3-41.
H. (pres.) 0.027. Th. 0.003. D. ca. 0.10(?)
Light gray clay with reddish yellow tinge. Flaky clay, worn surfaces. Frags. of light brown-black paint exterior and interior, Rim: Type B4.
L23 Top, level 3, lot 3405/6-9.

P610. 2 skyphos rim frags.
D. 0.10, 0.14.
Similar to **P609**. Rim: Type B4.
L23 Top, level 3, lot 3405/1-4.

P611. Upper profile (missing handles) of deep bowl. Fig. 3-31.
H. (pres.) 0.054. Th. 0.005. D. ca. 0.20.
Reddish yellow flaky clay. Broad band below rim; below, frags. of 2 sets of tangential accumbent semi-circles, possibly hand-drawn. Set to right has frags. of 6 arcs preserved; that to left, 1 frag. of arc. Good streaky black-brown coating on interior; reserved band inner rim. Wheel ridging on interior. Rim: Type C1.
L23 Top, level 3, lot 3405/6-9.

P612. 6 skyphos rim frags.
D. ca. 0.10-0.12.
Reddish yellow flaky clay. Frags. of black paint preserved on exterior and interior. One rim frag. has reserved band on inner rim. Rim: Type C1.
L23 Top, level 3, lot 3405/6-9.

P613. Upper profile (missing handles) of skyphos. Fig. 3-23.
H. (pres.) 0.034. Th. 0.004. D. ca. 0.12.
Very pale brown flaky clay. Thin black band under rim; below, frag. of set of piled triangles in black. Good black paint on interior. Rim: Type C3.
L23 Top, level 3, lot 3405/6-9.

P614. 3 skyphos rim frags.
D. ca. 0.14-0.15.
Reddish yellow flaky clay, worn surfaces. Frags. of black paint preserved on exterior and interior. One frag. has possible reserved band on inner rim; second frag. has 3 shallow incisions below rim on exterior. Rim: Type C2.
L23 Top, level 3, lot 3405/6-9.

P615. Profile of skyphos. Figs. 3-16, 3-23; Pl. 3-42.
D. rim ca. 0.09. D. base 0.041.
Reddish yellow clay. Good monochrome streaky black coating on exterior and interior. Rim: Type C3; Base: Type C.
L23 Top, level 3, lot 3405/6-9.

P616. Rim frag. of skyphos.
H. (pres.) 0.016. Th. 0.003. D. ca. 0.09.
Reddish yellow flaky clay. Streaky black-brown paint on exterior and interior. Rim: Type C3.
L23 Top, level 3, lot 3405/6-9.

P617. Rim frag. of skyphos. Fig. 3-16; Pl. 3-42.
H. (pres.) 0.024. Th. 0.005. D. ca. 0.20.
Reddish yellow clay with orange-pink core. Frags. of streaky brown paint preserved on exterior and interior. Rim: Type D.
L23 Top, level 3, lot 3405/6-9.

P618. Rim frag. of skyphos. Fig. 3-16; Pl. 3-42.
H. (pres.) 0.023. Th. 0.005. D. ca. 0.18(?)
Reddish yellow clay. Faint frags. of black paint on exterior and interior. Rim: Type D.
L23 Top, level 3, lot 3405/6-9.

P619. 3 skyphos rim frags.
Similar to **P617**, **P618**. Rim: Type D.
L23 Top, level 4C and S, lot 3408/2.

P620. 7 decorated body frags. of skyphoi or deep bowls. Pl. 3-53.
Reddish yellow clay. Frags. of arcs of compass-drawn accumbent semi-circles in black. Three body sherds contain frags. of 2 adjacent sets of semi-circles. On 3 sherds, central compass dot is linked to the nearest semi-circle in the form of a spiral. Frags. of streaky brown-black paint on interior.
L23 Top, level 3, lot 3405/6-9.

P621. 6 decorated body frags. of skyphoi.
Reddish yellow flaky clay; decoration quite worn. Frags. of arcs of compass-drawn (?) accumbent semi-circles in black. Frags. of 1 or 2 sets of semi-circles preserved. Frags. of streaky brown-black paint on interior.
L23 Top, level 3, lot 3405/6-9.

P622. Decorated skyphos body frag. Fig. 3-33.
H. (pres.) 0.043. Th. 0.0045-0.005.
Reddish yellow clay, worn surfaces. Decoration of wavy line flanked by 2 black bands; lower band drawn in heavier black paint. Good smooth black coating on interior.
L23 Top, level 3, lot 3405/6-9.

P623. Decorated skyphos body frag. Fig. 3-33.
H. (pres.) 0.038. Th. ca. 0.005.
Reddish yellow clay. Frags. of crosshatched triangles; below, black coating. Faint traces of black paint preserved on interior.
L23 Top, level 3, lot 3405/6-9.

P624. Decorated skyphos body frag. Fig. 3-33.
H. (pres.) 0.015. Th. 0.004.
Reddish yellow clay. Frags. of a crosshatched triangle in black. Fine black coating on interior.
L23 Top, level 3, lot 3405/6-9.

P625. Decorated skyphos body frag. Fig. 3-33.
H. (pres.) 0.0032. Th. 0.004.
Reddish yellow clay. Frag. of metope-triglyph motif; in metope a crosshatched diamond; 2 frags. of vertical lines of triglyph preserved on either side. Fine black coating on interior; slight wheel ridging on interior.
L23 Top, level 3, lot 3405/6-9.

P626. Decorated skyphos body frag. Fig. 3-33.
H. (pres.) 0.048. Th. 0.005.
Reddish yellow clay. Decorated zone of fragmentary wavy line in field between handles; above and below, black coating. Good streaky black-brown paint on interior.
L23 Top, level 3, lot 3405/6-9.

P627. Profile of skyphos (missing handles). Fig. 3-24.
H. (pres.) 0.08. D. rim 0.104. D. base 0.036.
Reddish yellow clay with orange pink core. Monochrome streaky black-brown coating on exterior and interior. Carinated body. Rim: Type C1; Base: Type C.
L23 Top, level 3, lot 3405/6-9.

P628. Rim and body frag. of skyphos.
H. (pres.) 0.042. Th. 0.004. D. ca. 0.18.
Reddish yellow clay. Broad black band under rim; below, frags. of 3 arcs of concentric semi-circles. Frags. of streaky black paint preserved on interior. Rim: Type B3.
L23 Top, level 3, lot 3405/1-4.

P629. Upper profile (missing handles) of skyphos. Fig. 3-24; Pl. 3-67.
H. (pres.) 0.045. Th. 0.004. D. ca. 0.12.
Metope-triglyph motif in handle zone; 4 vertical lines of triglyph preserved; above, streaky black coating. Good streaky black-brown coating on interior. Possible reserved band on inner rim. Rim: Type C1.
L23 Sop, level 2, lot 3403/1.

P630. Upper profile (missing handles) of skyphos. Fig. 3-22.
H. (pres.) 0.063. Th. ca. 0.003-0.004. D. ca. 0.09.
Broken just above base. Light red flaky clay, worn surfaces. Traces of monochrome black coating on exterior and interior. Rim: Type A2.
L23 Sop, level 2, lot 3403/1.

P631 (NP76). Profile of cup. Fig. 3-34; Pl. 3-68.
H. 0.063. D. rim ca. 0.073. D. base ca. 0.061. W. handle 0.012.
Munsell 5YR 7/8 reddish yellow. Flaky clay, worn surfaces. Frags. of reddish brown coating preserved on exterior and interior. String marks on exterior. Rim: similar to skyphos A4.
L23 Top, level 3, lot 3405/6-9.

P632. Upper profile of cup.
H. (pres.) 0.023. Th. 0.004. D. ca. 0.09.
Similar to **P631**.
L23 Top, level 3, lot 3405/6-9.

P633. Profile of cup. Fig. 3-35.
Th. 0.0035. D. ca. 0.09-0.095.
Reddish yellow clay, worn surfaces. Frags. of black coating preserved on exterior and interior. Rim: similar to skyphos B2.
L23 Sop, level 2, lot 3403/1.

P634. Rim and wall frag. of krater. Fig. 3-33.
H. (pres.) 0.059. Th. 0.005. D. ca. 0.28.
Reddish yellow clay with orange-pink core. Decoration very worn but seems to be vertical lines alternating with squares, one of which may have in it a large black dot. Very thin black band below rim. Frags. of black paint preserved on interior. Inner lip of rim fluted for holding lid. Rim: similar to skyphos B1.
L23 Top, level 3, lot 3405/6-9.

P635. Rim and wall frag. of krater. Fig. 3-16.
H. (pres.) 0.03. Th. 0.004. D. ca. 0.24.
Light gray brittle clay with pinkish tinge. Thin band below rim; below, wolf's tooth and frags. of 4 arcs of concentric semi-circles. All decoration in faded brown paint. Stripes on top of rim. Fine washy black paint on interior. Rim: Type A.
L23 Top, level 3, lot 3405/6-9.

P636. Rim frag. of krater.
Similar to **P635**, but only frags. of black paint preserved. Rim: Type A.
L23 Top, level 3, lot 3405/6-9.

P637. Rim frag. of krater.
D. ca. 0.28.
Reddish yellow clay. Frags. black paint. Rim: Type B2.
L23 Top, level 3, lot 3405/6-9.

P638. Rim and wall frag. of krater. Fig. 3-16; Pl. 3-72.
H. (pres.) 0.0345. Th. 0.008. D. ca. 0.29.
Reddish yellow clay. Thin black band under rim; below, frags. of wavy line in black with second band below. Good streaky black paint on interior; reserved band inner rim. Rim: Type F.
L23 Top, level 3, lot 3405/6-9.

P639. 2 krater wall frags.
Reddish yellow clay. Frags. of washy black paint on exterior and interior. One frag. has possible end of arc of concentric semi-circle. White slip.
L23 Top, level 3, lot 3405/6-9.

P640. 5 skyphos bases.
D. 0.03, 0.035, 0.038, 0.04, 0.056.
Frags. black paint exterior and interior. Base: Type A1.
L23 Top, level 3, lot 3405/6-9.

P641. 4 skyphos bases.
D. ca. 0.056, 0.058, 0.062, 0.08.
Black-brown paint exterior and interior. One base has wheel ridging on interior and concentric incisions on underside. Base: Type B.
L23 Top, level 3, lot 3405/6-9.

P642. 6 skyphos bases.
D. 0.036, 0.04, 0.041, 0.045, 0.05, 0.055.
Frags. black paint exterior and interior. Base: Type C.
L23 Top, level 3, lot 3405/6-9.

P643. Base frag. of skyphos.
D. ca. 0.061.
About ½ preserved. Reddish yellow clay. Good streaky black-brown paint on exterior and interior. Concentric incisions on underside of base. Base: Type D.
L23 Top, level 3, lot 3405/6-9.

P644. 5 flat bases of cups.
D. 0.046-0.05.
Reddish yellow clay. Frags. of washy black paint on exterior and interior.
L23 Top, level 3, lot 3405/6-9.

P645. Lower profile of cup. Fig. 3-18.

D. base 0.05.
Flat base. Shape like **P631** (NP76).
L23 Top, level 3, lot 3405/6-9.

P646. 12 skyphos handle frags. Fig. 3-32.
One frag. has preserved handle stump and undecorated zone with black coating above and below (Fig. 3-31). Type A.
L23 Top, level 3, lot 3405/6-9.

P647. 4 skyphos handle frags.
Type C.
L23 Top, level 3, lot 3405/6-9.

P648. 5 cup handles.
Type A.
L23 Top, level 3, lot 3405/6-9.

P649. 2 cup handles.
Type B.
L23 Top, level 3, lot 3405/6-9.

P650. 2 cup handles.
Type C.
L23 Top, level 3, lot 3405/6-9.

Closed Shapes

P651. Rim and neck frag. of oinochoe.
H. (pres.) 0.045. Th. neck ca. 0.005.
Very pale brown flaky clay, worn surfaces. Washy black paint exterior and top of rim. Rim: Type A1.
L23 Top, level 3, lot 3405/6-9.

P652. Rim and neck frag. of oinochoe.
Similar to **P651**.
Rim: Type B.
L23 Top, level 3, lot 3405/6-9.

P653. Decorated shoulder frag. of oinochoe.
H. (pres.) 0.063.
Reddish yellow clay. At top of frag. 2 grooves mark transition from shoulder to neck. Below grooves is a broad black band, followed by frags. of 2 sets of tangential semi-circles.
L23 Top, level 3, lot 3405/6-9.

P654. 3 decorated shoulder frags. of oinochoai.
Very pale brown to reddish yellow clay. Decoration consists of frags. of 2 sets of concentric semi-circles in black and frags. of 2 arcs of one set of semi-circles; groove at transition from neck to shoulder with 2 frags. of arcs of semi-circles below.
L23 Top, level 3, lot 3405/6-9.

P655. Decorated shoulder frag. of oinochoe.
H. (pres.) 0.057. Th. 0.005.
Reddish yellow flaky clay. Alternating thin (3) and broad (2) bands at beginning of shoulder; below, very worn set of cross-hatched triangles.
L23 Top, level 3, lot 3405/6-9.

P656. Frag. of neck handle, probably from amphora.
W. 0.04.
Handle: Type A1.
L23 Top, level 3, lot 3405/6-9.

P657. 2 handle frags. of oinochoai or jugs.
W. 0.018.
Handle: Type A2.
L23 Top, level 3, lot 3405/6-9.

P658. Handle and body frag., probably from oinochoe. Fig. 3-20; Pl. 3-85.
W. 0.025. Th. body 0.005.
Reddish yellow clay. Fine black paint on handle and body frag. Handle: Type A4 (with flute down center of top).
L23 Top, level 3, lot 3405/6-9.

Coarse Ware

P659. 2 rim frags.
D. ca. 0.20(?)
Burned. Rim: Type A.
L23 Top, level 3, lot 3405/6-9.

P660. 2 rim frags.
D. ca. 0.18(?)
Burned. Rim: Type B.
L23 Top, level 3, lot 3405/6-9.

P661. Handle frag.
W. 0.064.
Burned. Handle: Type A2 (with rib).
L23 Top, level 3, lot 3405/1-4.

P662. Body frag. of pithos. Pl. 3-113.
H. (pres.) 0.074. Th. body 0.022. Th. raised band 0.027.
Light red coarse clay. Raised band contains decoration of 3 rows of incised dots (D. ca. 0.006).
L23 Top, level 3, lot 3405/1-4.

Section D

From Area IVNW. Scattered groups of DAII sherds were found below the floor level of Unit IV-2 (Byzantine) and Unit IV-5 (DAIII). Perhaps the best of these groups comes from level 3 of L23 Rjk.

Open Shapes

P663. Rim frag. of skyphos.
D. ca. 0.09.
Very pale brown to reddish yellow clay. Rim: Type A1.
L23 Si/Sj baulk, level 2, lot 4128/2-3.

P664. Upper profile of skyphos. Fig. 3-22.
H. (pres.) 0.052. Th. 0.003. D. ca. 0.08.
Reddish yellow clay. Streaky monochrome black-brown paint on exterior and interior. Reserved band inner rim. Rim: Type A2.
L23 Skl, level 4, lot 4519/1.

P665. 2 skyphos rim frags.
Similar to **P664**. Rim: Type A2.
L23 Smn, level 4, lot 3416/1-3; L23 Sq, level 5N, lot 3432/4-5.

P666. Rim frag. of skyphos.
Type A4.
L23 Smn, level 4, lot 3416/1-3.

P667. Rim and body frag. of skyphos.
D. ca. 0.20.
Very pale brown to reddish yellow clay. Frags. of brown paint preserved on exterior and interior. Rim: Type B3.
L23 Si/Sj baulk, level 3, lot 4128/2-3.

P668. Rim and body frag. of skyphos.
D. ca. 0.15.
Very pale brown to light gray clay. Frags. of black paint preserved on exterior and interior. Rim: Type B4.
L23 Rj, level 1, lot 4142C.

P669. 4 skyphos or deep bowl rim frags.
D. ca. 0.18.
Reddish yellow clay. Rim: Type C1.
L23 Smn, level 4, lot 3416/1-3; L23 Rkl, test cut, Unit IV-2, lot 5041.

P670. 4 skyphos or deep bowl rim frags.
D. ca. 0.17-0.20.
Rim: Type C2.
L23 Smn, level 4, lot 3416/1-3; L23 Si/Sj baulk, level 2, lot 4128/2-3; L23 Rkl, test cut, Unit IV-2, lot 5041.

P671. Rim and body frag. of skyphos.
D. ca. 0.10(?)
Reddish yellow clay. Fine black coating exterior and interior. Reserved band inner rim(?). Rim: Type C3.
L23 Skl, level 4, lot 4519.

P672. 2 decorated skyphos body frags.
Reddish yellow clay. One had ends of arcs of concentric semi-circles; other has frags. of 3 arcs of concentric semi-circles. Streaky black-brown paint on interior.
L23 Si/Sj baulk, level 2, lot 4128/2-3; L23 Sm, level 4, lot 3416/1-3.

P673. Decorated skyphos body frag.
H. (pres.) 0.048. Th. 0.004.
Reddish yellow clay. 4 arcs and central dot of accumbent compass-drawn concentric semi-circles; to left, 3 frags. of arcs of second set preserved; below, streaky black-brown coating. Frags. streaky black-brown paint on interior.
L23 Rkl, test cut, Unit IV-2, lot 5041.

P674. Decorated skyphos body frag.
H. (pres.) 0.036. Th. 0.003.
Reddish yellow clay. 5 arcs and central dot of compass-drawn concentric semi-circles in black; to left, frags. of 3 arcs of second set; below, black coating. Good streaky black paint on interior.
L23 Rkl, test cut, Unit IV-2, lot 5041.

P675. 3 decorated skyphos body sherds.
Very pale brown clay. Frags. of arcs of concentric semi-circles. Frags. of black coating on interior.
L23 Rkl, test cut, Unit IV-2, lot 5041.

P676. Decorated skyphos body frag.
H. (pres.) 0.023. Th. 0.003.
Very pale brown flaky clay. 2 adjacent sets of piled triangles in brown, flanked by frags. of 2 brown bands. Good streaky black paint on interior.
L23 Rkl, test cut, Unit IV-2, lot 5041.

P677. Decorated skyphos rim and body frag. Fig. 3-24; Pl. 3-47.
H. (pres.) 0.033. Th. 0.0035. D. ca. 0.15.
Light gray clay. 2 thin bands below rim; below, frag. of cross-hatched triangle in black. Streaky black paint on interior; reserved band inner rim. Rim: Type A3.
L23 Rjk, level 3, lot 4149/1-3.

P678. Decorated skyphos rim and body frag. Pl. 3-47.
Similar to **P677**, but decoration more fragmentary. Rim: Type A3.
L23 Rjk, level 3, lot 4149/1-3.

P679. 3 skyphos rim frags.
D. ca. 0.12.
Reddish yellow clay. Rim: Type A4.
L23 Rjk, level 3, lot 4149/1-3.

P680. 10 skyphos or deep bowl rim frags.
D. ca. 0.15-0.20.
Reddish yellow clay. Frags. streaky black-brown coating preserved on exterior and interior; reserved band inner rim. Rim: Type B1.
L23 Rjk, level 3, lot 4149/1-3.

P681. Rim frag. of skyphos.
Similar to **P683.**
L23 Rjk, level 3, lot 4149/1-3.

P682. Decorated rim and body frag. of skyphos. Fig. 3-32; Pl. 3-47.
H. (pres.) 0.056. Th. 0.004. D. ca. 0.14(?)
Tip of rim missing. Very pale brown clay. Decoration of 2 wavy lines between 2 black bands. Good streaky black paint on interior. Rim: Type B2(?)
L23 Rjk, level 3, lot 4149/1-3.

P683. 3 skyphos rim and body frags.
D. ca. 0.14.
Reddish yellow clay. Frags. of black coating exterior and interior. Possible undecorated zone in field between handles. Rim: Type B2.
L23 Rjk, level 3, lot 4149/1-3.

P684. Rim and body frag. of skyphos or deep bowl.
D. ca. 0.19.
Reddish yellow clay. Fine black paint on exterior and interior; reserved band inner rim. Rim: Type B3.
L23 Rjk, level 3, lot 4149/1-3.

P685. 8 skyphos rim frags.
D. ca. 0.10-0.14. Th. 0.003-0.004.
Reddish yellow to gray clay. 2 rims have reserved band on inner rim. Rim: Type B4.
L23 Rjk, level 3, lot 4149/1-3.

P686. 5 decorated skyphos body frags.
Reddish yellow clay. Preserved frags. of arcs of accumbent concentric semi-circles. Black paint on interior.
L23 Rjk, level 3, lot 4149/1-3.

P687. Decorated body and handle frag. of skyphos. Fig. 3-32.
H. (pres.) 0.044.
Decoration is in zone between handles; possible metope-triglyph (vertical lines) motif, with end of crosshatched triangles preserved in metope; below, fine black coating. Good black paint on interior.
L23 Rjk, level 3, lot 4149/1-3.

P688. Decorated skyphos body frag. Pl. 3-47.
H. (pres.) 0.024.
Reddish yellow clay. Frag. of small crosshatched half-triangle between 2 black bands. Black coating on interior.
L23 Rjk, level 3, lot 4149/1-3.

P689. Decorated skyphos body frag.
H. 0.023.

Broken just short of rim. Similar to **P688**.
L23 Rjk, level 3, lot 4149/1-3.

P690. Decorated skyphos body frag. Pl. 3-47.
H. (pres.) 0.028.
Very pale brown clay. Frag. of wavy line in faded brown paint preserved; below, solid black-brown coating. Black paint on interior.
L23 Rjk, level 3, lot 4149/1-3.

P691. 3 skyphos rim frags.
D. ca. 0.14-0.18.
Rim: Type A2.
L23 Qij, level 2, lots 4129, 4148; L23 Pk and Qk, level 2, lot 4145.

P692. 2 deep bowl rim frags.
D. ca. 0.18-0.20.
Rim: Type B1.
L23 Pij, level 2, lot 4117/6; L23 Pk and Qk, level 4, lot 4522/1-2.

P693. 2 skyphos rim frags.
D. ca. 0.13.
Rim: Type B4.
L23 Qij, level 2, lots 4129, 4148; L23 Pij, level 2, lot 4117.

P694. 9 skyphos rim frags.
D. ca. 0.10-0.12.
Rim: Type C1.
L23 Pk and Qk, level 4, lot 4522/1-3; L23 Pij, level 2, lot 4117/6.

P695. 8 skyphos or deep bowl rim frags.
D. ca. 0.13-0.18.
Rim: Type C2.
L23 Qij, level 2, lots 4129, 4148; L23 Pk and Qkl, level 2, lot 4145.

P696. Rim and body frag. of skyphos.
Type C3.
L23 Qij, level 2, lots 4129, 4148.

P697. Profile of flat based skyphos. Fig. 3-26; Pl. 3-46.
H. (pres.) 0.068. Th. 0.003 (top)-0.005 (bottom). D. rim. ca. 0.065(?). D. base ca. 0.06. D. handle 0.008.
Reddish yellow clay with orange-pink core. Fine black coating on exterior and interior. Shallow concentric incisions on underside of base.
L23 Pkl and Qkl, level 2, lot 4145.

P698. 4 decorated skyphos body sherds.
Reddish yellow clay. Preserved frags. of arcs of accumbent concentric semi-circles. Frags. of black paint on interior.
L23 Pk and Qk, level 4, lot 4522/1-2; L23 Pk and Qkl, level 2, lot 4145; L23 Qij, level 2, lots 4129, 4148.

P699. Decorated skyphos body frag. Fig. 3-32; Pl. 3-52.
H. (pres.) 0.043. Th. 0.005.
Gray clay with orange-pink core. 2 adjacent sets of accumbent compass-drawn semi-circles in black; below, black coating. Fine black paint on interior.
L23 Pkl, level 2.

P700-701. Decorated body frags. of skyphoi.
Reddish yellow clay. **P700** has frags. of 2 overlapping sets of concentric semi-circles; **P701** has 1 set of compass-drawn semi-circles in faded brown; 3 drip marks on topmost arc. Both body frags. have streaky black-brown paint on interior.
L23 Pk and Qkl, level 2, lot 4145; L23 Pk and Qk, level 4, lot 4522/1-2.

P702. Decorated skyphos body frag.
H. (pres.) 0.023. Th. 0.0035.
Reddish yellow clay. Metope-triglyph motif with fragmentary crosshatched triangle in metope(?); below, black-brown coating. Same coating on interior.
L23 Pk and Qkl, level 2, lot 4145.

P703. Decorated body frag. of skyphos or krater. Pl. 3-66.
H. (pres.) 0.047. Th. 0.005.
Very pale brown clay with pinkish tinge. 10 short horizontal stripes flanked by vertical lines, 4 preserved on one side, 2 on other. To right is frag. of handle.
L23 Pij, level 2, lots 4117/6, 4119, 4121/1 (combined).

P704. Decorated skyphos rim and body frag.
H. (pres.) 0.042. Th. 0.003. D. ca. 0.10-0.12.
Very pale brown clay. Decorated zone, possibly in field between handles, has wavy line in black; below, black coating. Frags. of black paint preserved in interior.
L23 Pij, level 2, lots 4117/6, 4119, 4121/1 (combined).

P705. Profile of cup. Fig. 3-34.
H. (pres.) 0.0345. D. rim ca. 0.092. D. base 0.05.
Reddish yellow clay. Streaky black coating on exterior and interior. Rim: skyphos C1.
L23 Smn, level 4, lot 3416/1-3.

P706. 3 rim frags. of kraters.
D. ca. 0.20, 0.25, 0.29-0.30.
Very pale brown flaky clay, worn surfaces. Rim: Type D.
L23 Pk and Qk, level 4, lot 4522/1-2.

P707. Decorated wall frag. of krater. Fig. 3-33; Pl. 3-74.
H. (pres.) 0.058. Th. 0.008.
Reddish yellow clay, worn surfaces. Possible metope-triglyph (3 vertical lines preserved) motif, with decoration in metope of black dots in squares; above, ends of crosshatched triangles. Frags. of black paint on interior.
L23 Rjk, level 2, lot 4135/2.

P708. 4 skyphos bases.
D. 0.04-0.06.
Type A1.
L23 Rjk, level 3, lot 4149/1-3.

P709. 9 skyphos bases.
D. 0.06-0.075.
Type A2.
L23 Rjk, level 3, lot 4149/1-3.

P710. 7 skyphos bases.
D. ca. 0.04-0.06.
Type B.
L23 Rjk, level 3, lot 4149/1-3.

P711. 12 skyphos bases.
D. ca. 0.06-0.075.
Type C.
L23 Rjk, level 3, lot 4149/1-3.

P712. 6 flat bases of cups.
D. ca. 0.05-0.06.

L23 Pk and Qkl, level 2, lot 4145; L23 Pk and Qk, level 4, lot 4522/1-2; L23 Rjk, level 3, lot 4149/1-3.

P713. 22 skyphos handles. Fig. 3-32.
Type A.
L24 Rkl, test cut, Unit IV-2, lot 5041.

P714. 8 skyphos handles.
Type C.
L23 Rkl, test cut, Unit IV-2, lot 5041.

P715. Handle of shallow bowl or plate. Fig. 3-17.
W. 0.017.
Very pale brown flaky clay, worn surfaces. Rib down center of top. Frags. of black paint preserved. Handle: Type B.
L23 Rjk, level 3, lot 4149/1-3.

P716. Handle of shallow bowl or plate.
W. 0.013.
Very pale brown flaky clay, worn surfaces. Frags. of black paint preserved. Handle: Type B.
L23 Pk and Qk, level 4, lot 4522/1-2.

P717. Rim and handle frag. of cup.
W. handle 0.014.
Reddish yellow flaky clay. Black paint on handle; streaky black paint on interior of rim. Handle: Type C.
L23 Pk and Qkl, level 2, lot 4145.

Closed Shapes

P718. 2 rim and neck frags. of oinochoai.
D. rim ca. 0.08.
Reddish yellow clay. Frags. of black paint preserved on exterior; one frag. has black paint on inner rim, other does not. Rim: Type A1.
L23 Smn, level 4, lot 3416/1-3.

P719. Rim frag. of oinochoe.
D. ca. 0.16.
Reddish yellow clay. Black band under rim; undecorated zone below. Black coating on inner rim. Rim: Type A3.
L23 Rjk, level 3, lot 4149/1-3.

P720. (NP111). Profile of oinochoe, missing handle and base. Fig. 3-37; Pl. 3-86.
H. (pres.) 0.204. D. rim ca. 0.101. D. neck 0.074.
Munsell 2.5YR 6/8 light red. Metope-triglyph motif on shoulder; large crosshatched triangle flanked by 5 vertical lines to right, 3 to left. Black coating on belly and on inside of rim and neck. Mending hole (D. 0.004) in lower belly. Handle restored; possible Type A1. Rim: Type B.
L23 Pk and Qkl, level 2, lot 4145.

P721. Rim and neck frag. of small oinochoe. Fig. 3-39.
H. (pres.) 0.0375.
Reddish yellow flaky clay, worn surfaces. 3 shallow incisions on neck. Faint frags. of black paint preserved on neck only. Rim: Type B.
L23 Rj, level 2, lot 3445/5.

P722. Rim frag. of oinochoe.
H. (pres.) 0.03. Th. 0.0045.
Reddish yellow flaky clay, worn surfaces. No traces of paint preserved. Rim: Type C.
L23 Si/Sj baulk, level 2, lot 4128/2-3.

P723. Rim and handle frag. of small jug. Fig. 3-39.
D. 0.05. Th. 0.003.
Reddish yellow clay. Streaky black-brown paint on exterior; brown paint on inner rim. Rim: Type D.
L23 Si/Sj baulk, level 2, lot 4128/2-3.

P724. 3 decorated oinochoe shoulder frags.
Reddish yellow clay. Preserved frags. of arcs and central dot of compass-drawn concentric accumbent semi-circles.
L23 Si/Sj baulk, level 2, lot 4128/1-2.

P725. Decorated neck and shoulder frags. of oinochoe. Fig. 3-40; Pl. 3-93.
H. (pres.) 0.146. Th. neck 0.005. Th. shoulder 0.008.
Reddish yellow clay with tan tinge. 5 incisions at transition from neck to shoulder. On shoulder, metope-triglyph motif of cross-hatching flanked by 3 vertical lines of triglyph in black.
L23 Rj, level 2, lot 3445/1-4.

P726. Oinochoe base.
D. 0.097.
Gray clay. Frags. black paint. Base: Type A.
L23 Sq, level 5N, lot 3432/4-5.

P727. Base of possible amphora.
D. ca. 0.16.
Reddish yellow clay. Frags. black paint preserved. Base: Type B.
L23 Si/Sj baulk, level 2, lot 4128/2-3.

P728. Handle of oinochoe attached to rim.
W. 0.027.
Gray flaky clay. Frags. of black paint. Handle: Type A1.
L23 Qij, level 2, lot 4129.

P729. 3 oinochoe handle frags.
W. 0.016.
Reddish yellow to gray clay. Frags. of black paint. Handle: Type A4.
L23 Pkl, Qkl, Rkl, Skl, Rj, Sj, level 2, lot 4127 (cleaning inside Unit IV-2).

P730. Rope handle frag. from oinochoe. Fig. 3-20; Pl. 3-85.
D. ca. 0.02.
Clay fired to brittle blue-gray; flaky surfaces. No traces paint preserved. Handle: Type A5.
L23 Skl, level 4, lot 4519/1.

P731. Belly handle of amphora.
Reddish yellow flaky clay. No traces paint preserved. Handle: Type B (round).
L23 Pk and Qk, level 4, lot 4522/1-2.

Coarse Ware

P732. 2 rim frags. of probable bowls.
D. ca. 0.15, 0.17. Th. 0.007.
Clay burned to black and light gray. Rim: Type A.
L23 Skl, level 4, lot 4519/1; L23 Pk and Qkl, level 2, lot 4145.

P733. Rim of probable bowl.
D. ca. 0.18.
Burned. Rim: Type B.
L23 Pk and Qkl, level 4, lot 4522/1-2.

P734. Lower profile of probable jug. Fig. 3-41.

D. base 0.07 (uneven).

Frag. of handle stump preserved. Burned gray all over and black on underside of base. Base: Type A.

L23 Sq, level 5N, lot 3432/4-5.

P735. Base frag. of probable large bowl.

D. ca. 0.17.

Clay fired to a dark gray color with light gray-blue core. Base: Type A.

L23 Skl, level 4, lot 4519/1.

P736. Base frag.

D. ca. 0.10.

Light red clay. Base: Type B.

L23 Skl, level 4, lot 4519/1.

P737. Leg of cooking stand. Fig. 3-21; Pl. 3-112.

H. 0.055. D. base 0.050. D. stem 0.042.

One end broken. Munsell 2.5YR 6/8 light red; clay poorly fired.

L23 Smn, level 4, lot 3416/1-3.

P738. Handle frag.

W. 0.071.

Reddish yellow clay; burned black on top of handle. 5 grooves preserved. Handle: Type C.

L23 Pij, level 2, lots 4117/6, 4119, 4121/1 (combined).

Section E

From Area IVNW. A small number of DAII sherds were mixed with the DAIII lots just above the floor level of Room 2 of Unit IV-6. This Mycenaean house was reused in the DAIII period.

Open Shapes

P739. Rim and body frag. of skyphos.

H. (pres.) 0.042. Th. 0.003. D. ca. 0.14.

Reddish yellow clay. Streaky black-brown paint below rim; below, frags. of 4 vertical lines (from possible metope-triglyph motif?). Streaky black-brown paint on interior; possible reserved band inner rim. Rim: Type B2.

L23 Tj, level 2, lot 4417/3-4.

P740. Rim and body frag. of skyphos.

H. (pres.) 0.026. Th. 0.003. D. ca. 0.115.

Good reddish yellow clay. Fine smooth black coating on exterior and interior. Reserved band inner rim. Attic import? Rim: Type B4.

L23 Tj, level 2, lot 4417/3-4.

P741. Profile of skyphos. Fig. 3-25.

H. 0.118. D. rim 0.10. D. base 0.05. D. handle 0.011.

Munsell 10YR 7/4 very pale brown (with olive gray tinge) and orange-pink core. Flaky clay, worn surfaces. Frags. of monochrome black coating preserved on exterior and interior. Rim: Type B2; Base: Type B; Handle: Type A.

L23 Tj, level 2, lot 4417/3-4.

P742. Rim and body frag. of skyphos.

H. (pres.) 0.037. Th. 0.004. D. ca. 0.10.

Reddish yellow clay. Streaky black-brown paint below rim; below, frags. of 3 arcs of accumbent concentric semi-circles. Streaky black-brown paint on interior. Mending hole (D. 0.003) at top of frag. near rim. Rim: Type C1.

L23 Tj, level 2, lot 4417/3-4.

P743. Rim frag. of skyphos.

Reddish yellow clay. Fine smooth black paint on exterior and interior; reserved band inner rim. Rim: Type C1.

L23 Tj, level 2, lot 4417/3-4.

P744. Rim frag. of krater.

H. (pres.) 0.035. Th. 0.007. D. ca. 0.18.

White flaky clay, worn surfaces. Frags. of washy black paint preserved on exterior and interior. Rim: Type D.

L23 Tj, level 2, lot 4417/3-4.

P745. Skyphos base.

Reddish yellow clay. Type A1.

L23 Tj, level 2, lot 4417/3-4.

P746. 2 skyphos bases.

White flaky clay, worn surfaces. Type A2.

L23 Tj, level 2, lot 4417/3-4.

P747. Skyphos base frag.

About ⅛ preserved. Reddish yellow clay. Type B.

L23 Tj, level 2, lot 4417/3-4.

P748. Skyphos base.

Reddish yellow clay. Type C.

L23 Tj, level 2, lot 4417/3-4.

P749. 3 skyphos handles.

Reddish yellow clay. Black paint preserved. Type A.

L23 Tj, level 2, lot 4417/3-4.

P750. 2 skyphos handles.

Reddish yellow to gray clay. Frags. of black paint preserved. Type C.

L23 Tj, level 2, lot 4417/3-4.

Closed Shapes

P751. Rim and neck frag. of oinochoe.

H. (pres.) 0.07. D. rim ca. 0.08.

Reddish yellow clay. Good streaky black paint on exterior and interior of rim. Rim: Type A1.

L23 Tj, level 2, lot 4417/3-4.

P752(NP105). Decorated body frag. of pilgrim flask. Fig. 3-40; Pl. 3-100.

H. (pres.) 0.073. W. (pres.) 0.06. Th. 0.007-0.008.

Munsell 5YR 7/6 reddish yellow (with orange-pink core). Frag. belongs to central belly of flask. Decoration of 4 crosshatched triangles, each separated by crossing diagonal lines; entire decorated zone enclosed by a circular black band.

L23 Tj, level 2, lot 4417/3-4.

P753. Neck and handle frag. of oinochoe or jug.

W. handle 0.024.

Reddish yellow flaky clay, worn surfaces. Frags. of black paint on neck and handle. Handle: Type A1.

L23 Tj, level 2, lot 4417/3-4.

Coarse Ware

P754. Coarse rim. Fig. 3-20.

H. (pres.) 0.045. Th. 0.009. Th. raised band 0.018.

Reddish yellow clay. Below rim is a raised band decorated with finger impressions; 4 impressions preserved. Rim: Type A.

L23 Tj, level 2, lot 4417/3-4.

P755. 2 rim frags. Fig. 3-20.
D. ca. 0.26.
Reddish yellow clay, burned in places. One rim frag. has part of handle projecting from rim. Rim: Type A.
L23 Tj, level 2, lot 4417/3-4.

P756. 7 rim frags. Fig. 3-20.
D. ca. 0.12, 0.14, 0.19-0.20, 0.26.
Reddish yellow and light red clay; burned. Rim: Type B.
L23 Tj, level 2, lot 4417/3-4.

P757. Coarse base.
D. ca. 0.10.
Light red clay. Base: Type B.
L23 Tj, level 2, lot 4417/3-4.

P758. Coarse handle frag.
W. 0.039.
2 ribs. Burned dark gray. Handle: Type A2.
L23 Tj, level 2, lot 4417/3-4.

P759. Rim frag. of pithos. Fig. 3-21.
H. (pres.) 0.084. Th. ca. 0.027.
Reddish yellow clay, burned light gray at rim. Finger impressions (3 preserved) along top of rim.
L23 Tj, level 2, lot 4417/3-4.

P760. 2 incised body frags. of pithoi.
Th. body 0.025. Th. raised band 0.028.
Light red clay. Each frag. has a raised band with incised decoration of circles within triangles; additional row of incised circles above triangles at top of band.
L23 Tj, level 2, lot 4417/3-4.

P761. 2 body frags. of pithoi with rope band decoration.
Reddish yellow clay with inclusions; on interior, clay burned dirty white. Rim missing. Decoration of raised band with diagonal slashes (rope band).
L23 Tj, level 2, lot 4417/3-4.

Section F

From Area IVSW. Scattered DAII sherds were found in the predominantly Mycenaean levels associated with a curved terrace wall (A) spanning trenches L23 OPQefg. These sherds can be associated with no structure and are probably the result of hill-wash deposited against the terrace wall.

Open Shapes

P762. Profile of skyphos. Fig. 3-25.
H. (pres.) ca. 0.055. D. ca. 0.14. Th. 0.0035.
Reconstructed from 4 decorated frags. and 22 body sherds. Reddish yellow clay with pink tinge. Missing base and handles. Possibly 2 registers of decoration, 1 below rim and other in handle zone. Metope-triglyph motif in each register, with 3 vertical lines forming the triglyph and 3 piled triangles in the metope. Decoration in black paint; good black coating on interior; top of rim left unpainted. Laconian import? Rim: Type A2.
L23 Pfg, level 3, lots 938, 942, 1022 (combined).

P763. Rim frag. of skyphos.
D. ca. 0.12.
Reddish yellow clay. Frags. of streaky black paint on exterior and interior. Rim: Type B4.
L23 Pfg, level 3, lots 938, 942, 1022 (combined).

P764. Upper profile of deep bowl. Fig. 3-30.
H. (pres.) 0.106. Th. 0.005. D. ca. 0.185.
Very pale brown clay with orange-pink core; flaky clay, worn surfaces. Frags. of streaky black coating preserved on exterior and interior. Rim: Type C1; Handle: Type A (D. 0.011-0.012).
L23 PQh, level 2, lot 3260/2-3.

P765. Rim frag. of skyphos.
Th. 0.004. D. ca. 0.12.
Very pale brown clay. Frags. of washy black paint preserved on exterior and interior. Rim: Type C2.
L23 Pfg/Qfg baulk, level 2, pit 1, lot 3256/1.

P766(NP24). Decorated body frag. of skyphos. Fig. 3-32; Pl. 3-60.
H. (pres.) 0.046. W. 0.051. Th. 0.004.
Munsell 5YR 7/6 reddish yellow. On exterior, cross-hatching in faded black paint; to right, darker streak of black paint outlining junction of handle. Streaky black coating on interior.
L23 Pfg, level 2, lot 932.

P767. Decorated body frag. of skyphos.
H. (pres.) 0.029. Th. 0.004-0.005.
Reddish yellow clay with gray tinge. 3 frags. of arcs of accumbent concentric semi-circles in black; above, frag. of black band. Solid black coating on interior.
L23 Qfg, level 5, lots 771, 772, 774, 779, 780 (combined).

P768. Profile of cup. Fig. 3-35.
H. 0.079, D. rim ca. 0.115, D. base ca. 0.05.
2 nonjoining frags., rim with handle and base. Reddish yellow clay with pink core; flaky clay, worn surfaces. Monochrome black coating on exterior, interior, and on outer edges of underside of base. Concentric circular incisions on underside of base. Rim: skyphos A2 (?); cup handle: Type A (W. 0.011).
L23 Pfg/Qfg baulk, level 2, lot 3251/4.

P769. Frag. of flat base of cup.
D. ca. 0.05.
Only center of base preserved, missing edges. Reddish yellow clay. Frags. of black paint on exterior and interior. Concentric circular incisions on underside of base.
L23 Pfg, level 3, lots 938. 942, 1022 (combined).

P770. Handle of probable krater.
D. 0.19-0.20. (uneven).
Reddish yellow clay with pink core. Frags. of black paint preserved. Handle: Type A.
L23 Qfg, level 5, lots 771, 772, 774, 779, 780 (combined).

Closed Shapes

P771. Neck, belly, and base frags. of oinochoe.
D. base ca. 0.07.
All nonjoining frags. Reddish yellow clay. Remaining sherds have frags. of good black coating on exterior; interior of neck also coated black until point of transition from neck to shoulder. Base about ¼ preserved and burned light gray around foot on underside. Base: Type A.
L23 Pfg/Qfg, level 2, lot 3251/4.

P772. Rim, neck, shoulder, belly, and base frags. of oinochoe. Fig. 3-38.
D. base 0.076.
All nonjoining frags. Reddish yellow clay. Good monochrome black coating on neck and belly; possible decoration of 3 vertical stripes

(metope-triglyph motif?) on neck, but very faint; no paint on inner rim or neck. 4 wide grooves at transition from neck to shoulder. Base entirely preserved; frags. of black paint on exterior of base. Missing handle. Rim: Type B; Base: Type A.

L23 Pfg/Qfg baulk, level 2, pit 1, lot 3256/1.

P773. Rim, neck, and shoulder frags. of small jug. Fig. 3-37.

All nonjoining frags. Reddish yellow clay. Good streaky black coating on exterior and on top half of interior of neck. Small raised band on exterior at transition from neck to shoulder. Missing handle. Rim: Type B.

L23 Pfg/Qfg baulk, level 2, pit 1, lot 3256/1.

P774. Handle frag. of oinochoe or jug.

W. 0.022.

Reddish yellow clay. Frags. of black paint. Handle: Type A2 (with rib).

L23 OPe/OPf baulk, level 2, lot 4075/8.

P775. Handle frag. of oinochoe.

W. 0.03.

Reddish yellow clay with gray-blue core. Good black coating. Handle: Type A4 (with flute).

L23 Qfg, level 5, lots 771, 772, 774, 779, 780 (combined).

P776. Frags. of strainer with nipple decoration. Pl. 3-78.

H. (pres.) 0.056, W. (pres.) 0.046.

Light reddish yellow semi-coarse clay; flaky, worn surfaces. 5 well-preserved holes (D. 0.0035) around nipple. No traces of paint preserved.

L23 OPe/OPf baulk, level 2, lot 4075/8.

Coarse Ware

P777. Rim frag. of small pithos. Fig. 3-21.

H. (pres.) 0.047. Th. 0.018. D. ca. 0.30.

Pithos rim badly fired and warped. Reddish yellow clay with inclusions. White slip.

L23 Pfg/Qfg baulk, level 2, pit 1, lot 3256/1.

P778. Decorated body frag. of pithos. Pl. 3-119.

H. (pres.) 0.105. Th. 0.023. Th. raised band 0.029.

Coarse reddish yellow clay with inclusions. Raised band has row of 3 sets of incised piled triangles; 3 triangles in each set.

L23 OPe/OPf baulk, level 2, lot 4075/1-5E.

Section G

From Area IVSW. A moderately well-preserved group of DAII sherds comes from the area of Unit IV-9, a Mycenaean house, which appears to have been reused in the DAII period. Belonging in this section are walls P and L, associated with the reuse of Unit IV-9, the small Unit IV-10 to the east of Wall L, and the fragmentary Wall O to the north in grid L23 RSi. (See Chapter 2, pp. 44-46.

Open Shapes

P779. Rim frag. of skyphos.

D. ca. 0.105. Th. 0.004.

Rim: Type A2.

L23 Rfg, level 2, lots 1209, 1211-15.

P780. Rim frag. of skyphos.

D. ca. 0.10. Th. 0.0035.

Rim: Type B1.

L23 Rfg, level 2, lots 1209, 1211-15.

P781 (NP46). Upper profile of skyphos. Fig. 3-30; Pl. 3-57.

H. (pres.) 0.10. Th. 0.003 (top)-0.005 (bottom). D. ca. 0.18 (uneven).

Munsell 10YR 8/3 very pale brown. Decoration of 3 concentric semi-circles in handle zone; in the center of semi-circles there appears to be a small triangle rather than a dot or another semi-circle. Above and below decoration a dark streaky black coating is preserved, faded to a dark brown in places. Good black coating on interior. Rim: Type B3.

L23 Rfg, level 2, lots 1209, 1211-15.

P782. Upper profile of skyphos. Fig. 3-31.

Th. 0.004. D. ca. 0.18.

Two large sections from each side of base preserved. Munsell 5YR 7/8 reddish yellow. Traces of monochrome black coating preserved on exterior and interior. Rim: Type B3.

L23 Rfg/Rhi baulk, level 3, lot 4631/2.

P783. 4 skyphos rim frags.

D. ca. 0.12 (one frag.), 0.016.

Very pale brown to reddish yellow clay. Frags. of black paint preserved on exterior and interior. Rim: Type B3.

L23 RSfg, level 4, pit 1, lot 4628.

P784. Rim and body frag. of skyphos.

D. ca. 0.13.

Reddish yellow clay. Black paint. Rim: Type B4.

L23 RSfg, level 4, pit 1, lot 4628.

P785. Upper profile of skyphos or deep bowl. Fig. 3-26.

H. (pres.) 0.095. Th. 0.004. D. ca. 0.14.

Munsell 10YR 8/4 very pale brown (with pinkish core). Black coating preserved on exterior and interior. Rim: Type C1.

L23 STfg/SThi baulk, level 3, lot 4635/2-4.

P786. 2 skyphos or deep bowl rim frags.

D. ca. 0.18.

Similar to **P785**. Rim: Type C1.

L23 RSfg, level 4, pit 1, lot 4628.

P787. Rim frag. of deep bowl.

Th. 0.0045. D. ca. 0.18.

Frags. of washy black paint on exterior and interior. Rim: Type C2.

L23 Rfg, level 2, lots 1209, 1211-15.

P788. Rim frag. of skyphos.

Th. 0.004. D. ca. 0.09.

Reddish yellow clay with pink tinge. Rim: Type C3.

L23 RSfg, level 4, pit 1, lot 4628.

P789. 2 decorated skyphos body frags. Fig. 3-33.

Reddish yellow clay. Preserved frags. of arcs of accumbent concentric semi-circles with central dot for compass; below, frags. of black coating. Streaky black-brown paint on interior.

L23 RSfg, level 4, pit 1, lot 4628.

P790. Decorated skyphos body frag. Fig. 3-33.

Reddish yellow clay. Decoration, probably in handle zone, of wavy line in black; below, frags. of black coating. Streaky black-brown paint on interior.

L23 RSfg, level 4, pit 1, lot 4628.

P791. 5 decorated skyphos body frags. Fig. 3-33.

Reddish yellow clay. Preserved frags. of crosshatched triangles. Streaky black-brown paint on interior.

L23 Rfg, level 2, lots 1209, 1211-15; L23 RSfg, level 4, pit 1, lot 4628.

P792. Upper profile of skyphos. Fig. 3-22.

H. (pres.) 0.048. Th. ca. 0.003. D. ca. 0.09.

Reddish yellow gritty clay, worn surfaces. Probable monochrome black-brown coating on exterior and interior. Possible reserved band inner rim. Rim: Type A1.

L23 Shi, level 3, lot 1986.

P793. Rim frag. of skyphos.

Similar to **P792**. Rim: Type A1.

L23 Rhi, level 2, lot 1995.

P794. 4 skyphos rim frags.

D. ca. 0.08-0.12.

Rim: Type A2.

L23 Rhi, level 2, lot 1995.

P795. Rim frag. of skyphos.

D. ca. 0.12.

Rim: Type A3.

L23 Rhi, level 2, lot 1995.

P796. 4 skyphos rim frags.

D. ca. 0.10-0.14.

Rim: Type B1.

L23 Rhi, level 2, lots 2354, 2360, 2364, 2373, 2378-80 (combined).

P797. 5 skyphos or deep bowl rim frags.

D. ca. 0.16.

Reserved band inner rim. Rim: Type B2.

L23 Rhi, level 2, lots 2354, 2360, 2364, 2373, 2378-80 (combined).

P798. Rim frag. of skyphos.

D. ca. 0.12-0.14.

Reserved band inner rim. Rim: Type B3.

L23 Rhi, level 2, lots 2354, 2360, 2364, 2373, 2378-80 (combined).

P799. Rim frag. of skyphos.

D. ca. 0.10.

Rim: Type B4.

L23 Rhi, level 2, lot 1995.

P800. Upper profile of skyphos or deep bowl. Fig. 3-27.

H. (pres.) 0.084. Th. 0.005. D. ca. 0.152.

Munsell 5YR 7/8 reddish yellow. Flaky clay, worn surfaces. Possible monochrome black coating on exterior; too worn to tell if there is also an undecorated band in the handle zone. Black coating on interior. Rim: Type C1.

L23 Rhi, level 2, lots 2354, 2360, 2364, 2373, 2378-80 (combined).

P801. Upper profile of skyphos or deep bowl. Fig. 3-27.

D. ca. 0.15.

Similar to **P800** but with definite undecorated zone in field between handles. Munsell 5YR 7/8 reddish yellow. Rim: Type C1.

L23 Rhi, level 2, lots 2354, 2360, 2364, 2378-80 (combined).

P802-4. Upper profiles of skyphoi or deep bowls. Figs. 3-26 (**P804**), 3-27 (**P802**), 3-28 (**P803**).

D. ca. 0.165 (**P802**), 0.16 (**P803**), 0.14 (**P804**).

Reddish yellow flaky clay; worn surfaces. Monochrome black coating on exterior and interior. Rim: Type C1.

L23 Rhi/Shi baulk, level 2, lot 4097/2-3C; L23 Shi, level 3, lot 2357.

P805. Decorated skyphos body frag. Fig. 3-32; Pl. 3-64.

H. (pres.) 0.089.

Reddish yellow clay. Decoration, probably in handle zone, consists of framed crosshatched triangles; above and below, good streaky black coating; solid black coating on interior.

L23 Shi, level 3, lots 1986, 1996, 2357.

P806. Decorated skyphos body frag.

H. (pres.) 0.031. Th. 0.004.

Very pale brown clay. Frags. of crosshatched triangles in brown; frags. of streaky black paint on interior.

L23 Rhi, level 2, lots 2354, 2360, 2364, 2378-80 (combined).

P807. Decorated skyphos body frag.

H. (pres.) 0.046. Th. 0.004.

Reddish yellow clay. 6 frags. of arcs of concentric semi-circles with central dot in faded black; faint frags. of black paint on interior.

L23 Rhi, level 2, lots 2354, 2360, 2364, 2373, 2378-80 (combined).

P808. Profile of cup. Fig. 3-35.

H. (pres.) 0.065. Th. ca. 0.003. D. ca. 0.09.

Missing handle and base. Reddish yellow clay with tan tinge. Flaky clay, worn surfaces. Monochrome black coating on exterior and interior. Carinated body. Rim: skyphos A2.

L23 RSfg, level 4, lot 4095/1C.

P809. Upper profile of krater. Fig. 3-16.

H. (pres.) 0.139. Th. 0.007. D. ca. 0.28-0.30.

Reddish yellow clay. Good smooth monochrome streaky black paint on exterior and interior. White slip. Mending hole near rim. Rim: skyphos C1.

L23 Rhi, level 2, lots 2354, 2360, 2364, 2373, 2378-80 (combined).

P810. 3 skyphos bases.

Type A1.

L23 Rhi, level 2, lots 2354, 2360, 2364, 2373, 2378-80 (combined); L23 Shi, level 3, lots 1986, 1997, 2357.

P811. 4 skyphos bases.

D. ca. 0.04-0.05.

Base: Type A2.

L23 Rhi, level 2, lots 2354, 2360, 2364, 2373, 2378-80 (combined); L23 Rfg/Rhi baulk, level 3, lot 4631/2.

P812. Base of deep bowl.

D. ca. 0.07.

Base: Type B.

L23 Rhi, level 2, lots 2354, 2360, 2364, 2373, 2378-80 (combined).

P813. 5 skyphos bases.

D. ca. 0.05-0.10.

Type C.

L23 Rhi, level 2, lots 2354, 2360, 2364, 2373, 2378-80 (combined); L23 Shi, level 3, lots 1986, 1997, 2357; L23 RSfg, level 4, lot 4095/1C,N,S.

P814. Flat base of cup.
D. ca. 0.05.
L23 Rhi, level 2, lots 2354, 2360, 2364, 2373, 2378-80 (combined).

P815. Decorated flat base of cup. Pl. 3-71.
D. 0.048.
Reddish yellow clay. Streaky black paint on exterior and interior of sides. Underside of base decorated with a large black cross surrounded by thin circular band (uneven) of black paint around outer edge.
L23 Rhi/Shi baulk, level 2, lot 4079/3C.

P816. Pedestal base of krater. Fig. 3-18.
D. base 0.108. D. stem 0.095.
About ½ preserved. Reddish yellow clay. Frags. of streaky black-brown paint preserved on exterior and inside of base.
L23 Rfg, level 2, lot 1209.

Closed Shapes

P817 (NP74). Profile of oinochoe. Fig. 3-37; Pl. 3-87.
H. (pres.) 0.19. D. neck 0.065. D. belly 0.18. W. handle 0.021.
Munsell 10YR 7/3 very pale brown. Flaky clay, worn surfaces. Decoration of wavy line in black at shoulder; undecorated (or reserved) band at belly; rest of vase coated with monochrome black paint. Black paint also on inside of rim. Interesting feature of construction is that the neck has been made separately and fitted into slot at top of shoulder. Rim: Type A1; Handle: Type A1.
L23 Rhi, level 2, lot 2360.

P818. Profile of oinochoe. Fig. 3-33.
D. base ca. 0.06.
Preserved are rim, neck, shoulder, and base frags. Very pale brown flaky clay; worn surfaces. Transition from neck to shoulder marked by 3 grooves. Decoration on shoulder of accumbent concentric semi-circles (preserved are frags. of 6 arcs with central spiral); below, 2 black bands. Neck and belly coated with monochrome black paint. Black paint on inner lip of rim. Similar to **P817** in shape. Rim: Type A1.
L23 Rhi/Shi baulk, level 2, lot 4097/3C; level 3, lot 4627/1S.

P819. 2 oinochoe rim frags.
Similar to **P817**, **P818**. Type A1.
L23 Rhi, level 2, lots 1995, 2354, 2360, 2364, 2373, 2378-80 (combined).

P820. 2 oinochoe neck and shoulder frags.
Munsell 5Y 8/3 pale yellow. Frags. of washy black paint preserved. On one frag., transition from neck to shoulder is marked by 2 incisions; on other by 3 raised bands.
L23 Rhi, level 2, lots 1995, 2354, 2360, 2364, 2373, 2378-80 (combined).

P821. Rim and neck frag. of amphora. Fig. 3-19.
H. (pres.) 0.035. D. 0.144.
About ⅔ preserved. Reddish yellow flaky clay, worn surfaces. Frags. of black paint preserved.
L23 Rhi/Shi baulk, level 2, lot 4097/2-3C.

P822. Rim and neck frag. of amphora.
Similar to **P821**.
L23 Shi, level 3, lots 1986, 1997, 2357.

P823. Base of oinochoe or jug.
D. ca. 0.075.
Light gray clay. Frags. of brown paint. Base: Type A.
L23 RSfg, level 4, pit 1, lot 4628.

P824. Base of oinochoe or jug. Fig. 3-20.
D. ca. 0.07.
Reddish yellow flaky clay. Frags. of black paint. Base: Type C.
L23 STfg/SThi baulk, level 2, lot 4635/2-4.

P825. Flat base, possibly of amphora.
D. ca. 0.09.
Flat base: Type B.
L23 Rhi, level 2, lots 1995, 2354, 2360, 2364, 2373, 2378-80 (combined).

P826. 2 handles from small oinochoai or jugs.
W. 0.0165-0.017.
Flaky gray clay. Frags. of black paint. Handle: Type A1.
L23 Rfg, level 2, lot 1209; L23 RSfg, level 4, pit 1, lot 4628.

P827. Handle frag. of small oinochoe or jug.
W. 0.016.
Brittle gray clay. Frags. of black paint. Handle: Type A4 (fluted).
L23 STfg/SThi baulk, level 3, lot 4635/2-4.

P828. Rope handle of oinochoe.
D. 0.02.
Reddish yellow clay with gray-blue core. No paint preserved. Handle: Type A5 (rope).
L23 RSfg, level 4, lot 4095/1C,N,S.

P829. Handle frag. of small oinochoe or jug.
Reddish yellow clay. Brown paint. Handle: Type A6 (small round).
L23 Rhi, level 2, lots 1995, 2354, 2360, 2364, 2373, 2378-80 (combined).

Coarse Ware

P830 (NP75). Coarse mug. Fig. 3-41; Pl. 3-107.
H. 0.058-0.068 (uneven). Th. body ca. 0.007. D. rim 0.11. D. base 0.078.
Munsell 10YR 6/4 light yellowish brown. Clay fired to a light gray-blue in places around rim and to a light orange red in places at base. About ½ of rim restored. Rim is uneven.
L23 Sfg, level 3, lot 2396.

P831. Frag. of rim with attached lug handle. Pl. 3-108.
H. (pres.) 0.07. D. ca. 0.35.
Reddish yellow clay with dark gray core, burned in places. Semicircular lug built into body just below rim. Rim: Type A.
L23 Rhi, level 2, lots 1995, 2354, 2360, 2364, 2373, 2378-80 (combined).

P832. Coarse rim frag.
D. ca. 0.12.
Reddish yellow clay, slightly burned. Rim: Type B.
L23 Rhi, level 2, lots 1995, 2354, 2360, 2364, 2373, 2378-80 (combined).

P833. Tripod foot. Fig. 3-21.
H. 0.0525.
Coarse light red clay with inclusions. Rectangular in shape.
L23 Rhi, level 2, lots 1995, 2354, 2360, 2373, 2378-80 (combined).

P834. Coarse handle frag.

W. 0.042.

Burned. Handle: Type A1.

L23 Rhi, level 2, lots 1995, 2354, 2360, 2364, 2373, 2378-80 (combined).

P835. Coarse handle frag. badly warped in firing. Fig. 3-21; Pl. 3-105.

L. (pres.) 0.062. W. 0.042.

Brittle gray clay, burned. Handle has 5 grooves extant, 2 of which are badly chipped and worn. Handle: Type C(?)

L23 Rhi, level 2, lots 1995, 2354, 2360, 2364, 2373, 2378-80 (combined).

P836. Coarse handle frag. Fig. 3-21; Pl. 3-106.

L. (pres.) 0.072. W. 0.055.

Large handle badly fired to a light gray-blue color. Handle has 4 deep grooves, 2 at top and 2 at sides, with underside rounded. Handle: Type C(?)

L23 Rhi, level 2, lot 1995.

P837. Rim and body frag. of pithos. Fig. 3-21.

H. (pres.) 0.068. Th. 0.018. Th. with band 0.026.

Coarse reddish yellow clay. Raised band with diagonal slashes (rope decoration) at rim; second rope band just below first. Slashes in both bands go in same direction.

L23 Qfg/Rfg baulk, level 2, lot 4085.

P838. Rim frag. of pithos.

D. ca. 0.36.

Reddish yellow clay with inclusions, burned in places. Below rim is band of finger impressions.

L23 Qfg/Rfg baulk, level 2, lot 4085.

P839. Decorated pithos body frag. Pl. 3-117.

H. (pres.) 0.085.

Reddish yellow clay with inclusions, burned in places. Raised band with incised hatched triangles with impressed dots (made with end of twig) in between.

L23 Rfg/Rhi baulk, level 3, lot 4631/2.

P840. Incised body frag. of pithos.

H. (pres.) 0.058.

Coarse light red clay with inclusions. Decoration similar to **P839**.

L23 STfg/SThi baulk, level 3, lot 4535/2-4.

P841. Decorated body frag. of pithos. Pl. 3-120.

H. (pres.) 0.107.

Coarse reddish yellow clay fired a gray-blue color on exterior. Decoration of rope band with thumb impressions above.

L23 Rhi/Shi baulk, level 2, lot 4097/2C.

Section H

From Area IVSE. A few DAII sherds come from the bottom of a good DAIII deposit. These sherds are not associated with any architecture and are probably the result of hill-wash. They occur in lots mixed with Mycenaean and DAIII.

Open Shapes

P842. Upper profile of skyphos. Fig. 3-28.

D. ca. 0.164(?) Th. 0.004.

Very pale brown flaky clay. Good monochrome washy black coating on exterior and interior; reserved band inner rim. Rim: Type A2.

L23 UVc and ext., level 4, lot 4027/7-8W.

P843. Rim frag. of skyphos.

D. ca. 0.07-0.08.

Reddish yellow clay with red core. Frags. of brown paint preserved on exterior and interior; reserved band inner rim. Rim: Type C1.

L23 UVc and ext., level 4, lot 4027/7-8W.

P844 (NP108). Complete profile of flat-based skyphos. Fig. 3-26; Pl. 3-45.

H. 0.085. Th. 0.004-0.005. D. rim ca. 0.12. D. base ca. 0.08. D. handle ca. 0.013.

Munsell 10YR 8/4 very pale brown. Flaky clay, worn surfaces. Frags. of monochrome black coating preserved on exterior and interior. Wheel ridging both exterior and interior. Rim: Type C1; Handle: Type A.

L23 Sc, level 2, lot 4528/3-4.

P845. Decorated deep bowl rim and body frag. Fig. 3-31; Pl. 3-52A.

H. (pres.) 0.061. Th. 0.005 (top)-0.007 (bottom). D. ca. 0.24.

Munsell 7.5YR 7/6 reddish yellow (with orange-pink core and interior). Thin black band under rim; below, set of accumbent compass-drawn semi-circles with central dot; to left, broad diagonal band of streaky black paint, probably outlining point where handle joins body. Frag. of streaky black band below semi-circles. Good streaky black-brown paint on interior; reserved band inner rim. Rim: Type B2.

L23 Xd, level 4, lot 4031/5-9.

P846. 2 decorated skyphos body frags.

Reddish yellow clay, fired to an orange-red on interior. Frags. of arcs of accumbent concentric semi-circles; below, fragmentary band in faded black paint; good streaky black coating on interior.

L23 Sc, level 2, lot 4528/3-4; L23 UVc and ext., level 4, lot 4027/7-8W.

P847. Complete profile of cup. Fig. 3-35.

H. 0.057. D. rim ca. 0.12. D. base ca. 0.054. W. handle 0.013.

Very pale brown clay. Monochrome black coating on exterior, interior, and on underside of base. Rim: skyphos B2; Handle: cup B.

L23 UVc and ext., level 4, lot 4027/9N.

P848. Upper pofile of cup. Fig. 3-34.

H. (pres.) 0.044. Th. 0.003. D. ca. 0.075.

7 nonjoining body frags. Very pale brown flaky clay. Undecorated (reserved) band on exterior under rim; below, monochrome black coating. Same coating on interior; reserved band inner rim. Rim: skyphos B2.

L23 UVc and ext., level 4, lot 4027/9W.

Closed Shapes

P849. Decorated neck and shoulder frag. of oinochoe.

H. (pres.) 0.065.

Reddish yellow clay. On neck, ends of 5 arcs of accumbent concentric semi-circles in black; below, 2 grooves marking transition from neck to shoulder with frags. of black coating.

L23 UVc and ext., level 4, lot 4027/7-8W.

P850. 2 neck and shoulder frags. of oinochoai.

Reddish yellow clay. 2 grooves at transition from neck to shoulder. Frags. of black paint preserved.

L23 UVc and ext., level 4, lot 4027/7-8W.

P851. Decorated oinochoe shoulder frag. Pl. 3-92.

H. (pres.) 0.06.

Reddish yellow clay. 2 grooves mark transition from neck to shoulder; black coating in and above grooves. On shoulder, decoration of accumbent concentric semi-circles; to right, 6 arcs of semi-circles; to left, a ghost set of semi-circles with 7 very faded arcs preserved. At least 3 arcs of semi-circles to right have been painted over ghost set, so the oinochoe shoulder was repainted (but with same decoration). Below semi-circles, fragmentary band of black coating.
L23 UVc and ext., level 4, lot 4027/7-8W.

P852. Decorated shoulder frag. of oinochoe.
H. (pres.) 0.029.
Reddish yellow clay. Ends of arcs of accumbent concentric semi-circles with central dot.
L23 UVc and ext., level 4, lot 4027/7-8W.

P853. Decorated shoulder frag. of oinochoe.
H. (pres.) 0.03.
Reddish yellow clay, very worn. Possible metope-triglyph motif with 3 vertical lines of triglyph preserved.
L23 UVc and ext., level 4, lot 4027/7-8W.

P854. Decorated shoulder and belly frag. of oinochoe or jug. Pl. 3-89.
H. (pres.) 0.0455.
Reddish yellow clay; pale gray slip. On shoulder, ends of 6 arcs of accumbent concentric semi-circles; below, 2 black bands separate shoulder from belly. Decoration of wavy line on belly; below, black band.
L23 Xd, level 4, lot 4031/5-9.

P855. Base of probable amphora.
D. ca. 0.12.
Reddish yellow clay with gray-blue core. Frags. of black paint preserved. Base: Type B.
L23 Xd, level 4, lot 4031/5-9.

P856. 2 handle frags. of oinochoai or jugs.
Types A4 and A6.
L23 Sc, level 2, lot 4528/3-4; L23 Xd, level 4, lot 4031/5-9.

P856a. Pierced string-holed lug and rim frag. Fig. 3-33; Pl. 3-103.
H. (pres.) 0.05. Th. 0.004. Th. lug 0.014.
Reddish yellow clay. Worn surfaces. Lug is broken, but originally pointed; pierced for string hole. Above lug, frags. of black coating; below lug, frags. of cross-hatching. Light brown slip.
L23 UVc and ext., level 4, lot 4027/5W.

Coarse Ware

P857. Rim frag.
D. ca. 0.15.
Burned. Rim: Type A.
L23 Xd, level 4, lot 4031/5-9.

P858. 2 rim frags.
D. ca. 0.28-0.30.
Reddish yellow clay, burned gray in places. Rim: Type B.
L23 Xd, level 4, lot 4031/5-9.

P859. Base.
D. ca. 0.20 (uneven).
Burned. Base: Type A.
L23 Xd, level 4, lot 4031/5-9.

P860. Tripod foot. Fig. 3-21: Pl. 3-109.
H. (pres.) 0.058. D. top 0.035. D. bottom 0.02.
Reddish yellow clay, burned dark gray in places. Foot is round in shape with pointed base.
L23 Xd, level 5, lot 4527/1.

P861. Body frag. of pithos.
H. (pres.) 0.084. Th. 0.025. Th. raised bands 0.038.
Coarse reddish yellow clay with small inclusions. Body frag. has 2 undecorated raised bands or ribs.
L23 Sc, level 2, lot 4528/3-4.

Section I

From Area III. A very worn and scrappy group of DAII sherds is associated with Unit III-1. A great many of the sherds are too scrappy to be diagnostic; those that are, however, are listed below.

Open Shapes

P862. Rim frag. of skyphos.
D. ca. 0.08.
Reddish yellow clay. Rim: Type A1.
K25 Rg, level 2, lot 1653.

P863. Rim frag. of skyphos.
D. ca. 0.08.
Type A2.
K25 Rg, level 2, lot 1653.

P864. Rim frag. of skyphos.
D. ca. 0.08-0.09.
Type A3.
K25 Rg, level 2, lot 1653.

P865. 2 skyphos rim frags.
D. ca. 0.10-0.12.
Type A4.
K25 Rg, level 2, lot 1653.

P866. Rim frag. of skyphos.
D. ca. 0.12.
Shallow circular incision below rim. Type B2.
K25 Rg, level 2, pit, lot 1659.

P867. Rim frag. of skyphos.
D. ca. 0.12.
Type B4.
K25 Rg, level 3, pit, lot 1659.

P868. Rim frag. of skyphos.
Type C1.
K25 Rg, level 3, pit, lot 1659.

P869. Rim frag. of skyphos.
D. ca. 0.12.
Type D2.
K25 Rg/Sg baulk, level 2, lot 1664.

P870. Rim frag. of skyphos.
D. ca. 0.09.
Type C3.
K25 Rg, level 3, pit, lot 1659.

P871. 3 rim frags. of skyphoi or deep bowls.
D. ca. 0.16-0.18.
Type D.
K25 Rg, level 2, lot 1653.

P872. Rim of shallow bowl.

H. (pres.) 0.03. Th. 0.004. D. ca. 0.10.

Reddish yellow clay with pinkish tinge. Flaky clay, worn surfaces. Faint frags. of black paint preserved on exterior; none on interior.

K25 Rg, level 2, lot 1653.

P873. Rim frag. of krater.

D. ca. 0.20.

Reddish yellow flaky clay, worn surfaces. Faint frags. of black paint preserved on exterior and interior. Rim: Type D.

K25 Rg, level 3, pit, lot 1660.

P874. Base frag. of skyphos.

Type A1.

K25 Rg, level 2, lot 1653.

P875. 2 skyphos base frags.

Type C.

K25 Rg, level 2, lot 1653; level 3, pit, lot 1659.

P876. Flat base of cup or skyphos.

Base, because of its thickness, could belong to a skyphos. Reddish yellow clay; no traces of paint preserved.

K25 Rg, level 3, pit, lots 1659, 1660.

P877. 4 skyphos handle frags.

Type A.

K25 Rg, level 2, lot 1653; K25 Rg/Sg baulk, level 2, lot 1664.

P878. 2 skyphos handle frags.

Type C.

K25 Rg, level 2, lot 1653; level 3, pit, lot 1659.

Closed Shapes

P879. 3 rim frags. of oinochoai or jugs.

Reddish yellow clay; no traces of paint preserved. Rim: Type A1.

K25 Rg, level 2, lot 1653; level 3, pit, lots 1659, 1660.

P880. Strainer frag.

H. (pres.) 0.0515. Th. 0.006.

Reddish yellow clay, worn surfaces. Possible frags. of black paint on exterior. 8 complete holes (D. 0.004), 10 partially preserved holes.

K25 Rg, level 3, pit, lots 1659, 1660.

P881. Flat base of amphora.

D. ca. 0.13.

About ⅓ preserved. Very pale brown flaky clay, worn surfaces. No traces of paint preserved. Flat base: Type B.

K25 Rg/Sg baulk, level 2, lot 1664.

P882. Handle of oinochoe or jug.

W. 0.024.

Flaky gray clay. Possible frags. of black paint preserved. Handle: Type A4 (with flute).

K25 Rg, level 3, pit, lots 1659, 1660.

Coarse Ware

P883. 2 coarse rim frags.

D. ca. 0.16 (uneven).

Burned. Type A.

K25 Rg, level 3, pit, lots 1659, 1660.

P884. Coarse rim frag.

D. ca. 0.20.

Burned. Type B.

K25 Rg, level 3, pit, lots 1659, 1660.

Section J

From Area III. This section comprises the important sherds associated with the DA levels of Unit III-3, i.e., the upper DA field horizon, the lower DA field horizon, the DA backfill of robber pits, and the upper debris within the house.

Upper DA Horizon:

Open Shapes

P885. Body frag. of skyphos.

H. (pres.) 0.046.

Reddish yellow clay. On exterior, frags. of solid black coating; below, 3 black-brown bands. Streaky black coating on interior.

K24 Uv/Uw baulk, level 3, lot 4221.

Lower DA Horizon:

Open Shapes

P886. Rim and body frag. of skyphos.

D. ca. 0.10. Th. 0.0035.

Very pale brown clay. 2 black bands at rim, followed by undecorated zone (reserved band) in field between handles. Frags. of black coating on interior. Rim: Type C1.

K23 Uv/Uw baulk, levels 4 and 6, lots 4251, 4254.

P887. Decorated rim frag. of krater.

H. (pres.) 0.044. D. ca. 0.25.

Reddish yellow clay. Streaky black band at rim; below, wavy line in black. Frags. of black coating on interior. Rim: Type F.

K24 Uv/Uw baulk, level 4, lot 4252.

P888. Base frag. of skyphos.

D. ca. 0.037.

Flaky gray clay; frag. of black paint preserved. Base: Type A1.

K24 Uv/Uw baulk, levels 4 and 6, lots 4251, 4254.

P889. Base frag. of skyphos or deep bowl.

D. ca. 0.07.

Reddish yellow clay. Black paint on exterior and interior. Wheel ridging on interior. Base: Type B.

K24 Uv/Uw baulk, levels 4 and 6, lots 4251, 4254.

Closed Shapes

P890. Handle frag. of small oinochoe or jug.

W. 0.0125.

Flaky gray clay; frag. of black paint preserved. Handle: Type A2 (with flute).

K24 Uv/Uw baulk, level 4, lot 4281.

Backfill of DA Robber Pits:

Open Shapes

P891. Upper profile of skyphos. Fig. 3-24; Pl. 3-48.

H. (pres.) 0.075. Th. 0.006. D. ca. 0.11.

Reddish yellow clay. Decoration of wavy line in handle zone; above, streaky black coating. Below handle zone is thin black band, followed by streaky black coating. Good streaky black paint on interior. Rim: Type C1.

Robber pit, interior of apse (1975 probe), lot 5017.

P892. Profile of skyphos. Fig. 3-24.

H. 0.091. D. rim 0.093. D. base 0.035.

Very pale brown clay with pinkish tinge. Possible undecorated zone (reserved band) in field between handles; above and below, monochrome black paint. Good black coating on interior. Rim: Type C1; Base: Type A1; Handle: Type C.

K24 Uw, level 3, lot 3136/1-4.

P893. Decorated body frag. of skyphos or deep bowl. Pl. 3-51.

H. (pres.) 0.075. Th. 0.006.

Reddish yellow clay. Lower half of set of compass-drawn concentric circles preserved, probably in handle zone; frags. of 8 thin black arcs. Below, 3 thick black bands, followed by good monochrome black coating on belly of vase; similar coating on interior. 2 mending holes (D. 0.004), one in middle of concentric circles, other in black coating on belly.

K24 Vw, level 5, lots 4203/1, 4206/7, 4209.

P894. Decorated skyphos body frag.

H. (pres.) 0.039. Th. 0.005.

Very pale brown clay. Frags. of arcs of set of concentric semicircles with central dot (hand drawn?); below, 2 black bands, followed by black coating. Solid black paint on interior.

K24 Vw, level 5, lots 4203/1, 4206/7, 4209.

P895. Profile of cup (missing handle).

H. 0.059. D. rim ca. 0.10. D. base ca. 0.044.

Gritty and flaky reddish yellow clay, worn surfaces. Frags. of black paint preserved on exterior and interior. Rim: skyphos B2(?)

K24 TUv, level 3, lot 3124/1-2.

P896. Upper profile of large cup.

H. (pres.) 0.615. Th. 0.0045. D. rim ca. 0.15. W. handle 0.0125.

Reddish yellow gritty clay with tan tinge; worn surfaces. Frags. of black paint preserved on exterior and interior. Carinated body. Rim: skyphos C1; Handle: Type B(?)

K24 Uw, level 3, lot 3136/1-4.

P897. Pedestal base, possibly of krater. Fig. 3-18.

D. ca. 0.12.

About ¼ preserved. Reddish yellow clay with gray-blue core. High foot with rib in center. Frags. of black-brown paint preserved.

K24 Vw, level 5, lot 4203/1.

Closed Shapes

P898. Decorated shoulder frag. of oinochoe or jug.

H. (pres.) 0.03.

Reddish yellow clay. Black band marks transition from neck to shoulder; below on shoulder, 5 frags. of arcs of concentric semicircles in black.

K24 TUv, level 3, lot 3124/1-2.

P899. Decorated shoulder frag. of oinochoe. Pl. 3-90.

H. (pres.) 0.0445.

Reddish yellow clay. Black band marks transition from neck to shoulder; below on shoulder, 4 frags. of arcs of accumbent concentric semi-circles; to right, vertical band of cross-hatching in black.

K24 TUv, level 2, lot 3121/2-4.

P900. Decorated shoulder frag. of oinochoe. Pl. 3-94.

H. (pres.) 0.058.

Reddish yellow clay. Black band marks transition from neck to shoulder; below on shoulder, metope-triglyph motif with 3 frags. of vertical lines of triglyph preserved; to right, frag. of hatched triangle in metope.

K24 Vv/Vw baulk, level 4, lot 4252.

P901. 2 rope handle frags. of oinochoai.

D. 0.02-0.025.

Very pale brown flaky clay. Frags. of black paint preserved. Handle: Type A5.

K24 TUv, level 2, lot 3121/2-4; K24 Vv/Vw baulk, level 4, lot 4252.

P902. Handle frag. of oinochoe.

W. 0.026.

Reddish yellow clay. Frags. of black paint. Handle: Type A4 (with flute).

K24 TUv, level 3, lot 3124/1-2.

Coarse Ware

P903. Body frag. of pithos. Pl. 3-114.

H. (pres.) 0.065. Th. body 0.03. Th. raised band 0.04.

Gritty reddish yellow clay with inclusions. White slip(?) Raised band decorated with row of incised circles. One circle has 2 lines and was probably redrawn to correct a mistake.

K24 TUv, level 3, lot 3124/1-2.

Upper Debris within House:

Open Shapes

P904. Upper profile of skyphos. Fig. 3-24.

H. (pres.) 0.054. Th. ca. 0.003. D. ca. 0.12.

Very pale brown flaky clay, worn surfaces. Possible undecorated zone (reserved band) in field between handles and extending to neck of vase; above and below, streaky black coating. Streaky black paint on interior; reserved band inner rim. Rim: Type A3.

K24 TUu/Tuv baulk, level 6, lot 3146.

P905. Upper profile of skyphos or deep bowl. Fig. 3-28.

H. (pres.) 0.096. Th. 0.005. D. ca. 0.16.

Reddish yellow flaky clay, worn surfaces. Possible undecorated zone (reserved band) in field between handles; above and below, streaky black coating. Streaky black coating on interior; reserved band inner rim. Rim: Type C1.

K24 TUu/Tuv baulk, level 3, lot 3147.

P906. Decorated skyphos body frag. Fig. 3-32.

H. (pres.) 0.03.

Very pale brown clay with greenish tinge. Decoration of thin wavy line with frags. of black coating above and below. Frags. of black paint on interior.

K24 Uv/Uw baulk, level 6, lot 4286.

P907. Profile of cup. Fig. 3-34.

H. 0.065. D. rim 0.095. D. base 0.05. W. handle 0.013.

Reddish yellow clay with gray tinge. Frags. of streaky black coating preserved on exterior and interior. White slip. Rim: skyphos B4; Cup handle: Type B.

K24 Uv/Uw baulk, level 6, lot 4286.

P908. Pedestal base of possible krater. Fig. 3-18.

D. ca. 0.09.

Very pale brown flaky clay. Conical base, missing tip of foot. Frags. of black paint preserved on exterior.

K24 TUu/Tuv baulk, level 3, lot 3147.

Closed Shapes

P909. 4 decorated shoulder frags. of oinochoai.

Reddish yellow to very pale brown clay. Preserved frags. of arcs

of accumbent concentric semi-circles in black, probably hand-drawn.
K24 TUv/Tuv baulk, level 3, lot 3147; K24 Uv/Uw baulk, level 6, lot 4285.

P910. Decorated shoulder frag. of oinochoe. Pl. 3-88.
H. (pres.) 0.0625.
Frag. of black band at transition from neck to shoulder; below, metope-triglyph motif, with frag. of thick vertical band preserved for triglyph and frags. of thin concentric circles (5 arcs) in metope.
K24 Uv/Uw baulk, level 6, lot 4285.

Section K

From Area III. A good group of DAII sherds is associated with the upper levels of Unit III-4, with the lower hill-wash, rubbish tip, and debris over roadway.

Lower Hill-Wash:

Open Shapes

P911. 2 decorated skyphos body frags. Fig. 3-32.
Reddish yellow clay. One frag. has hatched triangles in black with 3 thin bands below; to left of bands is diagonal band of paint, probably representing outline of handle junction. Main body of decoration, therefore, is above handle zone. Other frag. has only 3 sides of hatched triangles preserved. Black paint interior.
K24 Wy/K25 Wa, level 3, lot 4381/3.

P912. Decorated skyphos body frag.
H. (pres.) 0.033.
Reddish yellow clay. Frag. of crosshatched triangles in black; below, frag. of black coating. Black paint on interior.
K24 Xa, level 2, lots 4363, 4364.

P913. Decorated skyphos body frag. Fig. 3-32.
Reddish yellow clay. Frags. of arcs of accumbent concentric semi-circles; below, black band and frag. of black coating. Black paint interior.
K24 Wy/K25 Wa, level 3, lot 4381/3.

P914. Body frag. of skyphos.
Reddish yellow clay. Undecorated zone, probably in field between handles; below, 2 brown bands followed by brown coating. Frags. of brown paint on interior.
K24 Wy/K25 Wa, level 3, lot 4381/3.

P915. Upper profile of skyphos, missing tip of rim and base.
H. (pres.) 0.06. D. ca. 0.13.
Reddish yellow flaky clay, very worn surfaces. Possible monochrome black coating on exterior and interior. Rim: Type C1(?); Handle: Type A (D. 0.01).
K24 Wy/K25 Wa, level 3, lot 4381/3.

P916. Upper profile of skyphos. Fig. 3-32.
H. (pres.) 0.023. D. ca. 0.09. D. handle 0.008.
Reddish yellow clay. Possible undecorated zone in field between handles; above and below, monochrome black coating; same coating on interior. Rim: Type A3(?); Handle: Type C.
K24 Wy/K25 Wa, level 3, lot 4381/3.

P916a. Upper profile of skyphos. Fig. 3-22.
H. (pres.) 0.04. D. ca. 0.08.
Reddish yellow clay. Frags. of monochrome black coating preserved on exterior and interior. Preserved band inner rim. Rim: Type B2(?); Handle: Type C.
K24 Wy/K25 Wa, level 3, lot 4381/3.

Closed Shapes

P917. 3 decorated shoulder frags. of oinochoai. Fig. 3-39.
Very pale brown flaky clay. Frags. of arcs of accumbent concentric semi-circles in brown-black paint.
K24 Wy/Xy / K25 Wa/Xa, level 3, lot 4390.; K24 Wy/K25 Wa, level 3, lot 4381/3.

P918. Frag. of strainer. Pl. 3-79.
H. (pres.) 0.041. Th. 0.005 (top)-0.008 (bottom).
Reddish yellow flaky clay, worn surfaces. 3 complete holes (D. 0.0035) preserved, 1 fragmentary hole. No paint preserved.
K24 Wy/Xy / K25 Wa/Xa, level 3, lot 4390.

P919. Handle of oinochoe.
W. 0.024.
Very pale brown flaky clay. Frags. of black paint. Handle: Type A2 (with rib).
K24 Wy/Xy / K25 Wa/Xa, level 3, lot 4390.

P920. Rope handle frag. of oinochoe.
D. 0.02.
Reddish yellow clay with gray core. Good black paint preserved. Handle: Type A5.
K24 Wy/Xy / K25 Wa/Xa, level 3, lot 4390.

Coarse Ware

P921. Body frag. of pithos.
H. (pres.) 0.04. Th. body 0.018. Th. raised band 0.026.
Coarse light red clay with small inclusions. Raised band with incised rope decoration.
K24 Wy/Xy / K25 Wa/Xa, level 3, lot 4390.

Rubbish Tip:

Open Shapes

P922 (NP94). Upper profile of skyphos or deep bowl. Fig. 3-29; Pl. 3-61.
H. (pres.) 0.107. Th. 0.004. D. ca. 0.17.
Munsell 5YR 7/6 reddish yellow. Handle zone contains decoration of overlapping crosshatched triangles in reddish brown paint; above and below, good streaky reddish brown coating. Thin reserved band on lower belly. Frags. of streaky reddish brown paint on interior. Carinated body; string marks on lower belly; wheel ridging on interior. Rim: Type B4.
K24 Xy, level 2, lot 4369/2(b).

P923. Upper profile of deep bowl. Fig. 3-30; Pl. 3-50.
H. (pres.) 0.058. Th. 0.004. D. ca. 0.18.
Reddish yellow clay. Decoration of sharp wavy line flanked by two black bands, probably in handle zone; above and below, monochrome black coating; same coating on interior. Reserved inner band.
K24 Yy, level 2, lots 4355-59.

P924. Upper profile of deep bowl. Fig. 3-28.
H. (pres.) 0.055. Th. 0.004. D. ca. 0.17.
Reddish yellow clay. Decoration and paint like **P923**, but more fragmentary and worn. Rim: Type B4(?)
K24 Yy, level 2, lots 4355-59.

P925. Upper profile of skyphos. Fig. 3-24.
H. (pres.) 0.053. D. ca. 0.10.
Reddish yellow flaky clay, worn surfaces. Possible undecorated zone in field between handles; above and below, streaky black

coating; same coating on interior. Light gray slip. Rim: Type C1; Handle: Type C (D. 0.008).
K24 Yy, level 2, lots 4355-59.

P926. Decorated skyphos body frag. Pl. 3-65.
H. (pres.) 0.053. Th. 0.005.
Reddish yellow clay with orange-pink core. Decoration consists of sets of 2 piled triangles in brown paint; above and below, monochrome brown coating; same coating on interior. Slight wheel ridging on exterior, heavy on interior.
K24 Yy, level 2, lots 4355-59.

P927. Decorated skyphos body frag.
H. (pres.) 0.057. Th. ca. 0.005.
Reddish yellow clay. Frag. of crosshatched triangle; above and below, monochrome black coating. Streaky black paint on interior.
K24 Yy, level 2, lots 4355-59.

P928. 3 skyphos body frags.
Very pale brown to reddish yellow clay. Flaky clay, worn surfaces. Frags. of arcs of accumbent concentric semi-circles in black, probably in handle zone. One frag., better preserved, has central spiral instead of dot.
K24 Yy, level 2, lots 4355-59.

P929. Profile of cup (missing handle). Fig. 3-34.
H. 0.067. D. rim ca. 0.075. D. base ca. 0.06.
Reddish yellow clay. Streaky monochrome black-brown coating on exterior and interior. Rim: skyphos C3.
K24 Yy, level 2, lots 4355-59.

P930. Profile of cup (missing handle and base).
H. 0.059. D. rim ca. 0.115. D. base ca. 0.034.
Shape and decoration similar to **P929**.
K24 Yy, level 2, lots 4355-59.

P931. Decorated krater wall frag. Fig. 3-33.
H. (pres.) 0.097. Th. 0.01-0.011.
Reddish yellow clay fired to a light gray in places. Decoration very faded and worn, but appears to consist of half-chevrons in three registers in faded black-brown paint. Good streaky black-brown coating on interior.
K24 Yy, level 2, lots 4355-59.

P932. Pedestal krater base. Fig. 3-18.
D. ca. 0.08.
About ⅓ preserved. Reddish yellow clay. Good streaky black paint on exterior and interior. Semi-conical in shape with rib in center of foot.
K24 Yy, level 2, lots 4355-59.

P932a. Pedestal krater base. Fig. 3-18.
D. ca. 0.075.
About ⅔ preserved. Reddish yellow clay. Good monochrome coating preserved on exterior and interior. High conical foot with rib in center of foot.
K24 Yy, level 2, lots 4355-59.

Closed Shapes

P933. 2 decorated oinochoe shoulder frags.
Reddish yellow clay. Frags. of arcs of accumbent concentric semi-circles in black. Central spiral instead of dot.
K24 Yy, level 2, lots 4355-59.

P934. Decorated oinochoe shoulder frag.
Reddish yellow clay. 2 adjacent sets of accumbent compass-drawn concentric semi-circles; 7 frags. of arcs in one set, 3 in the other.
K24 Yy, level 2, lots 4355-59.

P935. Decorated oinochoe shoulder frag.
H. (pres.) 0.039.
Reddish yellow clay. Ends of arcs of accumbent concentric semi-circles; below, monochrome black coating.
K24 Yy, level 2, lots 4355-59.

P936. Decorated oinochoe shoulder frag. Fig. 3-40; Pl. 3-96.
H. 0.04.
Very pale brown clay. Metope-triglyph motif with 2 vertical lines in black forming the triglyph and framed crosshatched triangle in the metope.
K24 Yy, level 2, lots 4355-59.

P937. 2 oinochoe handles.
W. 0.025.
Type A1.
K24 Xy, level 2, lot 4369/1-2; K24 Yy, level 2, lots 4355-59.

P938. Handle of oinochoe.
W. 0.026.
Type A4 (with flute).
K24 Xy, level 2, lot 4369/1-2.

P939. 2 rope handle frags. of oinochoai.
D. 0.016-0.018.
Type A5.
K24 Xy, level 2, lots 4355-59.

P940. Handle frag. of small oinochoe or jug.
W. 0.013.
Type A6.
K24 Yy, level 2, lots 4355-59.

Coarse Ware

P941. 3 rim frags.
D. ca. 0.20-0.26 (uneven).
Fired to dark gray. Rim: Type A.
K24 Yy, level 2, lots 4355-59.

P942. Rim frag.
D. ca. 0.19-0.20.
Fired to a dark gray color. Rim: Type B.
K24 Yy, level 2, lots 4355-59.

P943. Rim frag. of probable coarse oinochoe.
Light red clay with inclusions. Shape similar to rim Type A1 of fine ware.
K24 Yy, level 2, lots 4355-59.

Debris over Roadway:

Open Shapes

P944. Profile of skyphos.
H. (pres.) 0.026. D. rim ca. 0.085. D. base ca. 0.036. D. handle 0.075.
Reddish yellow clay. Possible monochrome black coating exterior and interior. Handle: Type C.
K25 Xb, level 3, lot 4378.

Coarse Ware

P945. Decorated body frag. of pithos.

H. (pres.) 0.083. Th. body 0.023. Th. raised band 0.031.

Light red coarse clay with inclusions. Raised band with incised circles.

K25 Xb, level 3, lot 4375.

P946. Decorated body frag. of pithos.

H. (pres.) 0.063. Th. body ca. 0.026. Th. raised band ca. 0.029.

Interior of body frag. broken off. Reddish yellow coarse clay with inclusions. Raised band with diagonal slashes (imitation rope decoration).

K25 Xb, level 3, lot 4375.

Section L

From Area III. This section is composed of sherds associated with terrace walls A-C in the south of Area III.

Upper Hill-Wash (over Walls A-C):

Open Shapes

P947. Rim and body frag. of skyphos. Fig. 3-33.

H. (pres.) 0.051.

Tip of rim missing. Reddish yellow clay. Black coating under rim. 4 frags. of vertical lines (triglyph?) below, probably in handle zone. Good streaky black paint on interior. Rim: Type C1(?)

L24 BCu, level 2, lot 4367.

P948. Decorated skyphos body frag. Fig. 3-33.

Reddish yellow clay. Decoration similar to **P926**, but more fragmentary.

L24 BCu, level 2, lot 4367.

P949. Decorated skyphos body frag. Fig. 3-33.

Reddish yellow clay. Frag. of ends of crosshatched triangle. Decoration similar to **P603**.

L24 BCu, level 2, lot 4371/1-2.

P950. Decorated skyphos body frag. Fig. 3-33.

Reddish yellow clay. Frag. of cross-hatching preserved; below, reserved band followed by black coating. Faded frags. of black paint on interior.

L24 BCu, level 2, lot 4367.

P951. Decorated krater wall frag. Fig. 3-35; Pl. 3-75.

H. (pres.) 0.051. Th. 0.008.

Reddish yellow clay with orange-pink core. 3 narrow vertical panels of decoration consisting of cross-hatching, squares, and diagonal lines; below, frag. of black coating. Streaky black-brown paint on interior.

L24 BCu, level 1, lot 4377.

Closed Shapes

P952. Decorated shoulder frag. of oinochoe.

H. (pres.) 0.032.

Broad black band marks transition from neck to shoulder; below, 4 frags. of arcs of accumbent concentric semi-circles in faded black-brown paint.

K24 Xt, level 3, lot 3163.

P953. Decorated neck frag. of oinochoe. Pl. 3-97.

H. (pres.) 0.03.

Reddish yellow clay. Metope-triglyph motif between 2 black bands. 3 vertical lines for triglyph with frag. of hatched triangle in metope.

K24 Ytu, level 2, lot 3151/4.

P954. Profile of jug. Fig. 3-36.

D. rim ca. 0.17. D. base 0.125. W. handle 0.028.

Reddish yellow clay. No decoration, but solid monochrome brown coating on exterior. 3 raised bands mark transition from neck to shoulder. Rim: Type A1; Base: Type C; Handle: Type A2 (with rib).

L24 Atu, level 2, lots 3172/2-7, 3173.

P955. Decorated handle of small jug. Fig. 3-33.

W. handle 0.024.

Attached to rim. Very pale brown clay. Top of handle decorated with alternating sets of horizontal and vertical stripes.

L24 BCu, level 2, lots 4367, 4371/1-2.

P956. 2 handle frags. of oinochoai.

W. 0.025.

Type A2 (with rib).

L24 BCu, level 2, lots 4367, 4371/1-2.

Lower Hill-Wash (Mainly between Walls A and B):

Open Shapes

P957. Decorated skyphos body frag. Fig. 3-32; Pl. 3-54.

H. (pres.) 0.057.

Reddish yellow clay. 2 adjacent sets of concentric semi-circles, probably in handle zone. To left, set almost complete with central spiral; to right, frags. of 3 arcs preserved. Below, streaky black coating; same coating on interior.

L24 Atu, level 3, lot 4392.

P958. Decorated skyphos body frag. Fig. 3-32; Pl. 3-54.

H. (pres.) 0.024.

Frags. of hatched triangle (4 oblique lines preserved); above, frag. of black coating. Washy black paint on interior.

L24 Atu, level 3, lot 4392.

Associated with Walls A, B, C:

Open Shapes

P959. Base frag. of krater.

D. ca. 0.09-0.10.

Streaky black-brown frags. preserved. Ringed base; similar in shape to skyphos Type C.

K24 Xtu, level 3, lot 3188.

P960. Pedestal base of krater. Fig. 3-18.

H. (pres.) 0.054. D. foot ca. 0.04. D. stem 0.022.

Munsell 2.5YR 6/8 light red. Flaky, worn surfaces. Hollow in underside of base. No traces of paint preserved.

K24 Wu, level 3, lot 3182N.

Closed Shapes

P961. Decorated rim and neck frag. of oinochoe.

H. (pres.) 0.0695.

Reddish yellow clay. Good streaky black paint on neck; stripes (5 preserved) on top of rim. Rim: Type D.

K24 Xtu, level 3, lot 3189.

P962. Base frag. of oinochoe.

D. ca. 0.07-0.08.

Reddish yellow clay. Base: Type C.

K24 Wu, level 3, lot 3180/2.

P962a. Base frag. of oinochoe. Fig. 3-20.
Similar to **P962**.
K24 Wu, level 3, lot 3180/2.

Coarse Ware

P963. Flat base.
Coarse reddish clay with inclusions. Base: Type A.
K24 Wu, level 3, lot 3180/2.

P964. Body frag. of pithos.
H. (pres.) 0.075. Th. body 0.028. Th. raised band 0.035.
Coarse light red clay with inclusions. Frag. of incised hatched triangle on raised band.
K24 Wu, level 3, lot 3180/2.

P965. Frag. of grill(?)
H. (pres.) 0.043.
Coarse gritty reddish yellow clay. Frag. has raised knob forming flutes on either side in which to place a spit.
K24 Xuv, level 3, lot 3187.

Section M

From Area III. This section contains good DAII sherds from trenches of little importance architecturally.

Open Shapes

P966. Upper profile of deep bowl. Fig. 3-31.
H. (pres.) 0.126. D. ca. 0.21.
Reddish yellow flaky clay, worn surfaces. Possible monochrome brown coating on exterior and interior. Rim: Type C2; Handle: Type C (D. 0.007).
K25 Tab, level 3, lot 1437.

P967. Rim and body frag. of skyphos.
H. (pres.) 0.051. Th. 0.005. D. ca. 0.18.
Reddish yellow clay with orange-pink core. Decoration of concentric semi-circles (5 frags. of arcs preserved) probably in handle zone; above, black coating. Faint frags. of black paint preserved on interior. Rim: Type C2.
K25 Tab, level 2, lots 1427, 1441.

P968. 2 decorated skyphos body frags.
Reddish yellow clay. Frags. of arcs of accumbent concentric semi-circles in black. Streaky black paint on interior.
K25 Tab, level 2, lots 1427, 1441.

P969. Upper profile of skyphos.
H. (pres.) 0.066. D. ca. 0.14.
Tip of rim and base missing. Reddish yellow clay. Possible monochrome black-brown coating on exterior and interior. White slip(?) Rim: Type C1(?)
K25 Uab, level 5, lots 4432, 4435.

P970. Decorated skyphos body frag.
H. (pres.) 0.0465.
Reddish yellow clay. Decoration (in handle zone?) of crosshatched triangles; below, 2 black bands followed by black coating. Good black paint on interior.
K24 Vw, level 2, lot 3654/1-2.

P971. Decorated skyphos body frag. Pl. 3-62.
Tip of rim missing. 3 small incisions under rim; decoration of crosshatched triangles begins at incisions. Good streaky black paint on top of rim and on interior; wheel ridging on interior.
L24 Cvw, level 1, lot 4562.

P972 (NP56). Profile of cup (missing handle). Fig. 3-34; Pl. 3-70.
H. 0.06-0.064 (uneven); D. rim 0.09. D. base 0.04. W. restored handle 0.013.
Munsell 10YR 7/3 very pale brown. Monochrome washy black coating on exterior and interior. Small reserved band under rim on exterior; band varies in width around vase. Rim: skyphos C3.
K25 Tab, level 3, lot 1437.

P973. Rim frag. of krater.
D. ca. 0.16.
Reddish yellow clay. Black stripes on top of rim; frags. of streaky black paint on exterior and interior. Rim: Type A.
L24 Cvw, level 2, lot 4568 SW½.

P974. Rim frag. of krater.
D. ca. 0.20.
Very pale brown clay. Thick black stripes on top of rim. Frags. of black paint preserved on exterior and interior. Rim: Type D.
K25 Tab, level 3, lot 1437.

P975. Decorated wall frag. of krater. Fig. 3-33; Pl. 3-76.
H. (pres.) 0.095.
Reddish yellow clay with gray-blue core. Decoration of checkerboard pattern with black circles in some of the squares. To left, frag. of arc of concentric semi-circle(?) Small raised band at top of frag. Good frags. of black paint on interior.
K25 Uab, level 2, lot 3102.

Closed Shapes

P976. Decorated shoulder frag. of oinochoe.
H. (pres.) 0.037.
4 frags. of arcs of accumbent concentric semi-circles in faded black-brown paint.
K24 Vw, level 2, lot 3650/3-4.

P977. 4 oinochoe shoulder frags.
Frags. of concentric semi-circles. One frag. has parts of 2 adjacent sets of semi-circles preserved.
K25 Tab, level 3, lot 1437; K25 Tcd, level 5, lots 1182, 1183.

P978-79. 2 decorated oinochoe shoulder frags. Pl. 3-91.
Reddish yellow clay. Frags. of arcs of accumbent concentric semi-circles. **P978** has 3 frags. of thin arcs with large diagonal band of paint to left, probably outlining point where handle joins shoulder.
K25 Uab, level 2, lot 3102.

P980. Possible frag. of lid. Pl. 3-102.
H. (pres.) 0.082. W. 0.059. Th. 0.005.
Reddish yellow clay with gray-blue core. Possible stump of loop handle at top edge of sherd. Black paint outlining junction of handle, followed by 3 faint black bands and frags. of 6 oblique lines in black. Frags. of black paint on underside. Grayish white slip.
K25 Uab, level 2, lot 3102.

Coarse Ware

P981. 5 rim frags.
D. ca. 0.28.
Burned. Rim: Type B.
K25 Tab, level 4, lot 1911.

P982 (NP197). Profile of round-based jug (dipper). Fig. 3-41.

H. (pres.) 0.131. Th. 0.008. D. ca. 0.14. W. handle 0.038.

Broken at rim and missing most of handle except for stump. Munsell 2.5YR 6/8 light red; fired to 7.5YR N7/0 light gray on ½ of exterior; rest of exterior and all of interior light red. Rim: Type B(?); Handle: Type A1.

K25 Tcd, level 4, lot 1179.

P983. Profile of rim and neck of neck-handled amphora. Fig. 3-42.

H. (pres.) 0.10. Th. 0.009. D. ca. 0.20. W. handle 0.0425.

Munsell 2.5YR 6/8 light red, burned dark gray in places. Rim: Type B; Neck handle: Type A1.

K25 Tab, level 4, lot 1911.

P984. Body frag. of pithos. Pl. 3-118.

H. (pres.) 0.108. Th. body 0.029. Th. raised band 0.035.

Coarse reddish yellow clay with inclusions. Raised band has row of incised hatched triangles, alternating right side up and upside down.

K25 Tab, level 3, lot 1437.

Section N

From the 1969 test trenches. There is little of architectural importance belonging to the DAII period from the trial trenches dug in 1969. In some trenches in Areas III, IIISE, IV, and VII, DAII sherds were found; those of note are cataloged below.

From Area III:

Closed Shapes

P985. Decorated shoulder and belly frags. of oinochoe.

4 nonjoining frags. from same vase. Reddish yellow clay; light gray slip. 1 neck and shoulder frag. has black band to mark transition from neck to shoulder; below on shoulder, frags. of arcs of accumbent concentric semi-circles in faded black paint. 2 shoulder frags. One has frags. of arcs of overlapping concentric semi-circles with frag. of black coating below marking beginning of belly; other has almost complete set of accumbent concentric semi-circles with central dot (compass-drawn) with black coating below. 1 belly frag. with tail ends of 2 adjacent sets of concentric semi-circles with central dots and heavy streaky black coating below on belly.

K25-III, level 2, lots 46, 49, 58, 63.

From Area IIIS:

Open Shapes

P986. Double handle of deep bowl. Fig. 3-31; Pl. 3-43.

D. 0.0085.

One complete handle and frag. of second one preserved. Munsell 10YR 7/3 very pale brown. Black stripes on complete handle; frag. of stripe on adjacent handle stump. Frags. of streaky black paint on exterior and interior of body frag. between handles. Handle: Type C.

K24-III, level 4, lots 98, 100.

From N Veves:

Open Shapes

P987. Upper profile of skyphos (missing handles). Fig. 3-26.

H. (pres.) 0.068. D. ca. 0.14.

Reddish yellow flaky clay, worn surfaces. Possible monochrome washy black coating on exterior and interior. Rim: Type C1.

L24-IV, level 2, lot 82.

P988. Decorated skyphos body frag.

H. (pres.) 0.026.

Reddish yellow clay. Tail end of cross-hatching preserved (cf. **P603**); below, small raised band to mark end of decoration zone (in field between handles?); below raised band are frags. of black coating. Fine black paint on interior.

L24-VII, level 2, lots 501, 503.

P989. Rim frag. of krater.

D. ca. 0.20.(?)

Rim: Type E.

L24-IV, level 2, lot 82.

P990. Decorated rim and body frag. of krater. Fig. 3-33.

H. (pres.) 0.065. Th. 0.007. D. ca. 0.24.

Very pale brown clay. Slight raised band under tip of rim; broad streaky black-brown band below rim followed by decoration zone. Frag. of framed, hatched triangle in reddish brown paint. Black paint on interior of rim only; no coating on rest of interior. Rim: Type F.

L24-IV, level 2, lot 82.

P991. Decorated body frag. of krater. Fig. 3-35; Pl. 3-77.

H. (pres.) 0.06. Th. 0.008.

Handle zone and lower body preserved. Reddish yellow clay. Metope-triglyph motif in handle zone; 9 vertical lines form triglyph, no decoration in metope; below, 3 black bands marking end of decoration zone followed by streaky black-brown coating on belly of vase. Handle: Type A(?)

L24-IV, level 2, lot 82.

Closed Shapes

P992. Decorated handle, probably of small jug. Fig. 3-40; Pl. 3-98.

W. 0.0155.

Elliptical handle. Very pale brown clay. Small black triangular stripes (like wolf's tooth) on top of handle; black at sides, no paint underneath.

L24-II, level 3, lots 187, 189, 190, 195.

From Area IVS:

Open Shapes

P993. Upper profile of skyphos. Fig. 3-26.

H. (pres.) 0.081. Th. ca. 0.0035. D. ca. 0.14.

Very pale brown clay, fired gray around edges and on interior. Possible undecorated zone in field between handles; above and below, monochrome black coating; same coating on interior. Rim; Type B2.

L23-VIII, level 2, lots 298, 300.

P994. Profile of deep cup.

H. 0.083. D. rim ca. 0.12. D. base 0.05.

Reddish yellow flaky clay, worn surfaces. Possible monochrome black coating on exterior and interior. Rim: similar to skyphos C1(?)

L23-V, level 3, lot 325.

Closed Shapes

P995. Frags. of oinochoe.

Munsell 7.5R N6/0 gray on exterior and 5YR 6/3 light reddish brown on interior; orange-pink core. Clay fired to a hard, brittle texture, warped in firing; worn surfaces. 1 neck frag., 3 neck-shoulder frags., 7 decorated shoulder frags., 1 lower shoulder-belly frag., 1 lower belly frag., 1 handle frag. Accumbent semi-circles on neck; grooving at transition from neck to shoulder. Shoulder decoration consists of both accumbent and pendent semi-circles on either side of black band. Accumbent semi-circles on shoulder; pendent semi-circles on lower shoulder-upper belly. Black bands at lower belly. Black bands at lower belly. Handle: Type A1. (W. 0.016).

L23-V, level 2, lot 226.

P996. Frags. of oinochoe.

Reddish yellow to very pale brown flaky clay, worn surfaces. 3 rim frags., 6 neck-shoulder frags., handle and base frags. Black coating on neck; 2 grooves at transition from neck to shoulder; faint frags. of accumbent concentric semi-circles on shoulder; probably monochrome black coating on belly. Rim: Type A1; Handle: Type A1 (W. 0.022); Base: almost flat, similar to skyphos Type D.

L23-V, level 2, lot 226; level 3, lots 227, 250.

P997. Frags. of jug.

Reddish yellow flaky clay, worn surfaces. 2 rim frags., 1 neck frag. 4 neck-shoulder frags., 1 handle frag. Probable black coating on neck; 3 grooves at transition from neck to shoulder. Surfaces too worn to discern decoration on shoulder. Rim: Type A1; Handle: Type A1 (W. 0.018).

L23-V, level 2, lots 225, 226; level 3, lot 250.

P998. Profile of rim and neck of neck-handled amphora. Fig. 3-19; Pl. 3-99.

H. (pres.) 0.093. D. ca. 0.12 (uneven). W. handle 0.035.

Munsell 2.5YR 6/8 light red. Flaky clay, worn surfaces. Faint frags. of black paint preserved on handle and in places on neck. Rim: Type A1; Handle: Type A1.

L23-VIII, level 2, lots 296, 297.

Coarse Ware

P999. Rim frag.

D. ca. 0.20 (uneven).

Burned. Rim: Type A.

L23-V, level 3, lot 324.

P1000 (NP198). Flat-based neck-handled amphora. Fig. 3-42; Pl. 3-110.

H. (pres.) 0.213. Th. body 0.01-0.012. D. base 0.082-0.083 (uneven).

Missing neck and rim. Munsell 5YR 5/4 reddish brown to 5YR 7/8 reddish yellow around neck. Munsell 2.5YR N3/0 very dark gray to 2/5YR N5/0 gray on interior. Coarse clay with inclusions and reddish core in places. Handle stub at base of neck. Handle: Type A1 (W. ca. 0.029); Flat base: Type B.

L23-VIII, level 2, pit, lot 301.

P1001. 2 handle and body frags.

W. 0.031-0.033 (uneven).

Light red to reddish yellow clay with inclusions. Handle: Type A1.

L23-VIII, level 2, lots 293, 294, 295.

P1002. Handle frag. Fig. 3-21.

W. 0.0245.

3 shallow grooves. Burned. Handle: Type C.

L23-V, level 3, lots 227, 250, 325, 326.

P1003. Body frag. of pithos.

H. (pres.) 0.047. Th. body 0.024 (very worn). Th. raised band 0.034.

Reddish yellow clay with inclusions. Raised band with row of finger impressions.

L23-V, level 3, lot 324.

P1004. Body frag. of pithos.

H. (pres.) 0.076. Th. body 0.021. Th. raised band 0.027.

Reddish yellow clay with inclusions. Raised band of diagonal slashes (imitation rope decoration).

L23-V, level 3, lot 324.

From Area VII:

Open Shapes

P1005. Decorated rim and body frag. of skyphos. Fig. 3-22; Pl. 3-63.

H. 0.035. D. ca. 0.0085.

Munsell 10YR 6/2 light brownish gray. Thin black band at rim; below, metope-triglyph motif; 5 vertical lines form triglyph with crosshatched triangle in metope. Frags. of 2 metopes preserved; below, frag. of black coating. Good streaky black paint on interior; wheel ridging on interior. Rim: Type A2.

N22-XV, level 4, lot 418.

P1006. Decorated skyphos body frag. Fig. 3-32; Pl. 3-63.

H. (pres.) 0.03.

Reddish yellow clay. Metope-triglyph motif; frags. of 3 vertical lines form triglyph with end of crosshatched(?) triangle in metope; below, frag. of black coating. Streaky black-brown paint on interior.

N22-XV, level 4, lot 418.

P1007. Rim of shallow bowl. Fig. 3-41.

H. (pres.) 0.0325. Th. 0.006. D. ca. 0.20.

Very pale brown gritty clay. Frags. of black paint preserved on exterior and interior.

N22-XIX, level 1, lot 572.

P1008. Upper profile of cup (missing handle).

H. (pres.) 0.048. D. ca. 0.08.

Very pale brown clay, worn surfaces. Possible monochrome black coating on exterior and interior. Light brown slip. Rim: skyphos C3.

N22-XVII, level 3, lots 437, 440, 457.

Closed Shapes

P1009. Decorated oinochoe neck and shoulder frag. Fig. 3-39; Pl. 3-95.

H. (pres.) 0.087. Th. 0.005-0.006.

Clay fired to a gray color. 2 broad incisions mark transition from neck to shoulder; below on shoulder, metope-triglyph motif. Frag. of single vertical line preserved of triglyph; to right, crosshatched triangle in black. Below, 2 thin black bands mark end of decoration zone. Solid black coating on neck frag. and in incisions.

N22-XVII, level 1, lots 424, 428, 436, 456.

P1010. Decorated oinochoe shoulder frag. Fig. 3-39; Pl. 3-95.

H. (pres.) 0.03.

Reddish yellow flaky clay. Frags. of ends of arcs of accumbent concentric semi-circles; below, frags. of 2 black bands to mark end of shoulder decoration. Light brown slip.

N22-XVII, level 1, lots 424, 428, 436, 456.

Coarse Ware

P1011. 2 rim frags.

D. ca. 0.12.

Burned. Rim: Type A.

N22-XVII, level 1, lots 424, 428, 436, 456.

P1012. Rim frag.

D. ca. 0.12-0.13.
Reddish yellow clay with black core. Rim: Type B.
N22-XVII, level 1, lots 424, 428, 436, 456.

P1013. Body frag. of pithos.
H. (pres.) 0.163. Th. body 0.034. Th. raised band 0.043.
Coarse reddish yellow clay with inclusions. Raised band is concave in shape (fluted).
N22-XV, level 3, lot 417.

Section O

Ribbed kylix stems. These continue into the DAII period. The types remain essentially similar to those of DAI. Hence, in the catalog below, the ribbed stems are typed by the same criteria as were used for the earlier period, and the same lettering for each type is followed. Again, the stems are scattered in various trenches throughout the site.

P1014. Kylix stem. Fig. 3-19; Pl. 3-80.
H. 0.07. D. stem ca. 0.022. D. ribs ca. 0.026.
Munsell 7.5YR 7/4 pink. Flaky clay, worn surfaces. Stem broken at bottom, missing foot. Ribs consist of 3 gentle swellings moving diagonally across stem. Coated with monochrome black paint. Type A.
K24 TUv, level 3, lot 3130/2.

P1015. Kylix stem. Pl. 3-80.
H. (pres.) 0.075. D. stem ca. 0.023. D. ribs ca. 0.025.
Flaky gray clay with orange-red core. Frag. of conical foot preserved; no traces of paint remaining. Shape similar to **P1014**. Type A.
L23 Tmn, level 5, lot 1487.

P1016. Frag. of kylix stem. Pl. 3-81.
H. (pres.) 0.048. D. stem 0.02. D. rib 0.032.
Reddish yellow clay with gray core, worn surfaces. Possible frags. of black paint preserved on exterior. Missing foot; one rib. Type B.
L23 Vmn, level 2S, lot 4333/1-3.

P1017. Kylix stem. Fig. 3-19; Pl. 3-81.
H. (pres.) 0.0435. D. stem 0.019. D. rib 0.025.
Foot missing. Reddish yellow clay with pinkish tinge, worn surfaces. Frags. of brown coating preserved on exterior. One rib. Type B.
L23 Rhi, level 2, lot 2364.

P1018. Kylix stem frag. Pl. 3-82.
H. (pres.) 0.045. D. stem 0.02. D. rib 0.03.
Broken at foot and at top where body joins. One rib. Very pale brown flaky clay; possible monochrome black coating on exterior. Type C.
K24 Xy, level 2, lot 4369/1-2.

P1019. Kylix stem. Fig. 3-19; Pl. 3-82.
H. (pres.) 0.032. D. stem 0.02. D. ribs 0.027.
Broken at foot and at top where body joins. 2 ribs. Gray-blue flaky clay. Frags. of black coating preserved. Type C.
K24 Vw, level 2, lot 3654/1-2.

P1020. Kylix stem. Fig. 3-19, Pl. 3-82.
H. (pres.) 0.035. D. stem 0.02. D. rib 0.025.
Complete foot, but broken at top. Reddish yellow flaky clay, worn surfaces. Frags. of black coating. Type C.
M23 Akl, level 2, lot 3384.

P1021. Kylix stem frag. Fig. 3-19.
H. (pres.) 0.035. D. stem 0.016. D. rib 0.026.
Broken at foot and at top. Small conical foot. Reddish yellow flaky clay, worn surfaces. Frags. black paint. Type F.
L23 We, level 2, lot 4036.

P1022-24. Kylix stem frags.
Reddish yellow flaky clay, worn surfaces. Ribs once sharp points but now quite worn. Frags. of black paint. Type F.
L23 Xklm-W1/3, level 2, tree pit, lots 2150, 2503 (**P1022**); L23 Vkl, level 3, lot 4338 (**P1023**); L23 Umn, level 2, lot 1118 (**P1024**).

P1025. Kylix stem. Fig. 3-19; Pl. 3-83.
H. (pres.) 0.045. D. stem 0.02. D. rib 0.023.
Broken at tip of foot and at top. High conical foot. Munsell 7.5YR 7/4 pink. Flaky clay, worn surfaces. Faint traces of black coating preserved. Type F.
K25 Tef, level 2, lot 1675.

P1026. Kylix stem. Pl. 3-83.
H. (pres.) 0.049.
Reddish yellow clay. Similar to **P1025**. Type F.
K24 Yy/K25 Yab, level 2, lot 4352 (Unit III-4, lower hill-wash).

P1027. Kylix stem. Fig. 3-19; Pl. 3-84.
H. (pres.) 0.058. D. stem 0.027-0.03. D. ribs 0.03-0.036.
Broken at foot and at top. Very pale brown clay. Frags. of black paint preserved. Type F.
L23 UVo, level 4b, lots 1467, 1472-3, 1477, 1479.

P1028. Kylix stem frag. Pl. 3-84.
Very worn and broken. Reddish yellow flaky clay. Appears to be similar to **P1027**. Type F.
L23-IX, level 2.

DARK AGE II/III TRANSITIONAL

A group of pottery, still basically DAII in character but containing features later developed in DAIII, was found associated with the second building phase of Unit IV-1, i.e., with the floors in L23 Tk1 and Uk1 and with the second (later) floor in L23 Vk1. Such a group can be considered transitional in nature.

Section A

From Area IVNE. The pottery in this section comes from the floor in L23 Tkl.

Open Shapes

P1029. Rim frag. of skyphos. Figs. 3-44, 3-46; Pl. 3-121.
H. (pres.) 0.055. Th. 0.003. D. ca. 0.09(?)
Munsell 10YR 8/4 very pale brown. Flaky clay, very worn surfaces. Frags. of streaky black paint preserved on exterior and interior; wheel ridging on interior. Rim: Type A.
L23 Tk1, level 3, floor lots 4322/1-3, 4304.

P1030. Rim frag. of skyphos. Fig. 3-44; Pl. 3-121.
H. (pres.) 0.029. Th. 0.003. D. ca. 0.10(?)
Munsell 10YR 7/4 very pale brown. Flaky clay, worn surfaces. No traces of paint preserved. Rim: Type B1.
L23 Tk1, level 3, floor lots 4322/1-3, 4304.

P1031. Rim frag. of skyphos. Pl. 3-121.
H. (pres.) 0.025. Th. 0.003. D. ca. 0.10(?)
Very pale brown flaky clay; worn surfaces. Faint traces of black paint preserved on exterior and interior. Rim: Type B2.
L23 Tk1, level 3, floor lots 4322/1-3, 4304.

P1032. Rim. frag. of skyphos. Fig. 3-44; Pl. 3-121.

H. (pres.) 0.02. Th. 0.003. D. ca. 0.10(?)

Munsell 2.5YR 6/8 light red. Faint traces of black paint preserved on interior and exterior. Rim: Type B2.

L23 Tk1, level 3, floor lots 4322/1-3, 4304.

P1033. Rim frag. of skyphos. Fig. 3-44; Pl. 3-121.

H. (pres.) 0.023. Th. 0.003. D. ca. 0.08.

Munsell 10YR 7/4 very pale brown (on exterior) to 2.5 YR 6/8 light red (on interior). Good monochrome black coating on exterior, monochrome brown on interior. Rim: Type C1.

L23 Tk1, level 3, pit 2, lot 4336.

P1034. Rim frag. of skyphos.

Similar to **P1033**. Rim: Type C1.

L23 Tk1, level 3, floor lots 4322/1-3, 4304.

P1035. Rim frag. of skyphos. Fig. 3-44; Pl. 3-121.

H. (pres.) 0.016. Th. 0.003. D. ca. 0.09.

Very pale brown flaky clay, worn surfaces. Traces of black paint preserved on exterior and interior. Rim: Type C2.

L23 Tk1, level 3, pit 2, lot 4336.

P1036. Rim and body frag. of skyphos. Figs. 3-44, 3-46; Pl. 3-122.

H. (pres.) 0.045. Th. 0.003. D. ca. 0.08.

Munsell 7.5YR 7/4 to 7/6 pink to reddish yellow. Flaky clay, worn surfaces. Frags. of black paint preserved on exterior and interior. Rim: Type D1.

L23 Tk1, level 3, floor lots 4322/1-3, 4304.

P1037. Rim frag. of skyphos.

Similar to **P1036**. Rim: Type D1.

L23 Tk1, level 3, floor lots 4322/1-3, 4304.

P1038. Profile of skyphos. Fig. 3-46.

H. (pres.) 0.08. D. rim 0.13. D. base 0.061.

Munsell 7.5YR 7/6 reddish yellow. Flaky clay, worn surfaces. Monochrome black coating on exterior and interior. Rim: Type E1.

L23 Tk1, level 3, floor lots 4322/1-3, 4304.

P1039. Rim and body frag. of skyphos or deep bowl. Figs. 3-44, 3-46; Pl. 3-122.

H. (pres.) 0.042. Th. 0.0035. D. ca. 0.20.

Munsell 5YR 7/8 reddish yellow. Broad black band under rim; below, frag. of diagonal line (wolf's tooth?). Good black coating on interior; wheel ridging on interior. Rim: Type E1.

L23 Tk1, level 3, floor lot 4322/1-3; level 3, pit 2, lot 4336.

P1040. Rim frag. of skyphos.

Similar to **P1039**. Rim: Type E1.

L23 Tk1, level 3, pit 2, lot 4336.

P1041 (NP97). Skyphos. Fig. 3-46; Pl. 3-123.

H. 0.105. D. (restored) ca. 0.118-0.120. D. handle 0.009. D. base 0.051.

⅔ preserved, ¾ of rim restored. Munsell 5YR 7/6 reddish yellow. Streaky black-brown coating exterior and interior; reserved band in handle zone and on inner rim. 2 mending holes, one below rim, other at belly. Rim: Type E2; Base: Type A; Handle: Type C.

L23 Tk1, level 3, floor lot 4322/2.

P1042. Rim and body frag. of skyphos. Fig. 3-44; Pl. 3-122.

H. (pres.) 0.025. Th. 0.003. D. ca. 0.12(?).

Reddish yellow flaky clay, worn surfaces. Frags. of black paint preserved on exterior and interior. Rim: Type E2.

L23 Tk1, level 3, pit 2, lot 4336.

P1043. Rim and body frag. of deep bowl. Fig. 3-45.

H. (pres.) 0.099. Th. ca. 0.005. D. ca. 0.18.

Munsell 7.5YR 7/6 reddish yellow (with orange-pink core). Decoration of crosshatched squares, probably in handle zone; above and below, black coating. Black coating on interior. Rim: similar to Type B2 of DAIII.

L23 Tk1, level 4S, lot 4342/1-4.

P1044. Rim and body frag. of skyphos.

D. ca. 0.10.

Rim: Type B1.

L23 Tk1, level 4S, lot 4342/1-4.

P1045. Rim and body frag. of skyphos.

D. ca. 0.09.

Black exterior and interior. Rim: Type B2.

L23 Tk1, level 4S, lot 4342/1-4.

P1046. Rim frag. of skyphos.

Munsell 2.5YR N5/0 gray. Black on exterior and interior. Rim: Type E2.

L23 Tk1, level 4S, lot 4342/1-4.

P1047. Rim and handle frag. of cup.

H. (pres.) 0.027. Th. 0.004. D. ca. 0.09.

Munsell 7.5YR 7/6 reddish yellow. Flaky clay, worn surfaces; no traces of paint preserved. Cup rim: Type A.

L23 Tk1, level 3, pit 2, lot 4336.

P1048. Rim and body frag. of cup.

H. (pres.) 0.034. D. ca. 0.09.

Munsell 10YR 8/4 very pale brown. Flaky clay, worn surfaces. Black paint on exterior and interior. Cup rim: Type A.

L23 Tk1, level 4S, lot 4342/1-4.

P1049. Rim frag. of krater. Fig. 3-44.

H. (pres.) 0.03. Th. ca. 0.008-0.01. D. ca. 0.23.

Munsell 7.5YR 7/6 reddish yellow. Flaky clay, worn surfaces. Traces of streaky black-brown paint preserved on exterior and interior. Pale light brown slip. Krater rim: Type A1.

L23 Tk1, level 3, floor lots 4322/1-3, 4304.

P1050. 5 frags. of strainer.

Th. body 0.005. D. strainer holes ca. 0.004.

Munsell 7.5YR 7/6 reddish yellow. Flaky clay, worn surfaces. Possible frags. of black paint preserved on exterior.

L23 Tk1, level 3, floor lots 4322/1-3, 4304.

P1051. Skyphos base. Fig. 3-44.

D. 0.062.

Munsell 10YR 8/3 very pale brown. Flaky clay, worn surfaces. Traces of black paint preserved on exterior and interior. Base: Type A1.

L23 Tk1, level 3, floor lots 4322/1-3, 4304.

P1052-53. 2 skyphos bases. Fig. 3-44 (**P1053**).

D. 0.056 (**P1052**), 0.04 (**P1053**).

Munsell 7.5YR 7/4 pink. Frags. of black paint preserved on exterior and interior. Base: Type A1.

L23 Tk1, level 3, floor lots 4322/1-3, 4304.

P1054-55. 2 skyphos bases.

D. 0.04.

Munsell 5Y 8/3 pale yellow. Flaky clay, worn surfaces. Frags. of black paint preserved on exterior. Base: Type B.

L23 Tk1, level 3, floor lots 4322/1-3, 4304.

P1056. 2 skyphos bases.
D. 0.04.
Munsell 10YR 8/4 very pale brown. Frags. of black paint preserved. Base: Type B.
L23 Tk1, level 4S, lot 4342/1-4.

P1057. 18 skyphos handles.
D. over 0.01.
Munsell 10YR 8/4 very pale brown to 7.5YR 7/6 reddish yellow. Flaky clay, worn surfaces. Frags. of black paint preserved. Handle: Type A.
L23 Tk1, level 3, floor lot 3552/1.

P1058. 14 skyphos handles.
D. under 0.01.
Clay and paint like **P1057**. Handle: Type C.
L23 Tk1, level 3, floor lots 4322/1-3, 4304.

Closed Shapes

P1059. Rim and neck frag. of amphora. Fig. 3-45.
D. ca. 0.20.
Munsell 10YR 8/4 very plae brown. Frags. of black paint preserved on exterior, top, and interior of rim.
L23 Tk1, level 3, floor lots 4322/1-3, 4304.

P1060. Hollow rim frag. of jug. Fig. 3-45.
H. (pres.) 0.03. D. ca. 0.17.
Munsell 2.5YR 8/4 pale yellow. Faint frags. of black paint on exterior and in hollow on interior. Hollow designed for placement of lid. Rim: variant of Type C.
L23 Tk1, level 3, floor lots 4322/1-3, 4304.

P1061-62. Rim frags. of small jug. Fig. 3-45 (**P1061**).
D. ca. 0.08.
Munsell 7.5YR 7/6 reddish yellow. Frags. of black paint on exterior and on interior of rim. Rim: Type A.
L23 Tk1, level 3, floor lots 4322/1-3, 4304; level 4S, lot 4342/1-4.

P1063. Rim and neck frag. of small jug. Fig. 3-45.
Reddish yellow flaky clay, worn surfaces. No traces of paint preserved. Rim: Type B.
L23 Tk1, level 3, floor lots 4322/1-3, 4304.

P1064. 2 belly handle frags. of amphorae. Fig. 3-45.
D. 0.023-0.025.
Munsell 10YR 8/4 very pale brown. Black paint. Handle: Type A (round).
L23 Tkl, level 4S, lot 4342/1-4.

P1065. Neck handle frag. of amphora. Fig. 3-45.
W. 0.031.
Very pale brown flaky clay, worn surfaces. Possible frags. of black paint. Handle elliptical in shape. Handle: Type B (flat to elliptical).
L23 Tkl, level 4S, lot 4342/1-4.

Coarse Ware

P1066. Rim and body frag. of bowl. Fig. 3-45.
H. (pres.) 0.047. Th. 0.008.
Munsell 7.5YR 7/6 reddish yellow. Burned in places. Finger ridging on interior. Rim: Type A1.
L23 Tkl, level 3, pit 2, lot 4336.

P1067. Rim of possible bowl. Fig. 3-45.
H. (pres.) 0.059. Th. 0.007.
Reddish yellow clay, burned in places. Slight ribbing on interior. Rim: Type A2.
L23 Tkl, level 4S, lot 4342/1-4.

P1068 (NP95). Coarse lid. Pl. 3-127.
D. 0.13. H. handle 0.045. Th. lid ca. 0.01.
Munsell 5YR 7/8 reddish yellow with orange tinge. Burned dark gray on underside of lid. 11 small holes at irregular intervals on upper surface of lid.
L23 Tkl, level 3, floor lot 4322/2.

P1069 (NP196). Frag. of coarse grill. Fig. 3-47.
H. 0.089. W. 0.087. Th. 0.032.
Munsell 2.5YR 6/8 light red. One surface burned black. Raised rim; knob-like projection.
L23 Tkl, level 3, floor lot 4322/2.

P1070. Body frag. of pithos.
H. (pres.) 0.068. Th. body 0.021. Th. raised band 0.029.
Munsell 7.5YR 7/6 reddish yellow. Coarse gritty clay with inclusions. 3 round fingertip impressions preserved on raised band.
L23 Tkl, level 4S, lot 4342/1-4.

Section B

From the floor in trench L23 Ukl. The floor lots here also contain some Mycenaean admixture.

Open Shapes

P1071. Rim and body frag. of skyphos.
H. (pres.) 0.028. Th. 0.0025. D. ca. 0.09.
Munsell 5Y 6/1 light gray. Flaky clay, worn surfaces. Black paint. Rim: Type B1.
L23 Ukl, level 3b, lot 3386.

P1072. Rim and body frag. of skyphos.
H. (pres.) 0.035. Th. 0.0035.
Reddish yellow clay. Broad band of black paint under rim; below, frags. of 4 vertical lines (metope-triglyph motif?); good black coating on interior; reserved band on inner rim. Rim: Type B2.
L23 Ukl, level 3E, lot 3373.

P1073-74. Rim and body frags. of skyphoi.
D. ca. 0.13.
Munsell 5YR 7/6 reddish yellow. Streaky black-brown paint on exterior and interior. Rim: Type E1.
L23 Ukl, level 3, lot 3373.

P1075-76. Rim frags. of skyphoi.
D. ca. 0.10. Th. 0.0035.
Reddish yellow clay. Black exterior and interior. Rim: Type E2.
L23 Ukl, level 3E, lot 3373.

P1077. Rim and body frag. of cup. Fig. 3-44.
H. (pres.) 0.037. D. ca. 0.08.
Reddish yellow clay. Faint frags. of black paint preserved on exterior and interior. String marks on exterior. Cup rim: Type A.
L23 Ukl, level 3E, lot 3373.

P1078. 2 rim frags. of cup.
Similar to **P1077**. Cup rim: Type A.
L23 Ukl, level 3, lot 3373.

P1079. Rim and body frag. of cup. Fig. 3-44.
H. (pres.) 0.051. D. ca. 0.08. Th. 0.003.

Munsell 10YR 7/4 very pale brown. Black frags. on exterior and interior. Cup rim: Type B.
L23 Ukl, level 3, lot 3373.

P1080. Skyphos base.
D. 0.069.
Base: Type A1.
L23 Ukl, level 3, lot 3373.

P1081-82. Skyphos bases. Fig. 3-44 (**P1081**).
D. 0.063 (**P1081**), 0.043 (**P1082**).
High conical foot. Reddish yellow clay. Black paint on exterior and interior. Base: Type B.
L23 Ukl, level 3E, lot 3373; level 3, N trial, lot 4316.

P1083. 6 skyphos handles.
Type A.
L23 Ukl, level 3, lot 3373.

P1084. 3 skyphos handles.
Type C.
L23 Ukl, level 3, lot 3373.

P1085. 4 cup handles.
W. 0.01-0.12.
Flat handles. Reddish yellow clay. Black paint.
L23 Ukl, level 3, lot 3373.

Closed Shapes

P1086. Rim and neck frag. of jug. Fig. 3-45.
H. (pres.) 0.016. D. rim ca. 0.08.
Reddish yellow clay with pinkish tinge. Good frags. of black paint preserved on exterior and on top of rim. Rim: Type C.
L23 Ukl, level 3b, lot 3386.

P1087. Jug rim.
D. ca. 0.09.
Type B.
L23 Ukl, level 3b, lot 3386.

P1088. 2 belly handles of amphorae.
D. 0.018-0.023.
Handle: Type A (round).
L23 Ukl, level 3b, lot 3386.

P1089. Neck handle of amphora.
W. 0.021.
Handle: Type B.
L23 Ukl, level 3, lot 3386.

P1090. Handle of oinochoe or jug.
W. 0.022.
Very pale brown clay. Frags. of black paint preserved. Handle: Type B.
L23 Ukl, level 3b, lot 3386.

Coarse Ware

P1091. Coarse rim. Fig. 3-45.
H. (pres.) 0.041. D. ca. 0.14.
Reddish yellow clay, burned in places. Rim: Type A2.
L23 Ukl, level 3E, lot 3373.

P1092. Coarse rim. Fig. 3-45.
H. (pres.) 0.071. Th. 0.012. D. ca. 0.17.
Reddish yellow clay, burned in places on exterior. Rim: Type B1.
L23 Ukl, level 3E, lot 3373.

P1093. Coarse rim. Fig. 3-45.
H. (pres.) 0.024. Th. 0.007. D. ca. 0.15.
Burned. Rim: Type B2.
L23 Ukl, level 3E, lot 3373.

P1094. Coarse rim. Fig. 3-45.
H. (pres.) 0.042. Th. 0.0075. D. ca. 0.16.
Reddish yellow clay, burned in places. Rim: Type B3.
L23 Ukl, level 3E, lot 3373.

P1095. 2 bases of probable bowls or jugs.
D. ca. 0.08, 0.15.
Reddish yellow clay, burned in places. Base: Type B.
L23 Ukl, level 3, N trial, lot 4316.

P1096. Coarse handle frag.
W. 0.025.
Burned. Handle: Type A (flat-elliptical).
L23 Ukl, level 3, lot 3373.

P1097 (NP195). Incised lid. Pl. 3-128.
D. 0.125-0.128 (uneven). Th. 0.013-0.015.
Missing handle. Munsell 5YR 6/6 reddish yellow. Burned dark red on top and dark gray on underside. Slightly curved with pattern of random incisions on convex side (top). Slight ridge around perimeter.
L23 Ukl, level 3E, lot 3373.

P1098. Frag. of cooking stand. Pl. 3-129.
H. (pres.) 0.092. Th. 0.027 (top)-0.017 (bottom). D. ca. 0.11.
About ⅓ preserved. Reddish yellow clay, burned slightly on interior. Top preserved, broken at bottom. Holes preserved at sides to let in oxygen for fire. Frag. is curved in shape and would originally have been round to hold pot.
L23 Ukl, level 3, lot 3373.

Section C

Pottery from the second (later) floor in L23 Vkl and in L23 Xklm-E2/3.

Open Shapes

P1099. 2 skyphos rim frags.
D. ca. 0.10.
Reddish yellow clay. Black paint. Rim: Type B1.
L23 Vkl, level 3, floor lot 3385/1.

P1100. 4 skyphos rim frags.
D. ca. 0.09-0.10.
Reddish yellow clay. Black paint. Rim: Type B2.
L23 Vkl, level 3, floor lot 3385/1.

P1101. Rim and body frag. of skyphos. Figs. 3-44, 3-46; Pl. 3-121.
H. (pres.) 0.047. Th. 0.0045. D. ca. 0.16.
Reddish yellow clay. Streaky brown bands under rim; decoration in handle zone of wolf's tooth; below, black-brown coating. Same coating on interior; reserved band inner rim. 2 small circular incisions under rim. Rim: Type B3.
L23 Vkl, level 3, floor lot 3385/1.

P1102. Rim frag. of skyphos.
Similar to **P1101**. Rim: Type B3.
L23 Vkl, level 3, floor lot 3385/1.

P1103. 5 skyphos rim frags.
D. ca. 0.07-0.10. Th. 0.0025-0.003.
Reddish yellow clay. Black paint on exterior and interior. Rim: Type C1.
L23 Vkl, level 3, floor lot 3385/1.

P1104. 6 skyphos rim frags.
D. ca. 0.07-0.10. Th. 0.003.
Rim: Type C2.
L23 Vkl, level 3, floor lot 3385/1.

P1105. Rim frag. of deep bowl.
D. ca. 0.17-0.18.
Reddish yellow clay. Streaky black paint on exterior and interior. 2 small circular incisions under rim. Rim: Type D1.
L23 Vkl, level 3, floor lot 3385/1.

P1106. Rim and body frag. of skyphos. Fig. 3-44; Pl. 3-122.
H. (pres.) 0.033. Th. 0.004. D. ca. 0.10.
Clay fired to a dark gray-blue color; worn surfaces. Traces of black paint on exterior and interior. Rim: Type D2.
L23 Vkl, level 3, floor lot 3385/1.

P1107. Rim frag. of skyphos.
Similar to **P1106**. Rim: Type D2.
L23 Vkl, level 3, floor lot 3385/1.

P1108. Rim frag. of skyphos.
H. (pres.) 0.027. Th. 0.004. D. ca. 0.08.
Reddish yellow flaky clay; worn surfaces. Undecorated band in handle zone; above and below, black coating. Black coating on interior; reserved band on inner rim. Rim: Type E1.
L23 Vkl, level 3, floor lot 3385/1.

P1109. 3 skyphos rim frags.
Reddish yellow clay. Flaky, worn surfaces. Frags. of black paint preserved on exterior and interior. Rim: Type E2.
L23 Vkl, level 3, floor lot 3385/1.

P1110. 2 decorated skyphos body frags.
Reddish yellow clay. Frags. of arcs of accumbent concentric semicircles; below, black coating; same coating on interior.
L23 Vkl, level 3, floor lot 3385/1.

P1111. Upper profile of skyphos.
H. (pres.) 0.043. Th. 0.0025. D. ca. 0.08-0.09.
Munsell 7.5YR 7/4 pink. Flaky clay, worn surfaces. Frags. of black-brown paint preserved on exterior and interior. Rim: Type A; Handle: Type C (D. 0.09).
L23 Xklm-E2/3, level 2, lot 3356/1-4.

P1112. Rim and body frag. of cup.
H. (pres.) 0.027. Th. 0.003. D. ca. 0.09.
Reddish yellow clay. Black paint on exterior and interior; possible reserved band on inner rim. Cup rim: Type A.
L23 Vkl, level 3, floor lot 3385.

P1113. Rim frag. of cup.
H. (pres.) 0.012. Th. 0.0045. D. ca. 0.12.
Reddish yellow clay. Streaky black-brown paint on exterior and interior. Cup rim: Type B.
L23 Vkl, level 3, floor lot 3385.

P1114. Rim frag. of cup. Fig. 3-44.
H. (pres.) 0.013. D. ca. 0.07.
Reddish yellow clay. Frags. of black paint preserved on exterior and interior. 2 deep incisions under rim. Cup rim: Type C.
L23 Vkl, level 3, floor lot 3385.

P1115. Rim frag. of krater.
D. ca. 0.28.
Reddish yellow flaky clay, worn surfaces. No traces of paint remaining. Krater rim: Type A1.
L23 Vkl, level 3, floor lot 3385.

P1116 (NP85). Krater rim and wall frag. Fig. 3-47; Pl. 3-124.
H. (pres.) 0.146. Th. 0.006 (top)-0.008 (bottom). D. ca. 0.35.
Munsell 7.5YR 7/6 reddish yellow. Metope-triglyph motif; 6 vertical lines form triglyph with metope decoration consisting of pendent crosshatched triangles from rim with 4 crosshatched triangles surrounded by a circle. Frags. of crosshatched triangles also visible in metope fragment to right. Below, frag. of black coating. Streaky black-brown paint on interior and on top of rim. Krater rim: Type A2.
L23 Vkl, level 3, floor lot 3385.

P1117. Rim frag. of krater. Fig. 3-44.
H. (pres.) 0.019. Th. 0.006. D. ca. 0.20.
Light reddish yellow flaky clay, worn surfaces. No traces of paint preserved. Krater rim: Type A2.
L23 Vkl, level 3, floor lot 3385.

P1118. Rim frag. of krater.
D. ca. 0.22.
Frags. of black paint. Krater rim: Type A2.
L23 Xklm-E2/3, level 2, lot 3356/1-4.

P1119. Rim frag. of krater. Fig. 3-44.
H. (pres.) 0.037. Th. 0.005. D. ca. 0.30.
Clay fired to a light gray color; worn surfaces. Frags. of black coating preserved on exterior and interior. Krater rim: Type B.
L23 Xklm-E2/3, level 2, lot 3356/1-4.

P1120. 2 skyphos bases.
D. 0.06, 0.075.
Reddish yellow clay. Black paint. Base: Type A1.
L23 Vkl, level 3, floor lot 3385.

P1121. Skyphos base. Fig. 3-44.
D. 0.04.
Reddish yellow flaky clay. Ringed foot. ½ of exterior paint is light brown, other ½ is black. Hub in center of underside. Base: Type A2.
L23 Vkl, level 3, floor lot 3385.

P1122. 4 skyphos bases. Fig. 3-44.
D. 0.04-0.06.
Reddish yellow clay. Black paint. Base: Type B.
L23 Vkl, level 3, floor lot 3385.

P1123. Skyphos base. Fig. 3-44.
D. 0.05.
Reddish yellow clay. Frags. of black paint on exterior, interior, and on underside of base. Spiral grooving on interior; string marks on exterior. Base: Type C.
L23 Vkl, level 3, floor lot 3385.

P1124. 4 skyphos bases.
Similar to **P1123**. Base: Type C.
L23 Vkl, level 3, floor lot 3385.

P1125. Conical pedestal base, probably of krater. Fig. 3-44.
H. 0.03. D. ca. 0.07.
Munsell 7.5YR 7/4 pink to 7/6 reddish yellow. About ⅓ preserved. Frags. of black paint on exterior; incisions in foot.
L23 Xklm-E2/3, level 2, lot 3356/1-4.

P1126. Pedestal base of krater. Fig. 3-45.
H. (pres.) 0.052. D. 0.06.
Reddish yellow flaky clay, worn surfaces. Traces of black paint on exterior, interior, and on underside of base. String marks on exterior.
L23 Xklm-E2/3, level 2, lot 3356/1-4.

P1127. Large krater base. Fig. 3-45.
D. ca. 0.10.
Ringed base, about ⅓ preserved. Reddish yellow clay with gray-blue core. Flaky clay, worn surfaces. Good black paint preserved on exterior and interior.
L23 Xklm-E2/3, level 3, lot 3356/1-4.

P1128. 5 flat bases of cups.
D. 0.056, 0.060, 0.070.
Munsell 10YR 7/4 very pale brown and 2.5YR 6/8 light red (with pink core). Frags. of black paint preserved on exterior. Circular incisions on underside of base.
L23 Vkl, level 3, floor lot 3385/1.

P1129. 12 skyphos handles.
Includes 3 probable krater handles, D. 0.015-0.016. Type A.
L23 Vkl, level 3, floor lot 3385; L23 Xklm-E2/3, level 2, lot 3356/1-4.

P1130. 14 skyphos handles.
Type C.
L23 Vkl, level 3, floor lot 3385.

P1131. 4 flat cup handles.
W. 0.014.
Reddish yellow clay. Frags. of black paint preserved.
L23 Vkl, level 3, floor lot 3383; L23 Xklm-E2/3, level 2, lot 3356/1-4.

Closed Shapes

P1132. 3 jug rims.
Reddish yellow flaky clay; worn surfaces. No traces of paint preserved. Rim: Type B.
L23 Vkl, level 3, floor lot 3385.

P1133. Rim and neck frag. of oinochoe. Fig. 3-45.
H. (pres.) 0.068. D. ca. 0.13.
Reddish yellow flaky clay; worn surfaces. No traces of paint preserved. Rim: Type D.
L23 Xklm E2/3, level 2, lot 3356/1-4.

P1134. Rim of squat amphora. Fig. 3-45.
H. (pres.) 0.031. Th. 0.009. D. ca. 0.25.
Reddish yellow clay. Good black coating on exterior; black on interior of rim only.
L23 Vkl, level 3, floor lot 3385.

P1135. 2 amphora base frags.
D. ca. 0.10.
Very pale brown flaky clay, worn surfaces. Traces of black paint preserved. Mending hole at top of lower belly frag. (D. hole 0.005). Flat base with concave profile at sides: Type A (cf. Type A of DAII shapes).
L23 Vkl, level 3, floor lot 3385; L23 Xklm-E2/3, level 2, lot 3356/1-4.

P1136. 2 amphora base frags.
D. ca. 0.10.
Pale yellow flaky clay, worn surfaces. Traces of black paint preserved; wheel ridging on interior. Flat base with straight sides: Type B (cf. Type B of DAII shapes).
L23 Vkl, level 3, floor lot 3385; L23 Xklm-E2/3, level 2, lot 3356/1-4.

P1137. 2 base frags. of oinochoai or jugs.
D. ca. 0.085.
Reddish yellow flaky clay, worn surfaces. Traces of black paint preserved. Ringed foot.
L23 Vkl, level 3, floor lot 3385.

P1138. Neck handle of amphora.
Light brown to olive gray clay. Black paint. Handle: Type B.
L23 Vkl, level 3, floor lot 3385.

P1139. 2 belly handles of amphorae.
D. 0.02.
Light red flaky clay. Black paint. Handle: Type A.
L23 Vkl, level 3, floor lot 3385; L23 Xklm-E2/3, level 2, lot 3356/1-4.

P1140. Handle of oinochoe or jug.
W. 0.012.
Very pale brown clay. Black paint. Handle: Type B.
L23 Vkl, level 3, floor lot 3385.

P1141. 2 handles of oinochoai or jugs. Fig. 3-45.
W. 0.021-0.025.
Reddish yellow flaky clay. Black paint. Handle: Type B.
L23 Xklm-E2/3, level 2, lot 3356/1-4.

Coarse Ware

P1142. 8 rim frags.
D. ca. 0.18-0.20.
Reddish yellow clay, slightly burned in places. Rim: Type A1.
L23 Vkl, level 3, floor lot 3385; L23 Xklm-E2/3, level 2, lot 3356/1-4.

P1143. 5 rim frags.
D. ca. 0.18.
Reddish yellow clay, slightly burned. Rim: Type A2.
L23 Xklm-E2/3, level 2, lot 3356/1-4.

P1144. 3 rim frags.
D. ca. 0.17.
Burned. Rim: Type B1.
L23 Xklm-E2/3, level 2, lot 3356/1-4.

P1145. 2 rim frags.
D. ca. 0.15.
Burned. Rim: Type B3.
L23 Xklm-E2/3, level 2, lot 3356/1-4.

P1146. 2 flat bases.
D. ca. 0.15.

Burned. Base: Type A (cf. Type A of DAII shapes).

L23 Xklm-E2/3, level 2, lot 3356/1-4.

P1147. 2 flat bases.

D. ca. 0.12.

Reddish yellow clay, burned slightly in places. Base: Type B (cf. Type B of DAII shapes).

L23 Xklm-E2/3, level 2, lot 3356/1-4.

P1148. Tripod foot.

H. (pres.) 0.079. W. 0.055. Th. 0.021-0.022.

Reddish yellow to light red clay with inclusions. Burned at bottom of foot. Rectangular. Similar to **P408**.

L23 Xklm-E2/3, level 2, lot 3356/1-4.

P1149. 6 coarse handle frags. Fig. 3-45.

W. 0.02-0.03.

Reddish yellow clay, burned in places. Handle: Type A (flat to elliptical).

L23 Vkl, level 3, floor lot 3385; L23 Xklm-E2/3, level 2, lot 3356/1-4.

P1150. Coarse handle. Fig. 3-45.

D. 0.02.

Burned. Handle: Type B (round).

L23 Vkl, level 3, floor lot 3385.

P1151. 5 handle frags.

Similar to **P1150**. Handle: Type B.

L23 Xklm-E2/3, level 2, lot 3356/1-4.

P1152. Coarse handle frag. Fig. 3-45.

W. 0.043.

Reddish yellow clay. Handle: Type C (ribbed).

L23 Xklm-E2/3, level 2, lot 3356/1-4.

P1153. Coarse handle frag., perhaps of jug.

D. ca. 0.035.

Reddish yellow clay, burned slightly in places. Diagonal incisions across top in imitation of rope decoration. Handle: Type D.

L23 Xklm-E2/3, level 2, lot 3356/1-4.

P1154. Body frag. of pithos.

Reddish yellow clay, burned on exterior. Plain raised band, undecorated.

L23 Xklm-E2/3, level 2, lot 3356/1-4.

P1155. 3 body frags. of pithoi.

Reddish yellow gritty clay with inclusions. Raised bands with diagonal slashes in imitation of rope decoration.

L23 Xklm-E2/3, level 2, lot 3356/1-4.

P1156. Body frag. of pithos with nipple decoration.

H. (pres.) 0.063. Th. 0.009-0.01. Th. with nipple 0.022.

Reddish yellow clay, burned slightly in places. Nipple is blunt and rounded.

L23 Xklm-E2/3, level 2, lot 3356/1-4.

Section D

3 ribbed kylix stems were found associated with the second floor level of Unit IV-1. These are listed below and cataloged according to the typology established for DAI.

P1157. Ribbed stem, broken at top. Fig. 3-45; Pl. 3-125.

H. (pres.) 0.035. D. foot 0.053. D. stem 0.025. D. rib 0.033.

Munsell 5YR 7/6 reddish yellow. Slight conical foot. Incisions in flutes between rib; large angular rib preserved. Good streaky black paint on exterior and underside of foot. Type B.

L23 Vkl, level 3, floor lot 3385/1.

P1158. Ribbed stem, broken at foot. Fig. 3-45; Pl. 3-126.

H. (pres.) 0.055. D. stem 0.023. D. rib 0.028.

Munsell 7.5YR 7/6 reddish yellow. 2 sharp ribs preserved. Good black paint preserved. Type F.

L23 Tkl, level 3, floor lot 4322/1-3.

P1159. Ribbed stem, broken at top and at foot. Fig. 3-45; Pl. 3-126.

H. (pres.) 0.06. D. stem ca. 0.02-0.023. D. ribs ca. 0.025-0.028.

Reddish yellow clay. 3 ribs preserved, quite worn. Frag. of slight conical foot. Frags. of black paint preserved. Type F.

L23 Xklm-W1/3, level 2, lot 2502.

DARK AGE III

Section A

From Area IVNE. Section A consists of ceramic material in the upper occupational debris of Unit IV-1 after the abandonment of that building, when its W end was used as a storage area.

From L23 Tkl:

Open Shapes

P1160. Rim and body frag. of large skyphos or deep bowl. Fig. 3-48.

H. (pres.) 0.044. Th. 0.004. D. ca. 0.17.

Munsell 5YR 7/6 reddish yellow. Flaky clay, very worn surfaces. Perhaps once coated with monochrome black paint on exterior and interior but no traces of paint survive. Rim: Type A1.

L23 Tkl, level 2, lots 1853, 1856, 1861, 1875, 1879 (combined).

P1161. Rim and body frag. of skyphos. Fig. 3-48.

H. (pres.) 0.037. Th. 0.005. D. ca. 0.14.

Munsell 10R 6/8 light red. Flaky clay, very worn surfaces. Possible traces of black paint on exterior and interior. Rim: Type A2.

L23 Tkl, level 2, lots 1853, 1856, 1861, 1875, 1879 (combined).

P1162. Rim and body frag. of skyphos. Fig. 3-48.

H. (pres.) 0.032. Th. 0.004. D. ca. 0.12.

Munsell 7.5YR 7/4 pink. Flaky clay, very worn surfaces. No paint preserved. Rim: Type B.

L23 Tkl, level 2, lots 1853, 1856, 1861, 1875, 1879 (combined).

P1163. Rim frag. of skyphos. Fig. 3-48.

H. (pres.) 0.022. Th. 0.003. D. ca. 0.10.

Munsell 7.5YR 7/4 pink. Flaky clay, very worn surfaces. No paint preserved. Rim: Type C1.

L23 Tkl, level 2, lots 1853, 1856, 1861, 1875, 1879 (combined).

P1164. Rim frag. of skyphos.

H. (pres.) 0.024. Th. 0.003. D. ca. 0.10.

Similar to **P1163**. Rim: Type C1.

L23 Tkl, level 2, lots 1853, 1856, 1861, 1875, 1879 (combined).

P1165. Rim frag. of skyphos. Fig. 3-48.

H. (pres.) 0.021. Th. 0.003. D. ca. 0.10.

Munsell 10YR 6/4 light yellowish brown. Flaky clay, very worn surfaces. No paint preserved. Rim: Type C2.

L23 Tkl, level 2, lots 1853, 1856, 1861, 1875, 1879 (combined).

P1166. Rim and body frag. of skyphos. Fig. 3-48.

H. (pres.) 0.036. Th. 0.002-0.0025. D. ca. 0.09-0.10.

Munsell 7.5YR 7/4 pink. Flaky clay, very worn surfaces. No paint preserved. Rim: Type C3.

L23 Tkl, level 2, lots 1853, 1856, 1861, 1875, 1879 (combined).

P1167. Rim frag. of skyphos.

H. (pres.) 0.016. Th. 0.003. D. ca. 0.09.

Similar to **P1166**. Rim: Type C3.

L23 Tkl, level 2, lots 1853, 1856, 1861, 1875, 1879 (combined).

P1168. Rim frag. of skyphos.

H. (pres.) 0.02. Th. 0.003. D. ca. 0.10.

Munsell 5YR 7/8 reddish yellow. No paint preserved. Rim: Type C3.

L23 Tkl, level 3, lots 1884, 1889.

P1169. Rim and body frag. of skyphos or deep bowl.

H. (pres.) 0.044. Th. 0.004. D. ca. 0.23.

Munsell 7.5YR 8/6 reddish yellow with orange-pink core. Possible frags. of black paint on interior; none on exterior. Rim: Type C3.

L23 Ukl/Umn baulk, level 2, lot 3383/1-2.

P1170. Rim and body frag. of skyphos. Fig. 3-48.

H. (pres.) 0.027. Th. 0.003. D. ca. 0.10.

Munsell 7.5YR 7/4 pink. Black paint preserved on interior; none on exterior. Rim: Type C3.

L23 Ukl/Umn baulk, level 2, lot 3383/1-2.

P1171. Rim frag. of skyphos. Fig. 3-48.

H. (pres.) 0.027. Th. 0.0045. D. ca. 0.10(?)

Reddish yellow flaky clay, very worn surfaces. No paint preserved. Slight swelling (raised band?) at point of transition from rim to body. Rim: Type C4.

L23 Tkl, level 2, lots 1853, 1856, 1861, 1875, 1879 (combined).

P1172. Rim and body frag. of skyphos. Fig. 3-48; Pl. 3-130.

H. (pres.) 0.039. Th. 0.002-0.0025. D. ca. 0.14.

Munsell 10YR 6/4 light yellowish brown. No traces paint preserved. Rim: Type D1.

L23 Tkl, level 2, lots 1853, 1856, 1861, 1875, 1879 (combined).

P1173. Rim frag. of skyphos. Fig. 3-48.

H. (pres.) 0.028. Th. 0.003. D. ca. 0.12.

Light yellowish brown clay. Very worn surfaces. No paint preserved. Rim: Type D1.

L23 Tkl, level 3, lots 1884, 1889.

P1174. Rim frag. of skyphos.

Similar to **P1173**. Faint traces of black paint on exterior. Rim: Type D1.

L23 Tkl/Ukl baulk, level 2, lot 3392/1-3.

P1175. Rim and body frag. of skyphos. Fig. 3-48; Pl. 3-130.

H. (pres.) 0.032. Th. 0.003. D. ca. 0.09.

Light yellowish brown clay. Possible traces of black paint on exterior and interior. Rim: Type D2.

L23 Tkl, level 2, lots 1853, 1856, 1861, 1875, 1879 (combined).

P1176. Rim frag. of skyphos.

Similar to **P1175**. Rim: Type D2.

L23 Tkl, level 2, lots 1853, 1856, 1861, 1875, 1879 (combined).

P1177. Rim frag. of skyphos. Fig. 3-48; Pl. 3-130.

H. (pres.) 0.019. Th. 0.004. D. ca. 0.10.

Munsell 10YR 6/4 light yellowish brown, but fired to a gray color in places on exterior. Very worn surfaces. No paint preserved. Rim: Type D3.

L23 Tkl, level 2, lots 1853, 1856, 1861, 1875, 1879 (combined).

P1178. Rim and body frag. of skyphos. Fig. 3-48.

H. (pres.) 0.041. Th. 0.005. D. ca. 0.14.

Light yellowish brown clay. Faint traces of streaky black-brown paint on interior; none on exterior. Rim: Type D3.

L23 Tkl, level 3, lots 1884, 1889.

P1179. Upper profile of skyphos. Fig. 3-55; Pl. 3-130.

H. (pres.) 0.031. Th. 0.0025. D. rim ca. 0.07. D. handle 0.08.

Munsell 10YR 6/2 light brownish gray with orange-pink core. Worn surfaces, but frags. of monochrome black coating preserved on exterior and interior. Rim: Type C3.

L23 Tkl, level 3a, lots 1890, 1895, 3359 (combined).

P1180. Rim frag. of skyphos. Fig. 3-48.

H. (pres.) 0.023. Th. 0.003. D. ca. 0.10.

Munsell 10YR 7/4 very pale brown. Flaky clay, worn surfaces. No paint preserved. Rim: Type E1.

L23 Tkl, level 2, lots 1853, 1856, 1861, 1875, 1879 (combined).

P1181. Rim frag. of deep bowl. Fig. 3-48.

H. (pres.) 0.039. Th. 0.005. D. ca. 0.17-0.18.

Munsell 10YR 6/4 light yellowish brown. Flaky clay, very worn surfaces. No paint preserved. Rim: Type E2.

L23 Tkl, level 2, lots 1853, 1856, 1861, 1875, 1879 (combined).

P1182. Rim frag. of skyphos. Fig. 3-48.

H. (pres.) 0.026. Th. 0.0035.

Munsell 10YR 6/4 light yellowish brown. Flaky clay, very worn surfaces. No paint preserved. Slight hollow at inner rim. Rim: Type F.

L23 Tkl, level 2, lots 1853, 1856, 1861, 1875, 1879 (combined).

P1183. Rim frag. of cup. Fig. 3-48.

H. (pres.) 0.023. Th. 0.005. D. ca. 0.09.

Munsell 7.5YR 7/4 pink. Flaky clay, very worn surfaces. Faint traces of black paint on exterior, none on interior. 3 small incisions at base of rim. Cup rim: Type A.

L23 Tkl, level 2, lots 1853, 1856, 1861, 1875, 1879 (combined).

P1184. Rim frag. of cup. Fig. 3-48.

H. (pres.) 0.016. Th. 0.0025. D. ca. 0.08-0.09.

Munsell 7.5YR 7/6 reddish yellow. Flaky clay, worn surfaces. Good monochrome black paint on exterior; fainter frags. on interior. Deep incision at base of rim followed by 2 shallower incisions. Cup rim: Type B.

L23 Ukl/Umn baulk, level 2, lot 3383/1-2.

P1185. Rim and wall frag. of krater. Fig. 3-48; Pl. 3-134.

H. (pres.) 0.033. Th. 0.007. D. ca. 0.20.

Munsell 5YR 7/8 reddish yellow. Very worn surfaces; faint traces of black paint on exterior, none on interior. Krater rim: Type A1.

L23 Tkl, level 3, lots 1884, 1889.

P1186. Rim and wall frag. of krater. Fig. 3-49; Pl. 3-134.

H. (pres.) 0.056. Th. 0.007. D. ca. 0.26.

Munsell 7.5YR 7/6 reddish yellow. Good monochrome black on interior, fainter traces of black on exterior. Wheel ridging on interior. Krater rim: Type B1.

L23 Tkl, Unit IV-1, between walls A and B.

P1187. Rim and wall frag. of large krater. Fig. 3-49; Pl. 3-135.

H. (pres.) 0.052. Th. 0.012. D. ca. 0.30(?)

Munsell 10YR 8/4 very pale brown (with reddish core). Good traces of black on exterior and top of rim, fainter traces on interior. Raised band with rope decoration below rim. Slight flute (for placement of lid?) on top of rim. Wheel ridging on interior. Krater rim: Type C.

L23 Tkl/Ukl baulk, level 2, lot 3399/1-3.

P1188. Base and lower profile of skyphos. Fig. 3-49.

H. (pres.) 0.052. D. 0.063.

Munsell 7.5YR 7/6 reddish yellow (with orange-pink core). Very worn surfaces. Faint traces of black paint on exterior and interior. Base: Type A1.

L23 Ukl/Umn baulk, level 2, lot 3383/1-2.

P1189. Base of skyphos. Fig. 3-49.

D. 0.048.

Reddish yellow flaky clay, worn surfaces. Faint traces of black paint preserved on exterior and interior. Spiral grooving on interior. Base: Type A1.

L23 Tkl, level 3, lots 1884, 1889.

P1190. Base frag. of skyphos. Fig. 3-49.

D. ca. 0.08.

About ⅓ preserved. Munsell 10YR 7/4 very pale brown (with gray-blue core). Very worn surfaces. No paint preserved. String marks on exterior; incisions on underside of base. Base: Type A1.

L23 Tkl, level 2, lots 1853, 1856, 1861, 1875, 1879 (combined).

P1191. 3 frags. of skyphos base.

D. ca. 0.046.

Similar to **P1190**. Base: Type A1.

L23 Tkl, level 2, lots 1853, 1856, 1861, 1875, 1879 (combined).

P1192. Skyphos base. Fig. 3-49.

D. 0.05.

Munsell 5YR 7/8 reddish yellow. Very worn surfaces. Possible frags. of black paint preserved on exterior and interior. Slight rib at base of foot. Base: Type A2.

L23 Tkl, level 2, lots 1853, 1856, 1861, 1875, 1879 (combined).

P1193. Base frag. of skyphos. Fig. 3-49.

D. ca. 0.06.

About ⅓ preserved. Reddish yellow clay; very worn surfaces. Faint frags. of black paint preserved on exterior. Possible white slip. Base: Type A2.

L23 Tkl, level 3, lots 1884, 1889.

P1194. Skyphos base. Fig. 3-49.

D. 0.03.

Reddish yellow clay; very worn surfaces. No paint preserved. Base: Type A3.

L23 Tkl, level 2, lots 1853, 1856, 1861, 1875, 1879 (combined).

P1195. Skyphos(?) base. Fig. 3-50.

D. 0.068.

Munsell 10YR 7/6 yellow. Very worn surfaces; possible frags. of black paint preserved on exterior. Base: Type B.

L23 Tkl/Ukl baulk, level 2, lot 3392/1-3.

P1196. Skyphos(?) base. Fig. 3-50.

D. 0.07.

Similar to **P1195**. Base: Type B.

L23 Tkl, level 2, lots 1853, 1856, 1861, 1875, 1879 (combined).

P1197. Skyphos(?) base. Fig. 3-50.

D. 0.07.

About ½ preserved. Munsell 10YR 7/6 yellow. Very worn surfaces. Frags. of black paint on exterior and underside of base. Incisions at point of transition from base to lower body. Base: Type C.

L23 Ukl/Umn baulk, level 2, lot 3383/1-2.

P1198. Skyphos base. Fig. 3-50.

D. 0.056.

Munsell 7.5YR 7/6 reddish yellow (with reddish pink core). Very worn surfaces. Frags. of black paint preserved on exterior and interior. Spiral grooving on interior. Base: Type D1.

L23 Tkl, level 3, lots 1884, 1889.

P1199. 2 skyphos bases.

D. 0.048, 0.075.

About ½ preserved. Reddish yellow clay. No traces paint preserved. Wheel ridging on interior. Base: Type D1.

L23 Tkl/Ukl baulk, level 2, lot 3392/1-3.

P1200. Skyphos base. Fig. 3-50.

D. ca. 0.04.

About ½ preserved. Reddish yellow clay; very worn surfaces. Possible traces of black paint preserved on exterior. Base: Type D2.

L23 Tkl, level 3, lots 1884, 1889.

P1201. 3 skyphos base frags.

Similar to **P1200**. Base: Type D2.

L23 Tkl, level 3, lots 1884, 1889.

P1202. Base frag. of cup. Fig. 3-50.

D. ca. 0.04.

About ½ preserved. Munsell 7/5YR 7/6 reddish yellow. Worn surfaces. No paint preserved. Hub in center of interior. Cup base: Type A1.

L23 Tkl, level 2, lots 1853, 1856, 1861, 1875, 1879 (combined).

P1203. 2 cup base frags.

D. ca. 0.06.

Similar to **P1202**. Cup base: Type A1.

L23 Ukl/Umn baulk, level 2, lot 3383/1-2.

P1204. Base frag. of cup. Fig. 3-50.

D. ca. 0.04.

About ¼ preserved. Reddish yellow flaky clay; very worn surfaces. No paint preserved. Cup base: Type A2.

L23 Tkl, level 2, lots 1853, 1856, 1861, 1875, 1879 (combined).

P1205. Base frag. of cup.

Similar to **P1204**. Cup base: Type A2.

L23 Ukl/Umn baulk, level 2, lot 3383/1-2.

P1206. Base frag. of cup. Fig. 3-50.

D. ca. 0.05.

About ⅕ preserved. Munsell 10YR 7/4 very pale brown. String marks on exterior. No paint preserved. Cup base. Type B.

L23 Tk1, level 2, lots 1853, 1856, 1861, 1875, 1879 (combined).

P1207. Base frag. of krater. Fig. 3-50.

D. ca. 0.10.

About ¼ preserved. Munsell 10R 8/4 very pale brown. Flaky clay, very worn surfaces. Good frags. of black paint on exterior; very faint frags. on interior. Krater base: Type A.

L23 Tk1/Uk1 baulk, level 2, lot 3392/1-3.

P1208. Skyphos handle.

D. 0.013.

Munsell 7.5YR 7/6 reddish yellow. Frags. of black paint preserved. Handle: Type A (D. over 0.01).

L23 Tk1, level 2, lots 1853, 1856, 1861, 1875, 1879 (combined).

P1209. 8 skyphos handle frags.

Type A.

L23 Tk1, level 2, lots 1853, 1856, 1861, 1875, 1879 (combined); L23 Tk1/Uk1 baulk, level 2, lot 3392/1-3; L23 Uk1/Umn baulk, level 2, lot 3383/1-2.

P1210. Skyphos handle.

W. 0.012.

Munsell 10YR 8/4 very pale brown. Frags. of black paint preserved. Handle: Type B (rectangular).

L23 Tk1/Uk1 baulk, level 2, lot 3392/1-3.

P1211. 4 skyphos handle frags.

Type B.

L23 Tk1, level 2, lots 1853, 1856, 1861, 1875, 1879 (combined).

P1212. Skyphos handle.

D. 0.006.

Munsell 7.5YR 7/6 reddish yellow. Frags. of black paint preserved. Handle: Type C (D. under 0.01).

L23 Tk1/Uk1, baulk, level 2, lot 3392/1-3.

Closed Shapes

P1213 (NP80). Upper profile of oinochoe. Fig. 3-60; Pl. 3-137.

H. (pres.) 0.25. D. rim 0.125. D. belly 0.23.

Missing lower belly and base. ⅔ rim restored. Munsell 10YR 6/1 light gray. Flaky clay, very worn surfaces. Traces of cross-hatching on neck; possible black bands on shoulder; monochrome black coating on belly and on inner rim. 2 incisions at transition from neck to shoulder. Rim: oinochoe Type A.

L23 Tk1, level 2, lot 1879.

P1214. Rim and neck frag. of jug. Fig. 3-51.

H. (pres.) 0.04. Th. body 0.004. D. ca. 0.15-0.16(?)

Munsell 7.5YR 7/6 reddish yellow. No paint preserved. Rim: jug Type A.

L23 Tk1/Uk1 baulk, level 2, lot 3392/1-3.

P1215. Neck and rim of amphora. Fig. 3-52.

H. (pres.) 0.068. D. ca. 0.14.

Munsell 7.5YR 7/6 reddish yellow. Black paint preserved on exterior and on interior of rim. Wheel ridging on interior.

L23 Tk1, level 3, lots 1884, 1889.

P1216. Base of oinochoe or jug. Fig. 3-52.

D. ca. 0.10.

Munsell 10YR 7/4 very pale brown (with orange-pink core). Semiconical foot. Traces of black paint on exterior and on underside of base. String marks and wheel ridging on exterior. 3 incisions at point of transition from lower belly to foot. Base: Type A1.

L23 Tk1, level 2, lots 1853, 1856, 1861, 1875, 1879 (combined).

P1217. Base of oinochoe or jug. Fig. 3-52.

D. ca. 0.08.

Munsell 10YR 8/4 very pale brown. Traces of black paint on exterior. String marks on exterior. Base: Type B.

L23 Tk1, level 2, lots 1853, 1856, 1861, 1875, 1879 (combined).

P1218. Base of oinochoe or jug. Fig. 3-52.

D. ca. 0.08(?)

½ preserved. Munsell 2.5YR 6/8 light red. Incisions on underside of base. No paint preserved. Base: Type C.

L23 Tk1, level 2, lots 1853, 1856, 1861, 1875, 1879 (combined).

P1219. Base frag. of amphora (?). Fig. 3-53.

D. ca. 0.10.

Munsell 10YR 7/4 very pale brown. Very worn surfaces. No paint preserved. Base: Type D1.

L23 Uk1/Umn baulk, level 2, lot 3383/1-2.

P1220. Base frag. of amphora. Fig. 3-53.

D. ca. 0.16.

About ½ preserved. Munsell 7.5YR 7/6 reddish yellow. Very worn surfaces. No paint preserved. Base: Type D2.

L23 Tk1/Uk1 baulk, level 2, lot 3392/1-3.

P1221. Belly handle of amphora.

D. ca. 0.023.

Munsell 7.5YR 7/6 reddish yellow. Faint traces of black paint preserved. Belly handle: Type A (round).

L23 Tk1, level 2, lots 1853, 1856, 1861, 1875, 1879 (combined).

P1222. Handle of large oinochoe. Fig. 3-52.

W. 0.028.

Munsell 5YR 7/8 reddish yellow. Very worn surfaces. Black-brown paint preserved. Oinochoe handle: Type A1.

L23 Tk1, level 2, lots 1853, 1856, 1875, 1879 (combined).

P1223. Handle of small oinochoe. Fig. 3-52.

W. 0.01.

Munsell 10YR 7/4 very pale brown. Very worn surfaces. Frags. of black paint preserved. Oinochoe handle: Type A3.

L23 Tk1, level 2, lots 1853, 1856, 1861, 1875, 1879 (combined).

Coarse Ware

P1224. Rim frag. Fig. 3-53.

H. (pres.) 0.042. Th. 0.008.

Munsell 2.5YR N3/0 very dark gray. Coarse gritty clay. Rim: Type A1.

L23 Tk1, level 2, lots 1853, 1856, 1861, 1875, 1879 (combined).

P1225. Rim frag. Fig. 3-53.

H. (pres.) 0.03. Th. 0.007.

Munsell 7.5YR 7/6 reddish yellow. Coarse gritty clay. Rim: Type A2.

L23 Tk1, level 2, lots 1853, 1856, 1861, 1875, 1879 (combined).

P1226. Rim frag. Fig. 3-53.

H. (pres.) 0.053. Th. 0.008.

Burned. Rim: Type B.

L23 Tk1, level 2, lots 1853, 1856, 1861, 1875, 1879 (combined).

P1227. Rim frag. Fig. 3-53.

H. (pres.) 0.054. Th. 0.009.

Reddish yellow clay, burned in places. Rim: Type C1.

L23 Tk1, level 2, lots 1853, 1856, 1861, 1875, 1879 (combined).

P1228-29. Rim frags.

Th. 0.007-0.008.

Burned. Rim: Type C1.

L23 Tk1, level 3, lots 1884, 1889.

P1230. Rim frag. Fig. 3-53.

H. (pres.) 0.045. Th. 0.0085.

Burned. Rim: Type C2.

L23 Tk1, level 2, lots 1853, 1856, 1861, 1875, 1879 (combined).

P1231. Tripod foot. Fig. 3-54; Pl. 3-143.
H. (pres.) 0.055. W. 0.044. Th. 0.017.
Munsell 5YR 7/6 reddish yellow with red core. Burned on inside. Coarse gritty clay. Broken at top. Rectangular in shape.
L23 Tk1, level 2, lots 1853, 1856, 1861, 1875, 1879 (combined).

From L23 Uk1:

Open Shapes

P1232. Rim frag. of skyphos. Fig. 3-48.
H. (pres.) 0.046. Th. 0.004. D. ca. 0.13.
Munsell 7.5YR 7/6 reddish yellow. Very worn surfaces. No paint preserved; probably coated in monochrome black on exterior and interior. Rim: Type A2.
L23 Uk1, level 2, lots 1900, 2103.

P1233. 2 skyphos rim frags.
D. ca. 0.09.
Similar to **P1232**. Rim: Type A2.
L23 Uk1, level 2, lots 1900, 2103.

P1234. 4 skyphos rim frags.
D. ca. 0.10. Th. 0.002-0.003.
Rim: Type C1.
L23 Uk1, level 2 lots 1888, 1897, 2109, 2113 (combined).

P1235. Rim frag. of skyphos.
H. (pres.) 0.037. Th. 0.004. D. ca. 0.12.
Munsell 10YR 7/4 very pale brown, fired in places to light gray. Very worn surfaces. No paint preserved. Rim: Type C2.
L23 Uk1, level 2, lots 1900, 2103.

P1236. Rim frag. of skyphos. Fig. 3-48.
H. (pres.) 0.043. Th. 0.004. D. ca. 0.11.
Very pale brown clay, fired in places to gray. No paint preserved. Rim: Type C2.
L23 Uk1, level 2, lots 1900, 2103.

P1237. Rim frag. of skyphos. Fig. 3-48.
H. (pres.) 0.044. Th. 0.0035. D. ca. 0.11.
Munsell 7.5YR 7/6 reddish yellow on exterior to 2.5YR 6/8 light red on interior. Flaky clay, very worn surfaces. Frags. of dark brown paint preserved on exterior; traces of black-brown paint on interior. Rim: Type C2.
L23 Uk1, level 2, lots 1900, 2103.

P1238. 3 skyphos rim frags.
Similar to **P1236**. Rim: Type C2.
L23 Uk1, level 2, lots 1900, 2103.

P1239. 3 skyphos rim frags. Fig. 3-48.
D. ca. 0.13.
Reddish yellow clay. No traces of paint. Rim: Type C3.
L23 Uk1, level 2, lots 1900, 2103.

P1240 (NP61). Upper profile of skyphos. Fig. 3-55; Pl. 3-131.
H. (pres.) 0.058. Th. 0.002-0.0025. D. ca. 0.073.
Missing base. Munsell 2.5YR 6/8 light red (with orange tinge). Very worn surfaces. Frags. of black paint on exterior and interior. Rim: Type C5; Handle: Type C (D. 0.006).
L23 Uk1, level 2a, lot 2125.

P1241. Rim frag. of skyphos. Fig. 3-48.
H. (pres.) 0.029. Th. 0.0025-0.003. D. ca. 0.09.
Munsell 5YR 7/6 reddish yellow. Worn surfaces. Frags. of black coating on exterior and interior. Rim: Type C5.
L23 Uk1, level 2a, lots 2125, 2130, 2137.

P1242. 2 skyphos rim frags.
Similar to **P1241**. Rim: Type C5.
L23 Ukl, level 2a, lots 2125, 2130, 2137.

P1243. Rim frag. of skyphos. Fig. 3-48.
H. (pres.) 0.021. Th. 0.003. D. ca. 0.09.
Munsell 5YR 7/6 reddish yellow. Worn surfaces. Frags. of black coating on exterior and interior. Rim: Type C6.
L23 Ukl, level 1, lots 1863, 1873, 1885.

P1244. Rim frag. of skyphos or deep bowl. Pl. 3-130.
H. (pres.) 0.062. Th. 0.005. D. ca. 0.24.
Reddish yellow clay. No paint preserved. Rim: Type D1.
L23 Ukl, level 2a, lots 2125, 2130, 1237.

P1245. Rim and body frag. of skyphos or deep bowl. Fig. 3-55; Pl. 3-130.
H. (pres.) 0.041. Th. 0.003. D. ca. 0.14-0.15.
Reddish yellow on exterior to light red on interior. Flaky clay, very worn surfaces. Traces of dark brown paint on exterior and interior. On exterior black band under rim with 5 frags. of vertical raised ribs below. Rim: Type D1.
L23 Ukl, level 2, lot 1888.

P1246. 5 skyphos or deep bowl rim frags. Fig. 3-48.
D. ca. 0.12-0.13.
Similar to **P1244**. Rim: Type D1.
L23 Ukl, level 1, lots 1863, 1873, 1885.

P1247. Rim frag. of skyphos.
H. (pres.) 0.038. Th. 0.005.
Reddish yellow clay, very worn surfaces. No paint preserved. Rim: Type D3.
L23 Ukl, level 2, lots 1897, 1900, 2103, 2109, 2113 (combined).

P1248. 2 skyphos rim frags.
Similar to **P1247**.
Rim: Type D3.
L23 Ukl, level 2, lots 1897, 1900, 2103, 2109, 2113 (combined).

P1249. 2 skyphos rim frags.
D. ca. 0.09-0.10.
Reddish yellow clay. No paint preserved. Rim: Type E1.
L23 Ukl, level 2, lots 1897, 1900, 2103, 2109, 2113 (combined).

P1250. 3 skyphos or deep bowl rim frags. Fig. 3-48.
D. ca. 0.20.
Reddish yellow clay; very worn surfaces. No paint preserved. Rim: Type E2.
L23 Ukl, level 2, lot 1888.

P1251. 3 rim and body frags. of skyphoi or deep bowls. Fig. 3-48.
Th. 0.0035-0.004. D. ca. 0.17.
Reddish yellow clay. Faint traces of black coating on exterior and interior. Rim: Type F.
L23 Ukl, level 2, lots 1888, 2109, 2113.

P1252. Rim and body frag. of skyphos.
H. (pres.) 0.034. D. ca. 0.12.
Reddish yellow clay. Very worn surfaces. Black band under rim; frags. of shallow vertical ribs below. Ribbed decoration similar to **P1245**. Frags. of black coating on interior. Rim: Type C2.

L23 Ukl, level 2, lot 1888.

P1253. Rim and body frag. of skyphos. Fig. 3-48.
H. (pres.) 0.043. Th. 0.004. D. ca. 0.10-0.11(?)
Munsell 10YR 6/3 pale brown. 2 raised horizontal bands below rim; frags. of black coating on exterior and interior. Rim: Type C5.
L23 Ukl, level 2, pit 1 (for pithos 1), lots 3362/1-3, 4340.

P1254. 3 skyphos rims. Fig. 3-48.
Th. 0.003. D. ca. 0.15.
Munsell 7.5YR 7/6 reddish yellow. Frags. of black paint preserved on exterior and interior. Rim: Type C6.
L23 Ukl, level 2 (inside pithos 1), lot 3360.

P1255. Rim frag. of skyphos.
Th. 0.003. D. ca. 0.12.
Very pale brown clay. Frags. of black paint. Rim: Type D1.
L23 Ukl, level 2 (inside pithos 1), lot 3360.

P1256. Rim frag. of skyphos or deep bowl.
Th. 0.005. D. ca. 0.15.
Reddish yellow clay. Frags. of black paint. Rim: Type D2.
L23 Tkl/Ukl baulk, level 2 (pit 2 for pithos 2), lots 3363/1-2, 3551.

P1257. Rim frag. of skyphos or deep bowl. Fig. 3-48.
H. (pres.) 0.056. Th. 0.006. D. ca. 0.17.
Reddish yellow clay with orange pink core. Flaky clay, very worn surfaces. Frags. of black coating preserved on exterior and interior. Rim: Type E1.
L23 Ukl, level 2 (pit 1 for pithos 1), lots 3362/1-3, 4340.

P1258. Rim frag. of skyphos or deep bowl.
H. (pres.) 0.0175. Th. 0.0035. D. ca. 0.15.
Munsell 5YR 7/6 reddish yellow. Frags. of black coating preserved on exterior and interior. Rim: Type E1.
L23 Ukl, level 2 (pit 1 for pithos 1), lots 3362/1-3, 4340.

P1259. Rim frag. of skyphos or deep bowl.
H. (pres.) 0.043. Th. 0.005. D. ca. 0.20.
Reddish yellow clay, worn surfaces. Frag. of arc of concentric semi-circle in black. Frags. of black coating on interior; reserved band inner rim. Rim: Type E2.
L23 Ukl, level 2 (pit 1 for pithos 1), lots 3361/1-3, 4340.

P1260. Skyphos or deep bowl rim frag.
Similar to **P1259** but no traces of decoration preserved. Rim: Type E2.
L23 Ukl, level 2 (pit 1 for pithos 1), lots 3362/1-3, 4340.

P1261. 3 cup rims.
Th. 0.003-0.0035. D. ca. 0.12-0.13.
Munsell 7.5YR 7/6 reddish yellow. Horizontal incision at base of rim. Worn surfaces. Frags. of black coating preserved on exterior and interior. Cup rim: Type A.
L23 Tkl/Ukl baulk, level 2 (pit 2 for pithos 2), lots 3363/1-2, 3551.

P1262. 2 rim and body frags. of cups. Fig. 3-48.
Th. 0.0035. D. ca. 0.12.
Reddish yellow clay. No incisions under rim. Frags. of black coating preserved on exterior and interior. Cup rim: Type A.
L23 Tkl/Ukl baulk, level 2 (pit 2 for pithos 2), lots 3363/1-2, 3551.

P1263. Rim and wall frag. of krater. Fig. 3-49; Pl. 3-135.
H. (pres.) 0.072. Th. 0.007. D. ca. 0.26.
Munsell 10YR 8/4 very pale brown. Very worn surfaces. No paint preserved. Krater rim: Type D.
L23 Ukl, level 2, lots 1900, 2103.

P1264. Base of skyphos(?) or deep bowl.
D. ca. 0.068-0.069.
Munsell 5YR 7/6 reddish yellow. Very worn surfaces. No traces paint. String marks on exterior; wheel ridging on interior. Base: Type A1.
L23 Ukl, level 2, lots 1900, 2103.

P1265. Base of skyphos or deep bowl. Fig. 3-49.
D. ca. 0.062.
Munsell 7.5YR 7/6 reddish yellow. Very worn surfaces. Traces of black paint on exterior and interior. Incisions at point of transition from lower belly to foot; small ribs on underside of base. String marks on exterior; hub in center of interior. Base: Type A1.
L23 Ukl, level 2, lots 1900, 2103.

P1266. 7 skyphos bases. Fig. 3-24.
D. 0.05, 0.06, 0.063.
Munsell 2.5YR 6/8 light red to 5YR 7/6 reddish yellow to 5Y-8/3 pale yellow. Very worn surfaces; frags. of black paint on exterior. String marks on exterior; slight wheel ridging on interior. Base: Type A1.
L23 Ukl, level 2, floor lots 2117, 2120.

P1267. Base of skyphos. Fig. 3-49.
D. ca. 0.04.
Very pale brown clay. Frags. of black-brown paint on exterior and interior. String marks on exterior; hub in center of interior. Base: Type A2.
L23 Ukl, level 2, lots 1900, 2103.

P1268. Base of skyphos. Fig. 3-49.
D. 0.035.
Reddish yellow clay. No paint preserved. Slight hub on underside of base. Base: Type A3.
L23 Ukl, level 2, lots 2109, 2113.

P1269. 3 skyphos bases.
D. 0.04.
Very pale brown to light red clay. No paint preserved. Base: Type A3.
L23 Ukl, level 2, lots 1900, 2103.

P1270. Base of skyphos or deep bowl. Fig. 3-50.
D. 0.066.
Reddish yellow clay with orange-pink core. Frags. of brown paint on exterior. Rib on outside of foot; string marks on exterior. Base: Type B.
L23 Ukl, level 2, lots 1900, 2103.

P1271. 3 skyphos or deep bowl bases.
D. 0.056, 0.066, 0.075.
Reddish yellow clay. Black paint; string marks on exterior. Base: Type B.
L23 Ukl, level 2, lots 1900, 2103.

P1272. Skyphos base.
D. ca. 0.07.
About ½ preserved. Munsell 10YR 7/4 very pale brown. Very worn surfaces. No paint preserved. String marks on exterior. Base: Type C.
L23 Ukl, level 2, lots 2109, 2113.

P1273. Skyphos(?) base.
D. ca. 0.06.
Reddish yellow clay, fired in places to a light olive gray. Very worn surfaces. No paint preserved. Base: Type D1.
L23 Ukl, level 2, lots 2109, 2113.

P1274. Skyphos base. Fig. 3-50.
D. ca. 0.06.
About ¾ preserved. Munsell 2.5YR 6/8 light red. Very worn surfaces. No paint preserved. String marks on exterior. Base: Type D1.
L23 Ukl, level 2, lots 1900, 2103.

P1275. 3 skyphos base frags.
D. ca. 0.048, 0.065.
No paint. Base: Type D1.
L23 Ukl, level 2, lots 1900, 2103.

P1276. Skyphos base. Fig. 3-50.
D. ca. 0.06.
About ⅓ preserved. Reddish yellow clay. No paint preserved. String marks on exterior. Base: Type D2.
L23 Ukl, level 2, lot 1888.

P1277. Skyphos base. Fig. 3-50.
D. 0.035.
Small high conical foot. Munsell 7.5YR-7/6 reddish yellow. Flaky clay, very worn surfaces. Traces of black paint on interior; none on exterior. Base: Type E1.
L23 Ukl, level 2, lots 1900, 2103.

P1278. Skyphos base. Fig. 3-50.
D. 0.05.
High conical foot. Reddish yellow flaky clay, worn surfaces. Good frags. of streaky black paint on exterior and interior. Hub in center of interior; wheel ridging on interior. Base: Type E1.
L23 Ukl, level 2 (inside pithos 1), lot 3360/1-4.

P1279. Skyphos base. Fig. 3-50.
D. ca. 0.04.
About ½ preserved. Munsell 10YR 7/2 light gray to 10YR 7/3 very pale brown. Very worn surfaces. No paint preserved. Base: Type E2.
L23 Ukl, level 2, lots 2109, 2113.

P1280. 2 flat bases of cups.
D. 0.05.
Reddish yellow clay. Frags. of black paint preserved on interior; none on exterior. Cup base: Type A.
L23 Ukl, level 2, lots 2109, 2113.

P1281. Base frag. of krater. Fig. 3-50.
D. ca. 0.10.
About ⅙ preserved. Munsell 10R 8/4 very pale brown. Black paint on exterior and interior. Light brown slip(?). Krater base: Type A.
L23 Ukl, level 1, lots 1863, 1873, 1881, 1885 (combined).

P1282. Krater base.
D. ca. 0.08.
Munsell 10YR 7/3 very pale brown. Frags. of black paint on exterior and interior. Krater base: Type B.
L23 Ukl, level 2, lots 2109, 2113.

P1283. 2 krater base frags.
Similar to **P1282**. Type B.
L23 Ukl, level 2, lots 1900, 2103.

P1284. Krater base. Fig. 3-51.
D. ca. 0.14.
Ringed foot. Munsell 7.5YR 7/6 reddish yellow. Frags. of black paint preserved on exterior and interior; wheel ridging on interior. Krater base: Type C1.
L23 Ukl, level 1, lots 1863, 1873, 1881, 1885 (combined).

P1285. 46 skyphos handles.
Type A.
L23 Ukl, level 2, lots 1900, 2103, 2109, 2113.

P1286. Skyphos handle.
W. ca. 0.016-0.017.
Reddish yellow clay. Black paint. Handle: Type B.
L23 Tkl/Ukl baulk, level 2 (inside pithos 2), lot 3550/1-4.

P1287. 23 skyphos handles.
Type C.
L23 Ukl, level 2, lots 1900, 2103, 2109, 2113.

P1288. 4 cup handles.
W. 0.012-0.013.
Munsell 10YR 7/3 to 8/4 very pale brown. No paint preserved. Cup handle: Type A.
L23 Ukl, level 2 (pit 1 for pithos 1), lots 3362/1-3, 4340.

P1289. Cup handle. Fig. 3-49.
W. 0.009.
Almost rectangular in shape. Reddish yellow clay. Frags. of black paint. Cup handle: Type B.
L23 Ukl, level 1, lots 1863, 1873, 1881, 1885 (combined).

Closed Shapes

P1290. Neck, handle, and rim frag. of neck-handled amphora. Fig. 3-52.
H. (pres.) 0.063. D. rim ca. 0.17-0.18. D. handle ca. 0.03.
Munsell 5YR 7/6 reddish yellow. Handle attached to neck below rim. Frags. black paint preserved on exterior.
L23 Ukl, level 2, lot 1888.

P1291. Rim and neck frag. of oinochoe. Fig. 3-51.
H. (pres.) 0.062. Th. 0.005.
Munsell 10YR 7/4 very pale brown. Black paint. Rim: Type A.
L23 Ukl, level 2, lot 1888.

P1292. 3 oinochoe rim frags. Fig. 3-51.
Similar to **P1291**. Rim: Type A.
L23 Ukl, level 2a, lots 2125, 2130, 2137; level 2, lots 1900, 2103.

P1293. Rim frag. of oinochoe. Fig. 3-51.
H. (pres.) 0.018.
Light reddish yellow clay. No paint preserved. Rim: Type B.
L23 Ukl, level 2, lots 2109, 2113.

P1294. Rim frag. of oinochoe.
Very pale brown clay. No paint preserved. Rim: Type B.
L23 Ukl, level 2, lots 2109, 2113.

P1295. Rim and neck frag. of jug. Fig. 3-51.
H. (pres.) 0.038. D. ca. 0.12(?)
Reddish yellow clay. Very worn surfaces. No paint preserved. Jug rim: Type B.
L23 Ukl, level 2, lot 1888.

P1296. Rim of jug.
Similar to **P1295**. Jug rim: Type B.
L23 Ukl, level 2, lots 1900, 2103.

P1297. Rim of jug. Fig. 3-51.
H. (pres.) 0.03. D. ca. 0.10(?)
Munsell 7.5YR 7/8 reddish yellow. No traces of paint. Jug rim: Type C.
L23 Ukl, level 2, lots 2109, 2113.

P1298. 3 jug rim frags. Fig. 3-51.
D. ca. 0.008(?)
Similar to **P1297**. Jug rim: Type C.
L23 Ukl, level 1, lots 1863, 1873, 1881, 1885 (combined).

P1299. Rim frag. of jug. Fig. 3-52.
H. (pres.) 0.03. Th. 0.003. D. ca. 0.07(?)
Reddish yellow clay. Very worn surfaces. 5 incisions under rim on exterior; wheel ridging on interior. Black paint on exterior and on inner rim. Jug rim: Type D.
L23 Ukl, level 2, pit 1 for pithos 1, lots 3362/1-3, 4340.

P1300. Base frag. of oinochoe or jug. Fig. 3-52.
D. ca. 0.11.
About ¼ preserved. Reddish yellow clay. Good black paint on exterior. String marks. Base: Type B.
L23 Tkl/Ukl baulk, level 2, inside pithos 2, lot 3350/1-4.

P1301. Base of oinochoe or jug. Fig. 3-53.
D. 0.077.
Very pale brown clay. Traces of brown paint on exterior and on outer ⅓ of underside of base. Slight hub in center of interior. Base: Type C.
L23 Tkl/Ukl baulk, level 2, pit 2 for pithos 2, lots 3363/1-2, 3551.

P1302. 2 frags. of flat bases, probably from oinochoe and amphora.
D. ca. 0.09 (oinochoe), 0.17 (amphora).
Reddish yellow clay. No paint preserved. Wheel ridging on interior. Base: Type D1.
L23 Ukl, level 2, pit 1 for pithos 1, lots 3362/1-3, 4340.

P1303. Flat base, probably from oinochoe. Fig. 3-53.
D. ca. 0.10.
Reddish yellow clay, fired to olive gray in places. Worn surfaces; possible frags. of black paint on exterior. Wheel ridging on interior. Base: Type D2.
L23 Ukl, level 2, lot 1897.

P1304. Belly handle of amphora.
D. 0.025.
Very pale brown clay. Possible frags. of black paint preserved. Belly handle: Type A (round).
L23 Ukl, level 2, lots 1900, 2103.

P1305. 3 belly handle frags. of amphorae.
D. ca. 0.019 (2 frags.)-0.02 (1 frag.).
Reddish yellow clay. No paint preserved. Belly handle: Type A.
L23 Ukl, level 2, lots 2109, 2113.

P1306. Belly handle of amphora.
W. 0.0285.
Reddish yellow clay. No paint preserved. Belly handle: Type B (elliptical).
L23 Ukl, level 2, lots 2109, 2113.

P1307. Handle of small oinochoe or jug. Fig. 3-52.
W. 0.017.
Munsell 7.5YR 7/6 reddish yellow. Black paint. Oinochoe handle: Type A2.
L23 Ukl, level 2, lots 1900, 2103.

P1308. Handle of small oinochoe or jug.
Similar to **P1307**. Oinochoe handle: Type A2.
L23 Ukl, level 2, lots 1900, 2103.

P1309. 2 handle frags. of small oinochoai or jugs.
Type A2.
L23 Ukl, level 2, lots 2109, 2113.

P1310. 2 handle frags. of small oinochoai or jugs.
W. 0.01-0.013.
Very pale brown clay. No paint preserved. Oinochoe handle: Type A3.
L23 Ukl, level 2, lots 1900, 2103.

P1311. Lid of closed vase. Fig. 3-53; Pl. 3-138.
H. 0.0325. Th. lid 0.003. W. handle 0.013.
Lid about ½ preserved; attached handle, complete. Handle rectangular. Munsell 5YR 7/6 reddish yellow; clay fired to light gray on underside of lid. Very worn surfaces. Frags. of black coating preserved on lid and handle. On exterior of lid beneath handle are 4 incised concentric circles, 3 in center of lid, 1 in middle. Hub on underside of lid.
L23 Tkl/Ukl baulk, level 2, pit 2 for pithos 2, lots 3363/1-2, 3551.

Coarse Ware

P1312 (NP79). Profile of round-based jug or dipper. Fig. 3-61; Pl. 3-142.
H. (pres.) 0.165. D. rim ca. 0.12. W. handle 0.028.
About ⅓ preserved. Munsell 10YR 5/1 light gray to 10YR 6/1 gray; varies to reddish yellow under handle. Handle has flute down center of top. Rim: Type A1; Handle: Type A3.
L23 Ukl, level 2, inside pithos 1, lot 3360/3-4.

P1313. 3 frags. of large coarse tripod vase. Fig. 3-62.
3 nonjoining frags. of rim, body, and foot. Reddish yellow clay. Rim: H. (pres.) 0.132, D. ca. 0.40 (?). Type A1. Body frag.: H. (pres.) 0.12. Undecorated raised band; frag. curves outwards. Tripod foot: H. (pres.) 0.072. Has orange-red core; burned at bottom. Elliptical in shape.
L23 Ukl, level 2, inside pithos 1, lot 3360/3-4.

P1314. Rim frag. Fig. 3-53.
H. (pres.) 0.042. Th. 0.007. D. ca. 0.15.
Munsell 2.5YR 6/8 light red, burned gray at tip of rim and on interior. Rim: Type A1.
L23 Ukl, level 2, lots 1900, 2103.

P1315. Rim frag. Fig. 3-53.
Reddish yellow clay. Similar to **P1314**. Rim: Type A1.
L23 Ukl, level 2, lots 2109, 2113.

P1316. Rim frag. Fig. 3-53.
H. (pres.) 0.047. Th. 0.007. D. ca. 0.16.
Light gray exterior, light red interior. Rim: Type A1.
L23 Ukl, level 2, lots 1900, 2103.

P1317. Rim frag. Fig. 3-53.
Similar to **P1314**. Rim: Type A1.
L23 Ukl, level 2, lots 1900, 2103.

P1318. Rim frag. Fig. 3-53.
H. (pres.) 0.054. Th. 0.01. D. ca. 0.20(?)
Reddish yellow clay. Rim: Type A2.
L23 Ukl, level 2, lots 1900, 2103.

P1319. Rim frag. Fig. 3-53.
Similar to **P1318**. Rim: Type A2.
L23 Ukl, level 2, lots 1900, 2103.

P1320. Rim frag. Fig. 3-53.
H. (pres.) 0.052. Th. 0.011.
Reddish yellow clay, burned in places. Rim: Type D.
L23 Ukl, level 2, lots 1900, 2103.

P1321-22. 2 rim frags. Fig. 3-53.
D. ca. 0.11.
Munsell 10YR 6/1 light gray (with gray-blue core.) Rim: Type A1.
L23 Ukl, level 2, inside pithos 1, lot 3360.

P1323. Rim frag. Fig. 3-53.
H. (pres.) 0.067. Th. 0.009. D. ca. 0.14-0.15.
Munsell 2.5YR N5/0 gray. Rim: Type A2.
L23 Ukl, level 2, inside pithos 1, lot 3360.

P1324. Flat base. Fig. 3-54.
D. ca. 0.14.
Light red clay, burned in places. Base: Type A.
L23 Ukl, level 2, lots 1900, 2103.

P1325. Flat base. Fig. 3-54.
D. ca. 0.15.
Burned. Base: Type A.
L23 Ukl, level 2, lots 1900, 2103.

P1326. Flat base. Fig. 3-54.
D. ca. 0.10.
Reddish yellow clay. Base: Type B.
L23 Ukl, level 2, lots 1900, 2103.

P1327. Coarse leg or pestle (?) Fig. 3-54; Pl. 3-143.
H. 0.06. D. base 0.025. D. top 0.015.
Broken at top. Munsell 2.5YR 6/8 light red. Coarse micaceous gritty clay. Conical in shape with flat base.
L23 Ukl, level 2, lot 1897.

P1328. Handle frag. (of jug?) Fig. 3-53.
W. 0.03.
Reddish yellow gritty clay. Handle: Type A1 (elliptical).
L23 Ukl, level 2, lot 1888.

P1329. Handle (of jug?). Fig. 3-53.
W. 0.0315.
Reddish yellow clay with dark core. Handle: Type A1.
L23 Ukl, level 2, lot 1888.

P1330. Handle (of jug or amphora?) Fig. 3-53.
W. 0.042.
Burned. Handle: Type A2 (rectangular).
L23 Ukl, level 2, lot 1888.

P1331-32. Handle frags. Fig. 3-54 (**P1331**).
W. ca. 0.04.
Burned. Handle: Type A4 (ribbed).
L23 Ukl, level 2, lot 1888.

P1333. Handle frag. (of amphora?) Fig. 3-53.
W. 0.042.
Reddish yellow clay, burned in places. Handle: Type A3 (fluted).
L23 Ukl, level 2 (inside pithos 1), lot 3360.

P1334. Handle frag. Fig. 3-54; Pl. 3-140.
W. 0.061.
Burned. Handle has raised edges with 2 grooves down center of top; additional groove along side. W. grooves ca. 0.002. Handle: Type B1.
L23 Ukl, level 2, lot 1888.

P1335. Handle frag. Fig. 3-54; Pl. 3-140.
W. 0.024.
Reddish yellow clay, burned in places. Smaller than **P1334** with only one groove. Handle: Type B2.
L23 Ukl, level 2, lot 1888.

P1336. Pithos no. 1. Fig. 3-54; Pls. 3-150, 3-151. ½ preserved (*in situ*).
5 cataloged frags.: 2 rim frags., 2 wall frags., base. Rim: D. ca. 0.90; varies from Munsell 7.5YR 7/6 reddish yellow to 2.5YR 6/8 light red. Coarse gritty clay with inclusions. Wall: Th. 0.04, Th. raised band 0.06. Raised band with rope decoration. Base: H. (pres.) 0.108, D. ca. 0.15-0.16; varies from Munsell 5Y 8/2 white (on exterior) to 7.5YR 8/6 reddish yellow (on interior). Rough rounded bottom. Probable height of pithos ca. 2.30; D. (max.) in middle ca. 1.05. White slip.
L23 Ukl, level 2, pithos 1, lot 3360/1-4.

P1337. Pithos no. 2. Fig. 3-54; Pls. 3-152, 3-153. ⅓ preserved (removed).
5 cataloged frags.: 3 rim frags., 1 wall frag., base. Rim: D. ca. 0.75. Munsell 7.5YR 7/6 reddish yellow. Coarse gritty clay with inclusions. Wall: Th. 0.045, Th. raised band 0.052. Reddish to yellow clay, burned gray in interior. Undecorated raised band. Base: H. (pres.) 0.20, D. 0.145, D. with rib 0.175. Reddish yellow to light red gritty clay. Ribbed pedestal base. Probable height of pithos ca. 1.20-1.30; D. (max.) in middle ca. 0.90-0.95. White slip.
L23 Ukl, level 2, pithos 2, lot 3550.

P1338. Decorated pithos body frag.
H. (pres.) 0.109. Th. 0.027. Th. raised band 0.034.
Reddish yellow gritty clay. Raised band has incised decoration of circles inside triangle.
L23 Ukl, level 2, lots 1900, 2103.

P1339. 2 pithos body frags.
Reddish yellow gritty clay. Frags. have raised bands with rope decoration.
L23 Ukl/Umn baulk, level 2, lot 3383/1-2.

P1340. Handle frag. of pithos(?)
D. 0.042.
Coarse reddish yellow clay with red core. Large round belly handle.
L23 Ukl, level 2, lots 2109, 2113.

From L23 Vkl:

Open Shapes

P1341. Rim and body frag. of skyphos. Fig. 3-48.
H. (pres.) 0.044. Th. 0.004. D. ca. 0.10.
Munsell 10YR 7/4 very pale brown. Frags. of black paint preserved on exterior and interior. Rim: Type A1.
L23 Vkl, level 1, lots 2101, 2105, 2108, 2114 (combined).

P1342. Rim and body frag. of large skyphos or deep bowl.
H. (pres.) 0.068. Th. 0.005. D. ca. 0.20.
Reddish yellow clay. No paint preserved. Rim: Type A1.
L23 Vkl, level 1, lots 2101, 2105, 2108, 2114 (combined).

P1343. Rim and body frag. of skyphos. Fig. 3-48.
H. (pres.) 0.053. Th. 0.0045. D. ca. 0.10.
Reddish yellow clay. No paint preserved. Rim: Type A1.
L23 Vkl, level 2, lots 2115, 2122, 2127.

P1344. 3 skyphos rim frags.
D. ca. 0.09 (1 frag.), 0.13 (2 frags.).
Rim: Type A1.
L23 Vkl, level 2, lots 2115, 2122, 2127.

P1345. Rim frag. of skyphos.
H. (pres.) 0.032. Th. 0.004. D. ca. 0.25.
Reddish yellow clay. No paint preserved. Rim: Type A2.
L23 Vkl, level 1, lots 2101, 2105, 2108, 2114 (combined).

P1346. 3 skyphos rim frags. Fig. 3-48.
D. ca. 0.12.
Rim: Type A2.
L23 Vkl, level 2, lot 3365/1-2.

P1347. Rim frag. of skyphos. Fig. 3-48.
H. (pres.) 0.021. Th. 0.005. D. ca. 0.10.
Reddish yellow clay. Monochrome black coating on exterior and interior. Rim: Type B.
L23 Vkl, level 2, lots 2115, 2122, 2127.

P1348. Rim frag. of skyphos. Fig. 3-48.
H. (pres.) 0.04. Th. 0.003. D. ca. 0.10.
Munsell 10YR 7/4 very pale brown to 10YR 7/6 yellow. Traces of black paint preserved on exterior and interior. Rim: Type B.
L23 Vkl, level 2, lot 3369/1.

P1349. Rim and body frag. of skyphos.
H. (pres.) 0.033. Th. 0.003. D. ca. 0.10.
Munsell 10YR 7/4 very pale brown to 10YR 7/6 yellow. Traces of black coating preserved on exterior and interior. Rim: Type C1.
L23 Vkl, level 2, lots 2115, 2122, 2127.

P1350. Rim and body frag. of skyphos. Fig. 3-48.
H. (pres.) 0.028. Th. 0.004. D. ca. 0.07.
Reddish yellow clay. Black paint on exterior and interior. Rim: Type C1.
L23 Vkl, level 2, lots 2115, 2122, 2127.

P1351. 3 skyphos rims.
D. ca. 0.08.
Reddish yellow clay. No paint preserved. Rim: Type C1.
L23 Vk1, level 2, lots 2115, 2122, 2127.

P1352. Rim and body frag. of skyphos. Fig. 3-55.
H. (pres.) 0.031. Th. 0.005. D. ca. 0.11.
Munsell 10YR 8/4 very pale brown. Thin black band at rim; below, 3 frags. of arcs of accumbent concentric semi-circles; to left, frag. of diagonal band of paint outlining junction between handle and body. Monochrome black coating on interior; reserved band on inner rim. Rim: Type C2.
L23 Vk1, level 2, lot 3365/1-2.

P1353. Rim and body frag. of skyphos. Fig. 3-55.
H. (pres.) 0.051. Th. 0.005. D. ca. 0.12(?)
Tip of rim missing. Very pale brown clay. Undecorated band in handle zone; above and below, black coating. Monochrome black coating on interior. Rim: Type C2(?)
L23 Vk1, level 2, lot 3365/1-2.

P1354. 3 skyphos rim frags.
D. ca. 0.10-0.12.
Reddish yellow clay. Shallow incision at base of rim. Traces of black paint on exterior and interior. Rim: Type C2.
L23 Vk1, level 2, lot 3365/1-2.

P1355. Rim frag. of skyphos.
D. ca. 0.09.
Munsell 2.5YR N4/0 dark gray. Black paint on exterior and interior. Rim: Type C3.
L23 Vk1, level 2, lots 2115, 2122, 2127.

P1356. Rim and body frag. of skyphos.
H. (pres.) 0.04. Th. 0.05.
Reddish yellow clay. Very worn surfaces. Frags. of brown paint preserved on interior; none on exterior. Rim: Type C4.
L23 Vk1, level 2, lots 3365/1-2.

P1357. 3 rim and body frags. of skyphoi. Fig. 3-48.
Th. 0.003. D. ca. 0.09-0.10.
Reddish yellow clay. Frags. of black paint on exterior and interior. Rim: Type C5.
L23 Vk1, level 2, tumble, lot 3369/1.

P1358. Rim frag. of skyphos.
H. (pres.) 0.023. Th. 0.003. D. ca. 0.12.
Reddish yellow clay. Shallow incisions under rim. Frags. of black paint on exterior and interior. Rim: Type C6.
L23 Vk1, level 2, lots 2115, 2122, 2127.

P1359. 2 skyphos rim frags.
Th. 0.003. D. ca. 0.08.
Reddish yellow clay. No paint preserved. Rim: Type D1.
L23 Vk1, level 2, lot 3365/1-2.

P1360. 2 skyphos rim frags.
Th. 0.003.
Faint traces of black coating on exterior and interior. Rim: Type D2.
L23 Vk1, level 2, lots 2115, 2122, 2127.

P1361. 4 skyphos rim frags. Fig. 3-48.
Th. 0.003. D. ca. 0.09-0.10.
Black paint on exterior and interior. Rim: Type D3.
L23 Vk1, level 2, lots 2115, 2122, 2127.

P1362. Rim and body frag. of deep bowl. Fig. 3-48.
H. (pres.) 0.048. Th. 0.007. D. ca. 0.20-0.21.
Reddish yellow clay. Good streaky black-brown coating on exterior and interior. Possible reserved band on inner rim, but very worn. Rim: Type E1.
L23 Vk1, level 2a, lots 2116, 2123.

P1363. Rim frag. of skyphos.
Th. 0.004.
Very pale brown clay. Shallow incisions below rim. Traces of black paint on exterior and interior. Rim: Type E1.
L23 Vk1, level 2, lot 3365/1-2.

P1364. Rim frag. of skyphos.
Very pale brown clay. Shallow incision under rim. No paint preserved.

Rim: Type E2.
L23 Vk1, level 2, lots 2115, 2122, 2127.

P1365. Rim and body frag. of skyphos.
H. (pres.) 0.029. Th. 0.004. D. ca. 0.13.
Very pale olive gray clay. Very worn surfaces. No paint preserved. Rim: Type F.
L23 Vk1, level 2, lot 3365/1-2.

P1366. 4 rim frags. of cups.
D. ca. 0.12-0.13.
3 frags. with incisions below rim, 1 frag. without. Reddish yellow clay. No paint preserved. Cup rim: Type A.
L23 Vk1, level 2, lot 3365/1-2.

P1367. Rim frag. of cup.
H. (pres.) 0.02. Th. 0.0025. D. ca. 0.07(?)
Reddish yellow clay. Good black paint on exterior and interior. Raised band under rim. Cup rim: Type B.
L23 Vk1, level 2, lot 3365/1-2.

P1368. Rim and handle frag. of shallow bowl. Fig. 3-58.
H. (pres.) 0.042. D. ca. 0.25.
Munsell 2.5YR 6/8 light red. Fairly coarse flaky clay, worn surfaces. No paint preserved. Strap handle from rim.
L23 Vk1, level 1, lots 2101, 2105, 2108, 2114 (combined).

P1369. Rim frag. of krater. Fig. 3-48; Pl. 3-134.
H. (pres.) 0.019. D. Ca. 0.22.
Munsell 5YR 7/6 reddish yellow. Good black paint on exterior and interior. Black stripes on top of rim. Krater rim: Type A2.
L23 Vk1, level 2, lot 3365/1-2.

P1370. Rim frag. of krater.
Similar to **P1369**, but no paint preserved. Krater rim: Type A2.
L23 Vk1, level 2, lot 3365/1-2.

P1371. Rim. frag. of krater.
D. ca. 0.26.
Frags. of streaky black-brown paint preserved on exterior. Krater rim: Type D.
L23 Vk1, level 2, lots 2115, 2122, 2127.

P1372. Rim frag. of krater. Fig. 3-49.
Similar to **P1371**, but smaller. Krater rim: Type D.
L23 Vk1, level 2b, lots 2128, 2133.

P1373. Rim frag. of krater. Fig. 3-49; Pl. 3-135.
H. (pres.) 0.033. Th. 0.007. D. ca. 0.22.
Flaky gray clay. Traces of black paint preserved on exterior and interior. Krater rim: Type E.
L23 Vk1, level 2b, lots 2128, 2133.

P1374. Rim frag. of krater. Fig. 3-49; Pl. 3-135.
H. (pres.) 0.035. Th. 0.007. D. ca. 0.26.
Munsell 2.5YR 6/8 light red. Very worn surfaces. No paint preserved. Krater rim: Type E.
L23 Vk1, level 2b, lots 2128, 2133.

P1375. Skyphos base. Fig. 3-49.
D. 0.056.
Very pale brown clay. Frags. of black paint preserved on exterior and interior. Incisions on exterior; spiral grooving on interior. Base: Type A1.
L23 Vk1, level 2, lot 3365/1-2.

P1376. 3 skyphos bases.
D. 0.07.
Black paint; string marks. Base: Type A1.
L23 Vk1, level 2, lots 2115, 2122, 2127, 3374/1-2.

P1377. Base frag. of skyphos. Fig. 3-49.
D. 0.045.
About 1/2 preserved. Reddish yellow clay. Monochrome black exterior and interior. Rib on underside of foot. Base: Type A2.
L23 Vk1, level 2, lot 3365/1-2.

P1378. Base frag. of skyphos.
Very worn and broken. Base: Type A2(?)
L23 Vk1, level 2, lot 3365/1-2.

P1379. Base frag. of skyphos. Fig. 3-49.
D. 0.035.
About 2/3 preserved. Very pale brown clay. No paint preserved. Hub on underside of foot. Base: Type A3.
L23 Vk1, level 1, lots 2101, 2105, 2108, 2114 (combined).

P1380. 2 skyphos bases.
D. ca. 0.09.
Worn surfaces. No paint preserved. Base: Type B.
L23 Vk1, level 2, lot 3365/1-2; level 2, tumble, lot 3369/1.

P1381. Base frag. of skyphos. Fig. 3-50.
D. ca. 0.058.
About 2/3 preserved. Reddish yellow clay. Frags. of black paint on exterior and interior. String marks; wheel ridging. Base: Type C.
L23 Vk1, level 2, lot 3374/1-2.

P1382. 3 skyphos base frags.
D. ca. 0.07-0.08.
Reddish yellow clay. Frags. of black paint. Base: Type C.
L23 Vk1, level 2, lot 3365/1-2; level 2, tumble, lot 3369/1.

P1383. Skyphos base. Fig. 3-50.
D. 0.054.
Very pale brown clay. No paint preserved. Hub on underside of foot. Base: Type D1.
L23 Vk1, level 2, lot 3374/1-2.

P1384. 5 skyphos base frags.
D. ca. 0.06 (1 frag.), 0.07 (2 frags.), 0.08 (2 frags.).
Reddish yellow clay. No paint preserved. Base: Type D1.
L23 Vk1, level 2, lot 3365/1-2.

P1385. Base frag. of skyphos.
D. ca. 0.045.
About 1/8 preserved. Reddish yellow clay. No paint preserved. Base: Type D2.
L23 Vk1, level 2, lots 2115, 2122, 2127.

P1386-88. Skyphos bases. Fig. 3-50 (**P1387**).
D. 0.04 (**P1388**), 0.046 (**P1387**), 0.05 (**P1386**).
Reddish yellow clay. **P1388** only has traces of black paint preserved on interior, none on exterior. Base: Type E1.
L23 Vk1, level 1, lots 2101, 2105, 2108, 2114 (combined); level 2, lots 2115, 2122, 2127.

P1389. Flat base of cup.
D. ca. 0.05.
Incisions on underside of base. Frags. of black paint preserved on exterior and on underside. Cup base: Type A1.

L23 Vk1, level 2, tumble, lot 3369/1.

P1390. 3 flat base frags. of cups.
D. 0.05-0.06.
Reddish yellow clay. Possible frags. of black paint on exterior and interior. Cup base: Type B.
L23 Vkl, level 2, lot 3365/1-2.

P1391. Base of krater. Fig. 3-50.
D. ca. 0.09.
About ½ preserved. Reddish yellow clay. Frags. of black paint on exterior and interior. Krater base: Type B.
L23 Vkl, level 2, lot 3365/1-2.

P1392. Base of krater. Fig. 3-51.
D. ca. 0.125.
About ⅓ preserved. Ringed foot. Reddish yellow clay. Faint frags. of black paint on exterior and interior. Krater base: Type C1.
L23 Vkl, level 2a, lots 2116, 2123.

P1393. Pedestal base, possibly from krater. Fig. 3-51.
H. (pres.) 0.031. D. base 0.04. D. pedestal 0.022-0.026.
Munsell 5YR 7/8 reddish yellow. Very worn surfaces. Small conical foot. No paint preserved.
L23 Vkl, level 2, lot 3365/1-2.

P1394. 30 skyphos handles.
Type A.
L23 Vkl, level 2, lots 2115, 2122, 2127, 3365/1-2.

P1395. 18 skyphos handles.
Type C.
L23 Vkl, level 2, lots 2115, 2122, 2127, 3365/1-2.

P1396-97. Cup handles. Fig. 3-49.
W. 0.01 (**P1396**), 0.014 (**P1397**).
Munsell 10YR 7/4 very pale brown. Black paint. Cup handle: Type A.
L23 Vkl, level 2, lots 2115, 2122, 2127 (**P1396**), 3374/1-2 (**P1397**).

P1398. Cup handle frag.
W. 0.013.
Reddish yellow clay. No paint preserved. Cup handle: Type B.
L23 Vkl, level 2, lot 3365/1-2.

Closed Shapes

P1399. 2 oinochoe rim frags.
Reddish yellow clay. Black paint. Oinochoe rim: Type A.
L23 Vkl, level 2, lot 3365/1-2.

P1400. Rim and neck frag. of oinochoe. Fig. 3-51.
H. (pres.) 0.062.
Munsell 10YR 7/4 very pale brown. Black paint. Flute at inner lip of rim. Oinochoe rim: Type C.
L23 Vkl, level 2, lot 3365/1-2.

P1401. Rim frag. of oinochoe.
Similar to **P1400**. Oinochoe rim: Type C.
L23 Vkl, level 2, lot 3365/1-2.

P1402. 3 belly handles of amphorae.
D. 0.021-0.024.
Reddish yellow clay. No paint preserved. Belly handle: Type A (round).
L23 Vkl, level 2, lots 2115, 2122, 2127.

P1403. Neck handle of amphora. Fig. 3-52.
W. 0.034.
Very pale brown clay. No paint preserved. Neck handle: Type A (elliptical).
L23 Vkl, level 2, lots 2115, 2122, 2127.

P1404. Neck handle of amphora. Fig. 3-52.
W. 0.038.
Very pale brown clay. Black paint. Neck handle: Type B1 (convex).
L23 Vkl, level 2, lot 3365/1-2.

P1405. Neck handle of amphora. Fig. 3-52.
W. 0.035.
Very pale brown clay. Black paint. Neck handle: Type B2 (concave).
L23 Vkl, level 2, lot 3365/1-2.

P1406. 7 handles of small oinochoai or jugs.
W. 0.014.
Very pale brown clay. No paint preserved. Oinochoe handle: Type A2.
L23 Vkl, level 2, lots 2114, 2122, 2127, 3365/1-2.

Coarse Ware

P1407. Rim frag.
H. (pres.) 0.066. Th. 0.009. D. ca. 0.14.
Burned. Rim: Type A1.
L23 Vkl, level 2, lot 3365/1-2.

P1408. 2 rim frags.
Th. 0.007. D. ca. 0.11, 0.14.
Burned. Rim: Type A2.
L23 Vkl, level 2, lots 2115, 2122, 2127, 3365/1-2.

P1409. Flat base.
D. 0.10.
Burned. Base: Type B.
L23 Vkl, level 2, lot 3365/1-2.

P1410. 2 handle frags.
W. 0.025, 0.027.
Burned. Handle: Type A1.
L23 Vkl, level 2, lots 2115, 2122, 2127, 3365/1-2.

From L23 Wklm and L23 Xklm:

Open Shapes

P1411. Rim and body frag. of skyphos.
D. ca. 0.16.
No paint preserved. Rim: Type A1.
L23 Xklm-W1/3, level 1, lots 2140, 2142.

P1412. 3 skyphos rim and body frags.
D. ca. 0.13-0.15.
Rim: Type A2.
L23 Wklm, level 1, lots 2134, 2135.

P1413. Rim frag. of skyphos.
Very worn. No paint preserved. Rim: Type B.
L23 Wklm, level 1, lots 2110, 2124, 2129.

P1414. 7 skyphos rim frags.
D. ca. 0.09.
Rim: Type C1.
L23 Wklm, level 1, lots 2119, 2124, 2129; L23 Xklm-W1/3, level 1, lots 2140, 2142.

P1415. 4 skyphos rim frags.
D. ca. 0.12.
Rim: Type C2.
L23 Wklm, level 1, lots 2119, 2124, 2129; L23 Xklm-W1/3, level 1, lots 2140, 2142.

P1416. 3 skyphos rim frags.
D. ca. 0.10.
Rim: Type C3.
L23 Wklm, level 1, lots 2134, 2135; L23 Xklm-E2/3, level 1, lots 3352/1-4.

P1417. Upper profile of skyphos. Fig. 3-55.
H. (pres.) 0.029. Th. 0.0025-0.003. D. ca. 0.10.
Reddish yellow clay. Probable monochrome black coating exterior and interior. Rim: Type C5; Handle: Type C (D. 0.006).
L23 Wklm, level 2, lots 2135, 2139.

P1418. Upper profile of skyphos. Fig. 3-55.
H. (pres.) 0.034. Th. 0.003. D. ca. 0.09.
Missing ⅔ of handle. Reddish yellow clay. Probable monochrome black coating exterior and interior. Rim: Type C5; Handle: Type C.
L23 Wklm, level 2, lot 2141.

P1419. 11 skyphos rim frags.
D. ca. 0.09-0.10.
Rim: Type C5.
L23 Wklm, levels 1 and 2, lots 2124, 2129, 2134, 2135, 2136; L23 Xklm, levels 1 and 2, lots 2140, 2142, 2145, 2149, 2502, 2505.

P1420. Skyphos rim frag.
D. ca. 0.07-0.08.
Rim: Type C6.
L23 Wklm, level 1, lots 2119, 2124, 2129.

P1421. 6 skyphos or deep bowl rim frags.
D. ca. 0.15-0.18.
Rim: Type D1.
L23 Wklm, level 1, lots 2119, 2124, 2129; L23 Xklm-E2/3, level 1, lot 3352/1-4.

P1422. 4 skyphos rim frags.
D. ca. 0.10.
Rim: Type D.
L23 Wklm, level 1, lots 2119, 2124, 2129; L23 Xklm-W1/3, lots 2140, 2142.

P1423. 15 skyphos rim frags.
D. ca. 0.08-0.10.
Rim: Type D3.
L23 Wklm, level 1, lots 2119, 2124, 2129, 2134, 2135; L23 Xklm-E2/3, level 1, lot 3352/1-4.

P1424. 5 deep bowl rim frags.
D. ca. 0.20.
Rim: Type E1.
L23 Wklm, level 1, lots 2119, 2124, 2129; L23 Xklm, levels 1 and 2, lots 2140, 2142, 2145, 2149.

P1425. 4 skyphos rim frags.
D. ca. 0.10.
Rim: Type E2.
L23 Wklm, level 1, lots 2134, 2135; L23 Xklm-W1/3, lots 2140, 2142.

P1426. 7 skyphos rim frags.
D. ca. 0.12-0.13.
Rim: Type F.
L23 Wklm, level 1, lots 2119, 2124, 2129, 2134, 2135; L23 Xklm, levels 1 and 2, lots 2140, 2142, 2145, 2149.

P1427. 4 cup rims.
D. ca. 0.10.
Cup rim: Type A.
L23 Wklm, level 1, lots 2134, 2135; L23 Xklm, levels 1 and 2, lots 2140, 2142, 2145, 2149.

P1428. 7 krater rim frags.
D. ca. 0.22.
Krater rim: Type A2.
L23 Wklm, level 1, lots 2119, 2124, 2129, 2134, 2135; L23 Xklm, levels 1 and 2, lots 2140, 2142, 2145, 2149.

P1429. Rim frag. of krater. Fig. 3-49.
H. (pres.) 0.05. Th. 0.007. D. ca. 0.30.
Reddish yellow clay. Frags. of black coating preserved on exterior and interior. 2 shallow incisions under rim. Krater rim: Type B.
L23 Wklm, level 2, lots 2136, 2139.

P1430. 3 rim frags. of krater. Fig. 3-49.
H. (pres.) 0.068. Th. 0.008. D. ca. 0.30(?)
Munsell 10YR 8/3 very pale brown. Frags. of black paint preserved on exterior. Below rim is raised band with diagonal slashes in imitation of rope decoration; below rope decoration 2 shallow raised bands. Krater rim: Type C.
L32 Wklm, level 1, lots 2119, 2124, 2129.

P1431. Rim frag. of krater.
H. (pres.) 0.209. Th. 0.006. D. ca. 0.20.
Munsell 2.5YR 8/2 white. No paint preserved. Krater rim: Type E.
L23 Wklm, level 1, lots 2134, 2135.

P1432. Skyphos base.
D. ca. 0.052.
Base: Type A1.
L23 Wklm, level 2, lots 2144, 2147.

P1433. 12 skyphos bases.
D. ca. 0.04.
Base: Type A1.
L23 Wklm, levels 1 and 2, lots 2134, 2135, 2136, 2139; L23 Xklm, levels 1 and 2, lots 2140, 2142, 2145, 2149, 2502, 2505, 3352/1-4.

P1434. 8 skyphos bases.
D. ca. 0.035.
Base: Type A3.
L23 Xklm, levels 1 and 2, lots 2140, 2142, 2145, 2149, 2502, 2505, 3352/1-4.

P1435. 3 skyphos or deep bowl bases.
D. ca. 0.06 (2), 0.08 (1).
Base: Type B.
L23 Wklm, level 2, lots 2136, 2139, 2144, 2147.

P1436. Skyphos or deep bowl base.
D. ca. 0.07.
Base: Type C.
L23 Wklm, level 1, lots 2134, 2135.

P1437. 23 skyphos or deep bowl bases.
D. ca. 0.06-0.07.
Base: Type D1.
L23 Wklm, levels 1 and 2, lots 2119, 2124, 2129, 2134, 2136, 2139, 2141, 2144, 2147; L23 Xklm, levels 1 and 2, lots 2140, 2142, 2145, 2149, 2502, 2505.

P1438. 6 skyphos bases.
D. 0.035 (2), 0.04 (4).
Base: Type E1.
L23 Wklm, level 1, lots 2119, 2124, 2129, 2134, 2135; L23 Xklm, level 1, lots 2140, 2142, 3352/1-4.

P1439. Skyphos base frag. Fig. 3-50.
D. ca. 0.03.
Very pale brown clay. Very worn surfaces. No paint preserved. Base: Type E2.
L23 Wklm, level 2, lots 2136, 2139.

P1440. 5 flat cup bases.
D. ca. 0.05.
Cup base: Type B.
L23 Wklm, levels 1 and 2, lots 2134, 2135, 2136, 2139; L23 Xklm, levels 1 and 2, lots 2140, 2142, 2145, 2149, 2502, 2505.

P1441. Base of krater. Fig. 3-51.
D. ca. 0.088.
About ½ preserved. Munsell 7.5YR 7/4 pink to 7.5YR 7/6 reddish yellow with light gray core. Good frags. of black coating preserved on exterior and interior. String marks. Krater base: Type B.
L23 Wklm, level 2, lot 2141.

P1442. Base of krater. Fig. 3-51.
D. ca. 0.10.
About ⅓ preserved. Reddish yellow clay with gray-blue core. Good streaky black-brown coating on exterior; fainter traces of black coating on interior. Krater base: Type B.
L23 Wklm, level 2, lot 2144.

P1443. Base of large krater.
D. 0.16.
Ringed foot. Munsell 10YR 8/4 very pale brown. Frags. of black paint preserved on exterior and interior. Burned on underside of foot. Krater base: Type C1.
L23 Xklm-E2/3, level 1, lot 3552/1-4.

P1444. Base of large krater. Fig. 3-51.
D. ca. 0.16.
Munsell 5YR 7/4 pink. Very worn surfaces. Possible frags. of black paint preserved on exterior and interior. Krater base: Type C2.
L23 Xklm-E2/3, level 1, lot 3352/1-4.

P1445. 8 cup handles.
W. 0.012-0.014.
Cup handle: Type A.
L23 Wklm, level 1, lots 2134, 2135; L23 Xklm, levels 1 and 2, lots 2140, 2142, 2145, 2149.

Closed Shapes

P1446. 4 oinochoe rims.
D. ca. 0.10.
Oinochoe rim: Type A.
L23 Wklm, level 1, lots 2134, 2135.

P1447. Oinochoe rim.
Type B.
L23 Xklm-W1/3, level 1, lots 2140, 2142.

P1448. 4 oinochoe rims.
Type C.
L23 Xklm-W1/3, level 1, lots 2140, 2142.

P1449. 7 jug rims.
D. ca. 0.10-0.11.
Jug rim: Type C.
L23 Wklm, level 2, lots 2136, 2139, 2141; L23 Xklm, level 1, lots 2140, 2142, 3352/1-4.

P1450. Rim frag. of jug.
H. (pres.) 0.017. D. ca. 0.12.
Reddish yellow clay. Black paint. Jug rim: Type D.
L23 Wklm, level 2, lots 2136, 2139.

P1451. 3 bases of oinochoai or jugs.
D. ca. 0.072.
Base: Type A1.
L23 Xklm, level 1, lots 2140, 2142, 3352/1-4.

P1452. Base of large amphora. Fig. 3-52.
D. ca. 0.15.
Ringed foot. Reddish yellow clay. Very worn surfaces. No paint preserved. Base: Type A2.
L23 Wklm, level 2, lots 2136, 2139.

P1453. Base of amphora.
D. ca. 0.12.
Similar to **P1452**. Base: Type A2.
L23 Wklm, level 2, lot 2141.

P1454. Base of oinochoe or jug.
D. ca. 0.07.
Black paint. Base: Type B.
L23 Wklm, level 2, lots 2136, 2139.

P1455. Base of probable amphora.
D. ca. 0.12.
No paint preserved. Base: Type C.
L23 Wklm, level 1, lots 2119, 2124, 2129.

P1456. Flat base (of amphora?)
D. ca. 0.12.
No paint preserved. Base: Type D2.
L23 Wklm, level 2, lots 2141.

P1457. Belly handle of amphora.
D. 0.023.
Light red clay. No paint preserved. Belly handle: Type A.
L23 Xklm-W1/3, level 1, lots 2140, 2142.

P1458. Neck handle of amphora.
W. 0.032.
Very pale brown clay. No paint preserved. Neck handle: Type A.
L23 Wklm, level 1, lots 2119, 2124, 2129.

P1459. Handle of oinochoe or jug.

W. 0.027.

Reddish yellow clay. Streaky black-brown paint. Oinochoe handle: Type A1.

L23 Xklm-W1/3, level 1, lots 2140, 2142.

P1460. 5 handle frags. of oinochoai or jugs.

W. 0.027-0.031.

Oinochoe handle: Type A1.

L23 Wklm, level 1, lots 2119, 2124, 2129; L23 Xklm-W1/3, level 1, lots 2140, 2142.

P1461. Handle of oinochoe or jug.

W. 0.019.

Reddish yellow clay. No paint preserved. Oinochoe handle: Type A2.

L23 Wklm, level 1, lots 2119, 2124, 2129.

P1462. 3 handle frags. of oinochoai or jugs.

W. 0.02.

Oinochoe handle: Type A2.

L23 Wklm, level 1, lots 2119, 2124, 2129; L23 Xklm-W1/3, level 1, lots 2140, 2142.

P1463. 2 handle frags. of oinochoai or jugs.

W. 0.01.

Oinochoe handle: Type A3.

L23 Xklm-E2/3, level 1, lot 3352/1-4.

P1464. 2 handle frags. of oinochoai or jugs. Fig. 3-52.

W. ca. 0.023.

Rib down center of top. Oinochoe handle: Type B (ribbed).

L23 Xklm-W1/3, level 1, lots 2140, 2142.

P1465. Handle of oinochoe or jug. Fig. 3-52; Pl. 3-139.

W. 0.028.

3 shallow grooves along top. Munsell 10YR 8/3 very pale brown. Very worn surfaces. No paint preserved. Handle: Type D.

L23 Wklm, level 1, lots 2134, 2135.

P1466. 2 rope handle frags. of oinochoai.

D. ca. 0.02.

Reddish yellow clay with orange-pink and gray-blue cores. Frags. of black paint preserved. Oinochoe handle: Type E (rope).

L23 Wklm, level 1, lots 2134, 2135; L23 Xklm-W1/3, level 1, lots 2140, 2142.

Coarse Ware

P1467. 22 rim frags.

D. ca. 0.20-0.22.

Burned. Rim: Type A1.

L23 Wklm, level 1, lots 2134, 2135; L23 Xklm, level 1, lots 2140, 2142, 3352/1-4; level 2, lots 2145, 2149, 2502, 2505.

P1468. 7 rim frags.

D. ca. 0.18.

Burned. Rim: Type A2.

L23 Wklm, level 1, lots 2134, 2135; L23 Xklm, levels 1 and 2, lots 2140, 2142, 2145, 2149.

P1469. Rim frag. Fig. 3-53.

H. (pres.) 0.042. Th. 0.007. D. ca. 0.18(?)

Burned. Rim: Type C2.

L32 Wklm, level 2, lot 2141.

P1470. 6 flat bases (of bowls?).

D. ca. 0.15 (2), 0.18 (2), 0.20 (2).

Burned. Base: Type A.

L23 Wklm, level 2, lots 2136, 2139.

P1471. Flat base.

D. ca. 0.14-0.15 (uneven).

Gritty reddish yellow clay. Base: Type B.

L23 Wklm, level 2, lots 2144, 2147.

P1472. 3 handle frags.

W. 0.025-0.028.

Burned. Handle: Type A1.

L23 Wklm, level 1, lots 2134, 2135; L23 Xklm-W1/3, level 1, lots 2140, 2142.

P1473. 9 handle frags.

W. 0.045-0.051.

Burned. Handle: Type A2.

L23 Wklm, level 2, lots 2134, 2135; L23 Xklm-W1/3, level 1, lots 2140, 2142.

P1474. Handle frag.

W. 0.04.

Reddish yellow clay, burned in places. Handle: Type A3.

L23 Wklm, level 2, lot 2141.

P1475. Handle frag. Fig. 3-54.

W. 0.035.

2 ribs along top. Burned. Handle: Type A4.

L23 Wklm, level 2, lot 2141.

P1476. 7 handle frags.

W. 0.034-0.04.

1 rib along top. Burned. Handle: Type A4.

L23 Wklm, level 2, lot 2141; L23 Xklm-W1/3, level 1, lots 2140, 2142.

P1477. Handle frag. Fig. 3-54.

W. 0.055.

4 incisions along top. Burned. Handle: Type B1.

L23 Wklm, level 2, lot 2141.

P1478. Handle frag.

W. 0.032.

3 incisions along top. Burned. Handle: Type B1.

L23 Wklm, level 2, lot 2141.

P1479. 2 handle frags. Fig. 3-54.

D. 0.0145-0.015.

Round handles of coarse jugs(?) Burned. Handle: Type C (round).

L23 Wklm, level 2, lot 2141.

P1480. Frag. of coarse grill. Pl. 3-149.

H. (pres.) 0.066. Th. 0.036.

Munsell 2.5YR 6/6 light red. Broken at bottom. Side edge preserved and smooth; top edge rounded, forming groove in which to place bar of grill.

L23 Xklm-W1/3, level 2, lot 2149.

P1481. Decorated body sherd of coarse bowl(?) Pl. 3-144.

H. (pres.) 0.044.

Reddish yellow clay. Decorated with nipple surrounded by holes (7 preserved) which are pierced deeply but do not go through.

L23 Xklm-E2/3, level 1, lot 3352/1-4.

P1482. Body frag. of pithos.
H. (pres.) 0.084.
Raised band with rope decoration.
L23 Xklm-W1/3, level 2, lots 2145, 2149.

P1483. Body frag. of pithos.
H. (pres.) 0.052.
Raised band with row of finger impressions.
L23 Wklm, level 1, lots 2134, 2135.

P1484. Body frag. of pithos.
H. (pres.) 0.078.
Raised band with incised triangle; small incised circles both within and outside triangle.
L23 Wklm, level 2, lot 2141.

Section B

From Area IVNE. Hill-wash above the DAII reuse of Unit IV-7.

Open Shapes

P1485. Profile of skyphos. Fig. 3-56.
H. (pres.) 0.11. Th. 0.0035-0.004. D. 0.12. D. base 0.06.
Missing handles and lower body. Reddish yellow clay with pinkish core. Very worn surfaces. Frags. of monochrome black coating preserved on exterior and interior. Carination at point where handle joins body. Rim: Type D1; Base: Type A1; Handle: Type C(?)
L23 Tmn, level 4, lot 1465.

P1486. Profile of deep bowl. Fig. 3-56.
H. ca. 0.136. Th. 0.004-0.005. D. rim ca. 0.22. D. base 0.06.
Missing handles and lower body. Reddish yellow clay. Very worn surfaces. Frags. of monochrome black coating preserved on exterior and interior. Carination at point where handle joins body. Rim: Type E1; Base: Type A1; Handle: Type A(?).
L23 Tmn, level 4, lot 1465.

P1487. Profile of skyphos. Fig. 3-56.
H. (pres.) ca. 0.16. Th. 0.003-0.004. D. rim 0.13. D. base 0.04. D. handle 0.013.
Missing lower body. Clay is reddish yellow on interior, but fired to orange-red on exterior, with orange-pink core. Very worn surfaces. Good frags. of monochrome black coating on interior, fainter frags. on exterior. Carination at point where handles join body. Rim: Type D1; Base: Type E2; Handle: Type A.
L23 Umn, level 2, lot 1120.

P1488. Profile of skyphos. Fig. 3-55.
H. (pres.) ca. 0.12. Th. 0.0035-0.004. D. rim ca. 0.13. D. base 0.057. D. handle 0.01.
Missing lower body. Munsell 5YR 7/6 reddish yellow. Very worn surfaces. Frags. of metallic blue-black coating on exterior and interior. Rim: Type D3; Base: Type D1; Handle: Type A.
L23 Vo (exploratory), level 1, lots 1255, 1257.

P1489. Profile of skyphos. Fig. 3-58.
H. (pres.) ca. 0.125. Th. 0.003-0.004. D. rim ca. 0.18. D. base 0.075. D. handle 0.015.
Missing lower body. Reddish yellow clay. Very worn surfaces. Frags. of monochrome black coating preserved on exterior and interior. Rim: Type F; Base: Type D1; Handle: Type A.
L23 Tmn/Umn baulk, level 2, lots 3398/1-3, 4590.

P1490. Profile of cup. Fig. 3-58.
H. 0.07. Th. 0.003. D. rim 0.085. D. base ca. 0.055. W. handle ca. 0.01(?).
Missing handle, but stump preserved. Reddish yellow clay, fired light gray in places on exterior and interior. Very worn surfaces. Frags. of black paint preserved on exterior only. Probably once coated with black on interior.
L23 Umn, level 1, lots 1113, 1114.

P1491. Profile of cup. Fig. 3-58.
H. ca. 0.08. Th. 0.003. D. rim ca. 0.12. D. base ca. 0.05. W. handle 0.014-0.015.
Reddish yellow clay, fired light gray in places. Very worn surfaces. No paint preserved, but probably coated in monochrome black on exterior and interior. Carination at point where handle joins body. Cup rim: Type A; Base: Type A2; Handle: Type A.
L23 Umn, level 2, lot 1118.

P1492. Rim frag. of krater. Fig. 3-48; Pl. 3-134.
H. (pres.) 0.025. Th. 0.004-0.005. D. ca. 0.21.
Very pale brown clay. No paint preserved. Rim is everted toward interior instead of exterior, as usual. Rim: Type A1 (reversed).
L23 Umn, level 2, lot 1120.

P1493. Small conical pedestal base, perhaps of krater. Fig. 3-51.
H. (pres.) 0.03. D. ca. 0.045(?)
Reddish yellow clay, fired gray in places, with gray-blue core. Faint traces of black paint on exterior.
L23 Vmn, level 2, lots 1111, 1112.

P1494. Pedestal base of krater. Fig. 3-51.
H. (pres.) 0.045. D. base 0.053. D. stem 0.048.
Tip of foot missing. Reddish yellow clay. Frags. of black paint preserved on exterior.
L23 Vmn, level 1, lot 1109.

Closed Shapes

P1495. Rim and neck frag. of amphora. Fig. 3-52.
H. (pres.) 0.03. D. ca. 0.21.
Reddish yellow clay. Black paint. Interior of rim has ledge for placement of lid.
L23 Wmn, level 2, lot 4592/1.

P1496. Rim and neck frag. of jug. Fig. 3-52.
H. (pres.) 0.05. D. ca. 0.08.
Reddish yellow clay. Black paint. 2 raised bands under rim. Jug rim: Type E.
L23 Wmn, level 2, lot 4592/1.

P1497. Spout. Pl. 3-138.
L. (pres.) 0.04. D. top 0.012. D. bottom 0.017.
Munsell 5YR 7/6 reddish yellow. Dull metallic monochrome black paint. Spout hole widens as it nears junction with body.
L23 Umn, level 2, lot 1120.

P1498. Neck handle of amphora. Fig. 3-52.
W. 0.05.
Very pale brown clay. Frags. of black paint. Rib along center of top. Neck handle: Type B3 (ribbed).
L23 Vmn, level 2, lots 1115, 1117.

P1499. Handle of small oinochoe or jug. Fig. 3-52; Pl. 3-139.
W. 0.0135.
Very pale brown clay. Frags. of black paint. Flute down center of top. Oinochoe handle: Type C (fluted).
L23 Tmn, level 2, lots 1458, 1460.

P1500. Handle of small oinochoe of jug. Fig. 3-52.
W. 0.021.
Reddish yellow clay. Frags. of black paint. Double handle formed by deep groove down center of top and underside. Oinochoe handle: Type F (double).
L23 Wmn, level 2, lot 4592/1.

Coarse Ware

P1501. Coarse oinochoe rim. Fig. 3-53.
H. (pres.) 0.077. Th. 0.007.
Reddish yellow clay exterior, burned to light red on interior.
L23 Vmn, level 2, lots 1115, 1117.

P1502. Upper profile of neck-handled amphora. Fig. 3-63.
H. (pres.) 0.093. D. ca. 0.18-0.20. W. handle 0.04.
Burned. Rim: Type A1; Handle: Type A2.
L23 Umn, level 2, lot 1120.

P1503. Profile of rim, neck, and handle of coarse jug. Fig. 3-62.
H. (pres.) 0.092. D. ca. 0.16(?) W. handle 0.026.
Burned. Rim: Type B; Handle: Type A3 (fluted).
L23 Vmn, level 2, pit lot 1116.

P1504. Frag. of cooking stand. Pls. 3-146, 3-147.
H. 0.112. W. (pres.) 0.154. Th. 0.032.
Reddish yellow clay with inclusions. Frag. of curved stand for support of pot. Vertical and horizontal (broken) projections at one side for support of pot.
L23 Tmn, level 2, lot 1460.

P1505. 2 coarse strainer frags.
D. holes 0.006.
Reddish yellow clay. Slightly burned.
L23 Umn, level 2, lots 1118, 1120.

P1506. Strainer frag. with nipple decoration. Pl. 3-144.
Th. 0.01. Th. with nipple 0.003.
Reddish yellow clay with inclusions. Nipple very worn and most holes broken.
L23 Umn, level 2, lot 1120.

Section C

From Area IVNW. This section consists of DAIII sherds associated with Unit IV-5.

Open Shapes

P1507. Profile of skyphos. Fig. 3-57; Pl. 3-132.
H. 0.128. Th. 0.004-0.005. D. rim ca. 0.20. D. base 0.066.
Missing handles. Reddish yellow clay. Black band under rim; below, decoration of crosshatched triangles. Monochrome black coating on belly and base. Good black coating on interior. Carination below decoration zone at point where handles would have joined body. Rim is rectangular, a variation of Type E1; Base: Type D1; Handles: probably Type A.
L23 R1, test cut N of Room 2, Unit IV-2, lot 5042.

P1508. Rim and base frag. of skyphos.
D. rim ca. 0.12. D. base ca. 0.06.
Fired gray with orange-pink core. Frags. of black paint preserved on exterior and interior. String marks on base. Rim: Type C2; Base: Type B.
L23 R1, test cut N of Room 2, Unit IV-2, lot 5042.

P1509. Upper profile of cup. Fig. 3-58.
H. (pres.) 0.053. Th. 0.004-0.005. D. ca. 0.09.
Missing handles. Clay burned gray. Traces of monochrome black coating on exterior and interior. Carination at point where handle would have joined body. Cup rim: Type B.
L23 Smn, level 3, lot 3411/1-3.

P1510. Upper profile of deep bowl or small krater. Fig. 3-57.
H. (pres.) 0.082. Th. 0.006. D. ca. 0.23(?) D. handle ca. 0.013.
Tip of rim missing. Reddish yellow clay with gray-blue core. Broad raised band below rim. No paint preserved, but probably coated in monochrome black on exterior and interior. Handle: Type A.
L23 Smn, level 3, lot 3411/1-3.

Closed Shapes

P1511. Profile of small oinochoe. Fig. 3-59.
H. (pres.) 0.137. Th. ca. 0.004. D. ca. 0.09.
Missing handle, lower belly, and base. Burned dark gray on exterior, light gray on interior. Very worn surfaces. 7 ends of arcs of accumbent concentric semi-circles preserved on shoulder and upper belly. Above on neck, possible frags. of black coating. Below decoration on shoulder, 3 black bands followed by solid black coating, but very worn and hard to decipher. Oinochoe rim: Type C.
L23 Smn, level 3, lot 3411/1-3.

P1512. Handle of oinochoe or jug.
Reddish yellow clay. Black paint. Oinochoe handle: Type A2.
L23 T1, level 4, lot 4520/1.

P1513. Rope handle of oinochoe.
D. ca. 0.017.
Reddish yellow clay with gray-blue core. Frags. of black paint preserved. Oinochoe handle: Type E (rope).
L23 T1, level 4, lot 4520/1.

Coarse Ware

P1514. Rim frag., possibly from large amphora.
H. (pres.) 0.058. D. ca. 0.28.
Burned. Rim: Type A1.
L23 Smn, level 3, lot 3411/1-3.

P1515. Upper profile of belly-handled amphora. Fig. 3-63.
H. (pres.) 0.215. D. rim ca. 0.20. D. handle 0.03.
2 nonjoining frags., missing shoulder. Base probably like **P1564**. Reddish yellow clay with inclusions, burned in places on exterior and interior. Rim: Type A2.
L23 S1, level 3, lot 4509/1.

P1516. Upper profile of neck-handled amphora.
H. (pres.) 0.122. D. rim ca. 0.16-0.17. W. handle 0.04.
Similar in shape to **P1502**. Reddish yellow clay with inclusions, burned in places. Rim: Type A1; Handle: Type A2.
L23 Smn, level 3, lot 3411/1-3.

Section D

From Area IVNW. This section consists of sherds associated with the DAIII reuse of Unit IV-6.

Open Shapes

P1517. Upper profile of skyphos.
H. (pres.) 0.046. Th. 0.0035. D. ca. 0.08.
Fired gray. Frags. of black coating exterior and interior. Rim: Type A2; Handle: Type C(?).

L23 Ui, level 2, Room 3, lot 4421/1-4.

P1518. Decorated skyphos body frag.
H. 0.032.
Very pale brown clay. 4 arcs of accumbent concentric semi-circles with central dot; below, black coating. Faint frags. of black paint on interior.
L23 Tj, level 2, Room 2, lot 4417/1-2.

P1519. 2 krater rim and wall frags.
D. ca. 0.24.
Reddish yellow clay. Good black paint on exterior and interior. Stripes on top of rim. Krater rim: Type A2.
L23 Tj, level 2, Room 2, lot 4417/1-2.

P1520. Rim and wall frag. of krater. Fig. 3-49; Pl. 3-134.
H. (pres.) 0.036. Th. 0.005. D. ca. 0.24.
Good black paint preserved on exterior and interior. 3 incised bands under rim. Outer edge of top of rim left undecorated; inner edge painted black. Krater rim: Type B2.
L23 Tj, level 2, Room 2, lot 4417/1-2.

Closed Shapes

P1521. Upper profile of oinochoe. Fig. 3-60.
D. rim 0.10.
Missing lower belly and base. Fired gray. Flaky, worn surfaces. Probable monochrome black coating on neck and belly; too worn to tell what decoration, if any, was on shoulder. Black coating on top half of inner rim and neck. 3 incisions mark transition from neck to shoulder. 2 mending holes in handle. Oinochoe rim: Type A.
L23 Tj, level 2, Room 2, lot 4417/1-2.

P1522. Neck and shoulder frag. of oinochoe.
H. (pres.) 0.07.
Reddish yellow clay with gray-blue core. 3 grooves at transition from neck to shoulder. Below, on shoulder, ends of 4 arcs of accumbent concentric semi-circles in black.
L23 Tj, level 2, Room 2, lot 4417/1-2.

P1523. Rope handle frag. of oinochoe.
D. ca. 0.14-0.15.
Reddish yellow clay with gray-blue core. Frags. of black paint. Oinochoe handle: Type E (rope).
L23 Ui, level 2, Room 3, lot 4421/1-4.

P1524. Double handle of small oinochoe or jug. Fig. 3-52; Pl. 3-139.
D. each handle 0.01.
Reddish yellow clay with gray-blue core. Faint frags. of black paint. Oinochoe handle: Type F (double).
L23 Ui, level 2, Room 3, lot 4421/1-4.

Coarse Ware

P1525. Rim frag. of probable amphora. Fig. 3-53.
H. (pres.) 0.089. D. ca. 0.30(?)
Reddish yellow clay, burned in places. Rim: Type D.
L23 Tj, level 2, Room 2, lot 4417/1-2.

P1526. Rim frag. of oinochoe. Fig. 3-53.
H. (pres.) 0.037. D. ca. 0.16(?)
Burned.
L23 Tj, level 2, Room 2, lot 4417/1-2.

P1527. Body frag. of pithos. Pl. 3-156.
H. (pres.) 0.095. Th. body 0.025. Th. raised band 0.03.
Reddish yellow clay with inclusions and orange-pink core. Raised band had rope decoration at top with incised piled triangles below.
L23 Tj, level 2, Room 2, lot 4417/1-2.

Section E

From Area IVSW. Sherds associated with Walls M, N, and T and the possible apsidal building formed by Walls N and T.

Open Shapes

P1528. Upper profile of skyphos or deep bowl.
H. (pres.) 0.05. Th. 0.004. D. ca. 0.22(?).
Missing tip of handles and base. Fired to gray. Frags. of black paint preserved on exterior, none on interior. Rim: Type A2.
L23 Rfg, level 2, lots 1035, 1040, 1042, 1210 (combined).

P1529. 2 skyphos rim frags.
D. ca. 0.12.
Reddish yellow clay, burned gray in places. Very worn surfaces. No paint preserved. Rim: Type C2.
L23 Rfg, level 2, lots 948, 950, 1012 (combined).

P1530. Rim frag. of cup.
H. (pres.) 0.026. D. ca. 0.14.
Reddish yellow clay, fired gray in interior. Very worn surfaces; black frags. on interior only. Raised band under rim (instead of broad incision). Cup Rim: Type B.
L23 Pfg, level 2, lots 932, 937, 940, 946, 949, 1011 (combined).

Closed Shapes

P1531 (NP72). Upper profile of oinochoe. Fig. 3-59; Pl. 3-136.
H. (pres.) 0.125. Th. 0.005. D. neck 0.083. W. handle 0.034.
Missing belly and base. Munsell 5Y 7/3 pale yellow. Very worn surfaces. No paint preserved, but probably once coated with black paint. 3 incisions mark transition from neck to shoulder. Oinochoe rim: Type C; Handle: Type A1.
L23 Rhi, level 2, lots 1983, 1990.

P1532. Upper profile of small oinochoe. Fig. 3-59.
H. (pres.) 0.035. D. ca. 0.045.
Missing handle, belly, and base. Clay burned gray. No paint preserved, but probably coated in black on exterior. Oinochoe rim: Type C.
L23 Rhi/Shi baulk, level 1, lot 4093/3-4.

P1533. Decorated lower shoulder frag. of oinochoe.
H. (pres.) 0.031.
Fired to gray. Very worn surfaces. 5 frags. of ends of arcs of accumbent concentric semi-circles in black; below, frag. of thin black band.
L23 Pfg, level 1, lots 928, 931, 945 (combined).

Coarse Ware

P1534. Rim frag.
H. (pres.) 0.05. D. ca. 0.22.
Burned. Rim: Type B.
L23 Rfg, level 2, lots 948, 950, 1012 (combined).

P1535. Small tripod foot. Fig. 3-54.
H. (pres.) 0.027. W. top 0.017. W. bottom ca. 0.006.
Burned. Foot is broad at top (at point of junction with body) but narrows toward bottom.
L23 Rfg, level 2, lots 1035, 1040, 1042, 1210 (combined).

P1536. Frag. of leg of cooking pot. Fig. 3-54; Pl. 3-145.

H. 0.06. D. base 0.05. D. stem 0.038.

About ½ preserved, missing one side. Dark orange clay, burned on ⅔ of its surfaces, including break. Small hollow (0.005 deep) in underside of base. Leg is in the shape of a "spool."

L23 Rhi/Shi baulk, level 1, lot 4093/3-4.

P1537. Handle of possible jug or amphora. Fig. 3-54.

W. 0.042-0.004 (uneven).

Burned. One rib in center with flute on either side. Handle: Type A4.

L23 Rfg, level 2, lots 1035, 1040, 1042, 1210 (combined).

P1538. Body frag. of pithos.

H. (pres.) 0.096.

Coarse reddish yellow clay with inclusions. Decoration of row of incised circles (D. 0.005).

L23 Rfg, level 2, lots 948, 950, 1012 (combined).

P1539. Body frag. of pithos.

H. (pres.) 0.076. Th. body 0.024. Th. raised band 0.03.

Decoration of incised hatched triangles on raised band.

L23 Rfg, level 2, lot 1030.

P1540. Body frag. of pithos.

H. (pres.) 0.034. Th. body 0.01. Th. raised band 0.013.

Burned; worn. Raised band with decoration of diagonal slashes in imitation of rope band.

L23 Rfg, level 2, lots 1035, 1040, 1042, 1210 (combined).

P1541. 3 pithos body frags.

Raised band with imitation rope decoration. Similar to **P1540**.

L23 Thi, level 2, lots 1540, 1543, 1548.

P1542. Body frag. of pithos. Pl. 3-155.

H. (pres.) 0.205. Th. body 0.048. Th. raised band 0.058.

Reddish yellow clay with inclusions. Band decorated with row of raised triangles.

L23 Thi, level 2, lots 1540, 1543, 1548.

P1543. Base of pithos. Fig. 3-64; Pl. 3-154.

H. (pres.) 0.09. D. base 0.17.

Coarse light red clay with inclusions, very friable and crumbly. Flat base. Shows technique of making base: in middle is core (D. ca. 0.13), around which were applied coils of clay. With base were found 5 nonjoining frags. with raised band of diagonal slashes in imitation of rope decoration. Th. raised band 0.015. This decorative band was probably placed at point where base begins to flare into body in order to outline junction between base and lower body.

L23 Nfg, level 2, lot 4093/1-3.

Section F

From Area IVSE. A good DAIII deposit with little architectural association, except the fragment of an apsidal building.

Open Shapes

P1544. Profile of skyphos.

D. rim ca. 0.11. D. base ca. 0.036-0.04. D. handle 0.008.

Nonjoining frags. of rim, body, handle, and base. Munsell 5YR 7/8 reddish yellow. Very worn surfaces; no paint preserved. Rim: Type C2; Base: Type D1(?); Handle: Type C.

L23 Td, level 2, lot 4048/1-6.

P1545. Upper profile of skyphos. Fig. 3-55.

H. (pres.) 0.062. Th. 0.002-0.003. D. ca. 0.10.

Missing lower body and base. Munsell 10YR 8/3 very pale brown. Flaky clay; worn and incrusted surfaces. On exterior, two possible large piled triangles in black from rim; possible frags. of monochrome black coating on interior. Rim: Type C2.

L23 Td, level 2, lot 4048/1-6.

P1546. Decorated skyphos body frag.

H. (pres.) 0.025.

Reddish yellow clay, worn surfaces. Frags. of 2 arcs of accumbent concentric semi-circles in faded black paint. Good monochrome brown coating on interior.

L23 Wc, level 3, lot 4037/6-12.

P1547. Profile of deep bowl. Fig. 3-57.

H. (pres.) 0.154. D. ca. 0.195. D. base 0.08. D. handle ca. 0.012 (only handle stump preserved).

Missing lower body. Reddish yellow clay, fired to olive gray in places at rim. Frags. of streaky black-brown coating preserved on exterior, interior, and on handle stump and base frag. Base about ½ preserved. Rim: Type E1; Base: Type B; Handle: Type A.

L23 Xd, level 4, lot 4031/1W.

P1548. Rim frag. of skyphos or deep bowl.

H. (pres.) 0.025. D. ca. 0.15.

Reddish yellow clay. No paint preserved. Below rim, 3 mending holes (D. ca. 0.004). Rim: Type D1.

L23 Xd, level 3, lot 4030/4NE.

P1549 (NP87). Profile of cup. Fig. 3-58; Pl. 3-133.

H. 0.066. Th. 0.003. D. rim 0.083-0.09 (uneven). D. base (flat) 0.044.

About ⅓ preserved, rest restored. Munsell 10YR 7/4 very pale brown; clay fired to light gray in places around belly. Frags. of monochrome black coating preserved on exterior and interior. Cup rim: Type A.

L23 Wd, level 3a, lot 3603.

P1550. Rim frag. of krater.

H. (pres.) 0.033. Th. 0.006. D. ca. 0.15-0.16.

Clay fired gray. No paint preserved. Krater rim: Type B1.

L23 Wc, level 3, lot 4037/6-12.

P1551. Rim frag. of krater.

H. (pres.) 0.0435. Th. 0.006-0.007. Th. raised band 0.01. D. ca. 0.34.

Reddish yellow clay. Frags. of black paint on exterior and interior. Undecorated raised band below rim. Krater rim: Type C.

L23 Wc, level 3, lot 4037/6-12.

P1552. Decorated wall frag. of krater.

H. (pres.) 0.047. Th. 0.008.

Black band at top; below, ends of 4 arcs of accumbent concentric semi-circles in black; good streaky black-brown paint on interior.

L23 Wc, level 3, lot 4037/6-12.

P1553. Pedestal base of krater. Fig. 3-51.

H. (pres.) 0.062. D. foot 0.05. D. stem 0.022.

Munsell 5YR 7/8 reddish yellow. Very faint frag. of black paint on exterior only.

L23 Ude, level 2, lot 4041/2.

Closed Shapes

P1554. 2 rim and neck frags. of oinochoai.

Black paint. Oinochoe rim: Type A.

L23 UVc and extension, level 4, lot 4027/7-8W.

P1555. Rim frag. of small oinochoe.

Type B.
L23 UVc and extension, level 4, lot 4027/7-8W.

P1556. 3 neck and shoulder frags. of oinochoai.
Reddish yellow clay; black paint. 3 grooves mark transition from neck to shoulder.
L23 UVc and extension, level 4, lot 4027/7-8W.

P1557. Decorated oinochoe neck and shoulder frag.
1 groove marks transition from neck to shoulder; frags. of cross-hatching above groove on neck and below groove on shoulder.
L23 Wc, level 3, lot 4037/6-12.

P1558. Decorated oinochoe shoulder (?) frag.
5 vertical lines in black paint (metope-triglyph motif?); below, frag. of black band.
L23 Wc, level 3, lot 4037/6-12.

P1559. 2 rope handle frags. of oinochoai.
D. 0.023, 0.026.
Reddish yellow clay with gray-blue core. Frags. of black paint. Oinochoe handle: Type E (rope).
L23 Wc, level 3, lot 4037/6-12.

Coarse Ware

P1560 (NP174). Upper profile of neck-handled amphora. Fig. 3-63.
H. (pres.) 0.178. Th. 0.11-0.12. D. ca. 0.30. W. handle 0.044.
Handle stump preserved; missing tip of rim. Base probably like **P1563**. Munsell 10YR 6/2 light brownish gray to 10YR 4/1 dark gray (with dark gray core). Coarse gritty clay with inclusions. Rim: Type A2(?); Handle: Type A1.
L23 Wd, level 3a, lot 3603.

P1561. Upper profile of neck-handled amphora.
H. (pres.) 0.119. Th. 0.0065. D. ca. 0.18(?) W. handle 0.043.
Reddish yellow clay, burned on handle and tip of rim; gray core. Rim: Type A2; Handle: Type A2. Similar to **P1502**.
L23 Td, level 2, lot 4048/1-6.

P1562. Rim frag. of large amphora.
H. (pres.) 0.108. Th. 0.011. D. ca. 0.38.
Munsell 10YR 5/2 grayish brown. Rim: Type B.
L23 Ude, level 2, lot 4041/1.

P1563 (NP173). Lower profile of neck-handled(?) amphora. Fig. 3-64.
H. (pres.) 0.10. Th. body 0.012. D. base 0.113 (uneven).
Missing upper belly, neck, and rim, but probably like **P1560**. Munsell 2.5YR 6/6 light red; burned black in places on interior and underside of base; black core. Includes 3 small nonjoining base frags. and 11 nonjoining body frags. 1 body sherd has frag. of undecorated raised band, probably from upper belly. Base: Type A.
L23 Ude, level 2, lot 4041/4.

P1564 (NP175). Lower profile of belly-handled(?) amphora. Fig. 3-65.
H. (pres.) 0.142. Th. body 0.01. D. base 0.128.
Missing upper belly, neck and rim, but probably like **P1515**. Munsell 5Y 7/3 pale yellow. Burned dark gray on underside of base and on lower belly near base; burned on interior; dark gray core. Coarse clay with inclusions. Includes 7 nonjoining body frags. Base: Type A.
L23 Xd, level 4, lot 4031/1W.

P1565 (NP172). Lower profile of round-based jug or dipper(?). Fig. 3-61.
H. (pres.) 0.16. Th. body 0.01. D. belly 0.202.
Preserved to middle belly. Rim and shoulder similar to **P1312**, but larger. Munsell 5YR 5/6 yellowish red. Coarse gritty clay.
L23 Xd, level 3, lot 4030.

P1566. Incised frag. of base. Fig. 3-54; Pl. 3-141.
H. (pres.) 0.014. D. ca. 0.10.
Conical foot(?) Fired to red and burned black in places on exterior and underside. Incised decoration at tip of foot; incised wavy line with thin incised band below; at extreme tip of foot, row of dots.
L23 Uvc and extension, level 4, lot 4027/3W.

P1567. Tripod foot. Fig. 3-54.
H. (pres.) 0.05. W. 0.041. Th. 0.023.
Rectangular. Light red clay with inclusions, burned in places. At top is projection to fasten into slot at bottom of vase.
L23 Uvc and extension, level 4, lot 4027/5W.

P1568. Tripod foot. Fig. 3-54.
H. (pres.) 0.055. W. 0.0545. Th. 0.021 (top)-0.014 (bottom).
Rectangular. Reddish yellow clay with inclusions.
L23 Ude, level 2, lot 4041/6S.

P1569. Frag. of large leg of cooking pot.
H. (pres.) 0.044. D. foot 0.0455. D. stem 0.044.
About ½ preserved, missing top. Reddish yellow clay, burned gray-blue to black on one side. Probably similar to **P1536**, but much larger.
L23 Uvc and extension, level 4, lot 4027/7-8W.

P1570. Frag. of cooking stand. Fig. 3-54; Pl. 3-148.
D. ca. 0.07 (uneven). Th. 0.021.
Oval, about ½ preserved. Munsell 5YR 6/8 reddish yellow to 5YR 5/8 yellowish red. Clay contains stone inclusions; discolored on one side to Munsell 10YR 5/4 yellowish brown and also blackened on same side. Perhaps used as a stand for round-based jugs; cf. **P1312, P1565**.
L23 Uvc and extension, level 4, lot 4027/2W.

P1571. Rim frag. of small pithos. Fig. 3-54.
H. (pres.) 0.091. Th. body 0.012. Th. ribs 0.016.
Reddish yellow gritty clay with small inclusions; gray-blue core. 3 ribs preserved on body below rim.
L23 Ude, level 2, lot 4041/4.

P1572. Body frag. of pithos.
H. (pres.) 0.0385. Th. body 0.018. Th. raised band 0.024.
Reddish yellow clay with inclusions; burned light gray on interior. Raised band with decoration of row of finger impressions.
L23 UVc and extension, level 4, lot 4027/1.

P1573. Body frag. of pithos(?) with nipple decoration. Fig. 3-54.
H. (pres.) 0.06. Th. 0.024.
Reddish yellow clay with inclusions; orange slip on exterior. Nipple projects straight from body (as opposed to MH nipples which are curved) with worn handle stump adjacent.
L23 UVc and extension, level 4, lot 4027/1.

LATE GEOMETRIC

From trial trench L24-III, level 4, lots 508-10, in N Veves. 3 vases from a pithos burial discovered in 1969. Cf. *Hesperia* 41(1972):228, Pl. 40C.

Open Shapes

P1574 (NP12). Kantharos. Fig. 3-66; Pl. 3-157.
H. 0.137. Th. 0.004-0.005. D. rim 0.126. D. base 0.064. W. handles 0.021.

Munsell 2.5YR 6/8 light red. Paint varies from dark brown to black. 4 bands below rim; on neck, decoration of angular wavy line (like wolf's tooth). On shoulder at point where handle joins body, row of linked lozenges with central dots; below on belly, 1 thick band with thin bands above and below. Monochrome black coating on lower belly and base. Monochrome black coating on interior; reserved band inner rim. On handle, double "X" alternating with black bands. Straight rim, flat base, and flat, elliptical handle.

P1575 (NP11). Shallow bowl. Fig. 3-66; Pls. 3-158, 3-159, 3-160.

H. 0.063. Th. 0.005-0.006. D. rim 0.195. D. base 0.076.

Munsell 2.5YR 6/8 light red. Almost complete, only a few rim frags. missing. Paint varies from dark brown to black. Vertical stripes at rim in field between handles; below, 2 thick bands with alternating thin bands. Horizontal stripes on top of rim; thick bands on interior; handles monochrome black. Possible slip.

P1576 (NP4). Cup. Fig. 3-66; Pl. 3-161.

H. 0.092. D. rim 0.085-0.091 (uneven). D. base 0.06. W. handle 0.016.

Munsell 5YR 7/8 reddish yellow. Streaky monochrome black-brown paint on exterior and interior and on handle. Straight rim, flat base.

Coarse Ware

P1577. Pithos (restored). Fig. 3-66; Pl. 3-162.

H. 1.72. D. rim 0.63. D. base 0.12. H. base 0.11. D. (max.) 1.17.

Munsell 7.5YR 7/6 to 7/8 reddish yellow on body; 5YR 7/8 reddish yellow at rim. Coarse clay with inclusions; white slip(?); base in form of long stem.

POTTERY FROM CEMETERIES

DARK AGE I

From Nikitopoulos no. 6 in the area of Tourkokivouro. Profiles only are provided here, since photographs have already been published by Choremis (1973). His number = Kalamata Museum accession.

Open Shapes

P1578. Skyphos or deep bowl. Fig. 3-11.

Choremis no. 724, Pl. 19ε. H. 0.10. Th. 0.004-0.005. D. rim 0.145. D. base 0.05.

Munsell 5YR 7/8 reddish yellow. Undecorated zone in field between handles; above and below, streaky black coating; same coating on interior. 3 incisions on underside of base. Rim: Type A1; Base: Type A.

P1579. Skyphos or deep bowl.

Choremis no. 723, Pl. 18ς. H. 0.068. D. 0.104.

Similar in shape and decoration to **P1578**.

From the vicinity of Tsagdis nos. 1 and 2 in the area of Tourkokivouro.

Closed Shapes

P1580. Small oinochoe. Fig. 3-14.

Choremis no. 97, Pl. 38δ. H. 0.096. D. rim 0.05. D. base 0.036. W. handle 0.009.

Munsell 10YR 8/4 very pale brown to 10YR 7/2 light gray. Conical belly. Reserved band just above middle belly; above and below, monochrome black coating. Black paint on inner rim. Base: Type A; Handle: Type B1.

P1581. Belly-handled amphora. Fig. 3-15.

Choremis no. 158, Pl. 38ε. H. 0.405. D. rim 0.15. D. base 0.13. D. handle 0.02.

⅓ of rim and right handle restored. Munsell 5YR 7/8 reddish yellow. Monochrome black coating on neck; reserved band on shoulder; streaky black coating on upper and lower belly. At middle belly in field between handles, black band between 2 wavy lines. Handle: Type A.

DARK AGE II

From the DA tholos in the area of Lakkoules.

From Burial A:

Open Shapes

P1582. Skyphos or deep bowl. Fig. 3-29.

Choremis no. 622, Pl. 35γ. Missing base. H. (pres.) 0.165. D. rim 0.155. D. base ca. 0.065(?)

Munsell 5YR 7/8 reddish yellow. Paint varies from black on shoulder and upper belly to reddish brown on lower belly. Decoration of 2 wavy lines in handle zone; above and below, monochrome coating. Monochrome black-brown coating on interior; reserved band inner rim. Rim: Type B3; Base: Type C(?)

P1583. Skyphos. Fig. 3-23.

Choremis no. 624, Pl. 36γ. H. 0.114. D. rim 0.09. D. base 0.056. D. handle 0.01.

Reddish yellow clay; black paint. Metope-triglyph decoration on shoulder; 5 vertical lines for triglyph; metope left undecorated. Above and below, monochrome coating. Same coating on interior; reserved bands at inner rim and base of foot. Conical belly. Rim: Type B2; Base: Type A2.

From Burial B:

Open Shapes

P1584. Skyphos or deep bowl. Fig. 3-28.

Choremis no. 623, Pl. 35ξ. H. 0.144. D. rim 0.16. D. base 0.076.

Reddish yellow clay; streaky black paint. Decoration of 2 wavy lines in handle zone; above and below, monochrome coating. Monochrome black coating on interior. Rim: Type B3; Base: Type C.

P1585. Small skyphos. Fig. 3-23.

Choremis no. 626, Pl. 35δ. H. 0.076. D. rim 0.083. D. base 0.045.

Reddish yellow clay; streaky black-brown paint. Uneven reserved band in handle zone; above and below, monochrome coating. Monochrome black coating on interior. Rim: Type B3; Base: Type C.

Closed Shapes

P1586. Oinochoe. Fig. 3-36.

Choremis no. 618, Pl. 34α, β. H. 0.234. D. rim 0.09. D. base 0.086. D. handle 0.019.

Munsell 5YR 7/8 reddish yellow to 10YR 8/4 very pale brown. Good metallic blue-black paint on neck; faded to a washy black on belly. Monochrome coating on neck and inner rim; decoration of compass-drawn accumbent concentric semi-circles (5 sets in all) alternating with vertical wavy lines (6) and cross-hatching on shoulder. 1 thick and 6 thin uneven black bands on belly; monochrome coating below on lower belly and base. Rope handles; 3 pairs of mending holes around central trefoil lip. Rim: Type B; Handle: Type A5; Base: Type C.

P1587. Small oinochoe. Fig. 3-39.

Choremis no. 620, Pl. 34δ. H. 0.105. D. rim 0.04. D. base 0.04.

Reddish yellow clay; streaky black-brown paint, now faded to brown except on lower belly and base. 3 bands on neck; black coating on inner rim. Compass-drawn accumbent semi-circles on shoulder.

From Burial Γ:

Closed Shapes

P1588. Oinochoe. Fig. 3-38.

Choremis no. 617, Pl. 34γ. H. 0.225. D. rim 0.075. D. base 0.08. W. handle 0.021.

Reddish yellow clay; black-brown paint. 3 bands at top of neck and 2 at bottom; center of neck left undecorated; black coating on inner rim. Hand-drawn accumbent semi-circles on shoulder; below on belly and base, monochrome black coating. Rim: Type A1; Handle: Type A1; Base: Type C.

From Burial Δ:

Open Shapes

P1589. Small skyphos. Fig. 3-23.

Choremis no. 625, Pl. 36α. H. 0.078. D. rim 0.08. D. base 0.044.

Reddish yellow clay. Good streaky black paint. Reserved band in handle zone; drip mark in center of band on one side; above and below, monochrome coating. Same coating on interior; reserved band at inner rim and base of foot. Rim: Type B2; Base: Type C.

Coarse Ware

P1590. Coarse oinochoe. Fig. 3-41.

Choremis no. 621, Pl. 35β. H. 0.143. D. rim 0.065. D. base 0.055.

Munsell 2.5YR 6/8 light red to 5YR 7/8 reddish yellow. Coarse clay with inclusions. Possible slip.

Between Burials Γ and Δ:

Closed Shapes

P1591. Small oinochoe. Fig. 3-39.

Choremis no. 619, Pl. 35α. H. 0.114. D. rim 0.045. D. base 0.05.

Handle restored. Munsell 10YR 7/4 very pale brown to 5YR 7/6 reddish yellow. Black-brown paint. Monochrome coating on neck and lower belly; hatched triangles on shoulder and upper belly. Possible black coating on upper portion of inner neck and rim, but very worn. Rim: Type A2; Base: Type C.

LATE GEOMETRIC

From the Vathirema chamber tomb.

Open Shapes

P1592. Skyphos. Fig. 3-67; Pls. 3-166, 3-167.

Kalamata Museum no. 308. H. 0.073. D. rim 0.134. D. base 0.093.

Flat base. Munsell 5YR 7/8 reddish yellow. Black-brown and white paint. On neck, angular zigzag in white with 3 thin bands above and below; decoration of linked lozenges with central dots in field between handles; below, on lower belly, thick and thin black bands. Monochrome black-brown coating on interior; reserved band on inner rim. On underside of base, 6 concentric circles with central dot, faded to a brown color.

P1593. Skyphos. Fig. 3-67; Pl. 3-168.

Kalamata 309. H. 0.10. D. rim 0.10. D. base 0.07.

Munsell 2.5Y 8/2 white to 10YR 8/4 very pale brown. Black paint. Decoration of linked lozenges (drawn by 5-stroke brush) framed above and below by 2 thin bands in field between handles. Monochrome coating on exterior with reserved bands at rim and lower belly. Monochrome coating on interior; reserved band on inner rim. Carination at point where handle joins body.

P1594. Kotyle. Fig. 3-67; Pl. 3-165.

Kalamata 311. Imitation of Corinthian hemispherical kotyle. Munsell 2.5Y 8/2 white to 10YR 8/4 very pale brown. 3/4 of one side restored. Monochrome black coating on exterior and interior.

P1595. Deep lakaina-like skyphos. Fig. 3-67; Pls. 3-169, 3-170.

Kalamata 317. H. 0.108. D. rim 0.10. D. base 0.06.

Munsell 5YR 7/8 reddish yellow. Black paint. Below rim, decoration of linked lozenges with central dots, framed above and below by 2 thin bands. Main panel of decoration on shoulder and belly; hatched meander pattern with crosshatched lozenges below; to left by handle, piled short wavy lines in shape of "M" flanked by 3 vertical bands in metope-triglyph motif. In semi-circles formed by handles at side of vase are water birds (1 each side) with half-lozenges and circles of dots above. Thin and thick bands on lower belly and base. Monochrome coating on interior; reserved band on inner rim.

P1596. Cup. Fig. 3-67; Pl. 3-171.

Kalamata 310. H. 0.093. D. rim 0.10. D. base 0.055. W. handle 0.016.

Munsell 2.5YR 6/8 light red to 5YR 7/8 reddish yellow. Paint varies from black to dark brown. Monochrome coating on exterior and interior; reserved bands on exterior at rim and on inner rim.

P1597. Pyxis lid. Pls. 3-163, 3-164.

Kalamata 316. D. 0.36. H. lid 0.17. H. with horses 0.30.

Munsell 10YR 8/4 very pale brown to 5YR 7/8 reddish yellow. Dark brown paint with blackish tinge in places. On outer edge of top are alternating zones of vertical stripes, bands, and linked lozenges. 4 horses in center, 2 preserved, 2 missing.

STRAY FINDS

DARK AGE I

From the area of Lakkoules in the field of Christos Lambropoulos near the DA tholos. Found in the area of the 4 apsidal cists to the west of the DA tholos and perhaps from them (see Chapter 4, pp. 268-270).

P1598. Belly-handled amphoriskos. Fig. 3-14.

Choremis no. 102, Pl. 37β. H. 0.153. D. rim 0.105. D. base 0.055.

Munsell 2.5Y 8/2 white. Black-brown paint. Decoration of wavy line in handle zone; above and below, monochrome black coating. Black coating also on inner rim and neck.

P1599. Ribbed kylix stem. Fig. 3-5.

H. 0.053. D. stem 0.013. D. ribs 0.017-0.019.

Broken at foot. Munsell 2.5Y 8/2 white to 10YR 8/4 very pale brown. Black coating. Type D2 (cf. **P318**).

DARK AGE II

From the area of Lakkoules in the field of Christos Lambropoulos near the Dark Age tholos. Found in the area of the 4 apsidal cists to the W. of the DA tholos and perhaps from them. (see Chapter 4, pp. 268-270).

Open Shapes

P1600. 2 skyphos rims.
Type A1 (cf. **P341**).

P1601. 2 skyphos rims.
Type A2 (cf. **P762**).

P1602. 2 skyphos bases.
Type C (cf. **P402-3**).

P1603. Flat base of cup.
D. 0.045m. (cf. **P848**).

Closed Shapes

P1604. Small oinochoe. Fig. 3-39.

Choremis no. 99, Pl. 37*a*. H. 0.135. D. rim 0.058. D. base 0.052.

Handle restored. Munsell 10YR 8/4 very pale brown to 5YR 7/8 reddish yellow. Brown-black paint. Monochrome coating on neck and belly; compass-drawn accumbent semi-circles on shoulder and upper belly; black band below semi-circles. Black band at inner rim. Rim: Type D; Base: Type C.

P1605. Small oinochoe. Fig. 3-39.

Choremis no. 105, Pl. 37*a*. H. 0.138. D. rim 0.06. D. base 0.052. W. handle 0.016.

Munsell 10YR 6/1 light gray to 5YR 7/8 reddish yellow. Streaky black-brown coating on neck and belly; compass-drawn accumbent semi-circles on shoulder and upper belly. Rim: Type D; Handle: Type A6; Base: Type C.

P1606. Belly-handled amphora. Fig. 3-40.

Choremis no. 104, Pl. 36*θ*. Portion of rim, base, and right handle restored. H. 0.20. D. rim 0.12. D. base 0.132.

Munsell 10YR 8/4 very pale brown to 5YR 7/8 reddish yellow. Monochrome black coating on neck and belly; metope-triglyph motif on shoulder and upper belly (in handle zone); vertical cross-hatching for triglyph with crosshatched triangle in metope. Black band at inner rim.

Coarse Ware

P1607. 2 pithos body frags.

Reddish yellow to light red clay. One frag. has raised band with row of incised circles (cf. **P903**); other frag. has raised band decorated with row of finger impressions (cf. **P838**).

From the area of Tourkokivouro in the field of Anastasios Tsagdis near the two DAI apsidal cists.

Open Shapes

P1608. Skyphos base.
Type A1 (cf. **P389**).

P1609. Skyphos handle.
Type A (D. 0.011).

From the area of Trypetorachi to the SE of the Nichoria ridge in the field of Panayiotis Kanellopoulos. Good DAII sherds were found here, including some 25 monochrome coated body sherds and handle frags. not listed below.

Open Shapes

P1610. Skyphos rim.
Type A1 (cf. **P341**).

P1611. 2 skyphos rims.
Type A2 (cf. **P762**).

P1612. Decorated skyphos body and handle frag.

Reddish yellow clay; black paint. Handle stump to left with adjacent frags. of arcs of concentric semi-circles; monochrome black coating below on belly and on interior.

P1613. 5 decorated skyphos body frags.

Munsell 10YR 8/4 very pale brown to 5YR 7/8 reddish yellow. Black paint. Arcs of adjacent sets of compass-drawn accumbent semi-circles; frags. of streaky black coating above, below, and on interior.

P1614. Decorated skyphos body and handle frag. Pl. 3-55.

H. (pres.) 0.065. Th. 0.005. D. handle ca. 0.013 (uneven).

Munsell 5YR 7/6 reddish yellow. Streaky black paint. To left, handle frag. with adjacent frag. of concentric semi-circle with central spiral. Monochrome coating below and on interior. Handle: Type A.

P1615. Decorated skyphos body frag. Pl. 3-56.

H. (pres.) 0.05.

Same Munsell as **P1614**. Ends of arcs of concentric semi-circles with central spiral; black coating below and on interior.

P1616. Decorated skyphos body frag.

H. (pres.) 0.027. Th. 0.0045-0.005.

Munsell 5YR 7/6 reddish yellow. Ends of arcs of concentric semi-circles with large central dot; streaky black-brown coating below and on interior.

P1617. Decorated wall frag. of krater. Pl. 3-73.

H. (pres.) 0.067. Th. 0.006.

Munsell 7.5YR 7/4 pink. Streaky black paint. Possible metope-triglyph motif with cross-hatching flanked by 3 vertical lines forming triglyph. To right, diagonal band outlining junction between handle and body; streaky black coating on interior.

P1618. Decorated wall frag. of krater.

Fabric and decoration similar to **P1617**, but with 2 black bands and frag. of zigzag below triglyph; frag. of handle lining to left.

P1619. Skyphos base.
Type B (cf. **P400**).

P1620. Skyphos base.
Type C (cf. **P402**).

Closed Shapes

P1621. Rim and neck frag. of oinochoe.

H. (pres.) 0.07. Th. 0.004-0.005.

Munsell 5YR 7/6 reddish yellow to 7.5YR 7/4 pink. Monochrome black coating on exterior and on top half of neck on interior. Rim: Type A1.

DARK AGE III

From the area of Lakkoules in the field of Christos Lambropoulos. Here were found some 200 monochrome black-coated body sherds and handle frags. with DAIII characteristics. Some diagnostic pieces are listed below.

Open Shapes

P1622. 2 skyphos rim and body frags.
Type C2 (cf. **P1545**).

P1623. Skyphos rim and body frag.
Type C3 (cf. **P1170**).

P1624. Flat base of cup.

D. ca. 0.055.

Reddish yellow clay. Frags. of black paint exterior.

Closed Shapes

P1625. Base of oinochoe.

D. 0.055.

Reddish yellow clay. Frags. of black paint preserved. Oinochoe base: Type C (cf. **P1218**).

LATE GEOMETRIC

From the field of Georgios Papamichroulis at the village of Rizomilo.

Open Shapes

P1626. Decorated body sherd, perhaps from skyphos or kantharos. Pl. 3-172.

H. (pres.) 0.034.

Reddish yellow clay. Faded black-brown paint. Decoration of linked lozenges with 3 bands below.

4

The Burials

by

William D. E. Coulson

with contributions by Sara C. Bisel, William P. Donovan, and William Wade

The MME permit specifically prohibited any excavation in the cemetery areas surrounding the ridge. The Mycenaean burials in the tholos tomb and the contiguous Little Circle on the lowest NW slope (Area I) and a few scattered LH graves elsewhere on the ridge will be fully discussed in *Nichoria* II. Here we describe in detail the Late Geometric pithos grave (Nichoria Burial 1-1), which is the only certain DA grave discovered on the ridge itself. Donovan was the excavator and Bisel and Wade examined the relatively well-preserved skeleton from their somewhat different perspectives. Here, too, with the kind permission of the Greek authorities, Coulson reviews all of the known evidence resulting from salvage and scheduled excavation of DA burials in the immediate environs. Most of these graves are loosely grouped in what was obviously a large cemetery lying to NW of the Nichoria ridge.

Bisel was asked to summarize for this series pertinent sections of her doctoral dissertation on human bone mineral and nutrition. We regret the necessary fragmentation of her report. The introduction, description of methodology, and her analysis of Nichoria Burial 1-1 appear in this chapter. The "References" for both her text and Wade's appear at the end of this chapter only and are not repeated with their discussion of later burials in Chapter 11.

The Late Geometric Pithos Burial (Fig. 1-1)

During the 1969 season the position of most of the trial trenches was determined after studying the results obtained from geophysical exploration (*MME* 1972, pp. 236-39). The North Veves field slopes up from the modern path toward the NE edge of the ridge, where one has a superb view toward the head of the gulf (Pl. 4-1). No traces of broken pottery or building stones were visible on the surface here, although such traces were plentiful in the lower (SE) part of the same field. Nevertheless, geophysical tests were extended over the entire area. Magnetometer readings were quite uniform over most of the upper part of the field, but in two spots, side by side, there were indications of markedly increased magnetic disturbance (Rapp 1970, p. 62 and Fig. 4). These two anomalies were then checked by the use of the electrical resistivity meter which also indicated the presence below the surface of a rather solid barrier.

Since one of the two spots, thus discovered, lay under an olive tree and its excavation would have violated a pledge not to harm crops, it was decided to open a trench to test only one of the anomalies. Excavation of this test trench (L24-III) was begun in an area that measured 2.50 by 2.30 m (later extended to 3.70 m). Between 0.20 and 0.30 m below the surface stones were first encountered. It soon became clear that these stones formed a cairn which had been constructed over a pithos lying on its side with mouth to the S (for similar arrangements see Snodgrass 1971, pp. 155-72, especially pp. 171, 172). It was the stone cairn and the terra-cotta pithos that were responsible for the anomalies during the geophysical survey (Fig. 4-1).

The cairn was constructed of irregular blocks of limestone, identical in appearance to others found throughout the site and obviously used as building material. These were probably reused, but all such blocks on the ridgetop probably derive from limestone outcrops just NW of the ridge. The stones were not piled up haphazardly, but show clear evidence of rough courses toward the top (three were preserved). The shape of the cairn was apsidal, with the apse to the S. Its maximum length (NS) was 3.00 m

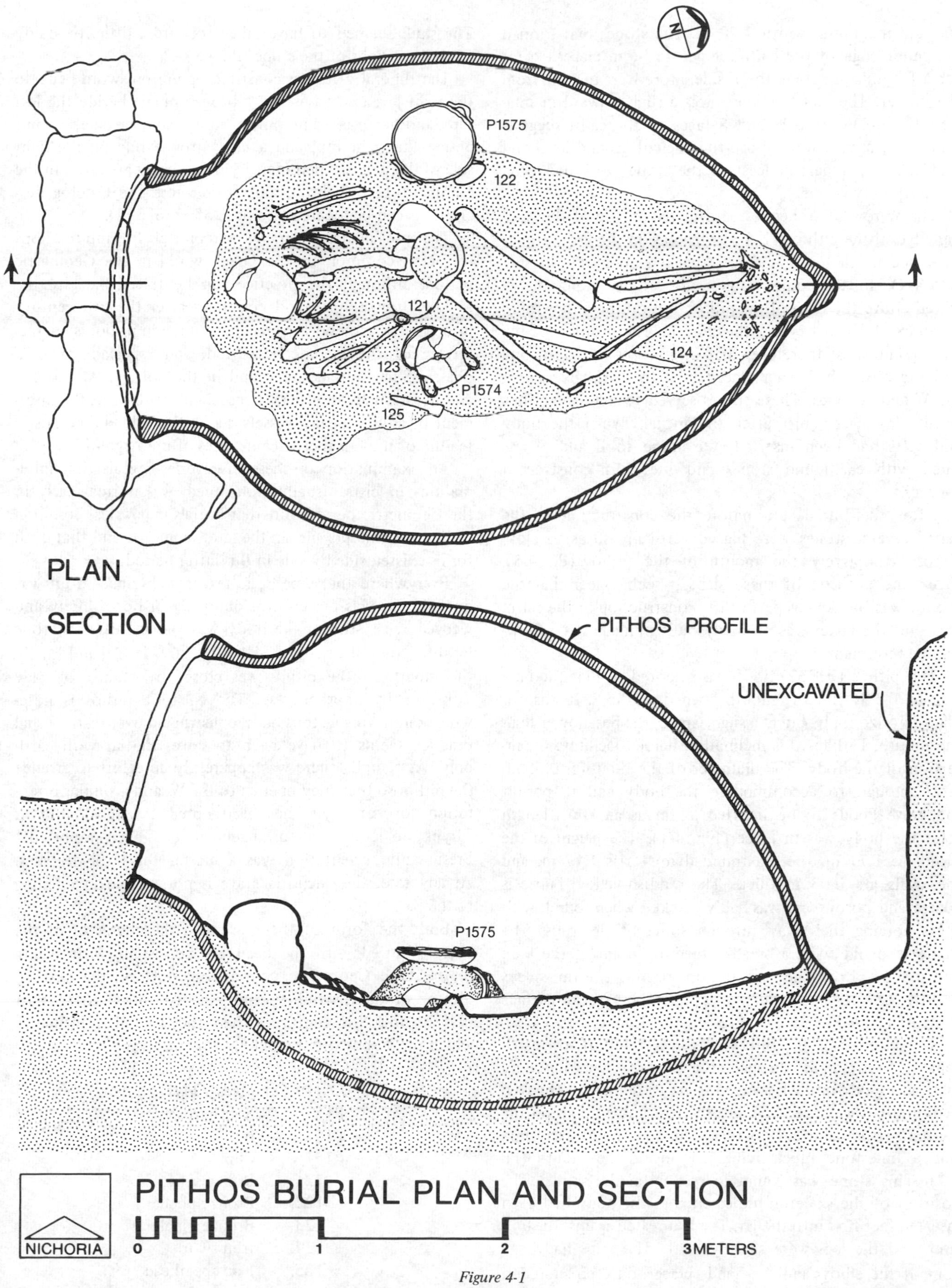

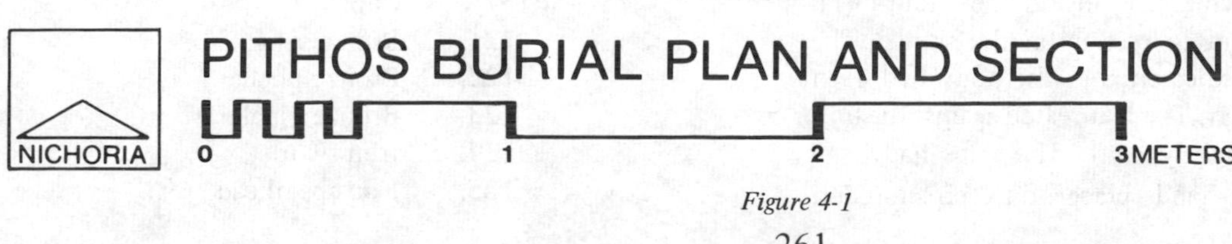
P1575
122
121
123
P1574
125
124
PLAN
SECTION
PITHOS PROFILE
UNEXCAVATED
P1575
NICHORIA
PITHOS BURIAL PLAN AND SECTION
0
1
2
3METERS

Figure 4-1

and the maximum width 1.70 m. The stones that formed the outer edge of the cairn seemed to be in place, except for a few missing along the E side. More were missing from the center. The fact that there was a slight inward inclination (Pl. 4-2) of the W and S faces of the cairn suggests that these stones were above the ancient ground level and that the upper part at least of the stone work had been left purposely visible.

The W row of stones rested directly on top of the sloping edge of the pithos (Pl. 4-3), whereas on the E the stones extended much lower and were packed up against its side (Pl. 4-4). In the same fashion, the stones along the N rested above the base of the pithos, but on the S the stones extended 1.10 m beyond the mouth. The position of the stones indicates, therefore, that a large pit had been dug and the pithos had been placed in it to fit snugly against the W and N edges. These stones served to hold the pithos firmly in place until after the burial. When the body and gifts had been inserted, the space to E and S was filled with earth and stones and the cairn constructed over all.[1]

After the burial, but before the construction of the cairn, several stones were placed vertically so as to close almost completely the mouth of the pithos (Pl. 4-5). From the position of these slabs it seems clear that the mouth was blocked as part of the construction of the cairn, and thus the latter was probably built immediately following the interment.

The pithos (**P1557**) itself was oriented so that the base was to the N and the mouth opened to the S. It was not placed horizontally, but at a slight angle, the base lower than the mouth. Perhaps this inclination helped facilitate the insertion of the body. The diameter of the mouth is 0.65 m, large enough to accommodate the body and to permit the grave goods to be inserted as far as an arm's length after the body was in place (Fig. 4-1). The height of the pithos is 1.71 m, the maximum diameter is 1.17 m, and the walls are 0.03 m thick. The reddish-yellow fabric is coarse and porous and was badly cracked when found, with roots forcing their way through some of the gaps. The shape is ovoid with a small projecting point at the base and a short, broad neck at the upper end. The rim splays slightly, and its upper surface is flat. The exterior surface is plain[2] (Pl. 4-5).

The interior of the pithos was nearly full of soft earth that had sifted in through the cracks. The only safe method of excavating it seemed to be to remove the broken sections of the upper side and then to come down on the contents from above (Pl. 4-6). The first item discovered was a limestone block lying just inside the mouth (Pl. 4-7). This stone was found to rest upon the skull.[3] The position of the skeleton indicated that the body had been inserted feet first into the jar. The feet rested against the bottom, and the legs were slightly bent. The arms had been bent at the elbow and the hands placed on each shoulder. The skull seemed to have fallen forward a little, probably from the weight of the stone (Pl. 4-8).

The funeral offerings consisted of an iron sword beneath the right leg, two vases and a bronze phiale beside the left hip, another vase and phiale above an iron spear point beside the right hip, and a large bronze ring on the right side of the pelvis. Their identifying numbers are given in the Summary List (below), and from these the Catalog descriptions can be located (see pp. 255, 256, 312).

The use of large jars as sarcophagi for inhumations was very common in the Greek world in the Geometric period, although the practice can be traced back to the Middle Bronze Age[4] and continues after the 8th century into Archaic times.[5] Nevertheless, burial in pithoi is characteristic of the Geometric period, and especially its late phases. Such burials are found in the north in Macedonia and occasionally in central Greece and Attica, but the interment of adults in such vessels is a particularly characteristic feature of the Geometric cemeteries of the Argolid.[6]

An examination of these discoveries reveals that inhumations in cists, usually stone-lined, was normal early in the Geometric period, but that burials in jars, less common earlier, became popular in the late Geometric and that both forms existed side by side in this latter period.

Everywhere the same basic features obtained: a pit was dug; the jar was placed in it obliquely or horizontally and wedged with stones; the body was slid in feet first (one head-first burial at Argos, *AAA* 2, 1969, Pl. 2); and finally the mouth of the pithos was closed by stones, by clay disks, or by another vase. The Nichoria pithos is noteworthy in having a stone cairn constructed over it; the usual practice seems to have been to cover the jar with earth only. At Nauplia there was apparently an effort to arrange the pithoi so that they opened to the W, and a similar orientation for some jars has been noted at Argos;[7] but at Tiryns no consistent arrangement has been reported.[8] Presumably, orientation was a matter for local decision. At any rate, the Nichoria grave is not unique in opening to the S.

Both the form of the grave and the character of the objects buried with the dead are consistent with a date in the Late Geometric period. The pottery, the best indicator of date, would permit an attribution to the last half of the 8th century, when the Laconian influence which the vases exhibit would not be surprising.

W.P.D.

List of Cataloged Finds

P1574.	Kantharos
P1575.	Bowl
P1576.	Cup
121.	Bronze ring
122.	Bronze phiale
123.	Bronze phiale
124.	Iron sword
125.	Iron spearhead

Analysis of Skeletal Material

NICHORIA BURIAL 1-1 (PITHOS BURIAL)

Provenience: Trial trench L24-III.
Chronology: Late Geometric (745-725 B.C.).
Sex: Male.
Age: Young adult (21-35 years).
Condition: The skeleton is represented by a cranium in fair condition, lacking the basilar area, the right side of the upper face, and much of the lower cranial vault on the right side (Pls. 4-9 to 4-12). The nasal and interior orbital areas are also missing, as well as the area surrounding the left pterion (Pl. 4-9). The dentition, well preserved, is complete except for the left lateral maxillary incisor, lost some time after death.

The postcranial skeleton is represented by the major long bones in fair condition with broken or eroded epiphyses; the left clavicle; fragments of the scapulae and innominates; fragmentary lower thoracic and lumbar vertebrae; a few fragmentary ribs; and most of the bones of the hands and feet, in poor to fair condition.

Observations: The skull (Pls. 4-10 to 4-12) is dolichocranic (cranial index = 72.2), with a broad forehead (fronto-parietal index = 70.7), and a wide jaw (fronto-gonial index = 104.0) with a low, broad ramus (ramus index = 58.9). In spite of strong gonial eversion and heavy muscle attachments in the mandible (Pl. 4-13), the cranium is not particularly robust for a male.

The stature is estimated to have been 1774 mm., on the basis of the left femur length according to the regression estimates of Trotter and Gleser (1958). The left clavicle is fairly thick (index of robustness = 26.5), but medium in lateral breadth (index = 15.6). The glenoid fossae of the scapulae are piriform in shape, but relatively narrow (glenoid index = 71.1, left side; 71.8, right side). The left humerus is slightly platybrachic (index = 76.2), although the right humerus (79.2) and the mean of the two (77.8) are eurybrachic. The relationship of the mid-diaphyseal circumference to the bicondylar length of the femur yields an index of 19.2 (left side). A similar relationship between the sum of the antero-posterior and medio-lateral mid-diaphyseal diameters and the bicondylar length of the femur is expressed as an index with the value 12.1. The lineae asperae of the femora have the form of a medium pilaster (index = 114.8, left side; 110.7, right side). Both femora are platymeric (index = 81.8, both sides). The left tibia is mesocnemic (index = 65.8), whereas the right tibia is mildly platycnemic (62.5). The right tibia is fairly slender (index of robustness = 19.7).

The only observable pathologies are relatively minor dental problems (Pl. 4-13). Of the 31 fully erupted teeth present, carious lesions were present only on the left maxillary first and third molars. Dental attrition is not particularly severe, consisting of enamel wear with partial dentine exposure in the earliest erupted teeth, except for the mandibular incisors, in which exposure of the dentine is complete.

Summary: This was a young adult male, probably about 25 to 30 years of age. He was fairly tall, even somewhat above the average stature of modern European males, and of medium build, with few really robust features. There is no evidence suggestive of a possible cause of death or of serious illness. The teeth are generally sound, with indications that they were subjected to moderately heavy use.

Table 4-1. Metric Data on Nichoria Burial 1-1

Measurement		
Cranial length	194 mm	
Cranial breadth	140 mm	
Minimal frontal diameter	99 mm	
Maximum circumference	538 mm	
Auricular height	114 mm	
Frontal arc	141 mm	
Parietal arc	126 mm	
Occipital arc	112 mm	
Frontal chord	121 mm	
Parietal chord	114 mm	
Occipital chord	97 mm	
Mandibular length	(100) mm	
Bigonial breadth	103 mm	
L. ramus height	56 mm	
L. ramus minimum breadth	33 mm	
L. ramus coronoid height	57 mm	
Symphyseal height	31 mm	
Inter-foraminal breadth	44 mm	
Humerus A-P mid-shaft diameter	16 mm	19 mm
Humerus M-L mid-shaft diameter	21 mm	24 mm
Humerus minimum shaft circumference	62 mm	69 mm
Radius maximum head diameter	. . .	23 mm
Radius minimum shaft circumference	39 mm	42 mm
Ulna minimum shaft circumference	38 mm	38 mm
Femur length	482 mm	. . .
Femur bicondylar length	480 mm	. . .
Femur A-P sub-trochanteric diameter	27 mm	27 mm
Femur M-L sub-trochanteric diameter	33 mm	33 mm
Femur A-P mid-shaft diameter	31 mm	31 mm
Femur M-L mid-shaft diameter	27 mm	28 mm
Femur mid-shaft circumference	91 mm	91 mm
Femur maximum head diameter	48 mm	. . .
Tibia length	. . .	411 mm
Tibia nutrient foramen A-P diameter	38 mm	40 mm
Tibia nutrient foramen M-L diameter	25 mm	25 mm
Tibia minimum shaft circumference	82 mm	81 mm
Clavicle length	(147) mm	. . .
Clavicle lateral breadth	(23) mm	. . .
Clavicle medial breadth	21 mm	. . .
Clavicle mid-shaft circumference	39 mm	. . .
Scapula glenoid height	38 mm	39 mm
Scapula glenoid breadth	27 mm	28 mm

NICHORIA BURIAL 6-1

Provenience: Grid J25 Jb (outside MME area; salvaged at ephor's request).
Chronological Note: Geometric?

Sex: Female.
Age: Young adult (21-35 years).
Condition: The cranium is represented merely by a badly eroded occipito-parietal region and a fragment of the right mandibular body, including the alveoli of the canine, premolar, and molar teeth. Only the molars were recovered, the other teeth probably being lost after death.

The post-cranial skeleton includes fragments, mostly very small and in no better than fair condition, of the major long bones; the lower cervical, thoracic, and upper lumbar vertebrae; ribs; the bones of the shoulder girdle; and the left innominate.

Observations: Very few observations are possible, other than the reliable estimate of sex based on pelvic morphology. It is also quite likely that this was a very young adult, probably between 20 and 25 years, as indicated by the relatively light occlusal enamel wear in the molars.

The diaphyseal index of the right humerus is 76.2, barely within the range of platybrachia. In the left femur, the platymeric index is an extreme 71.0, and the pilastric index, 108.3, is indicative of a moderately weak pilaster.

The only pathologies noted are occlusal caries in the first and third molars and a single carious lesion on the buccal surface of the second molar.

Summary: This was a young adult female whose remains are quite poorly preserved. Of three teeth recovered, all contained at least one carious lesion and were not severely worn.

W.W.

Table 4-2. Metric Data on Nichoria Burial 6-1

Parietal arc	121 mm	
Occipital arc	113 mm	
Parietal chord	106 mm	
Occipital chord	95 mm	
Humerus A-P mid-shaft diameter	. . .	16 mm
Humerus M-L mid-shaft diameter	. . .	21 mm
Ulna trochlear notch height	23 mm	. . .
Femur A-P sub-trochanteric diameter	22 mm	. . .
Femur M-L sub-trochanteric diameter	31 mm	. . .
Femur A-P mid-shaft diameter	26 mm	. . .
Femur M-L mid-shaft diameter	24 mm	. . .
Femur mid-shaft circumference	77 mm	. . .
Clavicle mid-shaft circumference	34 mm	34 mm

Human Bone Mineral and Nutrition

INTRODUCTION

The writer studied the Nichoria skeletal material in the fall of 1978 at the Benaki Museum in Kalamata.[9] The data obtained on morphology, gross appearance, and pathologies[10] were used to compare with data obtained in the mineral analysis of bone samples. The latter investigations were conducted at the Trace Metals Laboratory of the Mayo Clinic, Rochester, Minnesota.[11] Soil and water were also studied; these investigations will be reported in *Nichoria* II. All data were submitted to statistical analysis.[12]

A number of parameters can be used to assess nutritional status in skeletal populations. More reliable conclusions result from considerations of as many of the phenomena as are available to study.[13] The Nichoria skeletons, almost without exception, are fragmentary, eliminating much data on morphology and pathology which are usually available in skeletal populations and causing the bone mineral data to assume a greater relative importance in the analysis. With skeletal remains of only a few post-Mycenaean individuals, and these from different periods, few reliable trends can be noted; but perhaps remarks about each individual will be informative.

METHODOLOGY

Anthropological methods used in field study to indicate state of nutrition include estimation of stature (Trotter and Gleser 1958), pelvic brim index (Greulich and Thoms 1938; Nicholson 1945; Angel 1976), and indices of shafts and tibiae and femora (Adams 1969). Longevity as determined by epiphyseal closure (McKern and Stewart 1957), tooth eruption (Schour and Poncher 1940), change in the face of public symphyses (Todd 1920, 1921; McKern and Stewart 1957), general appearance of bones, skull suture closure (Todd and Lyon 1924) reflects nutrition among other factors. Dental health also has a nutritional factor. Dental lesions and enamel hypoplasia (Mellanby 1934) were observed and noted. Other conditions having at least a slight nutritional input include anemia (Angel 1966), arthritis, inflammation, and infections. Several additional conditions having a nutritional factor were not studied because of technical difficulties. These include cortical thickness and lines of growth arrest in long bones as determined by x-ray (Garn et al. 1964; Wells 1967).

Minerals studied up to this point are calcium, phosphorus, strontium, zinc, and magnesium in human bone, with animal bone as controls. Some data for modern Americans were available for comparison (Janes et al. 1975 for Ca, Zn, Mg; Zipkin 1970 for P). Strontium has been studied in several archaeological populations (Brown 1973; Schoeninger 1979). In order to overcome problems of differential leaching at different sites, elements are reported both as absolute values and as ratios with calcium. Strontium is also reported as a ratio of human Sr/Ca with the site-specific sheep-goat Sr/Ca, in order to be able to compare human values of an element dependent on the ecosystem at specific sites. Analysis of bone and soil was done by atomic absorption spectroscopy

Table 4-3. Specifications for Atomic Absorption Spectroscopy of Bone Mineral

Element	Total Dilution	Wavelength
Ca	1-75,000	422.6
Sr	1-150	460.7
Mg	1-1,500 and 1-7,500	285.2
Zn	1-150	213.8

(Fiske and Subbarow 1925; Perkin-Elmer Corp. 1971). Methods of analysis for the soil will be discussed in *Nichoria* II. Bone samples, mostly from tibial crest, were cleaned mechanically of surface dirt. Each sample, approximately 500 mg, was weighed to 10^{-4} g and dissolved in 3 ml concentrated HCl. For the determination of calcium, strontium, magnesium, and zinc, further dilutions for each mineral were made with distilled water as noted below. Each was analyzed with a 303 Perkin-Elmer atomic absorption spectrophotometer, using wavelengths noted below and an air-acetylene flame (Perkin-Elmer Corporation, 1971, Mayo Clinic adaptation). Values were then calculated as mg/g of calcium and magnesium and as ug/g of strontium and zinc.

For the determination of phosphorus in bone, the samples previously dissolved in concentrated HCl were further diluted 1-1000 in distilled water. Two ml each of the standard phosphorus reagents amino-naphthol-sulphonic acid and ammonium molybdate were added to 1 ml of dilute sample (Fiske and Subbarow, 1925). Values were read at 630 on a Perkin-Elmer Hitachi 200 spectrophotometer and calculated as mg/g.

NICHORIA BURIAL 1-1 (PITHOS BURIAL)

This is a male in his late twenties. At 179.4 cm, he was fairly well nourished and tall for his period. His long bone shafts were slightly flattened (average platymeric index = 81.2, average cnemic index = 62.3), indicating fairly heavy exercise together with slightly suboptimal nutrition. His generally excellent teeth (one antemortem loss and one caries in 32 alveolae present) show a slight degree of enamel hypoplasia on molars and canines, reflecting periods of suboptimal nutrition or severe illness in early childhood during the period of tooth development. A slight degree of alveolar resorption indicates some periodontal problems in adult life.

In the mineral analysis, calcium and phosphorus values are those to be expected in archaeological material. The collagen portion of the bone has disappeared, leaving relatively higher calcium and phosphorus values. The strontium value is low in this individual, indicating his reliance on terrestrial animal protein. Strontium in bone depends on the animal's position in the food chain, herbivores having a much higher value than carnivores (Brown 1973; Schoeninger 1979). Humans can be evaluated for their relative use of animal or vegetable protein by comparison with animal bone from the same soil system. This individual's magnesium value is low, as are all the others from Nichoria. These low values can be explained by the very low magnesium level of Nichorian soil. This aspect will be discussed more fully in *Nichoria* II.

All the above morphological data and mineral values are about what would be predicted for a rather well-off male of his period; but his zinc value presents a problem of interpretation. It is quite low, both in comparison with other ancient inhabitants of Nichoria and Athens and with modern Americans. Most archaeological individuals with low zinc have been female, reflecting the extra stress of childbearing. But what was the extra stress for this young man? Chronic debilitating illness or chronic alcoholism are possibilities. In addition, other culture factors, such as the use of unleavened bread and unrefined cereals, may play a part. These two foodstuffs decrease absorption of zinc by binding it in the gut (Brewer and Prasad 1977; Prasad 1978).

S.B.

The Nichoria Environs (Fig. 4-2)

This chapter, for the sake of completeness, contains a brief review of the DA tombs in the immediate environs of the Nichoria ridge. These graves have an important bearing on the MME results, since they obviously constitute a cemetery belonging to the DA settlement on the ridge. The pot-

Table 4-4. Bone Mineral in Nichoria Burial 1-1 Compared with Ancient Athens and U.S. Modern

	Sex	Ca (mg)	P (mg)	Sr (mg)	Sr/Ca	Site Corrected Sr/Ca	Mg (mg)	Mg/Ca	Zn (ug)	Zn/Ca
Nichoria Burial 1-1	♂	269.6	137.4	53.3	.198	.504	.47	.0017	80.0	.297
Athens av. N=7	♂	313.7	155.0	102.8	.333	.548	1.81	.0058	160.8	.513
U. S. Mod. N=40		220.4	102.5	. . .	. . .	. . .	2.81	.0127	147.1	.671

tery has been discussed in detail in Chapter 3, along with that from the settlement. It remains to assess the architectural importance of these tombs and to attempt to bring some order to a scattered body of material that was salvaged between 1959 and 1968. More precise information resulted from excavations in 1969 sponsored by the Greek Archaeological Service and directed by Angelos Choremis. Preliminary reports (Choremis 1968, 1970) were followed by a fuller publication (Choremis 1973).[14]

Evidence for DA tombs is found to the NW of the ridge in the areas of Lakkoules (Features 11, 12; *Nichoria* I, pp. 108, 109) and Tourkokivouro (Features 3, 30), and to the SE in the area of Trypetorachi (Feature 16). The pottery associated with these burials can be assigned to all three major DA periods which have been differentiated for the settlement on the Nichoria ridge. The graves will therefore be discussed in the chronological order thus established.

THE NIKITOPOULOS TUMULUS

In the area of Tourkokivouro (Fig. 4-2) in the field of Ioannis Nikitopoulos, Choremis excavated in 1969 a predominantly Mycenaean tumulus containing five small tholoi and an apsidal cist grave (Choremis 1973, p. 27, Fig. 2). One of these tholoi (Nikitopoulos no. 6) was evidently reused in the DAI period, since two of the seven vases (**P1578**, **P1579**) found within exhibit definite DAI characteristics. These two vases belonged to a burial, found in a disturbed condition, which had been made along the S side of the tomb (Choremis 1973, p. 46, Fig. 12); the larger (**P1578**) had been placed at the head, and the smaller (**P1579**) at the feet. Also associated with this burial were two bronze rings, fragments of an iron pin, and a clay whorl. Care had been taken to separate this burial from the earlier one, since it was ringed on the N and W by a simple row of irregular, rounded stones. The S and E sides were formed by the wall of the tomb itself. Entrance to the preexisting Mycenaean tholos may have been through the dromos where a pithos was placed. The previous contents were apparently swept aside, since several LHIIIB vases were found along the NW side, and the new burial was then placed in its own carefully delimited area along the S side.

In the dromos and occupying all the available space a pithos lay on its side with mouth toward the interior. It had a maximum preserved height of 1.14 m and a diameter at mid-belly of 0.95 m. Inside were found an additional bronze ring, a clay whorl, and a twisted bronze coil (ring?). Although there is no conclusive evidence to prove that the pithos dates from the Dark Age, the placing of a pithos burial at the entrance to stone-built tombs appears to be a DA feature at Nichoria (see p. 269). No bones or ashes are mentioned as having been associated with this pithos, and thus it is difficult to determine what type of burial it contained. If it was an inhumation, one would expect at least some traces of bones to survive, since fragments of the DA skeleton were preserved in the interior. Thus, the presence of a cremation burial here must remain a strong possibility.

If, as seems likely, later entrance to the tholos was through the dromos, the relatively well-preserved state of the pithos would indicate that the inhumation in the interior was made first. **P1578** and **P1579** date this inhumation to DAI, but there is no such ceramic evidence to provide a date for the pithos burial. Probably it also belongs to DAI, since the only tomb in the Nikitopoulos tumulus that was constructed in DA times is a small apsidal cist that is also DAI in date (see below). There is no evidence for subsequent DAII or DAIII activity in the tumulus, and hence we may consider that both DA burials in Nikitopoulos tholos no. 6 belong to DAI.

Some 18 m to the E of Nikitopoulos no. 6, a small apsidal cist (Nikitopoulos no. 1) appeared to be intact (Choremis 1973, p. 70, Fig. 26). Oriented in a N-S direction with the apse to the S, it was built with flat, partially dressed blocks of the type found in Mycenaean buildings on the ridge, perhaps indicating DA reuse of Mycenaean building material. The cover consisted of four large flat slabs placed along the N-S axis. The cist has a total length of 1.40 m, a width of 1.0 m, and a preserved height varying from 1.45 to 1.60 m. The contents indicate that, as with Nikitopoulos no. 6, there were two DA burials here. On the paved floor was found a partially preserved skeleton with head to the W. Farther S, the disarticulated fragments of a second skeleton indicate that it had been swept aside for the later burial.

The finds were quite meager, consisting of a bronze ring, a twisted coil, and a clay whorl similar to those from Nikitopoulos no. 6 and suggesting a parallel date. In general, the small size of the tomb, its relative lightness of construction, and the paucity of finds from within accord well with the evidence of a meager settlement on the ridge in DAI and further suggest a DAI date for Nikitopoulos no. 1.

It is interesting to note that both Nikitopoulos nos. 1 and 6 had two DAI burials, The fact that those in no. 6 were made in a reused Mycenaean tomb suggests that there could have been some continuity in family and/or cult here between the end of LHIIIB and DAI.

THE TSAGDIS CIST GRAVES (FIG. 4-2)

Also in the area of Tourkokivouro, some 300 m NE of the Nikitopoulos tumulus in the field of Anastasios Tsagdis, Choremis excavated in 1969 two apsidal cists (Fig. 4-2). The tombs had been accidentally discovered when the plow disturbed a cover slab, revealing two vessels (**P1580**, **P1581**), a bronze pin, and a bronze ring. Subsequent excavation showed that there were two small apsidal cists

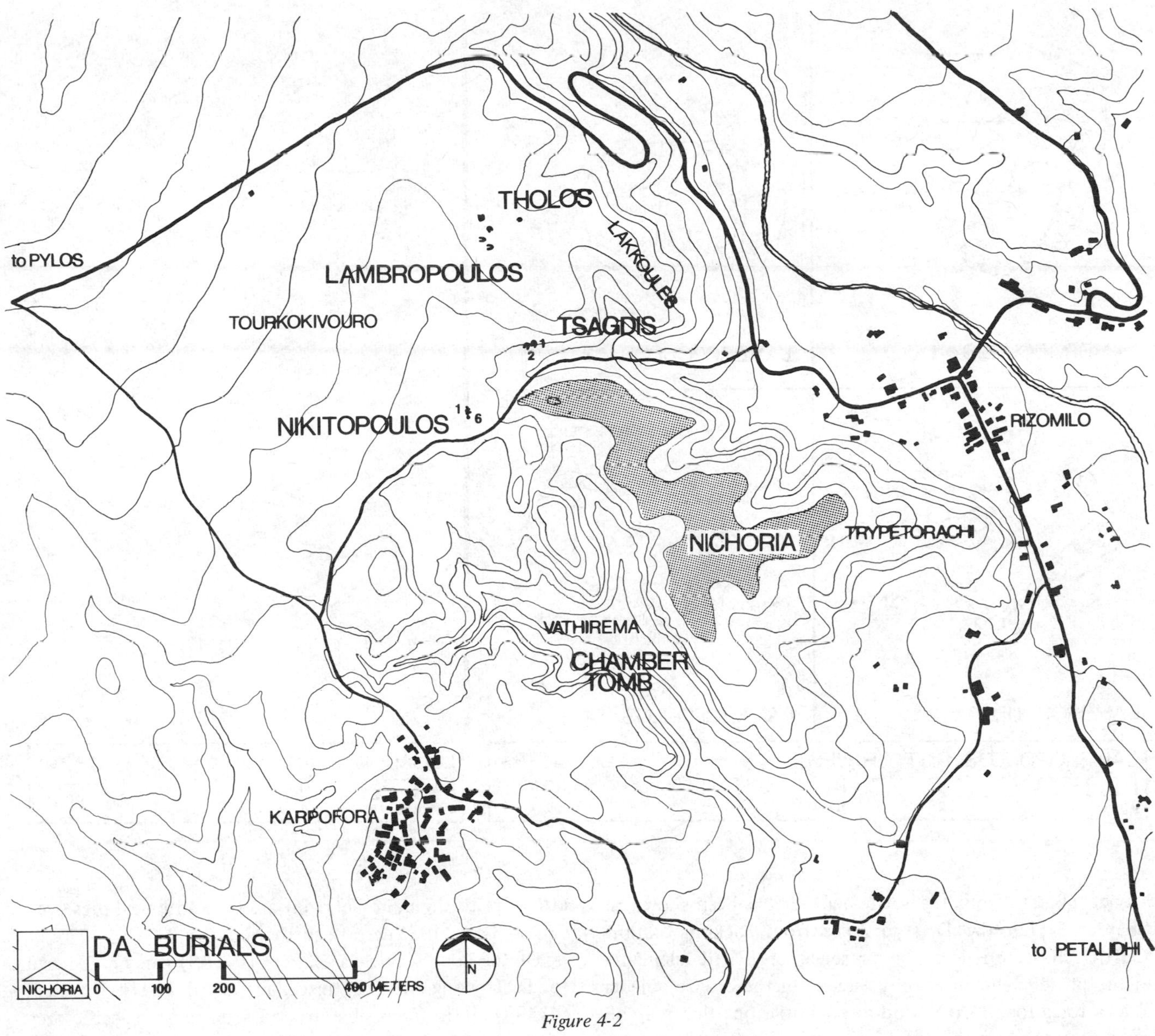

Figure 4-2

with the same approximate dimensions as Nikitopoulos no. 1 but with a NW × SE orientation and the apse to the NW (Choremis 1973, p. 72, Fig. 27). Tsagdis no. 1, to the E, was only partially preserved along its apse and W side, together with a small portion of the paved floor close to the apse. The long bones of a skeleton were also uncovered within the apse, and among these were found a bronze pin and two bronze rings. At a distance of only 0.70 m to the W, the second cist was discovered. Tsagdis no. 2 is better preserved than its counterpart, with the apsidal end reaching a height of 0.55 m. The only offerings recorded are two fragments (unspecified) of unpainted (coarse?) vessels, but on the floor there was a skeleton in good condition with feet toward the rectangular end.

Portions of the cover slabs lay between the two cists, similar in shape and size to those from Nikitopoulos no. 1. In the fill between the slabs Choremis records portions of the jaw and backbone of a bovine and a fragment from the jaw of a wild pig. He suggests that the area between the tombs had been used for sacrifice.

Unfortunately, owing to the circumstances of their discovery, it is impossible to tell from which of the two tombs **P1580** and **P1581** came. But it is clear that they should be associated with the cists, as they do provide a firm DAI date for them. Also, the similarity in size and construction between Tsagdis 1 and 2 and Nikitopoulos no. 1 indicates that all three belong to the same period. The pin found by Tsagdis (Choremis 1973, Pl. 38β) and the one from cist no. 1 (Choremis 1973, Pl. 38ξ) also provide evidence for an early date. Choremis cites Submycenaean parallels from the Argolid, and Catling in Chapter 5 also cites Submycenaean parallels for many of the DA

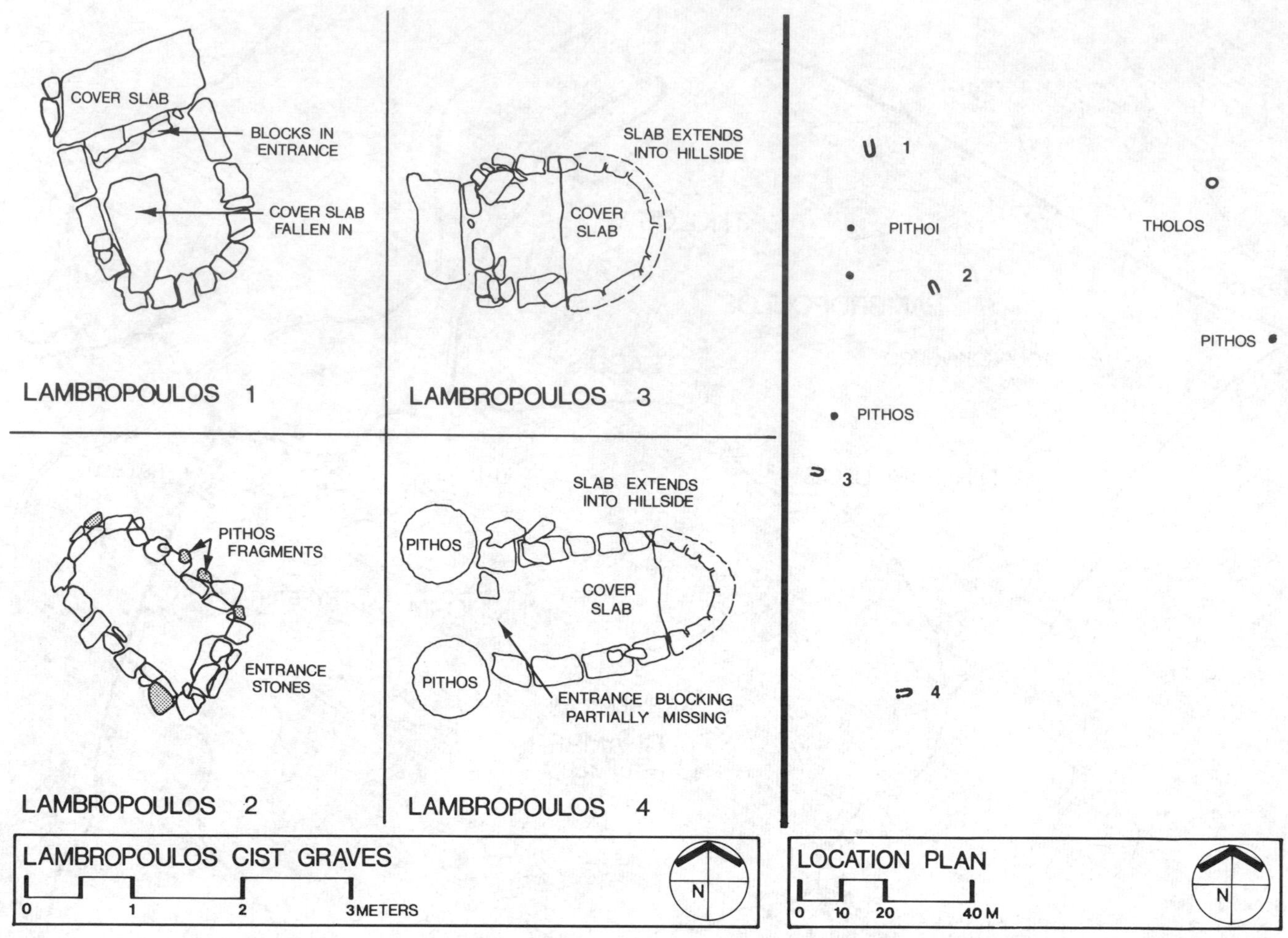

Figure 4-3

bronze objects from the settlement. It has been shown in Chapter 3 that the DAI ceramics from Nichoria exhibit LHIIIC characteristics. The presence of LHIIIC elements in the pottery and of Submycenaean in the bronze objects argues for a long DAI period at Nichoria, one that may be roughly equivalent in time to the late LHIIIC and Submycenaean phases elsewhere on the mainland, especially in Attica and the Argolid.

THE LAKKOULES CEMETERY (FIGS. 4-2, 4-3)

Evidence for a DA cemetery comes from the area of Lakkoules, in the field of Christos Lambropoulos to the W of the later DAII tholos. Here, between 1959 and 1961, the accidental discovery of six apsidal graves, along with various whole vases and numerous sherds, was reported (Daux 1960, 1961; Yalouris 1960). Much of the ceramic material was apparently lost before the remainder was turned over to representatives of the Greek Archaeological Service. In any case, all that now survives of what was once "a large quantity of vases" (Daux 1961; Desborough 1972, p. 252) are four vessels and a handful of sherds. Choremis dismisses the tombs as "ruined" and pays little attention to them; in fact, four are still quite well preserved (Fig. 4-3) and they deserve further comment.

Of the four whole vases, one **(P1598)** can be assigned to DAI along with a miscellaneous ribbed kylix stem **(P1599)**. It is impossible to tell from what specific area of Lakkoules **P1598** and **P1599** came or whether they should be associated with any of the four cists that can now be located. The latter exhibit different characteristics from the DAI cist in Tourkokivouro. They are larger both in length and in width and are constructed of larger, more regularly dressed blocks that are similar in shape to those of Wall A of Unit IV-1 on the Nichoria ridge (see p. 27). The hairpin apsidal shape with curving side walls is quite striking in the three Tourkokivouro tombs, whereas the Lambropoulos cists (Fig. 4-4) have straight side walls with a gently curving apse. In general, then, the Lambropoulos cists exhibit more sophistication in shape and construction, especially Lambropoulos no. 4 with its two pithoi flanking the entrance. The other three whole vases **(P1604-6)** and all the diagnostic sherds **(P1600-1603)** can be assigned to DAII, and it is likely that the cists also belong to this period, i.e., contemporary with the small tholos to the E. We may, therefore, with fair confidence associate the DAII pottery with them, although it is now impossible to assign any particular vase to a specific tomb. The presence of **P1598** and **P1599**, however, does indicate that the Lakkoules area was also used as a cemetery in DAI, although no cists of that period have yet been recovered there.

The four cist graves are located in a group some 75 m to the W of the small tholos and are labeled from N to S as Lambropoulos nos. 1 to 4. Lambropoulos no. 1, the farthest N, is oriented in a NNW × SSE direction, with the apse at the SE. It measures some 2.10 m in length and 1.10 m in width (Pls. 4-14, 4-15). The sides are preserved to a height of 0.33 m and consist of two courses of long, flat limestone blocks, now weathered gray. The apse has three courses of smaller stones, with an average size of 0.30 × 0.20 m. The straight end is formed by three courses of irregularly sized stones, carelessly laid; a large cover slab now blocks the entrance, and a second cover slab has fallen into the tomb at the rear and rests partially on the apsidal wall.

Lambropoulos no. 2, some 20 m to the SE of no. 1, is oriented NW × SE, with the apse at the NW. It measures 1.70 m in length and 0.80 m in width, being the smallest of the four (Pls. 4-16, 4-17). All sides are preserved to a height of 0.42 m (three courses) and are built of weathered limestone blocks. A large cover slab, measuring 1.30 × 0.95 m, lies to the E. An interesting feature is the presence of large pithos body fragments built into the walls.

Lambropoulos no. 3, some 50 m to the SW of no. 2, was cut into a slope, with the apse to the E (Pls. 4-18, 4-19). The deeper rear half is well preserved, since it is covered by the higher slope. A large cover slab, still in place, extends over the apse and half of the side walls; a second broken slab has slipped from the front and lies at an angle. The W end is quite disturbed, but the side walls and apse at the rear consist of four courses of long, flat, gray limestone blocks, preserving the original height of 0.50 m from floor to bottom of cover slab. The preserved length is 1.70 m (probably originally slightly longer), and the width is 1.15 m.

Lambropoulos no. 4, approximately 50 m to the SE of no. 3, is by far the most elaborate of the four (Pls. 4-20, 4-21). Like no. 3, it was cut into a slope, and the apse and cover slab over it are well preserved. It has the same orientation as no. 3 and is 2.20 m in length and 0.90 m at its widest point. It was constructed from long (0.20 to 0.40 m), flat, gray and white limestone blocks. The apse is intact, with 12 courses reaching a height of 0.75 m from floor to cover slab. At the point where the cover slab is broken, the side walls contain only seven courses, since the floor level slopes down toward the apse. As with no. 3, the W end has been disturbed, and only one stone remains in place. Two pithoi, now badly fragmented, flanked the entrance. Enough remains intact of the N pithos to determine that it had a diameter at mid-belly of 0.70 m, yielding an estimated height of 1.40 m. The fragments of the S pithos indicate that it had a somewhat similar diameter. Some 40 pithos body fragments lie scattered around the W end of the tomb. Most are plain, but a few contain decoration. Two fragments from the N pithos show a raised fluted band, and one from the S pithos a raised band with incised zigzags. Two pithos body fragments (**P1607**), now in the Kalamata Museum, have the same light red, coarse clay as do the pieces now in existence at the front of the tomb. These probably belonged to this grave and were selected from the rest of the fragments as being the most representative. One fragment of **P1607** has a raised band with a row of incised circles (cf. **P903** from the settlement), and the other has a raised band with a row of finger impressions (cf. **P838** from the settlement).

The shape of these structures has already been discussed in connection with their relationship to the DAI cists. There seems to be no standard orientation. In each case the long axis appears to have been determined by the nature of the terrain. It may be worth noting, however, that the two most elaborate cists, Lambropoulos nos. 3 and 4, are oriented in an E × W direction, with the apse to the E. In none of the Lambropoulos cists do traces of floor paving remain, not even in the well-preserved apsidal sections of nos. 3 and 4. There is no record now of what types of burial these Lambropoulos cists contained. An earth floor would be appropriate for cremations where there was no need to lay out a corpse. A large belly-handled amphora (**P1606**), found in the area of these cists, is the right size to contain ashes and charred bones. Thus, it is possible that some or all of these Lambropoulos cists contained cremations. Some weight may be added to the possibility by the landowner's affirmation that, although he was present when all cists were discovered, he saw no indication that they contained skeletal remains.

Pithos burials are also reported to have been found in the vicinity of the cists (Daux 1960, 1961; Yalouris 1960). The general location of these pithoi between the cists and to the S of the DA tholos has been indicated on the plan (Fig. 4-3) from information provided by the owner. The use of pithoi in conjunction with stone-built tombs has already been noted in connection with the reuse of Nikitopoulos no. 6 in DAI. This practice was continued in DAII on a more elaborate scale with the two pithoi at the entrance of Lambropoulos no. 4. The presence of pithos fragments built into the walls of Lambropoulos no. 2 is interesting, for it suggests the presence in the Lakkoules cemetery of broken pithoi that antedate the construction of the tomb. It may be that these fragments in the walls of no. 2 belong to DAI pithoi and were reused in DAII as building material. It is impossible now to determine the date of the pithos burials found between the Lambropoulos cists; all that can be said with assurance is that burials in pithoi and in stone-built tombs were made in both DAI and DAII.

In 1967, a small DA tholos (Fig. 4-2) about 2 m in diameter was discovered to the E of the Lambropoulos cists (Choremis 1968, 1973). Its architectural features have been reported in some detail by the excavator (Choremis 1973, Figs. 24, 25) and will not be repeated here. The good group of pottery recovered from it (**P1582-91**) dates the four burials in the tholos to DAII. Burials A, Γ, and Δ were made first; at some later date these were swept aside to make room for Burial B, for which the skeleton was found in an extended position. According to Choremis (1973, p. 64), the bones were lying on top of a layer of scattered ash and bone fragments. The extent of this deposit is not reported, nor are the bone fragments identified. Consequently, it is impossible to learn whether they were animal or human. If the former, the ash debris probably comes from sacrifices which took place in the tomb as part of the burial ceremony for the first inhumations (A, Γ, Δ); if the latter, it is likely that the tomb was used even earlier (but still within DAII) when cremation(s) had been the rite. **P1591**, found between Burials Γ and Δ, shows traces of burning and may belong to the ash debris.

ADDITIONAL DAII BURIALS

Elsewhere in the immediate environs (Fig. 4-2) miscellaneous sherds (**P1608**, **P1609**) were found near the abovementioned DAI Tsagdis apsidal cists, indicating that the Tourkokivouro area continued to be used as a cemetery in DAII times. And from the area of Trypetorachi to the SE of the ridge, throughout the field of Panayiotis Kanellopoulos, good decorated and diagnostic DAII sherds (**P1610-21**) occur in the plow soil, suggesting that there was an extensive DAII cemetery in this area.

DAIII BURIALS

For DAIII the evidence is less abundant. No pithos burials or stone-built tombs can be assigned to this period, but the plow soil in the field of Christos Lambropoulos, in which the DAII cists and tholos are located, yielded a group of diagnostic DAIII sherds (**P1622-25**) together with some 200 monochrome black-coated body sherds with characteristics similar to those of DAIII pottery on the ridge. This indicates that the major DAIII cemetery was also in Lakkoules and proves that burials were made here throughout the DA occupation of the Nichoria ridge.

LATE GEOMETRIC BURIALS

For the Late Geometric period, the evidence is confined to the pithos burial on the ridge (described on pp. 260-62) and a chamber tomb on the steep SW slope of the Vathirema ravine (Feature 1; Fig. 4-2). The chamber tomb was excavated in 1960 by Yalouris (Daux 1961, 1962; Yalouris 1960) and a plan was subsequently published by Papathanasopoulos (1961-62).[15] The tomb is apsidal in shape and is oriented in a NE × SW direction with the entrance to the NE (1.34 m wide) blocked with stones. The chamber measures 6.0 m in length and 3.7 m in width, with a height of 2.60 m. On the floor, four paving stones survive at the rear near the apse and in the center. To the NW of these stones was found a poorly articulated inhumation burial with its head toward the rear. Fragments of bones from a second burial were found between the paving stones by the rear wall, evidently having been swept there when the later burial was made. A Geometric bronze pin was found with the miscellaneous bones and may date the earlier burial. A second pin was found with the central burial, together with six Late Geometric vases (**P1592-97**) datable to ca. 745-725 (see Chapter 3, pp. 109, 110). Both inhumations appear to be Late Geometric. The tomb also contained a sequence of pottery continuing into Classical times, with late Classical pottery similar to that from the tholos (see Chapter 7, pp. 334-36). However, the date of the original construction of the tomb is unclear. It could be a Mycenaean chamber tomb that was cleared out and reused, as Coldstream (1977, p. 161) suggests. The character of the paving and blocking stones is of little help, since they consist of the same rounded limestone blocks as are used in all periods of construction on the ridge. After the Late Geometric burials, the tomb was probably used for a hero cult that lasted through late Classical times, with its last phase contemporary with the cult worship in the tholos in Area I (pp. 332-34). The person buried in the center of the tomb and possibly worshiped in subsequent periods must have been quite important, as is suggested by the fine pyxis lid (**P1597**). Whether it was imported from Attica or Boeotia is unclear, but so ornate an imported piece is unusual in Messenia during this period.

The final item of evidence in Late Geometric comes from the field of Georgios Papamichroulis in Rizomilo (Feature 52) where numerous stone blocks and sherds occur. The pottery is predominantly Mycenaean, but we identified one good Late Geometric piece (**P1626**). No DA sherds have been found here, and it is possible that this is the site of another (or several?) reused chamber tomb(s) similar to that at Vathirema.

W.D.E.C.

NOTES

1. The practice of using stones to wedge a jar firmly in place is common (e.g., at Nauplia, *Praktika* 1953:192; Tiryns, *AM* 78, 1963:47; Lerna, *Hesperia* 25, 1956:171). Charitonides also noted stones placed above the jars at Nauplia, although the purpose seems to have been to ensure stability rather than to erect a monument over the burial (*Praktika* 1953:192 and 1954:233, Fig. 1).

2. The pithos was removed in pieces, reconstructed, and is now displayed in the Benaki Museum, Kalamata. The shape is most closely paralleled, among published examples, by two from Argos (Courbin 1966, Pl. 106, GM1 and GR), but our pithos lacks their banded decoration. In the cemeteries in the Argolid three basic shapes seem to be represented: smaller, egg-shaped (Courbin 1966, Pl. 106, GR2); cylindrical (*BCH* 77, 1953:257, Fig. 47); and larger ovoid, to which class our pithos belongs.

3. Probably the stone had helped to block the mouth of the pithos and had accidentally fallen in. I am not aware of examples of such stones being intentionally placed over the dead to keep them down and prevent spirits rising as part of Greek burial practices. See Kurtz and Boardman (1971, p. 191).

4. In Middle Minoan Crete the bodies were interred head first (Mallia, *BCH* 94, 1970:875, 877); for Middle Helladic Messenia cf. Papoulia (*BCH* 79, 1955:248, 249, Fig. 2).

5. E.g., at Rhitsona in Boeotia, Kameiros in Rhodes, Pitane in Aeolis in Asia Minor (Kurtz and Boardman 1971, pp. 175, 177, 183); on Corfu (*AAA* 3, 1970:68-71).

6. At Vergina (*Deltion* 17, 1961-62, A 268) as many as 16 pithoi were uncovered in one tumulus; isolated burials of adults in jars occur at Thebes (*BCH* 94, 1970:1034, 1035, Fig. 313); Athens (*AM* 18, 1893:133); Thorikos (*Deltion* 22, 1967, B. 138); Argos (*BCH* 77, 1953:257, Fig. 47; 78, 1954:775 ff.; 94, 1970: 765, 766; 96, 1972:229-51; *AAA* 2, 1969:159-62, Fig. 2); Lerna (*Hesperia* 25, 1956:171, 172); Mycenae (*BSA* 49, 1954:265); Nauplia (an extensive cemetery excavated by Charitonides at Pronoia; *Praktika* 1953:191-204; 1954:232-41); Tiryns (two cemeteries, *Tiryns I*, 2:127-64 and AM 78, 1963:1-62).

7. *Praktika* 1953:192; 1954:232.

8. *BCH* 77, 1953:257.

9. Acknowledgments are owed to A. Triandi, ephor of West Peloponnese, and to P. Stephanou, head guard at the Kalamata Museum, for their courtesy and cooperation.

10. Readers may notice slight discrepancies in detail between this study and that of Dr. Wade, although the focus of the research is complementary and not overlapping.

11. Acknowledgments are owed to J. T. McCall, head of section, and to P. Hass and G. Mussman, technicians.

12. Acknowledgments are owed to W. M. O'Fallon, head of section and to G. Augustine, statistician of the Biostatistics Section of the Mayo Clinic.

13. Partial support for the research was obtained from a Smithsonian Institute Research Fellowship in 1977 and a University of Minnesota Doctoral Research Fellowship in 1977-78.

14. The author is indebted to Dr. Choremis for permission to study and comment on this DA material.

15. The author is indebted to Drs. Yalouris and Papathanasopoulos for permission to study and comment on the Late Geometric material from the Vathirema chamber tomb.

REFERENCES

Adams, P. 1969. "The Effects of Experimental Malnutrition on the Development of Long Bones," *Biblioteca Nutritio et Dieta* 13:69-73. Basel.

Angel, J. L. 1966. "Porotic Hyperostosis, Anemias, Malarias, and Marshes in the Prehistoric Eastern Mediterranean," *Science* 153:760-63.

______. 1976. "Colonial to Modern Skeletal Change," *Journal of the Association of Physical Anthropology* 45:723-35.

Brewer, G., and Prasad, A. S., eds. 1977. *Zinc Metabolism in Health and Disease*. New York.

Brothwell, D. R. 1959. "The Use of Non-metrical Characters of the Skull in Differentiating Populations," *Bericht über die 6 Tagung der Deutschen Gesellschaft für Anthropologie*:103-9.

Brown, A. B. 1973. "Bone Strontium as a Dietary Indicator in Human Skeletal Populations." Ph.D. dissertation, University of Michigan, Ann Arbor.

Choremis, A. 1968. "A Tholos Tomb in Karpofora, Messenia," *AAA* 1:205-9. In Greek.

______. 1970. "Rizomilo, Karpofora," *Deltion* (Chronika) 25: 179-81. In Greek.

______. 1973. "Mycenaean and Protogeometric Tombs in Karpofora, Messenia," *Arch Eph*:25-74. In Greek.

Coldstream, J. N. 1977. *Geometric Greece*. London.

Courbin, P. 1966. *La céramique geométrique de l'Argolide*. Paris.

Daux, G. 1960. "Chronique de fouilles 1959," *BCH* 84:700.

______. 1961. "Chronique de fouilles 1960," *BCH* 85:697.

______. 1962. "Chronique de fouilles 1961," *BCH* 86:725.

Desborough, V. R. D'A. 1972. *The Greek Dark Ages*. London.

Fiske, C. H., and Subbarow, Y. 1925. "The Colorimetric Determination of Phosphorus," *Journal of Biologic Chemistry* 66: 375-400.

Garn, S. M., et al. 1964. "Compact Bone Deficiency in Protein-Caloric Malnutrition," *Science* 145:1444.

Gilbert, B. Miles, and McKern, Thomas W. 1973. "A Method for Aging the Female Os pubis," *American Journal of Physical Anthropology* 38:31-38.

Greulich, W., and Thoms, H. 1938. "The Dimensions of the Pelvic Inlet of 789 White Females," *Anatomical Record* 72:45-51.

Janes, J. M., McCall, J. T., Kniseley, R. N. 1975. "Osteogenic Sarcoma: Influence of Trace Metals in Experimental Induction," *Trace Substances in Environmental Health*:433-39. University of Missouri.

Kurtz, D. C., and Boardman, J. 1971. *Greek Burial Customs*. London and Ithaca, N. Y.

Lukermann, F. E., and Moody, J. 1978. "Nichoria and Vicinity: Settlements and Circulation." In Rappand Aschenbrenner 1978, pp. 78-107.

McDonald, W. A., and Rapp, G., Jr., eds. 1972. *Minnesota Messenia Expedition: Reconstructing a Bronze Age Regional Environment*. Minneapolis.

McKern, T. W., and Stewart, T. D. 1957. "Skeletal Age Changes in Young Males, Analyzed from the Standard of Age Identification." Quartermaster Research and Development Command, Environmental Protection Division, Technical Report EP-45, Natich, Mass.

Mellanby, M. 1934. "Diet and the Teeth: An Experimental Study," Medical Research Council, Special Report Series, no. 191, London.

MME 1972 = McDonald and Rapp 1972.

Nicholson, G. 1945. "The Two Mean Diameters of the Brim of the Female Pelvis," *Journal of Anatomy* 79:131-35.

Nichoria I = Rapp and Aschenbrenner 1978.

Papathanasopoulos, G. 1961-62. "Messenia," *Deltion* (Chronika) 17:95. In Greek.

Perkin-Elmer Corporation. 1971. *Analytical Methods for Atomic Absorption Spectrophotometry*. Norwalk, Conn.

Prasad, A. S. 1978. *Trace Elements and Iron in Human Metabolism*. New York.

Rapp, G., Jr. 1970. "Geology in Aid of Archaeology: Investigations in Greece," *Journal of Geological Education* 18:59-65.

______, and Aschenbrenner, S. E., eds. 1978. *Excavations at Nichoria in Southwest Greece* I: *Site, Environs, and Techniques*. Minneapolis.

Schoeninger, M. J. 1979. "Dietary Reconstruction at Chalcatzingo, a Formative Period Site in Morelos, Mexico," Technical Report no. 9, University of Michigan, Ann Arbor.

Schour, I., and Massler, M. 1941. "The Development of the Human Dentition," *Journal of the American Dental Association* 28:1153-60.

———, and Poncher, H. G. 1940. *Chronology of Tooth Development*. Mead Johnson Company.

Snodgrass, A. M. 1971. *The Dark Age of Greece*. Edinburgh.

Todd, T. W. 1920. "Age Changes in the Pubic Bone; Part I, the Adult White Male Pubis," *American Journal of Physical Anthropology* 3:285-334.

———. 1921. "Age Changes in the Pubic Bone; Part 3, the Pubis of the White Female," *American Journal of Physical Anthropology* 4:1-70.

———, and Lyon, D. W. 1924. "Endocranial Suture Closure, Its Progress and Age Relationship; Part 1, Adult Males of White Stock," *American Journal of Physical Anthropology* 7:325-85.

Trotter, M., and Gleser, G. 1952. "Estimation of Stature from Long Bones of American Whites and Negroes," *American Journal of Physical Anthropology* 10:463-514.

———. 1958. "A Re-evaluation of Estimation of Stature Taken during Life and of Long Bones after Death," *American Journal of Physical Anthropology* 16:79-124.

Wells, G. 1967. "A New Approach to Paleopathology: Harris' Lines." In *Diseases in Antiquity*, ed. D. Brothwell and A. T. Sandison, pp. 390-404. Springfield, Ill.

Woo, T. L., and Morant, G. M. 1936. "A Biometric Study of the Flatness of the Facial Skeleton in Man," *Biometrika* 26:196-250.

Yalouris, N. 1960. "Messenia" *Deltion* (Chronika) 16:108. In Greek.

Zipkin, I. 1970. "The Inorganic Composition of Bones and Teeth." In *Biological Calcification: Cellular and Molecular Aspects*, ed. H. Schrar, pp. 69-103. New York.

5
The Small Finds

by

Hector Catling, Jill Carington Smith, and Helen Hughes-Brock

The organization of this chapter has been particularly complex and difficult. During the course of the excavation Dr. Hector Catling agreed to publish all metal items, and his account of the certain or probable DA finds in this category appears first. This segment is followed by Dr. Jill Carington Smith's account of the objects that constitute evidence for spinning and weaving (presumably a "cottage" craft). Then we publish a few paragraphs written by Harriet Blitzer, who is in general charge of the tools and implements made of stone and bone. She explains her reasons for publishing in *Nichoria* II (Bronze Age occupation) even the objects in these categories that were recovered from predominantly DA contexts. Helen Hughes-Brock, who was in general charge of the small finds during the last three campaigns, contributed materially to this chapter by checking the references, revising the Catalog for the metals section (where information originally supplied to Catling has been inadequate or outdated), and consulting with the editor on the catalog format and other details of organization. Finally, Hughes-Brock and Coulson discuss a very few DA items that seemed worthy of inclusion in this chapter but do not belong in the above categories.

Vicky Walsh is conducting an intensive study to determine whether there is a statistically significant clustering of small finds within the excavated areas. Since a very high proportion of the items involved is certainly or probably to be assigned to the Bronze Age, the results will appear in *Nichoria* II. Any information coming out of her study that is relevant to the DA small finds will be included there.

The Metal Objects

On a long-lived site like Nichoria the evaluation of material such as the metal objects is subject to a procedural problem that has not been wholly overcome here. This is the basic difficulty of isolating older material in deposits of obviously mixed origin where there are no intrinsic typological indicators to assist in an identification. The problem is less serious in dealing with pottery, where the material for the most part is self-revealing, and where it is not, little is lost by ignoring it. As the catalog of the metal objects (pp. 305-12) shows, the material is in general of so scrappy a nature that only a limited amount of it can safely be dated to the Bronze Age or the Dark Age on form alone. Contextual evidence is essential.

This has led to a rather crude rule-of-thumb for selecting metal objects for inclusion in this DA section. All material from deposits identified as purely DA is included, unless an object is self-evidently of Bronze Age type. All material that is self-evidently of DA date is included, irrespective of the (ceramic) date of its deposit (e.g., **85**, **105**). Some objects from deposits that are ceramically ambiguous and are themselves typologically ambiguous have been included in the DA section, though not without some misgivings. Such misgivings are of less importance in the case of iron objects (e.g., **96**, **100**, **106**) than in dealing with the bronzes. The ambiguity is stated in the catalog in the description of context, but degrees of certainty have not been evaluated in the rough-and-ready statistical summaries that follow. As an indicator of the degree of reliability of this procedure, it should be noted that 43 of the 79 objects in bronze (about 54%) come from mixed or otherwise ambiguous contexts, whereas 22 of the 32 iron objects (about 68%) come from similar contexts. The figures for lead are five out of eight (about 62%).

An exception to the procedure outlined above has been made for scrap waste metal. Material of this kind from ambiguous contexts will be considered separately in Volume II, where some attempt will also be made to assess the statistical significance of the un-inventoried metal objects (not seen by the writer) that were taken for analysis in the course of study of the site's metallurgical achievement. This material will be found tabulated and discussed in *Nichoria* I, pp. 166-81, with particular reference to Tables 11-1, 11-2, 11-4 and 11-5.

It will be convenient to make some general observations about the objects cataloged above before any dicussion is undertaken of individual categories of material or of specific objects. With very few exceptions (**5**, **6**, **52**, **57**, **58**), the bronze, iron, lead, and gold objects are of very slight intrinsic importance. Their combined testimony, nevertheless, is of some interest for the information offered concerning both metal technology and the technologies that may be inferred from the use to which the objects themselves were put. The material is also briefly considered in relation to find contexts in an attempt to isolate any evidence of area-specialization there may be. Some of these categories of information are summarized in tabular form below.

Seventy-nine bronze objects are cataloged, of which 16 (about 10%) are made up of formless pieces of scrap or small droplets of waste metal spilled in the work of melting or casting bronze. There remain 63 pieces that can be identified, with varying degrees of confidence. Only a minority was found complete. With rare exceptions (e.g., **57**), the objects are very small, and it is not surprising that they were overlooked or ignored at the time of their original loss. Twenty-five (about 40%) of these consist of such personal objects as dress pins, fibulae, finger rings, and beads. Twenty-one (about 33%) are in the general category of small tools (including needles) and rivets probably used for hafting knives. The remaining categories are represented by only a few examples each. Statuettes, for instance, amount to less than 4% of the total, and the rather heterogeneous category of miscellaneous "Trappings" accounts for another 6%.

The contextual evidence obtained for this material during excavation allows the following chronological summary (Table 5-1) for the use of bronze in the DA settlement.

The evidence on which this summary is based is presented in Table 5-2. Little comment is required. The very limited DAI representation may be significant, including as it does only the very simplest objects. If scrap is ignored, indeed, only three categories are recorded. DAII, by contrast, is the most important period not only for the number of objects found, but also for their diversity. If the bronzes of DAII and DAIII are compared, the latter period, although it accounts for less than half the number of the former, nevertheless includes examples of nearly all the categories well represented in the earlier period.

A similar analysis of the much smaller total of 32 iron objects may be attempted (see Table 5-4). Nine of the cataloged pieces (about 28% of the total) consist of unidentified scrap. Of the remaining 23 items, seven (about 30%) were personal items (pins, etc.) and seven were one-edged knives. Six more (about 26%) consist of the so-called "nails," incomplete objects that do not necessarily all belong to the same category. The number of objects in the remaining categories is too insignificant for separate consideration.

The contextual evidence for this material allows a tabular summary (Table 5-3) of its chronological significance. The evidence upon which this is based is presented in Table 5-4.

The sample of iron objects (Table 5-4) is probably too small for much significance to attach to these figures, although in general they offer a reasonably faithful approximation to the ordering observed in the figures obtained for the bronzes. DAII again appears as the peak period for use and variety of types available.

Only eight lead objects were recorded in DA contexts (Table 5-5). Half of these occurred in DAII, a hint of confirmation of that phase's relative importance. The amounts of metal involved are very small.

One gold object (**120**)—a twist of wire—was found in a DAIII context. This may have been a goldsmith's stock-in-trade rather than the remains of a manufactured object.

Table 5-1. Chronological Distribution of Cataloged DA Bronze Objects

Bronze	DAI	DAI-II	DAII	DAII-III[a]	DAIII	DA
Total no. of objects (79)	7	17	32	5	14	4
Percent of total	8.9	21.5	40.5	6.3	17.7	5.0

[a]This rubric in Tables 5-1 to 5-5 indicates a mixed DAII *and* DAIII pottery context; it is *not* equivalent to the transitional DAII/III ceramic phase of Chapter 3.

Table 5-2. Chronological Breakdown of Cataloged DA Bronze Objects by Category

Bronze	DAI	DAI-II	DAII	DAII-III	DAIII	DA
Pins		1	3, 4, 6	5	2, 7	
Fibulae		8		10	9	
Rings	15	16	12, 13		11, 14	
Spirals		17, 23	18, 22	19	20	21
Earring			24			
Bead			25			
Weapon			26			
Awls/Gravers	27, 34	32, 33, 35	28, 29, 30		31	
Needles	36, 44	38, 40, 42	37, 39, 41 43			
Tools/Rivets		46	45, 47			
Vessels/Rivets		51	48, 49, 50			
Trappings			52, 55	54	53, 56	
Fitting			57			
Statuettes	59, 60				58	
Incomplete		61, 63	62			
Scrap		64, 65	66, 67, 68, 69, 70, 75		71, 72, 73	74
Waste				76	78	77, 79
TOTALS: 79	7	17	32	5	14	4

It is natural that the largest single concentration of metal objects should be associated with Unit IV-1, the most important DA building uncovered on the site. Bronze, iron, and lead are all represented, and there is a fair cross-section of the main categories of objects found on the site as a whole (see pp. 19-42 and Fig. 2-11). The evidence of these objects does not prove any special role for the building. Objects of personal use, small tools and implements, waste bits and pieces are quite appropriate for routine secular and domestic use.

THE BRONZE OBJECTS

PINS (CATALOG NOS. 1-7)

Among the objects of a personal nature, seven dress pins were identified, one (7) with less confidence than the remainder. Almost as many types are represented. Only the roll-top variety appears more than once (3 and 4); both come from DAII contexts, although in the case of 3 LH material was also associated. Such pins could be imported, although the design is so simple that it could easily have been imitated in Greece. The type appears in Early Bronze Age Europe and in the Bronze Age in the Near East (Jacobsthal 1956, pp. 122 ff.). Its Late Bronze Age occurrences include Enkomi (Dikaios 1969, Pl. 163) and Troy (Catling 1964, p. 238, n. 8). Nearer home, one was found by Tsountas (1888, Pls. 9, 25) in his Tomb 25 at Mycenae. From Nichoria itself comes another roll-top pin (N1898; to be published in *Nichoria* II) in a LH context, associated with pottery of LHIIA-IIIA date. There are several occurrences in Dark Age Greece. T.85 in the Kerameikos cemetery in Athens contained two pins that lay on the left shoulder of the skeleton of a girl, of which one (1.096) was a roll-top; the type of the second is not mentioned in the publication (Kraiker and Kübler 1939, p. 40). The grave cannot be closely dated, since it contained no other objects. Another roll-top pin was found in Kerameikos T.104, 1.136, a grave dated Submycenaean by Styrenius (1967, pp. 31, 46). Two others were found in the Salamis Submycenaean cemetery, one of them illustrated by Wide (1910, pp. 29, 30; Fig. 13). These pins were

Table 5-3. Chronological Distribution of Cataloged DA Iron Objects

Iron	DAI	DAI-II	DAII	DAII-III	DAIII	DA	"BA"
Total no. of objects (32)	1	3	11	4	6	3	4
Percent of total	3.1	9.4	34.3	12.5	18.8	9.4	12.5

Table 5-4. Chronological Breakdown of Cataloged DA Iron Objects by Category

Iron	DAI	DAI-II	DAII	DAII-III	DAIII	DA	"BA"
Pins			**80**		**81**		**82**
Rings				**84**	**83**		
Tweezer					**86**		
Bracelet							**85**
Weapons			**87, 88**				
Tools			**89**				
Knives		**90, 93**	**91, 92** **95, 96**		**94**		
"Nails"	**97**		**98**	**99, 100**	**101**	**102**	
Scrap		**107**	**108, 110**	**103**	**111**	**104, 106**	**105, 109**
TOTALS: 32	1	3	11	4	6	3	4

0.165 and 0.125 m long respectively. Later than these is a roll-top pin from Lefkandi, Palaea Perivolia Tomb 21, no. 11 (Popham, Sackett, and Themelis 1979-80, pp. 149, no. 11, 245; Pls. 136, 242F), dated Sub-Protogeometric II (roughly equivalent to Attic EG II, 875-85). The Lefkandi pin is thus approximately contemporary with our **3** and **4**.

Our fragmentary **1**, found without its head, recalls another type of Lefkandi pin,[1] this time characteristic of Submycenaean burial groups. This is a relatively small pin, with small nail-like head, usually flat, occasionally slightly domed. The head is separated by a slim neck from an oval swelling, more pronounced in some cases than others. There is no decoration. These Lefkandi pins recall an early Submycenaean pin from Kerameikos Tomb 16 (Styrenius 1967, p. 42); not dissimilar are two pins in the Kerameikos Middle Submycenaean Tomb 42 (Styrenius 1967, p. 43). These pins, and the Nichoria example, are very modest versions of the larger disk-topped, long-shafted pins with large globes on the shafts below the heads that are more characteristic of Athenian Submycenaean than the examples cited above.[2] The most that can be said of the Nichoria pin is that it belongs to a relatively common type of dress fastener that was current in the Peloponnese, Attica, and Euboea in the early part of the Dark Age. The finest examples of the series were produced in Athens (Catling in Popham et al. 1979-80, p. 245).

The decorated, cast pin **5** raises an interesting problem of attribution, although, as will be seen, its most likely identification is with a distinctive, not very common pin type, datable to Submycenaean/Subminoan in normal parlance. The pin is distinguished by a small nail-like head, a fusiform swelling on the upper part of the shaft, and the space between the swelling and the head picked out by a succession of evenly sized and spaced bead moldings, of which there are a few more on the shaft below the swelling. This recalls a pin type that has been discussed quite frequently, notably by Sandars (Hood et al. 1958-59, pp. 235-37), Desborough (1964, pp. 53 ff.; 1965, p. 226; 1972, p. 297), Deshayes (1966, pp. 204 ff.), and Snodgrass (1971, pp. 226 ff.). Desborough (1964, p. 53) quotes Sandar's definition: "an elongated globe-like swelling in the upper part of the shank with zones of simple moulding above and below it." He further adds that the pins have "a tapered-off moulded head with no enlargement." It will be noted, of course, that this latter element in the definition already distinguishes the Nichoria pin, with its nail-like head, from the type under discussion. It may be useful to list those known to me; there are surely others.

1. Crete, Knossos, Gypsadhes, Tomb VII:13. L. 0.26 m (Hood et al. 1958-59, pp. 249, 257, Fig. 34, Pl. 60a)

Table 5-5. Chronological Breakdown of Cataloged DA Lead Objects by Category

Lead	DAI	DAI-II	DAII	DAII-III	DAIII	DA
Whorl			**112**			
Sinkers			**113, 114**			
Clamps	**117**					**115, 116**
Scrap					**118**	
Waste		**119**				
TOTAL: 8	1	1	3		1	2

2. the same, no. 14. L. ca. 0.107 m
3. the same, no. 15. L. 0.07 m
4. Argos, Deiras cemetery, Tomb XVIII, no. DB2. L. 0.184 m (Deshayes 1966, pp. 44, 54, Pls. 24, 54, and C)
5. the same, Tomb XIV, no. DB3. L. 0.378 m
6. Messenia, Nichoria, Tourkokivouro, Tsagdis Tomb I. L. 0.14 m (Choremis 1973, pp. 71-73, Pl. 38)
7. the same, perhaps from the same tomb. L. 0.221 m

The contexts of these pins are closely comparable. The Gypsadhes tomb contained pottery of LMIIIB2-Subminoan types. No. 4 was associated with pottery datable to the LHIIIC/Submycenaean transition, and no. 5 was found with Submycenaean pottery. The context of nos. 6 and 7 is less certain, as the graves had been disturbed by cultivation before excavation. However, the only pottery from the site was identified by Choremis (1973, p. 73) as LHIIIC-PG and by Coulson (pp. 266-68) as DAI.

The seven pins listed above all have the fusiform swelling on the upper shaft, but they vary a good deal in the extent and emphasis of the moldings; their heads are in no way enlarged. With these examples Desborough compares two very large pins now in Mainz (Hampe and Simon 1959, p. 13, Figs. 1, 2), said to have been found with late PG pottery, bronze bracelets, and three fibulae with swollen arch, allegedly from a tomb group found somewhere in the Peleponnese. He implies that the very different treatment of the shank above and below the fusiform swelling—groups of traced encircling lines and a different linear pattern traced on the head—was the natural evolution of the type. This may well be right, but this supposed development from the variety is so rare that it is difficult to attach great weight to the suggestion.

Scholars have distinguished between the headless molded pins described above and a series of Submycenaean pins, some of them very large, with a relatively elongated fusiform swelling, nail-like head and groups of traced encircling bands above and below the swelling.[3] Styrenius (1967, p. 159) shows reason to believe that, in Athens at least, this type of pin was introduced somewhat later than the alternative Submycenaean type with globe swelling on the shank and fairly prominent head (Müller-Karpe 1962, p. 83, Fig. 1, nos 1, 7, 8). It is certainly not confined to Athens; for there is, for instance, a pair in a late Submycenaean context at Mycenae itself, illustrated by Desborough (1965, Pl. 33e; 1972, pp. 67 ff.). Styrenius identifies as pins of this type a pair found in the Submycenaean cemetery at ancient Elis (Leon 1961-63, Fig. 25a).

In publishing her nos. VII 13-15, Sandars (Hood et al. 1958-59, p. 236) considered the possibility that a pin with globe and shank moldings from Mouliana Tomb A (Xanthoudides 1904, p. 31, Fig. 7) was of the same type. She also refers to a Macedonian pin, found at Boubousti,[4] with the same features, although the shank is square in section. Jacobsthal, who did not know of the Gypsadhes pins, classed the Mouliana pin as "Sub-Mycenaean-Proto-Geometric";[5] he rejected (Jacobsthal 1956, p. 2, note 3 and p. 16) Heurtley's suggestion that the Boubousti pin is also Submycenaean and was surely right. Although the Mouliana pin is probably contemporary with ours, its more massive globe clearly distinguishes it from the rest.

To sum up, it seems that the Nichoria pin **5** incorporates features found in two varieties of Submycenaean/Subminoan pins; it has the nail-like head of one variety, the bead moldings of the other. Such a fusion is inherently likely, and there is probably no need to look further for the pin's identity. It seems very probable that it should itself be dated to the local equivalent of Submycenaean elsewhere in Greece.

It has been necessary to review a considerable body of evidence in attempting to identify our pin **5**. It is very important, however, that this pin be correctly assigned. Had it not found its place within this Submycenaean series, it could only have been regarded as a rather provincial version of Jacobsthal's Group 3 of Geometric pins, the final step in the development of the Greek pin before the appearance of the Orientalizing series (Jacobsthal 1956, pp. 12 ff.). Pins of this type figure predominantly among early votives at Artemis Orthia (Dawkins 1929, p. 197, Pl. 75); an equally rich series was found at the Argive Heraion (Waldstein et al. 1905, Pls. 78, 79). The chronological evidence of Artemis Orthia, recently reinterpreted by Boardman (1963, pp. 1-7), would make a date for such pins unlikely before the last quarter of the 8th century; and they could be still later. Such a result would not be in keeping with the main body of Dark Age evidence at Nichoria. In any event, pin **5** appears to be out of chronological context in its cranny in the west wall of Unit IV-9, and it is probably idle to speculate on how it got there.

The fine fragment of a cast pin (**6**) belongs to a more sophisticated tradition of metal working and must be compared with material from the full Geometric period elsewhere in Greece. It is probably the finial of an elaborately decorated pin of the second group of Jacobsthal's Group 2 pins, all of which he assigned to the Geometric period (Jacobsthal 1956, pp. 9 ff.). Whereas some of the most magnificent of these Geometric pins have been reported from Corinth (Davidson 1952, Pl. 117; Jacobsthal 1956, Fig. 33) or from the Hera Akraia votive deposits at Perachora (Payne et al. 1940, p. 70, Fig. 11, Pl. 17), others, perhaps a little less sophisticated, were found rather nearer Nichoria in the sanctuary of Athena Alea at Tegea (Dugas 1921, pp. 335-435, Figs. 39-41). Jacobsthal (1956, Figs. 26-28) illustrated three of the finest, whose elongated finials, though not an exact parallel for our fragment **6**, are sufficiently close to suggest the attribution. The Tegea finds are not closely datable by context, but the Perachora deposit must belong to the earlier 8th century (Coldstream 1968, pp. 352-53, 404). The Corinth tomb groups containing the pins mentioned above are to be dated ca. 750 (Coldstream 1977, p. 174). On the face of it, our pin no. **6** ought to be no earlier than ca. 800, and it could be a good deal later.

FIBULAE (CATALOG NOS. 8-10)

The remains of fibulae are very scrappy. Parts of two, perhaps three brooches are preserved, of which only one (**8**) can be identified with some confidence. This is most of the bow and the spring of a symmetric arched bow fibula corresponding to Blinkenberg's type II.1 or II.2 (Blinkenberg 1926, pp. 60-62). The form is typical of the Submycenaean and earliest Protogeometric periods and has been found fairly widely distributed within Greece and the Aegean.[6] An important series has been found among the fibulae from the DA cemeteries at Lefkandi in Euboea (Popham et al. 1979-80, pp. 233 ff., Pls. 238, 247). A particularly fine group was found in Skoubris Tomb 16 (Popham et al. 1979-80, pp. 114 ff., Pls. 95, 207) whose 11 arched bow fibulae recall the better known Late Submycenaean Grave 108 in the Kerameikos with its total of 13 fibulae, the majority of which are of symmetric arched bow type (Kraiker and Kübler 1939, Pl. 28; Desborough 1964, Pl. 21). The appearances of this type of fibula are, in general, coterminous with the incidence of Submycenaean or Subminoan burial; this is not the place, however, to review the full distribution of the type. Among sites within significant distance of Nichoria mention may be made of four fibulae from the group of Submycenaean graves at ancient Elis, of which a pair from Grave 1961:6 are closely comparable to the Nichoria piece.[7]

Our **9** is certainly a fibula pin, but it is probably futile to try to conjecture the type of brooch to which it once belonged. Its size is consistent with a Submycenaean or early Protogeometric type and is comparable to **8**. I cannot place **10**.

RINGS (CATALOG NOS. 11-23)

This is an unsatisfactory collection of material, partly because of the indifferent state of preservation, partly because of its heterogeneity. With the exception of **11**, which has a pronounced thickening at one point suggesting a bezel, the other closed rings, **12-14**, are very slight, plain objects, all of plano-convex section. Two come from DAII contexts, two from DAIII. They seem to be slimmer versions of a ring type that appears in Submycenaean and Protogeometric graves in Athens (Styrenius 1967, pp. 48, 70, 109) and Euboea (Catling in Popham et al. 1979-80, pp. 247 ff.), for instance. In grave groups at least, the use of closed bronze rings seems to diminish from PG onward.[8] Our **15**, and probably **16** too, are examples of a very simple open ring made by rolling a hammered strip to the shape of the finger—about as basic an ornament as may be imagined. The context for **15** is DAI; for **16** it is predominantly DAII. Elsewhere in Greece open-ended rings occur together with the closed hoop variety in Submycenaean and, to a lesser extent, in PG contexts. There is slight variety—rounded, tapering, or squared-off terminals, hoops plain or picked out with a slightly raised ridge. They have yet to be the subject of a separate study.

The spiral rings **17-23** differ a good deal in their form. Only one (**19**) has a diameter of 0.02 m or more; the remainder vary between 0.015 and 0.017 m, which is on the small side to have been used as finger rings. They vary, too, in the number of turns of metal of which they are composed, from the three-and-a-quarter turns of **17** to the one-and-three-quarter turns of **20**. The metal width also varies between 0.0015 m and 0.003 m. Unfortunately, the Nichoria find circumstances provide no clue to their function(s); only when they are grave goods is there likelihood of determining that problem. Their narrowness suggests, perhaps, that they were used in dressing the hair, but the find circumstances of bronze spirals in five Kerameikos tombs (nos. 43, 47, 52, 104, 108) are equivocal, and some positions seemed more appropriate to finger rings than hair fasteners (Kraiker and Kübler 1939, pp. 85 ff., Fig. 4, Pl. 28). Use of spiral rings continues into the PG period. A bronze example was found by Verdelis (1963, p. 32, Fig. 11.5) in Tomb XV at Tiryns along with a gold pair; a second gold pair was found in Tomb VII at the same site (Verdelis 1963, p. 30, Fig. 11.3). Other gold spirals came from the Lefkandi cemetery (Popham et al. 1979-80, p. 220, Pl. 230).

EARRING(?) (CATALOG NO. 24)

The Nichoria spirals are evenly distributed throughout the DA period. No. **24**, a twist of very thin wire from a DAII context, has been tentatively identified as an earring. The context tells us nothing of its function. Earrings in the Dark Age are uncommon. Styrenius in his survey (1967, p. 48) of the earlier part of the period mentions only one, i.e., in Kerameikos Tomb 583; and the identity of even that is uncertain. I feel more confident about identifying as earrings two Lefkandi objects from the Submycenaean tombs 19 and 22 (Popham et al. 1979-80, Pl. 98—Skoubris 19.9 and Pl. 99—Skoubris 22.4). The Nichoria piece is very similar. All alike are essentially featureless.

BEAD (CATALOG NO. 25)

The bead (**25**) comes from a DAII context. It is composed of a tight coil of wire which may not be complete. It could be a fragment of a much larger tight coil of the type found in great abundance at the Vergina cemetery in west Macedonia (Andronikos 1969, esp. pp. 225-27 and Pl. 126). The diameter of these Macedonian spirals is in the range of 0.05-0.07 m, which harmonizes with **25**. It seems, however, that such ornaments have been identified only on Aigina (Furtwängler 1906, pp. 53, 54, Pls. 115, 116) in south Greece, and the suggested identification must be very tentative.

WEAPON (CATALOG NO. **26**)

The only bronze weapon is **26**, a small fragment from the extreme tip of what could be any of the stabbing/thrusting weapons. It comes from an ambiguous context where LH and DAII material was mixed and so might be thought more naturally to be of Late Bronze date. But it must be remembered that bronze continued to be used for some weapons, particularly spearheads, well into the DA period. Unfortunately, the lightly traced parallel lines detectable on either side of the blade do not assist the attribution, since all three categories of weapon mentioned above share this feature.

SMALL TOOLS (CATALOG NOS. **27-35**)

For the categories of bronze objects from Nichoria that have so far been discussed, it has been possible to turn to the evidence of DA cemeteries elsewhere in Greece for parallels and chronological confirmation of the correctness of the attributions proposed here. With small tools, however, we move into largely uncharted waters. Very little material from contemporary settlements has been published, while tools virtually never found their way into DA graves. The difficulty is intensified by the extreme simplicity of the instruments themselves and by the fact that few of them are complete. It is an interesting side light upon the systematic fashion in which worn or damaged metal objects were recycled at Nichoria that the only traces of the bronze tool kit that must have been in use are a few tiny instruments and fragments of others. Although the identifications suggested in the catalog are in several cases tentative, the general character of this fragment of a tool kit is not in doubt. We have tools for boring or drilling (**27-33**), a very small chisel (**34**), and scraps of a rather larger chisel (**35**). Some of these implements would be useful in leather working (for piercing stitch holes, etc.) or in light carpentry in conjunction with a bow-drill. The light chisel (**34**) might have been of use to a wood carver, but only for very delicate work. All the tools could have been of use to a sculptor in metal, working over his wax cartoon in preparation for making an investment mold for a bronze statuette or for the decorated elements in tripod caldrons or other large embellished objects.

One of the few collections of bronze tools from a DA site is that from Karphi (Pendlebury 1940, pp. 112 ff., Pls. 28, 29), which includes awls, gravers, and small chisels of the same general character as the Nichoria pieces. That the small tool kit changed relatively little over a considerable period and was remarkably similar within the limits of an extensive geographical region can be seen by comparing the Nichoria series with material from Late Bronze Age Cyprus (Catling 1964, Fig. 10) and with recent finds from Late Minoan II Knossos (Catling and Jones 1977, p. 60, Fig. 1).

NEEDLES (CATALOG NOS. **36-44**)

Nine needles come from contexts throughout the DA period, the majority being of DAII date. Their interest lies in their presence rather than their typology. Only two (**42** and **44**) are complete, and even those have nothing distinctive about them. The Karphi group of tools and implements is said to include two needles (Pendlebury 1940, pp. 38, 115, Pl. 28), but one of them (their no. 171) must surely be an eyelet pin.

RIVETS (CATALOG NOS. **45-47**)

Among a number of miscellaneous rivets, three from DA contexts are of the type used to secure hilt plates of organic material to the butts of hand-held tools or weapons. There is nothing in the objects themselves to ensure that they were manufactured after the Late Bronze Age. It will be remembered, of course, that during the initial stages of the introduction of iron to Greece it was quite common for bronze rivets to be used in conjunction with iron blades. The phenomenon has been discussed by Snodgrass (1971, pp. 217-29) and Desborough (1972, p. 308). This feature is almost certainly confined to knives and swords; in some cases the habit persisted until the 9th or even the 8th century.

VESSELS (CATALOG NOS. **48-51**)

The material is very scrappy, and nothing approaching a complete vessel shape was found. It could be objected that any or all of the items might be appreciably earlier than the primarily DA deposits with which they were associated. In all four cases LH pottery was found with the DA material.

The two rivets **50** and **51** represent different types. No. **50** is typical of the method adopted by bronzesmiths building up a large or very large vessel from a number of different pieces of sheet metal. This technique is better attested among the bronze vessels of LM/LH than DA times (Catling 1964, pp. 166-88; Catling and Catling 1974, pp. 231-51); but caldrons and tripod caldrons alone act as a reminder that major bronze vessels were a feature of DA metalwork (Benton 1938, pp. 74 ff.), even if there may not be general agreement on the early history of the series (see in particular Snodgrass 1971, pp. 281-86). If correctly identified as a component of a vessel, **51** was clearly used for a different purpose. This should have been to secure some large heavy cast component, such as a handle escutcheon or leg of a tripod caldron, to the rim or wall of the vessel.[9]

The handle fragment **49** is anonymous, although it clearly formed part of a small vessel, cup, or something of the kind. The handle will have been fabricated rather than cast; the type is illustrated by two cups from the LMIIIA1 Sellopoulo Tomb 4, at Knossos (Catling and Catling 1974, p. 235, Fig. 22). Relatively little is known of the smaller DA bronze vessels. Some might argue that, particularly in the period between ca. 1025 and ca. 950, there was so serious a shortage of bronze in a large area of Greece and the Aegean as to provide a signal stimulus to the development of iron technology.[10] If this suggestion is correct, it should be vain to search for bronze vessels at this period. Although I recognize the strength of the argument for bronze shortage, I see it suffers from the weakness of all arguments *e silentio*, particularly when in this case the period during which evidence is lacking is succeeded by one in which there is once more evidence not only for the existence of the metal but also for the very particular skills in its working. Perhaps the clearest illustration comes from the Lefkandi workshop, evidence that cannot be dated much later than ca. 900, where it is evident from the debris of quite sophisticated investment casting that a very experienced bronze founder had been active at Lefkandi at the end of the 10th century.[11] This problem must be seen against the general background of knowledge of the Greek Dark Age that is dominated by cemetery evidence and a burial rite that was particularly conformist. The Lefkandi evidence suddenly opened a window upon a prospect of DA activity of which we had been hitherto in almost complete ignorance.

The most tendentious attribution is **48**, small scraps of sheet metal, two of which bear *pointillé* linear ornament; one of the latter consists of two pieces of sheet, decorated, and pinned together by a rivet. The suggestion is here made that this could be part of a small hammered bronze vessel, composed of more than one metal sheet. There are difficulties in this explanation, not least of which is the lack of closely parallel vessels from which such fragments could have come. Small sheet metal vessels decorated *en pointillé* are well represented in Italy,[12] but their use of rivets seems largely to be confined to the attachment of handles. This is not at issue with **48**, where the rivet is joining two pieces of metal of equal thickness. That **48** is not necessarily the remains of a vessel can be illustrated by reference to a fine bronze diadem of sheet metal with *pointillé* ornament found by Andronikos (1969, pp. 51, 52, 251-54, Figs. 15, 18, Pls. 16, 101) in Vergina Tomb Y III. Here the terminals overlap and are secured by rivets. In my view, the balance is slightly in favor of the identity of our fragments as from a vessel, but the evidence is very weak.

TRAPPINGS (CATALOG NOS. 52-56)

The phalaron (**52**) is an object of great interest, for the class to which it belongs has been the source of a considerable controversy that has not yet been resolved. The most recent discussion has been that of Snodgrass (1973). The same scholar was earlier responsible for one of the most comprehensive surveys of the Greek material (Snodgrass 1964, pp. 37-51); both his studies are fundamental for an understanding of the issues involved. In view of the clarity and thoroughness with which he has set out the evidence and arguments, it will not be necessary to review the matter in full. The controversy, in essence, is one concerning identity—the identity of a considerable number of bronze (much less frequently, iron) discs with raised centers, sometimes with a separate spike protruding from this center, sometimes (as with our **52**) with no other feature on the raised center than a small hole pierced in it. Some examples have simple *pointillé* decoration; the best illustration of this is the Vergina series (Andronikos 1969, pp. 243-47, Figs. 84, 85, Pls. 127, 128). The spikes with which a majority are equipped come in a good many forms, varying from somewhat nipple-like tips seen on the Vergina series to very prominent and elaborately molded projections, illustrated by a phalaron in Tiryns Tomb XXVIII (Submycenaean; Verdelis 1963, p. 13, Fig. 6), another in Kerameikos Grave 24 (Kübler 1943, Pl. 37), one from Kaloriziki Tomb 40 (McFadden 1954, Pl. 25), and a very elaborate example in an 8th century tomb (T.34) at Vitsa Zagoraiou (Epirus) recently illustrated by Vokotopoulou (1967, p. 348, Pl. 251α,β) and repeated by Snodgrass (1973, Pl. 1).

At least five explanations of the identity of these phalara have been offered over more than a century of scholarship. These include breastplate attachments, shield bosses, cymbals, belt ornaments, and horse trappings. One of the most valuable contributions made by Snodgrass has been the assurance that no single explanation fits the whole body of material. For instance, the excavation by Andronikos in the Vergina tumulus field uncovered several female inhumations where phalara were found in such a position that the correct explanation for their use can only be that they were part of a woman's costume, perhaps belt attachments.[13]

This explanation is inappropriate in many cases, however, especially where a single phalaron with prominent central spike is part of a burial complex otherwise appropriate to a warrior. Tiryns Tomb XXVIII has already been mentioned; in that case the phalaron was found with an iron dirk, another iron blade, a bronze spearhead, and bronze facings for a helmet (Verdelis 1963, pp. 10-24). Recent excavation in the University cemetery at Knossos brought two more phalara to notice, both with central spike (Catling 1978-79, pp. 45, 46). One, in T.186, was accompanied by an iron dirk, an iron knife, a large bronze spearhead and two whetstones. The second, in T.201, was found with a bronze sword of type II, a bronze spearhead, and five large bronze arrowheads. For these three complexes at Tiryns and at Knossos, the shield boss explanation is more plausible, although the Knossian burial chambers were so small (the rite was cremation) that the bosses must have been dismounted from the shields to fit in the grave. This is not as artificial an explanation as it may sound, since in both graves the spearheads had been detached from their shafts and the bronze type II sword was broken in pieces.

Snodgrass (1973, pp. 42-44) has thrown considerable doubt on the identification of any of the Greek phalara as horse trappings; nor is he particularly impressed by the arguments in support of the identification as cymbals. I agree fully with his position as far as it affects the types of associations so far considered, namely Macedonian female burials and Argive and Knossian warrior graves. The Nichoria piece, however, is in a different category, since it was found in a neutral context—alone on a house floor—that can say nothing of its function. Lacking any kind of central spike, it is equally neutral in its own design. At 0.11 m in diameter, it is in the smaller range of those included in Snodgrass's list (1964, pp. 39-41). The stilted profile of the raised central part distinguishes it from the Mouliana phalara (Xanthoudides 1904, p. 46, Fig. 11) and from the two smaller Kaloriziki phalara (McFadden 1954, Pl. 25) whose central parts leave the flat of the disc in an immediate curve. In this respect, the structure of **52** resembles the majority of the Vergina phalara (Andronikos 1969, Figs. 84, 85), although there is no other feature of close resemblance.

The DAII date of the context in which **52** was found suits the fairly wide range of dates from Submycenaean/Subminoan until at least the 8th century for the contexts in which the phalara described above have severally been found.

Finally, in its spikeless state, **52** is unlikely to have been a shield boss on its own. It might once have been part of a set fixed on a shield, as I believe the Kaloriziki trio to have been (Catling 1964, pp. 142-46; Catling and Catling in Benson 1973, pp. 130 ff.). In fact, it is scarcely possible to learn what its function can have been, although I suspect a decorative rather than a functional role.

It is unfortunate that the identity of the "collar," **53**, should be so inscrutable; technically, it is one of the more sophisticated Nichoria pieces. Its context is DAIII. It must have formed part of a much larger object at the identity of which I cannot even guess. It will have been made by lost wax. The mold in which it was cast must have required skill and experience to make.

The fragment **54**, from a DAII-III context, appears to be part of the circumference of a flat open circle with the start of an internal "spoke." It is possibly a scrap broken from a wheel pendant of some kind and could, when complete, have been comparable to a Perachora piece from the Hera Limenia deposit (Payne et al. 1940, Pl. 78.16).

The remains of a hollow boss, **55**, from a DAII context, are insufficiently distinctive to allow identification. The object doubtless originally formed part of something more complicated at whose identity it is hardly possible to guess. The elaborate bracelets (decked with threaded hemispheres) from the votive deposits at the Argive Heraeum (Waldstein et al. 1905, Pl. 89) may suggest the type of complicated object that could have been involved.

From a DAIII context, another scrap, **56**, may once have formed part of a pendant in the form of a double ax, a type of ornament popular as a votive at sanctuaries in many parts of Greece.[14]

UNIDENTIFIED FITTING (CATALOG NO. 57)

The solid cylindrical bar, **57**, with its oblique holes pierced in the face of each end to emerge nearby on the curved face of the bar, is at once the most substantial DA bronze object recovered and the most enigmatic. It was found on the floor of the DA building, Unit IV-1, in a DAII context and in close juxtaposition with the iron tool **89**. It is tempting to see the latter as in some way connected with the making of textiles—even having been used in the working of a loom. This suspicion, in turn, raises the possibility that the bronze bar formed part of a loom. The difficulty in accepting such a suggestion lies in attempting to see why a relatively simple working part that could have been made of wood or bone should have been so expensively manufactured. A different explanation must almost certainly be sought; but the problem of identification is such that, unless one had the good fortune to encounter the complex of which such an item formed part, the likelihood of providing the solution is not strong.

STATUETTES (CATALOG NOS. 58-60)

The quadruped **58** is a relatively undistinguished piece on its own. Its interest lies in its relationship to the great DAIII building that presumably had (at least in part) a domestic function. The vast majority of animal statuettes of the Geometric period have been found in sanctuary deposits or, very much less frequently, as grave offerings. A new study of the material from Olympia by Heilmeyer (1979) emphasizes how substantial was the output of small animal figures, either free-standing or, like our piece, set on a stand. Even within a milieu conspicuous for summary modeling, our figure has been modeled in an exceptionally summary fashion, so that the animal's identity is far from clear. It could have been meant to represent a deer; but a horse is not impossible.

The form of the stand on which our animal is set is unusual. Most stands are rectangular, hollow beneath, with a design in relief or intaglio; more rarely, they are oval or round. A beetle from Olympia (Kunze and Schleif 1937-38, no. 950, Pl. 121) stands on a round *ajourée* rayed base, perhaps representing a wheel, and recalling a trifle the incised pattern on our stand. Roughly the same design is repeated on the stand for a horse, also from Olympia (Kunze and Schleif 1937-38, no. 326, Pl. 38) dated to the middle of the 8th century. Also on a rayed *ajourée* base is a rather featureless creature from Artemis Orthia, whose date of deposition is unlikely to be earlier than the late 8th century.[15] A stand of the same type, whose animal figure is broken away and lost, was found at Delphi (Rolley 1969, p. 93, no. 152, Pl. 23). Two birds mounted on similar stands were reported from the Argive Heraion (Waldstein et al. 1905, pp. 11, 42, 43, Pl. 77). Although the recent publication of the Olympia material has provided an invaluable insight into the nuances of variety in this somewhat intractable material, nothing emerges but general similarities with the Nichoria piece. It is tempting to see it more as a bronze seal with zoömorphic handle than as an animal on a stand.

The fragments **59** and **60** are likely to have come from objects of a class similar to that for **58**. It is suggested that **60** could have been part of the tail of an animal figurine, perhaps a horse. The rather puzzling fragment **59** might have formed part of a stand for an animal figure, although it is not wholly clear how the piece should be restored.

INCOMPLETE OBJECTS (CATALOG NOS. 61-63)

Nos. **62** and **63** appear to be largely unworked fragments of rough billets of metal of the kind bronzesmiths will have used for a variety of purposes, including the preparation of hafting rivets and for working into small tools like the awls/drills/gravers/chisels described above. Several billets of this kind are among the waste metal found in a LMII context in the Unexplored Mansion at Knossos (Popham and Sackett 1973, pp. 50-71).

SCRAP (CATALOG NOS. 64-75)

These objects, all comparatively small and insignificant, come from a succession of contexts that cover the whole of the DA occupation of the site. Many of them are fragments of sheet metal that might once have been parts of small vessels or decorative overlays or affixes. Other pieces might have come from knife blades or small tool shafts. The generic description of "scrap" has been given to this material in the belief that some of it, at least, came from the remelting boxes of a bronzesmith's workshop, after being broken up and thrown away for recycling through wear or damage or mere desuetude. The site had clearly been too well scoured, both during and following occupation, for there to be much hope that less equivocal material of this kind might survive.

MELTING OR CASTING WASTE (CATALOG NOS. 76-79)

Pellets of bronze found in contexts covering the whole DA occupation were evidently the result of handling molten metal at the moment of pouring from the crucible into the mold or removing a charged crucible from the furnace in preparation for such casting. One piece of waste (SF 462) used for analysis was more substantial than the rest and different in shape. It may have been the product of casting in a two-piece mold, representing the excess metal projecting as a riser beyond the limit of the vent cut in the material of the mold to allow the escape of gases during the moments of casting. None of this material, obviously, has any intrinsic interest, but it is of great importance for the evidence it provides of industrial activity on the site. Again, the quantity of waste surviving, the identity of the types, and the minute size of the individual items are a reminder of the care with which metal was conserved. Substantial pieces of waste, such as the jets that represent the filling cups/pouring funnels of two-piece lost wax molds, have not survived. Their absence is quite understandable, since on removal of a cast from its mold after cooling, the jet would be the first piece to be broken off and thrown into a box for recycling.

PRELIMINARY ANALYTICAL RESULTS

Catling and Jones (1977, pp. 57-66) have published the results of XRF analysis on a significant number of LMII bronzes from the Unexplored Mansion at Knossos. The prime interest of this work had been to determine the principal constituents of each piece analyzed, and in particular the changing proportion of tin added to the major copper constituent of the bronze alloy. Study of the analyses pointed to a fairly consistent correlation between the amount of tin involved and the identity/function of the artefact sampled. In certain cases it was observed that the amount of tin present was much in excess of the optimum (about 10%) for practical reasons. The authors suggested that such results might be explicable in cosmetic terms: the color change in the alloy brought about by the addition of an impractical amount of tin may have been the main, if not the sole, objective. Otherwise, such a departure from careful control over the properties of the mixture would be inexplicable.

Several of the Nichoria objects cataloged and discussed here have also been analyzed, either by OES or by XRF. The results are presented by G. Rapp, R. E. Jones, S. R. B. Cooke, and E. L. Henrickson in *Nichoria* I, pp. 166-81. Of the material under review, nos. **2**, **3**, **4**, **5**, **6**, **9**, **13**, **17**, **18**, **19**, **20**, **26**, **28**, **30**, **32**, **33**, **35**, **47**, **52**, **53**, **57**, **58**, **62**, and **71** were analyzed. In the Catalog, note has been made of those analyses; figures for Arsenic (As), Tin (Sn), and Lead (Pb) are quoted. The roll-top pin, **3**, has an exceptional quantity of tin (16.5%). The Submycenaean pin, **5**, has the even higher figure of 25% tin. The fragment of Geometric decorated pin, **6**, is also very high at 17%. The only fibula analyzed, **9**, is also very rich in tin, at 20%. The finger ring, **13**, is high, at 17.1%, almost exactly the same proportion (17%) as for the spirals, **19** and **20**. Higher again is the phalaron, **52**, at 25%. The "collar," **53**, at 16% is still much higher than the optimum, and it is made more remarkable by the presence of 20% lead. The remaining results are less noteworthy. If we ignore **53** for the moment, since its function is uncertain, a significant correlation seems clear between bronzes with very high tin content and their decorative function. Not excepting the phalaron, **52**, all these objects were part of dress (fibulae, pins) or more directly on the person (finger rings, hair spirals). The higher the content of tin, the lighter and doubtless more silvery the color of the metal. The figures speak for themselves.

The case of **53**, the so-called "collar," with its 20% of lead in addition to 16% tin, is of interest in a different context. The addition of so much lead must have been deliberate, its effect being to enhance the fluidity of the molten metal during the cast. This lends support to the view that our fragment is but a small part of a complex object produced in a lost wax mold, where the effect introduced by the lead would have been of particular importance in casting.

It may be noticed that **26**, a fragment identified as part of a weapon, has only 10.5% tin in its composition. This contrast illustrates the bronze-founder's use of the optimum proportions in making an object whose function was entirely practical. Among the DA objects analyzed by XRF, this was the only one where the optimum was attained.

Analysis of the animal figure, **58**, showed 3.7% tin content. This result may be compared with the analyses published very recently by Heilmeyer (1979, pp. 276-83) of 19 bronzes, many of them animal statuettes contemporary with ours, that come from several different groups or workshops. The great variety of the results, particularly in tin content, is striking.

THE IRON OBJECTS

PINS (CATALOG NOS. 80-82)

The material is, unfortunately, too poorly preserved to be particularly informative. The DAII context for **80** and DAIII for **81** provide satisfactory associations, but the evidence for **82** ("LH and Modern") is ambiguous. No pins with heads survive; nor is there any sign of pins whose upper shafts are picked out by a globe, either of iron or of bronze, features that are well represented elsewhere in Greece, particularly in cemetery finds.[16] The frequent adoption of iron for pins from Late Submycenaean times onward has been interpreted as evidence consistent with the theory of bronze shortage, to which reference was made above. This argument is persuasive, but not fully convincing. The existence, notably in Attic Protogeometric and early Geometric grave groups, of pins whose heads and shafts are of iron, with the boss made separately of bronze and slipped on the shaft, suggests much more a delight in the decorative quality in terms of color, first, of the iron, then of the strong contrast offered by the copper/bronze of the boss.

The way back to bronze may have been shown by the interest in the modeling of the pin seen in the overlaying of Geometric iron pins with gold sheet. Once this move had been made, a return to the plastic advantages of bronze was inevitable.

RINGS (CATALOG NOS. 83-84)

These two rings are similar in type and resemble the basic bronze finger ring with closed hoop and plano-convex in section that was described above. In the Kerameikos and Salamis cemeteries at least, iron rings appear from Submycenaean times onward, and they are, in general, found earlier than iron pins. Of the four Kerameikos Submycenaean graves in which iron rings were found, one (their no. 83) contained three rings. One ring had been on the one hand of the deceased, two on the other. Tombs 20, 84, and 108 each had one ring; that in Tomb 108 was isolated among a large number of bronze rings (Kraiker and Kübler 1939, pp. 1, 16, 39, 47, 87). No iron rings, it seems, were found in the Protogeometric graves in the Kerameikos (Kraiker and Kübler 1939, p. 220; Kübler 1943, p. 26). They seem never to have been as popular a substitute for bronze rings as the iron pins became for a time in relation to their bronze equivalents. Iron and bronze rings are occasionally found in the same grave (see in particular Styrenius 1967, pp. 22, 48, 67, 70, 75, 156). Surprisingly, no iron rings occurred in the Lefkandi grave groups, although 21 bronze finger rings, of three different types, were found in the cemetery.

BRACELET (CATALOG NO. 85)

This object comes from a very ambiguous context, described as "LHI-LHII." It seems unlikely (though not impossible)[17] that it can be so early, and I have therefore assumed that it is an object of DA or later date that somehow got out of context. An iron bracelet was found by the Italians in Tomb XVII at Ialysos, dated LHIIIC (Maiuri 1926, p. 127; cf. Snodgrass 1971, p. 229), which shows that an object such as **85** *could* be found in a Bronze Age context, although this example is much later than the contextual material with which **85** was associated. DA bracelets in other materials seem never to have been very common. Three bronze examples have been recorded in Submycenaean Athens.[18] They were rarely deposited in Protogeometric graves, at least in Athens. Styrenius (1967, p. 108) notes two in Agora XLII, a child's grave; there is also a bracelet in Heidelberg B (transitional Submycenaean/Protogeometric; Styrenius 1967, p. 83). The Lefkandi graves contained a relatively larger number of bracelets than Athens; nine were found, none of them earlier than Late Protogeometric and the majority from Subprotogeometric contexts.[19] If the Vergina cemetery may be taken as representative, bracelets of a variety of types were a more common ornament and hence a natural grave offering in the North; Andronikos (1969, pp. 241-43, Figs. 82, 83) reports 45 in the graves he excavated. The least elaborate form of bracelet, consisting of a simple strap with open end like our **85**, was the most frequent variety.

TWEEZER(?) (CATALOG NO. 86)

The identification of **86** as fragments of a small pair of tweezers, though probable, is not absolutely certain. Such objects are not found in DA burials in other parts of Greece, although bronze specimens were not uncommon in the Late Bronze Age (Catling 1964, p. 229 and references there); their use certainly continued as late as LHIIIC, as four examples from Perati show (Iakovidis 1970, pp. 284-85). Another pair from Fortetsa Tomb P (Brock 1957, p. 137, no. 1597) is almost certainly later than our **86**.

AX (CATALOG NO. 87)

The fragmentary **87** was found in a DAII context, closely associated with Unit IV-1. Neither its place of discovery nor its form determines whether it was a tool or a weapon; it could have been either and it may very probably have been both. Its original form is unclear, but it could have been a double ax. Axes, shafted or otherwise, are not very common DA finds; after the end of the Bronze Age they appear to be made of iron only. They occur in the shaft-hole version of **87**, as lugged (or trunnion) axes and as double axes. The most notable instance of the last category is the pair found in the Panoply Tomb at Argos (Courbin 1957, pp. 367-68, Figs. 50, 51), whose warlike character must surely be conceded, despite the deprecatory remarks of Courbin and, still more, of Coldstream (1977, p. 146). At least three trunnion axes are known to me from Late Protogeometric to Subprotogeometric contexts, two from Athens and one from Lefkandi.[20] Axes were a more frequent grave offering in Crete, to judge from finds in the Fortetsa cemetery (Brock 1957, p. 202, Pl. 172).

BLADE FRAGMENT(?) (CATALOG NO. 88)

I have no comment to offer on the possible "blade" fragment **88**, found in an ambiguous context (DA with LH).

SMALL TOOLS (CATALOG NOS. 89-96)

The most interesting iron object from DA Nichoria, **89**, is also the least easily identified. From a DAII context, found in Unit IV-1 in association with the puzzling bronze object **57**, this socketed tool with pierced, lozenge-shaped working end is self-evidently a piece of specialized equipment. If it indeed belonged to the same mechanism as the heavy bronze rod **61**, the difficulty of identification is increased. An instinctive feeling that **89** was in some way involved with weaving is probably wrong, for it can hardly be a shuttle, or part of a shuttle; and in default of such a function, there is really no place for it in the equipment for a loom. Explanation of its identity must take account of the very narrow socket, whose internal diameter as preserved is only 0.005 m. Even allowing for the distortion created by oxidation, it is unlikely to have been over 0.0075 m at most. It is thus strangely long at 0.197 m to have been mounted on so slight a shaft; it can hardly have been a projectile of some kind. The pierced head cannot be ignored in attempting to identify its function. It could have been used, needle-fashion, to deliver a filament of material of some kind, a supply of which was wrapped round the shaft (hence the unworkable suggestion that this is a shuttle).

Alternatively, the hole in the point might have been used to pin this to some other component, perhaps made of a different material. A possible explanation for **89** and **57** could be that, in combination, they formed part of a locking mechanism. In that case, **57** would have been employed as a counterweight that normally held the actual lock in position, whereas **89** was the activating rod connecting the lock itself with whatever handle or key was used to open it. I have no parallel with which to justify this suggestion.

The iron knives, nos. **90-96**, form the largest single class of identifiable DA material, distributed throughout the period but most strongly represented during DAII. Two, at least, were closely associated with Unit IV-1. It must be remembered that their appearance and size may have been considerably altered by whetting during their periods of use, but in their present form they are all small knives with stubby butts. Most have short, convex-backed blades, making them ideal general purpose personal implements that would be useful for cutting food, cleaning game, pruning, whittling, and—conceivably—for shaving. They all had hafts of bone or wood, less probably of ivory.

The true knife, with single cutting edge, has a shorter history than the dagger, with its two edges. Knives in use during the Bronze Age were studied some time ago by Sandars.[21] Iron knives, usually with bronze rivets in the butt, document the first systematic usage of iron in the Aegean before the end of the Late Bronze Age, and as such they have attracted considerable interest. Sandars published an iron knife with bronze rivets from the Subminoan Tomb VII at Gypsadhes and commented upon the developed state of its design in relation to the bronze series.[22] Iakovidis drew attention more recently to the great interest attaching to the two iron knives found in the LHIIIC cemetery at Perati.[23] It is of equal interest that an iron knife with bronze rivets should have been found at Lefkandi in a context of Phase II of the LHIIIC occupation (Popham and Sackett 1968, p. 14, Fig. 22; Popham et al. 1979-80, pp. 170, 257, Pl. 245F).

Desborough has commented upon these finds, which have now been augmented by the new discoveries in the University cemetery at Knossos, where iron knives were found in the Subminoan Tombs 186 and 201 (Catling 1978-79, p. 46). He considered it probable that, during this period, the objects had probably been imported from

Cyprus, where several iron knives of this general description have been found in Late Cypriot IIIA and IIIB contexts.[24] For the Late Cypriot IIIA period, note may be made of unpublished knives from the Kouklia cemeteries (Catling 1968b, p. 168; two examples in Evreti Tomb VIII, one in Asproyi Tomb IV). There are many more from LCIIIB contexts, including two from Kaloriziki (Benson 1973, p. 124, Pl. 40) and another two from Salamis (Yon 1971, pp. 18, 19, Pls. 15, 18). The series continues into Cypro-Geometric (see, for instance, Catling 1964, p. 104) but need not be pursued beyond that point.

It is interesting that in none of those cases at Nichoria where rivets are preserved (**90, 91, 95**) are they of bronze. Evidence at Lefkandi shows that this feature, characteristic of the LHIIIC and Submycenaean periods, could persist as late as Subprotogeometric times (Popham et al. 1979-80, pp. 170, 257, Pls. 170, 246e = Toumba T.3:11). The technical explanation for the reluctance to use iron rivets has been given by Snodgrass (1971, p. 217) and is wholly convincing.

In attempting to assess the role of the knife during this period, it is interesting to contrast the DA evidence from Athens with that from Lefkandi; the result is equivocal. In Athens, many of the knives found in PG and EG burial contexts were associated with obvious warrior graves. These may be summarized as follows (the weapons mentioned are of iron, unless stated):

Kerameikos PG A	Two bronze spearheads, dagger
Kerameikos PG B	Sword
Kerameikos PG 17	Spearhead
Kerameikos G 13	Sword
Kerameikos G 38	Sword, spearhead
Agora T. XXVII	Sword, spearheads, axes
Areopagus 1944 T.	Sword
Agora cremation	Sword

In fact, the only Athens knife of which I have note that was found without weapons is that from Agora Tomb XXVI (Young 1949, p. 297, Pl. 72; Müller-Karpe 1962, pp. 111, 127, Fig. 29.4). In the case of Lefkandi, from whose tombs and pyres five, perhaps six, knives were recovered,[25] there was only one instance (P Pyre 16, 2) of an association with weapons. Three of the knives were the only metal objects in their groups; the remaining two were found, in one case certainly, in the other possibly, with a bronze fibula.

Müller-Karpe (1962, pp. 65 ff.) picked upon iron knives as one of the hallmarks of the grave inventories in his stage III (contemporary with Attic EG) in the use of metal objects as grave offerings in the Dark Age. In adopting this position, he is not taking account of at least three PG instances of knives as grave goods (Kerameikos PG A, PG 17, PG 28), while the EG instances are hardly so frequent as to make this a very compelling item in his equation, Stage III = EG. His argument, it seems, is further weakened by the Lefkandi evidence.

"NAILS" AND SCRAP (CATALOG NOS. 97-111)

The iron pieces tentatively called "nails" in the Catalog (nos. **97-102**) are not susceptible to identification, and no discussion is called for. It may be noted in passing that they cover the whole DA occupation of the site.

Similarly, no significant comment can be made on Catalog nos. **103-11**, described as "scrap." Each piece is too small and too anonymous for further consideration. Much of this material came from ambiguous contexts and is of little help in reconstructing the history of the DA use of metals at Nichoria.

THE LEAD OBJECTS (CATALOG NOS. 112-19)

Nine lead objects came from DAII and DAIII contexts, with several (**114-17**) from ambiguous associations. The categories represented (button/whorl; net sinkers; repairing clamps) are of simple kind and, like nearly all the metal objects, are small in size and weight. It would be a mistake to necessarily deduce from this that lead was available only in very small quantities. Both during occupation and after abandonment, the site was kept scoured of anything of value, leaving only "halves and skinny bits" for archaeological recovery. The largish lump of lead waste, **119**, however, corrects the balance somewhat, since it clearly suggests that lead was worked on the site. The clamps, **115-17**, though hardly lending themselves to close typological analysis, are of some economic interest in offering insight into the relationship between, let us suppose, the sentimental value of a household vessel or a pottery vase, the expense and trouble of replacing such a vessel when broken, and the expertise needed to fabricate the rivets *in situ* in the broken fragments.

The function of **112** is uncertain, but in size and shape, at least, it can be referred to one category of buttons—or *conuli* as Iakovidis (1977, pp. 113-19) would prefer to call them—that were used throughout the LH period. Iakovidis has suggested with some conviction that they were used as dress weights, being attached to the hems of long dresses. A similar use would have been possible for **112**. In that case, it may once have been covered by gold foil, which the ridges on the surface would have helped hold in place.

Nos. **113** and **114** would have been suitable as net sinkers. A rather different type is reported from the LHIIIC cemetery at Perati (Iakovidis 1969-70, I, p. 453; II, pp. 355-56; III, Pl. 135) and is encountered again in Attica in a LHIII tomb at Brauron (Papadimitriou 1961, p. 86, Pl. 24*a*).

As Buchholz showed in his classic study (1972) of lead in the prehistoric Aegean, lead was used throughout the Helladic period, most liberally in the Late Bronze Age when it was possible for large vessels to be made in this material (e.g., Buchholz 1972, p. 32, nos. 117-22, 129-33). It was also used widely for weights (Caskey 1969, pp. 95-106; also Marinatos 1974, p. 34, Pl. 83d).

The evidence for its DA use is on a very much smaller scale. With one very doubtful exception in the Submycenaean cemetery at Salamis (Styrenius 1967, p. 48), lead makes no appearance in the grave inventories in Submycenaean Athens; and there is little or no sign of it during the PG period in Athens. The Lefkandi evidence agrees closely with the Athenian. The cemeteries produced 262 metal objects from the tombs and pyres combined. Of these, 179 were bronze, 71 iron, six iron and bronze in combination, and only six were lead—i.e., 2% of the total. Two of these came from undatable contexts, one from the transitional Sub-PG I-II, the remainder from Sub-PG III, the last period in the use of the site. This is of particular interest in view of Lefkandi's relative proximity to the Laurion area, since there is evidence for silver and lead extraction at Thorikos as early as Protogeometric times (Mussche 1967a, pp. 29, 30; 1965, pp. 34-42, Figs. 44-48; Snodgrass 1971, p. 248; Coldstream 1977, pp. 70, 71).

GOLD (CATALOG NO. **120**)

The twist of fine wire, **120**, from a DAIII context, calls for no special comment. Recent finds in the DA cemeteries of Lefkandi and Athens, in particular in the Tomb of a Rich Athenian Lady found in the north slope of the Areopagus (Smithson 1961, pp. 77-116), have emphasized the relative prosperity of the later Dark Age. This is indicated not only by the amount of gold jewelry that might be buried with the dead, but also by the high quality of craftsmanship occasionally found in some of the items, of which the earrings in the north slope grave are merely the most outstanding. The presence of our scrap of gold suggests a goldsmith's stock-in-trade, rather than the remains of an item of jewelry. Such lengths of wire could have been used, for example, in the application of granulation. (For the technique see, e.g., Higgins 1961, pp. 18 ff.)

THE PITHOS BURIAL[26]

The warrior (it seems fair to describe him as such) was buried with bronze ring, iron sword, iron spear, and two bronze bowls. These offerings suggest his wealth and importance, for the burial of metal vessels with the dead, although attested in the Dark Age, was not a common phenomenon. The bronze ring, **121**, was found over the pelvis and has an internal diameter of nearly 0.03 m. It seems too large for a finger ring, although there is no very obvious alternative explanation for its presence unless it was in some fashion attached to belt or baldric used to gird his sword.

The badly oxidized iron sword, **124**, ca. 0.48 m long, is a rather poorly preserved example of a weapon type that seems to have been standard throughout much of Greece during the Dark Age, an iron version of a bronze weapon introduced to Greece before 1200 from barbaric Europe. The suggested typology of the bronze weapons (Catling 1968a, pp. 95-104 and references) does not hold good for the evolution of the iron weapons; this was pointed out some time ago by Snodgrass (1964, pp. 94, 106 ff.). The use of this type of sword evidently lasted throughout the 8th century, and perhaps longer.[27] One of the later instances is the series from the West Gate cemetery at Eretria, where at least six swords were found in a cremation grave complex dated 720-680 (Bérard 1970, pp. 16, 22, 32). Notice also the sword in a Geometric pithos burial at Drepanon in Achaea (Dekoulakou 1973, pp. 23-25). The chronology of the tumulus cemetery at Vergina is insufficiently secure to place much reliance upon that site as an index of the latest use of type II iron swords, although it is notable for having produced the largest number from any site yet known in Greece.[28]

The spearhead, **125**, was found in very poor condition, too poor for it to be closely referable to Snodgrass's typology (1964, pp. 115 ff.), although it may be related to his type D. It is not unlike the basic spear type found in the cemeteries of Lefkandi (Popham et al. 1979-80, Pl. 244). The association of sword and spear in the same group is quite frequent in DA warrior burials, but not an unvarying rule. According to the Athenian evidence, as summarized by Müller-Karpe (1962, p. 114, Fig. 33), it is not until the EG period that both weapon types are found in the same group. The Lefkandi evidence suggests a closer sword-spear relationship, since three of six spearheads from the whole cemetery were found with swords. Another spearhead was found with a (battle?) ax, a fifth with a very large knife, and only one without other weapon or tool association. Of the sword-spear associations at Lefkandi, one is dated to Late PG, another to the transitional Sub-PG I-II. The same association occurs in the Drepanon pithos burial already referred to, involving a spearhead not dissimilar in type from ours, although the group in question must be a good deal later (Dekoulakou 1973, Fig. 3, Pl. IΔ).

I have discussed in some detail (Popham et al. 1979-80, pp. 248-251) the DA appearance and usage of bronze bowls, with reference to their occurrence at Lefkandi. No bronze vessel of any kind was found there earlier than Sub-PG I; most belonged to the final phase in the use of the cemetery. Their use at Lefkandi was in striking contrast with practice in the Athenian and nearby cemeteries. One bowl was found in the Salamis cemetery, the only Submycenaean occurrence. A bowl was found in PG Tomb 48 in the Kerameikos, where it was serving as the cover of the ash urn. This practice became relatively common there in EG and MGI, with at least ten recorded instances (Kübler 1954, pp. 209 ff., Pl. 163). A similar use for a bowl was reported at Eleusis (Philios 1889, p. 178). Beyond Athens-Attica, similar bronze bowls have been found in 9th- and 8th-century graves at Argos, where they were deposited with the other offerings, not used as lids (Courbin 1974, pp. 129 ff. and references).

The "raised hump" in the floor of **122** (and probably in the fragmentary **123** as well) marks it as an early example of a phiale mesomphalos. One of the very earliest must be a vessel said to have come from a grave in Athens near Piraeus Street, dated by Blegen (1952, pp. 287-88, 293, Fig. 4, Pl. 77b) to ca. 900. The origin of the shape is almost certainly foreign; one possible source is suggested by a pottery version in Tomb 5 at Amathus in Cyprus (Gjerstad et al. 1935, p. 26, no. 37, Pl. 8) datable to the mid-9th century in Birmingham's revised chronology (1963, pp. 15-42). A very flat-profiled phiale mesomphalos was found at Lefkandi in Toumba Tomb 31, no. 20, from the last phase in the use of the cemetery, Sub-PG III, which is equivalent to MG I and II in Attic terms (Popham et al. 1979-80, pp. 186, 250 ff., Pls. 186, 243e). Other early instances include a phiale of ca. 750 from Corinth (Davidson 1952, p. 69, no. 517, Fig. 1), another from Delphi (Demangel 1926, p. 3, Fig. 56), and two from Perachora (Payne et al. 1940, p. 155, Pl. 55.1).

The general character of the metal offerings in our pithos grave distinguishes it from Athenian practice. A much closer comparison is found in the rather later Geometric pithos burials from Drepanon in Achaea, published by Dekoulakou (1973 supplement, pp. 15-29, Pls. I-IE). One of these contained two bronze vessels with the grave offerings, a second yielded an iron sword and spear. The associated pins and other finds suggest dates in the 8th and 7th centuries for this material. Other later pithos burials associated with bronzes are referred to by Coldstream (1977, p. 162 and references).

H.C.

The Evidence for Spinning and Weaving

THE WHORLS (PLS. 5-15 to 5-37)

The Nichoria DA whorls are numerous in proportion to the area of settlement excavated. Forty-four whorls are certainly of DA date, and another 34 probably are, making a total of 78. A further 26 whorls may possibly belong to the period.

The architectural remains of most of the buildings are fragmentary, but in the best-preserved structure, Unit IV-1, ten whorls were in use in the DAII/III (phase 2) period of occupation (nos. **143, 144, 145, 147, 148, 149, 150, 151, 161**, and **165**). A further five or six (nos. **132, 134, 137, 138, 146**, and perhaps **133**) were found in the DAIII reuse of this immediate area.

One gets the impression that spinning was very much a home industry, and this is borne out by the appearance of the whorls. Their formation is often clumsy and asymmetrical (which would not materially have affected their efficiency in spinning) and all appear to be handmade. In an age when whorls were very often decorated, all save two (**159, 159A**) of our whorls are plain. One or two have lightly burnished surfaces; others have been slipped and smoothed, and, very rarely, painted. The majority (just over 50% in both the certain and the probable groups) merely have a fire-blackened or dark exterior. The fabric—buff, beige, pink, orange, and, less often, brown or red—is frequently somewhat coarse and gritty, and in more cases than not the firing is poor and uneven and the consistency crumbly. This, combined with the fire-blackened surfaces, suggests that all the firing that most whorls received was in the family oven, or perhaps merely in the family hearth. The blackened surface is so typical of the certain DA whorls that it is a useful factor in helping to decide whether a whorl from a mixed context is DA (another criterion is shape—see below).

The weights of the whorls are moderate. Many are so broken that it was not possible to weigh them; but a sample of 34 whorls, either whole or broken in such a manner that their weight could be reasonably estimated, was selected from the whorls of certain DA date. The lightest of these (**141, 149**) weigh 7.6 and 8 grams, the heaviest (**158**) a massive 76 grams, and the average weight is 20 grams. If, however, we except two unusually large and heavy whorls, **158** (above) and **169** (40 grams), the average weight drops to 18 grams.

This comparatively light weight suggests that the raw material being spun was wool. Since much more always depends on the skill of the spinner than on the type or weight of the whorl, certainty is impossible; but, generally speaking, lighter-weight whorls are more appropriate for the elastic and cohesive fibers of wool, whereas heavier whorls are better suited to the smoother, stronger flax fibers. The two very heavy whorls mentioned above would have been suitable for flax spinning, however, and both fibers may have been in use. Messenia has some of the most suitable conditions for flax-growing to be found in Greece and was in 1968 the country's major flax-growing center (Loy 1970, pp. 24, 25, Fig. 9).

In any collection of whorls there will always be some that are suspected of being beads, and there is no certain method of distinguishing the two classes of object. Unless the perforation is too small to receive a spindle, it is perfectly possible to use a large bead as a whorl in spinning. Objects of light weight (less than 10 grams) and/or approximately round shape may be either whorls or beads. Into this category fall **126, 146**, and **160** of certain DA date; **181, 183**, and **193**, which are probably DA; and **206, 207, 209**, and **226**, which are of possible DA date. Of these, **181** is certainly too small to be a whorl; **146** was once painted red, and surely the whole point of a bead is that it should be decorative; **206** and **207** are of much finer and better-fired fabric than the usual whorls, and the latter's perforation is probably too small for a spindle; and **226** actually has signs of string-wear in its hole. Three other pieces (**141**, **149**, **164**), all certainly DA, have a somewhat convex-conical profile and hollow top (Type G) and would seem too small and light to be whorls. They may have been beads, or perhaps garment weights (Iakovidis 1977). It is just possible that **149**, weighing 8 grams but found with three whorls of different types, was a whorl.

The shapes found among the certain or possible DA whorls are set out in Figure 5-64. Type A is an asymmetrical bicone, Type B a symmetrical bicone, Type C a sphere, and Type D a flattened version of Type B. Type E is a straight-sided cone, Type F the same, but with a truncated base; Type G is also conical, but with a hollow top and somewhat convex sides. Types H, I, and J are conical too, but their sides are to greater or less degree concave, giving them a campaniform outline. Type H has a flat top, Type I a hollow top, and Type J a domed top. Type K, a unique reel-shaped whorl, is probably an eccentric version of H. Type L, a cylindrical whorl with a hollowed top, also occurs in only one example and is not certainly assignable to the Dark Age (see Fig. 5-65).

If we ignore the oddities (Types K and L), the ten remaining whorl types resolve themselves into three groups: Types A, B, C, and D are rounded, for DA biconical whorls are seldom well defined in profile; Types E, F, and G are conical; and Types H, I, and J are campaniform.

As will be seen from Tables 5-6, 5-7, and 5-8, the campaniform whorls in both the certain and the probable categories are the most numerous, and the conical whorls occur least often. Naturally, such irregularly shaped objects are often intermediate between two types, and one or two whorls assigned to Types E and F have a slight tendency toward the popular concave profile (**134**) and/or the domed top (**143**). Therefore, when a whorl is both campaniform in outline and has a blackened surface, it may very well be assigned to the Dark Age, even if it comes from a mixed context (e.g., **203** on Table 5-8).

The fact that the relative percentages of round, conical and campaniform whorls are so similar in Tables 5-6 and 5-7 makes it likely that those in Table 5-8 are distorted. As stated above, some of the objects in Types A, B, and C may be beads.

The sherd whorls are not numerous. One, **131** (kylix foot), is from Table 5-6; two, **192** (stirrup jar spout?) and **195** (bored kylix stem), are from Table 5-7; the remaining four are **220, 221, 222** (kylix feet?), and **228** (body sherd with *two* drilled holes–whorl or button?). Those from Tables 5-6 and 5-7 constitute only 4% of the total of those two groups. The practice of reusing sherds in such a manner is common to almost all periods.

Table 5-6. Whorls from "Certain" DA Contexts

Type	No.	%
A	6	14.3
B	5	11.9
C	3	7.1
D	. . .	. . .
Subtotal	**14**	**33.3**
E	4	9.5
F	1	2.4
G	3	7.1
Subtotal	**8**	**19.0**
H	13	30.9
I	. . .	. . .
J	6	14.3
Subtotal	**19**	**45.2**
K	1	2.4
L	. . .	. . .
Subtotal	**1**	**2.4**
fragment **138**	1	
sherd whorl	1	
TOTAL	**44**	99.9

An attempt to subdivide the certain DA whorls of Table 5-6 according to the ceramic phases adopted in Chapter 3 did not prove useful. Types A, B, C, H, and J are represented in DAII, DAII/III, and DAIII; Type F in DAI and again in DAIII (the gap surely being fortuitous); and Type E in DAII/III and DAIII. The three representatives of Type G, all doubtful as whorls, are from DAII/III. That there are no Type I whorls in Table 5-6 is again likely to be fortuitous, since there are five in Table 5-7, all of them probably from the earlier part of the period.

Plain spherical and biconical whorls were in use in other parts of Greece during the same period as they were at Nichoria, but a list of comparanda would be profitless since these whorl types are very obvious ones. They are found in the Neolithic period and throughout the Bronze Age, except for a hiatus in central Greece and the Peloponnese in the Early Helladic period. Our round Type C whorls/beads differ from many of their contemporaries in being plain. In Attica and Crete particularly,[29] numerous round clay objects are usually and not unreasonably (despite considerable size in some) identified as beads. They regularly bear incised decoration composed of lines, circles, dots, dashes, etc., although plain examples are sometimes found with them. They are usually of fine clay and well fired. Our biconical Type B whorl **159A**, perhaps assignable to DAII, has only a simple and irregular *pointillé* decoration that is quite unlike these. The nearest parallels are from a much earlier period in the north (Mylonas 1929, p. 80, Figs. 91a, b; Tsountas 1908, p. 343, Pl. 44, no. 14), from the beginning of the Mycenaean Age at Mycenae (Mylonas 1973, pp. 188, 207, Pl. 189β), and from the palace at Ano Englianos (Blegen and Rawson 1966, p. 286; cf. *B.C.H.* 1936, p. 270 for Geometric piece).

The hollow tops displayed by Types G and I were introduced into Greece at the very end of the Early Helladic period and were popular throughout the Middle Helladic period. They are usually found on asymmetrical biconical whorls which often have incised decoration on the upper half. The hollow top, in modified form, continued to appear sporadically throughout the Late Bronze Age, in both conical and biconical whorls.[30]

Straight-sided conical whorls of various kinds were used in the Neolithic period and throughout the Bronze Age, and again the shape is an obvious one for a whorl. But the distinctive variation in the campaniform Type H is a different matter. Apart from one large and perhaps irrelevant example from the Early Bronze Age in the north (Heurtley 1939, p. 87, Figs. 67 ff.), the type is not seen before the Middle Helladic period, during which examples occur at Prosymna (Blegen 1937, p. 45, Fig. 79, no. 669, Grave 26), Asine (Frödin and Persson 1938, pp. 250-52, Fig. 177), and Asea (Holmberg 1944, p. 117, Fig. 113, nos. 15, 16). There is no question that campaniform whorls were found at Malthi,[31] but there is little guidance as to the period in which they belong. The site was occupied both in the Middle and Late Bronze Age, with occupation probably continuing until late in LHIIIC and possibly into the Protogeometric period.[32]

Table 5-7. Whorls from "Probable" DA Contexts

Type	No.	%
A	3	9.4
B	3	9.4
C	5	15.6
D	. . .	. . .
Subtotal	**11**	**34.4**
E	3	9.4
F	3	9.4
G	. . .	. . .
Subtotal	**6**	**18.8**
H	6	18.7
I	5	15.6
J	4	12.5
Subtotal	**15**	**46.8**
K	. . .	. . .
L	. . .	. . .
Sherd whorls	2	
TOTAL	34	100

Table 5-8. Whorls from "Possible" DA Contexts

Type	No.	%
A	4	18.2
B	3	13.6
C	4	18.2
D	4	18.2
Subtotal	**15**	**68.2**
E	1	4.5
F	. . .	. . .
G	. . .	-
Subtotal	**1**	**4.5**
H	2	9.1
I	. . .	. . .
J	3	13.6
Subtotal	**5**	**22.7**
K	. . .	. . .
L	1	4
Subtotal	**1**	**4.5**
Sherd whorls	4	
TOTAL	26	**99.9**

Once established, Type H whorls continued into the Mycenaean Age,[33] being used at Kythera (Coldstream and Huxley 1972, p. 210, π39, Pl. 59, Fig. 60), Pylos (Blegen and Rawson 1966, p. 286; Blegen et al. 1973, p. 50, Fig. 113), Mycenae (Mylonas 1973, pp. 188, 207, Pl. 189β; Wace 1932, p. 218, conical whorls with "splayed bases"), Korakou (Blegen 1921, p. 109), Eutresis (Goldman 1931, p. 192, Fig. 265, no. 7, row 3), and Perati (Iakovidis 1970, p. 388; p. 280, Fig. 123, Type 8). A painted whorl from Mycenae provides an extreme example (Wace 1932, p. 217, Tomb 515, no. 16, Pl. 28). The type does not seem to have been in favor in the non-Mycenaean north.

In Mycenaean times, Type H was only one among many, whereas the DA people adopted it and made it peculiarly their own. And the variation, Type J, with its slightly domed top does seem to have been a DA innovation.[34]

As with the round Protogeometric beads and whorls, so campaniform whorls from the cemeteries of Athens were usually of fine, well-fired clay, and they often bore incised decoration.[35] Only one of our campaniform whorls (**159**) is decorated, again only with incised dots arranged in irregular patterns (Pl. 5-38). In this respect it is not unlike two presumably earlier whorls from nearby Malthi (Valmin 1938, pp. 335-36, Fig. 71, A2, 3).

As well as incised campaniform whorls, Athenian cemeteries were furnished with painted ones (Kübler 1943, pp. 40, 45, Pl. 32, nos. 2130a, 2045, 2046). Those of somewhat later date sometimes show eccentric variations, no doubt created especially for the tomb (Kübler 1954, Pl. 146; two have hollowed tops). Painted campaniform whorls were also in use at Corinth (Williams 1970, pp. 19, 20, Pl. 9, nos. 29-32). It is interesting to note, however, that plain campaniform whorls, not so far removed from ours, were sometimes found in Athenian burials.[36] This suggests that the homely appearance of the Messenian whorls might not be entirely owing to their provincial origin, but partly to the fact that they were objects of daily use and not grave goods. A whorl of Type J, however, from one of the tombs near the Nichoria ridge is also plain (Choremis 1973, p. 48, no. 727, Pl. 19).

Lefkandi in Euboea yielded several of these whorls in its DA cemetery, one incised, the others plain (Popham et al. 1979-80, Pls. 65 p, q, 236j). Among over 100 clay whorls found in the DA settlement of Karphi in Crete, only two were of this type (Pendlebury et al. 1940, pp. 129, 131).

Long after the DA settlement at Nichoria had been abandoned, campaniform whorls, plain and painted, continued in use elsewhere in Greece. A handsome painted example was found in a Late Geometric context at Zagora on Andros (Cambitoglou et al. 1971, p. 61, Fig. 61); others of Geometric and Archaic date are known from Rheneia and Delos (Deonna 1938, p. 270, Fig. 309, Pl. 711); and yet another "de style Corinthien," is from Thorikos in Attica (Mussche et al. 1967a, p. 60, Fig. 61). A plain example came from a 7th-century house on Siphnos (Brock and Mackworth Young 1949, p. 30, II 6b); and others, plain save for a coating of black glaze, are from 5th-century Corinth (Davidson 1952, p. 175, no. 1219, Pl. 78, no. 1219) and early 4th-century Athens (Schlörb-Vierniesel 1966, Grave 104.9, Fig. 41.1). They became "the typical Athenian spindle whorl of the classical period" (Davidson 1952, p. 175, no. 1219), and it has been pointed out that they are "clearly pictured [in use] on vases and other contemporary monuments" (Davidson and Thompson 1943, p. 95). An elegant selection of 5th- and 4th-century whorls from the Pnyx, wheel-made, of fine Attic clay, glazed, with painted or, in one case, stamped decoration, may seem remote from our humble Type J whorls; but a comparison of the two can leave little doubt as to the origin of the classical whorls (Davidson and Thompson 1943, pp. 94, 95, Fig. 43).

NOTE ON THE CLAY "SPOOLS"

Six complete or partially preserved objects are relevant here. They were originally inventoried as "small finds" but were later de-cataloged and included in the pottery classification. Thus, the four recovered in predominantly DAII contexts are published in Chapter 3 as **P570**, **571**, **572**, **737** (Fig. 3-21; Pls. 3-111, 112) and two from DAIII contexts, **P1536** (Fig. 3-54; Pl. 3-145) and **P1569**. There they are called "cooking supports"; but a more thorough review of comparanda and rival theories about their use seems to be in order here.

Very similar small, rough spools were already in use in the Early Neolithic period in northern Greece,[37] and they continued through the Middle and Late Neolithic phases in the north only.[38] In the Early Bronze Age one or two examples of somewhat better manufacture occur at Peloponnesian sites,[39] but they are by no means common. (They are not to be confused with the much larger EBA cylindrical loomweight which was pierced once or twice along its longest axis.) Thereafter they drop from the record until, at the very end of the Late Bronze Age, very similar objects suddenly turn up at widely scattered sites. The list includes Boubousti in far western Macedonia, which was inhabited at the end of the Bronze Age and the beginning of the Iron Age (Heurtley 1926-27, p. 174.3, Fig. 31, nos. 1, 2); a LHIIIC house at Lefkandi in Euboea (Popham and Sackett 1968, p. 13, Fig. 16); an unspecified Mycenaean context at Delphi (Demangel 1926, p. 10, Fig. 11); an 11th- or 12th-century tomb on Kefallenia (Marinatos 1933, p. 80, Fig. 38); the LHIIIC Granary at Mycenae (Wace 1925, pp. 41, 54); House I at Asine (Frödin and Persson 1938, p. 310, Fig. 213, no. 7), which may well be of LHIII date (Desborough 1964, p. 82); the Teichos Dymaion site in NW Peloponnese (Mastrokostas 1965, p. 136, Pl. 180*a*); a late context in the Palace at Knossos (Evans 1901-2, p. 94); LMIIIC levels at Palaikastro in E Crete (Sackett and Popham 1965, p. 305, nos. 45-50, Fig. 19, nos. 46, 47, 50); and grouped in numerous rooms at the sub-Minoan site of Karphi (Pendlebury et al. 1940, pp. 70ff.).

The spools from Karphi and Nichoria prove that the use of these objects continued into the Dark Age, although there is much less information about them in this period. The explanation may be that they are usually found in settlements, not in tombs, and very few DA settlements have been excavated. Comparable spools were numerous on the surface at Palaikastro (Thessaly) which was inhabited in the Early and Middle Bronze Ages, abandoned, and then reoccupied in the sub-Mycenaean, Protogeometric, and possibly Geometric periods (Béquignon 1932, pp. 113, 114, Figs. 14, 15). The nearby site of Ktouri produced similar spools from an apparently Archaic context, although the site had been occupied since LHIII, except for a gap during the Geometric period (Béquignon 1932, pp. 145, 189, Fig. 40, no. 11). At Delphi, they continued to be found in 8th- and 7th-century levels; but those from the 7th-century context are much more neatly formed, have a painted cross on the ends, and should probably be excluded from the discussion (Lerat 1961, pp. 338-40, Figs. 24c, 26; Perdrizet 1908, p. 199, no. 625, Fig. 888). After this the spools are seen no more, unless their descendants are the well-formed, well-fired, often stamp-decorated reel-shaped objects found in Classical and particularly in Hellenistic levels (Davidson 1952, p. 175).

There have been various suggestions as to the use of these enigmatic objects. The clues are that they are very often found in groups, sometimes near hearths, and that they are often very poorly fired and have a partially-burned surface. This rough surface, plus the very slight "waist," renders them ineligible for the actual winding of thread. It has been proposed that they were supports for cooking pots (Heurtley 1926-27, p. 174, n. 2; Lamb 1936, p. 164), or that they might be separators or supports used in firing pottery or other terra-cotta objects in a kiln or even an open hearth.[40] But might it not be that they have partially burned surfaces and are sometimes found near hearths because they themselves were "fired" in or near the hearths? Schliemann (1886, p. 146) was probably the first to suggest that objects of similar type but larger size which he found at Tiryns were loomweights; and others, admittedly with rather more pronounced "waists," were certainly used as such in early Bulgaria. In these, the warp threads, in bunches, were tied round the waists (Detev 1968, p. 24, Fig. 16). The weight of our spools would be quite appropriate to their use as loomweights. The fact that spools are so often found in groups is a point in favor of their being loomweights; also, in the palace at Knossos and in the two later instances at Delphi, they were actually found with certain loomweights. It is quite possible to use different kinds of loomweights on the same loom at the same time, and the roughly formed spools may have been homely replacements for breakages among the more professional weights.

If these objects are loomweights, their sudden appearance at the very end of the Late Bronze Age and their continuation into the Dark Age suggest that they are symptoms of hard and troubled times. Like many of the Nichoria DA whorls, they are rough objects, easily made at home and easily replaced when broken. In the more settled conditions that were to follow in Greece, the need for the rude, homemade "spools" would have been a thing of the past. Loomweights were professionally made in standard shapes, with potters' trademarks and sometimes with the impression of their owner's ring, as though they were commissioned (Davidson 1952).

J.C.S.

A Note on Stone and Bone Artefacts

CHIPPED STONE

Implements and *débitage* of chert and obsidian numbering into the thousands were collected in the excavation of the settlement at Nichoria.[41] Of this substantial evidence for the manufacture of chipped stone implements at the site, a major percentage was recovered from the Middle Helladic levels. In addition, Late Helladic occupation produced evidence of a somewhat limited, but uninterrupted, tradition in the manufacture and use of chipped stone tools. Worked chert and obsidian were much more rarely recovered from the predominantly Dark Age deposits. The morphological and technological characteristics of these few later-occurring chipped stone artefacts do not differ substantially from those uncovered in the excavation of the Bronze Age deposits.

The limited occurrence of chipped stone in both the Dark Age and Byzantine levels could imply that the movement of earth, reuse of building materials, and leveling which generally accompany the construction of new buildings at a multiperiod site such as Nichoria may have had some effect on any possible DA record of chipped stone manufacture and use.[42]

This possibility was remarked upon by Carl Blegen (in Blegen and Rawson 1966, p. 37) in discussing the clay building material found throughout the Englianos palace. He wrote: "As we observed, it was often mixed with bits of crushed stone, potsherds, bones, plaster, and other matter, evidently added to promote cohesion. Perhaps, in some instances, the clay came from deposits which had been previously used and already possessed these extraneous elements."[43] For the study of later prehistoric artefacts such as chipped stone, whose typology and chronological range are not yet well established in the archaeological record, the random movement of materials is an important consideration.

Thus, from the artefactual evidence at hand, it is not possible to state that the manufacture of chipped stone implements at Nichoria continued undisturbed as a flourishing cultural tradition into the Dark Age. Nor may one insist that all knowledge of chipped stone manufacture ceased at this site with the establishment of DA habitation. Such secure evidence for the continuity or cessation of a chipped stone tradition must be sought at a DA site where there is no possibility of contamination from earlier deposits.

GROUND STONE AND WORKED BONE

Approximately 200 ground stone objects, including querns and hand-size or smaller tools of various kinds, were recovered at Nichoria. Forty examples of worked bone (including horn core and ivory) were also found.[44] Almost all these objects were found in deposits of Bronze Age date, or they were recovered in a fragmentary or reused state in the Dark Age and Byzantine levels. Given the relative anonymity of these artefact categories in the Aegean Bronze Age record[45] and the mixed nature of the deposits in which most of them were found, it seems wise to present all the Nichoria ground stone and worked bone objects in Volume II of the Nichoria series. In this way, changes or continuities in the techniques of manufacture, in materials, and in morphology can be traced more clearly.

H.B.

Editor's Note

Few excavators would disagree with Harriet Blitzer's comments about the problems posed by mixed deposits in multiperiod habitation sites. It is always tricky and sometimes impossible to detect specific items of pottery and other artefacts that may be intrusive in an otherwise more or less homogeneous context; and the difficulty is compounded when, as is typical of many of our lots, the pottery is definitely mixed. Yet to consider seriously the possibility that the DA inhabitants of Nichoria may not have made or used chipped or ground stone tools seems to me somewhat perverse. Reasonable inference surely points in the opposite direction. The carry-over of other craft traditions in the Aegean context from Late Bronze to Protogeometric times seems clear, and the apparent fluctuation in the availability of metals would be expected to make stone tools, if anything, *more* basic in DA times than earlier. Snodgrass (1971, p. 384) is also perhaps overcautious and too dependent on data from burials when he speaks of the "occasional resort to obsidian, bone and stone implements in the early Iron Age." In the case of imported obsidian, "occasional" use may be correct; but local stones such as cherts are scarcely to be considered in the same context. The apparent fact that there are no easily discernible differences in stone-chipping technique between artefacts found in predominantly LH versus predominantly DA contexts at Nichoria could indeed serve as confirmation for a relatively uninterrupted craft tradition. Nor can the possibility of fairly large-scale DA reuse of LH stone tools be ignored.

In spite of such arguments, however, Blitzer decided to publish here none of the stone artefacts, whatever the circumstances of their recovery. This is, of course, her prerogative; and the information on provenience to be provided for these objects in the larger context of *Nichoria* II will serve to identify them as possibly of DA manufacture and/or use. See now *JFA* 9 (1982):363-73.

W.A.M.

Miscellaneous Small Finds

Apart from metal, chipped stone and spindle whorls, the DA levels at Nichoria yielded few small finds, and of these, fewer still can be regarded with any certainty as being of DA manufacture. The DA inhabitants must frequently have found small Mycenaean objects, whole or broken, lying underfoot, just as they did Mycenaean potsherds. When such objects occurred in good DA contexts, we may suppose that they had perhaps been picked up and reused. The clearest examples are a stone celt (**239**) found lying on the floor of the second phase of Unit IV-1 and three spindle whorls. Of the latter, two (**131**, **195**) were made from kylix feet, and the third (**192**) from the top of a stirrup jar.

Furthermore, at least five "steatite" conuli (Boardman 1963b, pp. 15-16; Warren 1969, p. 138; Iakovidis 1977) were found unbroken in levels not containing LH pottery. Two of them were found on the floor of Room 1 in Unit IV-1, a third with DA sherds lying outside the building, a fourth in the good DAII deposit in the refuse dump in L23 Top, and the fifth was apparently associated with the DA reuse of Unit IV-9. Another four unbroken conuli may also have been reused, but they come from contexts where DA pottery was mixed with LH and may simply have formed part of the LH rubbish, as did most probably a further seven found as fragments. One more or less whole conulus and one fragment were found in levels near the surface where DA pottery was mixed with Byzantine, and a final small fragment was found in what seemed to be an otherwise Byzantine context. All will be published in *Nichoria* II. Of the total of 84 conuli, whole and fragmentary, most come from unequivocally LH levels; but the fact that the 19 here mentioned amount to nearly 23% of the total is a strong indication of how much the debris of Mycenaean life was still visible in succeeding periods.

The stone finds present the same problem of ambiguous connections. A full treatment of all the chipped and ground stone objects recovered in the excavation will appear in *Nichoria* II, since it is clear that the vast majority were made and used in the Bronze Age. We include here, however, seven items that appear most likely to have been associated with buildings or other activities that we can confidently connect with the DA occupation, particularly during the DAII period. Perhaps the most intriguing of these stone objects is a schist plaque (**243**) found in the LH stone rubble from the N wall of Unit IV-9, but lying a little outside the building. The plaque bears an incised design of a rectangle with a central vertical division crossed by eight more lightly incised parallel lines (Pl. 5-46). The design appears to be more decorative than a mere doodle but too small for use in counting or a game. Its use must, for the time being, remain an enigma; but it probably does not represent a schematic drawing of a "tent-like structure," as was suggested in a preliminary report (*Hesperia* 41, 1972, p. 264). A second fragment of worked stone (**238**; Pl. 5-41) was found where the DA Unit III-1 overlay the LH street and where pottery of both periods was present. It is not an ordinary building stone and perhaps had attracted the notice of the ancient inhabitants (as it did that of the excavators) simply because of its shape and the two curious holes.

The limestone fragment **237**, if it functioned as a bead, cannot have been in use for very long. The calcium carbonate of which it is made dissolves easily, and the hole could as easily be natural as manmade. It is a humble pebble that someone might have picked up and formed into a bead, either using the natural hole or making one.

Lying about as rubbish, it would probably have suffered damage, so that it seems more likely to have been associated with the latest pottery found with it. Two whetstones (**240**, **242**) come from the dump to N of Unit IV-1 (Pls. 5-43, 5-45). From the rectangular enclosure at the bottom of the same dump (see p. 43) comes a pair of objects (**241**), apparently a grinder and palette set (Pl. 5-44).

The four terra-cotta objects are published here without reservations on context. The figurine head (**232**) comes from DAIII levels above Unit IV-1 (Pl. 5-39). Like the bronze figurine (**58**), this animal appears to represent a deer, fawn, or horse. The latter may be the most likely, both because of the shape and on the general grounds that deer are known mostly in bronze and from sanctuaries (Brein 1969, pp. 147-54) and fawns in particular are rare (Lamb 1926-27, p. 99, no. 10; Hill 1955, p. 40). Both **58** and **232** were found in association with buildings that appear to have had at least some religious function; and, indeed, the chief interest of both objects lies in their findspots.

What the horse can have meant in such a context is in the realm of speculation. Horse figurines have been variously interpreted—e.g., as firstlings (Rouse 1902, p. 298), as having a solar or chthonic significance (Roes 1933, p. 82), as connected with the idea of mastery (Kübler 1954, p. 27), and with the dead (Furtwängler 1883-87, p. 27). All such theories should be seen against the background of Snodgrass's perceptive remarks on the role and symbolic value of the horse in early Greek society (Snodgrass 1971, pp. 414-15). But which explanation, if any, might suit **232** is impossible to determine. We do not even know whether the head belonged to a free-standing figure or group, to an attachment like the horses on pyxis lids, or to a toy with bored legs (Kübler 1954, p. 69, Pl. 142).

The animal leg (**231**) is from a mixed level but almost certainly belongs with the LH debris. Overall, the recovery of less than ten figurines (or fragments thereof) that might have some association with the DA settlement at Nichoria clearly underlines a notable difference in custom between the Bronze and Iron Ages. The Mycenaean levels here produced over ten dozen human and animal figurine fragments from all over the site.

An undistinguished object (**233**) appears to be a clay pendant. It may not even have been painted. The shape is not peculiar to any period. A good parallel, though slightly smaller, was found at Knossos and dated some centuries later (Hughes-Brock 1973, p. 118, no. 25).

The enigmatic fragment (**234**) cannot have been a spindle whorl, because its wide central cavity would not grip a spindle. The cataloged fragment of mudbrick (**235**) comes from the porch of Unit IV-1 (see Ch. 2, p. 24).

With the bone bead (**236**) we return to the problem of mixed contexts (Pl. 5-40). This item was found in the DA refuse dump in L23 Top, but in a lower stratum where LH sherds were beginning to appear. It is difficult to find published parallels in either LH or DA contexts. Considering that the raw material was so easy to come by, it is perhaps surprising that bone beads are so uncommon in the Aegean. They would have required some trouble to make and perhaps were considered not worth the effort when a much gayer effect could be created with colored materials like stone, glass, faience, and gold, particularly against drab garments of undyed wool.

The closest in shape to **236** would seem to be two beads from Karphi, a "pear-shaped" or "drop-shaped" bead from the Temple dependencies and a "tubular" bead from tomb 8 (Pendlebury 1940, pp. 76, 133, no. 262; pp. 104, 133, no. 165). Both are smaller than ours. Back in LHI, Blegen reports from Korakou "a small spool, or spool-shaped bead" with a large hole and a ridge around the middle (Blegen 1921, p. 105, Fig. 130:10); and from a tomb at Prosymna used in LHII and III he records a "spool or bobbin . . . . made from a vertebra" (Blegen 1937, pp. 121, 123, 286). The LH settlement at Asine produced "beads in the form of gourd pips," with or without incised lines along the string-hole and along the edges (Frödin and Persson 1938, p. 311, no. 4). The large cemetery at Perati yielded only two bone beads, one discoid, one globular; the first was probably, the second possibly associated with the burial of a young person or child (Iakovidis 1969-70, pp. 46, 49, 159-60, 165).

Whole necklaces of bone beads do not appear until toward the end of the Late Bronze Age. One is reported, but without details, from a mainly LHIIIC cemetery of small chamber tombs (Leekley and Noyes 1976, p. 35), dug by Yalouris on the road between Kangadhi and Riolo in the district of Patras (Hood and Boardman 1956, p. 17; Papadopoulos 1979, pp. 141, 223). Courbin speaks of Protogeometric necklaces of "rondelles d'os" at Argos but remarks that they are not found in the Geometric graves. Three or four such "rondelles" are recorded from tomb 37 there, probably a woman's grave (Courbin 1974, pp. 38, 119). The earlier Swedish excavators at Asine found one bone "whorl," described as "carinated," in a PG cist grave in the Lower City (Frödin and Persson 1938, pp. 131, 425). The five or six bone beads from grave XXIII at Tiryns are problematical (Verdelis 1963, pp. 36-37). They are carefully made cylinders with a "collar" at each end and a central midrib, a shape not unlike that of certain amber beads found mostly around the Adriatic but also on the gold wheels of the Tiryns hoard (Harding and Hughes-Brock 1974, pp. 155, 158). They were found with beads of faience. The date of the beads is, as Snodgrass puts it, "mysterious," since parallels given for the various grave goods range from Submycenaean to Early Geometric (Snodgrass 1971, pp. 248, 333, 382).

Snodgrass sees the bone beads as a substitute for amber

and places bone beads and finger rings in the general context of DA poverty, in which "primitive materials re-appear as apparent substitutes." The 42 discoid bone beads from eight burials at Vergina would seem to fit in with this view, since they come mostly from poor tombs with few gifts, generally those of women (Andronikos 1969, pp. 160, 225). It may well be that bone beads were more apt to be worn by women and children, but the evidence is meager and hard to evaluate. An Early Geometric grave near the Athenian Agora may have included a woman, but the excavator puts forward the suggestion as "pure hypothesis" (Young 1949, pp. 288-89, 297). It contained a single bone cylinder decorated with incised rings. The object was perhaps a clasp to fasten the ends of a string of beads made of some perishable material. Only later, at the sanctuary of Artemis Orthia, do we meet with bone beads in any quantity. Dawkins dates them from the 8th down through the 7th and 6th centuries. He reasons that, toward the end of that period, bone was being adopted specifically as a substitute for ivory when supplies of the latter had ceased (Dawkins 1929, pp. 204, 227-28).

H.H.-B.
W.D.E.C.

NOTES

1. See Popham, Sackett, and Themelis 1979-80, Pl. 242, nos. A-C; Skoubris Tomb 62.2 and 3, p. 134, nos. 2, 3; Pls. 111, 242A, 250:2. Skoubris Tomb 63.1 and 2, p. 134, Pls. 111, 242B, 250:3. Skoubris Tomb 38.6 and 7, p. 123, Pls. 103, 204d, 242c.

2. On this type of pin, see Desborough 1964, pp. 53 ff., Pl. 24b, and Desborough 1972, pp. 294-300, Fig. 33.

3. See, for example, Müller-Karpe 1962, especially p. 86, Fig. 4, nos. 1, 2, 10, 11. Compare also Desborough 1972, p. 296, Figs. 33 B, C, and Snodgrass 1971, p. 227, Fig. 81.

4. Heurtley 1926-27, p. 175, Fig. 31.4; Heurtley 1939, p. 231, Fig. 104z; Jacobsthal 1956, Fig. 47.

5. Sandars (Hood et al. 1958-59, p. 236) seems to believe that Jacobsthal considers the Mouliana pin to be of Geometric date, but this is not what he says in *Greek Pins*, pp. 1, 2.

6. See also Sapouna-Sakellarakis 1978. Our brooch corresponds to her Type IIa (pp. 42 ff.; Pl. 3). Most of her examples that closely resemble 8 come from Crete.

7. Leon 1961-63, pp. 46, 47, 51, Fig. 25e. I am very grateful to Dr. V. Mitsopoulou-Leon for invaluable help with the material from ancient Elis.

8. See also Verdelis 1963, p. 7, Fig. 3, a typology worked out for his Tiryns graves.

9. Notice the size of the securing rivet head on the inside of some tripod legs, as in Benton 1938, Pls. 14c, 23.2.

10. See, in particular, Snodgrass 1971, pp. 237-39; Desborough's comments (1972, pp. 316-18) should be considered in conjunction with this exposition.

11. See Catling in Popham and Sackett 1968; Popham et al. 1979-80, pp. 93-97, Pls. 12, 13a.

12. The Italian material is very conveniently collected by Müller-Karpe 1959, e.g., Pls. 9, 18, 28, 29, 31-35, 46.

13. They are seen most clearly with the group Tomb AZ VII (Andronikos 1969, Pls. 27-29) where a set of three phalara were found *in situ* in the area of the lower body. A pair of phalara was *in situ* in Grave Yl (Andronikos 1969, Pl. 16).

14. See, for example, the nearby Artemis Orthia votives (Dawkins 1929, Pl. 85β, γ); also those from Athena Alea at Tegea (Dugas 1921, p. 379, Fig. 41), from Olympia (Furtwängler 1890, Pl. 26), and from Delphi (Perdrizet 1908, p. 121, Figs. 441-45).

15. See Dawkins 1929, Pl. 76; the stand is drawn in Heilmeyer 1979, p. 123, Fig. 9.

16. For iron pins in Submycenaean-Geometric contexts, see Styrenius 1967, pp. 70, 156; Desborough 1972, pp. 294ff.; Snodgrass 1971, pp. 225-26; Coldstream 1977, pp. 32 ff.

17. The occurrence of iron objects in the full Bronze Age is a familiar phenomenon. Lorimer (1950, pp. 111, 112) published a list of Minoan/Mycenaean instances known to her; a valuable summary, including more recent discoveries, is also given by Iakovidis (1970, pp. 376-78). See also Desborough 1964, pp. 25 ff.; Snodgrass 1971, pp. 221 ff.; Drower 1973, pp. 513 ff. Note that Rosser regards the same item (his **528**) as possibly of Byzantine date (p. 407).

18. Kraiker and Kübler 1939, pp. 18 (Grave 27), 48 (Grave 108). Styrenius (1967, pp. 22, 48) is referring to a bracelet from one of the eight Submycenaean graves dug by M. Mitsos in 1939-40, SW of the Olympieion.

19. Popham et al. 1979-80, pp. 246 ff., Pls. 134 (P. Tomb 14), 148 (P. Tomb 43), 167 (T. T. 1), 173 (T. T. 13), 187 (T. T. 33), 188 (T. T. 36).

20. In Athens, the Late Protogeometric Grave 40 in the Kerameikos (Kübler 1943, Pl. 38, M9) and the Late Protogeometric/Early Geometric Grave 27 in the Athenian Agora (Blegen 1952, pp. 280 ff., esp. p. 287). At Lefkandi, Palaia Perivolia T. 13, no. 22 (Popham et al. 1979-80, pp. 147, 256, Pls. 133, 244F).

21. Sandars 1955, pp. 174 ff.; Hood et al. 1958-59, pp. 232-34. See also Deshayes 1960, pp. 302-30; Harding 1975, pp. 195-202.

22. Hood et al. 1958-59, p. 234 and references, pp. 248 ff. (VII: 12), Fig. 32 (top left), Pl. 60a.

23. Iakovidis 1970, p. 342, Fig. 147 (M75); p. 344, Fig. 149 (M85); also pp. 376-78.

24. See, for example, Schaeffer 1936, p. 137, Enkomi Tomb 6, no. 13 – possibly the same as Catling 1964, p. 103.

25. Popham et al. 1979-80, pp. 138 (S Pyre 1, 2), 148 (P 16, 7), 155 (P 31, 7), 163 (P Pyre 16, 2), 170 (T 3, 11); Pls. 245-46.

26. This account is not based on autopsy of the metal objects discussed below. For a full account of the ceramic grave goods, see Chapter 3, p. 109. See also excavation report, Chapter 4, pp. 260-62.

27. Note the 11 weapons from cremations in the Halos tumulus (Wace and Thompson 1911-12, pp. 1-29, Fig. 15); cf. Coldstream 1977, pp. 87 ff.

28. Andronikos 1969, pp. 262-65, Figs. 101, 102; Petsas 1963, especially p. 242 and Pl. 146a, for the only *bronze* type II sword yet found there.

29. For Athens, see Smithson 1961, p. 172, Pl. 30 (55a, b); Young 1949, p. 297, Pl. 72; Kraiker and Kübler 1939, pp. 98, 194, Pls. 70 (no. 729), 74 (no. 764); Kübler 1943, pp. 39, 40, 42, 45, Pl. 32 (nos. 2117, 2118, 2120, 2154, 2090); Kübler 1954, pp. 215, 262, Pl. 157 (nos. 245, 901); Charitonidis 1973, p. 28, Pl. 17a, b.

For Asine, see Frödin and Persson 1938, p. 251, Fig. 177 (far right in row 4). For Lefkandi, see Popham and Sackett 1979, pp. 83, 87, 143, 165, Pls. 65 o, 125, 236 k.

For Crete, see Boardman 1960, pp. 146-48, Fig. 10, Pl. 39, and references; van Effenterre 1948, p. 66, Pl. 42 (D71); Marinatos 1936, p. 270, Fig. 33 (nos. 10, 11); Rizza and Scrinari 1968, pp. 5, 17, Figs. 4 (no. 2), 34 (no. 1); Rizza 1969, pp. 21, 25, 28, Pls. 13 (2), 18 (3); Hall 1914, pp. 121-22, Fig. 73.

30. Cf. Wace 1932, pp. 73, 217, Tomb 517, Pl. 35 (no. 35, bottom right); Goldman 1931, p. 192, Fig. 265 (no. 6, row 3); Iakovidis 1969, p. 40, π9, Pl. 10β, p. 93, π4, Pl. 29β, p. 461, π8, Pl. 138ε;

Iakovidis 1970, p. 388, Fig. 123, Type 6; Blegen 1937, p. 313; Blegen and Rawson 1966, pp. 297, 322; Valmin 1938, pp. 355-56, Fig. 71D (but these may be either MH or LH).

31. Valmin 1938, pp. 335-36, Fig. 71E, Pl. 25 (1) (third from left and far right in second row).

32. For serious doubts about occupation at Malthi before advanced MH, see Howell in McDonald et al. 1975, p. 111. For the possible late occupation at Malthi, see Desborough 1964, p. 94.

33. Blegen (1928, p. 190) compared his Zygouries EBA "plump cones" (to their disadvantage) with "Mycenaean examples with their . . . almost straight or concave line of profile."

34. The "bottle-shaped" whorls from Malthi are somewhat similar, but these do seem to have belonged to the MH period there. See Valmin 1938, pp. 335-36, Fig. 71 F4, 5, 6; also p. 29, Fig. 8 (no. 3) and p. 31.

35. Smithson 1961, pp. 172-73, Pl. 30 (56a, b, c); Kübler 1943, pp. 40, 45, Pl. 32, nos. 2128, 2130, 2059, 2062; Kübler 1954, pp. 214, 218, 235, Pl. 157 (nos. 900, 1179, 1222).

36. Kraiker and Kübler 1939, p. 98, Pl. 74, nos. 757, 758, 760, 763 (stone?); Kübler 1943, pp. 43, 45, Pl. 32, no. 2064, Pl. 33, no. 1107; Smithson 1961, p. 173, Pl. 30, no. 56d.

37. Milojčić and Milojčić 1971, Teil I, pp. 26, 31, Pls. D. 13-15, 10.25-27, 19.23, 24, 8-9, Fig. 9; Teil II, pp. 9, 15, 27, 50. See also Weinberg 1962, pp. 165, 203, 204, Pl. 69a, b.

38. Weinberg 1962, p. 203; Wace and Thompson 1912, p. 149; Tsountas 1908, p. 346, Figs. 278-79.

39. Blegen 1928, pp. 190 ff., Fig. 179, nos. 4, 5; Holmberg 1944, pp. 120-21, Fig. 114, nos. 13-15, 17-19; Säflund 1965, p. 127, no. 22. Some of the Asea objects are of stone and unrelated; dates are doubtful because of the disturbed stratigraphy.

40. Karageorghis 1969, pp. 467-69 and note 1, Fig. 55; but many of the Greek examples are too poorly fired for this purpose.

41. Complete data on the quantities, types, and findspots of chipped stone implements will appear in Volume II of the excavation reports.

42. The movement of materials at archaeological sites has been discussed in various field reports. A classic case should be noted at the site of Tell Fakhariyah (Syria), where large quantities of prehistoric chert implements were recovered in well-defined Iron Age levels yielding Hellenistic and Roman pottery (cf. L. S. Braidwood, "Stone Implements," Chapter V, in *Soundings at Tell Fakhariyah*, Oriental Institute Publications, Volume LXXIX, Univ. of Chicago Press, 1958). Another useful discussion of this problem occurs in N. Stanley Price and D. Christou, "Excavations at Khirokitia, 1972," *Report of the Department of Antiquities in Cyprus*, 1973, p. 27.

43. A personal examination of the chipped stone artefacts found at the palace adds strength to Blegen's thoughtful discussion. Both Middle and Late Helladic chipped stone implements were recovered in the excavation. I wish to acknowledge the courtesy of the late Professor J. L. Caskey for permission to study this comparative material.

44. In Volume II, each of the objects in these categories will be accompanied in the Catalog description with its specific ceramic context.

45. As Warren (1972, p. 225) has noted: "Quernstones have not been loved by Cretan archaeologists." This statement applies also to those of us working elsewhere in the Aegean. Worked bone objects of Bronze Age date have received more attention than stone artefacts, although even these deserve greater emphasis.

REFERENCES

Andronikos, M. 1969. *Vergina I – The Cemetery of the Mounds*. Athens. In Greek.

Benson, J. L. 1973. *The Necropolis of Kaloriziki*. Studies in Mediterranean Archaeology 36. Göteborg.

Benton, S. 1938. "The Evolution of the Tripod-Lebes," *BSA* 35:74-130.

Béquignon, Y. 1932. "Études Thessaliennes," *BCH* 56:89-191.

Bérard, C. 1970. *Eretria, fouilles et recherches, III: L'Héröon à la porte de l'ouest*. Bern.

Birmingham, J. 1963. "The Chronology of Some Early and Middle Iron Age Cypriot Sites," *AJA* 67:15-42.

Blegen, C. W. 1921. *Korakou: A Prehistoric Settlement near Corinth*. Boston and New York.

——. 1928. *Zygouries: A Prehistoric Settlement in the Valley of Cleonae*. Cambridge, Mass.

——. 1937. *Prosymna, the Helladic Settlement Preceding the Argive Heraeum*. 2 vols. Cambridge, Mass.

——. 1952. "Two Athenian Grave Groups of about 900 B.C.," *Hesperia* 21:279-94.

——, and Rawson, M. 1966. *The Palace of Nestor at Pylos in Western Messinia*, Vol. I. 2 parts. Princeton.

——, Rawson, M., Taylour, Lord, W., Donovan, P. 1973. *The Palace of Nestor at Pylos in Western Messenia*, Vol. III. Princeton.

Blinkenberg, C. 1926. *Fibules grecques et orientales*. Lindiaka, V. Copenhagen.

Boardman, J. 1960. "Protogeometric Graves at Agios Ioannis near Knossos (Knossos Survey 3)," *BSA* 55:128-48.

——. 1963a. "Artemis Orthia and Chronology," *BSA* 58:1-7.

——. 1963b. *Island Gems: A Study of Greek Seals in the Geometric and Early Archaic Periods*. Society for the Promotion of Hellenic Studies, Supplementary Paper no. 10. London.

Bouzek, J. 1974a. "The Attic Dark Age Incised Ware," *Sbornik Národního Muzea v Praze* A, 28, 1:1-56.

——. 1974b. "Bulgaria and the Greek Dark Age Incised Ware," *Listy Filologické* 102:8-11.

Brein, F. 1969. "Der Hirsch in der griechischen Frühzeit." Dissertationen d. Univ. Wien, 34. Vienna.

Brock, J. K. 1957. *Fortetsa: Early Greek Tombs near Knossos. BSA* Supplementary Paper No. 2. Cambridge.

——, and Mackworth Young, G. 1949. "Excavations in Siphnos," *BSA* 44:1-92.

Buchholz, H.-G. 1972. "Das Blei in der mykenischen Kultur und in der bronzezeitlichen Metallurgie Zyperns," *JDAI* 87:1-59.

Cambitoglou, A., Coulton, J. J., Birmingham, J., and Green, J. R. 1971. *Zagora* 1: *Excavation Season 1967; Study Season 1968-9*. Australian Academy of the Humanities, Monograph 2. Sydney.

Caskey, J. L. 1969. "Lead Weights from Ayia Irini in Keos," *Deltion* 24, A':95-106.

——, and Caskey, E. G. 1960. "The Earliest Settlements at Eutresis: Supplementary Excavations, 1958, *Hesperia* 29:126-67.

Catling, E. A., and Catling, H. W. 1974. "Sellopoulo Tombs 3 and 4: The Bronzes," *BSA* 69:225-54.

Catling, H. W. 1964. *Cypriot Bronzework in the Mycenaean World*. Oxford.

——. 1968a. "Late Minoan Vases and Bronzes in Oxford," *BSA* 63:89-131.

——. 1968b. "Kouklia: Evreti Tomb 8," *BCH* 92:162-69.

——. 1978-79. "Knossos, 1978," *AR*:43-58.

——, and Jones, R. E. 1977. "Analyses of Copper and Bronze Artefacts from the Unexplored Mansion, Knossos," *Archaeometry* 77:57-66.

Charitonidis, S. I. 1973. "Finds of the Protogeometric and Geometric Period from the Excavation South of the Acropolis," *Deltion* 28, A':1-63. In Greek.

Choremis, A. 1973. "Mycenaean and Protogeometric Graves at Karpofora in Messenia," *Arch Eph*:25-74. In Greek.

Coldstream, J. N. 1968. *Greek Geometric Pottery: A Survey of Ten Local Styles and Their Chronology*. London.

——. 1977. *Geometric Greece*. London.

——, and Huxley, G. L., eds. 1972. *Kythera: Excavations and Studies Conducted by the University of Pennsylvania Museum and the British School at Athens.* London.

Courbin, P. 1957. "Une tombe géométrique d'Argos," *BCH* 81:322-86.

——. 1974. *Tombes géométriques d'Argos, I (1952-1958).* Études Péloponnésiennes VII. Paris.

Davidson, G. R. 1952. *Corinth, Vol. XII: The Minor Objects.* Princeton.

——, and Thompson, D. B. 1943. "Small Objects from the Pnyx: I," *Hesperia* Supplement VII. Baltimore.

Dawkins, R. M., ed. 1929. *The Sanctuary of Artemis Orthia at Sparta. JHS* Supplementary Paper No. 5. London.

Dekoulakou, I. E. 1973. "Geometric Burial Pithoi from Achaea," *Arch Eph* (supplement):15-29. In Greek.

Demangel, R. 1926. *Fouilles de Delphes, II, 5: Le sanctuaire d'Athèna Pronoia – Topographie du sanctuaire.* Paris.

Deonna, W. 1938. *Exploration archéologique de Délos, XVIII: Le mobilier Délien.* 2 vols. École Française d'Athènes. Paris.

Desborough, V. R. d'A. 1964. *The Last Mycenaeans and Their Successors.* Oxford.

——. 1965. "The Greek Mainland, c. 1150-c. 1100 B.C.," *PPS* 31: 213-28.

——. 1972. *The Greek Dark Ages.* London.

Deshayes, J. 1960. *Les outils de bronze, de l'Indus au Danube (IVe au IIe millénaire)*, Vol. I. Paris.

——. 1966. *Argos: Les fouilles de la Deiras.* Études Peloponnésiennes IV. Paris.

Detev, P. 1968. "La Localité préhistorique près du village Mouldava," *Annuaire du Musée National Archéologique Plovdiv* VI:9-48.

Dikaios, P. 1969. *Enkomi: Excavations 1948-1958*, Vol. IIIa. Mainz.

Drower, M. S. 1973. "Syria c. 1550-1400 B.C.," *Cambridge Ancient History*, 3rd ed., II:1, Ch. X, pp. 417-525. Cambridge.

Dugas, C. 1921. "Le sanctuaire d'Aléa Athéna à Tégée," *BCH* 45:335-435.

Evans, A. J. 1901-2. "The Palace of Knossos: Provisional Report of the Excavations for the Year 1902," *BSA* 8:1-124.

Frödin, O., and Persson, A. 1938. *Asine: Results of the Swedish Excavations, 1922-1930.* Stockholm.

Furtwängler, A. 1883-87. *La collection Sabouroff: monuments de l'art grec*, Vol. I. Berlin.

——. 1980. *Olympia IV: Die Bronzen und die übrigen kleineren Funde von Olympia.* Tafelband. Berlin.

——. 1906. *Aegina: Das Heiligtum der Aphaia.* 2 vols. Munich.

Gjerstad, E., Lindros, J., Sjöquist, E., Westholm A., 1935. *The Swedish Cyprus Expedition: Finds and Results of the Excavations in Cyprus, 1927-1931, II.* 2 vols. Stockholm.

Goldman, H. 1931. *Excavations at Eutresis in Boeotia.* Cambridge, Mass.

Hall, E. H. 1914. *Excavations in Eastern Crete – Vrokastro.* Univ. of Pennsylvania, The Museum: Anthropological Publications III:3. Philadelphia.

Hampe, R., and Simon, E. 1959. *Corpus Vasorum Antiquorum.* Mainz Universität 1. Munich.

Harding, A. 1975. "Mycenaean Greece and Europe: The Evidence of Bronze Tools and Implements," *PPS* 41:183-202.

Harding, A., and Hughes-Brock, H. 1974. "Amber in the Mycenaean World," *BSA* 69:145-72.

Heilmeyer, W.-D. 1970. *Frühe Olympische Bronzefiguren: Die Tiervotive.* Olympische Forschungen XII. Berlin.

Heurtley, W. A. 1926-27. "A Prehistoric Site in Western Macedonia and the Dorian Invasion," *BSA* 28:158-94.

——. 1939. *Prehistoric Macedonia: An Archaeological Reconnaissance of Greek Macedonia (West of the Struma) in the Neolithic, Bronze, and Early Iron Ages.* Cambridge.

Higgins, R. A. 1961. *Greek and Roman Jewellery.* London.

Hill, D. K. 1955. "Six Early Greek Animals," *AJA* 59:39-44.

Holmberg, E. J. 1944. *The Swedish Excavations at Asea in Arcadia.* Lund.

Hood, M. S. F., and Boardman, J. 1956. "Archaeology in Greece," *AR* 1955:3-38.

Hood, S., Huxley, G., and Sandars, N. 1958-59. "A Minoan Cemetery on Upper Gypsades," *BSA* 53-54:194-262.

Hughes-Brock, H. 1973. "The Beads, Loomweights, etc." In Coldstream, J. N., *Knossos: The Sanctuary of Demeter*, pp. 114-23. BSA Supplement 8. London.

Iakovidis, S. E. 1969-70. *Perati: The Cemetery.* 3 vols. Athens. In Greek.

——. 1977. "On the Use of Mycenaean 'Buttons'," *BSA* 72: 113-19.

Jacobsthal, P. 1956. *Greek Pins and Their Connexions with Europe and Asia.* Oxford.

Karageorghis, V. 1969. "Chronique des fouilles et découvertes archéologiques à Chypre en 1968," *BCH* 93:431-569.

Kraiker, W., and Kübler, K. 1939. *Kerameikos: Ergebnisse der Ausgrabungen, I: Die Nekropolen des 12 bis 10 Jahrhunderts.* Berlin.

Kübler, K. 1943. *Kerameikos: Ergebnisse der Ausgrabungen, IV: Neufunde aus der Nekropole des 11 und 10 Jahrhunderts.* Berlin.

——. 1954. *Kerameikos: Ergebnisse der Ausgrabungen, V, 1: Die Nekropole des 10 bis 8 Jahrhunderts.* 2 vols. Berlin.

Kunze, E., and Schleif, H. 1937-38. *II. Bericht über die Ausgrabungen in Olympia.* Berlin.

Lamb, W. 1926-27. "Excavations at Sparta, 1906-1910: Notes on Some Bronzes from the Orthia Site," *BSA* 28:96-106.

——. 1936. *Excavations at Thermi in Lesbos.* Cambridge.

Leekley, D., and Noyes, R. 1976. *Archaeological Excavations in Southern Greece.* Park Ridge, N.J.

Leon, V. 1961-63. "Zweiter vorläufiger Bericht über die Ausgrabungen in Alt-Elis," *Jahreshefte der Österreichischen Archäologischen Institutes in Wien* 46, Beiblatt:33-58.

Lerat, L. 1961. "Fouilles à Delphes, à l'est du grand sanctuaire (1950-1957)," *BCH* 85:316-66.

Lorimer, H. L. 1950. *Homer and the Monuments.* London.

Loy, W. G. 1970. *The Land of Nestor: A Physical Geography of the Southwest Peloponnese.* Nat. Acad. of Sciences Office of Naval Research, Report No. 34. Washington, D.C.

Maiuri, A. 1926. "Jalisos: Scavi della Missione Archeologica Italiana a Rodi – Parte I: La Necropoli Micenea," *Annuario della R. Scuola Archeologica di Atene* 6-7 (1923-24):86-256.

Marinatos, S. 1933. "The Goekoop Excavations in Kephallenia, 2" *Arch Eph*:68-100. In Greek.

——. 1936. "Le temple géométrique de Dréros, II," *BCH* 60: 257-85.

——. 1974. *Excavations at Thera VI (1972 Season).* Athens.

Mastrokostas, E. I. 1965. "Excavation of the Teichos Dymaion," *Praktika*:121-36. In Greek.

McDonald, William A., et al. 1975. "Excavations at Nichoria in Messenia: 1972-1973," *Hesperia* 44:71-141.

McFadden, G. H. 1954. "A Late Cypriote III Tomb from Kourion: Kaloriziki No. 40," *AJA* 58:131-42.

Milojčić-von Zumbusch, J., and Milojčić, V. 1971. *Die Deutschen Ausgrabungen auf der Otzaki-Magula in Thessalien I: Das frühe Neolithikum.* Beiträge zur Ur- und Frühgeschichtlichen Archäologie des Mittelmeer-Kulturraumes für das Institut für Ur- und Frühgeschichte der Universität Heidelberg. 2 vols. Bonn.

Müller-Karpe, H. 1959. *Beiträge zur Chronologie der Urnenfelder-*

zeit nördlich und südlich der Alpen. Römisch-Germanische Forschungen 22. 2 vols. Berlin.

——. 1962. "Die Metallbeigaben der früheizenzeitlichen Kerameikos-Gräber," *JDAI* 77:59-129.

Mussche, H. F., et al. 1967a. *Thorikos II (1964).* Brussels.

——. 1967b. *Thorikos V (1965).* Brussels.

Mylonas, G. E. 1929. *Excavations at Olynthus Part I: The Neolithic Settlement.* Baltimore.

——. 1972-73. *Grave Circle B at Mycenae.* 2 vols. Athens. In Greek.

Nichoria I = Rapp and Aschenbrenner 1978.

Papadimitriou, I. 1961. "Excavations at Brauron," *Praktika* 1956: 72-89. In Greek.

Papadopoulos, T. J. 1979. *Mycenaean Achaea.* Studies in Mediterranean Archaeology 55. Göteborg.

Payne, H. et al. 1940. *Perachora: The Sanctuaries of Hera Akraia and Limenia,* Vol. I. Oxford.

Pendlebury, J. D. S., et al. 1940. "Excavations in the Plain of Lasithi. III. Karphi: A City of Refuge of the Early Iron Age in Crete," *BSA* 38:57-145.

Perdrizet, P. 1908. *Fouilles de Delphes V: Monuments figurés, petits bronzes, terre-cuites, antiquités diverses.* Paris.

Petsas, P. M, 1963. "Excavation of an Archaic Cemetery at Vergina (1960/61)," *Deltion* 17 (1961/62):218-88. In Greek.

Philios, D. 1889. "Excavation of Archaic Graves at Eleusis, *Eph Arch*:171-94. In Greek.

Popham, M. R., and Sackett, L. H., eds. 1968. *Excavations at Lefkandi, Euboea, 1964-66: A Preliminary Report.* British School of Archaeology at Athens. London.

——. 1973. "The Unexplored Mansion at Knossos: A Preliminary Report on the Excavations from 1967 to 1972," *AR* 1972-73: 50-71.

——, and Themelis, P. G. 1979-80. *Lefkandi I: The Iron Age.* British School at Athens Supplementary Vol. 11. 2 parts. London.

Rapp, G., Jr., and Aschenbrenner, S. E., eds. 1978. *Excavations at Nichoria in Southwest Greece I: Site, Environs, and Techniques.* Minneapolis.

Rizza, G. 1969. "Nuove ricerche sulla Patela e nel territorio del Prinias. Relazione preliminare degli scavi del 1969," *Cronache di Archeologia e di Storia dell'Arte*:7-32.

——, and Santa Maria Scrinari, V. 1968. *Il Santuario sull'Acropoli di Gortina I.* Monografie della Scuola Archeologica di Atene II. Rome.

Roes, A. 1933. *Greek Geometric Art: Its Symbolism and Its Origin.* Haarlem and London.

Rolley, C. 1969. *Fouilles de Delphes V: Monuments figurés, Les statuettes de bronze.* École Française d'Athènes. Paris.

Rouse, W. H. D. 1902. *Greek Votive Offerings: An Essay in the History of Greek Religion.* Cambridge.

Sackett, L. H., and Popham, M. R. 1965. "Excavations at Palaikastro, VI," *BSA* 60:248-305.

Säflund, G. 1965. *Excavations at Berbati, 1936-1937.* Stockholm.

Sandars, N. K. 1955. "The Antiquity of the One-Edged Bronze Knife in the Aegean," *PPS* 21:174-97.

Sapouna-Sakellarakis, E. 1978. *Die Fibeln der griechischen Inseln.* Prähistorische Bronzefunde XIV, 4. Munich.

Schaeffer, C. F. A. 1936. *Missions en Chypre, 1932-1935.* Paris.

Schliemann, H. 1886. *Tiryns: The Prehistoric Palace of the Kings of Tiryns.* London.

Schlörb-Vierneisel, B. 1966. "Eridanos-Nekropole I. Gräber und Opferstellen ns. 1-204," *JDAI* 81:4-111.

Smithson, E. L. 1961. "The Protogeometric Cemetery at Nea Ionia, 1949," *Hesperia* 30:147-78.

Snodgrass, A. M. 1964. *Early Greek Armour and Weapons from the End of the Bronze Age to 600 B.C.* Edinburgh.

——. 1971. *The Dark Age of Greece: An Archaeological Survey of the Eleventh to the Eighth Centuries B.C.* Edinburgh.

——. 1973. "Bronze 'phalara' – a Review," *Hamburger Beiträge zur Archäologie* III:41-50.

Styrenius, C.-G. 1967. *Submycenaean Studies: Examination of Finds from Mainland Greece, with a Chapter on Attic Protogeometric Graves.* Lund.

Tsountas, C. D. 1888. "Excavations of Tombs at Mycenae," *Eph Arch* 3:119-80. In Greek.

——. 1908. *The Prehistoric Acropoleis of Dimini and Sesklo.* Athens. In Greek.

Valmin, M. N. 1938. *The Swedish Messenia Expedition.* Lund.

van Effenterre, H. 1948. "Necropoles du Mirabello." Études Crétoises VIII. Paris.

Verdelis, N. M.1963. "Neue geometrische Gräber in Tiryns," *JDAI* 78:1-62.

Vokotopoulou, I. P. 1967. "Antiquities and Remains of Epirus-Vitsa Zagoriou," *Deltion* 22 B'2:346-49. In Greek.

Wace, A. J. B. 1925. "Excavations at Mycenae," *BSA* 25:1-126.

——. 1932. *Chamber Tombs at Mycenae.* Archaeologia 82. Oxford.

——, and Thompson, M. S. 1911-12. "Excavations at Halos," *BSA* 18:1-29.

——. 1912. *Prehistoric Thessaly.* Cambridge.

Waldstein, C. et al. 1905. *The Argive Heraeum, II.* Boston and New York.

Warren, P. M. 1969. *Minoan Stone Vases.* Cambridge.

——. 1972. *Myrtos. An Early Bronze Age Settlement in Crete. BSA* Supplement 7. Oxford.

Weinberg, S. S. 1962. "Excavations at Prehistoric Elateia, 1959," *Hesperia* 31:158-209.

——. 1970. "The Stone Age in the Aegean," *Cambridge Ancient History,* 3rd ed., I:1, Ch. X, pp. 557-618.

Wide, S. 1910. "Gräberfunde aus Salamis," *AM* 35:17-36.

Williams, C. K., II. 1970. "Corinth, 1969: Forum Area," *Hesperia* 39:1-39.

Xanthoudides, St. A. 1904. "From Crete," *Eph Arch*:1-56. In Greek.

Yon, M. 1971. *Salamine de Chypre II: La tombe T.1 du XIe siècle av. J.-C.* Paris.

Young, R. S. 1949. "An Early Geometric Grave near the Athenian Agora," *Hesperia* 18:275-97.

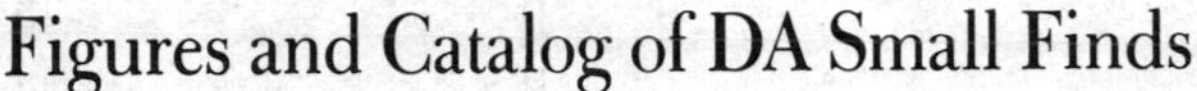

Figures and Catalog of DA Small Finds

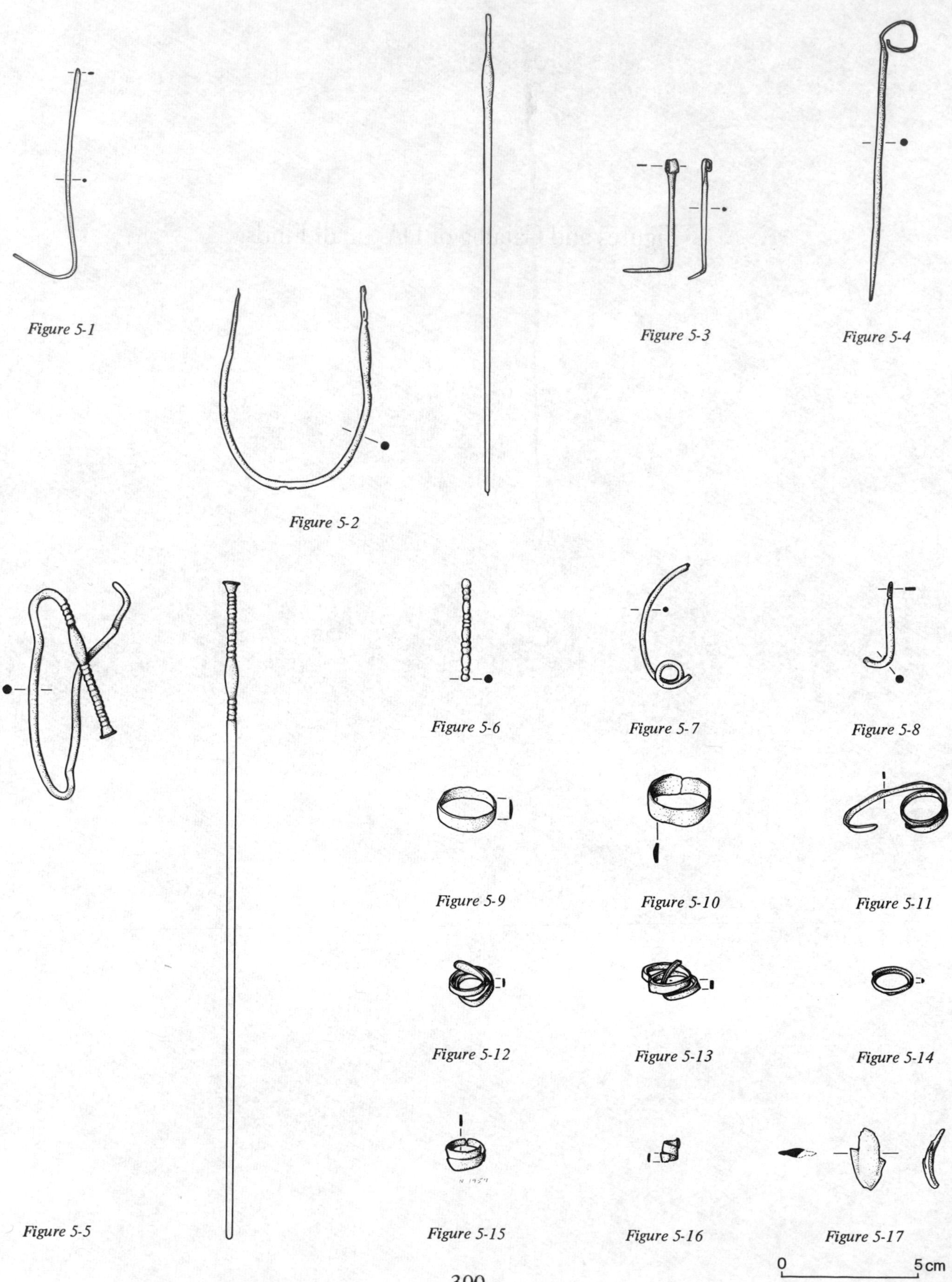

Figure 5-1

Figure 5-2

Figure 5-3

Figure 5-4

Figure 5-5

Figure 5-6

Figure 5-7

Figure 5-8

Figure 5-9

Figure 5-10

Figure 5-11

Figure 5-12

Figure 5-13

Figure 5-14

Figure 5-15

Figure 5-16

Figure 5-17

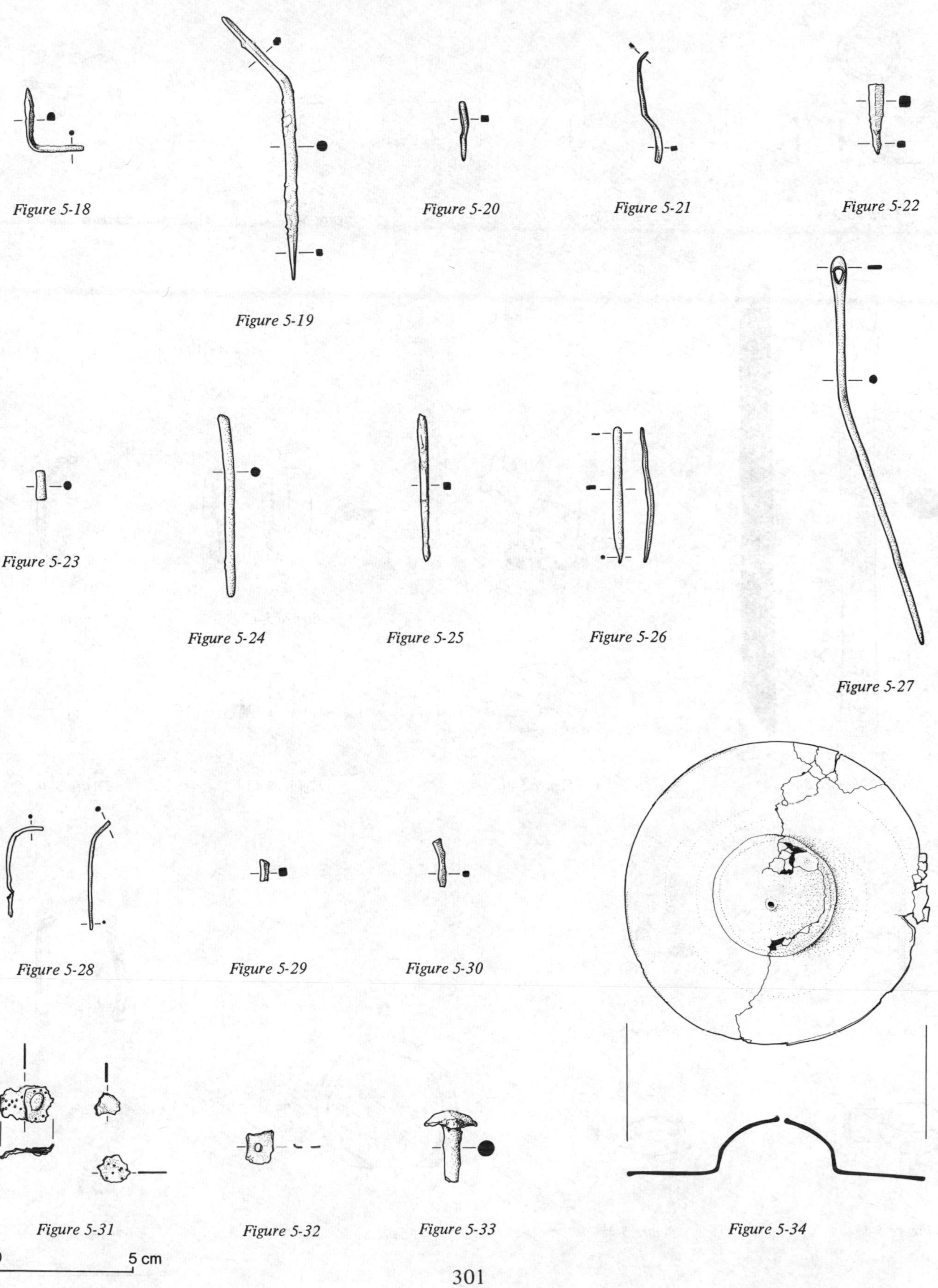

Figure 5-18

Figure 5-19

Figure 5-20

Figure 5-21

Figure 5-22

Figure 5-23

Figure 5-24

Figure 5-25

Figure 5-26

Figure 5-27

Figure 5-28

Figure 5-29

Figure 5-30

Figure 5-31

Figure 5-32

Figure 5-33

Figure 5-34

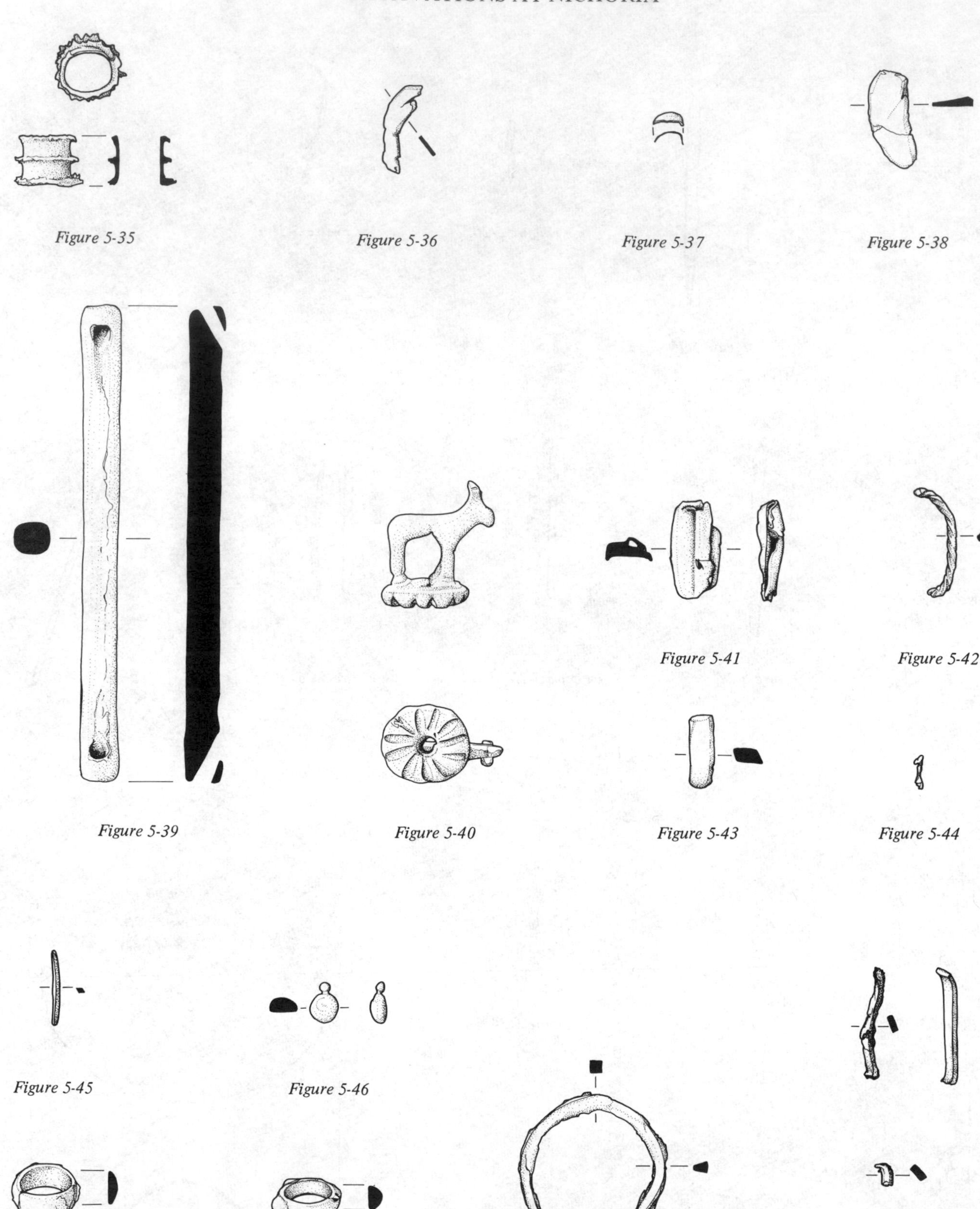

Figure 5-35

Figure 5-36

Figure 5-37

Figure 5-38

Figure 5-39

Figure 5-40

Figure 5-41

Figure 5-42

Figure 5-43

Figure 5-44

Figure 5-45

Figure 5-46

Figure 5-47

Figure 5-48

Figure 5-49

Figure 5-50

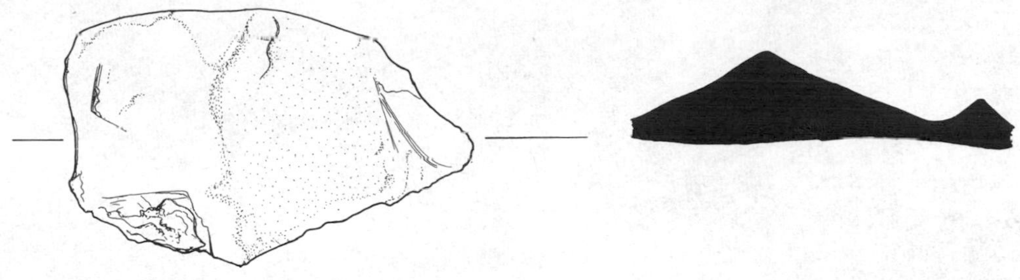

Figure 5-51

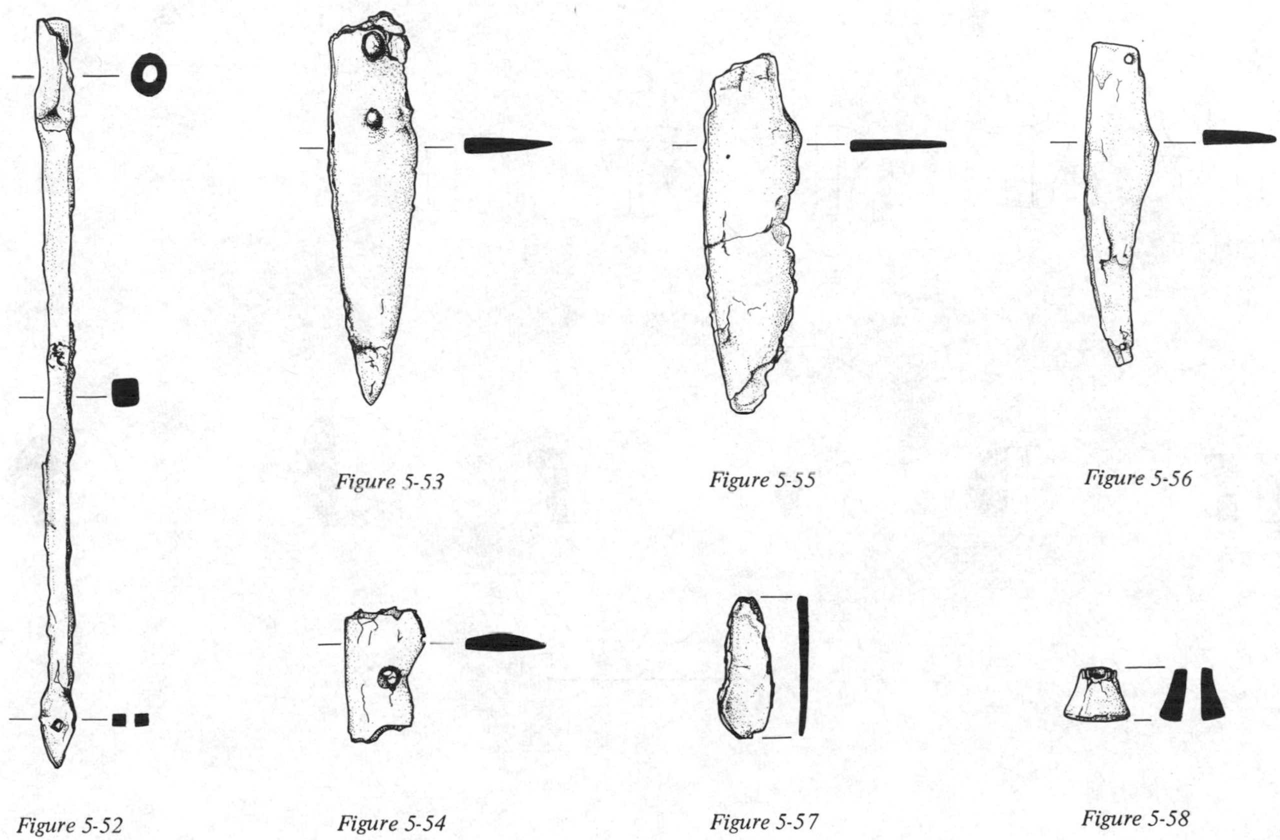

Figure 5-53 *Figure 5-55* *Figure 5-56*

Figure 5-52 *Figure 5-54* *Figure 5-57* *Figure 5-58*

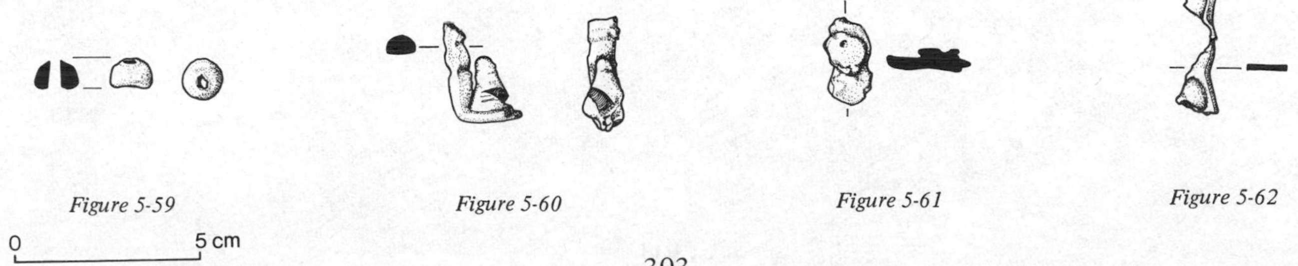

Figure 5-59 *Figure 5-60* *Figure 5-61* *Figure 5-62*

Figure 5-63

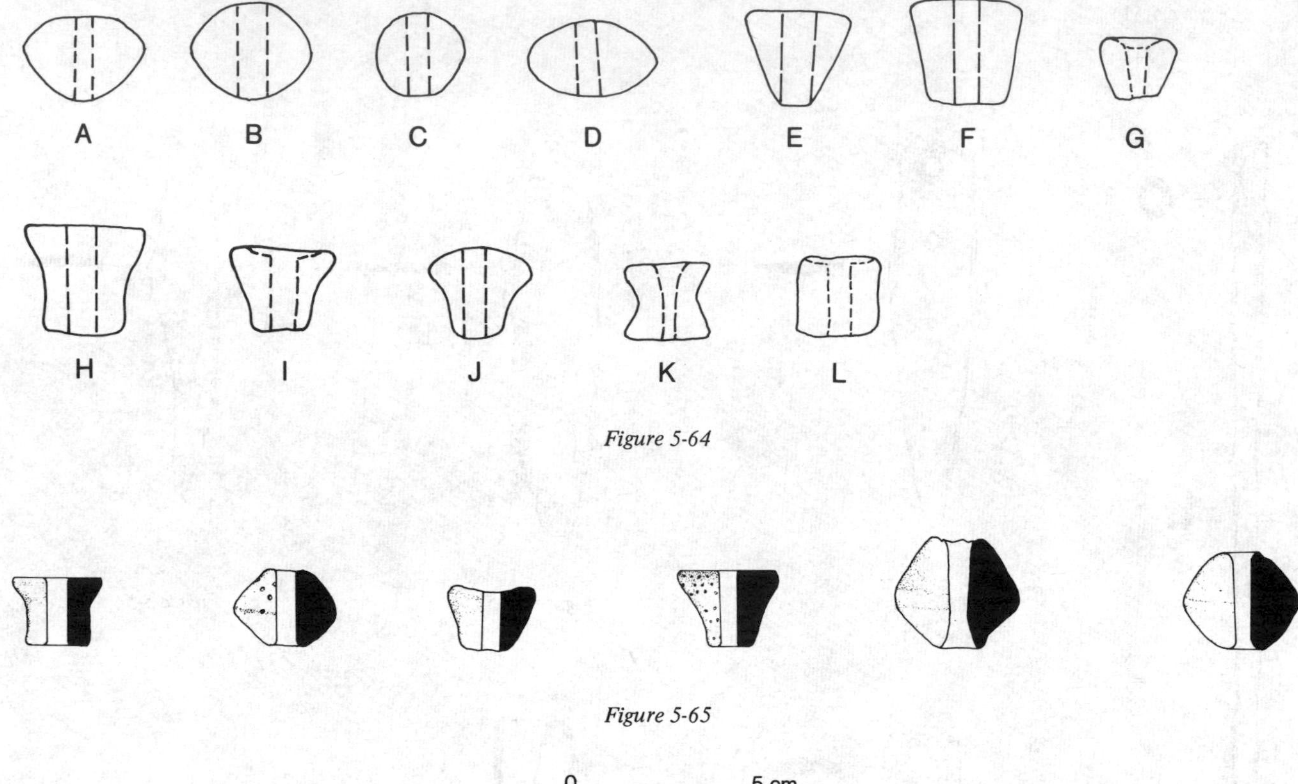

Figure 5-64

Figure 5-65

CATALOG OF DA SMALL FINDS

Bronze

PINS (NOS. **1-7**)

1 (N1916). Plain head. Fig. 5-1.
L. 0.10. D. 0.0015.
Lightly oxidized; complete, though bent. Slightly flattened head with fine point to slim shaft, which has traces of hammer marks. Found with **46** and **42** in LH context (Unit III-4).
DAI-II (with more LHIIIA2-B2).
Area III N, K24 Wy/K25 Wa baulk, level 5, lot 4383.

2 (N1944). Single beaded shaft. Fig. 5-2.
L. (pres.) 0.175. D. bead 0.004. L. bead 0.018. D. shaft 0.002.
Heavily oxidized, bent double, head lost. Bead is slight elliptical swelling just below missing head.
DAIII. *Hesperia* 44 (1975):118.
Analyzed (XRF)–*As*:nd, *Sn*:3%, *Pb*:nd. *Nichoria* I:173.
Area IV NE, L23 Vmn E extension, level 2, lot 4576.

3 (N1838). Roll-top. Fig. 5-3.
L. 0.064. Head 0.004 × 0.0028. D. shaft 0.0015.
Lightly oxidized. Complete, but lower shaft bent at right angles to upper. Head hammered flat and rolled for 1½ turns. (Could have been used as needle.)
DAII (with LH). *Hesperia* 44 (1975):118, Pl. 32g.
Analyzed (XRF)–*As*:nd, *Sn*:16.5%, *Pb*:nd. *Nichoria* I:173.
Area III S, L24 BCu, level 2, lot 4371/2.

4 (N768). Roll-top. Fig. 5-4.
L. 0.102. Head 0.013 × 0.01. D. shaft 0.003.
Complete and cleaned. Surface pitting. Top hammered flat and rolled into wide head for just over one turn. Shaft round in section.
DAII (with LHIII). *Hesperia* 41 (1972):263, Pl. 51g; *Hesperia* 44 (1975):118.
Analyzed (XRF)–*As*:1%, *Sn*:nd, *Pb*:nd. *Nichoria* I:173.
Area III N, K25 Uab, level 2, lot 2216.

5 (N1789). Bead-and-moldings. Fig. 5-5; Pl. 5-1.
L. (original) 0.224. D. head 0.0055. D. bead 0.006. D. shaft 0.003.
Cast; a very solid pin only lightly oxidized. Complete but crumpled; tip reattached. Plain disc head above 13 bead moldings, separated by long oval bead from 4 more moldings.
DAII-III. *Hesperia* 44 (1975):106, 117-18, Pl. 27a.
Analyzed (XRF)–*As*:tr, *Sn*:ca. 25%, *Pb*:nd. *Nichoria* I:173.
Area IV SW, L23 Qfg/Rfg baulk, level 2, lot 4082.

6 (N464). Bead-and-rod moldings. Fig. 5-6.
L. (pres.) 0.037. D. shaft 0.004-0.0025.
Cast. Lightly oxidized; pale green patina. Head and upper shaft only; succession of moldings from head to break.
DAII (with LHIII). *Hesperia* 41 (1972):263, Pl. 51d.
Analyzed (XRF)–*As*:1%, *Sn*:17%, *Pb*:nd. *Nichoria* I:173.
Area III, K25 Rg, level 3, lot 1660. Unit III-I, pit deposit.

7 (N56). Fragment.
L. (extended) 0.073. D. shaft 0.002.
Identification as pin uncertain. Oxidized, bent. Head and tip lost. Shaft round in section.
DAIII.
Area IV SW, L23-IV (trial), level 2, lot 280.

FIBULAE (NOS. **8-10**)

8 (N1561). Arched bow. Fig. 5-7; Pl. 5-2.
L. (pres.) 0.057. H. 0.034. Th. bow 0.002.
Much oxidized. Spring and most of bow in two joining pieces. Wire of round section and even thickness. Spring to left, one turn. Perhaps Blinkenburg type II.1.
DAI-II (with LHIII).
Area IV SW, L23 Ocd, level 2, lot 4104/3N.

9 (N935). Pin only.
L. 0.044. Th. 0.002.
Oxidized. Complete from tip to start of spring.
DAIII.
Analyzed (XRF)–*As*:nd, *Sn*:ca. 20%, *Pb*:nd. *Nichoria* I:173.
Area IV NE, L23 Vk1, level 2, lot 3365/2.

10 (N1620). Fragment of pin(?) Fig. 5-8.
L. 0.026. Th. 0.0025.
Oxidized. Fine rod of round section; flattened at one end. Perhaps part of pin and spring of fibula.
DAII-III.
Area IV SE, L23 Wc, level 3, lot 4037/6. DA fill, Unit IV-4.

RINGS (NOS. **11-23**)

11 (N589). Finger ring with bezel.
0.024 × 0.023. Th. 0.003.
Oxidized. Complete. Hoop of plano-convex section. Bezel undecorated.
DAIII.
Area IV SW, L23 Rhi, level 1, lot 1789.

12 (N1777). Finger ring. Fig. 5-9.
D. 0.021. W. 0.006. Th. 0.001.
Much oxidized and chipped. Plain hoop, very flat plano-convex section.
DAII. *Hesperia* 44 (1975):89.
Area IV NE, L23 Vkl/Vmn baulk, floor level 3, lot 4324. Unit IV-1, Phase 1.

13 (N1401). Finger ring. Fig. 5-10.
D. 0.022. W. 0.007. Th. 0.002.
Lightly oxidized. Complete, intact. Plain hoop, plano-convex section. Rather roughly made.
DAII. *Hesperia* 44 (1975):89.
Analyzed (XRF)–*As*:nd, *Sn*:17.1%, *Pb*:nd. *Nichoria* I:173.
Area IV NE, L23 Vkl, floor level 3, lot 3385/1. Unit IV-1, Phase 2.

14 (N594). Finger ring(?)
D. (restored) 0.016. W. 0.004. Th. 0.0015.
Much oxidized; reconstructed as slim closed hoop of slightly convex section.
DAIII. *Hesperia* 41 (1972):264, no. 3.
Area IV NE, L23 Ukl, level 2, lot 1888.

15 (N134). Open-ended ring.
D. (restored) 0.018. W. 0.007. Th. 0.0005.
Lightly oxidized. Rectangular strip with rounded terminals. Crushed out of shape.
DAI (with LHIII).
Area IV SW, L23-V (trial), level 5, lot 329.

16 (N1632). Fragment of open ring(?)

0.02 × 0.003 × 0.002.

Completely oxidized. Thickness and width tapering to rounded terminal.

DAI-II (with LH).

Area IV SW, L23 Nc, level 3, lot 4112/1E.

17 (N1829). Spiral ring. Fig. 5-11.

D. 0.017. W. 0.0025. Th. 0.0005.

Lightly oxidized. Complete but partly untwisted. Spiral of fine flat strip. Pointed terminals. Probably originally 3¼ turns.

DAI-II (with LHIII). *Hesperia* 44 (1975):106, Pl. 27c.

Analyzed (XRF)–*As*:tr, *Sn*: 5.8%, *Pb*:1%. *Nichoria* I:173-74.

Area IV SW, L23 OPe/OPf baulk, level 2, lot 4075/8.

18 (N1206). Spiral ring. Fig. 5-12.

D. ca. 0.0165. W. 0.003. Th. 0.001.

Oxidized. Complete. Coil of flat strip with rounded terminals. 2¼ turns, now slightly distorted.

DAII (with LH).

Analyzed (XRF)–*As*:nd, *Sn*:16.5%, *Pb*:0.5%. *Nichoria* I:173-74 (first reference to "N294" on p. 173 should read "N1206").

Area III S, K24 Ytu, level 3, lot 3179. Sector 3, terrace walls.

19 (N294). Spiral ring. Fig. 5-13.

D. 0.021. W. 0.003. Th. 0.001.

Lightly oxidized. Tip gone; terminal lost; crushed. Flat strip with blunt terminals. 2¼ turns.

DAII-III (with some LHIII).

Analyzed (XRF)–*As*:nd, *Sn*:17%, *Pb*:5%. *Nichoria* I:173-74 (second reference to "N294" on p. 173 is correct).

Area IV SW, L23 Pfg, level 2, lot 940.

20 (N618). Spiral ring. Fig. 5-14.

D. 0.015-0.014. W. 0.0015. Th. 0.001.

Lightly oxidized. Complete (repaired). Plano-convex section. 1¾ turns.

DAIII. *Hesperia* 41 (1972):264, no. 4.

Analyzed (XRF)–*As*:nd, *Sn*:17%, *Pb*:nd. *Nichoria* I:173-74.

Area IV NE, L23 Ukl, level 2, lot 1900.

21 (N1957). Spiral ring. Fig. 5-15.

D. 0.015. W. 0.003. Th. 0.001.

Oxidized; incomplete (terminals lost). Flat strip at least 1½ turns.

Mainly DA (but mixed).

Area IV SW, L23 Rab, level 2, lot 4571.

22 (N910). Spiral(?) ring.

D. (restored) 0.012. W. 0.002. Th. 0.0005.

Wholly oxidized; in 5 possibly joining fragments. Flat strip.

DAII (with some LHIII).

Area IV SW, L23 OPe, level 2, pit 1, lot 3270.

23 (N1890). Spiral ring(?)

L. (extended) 0.035. W. 0.002. Th. 0.001.

Lightly oxidized fragment of flat strip; both ends broken away.

DAI-II (with LH).

Area III N, K24 Wy/K25 Wa baulk, level 3, lot 4381/2.

EARRING(?)

24 (N1665). Open ring.

D. 0.01. Th. 0.001.

Much oxidized; open ring of horseshoe shape in fine wire, round in section. One end may be incomplete.

DAII. *Hesperia* 44 (1975):89.

Area IV NE, L23 Vkl, floor level 3, lot 4301. Unit IV-1, Phase 1.

BEAD

25 (N1711). Spiral. Fig. 5-16.

L. (pres.) 0.008. D. 0.006. W. 0.0033. Th. 0.0005.

Much oxidized. Fine strip of flat section. Incomplete. Tightly coiled into spiral of 1⅓ turns.

DAII.

Area IV S, L23 Sc, level 2, lot 4528/3 NE.

WEAPON

26 (N1832). Fragment. Fig. 5-17.

0.022 × 0.0125.

Heavily oxidized and split. Tip of sword, dagger, or spearhead. Remains of traced lines on either side of vanishing broad, flat midrib.

DAII (with LH). This could be a Bronze Age survivor.

Analyzed (XRF)–*As*:1%, *Sn*:10.5%, *Pb*:nd. *Nichoria* I:173.

Area III S, L24 BCu, level 2, lot 4371/2. Sector 3, terrace walls.

SMALL TOOLS (NOS. **27-35**)

27 (N135). Graver or awl(?) Fig. 5-18.

L. (extended) 0.042. Th. 0.0015-0.0025.

Much oxidized. Shaft and point. Rectangular in section. Bent at right angle in middle.

DAI (with LHIII).

Area IV SW, L23-V (trial), level 5, lot 327.

28 (N1466). Awl. Fig. 5-19.

L. 0.11. Th. 0.004.

Heavily oxidized. Complete but bent. Shaft round in section, butt roughly square, and square again immediately adjacent to working point.

DAII (with some LH). *Hesperia* 44 (1975):118, Pl. 32g.

Analyzed (XRF)–*As*:1%, *Sn*: 10.1%, *Pb*:tr. *Nichoria* I:173.

Area III S, K24 Yuv, level 4, lot 3683N.

29 (N228). Fragment of graver or awl(?) Fig. 5-20.

L. 0.022. Th. 0.003.

Much oxidized. Slightly bent. Shaft rhomboidal in section, tapering to fine point.

DAII (with LHIIIA-B).

Area III N, K25 Sef, level 2, lot 805. Mycenaean street.

30 (N831). Graver(?) Fig. 5-21.

L. 0.042. Th. 0.003 × 0.002.

Broken at one end; otherwise well preserved. Shaft rectangular in section; twisted; tapers evenly to tip.

DAII (with mainly LHIIIA-B).

Analyzed (XRF)–*As*:0.8%, *Sn*:6.8%, *Pb*:1%. *Nichoria* I:173 (where date should be "LHIII-DA").

Area IV SW, L23 Ofg/Pfg baulk, level 3, lot 3257/2.

31 (N359). Fragment of awl(?) Fig. 5-22.

L. 0.026 Th. 0.001 0.004.

Much oxidized. Remaining part of shaft square in section, tapering to point.

DAIII.

Area IV NE, L23 Umn, level 2, lot 1120.

32 (N1904). Fragment of awl(?) Fig. 5-23.

L. 0.024. D. shaft 0.004.

Lightly oxidized. Shaft round in section. Unbroken end rounded.

DAI-II (with LH). *Hesperia* 44 (1975):118, Pl. 32g, where it is shown as part of no. 33 (N1906).

Analyzed (OES)–*As*:0.20%, *Sn*:4.4%, *Pb*:0.30%. *Nichoria* I:169, 181 (SF4839). Also analyzed (NAA), *Nichoria* I:178 (where "N904" should be "N1904").

Area III N, K24 Wy/K25 Wa baulk, level 3, lot 4381/3.

33 (N1906). Fragments of awl(?) Fig. 5-24.

(a) L. 0.0062. D. shaft 0.0035, (b) L. 0.0023. D. shaft 0.0035.

Shaft of (a) lightly oxidized, round in section, with blunt point. Fragment (b), numbered SF4842, used for analysis.

DAI-II (with LH). *Hesperia* 44 (1975):118, 131.

Analyzed (OES)–*As*:0.14%, *Sn*:25%, *Pb*:0.76%. *Nichoria* I:169. Also analyzed (NAA), *Nichoria* I:169, 178 (SF4842).

Area III N, K24 Wy/K25 Wa baulk, level 3, lot 4381/2. Found with no. **32**. Impossible to determine whether **32** and **33** are parts of same tool.

34 (N547). Chisel. Fig. 5-25.

L. 0.053. Th. 0.0035-0.002.

Heavily oxidized. Tip damaged; extreme end of butt broken. Shaft square in section. Working tip of fine chisel type.

DAI (with mainly LHII-III).

Area II, K25 If, level 2, lot 1809.

35 (N1907). Fragment of chisel. Fig. 5-26.

L. 0.049. W. 0.0033. Th. 0.0017.

Lightly oxidized. Slim bar, rectangular in section, with pointed "butt" and slightly expanded working tip.

DAI-II (with LH). *Hesperia* 44 (1975):118, Pl. 32g (bottom right).

Analyzed (XRF)–*As*:1%, *Sn*:nd, *Pb*:1%. *Nichoria* I:173-74.

Area III, K24 Wy/K25 Wa baulk, level 3, lot 4381/2.

NEEDLES (NOS. **36-44**)

36 (N125). Fragments.

(a) L. 0.003. D. 0.001. (b) L. 0.0055. D. 0.001.

Oxidized. Two fragments of needle shaft.

DAI (with LHIII).

Area IV SW, L23-V (trial), level 5, lot 329.

37 (N1779). Fragments.

(a) L. 0.019. D. 0.001. (b) L. 0.009. D. 0.001.

Heavily oxidized. Two fragments of needle shaft. Round in section, bent and broken at both ends.

DAII.

Area IV NE, L23 Xm, level 4N, lot 4321.

38 (N1844). Fragments.

L. 0.024 (total for 2 pieces). D. 0.001.

Much oxidized. Bent. Probably nonjoining.

DAI-II.

Area III N, K24 Xy, level 2, lot 4370/4. Unit IV-4, rubbish tip.

39 (N1793). Fragment.

L. 0.018. D. 0.0013.

Lightly oxidized. Shaft round in section, broken top and bottom.

DAII?

Area IV SW, L23 STfg/SThi baulk, level 3, lot 4635/4.

40 (N1841). Fragment.

L. (pres.) 0.054. D. 0.001.

Lightly oxidized. Point and shaft round in section.

DAI-II.

Area III N, K24 Xy, level 2, lot 4370/3. Unit III-4, rubbish tip.

41 (N1949). Fragment.

L. (pres.) 0.019. D. 0.0015.

Oxidized. Point and shaft round in section. Two other minute, formless scraps may belong.

DAII (with LHII-IIIA).

Area IV S, L23 Xd, level 5, lot 4527/1.

42 (N1919). Needle. Fig. 5-27.

L. 0.142. W. head 0.005. D. 0.003. Eyelet 0.003 × 0.004. Complete and in good condition. Cleaned. Upper end of shaft (round in section) hammered flat and pierced. Ovoid eyelet.

DAI-II (with more LHIIIA2-B2).

Area III N, K24 Wy/K25 Wa baulk, level 5, lot 4383.

43 (N308). Fragment.

L. 0.012. D. 0.0025.

Much oxidized. Scraps of shaft, round in section.

DAII (with more LHIIIA-B).

Area III N, K25 Se, level 3, lot 826.

44 (N1993). Needle. Fig. 5-28.

L. 0.085. D. 0.0013.

Two joining fragments. Very fine needle with damaged eyelet. Extreme point lost.

DAI (with LH).

Area IV NW, L23 Sk, level 5, lot 4521.

RIVETS (NOS. **45-47**; PROBABLY FROM KNIFE HAFTS)

45 (N1207). Fragment.

L. (pres.) 0.006. D. head 0.005. D. shaft 0.003.

Well preserved but probably incomplete. One end burred, other rough and unburred.

DAII (with LH).

Area III S, K24 Ytu, level 3, lot 3179. Sector 3, terraces.

46 (N1916–part only). Rivet. Fig. 5-29.

L. 0.008. D. 0.003.

Slightly oxidized. Complete. Roughly square heads. Found with no. 1.

DAI-II (with more LHIIIA2-B2).

Area III N, K24 Wy/K25 Wa baulk, level 5, lot 4383.

47 (N459). Rivet. Fig. 5-30.

L. 0.022. W. 0.002. D. head 0.003.

Oxidized. Complete. Slightly bent.

DAII (with mainly LHIII).

Analyzed (OES)–*As*:tr, *Sn*:0.035%, *Pb*:0.35%. *Nichoria* I:169. Also analyzed (NAA), *Nichoria* I:178.

Area III, K25 Pgh, level 2, lot 1405.

VESSELS (NOS. **48-51**)

48 (N627). Body fragments. Fig. 5-31.

(a) 0.019 × 0.013 × 0.0005. (b) 0.009 × 0.01. (c) 0.007 × 0.007.

3 fragments of lightly oxidized sheet metal; (b) and (c) broken all round; (a) made up of 2 overlapping pieces joined by a rivet; (a) and (b) decorated *en pointillé*; (a) has design of St. Andrew's cross, possibly repeated on (b).

DAII? (with mainly LHIIIB). Cf. composite sheetmetal vessels from Italy and barbarian Europe.

Area II, K25 Lfg, level 2, lot 1831.

49 (N1287). Handle fragment. Fig. 5-32.

0.012 × 0.009. Th. 0.001. D. hole 0.0025.

Smooth green patinated surface. Apparently broken from one terminal of ribbon handle of vessel. Curve on one edge indicates handle could have been horizontally mounted under lip.

DAII (with LH).

Area III N, K24 Uw, level 3, lot 3135/1.

50 (N1708). Rivet.

D. 0.023. H. 0.005.

Lightly oxidized. Very flat head; edges chipped; shaft chipped off short.

DAII.

Area III N, K24 Yy, level 2, lot 4358. Unit III-4, rubbish tip.

51 (N1060). Rivet. Fig. 5-33.

L. 0.026. D. head 0.018. H. head 0.006. D. shaft 0.006.

Lightly oxidized. Shaft probably complete. Could have served to attach large handle to thick rim. Head almost certainly on inside.

DAI-II (with LHIII).

Area IV SW, L23 OPe, level 3, lot 3272/4.

MISCELLANEOUS TRAPPINGS (NOS. **52-56**)

52 (N1833). Shield boss/phalaron. Fig. 5-34; Pl. 5-3.

D. 0.11. H. 0.03. D. boss 0.045. Th. metal 0.001. D. hole in center of boss 0.015.

Heavily oxidized. Repaired from fragments; almost complete, save chips. Raised from disk casting. Boss stilted. Hole pierced at top is off-center. Undecorated. No stitch-holes.

DAII. *Hesperia* 44 (1975):91, 118, Pl. 22d; *Nichoria* I:261 ff., Pls. 15-6, 15-7.

Analyzed (XRF)–*As*:0.5%, *Sn*:ca. 25%, *Pb*:0.5%. *Nichoria* I:173.

Area IV NW, L23 Tkl/Ukl baulk, floor level 3, lot 4322/3. Unit IV-2, Phase 2.

53 (N1335). "Collar." Fig. 5-35; Pls. 5-4, 5-5, 5-6.

L. (pres.) 0.0175. D. 0.026. Th. metal 0.004.

Heavily oxidized. Cylinder with three ridges. Bottom ridge seems broken away all round. Center ridge, with symmetrical "cogs," may be complete. Top ridge has a few long "cogs," but this might be remains of *ajourée* stand completely broken away. Unidentified component of complex object. Suggestion that it was collar for human use (*Nichoria* I:174) based on misunderstanding.

DAIII.

Analyzed (XRF)–*As*:nd, *Sn*:16%, *Pb*:ca. 20%. *Nichoria* I:173-74.

Area IV SE, L23 Wd, level 2, lot 3348/3.

54 (N1623). Fragment. Fig. 5-36.

L. (pres.) 0.034. W. 0.008. Th. 0.001.

Heavily oxidized. Arc of open circle, including start of one "branch" from internal circumference. Broken away at each end. Form and function of complete object unknown.

DAII-III.

Area IV SE, L23 Wc, level 3, lot 4037/6.

55 (N1776). Boss. Fig. 5-37.

L. 0.013. W. 0.0075. Th. metal 0.0005.

Much oxidized. Less than half of hemisphere with traces of a tongue at edge. Complete piece perhaps had 2 tongues with which boss attached to leather or cloth.

DAII.

Area IV N, L23 Tkl, floor level 3, lot 4322/2. Unit IV-1, Phase 1.

56 (N1893). Double-ax pendant(?) Fig. 5-38.

0.014 × 0.015 × 0.003.

Much oxidized. Tip of lunate blade, possibly from an ornamental ax or double ax.

DAIII.

Area IV SW, L23 Rfg/Sfg baulk, level 2, lot 4091/3.

UNIDENTIFIED FITTING

57 (N1283). Component of larger object. Fig. 5-39; Pl. 5-7.

L. 0.161. D. 0.012. D. holes 0.0065.

Some surface oxidation. Solid bar, round in section. Hole pierced obliquely at each end, to emerge ca. 0.012 into length of bar. Probably component of much larger object that was not necessarily of same material.

DAII. Found with **89**.

Analyzed (XRF)–*As*:nd, *Sn*:3.8%, *Pb*:1%. *Nichoria* I:173.

Area IV NE, L23 Vkl, floor level 3, lot 3385/1. Unit IV-1, Phase 2.

STATUETTES (NOS. **58-60**)

58 (N1723). Quadruped on Stand. Fig. 5-40; Pl. 5-8, 5-9.

H. 0.042. Base 0.032 × 0.027 × 0.007.

Lightly oxidized. Cleaned. Complete except chip from ear (old break). Made by lost wax process. Very summarily modeled; ears (or horns) but no eyes; snout but no mouth; forelegs partly divided, hind legs in one piece; no tail. Set on oval stand with central hole and 11 deep incisions in form of rough rosette on underside. Animal (deer? horse?) stands crooked on base, probably result of clumsy wax-work. Perhaps used as stamp seal.

DAIII. *Hesperia* 44 (1975):118, Pl. 31e, f; *Nichoria* I:261, Pls. 15-4, 15-5.

Analyzed (XRF)–*As*:nd, *Sn*:3.7%, *Pb*:nd. *Nichoria* I:173.

Area IV NW, L23 Sl, level 1, lot 4123/1. Room 1 of Unit-IV-5.

59 (N1784). Fragment. Fig. 5-41.

L. (pres.) 0.0335. W. (pres.) 0.0165.

Lightly oxidized. Part of unidentified object made by lost wax process. When complete, possibly oval plinth over 0.006 high with something now broken and crushed standing along its median line.

DAI (with LH).

Area III, K24 Vy, level 4, lot 4444.

60 (N1850). Fragment.

L. 0.028. D. 0.0075.

Lightly oxidized. Circular in section, broken at one end. Perhaps tail of bull or horse figurine. Made by lost wax process.

DAI (with LHIII).

Area III, K24 Vy, level 4, lot 4458.

INCOMPLETE OBJECTS (NOS. **61-63**)

61 (N788). Twisted rod. Fig. 5-42.

L. (pres.) 0.038. D. 0.003.

Slightly oxidized; otherwise well preserved. Could be part of bracelet or fibula bar or possibly of vessel handle.

DAI-II.

Area IV, L23 Shi, level 7, lot 2408.

62 (N399). Billet. Fig. 5-43.

L. 0.025. Section 0.0085 × 0.006.

Oxidized. One end unbroken. Rectangular but asymmetric in section. Part of unworked rough billet casting.

DAII (with LHIII).

Analyzed (XRF)–*As*:ca. 1%, *Sn*:ca. 20%, *Pb*:ca. 1%. *Nichoria* I:173 (where date should be emended to "LHIII-DA").

Area III N, K25 Tcd, level 4, lot 1180.

63 (N775). Billet.

L. 0.051. Section 0.002 × 0.0015.

Heavily oxidized. Rectangular in section. Fine bar, broken top and bottom.

DAI-II.

Area IV NW, L23 Thi, level 5, lot 2381.

SCRAP (NOS. 64-75)

Many of these objects are barely recognizable fragments of categories described above.

64 (N1714). Ring?
0.012 × 0.007 × 0.001.
Heavily oxidized. Bent fragment, possibly from an open-ended ring or spiral ring. One rounded terminal preserved.
DAI-II (with LH).
Area IV NE, L23 Xklm, level 4, lot 4311/2W.

65 (N1538). Billet fragment.
0.011 × 0.003 × 0.002.
Completely oxidized. Rectangular; broken at both ends.
DAI-II (with LH).
Area IV SW, L23 Ocd, level 1, lot 4103/5 C and N.

66 (N827). Sheet metal.
0.027 × 0.019 × 0.001.
Lightly oxidized. Broken all round, with possible exception of slightly wavy edge. Trace of engraved line at one broken edge.
DAII.
Area IV NW, L23 Top, level 3, lot 3405.

67 (N844). Sheet metal.
0.041 × 0.009 × 0.001.
Lightly oxidized. Fragment of crumpled sheet; more likely part of strip than of vessel wall.
DAII.
Area IV NW, L23 Top, level 3, lot 3045/6.

68 (N1853). Unidentified.
0.03 × 0.025. Th. 0.005.
Lightly oxidized. Tip of unknown object; unlikely to be tool or weapon in view of plano-convex section. Possibly broken away from bar ingot.
DAII.
Area IV NW, L23 Tj, level 2, lot 4417/4. Unit IV-6, Room 2.

69 (N1215). Unidentified. Fig. 5-44.
L. 0.012. D. 0.001.
Slightly oxidized. Fine wire, round in section, with "bunch" of threads at one end, "hook" at other. Possibly an unusually shaped riser.
DAII (with LH).
Area III S, K24 Ytu, level 3, lot 3175/2. Sector 3, terraces.

70 (N1208). Sheet metal.
(a) 0.016 × 0.006 × 0.001; (b) 0.011 × 0.004 × 0.0005.
Oxidized. Formless scraps of thin sheet, broken all round.
DAII (with LH).
Area III S, K24 Ytu, level 3, lot 3179. Sector 3, terraces.

71 (N483). Unidentified.
0.02 × 0.016 × 0.005.
Lightly oxidized. Formless, broken all round.
DAIII.
Analyzed (OES)—*As*:0.15%, *Sn*:3.1%, *Pb*:0.30%. *Nichoria* I:169; also analyzed (NAA). *Nichoria* I:178 (where date should be "DAIII").
Area IV NW, L23 Thi, level 2, lot 1543.

72 (N694). Sheet metal.
0.013 × 0.008 × 0.001 (largest of 3 fragments).
Much oxidized. Fragments of fine sheet, broken all round.
DAIII.
Area IV NE, L23 Ukl, level 2a, lots 2125, 2130.

73 (N705). Sheet metal.
0.018 × 0.008 × 0.001.
Lightly oxidized. Small piece of thin sheet, broken all round.
DAIII.
Area IV NE, L23 Wklm, level 2, lot 2136.

74 (N1958). Billet. Fig. 5-45.
L. 0.026. Section 0.0018.
Lightly oxidized. Very roughly made billet, rhomboidal in section. Clear signs of hammering.
DA.
Area IV SW, L23 Rab, level 2, lot 4571.

75 (N806). Unidentified.
L. 0.011. D. 0.001.
Lightly oxidized. Bent; broken away at both ends. Possibly part of fine needle or coil ring.
DAII.
Area IV NW, L23 Rhi, level 3, lot 2412.

MELTING OR CASTING WASTE (NOS. 76-79)

76 (N377). Droplet.
0.007 × 0.005.
Lightly oxidized. Rounded pellet.
DAII-III (with LH).
Area IV NE, L23 Umn, level 4, lot 1127.

77 (N851). Droplet.
0.0035 × 0.0035.
Completely oxidized. Minute pellet.
DA (with some LH).
Area IV NE, L23 Xklm, level 2, lot 3356/3.

78 (N681). Double droplet. Fig. 5-46.
0.014 × 0.01 × 0.005.
Lightly oxidized.
DAIII. *Hesperia* 41 (1972):264, no. 6 (where called "earring").
Area IV NE, L23 Ukl, level 2a, lot 2125.

79 (N1533). Droplet.
0.017 × 0.01 × 0.0055.
Lightly oxidized. Oval pellet of rather spongy metal.
DA.
Area IV SE, L23 UVc, level 3, lot 4026/1.

Iron

PERSONAL OBJECTS (NOS. 80-86)

80 (N1465). Pin.
L. 0.15. D. 0.002-0.0045.
Much oxidized. 5 fragments; head and upper part lost. Shaft, round in section, tapers evenly to point.
DAII? (with mainly LHIII).
Area III S, K24 Xuv, level 4, lot 3195. Terrace walls.

81 (N667 – part only). Pin.
L. 0.028. D. 0.0025.
Much oxidized. Two joining pieces of shaft, round in section.
DAIII. *Hesperia* 41 (1972):264, no. 5.

Area IV NE, L23 Ukl, level 2, lot 2109.

82 (N70–part only). Pin.
L. 0.147. D. 0.007-0.004.
Oxidized. Bent. Shaft round in section.
LH and modern.
Area VII, N22-XIII (trial), level 1, lot 402.

83 (N1559). Ring. Fig. 5-47.
D. 0.024. W. 0.012. Th. 0.005.
Heavily oxidized. Plain hoop, plano-convex in section. Broken open but complete.
DAIII (with LH).
Area IV SE, L23 UVc and extension, level 4, lot 4027/3E.

84 (N1828). Ring. Fig. 5-48.
D. (out) 0.025; (in) 0.016. W. 0.008. Th. 0.005.
Much oxidized. Plain closed hoop, plano-convex in section.
DAII-III.
Area IV NW, L23 Tj, level 2, lot 4417/2. Unit IV-6, Room 2.

85 (N236). Bracelet. Fig. 5-49.
D. 0.053. Th. 0.006.
Heavily oxidized and disintegrating. Open ring, rectangular in section. Flattened terminals.
LHI-LHII (bulk LHI).
Area III, K25 Rd, level 2, lot 710.

86 (N807). Tweezer(?) Fig. 5-50; Pl. 5-10.
L. (pres.) 1.09. W. 0.016.
Completely oxidized. 5 fragments of bar and strip probably compose one arm of pair of tweezers with narrow pinched spring and relatively broad blade.
DAIII.
Area IV NE, L23 Wklm, level 2, lot 2141.

WEAPONS (NOS. 87, 88)

87 (N1834). Fragment of ax head. Fig. 5-51; Pl. 5-11.
L. (pres.) 0.107. W. 0.065. Th. 0.025.
Much oxidized. Remains of shafted ax blade. Diagonal split across shaft-hole leaves it doubtful whether a double ax, a hammer ax, or a single-bladed shaft-hole ax.
DAII. *Hesperia* 44 (1975):91, 118.
Area IV NE, L23 Tkl, floor level 3, lot 4322/2. Unit IV-1, Phase 2.

88 (N489). Fragment of blade(?)
L. (pres.) 0.126. W. 0.015. Th. 0.009.
Completely oxidized. In many flakes. Original form not recognizable but more likely a weapon than a tool.
DAII (with LH).
Area III, K25 Rg/Sg baulk, level 2, lot 1664. Unit III-1.

SMALL TOOLS (NOS. 89-96)

89 (N1282). Weaving instrument(?) Fig. 5-52; Pl. 5-12.
L. 0.197. L. working point 0.022. W. 0.01. Th. 0.004. Hole in tip 0.003. L. socket 0.026. D. 0.01 (out); 0.005 (in). Shaft at socket rectangular, 0.006 × 0.04. Shaft rectangular at point, 0.006 × 0.006.
Much oxidized. Made from rectangular billet. One end wrought into flat snake head, the point pierced. Other end hammered flat and rolled into socket open at both ends.
DAII. Found with **57**. *Hesperia* 44 (1975):89.
Area IV NE, L23 Vkl, floor level 3, lot 3385/1. Unit IV-1, Phase 2.

90 (N1669). Knife. Fig. 5-53.
L. 0.102. W. 0.023. Th. 0.005. D. rivet heads 0.005 and 0.006.
Much oxidized. Complete except for part of butt. One edged. Convex back, straight cutting edge. Two iron rivets, 0.02 apart, in butt.
DAI-II (with LH).
Area IV NE, L23 Xklm, level 4, lot 4312/E.

91 (N1429). Fragment of knife. Fig. 5-54.
L. 0.034. W. 0.021. Th. 0.006.
Wholly oxidized. Scrap of blade and butt with single iron rivet.
DAII. *Hesperia* 44 (1975):91.
Area IV NW, L23 Tkl, floor level 3, lot 3352/1. Unit IV-1, Phase 2.

92 (N853). Knife. Fig. 5-55.
L. 0.093. W. 0.02. Th. (back) 0.009; (edge) 0.002.
Much oxidized. Part of butt and chips of cutting edge lost. Convex back, wedge section to blade. No trace of rivet.
DAII (with LHIII). *Hesperia* 44 (1975):118.
Area IV NW, L23 Top, level 4, lot 3408/1.

93 (N375). Knife. Fig. 5-56.
L. (pres.) 0.085. W. 0.019. Th. 0.004.
Much oxidized. Only tip missing. One edged. Convex back and well-ground concave cutting edge. No trace of rivet.
DAI-II (with LHIII).
Area III N, K25 Ucd, level 4, lot 1172.

94 (N749). Fragment of knife.
L. 0.021. W. 0.011. Th. 0.005.
Much oxidized. Part of slim blade with parallel edges.
DAIII. This piece is possibly post-DA. *Hesperia* 41 (1972):264, no. 7.
Area IV NE, L23 Xklm W 1/3 and baulk, level 2, lot 2145.

95 (N1802). Fragment of knife.
L. 0.033. W. 0.021. Th. 0.005.
Much oxidized. Part of butt, including half of rivet.
DAII.
Area IV NW, L23 Tk, level 3, lot 4412. Outside (SW) of Unit IV-1, Phase 1.

96 (N1422). Fragment of knife(?)
0.032 × 0.14 × 0.004.
Much oxidized. Wedge-shaped section. Probably tip of knife.
DAII (with mainly LHIII).
Area III S, K24 Tu, level 3, lot 3147. Upper debris over Unit III-3.

"NAILS" (NOS. 97-102)

97 (N126). Shaft fragment.
L. 0.035. W. 0.0003.
Completely oxidized. Broken at both ends.
DAI (with mainly LH).
Area IV SW, L23-V (trial), level 5, lot 327.

98 (N1854). Shaft fragment.
L. 0.048. Th. 0.003-0.007.
Much oxidized. Broken at both ends. Perhaps rectangular in section.
DAII.
Area IV NW, L23 Tj, level 2, lot 4417/4. Unit IV-6, Room 2.

99 (N622). Shaft fragment.
0.029 × 0.005 × 0.004.
Completely oxidized. Broken at both ends.
DAII-III (with LHIII).

Area IV SW, L23 Thi, level 4, lot 1791.

100 (N438). Shaft fragment.
L. 0.041. W. 0.007. Th. 0.006.
Completely oxidized. Broken at both ends.
DAII-III (with some LHIII).
Area III, K25 Rg, level 2, lot 1653. Unit III-1.

101 (N1728 – part only). Shaft fragment.
L. 0.03. D. 0.004.
Oxidized.
DAII (with MH and LH).
Area IV S, L23 Ude, level 2, lot 4041/4. Upper debris over Unit IV-4.

102 (N1831). Shaft fragments.
L. 0.027. W. 0.003.
Oxidized. Three joining pieces.
DA.
Area III N, K25 Va, level 2, lot 4442.

SCRAP AND UNIDENTIFIED (NOS. **103-11**)

103 (N538). Bar(?)
0.052 × 0.011 × 0.008.
Oxidized. Rough billet, misshapen and broken at both ends.
DAII-III (with LHIIIB).
Area IV NE, L23 UVo, level 5a, lot 1491. Unit IV-7.

104 (N999). Fragment of handle or spatula(?) Fig. 5-57.
L. 0.037. W. 0.014. Th. 0.004-0.006.
Oxidized. Could be part of vessel handle or lunate working point.
DA (with LHIII).
Area III S, K24 TUv, level 2, lot 3118/3.

105 (N292). Scrap.
0.018 × 0.012 × 0.001.
Much oxidized. Shapeless and broken all round.
MH (with LHI-II).
Area III N, K25 Ref, level 3, lot 823. Vicinity of Mycenaean street.

106 (N789). Slag.
0.036 × 0.036 × 0.018.
Lump of slag with clear flow lines.
DA (with LHIIIA2-B).
Area III N, K25 Sef/Tef baulk, level 3, lot 2050. Mycenaean street.

107 (N388). Scrap.
0.026 × 0.011 × 0.004.
Oxidized. Roughly rectangular fragment. Could have been part of vessel rim or working point of tool.
DAI-II (with LHIIIA-B).
Area III N, K25 Ucd, level 4, lot 1175.

108 (N382). Scrap.
Largest of several fragments 0.02 × 0.02 × 0.004.
Completely oxidized. Joining fragments include short butt pierced by rivet hole (D. 0.004) and blade piece.
DAII (with LH).
Area IV NE, L23 Vmn, level 2, lot 1135.

109 (N70 – part only). Scrap.
0.043 × 0.038.
Oxidized. Flat piece of sheet, folded.
LH and modern.
Area VII, N22-XIII (trial), level 1, lot 402.

110 (N1120). Scrap.
L. 0.053. W. 0.025. Th. 0.004.
Lump of longitudinally curved, thick-walled metal. Probably broken all round.
DAII (with LH).
Area IV NW, L23 Sq, level 4, lot 3431/1.

111 (N1728 – part only). Scrap.
L. 0.009. W. 0.007. Th. 0.004.
Oxidized. Groove across top. Rough on underside (broken?). Identification as iron may be doubtful.
DAIII (with MH and LH).
Area IV SE, L23 Ude, level 2, lot 4041/4S. Fill over Unit IV-4.

Lead

112 (N1821). Button or whorl. Fig. 5-58.
D. base 0.017. H. 0.014. D. hole 0.0043 (top); 0.0055 (bottom).
Much oxidized. Truncated cone. Surface divided into quadrants by 4 evenly spaced ridges.
DAII. *Hesperia* 44 (1975):91.
Area IV N, L23 Tkl, floor level 3, lot 4322/2. Unit IV-1, Phase 2.

113 (N1820). Net sinker(?)
D. 0.026. Th. 0.009. D. hole 0.003 × 0.004.
Lightly oxidized. Rather battered thick round disc of convex/concave profile.
DAII. *Hesperia* 44 (1975):91.
Area IV N, L23 Tkl, floor level 3, lot 4322/2. Unit IV-1, Phase 2.

114 (N443). Net sinker(?) Fig. 5-59.
D. base 0.011. H. 0.007. D. hole ca. 0.004 (irregular).
Lightly oxidized. Roughly hemispherical; pierced.
DAII (with LHIII).
Area III N, K25 Sg, level 1, lot 1654. Unit III-1.

115 (N543). Clamp. Fig. 5-60.
L. (extended) 0.041. W. bar 0.0075. Th. bar 0.005. D. base 0.011. H. "peg" 0.014.
Lightly oxidized. Part of clamp bent out of shape. Only one rivet preserved; shape indicates that it was imbedded into a conical hole in fabric of repaired pot.
DA (with more LHIIIA1-B).
Area III N, K25 Tef, level 3, lot 1676. Mycenaean street.

116 (N499). Clamp. Fig. 5-61.
L. 0.023. W. 0.011. Th. 0.006.
Lightly oxidized. Complete; roughly made. Used to repair some very slim object.
DA(?) (predominantly LHIIIA2-B).
Area II, K25 Gf, level 2, lot 1584. Vicinity of NW gate.

117 (N638). Clamp. Fig. 5-62.
L. 0.035. W. 0.012. Th. strip 0.0015. H. rivet 0.006.
Lightly oxidized. Only half preserved.
DAI (with LHI-III).
Area II, K25 Lfg, level 2, lot 1845.

118 (N655). Scrap.
L. 0.028. W. (extended) 0.027. Th. 0.002.
Slightly oxidized. Bent scrap of sheet, broken all round.

DAIII.
Area IV N, L23 Ukl, level 2, lot 2113.

119 (N467). Waste.
0.053 × 0.035 × 0.021.
Oxidized. Shapeless mass. Probably spill from crucible.
DAI-II (with mainly LH).
Area IV NE, L23 UVo, level 4a, lot 1471.

Gold

120 (N566). Wire twist. Fig. 5-63.
L. (extended) 0.074. D. 0.001.
Round in section. Each end broken off. Appears to have been hammered.
DAIII. *Hesperia* 41 (1972):264, no. 2, Pl. 51f.
Area IV N, L23 Ukl, level 1, lot 1881.

Pithos Burial (Fig. 4-1; Pl. 4-8)

BRONZE

121 (N345). Finger ring. Pl. 4-8.
D. 0.039. Th. 0.005.
Lightly oxidized. Well-preserved closed hoop, round in section.
LG.
L24-III (trial).

122 (N372). Phiale. Pl. 5-13.
D. 0.15. H. 0.048. Th. rim 0.002. Th. wall 0.001.
Much oxidized. Rim complete; parts of body disintegrated. Omphalos at center. Raised from disk cutting.
LG.
L24-III (trial).

123 (N469). Phiale. Pl. 4-8.
D. ca. 0.16.
Severely oxidized. Found in many fragile pieces; not capable of restoration. Apparently twin of 135.
LG.
L24-III (trial).

IRON

124 (N475). Sword. Pl. 5-14.
L. 0.48. W. 0.035. Th. 0.005.
Much oxidized. Three joining pieces. Edges of blade broaden below hilt and then narrow to point (so-called leaf shape). One rivet at top of grip, two in guard.
LG.
L24-III (trial).

125 (N434, 435). Spearhead. Pl. 4-8.
L. ca. 0.23. L. blade 0.134. W. 0.029. Th. 0.016.
Much oxidized. Open socket. Slight midrib to blade of trapezoidal section.
LG.
L24-III (trial).

Terra-Cotta Whorls (Selected Items from Nos. **126-230***)*

126 (N360). Whorl. Pl. 5-22.
H. 0.023. D. (max.) 0.026. D. hole 0.006. Wt. 12.45 gr.
Coarse pink-brown gritty fabric. Crumbly condition. Remaining surface fired black. Type C.
DAIII.
Area IV NE, L23 Umn, level 3, lot 1126.

141 (N888). Whorl(?) Pl. 5-28.
H. 0.018. D. (max.) 0.023. D. hole 0.003. Wt. 7.6 gr.
Fairly fine buff fabric. Slightly broken at small end. Type G. Size and weight suggest it may have been a bead or garment weight.
DAII-III.
Area IV NW, L23 Top (N), level 2, lot 2302/2.

144 (N970). Whorl. Pl. 5-25.
H. 0.026. D. (max.) 0.032. D. hole 0.007. Wt. 18.35 gr.
Good condition. Well-fired red fabric. Surface almost wholly blackened. Type E.
DAII (with LHIII).
Area IV NE, L23 Ukl, level 3, lot 3373. Unit IV-1, Phase 2.

148 (N1342A). Whorl.
H. 0.029. D. (max.) 0.031. D. hole 0.006. Wt. 22.2 gr.
Good condition. Gray-brown slightly gritty fabric. Type B. Found with **149, 150, 151**.
DAII-III.
Area IV NE, L23 Vkl, level 3, lot 3385/1. Unit IV-1, Phase 2.

149 (N1342B). Whorl(?)
H. 0.016. D. (max.) 0.022. D. hole 0.005. Wt. 8 gr.
Good condition. Pink-brown gritty fabric. Type G. Found with **148, 150, 151**. Very small and light for a whorl.
DAII-III.
Area IV NE, L23 Vkl, level 3, lot 3385/1. Unit IV-1, Phase 2.

150 (N1342C). Whorl.
H. 0.019. D. (max.) 0.025. D. hole 0.006.
Good condition. Gray-brown gritty fabric. Type H. Found with **148, 149, 151**.
DAII-III.
Area IV NE, L23 Vkl, level 3, lot 3385/1. Unit IV-1, Phase 2.

151 (N1342D). Whorl.
H. 0.026. D. (max.) 0.033. D. hole 0.005.
Good condition. Red-brown core, dull black surface. Type C. Found with **148, 149, 150**.
DAII-III.
Area IV NE, L23 Vkl, level 3, lot 3385/1. Unit IV-1, Phase 2.

154 (N1614). Whorl. Pl. 5-30.
H. (pres.) 0.03. D. (max.) 0.035. D. hole 0.008.
Broken in 2 pieces. Buff-brown fabric with small white inclusions. Carelessly formed with perforation slightly off-center. Surface smoothed. Type H.
DA.
Area IV SE, L23 Wc, level 2, lot 4036.

155 (N1656). Whorl. Pl. 5-31.
H. 0.023. D. (max.) 0.033. D. (min.) 0.023. D. hole 0.007-0.008.
Mended from 5 fragments. Brown fabric. Type H.
DAII.
Area IV NE, L23 Vkl, level 3, lot 4301 (cleaning floor of Unit IV-1).

156 (N1667). Whorl.
H. 0.032. D. (max.) ca. 0.027. D. (min.) 0.019. D. hole 0.006.
Bottom half badly disintegrated. Very poorly fired, rather gritty fabric. Black and crumbly interior. Type H.
DAII.

Area IV NE, L23 Vkl, level 3, lot 4301 (cleaning floor of Unit IV-1).

157 (N1668). Whorl. Pl. 5-21.
H. 0.026. D. (max.) 0.029. D. hole 0.006. Wt. (half) 8 gr.
Only half preserved. Light brown gritty fabric. Type C.
DAII (with LH).
Area IV NE, L23 Wmn, level 2, lot 4592/2.

158 (N1690). Whorl. Pl. 5-29.
H. 0.048. D. (max.) ca. 0.052. D. hole 0.011. Wt. 76 gr.
Poorly fired brown-black fabric. Shape somewhat irregular. Type H.
DAIII.
Area IV SE, L23 Ude, level 2, lot 4041/1.

159 (N1692). Whorl. Pl. 5-38.
H. 0.024. D. (max.) 0.0275. D. hole 0.0055. Wt. 12.55 gr.
Slightly crumbly fabric. Surface burned dark brown-black. *Pointillé* decoration of small incised dots randomly disposed on top and arranged in bands around sides. Type H. *Hesperia* 1975, p. 120, Pl. 32f.
DAII (with LH).
Area IV NE, L23 Wmn, level 2, lot 4592/2.

159A (N1286). Whorl.
H. 0.02. D. (max.) 0.27. D. hole 0.006. Wt. (pres.) 12.05 gr.
Broken and mended. Fine, dark gray fabric, brownish on exterior. *Pointillé* decoration of small incised dots, apparently made randomly on upper surface only. Type B.
DAII (with LH).
Area III S, K24 Uw, level 3, lot 3136.

160 (N1706). Whorl. Pl. 5-15.
H. 0.018. D. (max.) 0.024. D. hole 0.005. Wt. 8.7 gr.
Slightly crumbly fabric (stabilized). Type A.
DA.
Area IV NW, L23 Pij, level 2, lot 4119/1.

161 (N1721). Whorl.
H. 0.023. D. (max.) 0.028. D. hole 0.006.
Poorly fired black fabric. Type J.
DAII (with LHIII).
Area IV NE, L23 Ukl, level 3, lot 4316. Unit IV-1, Phase 2.

162 (N1722). Whorl.
H. (pres.) 0.027. D. (max.) 0.038. D. hole 0.006.
Broken at smaller end. Pinkish-orange gritty fabric. Hole slightly off-center. Type J.
DAII (with LHIII).
Area IV NE, L23 Umn, level 3, lot 4316.

163 (N1787). Whorl. Pl. 5-19.
H. 0.02. D. (max.) 0.03. D. hole 0.006. Wt. 15.2 gr.
Unevenly fired, somewhat gritty, brown-black fabric. Type B.
DAIII.
Area IV SW, Rhi, level 2, lot 4093/3C.

166 (N1882). Whorl. Pl. 5-16.
H. (pres.) 0.021. D. ca. 0.03. D. hole ca. 0.006.
Less than half preserved. Gray-black fabric. Type A.
DAI-II (with LH).
Area IV NE, L23 Vmn, level 2, lot 4333/1.

167 (N1945). Whorl. Pl. 5-36.
H. 0.03. D. (max.) 0.041. D. hole 0.0075.
Slightly irregular shape at smaller end. Orange fabric. Type J. Found with **168**.
DAI-II (mainly LH).
Area IV NE, L23 Vmn, level 3, lot 4578/2.

168 (N1946). Whorl. Pl. 5-27.
H. 0.024. D. (max.) 0.024. D. hole 0.0065. Wt. 10.8 gr.
Surface blackened. Type F. Found with **167**.
DAI-II (mainly LH).
Area IV NE, L23 Vmn, level 3, lot 4578/2;

169 (N2089). Whorl. Pl. 5-17.
H. 0.032. D. (max.) 0.043. D. hole 0.0115. Wt. 40 gr.
Mended from 2 fragments. Part still missing. Softish orange fabric. Top of hole slightly contoured (worn?). Type A.
DAI-II.
Area III, trial trench K24-III, level 4, lot 100.

171 (N472). Whorl.
H. (pres.) 0.0215. D. ca. 0.045. D. hole ca. 0.008.
Less than half preserved. Soft dark-orange fabric burned black on outer surface. Type J.
DAII (mainly LHIIIA2-B).
Area II, K25 Ff, level 2, lot 1577.

173 (N556). Whorl. Pl. 5-32.
H. 0.026. D. (max.) 0.027. D. (min.) 0.017.
Orange fabric. Surface partly blackened. Type H.
DAII (mainly LH).
Area III N, K25 Tde baulk, level 2, lot 1690.

190 (N1212). Whorl. Pl. 5-33.
H. 0.025. D. (max.) 0.029. D. (min.) 0.017. D. hole 0.006.
Gray-black fabric with some grit. Polished surface. Type I.
DAI-II (with some LHIII).
Area III S, K25 Uab, level 2, lot 3102.

194 (N1641). Whorl. Pl. 5-20.
H. 0.028. D. (max.) 0.027. D. hole 0.007. Wt. 14.2 gr.
Reddish yellow fabric. Surface flecked with black. Type B. DAII (with LHII-III).
Area IV SW, L23 Nc, level 3, lot 4112/3E.

196 (N1705). Whorl.
H. 0.018. D. (max.) 0.025. D. hole (min.) 0.0045.
Crumbly fabric. Hole wider at both ends (wear?). Type I.
DAII (mainly LHIIIA2-B2).
Area III S, K24 Uuv, level 16, lot 4428.

201 (N2096). Whorl. Pl. 5-34.
H. 0.0275. D. (max.) 0.0275. D. (min.) 0.017. D. hole 0.007.
Reddish brown somewhat gritty fabric. Type J.
DAII (with LHIII).
Area IV NW, L23 Top, level 4, lot 3408/2.

215 (N1124). Whorl. Pl. 5-24.
H. 0.0155. D. (max.) 0.025. D. hole 0.004. Wt. 14.45 gr.
Brownish surface (gray at center) with some grits. Type D.
DAI-II (with LHIIIA2-B).
Area IV NW, L23 Sq, level 5, lot 3432/1.

217 (N1461). Whorl. Pl. 5-37.
H. 0.02. D. 0.022. D. hole 0.005.

Fine powdery buff fabric. Type L.

DAII (with LHIII).

Area III S, K24 Vw, level 2, lot 3654.

218 (N1462). Whorl. Pl. 5-26.

H. 0.022. D. (max.) 0.027. D. hole 0.006. Wt. 12.2 gr.

Fine orange-buff fabric. Type E.

DAII (with LHIII).

Area III S, K24 Vuv, level 2, lot 3137/8.

225 (N1697). Whorl. Pl. 5-35.

H. 0.027. D. (max.) 0.036. D. (min.) 0.02. D. hole 0.006.

Poorly fired dark fabric. Mended but some fragments missing. Type J.

DA (mainly LHIIIA-B).

Area III N, K25 Vb, level 3, lot 4298.

226 (N1707). Whorl(?) Pl. 5-23.

H. (max.) 0.027. D. 0.021. D. hole 0.003-0.004. Wt. 9.3 gr.

Poorly fired red-brown fabric. Clear signs of wear. Type C. Possibly a bead.

DA (with Byzantine).

Area IV NW, L23 Pij, level 1, lot 4120.

230 (N1979). Whorl. Pl. 5-18.

H. 0.026. D. (max.) 0.032. D. hole 0.008.

Poorly fired, crumbly, brown-black fabric. Type A.

DAI-II (mainly LHIII).

Area III N, K25 Wa, level 4, lot 4393/1.

Miscellaneous Objects (Nos. 231-43*)*

TERRA-COTTA

231 (N1664). Leg of animal figurine.

H. (pres.) 0.028. D. tapering end 0.013.

Broken at top and worn at bottom. Light gray fabric. Worn surface with no trace of paint.

DAII (with LH).

Area III S, K24 Vw, level 5, lot 4206. DA backfill over Unit III-3.

232 (N792). Head of animal. Pl. 5-39.

H. (pres.) 0.05. L. neck to muzzle 0.041. W. neck 0.019 × 0.015.

Broken at base of neck. Reddish yellow fabric. Surface worn and flaky but faint fragments of black paint preserved in places. Short, pointed ears, blunt nose.

Hesperia 41 (1972), p. 264, no. 8.

DAIII.

Area IV NE, L23 Xklm-W 1/3 and baulk, level 2, lot 2149.

233 (N766). Pendant(?)

L. (pres.) 0.029. D. (max.) 0.015, D. at top 0.01.

Top broken away at perforation. Surface mostly worn away. Teardrop shape. Reddish yellow fabric.

DAIII (with a little DAII).

Area IV SW, L23 Sfg, level 3, lot 2396.

234 (N324). Enigmatic fragment.

D. 0.0023. H. (max. pres.) 0.022. D. of hole 0.0085.

Apparently about one-third pres. The small end and half of the body missing. From a hollow object of conical shape, the base of the cone being slightly rounded. Conceivably a Type G spindle whorl with part of the hole accidentally enlarged by a strange fracture? Fine soft pink-orange clay.

DAIII.

Area IV N, L23 Vmn, level 2, lot 1111.

235 (N1835). Mudbrick fragment.

L. (pres.) 0.15. W. (pres.) 0.14. Th. (pres.) 0.05.

Mudbrick no. 1. Fragment of mudbrick from the fence of the porch of Unit IV-1.

DAII.

Area IV NE, L23 Wklm, level 3, entrance, lot 4306.

BONE

236 (N866). Bead. Pl. 5-40.

L. 0.014. D. 0.01. D. hole 0.004.

Intact. Cylinder sawn neatly from animal long bone. Surface polished. *Hesperia* 44 (1975), p. 95; *Deltion* 28, p. 190.

DAII (with some LHIII).

Area IV NW, L23 Top, level 4, lot 3408/1. Dump to N of Unit IV-1.

STONE

237 (N858). Bead(?)

L. (pres.) 0.007. W. (pres.) 0.006. Th. (pres.) 0.004.

Very small piece of weathered calcium carbonate. Apparently ovoid in shape. Flattened cylindrical in section. Small hole preserved.

Deltion 28, p. 185.

DAII-III (with some LHIII).

Area IV NE, L23 Xklm-E 2/3, level 2, lot 3356/2. Unit IV-1, Phase 2.

238 (N699). Worked fragment. Pl. 5-41.

H. (pres.) 0.035. W. (pres.) 0.021. Th. (max.) 0.006.

Much weathered and broken on all sides. Roughly rectangular plaque of argilite-sandstone. Two holes at one end; one is pierced through, the other merely a conical depression.

DAII (with LHIIIA-B).

Area III N, K25 Rg, level 3, lot 2019. Unit III-1.

239 (N1819). Celt. Pl. 5-42.

L. 0.06. W. sharp end 0.031. Th. 0.032.

Celt of mica schist. One end roughened for hafting. Probably reused in DA.

DAII.

Area IV NE, L23 Tkl, level 3, lot 4322/1. Unit IV-1, Phase 2.

240 (N867). Whetstone or pendant. Pl. 5-43.

L. (pres.) 0.04. W. (pres.) 0.037. Th. 0.01. D. hole 0.004-0.007.

Broken slightly(?) at bottom. Flat, smooth sandstone plaque. One side noticeably worn. At one end hole drilled from both sides.

DAII (some LHIII).

Area IV NW, L23 Top, level 4, lot 3408/2. Dump to N of Unit IV-1.

241 (N871a-b). Grinder and palette(?) Pl. 5-44.

Grinder: L. 0.065. W. 0.048. Th. 0.039. Palette: L. 0.111. W. 0.06. Th. (max.) 0.018.

Grinder is large chert pebble with white band around center. Palette is flat sandstone, slightly(?) broken and thinner at one end. Traces of red coloring matter (probably iron oxide) at broken end. Found close together but geologists' opinion that difference in hardness of two pieces makes it unlikely that they were used as a pair.

DAII (with LHIII).

Area IV NW, L23 Sop, level 3, lot 3404/5-6. Dump to N of Unit IV-1.

242 (N826). Whetstone or pendant. Pl. 5-45.

L. (pres.) 0.037. W. top 0.022. Th. 0.01. D. hole 0.009.

Fine grayish brown siltstone. One surface slightly concave. Slightly polished. Hole drilled from both sides and not exactly opposite.

DAI-II (with LHIII).

Area IV NW, L23 Sop, level 3, lot 3404/5-6. Bottom of dump to N of Unit IV-1.

243 (N701). Incised plaque. Pl. 5-46.

L. 0.083. W. (max.) 0.064. W. (min.) 0.045. Th. (max.) 0.011.

Trapezoidal schist plaque. Top (incised) surface flat, bottom slightly concave. Design consists of a rough rectangle with a central vertical division crossed by 8 parallel lines much more lightly incised. *Hesperia* 41 (1972), p. 264, Pl. 52e. (See Chapter 2, p. 16).

DAI-II.

Area IV NW, L23 Shi, level 3, lot 2351. LH stone rubble from N walls of Unit IV-9.

6

The Dark Age at Nichoria: A Perspective

by

William A. McDonald and William D. E. Coulson

We begin this review with a synopsis of current opinion on developments during the Dark Age in mainland Greece and particularly in Messenia and bordering regions in West and South Peloponnese. This overview is intended as a base against which to assess local conformities and contrasts. The reader might also wish to review the topical summaries of the Nichoria evidence on the architecture and pottery that are appended to the relevant chapters. Then we attempt to coordinate the highlights of the evidence previously presented in this volume with supplementary data, much of it already published in *Nichoria* I. That is, we look at the "orthodox" kinds of cultural remains in the context of other categories of information. For example, the animal bones found on an excavated site are also undeniably cultural, i.e., "fossilized remains of human behavior." We also hope to demonstrate that, by taking into consideration MME-generated information that bears on the local physical environment, we can begin to reach a more balanced understanding of the complex and subtle interplay between this particular human community and its available natural resources. Limitations of space severely restrict this approach here and in Volume II; but in Volume IV of the series we will focus primarily on the cultural and environmental interaction.

General Trends

Whatever the cause or causes of the collapse of the highly organized and strikingly homogeneous Mycenaean kingdoms, their disintegration in the late 13th century (LHIIIB2) ushered in a century or more of shock and insecurity, followed by a slow and uneven rebuilding of Greek society on a much simpler and more diversified pattern. In Messenia, perhaps more notably than in some of the other regions where Mycenaean culture had flourished, there was a drastic reduction in number and size of settlements. In at least a few of the formerly important centers, especially in east central Greece, survivors tried to maintain Mycenaean customs for several generations; other sites were immediately deserted in favor of more isolated regions (some of them overseas) where refugees perpetuated for a while recognizable elements of their ancestral way of life. But almost every material manifestation in these LHIIIC communities shows that craft traditions were stagnating and that local diversity was replacing the formerly standardized way of life. It is usually assumed that most of these struggling and dispirited little settlements had been destroyed or abandoned by the late 12th century and that the sites themselves were not reoccupied (if at all) for a century or more.

There are, however, a number of communities, particularly in east central Greece, that represent what might be called the wave of the future, rather than the end of an era. Developing in the late 12th and earlier 11th centuries, these so-called Submycenaean settlements seem to overlap with, rather than succeed, their LHIIIC counterparts in time. "Submycenaean" is a somewhat misleading term, since the important characteristic of these communities is not so much that they perpetuate Mycenaean culture traits but that they display definite innovations. Individual burials in earth-cut pit graves or stone-lined cists replace multiple family or clan burials in chamber tombs; garments are secured with long pins instead of buttons; new or modified vase shapes and decorative motifs are added to the tired Mycenaean repertory; and in places cremation burial gradually rivals inhumation in popularity. Before 1050 B.C. these communities were in active contact eastward across the Aegean as far as Cyprus, whence they seem to have borrowed vital expertise in iron technology.

Although no one claims that this congeries of novel culture traits reflects a real recovery from the Mycenaean collapse, it remains true that east central Greece continued to set the pace in later DA developments which did gradually revitalize Greek culture. It was in this same Submycenaean orbit around the mid-11th century that the severe and disciplined Protogeometric pottery style emerged; and Protogeometric conventions eventually reached nearly everywhere in the Greek world, continuing in the more isolated regions long after the fully developed Geometric styles were popular in the "heartland."

It is quite unclear as yet how we are to explain the amalgam of old and new culture traits in the early Dark Age. Desborough (1964, 1972) consistently held that actual invaders–or at least outsiders–must have been involved. He conceded that there may have been relatively few newcomers, and he believed that they probably came from the northwest. Northern ceramic influence has also been claimed recently in early LHIIIC contexts in southern Greece (Rutter 1975; Sanders 1978, pp. 191, 192). Snodgrass (1971), on the other hand, views the evidence for external influence as so diffuse that it is unlikely that sizable groups of newcomers from any single direction were involved. Very few authorities would now connect these Sybmycenaean/Protogeometric traits with the elusive Dorian Invasion which Greek tradition firmly held to have bypassed the very region where they appear to have emerged. Indeed, a current theory would explain at least some of the DA cultural novelties (e.g., apsidal house plans) as the re-emergence of Middle Bronze traits that were submerged by Mycenaean fashions but never totally abandoned by the substrate population (Deshayes 1966, pp. 240-42, 249, 250; Snodgrass 1971, pp. 184, 186).

In any case, beginning around the mid-11th century, a more organized and confident way of life is apparent. The new spirit is particularly noticeable in the Protogeometric pottery styles. The potters infused a fresh crispness to shapes that are still largely traditional, and they decorated their work with very limited and austere "geometric" motifs, mostly rectilinear but including circles and semicircles neatly drawn with a pair of dividers and multiple brushes. Iron technology was relatively well understood, and iron seems to have been generally preferred for weapons and tools, perhaps because of uncertain supplies of imported copper and tin rather than any inherent superiority of iron as it was then worked.

Settlements tended to be located in naturally strong but unfortified spots on or near the sea. Former Mycenaean sites were favored, but the ruined townsites were often re-used as DA cemeteries, with the new living area nearby. DA settlements were apparently being founded as late as the 10th century, and in very few cases can LH-DA continuity be proved. The meager evidence for DA domestic architecture indicates that the Mycenaean tradition of rectangular, flat-roofed houses was largely replaced by apsidal or oval structures with pitched roofs. No building remains are associated with what are occasionally interpreted as open-air DA shrines. Individual graves are the rule, frequently with cremation and inhumation rites alternating in no detectable pattern. Pottery and other grave goods are not rich or varied, suggesting a relatively unstratified economic and social situation. Long dress pins, arched fibulae, and rings are typical items of metal buried with the dead. Weapons are uncommon in the graves, and, when they occur, their Mycenaean ancestry is usually clear. Their rarity may indicate that organized warfare was not endemic, although their increased value may have made the living hesitate to surrender them for the benefit of departed kinsmen.

There is no evidence to suggest that political power extended beyond the small individual settlements. Presumably each had its hereditary leader or chief, but (as with the graves) few DA houses known before the Nichoria excavation seem to reflect exceptional wealth or privilege. Very little can be said with any confidence about continuity or discontinuity in religious practices, either in terms of structures or cult objects, although the disappearance of the formerly ubiquitous Mycenaean female figurines may be significant.

In the second half of the 10th century there was, at least in east central Greece, a noticeable quickening of cultural development that marks the watershed between the Protogeometric and full Geometric periods. Desborough chose to consider this as the end of his "Late Dark Ages," but the Protogeometric tradition continues to characterize many outlying regions throughout the 9th and 8th centuries and even later. The new Geometric pottery styles show continuous development in shape and particularly in increasingly complex and ambitious decorative motifs. Domestic architecture improved notably, or at least its development is much better documented. The apsidal plan continued to be typical, but rectangular buildings increased in proportion as time went on. The remains of several structures as well as terracotta models are apparently to be recognized as ancestors of the canonical Greek temple. Population appears to have increased, individual communities were less isolated, overseas trade was much more regular, and Greek colonies sprang up on the eastern Aegean seaboard.

In the 8th century the pace of this renewal accelerated and its scope broadened. Whole regions were coalescing into larger political entities, and rivalries intensified. Closer communication lessened cultural disparity between advanced and backward regions as well as between individual centers within regions. Interregional religious festivals, like the Olympic Games, were instituted–or were perhaps in some cases revived after a long interval. Increasing population led to the founding of many new towns at home and to a second wave of colonization abroad. Imported goods were more common, and exotic prototypes naturally affected local tastes. Experimentation with alphabetic writing led to at least limited literacy after a gap of 400 years. There was a notable tendency to reestablish links with a heroic past, of which literacy brought renewed awareness and nurtured local, regional, and even national pride. Burials were made and sacrificial rites performed in reused Mycenaean tombs, in many cases structures that show very little evidence of pious care in the long interval. Representational art became popular in Late Geometric pottery and in other media such as engraved and embossed metal.

Trends in Messenia and Neighboring Regions

Messenia, Laconia, and West Greece constitute one of the most poorly documented of all the major mainland sectors in DA times. In the 13th century Messenia and Laconia had been among the most flourishing and populous regions of the Greek world. Although surface survey in Elis, Achaea, Aetolia, and the Ionian islands has been much less thorough, there is reason to assume that they had been less heavily populated. In the 12th and earlier 11th centuries, however, the situation was apparently reversed. Population was drastically reduced in the south, while significant numbers of Mycenaean refugees fled to isolated western regions like Achaea and Kephallenia and merged to some extent with indigenous elements (Hope Simpson and Dickinson 1979, Maps C, D, E). Clear Mycenaean culture traits like LHIIIC pottery and multiple burials persist in the west for two centuries or more.

On present evidence, Ithaca is the only locality in this whole area where an uninterrupted ceramic sequence attests to the derivation of a sturdily independent Protogeometric style from the local LHIIIC tradition. The transition, which may have taken place as late as the 10th century, seems to owe very little to earlier developments in east central Greece. Direct Ithacan contacts with that area are not proved before the import of Middle Geometric Corinthian pottery. But at ancient Elis a group of graves with Submycenaean analogies suggests that the west was not totally isolated from outside contacts.

For developments in South Peloponnese in the 12th through the 10th centuries, the evidence is extremely thin and ambiguous. Only a handful of sites in Messenia and Laconia can be shown to have survived the Mycenaean collapse (*MME* 1972, pp. 142-44; Hope Simpson and Dickinson 1979, Map E). A few formerly important Mycenaean centers appear to have retained a diminished form of the LHIIIC culture through this "dark" interval. But the main evidence, such as it is, in Messenia consists of occasional reuse of Mycenaean tholos tombs, construction of small tholoi in the same tradition, and scattered individual graves.

The known Protogeometric pottery in South and West Peloponnese, with the possible exception of Laconia, seems to reflect a certain amount of internal contact, no doubt mainly by sea. Common features point to a "provincial" style which owes little to Aegean influences from its inception down through the 9th century. It appears that the Mycenaean tradition persisted longer in these relatively isolated and conservative regions, and it is virtually certain that the same "lag" continued during the long Protogeometric phase. The above-mentioned Ithacan transition from LHIIIC to Protogeometric, which apparently took place as late as the 10th century, may perhaps serve as a general chronological guide. And, although evidence to date is exceedingly scarce, the Ithacan continuity tends to throw doubt on any general theory of an absolute "habitation gap" elsewhere in the area during LHIIIC and earlier Protogeometric times.

To sum up, then, the ceramic record suggests that there was in the South and West a particularly tenacious Mycenaean tradition, followed—or overlapped—by a quite recognizable but largely independent Protogeometric phase which persisted here long after this style had developed into the full Geometric in the Aegean orbit. Burial customs and metal grave goods generally confirm this sketchy reconstruction; yet it would be misleading to overemphasize the conservative element. For in the South and West, too, notable DA innovations—individual graves, new types of dress pins, fibulae, iron technology, and at least occasional cremation—do gradually appear. It is safest at present to regard these regions, peripheral as they were geographically to mainstream developments in the Aegean heartland, as provincial cousins—but certainly not totally isolated cultural backwaters. And what is now known about the situation at DA Nichoria must be considered as incomparably the most dependable record that has so far been recovered.

Chronology

Since practically all material remains from the Greek Dark Age derive from graves, the establishment of a dependable overall chronological sequence is notoriously difficult. In the case of Nichoria, we are fortunate to have recovered stratified habitation debris covering most of the period and to be able to correlate it with more complete objects from the associated cemetery. Thus, our typological series for the major phases of occupation provides a firm relative chronology for the local situation; and this can, in turn, be usefully correlated with the known grave deposits from elsewhere—particularly those from western Greece. On this basis we have, for convenience, divided the known span of DA habitation at Nichoria into three major phases, i.e., DAI, II, III, with a distinguishable transitional situation labeled DAII/III.

Although the relative chronology of the DA occupation of the Nichoria ridge is thus reasonably secure, the establishment of even approximate absolute limits for the DA subphases must for the present remain extremely risky and imprecise. And here even the closest parallels from other sites are of little help, since they themselves lack precise definition in absolute terms. Nevertheless, we feel compelled to offer a first, tentative estimate of absolute dating brackets for our suggested subphases, and we trust that the proposed dates will be recognized as approximations at best. The scheme appears below and is followed by an explanation and discussion:

DAI	ca. 1075-975 B.C.
DAII	ca. 975-850 B.C.
DAII/III	ca. 850-800 B.C.
DAIII	ca. 800-750 B.C.
Late Geometric	ca. 750-700 B.C.

DAI is the most elusive of the four phases because of the meager nature of both pottery and small finds and because of uncertain stratigraphic contexts. The latter problem is compounded by the fact that we recovered very little in the way of associated architectural remains. The only DAI wall fragment (G) is in trial trench N22-XVII. The associated pottery represents a group that is essentially different from the large deposits connected with the later Units IV-1 and IV-5. The deposit from N22-XVII has affinities with pottery from elsewhere in western Peloponnese that has been assigned to the early Dark Age. These characteristics serve as the primary base for identifying DAI sherds when they occur in mixed lots. Additional criteria noted in deposits elsewhere on the ridge include shapes and motifs commonly associated with LHIIIC pottery and, in particular, a grainy white clay with a tendency to flake from the surface.

Thus, in assessing the context of the DAI material, we are forced to depend heavily on the comparative material which itself is from uncertain or unsatisfactory contexts. The loss of the later vases from Malthi and Tragana excludes reexamination of those important groups. The best existing evidence that can now be cited from Messenia comes from a LHIIIC deposit at Ramovouni-Dorion. Comparisons with vases from Kephallenia and Ithaca suggest a date at the end of the 12th or the beginning of the 11th century for the Ramovouni material, although it must be emphasized that the sequences on both islands are unclear. Still, the Ramovouni material does provide a valuable frame for the beginning of our earliest DA phase.

The relative chronology for DAII is much better documented, since it depends for the most part on clear stratigraphic and architectural associations. The major deposit comes from the floor of the first phase of Unit IV-1. Distinctive characteristics of shape, decoration, and clay type in the pottery from this level are used to identify DAII material from elsewhere on the ridge, notably in Area IVSW and in Area III. Shape and clay type were the criteria used, for example, in assigning Unit III-1 to DAII, since this building yielded only a meager amount of very worn ceramic material.

As for absolute chronology, the amount of comparative material from Messenia and neighboring regions is greater than for DAI (see the following chart); but again the lack of firmly dated contexts elsewhere prevents the construct of anything but a very general framework. Nichoria shapes are represented at Antheia, Kardamyla, Kokevi, Rizes—and perhaps also at Malthi and Tragana, although the comparable material from these sites has been lost. Nichoria decorative motifs are also found at the above sites, plus Kaphirio where no whole shapes were recovered.

We have used the designation DAII/III to categorize the pottery associated with the second phase of Unit IV-1. This transitional material really represents a last stage of DAII, but certain features occur that foreshadow the thin monochrome vessels of DAIII. Such subtle distinctions, though discernible in material associated with the later floor of this building, could not be confidently made in the mixed lots from other areas. Comparative material for this transitional phase is nonexistent in Messenia and scarce throughout the rest of the Peloponnese. Closest decorative parallels appear to be the thick and crowded hatched triangles that are common in Achaea in the 9th century, occurring specifically on a kantharos from grave 2 at Drepanon and on sherds from Neos Erineos.

Our DAIII material comes almost exclusively from Area IV, although a few comparable sherds were found in the levels above Unit III-1. The major deposits occurred in Unit IV-5, which is the successor to Unit IV-1, and in the levels above the debris of Unit IV-1 in association with the later storage area. Thus there is a clear stratigraphic distinction between DAII and DAIII. The later material is easily distinguished in shape and decoration, consisting for the most part of vessels with thin fabric and a monochrome coating on both exterior and interior. Similar material has been identified elsewhere in Area IV, particularly in the S segment. Little comparative material exists at other known sites. A few miscellaneous vases from Ano Englianos are similar, but they occur in undated contexts and provide no help in establishing an absolute chronology. More useful for postulating a *terminus ante quem* is the evidence from the Late Geometric vases in the pithos burial on the ridge and in the Vathirema chamber tomb, since it appears that those burials were made after the DAIII village had ceased to exist.

The range of find-spots of the most important comparative material and the general chronological frame are summarized in the accompanying chart.

It is obvious that the chart provides only the broadest framework for an absolute chronology. For DAI, perhaps the major problem concerns the beginning of the period, i.e., the local transition from the Late Bronze to the Early Iron Age. Comparisons with vases from Kephallenia (Lakkithra and Mazarakata) and Ithaca suggest a date at the end of the 12th or the beginning of the 11th century for the

Ramovouni-Dorion deposit and thus a tentative *terminus post quem* for the beginning of DAI at Nichoria. Specifically, the deep shape of the Ramovouni skyphos with its high up-swung handles and isolated spiral as a decorative motif is found on Kephallenia, and there are parallels from Korakou, Lefkandi, and Perati, with especially good examples from Teichos Dymaion. Similarly, the ovoid shape of the Ramovouni amphora is paralleled by those from the pit graves under the theater parodos at Elis.

The Tragana material, although somewhat more controversial, is also important for establishing an absolute date for DAI. Of the probable three periods connected with the use of the tomb (LHIIA-IIIA2, LHIIIC, and DAII), it is burials α and β, of the LHIIIC period, that concern us here, specifically whether a distinction can be made between the vases associated with the two burials. Those associated with burial β, most notably the krater of panel style, the stirrup jar top of close style, and the pyxis with representations of ship and tree, are certainly different from the simpler concentric loops and globular bodies of the vases from burial α. The affinities that the vases of burial β exhibit with LHIIIB vessels suggest that this burial is earlier than its counterpart,

Nichoria Phases	*Regions*	*Sites*	*Absolute Chronology* (estimated)
DAI	*Messenia*	Ramovouni-Dorion Malthi Tragana (burial α)	Late LHIIIC, 12th 11th century B.C.
	W. Peloponnese and Islands	Kephallenia (Lakkithra and Mazarakata) Ithaca (Polis) Elis Teichos Dymaion	Late 12th to early 11th century B.C.
	E. Central Greece	Korakou Lefkandi Perati	Late LHIIIC
DAII	*Messenia*	Antheia Kaphirio Kardamyla Kokevi Malthi Rizes Tragana Volimnos	All material falls within the 10th century B.C.
	Peloponnese and Islands	Ithaca (Polis, Aetos) Achaea Asine	10th century B.C.
	Aetolia	Agrinion Astakos Kalydon Kryoneri	10th century B.C.
	Laconia	Amyclae Heroön Sparta (Acropolis)	10th-9th century B.C.
	W. Crete	Modi Vryses	10th-9th century B.C.
DAII/III (transitional)	*Messenia*	No comparative material	
	Achaea	Drepanon Neos Erineos	9th century B.C.
DAIII	*Messenia*	Ano Englianos	Perhaps 8th century, although dated by excavators to 600 B.C.
LG	*Messenia*	Volimidia	2nd half of the 8th century B.C.
	Peloponnese	Argos Corinth	

whereas the vases from burial α appear to share characteristics with those from Ramovouni Dorion and with our DAI material. The difference in the character of the vases from the two burials suggests that two phases of LHIIIC may be represented in the Tragana tholos.

The possibility of distinguishing an early and late LHIIIC period in Messenia is important for the sequence of events at Nichoria. If the Ramovouni, Tragana (burial α), and perhaps also the Malthi vases do represent a late LHIIIC phase, our DAI material appears to be only slightly later. We can thus hypothesize that DAI may represent the very last stage of the LHIIIC regional pattern. The same conclusion may be drawn from the Submycenaean character of some of the small finds of both the DAI and DAII periods, from the presence of a DAI apsidal cist (Nikitopoulos no. 1) in a predominantly Mycenaean tumulus, and, more specifically, the reuse in DAI of a small Mycenaean tholos (no. 6) in the same tumulus. Such a reuse is paralleled elsewhere in Messenia by the DA reuse of the Tragana tholos. Material belonging to the earlier stage, represented by the vases from burial β at Tragana, has not yet been found at Nichoria.

The comparative material, therefore, seems to justify our placing the earliest DA material at Nichoria sometime in the 11th century. The length of the DAI phase is also in question, but there is slightly more evidence for the transition to DAII, since the latter phase is much better documented both at Nichoria and in the rest of Messenia. The bell-shaped skyphoi and S-shaped cups have parallels tentatively dated to the 10th century, as do the decorative motifs of cross-hatching, crosshatched triangles, and concentric semicircles. More particularly, parallels to our DAII material from Ithaca, Rizes, and Laconia suggest that our DAI did not extend too much into the 10th century, perhaps not beyond the first quarter.

It seems clear from the scanty comparative material known at present that there was a common ceramic style in Messenia during the DAII period. That this style also extended beyond Messenia to Ithaca, Achaea, and Aetolia is indicated by parallels from these regions. Even closer ties between eastern Messenia and Laconia are suggested by the appearance at Nichoria and Kaphirio of decorative motifs hitherto associated with Amyclae, the Heroön, and the Acropolis of Sparta. Indeed, so strong is the similarity in shape and decoration between Heroön 2577 and our **P602** that they may have originated from the same workshop. The discovery of sherds with crosshatched triangles at the Volimnos shrine, near the Langadha pass that connects Messenia and Laconia, is an important indication that Volimnos may have acted as a common meeting place.

The comparative material does not establish a secure absolute dating for our DAII, but it does at least provide a broad chronological frame in the 10th and 9th centuries. The S-shaped cups from Rizes and Antheia seem to belong in the 10th century. The material from Ithaca, Laconia, and West Crete spans the 10th and 9th centuries. The Laconian parallels do not allow for a date earlier than the mid-10th century. Although some of the Modi vases belong to the 10th century, the majority can be dated to the 9th. Any further refinements in this broad chronological frame are difficult to make.

If we accept the premise that DAI did not continue too far into the 10th century and that the comparative material for DAII spans the 10th and 9th centuries, we can tentatively assign DAII to between 975 and 800 B.C. This leaves the problem of where DAII/III fits into the scheme. The scanty decorated sherds of this transitional period, in particular the circle with crosshatched quadrants of **P1116**, show a greater sophistication than the simple cross-hatching and concentric semicircles used in DAII, and the parallels from Drepanon and Neos Erineos suggest a date in the second half of the 9th century for our transitional material. At the very least, the comparative material provides a *terminus ante quem* of the end of the 9th century for the transitional stage and, hence, for the DAII period as a whole.

The lack of comparative evidence for our DAIII material seems to indicate that in this period Nichoria was considerably more isolated from developments elsewhere in Messenia and in neighboring regions. It is a paradox, however, that striking novelties occur in both the local architecture and pottery. For instance, the apparent preference for N-S orientation in DAIII buildings and the great variation in DAIII ceramic shapes are features that scarcely fit an introverted and declining community. The variety of rim forms and vessel shapes is greater than that of DAII; and the concentration on small vases with paper-thin fabric surely argues for considerable technical expertise. On the other hand, there was a sharp drop in the range of decorative motifs. A few examples of accumbent concentric semicircles and cross-hatching carry over from DAII, but for the most part the vases are simply monochrome coated with a metallic black paint on both exterior and interior. There are, at present, practically no parallels to our DAIII vases in Messenia or elsewhere in West Greece or Laconia. The only comparative material in Messenia comes from the undated level above the palace at Ano Englianos and from the lower town.

The lack of comparative material makes it difficult to establish a reliable span for the DAIII phase. If we accept as a *terminus post quem* the end of the 9th century (suggested above for the end of DAII/III), the upper limit has still to be sought. The only usable indication here seems to be the firm date of the mid-8th century that is provided by the imported vases from the pithos burial on the ridge and from the Vathirema chamber tomb. We are reasonably confident that these burials were made after the DAIII village was burned and abandoned, but it must be admitted that the argument is based on inference. In that case, the chronological frame for DAIII becomes the first half of the 8th century. Such a relatively short life for the latest phase of the DA village on the ridge is generally supported by the overall character of the archaeological evidence.

The Nichoria Community in the Dark Age

In view of the general ambiguities and obscurities outlined earlier in this chapter, it is natural to expect crucial new evidence to emerge from the first intensively excavated DA settlement on the mainland; and we may fairly claim that the results reported in the preceding chapters have justified such expectations. At the same time, we are very much aware of limitations imposed not only by serious gaps in the recovered data but also by our imperfect grasp of important implications that the available data may contain. When other scholars as well as MME authors have time to digest the new evidence more thoroughly, modifications will no doubt be required. But all of us must face the stark fact that, at least until additional carefully planned excavation has been done at Nichoria and contemporary sites, no one can speak with assurance about numerous aspects of the local DA life-style.

A strong case can be made for the proposition that our ridgetop was the site of Mycenaean TI-MI-TO-A-KE-E. But, regardless of whether this claim is eventually proved, Nichoria was certainly one of the important subregional centers of the Pylian kingdom. Contrary to some published reports, the LHIIIB houses so far excavated were not destroyed by fire nor did they suffer from other obvious violence. The remains point instead to their being left to disintegrate after valuables had been thoroughly cleared out. While hostile action from outside is not excluded, the condition of the ruins could be equally the result simply of panic caused by anticipation of attack. Indeed, our evidence does not rule out any one (or a combination) of the human and ecological factors variously alleged to have been responsible for the general Mycenaean collapse, although the civil war theory seems unlikely to explain the desertion of such middle-level towns.

Unless the entire population was wiped out by warfare or pestilence or all survivors were carried off into slavery, it is difficult to understand the total abandonment of such an attractive and productive environment. It is reasonable, on the contrary, to suppose that there were *some* survivors. And even if they had to live under the threat of repeated raids from sea or land or to suffer the privations caused by a long-term drought or other ecological threat, one would expect at least a few families to cling to the fields and graves of their ancestors. A disastrous blight on one of the staple crops or disease affecting one species of domesticated animals could hardly wipe out as diversified an agricultural economy. If there was a total interruption of internal and overseas trade, the natural reaction would be a return to a simpler subsistence system.

There is, then, at least a theoretical possibility that a few people continued to live in some unexcavated section of the Nichoria acropolis or in the immediate environs. Very tentative support for such a theory may be provided by scattered finds that would normally be assigned to early LHIIIC (see comparanda for various metal objects and terra-cotta spools cited in Chapter 5, as well as ceramic evidence treated by Shelmerdine in Chapter 12 of forthcoming Vol. II). Perhaps a somewhat stronger possibility is that the survivors retreated only temporarily to some refuge site in the mountains but returned to their old home within a generation or less, when the original threat had disappeared or diminished. This in a sense would simply mean the extension of seasonal transhumance, which may have been practiced by shepherds in normal times. A useful modern analogy to such a short-term abandonment and resettlement might be the behavior of many Messenian villagers in the years just before and after the War of Independence in the early 19th century A.D. (see p. 429).

In such a drastically simplified way of life skilled artisans who survived might have become superfluous. Containers of wood and basketry and leather could have replaced pottery; stone tools and implements (reused or copied) could have served instead of metal; and temporary shelters instead of permanent houses are a distinct possibility. This kind of existence would not have left much in the way of an enduring and distinguishable material record. Thus, a relatively brief abandonment of the site—or even marginal continuity—is not ruled out by our evidence; in fact, the scanty indications of LHIIIC presence elsewhere in Messenia (*MME* 1972, pp. 142, 143) almost guarantee that this is what happened at a few comparable sites.

It is very difficult to estimate the rate of deterioration when an inhabited site is totally or largely deserted. Our observation of regeneration of vegetation and dilapidation of both stone and mudbrick buildings in recently abandoned Messenian villages would suggest that after more than two or three generations the DA reuse of Mycenaean houses and building material that we detect at Nichoria (see Chapter 2) would have been most unlikely. That is, it looks as if at least the lower walls of LH buildings could still be easily detected above ground when the people making and using what we call DAI pottery chose to patch up at least a few of them in Area IV (Units 6, 7, and 9) for their own shelter. And in the preserved foundations of DAII buildings the settlers utilized big weathered blocks that we believe were originally quarried by the Mycenaean inhabitants, were exposed to the elements in dilapidated and tumbled LH house walls, and so were readily available above ground on-site.

The ceramic evidence presented in Chapter 3 does indicate, however, that the earliest post-LHIIIB2 pottery recovered at Nichoria belongs to a somewhat later stage of

LHIIIC than that, for example, from Messenian sites like Tragana and Ramovouni; and these in turn seem to reflect a relatively advanced stage of LHIIIC development. So it may be safest on present evidence to view Messenia as particularly slow in recovering from the Mycenaean collapse and *not* to consider Nichoria as one of the very first settlements in the region to rebound from the shock.

Even if this reconstruction is correct in relative terms, its transfer to even the loosest sort of absolute dating is extremely risky. No structure associated with DAI pottery survives, and the architectural evidence from DAII and III lacks close parallels on the mainland. Because the chronology is uncertain, we used particular care to recover samples of carbonized wood in what seemed to be secure DA contexts, but the wide spread of the resulting radiocarbon analyses is not particularly helpful (*Nichoria* I, p. 5). If one eliminates the three samples in that chart which are clearly vitiated by contamination or other factors, the most that can be said about the dates yielded by the remaining seven samples is that they cluster around the 10th century B.C. for DAII and III. Although this bracket is roughly compatible with independent estimates based mainly on ceramic evidence (see pp. 318-21), it is of very limited value in establishing an upper or lower limit for the DA settlement.

The parallels cited in Chapter 5 for some of the metal objects may perhaps be claimed to indicate a relatively early date. There are close similarities between objects from Nichoria and from LHIIIC and Submycenaean cemeteries of fairly secure 12th- and 11th-century date in east central Greece. But, again, the rarity of such objects with firm DAI proveniences is a limitation, the problem of heirlooms, and the probable conservatism or "lag" in regions like South and West Greece renders risky the chronological equation of closely similar objects from Nichoria and the vicinity of Athens.

With all due caution, then, we propose that our poorly documented DAI village was in existence no later than some time in the 11th century. It is clear from their pottery and some of the metal objects that the inhabitants were still familiar with residual Mycenaean traits. Furthermore, their reuse of the Mycenaean cemetery and townsite strongly suggests Mycenaean roots for at least some of the DAI people. And the little tholos tomb built for a series of DAII burials surely betrays an unbroken cultural thread. Yet, somehow and somewhere, the earliest documented DA settlers must have come in contact with people and/or ideas of a non-Mycenaean tradition. Although independent local innovation must always be kept in mind as a contributing factor, new ceramic features point to outside influence. An even clearer "break" with Mycenaean tradition is seen in the individual apsidal cists in the Lakkoules cemetery, and the contemporaneity of the earliest of them with the DAI pottery recovered on the ridge is secure.

Another sharp contrast with the Mycenaean way of life seems to be emerging from the study of the Nichoria animal bones (*Nichoria* I, Chapter 6, especially p. 74 and Table 6-1). If Sloan and Duncan are right, there was a shift between LH and DA from a mixed economy in which agriculture had precedence to one based much more heavily on herding, with the emphasis on cattle raising. Basing their conclusions on the analyses of bones from "pure" contexts only, they find that beef comprised on the average 15 to 20% of the meat diet through the Middle and Late Bronze Age, dropped to only 11% at the very end of LH, and then rose to 29% in DAI, 35% in DAII, and 40% in DAIII. Also, from their calculations on average age at slaughter of both cattle and caprovines, they project a change from a spread-out pattern in LH, typical of a regime favoring use of milk products, to the DA habit of earlier butchering which is characteristic of meat ranching.

It is clear that in the carefully controlled LH economy different production centers within the Pylian kingdom specialized in different products and that herding was one of the major specialized activities (Carothers and McDonald 1979). But that was a regionally balanced system, and the herds consisted mainly of sheep for wool production. Futhermore, if the equation of Nichoria with TI-MI-TO-A-KE-E is accepted, this particular center did not specialize in animal husbandry (Shelmerdine 1981). We cannot agree with the position taken by Snodgrass (1971, p. 385) that the apparent DA emphasis on herding was "another Mycenaean legacy, making a contrast with the crop-raising communities of M.H." We believe that, if concentration on cattle raising in the DA community can be conclusively proved, it would reflect a rather drastic shift in economic base. Cattle do not do well on marginal pasturage in the long Mediterranean dry season. Their presence in relatively large numbers in the Nichoria environs strongly suggests that the extensive bottomlands to E and SE of the ridge were used mainly to furnish pasture and fodder. Even if Vita-Finzi and his supporters are correct in attributing to such valleys a less fertile, pre-Roman "Older Fill," the soil in LH times would still have been relatively well watered and more valuable for intensive agriculture. On the other hand, much less labor is required for large-scale cattle raising, and such a regime fits in well with our impression that Nichoria's DA population was small and that there was little pressure on good land.

Perhaps, as methods improve and concerns broaden, archaeologists may learn to tie in known food regimes with shapes and types of ceramic vessels. For the present, we simply raise the possibility that the DA pottery at Nichoria may support other evidence of a shift from a predominantly cereal diet to a notable increase in meat consumption. Cereals in the form of porridges and gruels were presumably eaten from roomy, open containers like deep bowls; and the popularity of such dishes declined notably, especially in DAII, in proportion to smaller vessels. Furthermore, grills for roasting meat on spits or skewers were apparently more common in the DA repertory.

The animal bones in the "pure" lots that have so far been analyzed may reveal additional, though less striking novelties in the DA way of life. The percentage of sheep and goats is down somewhat when compared with the Bronze Age statistics; and the same is true of pigs which in DAII contributed an all-time low percentage to the meat diet. On the other hand, the percentage of domestic dogs increased notably, a characteristic that fits neatly with a regime that stressed cattle raising and hunting. In the latter connection, the percentage of red deer consumed was higher in DAI than in any period before or after; and the smaller roe deer apparently became the major source of wild meat in DAII. Indications are that hunting pressure on deer was so intense that by DAIII the herds within range of the village had been either exterminated or driven away.

Although there is some evidence for the taking of smaller game such as hare and tortoise, the DA settlers appear to have been uninterested in or unsuccessful at hunting winged game. At any rate, only one fragment of an unidentified bird was recognizable. In the lots that were carefully analyzed (*Nichoria* I, p. 70) only a few remains of cockle, oyster, and scallop were identified, and shells of land snails were infrequent. Lack of sophistication or care in recovery techniques cannot be the explanation for the dearth of delicate bones or shells, since there is a striking variation in the bulk of identified remains from other prehistoric sites (Reese, personal communication). Perhaps the inhabitants of villages where remains are few may have consumed marine food on or near the beach; or certain soils may have caused the disintegration of fragile bones; or preferred foods may have been more abundant in some localities than in others. Bisel's research on trace minerals in human bone (pp. 264, 265; to be reported in greater detail in *Nichoria* II) may provide some support for the last-named explanation, since it suggests that the Nichoria inhabitants consumed significantly less seafood than their Athenian counterparts.

The numerous analyses of carbonized plant and wood remains yielded such meager results that the Shays make no claim for their statistical relevance (*Nichoria* I, Chapter 5, especially Tables 5-7 to 5-10). But at least the results provide hard evidence to support the natural inference that the DA villagers also practiced a varied agricultural regime that supplied an important part of the diet. Among the seeds recovered in DA contexts, the following typical food plants have been identified: cereal grain (wheat and probably barley), grape, olive (apparently both eating and oil varieties), and legumes of the pea family. Thus we have confirmation of the continuing cultivation of Renfrew's basic "Mediterranean triad," i.e., cereals, olives, and grapes. Acorns and what are probably wild cherries were collected and eaten. A deposit of charred acorns was recovered in Unit IV-1; and substantial deposits of charred grain and grape seeds were discovered in and near Unit IV-5. Indeed, there appears to have been an unusual concentration of stored food in these major buildings, especially in the DAIII period.

From the carbonized woods comes further confirmation that another LH food, the fig, was still being cultivated. But our tiny samples allow no dependable inferences about the relative proportions of these staples in the vegetable and fruit diet. On general grounds it may perhaps be inferred that the LH profusion of somewhat exotic garden plants, such as the sesame documented in the Linear B tablets, was considerably less and that, conversely, the bulk of wild plants and fruits in the diet may have been greater.

Jennifer Shay's painstaking analysis of some 100 samples of wood charcoal from DA contexts provides useful hints not only about foods but about forestation, construction, and sources of fuel. Approximately 45% of the samples are oak, 30% olive, 6% maple, with a scattering of such additional species as pine, fig, grape, and pistacia. With so few samples, it is doubtful whether any valid conclusions can be drawn from apparent variations between subperiods, such as a drop in oak from 54% in DAI-II to 31% in DAIII. And it is seldom possible to be precise as to whether a given fragment belonged to a good-sized timber that may have been used in house construction, to relatively small wooden objects such as implements, furniture, and containers, or to branches and twigs used for fodder and firewood. It is likely, however, that most samples were the scattered remains of fires in hearths and ovens in which prunings from vines and olives are a common modern fuel. On the other hand, most of the oak and perhaps some of the olive had almost certainly been used for other purposes.

The comparative abundance of oak and acorns may be seen as some confirmation of the contention that these hardy and useful trees covered much of Messenia in prehistoric times; and we are informed that large oak groves and forests existed even as late as the 19th century A.D. (*MME* 1972, pp. 246, 247). The intensification of deer hunting in DA times may point to a rejuvenation of nearby woodlands that had suffered somewhat from more intensive use in Mycenaean times. Yassoglou and Nobeli argue that the area of the DA cemetery was forested until comparatively recent times (*MME* 1972, p. 175). In the case of the olive, regardless of the reason it was brought into the settlement, the proportion of charred wood suggests that this remarkable tree was still an agricultural staple. Olive culture would have been popular in DA times for the same reason as cattle raising, i.e., that its cultivation requires proportionately less intensive labor than annual or shorter-lived plants and tree crops. And olives adapt well to poorer soil that is not suited to cattle grazing or to interculture with cereals. The heavy DA terrace wall at the lower S end of Area III probably delimits a good-sized field on the sparsely inhabited ridgetop that may have been planted to olives. They flourish now on the ridge and would have provided welcome shade in and near inhabited areas.

Indeed, it is quite possible that olive trees planted before the end of the Bronze Age could have been utilized by DA farmers. It is no longer necessary, however, to interpret Wright's pollen cores from Osmanaga lagoon as evidence for an olive peak in DA rather than LH times (*MME* 1972, p. 195; *Nichoria* I, p. 94). Calibration with the recent dendrochronological data (*Nichoria* I, p. 4) now indicates that the Osmanaga olive peak occurred in the later Mycenaean context, where other factors would indicate it should be expected. This is not to deny, of course, that per capita consumption of olives and olive oil in DA communities like Nichoria may have been as high as before.

Among the crafts certified to have been carried on in the DA village we may cite house construction, pottery making, textile manufacture, and metallurgy. Others that can safely be inferred include the production of stone tools (Chapter 5, pp. 291, 292) and leather working. The latter doubtless assumed unusual importance in an economy where cattle raising appears to have been so basic. In contrast to the well-documented craft specialization in the highly organized Mycenaean society, household self-sufficiency would have been the DA norm. But, at least in the case of fine pottery and metallurgy, production for the needs of the whole village must have been handled by specialists. Within the village, barter would have gone on in a limited way, with manufactured items exchanged for services or agricultural products. We have no way of inferring at present whether local products reached a wider market, but some kind of goods and/or services must have served in a barter system for the procurement of metals, obsidian(?), and perhaps a very limited supply of luxury items for cult and personal adornment. The recovery of a twisted piece of gold wire (**N566**) in Unit IV-1 shows that at least one individual in the village had the means to acquire and/or the skill to work such a precious possession.

In Chapter 2 of this volume Coulson reports in detail on the architectural evidence, and in *Nichoria* II Walsh will publish some of the results of her research on house construction. There can be no doubt that the work force available in an individual family could have collected the material and built and kept in repair the simpler huts or houses. But, in the case of Units IV-1 and IV-5, wider communal effort was presumably required, and their construction may have involved an imported "master" who had considerable experience in planning and erecting major buildings. The construction of the graves described in Chapter 4 was probably a routine family responsibility.

On the other hand, the manufacture of the better grade of pottery vessels surely involved specialist skills. And it is our impression, although not supported by exact statistical proof, that the quantity of DAII and III pottery recovered from the limited areas of the ridgetop that were intensively excavated could hardly be accounted for by the output of one family, even if they worked full time in suitable weather. We discovered no remains of kilns or concentrations of misshapen or misfired pottery that would indicate where the pottery was manufactured. Matson's analyses show that there are usable clay deposits on the ridge and still better sources elsewhere in the environs (*Nichoria* I, pp. 229-31). Notable differences in fabric between late Mycenaean and DAI wares (as well as those of later DA times) show that clay sources and/or mixtures shifted over time (see Chapter 3, pp. 110, 111). Workshop and kiln sites could also have shifted, their location being governed mainly by accessibility to preferred clay components, adequate fuel, water, and perhaps to the potter's home. A distinct possibility is a location down in the Karia valley where a tile factory was located less than a century ago.

The working of copper, bronze, and iron, however, was certainly carried on, in part at least, on the ridgetop. This is proved by the melting slags, prills, and spatters from the casting process that were recovered in the excavations (*Nichoria* I, pp. 166-224). The manufacture of unalloyed copper artefacts decreased in DA as compared to LH times; and there is a corresponding (and quite unexpected) increase in the tin content in several DA bronze objects. Catling reports the results of some of the individual analyses in the catalog of metal objects (Chapter 5). Although the percentage of tin is variable, its generally liberal use argues against any theory of near-total isolation of SW Peloponnese from distant trade routes. The high tin content in items like rings which are worn next to the skin may reflect an intentional precaution against the deterioration of copper when in contact with skin acids and oils. The overall similarity of DA to LH bronze metallurgy, both in techniques and in the apparent provenience of the raw metals themselves, strengthens the case for cultural continuity in the transition period, although it does not necessarily imply continuous occupation at a particular site such as Nichoria.

The local smiths usually remelted imported copper/bronze ingots that had been smelted/alloyed elsewhere, no doubt close to the mines. Again, there is no obvious clustering in the excavated areas that would indicate the precise location of the DA furnaces or hearths in which the melting was done; nor can we be sure that all of the bronze artefacts recovered were made locally.

Of the six certain or probable DA slags that were prepared for detailed analysis, two were "bronze crucible," two "copper crucible," and two "iron smelting" (*Nichoria* I, Table 1-1, nos. 32, 34-38). Cooke and Nielsen (*Nichoria* I, Chapter 12) believe that a very modest DA operation was conducted somewhere on-site in which iron ore was smelted into metallic iron suitable for forging. Iron slag was recovered only in Areas III and IV, where the pottery documents the main DA habitation. The iron ore may have been imported from the nearby Mani on the E side of the Messenian gulf, and it is possible that local workmen actually did the mining. The best available fuel would have been charcoal made from the oak that is known to have been available locally.

A phenomenon noted by all trenchmasters who worked in Areas III and IV, where DA remains seem to be concentrated, is the dark color and fine texture of the soil and its tendency to be very sticky in spring and rock-hard in summer. The occurrence in these levels of a good deal of fine charred material plus the dark color led to the natural inference that these levels contain a concentration of occupationally derived humus. Stein and Rapp carried out a number of experiments to check the validity of this hypothesis (*Nichoria* I, pp. 250, 251). Their conclusion is that the dark color is produced naturally by a concentration in clay content, usually to a depth of ca. 1.0 m below the modern surface.

The DA deposits broadly correspond with what soil scientists call an argillic horizon, i.e., one in which "clay materials have been concentrated through trans-location from overlying horizons" (*Nichoria* I, p. 39). Yassoglou and Haidouti deduce that this phenomenon indicates that the minimum time for the formation of an argillic horizon under the xeric conditions of southern Greece is about 2,000 years, and they point to the fact that, without chronological data supplied by archaeology, it would have been impossible to shed light on a lively controversy among soil scientists concerning the time required for the development of such a soil profile. Since the debt in such interdisciplinary projects seems usually to be one-sided, it is reassuring to be reminded that cooperation between archaeologists and natural scientists can sometimes work to the advantage of both.

In their chapter on the "archaeological geology" of the site, Stein and Rapp show that, in comparison with the significant Bronze Age changes in the ridge contours due to a combination of natural and man-made factors, DA habitation had relatively slight effects (*Nichoria* I, p. 256). There is a marked decrease in DA sedimentation, with cultural deposits generally spread thinner over artificially leveled limestone blocks and rubble from earlier structures. They attribute the contrast mainly to the much smaller DA population which may have left large areas of the surface relatively undisturbed and allowed natural stabilization of the surface with a heavier vegetation cover. They also suggest that the DA shift to cattle raising may have resulted in less on-site destruction of trees and shrubs by sheep and goats.

The end of DA habitation on the Nichoria ridge is better documented than the beginning. In the DAIII period the community was definitely smaller and apparently more isolated than it had been in DAII. In view of the newly revealed cultural association of eastern Messenia with Laconia in DAII (see Chapter 2, pp. 78, 111), it is tempting to see in the later situation a growing estrangement between the neighboring regions—and perhaps even actual or anticipated Spartan aggression. In that context, one could easily see a possible connection between the semi-legendary and imprecisely dated First Messenian War and the concentration of population and food storage in Area IV, the burning of the community center (Unit IV-5), the ubiquitous ash in late DA levels, and the abandonment of the ridge before mid-8th century.

The literary and mythological tradition concerning early Messenia is admittedly corrupt and may have been in large part the product of a rewriting of Messenian history following the foundation of the federal capital at Messene in 369 B.C. (Pearson 1962). At the same time, the written record cannot be totally ignored, especially when archaeological evidence may be interpreted as offering possible confirmation. Pausanias (4.4.1) states that the first dispute between Messenia and Sparta occurred in the time of Phintas, the descendant of Kresphontes, chief of the Messenians. The outcome was a Spartan expedition into Messenia, led by King Teleklos. Both Huxley (1962, p. 31) and Coldstream (1977, p. 163) reckon that Teleklos was active in Messenia in the mid-8th century B.C. This date accords well with the *terminus ante quem* for the DAIII settlement on the Nichoria ridge (see the discussion of the vases from the pithos burial and the Vathirema chamber tomb in Chapter 3, pp. 109, 110 and in the chronology section above).

In the same frame of reference, Pausanias (4.3.6) mentions that Kresphontes married Merope, the daughter of the king of Arcadia. Such an early dynastic alignment—or even the tradition that it had happened—would provide an understandable motivation for the later Arcadian alliance with Messenia against the Spartan aggressor (Pausanias 4.11.1). In addition, the relationship might well have promoted the movement of settlers to Messenia from the more austere Arcadian environment. The resettlement of the modern village of Karpofora by Arcadians in the 1870s could be adduced as a parallel (see Chapter 14, p. 429). In this connection it would be perverse to deny the possibility that the shift in orientation from E-W to N-S in DAIII buildings at Nichoria (especially the crucial Unit IV-5) may have been due to the influence of Arcadian allies or settlers, since Arcadian buildings, more than any others on the Greek mainland, are characterized by a N-S orientation.

We do not know where the local inhabitants lived in Late Geometric times; but two known LG graves prove that the environs of the ridge were still in use and indicate that an LG village was not far away. Furthermore, the contents of the burials indicate that at least some of the inhabitants were reasonably prosperous. The pithos burial on the ridge suggests that this ground had precious associations for the descendants of those who had lived there for some 300 years. The grave's striking location, on a high point with an all-embracing view to east and south (Pl. 4-1), may reflect a conscious wish by the living to enlist the dead hero's continued vigilance to help them ward off the incursions of the hated foe from across Taygetos.

Village Life in the Dark Age

To conclude this summary chapter, we attempt a reconstruction of the kind of life that was led by the inhabitants of this little DA community. The perils of such an enterprise are obvious. Some of the points made in the previous section depend on fairly "soft" data; but most of the following inferences have to be based on evidence that is equivocal at best. For some of the most important aspects, particularly those that Renfrew terms the projective or symbolic activities, our data provide little or no basis even for inference. And yet the search for a balanced view of past life-styles is surely the proper goal of humanistic archaeology, and archaeologists should not shirk the responsibility of reviewing what is known or can reasonably be reconstructed about one of the "darkest" episodes in the last 4,000 years of Greek history.

First, we might take a close look at the geographical setting of the village. Even if there was no settlement on or near the ridge in the immediate post-LHIIIB2 years, the site itself could scarcely be forgotten. It lies squarely at the crossroads of two major perennial land routes, i.e., the E-W road from Kalamata to Pylos and the N-S route along the E side of the peninsula and northward beyond Nichoria to Ithome in central Messenia (Fig. 1-2; cf. *Nichoria* I, Fig. 7-8, p. 91). Unless the whole subregion was totally depopulated, these routes must have continued in at least local use; and the ridgetop where they converged would be a well-known landmark, even if it was no longer considered important for strategic or other reasons. It is noteworthy, for instance, that a concentration of DA burials occurs along the N-S road, just beyond the main intersection. And when settlement on the ridge was resumed (if in fact there was a hiatus), the DA people always preferred to live in the more secluded Areas III, IV, and VII rather than on the exposed heights (Areas II, VI). This surely points to a less outward-looking and confident era than was the case in the Late Bronze Age.

In DA times even more than in most periods of Greek history, such long-distance travel as there was would have been mainly by sea. But it is a long and often dangerous voyage from the Messenian gulf around Cape Akritas to the west coast or around Cape Malea to the Aegean orbit. Although close to the gulf and within easy reach of the protected little harbor at modern Petalidhi, Nichoria's rather secluded position vis-à-vis the main sea routes would afford a fair amount of protection in those troubled times. But this location also imposed certain limitations. A village so situated would have minimal direct cultural contact with the Aegean; and interrelations with less distant regions like West Peloponnese might be slow and spasmodic. Far more natural and likely would be direct communication across the gulf to spots that were gradually coming under Laconian control as Spartan forces breached the less formidable southern passes of the Taygetos chain. This situation almost surely explains why ceramics from Nichoria and her southern neighbor Kaphirio show unmistakable Laconian influence in the DAII period (see pp. 78, 111).

Perhaps the main advantage of the Nichoria vicinity for the DA settlers was the large and relatively fertile lowland immediately to S and E of the ridge (see pp. 6-8). Here the coastal valleys formed by the two perennial rivers, the Karia and the Velika, practically coalesce. Yassoglou and Nobeli emphasize how valuable these bottomlands would have been in providing pasture and fodder for large ruminants like cattle and horses (*MME* 1972, p. 175). One can be reasonably sure that the heaviest village traffic pattern would have been that connecting the ridgetop with these handy pastures.

Circulation on the ridgetop itself can be reconstructed with some assurance, even though no actual street or path of DA date has been identified. The modern path (see Fig. 1-1) fits the natural contours of the site, and this general line must always have been the main NW-SE traffic artery. It leads up from the highway through the Tourkokivouro ravine, past Area I, and onto the NW acropolis (Area II). From there it skirts the N edge of Area III, angling down the slope and running between the N and S Veves fields. Here the present route begins a sunken course, crowned on each side by field walls built of limestone blocks gathered by modern farmers from tumbled prehistoric house walls. It continues past Areas V and IV (which lie to the S), onward through a deep cut in a hillock just E of Area IV, and becomes less distinct as it reaches Areas VI and VII.

Pockets of what appears to have been minor DA occupation fit neatly along this artery in Areas III, the N Veves field, and Area VII (Fig. 1-1). In Area IV, Units IV-1 and IV-5 are contiguous to the main path, but at least for this focal area of the village we must postulate the existence of alleys branching to the S and SW that gave access to the houses which seem to have formed a considerable cluster. An important branch must have diverged from the main artery so as to lead past the main east entrance of Unit IV-1, and there may have been the equivalent of the modern *plateia* or open "village square" here. On the opposite (NE) side of the main artery a steep path now leads down through a deeply eroded gully to the village of Rizomilo and the Karia valley. Although there are a few other points where the ridgetop may be approached with some difficulty, it is fair to conjecture that, depending on where they had been working, the villagers would come back to their homes on the ridge either by the NW approach or by this steeper NE path.

It is interesting to speculate on their reasons for living on the waterless ridgetop rather than in the valley. Probably they felt safer on the height and (like the villagers of modern Karpofora which is built on a nearby ridge) they would find the summer air cooler and mosquitoes less bothersome.

What kind of settlement would one see on reaching the ridgetop? Most people seem to have lived in one-roomed apsidal huts, not much larger on the average than Unit III-1, with stone foundations, wattle and daub or mudbrick walls, and pitched roofs of thatch. These simple dwellings were strung along the main path, with the largest concentration in Area IV. This was no doubt the favored neighborhood because of the presence of the chieftain's home in which the political, religious, and social life of the community was centered. To ensure fertility of herds and crops, the villagers may have offered first-fruits in Unit IV-1 and its successor, Unit IV-5, believing that the chieftain was the ordained intermediary between them and their gods. Perhaps they also stored surplus food in or near these buildings for safekeeping and some kind of communal distribution.

How may we visualize the work regime? The women would spend most of their time on the ridgetop, except when carrying out the age-old female task of bringing water up from the river or perhaps from a couple of closer springs (one now flows very slowly, and the other has recently ceased flowing). Preparation of food and the various home crafts would be carried out in or near their huts. Since the latter occupied only a small part of the ridgetop, a good deal of land was available on the ridge for tree crops, pasture for sheep and goats, and for gathering plants and fuel. Summer kitchen gardens, if such were cultivated, would have had to be situated nearer water. Most of the men no doubt worked farther from home, tending cattle in the bottomlands and crops on the slopes that were safe from seasonal floods. Hunting was probably a part-time occupation in seasons when the major tasks were lighter.

It is doubtful if the cattle were ever driven up on the ridge, unless in times of danger. A few attendants could normally guard them in stockades during the night. Probably the calves consumed most available cow's milk, and cheese and other milk products were made mainly from sheep and goat milk. Butchering would be done near the stockades. Tanned leather must have been proportionately more abundant than in LH times, and skins may have been more common than textiles for garments and coverlets. The presence in the settlement of whorls, loomweights, and sheep bones proves, however, that some wool was woven; but it is possible that the fine linen fabrics of LH times were no longer produced. (See Chapter 5, p. 287.)

One of our major aims in the Nichoria excavations was to try to ascertain fairly closely the size and layout of the settlements in the various periods of prehistoric habitation. But the extent of the ridge and our limited time and budget proved frustrating. Furthermore, it is not easy to estimate how many of the limited number of DA houses that we can document were occupied at the same time. And, even if we had accurate gross weights for the pottery recovered from distinct subperiods, we could not claim that the proportions would be representative of the site as a whole. Similarly, the overall size of the DA cemetery is unknown.

It is quite safe to conclude, however, that throughout the DA period inhabitants were much fewer than in LH times, and probably fewer than in the more prosperous MH phases. On the other hand, they were certainly more numerous than the Byzantine settlers. We can also be reasonably sure that, within the DA period, the population was larger in DAII than in DAI or III. But, as with absolute chronology, any estimates of specific population totals are extremely shaky. Some 40 families, amounting to about 200 souls, may be a reasonable figure for DAII–and for DAI perhaps one-third and for DAIII one-half that number.

It is even more risky to estimate gross DA population for the environs or for the whole region. If one is to take seriously the scale implied in the traditional accounts of the Messenian Wars, Nichoria must have been a very minor village or else small villages were the rule. Possibly the population in east Messenia was smaller and more scattered –at least in DAIII times–because of its position as a buffer zone exposed to Spartan threat and ultimate invasion. But the traditional picture of a region that could muster large forces time after time to resist Spartan domination is at serious variance with the evidence furnished by archaeological field survey. A decade of regional search pointed to Nichoria as the most promising known DA habitation site, and it is clear now that we must scale down any expectations of its importance as a substantial population center. So, for the present, it appears that the population levels implied in the quasi-historical tradition must be even more wildly exaggerated than usual. Indeed, Messenia seems to have been very sparsely populated in Protogeometric times and not at all intensively inhabited even as late as the 8th century B.C.

REFERENCES

Carothers, J., and McDonald, W. A. 1979. "Size and Distribution of the Population in Late Bronze Age Messenia: Some Statistical Approaches," *JFA* 6:433-54.

Coldstream, J. N. 1977. *Geometric Greece*. London.

Desborough, V. R. D'A. 1964. *The Last Mycenaeans and Their Successors*. Oxford.

———. 1972. *The Greek Dark Ages*. London.

Deshayes, J. 1966. *Argos, les fouilles de la Deiras*. Paris.

Hope Simpson, R., and Dickinson, O. T. P. K. 1979. *A Gazetteer of Aegean Civilization in the Bronze Age I: The Mainland and Islands*. Göteborg.

Huxley, G. L. 1962. *Early Sparta*. London.

McDonald, W. A., and Rapp, G., Jr., eds. 1972. *Minnesota Messenia Expedition: Reconstructing a Bronze Age Regional Environment*. Minneapolis.

MME 1972 = McDonald and Rapp 1972.

Nichoria I = Rapp and Aschenbrenner 1978.

Pearson, L. 1962. "The Pseudo-History of Messenia and Its Authors," *Historia* 11:397-426.

Rapp, G., Jr., and Aschenbrenner, S., eds. 1978. *Excavations at Nichoria in Southwest Greece I: Site, Environs, and Techniques*. Minneapolis.

Rutter J. 1975. "Ceramic Evidence for Northern Intruders in Southern Greece at the Beginning of Late Helladic IIIC," *AJA* 79:17-32.

Sandars, N. 1978. *The Sea Peoples: Warriors of the Ancient Mediterranean, 1250-1150 B.C.* London.

Shelmerdine, C. W. 1981. "Nichoria in Context: a Major Town in the Pylos Kingdom," *AJA* 85:319-25.

Snodgrass, A. M. 1971. *The Dark Age of Greece*. Edinburgh.

II. Archaic to Roman Times

7
The Site and Environs

by
William D. E. Coulson
with a contribution by Nancy C. Wilkie

The purpose of this chapter is to set out the data we have recovered that throw a little light on the history of the site in the long interval between Late Geometric and Late Roman/Early Byzantine times. The evidence is sparse and for the most part limited to the Late Classical period. In order to see the remains at Nichoria in somewhat wider perspective, this chapter will also include a brief description of some contemporary features in the immediate environs. Considerable information, derived from MME and earlier research, has already been published on Messenia in general[1] and on Nichoria and vicinity in particular.[2] Consequently, we include here only selected surface finds that seem to bear most directly on the evidence recovered on the ridge itself (Fig. 1-4). Nancy Wilkie describes here the digging of the later levels in the tholos tomb.

The Archaic Period

There are no finds from the ridge itself that document its use in Archaic times and very little to shed light on the environs. The only definite evidence is a thick deposit of black-glazed Archaic pottery from a chapel-crowned hill called Panayitsa, near Neromilo (*Nichoria* I, p. 112, Feature 517).[3] Lukermann and Moody (*Nichoria* I, p. 95) postulate that in Archaic times the Spartans divided this part of Messenia into farmsteads (*klēroi*) and that these, rather than villages, represented the normal tiny nuclei of habitation. The presence of scattered farmsteads with a predominantly rural population may explain the paucity of preserved surface material. The pottery from Panayitsa could represent one such farmstead, although its concentration in relatively unworn condition might argue for a ritual deposit (*apothetis*) connected with a small local shrine on the hilltop. Shrines do occur in the Archaic period, the most notable found in the district being that of Apollo Korythos at Ayios Andreas (Feature 504). Earlier tombs were occasionally reused in this period. Those at Koukounara produced a good group of decorated Archaic pottery. There is no evidence, however, that the Vathirema chamber tomb (Feature 1) was reused at this time. The pottery dates from the Late Geometric period (for a detailed discussion, see Chapter 3, pp. 109, 110) and subsequently from Classical and Hellenistic times. There is nothing from the black-glazed contents that is definitely Archaic; and the lack of material here confirms our impression that the Nichoria ridge and its immediate environs were essentially unused in Archaic times.

The Classical Period

There is rather sparse evidence, however, for activity on the ridge during Classical times. The Mycenaean tholos tomb in Area I (Fig. 2 in McDonald et al. 1975) was reused for what was presumably a hero cult; two rather fragmentary walls associated with diagnostic Classical sherds were found in Area IV; and a considerable section of the podium of a large structure (Unit L21-2) located to the S of Area IV, in grid L21 STabc, was cleaned (but not excavated) and may be Classical in date (Fig. 7-2).

W.D.E.C.

THE HERO CULT IN THE THOLOS

The pottery associated with the floor deposits in the tholos tomb dates its principal use to LHIIIA2-B1, with the final burial being made in LHIIIB2.[4] Subsequently the tomb was reentered by looters who gained access by removing stones from the upper portion of the blocking wall and pushing many of them into the stomion.[5] This resulted in a gap ca 0.35 m high between the underside of the lintel and the remaining portion of the blocking wall through which material from the upper dromos and its immediate vicinity could enter the tomb. In time, a layer of reddish brown sand accumulated over the entire stomion and extended a short distance into the tomb chamber, following the general contours of the stone tumble from the blocking wall that lay beneath it (Fig. 7-11). Fragments of carbonized olive wood and a few nondescript sherds, all similar in character to those from the unstratified dromos fill, were found in this layer.

In the stomion a thin layer of red sand, similar to that which comprised the dromos fill and which covered the Mycenaean deposits on the floor of the tomb chamber, lay directly above the reddish brown sand (Fig. 7-11). Objects that must have belonged to the original grave goods were found in this layer, including fragments from several Mycenaean vases which joined with sherds from those on the stomion and dromos floors. This stratigraphic discontinuity can only have resulted from human activity within the tomb. It is possible that in plundering the grave goods the robbers removed material from the tomb chamber and threw it into the stomion. But the disturbance might also have taken place in the Classical period when the tomb was reused as a cult center.

During the Classical period, access to the tomb could scarcely have been through the gap at the top of the blocking wall made by the earlier tomb robbers. This opening was far too small for the repeated entrances and exits which are indicated by the amount of Classical material recovered in the chamber. Nor is there evidence to suggest that acesss was through a hole in the upper portion of the dome. The use of the central area of the tomb chamber as a hearth, presumably in connection with the rites conducted within the tomb, would seem to argue against access through the top of the dome.

Another possibility is that the space created by a relieving triangle above the lintel blocks was used as an entrance. Since the stomion is not preserved above the level of the lintel blocks, it is presently impossible to determine whether a relieving triangle was included in the original design and construction of the tomb. The three short, roughly worked lintel blocks that are still in place would not require such a device to keep them from cracking under the weight of the dome.

The likeliest access in the Classical period, however, was through an opening in the roof of the stomion created by the removal of two interior lintel blocks which are presently missing and of which no trace was detected in the course of the excavation. Judging from the size of the three blocks that remain, two additional blocks would have been required to fill the 1.50 m gap in the center of the stomion roof. Their removal would have entailed a partial destruction of the segment of the dome directly above the stomion, but for the short term this probably would not have affected the integrity of the structure.

The use of the tomb as a cult center is shown by a black stratum that covered the N end of the stomion and most of the tomb chamber floor, except for a small area beside the W portion of the tholos wall (Fig. 7-11). This black layer ranged in thickness from 0.20 to 0.40 m and sloped downward S to N, following the general direction of the material that gradually sifted into the chamber through gaps in the blocking and stomion walls. The dark color resulted from repeated fires that were lit near the center of the tomb, where there was a particularly heavy concentration of ash and charcoal. Among the charcoal fragments, oak, olive, grape, *Pistacia* and *Acer* type maquis, and *conifer* (probably pine) have been identified (*Nichoria* I, pp. 55-57). In this stratum there was also a large quantity of bones, mainly of small mammals. Particularly noteworthy are the teeth, tusks, and limb fragments of pig, a common sacrificial animal. The majority of the pottery associated with this burned level (discussed on pp. 334-36) dates from the late 5th to early 4th centuries B.C., although a small number of earlier sherds, both MH and Mycenaean, were included in the deposit.

The reuse of Mycenaean tombs as cult centers seems to have been a common practice in Messenia and much of the rest of Greece.[6] Two Mycenaean tombs at Koukounara contained pottery from the 7th century B.C. onward, accompanied by animal sacrifices, particularly deer; and a whole ox was offered in the tholos at Voïdhokoilia, near classical Pylos. Near Dhafni, some 3 km N of the Nichoria acropolis (Figs. 1-4, 7-1), a tholos tomb (Feature 113 A) that was first identified by MME was excavated by Styliana Parlama in 1973.[7] Like our tholos, it contained in its upper fill vases of the late Classical period, along with evidence of burning. The Vathirema chamber tomb (Feature 1) also produced a good group of black-glazed Classical pottery. These examples, together with our tholos, provide clear evidence for the practice of hero worship in this part of Messenia in Classical times. Perhaps this was a way of perpetuating local traditions in the face of Spartan occupation. In none of the local tombs, however, is there evidence to support any theory of unbroken cult continuity from Mycenaean into Classical times.

While our tholos was in use as a cult center, some deterioration of the structure seems to have been occurring, since numerous small stones were found scattered throughout the black stratum. They probably served originally as chinking stones, set in the spaces between the larger blocks comprising the dome in order to keep them from shifting. Their gradual loss must have contributed to the eventual collapse of the dome.

Above the black stratum there was a layer of dark yellow sand ca. 0.30-0.40 m thick. Since it also contained an assortment of charcoal, bone, and pottery fragments, it must likewise be associated with the reuse of the tomb as a cult center (Fig. 7-11). Unlike the black stratum beneath it, this dark yellow layer contained many large blocks. It is clear that they must have become dislodged from the dome following the loss of the chinking stones. Through holes thus created the yellow sand must have gradually filtered into the chamber from the earth mound that covered the tholos. Thus, the tomb became increasingly unsafe, and it is not surprising that it was abandoned as a cult center. Before the total collapse of the dome, some disturbance or sporadic use of the tomb seems to have occurred, since joining fragments of vases used in the cult were found widely scattered throughout the chamber. However, there is no way of calculating the length of time between the abandonment of the tomb as a cult center and the collapse.

N.C.W.

THE THOLOS POTTERY

The Classical pottery from the tholos in Area I consists of both fine black-glazed pieces and coarse ware. The best-preserved piece is a fine black-glazed mug with a double roll handle and two broad circles of black glaze on the underside of the base (**P1627**; Fig. 7-3; Pl. 7-1). The squat shape with its sharply everted lip is especially common in Attica in the second half of the 5th century B.C. (Sparkes and Talcott 1970, pp. 71-73).[8] The decorative circles on the underside of the base, however, are closely paralleled by examples discovered at Olympia (Mallwitz and Schiering 1964, Pls. 64, 1 and 65, 1-5) from the last quarter of the 5th century B.C.;[9] and it may be that **P1627**, on the basis of its fine black glaze, is an import from Olympia or from the place of manufacture of comparable vases found at Olympia. An interesting feature is the reserved band on the base, a decorative motif which does not occur frequently at Olympia.

A second Olympian parallel is seen in our **P1628** (Fig. 7-3), a ribbed mug which recalls the Phidias shape, so called from the mug of this shape found in the "Workshop of Phidias" at Olympia and inscribed with his name (Mallwitz and Schiering 1964, Pl. 64). The characteristics of this shape are a fat body, a double handle with shouldering, and the junction of the neck and wall emphasized by a thin line of notching. There is usually a ringed foot, although this feature is missing in the Nichoria example. Again, the shape was very popular in Athens during the second half of the 5th century B.C. (Sparkes and Talcott 1970, p. 72), but the wall there is much straighter than in either the Olympia or the Nichoria examples. Our vase has a wide, globular body which distinguishes it from the parallels at Olympia. It is also coated on both exterior and interior with a rather dull paint, varying from red to black and unevenly applied, thus lacking the fine black glaze found at Olympia. **P1628**, then, can be considered as a local imitation of the popular Phidias shape.

Also coated with a dull, washy black paint and thus possibly another local product is a one-handled cup (**P1629**; Fig. 7-3; Pl. 7-2) with a slightly everted rim and vertical handle. The Attic one-handled cups all have straight rims and slightly oblique handles. Closer parallels with vertical handles are again seen from the "Workshop of Phidias" (Mallwitz and Schiering 1964, Pl. 68, 1-6),[10] but all have straight rims. The S-shaped profile and carinated body of **P1629** do not occur at Olympia. Again, on the basis of its profile and dull paint, the Nichoria example can be considered as a local imitation of the one-handlers of the last quarter of the 5th century B.C. known from Olympia.

A large skyphos (**P1630**; Fig. 7-3), restored from many small pieces and missing both handles and base, is directly paralleled by a good example from the "Workshop of Phidias" (Mallwitz and Schiering 1964, Pl. 67, 1). Like **P1627, P1630** is covered on the exterior and interior by a fine black glaze and not by the dull paint that characterizes the local imitations (**P1628, P1629**); consequently, our skyphos may be considered as an import.

The four more or less complete open vases from the reuse of the Nichoria tholos, then, show close affinities with similar vases from Olympia. Two (**P1627, P1630**) may be imports from Olympia or a common source; and two (**P1628, P1629**), on the basis of their dull, washy paint, are more likely local imitations of popular shapes recovered at Olympia. All four Nichoria vases, on the basis of the parallels from Olympia, can be dated to the last quarter of the 5th century. B.C., indicating that this was the time when the tholos began to be used for a hero cult.

In addition to the whole (restored) vases discussed above, the burned level within the tholos yielded various diagnostic fragments of mugs and skyphoi. **P1632** and **P1633** (Fig. 7-4) are everted rims of the type belonging to mugs; both are coated with a fine black glaze and may be considered as imports from Olympia or a common source. Conversely, **P1634** to **P1637** (Fig. 7-4), also mug rims, have a dull black glaze, fired in places to a brown color; the sloppy and unevenly applied glaze points to a local product. **P1638** (Fig. 7-4) has an incision below the rim, outlining the transition between rim and neck. It may thus belong to a ribbed mug, where such incisions commonly occur. **P1641** and **P1642** (Fig. 7-4; Pl. 7-3) are bases belonging to mugs, perhaps also imported from Olympia or a common source on account of their fine black glaze. The underside of **P1641** is decorated with two black circles in a similar manner to that of **P1627**, and **P1641** probably belongs to a vase of similar shape and size. **P1639** (Fig. 7-4) is a straight rim, probably belonging to a local skyphos, whereas **P1643** and **P1644** (Fig. 7-4) are large, angular ringed bases of the type that appear on skyphoi from the "Workshop of Phidias."

P1631 (Fig. 7-3), missing a portion of its lower belly and the majority of the handle, represents a curious shape that combines elements of both skyphos and mug. The base is a ringed foot of the type frequently occurring on skyphoi, and the straight rim and handle are typical of the body of a mug. The resulting hybrid, a rather deep "skyphos-mug," is probably a local creation, since there are no direct parallels to this shape. Another rim fragment, **P1640** (Fig. 7-4), may possibly come from a second skyphos-mug. Four bases of saltcellars (**P1645-48**; Fig. 7-4) end the list of cataloged fine open vases from the tholos. Such saltcellars have parallels both in Attica (Sparkes and Talcott 1970, Pl. 34, 944-50) and Olympia (Mallwitz and Schiering 1964, Pl. 68, 1-4), but the soft, flaky state of the fired clay and the worn surfaces on these bases suggest that they are local imitations.

Of the fine closed shapes, a lekythos (**P1649**; Fig. 7-6; Pl. 7-4) is the only shape represented in our group. It has an ovoid body, strap handle, flat base, and a drip band at the junction of neck and shoulder, with further raised bands and incisions on the shoulder. In places on the body the glaze has fired brown, with additional black glaze on the interior of the neck. It is paralleled by a series of lekythoi from the Athenian Agora,[11] dating to the last quarter of the 5th century B.C. This suggests a similar date for our lekythos, although its body has a more globular shape than those from the Athenian Agora and the base is quite flat compared with the disk feet of the Athenian examples. It may be supposed that **P1649** is a local variation of a popular Athenian form.

The burned level in the tholos also produced a small but interesting series of household wares, no doubt used for the actual sacrifices. The best preserved is a chytra (**P1650**; Fig. 7-6) with a single handle and raised bands on the exterior below the rim. Again, a series of parallels are found at Olympia (Kunze and Schlief 1944, pp. 98, 99, Fig. 76, 77).[12] Although larger in size, the Olympia examples have the same shape as our vessel. Such chytrai continue into the mid-4th century B.C. (Jones, Graham, and Sackett 1973, pp. 386-88) and suggest that use of the tholos as a cult center may have continued well into the 4th century B.C. Rims of three other chytrai (**P1651-53**) were also recovered.

The ceramic finds include a series of interesting fragments of cooking pots, all showing traces of secondary burning. The best is the rim of a lopas (**P1654**; Fig. 7-4) with flaring lip and inner falange. The shape is paralleled by examples belonging to the first half of the 4th century B.C. from both the Athenian Agora (Sparkes and Talcott 1970, Fig. 18)[13] and the Vari house (Jones, Graham, and Sackett 1973, p. 388). Remains of other cooking vessels include two angular everted rims with extraordinarily long lips (**P1655**, **P1656**; Fig. 7-4) and two straight rims with attached strap handles (**P1657**, **P1658**; Fig. 7-4) and with a flute at the junction between handle and rim for the placement of a lid.

In addition, four varied lekane bases were recovered. One (**P1659**; Fig. 7-5) has a very ornate and unusual ring foot, whereas two others (**P1660**, **P1661**; Fig. 7-5) have simple ring feet of the type common in the late 5th to early 4th centuries B.C. (Sparkes and Talcott 1970, Fig. 15). The remaining two pieces (**P1662**, **P1663**; Fig. 7-5) are simple flat bases. The chronological range of the household wares suggests that the tholos was used as a cult center at least until the end of the first quarter of the 4th century B.C., perhaps terminating at about the time of the final expulsion of the Spartans in 369 B.C.

Amphorae were also used in the cult. At least five different types can be distinguished, all local products. The first is a small squat amphora (**P1664**; Fig. 7-7) of coarse red clay with secondary burning in places. The handles are missing; but, given the presence of nipples on the shoulder, they should probably be restored at mid-belly. The presence of nipples on the shoulder is an interesting feature, recalling the nippled vases of the DAII period. There are no direct parallels for either shape or nipple decoration, and thus **P1664** may be considered a local product.

P1665 (Fig. 7-8) is a tall amphora with long neck and pointed base, made with a clay that has fired to a pale yellow color and has a soft, flaky texture. The fabric recalls that of the DAI and II periods and suggests a local origin for the amphora. Its shape, especially the angular rim, has no 4th century B.C. parallels, which strengthens the likelihood that it is a local product. An interesting feature is that the pierced toe would allow the contents to seep into the ground. The toe is in such a worn state that it is impossible to tell whether the hole was made before or after firing. Hence, it is uncertain whether the amphora was made specifically for sacrificial use or was reused for this purpose. In any case, the presence of the pierced toe suggests that the amphora was used for sacrificial purposes[14] and that it was partially buried in the floor. Liquid sacrifices could then be poured into the vase and trickle down to nourish the buried hero.

The other three amphorae are poorly preserved. **P1666** and **P1667** were made with a light red, micaceous clay, perhaps also local. **P1666** (Fig. 7-5) is the best preserved and consists of a complete rim and neck fragment with preserved handle stumps. The rim has a rounded shape in contrast to the angular form of **P1665**. **P1667** (Fig. 7-5), consisting only of a rim fragment, belonged to a slightly larger neck than **P1666** and is burned in places on the exterior. **P1668** (Fig. 7-5) is a short button toe of light red clay without mica flakes and thus belongs to a different vessel from **P1666** and **P1667**. The shape indicates that it comes from a fairly squat amphora. Since the toes of **P1666** and **P1667** do not survive, it is impossible to tell whether they belonged to sacrificial or storage amphorae. **P1668**, however, is not pierced and should belong to a storage vessel.

Fragments of at least two pithoi were also found. In

one case (**P1669**; Fig. 7-9), the rim, neck, handle, shoulder, and base are preserved, presenting altogether a globular shape. The other (**P1670**; Fig. 7-5) is represented only by a rim which has the same angular shape as that of **P1669** but a horizontal top rather than the oblique one of **P1669**. The pithoi would have been used for storage of liquids and foods used for the sacrifices.

Thus, the later (Classical) levels in the tholos yielded valuable evidence for some of the details connected with local hero worship. The person so revered was obviously considered to have been buried in this monumental tomb, and liquid offerings were poured into a sacrificial amphora with a pierced toe. The consecrated liquids and other foods were stored in amphorae and pithoi within the tomb itself. Mugs, skyphoi, saltcellars, a cup, and a lekythos were used in these rites. Pigs appear to have been sacrificed and cooked, perhaps on the fires in the center of the tomb. Chytrai, lekanai, a lopas, and coarse cooking pots with lids were used in the preparation of the banquet. It is interesting to note that the worshipers used ordinary household pots, not specially formed ritual vessels, in these memorial ceremonies.

ADDITIONAL FINDS OF CLASSICAL DATE

Areas II and III produced little evidence for a Classical presence associated with the reuse of the tholos in Area I. This could be due in part to the eroded and disturbed nature of the surface levels here, but the worshipers in the tholos almost certainly came from farther away. In Area II (K25 Gbc, level 3) a bronze coin of Messene (**244**) was found (Fig. 7-12). No inscription survives, but the presence of Zeus Ithomatas on the reverse (Pl. 7-5) probably dates the coin to the 4th century B.C.[15] From Area III (K25 Ue, level 1) comes a very badly worn bronze coin (**245**), possibly of the same period (Fig. 7-12).

In Area IV the evidence for activity in Classical times is somewhat more substantial. Close to the modern surface in grid L23 Rf a wall fragment (Q) is associated with late Classical pottery. This wall measures approximately 1.0 m in length and has a maximum height of 0.20 m, with only one course preserved (Pl. 7-6). Its N and S ends seem to have been disturbed by the plow, but the preserved sector runs in a N-S direction. It is paralleled to the W in grid L23 Qg by a similar wall (U), preserved in only one row of fairly large blocks of white limestone. Its N and S ends have also been disturbed. Wall U measures 2.30 m in length and has a height of some 0.14 m. It is likely that Walls Q and U once belonged to a small structure in Area IV SW, perhaps a field house (Table 7-1). To the NE of Wall U in grid L23 Shi was found a bronze coin (**N579**) so completely worn that no stamp is preserved on either side. The weight (4.785 gr) and thickness (0.0025 m) indicate that it is probably a Greek coin; if so, it may belong to the same period of activity as Walls Q and U.

The pottery associated with Walls Q and U includes the complete rim and neck (**P1671**; Fig. 7-6) and two rim fragments (**P1672**, **P1673**; Fig. 7-5) of neck amphorae. **P1671** and **P1672**, with offset rims, are similar in shape, whereas **P1673** is straighter and much more angular. All can be dated to the first quarter of the 4th century B.C. and indicate that the building represented by Walls Q and U was in use at the same time as the later stages of the hero cult in the tholos. Miscellaneous body sherds with fragments of preserved black glaze were also found associated with these two walls.

In Area IV N scattered black-glaze body sherds with fragments of preserved paint were found in levels 1 and 2 of L23 Vkl, suggesting that there may have been a second field house here. Two relevant C14 dates were also obtained from this part of the hilltop (*Nichoria* I, p. 5). The first sample (no. 3536) comes from the baulk between L23 Tm and Um and was located 0.20 m N of Wall A of Unit IV-1 and 0.44 m below the surface. It yielded a MASCA-corrected date of 356 ± 88 B.C. The second sample (71-Coul-17) was found at the W end of L23 Uo at a distance of 0.83 m from the SW corner of the grid. It yielded a MASCA-corrected date of 320 ± 93 B.C. Both samples thus agree reasonably well with the evidence already cited for at least minimal utilization of this sector of the ridge in Classical times and perhaps testify to minor construction contemporary with the reuse of the tholos tomb. Another possible explanation is that the wood comes from trees that were part of a cultivated orchard. One can therefore hypothesize that in Classical times Area IV—and perhaps also Areas II and III where the stray coins were found—was planted in trees. They would have been tended by owners who lived elsewhere, as was the case before our excavation started in 1969. The structure

Table 7-1. Specifications of Late Classical Walls: Area IV SW

Wall and Date	Grid	Length	Width	Maximum Height	Maximum Number of Courses	Bond/Butt
Wall Q	L23 Rf	ca. 1.0	?	0.20	1	none
Wall U	L23 Qg	2.305	0.57 (max.)	0.14	1	none

represented by Walls Q and U could have been a field house for storage and for shelter in labor-intensive periods.

South of Area IV in grid L21 STabc there is a mound (perhaps at least partially artificial) which served as the platform or podium for a large building (Unit L21-2). Its ruins could not be excavated since they are on private property, but the owners allowed us to clear the brush for measuring and photography. The exposed foundations are roughly rectangular in shape, with perhaps the hint of a porch at one end (Fig. 7-2; Pl. 7-7). The large limestone blocks, now weathered gray, clearly belonged to the podium of a substantial structure, perhaps a temple, whose superstructure has completely disappeared.

The scattered sherds that can probably be associated with the podium appear to be contemporary with the pottery recovered from the reuse of the tholos and thus suggest a Classical date for the podium. They include a mug(?) rim, similar in shape to **P1627**, with fragments of black glaze preserved on the exterior and interior; a ribbed body sherd, possibly belonging to a mug, with good black glaze preserved on the exterior only; and an amphora(?) body fragment of the same light red micaceous clay as **P1666**.[16]

A somewhat similar situation to that of Unit L21-2 (above) is to be found at Soudhes (Feature 18), on top of a N-S ridge some 2 km SE of Nichoria (Fig. 7-1). Just W of the modern highway to Petalidhi there is a similar earth platform, though without evident limestone blocks. On its N slope were found a number of well-preserved tear bottles (Pl. 7-8) and fragments of Megarian bowls. The tear bottles may come from a ritual deposit (*apothetis*) that was connected with a Hellenistic temple or shrine on the summit.

Painted roof tiles of both Classical and Hellenistic date were found at Ayios Nikolaos (Feature 50), near Karpofora. They might indicate the presence of a small shrine (Fig. 7-1). Black-glazed sherds from SE of Velika (Feature 112), either Classical or Hellenistic in date, may come from a farmstead. And similar sherds from Petalidhi (Feature 502), which is the site of the important Classical town of Korone, document earlier stages of the development of Korone into the regional administrative and commercial center it was to become in Hellenistic and Roman times.

To recapitulate, the meager evidence from Nichoria and its environs indicates that throughout Classical times the local population was still mainly rural, with farmsteads and small shrines scattered about the countryside. If there was a major town in the immediate vicinity, Petalidhi is the likeliest candidate. A notable feature that seems to date from Classical times is the reuse of earlier tombs for hero worship. Perhaps, as has already been suggested, such practices became symbolic of the Messenian "resistance movement." The cult of Messenian heroes would be an effective way of perpetuating local traditions in the face of occupation by the hated Spartans.

The Hellenistic Period (Fig. 7-1)

The evidence for the use of the ridge in the Hellenistic period is poor, but there are clear indications of increased activity in the environs. The latest pottery from the tholos does not extend beyond the mid-4th century B.C., and the miscellaneous sherds from Area IV and the podium in L21 STabc are also Classical in date. One C14 sample (71-Coul-17) from Area IV did yield a MASCA-corrected date of 320 ± 93 B.C. It has already been suggested (p. 336) that the wood in both C14 samples may have belonged to trees that were part of a cultivated orchard, and it can be assumed that the farming activities that took place on the ridge in Classical times continued into the Hellenistic period. It has also been assumed (p. 336) that the coins from Areas II and III belong to Late Classical times, but they are very badly worn and the possibility of a Hellenistic date cannot be entirely dismissed.

The only tomb that is known to have continued in use for cult worship is the Vathirema chamber tomb (Feature 1), with its Classical and Hellenistic pottery. Shrines continued to dot the countryside; the most important of these is the one at Soudhes, already mentioned (Feature 18), represented by a deposit of tear bottles and Megarian bowls. Elsewhere in the environs, Lukermann and Moody (*Nichoria* I, pp. 108-12) list eight sites, including Petalidhi (Feature 502), that produced as surface material good black-glazed Hellenistic pottery. Except for Petalidhi, which developed into a town of importance, the other seven sites could all represent farmsteads. If so, present evidence indicates that the rural and agricultural nature of activities on the ridge and environs continued into the Hellenistic period but that there was an increased tempo, no doubt owing to the nationalistic euphoria following the expulsion of the Spartans.

The Roman Period (Fig. 7-10)

There is considerably more evidence for activity in Roman times, especially in the environs. On the ridge itself, the finds continue to be rather meager. In the stomion of the tholos, we came upon the burial of a young adult female (see p. 399). Since no objects were placed with this burial, its date is uncertain. A Roman context would be consistent with the stratigraphy in the stomion, since the burial was probably made after the collapse of the tomb, which seems to have occurred soon after Late Classical times (see pp. 333, 334).

Elsewhere on the ridge, only Area IV produced a few stray finds from the Roman period. **P1674** (Fig. 7-6; Pl. 7-9) is the fragment of a bowl rim with relief decoration, perhaps belonging to part of a garland, and possibly from an Arretine bowl of the 1st century A.D. (Robinson 1959, p. 26, G38). **P1675** may be part of a Roman plaque. It is rectangular with red glaze on the exterior and relief decoration, perhaps representing part of a human leg. Its fragmentary nature makes it difficult to date. A lamp handle (**P1676**; Pl. 7-10) of oval shape and with incised lines on the top and bottom surfaces belongs to the second half of the 2nd or early 3rd century A.D. (Perlzweig 1961, p. 108, no. 454).[17] These stray finds at least suggest that the ridge continued to be cultivated in Roman times as late as the 3rd century A.D. Similar activities may well have continued without interruption until the late 5th century A.D., when a fine large storage building was constructed in Area IV (for detailed discussion, see pp. 364-68).

In the environs, on the other hand, evidence for habitation, baths, and cemeteries is quite abundant (Fig. 7-10). Perhaps the most impressive site is at Mandritsa (Feature 15) at the S foot of the Nichoria ridge on both sides of the Rizomilo-Karpofora road. Debris here is scattered over an area 300 m in diameter and includes walls with mortar, a kiln, tile, graves, and a fragment of relief sculpture. This appears to be the site of a large villa, located in a particularly pleasant and sheltered spot. Its proximity to the ridge strongly suggests that the cultivated fields and orchards on the ridge belonged to its owners. Similar debris scattered over a wide area was found at six other sites (Features 31, 33, 40, 131, 503, 519), indicating the presence of numerous villas in the environs. Lukermann and Moody (1978, pp. 108-12) list surface finds that can clearly be identified as Roman from ten additional sites, including Petalidhi, and possible Roman material from 14 others. Villas were scattered along or near the shore with their fields farther inland, as at Mandritsa. The fortifications, bath, and acqueduct at Petalidhi-Korone (Feature 502) and the numerous fragments of architecture, sculpture, mosaics, and inscriptions found there support other indications that it was an important regional center in Roman times (*MME* 1972, pp. 312-13).

Summary

When the evidence from both ridge and environs is considered together, the one will be found to complement the other to provide at least an outline of what was happening in the Nichoria subregion from Late Geometric until Late Roman times. There are no finds from the ridge belonging to the Archaic period and few in the environs. The paucity of finds perhaps indicates the presence of isolated farmsteads scattered over the countryside. That the ridge was cultivated in Classical times is made likely by the presence of what may be the foundations of a field house in Area IV and of a possible orchard, dated by two isolated charcoal deposits. During this period of Spartan occupation local traditions were evidently kept alive through hero worship which took place in tombs of earlier date. Most of the pottery associated with the cult in the Nichoria tholos is, as might be expected, of local manufacture; but several fine black-glazed vases find close parallels in vessels recovered at Olympia. This suggests that Spartan control of E Messenia was not totally rigid and that some outside contact was possible.

Virtually no Hellenistic material was recovered on the ridge but surface finds in the environs suggest increased activity, no doubt owing to liberation from Spartan control. In Roman times, the agricultural regime appears to have changed, with extensive landholdings replacing family farms. Large villas were scattered over the countryside, particularly along the coast. The fields on the Nichoria ridge may have belonged to one such villa at Mandritsa. Occasional finds from Area IV indicate that the ridge was cultivated at least until the beginning of the 3rd century A.D., and the existence of Unit IV-2 (late 5th/early 6th century A.D.) would argue for continued use up to the Slavic invasion (see p. 374).

W.D.E.C.

NOTES

1. From 1959 to 1968, MME conducted a surface survey of sites from all periods in Messenia (McDonald and Hope Simpson 1961, 1964, 1969). Description and references concerning these sites occur in Register B in *MME* 1972, pp. 310-21. Lazenby and Hope Simpson (*MME* 1972, pp. 81-99) have also reviewed the literary evidence on Messenia.

2. The results of a fairly intensive survey of the Nichoria environs were published by Lukermann and Moody (*Nichoria* I, pp. 78-112); they include an Appendix of specific features.

3. The Feature numbers designating sites are those used by Lukermann and Moody (*Nichoria* I, pp. 108-12). A group of sherds from this deposit was handed over to the Kalamata Museum (McDonald and Hope Simpson 1961, p. 246).

4. A definitive account of the LH stratigraphy of the tholos will be published in *Nichoria* II. For a preliminary report, see McDonald et al. 1975, pp. 73-79.

5. A similar situation was noted in Tholos IV at Pylos where the upper courses of the blocking wall were also thought to have been removed by looters who entered the tomb in antiquity (Blegen et al. 1973, p. 96).

6. References and bibliography are collected by Coldstream (1976, pp. 10, 11, and notes 24-26).

7. *Nestor* 4 (1974): 904.

8. For further parallels, see Sparkes 1968, pp. 3-15, esp. 14, 15.

9. For further parallels, see Kunze and Schleif 1939, p. 38, Fig. 24; Coldstream and Huxley 1972, Pl. 44, 14, 15 and Pl. 45, 39.

10. For further parallels, see Kunze and Schleif 1939, p. 53, Fig. 32 and Eilmann 1941, p. 56, Fig. 56.

11. The best of these is Agora P9499; cf. Sparkes and Talcott 1970, Pl. 38, no. 1111.

12. For another parallel, but with two handles, see Mallwitz and Schiering 1964, p. 233, Pl. 77, no. 1.

13. For another parallel, see Kunze and Schleif 1944, pp. 100, 101, Fig. 84.

14. For a good discussion of vases connected with the cult of the dead, see Oeconomos 1921, pp. 22-27.

15. The statue represented is that made by Agelades for the Messenians at Naupactus (BMC *Peloponnese*, p. 109, nos. 1, 2). Cf. Pausanias 4.33.2.

16. The clay of the possible mug fragments has been fired to

Munsell 7.5YR 8/6 reddish yellow and that of the possible amphora fragment to 2.5 YR 6/8 light red.

17. For additional parallels, see Broneer 1930, p. 90. Type. XXVII and Broneer 1977, Type XXV.

REFERENCES

Blegen C., et al. 1973. *The Palace of Nestor at Pylos in Western Messenia* III. Princeton.

Broneer, O. 1930. *Corinth* IV, 2: *Terracotta Lamps*. Cambridge, Mass.

———. 1977. *Isthmia* III: *Terracotta Lamps*. Princeton.

Coldstream, J. N. 1976. "Hero-Cults in the Age of Homer," *JHS* 96: 10, 11.

———, and Huxley, G. L. 1972. *Kythera: Excavations and Studies*. London.

Eilmann, R. 1941. "Olympiabericht III, Winter 1938/1939," *JDAI* 56:1-154.

Jones, J. E., Graham, A. J., and Sackett, L. H. 1973. "An Attic Country House below the Cave of Pan at Vari," *BSA* 68:355-452.

Kunze, E., and Schleif, H. 1939. *II. Bericht über die Ausgrabungen in Olympia, 1937-1938*. Berlin.

———. 1944. *IV. Bericht über die Ausgrabungen in Olympia, 1940-1941*. Berlin.

Lazenby, J. F., and Hope Simpson, R. 1972. "Graeco-Roman Times: Literary Tradition and Topographical Commentary." In McDonald and Rapp 1972, pp. 81-99.

Lukermann, F. E., and Moody, J. 1978. "Nichoria and Vicinity: Settlement and Circulation." In Rapp and Aschenbrenner 1978, pp. 78-107.

McDonald, W. A., and Hope Simpson, R. 1961. "Prehistoric Habitation in Southwestern Peloponnese," *AJA* 65:221-60.

———. 1964. "Further Explorations in Southwestern Peloponnese: 1962 1963," *AJA* 68:229-45.

———. 1969. "Further Explorations in Southwestern Peloponnese: 1964-1968," *AJA* 73:123-77.

———. 1972. "Archaeological Exploration." In McDonald and Rapp 1972, pp. 117-47.

McDonald, W. A., and Rapp, G., Jr., eds. 1972. *The Minnesota Messenia Expedition: Reconstructing a Bronze Age Regional Environment*. Minneapolis.

McDonald, W. A., et al. 1975. "Excavations at Nichoria in Messenia: 1972-1973," *Hesperia* 44:69-141.

Mallwitz, A., and Schiering, W. 1964. *Die Werkstatt des Phidias in Olympia (Olympische Forschugen V)*. Berlin.

MME 1972 = McDonald and Rapp 1972.

Nichoria I = Rapp and Aschenbrenner 1978.

Oeconomos, G. D. 1921. *De Profusionum Receptaculis Sepulchralibus*. Athens.

Perlzweig, J. 1961. *The Athenian Agora* VII: *Lamps of the Roman Period*. Princeton.

Rapp, G., Jr., and Aschenbrenner, S. E., eds. 1978. *Excavations at Nichoria in Southwest Greece* I: *Site, Environs, and Techniques*. Minneapolis.

Robinson, H. S. 1959. *The Athenian Agora* V: *Pottery of the Roman Period*. Princeton.

Shay, J. M., and Shay, C. T. 1978. "Modern Vegetation and Fossil Plant Remains." In Rapp and Aschenbrenner 1978, pp. 41-59.

Sloan, R. E., and Duncan, M. A. 1978. "Zooarchaeology of Nichoria." In Rapp and Aschenbrenner 1978, pp. 60-77.

Sparkes, B. A. 1968. "Black Perseus," *Die Antike Kunst* 11:3-15.

———, and Talcott, L. 1970. *The Athenian Agora* XII: *Black and Plain Pottery*. Princeton.

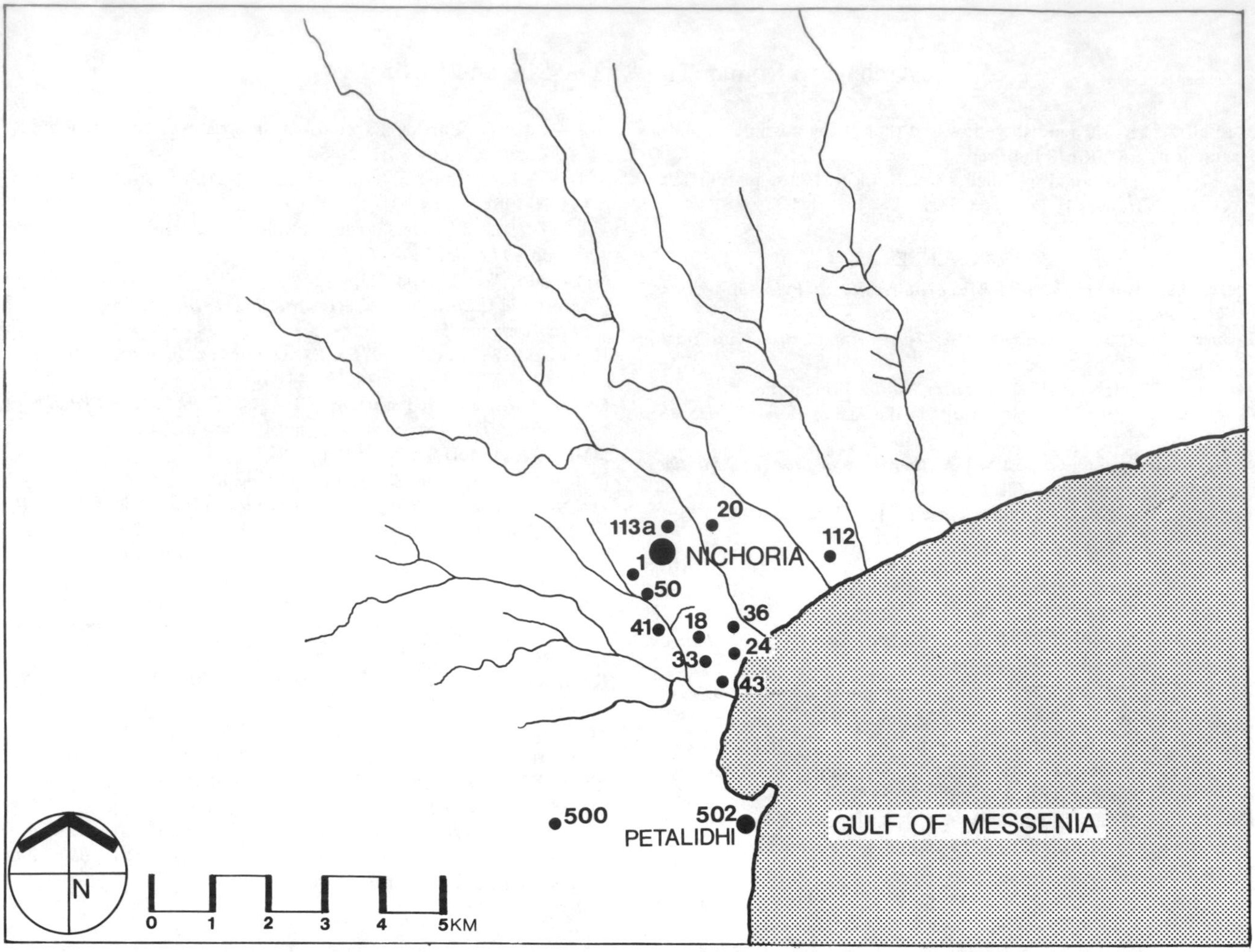

113a
20
112
NICHORIA
1
50
41
18
36
24
33
43
500
502
PETALIDHI
GULF OF MESSENIA
N
0
1
2
3
4
5KM

Figure 7-1. Classical and Hellenistic sites in environs

2100
7372
PODIUM: CLASSICAL TEMPLE?
0
2
4
8 METERS
N

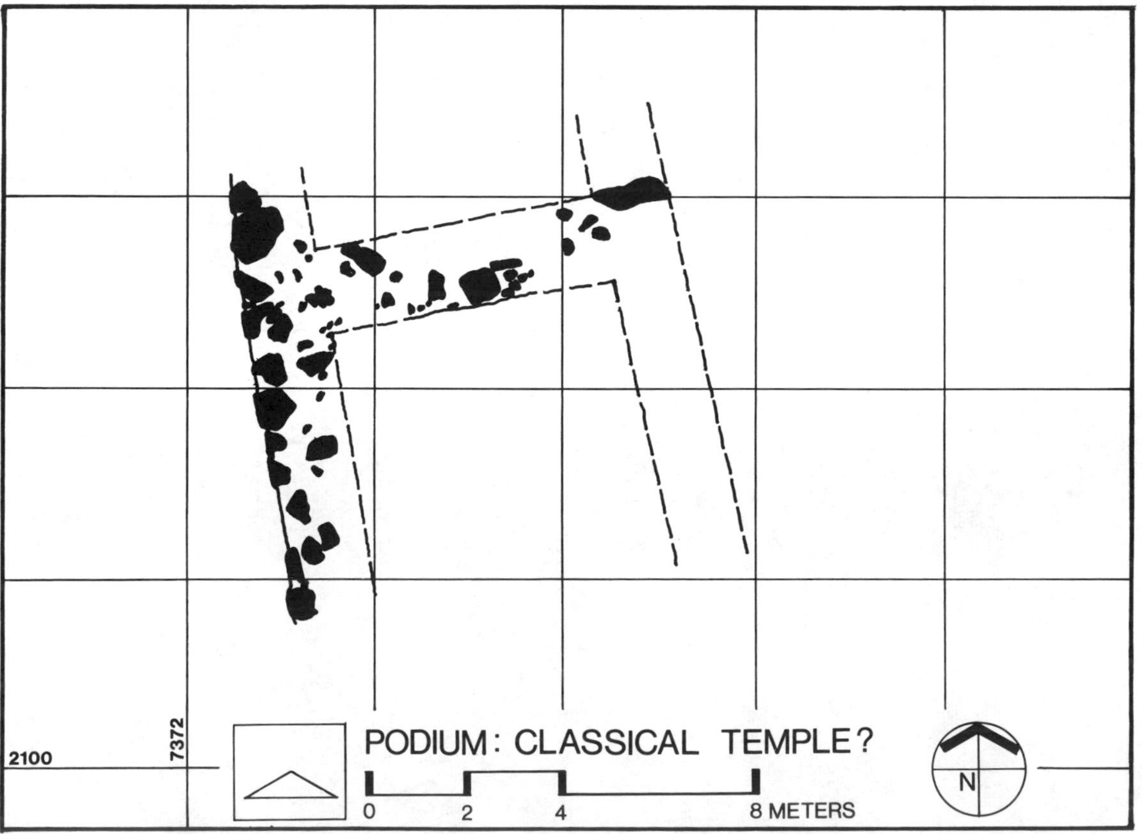

Figure 7-2. Podium: Classical temple (?)

FINE WARES

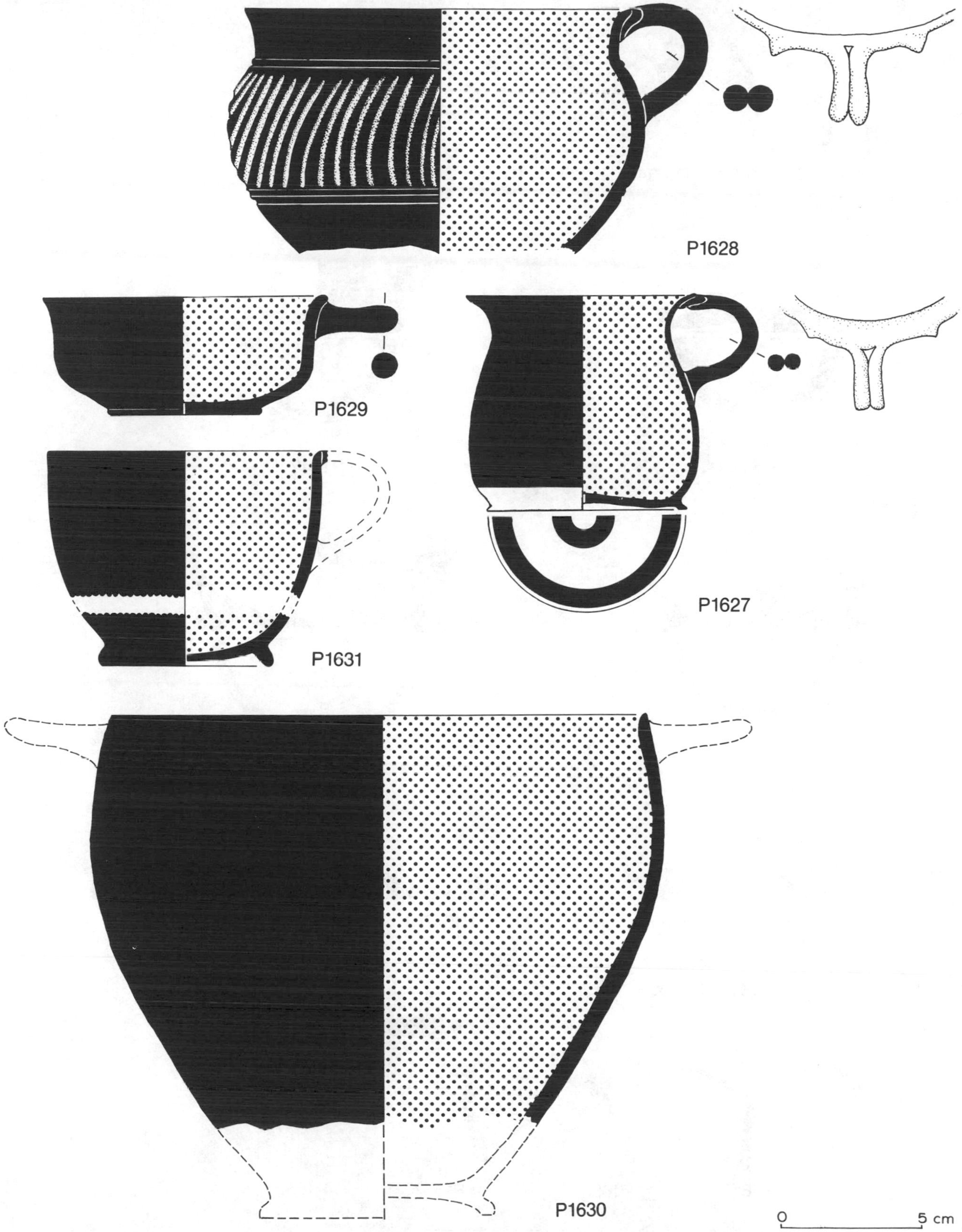

P1628

P1629

P1627

P1631

P1630

0 5 cm

Figure 7-3. Classical pottery from tholos

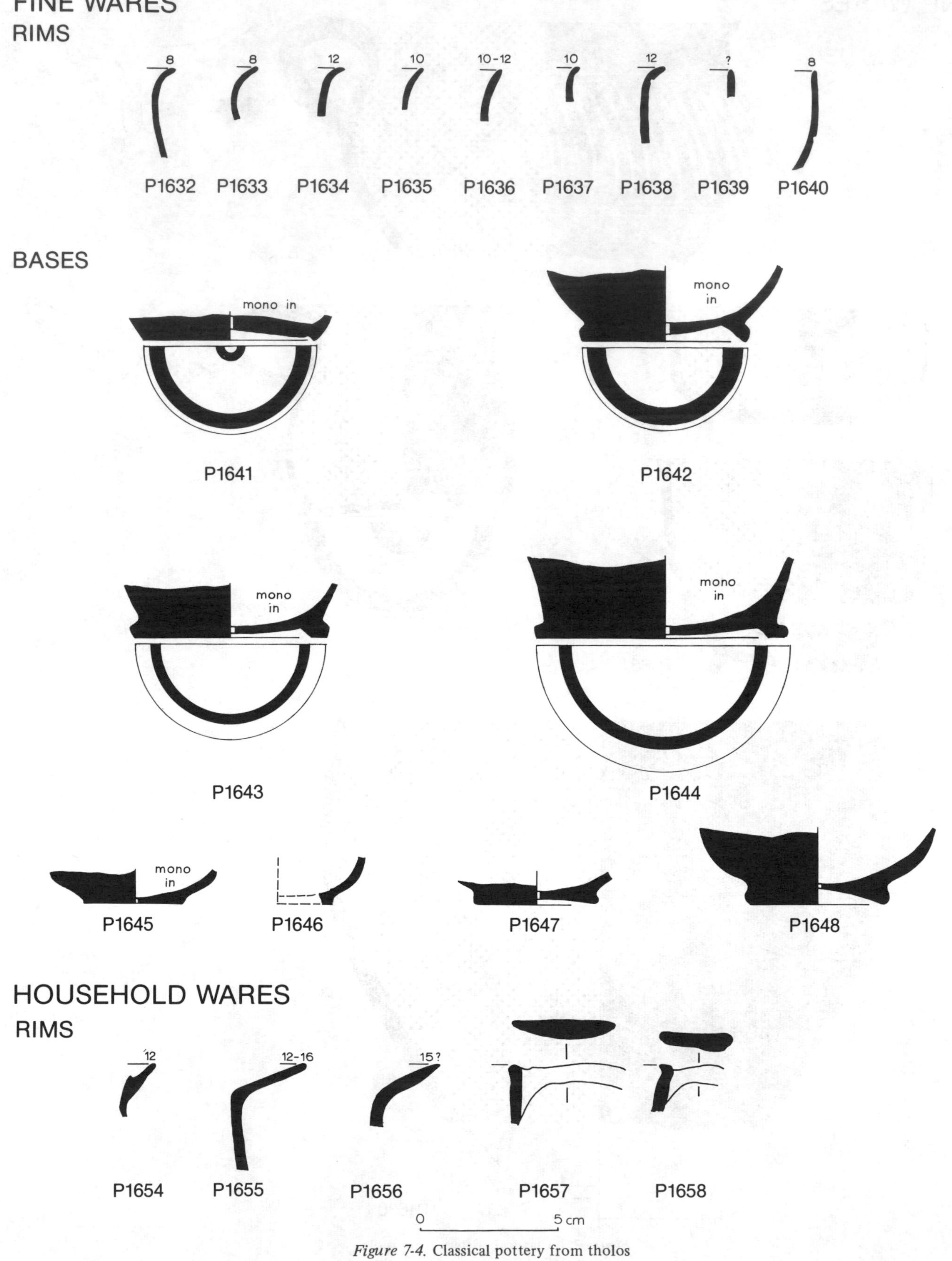

Figure 7-4. Classical pottery from tholos

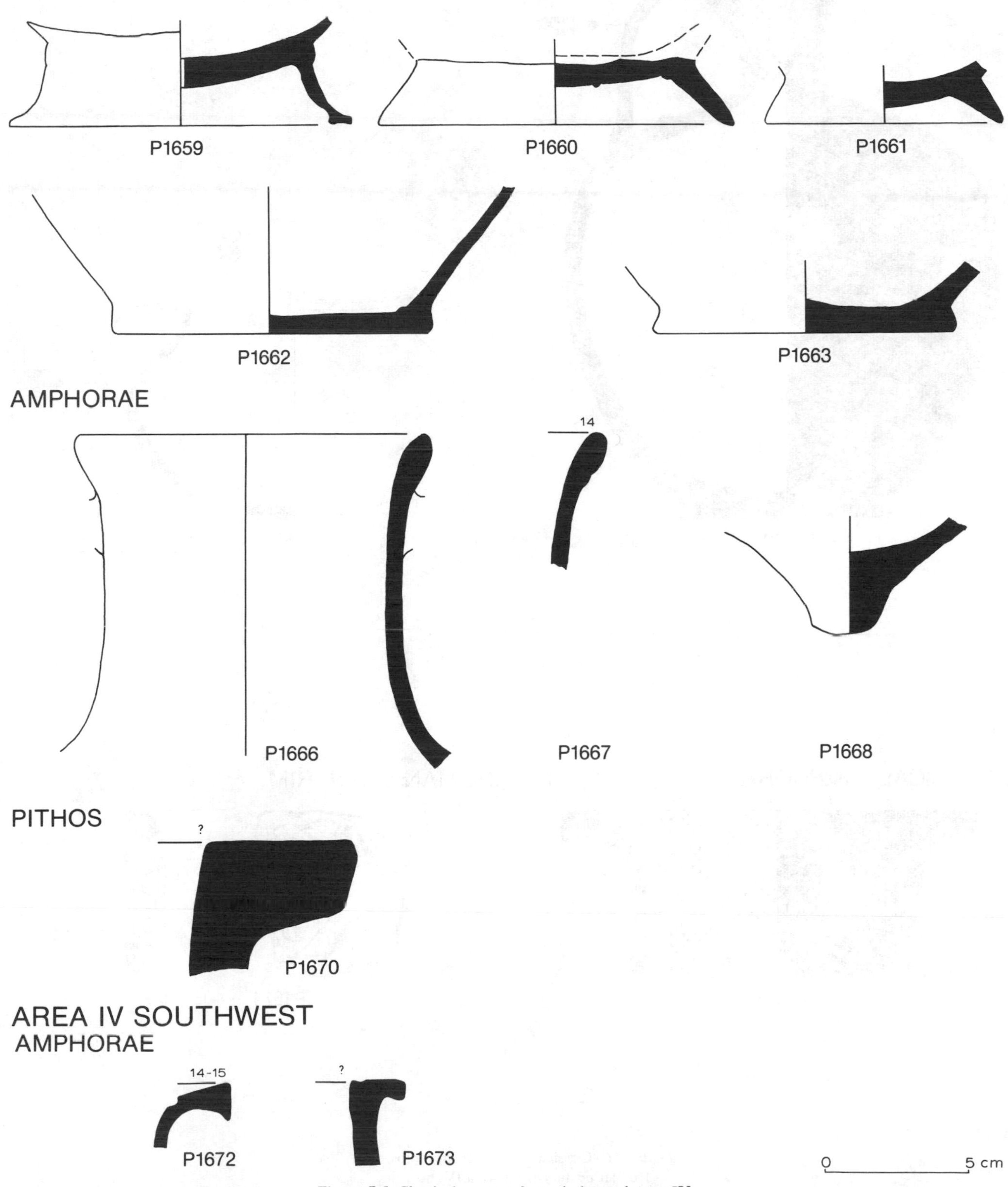

Figure 7-5. Classical pottery from tholos and Area IV

THOLOS

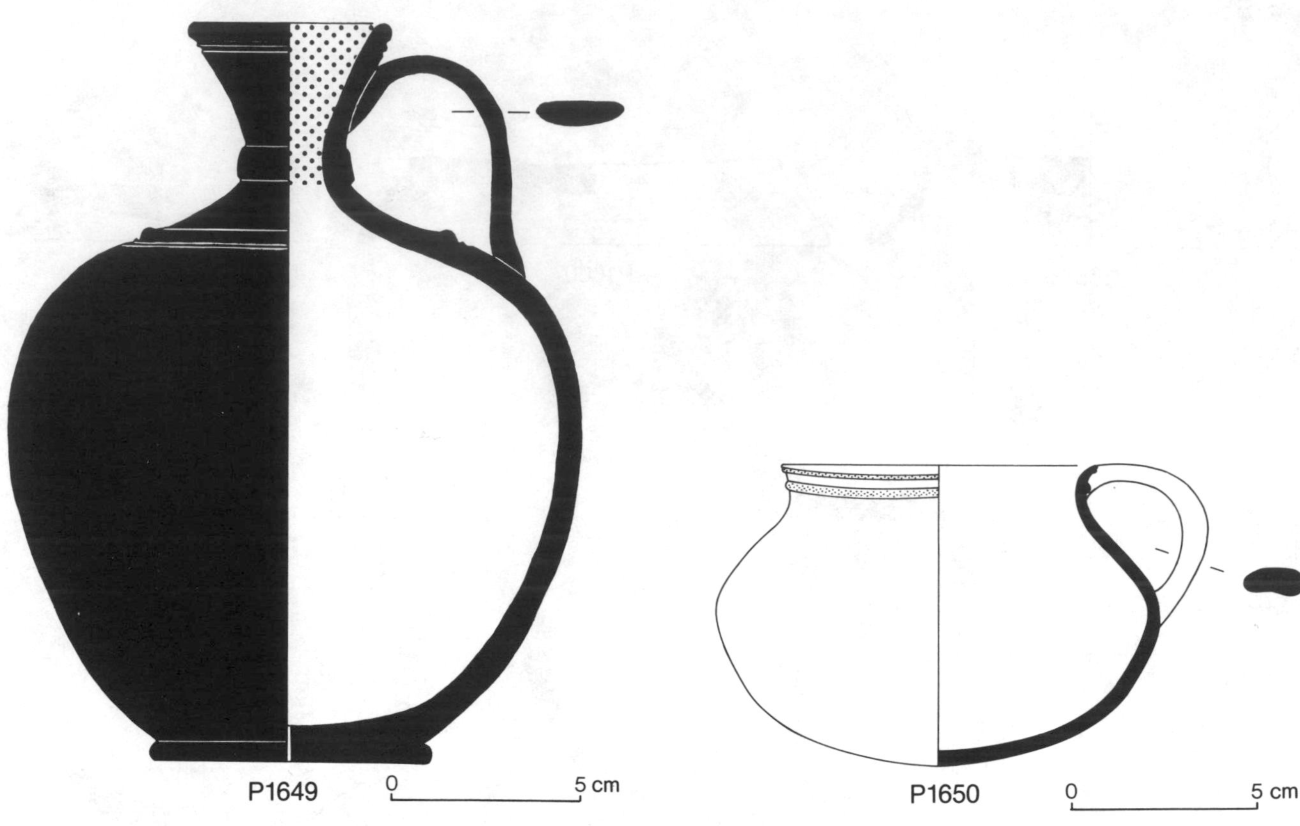

CLASSICAL AMPHORA

P1671

ROMAN BOWL RIM

P1674 FULL SIZE

0 5 cm

Figure 7-6. Classical pottery from tholos, top; Roman pottery from Area IV, bottom.

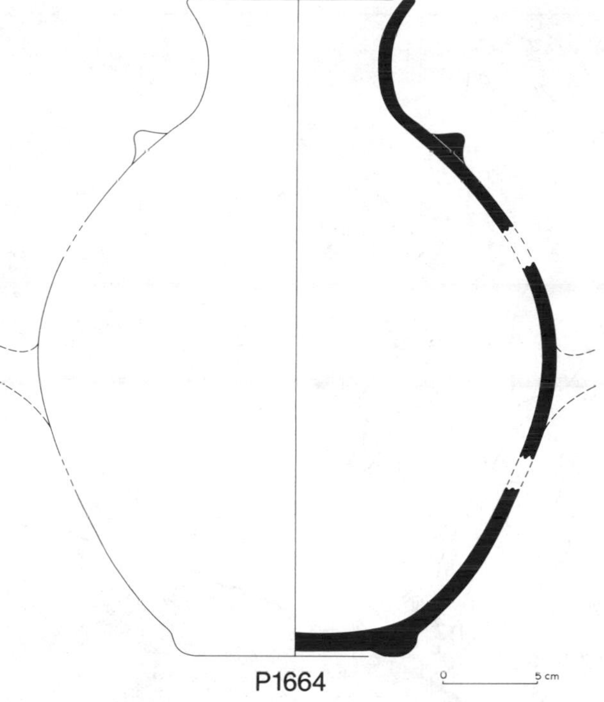

Figure 7-7. Classical amphora from tholos

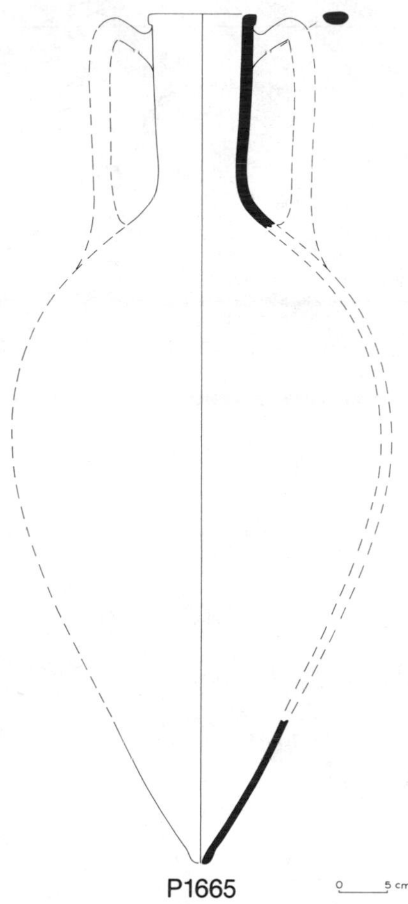

Figure 7-8. Classical amphora from tholos

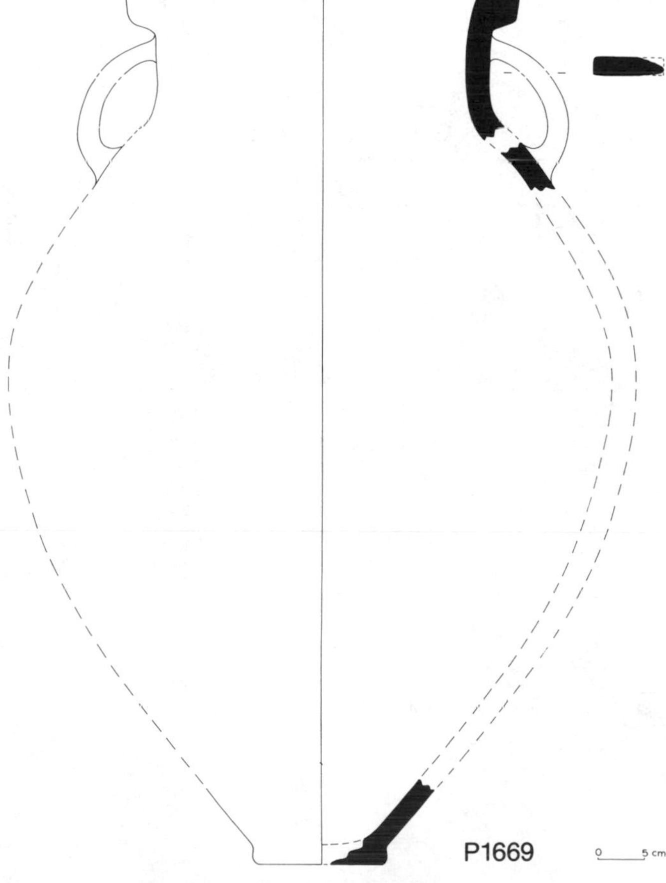

Figure 7-9. Classical pithos from tholos

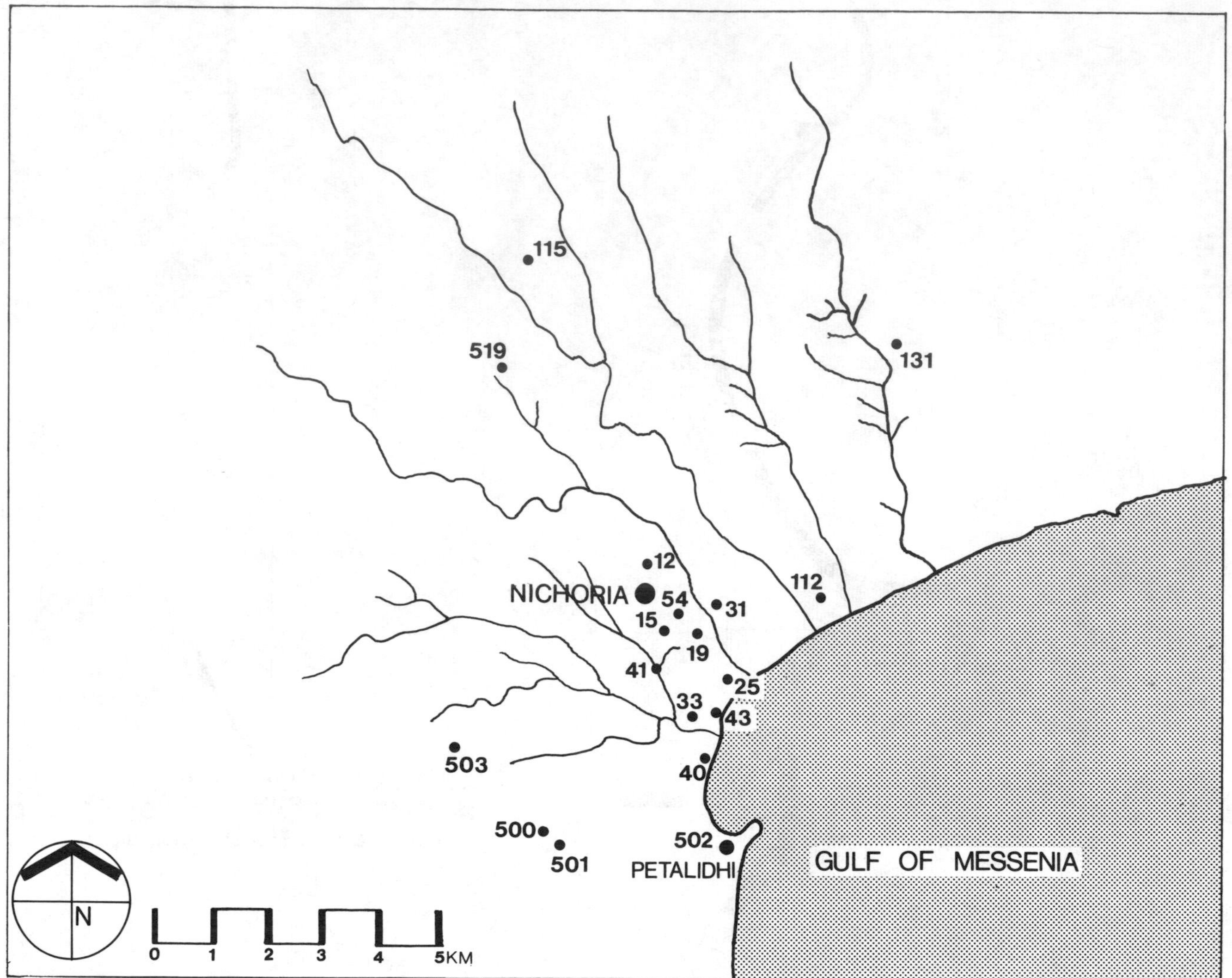

Figure 7-10. Roman sites in environs

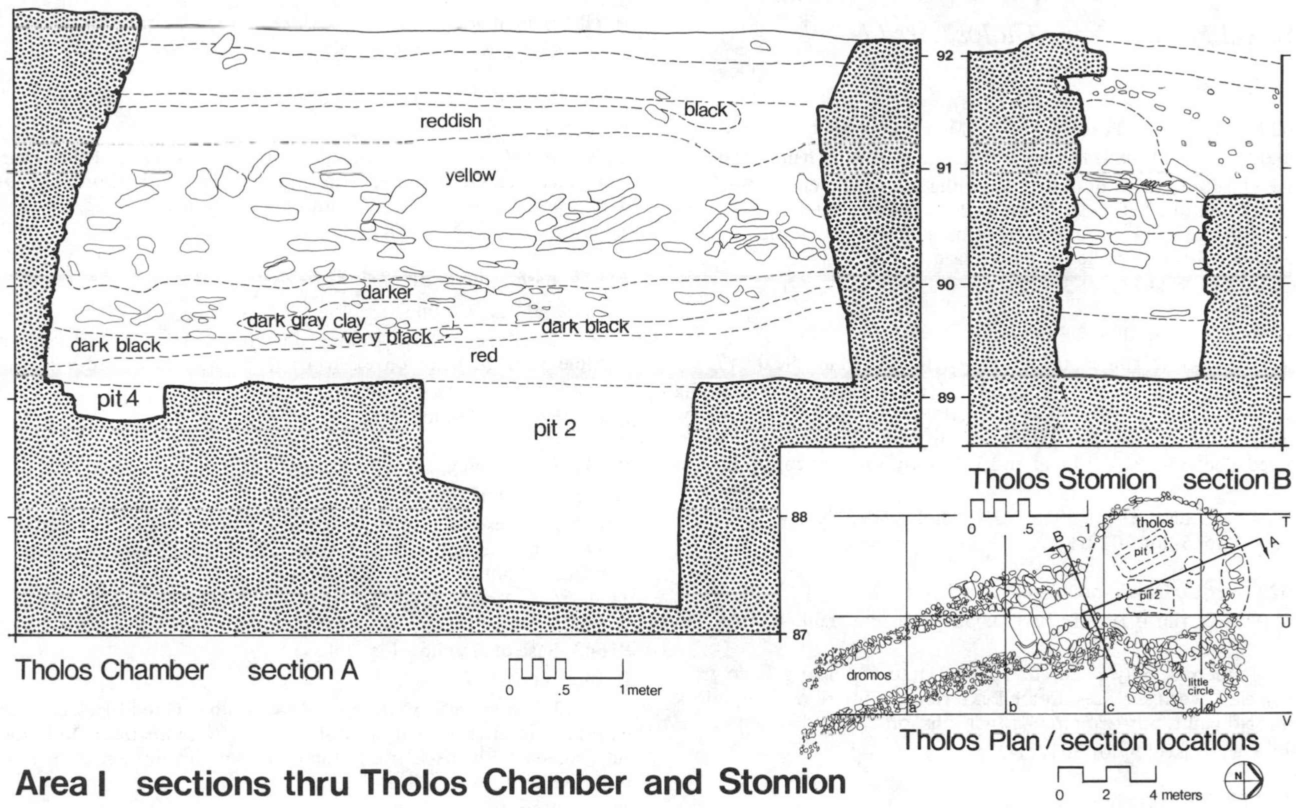

Figure 7-11.

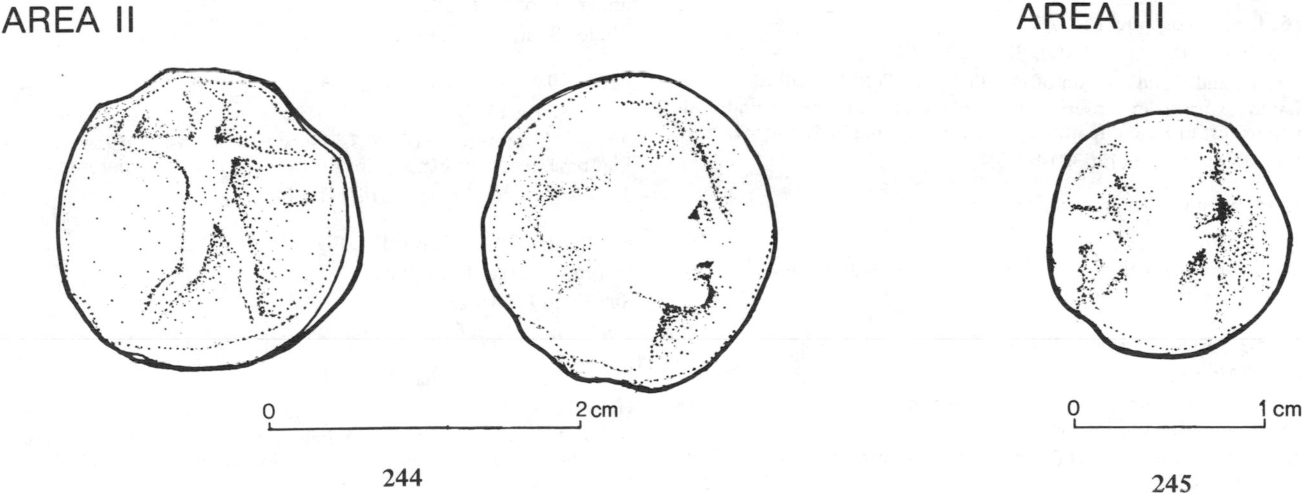

Figure 7-12. Classical coins from Areas II and III

CATALOG FOR ARCHAIC TO ROMAN TIMES

Classical Pottery from Tholos, Area I

Open Shapes

P1627 (TP = Tholos Pottery, No. 1). Mug. Fig. 7-3; Pl. 7-1.

H. 0.071. D. rim 0.088. D. base 0.071. Th. 0.003. W. handle 0.0125.

Black-glaze mug with double roll handle. Parts of rim and body restored. Munsell 5YR 7/6 reddish yellow. Coated exterior and interior. Very fine black glaze. Preserved band at base. Underside of base decorated with two circles of black glaze.

Tholos West, level 15, lot 3012/1-2.

P1628 (TP2). Mug. Fig. 7-3.

H. (pres.) 0.09. D. rim ca. 0.138. Th. ca. 0.004. W. handle 0.017.

Fluted mug with double roll handle. Missing base; one nonjoining frag. 5YR 7/6 reddish yellow. Coated exterior and interior. Color varying from red to black, unevenly applied. Fluting on shoulder, flanked above by raised band and below by two horizontal incised bands.

Tholos East, level 6, lot 3015/1-2N; Tholos West, level 4, lot 3007/1-2 and level 5, lot 3012/1-2.

P1629 (NP81). One-handled cup. Fig. 7-3; Pl. 7-2.

H. 0.043. D. rim 0.102. D. base 0.055. D. handle 0.008-0.0085. Th. 0.005.

Part of rim and belly restored. 10YR 7/1 to 6/1 light gray to gray. Flaky clay, worn surfaces. Coated exterior and interior. Washy black paint. No paint, but two circular incisions, on underside of base.

Tholos West, level 5, lot 3012/1-2.

P1630 (TP20). Skyphos. Fig. 7-3.

H. (pres.) 0.15. D. rim 0.207. Th. ca. 0.005.

Restored from many fragments; missing base and handles. Surface scratched in places. 5YR 7/6 reddish yellow. Coated exterior and interior. Black glaze, fired in places to blue-brown tinge.

Tholos East, level 5, lot 3013/1-2; Tholos West, level 4, lot 3007/1-2 and level 5, lots 3012/1-2, 3014/1-3N.

P1631. Skyphos-mug. Fig. 7-3.

H. ca. 0.078. D. rim ca. 0.098. D. base 0.061.

Missing handle and portion of middle belly. 5YR 7/6 reddish yellow. Coated exterior and interior. Plain black glaze. Glaze on underside of foot; rest of base unpainted. Seven nonjoining body fragments.

Tholos West, level 6, lot 3014/1-3N.

P1632, P1633. Two mug rims. Fig. 7-4.

D. ca. 0.08.

5YR 7/6 reddish yellow. Good black glaze on exterior and interior.

Tholos East, level 6, lot 3015/1-2N.

P1634-37. Four mug rims. Fig. 7-4.

D. ca. 0.10-0.12.

5YR 7/6 reddish yellow. Fired to brown in places on exterior. Black glaze on exterior and interior.

P1634: Tholos West, level 6, lot 3014/1-3N. **P1635-37:** Tholos East, level 6, lot 3021/13.

P1638 Rim of fluted mug(?) Fig. 7-4,

H. (pres.) 0.03. D. ca. 0.12.

5YR 7/6 reddish yellow. Black glaze on exterior and interior. Fired to brown in places on exterior. Horizontal incision under rim. Two nonjoining fragments.

Tholos East, level 6, lot 3015/1-2N.

P1639. Rim frag. of skyphos. Fig. 7-4.

H. (pres.) 0.012.

10YR 7/1 light gray. Good black glaze on exterior and interior.

Tholos East, level 6, lot 3015/1-2N.

P1640. Rim frag. of skyphos-mug. Fig. 7-4.

H. (pres.) 0.036. D. rim ca. 0.08.

5YR 7/6 reddish yellow. Flaky clay, worn surfaces. Paint varies from black to brown on exterior and interior. Carination at shoulder(?); horizontal incision at point of carination.

Tholos East, level 5, lot 3013/1-2.

P1641. Base of mug. Fig. 7-4; Pl. 7-3.

H. (pres.) 0.01. D. 0.063.

5YR 7/6 reddish yellow. Coated on interior with fine black glaze; possible reserved band on exterior. Underside decorated with two circles of black paint. Similar to base of **P1627**.

Tholos East, level 6, lot 3021/1S.

P1642. Base of mug. Fig. 7-4; Pl. 7-4.

H. 0.028. D. 0.061.

About 1/5 preserved. 5YR 7/6 reddish yellow. Good black glaze on exterior and interior. Glaze on underside of foot, rest of underside unpainted. Similar to base of **P1631**.

Tholos East, level 6, lot 3021/1S.

P1643. Base of skyphos. Fig. 7-4.

H. (pres.) 0.019. D. 0.07.

About 2/3 preserved. 5YR 7/6 reddish yellow. Good black glaze on exterior and interior. Ringed foot. Base of foot unpainted, but inner side coated with black glaze. Light brown slip on central part of underside.

Tholos West, level 6, lot 3014/1-3N.

P1644. Base of skyphos. Fig. 7-4.

H. (pres.) 0.03. D. 0.091.

About 1/2 preserved. 5YR 7/6 reddish yellow. Good black glaze on exterior and interior. Ringed foot. Base of foot unpainted, but inner side coated with black glaze. Light brown slip on central part of underside of base.

Tholos West, level 6, lot 3014/1-3N.

P1645. Base of saltcellar. Fig. 7-4.

H. (pres.) 0.015. D. 0.036.

About 1/2 preserved. 10YR 7/3 very pale brown. Hard, gritty clay. Flat base. Frags. of black paint preserved on exterior and interior.

Tholos West, level 6, lot 3014/1-3N.

P1646. Base frag. of saltcellar. Fig. 7-4.

H. (pres.) 0.016. D. ca. 0.04.

Similar to **P1645** above.

Tholos East, level 6, lot 3015/1-2N.

P1647. Base of saltcellar. Fig. 7-4.

H. 0.012. D. ca. 0.04.

About 1/5 preserved. 5YR 6/8 light red. Slightly conical. Frags. of good brown glaze preserved on exterior, interior, and underside of base.

Tholos West, level 6, lot 3014/1-3N.

P1648. Base of saltcellar. Fig. 7-4.

H. (pres.) 0.021. D. 0.05.

About 1/2 preserved. 10YR 7/1 light gray. Flaky clay, worn surfaces. Semi-conical foot. Frags. of black paint preserved on exterior and interior; none on underside of base.

Tholos East, level 6, lot 3015/1-2N.

Closed Shapes

P1649 (TP10). Lekythos. Fig. 7-6; Pl. 7-4.

H. 0.197. D. rim 0.056. D. neck 0.0285. D. belly ca. 0.14. D. base 0.076. W. handle 0.0225.

5YR 7/6 reddish yellow. Parts of lip, shoulder, lower belly, and base restored. Black glaze fired to brown in places on belly; black glaze on interior of neck. Wide drip band at base of neck. Three shallow horizontal incisions under rim. Raised band and two incisions on shoulder.

Tholos East, level 6, lot 3015/1-2N; Tholos West, level 5, lot 3012/1-2 and level 6, lot 3014/1-3N, 3016/1-2S.

Coarse Ware

P1650. Chytra. Fig. 7-6.

H. 0.08. D. rim ca. 0.082.

About 1/2 preserved. 2.5YR 6/8 light red to 5YR 4/1 dark gray at lower belly. Flaky, gritty clay. No evidence of slip. Wheel ridging on interior. Two horizontal raised bands on exterior below rim. One handle.

Tholos East, level 6, lots 3015/1-2N, 3021/1S.

P1651, P1652. Two chytra rims.

D. ca. 0.13.

5YR 6/8 light red. Flaky, gritty clay. Shape similar to **P1650** above. No bands or incisions below rim.

Tholos East, level 6, lot 3021/1S.

P1653. Rim and handle frag. of chytra.

5YR 6/8 light red. Flaky, gritty clay. Handle slightly misfired; otherwise shape like **P1650** above.

Tholos East, level 6, lot 3015/1-2N.

P1654. Rim of lopas. Fig. 7-4.

H. (pres.) 0.02. D. ca. 0.12 (uneven).

2.5YR 6/8 light red. Burned in places on exterior. Falange on interior. Eight nonjoining body frags.

Tholos East, level 4, lot 3011/1.

P1655. Rim of cooking pot. Fig. 7-4.

H. (pres.) 0.038. D. ca. 0.15.

2.5YR 6/8 light red. Flaky, gritty clay. Long, offset rim.

Tholos East, level 6, lot 3021/1S.

P1656. Rim of cooking pot. Fig. 7-4.

H. (pres.) 0.022. D. ca. 0.15.

7.5YR 7/4 pink. Shape similar to **P1655** above. About 75 nonjoining small body frags.

Tholos East and Tholos West, level 6, lots 3015/1-2N, 3021/1S, 3014/1-3N, 3016/1-2S.

P1657, P1658. Handle and rim frags. of cooking pots with lid. Fig. 7-4.

H. (pres.) 0.02. W. handle 0.038.

2.5YR 6/8 light red. Slight groove at junction of rim and handle for placement of lid.

P1657: Tholos West, level 5, lot 3012/1-2. **P1658**: Tholos East, level 6, lot 3021/1S.

P1659. Base of lekane. Fig. 7-5.

H. 0.04. D. 0.122.

5YR 7/6 to 7/8 reddish yellow. Well-fired hard clay. High ringed foot. Spiral grooving on interior. Circular incisions on underside of base. Ornate foot; white slip.

Tholos East, level 5, lot 3013/1-2.

P1660. Base of lekane. Fig. 7-5.

H. 0.03. D. 0.126.

5YR 7/6 reddish yellow. Coarse, gritty clay. Three joining frags. Circular incisions and wheel ridging on underside of base. Ringed foot.

Tholos West, level 5, lot 3012/1-2.

P1661. Base of lekane. Fig. 7-5.

H. 0.022. D. 0.085.

5YR 7/6 reddish yellow. Flaky clay, worn surfaces. Ringed foot.

Tholos West, level 5, lot 3012/1-2.

P1662. Base of lekane(?) Fig. 7-5.

H. 0.051. D. 0.11.

2.5YR 6/8 light red. Two joining frags. Coarse, gritty clay. Wheel ridging on interior. Flat base.

Tholos West, level 4, lot 3007/1-2.

P1663. Base of lekane(?) Fig. 7-5.

H. 0.025. D. 0.105.

5YR 7/6 reddish yellow. 1/2 of exterior slightly burned. Five nonjoining body frags. Hub in center of interior. Flat base.

Tholos West, level 5, lot 3012/1-2.

P1664. Amphora. Fig. 7-7.

H. ca. 0.34. D. rim 0.115. D. base 0.12.

Reconstructed from rim and neck frag., shoulder frag. with nipple, belly frag., and large base – all nonjoining. Missing handles. On exterior, color varies from predominant 7.5R N3/0 very dark gray to 10R 6/8 light red on lower belly and base. On interior, color varies from 2.5Y 7/4 pale yellow to 2.5Y 7/2 light gray. Flaky texture on interior, but hard and gritty on exterior. Light brown slip on exterior. Wheel ridging on interior. Nipple on either side of shoulder. One nipple completely preserved; other broken at tip.

Tholos West, level 6, lots 3014/1-3N, 3016/1-2S.

P1665. Amphora. Fig. 7-8.

H. (est.) 0.98. Rim and neck frag: H. 0.115. D. rim 0.11. Av. D. neck 0.10. Lower belly and toe: H. 0.155. Th. 0.007-0.008.

40 small nonjoining body frags. Reconstructed from rim and neck (preserved) and toe with lower belly. One handle preserved to point where it begins to turn downward toward shoulder; stump of other on neck. Preserved rim and neck 5Y 8/3 pale yellow. Nonjoining body frags. burned to 10YR 7/1 light gray. Lower belly and toe 5YR 7/6 reddish yellow with pinkish core. Flaky, gritty clay with small inclusions. Wheel ridging on interior. Center of toe pierced through.

Tholos East and West, levels 4-6, and level 5 of the stomion, lots 3011/1, 3020/1, 3012/1-2, 3016/1-2S, 4234.

P1666. Rim and neck of amphora. Fig. 7-5.

H. 0.116. D. rim 0.125. Av. D. neck 0.105.

16 nonjoining body frags. 2.5YR 6/8 light red. Gritty, micaceous clay. Wheel ridging on exterior and interior. Handle stumps preserved below rim on neck.

Tholos West, levels 5, 6, lots 3012/1-2, 3016/1-2S.

P1667. Rim frag. of amphora. Fig. 7-5.

H. 0.047. D. rim ca. 0.14

Ten nonjoining small body frags. 5YR 7/6 reddish yellow. Gritty, micaceous clay, burned gray in places on exterior. Shape of rim similar to that of **P1666** above.

Tholos East, level 6, lot 3015/1-2N.

P1668. Amphora toe. Fig. 7-5.

H. 0.04.

2.5YR 6/8 light red. Surfaces badly corroded. Short button toe.

Tholos West, level 6, lot 3014/1-3N.

P1669. Pithos. Fig. 7-9.

H. (est.) 0.93. Rim, neck, handle frag.: H. 0.15. D. rim 0.37. W. handle 0.075. Base: H. 0.09. D. 0.14.

Reconstructed from rim, neck, handle frag., and base. One handle almost completely preserved; other in two frags. About 2/3 of rim and 1/2 of base preserved. Part of shoulder missing. About 100 widely scattered nonjoining body frags. 5YR 7/8 reddish yellow varying to 5YR 7/6 reddish yellow in places.

Tholos East and West, levels 4-6, lots 3011/1, 3013/1-2, 3015/1-2N, 3012/1S, 3007/1-2, 3012/1-2, 3014/1-3N.

P1670. Rim frag. of pithos. Fig. 7-5.

H. 0.045. D. ca. 0.40.

2.5YR 6/8 light red. Coarse, gritty clay with inclusions. Seven nonjoining body frags.

Tholos West, level 4, lot 3007/1-2.

Classical Pottery from Area IVSW (Sherds Associated with Walls Q and U)

P1671 (NP107). Rim and neck frag. of neck amphora. Fig. 7-6.

H. 0.062. D. rim ca. 0.145. D. neck 0.105. Th. neck ca. 0.006.

About 1/3 preserved. Eight joining frags. and one nonjoining frag. 2.5YR 6/8 light red. Flaky clay, worn surfaces. Good, smooth, streaky black-brown glaze preserved in portions of exterior and interior of neck.

L23 Qfg/Rfg baulk, level 2, lot 4082/2.

P1672. Rim frag. of neck amphora. Fig. 7-5.

H. 0.02. D. ca. 0.14-0.15.

5YR 7/6 reddish yellow. Patches of good black glaze preserved on exterior and interior.

L23 Qfg/Rfg baulk, level 2, lot 4082/2.

P1673. Rim frag. of neck amphora. Fig. 7-5.

H. 0.03. D. ca. 0.15.

Color varies from 2.5YR 6/8 light red to 5YR 7/6 reddish yellow. Good black glaze preserved on exterior; none on interior. Two joining frags.

L23 Qfg, level 7, lot 781S.

In addition to the above sherds, some eight noninventoried body frags. were found in L23 Qfg, level 5, lots 771, 774, 779-80 and L23 Qfg, level 6a, lot 776. 2.5 YR-6/8 light red with frags. of black glaze preserved on exterior and interior. Some six noninventoried body sherds with the same Munsell color and preserved black glaze were found in levels 1 and 2 of L23 Vkl in Area IVNE.

Classical Coins

244 (N246). Bronze coin. Fig. 7-12; Pl. 7-5.

Wt. 6.71 gr. D. 0.02 m.

Quite worn on both faces.
Obverse: Head of bearded male (Zeus?) r.
Reverse: Zeus Ithomatas striding r., holding thunderbolt in r. hand.

K25 Gbc, level 3, lot 870.

245 (N734). Bronze coin. Fig. 7-12.

Wt. 1.455 gr. D. 0.013 m.

Obverse: Bearded head r., wreathed(?)
Reverse: Two striding figures(?)

K25 Ue, level 1, lot 1431.

Roman Finds from Area IV

P1674. Frag. of bowl rim. Fig. 7-6; Pl. 7-9.

H. 0.027. W. 0.030. Th. 0.007.

2/5YR 6/8 light red. Very fine, soft clay. No traces of paint preserved. Relief decoration may represent part f a garland. Probably 1st century A.D. Originally cataloged as **N944.**

L23 Tkl/Ukl baulk, level 1, lot 3390/1-2.

P1675 Frag. of plaque(?)

H. 0.037. W. 0.03. Th. 0.005.

5YR 8/4 pink. Rectangular frag. with relief decoration; perhaps representing part of human leg. Red glaze on exterior. 1st century A.D.(?) Originally cataloged as **N1876.**

L23 Smn/Tmn baulk, level 2, lot 4501/2.

P1676 Lamp handle. Pl. 7-10.

L. 0.033. H. 0.025. D. hole in handle 0.0075.

5YR 7/6 reddish yellow. Pair of incised lines on top and bottom surfaces. Second half of 2nd century A.D. to early 3rd century A.D. Originally cataloged as **N1954.**

L23 Rab, level 1, lot 4569.

III. The Byzantine Occupation

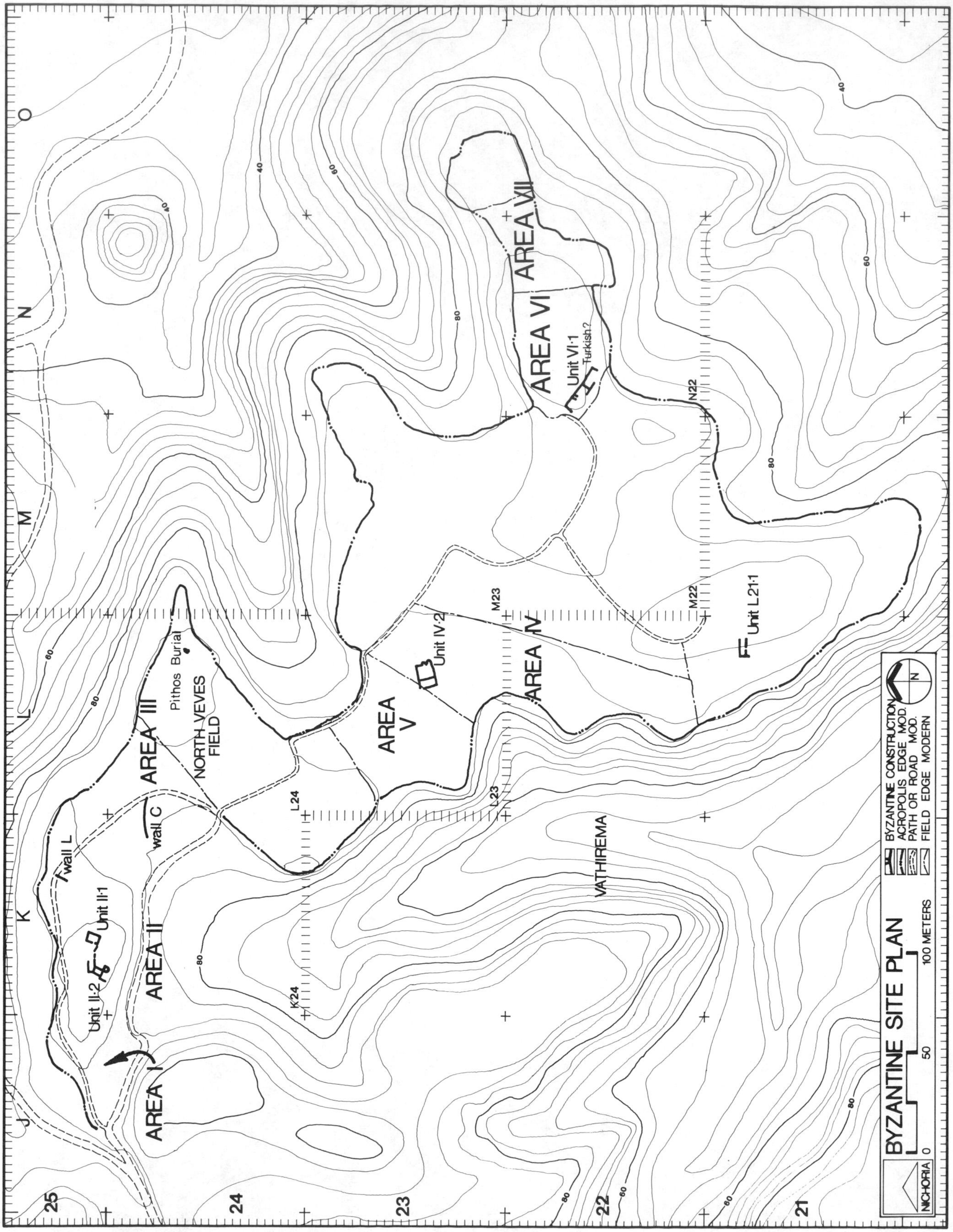
BYZANTINE SITE PLAN
NICHORIA
0
50
100 METERS
BYZANTINE CONSTRUCTION
ACROPOLIS EDGE MOD.
PATH OR ROAD MOD.
FIELD EDGE MODERN
AREA I
AREA II
AREA III
AREA IV
AREA V
AREA VI
AREA VII
Unit II·1
Unit II·2
wall L
wall C
Pithos Burial
NORTH VEVES FIELD
Unit IV·2
Unit VI·1
Turkish?
Unit L21·1
VATHIREMA
K24
L24
L23
M23
M22
N22
J
K
L
M
N
O
25
24
23
22
21
40
60
80

Figure 8-1

8

Introduction

by

John Rosser and William A. McDonald

The Byzantine Remains on the Ridge (Fig. 8-1)

The Byzantine occupancy is confined to the Late Roman/ Early Byzantine and to the Middle Byzantine periods. The former period is represented by a sturdy 9.70 X 12.13 m building in Area IV, designated Unit IV-2, Phases 1 and 2. Its ruins were discovered by William Donovan in 1972. Initially it was thought to be connected with the chapel which we now know was built over the SE corner of its ruins no later than the 12th and possibly as early as the 10th century. The chapel was therefore designated Unit IV-2, Phases 3 and 4.

The evidence for dating Phase 2 of Unit IV-2 is a single B-i type storage amphora (**P1756**) found on the floor under Phase 2 destruction debris. The amphora can be dated to ca. 460-520, which provides an approximate date for the use and abandonment of the Phase 2 building. The dates of the initial construction (Phase 1) and its enlargement (Phase 2) cannot be more closely determined.

The Middle Byzantine period is represented by Units II-1 and II-2 in Area II, firmly dated to the late 10th/early 11th century, and by the above-mentioned chapel, Unit IV-2, Phases 3 and 4, in Area IV. The use of the chapel is dated securely to the 12th century; it may have been built considerably earlier by the inhabitants of Area II.

Briefly, the history of the excavation of these structures is as follows. The foundations of Unit II-1 were partially visible above ground even before excavation. In 1969 Donovan's trial trench K25-I in grid K25 Jcd of Area II intersected its NW corner. In 1970 excavation of the building down to floor level was undertaken by Mark Ketcham, Donovan's assistant. Ketcham also worked in K25 Gbc, between the pair of fragmentary walls that run E-W and may originally have connected Unit II-1 with a larger building (Unit II-2) to the west. Donovan excavated the latter in 1970 and recovered some diagnostic glazed sherds (**P1677-79**) along with an important coin (**501**), a bronze issue of Basil II (976-1025). A. H. S. Megaw kindly identified both the glazed sherds and the coin (Megaw 1970).

In 1971 the excavation of Unit II-1 was completed, and its walls were dismantled in order to examine the Mycenaean building (Unit II-3) directly beneath it. The only new Byzantine remains discovered in Area II were those of a refuse dump in K24 Iy/K25 Ia, where quantities of iron slag and some glass fragments (including **551**, **552**) were found. Radiocarbon analysis provided confirmation of the late 10th/early 11th century date for the Middle Byzantine occupation (McDonald 1972, pp. 242-44; *Nichoria* I, Table 1-3, p. 5).

In 1972 Donovan turned his attention to Area IV, and in grids L23 PQRSkl and RSj he excavated all but the SW corner of Unit IV-2. The ruins were at first assumed to belong to a single complex, comprising a chapel and subsidiary rooms. In that year Rosser was invited to join the Nichoria staff and to take responsibility for publishing all the Byzantine pottery and small finds, as well as the architecture in Area IV.

In 1973 Rosser excavated the remaining SW corner of Unit IV-2 and began to sort out its various building stages. Angelos Choremis gave Rosser permission to publish the finds from graves that Choremis had excavated in 1969 on the hill of Trypetorachi, immediately SE of the Nichoria ridge (Pl. 8-2).

In 1974, the first of two study seasons, Rosser completed his analysis of the building phases of Unit IV-2 and compared notes on the Byzantine material with Donovan. They were aided by a visit from A. H. S. Megaw, who offered the suggestion that the deposit of pottery from the chapel narthex belonged to a floor packing that included material from the debris of a fire that destroyed part of the Phase 3 roof. John Hayes's identification of the B-i amphora recovered from the floor of the Phase 2 building provided an approximate *terminus post quem* for its abandonment (Hayes 1974). The task of sorting out the various Byzantine tile types from Areas II and IV was also undertaken.

In 1975 Rosser spent several weeks examining Byzantine pottery at Sparta, Mistra, Nauplion, Chora, Corinth, and Athens. Correspondence with Gladys Davidson Weinberg (1975a, 1975b) helped significantly in the study of the Byzantine glass fragments.[1]

Nichoria's Environs in the Byzantine Period

Basic to MME's strategy in the region of Messenia and in the Nichoria environs is the surface survey; and it is to the survey results that we now turn. To avoid a great deal of needless repetition, readers are referred to Pocket Map 1, Table 7-1, and to the Register of Archaeological Features (pp. 108-12) in *Nichoria* I where the known Byzantine features are documented. In 1975 some of the Roman and Byzantine remains in the environs were reviewed by Rosser, Howell, Aschenbrenner, and a visitor, Timothy Gregory. Gregory also helped to identify some of the pottery already collected. The following remarks constitute only additional observations (and in a few cases modifications or corrections) to the data presented by Lukermann and Moody in *Nichoria* I.

LATE ROMAN/EARLY BYZANTINE FEATURES (FIG. 1-2)

Almost half (34 of 72) of the features located and briefly described in *Nichoria* I are labeled "Roman" or "Roman?" A revisitation in 1975 to eight of the sites so identified showed that four (nos. 15, 19, 21, 31) continued in use into the Late Roman/Early Byzantine period. When we include the sites identified as "Roman and later" in *Nichoria* I, two inferences can be drawn. First, it is probable that much of the "Roman" occupation in the Nichoria environs lasted down into the 6th century, i.e., until the period of the Slavic invasions. Clearly, the well-documented Roman habit of establishing large country estates in attractive, productive, and well-watered areas of the provinces continued here until effective Roman political control had ended. And there is little doubt that the harbor town of Petalidhi-Korone (Feature 502) continued as the economic center of the Five Rivers subregion. Second, one should view Unit IV-2, Phases 1 and 2 on the Nichoria ridge as part of an extensive Late Roman/Early Byzantine presence along the coast of the Five Rivers area (*Nichoria* I, pp. 97-102).

To supplement the information in *Nichoria* I (p. 109), Feature 26 (Pl. 8-7) is a bronze issue, perhaps a follis of Constans I that was minted at Siscia between 337 and 341 A.D. (Carson, Hill, and Kent 1960, p. 782; Metcalf 1974).

MIDDLE/LATE BYZANTINE FEATURES

The survey of the Nichoria environs produced only a handful of Middle Byzantine sites. Habitation at these sites most likely continued into the Late Byzantine period, but no direct evidence for this was found. Undoubtedly, we did not discover every surviving Byzantine feature, probably not even half of them. This may have been due in part to deficiencies in survey techniques (*Nichoria* I, pp. 82-84), but it is also true that most Middle Byzantine remains do not lend themselves to easy identification (Bouras 1974, pp. 30, 31). On the Nichoria ridge the Byzantine occupation proved to be significant in size and importance; yet this phase was not recognized in MME's intensive surface survey at the site prior to actual excavation. No diagnostic Byzantine sherds were found on the surface. Ruined foundations still showed above ground in Area II, but it could not be determined by surface investigation to what period they belonged.

Probably the same limitations apply to the Nichoria environs. It is known, for example, that Messenia, like the rest of the Peloponnese, prospered from the late 10th until the 13th century. This situation is reflected in the numerous small churches that still survive (Bon 1951, pp. 138-42), yet where is the evidence for concomitant Byzantine domestic architecture? There are virtually no such identified remains, probably because the villages were modest in size and the houses were of simple construction which was easily destroyed and plowed over. Like Nichoria, too, such sites may not have much diagnostic surface pottery that documents Byzantine occupation.

For most of the following archaeological features, information concerning location, type of remains, and special characteristics may be found by consulting *Nichoria* I, pp. 108-12. Revisitation by Rosser and Gregory suggests, however, that a few of the "Byzantine" identifications on that list must be considered doubtful or possibly wrong. Such reservations will be pointed out below in individual cases, and some supplementary information is also included.

Feature 48 is given a Roman designation on the basis of its only identifiable fragment of pottery, the handle of an undated Roman lamp. It was tentatively labeled as continuing into Byzantine times, but the only basis for such a suggestion is the presence of copious tile fragments whose date and manufacture is uncertain.

Features 49 and *51* are confirmed as the sites of ruined churches of Middle Byzantine or later date.

Feature 45 is designated "Roman?, Byzantine," yet the only support for the Byzantine designation is the report by the present owner that occasional glazed sherds have been found in the topsoil. This site obviously had at least two or three periods of use, but none of them need be later than Late Roman/Early Byzantine times. There is a complex of walls that includes a probable well and what the owner described as a bathtub. The latter, about 1 × 1 × 2 m, and smoothly plastered on the sides with a stone spout at the bottom, might have been part of an olive or wine press. Some sheets of lead were found nearby. From the wall complex also came several Roman(?) coarse ware fragments and two column fragments (one marble, the other conglomerate). One cannot rule out the possibility of a Roman villa.

More certain, however, is the presence here of a pottery workshop. Just W of the above-mentioned complex of walls Lukermann and Moody report the remains of two kilns. Just to the E, however, and revealed by a recent road cutting, is the outline in the scarp of another kiln (Pl. 8-1). A jar rim of coarse ware from the scarp appears to be of Roman manufacture (2nd century?). The present owner reported having destroyed yet another kiln when a stable was built, which establishes the presence of a fourth kiln between the ones just described. Hence, it is reasonable to infer that the wall complex, with its "bathtub" and well, may have been part of a pottery workshop. The presence of at least four kilns indicates a larger than average operation.

The remains of several tile-covered graves are situated above and adjacent to the wall complex. They appear to date from a later time, when the pottery workshop was in ruins.

Feature 17 consists of two cist graves excavated by Angelos Choremis in 1969 on top of the conspicuous conical hill called Trypetorachi, located just below the SE tip of Nichoria ridge (Pl. 8-2; Choremis 1970; McDonald 1972, p. 238). One grave was covered by two large pan tiles, the other by slate slabs. The tile-covered grave is referred to in Choremis's notes as grave β, and that with slate slabs as grave στ. Both graves contained funeral offerings, mostly pottery.

Grave β is apparently the earlier of the two. It contained 14 coarse ware sherds, none diagnostic. There were also several glass fragments, including one piece of purplish glass and a green handle fragment from a small glass bowl (?). The glass could be Roman or possibly Byzantine, but it is not sufficiently diagnostic to date this grave. Much more helpful, however, are the two large pan tiles that covered the grave. The two are almost identical in size, though different in color. The tile of light red fabric is 0.45 m (tapering to 0.35 m) wide, 0.985 m long, and 0.03 m thick. The tile with white fabric is 0.425 m wide (tapering to 0.35m), 0.97 m long, and 0.04 m thick. A parallel for this tile type comes from Room 3 of Nichoria Unit IV-2. This tile (**P1757**), though more fragmentary, so closely resembles the two Trypetorachi tiles that we feel confident in dating grave β to the period of Unit IV-2, Phase 2, namely ca. 460-520. Incidentally, the tiles from grave β are not comparable to tiles from a late building (Unit VI-1) (McDonald 1972, p. 238; Chapter 14 of this volume) that was partially excavated on the Nichoria ridge in 1969.

Grave στ contained an altogether different array of grave goods, all pottery. These included base and rim fragments from at least two small coarse ware jugs and rim fragments from a glazed bowl. The coarse ware fragments resemble those of a small jug found in the floor deposit of the narthex of the Nichoria chapel (see, for example, **P1748-50**). The rim fragments from the glazed bowl are of a red fabric with a white slip on the interior. Over this a band of inward-slanting, short black stripes was then painted around the interior rim; and finally a yellow glaze was added over the interior rim, with occasional splotches on the exterior. These glazed sherds are not reminiscent of common Byzantine glazed-ware types. Some of the painted wares from the Nichoria chapel, however, are decorated in an unusual manner, probably representing a local style not known in Corinth; and it is possible to place the glazed bowl from grave στ within the context of this style, even though one can cite no specific parallels. In any case, the similarity of the coarse ware jugs in grave στ to the coarse ware jugs from the narthex floor deposit strongly suggests a 12th-century date for this second Trypetorachi grave.

Feature 58. About 500 m S of Paniperi, on the E side of the western of the two roads from Paniperi to the hamlet of Ayio Sotira and about 300 m E of the spring of Kephalovrysi, is the small church of the Panayia (Pl. 8-5), which was rebuilt about 1920. About 25 m NE of this church is a mound that local residents believe to have been the site of an earlier church. On the interior of the stone walls that can be seen jutting slightly from the mound, pieces of painted plaster were noted. Next to the road scarp was part of a skull. Pottery collected around the church and the mound included tile fragments and glazed bowl fragments. One of the latter was decorated in a Green and Brown Painted Ware style indicative of the first half of the 12th century. The above suggests that the mound contains the remains of a small Middle Byzantine church.

Feature 503. The description in *Nichoria* I (p. 112) should be modified to indicate that the name of the spring in question is Kephalovrysi and that the village of Paniperi is about 500 m NNE of it. The Roman (?) bath referred to is in the immediate vicinity of the spring. About 150 m N of the spring is the ruined church of Ayios Vasilios (Pl. 8-3). The roof has collapsed, along with its central dome, filling the interior with rubble. Very fragmentary painted plaster is still attached to the interior of the walls. The overall dimensions of the church are ca. 7 × 12 m. It is built of squared limestone blocks, each ca. 0.05 × 0.20 × 0.20 m, along with numerous smaller stones and tile fragments. Until recent years two glazed bowls could be seen on the exterior of the central apse.

The style of construction is typical of many small Middle Byzantine churches in Greece, namely a cross-in-square with a central dome. The exterior tile band of decadent Kufic design (Pl. 8-4), along with the overall construction style and presence of glazed pottery, suggests that this structure dates from the Middle Byzantine period, probably the 12th century.

Feature 502 designates modern Petalidhi (ancient Korone). The site is covered with extensive Roman ruins on and about its acropolis (Pl. 8-6; see *MME* 1972, p. 312 for the scholarly literature). A few glazed sherds of Byzantine manufacture, perhaps 12th century, were found on the acropolis in 1975 by Rosser and Gregory. This is the first indication of Middle Byzantine occupation here, although it would be surprising if the only reasonably safe harbor in the subregion had been deserted in medieval times.

The following chapters (9, 10, 11, 12) are concerned exclusively with Byzantine structures and materials recovered in the excavation of the Nichoria ridge. Chapter 13 summarizes the information now available about the Byzantine presence on and around the ridge.

NOTES

1. Our understanding of Byzantine Nichoria was facilitated by the help of many scholars. Mr. Angelos Liangkouras, Ephor of Antiquities for the western Peloponnese, gave us permission to examine Byzantine antiquities in the Archaeological Museum at Kalamata. Our visits there were expedited by Mr. Panayiotis Stephanou, the chief guard. Emily Bakuru, Curator of Byzantine Antiquities at the Archaeological Museum at Mistra, offered helpful advice about Byzantine finds stored there. Former Ephor D. I. Pallas helped to clarify certain points about our coarse pottery.

Permission to examine the Byzantine pottery from the Agora excavations in Athens was provided by Field Director T. Leslie Shear, Jr. Byzantine pottery from the Ayios Stephanos excavations was examined in the Archaeological Museum at Sparta with the permission of Lord William D. Taylour and the help of Jeremy Rutter. With the permission of Michael H. Jameson and the aid of James Dengate, the Byzantine pottery from the University of Pennsylvania Argolid Survey was examined in the Archaeological Museum at Nauplion. Also at Nauplion, the Byzantine pottery from recent German excavations at Tiryns was examined with the help of Christian Podzuweit. Several visits to the Archaeological Museum at Corinth were made especially pleasant by the hospitality that Charles K. Williams, II, Director of the Corinth excavations, extends to all visiting scholars.

Other specialists who helped with various aspects of the research include Gladys D. Weinberg, Assistant Director of the Museum of Art and Archaeology at the University of Missouri; William E. Metcalf and Michael Bates, curators at the American Numismatic Society; John Hayes of the Royal Ontario Museum; Timothy Gregory of Ohio State University; and Angelos Choremis, Epimeletis of Antiquities for Corfu.

A special dept to A. H. S. Megaw for his generous encouragement and help is here acknowledged.

REFERENCES

Bon, A. 1951. *Le Péloponnèse byzantin jusqu'en 1204*. Paris.

Bouras, C. 1974. "Houses and Settlements in Byzantine Greece." In *Shelter in Greece*, ed. B. Doumanis and P. Oliver, pp. 30-53. Athens. In Greek and English.

Carson, R. A. G., Hill, P. V., and Kent, J. P. C. 1960. *Late Roman Bronze Coinage, A.D. 324-498*. Part 1: *The Bronze Coinage of the House of Constantine. A.D. 324-346*. London.

Choremis, A. 1970. "Rizomilo-Karpofora," *Deltion* 25:179-81. In Greek.

Hayes, J. 1974. October 30, personal communication to J. Rosser.

McDonald, W. A. 1972. "Excavations at Nichoria in Messenia: 1969-71," *Hesperia* 41:218-73, Pls. 38-52.

———, and Rapp, G., Jr., eds. *The Minnesota Messenia Expedition: Reconstructing a Bronze Age Regional Environment*. Minneapolis.

Megaw, A. H. S. 1970. September 10, personal communication to W. A. McDonald.

Metcalf, W. E. 1974. December 3, personal communication to J. Rosser.

MME 1972 = McDonald and Rapp 1972.

Nichoria I = Rapp and Aschenbrenner 1978.

Rapp, G., Jr., and Aschenbrenner, S. E., eds. 1978. *Excavations at Nichoria in Southwest Greece* I: *Site, Environs, and Techniques*. Minneapolis.

Weinberg, G. D. 1975a. April 23, personal communication to J. Rosser.

———. 1975b. June 18, personal communication to J. Rosser.

9

The Architecture

by John Rosser and William P. Donovan

with contributions by Richard Hope Simpson, Dietmar Hagel, and William A. McDonald

The following features are included under the architectural rubric:

Area II.	Unit II-1
	Unit II-2
	Associated remains
Area III.	Field walls
Area IV.	Unit IV-2, Phases 1 and 2
	Unit IV-2, Phases 3 and 4
	Unit L21-1

Donovan discusses here the two buildings in Area II whose excavation he supervised in the campaigns of 1969, 1970, and 1971. Hope Simpson and Hagel then describe the meager Byzantine remains recovered in excavations under their supervision in Area III. Donovan also established in 1972 the main outlines of Unit IV-2 in Area IV. Its excavation was completed by Rosser in 1973, with minor additional tests during the 1974 study season. Rosser publishes here all architectural remains in Area IV and concludes the chapter with an analysis of the significance of Nichoria's Byzantine architecture.

Area II (Pl. 9-1)

The high flat-topped acropolis that is designated Area II has been described in *Nichoria* I (pp. 117, 118). Architectural remains dated to Middle Byzantine times were discovered there in 1969 test trenches K25-I and II and were fully explored during the seasons of 1970 and 1971. Although fragments of terra-cotta roof tiles and bits of broken pottery belonging to this period were found in surface levels over all of Area II, excavation suggests that Byzantine buildings occupied only a portion of this area. It is of course possible that even the foundations of further Byzantine structures that once stood in other parts of Area II have been obliterated by erosion or other factors.

Examination of the area plan (*Nichoria* I, Fig. 8-2, p. 118) reveals that the preserved foundations of Byzantine buildings were recovered only in the SW sector. Because some of these walls form two fairly widely separated rectangular rooms, one in grids K25 Fab and the other in K25 Jbc, they have been assigned to two different buildings, Units II-2 and II-1 respectively. It is clear, however, that extensive erosion as well as recent agricultural activity may have caused the disappearance or ruin of walls linking these two structures; and they may, in fact, be two parts of one very large complex structure. They are identical in construction, orientation, and date, and the surface deposit between them was particularly rich in the tiles, glass, pottery, and metallic slags belonging to this period.

Total or virtual ruin of Byzantine architectural remains seems to have occurred also both N and S of Unit II-2. In K25 FGd a jumbled mass of stones suggests a disturbed Byzantine foundation, and in K25 Ea a Byzantine wall is abruptly cut away by the erosion of the S edge of the acropolis. The S part of Unit II-1, in K25 Ja, seems to have suffered the same fate, since its E and W walls simply come to an end before they make a return for the S wall.

While it is clear, then, that a building or buildings occupied the S portion of Area II in Middle Byzantine times, it is not clear what use, if any, the inhabitants might have made of the N half. It may be stated with reasonable confidence, however, that this space was not covered with substantial buildings, since no traces of post-LH walls were found, nor any of the tumbled stones from the collapse of such structures. Further, all the Byzantine remains in Area II seem to belong to one, relatively brief, period of time.

The date of this occupation is securely based upon three mutually reinforcing items of evidence: (1) the recovery, immediately E of Unit II-2, of a coin of Basil II (976-1025); (2) a piece of carbonized wood, lodged between two stones of the much earlier (LH) Wall W of Unit II-1, which yielded a C^{14} date (MASCA corrected) of 946 ± 98 (*Nichoria* I, Table 1-3 DON 73, p. 5); and (3) three pieces of glazed pottery found E of Unit II-2 and dated by Rosser from the 10th to the late 11th or early 12th centuries (pp. 360, 379, 405). Finally, there are links between the remains in Area II and those in Area IV. The identical form of the roof tiles and similarities in construction (pp. 376, 380, 381) suggest a correspondence, or at least an overlap, in date for these two main areas of Byzantine occupation on the ridge.

In Area II, at any rate, the known structures seem to have been erected by the late 10th century and to have been abandoned a little more than a hundred years later. The gradual collapse of the structures is indicated by the absence of any signs of major conflagration, by the paucity of finds in the buildings, and by the general appearance of the debris over the remains of the walls. This dating also accords well with the architectural evidence, since what remains of the buildings shows no traces of extensive remodeling, rebuilding, or other signs of very long life.

This chronological homogeneity was matched by the homogeneity of the remains of the latest Byzantine occupation. Every location where walls appeared on or near the surface was marked by heaps of irregular field stones mixed with pieces of broken roof tiles and black, powdery humus (e.g., Pl. 9-9). These deposits were the favorite home for luxuriant vegetation and for scorpions. The sheer quantity of stone on or near the modern surface was enough to distinguish traces of Byzantine activity from that of any earlier period in this area.

Once the accumulated debris from the collapse of the buildings was cleared away, other characteristic features of this period were revealed. The foundations were constructed of stones usually arranged so as to form the two faces of the wall, with a fill between almost entirely made up of earth which measured from a few centimeters up to 0.20 m in thickness (Pl. 9-2). Sometimes the blocks that formed the faces in the lowest course were set upright upon one of their narrow edges to form crude orthostates. This feature, together with the thick earth fill, was especially useful in distinguishing the Byzantine walls from earlier ones. Many of the orthostates were propped into their vertical position by smaller stones which served as wedges beneath them (Pl. 9-3). Bits of pori, so accessible in Area II, were frequently utilized for this purpose, and rough blocks of the same material were occasionally used in the lowest foundation course. In earlier periods this material is not nearly as common in the construction of walls. Frequently, too, an orthostate alternated with several smaller stones laid flat to create a uniform height for this lowest part of the wall (Pl. 9-4). The quantities of fallen stones above and around the remains in place strongly suggest that the walls were carried up in a dry stone technique above this orthostate course, but no walls were in fact preserved to a sufficient height to prove this hypothesis; still less is it possible to prove that the walls were built entirely of stone.

A second characteristic of the construction is that the wall lines were not laid out with strings, as is proved by the fact that none of the faces are true and straight; nor are the angles formed by intersecting walls at the corners of rooms true right angles. It would appear that corners or ends of walls may have been marked by the placement of larger orthostates, since the largest blocks (e.g., 0.80 × 0.60 × 0.20 m) usually occur there. Possibly the rest of the walls were roughly laid in after the corners were in place. Whatever the method, it did not produce straight lines.

When the foundations of Unit II-1 were removed in 1971 in order to expose the remains of a Bronze Age structure directly beneath, it was definitely established that these Byzantine walls were built without any careful preparation of the ground surface. No footing trenches were dug, and indeed the ground was not even leveled; the lowest stones were simply placed upon the existing surface, however irregular. Despite the fact that stones of the two foundations actually touched one another in places, the Byzantine walls did not follow exactly the earlier, ready-made foundations. Thus, it seems evident that the Byzantine builders in Area II were not really aware of earlier foundations. If they had been, surely they would have constructed their walls upon them, as was essentially the technique in Area IV (see pp. 368, 369). In fact, the bottom of their orthostate walls rises and falls as determined by the level of the debris over which they were built (Pl. 9-5). From Unit II-1 there is additional evidence that these builders scarcely disturbed the soil as they laid out their walls. Stones in the E wall (A) rest directly upon a nearly complete, although broken, Mycenaean vase which seems not to have been touched by the later occupants (Pl. 9-6).

The casual preparation of the surface is also noticeable inside the buildings. There is no evidence of a carefully prepared floor; rather, the uneven ground together with stones from earlier structures appears to have formed the only floor on the ground level of the Byzantine units. There is not even any surviving indication that the earth was carefully trodden down to form a hard surface. The lack of a clearly defined floor might suggest that the ground level of these structures was used as shelter for animals or for storage, rather than for human habitation. In that case, the owners might have lived in a second story (as is a common modern practice), but there is no independent evidence of the existence of a second floor in these buildings.

UNIT II-1 (FIG. 9-1)

Before intensive excavation began in 1970, the remains of this structure appeared above the modern surface as a pile of stones covered with thick vegetation. During the 1970 season clearing and excavation revealed the partially preserved foundations of a rectangular room whose long axis extended from SW to NE in K25 JKbc. The three preserved walls (A, B, and C) were of the orthostate construction described above. Despite an effort at wedging, several of the orthostates had fallen over and some had apparently disappeared. The exterior face of Wall A was not preserved at its N end. There was a gap in Wall C where neither inner nor outer faces were preserved for about 1.50 m, although the latter gap may indicate the location of the doorway. These three walls bond together (Table 9-1) to form three sides of a rectangular room with an interior width of 4.15 m.

The S ends of Walls A and C were not preserved, so the original length of the room is unknown. At some point after the initial construction, a light wall (D) marked a division toward the S end. Its stones did not bond with the other walls, nor was its construction similar, as it was made up of a single row of stones laid flat. Only one course was preserved, and it broke off before butting against Wall A. That Wall D was a later construction is proved by the fact that it rested upon some of the broken Byzantine pottery on the floor of the room (Pl. 9-7). At any rate, the preserved length of the enclosed space varied from 5.40 to 5.70 m, since Wall D was not exactly parallel to Wall B (see Table 9-1).

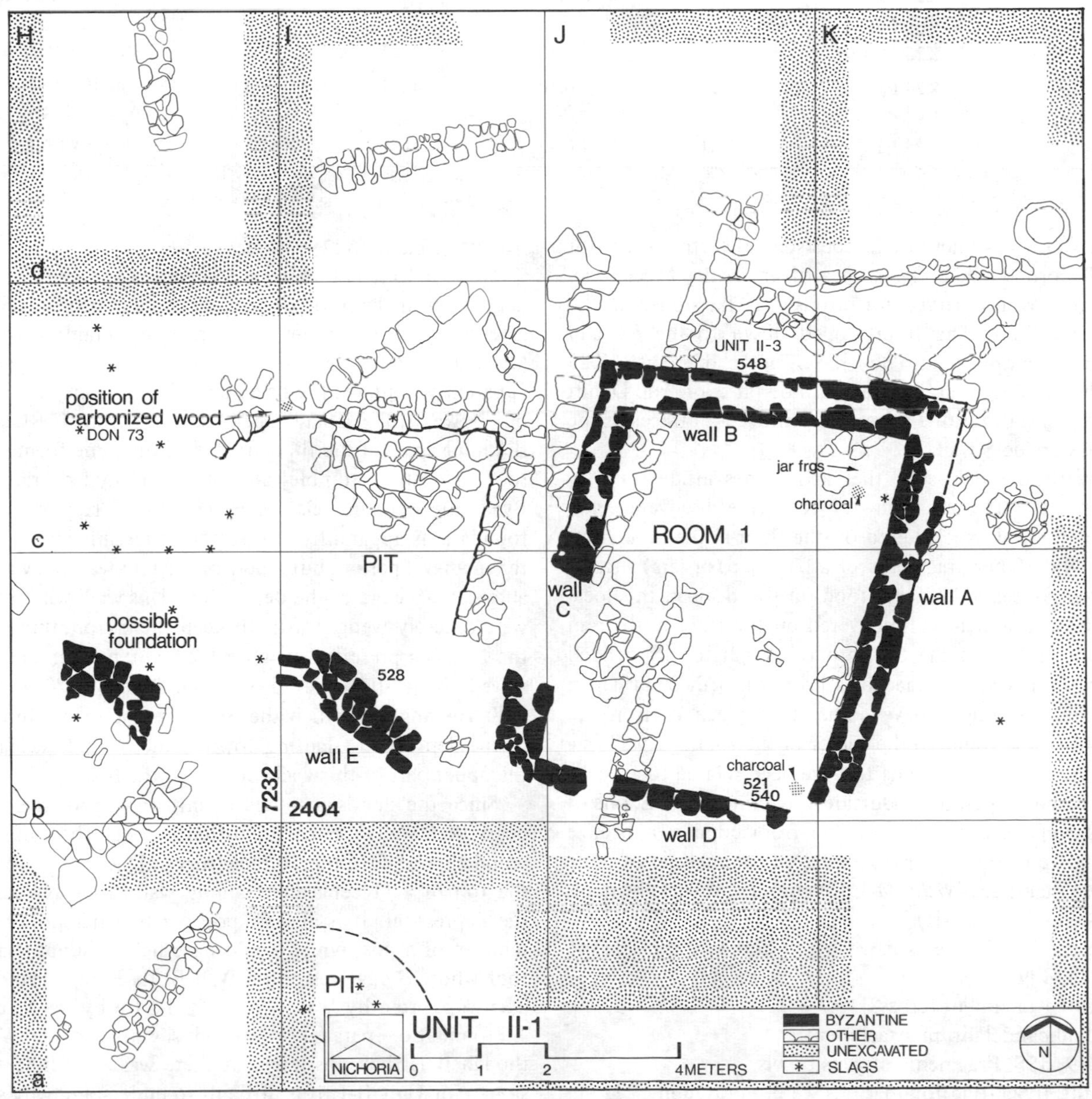

Figure 9-1

Table 9-1. Wall Specifications: Units II-1 and II-2

Wall	Grid	Length	Average Width	Maximum Height	Maximum Number of Courses	Bond/Butt
A	K25 Kbc	6.50	0.60	0.64	1	Bonds with B
B	K25 JKc	5.30	0.60	0.48	2	Bonds with A and C
C	K25 IJbc	6.10	0.55	0.35	2	Bonds with B
D	K25 Jb	5.20	0.28	0.20	1	Butts against C
E	K25 Ib	2.50	0.80	0.20	1	None
F	K25 Fc	1.93	0.75	0.40	2	Butts against B, bonds with G
G	K25 FGc	6.01	0.40	0.37	1	Bonds with F
H	K25 FGbc	6.25	0.62	0.48	4	Bonds with I and K
I	K25 Fb	6.20	0.60	0.40	1	Bonds with H and J
J	K24 Fy K25 Fa	6.44	0.60	0.47	4	Bonds with I, K, L, M
K	K25 FGab	6.20	0.55	0.55	3	Bonds with H and J
L	K24 Fy K25 Fa	. . .	0.40	0.61	3	Bonds with J
M	K25 Ea	2.16	0.45	0.40	5	Bonds with J

The floor was uneven and consisted of earth, except for the SW corner where flat stones of an earlier Mycenaean structure possibly served fortuitously as flagstones on the Byzantine floor. The floor sloped down to the SE and could not be traced into the next grid to the south (K25 Ja). The building may have ended not far S of Wall D, but erosion since Byzantine times has removed all traces of the original outside S wall.

Beneath the debris of tiles and stones inside this rectangular space (Room 1) few objects were discovered, and most of these were clustered on the floor in the SE corner. In the NE corner fragments of a large jar (or jars) suggest that such vessels may have stood on the floor in this location. Some charcoal was recovered on the floor both from this spot and from the SE corner immediately N of Wall D; but there was no trace of a proper hearth from which such charcoal might have come. One piece of iron ore (hematite) was found in the center of the room, as well as a chunk of iron which seems to have been related to a smelting or forging operation. Outside this unit to the E, bits of slag as well as part of a crucible from copper or bronze working were found (Figs. 9-1, 9-2). (For analyses of some of these slags, see *Nichoria* I, Chapter 12, especially items 39 to 49 in Table 12-1.)

The cataloged objects listed below come from inside the room (see Fig. 9-1):

521. Iron attachment (cross?)
540. Lead candelabrum attachment
548, 549, 555. Fragments of glass bowls

When the Byzantine foundations were removed in 1971, an iron knife blade (**522**) was recovered.

West of Unit II-1 there is a deep and apparently natural depression in the pori. This depression had been paved with several layers of stones and lined by retaining walls in Mycenaean times (Pl. 9-8). At the end of the Bronze Age it apparently contained considerable debris from that period, but it was still partially open, to judge from the fact that the upper part of the fill consisted of the same fragments of roof tiles, stone tumble, and black soil that characterized Byzantine remains elsewhere (Pl. 9-9). The Mycenaean foundations apparently still served as retaining walls during the medieval period, but a new orthostate wall (E) was built above the S edge of the depression. This wall, whose stones were securely wedged as if to keep them from tumbling to the N, has a preserved length of 2.50 m; neither end is preserved. It parallels the edge of the depression from SE to NW. The angle at which the Byzantine debris lay in the fill of the depression (slanting down to the N) makes clear that the upper part of this wall toppled to the N.

Since the debris included quantities of roof tiles, it appears that Wall E once supported a roof. The carbonized wood that yielded the 10th century A.D. date was found in the top of a Mycenaean retaining wall at the NW edge of the depression. It is at least possible that it represents the remains of a post which could have helped support a shed roof whose S edge rested on Wall E. Its E edge could have been supported by Wall C of Unit II-1 (or by the Mycenaean foundation parallel to it and slightly farther W). Although it is thus possible that there was a shedlike extension W of Unit II-1, it is difficult to understand why such a

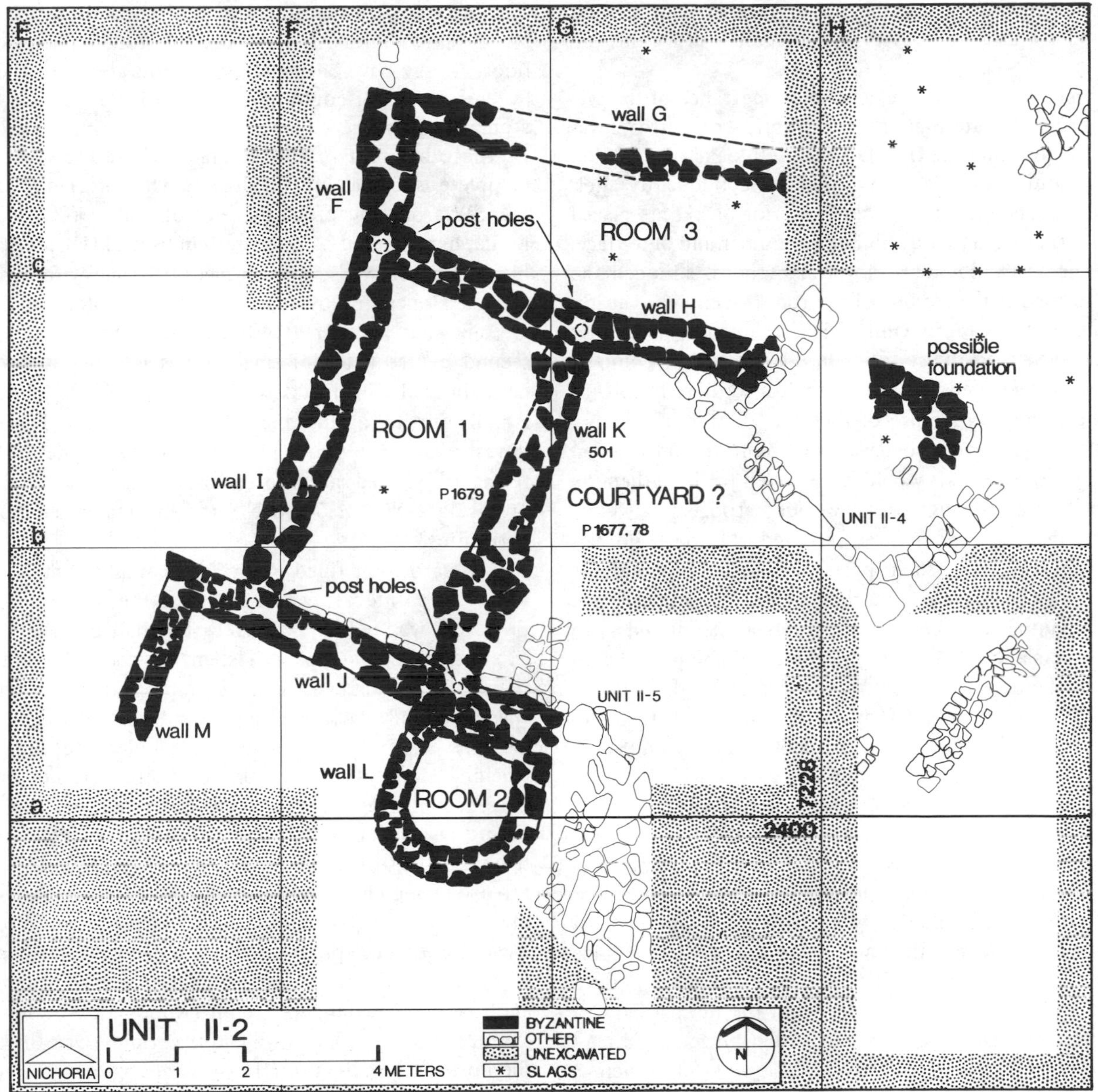

Figure 9-2

depression would have been roofed. Whatever the explanation, it is clear that a Byzantine structure collapsed into this space.

Some charcoal was found S of Wall E, but there were no samples of metallic slags nor charcoal from the Byzantine fill in the depression. In addition to the building debris and fragments of coarse pottery, the following cataloged objects were recovered (Fig. 9-1):

523. Iron blade
524. Iron bracelet(?)
526. Iron shaft

UNIT II-2 (FIG. 9-2)

Some eight or nine meters W of Unit II-1 a second concentration of Byzantine foundations was cleared in 1970 and 1971. Again the remains of a complete structure are not preserved, but since the walls certainly enclosed more than one room, this structure appears to have been more complex than II-1. Well-preserved foundations enclose a main, rectangular space (Room 1) and an apsidal oven or furnace (Room 2; Pl. 9-10); what appears to have been another rectangular room (Room 3) adjoining Room 1 to the N is only partially preserved. Yet another wall extends SW from the main room, but its function could not be determined (Table 9-1).

The same tumble of tile fragments, stones (the largest measured 0.60 × 0.40 × 0.25 m), and black earth filled these rooms and tumbled down the slope S and W of the structure. The original surface of the ground sloped down to the S and the accumulation of debris was thickest there.

The appearance of the tumbled stones shows that the walls collapsed toward the W as the structure fell into ruins (Pl. 9-11).

The nature of the debris and the appearance of the preserved walls indicate that the construction of Unit II-2 was similar to that of Unit II-1. Orthostate blocks were used in the first course, especially at corners, and frequently alternate with stones laid flat. Where exterior blocks are placed on edge, there is an earth fill between inner and outer face. Again the walls do not form straight lines, although the angles formed at the corners of the rooms seem more nearly 90° than is the case in Unit II-1. Presumably these walls were carried up to the roof line in the dry stone technique. The roof was covered with tiles identical to those from Unit II-1. An interesting feature of the construction of Room 1 is that the walls seem to have been built around wooden corner posts. The posts would have served to strengthen the walls and to anchor horizontal wooden stringers to which, in turn, the roof rafters were secured. Although no carbonized wood from such posts was actually found, its presence can be inferred from the fact that the stones in the preserved upper surface of the corners are so placed as to form sockets about 0.12 m in diameter and about 0.20 m in preserved depth.

The interior of Room 1 (formed by Walls H, I, J, and K) measures 5.10 by 2.56 m. Its long axis extends from SW to NE and is exactly parallel to the long axis of Unit II-1. The N wall (H) rests upon native pori at its W end and upon earth fill to the E. This wall continues at least 2.60 m E beyond the corner of Room 1, and its E end is not preserved. This extension, although it bonds with the rest of Wall H, may have been initially conceived as a separate wall since there is a large orthostate at the point where it joins the exterior of Room 1. The E wall (K) is marked by a distinct widening near its S end, from the normal 0.55 to about 0.70 m. This wider section is 0.90 m long and may mark the location of a doorway at this point. Since there is no sign of significant variation in the width of the foundations at any other place, the anomaly here does not seem to be due to sagging.

Wall K rests entirely upon earth fill, but the W wall (I) rests upon the pori at its N end and upon the deep layered fill formed by wash down the slope of the hill at its S end. The S wall (J) rests in large part upon the foundations of an earlier Mycenaean wall which continues to the E of Wall J. This probably fortuitous correspondence is not exact, since the earlier wall line is not exactly parallel and it projects slightly to the N. Wall J extends beyond the exterior line of Room 1 both to the W and the E and one cannot be sure that its preserved length of 6.44 m may not have originally been greater, since both ends seem to be broken off.

The uneven earth floor of Room 1 slopes down from the NW to the S and it was covered with the broken pieces of several large vessels of coarse fabric (Pl. 9-12). One sherd of finer glazed ware was found in the debris above the floor. Near Wall I there was a rectangular stone laid flat on the floor. It may have been simply incorporated into the floor by chance, but it could have served to support one of the storage amphoras.

The other part of this complex whose walls are nearly complete is a small apsidal chamber (Room 2) extending to the SW from the present E end of Wall J (Pl. 9-13). Its limits, here treated as one continuous wall (L), are formed, like the other walls, by two faces of stone with earth fill; but the stones employed are somewhat smaller and the wall is somewhat thinner (0.40 m). In many places, too, a second course made of small stones laid flat is preserved here above the orthostates. The straight N side of Room 2 is built directly against the S face of Wall J, and above the lowest course the two walls bond. The remainder of Wall L forms a U-shaped curve to enclose a small space that measures 1.35 E-W × 1.50 m N-S (to the maximum point of curvature).

The earth that filled Room 2 was unlike that from any other Byzantine deposit. Up against the inside of Wall L the earth was red, indicating that it had been repeatedly exposed to high temperatures. In the center of the room the soil was black because it was impregnated with charcoal fragments and black manganese oxides (Pl. 9-14). Analysis indicates that this enclosure was subject to high heat, reaching at times at least 800° C. There were no traces of slags or metal in the fill and the shape and location of the room suggest that, rather than a furnace for metal working, this was a very large domestic oven or (more likely) a kiln for producing charcoal. The only small find in the fill was the base of an EHII pot which had been pierced to serve as a whorl but whose presence here was probably accidental.

To N of Room 1 are partially preserved remains of another large rectangular room (Room 3). The long axis extends from E to W. The E end is not preserved since both the north (G) and south (H) walls are broken off. The west wall (F) does not bond with Wall I of Room 1, and its line runs much more nearly straight N. Wall I is particularly massive (0.75 m wide) and utilizes some large orthostates. The very ruined Wall G encloses Room 3 on the N. At its W end both faces are intact at the junction with Wall F but elsewhere only the S face is preserved. Since Wall G is not exactly parallel to the W sector of Wall H, the interior of Room 3 is only roughly rectangular, measuring 1.30 m wide at the W end and 2.15 m where Walls G and H peter out at the E. The preserved length is 5.50 m. The surface of the floor, if it may be called such, is as irregular as the width of the room. It consists of loose earth whose level slopes north quite steeply.

To judge from the tiles found here, one of which was nearly complete, Room 3 was roofed. Three samples of metallic slags were recovered from the fill, as well as many fragments of glass vessels. It is worth noting that the largest number of samples of Byzantine slags come from this room and from the space directly E of it in K25 Hc, i.e., between Room 3 and the depression just W of Unit II-1 (Figs. 9-1, 9-2).

The space E of Wall K and between Walls H and J was enclosed, at least in part, by these three walls. The paucity of stones and its position next to Room 1 make it unlikely that it was yet another roofed area. The quantities of tile fragments, broken Byzantine pottery, and animal bones from this space suggest the possibility that it served as an open courtyard in this complex. The species represented by the animal bones are cow, horse, pig, and deer (see *Nichoria* I, p. 75).

To the W of Room 1 there is a partially preserved, narrow wall (M) extending 2.10 m SW from the point at which it bonds with Wall J. This wall is not complete, nor can its original function be surmised. It may be noted that its width (0.40 m) is exactly the same as the apsidal wall (L), which may mean that it too did not serve as part of a wall of a major room. Any space that may once have been enclosed, in part, by Wall M would have been toward the west where erosion has been severe. The space between Walls M and L appears to have been outside the limits of Unit II-2 and to have served as the repository for debris such as pottery, glass, and small bits of metal.

The following cataloged objects were recovered in or near Unit II-2 (see Fig. 9-1):

P1677. Fragment of cup
P1678. Fragment of jug
P1679. Fragment of plate
501. Bronze coin
505. Bronze ring
527. Iron nail
530. Iron nail
545. Fragments of glass bottle(?)
546. Fragments of glass bowl(?)
550. Fragments of glass bowl(?)
556. Fragments of glass bottle(?)
557. Fragments of glass bottle(?)

W.P.D.

Area III (Figs. 2-1, 2-2; Table 9-2)

In the long gap between the end of the DA occupation and the Byzantine reoccupation (centered on Area II), a gradual accumulation of deposit in Area III was presumably the result mainly of natural processes. This intervening stratum (4 on Figs. 2-3, 2-4; 7 on Fig. 2-5; 3a on Fig. 2-6; and 7a on Sec. 3 of *Nichoria* I) is deeper toward the center of Area III and is not now present in most of the higher part on the NW and N. It was not always possible to distinguish it from the succeeding Byzantine stratum (5 on Figs. 2-3, 2-4; 8 on Fig. 2-5; 4 on Fig. 2-6; and 8 on Sec. 3 of *Nichoria* I), since the latter contained very little identifiable Byzantine material and the texture of the earth was often similar. The soil profiles (discussed in *Nichoria* I, pp. 34-40 and especially Table 4-2 and Fig. 4-3) were here of great assistance, providing a valuable overall check on the archaeological stratigraphy observed.

There is no evidence of actual dwellings in Area III during the Byzantine period. This is certainly true to the E of Wall L, a Byzantine field boundary (Pl. 9-16), of which a considerable length of foundations extended SSW to NNE through most of K25 Qef and Rfg. In K25 Qe and in the S part of Qf the foundations were set directly on the pori caprock, but in Rfg and in the N part of Qf they lay over a LHIII terrace wall and street as well as a DAII apsidal building (Unit III-1). Similar remains of another Byzantine terrace wall were found in K24 WXYu and L24 ABu, i.e., Wall C (with the associated level 4 on Fig. 2-6). Both walls incorporated several blocks of pori, often set orthostatically (Pl. 9-17). Wall C was built on footings that were set into a basinlike foundation trench and which at the N edge rest on top of a DAIII terrace wall (A) in grids K24 WXYu. The blocks vary considerably in size; limestone, cut and uncut, and pori are intermingled, and fragments of pithoi or tile are used in the fill. The arrangement of the building material is haphazard on the N uphill side where the orthostatic blocks occur. On the S side the wall line is clearly defined and shows a proper face. It is likely, therefore, that the retaining wall rose only slightly above the ground level on the uphill side. The curvature of the wall seems to have anticipated the greatest amount of downhill pressure in K24 XYu, roughly at the center of the field.

Byzantine finds were very sparse in the related stratum, which contained mainly mixed and heavily worn LH and DA pottery; but some tile fragments were found in Wall C and elsewhere in the stratum, and glass fragments occurred in K25 Wa and in K24 Vxy (**558**) at a depth of ca. 0.40 m below the modern surface. The amount of identified Byzantine pottery, apart from tile fragments, is exceedingly small. A few Byzantine sherds were found in K25 Tcd and

Table 9-2. Wall Specifications: Area III

Wall	Grid	Length	Average Width	Maximum Height	Maximum Number of Courses	Bond/Butt
L	K25 Qef/Rfg	9.0	0.55	0.30	2	Terrace wall
C	K24 WXYu/L24 ABu	19.50	0.90	0.35	2	Terrace wall

in nearby trenches (especially K24 Uy and K25 Uab; in level 8 on Sec. 3 of *Nichoria* I). The Byzantine stratum contained deposits of dark brown, manganese-stained earth of somewhat sticky consistency, which may have originated in Area II, where there are natural manganese deposits. Farther E, and especially in K24 WXYtu and L24 Atu, the earth in the Byzantine stratum is lighter in color and consistency, and in places it is either very thin or indistinguishable from the succeeding stratum.

It is clear, in any case, that Area III was used only for cultivation in the Byzantine period. Wall L was presumably part of a retaining wall to help stabilize the surface for the Byzantine settlement on the Area II "acropolis" above; and Wall C is clearly a retaining wall to inhibit erosion from the field that comprised the greater part of Area III.

Since the Byzantine period, further erosion took place along the upper edges of Area III on the NW, N, and E. Thus, Wall L was partly visible before excavation and formed part of the base of a modern field wall. The center of the field was further filled, causing the remains of Wall C to be covered by about a meter of deposit; and in trial trench K24-III, to the S of Wall C and near the edge of the modern field, the medieval and modern fill is at least 2.0 m thick. In modern times the area has been sparsely planted with figs and olives, whose roots have disturbed part of the Byzantine and earlier deposits. The modern plow soil is very thin, seldom more than 0.20 m.

R.H.S.
D.K.H.

Area IV (Pl. 9-18)

The foundations of Unit IV-2 (Figs. 9-3, 9-4, 9-5) were discovered by Donovan in 1972 when trenches L23 PQkl and RSjkl were excavated. Its main outlines were revealed and an ecclesiastical function was presumed because of the presence of the apses in the SE corner. The unraveling of the complex building phases and the completion of the excavation in L23 PQij was accomplished by Rosser in 1973. Certain aspects of the architectural history were further clarified during the study season of 1974, when minor additional tests were made and when the much earlier date for Phases 1 and 2 became apparent.

Table 8-3 in *Nichoria* I (p. 137) lists the above-mentioned trenches and the main cultural periods identified in each. The tops of the ruined walls of Unit IV-2 were encountered just below the modern surface (Fig. 8-1). Debris associated with this complex extended from 0.30 m to about 1.50 m below the surface. None of the trenches fully revealed the depth of the prehistoric habitation debris beneath Unit IV-2. To have done so would have necessitated at least some selective removal of the later remains. The deepest penetrations were three small trials, one of which is shown as level 1 in Fig. 9-6 (see Chapter 2, pp. 48, 51).

In the lowest levels of some trenches, however, LHIII sherds were predominant. They no doubt indicate the presence of a LHIII level of which Unit IV-6, which extends under the SE corner of Unit IV-2, is a part. Naturally, the remains of DA structures are more obvious immediately adjacent to and beneath Unit IV-2. A large apsidal DA building (Unit IV-1) was situated just to the NE, and the SW part of a somewhat later apsidal DA building (Unit IV-5), oriented roughly N-S, must have lain directly beneath the E sector of Unit IV-2. Immediately beneath the floors everywhere in Unit IV-2 we encountered tumbled DA debris (level 1 in Fig. 9-6), roughly leveled and packed down by the later builders (see Chapter 2).

UNIT IV-2, PHASES 1 AND 2: THE LATE ROMAN/EARLY BYZANTINE BUILDING

PHASE 1

This structure (Fig. 9-4) was exactly square, each of the outer walls (R, S, X, and Q) being 9.70 m in outside length. A single interior partition (T) on the N-S axis divided the enclosed space into two rectangular rooms of almost equal proportions. The western Room 1 is 3.70 × 8.33 m in inner dimensions, and the eastern Room 2 is 3.85 × 8.36 m.

The foundations are of local limestone blocks, quarried and hammer-dressed, and set in horizontal courses with a rubble core and careful chinking throughout. Although there is no obvious horizontal bonding, the walls are notably sturdy and bond tightly at the corners (Pls. 9-20, 9-21, 9-22). As can be seen from Table 9-3, their maximum preserved height varies from 0.42 to 0.80 m, their width is a uniform 0.70 m, and the number of preserved courses varies from three to six.

It was not possible to ascertain the location of any doorways, exterior or interior. The floors in Rooms 1 and 2 are both roughly at elevation 87.70 m, and the surrounding ground level is presently about the same. The outside ground level contemporary with the building must have been at least that high, perhaps up to 87.80 m in order to fully cover the earlier Wall V in Pjk, over which these builders constructed the NW corner of the new building (Figs. 9-4, 9-12). Thus, it seems likely that the door sills were *above* the preserved height of the walls. On the E side where Wall R intersects the later chapel Wall O, there is a structure that could be construed as an inner threshold in Room 2 (Figs. 9-4, 9-13). This feature may, however, belong to the underlying DA structure, Unit IV-5 (see Chapter 2, p. 51).

Wall R, at the NE exterior corner (Pl. 9-22), was set in a foundation trench 0.35 m below the elevation (87.70 m) that we believe characterized the area leveled for Phase 1. Presumably the other walls were set in foundation trenches to at least that depth, except in the NW corner, which was built over the earlier Wall V. The large amount of stone debris from the walls (X, T, and parts of Q and S) that collapsed into Room 1 (Figs. 9-6, 9-15, 9-16; Pl. 9-20)

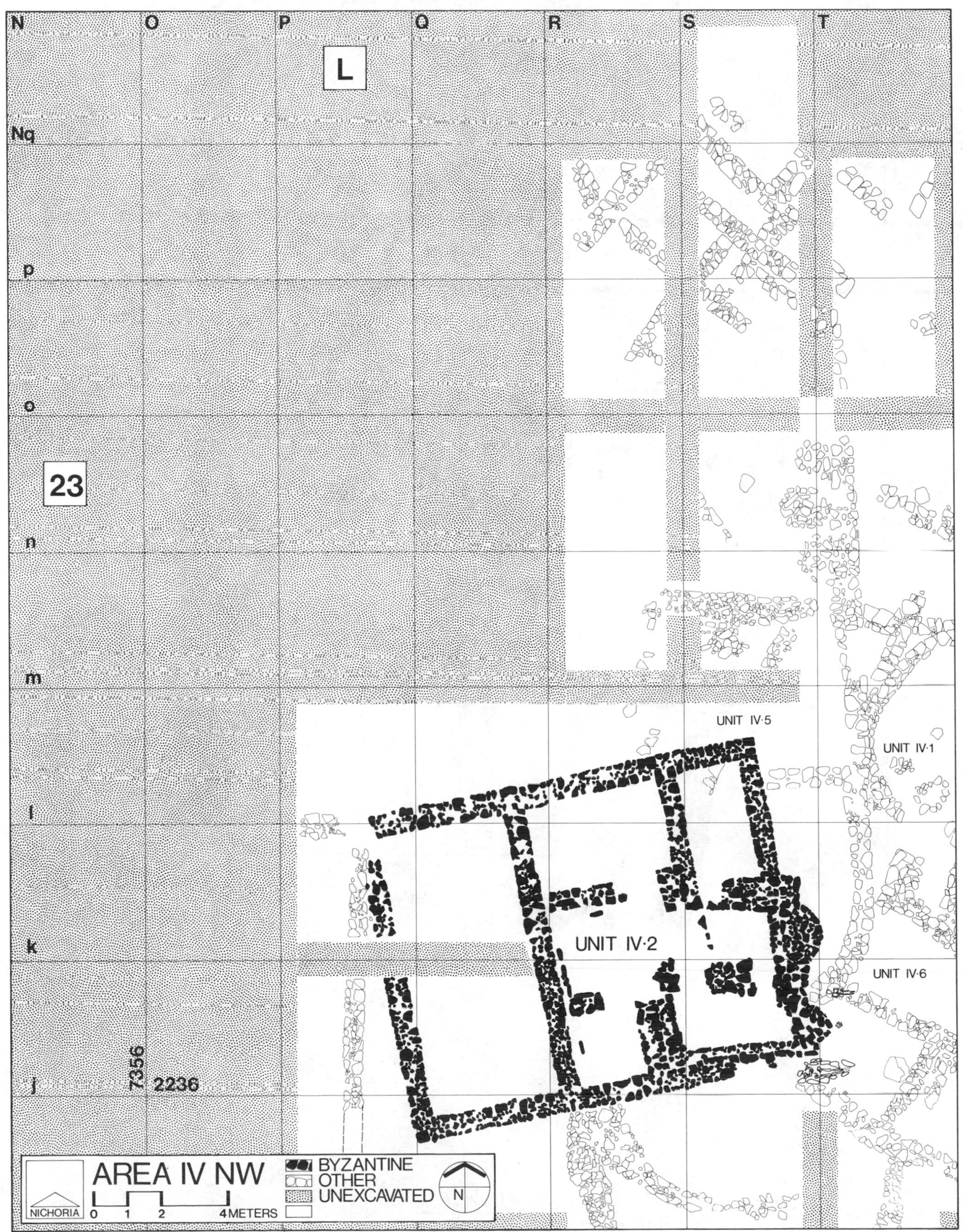
N
O
P
Q
R
S
T
L
Nq
p
o
23
n
m
l
k
j
7356
2236
UNIT IV·5
UNIT IV·1
UNIT IV·2
UNIT IV·6
AREA IV NW
NICHORIA
0 1 2 4 METERS
BYZANTINE
OTHER
UNEXCAVATED
N

Figure 9-3

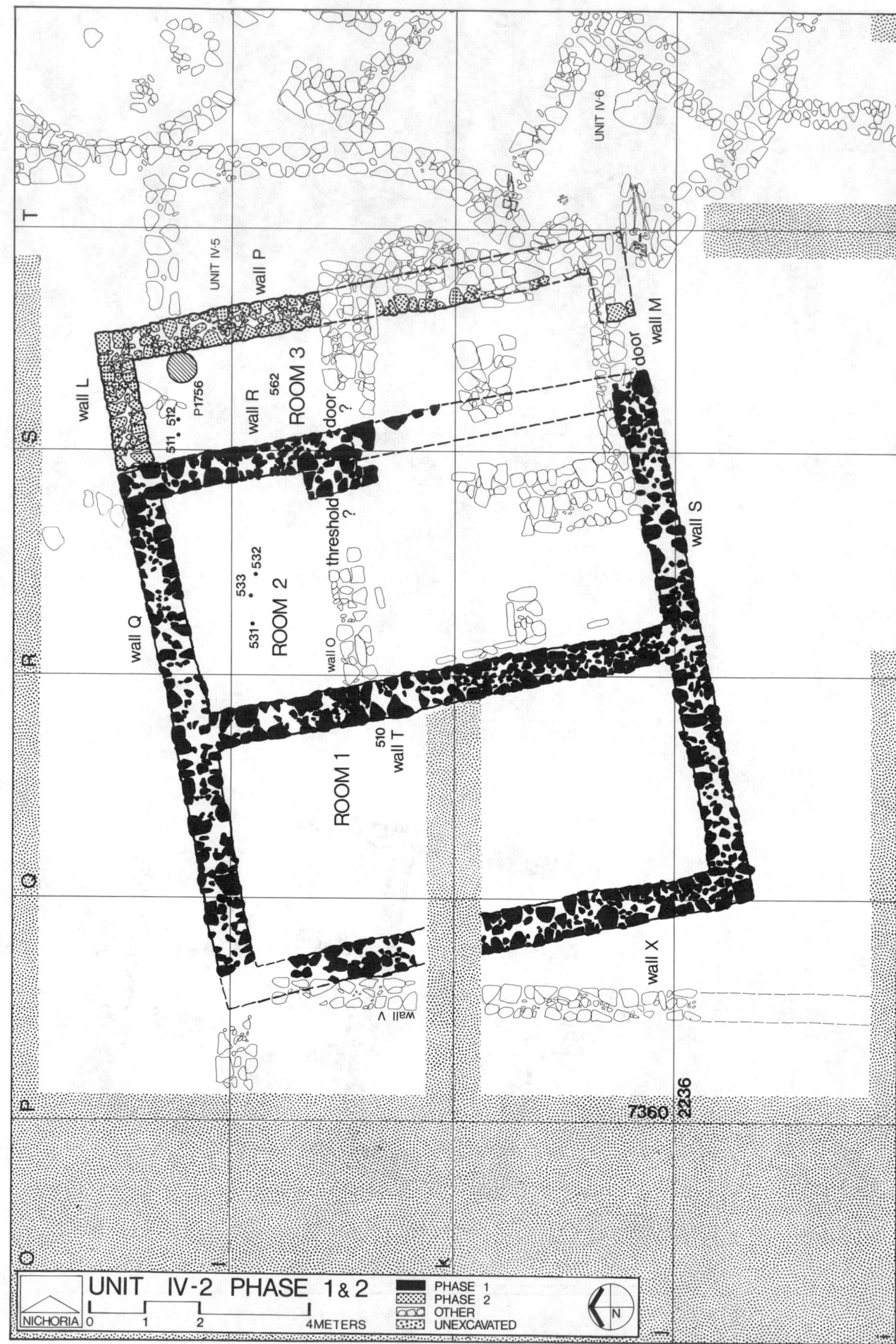
UNIT IV-2 PHASE 1 & 2
NICHORIA
0 1 2 4METERS
PHASE 1
PHASE 2
OTHER
UNEXCAVATED
N
ROOM 1
ROOM 2
ROOM 3
wall L
wall M
wall O
wall P
wall Q
wall R
wall S
wall T
wall V
wall X
door
door ?
threshold ?
UNIT IV-5
UNIT IV-6
P1756
510
511
512
531
532
533
562
7360
2236
O
P
Q
R
S
T
K

Figure 9-4

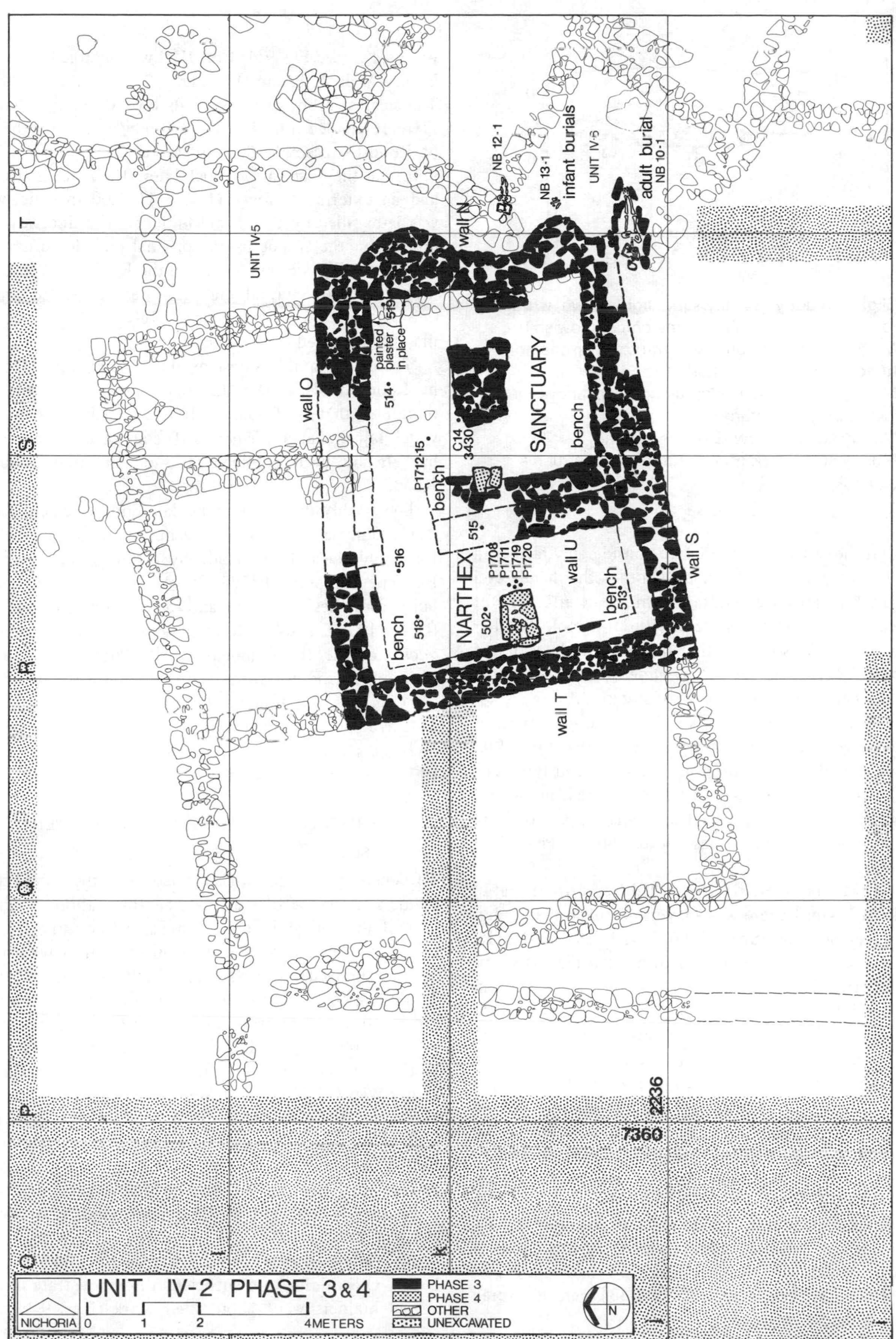
UNIT IV-2 PHASE 3 & 4
NICHORIA
0 1 2 4METERS
PHASE 3
PHASE 4
OTHER
UNEXCAVATED
N
SANCTUARY
NARTHEX
bench
wall O
wall N
wall U
wall S
wall T
painted plaster in place
infant burials
adult burial
UNIT IV-5
UNIT IV-6
NB 12-1
NB 13-1
NB 10-1
C14 3430
P1712-15
P1708
P1711
P1719
P1720
502
513
514
515
516
518
519
2236
7360

Figure 9-5

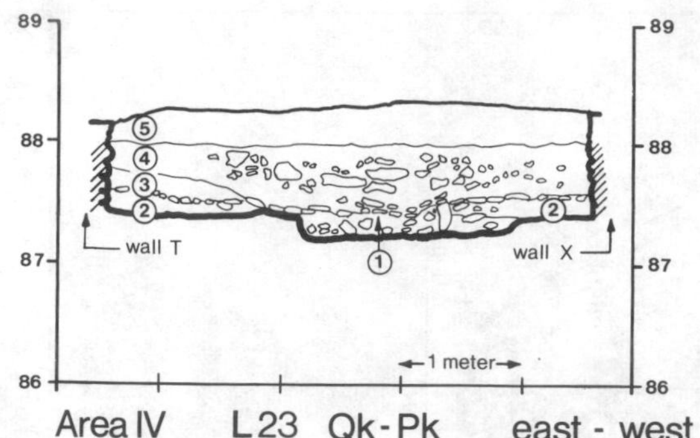

5. Slightly muddy gravelly sand: light brown, w/humus, roots, roof tiles, tumble, stone chips (plow soil)
4. Muddy sand: dark grey, w/humus, roots, charcoal, tumble, stone rubble (Early Byzantine)
3. Muddy sand: yellow, slightly compact above the tile layer (Early Byzantine)
2. Muddy sand: yellow (Early Byzantine)
1. Muddy sand: dark grey, w/tumble, stone rubble (Dark Age)

Figure 9-6

proves that the walls were carried up considerably farther in stone, possibly to their full height. On the other hand, level 3 in Fig. 9-6 might have resulted from the deterioration of mudbrick, once these walls were without a roof. Another interpretation of this level is that it represents deteriorated mud mortar. There is no other evidence, however, that these walls were built with mortar of any kind.

The fallen tiles in Rooms 1 and 2 (of the same types as those cataloged from Room 3 as **P1757-59**) prove that there was a tiled roof of the usual pan and cover type. The precise form of the roof cannot be determined. In modern buildings of this size throughout Messenia hipped roofs are commonly used, and this seems appropriate for Phase 1 of our building.

The destruction debris in Room 1 differed from that in Room 2. In Room 1 there was a layer of broken tiles underneath a layer of stone rubble (Figs. 9-4, 9-6, 9-15, 9-16; Pl. 9-21), in Room 2 only the layer of broken tiles. It seems likely that the chapel builders cleared the fallen stone in Room 2 and reused it in the new structure. Another possible explanation is that plowing and leveling began earlier in Room 2 and that this gradually cleared off the stone rubble but not the layer of tiles (see Pl. 9-19). Around Room 1, in any case, some portion of the walls must have remained standing long enough to allow a sunken trough to be formed by the weight of tiles on soil which was softened by collected rainwater. It was into this trough that the walls around Room 1 eventually collapsed. The layer of stone rubble here remained just beyond reach of the plow.

Very few objects were found in the destruction debris of these two rooms. From Room 1 came a bronze pin (**510**), and in Room 2 three iron nails (**531-33**) were recovered from under the fallen tiles.

PHASE 2

In Phase 2 (see Fig. 9-4) Unit IV-2 was enlarged toward the E. New Walls L, P, and M formed a 2.43 × 9.70 m addition. The clearest proof of the later date of Room 3 is that Wall L is not bonded into Wall Q. Yet in every respect the walls of Room 3 resemble those of the earlier phase (see Table 9-3), and they cannot be much later. The Phase 2 structure had an exterior doorway (Fig. 9-4), 1.00 m wide, which was later filled by the chapel builders. The doorway is delimited on the W side by the original outside corner made by Phase 1 Walls R and S, and on the E side by Wall M. The hipped roof of Phase 1 may have been extended over the new addition, or (perhaps less likely) a single-pitch roof may have covered it.

The chapel builders destroyed the S portion of the floor in Room 3 (Pl. 9-19). In what has survived, the floor resembles that in Room 2. It is of packed earth, upon which lay the fallen tile debris. The absence of stone rubble has already been commented upon in connection with Room 2.

Presumably Phase 1 is to be dated not long before Phase 2. Certainly all three rooms went out of use at the same time, and the building gradually disintegrated. A crushed B-i type amphora (**P1756**; Pl. 9-23) was found beneath fallen roof tiles in Room 3 and can be dated to ca. 460-520 (Hayes 1974). Thus we have an approximate *terminus post quem* for the abandonment of the Phase 2 building. In addition to the B-i storage amphora, the following cataloged objects were found in Room 3:

511, 512. Bronze game counters
562. Glass bead
P1757-59. Tile fragments

UNIT IV-2, PHASES 3 AND 4: THE CHAPEL

PHASE 3

To construct the chapel (i.e., Phase 3 of the complex), its builders made use of existing wall foundations in the SE part of the ruined Late Roman/Early Byzantine structure (Fig. 9-5). On the W side, their outer narthex wall (which has not survived) must have been built over the earlier Wall T. Moving counterclockwise around the exterior walls, the same is true for the wall built upon earlier Walls S and M, after first blocking the Phase 2 doorway. On the E side, two apses were built into the new Wall N, which overlies the earlier Wall P. At its S end, Wall N was destroyed by a later grave (see Chapter 11, p. 399). Wall O, the N exterior wall of the chapel, had no predecessor. It survives in only two segments, both of which are 0.60 m wide and two courses high (see Table 9-3). The W segment butts against the earlier Wall T, and the E segment bonds with the new chapel Wall N.

The only new exterior walls that survive, then, are Walls N and O, but they are sufficient to demonstrate how the chapel builders went about their work (Figs. 9-13, 9-14;

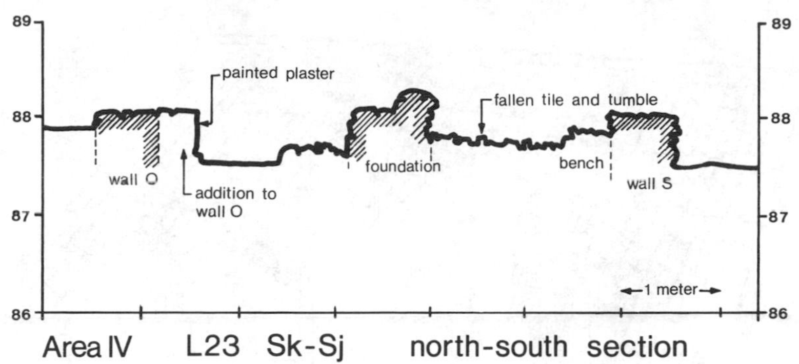

Figure 9-7

Pl. 9-24). The blocks vary widely in size, are not hammer-dressed, and no chinking is used. Wall O, the only exterior chapel wall that was not built on earlier foundations, does not even have a footing trench and is quite carelessly aligned. Compared with the walls of the underlying Late Roman/Early Byzantine building, the exterior chapel walls are of careless and flimsy construction.

The twin apses are actually extensions of Wall N (Pls. 9-25, 9-26). Three of the five preserved courses of Wall N were laid below the interior floor level and on top of previous Wall P (Figs. 9-13, 9-14; Pl. 9-27). The N apse is the larger of the two, occupying 1.71 m. (as opposed to 1.18 m) of Wall N. Both apses jut about a meter E from the outside wall line.

When the chapel was in use, the exterior ground level must have been between 87.60 and 88.00 m elevation, meaning that one would have stepped down slightly upon entering the chapel (note the elevation of the sanctuary floor in Fig. 9-14). No clear evidence of an exterior doorway was found, but its likeliest position is in the exterior narthex wall (T) at the W end of the chapel, as shown in Fig. 9-8 and in the cutaway perspective reconstruction (Fig. 9-9). Such is the case in numerous Byzantine churches.

There is every reason to suppose that all the interior wall surfaces were covered with painted plaster that bore religious scenes common to Byzantine fresco decoration (see Chapter 12, pp. 411, 412; 584-90). All that have survived from our chapel are some fragments found in place on the lowest parts of Walls N and O and numerous fresco fragments amid the narthex and sanctuary destruction debris.

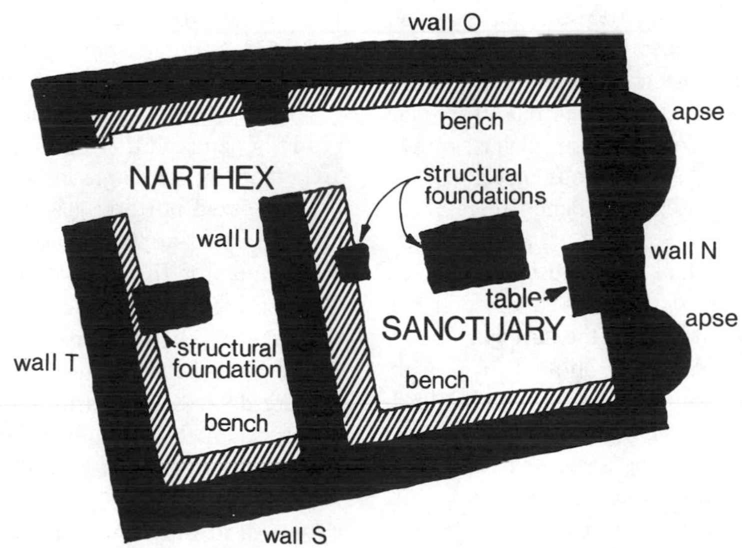

Figure 9-8

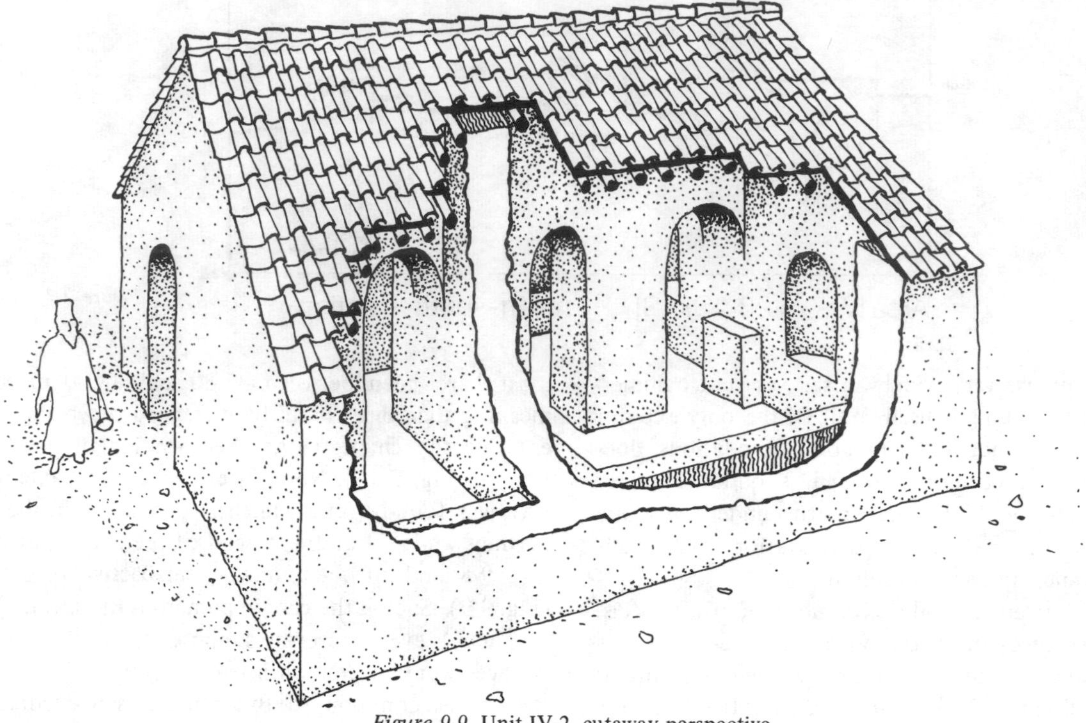

Figure 9-9. Unit IV-2, cutaway perspective of reconstructed chapel, Phases 3 and 4

A low bench, 0.40-0.60 m wide and about 0.30 m high (Fig. 9-7), is preserved along the S and W sides of the sanctuary (Figs. 9-8; Pl. 9-25). Originally, the bench probably also ran along the base of Wall O, although during Phase 4 it seems to have been continued up to roof level as further support for Wall O. Such benches are not uncommon in small Byzantine and post-Byzantine churches. In 1973 the author saw a similar arrangement in the ruins of a small church near Chora, in SW Peloponnese. Some upright stones (Pl. 9-28) along Walls O and T in our chapel narthex strongly suggest that there was also a bench there (Figs. 9-8, 9-14).

Although no evidence remains, there must have been an interior doorway through the partition Wall U (as in Fig. 9-8), which divided the sanctuary from the narthex. Wall U, of flimsy construction like Wall O, is about 0.70 m wide and is now preserved only in its S part. Perhaps the doorway was off-center toward the N end.

The altars must have been in the apses (as in Figs. 9-9, 9-10, 9-11) and were most likely built up to table height. Above the altars there would have been niches, as in the church of St. Mecurious on Corfu (Vokotopoulos 1967-68). The remains of three rubble-constructed piers survive along the E-W axis of the chapel (Figs. 9-5, 9-8, 9-14; Pl 9-18). These piers would have been connected by arches, thus forming one continuous central roof support. A structure that juts out from Wall N between the apses is not in line with the three piers and seems to have been a kind of table (as in Figs. 9-9, 9-10, 9-11, 9-14).

The roof of both the Phase 3 and Phase 4 chapel was probably hipped, as is indicated by the presence of fragments of ridge tiles (e.g. **P1760**) in the final destruction debris. Before the final destruction of the chapel, however, there seems to have been a fire in the Phase 3 narthex which necessitated some repair (Phase 4) at the W end of the chapel (Fig. 9-13).

The fire that gutted the narthex does not seem to have seriously damaged the remainder of the chapel. The cleanup after that fire left some important evidence in the form of broken glazed pottery, glass, and a coin (**502**) of Manuel I Comnenus (1143-80) in destruction debris which was used as packing for the new narthex floor. Destruction debris was also used to construct a new pier in the narthex (Figs. 9-8, 9-14; Pl. 9-28). Some of the glazed pottery (especially **P1708-10** and **P1712**) suggests a late 12th, even early 13th century date for the narthex fire. One particularly interesting aspect of the cleanup after the fire involves the bases of four glazed bowls (**P1708, 1711, 1719**, and **1720**), which were placed carefully next to one another, their bottoms upturned, in the deposit (Pl. 9-29). These glazed bowls may have come from above an entrance to the narthex, in the tympanum. The objects recovered from the Phase 3 chapel, then, belong to the destruction debris used to make a new (Phase 4) narthex floor. They include the following cataloged items:

502. Bronze coin of Manuel I Comnenus
513, 515, 516, 518. Bronze fillet fragments
543. Pierced stone slab

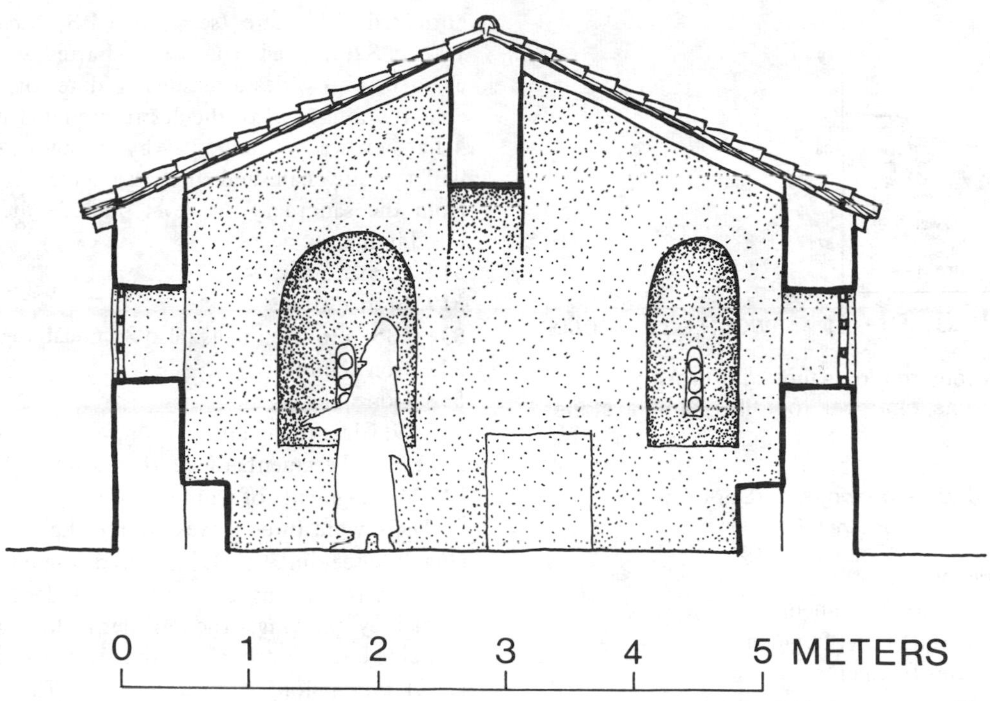

Figure 9-10. Unit IV-2, N-S elevation of reconstructed chapel

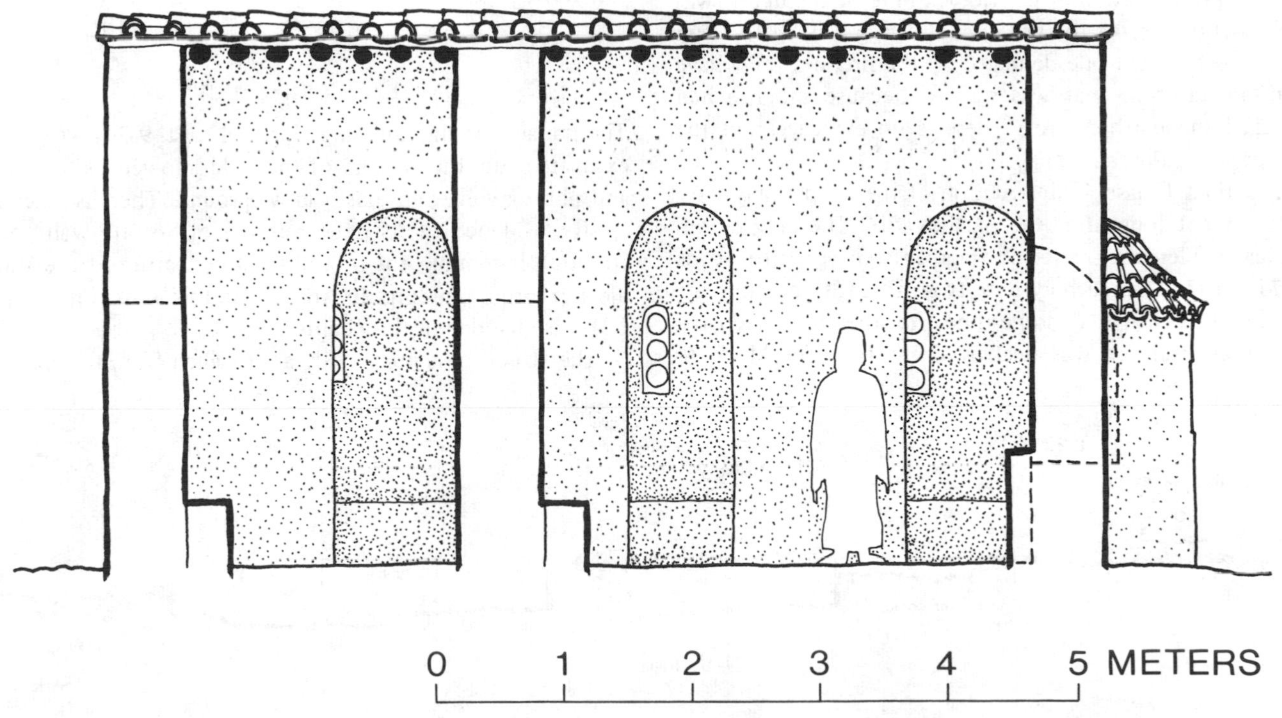

Figure 9-11. Unit IV-2, E-W elevation of reconstructed chapel

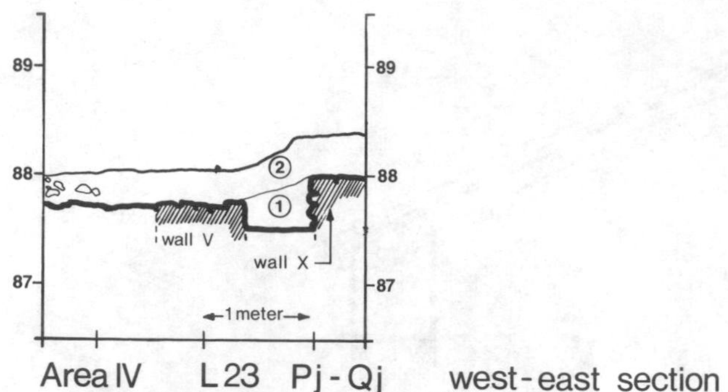

2. Slightly gravelly muddy sand: light brown, w/humus, roots, charcoal, roof tiles, tumble, stone chips (plow soil)
1. Muddy sand: dark brown, soft (Dark Age)

Figure 9-12

563-75. Glass fragments
P1707-11. Sgraffito bowl fragments
P1719-23. Painted ware bowl fragments
P1731, 1732. Brazier fragments
P1733-53. Fragments of coarse ware jugs

The only items recovered from the sanctuary that could belong to Phase 3 are painted plaster fragments **(584-90)**.

PHASE 4

The narthex fire made necessary rather extensive repairs at the W end of the chapel, although they probably did not alter the chapel's appearance. Destruction debris was leveled to create a new narthex floor. Some of the debris was used as chinking for the new pier abutting Wall T. This pier may have replaced one damaged by the fire, or it may have been an addition that was needed because the fire had damaged the narthex roof. There is no evidence that the fire spread to the sanctuary.

The final (Phase 4) destruction of the chapel may have occurred not long after the narthex fire. The only chronological evidence consists of fragments of sgraffito bowls **(P1712, 1713)** which may date from the 13th century. At any rate, it is clear that, some time after the Phase 4 repairs, the whole building was destroyed by fire. The MASCA-corrected C-14 date (see Table 1-3, *Nichoria* I, p. 5) of 1003 ± 82, derived from some charred wood in the sanctuary debris, provides a reasonable date for the initial chapel construction. Most of the destruction debris from the Phase 4 narthex was carried away by the plow, except for some undiagnostic nail and tile fragments. Objects recovered from the sanctuary, however, include the following cataloged items:

514. Bronze fillet
519. Bronze stylus
534, 535, 536. Iron nails (also 24 uncataloged iron nails)
537. Iron clamp
538. Iron spike
576-79. Glass fragments
P1712-15. Fragments of sgraffito ware
P1724. Fragments of painted ware

There were three graves around the exterior of the apses (Fig. 9-5; see pp. 398, 399). Two of the burials were of children, their remains close to the modern surface and disturbed by plowing. The northern child grave (NB 12-1) contained scattered faience beads **(583)** and a lead bead **(542)** that belonged to a necklace. The third burial (NB 10-1) was that of an adult female, placed in a stone-lined and slab-covered cist grave, with no grave goods. The space occupied by this grave robbed out part of the SE corner of the chapel wall (reused Wall M). Clearly, when this burial was made the chapel was already in ruins and the foundations of its E end were beneath ground level. Thus the memory of this holy place seems to have survived the structure itself.

J.R.

UNIT L21-1: GRID L21 UVWtu

The remains of this building (Fig. 9-17; Pl. 9-30) were not excavated but the owners of the field allowed us to clean and photograph what exists above ground. There is no conclusive evidence of its date, but the orthostate wall construction is reminiscent of a distinctive feature of the Middle Byzantine buildings in Area II. On this basis alone, Unit L21-1 is included in this chapter.

The structure is most easily approached from the area of

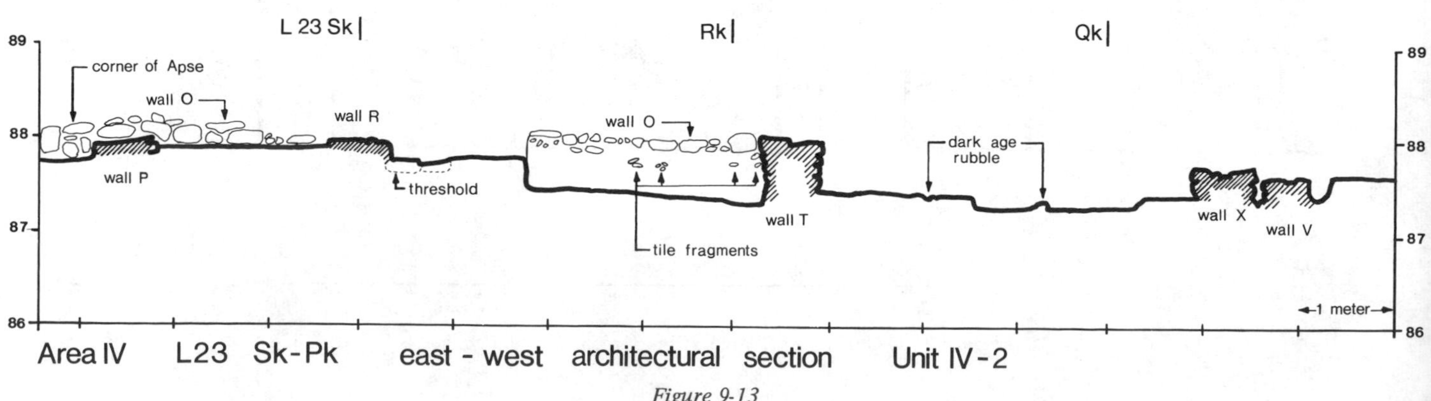

Figure 9-13

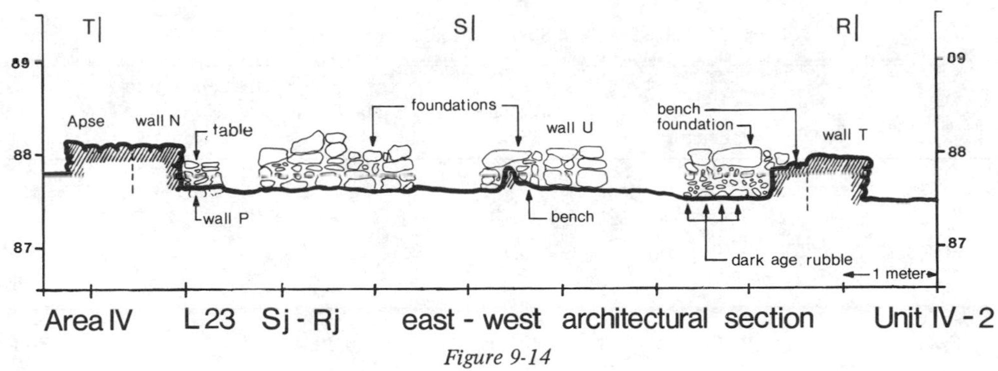

Figure 9-14

the chapel that lies about 150 m to the N. A gentle upward slope terminates in a knoll on whose other three sides the ground drops off more steeply. The foundations on top of the knoll consist of three walls (A, B, C), none of which is preserved to its original length. Walls A (present length 9.20 m) and B (present length 5.50 m) form the only visible exterior corner, presumably the NW corner of the whole structure. Both walls are 0.50-0.60 m wide and are composed of heavy orthostate blocks, some of which are 0.30-0.40 m thick. Wall C (present length 9.40 m) is 0.50 m wide and would appear to be an interior partition, since Wall B continues beyond their juncture. The room formed between Walls A, B, and C is 3.10 m wide, and its preserved length is 9.40 m. A probable interior doorway in Wall C is indicated by a vertical block about 4.50 m E of Wall B that may mark the E limit of the doorway.

Unit L21-1 must have been an impressive building, located on a knoll that affords excellent drainage and a commanding view over the ridge and beyond. The walls were carefully made of quarried and hammer-dressed limestone blocks, placed in two upright parallel rows with rubble fill and careful chinking. The orthostate construction, so similar to that of the Byzantine buildings in Area II, suggests a date in the late 10th or 11th century for the construction of Unit L21-1. The great orthostate blocks were probably reused from the monumental (classical?) podium whose ruins lie only some 30 m to the N (see Chapter 7, pp. 337, 340). Without excavation, we can only conjecture that Unit L21-1 was a storage building, like Phases 1 and 2 of Unit IV-2, rather than a proper dwelling of the type recovered in Area II.

J.R.

Analysis

Simple and unpretentious as these buildings may have been, the ruins of Late Roman and Byzantine date from Nichoria still provide precious evidence about the architecture of Greece during this period. For example, our knowledge of Roman houses and villas in Greece is "amazingly small" according to one authority, who further notes that the

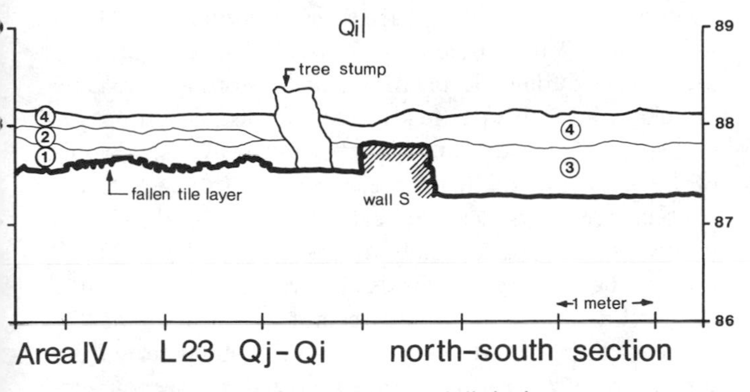

4. Slightly gravelly muddy sand: light brown, w/humus, roots, charcoal, roof tiles, tumble, stone chips (plow soil)
3. Muddy sand: dark brown, w/humus, slightly compact (Dark Age IIa)
2. Muddy sand: dark grey, w/humus, roots, charcoal, tumble, stone chips (Early Byzantine)
1. Muddy sand: yellow, slightly compact (Early Byzantine)

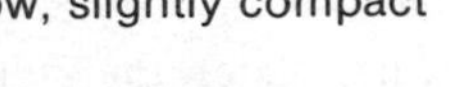

Figure 9-15

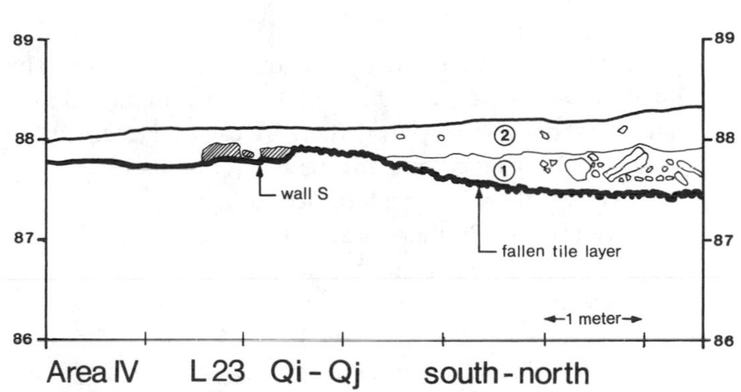

2. Slightly gravelly muddy sand: light brown, w/humus, roots, charcoal, roof tiles, tumble, stone chips (plow soil)
1. Muddy sand: dark grey, w/humus, roots, charcoal, tumble, stone chips, roof tile (Early Byzantine)

Figure 9-16

Table 9-3. Wall Specifications: Unit IV-2

Wall	Grid	Length	Average Width	Maximum Height	Maximum Number of Courses	Bond/Butt
			Phases 1 and 2			
X	PQijk	8.80 (pres.)	0.70	0.42	3	Bonds with S and Q
Q	PQRSkl	9.40 (pres.)	0.70	0.50	4	Bonds with R, T, X (originally); butts on L
P	Sjkl	9.60 (pres.)	0.70	0.70	5	Bonds with L, M
S	QRSij	9.70	0.70	0.60	5	Bonds with T, X; butts on U
R	RSkl	9.81	0.70	0.80	6	Bonds with Q, S (?)
T	QRjkl	9.66 (pres.)	0.70	0.65	5	Bonds with Q, S; butts on O
L	RSl	2.43 (pres.)	0.70	0.70	6	Bonds with P; butts on Q
M	Sj	1.47 (pres.)	0.70	0.50	4	Bonds with P
			Phases 3 and 4			
O	Sk	2.40; 2.33 (segments)	0.60	0.30	2	Bonds with N; butts on T; built over P
N	Sjk	5.25 (pres.)	0.60	0.58	5	Bonds with O; built over P
(apses) U	Rj	2.70	0.70	0.50	3	Butts on S

study of Roman surface remains "is desperately needed" (McKay 1975, p. 211). It is within this context that MME surface reconnaissance of Roman sites in the Five Rivers area and the excavation of Unit IV-2, Phases 1 and 2 should be viewed.

An approximate date for Unit IV-2, Phases 1 and 2 is provided by the B-i type storage amphora in Room 3. The building was in use from about 460 to 520, although it may have been built somewhat earlier. We cannot be sure of the function(s) it served and the reason(s) for its location in Area IV, but there is some basis for speculation.

Obviously this building was not a villa, or part of a villa complex. There are no baths, no evidence of marble and mosaic work, and the location would seem to be less than ideal for a villa (see *Nichoria* I, pp. 99, 100 where the criteria for villa sites are discussed; also Percival 1976, pp. 51-105). No other structures from this period are known to have existed on the Nichoria ridge. The building apparently stood alone in the late 5th/early 6th century in Area IV. It was a large and very carefully built structure. A storage amphora was the only object left in place when the building was abandoned. At least occasional domestic use is perhaps indicated by the few minor finds that were recovered. The building gradually disintegrated from disuse and neglect. That, in sum, is what is known about Phases 1 and 2 of Unit IV-2.

With these sparse facts in mind, we propose that the building was intended primarily as a large *apotheke,* a facility for processing and storing agricultural produce grown on the hilltop. One has also to consider the possibility that it was a kind of large-scale *agrospito,* or country field house. Much more modest mudbrick structures are used today during the planting and harvesting seasons by farmers who cultivate fields at some distance from the village, town, or estate in which they normally reside. Some of the modern buildings have an upper story, where the seasonal occupants sleep and eat. The space on the ground floor is then used exclusively for the storage of crops, tools and for the stabling of animals. The relative lack of household debris, however, would seem to cast doubt on the *agrospito* theory and to suggest that our building served as a simple *apotheke* for the processing and storage of agricultural produce.

The Phase 2 addition is so similar to Phase 1 in design and construction as to suggest that there was no radical alteration of the building's previous function. If it was simply more space that was needed, the addition may indicate increasing agricultural prosperity in the Nichoria locale during the late 5th/early 6th centuries.

Several centuries later the ruins of the Late Roman/

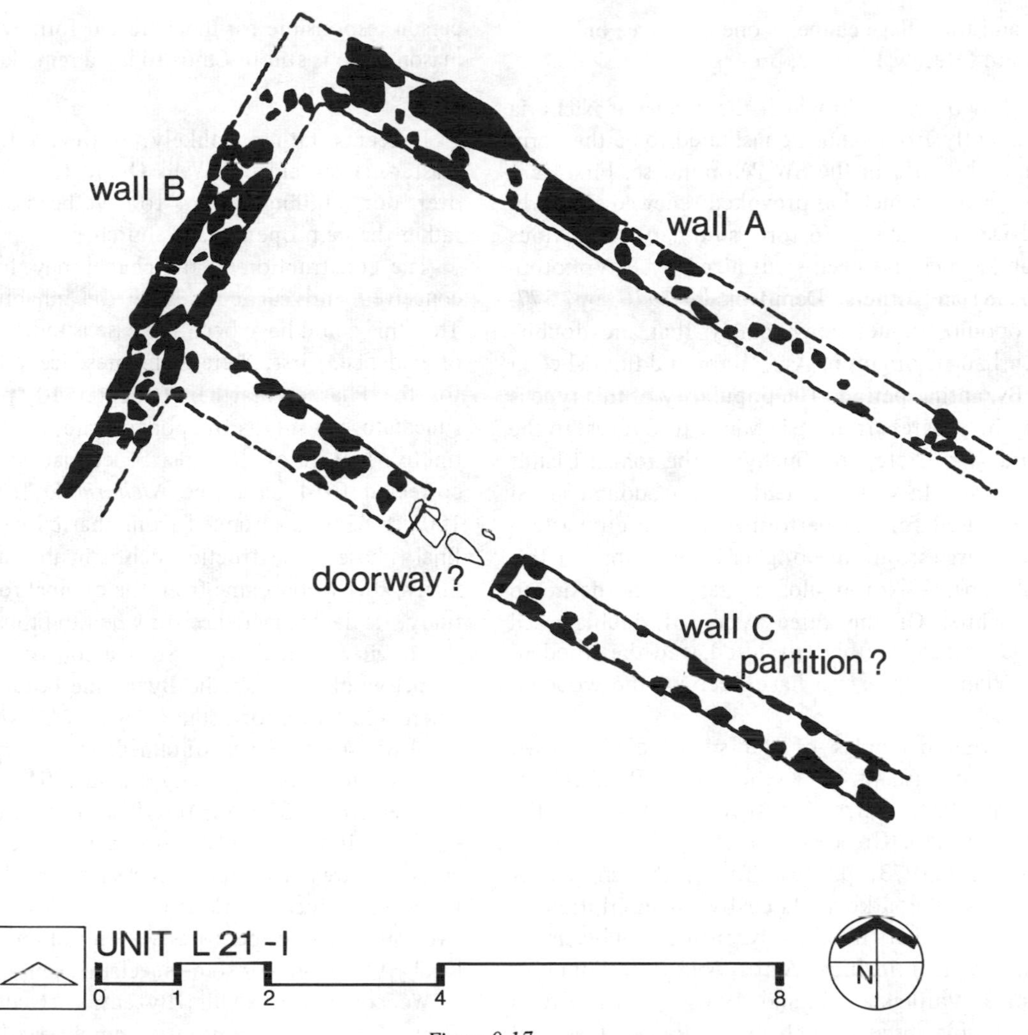

Figure 9-17

Early Byzantine building were apparently discovered in the early stages of the chapel construction. The deep and solid foundations would have suggested to the later builders that they should utilize them wherever possible. They did, in fact, build three of the exterior chapel walls over Walls P, S, and T of the Phase 2 structure. It is to this Middle Byzantine chapel, Unit IV-2, Phases 3 and 4, that we now direct our attention.

There are numerous small churches in the Peloponnese dating from the Middle Byzantine period (Bon 1951, pp. 138-42). Among the most impressive in Messenia are those at Samarina (*MME* 1972, Pl. 11-2) and at Kalamata (Kalokyres 1973). In the Mani there are, of course, many Middle Byzantine churches (see, e.g., Drandakis 1964, Megaw 1932-33). One can even speak of an independent Greek style of church construction during the two centuries prior to the Latin occupation (Megaw 1931-32, p. 90). The typical process by which churches were constructed during the Middle Byzantine period has been described as follows:

The craftsmen were organized in travelling Guilds (*Synergasiai*). This in itself would ensure unity of style over a given area at any time; while, on the other hand, new techniques whether due to isolated experiment or to external influence would with great difficulty replace the old, but once embodied in the general tradition would be universally employed.

The considerable variety of plan in churches approximately contemporary seems at first contradictory. The choice of plan was, however, by no means arbitrary; each church conformed to one or other of about half a dozen types, large and small, which at a given date varied but little through the whole of Greece. The builder no doubt chose from among these according to his resources, and perhaps his individual preference. But there his control ended; he could not break the continuity of a strong tradition. Together with diversity of type there was inevitably identity of structure. So in painting the Byzantine artist retained a single manner for a wide range of subjects. The humblest and most pretentious expressions were framed in a common medium; technique of structure and ornamentation united them. Architecturally the difference between the rich monastery church and the village chapel is one of degree only, not one of kind (Megaw 1931-32, pp. 99-100).

Yet there are two aspects in which the chapel at Nichoria differs significantly from what is considered to be the norm for Byzantine churches in the SW Peloponnese. First, it is double-apsed, a plan which has provoked renewed scholarly interest (see Demitrokalis 1976 for a summary of previous literature) and which has been scrutinized by P. Vokotopoulos (1967-68) and others (Demitrokalis 1976, pp. 377-83). Vokotopoulos argues convincingly that the double-apsed church had its origins in Asia Minor and flourished in the Middle Byzantine period. The popularity of this type is evidenced by its progress from Asia Minor to Cyprus, to the Aegean islands and Crete, and finally to the Ionian islands and southern Italy. In Venetian-held districts, double-apsed churches were used for the performance of both Eastern and Western liturgies; but the original motivation for this architectural type, Vokotopoulos argues, is the desire to honor two saints. Of the three types of double-apsed churches—the domed, the barrel-vaulted, and the wooden-roofed—our chapel appears to have been of the wooden-roofed variety.

Some surviving examples of the small, double-apsed church are on the island of Kythera (see Demitrokalis 1976, pp. 189-205), which "must have shared in the prosperity of southern Greece in the eleventh and twelfth centuries" (Herrin 1973, p. 46). There, the church of Ayios Demetrios at Pourko is dated by an inscription to the year 1100. Other Middle Byzantine double-apsed churches on Kythera include Ayios Nikon at Potamos, Ayios Blasios at Phriligkiankia, and Ayios Yiannis at Ayia Mone. The double-apsed church of Ayioi Kosmas and Damianos may be considerably earlier (Herrin 1973, pp. 43-46; Vokotopoulos 1967-68, p. 74). The several examples from Kythera are barrel-vaulted and domed, however, and they were probably more sumptuous than the wooden-roofed Nichoria chapel. Nevertheless, in view of the scarcity of Middle Byzantine churches and chapels of the double-apsed type reported for mainland Greece (Demitrokalis 1976, pp. 210-32; Vokotopoulos 1967-68, p. 74), our chapel merits scholarly interest.

Another characteristic in which our chapel deviates from the norm for known Byzantine churches in the SW Peloponnese is in its modest size and casual construction. It is hard to imagine that a traveling guild of craftsmen constructed this building. Rather, we are reminded of many simple Greek churches that are post-Byzantine in date. On the island of Chios, for example, in recent times simple village churches were built in the following way:

> The local priest, who in the villages was frequently a man with no special knowledge, was the chairman of a committee of village notables entrusted with the collection of the necessary funds; the labour was provided free by the villagers. No architect was employed and the person responsible for their present form was the master-mason, who is still in Chios today a remarkable figure (Smith 1962, p. 3).

It seems rather unlikely, however, that even a local master-mason laid out Walls O and U of our chapel. Moreover, our building appears to have been an isolated chapel rather than a proper village church.

The construction of the chapel may, in fact, have been conceived and carried out by the inhabitants in Area II. That this could have been the case is indicated by two kinds of evidence. First, there is the presence in the floor packing for the Phase 4 narthex (Chapter 10, p. 379) of a few (uncataloged) sherds of spongy ware, a fabric that is a distinctive feature of the Area II occupation. Also, a MASCA-corrected C-14 date (see *Nichoria* I, Table 1-3, p. 5) of 1003 ± 82 was obtained from charred wood found in the final (Phase 4) destruction debris in the sanctuary. If, as is likely, this wood came from the original roof over the sanctuary, its date is evidence for when the timbers were cut for the original chapel roof. Such a construction date for the chapel would overlap the Byzantine occupation in Area II, where a MASCA-corrected C-14 date (*Nichoria* I, Table 1-3, p. 5) of 946 ± 98 was obtained (see p. 358). The evidence from small finds, especially a coin (**501**), and pottery (see Chapter 10, pp. 379, 405) confirms this chronological bracket. Thus, it is certainly possible that the owner(s) or tenant(s) of Area II built the chapel, probably with the aid of friends and local workmen. The edifice was dedicated to two saints whose identities we do not know, but who were locally venerated for some special reason.

We come now to the Byzantine structures in Area II. First of all, it is important to emphasize how significant a report of *any* secular architecture from the Middle Byzantine period is. Much of what is known about such architecture is derived from urban sites excavated in Greece, especially from Corinth, Athens, and Thebes (see Bouras 1974, pp. 32-36, 50-52 for a full bibliography). Much less is known about village architecture during this period, although some information can be gathered from the study of still inhabited medieval villages of Chios (Kriesis 1965, pp. 131-34, 182-84), and to a lesser extent from available literary texts (see, for example, Laiou-Thomadakis 1977, pp. 36, 37).

Surface exploration and excavation demonstrate that our structures in Area II on the Nichoria ridge were not part of a proper "village," in the sense of a concentrated settlement. On the other hand, if one thinks of a Byzantine village as including the fields, fruit trees, gardens, mills, woods, and even swamps belonging to that settlement, then a village connection becomes possible. It is known that in Macedonia in the late 13th and early 14th centuries the Byzantine village was just such a geographical unity (Laiou-Thomadakis 1977, pp. 24-71). A village territory could vary considerably in size, but 5.5 km^2 might be considered moderately large. Villagers normally lived in a concentrated settlement, perhaps in a fortified enclosure (the *kastron*) or just outside it (Laiou-Thomadakis 1977, pp. 36, 37); but the village property on which subsistence depended extended considerably farther.

The eccentric location of our Area II structures may have been dictated by several factors, including those connected with known charcoal production and apparent metal working. One notes, for example, the handy transportation facilities for ore, the presence of hilltop drafts for the furnaces, and especially the availability of wood for making charcoal. Although it is often stated that by classical times much of Greece was deforested, this may not have been the case around Nichoria (see *MME* 1972, pp. 226, 247; *Nichoria* I, pp. 56, 57). The threat of malaria and the general dampness of the coast in the winter may also have favored hilltop locations, as they did until very recently in the Karpofora-Rizomilo locale (*MME* 1972, p. 61). The furnace in Area II, incidentally, was probably of the Catalan type, commonly used in the Mediterranean for the production of charcoal (Singer et al. 1957, pp. 41-80, Fig. 38B).

It is conceivable, then, that the Byzantine occupants of Area II were residents of a village, if the term is used to refer to the larger geographical entity and not just to a concentration of houses. The latter could have been in Petalidhi or Kastania (see *MME* 1972, Pocket Map 5-8), or perhaps closer at hand. For instance, the existence of the village of Karpofora can be traced back at least to the late 16th century, under the name "Caracasili" (Sauerwein 1969, No. 8 in the register under "Territorio di Coron"; see also *MME* 1972, p. 49).

So our residents in Area II may have had another house in the village center, wherever that center may have been (for an example of this practice, see Laiou-Thomadakis 1977, pp. 36, 37). Their inferred agricultural activity elsewhere on the ridge could have been seasonal, and Unit L21-1 may have played a part in it. Even if the Area II residents were responsible for the building of the chapel in Area IV, this would not necessarily indicate a year-round occupancy of Area II. In any case, the choice of Area II as a place of residence was probably dictated by factors having to do mainly with the apparent metallurgical activity, and the cultivation of foodstuffs on the ridge may have been subsidiary. Profits from both agricultural and industrial operations may have made possible the building of the chapel in Area IV.

J.R.
W.A.M.

REFERENCES

Bon, A. 1951. *Le Péloponnèse byzantin jusqu'en 1204*. Paris.

Bouras, C. 1974. "Houses and Settlements in Byzantine Greece." In *Shelter in Greece*, ed. B. Doumanis and P. Oliver, pp. 30-53. Athens. In Greek and English.

Demitrokalis, G. 1976. *Double-apsed Christian Churches*. Athens. In Greek.

Drandakis, N. B. 1964. *Byzantine Wall Paintings of the Middle Mani*. Athens. In Greek.

Hayes, J. 1974. October 30, personal communication to J. Rosser.

Herrin, J. 1973. "Byzantine Kythera." In *Kythera: Excavations and Studies*. ed. J. N. Coldstream and G. L. Huxley, pp. 41-51. Park Ridge, N.J.

Kalokyres, C. 1973. *Byzantine Churches of the Holy Metropolis of Messenia*. Thessalonika. In Greek.

Kriesis, A. 1965. *Greek Town Building*. Athens.

Laiou-Thomadakis, A. E. 1977. *Peasant Society in the Late Byzantine Empire. A Social and Demographic Study*. Princeton, N. J.

McDonald, W. A., and Rapp, G., Jr., eds. 1972. *The Minnesota Messenia Expedition: Reconstructing a Bronze Age Regional Environment*. Minneapolis.

McKay, A. G. 1975. *Houses, Villas, and Palaces in the Roman World*. London.

Megaw, A. H. S. 1931-32. "The Chronology of Some Middle-Byzantine Churches," *BSA* 32:90-130.

———. 1932-33. "Byzantine Architecture in Mani," *BSA* 33: 137-62.

MME 1972 = McDonald and Rapp 1972.

Nichoria I = Rapp and Aschenbrenner 1978.

Percival, J. 1976. *The Roman Villa: An Historical Introduction*. Berkeley and Los Angeles.

Rapp, G., Jr., and Aschenbrenner, S. E., eds. 1978. *Excavations at Nichoria in Southwest Greece* I: *Site, Environs, and Techniques*. Minneapolis.

Sauerwein, F. 1969. "Das Siedlungsbild der Peloponnes um das Jahr 1700," *Erdkunde* 23:237-44.

Singer, C., Holmyard, E. J., Hall, A. R., and Williams, T. I. 1957. *A History of Technology, II: The Mediterranean Civilizations and the Middle Ages, c. 700 B.C. to c. A.D. 1500*. Oxford.

Smith, A. C. 1962. *The Architecture of Chios*. London.

Vasiliades, D. 1955. "The Arch in Aegean Ecclesiastical Architecture," *Technica Chronika* 369-70:3-6. In Greek.

———. 1961. *Middle Byzantine Aegean Ecclesiastical Architecture*. Athens. In Greek.

———. 1962a. "Singly-Oriented Basilicas with Two Sacred Apses," *Zigos* 78:3-7. In Greek.

———. 1962b. *The Flat-Roofed Middle Byzantine Churches of the Cyclades*. Athens. In Greek.

Vokotopoulos, P. 1967-68. "A Contribution to the Study of Single-Room Churches with Two Sacred Apses." *Festschrift for Anastasios K. Orlandos* 4: 66-74. Library of the Athenian Archaeological Society, no. 54. Athens. In Greek.

10
The Pottery

by
John Rosser

Our knowledge of Byzantine pottery from Greece has its origins in the 1910-11 publication of Byzantine glazed pottery from the British School's excavations at Sparta. The authors of that publication, R. M. Dawkins and J. P. Droop, laid "no claim to speak as experts" about pottery "whose date and general relations are still matters of some doubt" (Dawkins and Droop 1910-11, p. 23). Not until considerably later was a sound basis laid for the study of Byzantine glazed pottery (Rice 1930), and subsequently much work has been done to create a sound typology and chronological framework (see MacKay 1967, p. 249 and Megaw 1975, p. 34 for the basic bibliography).

However much we may owe to the study of glazed wares from outside Greece (e.g., Peschlow 1977-78 for Istanbul and Yakobson 1959 for Cherson), it is nonetheless true that we are most indebted to the studies of wares recovered from Athens, Corinth, and elsewhere in Greece. Byzantine pottery from the Athenian Agora was published by F. O. Waagé in 1933 and A. Frantz in 1938. In 1942 C. H. Morgan published the corpus of Corinth's Byzantine glazed pottery and in so doing provided a basic chronological framework for Middle Byzantine glazed wares. Morgan's work has to some extent been clarified in recent years (e.g., Megaw 1968, 1975; Rice 1966), and an important study of Corinth's Byzantine coarse wares has appeared (MacKay 1967).

As a result, more is known about Byzantine pottery in Greece, and especially in the Peloponnese, than for any other part of the Byzantine empire. The importance of the Corinth material is particularly evident in dealing with Nichoria's Byzantine pottery. Our excavations produced parallels with Corinthian glazed wares, thus providing us with a useful chronological framework which was neatly confirmed by radiocarbon and numismatic evidence (see p. 358). The publication of our pottery will make a modest but important contribution to the knowledge of Byzantine glazed and coarse wares from the Peloponnese. Some of the Nichoria glazed wares are distinctive in their decoration and probably reflect an as yet unidentified local source of manufacture. The same can be said of our coarse wares, all of which are equally distinctive, firmly dated, and not like other published coarse wares from the Peloponnese.

The pottery was found almost exclusively within and immediately around the ruined Byzantine structures in Areas II and IV. In Area II, such pottery finds dwindled beyond about an eight-meter radius of Units II-1 and II-2. In Area IV, Byzantine tile and pottery fragments were spread over a slightly larger space, especially in the plowsoil N and S of the chapel (Unit IV-2, Phases 3-4) to about 20 m in either direction. Similar fragments were found to the E of the chapel, but not in such quantity or to such a distance. This probably indicates N to S plowing here in modern times. It is also worth noting that in Area II, where the Byzantine settlers built in part on prehistoric foundations, there is considerable mixing with prehistoric sherds. Nevertheless, the later pottery is almost always easily distinguished.

The reader should particularly notice the following points: (1) the importance of the few glazed sherds from Area II in providing information about date of occupation and standard of living; (2) **P1756** (NP104), the B-i amphora that dates Unit IV-2, Phases 1-2, to the late 5th/early 6th century; (3) the narthex floor packing in Unit IV-2, Phase 4, the pottery from which fixes the date of some important events in the architectural history of the chapel; and (4) the roof tiles, which are of interest primarily because so few such Byzantine tiles are properly published.

In Chapter 9 the pottery and minor objects from the rooms of Units II-1, II-2, and IV-2 are recorded within their broader architectural contexts (see pp. 360-63, 372). Here, however, we shall provide detailed descriptions of glazed and coarse wares, preceded by a general discussion of the pottery from each area, with emphasis on important problems, cataloged items of particular interest, and the connections between the pottery of the two areas. The catalog itself is organized primarily by area. Within each area, the glazed wares are first considered under the headings Sgraffito Wares and Painted Wares. Coarse wares are then treated, together by type if possible, followed by representative tiles. Entries that can be easily grouped by deposit are so grouped. Finally, Munsell Soil Color Chart designations are used throughout to describe more precisely glaze and fabric color (Munsell Products 1973).

Area II Glazed Wares

Fragments of a plate, a cup, and a small jug are all that comprise this category. A bronze coin (**501**) of Basil II (976-1025) is in general agreement with the date of these glazed sherds, except for **P1679**, the plate fragment, which may be late 11th or early 12th century.

P1677 (NP134). Cup. Fig. 10-1; Pl. 10-1.
D. rim 0.09.
Rim frag., body frag., and ring handle. Fine white fabric, thinly potted with small dark grits. On the exterior body, zigzag of yellow, red, and black. Yellow lip. On handle, alternating stripes of yellow, black and red. Thin, clear glaze on exterior.
Deltion 26 (1971), Pl. 115 a, c (lower right).
Constantinopolitan-type polychrome White Ware cup, probably imported. See *Corinth XI*, Pls. xii-xvii, perhaps 11th century; an unpublished Corinth example, C-38-286, has a similar handle and lip decoration and seems to come from a 10th-century context. See also Yakobson 1959, p. 356, Fig. 187, 1, and p. 358, no. 4, Pl. xviii, not later than the 10th century. A 10th-11th century date is assigned to polychrome wares from Istanbul; see Peschlow 1977-78, p. 376.
K25 Gbc, level 3, lot 876.

P1678 (NP135). Jug. Fig. 10-2; Pl. 10-2.
H. (pres.) base 0.045. D. base 0.045.
Button base. White fabric with small dark grits, similar to **P1677**. Mottled olive green glaze (Munsell 5Y 5/3 to 4/2) over interior and exterior.
Probably a type of Undecorated White Ware.
K25 Gbc, level 3, lot 993.

P1679 (NP138), Plate. Fig. 10-3; Pl. 10-3.
D. (est.) rim 0.23.
Nearly flat rim and lip. Black radial stripes along rim interior. Slip and thin green glaze on exterior and interior. Pink fabric (Munsell 5YR 8/4).
Deltion 26 (1971), Pl. 115 c (upper left).
See *Corinth XI*, Pl. xx, a and c, also Pl. xxi, a, for early 12th-century Green and Brown Painted plates with similar radial stripes along the rim. The form of the Nichoria rim frag. suggests a late 11th or early 12th century date.
K25 Fbc, level 2, lot 964.

Area II Coarse Wares

The coarse wares most characteristic of the Byzantine presence in Area II are the numerous tile and "spongy ware" fragments. The latter occur in most Area II Byzantine lots and in several Area IV lots (3433, 3440, 4114, 4115 and 4142, the last in the chapel narthex floor deposit). Our fragments appear to have come from modest jugs. They are contemporary with the three glazed pieces discussed above (**P1677-79**) and thus provide evidence for a contemporaneous occupation in Areas II and IV.

Spongy ware (**P1680-89**) is a distinctive Byzantine coarse ware. The fabric is hard, often reddish brown, but frequently showing various hues of gray as well. When gray, the color is probably due to reduction firing. This is a common cause of gray fabric color, although the presence of ferrous iron is another (Rhodes 1973, pp. 264, 265). The most characteristic feature of spongy ware, however, is its "pinholing" over the fabric surface. Pinholing can occur in both clay fabrics and glazes. Pinholes are small craters caused by bubbles of a gas, whatever its composition, rising during firing from the pores of the fabric, or in the case of a glaze from the glaze layer. Overfiring can be a cause of pinholing, although there are other possible causes (Cardew 1969, pp. 152, 153). A close examination of the spongy ware rims (Pl. 10-4) shows both the minute pinholes in the fabric and the characteristic grayer hues.

Another category of Byzantine coarse ware from Area II (**P1690-1701**) is similar to spongy ware in its shapes. The fabric, however, is not pinholed, nor is the color ever gray. Like the spongy ware, this coarse ware is presumed to be contemporary with the glazed wares (**P1677-79**).

AREA II SPONGY WARE JUG AND/OR JAR FRAGMENTS (PL. 10-4)

P1680. Fig. 10-4; Pl. 10-5.
H. (pres.) bottom 0.03. D. (est.) bottom 0.10.
Bottom frag. Flat bottom and deep body.
Pinkish fabric (Munsell 7.5YR 7/4).
J25 Ua, level 1, lot 1721.

P1681. Fig. 10-5.
H. (pres.) bottom 0.024. D. (est.) bottom 0.16.
Similar to **P1680**. Fabric light red on interior (Munsell 2.5YR 6/6), grayish brown on exterior (Munsell 2.5YR 5/2).
K25 Gbc, level 2, lot 871.

P1682. Fig. 10-6.
H. (pres.) bottom 0.024. D. (est.) bottom 0.12.
Similar to **P1680** and **1681**. Fabric very pale brown (Munsell 10YR 7/3) on interior, reddish yellow (Munsell 5YR 7/6) on exterior.
K25 Gbc, level 2, lot 868.

P1683. Fig. 10-7.
H. (pres.) rim 0.059. D. (est.) rim 0.14.

High, slightly outcurving vertical rim, typical for the spongy ware rims. Rounded lip. Light red fabric (Munsell 2.5YR 6/6).
K25 Ibc, level 2, lot 978.

P1684. Fig. 10-8.
H. (pres.) rim 0.034. D. (est.) rim 0.19.
Similar to **P1683**. Light red fabric (Munsell 2.5YR 6/8).
K25 JKbc, level 2, lot 1829.

P1685. Fig. 10-9.
H. (pres.) rim 0.027. D. (est.) rim 0.11.
Similar to **P1683** and **1684**. Light red fabric (Munsell 2.5YR 6/8) with white grits.
K25 Gbc, level 2, lot 863.

P1686. Fig. 10-10.
H. (pres.) rim 0.023. D. (est.) rim 0.155.
Similar to preceding rims. Light red fabric (Munsell 2.5YR 6/8) with infrequent white grits.
K24 Iy/K25 Ia, level 2, lot 1593.

P1687. Fig. 10-11.
H. (pres.) rim 0.018. D. (est.) rim 0.11.
Similar to preceding rims, except for its flat lip. Light red fabric (Munsell 2.5YR 6/8).
K25 Gc, level 5, lot 879.

P1688. Fig. 10-12.
H. (pres.) rim 0.031. D. (est.) rim 0.17.
High vertical rim, not outcurving. Light reddish brown fabric (Munsell 2.5YR 6/4).
J25 Ua, level 1, lots 1721 and 1726.

P1689. Fig. 10-13.
H. 0.022. D. (est.) rim 0.145.
Similar to **P1688**, except for a pointed lip. Light red fabric (Munsell 2.5YR 6/8).
K25 Ibc, level 2, lot 965.

AREA II: OTHER BYZANTINE COARSE WARE

P1690 (NP131). Jug(?) Fig. 10-14; Pl. 10-6.
H. (pres.) 0.085. D. bottom 0.069.
Flat bottom and deep body. Fine, very pale brown fabric (Munsell 10YR 7/4) with white and brown grits.
K25 IJc, level 1, lot 1086.

P1691 Jug(?) Fig. 10-15.
H. (pres.) 0.082. D. (est.) bottom 0.09.
Flat bottom and deep body, similar to **P1690**. Light red fabric (Munsell 2.5YR 6/8).
K25 Gbc, level 3, lot 885.

P1692. Jug(?) Fig. 10-16.
H. (pres.) 0.049. D. (est.) bottom 0.11.
Flat bottom with deep body. Very pale brown fabric (Munsell 10YR 7/4) with red grits. There are many fragmentary bottoms of this type from Area II, which vary only slightly in profile from each other. All are wheel-ridged on the interior.
K25 Gbc, level 2, lot 860.

P1693. Jug(?) Fig. 10-17.
H. (pres.) 0.047. D. (est.) bottom 0.10.
Flat bottom and deep body. Similar to **P1692**, except body is deeper and sides less vertical. Light red fabric (Munsell 2.5 YR 6/8) with white grits.
K25 Gbc, level 1, lot 859.

P1694. Jug(?) Fig. 10-18.
H. (pres.) 0.053. D. (est.) bottom 0.13.
Flat bottom and deep body. Similar to **P1693**, except body is more thinly potted and bottom diameter is slightly larger. Reddish yellow fabric (Munsell 5YR 6/8) with infrequent white grits.
K25 IJc, level 1, lot 1086.

P1695. Jug(?) Fig. 10-19.
H. (pres.) 0.06. D. (est.) bottom 0.10.
Flat bottom and deep body. Similar to **P1694**, except body is more thinly potted. Soft, very pale brown fabric (Munsell 10YR 8/4).
K25 Ibc, level 3, lot 992.

P1696 (NP136). Jug(?) Fig. 10-20; Pl. 10-7.
Dim. (max.) sherd 0.05 x 0.055
Nine body sherds. On the exterior, curving bands of impressed triangles and impressed dots forming chains of "V" and "T" shapes. Very pale brown fabric (Munsell 1YR 8/4) with red and white grits.
Deltion 26 (1971), Pl. 115b.
See A. Frantz, *Hesperia* 7 (1938), p. 449 (Fig. 10, A56) for a 12th-century amphora from Athens decorated with impressed triangles.
K25 Ibc, levels 1, 2, lots 952, 959, 961.

P1697 (NP132). Stand(?) Fig. 10-21; Pl. 10-8.
H. (pres.) 0.81. D. base 0.123.
Thick, conical base with a broken knob (?) on one side. Base of a stand? Through center of base is a hole, wide at the bottom, less than a centimeter wide at the top. Red fabric (Munsell 2.5YR 5/8) with red and white grits.
K24 Iy/K25 Ia, level 2, lot 1593.

P1698 (NP148). Amphora. Fig. 10-22; Pl. 10-9.
H. (pres.) 0.155. D. (est.) rim 0.125.
Vertical neck and circular handle of amphora. Reddish yellow biscuit (Munsell 7.5YR 7/6).
K24 Fy/K25 Fa, level 4, lot 1064.

P1699. Amphora. Fig. 10-23.
H. (pres.) 0.067. D. (est.) rim 0.06.
Frag. of amphora rim and handle. Dissimilar to **P1698**: rim D. is smaller and the handle, which arches sharply, is oval in section. Very pale brown fabric (Munsell 10YR 8/4).
K25 Ic, level 2, lot975.

P1700. Jug. Fig. 10-24.
H. (pres.) 0.03. W. (max.) 0.115.
Trefoil-shaped jug lip. Light red fabric (Munsell 2.5YR 6/8).
K24 Iy/K25 Ia, level 2, lot 1593.

P1701. Pithos. Fig. 10-25.
H. (pres.) 0.13. D. (est.) rim 0.50 (?) Th. rim 0.082.
Rim frag. Reddish yellow fabric (Munsell 5YR 7/8) with large stone grits.
K25 JKb, level 2, lot 852.

Area II Tiles

None of the individual tile fragments from Area II preserves an original length or width. There can be no question about their Byzantine origin, especially considering the total lack of evidence for the use of roof tiles in prehistoric contexts at Nichoria. Thus, these tiles are presumed to date from the late 10th to the early 12th century.

P1702. Cover tile. Fig. 10-26.
L. (pres.) 0.12. W. (pres.) 0.12. Th. (max.) 0.029.
Cover tile frag. W. was originally ca. 0.23. Soft reddish yellow fabric (Munsell 7.5YR 8/6) with large white and red grits.
K25 Fbc, level 2, lot 981.

P1703. Cover tile. Fig. 10-27.
L. (pres.) 0.11. W. (pres.) 0.13. Th. (max.) 0.023.
Cover tile frag. W. was originally ca. 0.20. Soft reddish yellow fabric (Munsell 7.5YR 7/6) with small white and red grits.
K25 Gbc, level 5, lot 884.

P1704. Pan tile. Fig. 10-28.
L. (pres.) 0.09. W. (pres.) 0.082. Th. (max.) 0.038.
Pan tile frag. Soft reddish yellow fabric (Munsell 5YR 7/8) with large white grits.
K25 Gbc, level 5, lot 884.

P1705. Pan tile. Fig. 10-29.
L. (pres.) 0.08. W. (pres.) 0.146. Th. (max.) 0.042.
Pan tile frag. Hard, pale yellow fabric (Munsell 2.5 YR 8/4) with large gray grits.
K26 Gbc, level 5, lot 884.

P1706. Stamped tile. Fig. 10-30.
L. (pres.) 0.113. W. (pres.) 0.059. D. palmette ca. 0.01.
Tile frag. with stamped palmette. Reddish yellow fabric (Munsell 5YR 7/8).
K25 Gbc, level 2, lot 868.

Area IV Glazed Wares

Most of the glazed pottery from Area IV comes from the construction of a new narthex floor for the chapel, i.e., for Phase 4 of Unit IV-2. The remaining glazed pottery, it seems certain, was disturbed from this floor deposit through action of the plow. The floor deposit was composed of collected debris from a fire that destroyed part of the Phase 3 chapel roof (see p. 372). It is this glazed pottery and a coin (**502**) of Manuel I (1143-80) from the floor deposit which dates the partial destruction of the chapel to some time between the late 12th and the early (?) 13th century. In the deposit four broken glazed bowls (Pls. 9-29, 10-12, 10-23, 10-24; **P1708, 1711, 1719, 1720**) were placed carefully next to one another, their bottoms upturned (see p. 370).

The quality and condition of most of the glazed pottery is poor. Of interest, however, are minor differences in shape and decoration which find no precise parallels in other published 12th-13th century Byzantine pottery from Greece. This is especially true of the painted wares. Thus, **P1719** is decorated with yellow and brown splotches of paint, reminiscent of Green and Brown Painted Wares, but otherwise unique. The range of colors used on our painted wares is wide: browns, yellows, greens, pinks, grays, and purples, in a variety of shades and mixtures. **P1711**, for example, is decorated with green and purple paint on a pale yellow glaze; and **P1725** is decorated with a pinkish gray paint.

Some of our glazed wares are difficult to date with any precision. Only one glazed pot, **P1707**, fits easily into the canon of glazed wares for Corinth. Perhaps **P1707** was imported from Corinth (if such pots were in fact manufactured there; see *Corinth XI*, p. 150 and Frantz 1938, pp. 437, 438). The remainder are of decidedly inferior manufacture, possessing a "freedom" in shape and decoration that could represent nothing more than a decline in ceramic technique. Such a decline at Corinth is associated with the 13th century, and thus the partial destruction of the Phase 3 chapel could be advanced at least into the early 13th century. On the other hand, such poor technique might document an out-of-the-way, local center of manufacture which produced during the reign of Manuel I glazed wares of poor quality, but with a certain flair. At any rate, **P1707** seems to belong in the late 12th century.

Area IV Sgraffito Wares

P1707 (NP89). Bowl. Fig. 10-31; Pl. 10-1.
H. (pres.) 0.095. D. (est.) rim 0.195. D. foot 0.12.
About a third is preserved in joining fragments, including a complete profile. High, flaring foot. Rather shallow body. Nearly vertical rim with rounded, slightly outcurving lip. On the interior, a central medallion with an interlace of imbricated ground, and a band of decadent Kufic below the lip. Slip over interior and exterior of rim. Cream glaze over interior and exterior of rim. Hard, pink fabric (Munsell 7.5YR 7/4) with white and pink grits.
Deltion 28 (1973), Pl. 159f.
Corinth XI, no. 1364 (Fig. 111, m) is vaguely similar in profile. However, one would hardly place this medallion-style bowl later than the reign of Manuel I (1143-80).
Unit IV-2, Phase 3, in narthex floor packing.

P1708 (NP128). Bowl. Fig. 10-32; Pl. 10-12.
H. (pres.) 0.10. D. (est.) rim 0.21. D. foot 0.094.
About a third is preserved in joining fragments. Flaring foot. Rather shallow body, rising without rim to a pointed lip. On the interior, a central medallion of three concentric circles, and a band of crude crosshatching below the lip. Slip over interior and upper exterior of rim. Pale yellow glaze over slip. Pink fabric (Munsell 5YR 7/6).
Corinth XI, no. 1324 (Fig. 111, g) is similar but with a deeper body. Our profile is late 12th, even 13th century, and the decadent style may indicate a date after the reign of Manuel I.
Unit IV-2, Phase 3, in narthex floor packing.

P1709 (NP122). Bowl. Fig. 10-33; Pl. 10-13.
H. (pres.) 0.095. D. (est.) rim 0.195. D. foot 0.09.
Fragmentary base and upper body, with nonjoining rim sherds. Profile similar to **P1708**, except for lower foot and slightly flaring body. On the interior, a band of crosshatching below lip. Slip all over. Yellowish brown glaze over interior. A streak of purplish brown glaze on exterior body and foot. Reddish yellow fabric (Munsell 5YR 7/6).
Corinth XI, no. 1324 (Fig. 111, g) has a vaguely similar profile, Like **P1708**, the profile of **P1709** could be late 12th, even 13th century. The simple, careless decoration may indicate a date after the reign of Manuel I.
Unit IV-2, Phase 3, in narthex floor packing.

P1710 (NP151). Bowl. Fig. 10-34; Pl. 10-14.

H. (pres.) 0.031. D. (est.) foot 0.08.

Low foot and part of lower body of bowl. On interior, a larger central medallion of two concentric circles, and a hatched band next to medallion. Slip on interior, under a white glaze. Pink fabric (Munsell 7/5YR 7/4).

The low foot is typical of sgraffito vessels of the mid-12th and 13th century. The crude decoration may indicate a late 12th, even 13th century date.

Unit IV-2, Phase 3, in narthex floor packing.

P1711 (NP127). Bowl. Fig. 10-39; Pl. 10-15.

H. (pres.) 0.048. D. foot 0.095.

Low, flaring foot. On the interior, traces of a simple, incised medallion band with a painted brown oval, bordered in yellow. Inside, a slip underneath a clear covering glaze. Pink fabric (Munsell 7.5YR 7/4).

Unit IV-2, Phase 3, in narthex floor packing.

P1712 (NP137). Bowl. Fig. 10-35; Pl. 10-16.

H. (pres.) 0.031. D. (est.) foot 0.11.

Base of bowl. Low foot. Originally a deep body. On the interior, a fragmentary split-palmette design (?). White slip on interior, under a very pale yellow glaze to which splotches of green and purple have been added. Reddish yellow biscuit (Munsell 5YR 7/6).

This is a type of painted sgraffito ware not encountered at Corinth. The crude decorative style may indicate a late 12th, even 13th century date.

Unit IV-2, Phase 4, chapel sanctuary.

P1713 (NP139). Bowl. Fig. 10-36; Pl. 10-17.

H. (pres.) 0.067. D. (est.) rim 0.23.

Rim sherd and two nonjoining body sherds. Rim vertical with pointed lip. On interior, a crude band of crosshatching below the lip. On the other two sherds, crude circular (?) lines. Slip on interior, under a green glaze. Very pale brown fabric (Munsell 10YR 8/4).

This vertical rim is characteristic of late 12th, 13th century sgraffito wares at Corinth. See *Corinth XI*, Fig. 111, j-m.

Unit IV-2, Phase 4, chapel sanctuary (rim sherd). The other two sherds are from L23 Qkl, level 1, lot 3441; and L23 Shi, level 1, lot 1757.

P1714 (NP147). Bowl. Fig. 10-37; Pl. 10-18.

H. (pres.) 0.039. D. rim impossible to est.

Rim and four body sherds. Rim outcurving with an exterior ridge. Pointed lip. On interior, a band of crosshatching below lip. Slip over interior and exterior of rim, under a thin white glaze. Pink fabric (Munsell 7.5YR 7/4).

Unit IV-2, Phase 4, chapel sanctuary.

P1715 (NP153). Bowl. Pl. 10-19.

H. (pres.) 0.052.

Single body sherd. Fragmentary central medallion with zigzag design. Slip over interior and exterior. Green glaze on interior. Traces of yellow and green glaze on exterior. Pink fabric (Munsell 7.5YR 7/4).

Unit IV-2, Phase 4, chapel sanctuary.

P1716 (NP145). Bowl(?) Pl. 10-20.

H. (pres.) 0.028.

Body sherd in four joining pieces. On interior a band with imbricated ground. Slip over interior and exterior. Glaze has deteriorated. Pink fabric (Munsell 7.5YR 7/4).

L23 Shi, Level 1, lot 1765.

P1717 (NP144). Bowl. Fig. 10-38; Pl. 10-21.

H. (pres.) rim 0.036. D. (est.) rim 0.24.

Three joining rim sherds, and four body sherds, one with an incised mark on interior. Vertical rim with pointed lip. Slip over interior and exterior of rim, under a pale yellow glaze (Munsell 5YR 8/3). Reddish yellow fabric (Munsell 5YR 7/6) with white grits.

L23 Rj, level 1, lot 3443.

P1718 (NP143). Bowl(?) Pl. 10-22.

Six body sherds, probably from same pot. Fragmentary concentric circles on one sherd. Slip over interior, under a white glaze. A splash of yellow glaze on one sherd. Pink fabric (Munsell 7.5YR 7/4).

L23 Rj, level 1, lot 3443.

Area IV Painted Wares

P1719 (NP129). Bowl. Fig. 10-40; Pl. 10-23.

H. (pres.) 0.03. D. foot 0.115.

Low foot and part of lower body preserved. White slip over interior, under streaks of brown and yellow paint mixed with glaze. No covering glaze. Pink fabric (Munsell 7.5YR 7/4). Three mending holes.

Unit IV-2, Phase 3, in narthex floor packing.

P1720 (NP126). Bowl. Fig. 10-41; Pl. 10-24.

H. (pres.) 0.043. D. foot 0.09.

Low, curving foot. White slip over interior, under patches of deteriorating yellow glaze. Reddish yellow fabric (Munsell 7.5YR 7/6).

Unit IV-2, Phase 3, in narthex floor packing.

P1721 (NP160). Bowl. Fig. 10-44; Pl. 10-25.

H. (pres.) 0.042. D. (est.) rim 0.21.

Two joining rim sherds. Vertical rim with flattened lip. White slip on interior and exterior of lip, under a light green glaze (deteriorated on interior). Reddish yellow fabric (Munsell 7.5YR 7/6).

One sherd is from Unit IV-2, Phase 3, in narthex floor packing; the other from L23 Qkl, level 1, lot 3441.

P1722 (NP154). Bowl. Fig. 10-48; Pl. 10-26.

H. (pres.) 0.03. D. (est.) rim 0.23.

Two joining rim sherds and two body sherds. Rim has rounded lip. Slip over interior and upper exterior of lip, under unevenly applied purple glaze. Pinkish fabric (between Munsell 7.5YR 7/4 and 8/6) with reddish yellow grits.

Unit IV-2, Phase 3, in narthex floor packing.

P1723 (NP130). Bowl. Fig. 10-50; Pl. 10-27.

H. (pres.) 0.062. D. (est.) rim 0.21.

Five rim sherds and eight body sherds, some joining. High, slightly flaring rim with pointed lip. Slip over interior and exterior upper rim. Pink glaze (Munsell 5YR 8/4) over slip, with brown paint dripped onto wet glaze. Reddish yellow fabric (Munsell 7.5YR 7/6).

Unit IV-2, Phase 3, in narthex floor packing, and sanctuary.

P1724 (NP83). Plate. Fig. 10-51; Pl. 10-28.

H. (pres.) 0.045. D. (est.) rim 0.30.

Three rim sherds, two joining. Shallow body with vertical rim and pointed lip. Slip over all. Wavy line of brownish yellow (Munsell 10YR 6/8) along interior lip over slip, under clear covering glaze. Hard, light red fabric (Munsell 2.5YR 6/5) with red and white grits.

Unit IV-2, Phase 4, sanctuary.

P1725 (NP150). Bowl. Fig. 10-42; Pl. 10-29.

H. (pres.) 0.032. D. foot 0.09.

Low foot, rather similar to **P1719** in profile. Slip over interior, under mottled/crackled yellow glaze. Reddish yellow biscuit (Munsell 7.5YR 7/6).

L23 Rj, level 1, lot 3443.

P1726 (NP123). Bowl. Fig. 10-43; Pl. 10-30.

H. (pres.) of largest rim sherd 0.065. D. (est.) rim 0.245.

Two rim sherds, eight body sherds, two joining. Shallow body curving out to low, upturned rim with flattened lip. Slip over interior, thin in places. Streaks of green and purple paint under light green glaze.

L23 Rj, level 1, lot 4142.

P1727 (NP159). Bowl. Fig. 10-45; Pl. 10-31.

H. (pres.) 0.042. D. (est.) rim 0.21.

Vertical rim sherd. Flattened lip. White slip over interior and splashed over exterior rim. Over interior a clear covering glaze onto which was dripped while wet a pinkish gray paint. Hard reddish yellow fabric (Munsell 7.5YR 7/6).

L23 PQij, level 1, lot 4136.

P1728 (NP157). Bowl. Fig. 10-46; Pl. 10-32.

H. (pres.) 0.035. D. (est.) rim 0.25.

Vertical rim sherd. Rounded lip. Slip over interior and exterior. On interior, splotches of green and purple glaze. Reddish yellow fabric (Munsell 7.5YR 8/6).

L23 Rj, level 1, lot 3443.

P1729 (NP146). Bowl. Fig. 10-47.

H. (pres.) 0.068. D. (est.) rim 0.20.

Three joining rim and body sherds. Shallow body curving out slightly to pointed lip. Slip over interior and exterior, under which on interior a light pink glaze (Munsell 5YR 8/2). Reddish yellow fabric (Munsell 5YR 7/6).

L23 Rj, level 1, lot 3443.

P1730 (NP133). Bowl. Fig. 10-49; Pl. 10-33.

H. (pres.) 0.06. D. (est.) rim 0.20.

Five joining rim sherds. Vertical rim, slightly outcurving with rounded lip. Slip over interior and exterior upper rim. Dark green glaze, very deteriorated, on interior. Pink fabric (Munsell 7.5YR 7/4).

L23 Rj, level 1, lot 3443.

Area IV Coarse Wares

A few uncataloged spongy ware sherds were found in the narthex floor deposit, and several other sherds of this fabric came from the topsoil above Unit IV-2. None of these sherds merit publication, nor do they demonstrate conclusively the use of the chapel while Area II was occupied by its Byzantine inhabitants. However, the presence of this pottery buttresses other evidence which indicates that the chapel was initially built (Phase 3 of Unit IV-2) when the Byzantine buildings in Area II were still in use (see p. 376).

Much coarse ware was found in the narthex floor deposit, but its fabric is quite different from the spongy ware. Nevertheless, there is some similarity between the predominant type, i.e., a small jug, found in both Areas II and IV. The jugs may well have contained oil for lamps. There is not enough variation in shape and decoration to warrant publishing more than a few examples of these jugs. Unless otherwise indicated, all of the following coarse ware vessels are from the narthex floor packing. As with the other material from this deposit, their date is middle 12th to early 13th century.

P1731 (NP120). Brazier. Fig. 10-52; Pl. 10-34.

H. (pres.) 0.058. L. (pres.) 0.21. D. receptacle 0.13.

Four joining fragments. Missing are part of receptacle and handle end. Thick, rectangular handle spreading into a circular, rimmed receptacle perforated by a dozen holes. Handle, rim, and rounded lip decorated by crude crisscrosses. Charcoallike stains in receptacle. Coarse, hard fabric, pale yellow (Munsell 2.5Y 8/4) with white and gray grits.

P1732 (NP121). Brazier. Fig. 10-53; Pl. 10-35.

H. (pres.) 0.053. D. receptacle 0.106.

Three joining fragments. Handle and part of receptacle missing. Receptacle similar in design to **P1731**, but smaller. Soft, fine pink fabric (Munsell 7.5YR 8/4).

P1733 (NP142). Jug. Fig. 10-54; Pl. 10-36.

H. (pres.) 0.091. D. (est.) rim 0.093.

Rim, handle, and body fragments in nineteen joining sherds. Bottom missing. Rounded body and shoulder. Vertical rim with groove around exterior middle. Flat lip. Handle oval in section. Shallow grooves around shoulder. Reddish yellow fabric (Munsell 7.5YR 7/6).

P1734. Jug. Fig. 10-55.

H. (pres.) 0.113. D. (est.) rim 0.14.

Rim, handle, and body fragment. Lower body and bottom missing. Similar in profile to **P1733**, except for rounded lip and absence of grooving around exterior rim. Reddish yellow fabric (Munsell 5YR 7/6).

P1735. Jug. Fig. 10-56.

H. (pres.) 0.048. D. (est.) rim 0.15.

Rim, shoulder, and handle fragment. Similar in profile to **P1733**, except for decorative plastic ridges from rim to shoulder. Reddish yellow fabric (Munsell 5YR 7/6).

P1736. Jug. Fig. 10-57.

H. (pres.) 0.043. D. (est.) rim 0.10 (?).

Rim, shoulder, and handle fragment. Similar in profile to **P1733**. Reddish yellow fabric (Munsell 5YR 6/8); exterior burned to dark gray.

P1737. Jug. Fig. 10-58.

H. (pres.) 0.195. D. (est.) rim 0.095.

Rim and shoulder fragment. Similar to **P1733**. Shallow grooving over entire shoulder below rim. Light red fabric (Munsell 2.5YR 6/8).

P1738. Jug. Fig. 10-60.

H. (pres.) 0.024. D. (est.) rim 0.14.

Rim fragment. Vertical rim, slightly outcurving, with flat lip. Reddish yellow fabric (Munsell 5YR 6/8), burned dark gray on exterior.

P1739. Jug. Fig. 10-61.

H. (pres.) 0.044. D. (est.) rim 0.12.

Rim and shoulder fragment. Vertical rim with flat lip. Shallow groove on shoulder. Reddish yellow fabric (Munsell 5YR 6/8).

P1740. Jug. Fig. 10-62.

H. (pres.) 0.045. D. (est.) rim 0.11.

Rim and shoulder fragment. Reddish yellow fabric (Munsell 5YR 7/8).

P1741. Jug. Fig. 10-64.

H. (pres.) 0.02. D. (est.) rim 0.14.

Rim fragment. Vertical rim with flat lip. Thinly potted, reddish yellow fabric (Munsell 5YR 7/6), blackened by fire, with small grits.

P1742. Jug. Fig. 10-65.
H. (pres.) 0.024. D. (est.) rim 0.12.
Rim fragment. Vertical rim with rounded lip. Reddish yellow fabric (Munsell 5YR 6/8) with white and red grits.

P1743. Jug. Fig. 10-66.
H. (pres.) 0.021. D. (est.) rim 0.12.
Rim fragment. Vertical rim with flat lip. Reddish yellow fabric (Munsell 7.5YR 7/6) with white and gray grits.

P1744. Jug. Fig. 10-67.
H. (pres.) 0.023. D. (est.) rim 0.13.
Rim fragment. Similar in profile to **P1733** and **P1735**, except for rounded lip. Pale brown fabric (Munsell 10YR 6/3).

P1745. Jug. Fig. 10-68.
H. (pres.) 0.026. D. (est.) rim 0.12.
Rim fragment. Vertical rim with rounded lip. Single deep groove just below exterior of lip. Gray fabric (Munsell 10YR 5/1).

P1746. Jug. Fig. 10-69.
H. (pres.) 0.027. D. (est.) rim 0.13.
Rim fragment. Vertical rim, slightly outcurving, with flat lip. Shallow groove on shoulder just below rim. Reddish yellow fabric (Munsell 5YR 6/8).

P1747. Jug. Fig. 10-70.
H. (pres.) 0.021. D. (est.) rim 0.095.
Rim fragment. Vertical, slightly outcurving rim with pointed lip. Shallow groove on shoulder just below rim. Light red fabric (Munsell 2.5YR 6/8) with white and red grits.

P1748. Jug. Fig. 10-72.
H. (pres.) 0.06. D. (est.) bottom 0.09.
Bottom fragment. Flat bottom, slightly concave toward center, with deep body. Red fabric (Munsell 2.5YR 5/6) with infrequent small white grits.

P1749. Jug. Fig. 10-73.
H. (pres.) 0.062. D. (est.) bottom 0.06.
Bottom fragment. Similar in profile to **P1748**. Reddish yellow fabric (Munsell 5YR 7/6).

P1750. Jug. Fig. 10-74.
H. (pres.) 0.04. D. (est.) base 0.08.
Base fragment. Flat base with flaring body. Reddish yellow biscuit (Munsell 5YR 7/6).

P1751. Jug. Fig. 10-75.
H. (pres.) 0.084. D. bottom 0.084.
Bottom fragment. Flat bottom with deep body. Reddish yellow fabric (Munsell 5YR 7/6).

P1752. Jug. Fig. 10-76.
H. (pres.) 0.019. D. bottom 0.054.
Bottom fragment. Similar in profile to **P1750**, but with smaller bottom diameter. Very pale brown fabric (Munsell 10YR 7/4).

P1753 (NP141). Jug. Fig. 10-71.
H. (pres.) 0.132. D. (est.) bottom 0.09.
Body and bottom fragments, in 12 joining sherds. Upper rim and handle(s) missing. Flat bottom. Deep body with almost vertical sides, gently curving shoulder and vertical rim. Light red fabric (Munsell 2.5YR 6/6). One of the few relatively complete profiles (see **P1733**) of this coarse ware.
Unit IV-2, Phase 4, sanctuary.

P1754. Jug. Fig. 10-63.
H. (pres.) 0.029. D. (est.) rim 0.10.
Rim and shoulder fragment. Vertical rim with rounded lip. Shallow grooving on preserved upper shoulder. Reddish yellow fabric (Munsell 5YR 6/8) with white and red grits.
L23 Rj, level 1, lot 3443.

P1755. Jug. Fig. 10-59.
H. (pres.) 0.029. D. (est.) rim 0.09.
Rim and shoulder fragment. Vertical rim with rounded lip. Two grooves around rim exterior; two grooves on shoulder. Reddish yellow fabric (Munsell 5YR 6/8) with white and red grits.
L23 Rj, level 1, lot 3443.

P1756 (NP104). Amphora. Pl. 10-10.
H. (pres.) 0.405. D. (est.) rim 0.11. W. (max.) ca. 0.30. W. (max.) handle 0.03.
Restored from fragments. Portions of rim and body missing. Deep body, with round bottom and button base. Two handles, round in section. Squat neck with vertical, slightly outcurving rim. Rounded lip. Fine, straight grooving from below handles to belly. Reddish yellow fabric (Munsell 5YR 6/8).
Hesperia 34 (1975), p. 98, Pl. 26a. See Robinson 1959, Pl. 40 (P4129). Late B-i amphora, very common in the Aegean. Ca 460-520 (Hayes 1974). Chapter 9, p. 368.
Unit IV-2, Phase 2, Room 3, on the floor.

Roof Tiles

UNIT IV-2, PHASES 1 AND 2

The broken tiles recovered from this Late Roman/Early Byzantine building represent a single type of large pan tile which was used with two distinct but similar types of cover tiles. The pan tiles are about 0.04 m thick, 0.43 m wide, and an estimated 0.80 m long. One type of cover tile is of soft fabric, about 0.025 m thick, 0.035 m wide, and about 0.52 m long. The second type is of harder fabric and slightly smaller dimensions, i.e., 0.02 m thick, 0.29 m wide, and about 0.50 m long. A sample of each of the three types is included in the catalog, all of them from Room 3 of this building.

P1757. Pan tile. Fig. 10-77.
L. (pres.) 0.58. W. 0.43. Th. 0.038.
Pan tile fragment. Original length ca. 0.80. Slightly convex with flat edges. Three finger-mark swirls on the interior surface. Hard reddish yellow fabric (Munsell 7.5YR 8/6) with large gray grits.

P1758. Cover tile. Fig. 10-78.
L. 0.52. W. (est.) 0.35. Th. 0.025.
Cover tile fragment. Slightly convex with flat, slightly thicker edges. Finger-mark swirls on interior surface. Soft, friable reddish yellow fabric (Munsell 5YR 6/6) with infrequent large white grits.

P1759. Cover tile. Fig. 10-79.
L. (pres.) 0.41. W. 0.29. Th. 0.02.
Cover tile fragment. Original length ca. 0.50. Similar in profile to **P1758**, but edges are rounded and not as thick. Hard reddish yellow fabric (Munsell 5YR 7/6) with infrequent small red grits.

UNIT IV-2, PHASE 4

Broken tiles from the Middle Byzantine chapel document three basic types: cover tile, pan tile, and ridge tile. The cover tiles are about 0.025 m thick, about 0.25-0.30 m wide, and about 0.40 m long. An occasional variant is thinner (rarely more than 0.02 m thick) and only 0.24 m wide. The lengths of both varieties are the same. The pan tiles are about 0.02 m thick, 0.37 m wide, and estimated to be as long as 0.80 m. They seem to be from the same workshop as the thinner variety of cover tile.

Only a few ridge tile fragments were recognized. The best example is **P1760** (below). All the ridge tiles are almost surely from the final, Phase 4 chapel, which was probably destroyed after the early 13th century (see p. 372). All cataloged tiles are from the roof of the sanctuary (not the narthex).

P1760. Ridge tile. Fig. 10-80.

L. (pres.) 0.415. W. 0.23. Th. 0.025.

Ridge tile fragment. Original length ca. 0.45. Sharply convex with flat edges. Hard, very pale brown fabric (Munsell 10YR 8/4) with infrequent small white grits. 2 finger-marks on exterior surface.

P1761. Cover tile. Fig. 10-81.

L. (pres.) 0.27. W. 0.23. Th. 0.025.

Cover tile fragment. Original length ca. 0.45. Convex with flat edges. Hard, very pale brown fabric (Munsell 10YR 8/4) with infrequent small white grits. Straw impressions on exterior surface.

P1762. Cover tile. Fig. 10-83.

L. (pres.) 0.185. W. (pres.) 0.175. Th. 0.015.

Cover tile fragment. Original length ca. 0.45. Estimated original width ca. 0.23. Convex with flat edges. Hard reddish yellow fabric (Munsell 7.5YR 7/6) with infrequent white grits. This is the thinner version of **P1761**.

P1763. Pan tile. Fig. 10-82.

L. (pres.) 0.12. W. 0.37. Th. 0.02.

Pan tile fragment. Original length ca. 0.80. Very slightly convex with round edges. Hard reddish yellow fabric (Munsell 7.5YR 8/6) with infrequent white grits.

For the purpose of comparison, a typical modern roof tile is included here. This particular tile comes from the nearby village of Petalidhi. The reconstructions of the chapel (Figs. 9-9, 9-10, 9-11) portray an even more modern arrangement of the roof tiles.

P1764. Modern roof tile. Fig. 10-84.

L. 0.40. W. 0.19. Th. 0.015.

Complete roof tile. Convex with flat edges. Hard reddish yellow fabric (Munsell 7.5YR 7/6) with infrequent small white grits.

REFERENCES

Cardew, M. 1969. *Pioneer Pottery*. New York.

Dawkins, R. M., and Droop, J. P. 1910-11. "Byzantine Pottery from Sparta," *BSA* 17:23-28.

Frantz, A. 1938. "Middle Byzantine Pottery in Athens," *Hesperia* 7:429-67.

McDonald, W. A. 1971. "Nichoria," *Deltion* 26:131-37.

MacKay, T. S. 1967. "More Byzantine and Frankish Pottery from Corinth," *Hesperia* 36:249-320.

Megaw, A. H. S. 1968. "Zeuxippus Ware," *BSA* 63:67-88.

———. 1975. "An Early Thirteenth-Century Aegean Glazed Ware." *Studies in Memory of David Talbot Rice*, 34-45. Edinburgh.

Morgan, C. H., II. 1942. *Corinth. American School Excavations XI: The Byzantine Pottery*. Cambridge, Mass.

Munsell Products. 1973. *Munsell Soil Color Charts*. Baltimore, Maryland.

Peschlow, U. 1977-78. "Byzantinische Keramik aus Istanbul. Ein Fundkomplex bei der Irenenkirche unter Mitarbeit von Gül und Samim Sismanoglu," *Deutsches Archäologisches Institut, Abteilung Istanbul* 27/28:363-414.

Rhodes, D. 1973. *Clay and Glazes for the Potter*, rev. edition. Philadelphia, New York, London.

Rice, D. T. 1930. *Byzantine Glazed Pottery*. Oxford.

———. 1966. "Late Byzantine Pottery at Dumbarton Oaks," *Dumbarton Oaks Papers* 20:209-19.

Robinson, H. S. 1959. *The Athenian Agora, V: Pottery of the Roman Period. Chronology*. Princeton, N.J.

Waagé, F. O. 1933. "The Roman and Byzantine Pottery" (Athenian Agora), *Hesperia* 2:279-328.

Yakobson, A. L. 1959. *Rannesrednovekovij Chersones = Materialy i issled. po. arch. SSSR* 63. In Russian.

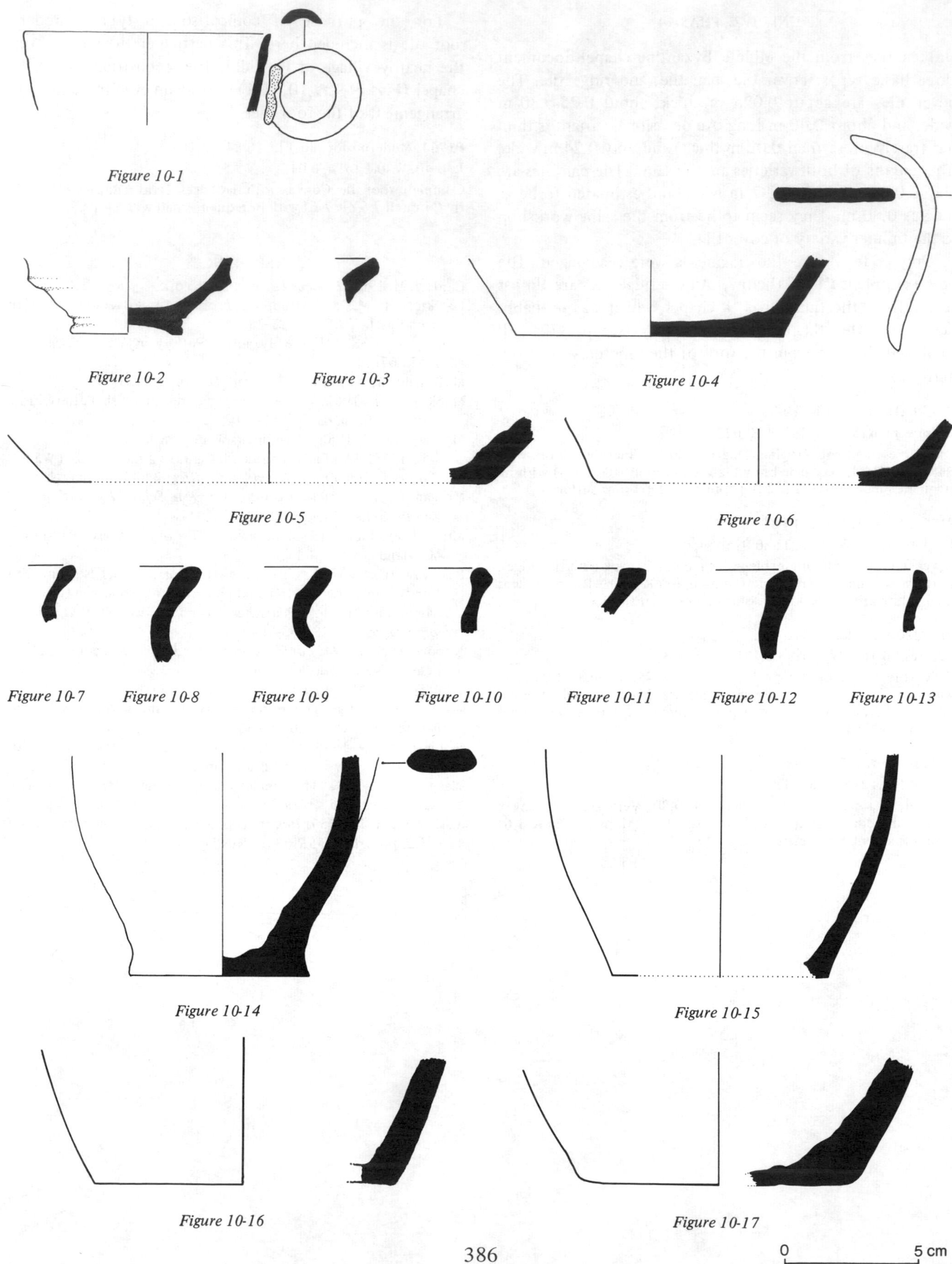

Figure 10-1

Figure 10-2

Figure 10-3

Figure 10-4

Figure 10-5

Figure 10-6

Figure 10-7

Figure 10-8

Figure 10-9

Figure 10-10

Figure 10-11

Figure 10-12

Figure 10-13

Figure 10-14

Figure 10-15

Figure 10-16

Figure 10-17

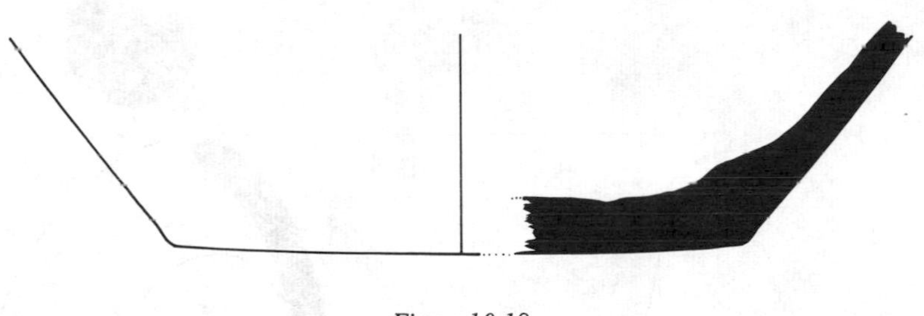

Figure 10-18

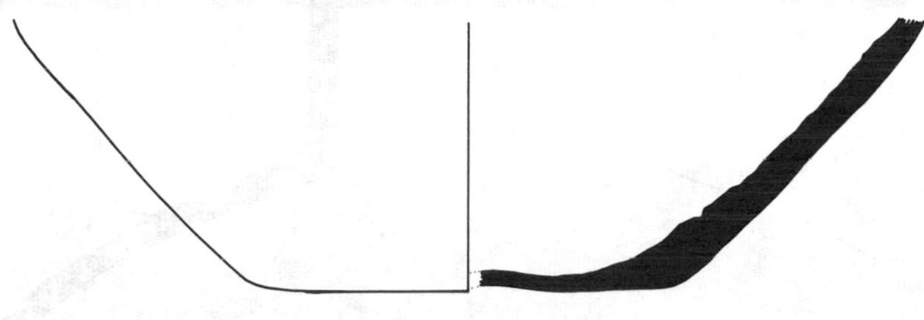

Figure 10-19

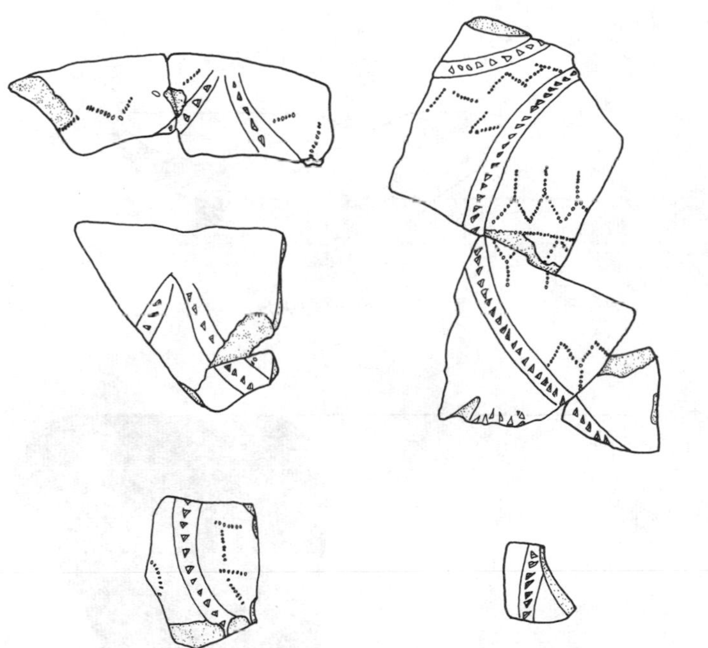

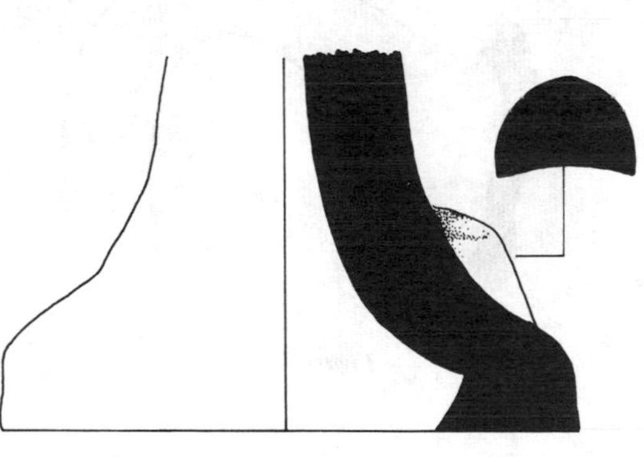

Figure 10-21

Figure 10-20

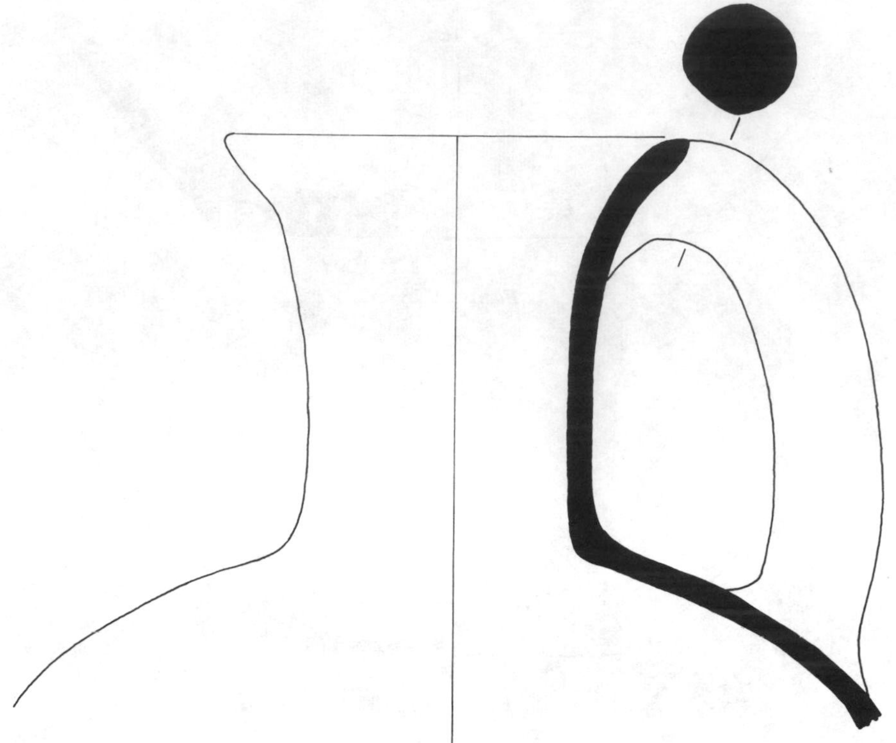

Figure 10-22

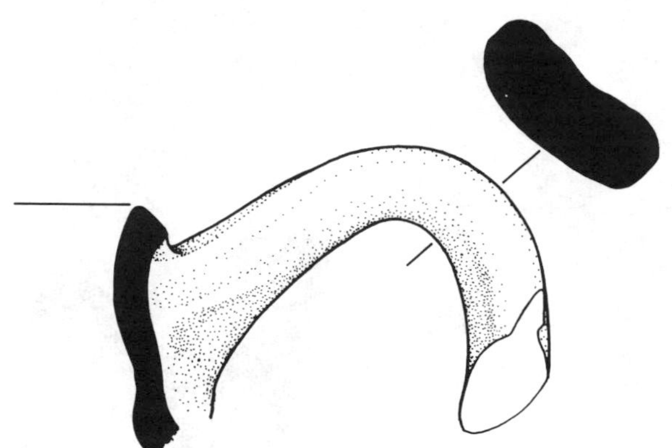

Figure 10-23

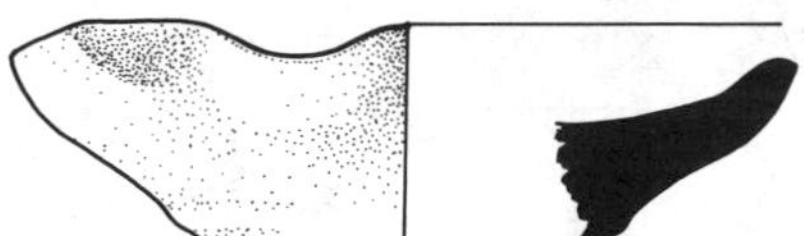

Figure 10-24

0 5 cm

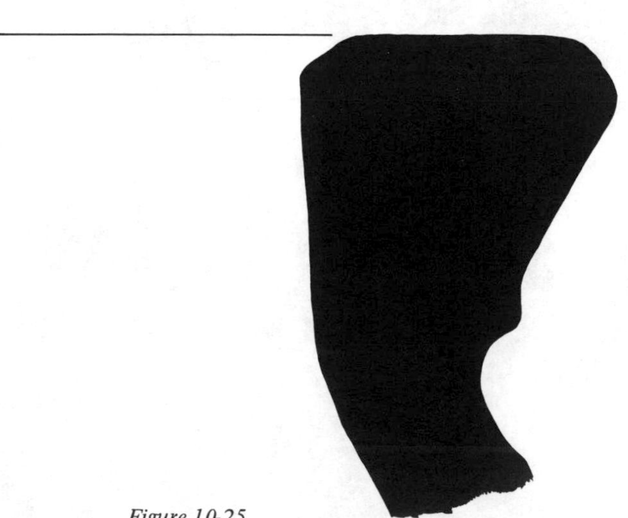

Figure 10-25

Figure 10-26

Figure 10-27

Figure 10-28

Figure 10-29

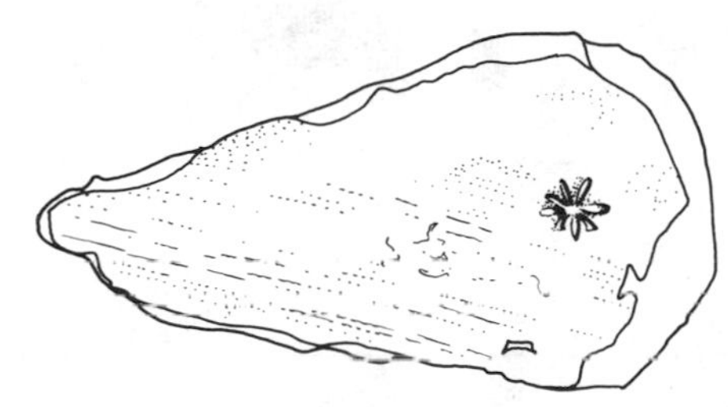

Figure 10-30

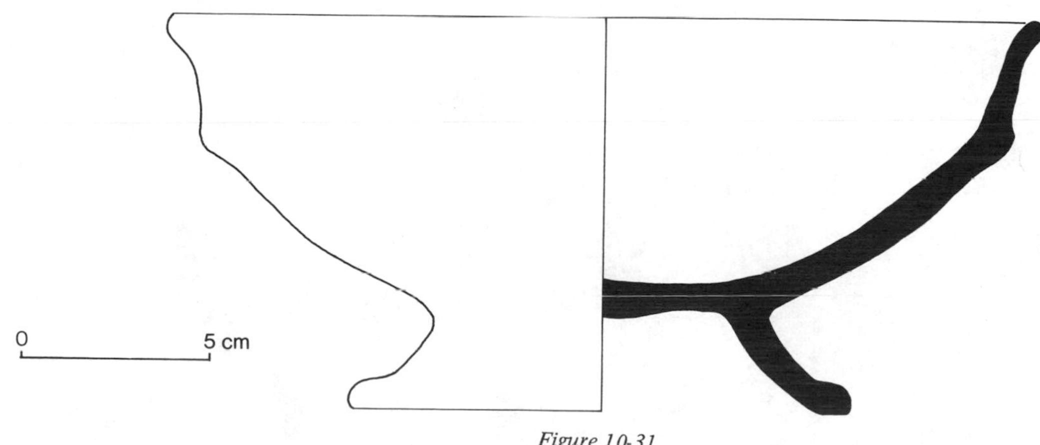

Figure 10-31

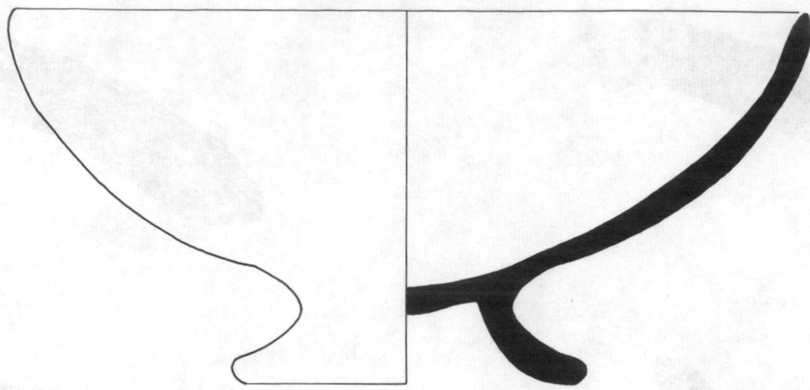

Figure 10-32

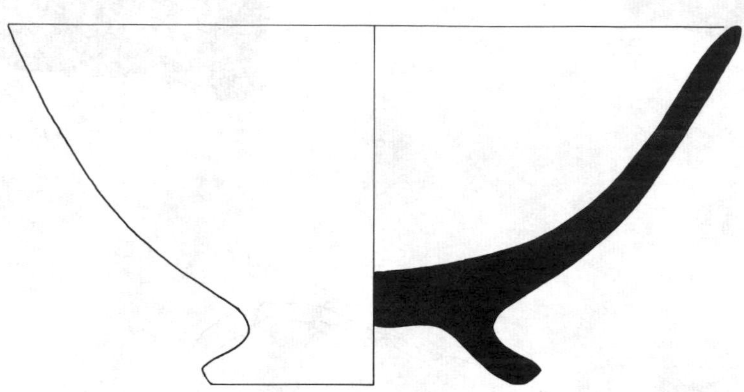

Figure 10-33

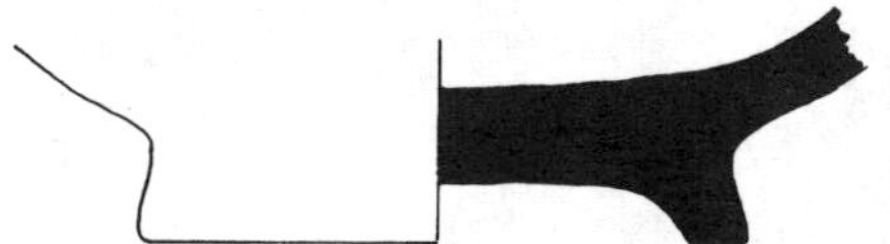

Figure 10-34

Figure 10-35

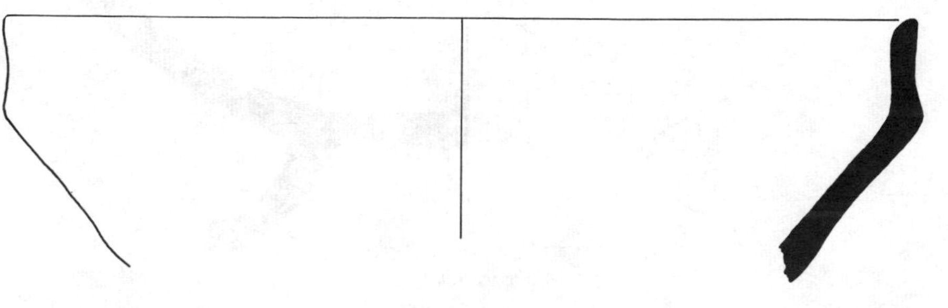

Figure 10-36

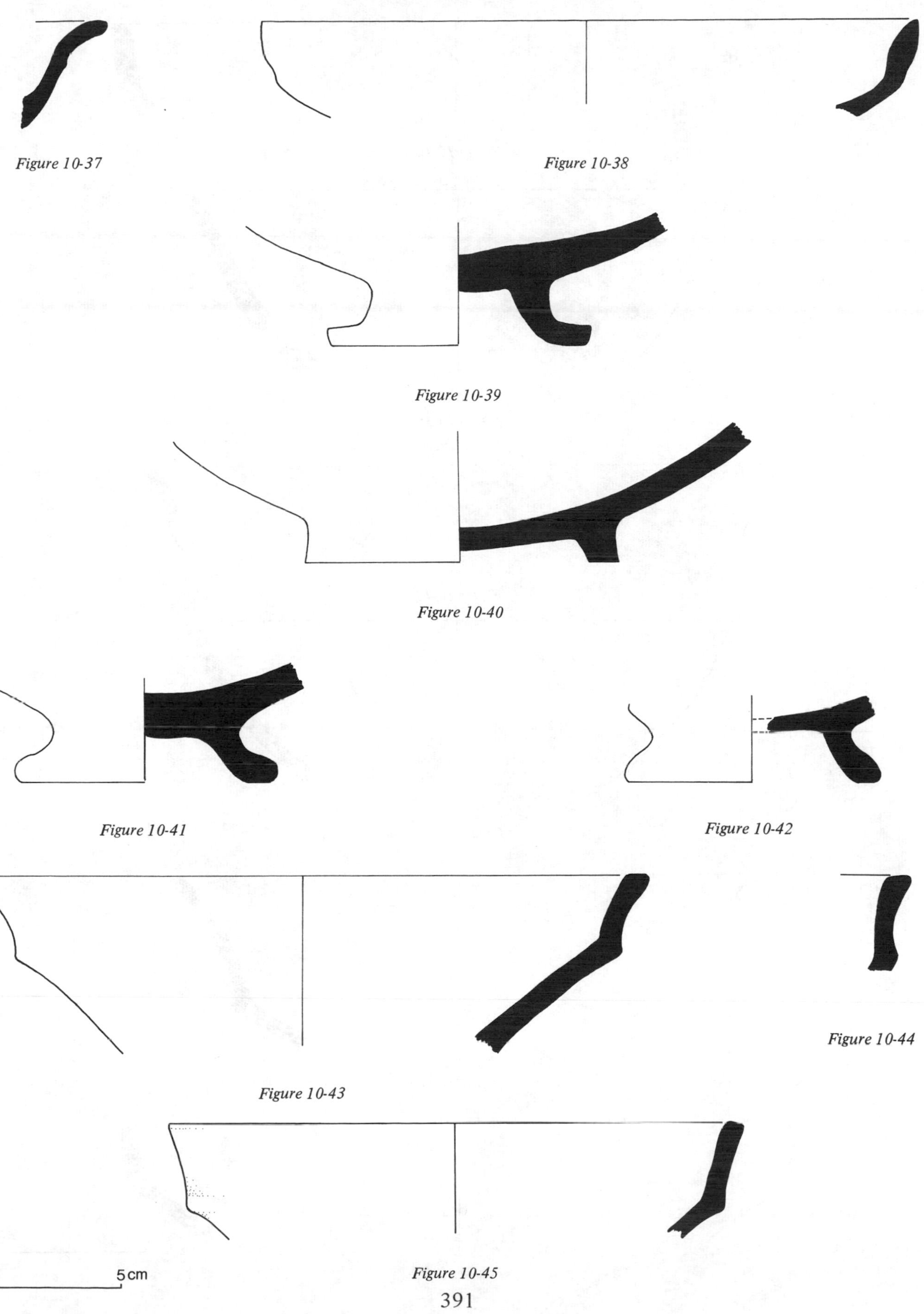

Figure 10-37

Figure 10-38

Figure 10-39

Figure 10-40

Figure 10-41

Figure 10-42

Figure 10-43

Figure 10-44

Figure 10-45

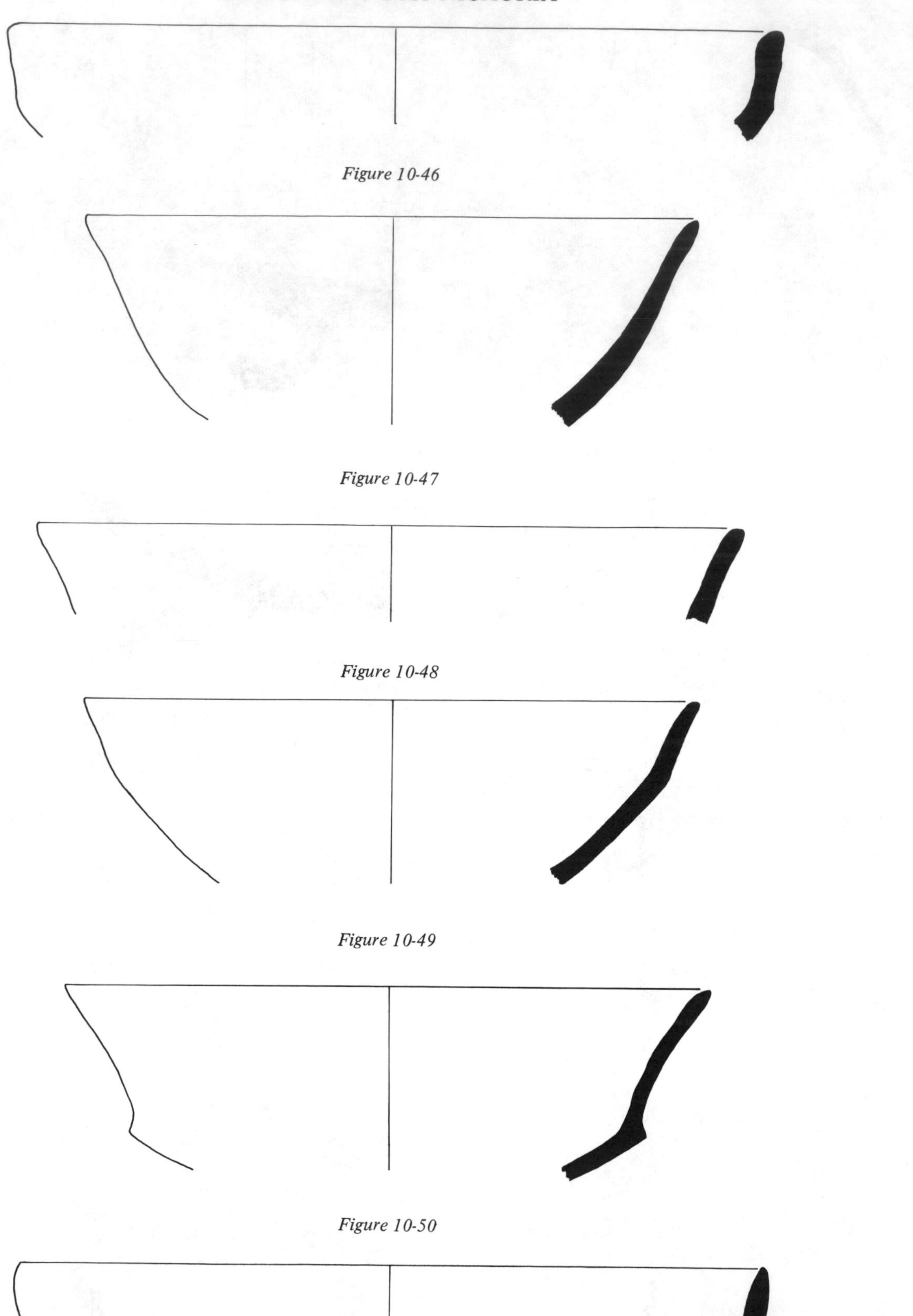

Figure 10-46

Figure 10-47

Figure 10-48

Figure 10-49

Figure 10-50

Figure 10-51

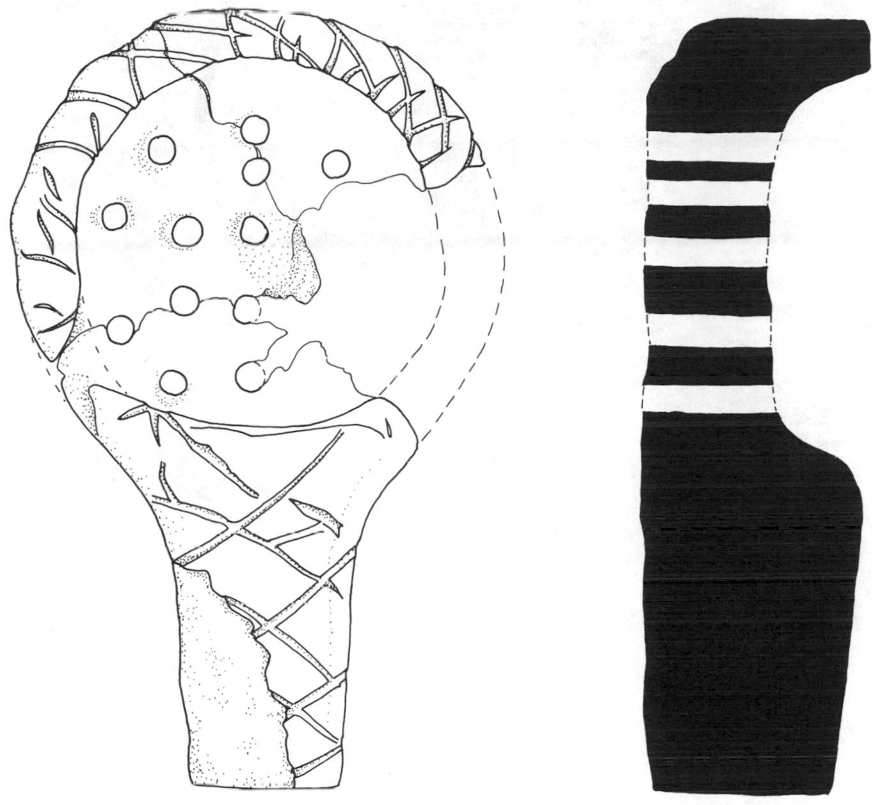

Figure 10-52

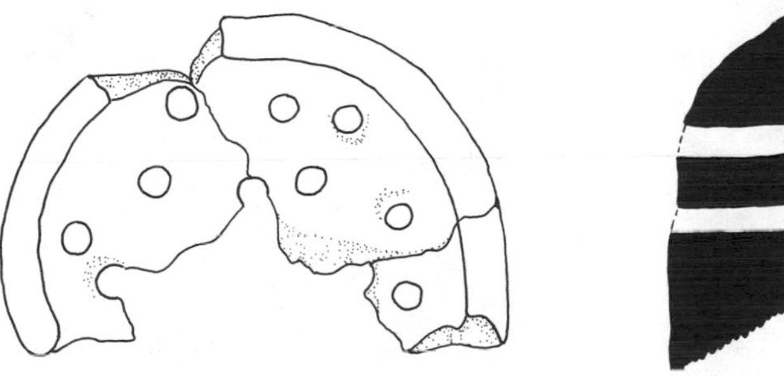

Figure 10-53

0 5 cm

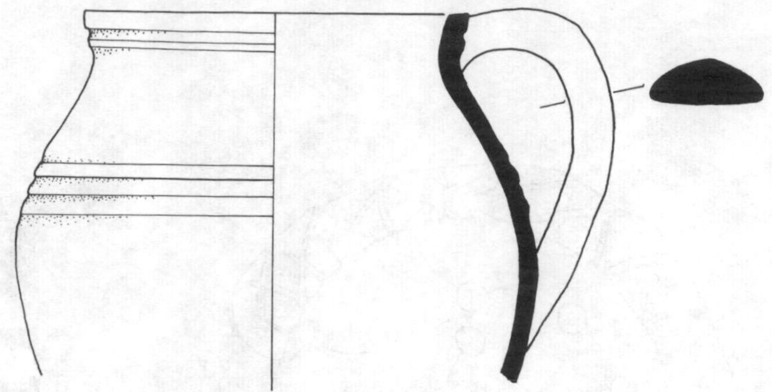

Figure 10-54

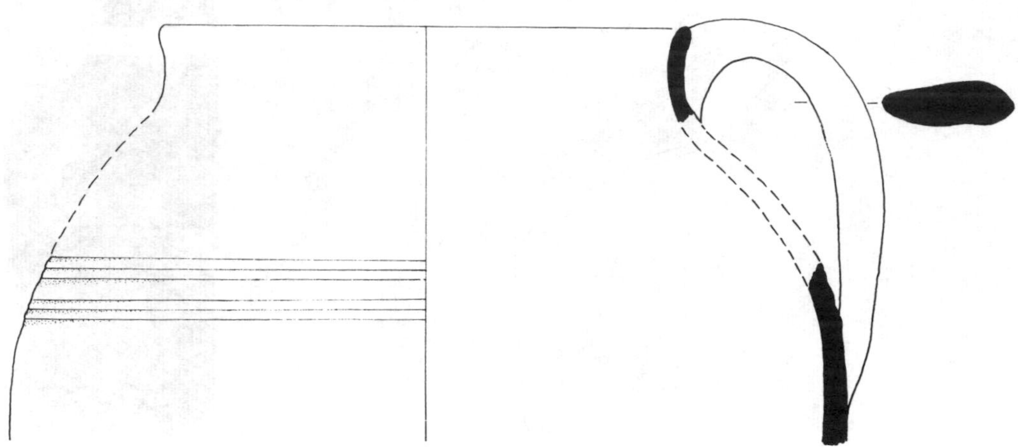

Figure 10-55

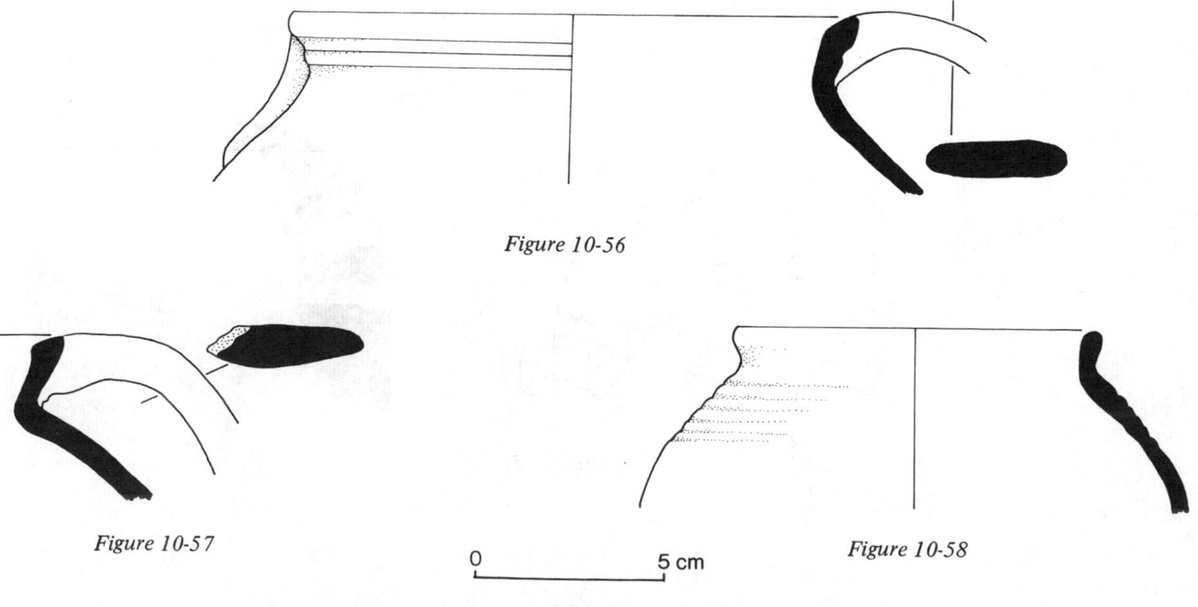

Figure 10-56

Figure 10-57

Figure 10-58

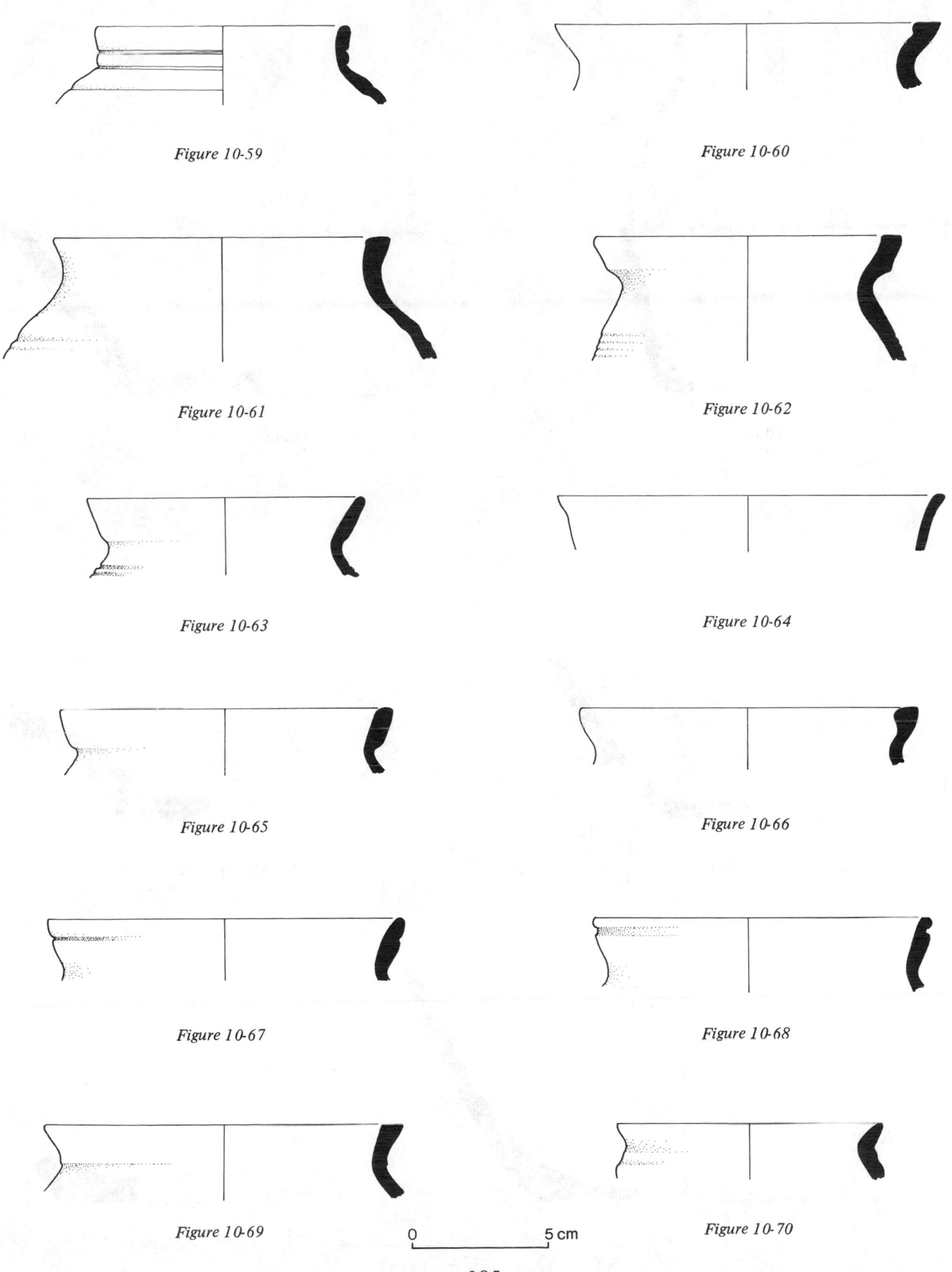

Figure 10-59

Figure 10-60

Figure 10-61

Figure 10-62

Figure 10-63

Figure 10-64

Figure 10-65

Figure 10-66

Figure 10-67

Figure 10-68

Figure 10-69

Figure 10-70

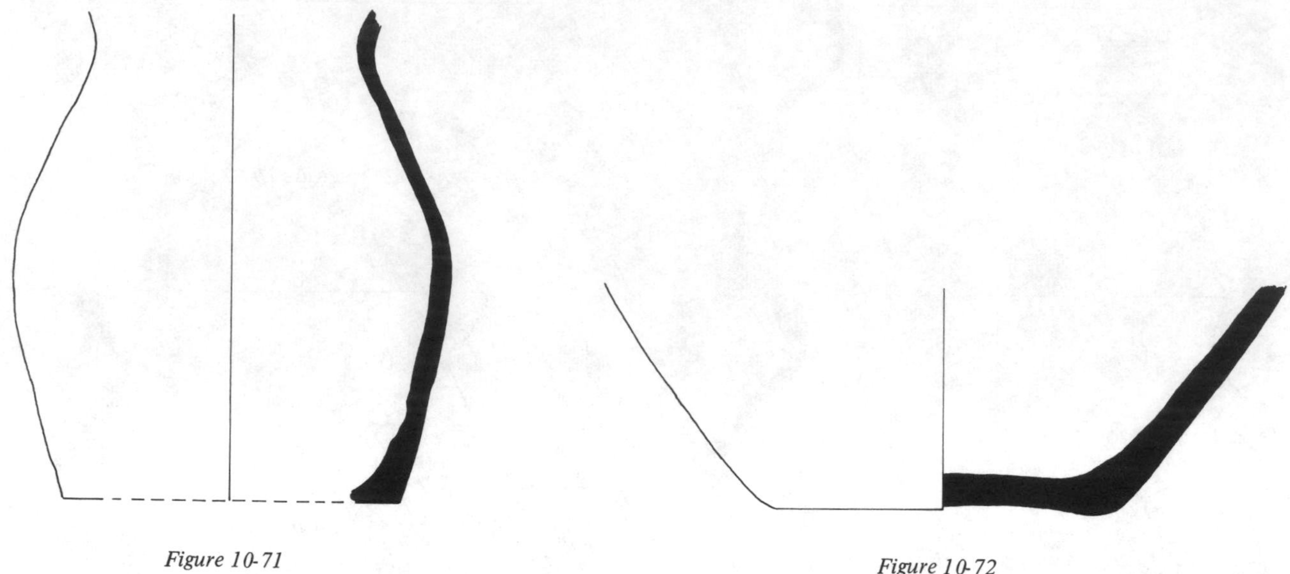

Figure 10-71

Figure 10-72

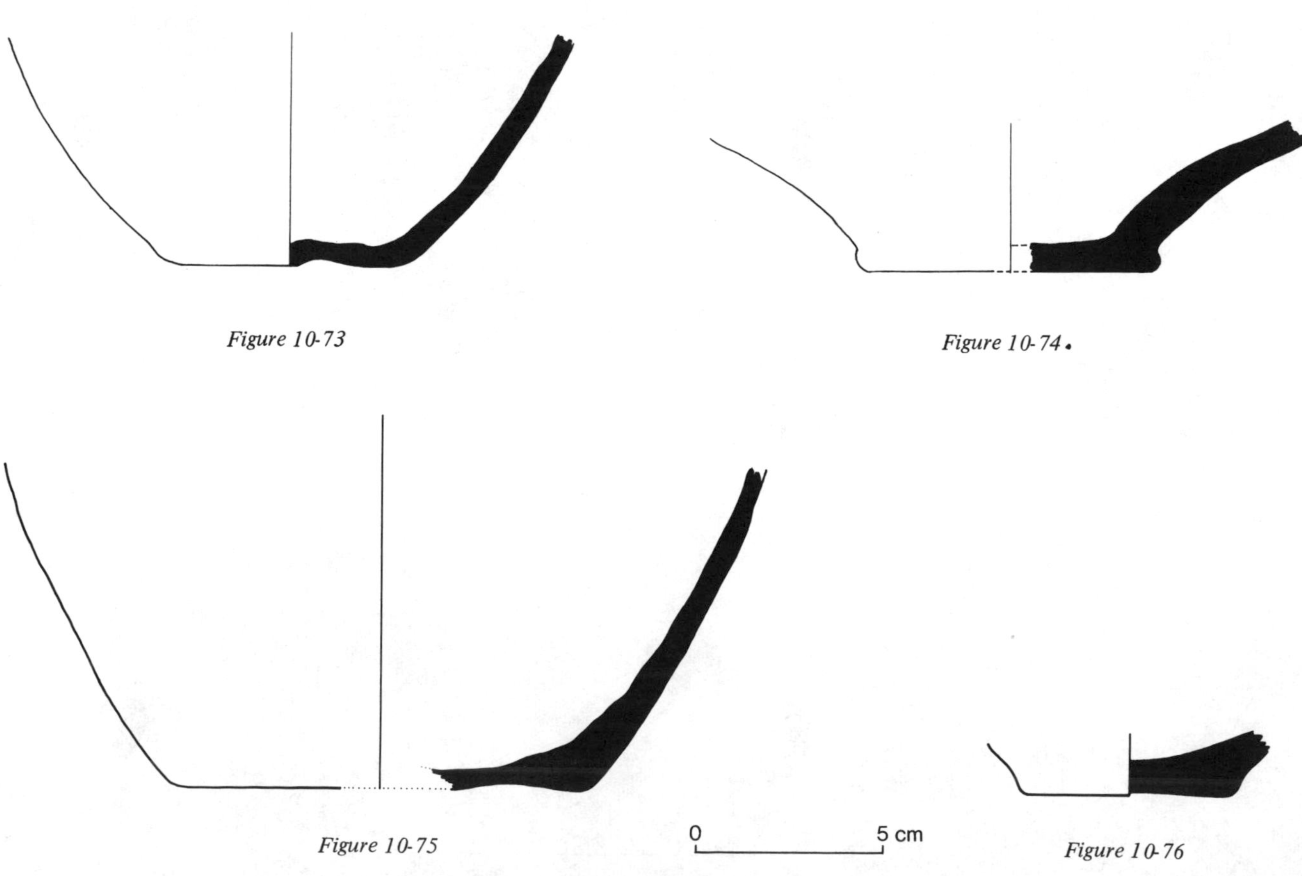

Figure 10-73

Figure 10-74

Figure 10-75

Figure 10-76

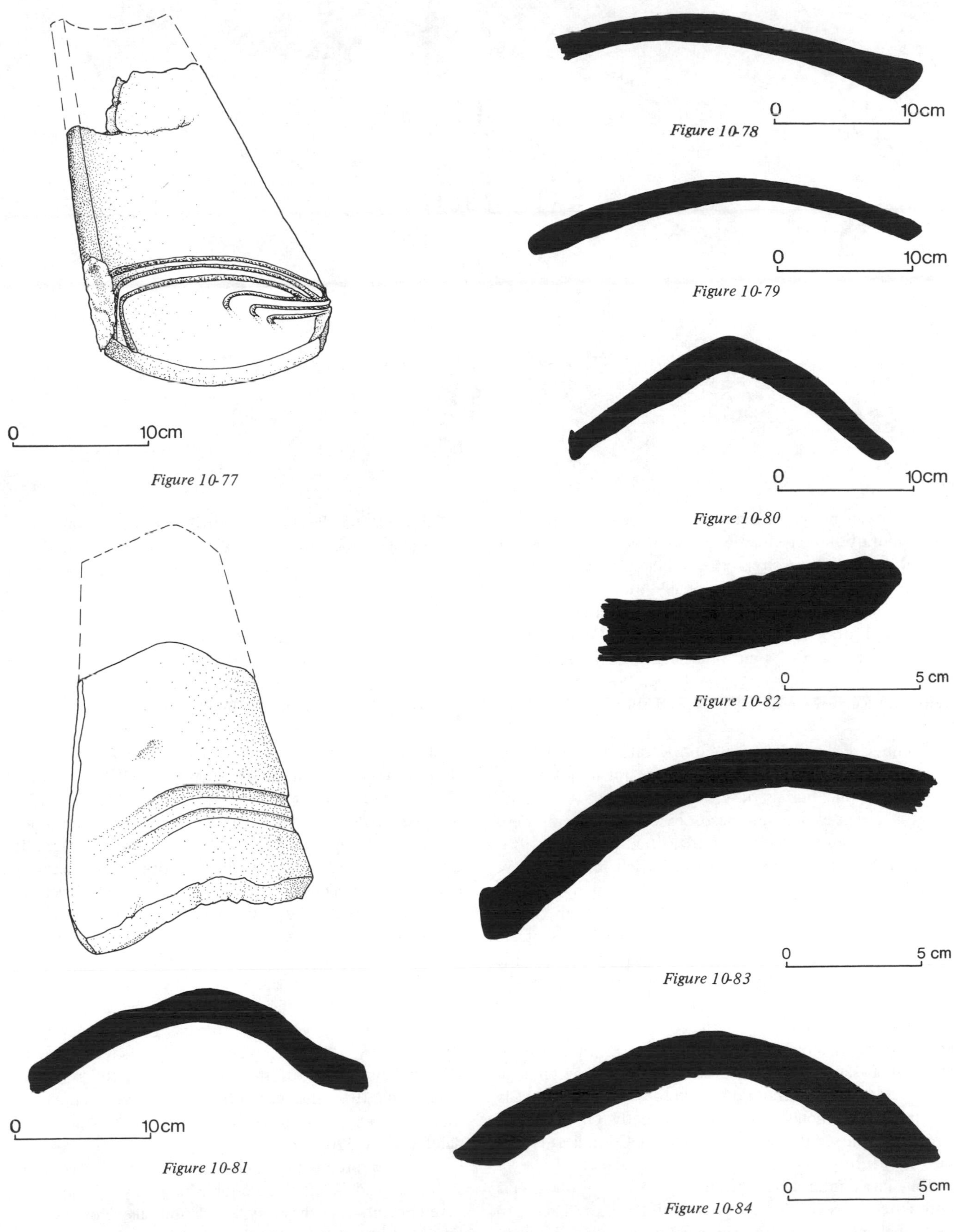

Figure 10-77

Figure 10-78

Figure 10-79

Figure 10-80

Figure 10-81

Figure 10-82

Figure 10-83

Figure 10-84

11
The Burials

by

William Wade

with contributions by Sara C. Bisel, John Rosser, and Nancy C. Wilkie

Much can be learned from Byzantine literature about contemporary burial practices. We have descriptions of funeral services, as well as the manner in which corpses were prepared for burial and finally buried. One of the most moving episodes in all Byzantine literature is about the funeral of the hero, Digenes Akrites (Mavrogordato 1956, p. 245). And of course burial scenes are represented in Byzantine art. Koukoules (1951, pp. 148-227) has gathered many such references and woven them into a lengthy essay.

For precise parallels to our burials, however, one must turn to the archaeological evidence. It is not surprising that many Byzantine burials have been recovered. At Corinth alone, at least seven cemeteries or extensive concentrations of Byzantine burials have been identified (Scranton 1957, pp. 29-31). The types of Byzantine burials in Greece have been discussed in detail by Soteriou (1942, pp. 61-79), Pallas (1950-51, pp. 163-81), and Scranton (1957, pp. 29-31, 126-28). The Corinth grave types include three that are represented at Nichoria and adjacent Trypetorachi: the simple interment without any cover or protection (except perhaps a winding sheet); burial in the earth with a covering of tiles arranged tentlike over the corpse; and the rectangular cist grave lined on the sides with stone slabs and covered with similar slabs. There is no evidence for any chronological development in these burial types at Corinth. Tile burials are commonly thought of as Early Christian, but Scranton points out that they occur at Corinth as late as the 12th century.

The simple interment without any cover or protection is represented at Nichoria by the two child burials adjacent to the chapel apses in L23 Tij that were excavated by Wilkie in 1973 (Fig. 9-5; Pl. 11-1). Both burials were considerably disturbed by plowing, but the N interment (NB 12-1) was intact enough to reveal that the child had been laid on its back with its head toward the W. The upper arms had been placed parallel to the body; the forearms were crossed over the chest. The scattered beads of a faience necklace (**583**) were recovered from the area of the neck (Chapter 12, p. 411). A meter to the S an infant burial (NB 13-1) was badly destroyed; no grave goods were found.

The two child burials were only 0.10-0.20 m below the modern ground surface and partially protected by tile and stone rubble from the destruction of the Phase 4 chapel. The N grave was at 87.97 m elevation, the other at 87.83 m. Elsewhere we have proposed that the ground level around the chapel during its use was about 88.00 m. The elevation of the N burial provides confirmation at least that it was not *below* this level. In fact, the ground level must have been at least 0.20-0.30 m higher in order to provide an adequate covering of earth for these otherwise unprotected graves. The child burials were probably made prior to the final destruction of the chapel.

The second type of burial, that covered with roof tiles or paving tiles, is represented by the Trypetorachi grave β excavated by Choremis (see p. 355). As discussed previously, this earlier of the two Trypetorachi graves was covered by two large pan tiles which are very similar to a tile recovered from Room 3 of Unit IV-2, Phase 2 and dated ca. 460-520.

It is important to emphasize Scranton's observation about the difficulty in establishing any chronological development for these types of burials. For example, Roman tile-covered burials are common (see Makaronas

1949-50, p. 10, Pls. 1-2), but such graves also date from classical Greek times (see Vavritsas 1969, p. 69, Pl. 90e). The covering tiles of the two periods, however, are usually quite different and should be helpful in making gross distinctions. But it is often difficult to compare published tiles because profiles and exact dimensions are not provided. For example, a grave from the Comnenian period or later (Pallas 1972, p. 234, Pl. 214a) had cover tiles which from the photographs alone appear to resemble the Trypetorachi cover tiles. The most carefully reported Byzantine tiles are still those from Cherson (Yakobson 1950, pp. 117-53).

The third type of burial, the cist grave with stone slabs lining the sides and covering the top, is represented by our NB 10-1 at the SE corner of the chapel (Fig. 9-5; McDonald et al. 1975, p. 99). It was 1.12 m in length, 0.35 m in average width, and covered by six large limestone slabs (Pl. 11-2). The skeleton was that of an adult female, lying on her back with head toward the W-NW. The upper arms were parallel to the body; the forearms and hands were crossed over the chest (Pl. 11-3). Although it was obviously unrobbed, no grave goods were associated with this burial. The fact that those who made the burial robbed out part of the SE corner of the chapel indicates that the chapel was already in ruins and at least some parts of its foundations were obscured when the burial was made. The small number of burials around the chapel might indicate that it was in use for a relatively brief period.

A less orthodox example of the third burial type is Choremis's Trypetorachi grave στ, which we have dated to the 12th century because of the similarity of fragments of coarse jugs found here and in the chapel (see p. 355). Although not stone-lined, this burial was covered with slabs of slate.

J.R.

Stomion Burial (NB 9-1)

When the tholos tomb collapsed some time in the 4th century B.C. or later, the large limestone blocks that comprised the dome and the coarse yellow sand that formed the mound over it filled most of the standing portion of the tomb chamber (Fig. 7-11). In the stomion, blocks from the collapsed dome were found only at the N end. Subsequent to the collapse, coarse reddish sand that was clearly slopewash from the hill to the NE gradually accumulated in both the stomion and the tomb chamber. This fill seems to have entered the stomion through an opening in the central part of the roof, where two of the five original lintel blocks are presently missing. These blocks were presumably removed to provide access to the tomb during its use as a cult center in the Classical period (see p. 333).

After the fill had built up throughout the stomion to a level of approximately 0.70 m below the bottom of the outermost lintel block, the burial of a young adult female (Nichoria Burial 9-1, see p. 337) was made at its N end (Pl. 11-4). The date of the burial cannot be closely determined since there were no associated grave goods. The burial was made after the dome collapsed, which probably occurred shortly after the chamber ceased to be used as a cult center. A Roman context would not be inconsistent with the stratigraphy.

At the time of the burial, the body was placed on its back, with head at the W side of the stomion, knees against the E stomion wall, and lower legs bent back. The burial was subsequently disturbed, since the long bones of the right leg and the cranium were found under the second lintel block, ca. 1.50 m S of the major portion of the skeleton. Since no attempt seems to have been made following the burial to seal off the N end of the stomion, either animals or humans could have caused this disturbance. Thereafter, no further activity seems to have taken place in connection with the ruined tomb until modern times.

N.C.W.

Analysis of Skeletal Material

NICHORIA BURIAL 9-1

Provenience: Stomion of tholos tomb (see Wilkie's account of excavation, pp. 332-34)

Chronology: Probably Roman or later. Apparently later than the collapse of the tholos dome, which took place after the 4th century B.C.

Sex: Female.

Age: Young adult (21-35 years).[1]

Condition: The cranium is in fair condition and lacks the temporal and basilar regions, the nasals, the interior orbital regions, pieces of the frontal bone, and both mandibular rami. All the teeth are present except the left third molars and, in the mandible, the central and right lateral incisors and right canine, all of these being lost after death. Also missing are the lateral incisors in the maxilla, but these appear not to have erupted.

The post-cranial skeleton, in fair to poor condition, includes the major long bones, most of the thoracic vertebrae and ribs, the right clavicle and scapula, the innominates, and the majority of the hand and foot bones.

Observations: Although the symphyseal faces of the pubes yield an age estimate of 32 years (Gilbert and McKern, 1973), this female shows moderately heavy wear of the teeth, with frequent partial exposure of the dentine and, in the maxillary incisors, complete dentine exposure. Contributing to the excessive wear in these central incisors may be the apparently congenital absence of the lateral incisors. The skull has an unfused metopic suture (Pl. 11-5), a trait that is fairly common among Europeans, according to Brothwell (1958).

The stature of this young woman is estimated to have

been 1516 mm (Trotter and Gleser, 1952), with 1.5 mm subtracted as a correction for age. This estimate is not likely to be very accurate since it is based on the length of the left humerus, which is not as strongly correlated with living stature as the bones of the leg. The left humerus distal end index is 20.1, the left index of humeral robustness is 19.4, and the diaphyseal indices of the humeri are 89.5 and 84.2 (left and right, respectively), both eurybrachic. The index of robustness of the right radius yields an extreme value, 14.9, and a more moderate 14.1 for the right ulna. The hyperplatymeric femora produce indices of 63.3 and 61.3. Both femora have very weak pilastric indices of 100.0. The tibiae are mesocnemic, with indices of 69.0 and 66.7.

Among the pathologies, the only caries are interproximal occurrences in the maxilla, involving the left premolars and first molar, and the right second premolar.

The interior aspect of the medial end of the right clavicle houses a prominent resorptive lesion (Pl. 11-6) that appears to be localized suppurative osteomyelitis.

Summary: This is a burial of a female who was probably approaching middle age. The skeleton has some interesting traits with probable genetic components, including metopic retention and congenitally absent maxillary lateral incisors. There is also some evidence of a fairly arduous life, including heavy dental wear and a serious, though apparently localized, infection.

Table 11-1. Metric Data: Nichoria Burial 9-1

Measurement	Left	Right
Cranial breadth	137 mm	
Nasal breadth	22 mm	
Frontal arc	129 mm	
Parietal arc	140 mm	
Occipital arc	93 mm	
Frontal chord	111 mm	
Parietal chord	121 mm	
Occipital chord	78 mm	
Biasterionic chord	103 mm	
Symphyseal height	25 mm	
Inter-foraminal breadth	44 mm	
Humerus length	279 mm	. . .
Humerus distal end breadth	56 mm	. . .
Humerus A-P mid-shaft diameter	17 mm	16 mm
Humerus M-L mid-shaft diameter	19 mm	19 mm
Humerus mid-shaft circumference	54 mm	53 mm
Ulna length		237 mm
Ulna shaft length		206 mm
Ulna trochlear notch height		20 mm
Ulna distal end breadth		16 mm
Ulna minimum shaft circumference		29 mm
Radius length		215 mm
Radius maximum head diameter		21 mm
Radius distal end breadth		30 mm
Radius minimum shaft circumference	33 mm	32 mm
Femur A-P sub-trochanteric diameter	19 mm	19 mm
Femur M-L sub-trochanteric diameter	30 mm	31 mm
Femur A-P mid-shaft diameter	25 mm	25 mm
Femur M-L mid-shaft diameter	25 mm	25 mm
Femur maximum head diameter	43 mm	45 mm
Femur mid-shaft circumference	78 mm	79 mm
Tibia nutrient foramen A-P diameter	29 mm	30 mm
Tibia nutrient foramen M-L diameter	20 mm	20 mm
Tibia minimum shaft circumference	69 mm	70 mm
Clavicle mid-shaft circumference		27 mm
Innominate height	184 mm	. . .

NICHORIA BURIAL 12-1

Provenience: Outside the E end of the Byzantine chapel, close to NB 13-1 (Pl. 11-1).

Chronology: Middle Byzantine (12th-13th century).

Sex: Undetermined.

Age: Young child (4-6 years).

Condition: Much of the cranium is present, but in very poor, badly fragmented condition. Twelve permanent and eleven deciduous teeth, all disarticulated, are associated.

The post-cranial skeleton includes the major long bones in fair to poor condition and missing most of the epiphyses. The vertebrae, ribs, clavicles, scapulae, and innominates are all badly fragmented.

Table 11-2. Metric Data: Nichoria Burial 12-1

Measurement	Left	Right
Humerus A-P mid-shaft diameter	8 mm	8 mm
Humerus M-L mid-shaft diameter	10 mm	10 mm
Humerus mid-shaft circumference	30 mm	30 mm
Radius minimum shaft circumference	20 mm	20 mm
Ulna minimum shaft circumference	14 mm	14 mm
Femur A-P mid-shaft circumference		11 mm
Femur M-L mid-shaft circumference		12 mm
Femur mid-shaft circumference		37 mm

Observations: There is fairly mild spongy hyperostosis in the superior margin of the right orbit (Pl. 11-7; left orbit missing). The teeth, in various degrees of development, show no evidence of pathology.

Summary: This burial is that of a young child about four years of age, according to the dental standards of Schour and Massler (1941). The condition of the skeleton is so poor that only very limited information can be obtained.

NICHORIA BURIAL 13-1

Provenience: Outside the E end of the Byzantine chapel, close to NB 12-1.

Chronology: Middle Byzantine (12th-13th century).

Sex: Undetermined.

Age: Infant (0-3 years).

Condition: Only very small fragments of the braincase, including no teeth or identifiable facial bones, and a few small fragments of the post-cranial skeleton were recovered.

Table 11-3. Metric Data: Nichoria Burial 10-1

Measurement		
Cranial length	182 mm	
Cranial breadth	132 mm	
Minimum frontal diameter	96 mm	
Basion-bregma height	140 mm	
Maximum circumference	509 mm	
Basion-porion height	22 mm	
Auricular height	114 mm	
Auricular breadth	116 mm	
Total facial height	120 mm	
Upper facial height	72 mm	
Bizygomatic diameter	125 mm	
Biorbital diameter	94 mm	
Protrusion of nasion	18 mm	
Nasal height	53 mm	
Nasal breadth	23 mm	
Nasion-basion length	100 mm	
Basion-prosthion length	93 mm	
Alveolar length	51 mm	
Alveolar breadth	60 mm	
Palatal breadth	41 mm	
Foramen magnum length	35 mm	
Foramen magnum breadth	30 mm	
Frontal arc	134 mm	
Parietal arc	121 mm	
Occipital arc	125 mm	
Biporial arc	312 mm	
Frontal chord	118 mm	
Parietal chord	110 mm	
Occipital chord	107 mm	
Simotic chord	10 mm	
Bidacryonic chord	21 mm	
Biasterionic chord	113 mm	
Mandibular length	99 mm	
Bicondylar breadth	121 mm	
Bigonial breadth	105 mm	
L. ramus height	61 mm	
L. ramus minimum breadth	29 mm	
L. ramus coronoid height	62 mm	
Symphyseal height	33 mm	
Inter-foraminal breadth	45 mm	
Humerus length	296 mm	303 mm
Humerus maximum head diameter	41 mm	40 mm
Humerus proximal end breadth	43 mm	44 mm
Humerus distal end breadth	58 mm	59 mm
Humerus A-P mid-shaft diameter	16 mm	15 mm
Humerus M-L mid-shaft diameter	20 mm	21 mm
Humerus mid-shaft circumference	55 mm	57 mm
Ulna length	240 mm	(245) mm
Ulna shaft length	215 mm	. . .
Ulna trochlear notch height	18 mm	17 mm
Ulna distal end breadth	16 mm	. . .
Ulna minimum shaft circumference	33 mm	34 mm
Radius length	(218 mm)	(224) m
Radius maximum head diameter	20 mm	. . .
Radius minimum shaft circumference	38 mm	38 mm
Femur length	417 mm	420 mm
Femur bicondylar length	413 mm	413 mm
Femur trochanteric length	404 mm	405 mm
Femur A-P sub-trochanteric diameter	24 mm	23 mm
Femur M-L sub-trochanteric diameter	31 mm	30 mm
Femur A-P mid-shaft diameter	29 mm	27 mm
Femur M-L mid-shaft diameter	26 mm	24 mm
Femur mid-shaft circumference	85 mm	79 mm
Femur maximum head diameter	41 mm	47 mm
Femur epicondylar breadth	80 mm	78 mm
Tibia length	360 mm	358 mm
Tibia maximum diameter proximal end	74 mm	74 mm
Tibia nutrient foramen A-P diameter	31 mm	31 mm
Tibia nutrient foramen M-L diameter	24 mm	24 mm
Tibia minimum shaft circumference	69 mm	69 mm
Fibula length	351 mm	352 mm
Clavicle length	125 mm	129 mm
Clavicle lateral breadth	22 mm	23 mm
Clavicle mid-shaft circumference	33 mm	35 mm
Scapula height	142 mm	. . .
Scapula breadth	96 mm	. . .
Scapular spine length	122 mm	. . .
Scapula glenoid height	32 mm	33 mm
Scapula glenoid breadth	24 mm	24 mm
Innominate height	201 mm	199 mm
Innominate breadth	159 mm	156 mm
Sacral height	99 mm	
Sacral breadth	110 mm	

Observations: Some of the cranial fragments are thickened and very porous, suggesting extensive hyperostotic involvement of at least the parietals.

Metric Data: None obtainable.

NICHORIA BURIAL 10-1

Provenience: At SE corner of Byzantine chapel in grid L23 Sj (Pl. 11-3).

Chronology: Middle Byzantine (13th century or not much later).

Sex: Female.

Age: Middle-aged (36-55 years).

Condition: This burial includes an intact, well-preserved cranium (Pls. 11-8 to 11-12) with only the right maxillary first molar lost after death.

The post-cranial skeleton is not so complete or well preserved but quite good, nonetheless. All the major long bones are present, in good to fair condition. The cervical, upper thoracic, lumbar, and sacral vertebrae are in good condition; the remaining thoracics (4-12) are fair to poor. The ribs are badly fragmented. All the bones of the pectoral and pelvic girdles, including the sternebrae, are present and in good condition, except for the poorly preserved right scapula. As well, nearly all the hand and foot bones are present, in good to fair condition.

Observations: The cranium is somewhat elongated, with an index of 72.5, and high, as indicated by both the height-length index, 76.9, and the height-breadth index, 106.1. Similarly, the face is high and narrow, as shown by the total facial index of 96.0 and the upper facial index of 59.2, with fairly prominent cheekbones (cranio-facial index = 94.7). The nose, also, is very narrow, with an index of 43.4. The forehead, however, is quite broad, with a fronto-parietal index of 72.7. The face is exceedingly orthognathic, yielding an index of 93.0 and an alveolar arch index of 117.6, although not at all flat in a transverse plane (index of Woo and Morant 1936 is 19.1). Most of these characteristics are consistent with and, in some cases, dependent upon, a short, high lower jaw (mandibular index = 81.8, ramus index = 47.5).

Stature is estimated to have been 1564 mm, based on femur length with 10.5 mm subtracted for age, which is thought to have been in the range of 45 to 50 years. The scapular index is 67.6 (left side only), and the glenoid index is 75.0 on the left side and 72.7 on the right. The claviculo-humeral index is 42.2 and 42.6, respectively. The clavicles are robust, with an index of 26.4 (left) and 27.1 (right). The innominate index is 126.4 (left) and 127.6 (right), and the sacral index is 111.1. To a minor extent, the lower limbs are proportionately longer than the upper limbs, as indicated by the humero-femoral index (71.0, left side; 72.1, right side) and the intermembral index (66.2, left side; 67.7, right side). The humerus head index is bilaterally 14.5. The distal end index of the humerus is 19.6 (left) and 19.5 (right). The index of humeral robustness is 18.6 (left) and 18.8 (right). The diaphyseal index of the humerus is quite asymmetrical, being 80.0 on the left side and only 71.4 on the right. The index of robustness is 17.4 (left) and 17.0 (right) in the radius and 15.3 in the left ulna. The femora are platymeric, with indexes of 77.4 and 76.7, respectively. The femora have medium pilasters (111.5 and 112.5, respectively). Femoral robusticity indices are 13.2 and 12.1, and the perimetral-length indices are 20.6 and 19.1. The crural index is 86.2 (left) and 85.7 (right). The tibiae are extremely broad, as defined by the cnemic index (77.4, both sides). The tibial index of robustness is 19.2 on the left side and 19.3 on the right. The superior epiphysis index is 20.6 in the left tibia and 20.7 in the right.

The only noteworthy cranial pathologies are dental. The teeth show extensive occlusal wear, with complete dentine exposure as a rule, excepting only the left third molar in the maxilla (Pl. 11-13). There is evidence of an active abscess in the region of the first two molars in the right maxilla. Teeth lost prior to death include the right second molar in the maxilla and, in the mandible, the left molars and distal premolar, as well as the right second and third molars. Only the maxillary third molars contain intact carious lesions.

Osteophytes are profuse in the apophyseal joints of the upper thoracic vertebrae, decreasingly so through the thoracic region. Moderate osteophytes are noted on the ventral margins of the lower lumbar and first sacral centra. The head of the right femur and the rims of both acentabula display moderate osteophytic lipping. The public symphyses exhibit multiple parturition scars. There is a healed fracture in the distal shaft of the left fibula (Pl. 11-14).

Summary: This burial is that of a rather slight female, well into middle age, who had borne several children, and whose teeth were not in the best condition during the latter part of her life. Other than these meager facts, there is little evidence of the events of her life, or death, other than that she suffered a minor fracture at some point.

NICHORIA BURIAL 8-1

Provenience: Trypetorachi (immediately SE of Nichoria ridge.[2]

Chronology: Early or Middle Byzantine.

Sex: Probably female.

Age: Young adult (21-35 years).

Condition: This cranium is in only fair condition, lacking the malar and basilar regions, the lower nasals, most of the interior structure of the orbits, the alveoli distal to the right first premolar, and the entire mandible. The skull is considerably compressed medio-laterally.

Observations: The single cranial index obtainable is the auricular height-length index, 61.0. The only other interesting observations are of the nine teeth recovered. The posterior teeth are relatively lightly worn and contain no caries. By contrast, the anterior teeth, which are too severely worn for any carious lesions to be present, show unusually heavy wear, ranging from exposure of the pulp chamber to the loss of the entire crown (see Pl. 11-15).

Summary: This burial was probably that of a young adult female, although an assessment of sex based solely on a poorly preserved cranium is not especially reliable. Since the molar teeth and second premolar show only enamel wear on their occlusal surfaces, the age of the individual is probably not over 35 years. The unusually heavy wear in the remaining teeth can probably be attributed to cultural use of the teeth, although nothing specific suggests itself.

W.W.

Table 11-4. Metric Data: Nichoria Burial 8-1

Cranial length	187 mm
Auricular height	114 mm
Nasal breadth	25 mm
R. orbital breadth	41 mm
Frontal arc	131 mm
Parietal arc	120 mm
Frontal chord	113 mm
Parietal chord	111 mm

Table 11-5. Bone Mineral in Nichoria Burial 9-1, Compared with U.S. Modern

	Sex	Ca (mg)	P (mg)	Sr (ug)	Sr/Ca	Site Corrected Sr/Ca	Mg (mg)	Mg/Ca	Zn (ug)	Zn/Ca
Nichoria Burial 9-1	♀	308.1	155.1	79.4	.258	.657	.51	.0017	76.2	.247
U.S. Mod. N=40		220.4	102.5	. . .	. . .	. . .	2.81	.0127	147.1	.671

Bone Mineral and Nutrition

NICHORIA BURIAL 9-1

At 1.5288 m, this female in her late twenties was shorter than the average Nichoria female in the Late Bronze Age. Her teeth, with three lesions, two suppressed eruptions, and rather poor occlusion, can be rated generally poor in spite of their being free of hypoplasia. The extreme flattening of the femur shafts as well as the hypertrophy of the deltoid tuberosities points to a life of heavy labor. Both of these phenomena are adaptations to the increasing musculature needed for hard work, particularly if the individual is small and/or malnourished. The left ulna and radius suggest a green-stick fracture, possibly from a fall when she was a child. The osteomyelitis of the right clavicle (reported by Dr. Wade; the bone was not examined by the writer) also points to a rigorous life-style; the infection was likely the result of injury, either traumatic or stress. Her right pubis, the only one present, suggests she did not endure the stress of parturition, since scars were absent.

Mineral analysis shows her to be rather similar to her Late Bronze predecessors. Calcium and phosphorus values are those expected in archaeological populations. Strontium level is moderate, indicating a diet that included terrestrial meat protein. Magnesium is low, as it is with all Nichorians. Zinc level is also quite low; the Zn/Ca ratio is less than half that of modern Americans. The use of unrefined cereals and unleavened bread can explain part of this problem, but she could have suffered a chronic debilitating illness as well. We have ruled out the stress of repeated pregnancies with the examination of the pubic symphysis.

NICHORIA BURIAL 10-1

This woman was in her late thirties. At 1.6039 m, she was fairly tall compared to Late Bronze females from Nichoria (av. = 1.5770 m) and from Byzantine Kalenderhane Camii at Istanbul (av. = 1.5436 m). Both her stature and her pelvic brim index at 94.57 indicate fairly good nutrition during her growth period. A moderate degree of enamel hypoplasia, however, suggests that she suffered periods of rather severe illness as a growing child. During her lifetime she endured heavy manual labor, as shown by the hypertrophy of the deltoid tubercles of the humeri. Repeated pregnancies, perhaps more than five, are suggested by scarring of the pubic symphyses. Arthritic changes at the left pubic symphysis and the right hip joint suggest more problems than the repeated pregnancies would indicate. Perhaps the trauma that resulted in the fracture of the left fibula also damaged the right hip and left pubic symphysis. Although the fibula fracture healed, some periostitis remained at the site of the injury as well as the inflammatory changes shown by the enlarged femur head, the acetabulum of the right hip, and enlarged left pubic symphysis. Her dental health was quite poor, with antemortem loss, caries, and moderate periodontal disease. She also had rather poor occlusion. Probably her health problems were related more to her very arduous life-style than to poor nutrition.

This woman's bone shows the typical Nichoria pattern

Table 11-6. Bone Mineral in Nichoria Burials 8-1 and 10-1, Compared with U.S. Modern

	Sex	Ca (mg)	P (mg)	Sr (ug)	Sr/Ca	Site Corrected Sr/Ca	Mg (mg)	Mg/Ca	Zn (ug)	Zn/Ca
Nichoria Burial 8-1	♀	334.4	138.3	47.6	.142	.426	.47	.0014	62.6	.187
Nichoria Burial 10-1	♀	317.11	173.7	31.6	.100	.299	.59	.0019	181.6	.573
U.S. Mod.		220.4	102.5	. . .	. . .	. . .	2.81	.0127	147.1	.671

of trace minerals. Calcium and phosphorus levels are normal for archaeological material. Strontium is very low, indicating that more than moderate amounts of terrestrial animal protein were habitually consumed. Zinc value is also fairly high because of the meat consumption; but it may also indicate consumption of somewhat refined cereals and leavened bread. Apparently, the repeated pregnancies and illnesses did not deplete her bones of zinc.

NICHORIA BURIAL 8-1

This woman was also in her late thirties. Little can be said about her health from morphological analysis. Her teeth were fairly good, certainly better than those of no. 10-1. In bone mineral analysis she is similar to no. 10-1 in calcium, phosphorus, magnesium, and strontium; but zinc is low. The strontium value indicates that she ate a moderate amount of meat, but perhaps she suffered chronic health problems.

NOTES

1. I pointed out to Professor Wade that, in terms of life expectancy in prehistoric or even medieval times, it is hazardous to link terms like "young" or "middle-aged" to absolute numbers of years. For example, an individual aged 35 can scarcely be considered "young" nor someone aged 55 as "middle-aged." He decided, however, to make no change in his text. The reader will also notice discrepancies in calculations of age between Wade's and Bisel's reports. (Ed.)

2. This cranium is from Angelos Choremis' 1969 excavation. When he handed it over to us at the end of the season he did not specify in which of the two graves it was discovered (see p. 355).

REFERENCES

(For Wade's and Bisel's bibliography, see References for Chapter 4, pp. 271, 272).

Koukoules, P. 1951. *Byzantine Life and Civilization*, Vol. 4. Athens. In Greek.

Makaronas, C. 1949-50. "Excavation of a Necropolis in Thessalonika," *Praktika:* 145-61. In Greek.

Mavrogordata, J. 1956. *Digenes Akrites*. Oxford.

McDonald, W. A., et al. 1975. "Excavations at Nichoria in Messenia: 1972-73," *Hesperia* 44: 69-141.

Pallas, D. 1950-51. "Salaminiaka," *Arch. Eph.*:163-81. In Greek.

———. 1972. "Excavation of the Basilica of Kraneos," *Praktika*: 205-50. In Greek.

Scranton, R. L. 1957. *Corinth. American School Excavations, XVI: Mediaeval Architecture in the Central Area of Corinth*. Princeton.

Soteriou, A. 1942. *Christian and Byzantine Archaeology*. Athens. In Greek.

Vavritsas, A. 1969. "An Excavation in Southern Thrace," *Praktika*: 59-69. In Greek.

Yakobson, A. L. 1950. *Srednevekosiyi Khersones = Materialy i issled. po. arch. SSSR* 17. In Russian.

12
The Small Finds

by
John Rosser

The Byzantine small finds have little intrinsic value. The largest categories are bronze, iron (especially nails), and glass. There are no gold or silver items. One's first impression is that they can all be easily accommodated to our picture of Nichoria's modest ecclesiastical and domestic architecture. Yet it is interesting that there is no significant difference between the quality of our objects and those of an important Byzantine site like Corinth. There are in fact several specific parallels with Corinthian minor objects which suggest imports to Nichoria from Corinth, or to both from a common source. Of course our assemblage is hardly as diverse as that of Corinth, but most of our minor objects are definitely products of the same milieu.

Despite the fact that no "treasures" were discovered, some of the minor objects will be of particular interest to Byzantinists. Most interesting are the enigmatic straps or fillets of bronze found in the floor deposit of the chapel narthex. Also, the function of some of the iron objects from Area II is uncertain and bears close scrutiny. Perhaps most important, however, is the fragmentary Byzantine glass, since surprisingly little Byzantine glass is published from excavations in Greece.

The following catalog is divided into these categories: Metal (Bronze, Iron, Lead), Stone, Glass, and Painted Plaster. Objects from Area II are usually listed first in a given category, followed by those from Area IV and a few items from Area III. Unless otherwise indicated, the date of the small finds from Area II can be bracketed in the late 10th to early 12th century, those from Unit IV-2, Phases 1-2, ca. 460-520, and those from Phases 3-4 of Unit IV-2 from the early 11th to the early 13th century. For reasons explained in the Preface, the catalog of Byzantine small finds is numbered consecutively, beginning with no. **501**, and all numbers are printed in **boldface.**

Metal Objects

BRONZE

Byzantine bronze coin finds were scarce. In fact, only two (**501**, **502**) were associated directly with the Byzantine architecture in Areas II and IV, but they are very useful in establishing the chronological framework for Byzantine Nichoria (see Chapter 9, pp. 358, 370). Both coins are from very common bronze issues.

Three bronze rings (**505-7**) were recovered from Byzantine contexts. They are in no way exceptional, and **505** and **506** find parallels at Corinth. Judging from the number of Byzantine bronze rings found both at Corinth and at Nichoria, such rings must have been popular with adults. Ring **505**, with the apparent "Chi-Rho" symbol, was discovered on the floor of Room 1 of Unit II-2. The other bronze objects are undistinguished, except for the enigmatic fillets found in the chapel.

501 (N242). Coin of Basil II and Constantine VII (976-1025). Pl. 12-1.

D. 0.03. Wt. 8.43 grams.

Worn, especially the obverse.

Obverse: visible only is bust of Christ, surrounded by a nimbus. *Reverse*: a four-line inscription.

This issue belongs to the anonymous bronze coinage instituted by John I in 972 and continued by his successors until Constantine X (1059-67) reintroduced the imperial name and portrait. See W. Wroth, *Catalogue of the Imperial Coins in the British Museum*, II p. 488, nos. 26-35, there attributed to Basil II.

Unit II-2, K25 Gb, fill in courtyard, E of Wall K.

502 (N1449). Coin of Manuel I Comnenus (1143-80). Pl. 12-2.

D. 0.017. Wt. 2.06 grams.

Very worn on both obverse and reverse.

Obverse: visible only is bust of Manuel, holding labarum in raised right hand and globus with cross on top in raised left hand. The inscription is worn away. *Reverse*: bust of St. George, beardless, with curly hair, facing, wearing a cuirass and cloak, holding in right hand a spear and (restored) in left hand an oval shield. The inscription is worn away.

See W. Wroth, *Catalogue of the Imperial Coins in the British Museum*, II. p. 579, Pl. 70, nos. 16-17. This tetarteron of Manuel I is attributed to the mint of Thessalonika by M. F. Hendy, *Coinage and Money in the Byzantine Empire, 1081-1261,* p. 120, Pl. 17.14.

Unit IV-2, Phase 3, in the narthex floor packing.

503 (N836). Coin of Constantine I (307-37). Pl. 12-3.

D. 0.017.

Worn.

Obverse: bust of Constantine with diadem, drape, and cuirass, facing right. Only the first five letters of Constantine's name visible. *Reverse*: two soldiers standing on either side of two standards. In the exergue, mint mark: CON(S), minted in Constantinople, probably about 330.

Area IV, L23 Top, N of chapel.

504 (N226). Buckle. Pl. 12-4.

L. 0.029. W. (max.) 0.026. Th. 0.003.

Tongue missing; there is, however, a slight depression where the tongue was attached. Cast, with one face rounded, the other flat. The flat face is broken.

See *Corinth XII*, no. 2202, which is dated "early 12th c., though probably not later than 10th c." (sic).

Area II, K25 Hc.

505 (N266). Finger ring. Fig. 12-1.

D. (inner) ca. 0.018. W. (max.) of bezel 0.009.

Flat hoop. Oval bezel with six-pronged design resembling the "Chi-Rho" symbol.

See *Corinth XII*, no. 1873 (Type G) which bears some resemblance to our ring; dated to 10th or 11th century.

Unit II-2, K25 Fbc, from floor in center of Room 1, amidst traces of burning.

506 (N230). Finger ring. Fig. 12-2; Pl. 12-5.

D. (inner) 0.01. Th. (max.) 0.002.

Bezel missing. Flat hoop of two outer pieces of thick wire, with three rows of spiral wire between.

Similar to *Corinth XII*, no. 1834 (Type D), dated to 11th century or later.

Area II, K25 Hbc.

507 (N520). Finger ring. Fig. 12-3.

D. impossible to est. W. of bezel 0.012. L. of bezel 0.015.

Hoop squashed flat against bezel. Rectangular, very thin bezel.

Area II, K24 Iy/K25 Ia.

508 (N487). Earring. Pl. 12-6.

D. (inner) ca. 0.014.

A simple round split hoop, with one end flattened. Whatever decorative wire or pendant was once attached is now lost.

See *Corinth XII*, no. 2026, dated not later than 11th century.

Area II, K25 Fe.

509 (N298). Tweezers. Pl. 12-7.

L. 0.0795. W. (max.) 0.011. Th. (max.) 0.002.

Half a pair of tweezers, with curving prong end.

See *Corinth XII*, no. 1465 for a somewhat similar example.

The pottery context is mixed Byzantine and LHIIIB2, so that this object could in fact be Mycenaean.

Area II, K25 Ibc.

510 (N1312). Pin. Fig. 12-4.

L. (pres., slightly bent) 0.046. D. (max.) 0.002.

Head missing; tip of other end broken.

Unit IV-2, Phase 1, Room 1, above layer of fallen tiles.

Ca. 460-520?

511 (N1934). Game counter. Fig. 12-5.

D. 0.008. Th. 0.0019. Wt. 0.55 grams.

Intact and in good condition. For a duplicate, see *Corinth XII*, no. 1712, dated to Late Roman or Byzantine period.

Unit IV-2, Phase 2, Room 3, in the floor.

512 (N1935). Game counter. Fig. 12-6.

D. 0.0075. Th. 0.0019. Wt. 0.57 grams.

Intact and in good condition.

See *Corinth XII*, no. 1712, and **511** (above).

Unit IV-2, Phase 2, in the floor, near **511.**

513 (N1452). Fillet. Fig. 12-7; Pl. 12-8.

L. (pres., if straightened) 0.085. W. (max.) 0.008.
D. (of tubular hole). 0.003. Th. (max.) 0.0005.

End opposite tubular end appears broken. Thin strap, bent, with one end twisted to form tubular hole.

Unpublished Corinth MF 5562 is exact parallel. Function uncertain.

Unit IV-2, Phase 3, in narthex floor packing.

514 (N1123). Fillet. Fig. 12-8.

L. (pres., if straightened) 0.15. W. (max.) 0.007.
Th. (max.) 0.0005.

One end appears broken.

Similar to **513**, lacking only tubular end.

Unit IV-2, Phase 3 sanctuary.

515 (N1444). Fillet. Fig. 12-9.

L. (pres., if straightened) 0.058. W. (max.) 0.01.
D. (of tubular hole) 0.004. Th. (max.) 0.0008.

End opposite tubular end appears broken.

Similar to **513**.

Unit IV-2, Phase 3, in narthex floor packing.

516 (N1451). Fillet. Fig. 12-10.

L. (pres.) 0.029. W. (max.) 0.007. Th. (max.) 0.001.

End opposite tubular end appears broken.

Similar to **513**, but with tubular end poorly formed.

Unit IV-2, Phase 3, in narthex floor packing.

517 (N1984). Fillet(?) Fig. 12-11.

L. (pres.) 0.059. W. (max.) 0.007.

A paper-thin strip folded in two; pointed at one end.

Area IV, L23 QRij, in topsoil above chapel narthex.

518. (N1426). Fillet frags.(?) Fig. 12-12.

(a.) L. (pres., if straightened) 0.045. W. (max.) 0.009. D. (of hole) 0.0025. Th. (max.) 0.004.

(b.) L. (pres., if straightened) 0.021. W. (max.) 0.12. Th. (max., where folded) 0.009.

(a.) End with hole intact, though bent; other end appears broken.

(b.) Both ends appear broken; one edge of width is folded over.

Unit IV-2, Phase 3, in narthex floor packing.

519 (N1927). Stylus(?) Fig. 12-13; Pl. 12-9.

L. 0.055. W. (max.) of head 0.011. W. and Th. (max.) of shaft 0.004.

Shaft square in section, tapering to point.

Unpublished Corinth MF 6881 and MF 3380 are similar and may be Late Roman/Early Byzantine or later.

Unit IV-2, Phase 3 or 4, in wall plaster of sanctuary.

520 (N449). Cup. Fig. 12-14.

D. (est.) of base 0.056. H. (est. original) 0.017.

Crushed, but otherwise in good condition. Walls originally slightly flaring.

H. W. Catling (personal communication) does not consider this object to be of prehistoric date. Possibly a hanging lamp from chapel. For analyses of metal, see *Nichoria* I, Tables 11-1 and 11-5 (3rd from bottom).

Area IV, L23 Tfg, near chapel in topsoil.

IRON

Most of the Byzantine iron comes from Area II, where it may have been produced in or near Unit II-2 (see *Nichoria* I, Table 12-1, slag samples 39-49). Nails make up the single largest category, although only samples of the various types are cataloged below. The majority of excavated nails come from the chapel sanctuary (Unit IV-2, Phase 3 or 4) and are generally divisible into two simple categories. *Type A* is the larger version, having a head diameter of at least 0.02 and a length about 0.08 m. The shank is about 0.006 m where it meets the head, and the head thickness is about 0.003-0.004 m. *Type B* is slightly smaller, having a head diameter of 0.02 m or less and a length of about 0.07 m. The shank is about 0.005 m where it meets the head, with a head thickness of about 0.003 m.

521 (N408). Attachment. Fig. 12-15; Pl. 12-10.

L. (pres.) of vertical bar 0.224. L. (pres.) of horizontal crossbar 0.151. W. (max.) of bars 0.023. Th. (max) 0.004. L. (pres.) of nails 0.067.

Much corroded. Vertical bar consists of two joining fragments. If conjectured restoration as a cross is correct, then crossbar lay over vertical bar. The nails, each with a square head, were inserted through holes in the bars.

See *Corinth XII*, no. 1505, an iron standard cross dated to the 10th or 11th century; also nos. 1057 and 1058, crosslike bronze attachments of Byzantine or later date, and of unknown purpose.

Unit II-1, on floor in SE corner.

522 (N641). Blade. Pl. 12-11.

L. 0.08. W. (max.) 0.012. Th. (max.) 0.005.

Corroded but otherwise intact. Seems triangular in section.

Unit II-1, in fill of Wall A.

523 (N240). Blade. Pl. 12-12.

L. (pres.) 0.067. W. (max.) 0.013. Th. (max.) 0.003.

Corroded; tip broken. Similar to **522.**

Area II, K25 Ib.

524 (N251). Bracelet(?) Fig. 12-16.

L. (max.) of arms 0.056. W. (max.) of bezel 0.017.
Th. (max.) of bezel 0.003.

Much corroded, but otherwise intact. Resembles a bracelet; much too large and clumsy to have been a fibula.

Area II, K25 Ibc, near Unit II-1 on what may have been Byzantine ground level.

525 (N591). Hook. Fig. 12-17.

L. 0.099 (0.116 if straightened). W. (max.) 0.006.
Th. (max.) 0.004.

Corroded but otherwise intact. Rectangular in section, tapering to bent, pointed end.

Area II, K25 Ia.

526 (N808). Shaft. Pl. 12-13.

L. (pres.) 0.065. W. (max.) 0.008.

Corroded, with both ends broken. Middle of shaft flares, then tapers; square to round in section.

Probably a spearhead, such as *Corinth XII*, no. 1559, dated not later than 11th century.

Area II, K25 HIb.

527 (N717). Nail. Pl. 12-14.

L. (pres.) 0.068.

Much corroded. Head missing and tip of shank broken. Rectangular in section.

Unit II-2, from amid building debris immediately W of Wall I.

528 (N236). Hoop. Fig. 12-19.

D. (max.) 0.053. Th. ca. 0.006.

Broken(?)

There are iron finger rings at Corinth, with diameters small enough to fit comfortably over a finger (see *Corinth XII*, no. 1841), but this is obviously not such a ring. Its context is obscure and it is also included as **85** in the Catalog of Chapter 5.

Area III, K25 Rcd.

529 (N1428). Attachment. Fig. 12-18.

L. (pres.) 0.039. W. (max. pres.) 0.015. Th. (max.) 0.006.
D. of hole 0.005.

Fragment. Cast, with concave underside having raised edge. The two holes no doubt received nails.

Perhaps part of handle, such as unpublished Corinth MF 1107, or part of hinge or binding, such as bronze examples, *Corinth XII*, nos. 904 (Byzantine) and 908 (Byzantine or later).

Area IV, L23 Pkl, in topsoil.

530 (N252). Nail. Fig. 12-20.

L. (pres.) 0.017. D. of head 0.02.

Most of shank missing. Oval, convex head.

Area II, K25 Gbc.

531. (N1827). Nail. Fig. 12-21.

L. (pres.) 0.072. D. of head 0.022.

Corroded. Intact except for missing tip of shank. Circular, convex head. Shank square in section.

Unit IV-2, Phase 1 (Room 2), from floor.

532 (N1825). Nail. Fig. 12-22.

L. (pres.) 0.081. D. of head 0.015.

Corroded. Intact except for missing tip of shank. Circular, convex head. Shank square in section.

Unit IV-2, Phase 1 (Room 2), from floor.

533 (N1826). Nail. Pl. 12-15.

L. (pres.) 0.021. D. of head 0.019.

Corroded and in two fragments. Circular, convex head. Shank square in section.

Dimensions vary slightly, but the three nails (**531, 532, 533**) basically similar.

Unit IV-2, Phase 1 (Room 2), from floor.

534 (N1478). Nail. Fig. 12-23; Pl. 12-16.
L. (slightly bent) 0.078. D. of head 0.022.
Corroded.
An intact example of nail *Type A*. Other *Type A* nails with same provenience are not listed separately in the catalog but bear the following inventory numbers: N1043, N1255, N1300, N1399 (only one of the two nails), N1727, and N1259.
Unit IV-2, Phase 3 or 4 sanctuary.

535 (N1454). Nail. Fig. 12-24; Pl. 12-17.
L. (pres.) 0.057. D. of head 0.019.
Corroded. Intact except for broken tip of shank.
This is best example of nail *Type B*. Others with same provenience are not cataloged separately but bear the following inventory numbers: N1045, N1116, N1117, N1256, N1258, N1299, N1397, N1399, N1453 (only one of the two nails), N1454, N1988, and N1989.
Unit IV-2, Phase 3 or 4 sanctuary.

536 (N1479). Nail. Pl. 12-18.
L. (pres., slightly bent) 0.024. D. of head 0.02. Th. of shank 0.005.
Corroded. Half of shank missing. Unique among chapel nails, insofar as the shank, which is square in section and uniformly 0.005 thick, goes through the head.
Unit IV-2, Phase 3 or 4 sanctuary.

537 (N1261). Clamp. Fig. 12-25.
L. 0.088. D. (max.) of head 0.017.
Corroded. Shank square in section, bent over and flattened at one end.
Unit IV-2, Phase 3 or 4 sanctuary.

538 (N1045). Spike. Fig. 12-26.
L. (pres.) 0.043. Th. (max.) of shank 0.16.
Corroded. Part of shank missing. Shank rectangular in section, much thicker than other nail shanks from sanctuary, and culminates in a flat end.
Unit IV-2, Phase 3 or 4 sanctuary.

LEAD

539 (N919). Candelabrum attachment(?) Pl. 12-19.
H. 0.018. D. 0.014. Wt. 14.9 grams.
Spherical body with projecting knob at top.
See Caskey, *Deltion* 1969, pp. 100, 101, Pl. 53, nos. 56-58, for three unidentified examples from Keos. Pallas found one of brass in the narthex of a Middle Byzantine church in Epirus and suggested it might be an attachment to a piece of ecclesiastical equipment, perhaps a candelabrum (*Praktika* 1971, p. 143, Pl. 178, B, b). At Corinth unpublished MF 6818 is from a Byzantine or later context. Our lead examples might be suspension weights.
Area IV, L23 VWkl, just E of chapel.

540 (N268). Candelabrum attachment(?) Fig. 12-27; Pl. 12-20.
H. 0.019. D. 0.009. Wt. 16.8 grams.
Part of body missing. Spherical body with projecting knob at top. Similar to **539** above.
Unit II-1, on floor in SE corner.

541 (N526). Button. Fig. 12-28.
D. 0.015. Th. 0.011. D. of hole 0.006.
Conical shape with vertical grooves around exterior. Pierced by an off-center hole.
See *Corinth XII*, no. 2634, dated to the Byzantine period.
Area IV, L23 Shi, S of chapel in topsoil.

542 (N1883). Bead. Fig. 12-29; Pl. 12-21.
L. 0.007. D. 0.011. Wt. 3.57 grams.
Conical shape with single pierced hole. Part of **583**, a necklace.
Area IV, L23 Tj, a child burial next to chapel.

Stone Objects

543 (N1987). Pierced slab. Pl. 12-22.
L. (pres.) 0.107. W. (max. pres.) 0.066. Th. (max.) 0.025. D. of hole 0.015.
Flat limestone slab, triangular-shaped at one end, with a single pierced hole. Broken at other end.
May have been used as weight.
Unit IV-2, in narthex floor packing.

Glass Objects

Despite its fragmentary state, the glass from Nichoria is the most important single category of Byzantine minor objects. If offers the first parallels in Greece for the Byzantine glass recovered at Corinth and published by Gladys Davidson Weinberg (Davidson 1940). Just as important are the independently dated contexts for our glass. The fragments from Area II are dated firmly in the late 10th to early 12th century. The fragments from the narthex floor packing of Unit IV-2 are dated from the early 11th to the early 13th century. This provides confirmation for Weinberg's initial assessment, which was not at first accepted, that the Corinth glass is Middle Byzantine, with a final date around the mid-12th century. The confirmation is of some importance, since among the parallels to the Corinth glass found outside Greece the contexts are mostly much later than the 12th century (Weinberg 1975b).

The discovery at Corinth in 1937 of two medieval glassmaking establishments of contemporaneous date was startling because glass manufacture was previously unknown in Greece for any period (Weinberg 1975c, p. 127). It soon became evident that Middle Byzantine Corinth was a center of glassmaking, producing a variety of vessels of excellent technique and elaborate decoration. Furthermore, the Corinthian vessels appear in Cyprus, Sicily, Italy, Dalmatia, Russia, and eventually in Germany where some types lasted for centuries (Weinberg 1977); yet since the Corinth glass was published there has been an astonishing absence of similar glass in excavation reports from Greece itself. Professor Weinberg commented upon this at the 15th International Congress of Byzantine Studies in Athens:

> The strange fact is that almost no similar glass has been recorded from elsewhere in Greece, although many churches have been excavated, and mosaics and frescoes studied. One cannot help supposing that the glass pieces have been neglected, as they were fragmentary and not considered worth noting. Some reports in recent issues of *Ergon* mention glass fragments from churches, without further details; the only glass vessels which I know

are being studied were found in the church of Nichoria, in Messenia.

Professor Weinberg concluded her paper by making a plea to archaeologists working on Byzantine remains in Greece to publish their glass finds, even though they may seem insignificant. "Such records," she said, "might have considerable effect on our knowledge of this period" (Weinberg 1977).

Of the Nichoria fragments with Corinthian parallels **544, 547, 556** and **559** are from Area II; and **561, 562, 567,** and **583** are from Area IV. As one might expect, the glass recovered in Area II differs from that of the Area IV chapel. Only one fragment from Area II (**545**, from a bottle) has a parallel profile (in **580**) from the chapel. Practically all of the estimated six vessels from the Area IV chapel consist of cups and bowls from the narthex floor packing. The glass from Area II, on the other hand, is more diverse. It includes fragments of a goblet, a bottle, of bowls, lamps, and jewelry. The diversity and quality of the Area II fragments are further indication of a relatively high standard of living.

The cups and bowls from the chapel may once have held oil, placed there by supplicants who desired some transference of the patron saint's power into the liquid. Thereafter, the oil could be used to anoint a sick friend or relative. An even more likely use for such glass containers would have been as lamps.

Faience beads are rarely found in Byzantine contexts. At Corinth only two were recovered (see *Corinth XII*, nos. 2424 and 2425), and they are regarded as "relics of an earlier age" still in use during the Byzantine period (Davidson 1952, p. 289). But our faience necklace (**583**) most certainly dates from the time the chapel was in use during the Middle Byzantine period.

Nos. **561** and **562** are the only glass objects from Phase 1-2 of Unit IV-2, the Late Roman/Early Byzantine structure.

It will be noticed in the following catalog that "N" designations are occasionally repeated for separate items. This is because a single "N" number was assigned to groups of fragments as they were excavated. Only upon later examination was it apparent that within these groups there were sometimes fragments from different vessels.

544 (N229). Lamp. Fig. 12-30; Pl. 12-23.
H. (pres.) of bulb 0.014. D. of bulb 0.021.
D. (est) of rim frag. 0.055.
Fragmentary bulb with small part of lower body; also rim fragment. Part of group of mostly rim and body fragments. Spherical bulb with body flaring widely as far as preserved. Lip of rim dark green, remainder pale green.
See *Corinth XII*, no. 802, for a lamp dated from the 11th to the mid-12th century. Such colored lips are found on vessels at the Corinth factory (Weinberg 1975a).
Area II, K25 Hc.

545 (N233). Bottle(?) Fig. 12-31.
H. (pres.) 0.011. D. of bottom 0.015.
Bottom fragment. Flat bottom, curving into sides which broaden as they ascend. Dark olive-green with large bubbles.
Area II, K25 Gbc.

546 (N254). Bowl(?) Fig. 12-32.
H. (pres.) 0.008. D. (est.) of base 0.035.
Base fragment. Slight enamel weathering. Small, thick tubular ring base. Blue.
Area II, K25 Gc.

547 (N718). Goblet. Fig. 12-33.
H. (pres.) 0.018.
Stem fragment with two coils, the larger a bright blue. Rest of fragment pale green.
Not dissimilar to *Corinth XII*, no. 723, dated to 11th or 12th century.
Unit II-2, Room 3.

548 (N328). Bowl(?) Fig. 12-34.
H. (pres.) 0.008. D. (est.) of base 0.033.
Base fragment. Crackled frabric, with slight enamel weathering. Small, thick tubular ring base. Dark green.
Similar to **546.**
Area II, K25 Kc.

549 (N328). Bowl(?) Fig. 12-35.
H. (pres.) 0.015. D. (est.) of rim 0.08.
Rim fragment with slight enamel weathering. Light green.
Area II, K25 Kc.

550 (N232). Bowl(?) Fig. 12-36.
H. (pres.) 0.014. D. (est.) of rim 0.085.
Rim fragment. Slight enamel weathering. Pale blue.
Area II, K25 Gbc.

551 (N495). Bowl(?) Fig. 12-37; Pl. 12 24 (right).
H. (pres.) 0.022. D. (est.) of rim 0.09.
Rim and upper body fragment. Rough surface. Pale green, except for dark green lip (cf. **544** above). Small bubbles and other impurities.
Area II, K24 Iy/K25 Ia.

552 (N495). Bowl(?) Fig. 12-38; Pl. 12-24 (left).
H. (pres.) 0.019. D. (est.) of rim 0.08.
Rim fragment. Pale green, except for dark green lip. Small bubbles and other impurities.
Area II, K24 Iy/K25 Ia.

553 (N370). Bowl(?) Fig. 12-39.
H. (pres.) 0.025. D. of rim impossible to est.
Rim fragment. Pale green, except for dark green lip (cf. **544, 551,** and **552** above). Small bubbles and other impurities.
Area II, K25 Jd, in topsoil.

554 (N232). Bowl(?) Fig. 12-40.
H. (pres.) 0.026. D. (est.) of rim 0.08.
Rim fragment. Slight enamel weathering. Pale green.
Area II, K25 Gbc.

555 (N328). Bowl(?) Fig. 12-41.
H. (pres.) 0.03. D. (est.) of rim 0.085.
Rim fragment. Pale green.
Area II, K25 Kc.

556 (N253). Bottle(?) Fig. 12-42.
H. (pres.) 0.012. D. (est.) of rim 0.016.
Rim fragment. Pale green with darker green lip.
See *Corinth XII*, no 773, with rounded rim and short neck.
Unit II-2, Room 3.

557 (N325). Bottle(?) Fig. 12-43; Pl. 12-25.
H. (pres.) 0.0185. D. of rim 0.017.
Rim fragment. Green; lip darker green. Bubbles. A larger version of **556.**
Area II, K24 Fy/K25 Fa.

558 (N785). Bowl(?) Fig. 12-44.
H. (pres.) 0.02. D. (est.) of rim 0.08.
Rim fragment. Yellow-green with small bubbles.
Area III, K24 Uxy.

559 (N560). Pellet. Pl. 12-26.
H. 0.013. D. (max.) 0.026.
A blob or pellet of some beauty. Turquoise. Surface slightly pitted.
Such pellets may have been used as insets for jewelry. A larger one, such as this, may have been used as a game counter. *Corinth XII*, nos. 1797-1801 are Byzantine.
Area III, K25 Ue.

560 (N731). Bead. Pl. 12-27.
H. 0.01. D. 0.015.
Half of bead preserved. Many small cracks throughout. Spherical, slightly flattened, and pierced. White, translucent.
Area III, K25 FGa.

561 (N1304). Bead. Pl. 12-28.
H. (pres.) 0.012. W. (max.) 0.009. D. of hole 0.002.
Double cone of transparent, dark green color.
See *Corinth XII*, no. 2471, for similar bead of Byzantine date or later.
Area IV, L23 Qk.

562 (N1119). Bead. Pl. 12-29.
H. (pres.) 0.01. W. (pres.) 0.009.
About half preserved. Originally probably a double cone. Opaque white.
Unit IV-2, Phase 2, Room 3.

563 (N1990). Bowl(?) Fig. 12-45.
D. of base 0.059.
Nearly complete base. Slight enamel weathering. Thick tubular ring base. Pale green.
Unit IV-2, Phase 3, in narthex floor packing.

564 (N1991). Cup(?) Fig. 12-46.
D. of base 0.037.
Complete base. Slight enamel weathering. Thick tubular ring base, similar to **563** but smaller. Pale green.
Unit IV-2, Phase 3, in narthex floor packing.

565 (N1931). Cup. Fig. 12-49.
H. 0.0215. D. (est.) of rim 0.13.
Handle and rim fragment. Slight enamel weathering. Coil handle attached to top of rim and side. Blue with many bubbles.
Unit IV-2, Phase 3, in narthex floor packing.

566 (N1930). Bowl. Fig. 12-50.
H. 0.046.
Large handle fragment with side attachment. Slight enamel weathering. Coil handle attached to thick oval side attachment over much thinner fragment of vessel wall. Pale green.
Unit IV-2, Phase 3, in narthex floor packing.

567 (N1448). Cup. Fig. 22-51.
H. 0.016. D. (est.) of rim 0.15.
Handle and rim fragment. Slight enamel weathering.
Coil handle attached to top of rim and side. Three threads are trailed horizontally around body, just below rim. Light blue with many bubbles.
See *Corinth XII*, no. 734, dated from 11th to mid-12th century.
Unit IV-2, Phase 3, in narthex floor packing.

568 (N1448). Cup. Fig. 12-52.
H. 0.022. D. (est.) of rim 0.08.
Handle and rim fragment. Slight enamel weathering. Coil handle attached to top of rim and side. Light blue.
Unit IV-2, Phase 3, in narthex floor packing.

569 (N1446). Handle. Fig. 12-53.
H. 0.021.
Handle fragment. Slight enamel weathering. Coil handle. Blue, with many bubbles.
Unit IV-2, Phase 3, in narthex floor packing.

570 (N1446). Cup(?) Fig. 12-54.
H. (pres.) 0.021. D. (est.) of rim 0.08.
Rim fragment. Blue, with many bubbles. Probably goes with **569.**
Unit IV-2, Phase 3, in narthex floor packing.

571 (N1448). Cup(?) Fig. 12-55.
H. (pres.) 0.032. D. (est.) of rim 0.09.
Rim and upper body fragment. Slight enamel weathering. Two pairs of horizontal threads are trailed around upper body. Pale green with few bubbles.
Unit IV-2, Phase 3, in narthex floor packing.

572 (N1448). Cup(?) Fig. 12-56.
H. (pres.) 0.016. D. (est.) of rim 0.08.
Rim fragment. Slight enamel weathering. Light blue with many small bubbles.
Unit IV-2, Phase 3, in narthex floor packing.

573 (N1658). Cup(?) Fig. 12-61.
H. (pres.) 0.02. D. (est.) of rim 0.08.
Rim fragment. Slight enamel weathering. Blue with many bubbles.
Unit IV-2, Phase 3, in narthex floor packing.

574 (N1658). Cup(?) Fig. 12-62.
H. (pres.) 0.041. D. (est.) of rim 0.165.
Rim fragment. Slight enamel weathering. Pale green.
Unit IV-2, Phase 3, in narthex floor packing.

575 (N1931). Cup(?) Fig. 12-58.
H. (pres.) 0.018. D. (est.) of rim 0.08.
Rim fragment. Slight enamel weathering. Light blue with many small bubbles.
Unit IV-2, Phase 3, in narthex floor packing.

576 (N1477). Cup. Fig. 12-48.
H. 0.034. D. (est.) of rim 0.13.
Handle and rim fragment. Slight enamel weathering. Coil handle attached to top of rim and side. Pale blue with small bubbles.
Unit IV-2, Phase 3 or 4 sanctuary.

577 (N1477). Cup(?) Fig. 12-59.
H. (pres.) 0.024. D. (est.) of rim 0.10.
Rim fragment. Slight enamel weathering. Dark blue with few bubbles.
Unit IV-2, Phase 3 or 4 sanctuary.

578 (N1477). Cup(?) Fig. 12-60.
H. (pres.) 0.039. D. (est.) of rim 0.10.
Rim fragment. Slight enamel weathering. Dark blue with few bubbles. Probably goes with **577.**
Unit IV-2, Phase 3 or 4 sanctuary.

579 (N1303). Cup(?) Fig. 12-57.
H. (pres.) 0.029. D. of rim impossible to est.
Rim fragment. Slight enamel weathering. Pale green with small bubbles.
Unit IV-2, Phase 3 or 4 sanctuary.

580 (N1044). Bottle(?) Fig. 12-47.
H. (pres.) 0.018. D. of bottom 0.012.
Bottom and part of lower body. Flat bottom curving into sides which slightly broaden as they ascend. Dark blue with small bubbles. Similar in profile to **545** from Area II.
Area IV, L23 Rk, in topsoil.

581 (N916). Goblet(?) Fig. 12-63.
D. 0.039.
Base, with fragmentary stem attachment. Thick tubular ring base. Pale yellow with few bubbles.
Area IV, L23 Sm.

582 (N427). Cup(?) Fig. 12-64.
H. (pres.) 0.01. D. (est.) of rim 0.075.
Rim fragments. Slight surface pitting and enamel weathering. Pale green with bubbles.
Area IV, L23 Sfg.

583 (N1883). Necklace. Fig. 12-65; Pl. 12-30.
Larger beads: L. 0.012-0.018. D. 0.004-0.007.
Smaller beads: L. 0.002-0.005. D. 0.002-0.004.
Intact, except for one broken red faience bead of the smaller type. The five large and 22 small faience beads are all "drawn beads" (see van der Sleen 1967: 23-26), pierced lengthwise, and cylindrical. Five are green, 18 red, three white, and one blue.
See *Corinth XII*, no. 2425, for an exact parallel to the larger faience bead type, from a Byzantine grave in Corinth. The beads forming the Nichoria necklace were from a child's grave, probably contemporary with use of chapel or at least soon afterward.
Area IV, L23 Tj, just outside E end of chapel.

Painted Plaster

Several hundred small fragments of painted plaster were found scattered amid the final destruction debris in the chapel sanctuary. Very few of the fragments are larger than about 0.02-0.03 m in maximum dimension, or thicker than about 0.005 m. The painted decoration to which these fragments belonged is presumably to be dated to the later use of the chapel (Phase 4), but one cannot rule out the possibility that they are part of the original decoration (Phase 3) that survived the narthex fire. As their thickness indicates, they rarely retained the mortar backing behind the painted stucco surface. A dozen larger fragments (maximum dimension about 0.30 m) still preserved evidence of the mortar backing, but they were in such a mashed, compressed state that it was impossible to recover the exact thickness of the backing. Near floor level along Walls N and O, however, as well as just above the bench along Wall S, several small patches of plaster were preserved in place (see Fig. 9-5).

Only one patch along Wall O showed any traces of paint, namely a red which serves as a frequent background color in many fragments. From these patches it could be determined that the mortar backing was about 0.044 m thick and consisted of a layer of mud mixed with small chips of limestone, some sand, straw, and lime. On top of this backing there was a thin layer of stucco, about 0.005 m thick. That at least the background colors were executed *al fresco* is indicated by the way these colors have permeated the thin layer of stucco. None of the fragments from the sanctuary are curved; nor did any show regular imprints of reed matting in the mortar (Clairmont 1975, pp. 109, 110).

The following cataloged items simply represent *types* of these painted plaster fragments. Nos. **584** and **585** are certainly garments, probably drapery fragments. Such garments in Byzantine wall paintings occur in approximately 17 colors or tones. Our **584** is from a light red garment, and **585** is from a gray garment; the white in both cases is used for highlighting (see Winfield 1968, p. 127 for this technique). Some uncataloged fragments suggest that light green drapery was also represented in our sanctuary.

In the finest Comnenian style the drapery clings to the body, the fabric seeming to be soaked in water. The chief impression is of graceful movement in line with the curves of the body (Djurić 1976, p. 22). Our fragments seem too linear and static for this style, and in any case Nichoria's modest chapel would scarcely be adorned in the finest style of 12th-13th century Byzantine wall painting. Yet it is apparent that the Nichoria drapery once covered the figure of at least one saint or holy personage. (For examples of similar drapery from the 13th-14th century church of St. Nicholas at Platsa in the Mani, see Mouriki-Charalambous 1975, Pls. 17 and 22.) Nos. **586-88** are not easily interpreted.

No. **589** comprises fragments that once belonged to the halo of a saint or other holy personage. The yellow oval halo surrounded by narrow bands of white and red (or umber) and set against a dark field of blue is typical of Byzantine wall painting (see Mouriki-Charalambous 1975, Pls. 1-3, 5, 7, etc.; Winfield 1968, p. 127). The Nichoria fragments, however, vary somewhat from this norm. Those in the lower right of Pl. 12-36 do not have an exterior field of dark blue; those in the upper left have the dark blue exterior field, but the bands around the oval are a darker blue and red, and without the white band. No. **590** is tantalizing to speculate about. The fragments belong to a lively ornamental design, only part of which is preserved.

The central motif, however, is vegetal with white blobs, sometimes in a row. It is possible that what is represented is embroidered cloth. No similar design is illustrated by Millet (1947), but the Nichoria fragments are reminiscent of the embroidered stole (*epitrachelion*) and cuffs worn by bishops and often portrayed in Byzantine wall paintings. There are several examples from Byzantine churches in the Mani, especially the church at Episcopi which dates from the end of the 12th century and is thus roughly contemporary with the Nichoria chapel. At Episcopi a similar vegetal embroidery decorates the cuffs and stoles of bishops (Drandakis 1964, Pls. 67-69), the border of an angel's garment (Pl. 74), a water basin (Pl. 79), and a pillow (Pl. 82). This embroidered design often appears surrounded by a line of pearls on the hems of garments, collars, and the cuffs of sleeves (Pls. 74, 79, 88, 89a).

No fragments of painted plaster were found in the chapel narthex; presumably it was undecorated. Yet why were relatively few fragments recovered even in the sanctuary? Perhaps the walls of the sanctuary did not immediately collapse in the fire that brought down the roof timbers and tiles. It is possible that the walls were later dismantled, or, if they had collapsed, that the stone rubble and with it the bulk of the painted plaster was removed to an as yet undiscovered dump. Compared to the innumerable tile fragments, relatively few plaster fragments were found in the topsoil in the vicinity of the chapel. Of course, the plaster fragments would have deteriorated and disintegrated more easily if exposed to plowing and weathering.

Many small, decorated Byzantine churches of the 12th and especially of the 13th century in the Peloponnese are either unpublished or inadequately published. The local painting styles have not been sufficiently studied, and their relationship to each other and to the great artistic centers of the Byzantine empire is not known (Djurić 1976, pp. 70-74). The surviving fragments of our wall paintings deserve further study within this larger context.

584 (N1125). Triangular designs of red, pink, and white. Pl. 12-31.

W. of stripes ca. 0.005.

Fragment. Striped, often curvilinear designs with triangular shapes. In the latter case, a triangular field of thick white paint is bordered by smaller pink and dark red stripes, the effect suggesting infolding drapery.

Unit IV-2, Phase 3 or 4 sanctuary.

585 (N1126). Stripes of black, gray, and white. Pl. 12-32.

W. of stripes ca. 0.005.

Fragment. Black stripes with adjacent stripes of white and/or gray, the effect suggesting infolding drapery.

Unit IV-2, Phase 3 or 4 sanctuary.

586 (N1125). Fields of red and blue. Pl. 12-33.

W. of stripes ca. 0.007.

Fragment. Probably from large fields of red and blue, which meet along rather straight lines, sometimes separated by a thick white stripe.

587 (N1126). Daubs of red, gray, and white. Pl. 12-34.

Fragment. Small, bustling daubs of red, gray, and white abutting in curvilinear borders.

Unit IV-2, Phase 3 or 4 sanctuary.

588 (N1042). Triangular fields of white on red. Pl. 12-35.

Fragment. Red background, with triangular-shaped fields of white, on which are occasional radiating spikes of blue.

Unit IV-2, Phase 3 or 4 sanctuary.

589 (N1042). Oval shapes defined by black, red, and white stripes. Pl. 12-36.

Fragment. Curving stripes of black, red, and white separate fields of yellow, sometimes blue. Larger shapes, probably ovals, suggest the halos of holy personages.

Unit IV-2, Phase 3 or 4 sanctuary.

590 (N1126). Blue field enclosing a decorated yellow triangle. Pl. 12-37.

W. of stripes ca. 0.005.

Fragment. A blue field borders a yellow rectangle. Around and just inside the rectangle runs a black stripe, enlivened by white dots. Short connecting and similarly decorated black stripes further decorate the interior of the rectangle. Part of a bishop's *epitrachelion* or ornate cuffs is suggested.

Unit IV-2, Phase 3 or 4 sanctuary.

REFERENCES

Caskey, J. L. 1969. "Lead Weights from Ayia Irini in Keos," *Deltion* 24: 95-106.

Catling, H. W. 1978. April 9, personal communication to J. Rosser.

Clairmont, C. W. 1975. *Excavations at Salona, Yugoslavia*. Park Ridge, N.J.

Davidson, G. R. 1940. "A Medieval Glass-Factory at Corinth," *AJA* 44: 297-324.

———. 1952. *Corinth. American School Excavations, XII: Mediaeval Architecture in the Central Area of Corinth*. Princeton, N.J.

Djurić, V. J. 1976. "La peinture murale byzantine: XIIe et XIIIe siècles," *XVe Congrès international d'études byzantines III: Art et Archéologie*. Athens.

Drandakis, N. B. 1964. *Byzantine Wall Paintings of the Middle Mani*. Athens. In Greek.

Hendy, M. F. 1969. *Coinage and Money in the Byzantine Empire, 1081-1261*. Dumbarton Oaks Center for Byzantine Studies, Washington, D.C.

Millet, G. 1947. *Broderies religieuses de style byzantine*. Paris.

Mouriki-Charalambous, D. 1975. *The Wall Paintings from the Church of St. Nicholas at Platsa in the Mani*. Athens. In Greek.

Nichoria I = Rapp and Aschenbrenner 1978.

Pallas, D. 1971. "Excavation of the Byzantine Church of Glykas in Epirus," *Praktika*: 130-45. In Greek.

Rapp, G., Jr., and Aschenbrenner, S. E., eds. 1978. *Excavations at Nichoria in Southwest Greece I: Site, Environs, and Techniques*. Minneapolis.

van der Sleen, W. G. N. 1967. *A Handbook on Beads*. Liège.

Weinberg, G. Davidson. 1975a. April 23, personal communication to J. Rosser.

———. 1975b. June 18, personal communication to J. Rosser.

———. 1975c. "A Medieval Mystery: Byzantine Glass Production," *Journal of Glass Studies* 17: 127-41.

———. 1977. "The Importance of Greece in Byzantine Glass Manufacture." In *XVe Congrès international d'études byzantines. Résumes des communications, III. Art et Archéologie. 5-11 September, Athens*, ed. Z. V. Udatsova. Moscow.

Winfield, D. C. 1968. "Middle and Later Byzantine Wall Painting Methods. A Comparative Study," *Dumbarton Oaks Papers* 22: 61-139.

Wroth, W. 1908. *Catalogue of the Imperial Coins in the British Museum*, Vol. II. London.

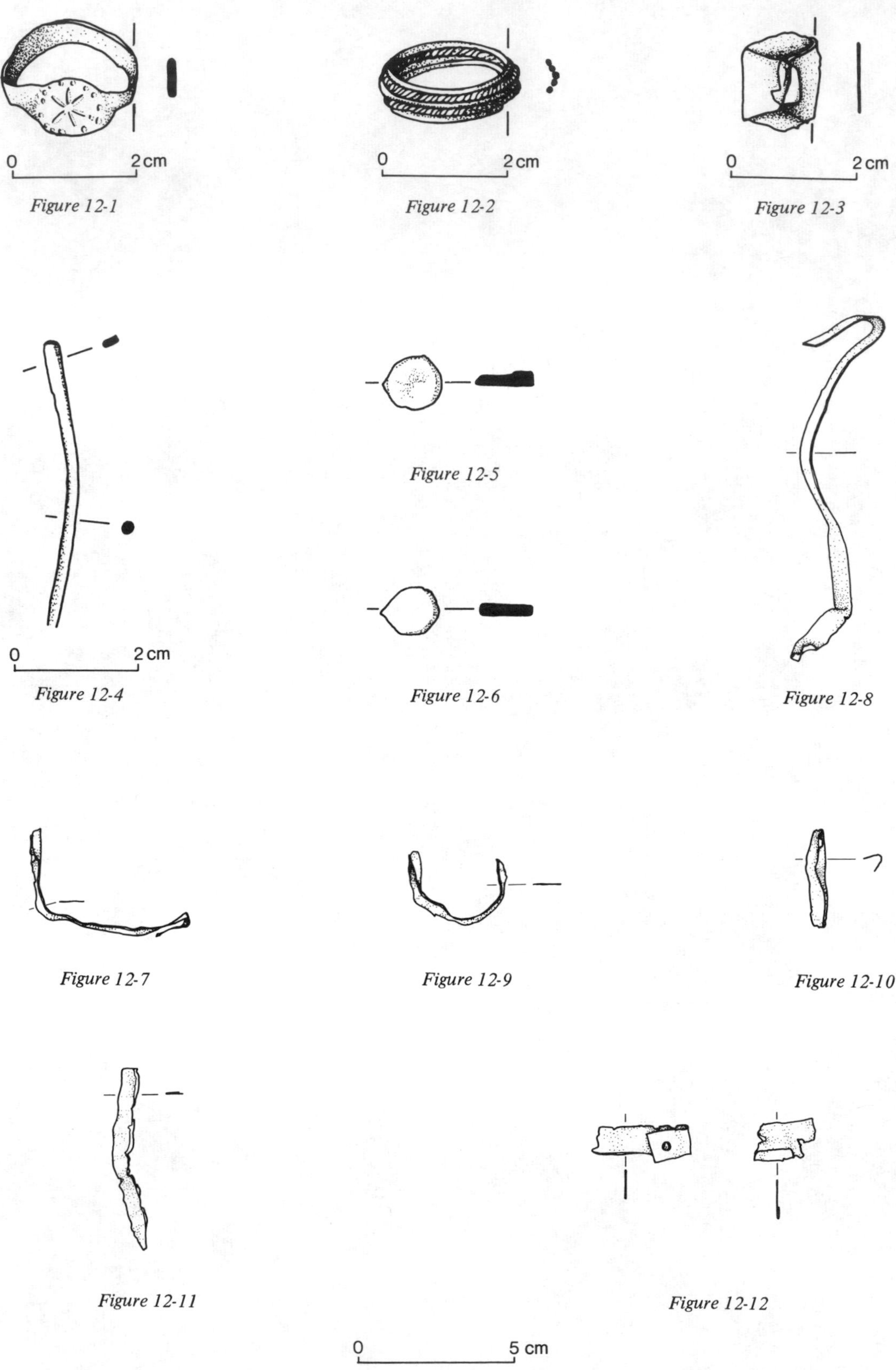

Figure 12-1

Figure 12-2

Figure 12-3

Figure 12-4

Figure 12-5

Figure 12-6

Figure 12-8

Figure 12-7

Figure 12-9

Figure 12-10

Figure 12-11

Figure 12-12

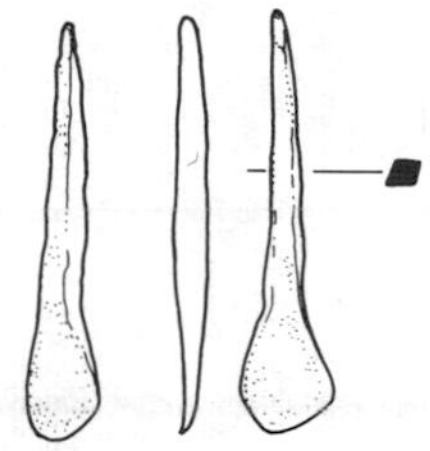

Figure 12-13

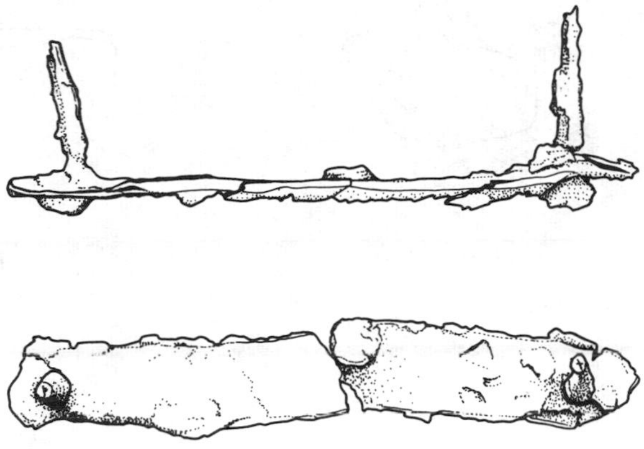

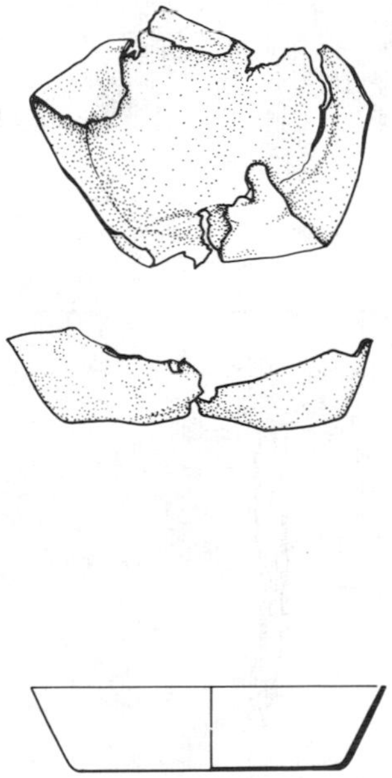

Figure 12-14

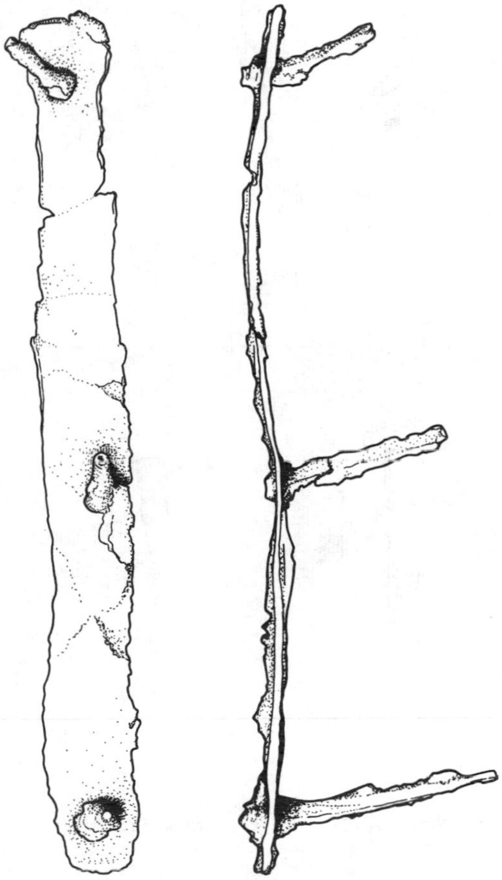

Figure 12-15

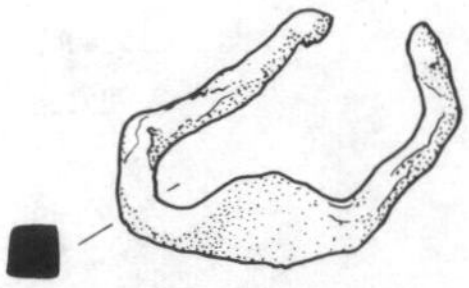

Figure 12-16 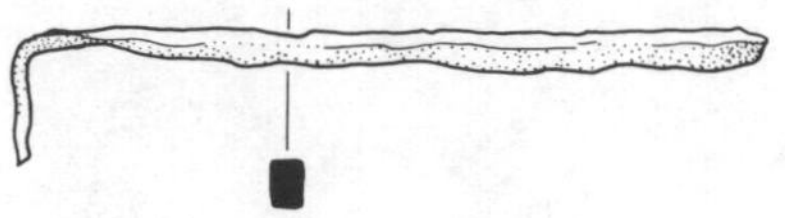 *Figure 12-17* 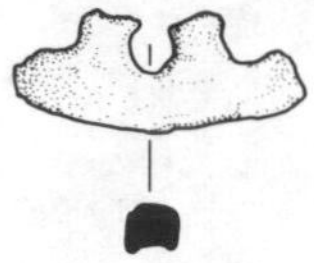 *Figure 12-18*

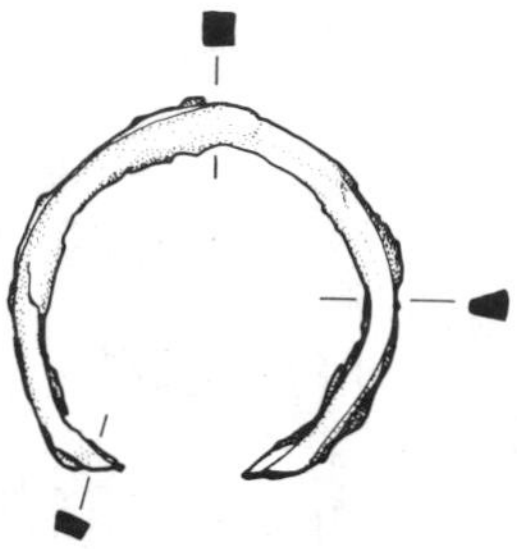

Figure 12-19 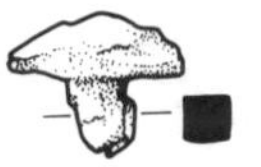 *Figure 12-20* 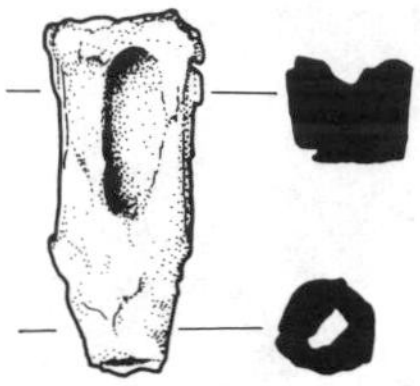 *Figure 12-26*

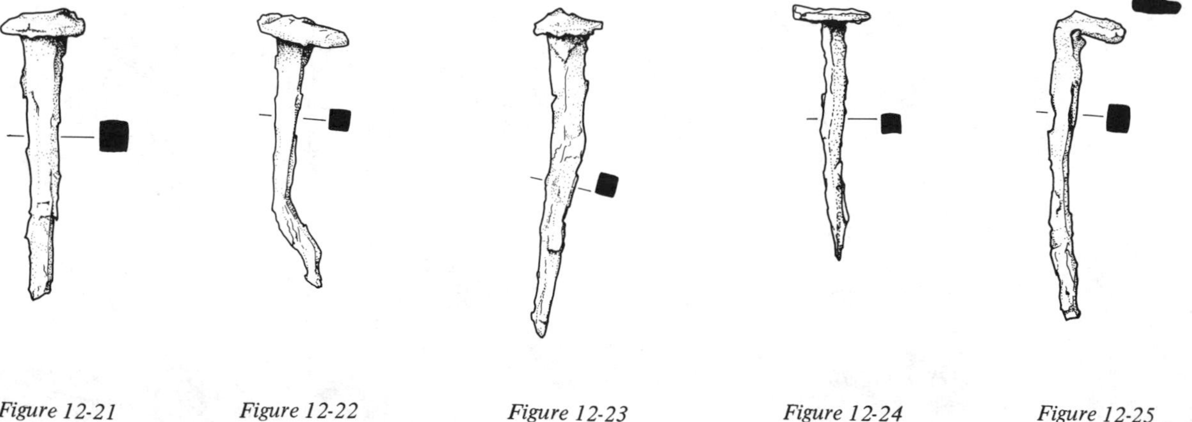

Figure 12-21 *Figure 12-22* *Figure 12-23* *Figure 12-24* *Figure 12-25*

0 5 cm

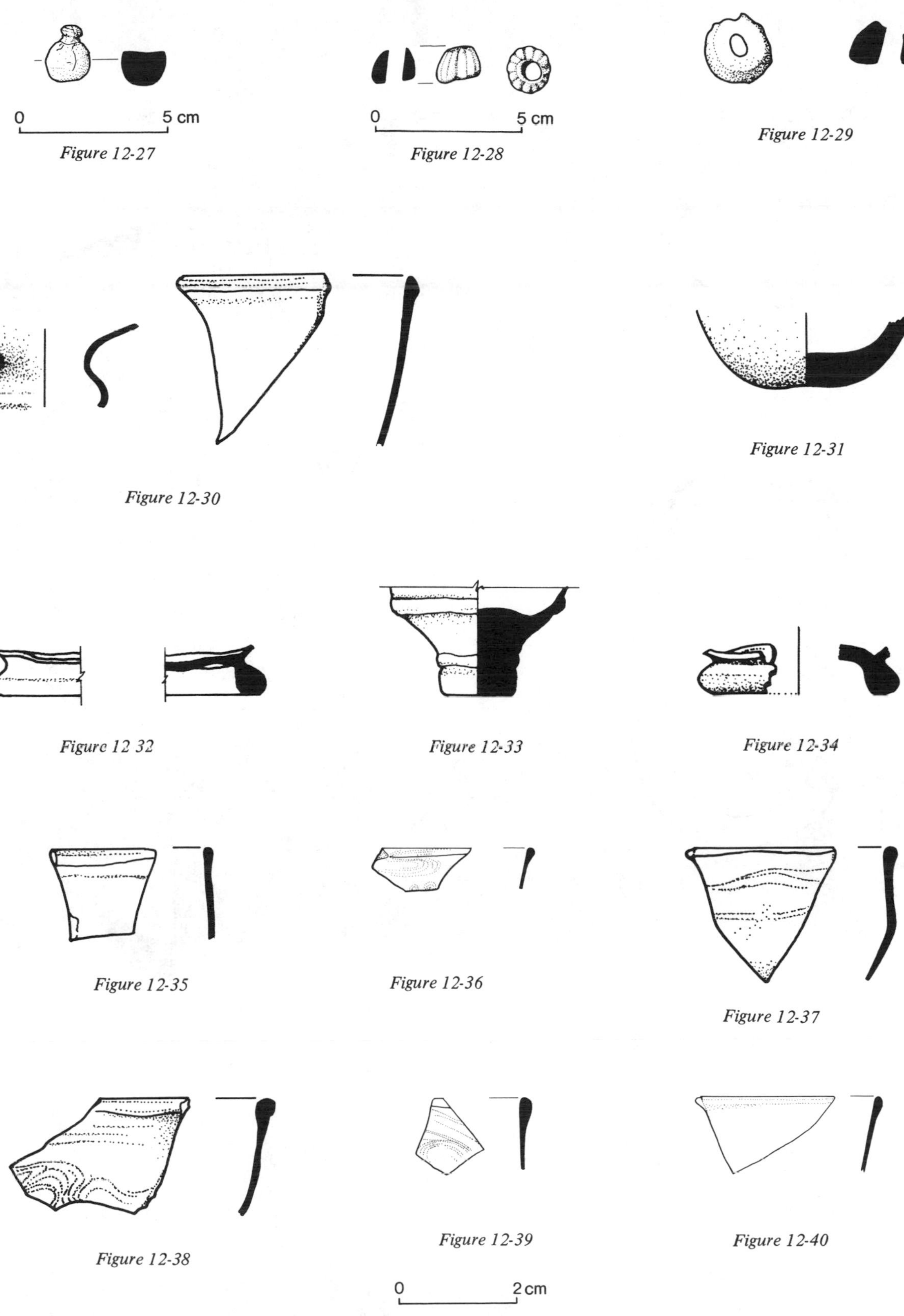

Figure 12-27

Figure 12-28

Figure 12-29

Figure 12-30

Figure 12-31

Figure 12 32

Figure 12-33

Figure 12-34

Figure 12-35

Figure 12-36

Figure 12-37

Figure 12-38

Figure 12-39

Figure 12-40

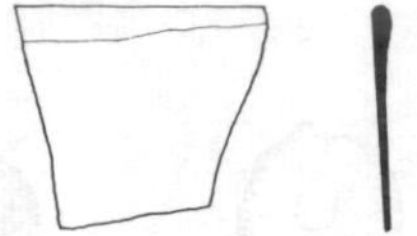

Figure 12-41

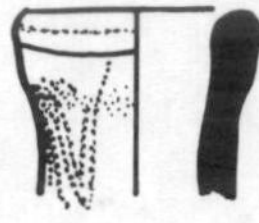

Figure 12-42

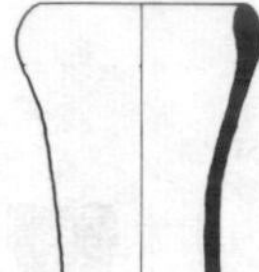

Figure 12-43

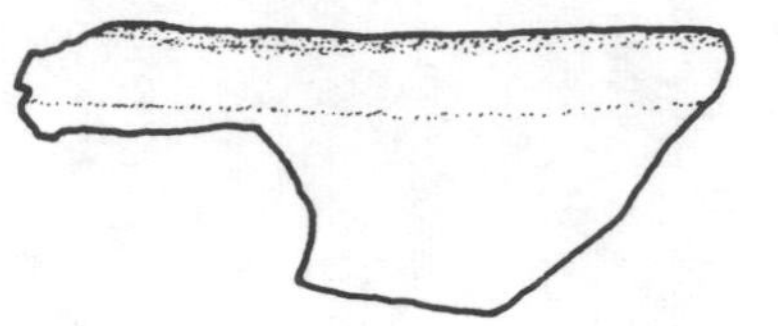

Figure 12-44

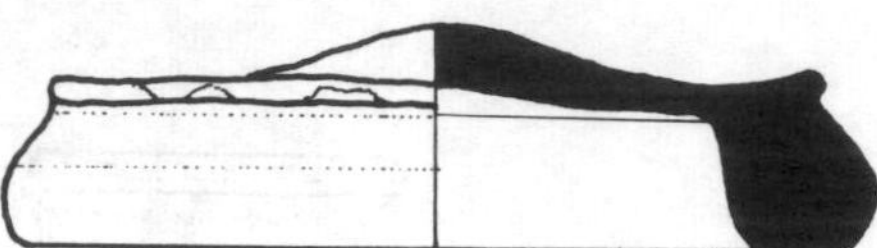

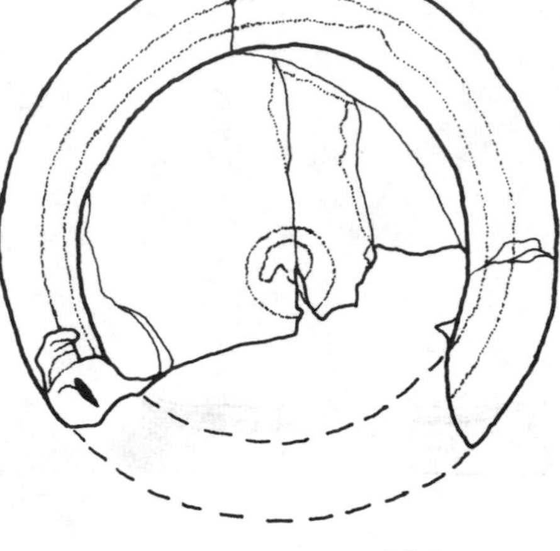

Figure 12-45

Figure 12-46

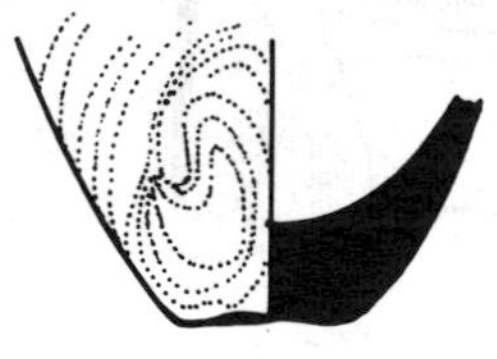

Figure 12-47

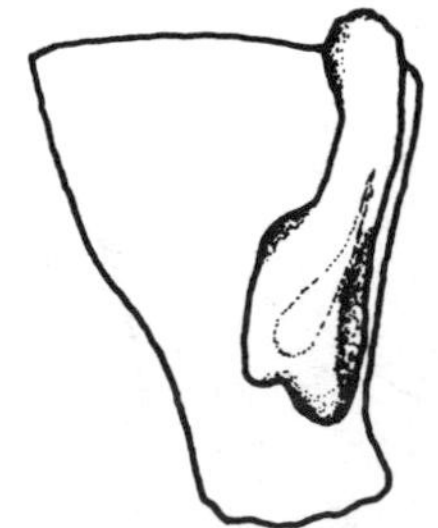

Figure 12-48

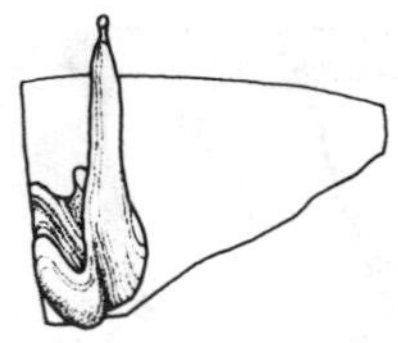

Figure 12-49

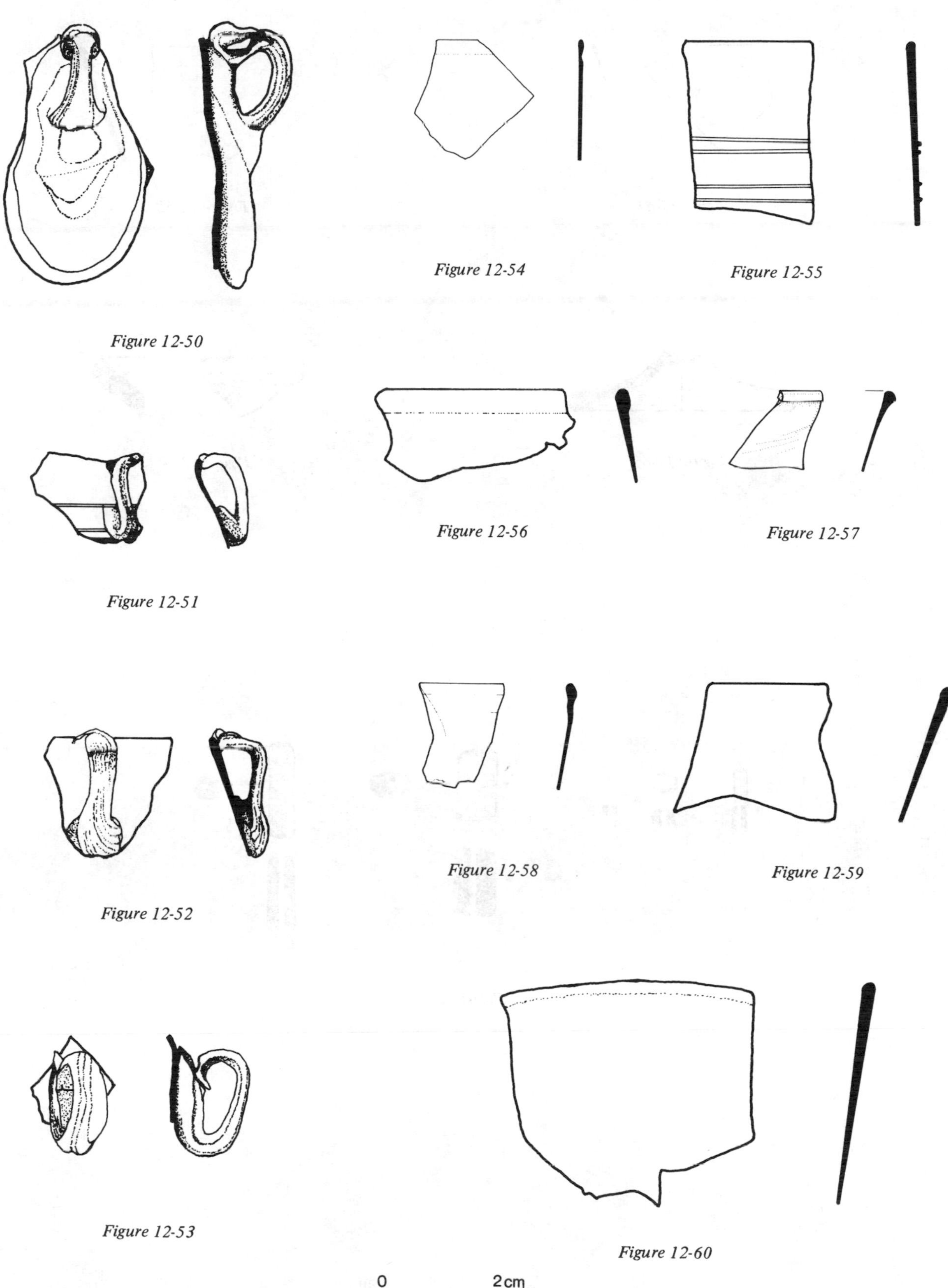

Figure 12-50

Figure 12-51

Figure 12-52

Figure 12-53

Figure 12-54

Figure 12-55

Figure 12-56

Figure 12-57

Figure 12-58

Figure 12-59

Figure 12-60

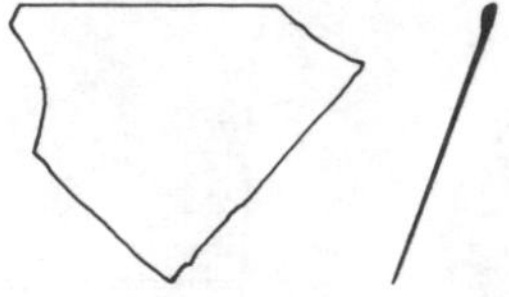

Figure 12-61

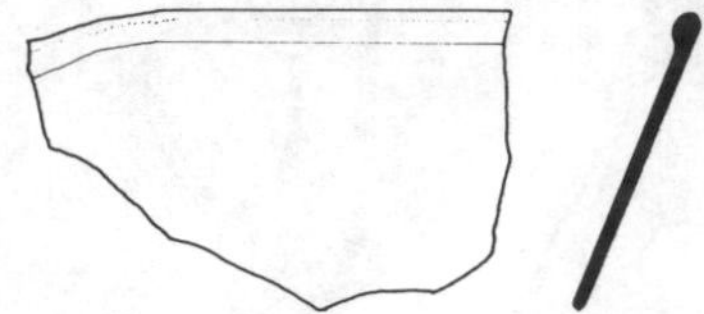

Figure 12-62

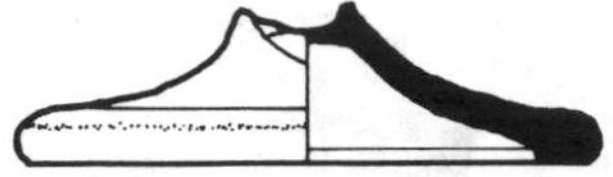

Figure 12-63

Figure 12-64

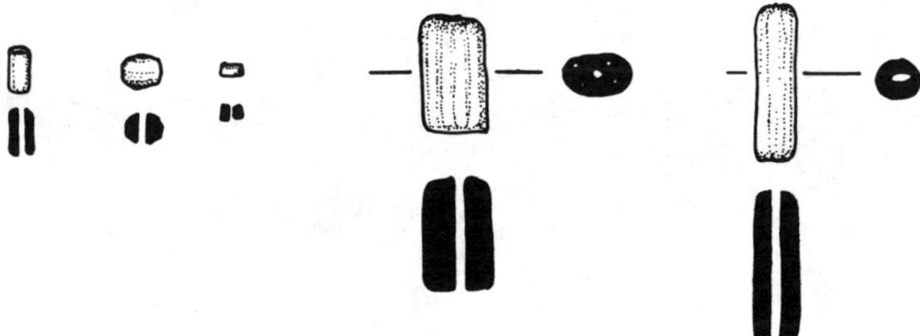

Figure 12-65

0 2 cm

13

Summary

by
John Rosser

The General Historical Situation

Unlike the earlier segments of Nichoria's past, the Late Roman and Byzantine habitation can be put in a fairly definitive historical context. The main outlines of what is known of the Peloponnese during the 5th and early 6th centuries A.D. have been traced by A. Bon (1951, pp.1-26), and his account is supplemented by several other modern writers (e.g., Charanis 1972, Study XVIII; Scranton 1957, pp. 6-26; *MME* 1972, pp. 64-66). For the Middle Byzantine period the best modern commentaries are by Bon (1951), Drandakis (1964), Herrin (1975), and for nearby Kythera by Herrin (1973, pp. 45-48).

The Late Roman/Early Byzantine period, when our Unit IV-2, Phases 1 and 2 was in use, represents simply a prolongation of the ancient world. The calm of the 4th century was broken in some places by natural disasters such as earthquakes and more importantly by German invasions. The most violent event took place in 395 when Visigoths under Alaric invaded the Peloponnese, sacking Corinth, Argos, and Sparta. The Peloponnese escaped invasion by the Huns in 447; but in 467, 474, and 477 parts of the Ionian islands and western Peloponnese were attacked by the seafaring Vandals. These attacks undoubtedly created apprehension, but they were only a prelude to the incessant invasions by Slavs and Avars which were to follow in the 6th century. On the whole, however, the Peloponnese experienced in the 5th century a relative calm before the real storm (Bon 1951, pp. 13, 14; Bury 1923, pp. 119, 120, 275, 276).

Also important in the 5th century was the increasingly rapid Christianization of the Peloponnese. This is demonstrated by the rise in the number of churches under construction. By mid-century ecclesiastical organization was well developed, with the seat of the metropolitan at Corinth. By 457 there were at least 20 bishoprics in the province, including one at Messini (Bon 1951, pp. 6-9).

The economic situation is much less clear. Bon claims that there was a general economic and demographic decline ever since the beginning of the Christian era, but the evidence he adduces is slender and some historians consider that during the 5th century Greece in general prospered markedly (Bon 1951, pp. 10-17; *MME* 1972, p. 64). Certainly, city and town life remained viable in the 5th century, as is attested by the *Synekdemos* of Hierokles, which enumerates 25 or 26 urban centers in the Peloponnese (Bon 1951, p. 21).

From the death of Justinian I in 565 until the early 9th century, the Peloponnese—indeed much of Greece—was enveloped by massive Slavic migrations. The few literary texts from this period have been fully exploited by modern scholars, notably P. Charanis (1972). Many inhabitants of the Peloponnese fled before the Slavs (Hood 1966, 1970). As a general indication of the low level of social and cultural life, in the whole Peloponnese no buildings are known that can be dated between the 7th and 9th centuries. Nor did any building erected prior to the 7th century survive intact (Bon 1951, p. 50). Western and central Peloponnese was one of the areas most affected by the Slavic invasions, as is attested by the great number of surviving place-names of Slavic origin (Charanis 1972, II, p. 40; Georgacas and McDonald 1969; Vasmer 1941); and from 587 to 805 the

Slavs were masters of all eastern Peloponnese (Charanis 1972, XIII, p. 81). Credit for the Byzantine recovery belongs to the emperor Nicephorus I (802-11) who refounded Patras in 805 and resettled the Peloponnese with Christian subjects from elsewhere in the empire (Charanis 1972, XIII, pp. 81-83). Thereafter the Peloponnese began to revive, as the Slavs were gradually Christianized and assimilated (Charanis 1972, XIII, p. 84 and XXI, p. 34).

This Middle Byzantine revival is represented by our Units II-1, II-2, and IV-2, Phases 3, 4 (the chapel), dating from the late 10th perhaps into the 13th century. In the first half of the 11th century Hellas and the Peloponnese were combined into one administrative unit and thereafter poorly governed by military and civilian officials who stayed in Constantinople and whose posts were bought, sold, and transferred as dowries and legacies (Herrin 1975, pp. 256, 266). Taxes were collected with great rapacity, but the upkeep of roads, bridges, government buildings, and especially defense, declined dramatically in the 12th century. Alexius Comnenus (1081-1118) had reorganized the naval forces in the maritime provinces around 1092, providing for a local naval squadron in every important port. Such squadrons probably consisted only of local captains and sailors enlisted for specific tasks when necessary, but even this defense declined when John II (1118-43) diverted tax revenues for this purpose away from the maritime provinces to Constantinople. Also, provincial militias were virtually nonexistent in the 12th century, and thus when the Normans raided Greece in 1147 they were able to march inland at will and even sack Corinth. What the Normans did in 1147, pirates repeated everywhere against coastal settlements, a constant threat that caused many coastal inhabitants to move inland to more inaccessible areas. In the absence of imperial administration, local magnates illegally occupied peasant holdings, driving farmers off the land and creating stretches of waste land everywhere. In what was essentially a lawless atmosphere, revolts against central authority erupted in the Argolid, Sparta, and Thessaly. It is no wonder that after 1204 knights from the Fourth Crusade had little difficulty in capturing the Peloponnese (see Herrin 1975, pp. 266-84).

Yet it is also true that during the late 10th and 11th centuries there was relative peace and prosperity in the Peloponnese, especially when compared with the centuries immediately preceding (Bond 1951, pp. 179, 180). The archbishopric of Christianoupolis in western Messenia was probably created some time in the early 11th century (Bon 1951, pp. 110-13), and the numerous churches of SW Peloponnese, especially those of the Mani, were mostly built from the 10th through the 11th centuries. Kalamata, for example, has numerous small churches dating from the 11th and 12 centuries; and the church of Samarina, not far north of Nichoria, is a fine example of 11th-century ecclesiastical architecture (Bon 1951, pp. 138-42; *MME* 1972, pp. 65, 66). Although one cannot safely generalize about prosperity solely on the basis of new ecclesiastical construction, the Orthodox Church was the only authority during these centuries that acted responsibly in the provinces. Through its charitable and educational work the Church contributed substantially to provincial life (Herrin 1975, p. 284), and doubtless the many new religious edifices reflect that contribution.

The Local Situation

During Roman times the fertile coastal region on the W and NW sides of the Messenian Gulf was a favored location for rural villas and manorial estates. This pattern of dispersed agricultural nuclei could flourish only in essentially peaceful and settled conditions. Modern Kalamata, Petalidhi, and Koroni seem to have been good-sized towns, with useable harbors and a productive countryside as a basis for local and foreign trade (*MME* 1972, pp. 96, 146; *Nichoria* I, pp. 97-103). Essentially peaceful conditions must have persisted until the death of Justinian I in 565. Until that date Justinian's wall across the Isthmus of Corinth effectively protected the Peloponnese from land-based barbarian incursions (*MME* 1972, p. 64).

That the Nichoria ridgetop was part of this productive countryside is demonstrated by Phases 1-2 of Unit IV-2, dated approximately 460-520 (see Chapter 9, p. 374). From its central position one may deduce that the building was a warehouse or storage facility for crops grown over the whole ridge. Its heavy and carefully built foundations (see Table 9-10), much the finest of any period in Nichoria's history, attest to settled conditions and high standards of workmanship. Good building stone was readily available from earlier ruined structures on the site, and our Late Roman builders put that stone to good use. Several small finds (see p. 368) suggest that the building also served as at least occasional living quarters for the agricultural workers who cultivated the ridgetop. That is, it may have had the same functions as a modern country field house or *agrospito*, though on a much larger scale. The plan of the building, however, with its three large rooms, none apparently intercommunicating, and the apparent absence of a second story, point to its major function as an *apotheke* for agricultural produce.

Except for certain periods of intensive and continuous work on the hilltop, the farmers probably lived in the vicinity of one of the nearby *mansiones* whose ruins occur down near the coast (*Nichoria* I, pp. 99, 100). Almost no indication survives of the crops processed and stored here, but they were probably those that we know were grown before and since in the same location, i.e., grain, olives, figs, and grapes (*Nichoria* I, Table 5-9). The addition of a third big room (Phase 2) to Unit IV-2 indicates that production was high and more storage space was needed. The contemporary grave β, discovered on the top of nearby Trypetorachi, may be that of one of these laborers; but its prominent location suggests that this spot was important enough for the burial of the owner and his family.

The B-i type storage amphora (**P1756**), found crushed by fallen roof tiles, indicates that the building was deserted sometime between 460 and 520, or shortly thereafter. In any case, it was abandoned, not destroyed by fire; and thereafter habitation at Nichoria appears to have ceased until the late 10th century. As we noted above, the cessation of monumental building activity is common to all of Greece during the period of the Slavonic invasions (Bon 1951, p. 50; Hood 1966, 1970). Our Late Roman farmers were doubtless affected by the unsettled times which overtook Messenia (*MME* 1972, p. 65).

What prompted the resettlement of the site in the late 10th century? The circumstance leading to general resettlement was no doubt the reestablishment of relative peace in the region following Byzantine recovery of the Peloponnese in the early 9th century (Charanis 1972, XIII). As for the specific site, a preference for a location somewhat removed from the coast when piracy may have been a problem (Herrin 1975, pp. 276-281) was probably a major factor. For the iron-working establishment in Unit II-2 (see Chapter 9, p. 363), handy transportation facilities for ore, hilltop drafts for the furnace, and the availability of wood for making charcoal may have been additional considerations. Although it is often stated that by Classical times most of Greece was deforested, this may not have been so around Nichoria; in any case, forests could have been rejuvenated in the interval (see *MME* 1972, pp. 226, 247; *Nichoria* I, pp. 56, 57). The threat of malaria and the general dampness of the coast in the winter may have also been factors favoring a hilltop site, even as they are today in the Karpofora-Rizomilo community (*MME* 1972, p. 61).

Ideally, an evaluation of the location of an individual site should be made within the broader context of the subregional settlement pattern. Unfortunately, the distribution of Byzantine sites is not well known for the Nichoria area (*Nichoria* I, p. 103) nor for the Peloponnese as a whole (*MME* 1972, p. 149). Petalidhi must have remained an important town (*MME* 1972, Table 5-8), but of other Middle Byzantine settlements around Nichoria we know too little to make general inferences (see Chapter 8, pp. 354-56). During the regional and subregional surface reconnaissance, efforts were made to identify Byzantine sites; but if the lack of evidence on the Nichoria ridge before excavation is typical, surface survey alone may fail to identify many sites (see Bouras 1974, pp. 30, 31; *Nichoria* I, p. 84).

As argued in Chapter 9, it is conceivable that the Byzantine occupants of Area II were residents of a village, if the term is used to refer to the larger geographical entity and not just to the nuclear grouping of houses. The latter could have been at Petalidhi or Kastania, or perhaps even Karpofora/Karacasili. In any case, Units II-1 and II-2 probably comprised the structures used by a single extended family. Domestic quarters were most likely confined to Unit II-1, whereas Unit II-2 served for storage and processing of agricultural products and for a modest metallurgical operation (see pp. 359-63; Figs. 9-1, 9-2).

That iron working was an important activity is suggested by the discovery of fragments of iron ore and iron slag around Unit II-2 (*Nichoria* I, pp. 212-22), along with numerous small finds of iron (**521-27**). The apsidal structure that was built onto the SW end of Unit II-2 seems to have been a charcoal furnace of the Catalan type, commonly used in the Mediterranean for this purpose.

It is probable that adjacent Area III was cultivated during Middle Byzantine times. Wall L may have served as a retaining wall for the Byzantine settlement on the Area II acropolis above, and Wall C was a heavier terrace wall to inhibit erosion of the soil at the bottom of a field that comprised most of Area III (see pp. 363, 364; Fig. 2-2). The Area II buildings could have provided processing and storage facilities for this agricultural produce. Unit L21-1, near the S end of the ridge, may have served the same purpose, and its presence indicates that more of the ridge than just Area III was cultivated in Middle Byzantine times.

We have suggested (see p. 376) that the construction of the chapel may have been undertaken by the inhabitants of Area II. The C-14 date from a chapel timber can be interpreted as pertaining to the original chapel construction. If this interpretation is correct, its origin overlaps with the C-14 date for the Byzantine occupation of Area II (see *Nichoria* I, Table 1-3, p. 5; also Chapter 9, pp. 358, 372). The evidence of pottery and small finds also indicates contemporary use. Thus, it is possible that the owner or tenant of Area II built the chapel, with its dual apses honoring two saints whom he particularly revered. The two children buried outside its apses may have been members of the family that lived in Area II. The 12th century grave στ on top of Trypetorachi may belong to one of the latest inhabitants of the ridge. More thorough exploration of this prominent hill could very well show the existence of additional burials contemporary with habitation in Area II. When the adult female was buried at the chapel's SE corner, however, the building was in ruins and Area II had been abandoned.

Nichoria's Middle Byzantine inhabitants had a relatively high standard of living, judging from the material remains that were left behind when they abandoned the ridge. They could afford fine imported pottery (**P1677-79**), jewelry (**505-8**) and elegant glass (**544-57**). Actually, the objects recovered here are hardly inferior in quality to those found in the large Byzantine metropolis of Corinth. Some of the Area II small finds may, in fact, have been imported from that city. It is often stated that from the 10th to the 12th centuries the Peloponnese enjoyed relative security and prosperity (e.g., *MME* 1972, p. 65). Now we can claim with some precision that, to judge from the Nichoria evidence, the standard of living in rural areas was not conspicuously inferior to that of large towns. Purchases were apparently made with cash (see **501**), probably derived from the sale of agricultural produce or manufactured iron objects.

The evidence of plant remains from Byzantine contexts is disappointingly meager. No identifiable seeds were recovered. Of the relatively few analyzed samples of charred wood, the majority were from olive and fig (*Nichoria* I, p. 56, Tables 5-9, 5-10). That olive production was high during this period is also supported by the report of the English pilgrim Benedict of Peterborough about the Koroni district (*MME* 1972, p. 66). The scanty available evidence may suggest that oak and maple were less abundant and that scrub (*Pistacia* type) was more common than previously.

The study of the animal bones produced some useful information about the Middle Byzantine meat diet (*Nichoria* I, pp. 76, 77, Table 6-10). Our Middle Byzantine farmers in Area II ate beef and pork, although meat consumption appears to have been modest. Sheep were reasonably abundant, and their wool may have been an important local product. Milk products were a major food use of cows, perhaps also of sheep and goats. Wild animals like the red deer were hunted, and even the occasional tortoise was consumed. The puzzling lack of evidence for the consumption of seafood is consistent with earlier periods of habitation. Bisel's evidence (Chapter 11, pp. 403, 404) on the scanty Byzantine skeletal material is important, since at present very little is known about the diet and health of the Middle Byzantine population in the Aegean (Brothwell 1968, p. 200).

Do the Nichoria results provide any useful guidelines for the future course of Byzantine archaeology in Greece? Byzantine archaeology can probably make its most significant contributions in the areas of demographic, social, and economic history. It is precisely such topics as the practice of agriculture, trade, metallurgy, diet, and health that require sophisticated archaeological investigation, since the literary sources concentrate on quite different matters. Prehistorians have been seeking solutions to problems like these for some time, and in fact Byzantine archaeology must to some extent adapt to its own needs the strategy and techniques of the prehistorian (Rosser 1979, pp. 157, 158). In conclusion, it is appropriate to stress the additional information about Byzantine Nichoria gained from the interdisciplinary investigation of the site. More traditional methods would have revealed the architecture and pottery, but it was the care taken to identify tiny objects like seeds that ensured the recovery of the very fragmentary glass. And, as it turned out, those bits of glass proved to be of real significance (Weinberg 1977).

REFERENCES

Bon, A. 1951. *Le Péloponnèse byzantin jusqu' en 1204*. Paris.

Bouras, Ch. 1974. "Houses and Settlements in Byzantine Greece." In *Shelter in Greece*:30-53, ed. B. Doumanis and P. Oliver, pp. 30-53. Athens. In Greek and English.

Brothwell, D. R. 1968. "Excavations at Saranchane in Istanbul: Fifth Preliminary Report," R. Martin Harrison and Nezih Firatli, *Dumbarton Oaks Papers* 22:195-216.

Bury, J. B. 1923. *A History of the Later Roman Empire from the Death of Theodosius I to the Death of Justinian (395-565)*, Vol. 1. London.

Charanis, P. 1972. *Studies on the Demography of the Byzantine Empire*. Variorum Reprint CS8. London.

Drandakis, N. B. 1964. *Byzantine Wall Paintings of the Middle Mani*. Athens. In Greek.

Georgacas, D. J., and McDonald, W. A. 1969. *The Place Names of Southwestern Peloponnesus*. Athens and Minneapolis. In Greek and English.

Herrin, J. 1973. "Byzantine Kythera." In *Kythera: Excavations and Studies*, ed. J. N. Coldstream and G. L. Huxley, pp. 41-51. Park Ridge, N.J.

———. 1975. "Realities of Byzantine Provincial Government: Hellas and Peloponnesos, 1180-1205," *Dumbarton Oaks Papers* 29:255-84.

Hood, M. S. F. 1966. "An Aspect of the Slavic Invasions of Greece in the Early Byzantine Period," *Sbornik Narodhino v Praze* 20:165-71.

———. 1970. "Isles of Refuge in the Early Byzantine Period," *BSA* 65:37-45.

McDonald, W. A., and Rapp, G., Jr., eds. 1972. *The Minnesota Messenia Expedition: Reconstructing a Bronze Age Regional Environment*. Minneapolis.

MME 1972 = McDonald and Rapp 1972.

Nichoria I = Rapp and Aschenbrenner 1978.

Rapp, G., Jr., and Aschenbrenner, S. E., eds. 1978. *Excavations at Nichoria in Southwest Greece I: Site, Environs, and Techniques*. Minneapolis.

Rosser, J. 1979. "A Research Strategy for Byzantine Archaeology," *Byzantine Studies/Études Byzantines* 6:152-66.

Scranton, R. L. 1957. *Corinth. American School Excavations, XVI: Mediaeval Architecture in the Central Area of Corinth*. Princeton, N.J.

Topping, P. 1972. "The Post-Classical Documents." In McDonald and Rapp, 1972, pp. 64-80.

Vasmer, M. 1941. *Die Slaven in Griechenland.* Abhandlungen der Preussischen Akademie der Wissenschaften, Jahrgang 1941. Phil.-hist. Klasse. No. 12. Berlin.

Weinberg, G. D. 1977. "The Importance of Greece in Byzantine Glass Manufacture." In *XVe Congrès international d'études byzantines. Résumés des communications, III. Art et Archéologie. 5-11 September, Athens*, ed. Z. V. Udatsova. Moscow.

IV. Post-Byzantine Times

14

The Site and Environs

by

Stanley E. Aschenbrenner, Richard Hope Simpson, and John Rosser

We here define "post-Byzantine" as the period following 1205 A.D., the year in which the Frankish Principality of Achaia (Morea) was established (Bon 1969; Longnon and Topping 1969; *MME* 1972, pp. 66-68). It is true that in 1262 the Byzantines reestablished themselves at Mistra and that from 1432 to 1460 Byzantine domination of the entire Peloponnese was briefly reaffirmed; yet such major political developments seem to have had little effect on rural localities like the one discovered on the Nichoria ridge. By the early 13th century our Byzantine farmstead in Area II (see pp. 375, 376) was already long in ruins and the life of the chapel in Area IV (see pp. 376, 377) was just ending.

Of the two known post-Byzantine structures on the ridge, one can be securely dated to the early 20th century and will be referred to later in this chapter. The other is Unit VI-1, once a quite substantial building whose foundations were discovered on the SE "acropolis" (Area VI) by Yalouris and McDonald in 1959 and partially excavated by Hope Simpson in the 1969 test campaign.

Unit VI-1. Grids N22 NOPQabcdef (Figs. 14-1 14-2; Pls. 14-1 to 14-6; Table 14-1)

It is reasonable to assume that the construction of Unit VI-1 involved both leveling of the site and reuse of stone from earlier structures. The building occupied the highest ground near the W edge of the SE acropolis (Area VI); and its builders would have presumably destroyed any walls that previously existed here. A "robber trench" immediately to the N, running roughly NNW to SSE and intersected by trial trenches N22-III, XI, I, and X, had been backfilled with unshaped stones, dark earth, and LHIII pottery with a few DAII sherds. This trench, which had shown up as a series of weak anomalies in the magnetometer survey, may represent one sector of the footings of a Mycenaean structure that once stood here.

The dense thicket within and around Unit VI-1 was only partially cleared, leaving the SE room (Room 3) still mainly obscured by bushes, and the SW sections of the other two rooms only partly explored (Pl. 14-1). The dimensions of the building are substantial, about 24 × 5 m (external measurements). The outer walls are 0.60-0.65 m wide, constructed of roughly squared and faced stones, with some tile fragments and fill of small stones and earth. The foundations rest on stereo, which also constituted the floors except for a large pit (3 on Fig. 14-2), filled with Mycenaean pottery, in the NE corner of the central room (Room 2).

Since the building was only partially explored, its function cannot be conclusively established, but the few known features suggest a secular purpose. All three rooms had separate points of access, and they were not interconnected. Rooms 1 and 2 had entrances, both about 0.85 m wide, along the NE side; and the situation was probably the same in Room 3, since the steep slope immediately below the SW wall of the building would preclude an entrance along this side. In Room 1 there is a circular depression, about 0.40 m in diameter and 0.05 m deep, which was filled with powdery gray ash. Although little more than a meter from the NE wall of the room, this may represent the position of a hearth.

Room 2 was furnished with a stone bench or platform (Pl. 14-2), which was laid directly on the earth floor and set against but not bonded with Wall C on the SE side of the

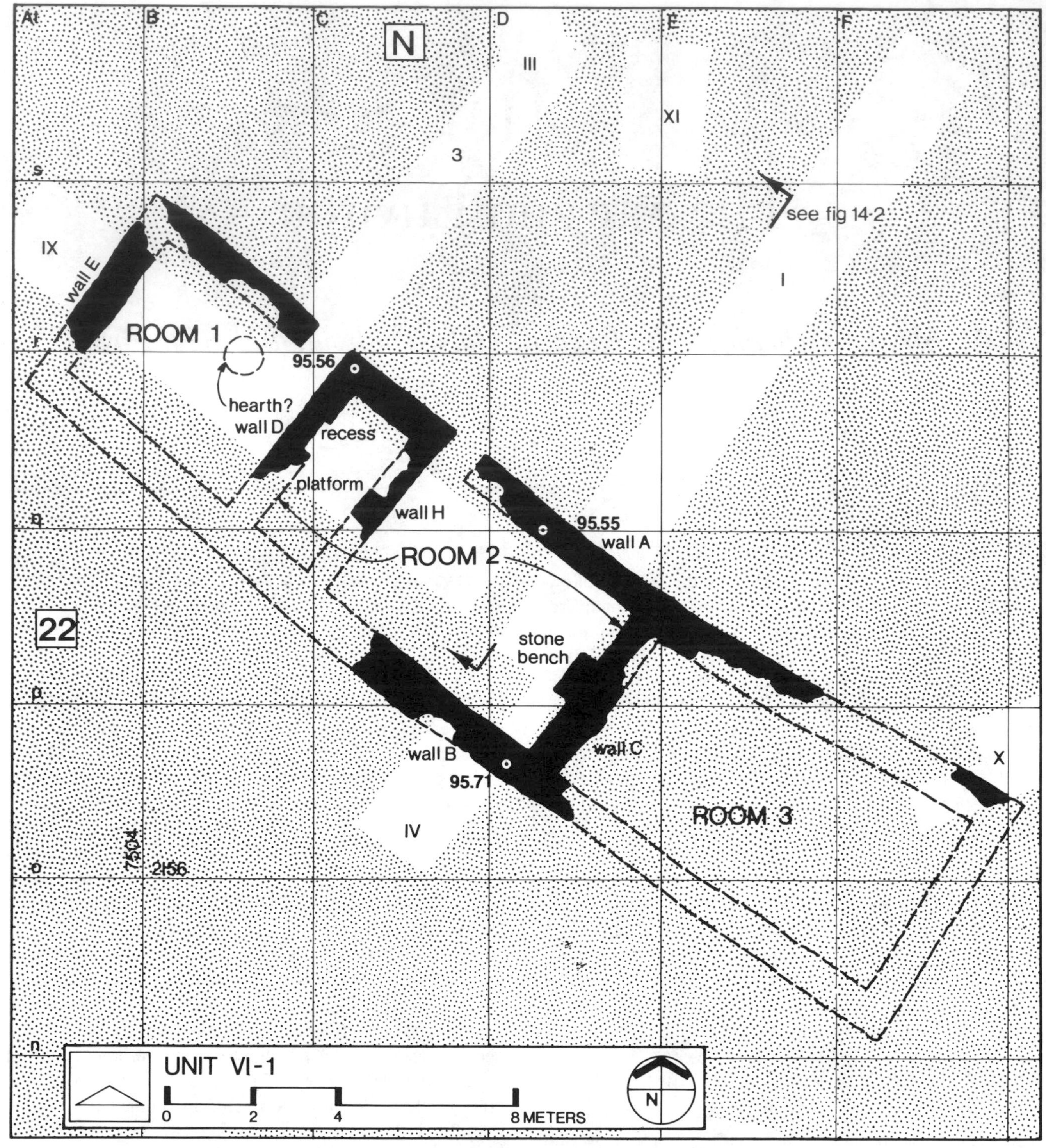

Figure 14-1

room. It was built in two courses of large and small stones and some small tile fragments. Its dimensions are ca. 1.0 m long, ca. 0.85 m wide, and 0.25 m in total height. It may have been the base for some wooden superstructure. At the opposite end of Room 2 and W of the entrance there is a much larger platform ca. 3.75 × 2.45 m and 0.30 m above floor level. Its surface is of orange clay, except for a stone border on the SE side which is formed by Wall H (Pl. 14-3), a structure with one face only and consisting of two to three ragged courses. Wall D, the partition at the back of the platform, contains a recess about 0.25 m deep, 0.65 m wide, and about 0.15 m above the flat surface of the platform. The sides and base of this recess are also coated in orange clay, and it was possibly a cupboard. The platform

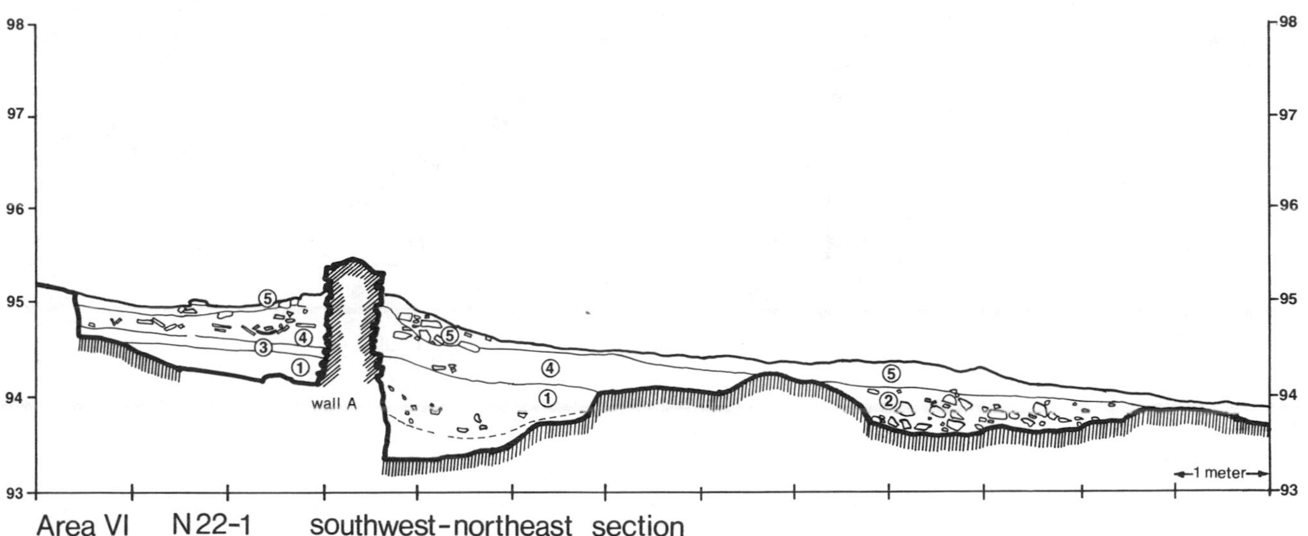

5. Plowed soil: dark brown, w/humus and roots (Modern)
4. Sandy mud: brown, w/tumble, charcoal and roof tiles (Post-Byzantine)
3. Slightly gravelly, sandy mud: brown, slightly compact (Post-Byzantine)
2. Slightly gravelly, sandy mud: brown, w/tumble (DA II w/LH)
1. Slightly gravelly, muddy sand: yellow, w/tumble (LH I - IIIA)

Figure 14-2

itself may have constituted a sleeping area, similar to the raised "Souphi" that is found in older houses in Karpathos and Kasos (Hope Simpson and Lazenby 1970, p. 73).

Unit VI-1 seems to have been abandoned to gradual decay. Within and immediately outside it, a layer of debris about 0.50 m thick (4 on Fig. 14-2) consisted of loose brown earth, many stones, a large quantity of tile fragments (e.g. **P1765**), and some carbonized wood. Five iron nails (**584, 585, 586, 587, 588**), squarish in section, were found in this layer in Room 2, and several glazed potsherds (**P1766**) from Room 1 may also belong to the building. But most of the pottery found in the debris consists of worn fragments of Mycenaean date.

R.H.S.

The fact that there is no tradition among the residents of the nearby village of Karpofora (Fig. 1-2) that a building once stood on the SE acropolis (Area VI) of the Nichoria ridge seems to argue for a date before ca. 1830. In every case so far investigated, contemporary families trace their history back to some ancestor who came to the village from elsewhere, especially from Arcadia and the slopes of the Taygetos range. In no case do oral history or genealogical reconstructions place the move any earlier than ca. 1830. How, then, is the known pre-1830 occupation of this village to be interpreted? One possibility is that Karakasili, as it was then called, was inhabited mainly or entirely by Turkish families and that Greeks resettled the village after the Turks departed. A second possibility is that the population of Karakasili was originally ethnically mixed and that the Greeks who came in after the War of Independence simply replaced the Turkish segment. In that case, the new Greek families were added to the indigenous ones and the latter subsequently died out. Thus far, ethnographic and historical research reveals no strong evidence to support one of these reconstructions over the other. Village records (which go back only to 1913) and oral history do reveal that several families have died out. Yet in every case known so far it turns out that the extinct family migrated from the more isolated areas referred to above after ca. 1830.

According to village oral history, however, there are in Karpofora the remains of four houses from the period of Turkish control (*epitourkokratia*). One of them, belonging to the present mayor, Panayiotis Perikli Sambaziotis, is still occupied, and the stone casement of its second-story southern windows bears a date to be interpreted as 1810 or 1840.

When one seeks information about habitation in the immediate environs before the 19th century, existing literary sources offer only vague help in explaining the presence of such a substantial structure as Unit VI-1. In 1927, at the height of the vogue to replace non-Greek place-names (Georgacas and McDonald 1969, pp. 10, 28), the name Karpofora was imposed on the old village of Karakasili. The earliest reference known to us that testifies to the existence of Karakasili is on a Venetian map dated about 1700 (Sauerwein 1969, No. 8 under "Territorio di Coron" in the Register). Thus, that village—presumably located on the same hilltop site as modern Karpofora—can be shown to go back at least as far as the period of

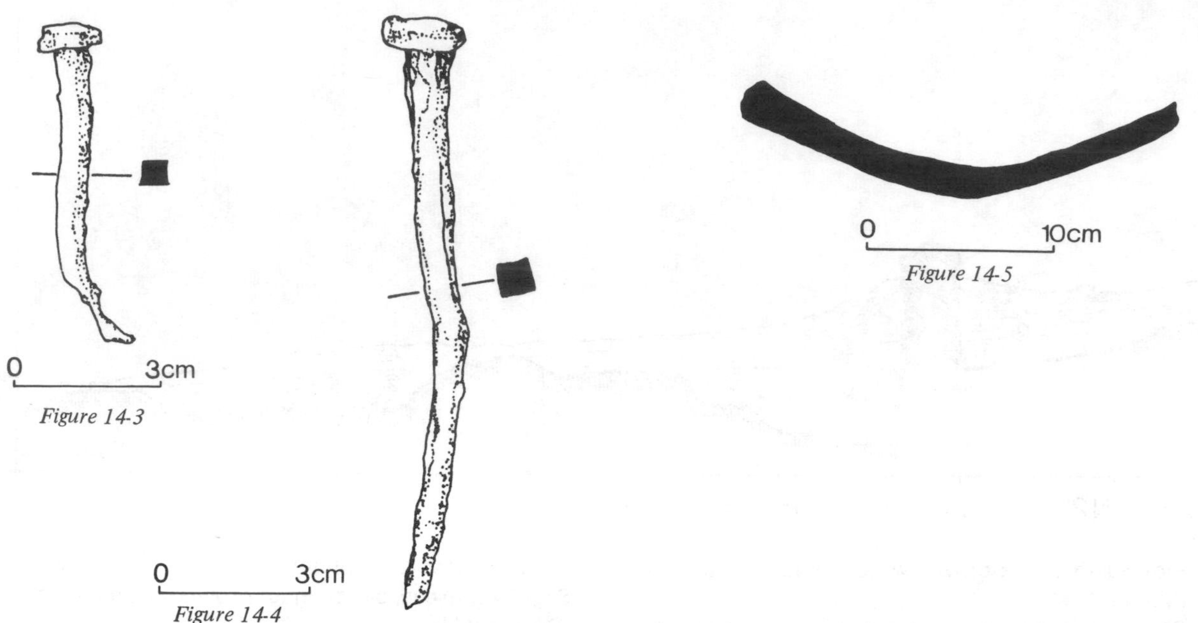

Figure 14-3

Figure 14-4

Figure 14-5

Venetian rule (1685-1715). A Venetian coin (**590**; Pl. 14-8) that cannot be exactly dated was found just S of Nichoria; a second was picked up on the opposite side of Karpofora. They constitute additional proof of the use of the immediate area at that time (Features 15 and 27, Fig. 1-4; *Nichoria* I, p. 109). And in the census list of 1815, i.e., near the end of the second Turkish occupation (1715-1821), Karakasili is reported to have consisted of 30 families (Poucqueville 1827, pp. 61, 62). A Turkish *akche* (**589**; Pl. 14-7) of Mehmet III (1595-1603), recovered in our excavations, might even be viewed as some confirmation that there was a village hereabouts during the earlier period of Turkish domination (1460-1685).

We do not know of any evidence that there was a village in the immediate environs during the unstable periods of Frankish control (1205-1432) and the brief revival of Byzantine rule (1432-60). But Petalidhi is known to have existed prior to about 1500 (*MME* 1972, p. 66; Pocket Map 5-8), and late medieval sources preserve the names of numerous villages in the region whose location cannot be established. Thus, it is probably safe to assume that throughout the post-Byzantine era there was nearly always at least one occupied spot within walking distance of the Nichoria ridge.

Unit VI-1 was apparently intended as a facility to process and store agricultural products cultivated on all or part of the ridgetop. The extreme scarcity of pottery and small finds would indicate that these farmers had their permanent dwellings elsewhere, although they would probably have used our building for shelter during labor-intensive seasons. Thus, the situation when Unit VI-1 was in use seems to have been very similar to that we have reconstructed for the Classical(?) building (see p. 337), and especially for the Late Roman/Early Byzantine Unit IV-2 (Phases 1, 2) which also had three rooms that may not have been interconnected (see pp. 364, 368). Unfortunately, specific evidence for dating Unit VI-1 is almost nonexistent, and speculation will have to be based almost entirely on the historical background sketched above.

We can begin by setting upper and lower limits for the date of the structure. For reasons already stated, the building may be presumed to be earlier than the mid-19th century; and it is almost certainly later than the Middle Byzantine period since the orthostate construction that is so distinctive of Units II-1, II-2, and L21-1 finds no parallel here. Also, the well-preserved roof tiles (e.g., **P1765**; Fig. 14-5; Pl. 14-6) do not resemble any of our Middle Byzantine tiles; and closer study requires us to correct the statement in a preliminary publication (McDonald 1972, p. 234) that tiles from Unit VI-1 are "very similar" to cover tiles from the Trypetorachi graves (see p. 355). Again, the nails from Unit VI-1 (**584-88**; Figs. 14-3, 14-4; Pl. 14-4) are unlike our Byzantine examples. Indeed, several rather nondescript scraps of glazed pottery (**P1766**; Pl. 14-5) that were apparently associated with Unit VI-1 might be considered generally comparable in their glazes to modern sherds recovered in surface levels elsewhere on the ridge (**P1767-70**; Figs. 14-7 to 14-10; Pls. 14-9 to 14-11).

Perhaps the safest course is to call Unit VI-1 (as we have done informally since 1969) the "Turkish building" and to suggest that it was built and used by residents of nearby Karakasili toward the end of the second period of Turkish control (1715-1821), when this region was generally prosperous and population was relatively high (*MME* 1972, p. 72).

The other post-Byzantine structure on the ridge is defin-

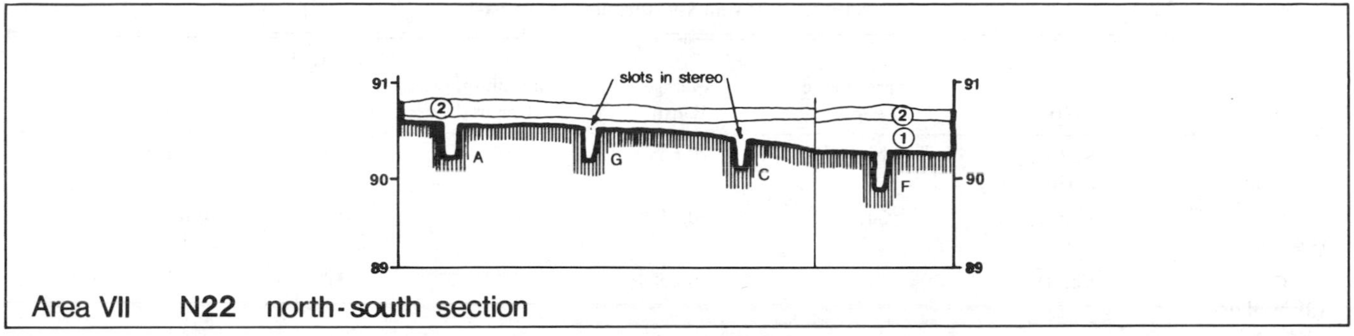

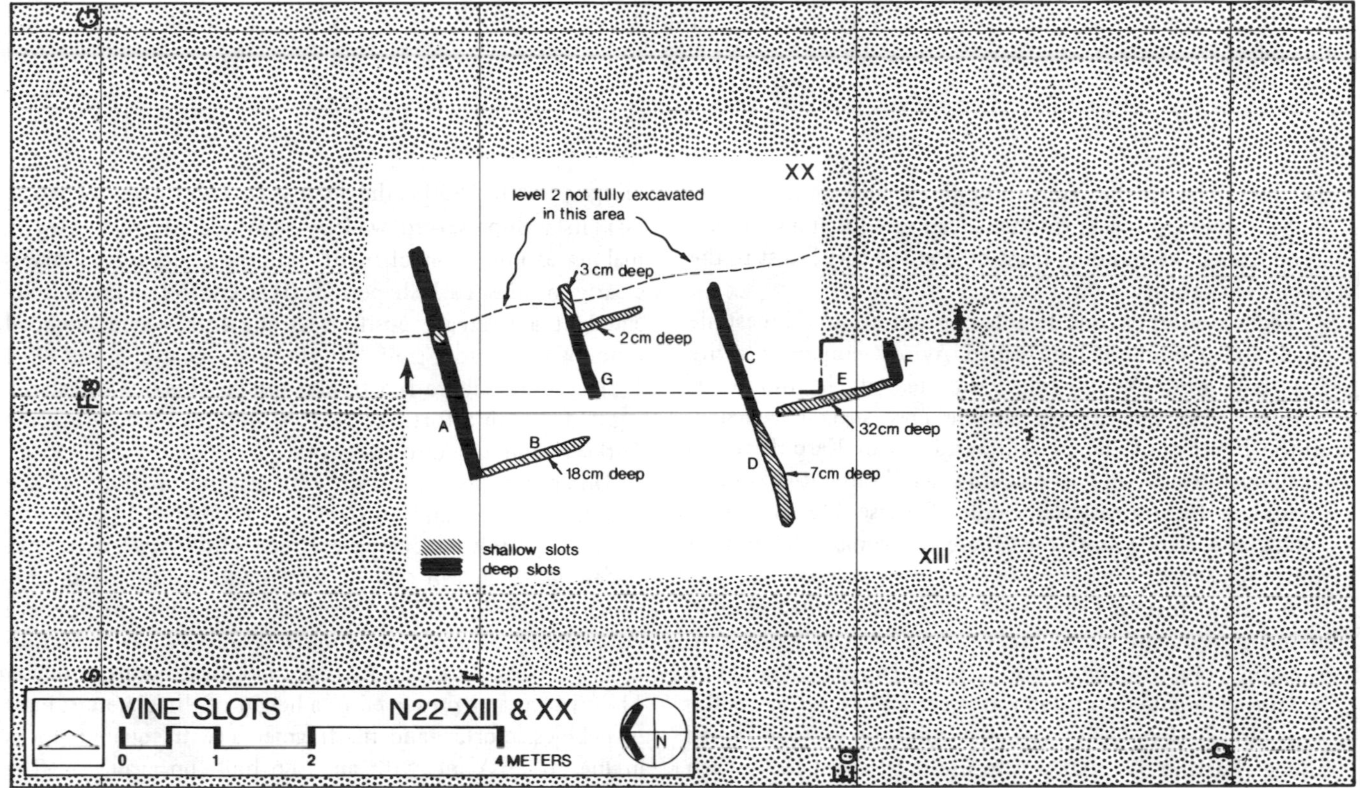

Figure 14-6

itely more recent. In Area I, grid J25 Sc the ruins of a sherherd's hut (*kalivi*) with a connected enclosure (*mandhri*) were encountered in the process of clearing around the tholos. According to villagers in Karpofora, this flimsy structure was built about 1920 of blocks taken from the collapsed tholos and it was abandoned about 1935. The same villagers report that the schoolhouse in Karpofora was constructed in 1923, using stone from the same source.

S.E.A.
J.R.

The only additional evidence for post-Byzantine activity on the ridge is a series of long, narrow slots of varying depth (Fig. 14-6) cut into the stereo or even into shallow prehistoric levels and now covered by plowsoil. They seem to have been most extensive in Area VII, but similar cuttings were encountered in Areas IV and V. The workmen identified these features as "vine slots," cut with a hoe (*axina*), along which in earlier times tendrils of sturdy plants were trained and brought to the surface to form new shoots at some distance from the original root. So it would appear that these features are relatively modern and reflect a system of viticulture in the decades 1870-1940 when farmers turned over large holdings, including much of the Nichoria ridge, to the commercial cultivation of currants.

R.H.S.

The Nichoria Environs (Fig. 1-2)

In the Nichoria environs we have noted a fair number of features that are of certain or probable post-Byzantine date (see *Nichoria* I, Chapter 7). At Ayios Ilias (Feature 60) there is a concentration of limestone blocks and a heavy scatter of roof tile fragments that are somewhat thicker than modern tiles. The place-name may give some weight to

Table 14-1. Wall Specifications: Unit VI-1

Wall	Grid	Approximate Length	Average Width	Maximum Height	Maximum Number of Courses	Bond/Butt
A (NE wall)	N22 Br to Go	24.0	0.65	1.30	12	Bonds with C
B (SW wall)	N22 Ag to Fn	24.0	0.65	1.40	12	Bonds with C, H, D, E
C (SE wall of Room 2)	N22 Dop	5.0	0.65	1.50	12	Bonds with A, B
D (SE wall of Room 1)	N22 BCg	5.0	0.60	0.95	8	Bonds with B

the theory that this ruined building may have been a chapel. Since no local informants can recall that a structure stood there, the building must date at the very latest to the early 19th century.

There is another considerable concentration of limestone blocks on a point of land called Ayios Georgios (Feature 59) that overlooks the vineyard area at the mouth of Vathirema. Again, the place-name may suggest a chapel, although none of the present residents of Karpofora can recall such a structure. The nearby field house of Nikos and Charikleia Chortareas was built of these blocks in the 1960s, and they report that there was some indication of wall stubs at that time.

At Ayios Ioannis (Feature 49) there is a ruined church, including remnants of walls, scattered stone and tiles, and a marble column (*Nichoria* I, p. 110). The church could be Byzantine in date, but if later, it is certainly prior to 1830.

In the Velika valley are the ruins of a stone-arched bridge (Feature 57) that was in use until about 1930 when it was destroyed by a flood. A strong reason for dating this bridge prior to 1830 is the nearby Turkish fortress (Feature 58). Its well-preserved walls are covered by thick growth, making examination difficult, but the style of masonry is clearly of the Turkish period. This control point was located at a strategic position at the fork where the road running north to Strefi left the main coastal route (Fig. 1-2). At Strefi there is a similar bridge, this one still standing, along with a fort. All these structures were part of the Turkish communication network.

Other remains from the Turkish occupation include Features 29, 33, and 56 (*Nichoria* I, pp. 109-11). Feature 29 is a narrow, stone-paved road (*kalderimi*), extensive traces of which can still be seen in the rough ground between the NW end of Nichoria ridge and the modern Kalamata-Pylos highway (*MME* 1972, Pl. 4-3; *Nichoria* I, p. 109). Feature 33 is a ruinous structure, roughly 11 × 14 m, and preserved to a height of three meters, built of pebbles, mortar, and tile fragments (with squared blocks in the corners) and with an oven built up against it. The style of masonry is quite unlike anything in the whole area

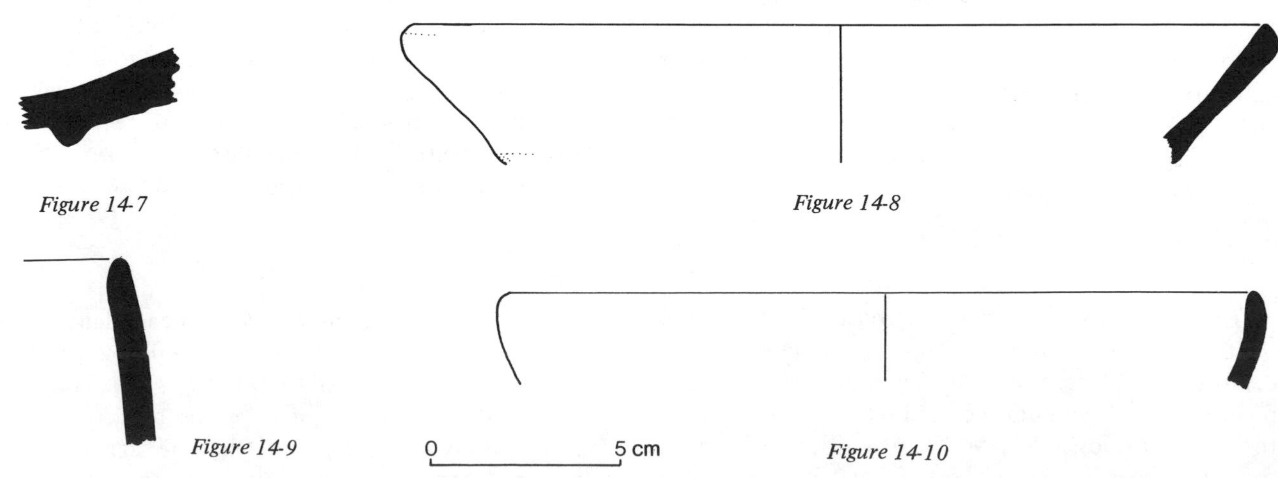

Figure 14-7
Figure 14-8
Figure 14-9
Figure 14-10

traceable to the post-1830 period. Feature 56 is located about 440 m S-SW of the Karia River, next to the house of Ioannis Troupakis, and consists of the remains of a ceramic kiln, two pithoi, and a mound of ceramic debris, all of which can probably be assigned to the Turkish period. Also, the flour mill still standing on the E side of the Rizomilo bridge and now owned by the Chronopoulos family is certainly to be dated long before 1880 (contrary to *MME* 1972, p. 59). Aschenbrenner now believes that it may prove to have been in use well before the end of the 18th century. Its existence presumably accounts for the name of the modern road junction, "Rizomilo." This toponym was already known in 1770.

A second water-powered flour mill was built on the W side of the Karia River about 1880. These mills were one response to the greatly expanded agricultural activity around Karakasili-Karpofora from 1880 to 1940. Land was also being cleared and planted to figs, olives, and currants. The farmers raised these as cash crops, and the local area was tied into the larger regional marketplace in 1925 by the construction of an all-season wagon road. Where this road crossed the Karia River a new settlement grew up at Rizomilo, just below and E-NE of the Nichoria ridge (*MME* 1972, p. 49).

S.E.A.
J.R.

To summarize, on the Nichoria ridge itself there is some evidence to indicate that Unit VI-1, which was probably used as a storage and processing facility for agricultural produce, may be of relatively recent origin, perhaps of late 18th or early 19th century date. The only other post-Byzantine structure on the site was a shepherd's hut built around 1920. In the Nichoria environs, most of the ruined structures identifiable from surface remains seem to be post-1460 in date, with the majority indicating activity during periods of Turkish control.

REFERENCES

Aschenbrenner, S. E. 1972. "A Contemporary Community." In McDonald and Rapp 1972, pp. 47-63.

Bon, A. 1969. *La Morée franque, Recherches historiques, topographiques, et archéologiques sur la principauté d'Achaïe (1205-1430)*. 2 vols., text and album. Paris.

Georgacas, D. J., and McDonald, W. A. 1969. *Place Names of Southwest Peloponnesus.* Athens and Minneapolis.

Hope Simpson, R., and Lazenby, J. 1970. "Notes from the Dodecannese II," *BSA* 65: 47-77.

Lazari, V. 1851. *Le monete dei possedimenti veneziani di oltremare e di terraferma, descritte ed illustrate*. Venezia.

Longnon. J., and Topping. P. 1969. *Documents sur le régime des terres dans la principauté de Morée au XIVe siècle.* Documents et recherches sur l'économie des pays byzantins, islamiques et slaves . . . IX. École pratique des hautes études, VIe section. Paris and The Hague.

Lukermann, F. E. 1972. "Settlement and Circulation: Pattern and Systems." In McDonald and Rapp 1972, pp. 148-70.

———, and Moody, J. 1978. "Nichoria and Vicinity: Settlements and Circulation." In Rapp and Aschenbrenner 1978, pp. 78-112.

McDonald, W. A. 1972. "Excavations at Nichoria in Messenia 1969-71," *Hesperia* 41: 218-73.

———, and Rapp, G., Jr., eds. 1972. *The Minnesota Messenia Expedition: Reconstructing a Bronze Age Regional Environment*. Minneapolis.

Metcalf, W. E. 1974a. October 17, personal communication to J. Rosser.

———. 1974b. December 3, personal communication to J. Rosser.

MME 1972 = McDonald and Rapp 1972.

Nichoria I = Rapp and Aschenbrenner 1978.

Pouqueville, F. C. H. L. 1827. *Voyage de la Grèce*, 2nd ed. Vol. 6. Paris.

Rapp, George, Jr., and Aschenbrenner, S. E., eds. 1978. *Excavations at Nichoria in Southwest Greece* I: *Site, Environs, and Techniques*. Minneapolis.

Sauerwein, F. 1969. "Das Siedlungsbild der Peloponnes um das Jahr 1700," *Erdkunde* 23: 237-44.

Topping, P. 1972. "The Post-Classical Documents." In McDonald and Rapp 1972, pp 64-80.

CATALOG FOR POST-BYZANTINE TIMES

Pottery

P1765. Tile. Fig. 14-5; Pl. 14-6.
L. ca. 0.50. W. ca. 0.25
Hard-fired, reddish yellow fabric (7.5YR 7/6). Not similar to other Nichoria tiles.
Unit VI-1, Room 1.
Turkish?

P1766. Glazed sherds. Pl. 14-5.
Various dimensions, from 0.01 to 0.029.
Three green, one light red (2.5YR 6/6) glazed sherds, each with white slip underneath. Another sherd has only slip remaining.
Unit VI-1, Room 1.
Turkish?

P1767. (NP124). Glazed sherd. Fig. 14-7.
D. of base impossible to est.
Base sherd frag. Very hard white fabric (2.5Y 8/2) with olive-yellow glaze (2.5Y 6/6) on interior. This particular sherd was judged to be about 30 years old by a potter at Vounari.
K25 Tcd in topsoil.
Modern.

P1768 (NP149). Glazed sherd. Fig. 14-8; Pl. 14-9.
D. (est.) of rim 0.19.
Rim frag. Yellow fabric (10YR 8/6) with some reddish yellow and white grits; white slip over interior and upper exterior rim. Thin, opaque, pinkish-gray (5YR 7/2) glaze over slip.
K25 Tcd in topsoil.
Modern.

P1769 (NP163). Glazed sherd. Fig. 14-9; Pl. 14-10.
D. (est.) of rim 0.23.
Joining rim and body sherds and nonjoining rim sherd. Hard-fired pink fabric (5YR 7/4) under opaque glaze appearing light red (2.5YR 6/8).
K25 Tcd in topsoil.
Modern.

P1770 (NP164). Glazed sherd. Fig. 14-10; Pl. 14-11.
D. (est.) of rim 0.28.

Rim frag. Pink fabric (7.5YR 7/4) under white slip, over which a thick pale yellow glaze (5Y 8/3) on exterior and interior.

K25 Tcd in topsoil.

Modern.

Small Finds

584 (N27). Nail. Fig. 14-3.

L. (pres.) 0.071. D. of head 0.016.

Corroded. Tip of shank broken off. Circular head. Shank rectangular in section.

Unit VI-1, Room 2.

Turkish?

585 (N28). Nail. Fig. 14-4.

L. (pres.) 0.12. D. of head 0.017.

Corroded. Circular head. Shank square in section. A resident of Karpofora claims that this type of long nail is used today to tie joining pieces of wood. This nail does not have a parallel among Byzantine nails from the site.

Unit VI-1, Room 2.

Turkish?

586 (N29). Nail. Pl. 14-4.

L. (pres.) 0.078. D. of head 0.015.

Corroded. Circular head. Shank square in section.

Unit VI-1, Room 2.

Turkish?

587 (N31). Nail.

L. (pres.) 0.07. W. of head 0.012.

Corroded. Square head. Shank rectangular in section.

Unit VI-1, Room 2.

Turkish?

588 (N32). Nail.

L. (pres.) 0.079. D. of head 0.01.

Corroded. Circular head. Shank square in section. Nails **584, 586,** and **588** resemble one another.

Unit VI-1, Room 2.

Turkish?

589 (N1048). Coin. Pl. 14-7.

D. (max.) 0.01. Th. ca. 0.0002. Wt. 0.26 grams.

Worn. Silver *akche* of Mehmet III (1595-1603) struck at Constantinople (Metcalf 1974a).

K24 TUu, level 2, lot 3126/1.

Turkish.

590 Coin. Pl. 14-8.

D. (max.) 0.017. Th. (max.) 0.0005.

Slightly worn. Bronze, undated issue of the Venetian colonies Isole and Armata, i.e., Ionian Islands and Fleet (Metcalf 1974b). See Lazari 1851, p. 88, Pl. 9.42.

From orchard of Argiris Dionysopoulos, located just S of Nichoria.

Venetian.

Plate 2-1. Unit III-1 and tumble in Mycenaean street (foreground), from S

Plate 2-2. Unit III-1 and underlying Mycenaean Wall R, from S

Plate 2-3. Unit III-1, Byzantine field Wall L over tip of apse, from E

Plate 2-4. Unit III-1, pit and posthole, from E

Plate 2-5. Unit III-1, from bipod

Plate 2-6. Modern shepherd's hut at Vrana, near Marathon (photograph courtesy of Hector Catling)

Plate 1-1. Vertical view of Nichoria ridge from balloon. North approximately at top of picture

Plate 1-2. Nichoria ridge seen in profile from NE, with Rizomilo in foreground

Plates

Plate 2-7. Wall H, K25 TUa, from NE

Plate 2-8. Unit III-3, DA surface over Mycenaean foundation, from NE

Plate 2-9. Unit III-3, DA surface over Mycenaean debris, from NE

Plate 2-10. Unit III-3, DA and LH deposits, from NE

Plate 2-11. Terrace walls, Area III SE, aerial view

Plate 2-12. Wall A, K24 Xtu, from N

Plate 2-13. Wall A partially dismantled, from N

Plate 2-14. Unit N Veves-1, Walls A and B, from S

Plate 2-15. Unit N Veves-1, stone platform against Wall B, from SW

Plate 2-16. Unit IV-1 with earlier and later contiguous structures, from balloon, N at top of picture

Plate 2-17. E end of Unit IV-1 with Mycenaean Unit IV-3, from balloon, N at top of picture

Plate 2-18. Unit IV-1, threshold in Wall F and porch, from S

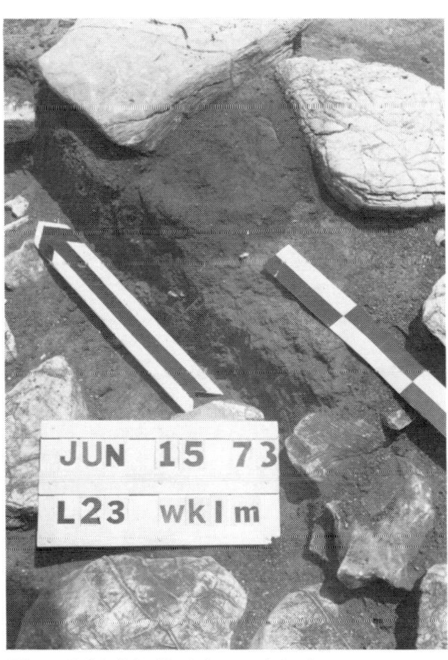

Plate 2-19. Mudbrick no. 1 before removal, from SW

Plate 2-20. Unit IV-1, cobbles in porch floor, from N

Plate 2-21. Unit IV-1, side doorway and block with cut hole, from W

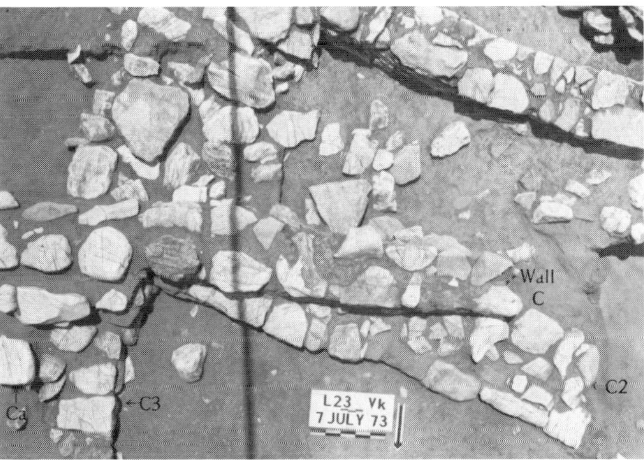

Plate 2-22. Unit IV-1, Walls C, Ca over Mycenaean foundations (C2, C3), from bipod

Plate 2-23. Unit IV-1, Walls C, Ca, C2, C3, from N

Plate 2-25. Unit IV-1, Walls D, E, and paved circle, from W

Plate 2-24. Unit IV-1, stones at bottom of pit hearth, from S

Plate 2-26. Unit IV-1, Wall D over Mycenaean Wall K, from SW

Plate 2-27. Unit IV-1, Walls D, E, and paved cricle, from bipod

Plate 2-28. Unit IV-1, bonded corner of Walls X and A over Mycenaean foundation, from S

Plate 2-29. Unit IV-1, packed earth between Walls A and B, from S

Plate 2-30. Unit IV-1, support Wall Y with posthole C (in foreground) and underyling Mycenaean foundation, from E

Plate 2-31. Unit IV-1, stone packing of Posthole C, from S

Plate 2-32. Unit IV-1, support Wall Z and Posthole D, from S

Plate 2-33. Modern shepherd's hut, Marathon

Plate 2-34. Modern shepherd's hut, Boeotia (along National Road)

Plate 2-35. "Window" in modern shepherd's hut, Boeotia

Plate 2-36. Unit IV-1, Wall G, from N

Plate 2-37. Unit IV-1, stone scatter on Phase 2 floor, from N

Plate 2-38. Unit IV-1, apsidal Room 3, from SSE

Plate 2-39. Unit IV-1, storage pit no. 1, from E

Plate 2-40. Unit IV-1, storage pit no. 2, from E

Plate 2-41. Unit IV-1, exterior Posthole a, from NE

Plate 2-42. Unit IV-1, animal bones behind paved circle, from N

Plate 2-43. Unit IV-1, exterior Posthole e, from N

Plate 2-44. Unit IV-1, exterior Posthole c, from S

Plate 2-45. N environs of Unit IV-1, from balloon

Plate 2-46. Curving Wall H, from bipod

Plate 2-47. Wall I, from bipod

Plate 2-48. Walls J and I, from bipod

Plate 2-49. Refuse dump, rectangular enclosure at bottom, from W

Plate 2-50. Area IVSW, S environs of Unit IV-1, from balloon

Plate 2-51. Wall L, reused Unit IV-9, from S

Plate 2-52. Oval pit, reused Unit IV-9, from bipod

Plate 2-53. Unit IV-10 and reused Unit IV-9, from bipod

Plate 2-54. Trial trench L23-VIII, from E

Plate 2-55. Trial trench L23-IX, from N

Plate 2-56. Unit IV-5 and contiguous structures, from balloon, N at top of picture

Plate 2-57. Unit IV-5. Wall A and floor of Room 1, overlain by apse of Unit IV-2, from N

Plate 2-58. Unit IV-5, detail of Wall A, from N

Plate 2-60. Unit IV-5, N end of Wall A, from S

Plate 2-59. Burned mudbrick from Unit IV-5 in test trench, Room 3, Unit IV-2

Plate 2-61. Unit IV-5, cobble paving and collapsed pithos, from NE

Plate 2-62. Unit IV-5, paved circle no. 2, from W

Plate 2-63. Pithos no. 1 **(P1336)** during excavation, from S

Plate 2-64. Pithos no. 1 **(P1336)** and no. 2 **(P1337)**, from S

Plate 2-65. Pithos no. 2 **(P1337)**, from NE

Plate 2-66. Pit for pithos no. 2, from N

Plate 2-67. Wall β, reused Unit IV-6, from bipod

Plate 2-68. Wall M, Area IVSW, from N

Plate 2-69. Walls T and N, Area IVSW, from bipod

Plate 2-70. Curving wall fragment, trial trench L22-V, from N

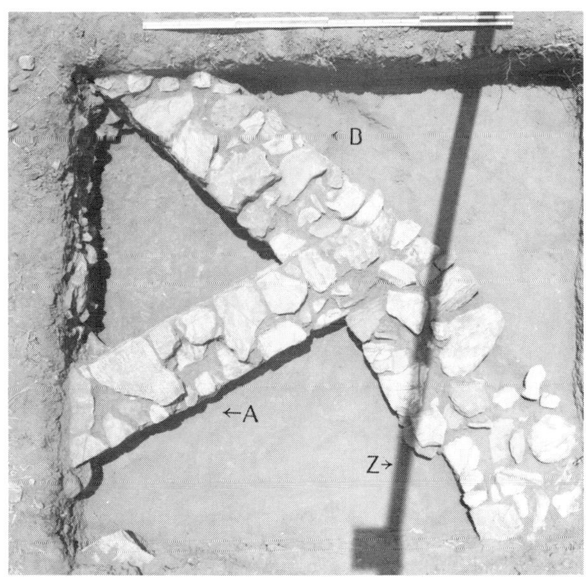

Plate 2-71. Walls, A, B, Z, trial trench L22-VII, from bipod

Plate 2-72. Wall Z, trial trench L22-VII, from SW

Plate 2-73. Wall A, Area IVSE, from SE

Plate 2-75. Area IVV, trial trench N22-XVII, Walls C, and D, and F

Plate 2-74. Apsidal Wall B, Area IVSE, from bipod

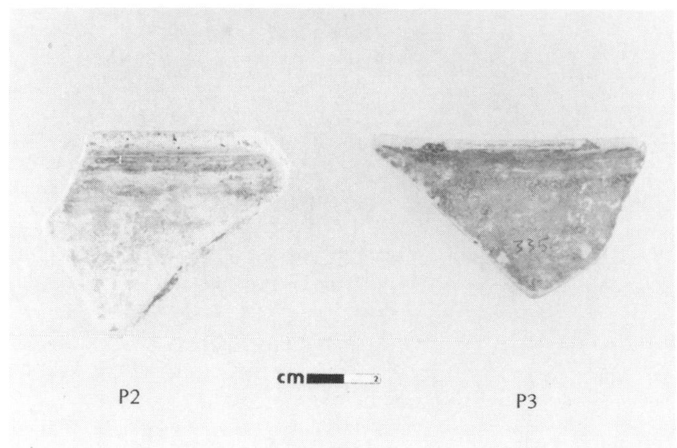

Plate 3-1. DAI rims

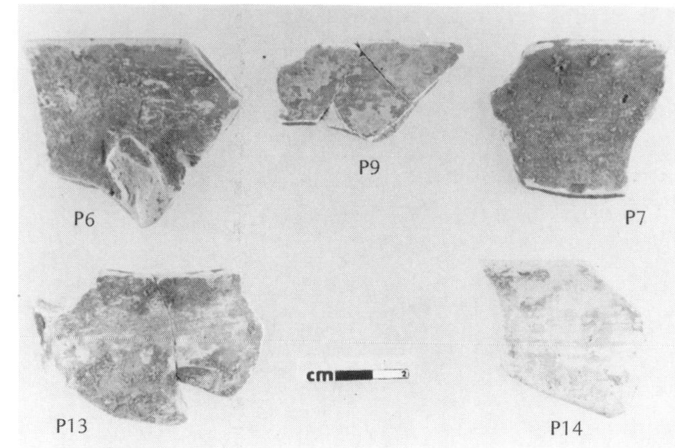

Plate 3-2. DAI rims

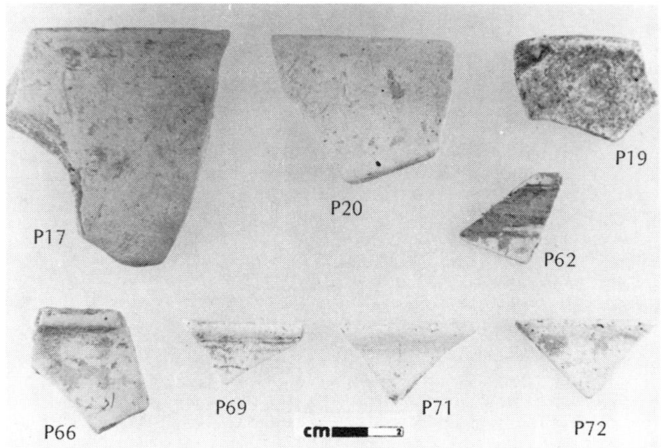

Plate 3-3. DAI rims

Plate 3-4. DAI rims

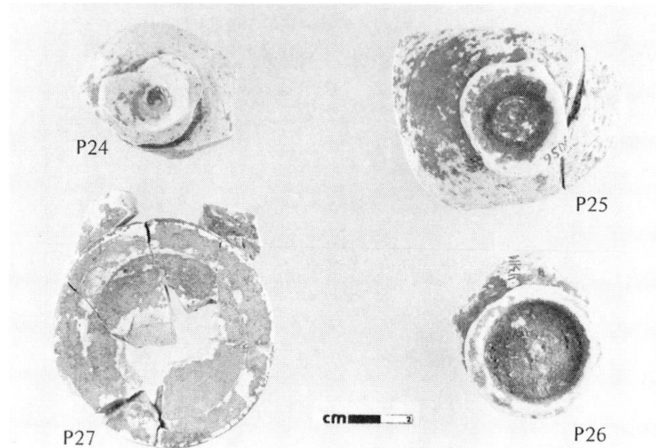

Plate 3-5. DAI bases

Plate 3-6. DAI, Shape 1

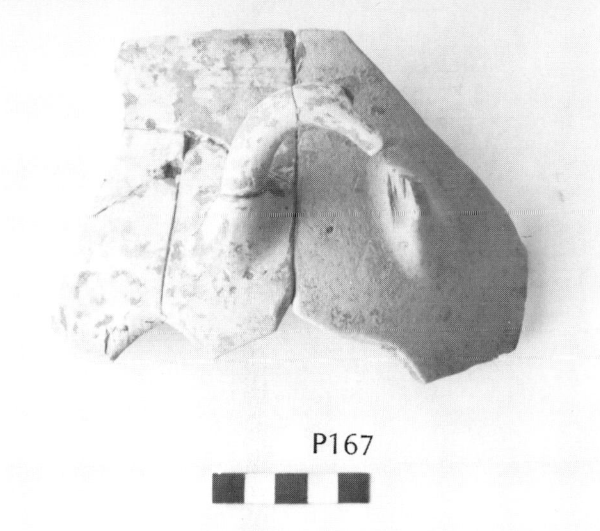

Plate 3-7. DAI, Shape 1

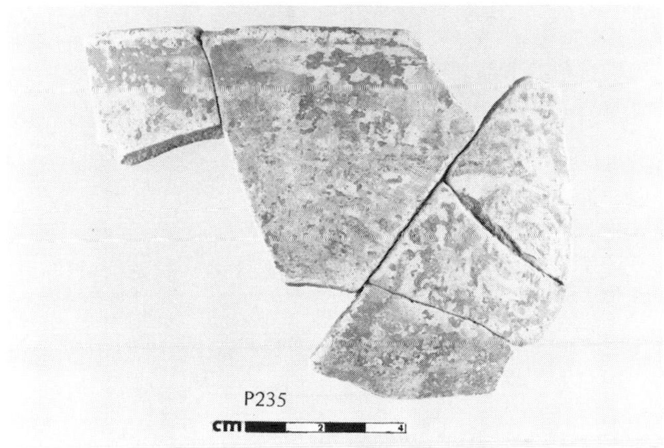

Plate 3-8. DAI, Shape 2

Plate 3-9. DAI, Shape 4

Plate 3-10. DAI, Shape 7

Plate 3-11. DAI, Shape 7

Plate 3-12. DAI, Motif 3a

Plate 3-13. DAI, Motif 3a

Plate 3-14. DAI, Motif 3a

Plate 3-15. DAI, Motif 3a.

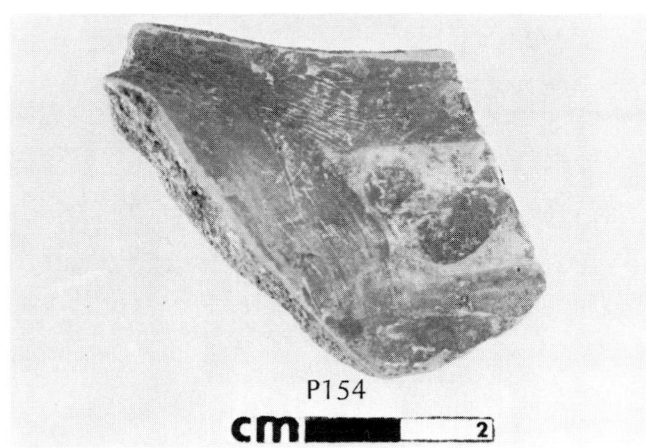

Plate 3-16. DAI, Motif 3a.

Plate 3-17. DAI, Motif 3a

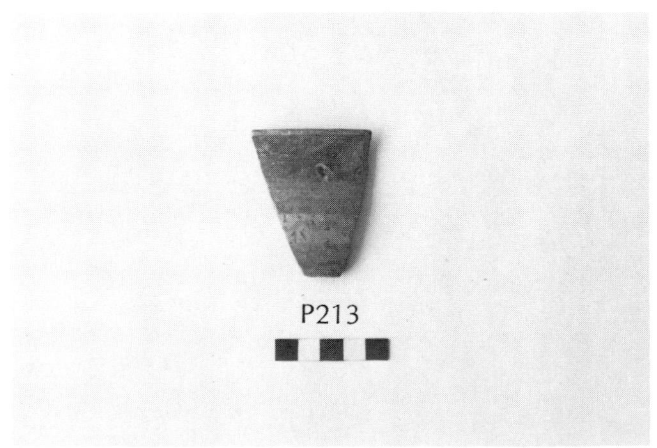

Plate 3-18. DAI, Motif 3a

Plate 3-19. DAI, Motif 3a (left); decorated oinochoe/jug sherd (right)

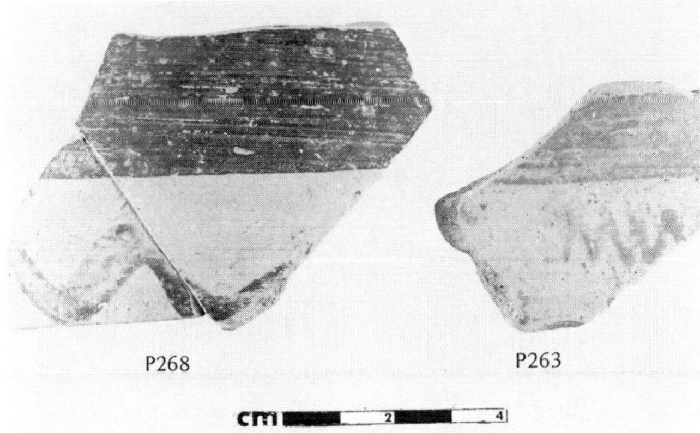

Plate 3-20. DAI, Motif 3a

Plate 3-21. DAI, Motif 3a

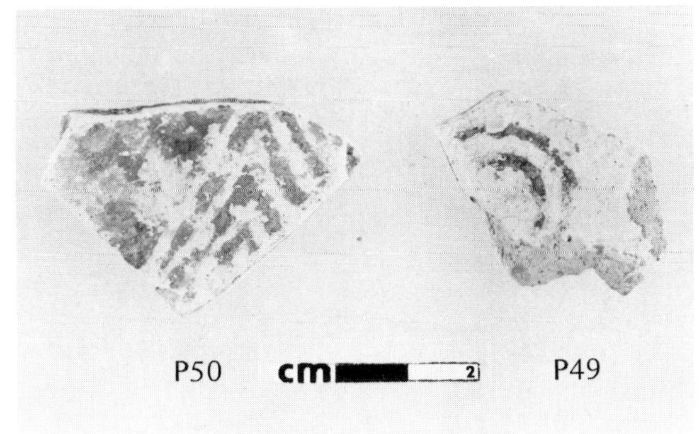

Plate 3-22. DAI, Motifs 6 (left) and 7 (right)

Plate 3-23. DAI, decorated krater fragment

Plate 3-24. DAI, zoomorphic handles

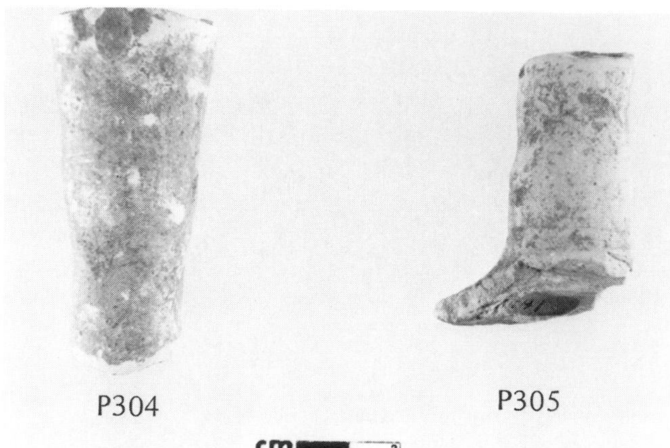

Plate 3-25. DAI, ribbed stems, Type A

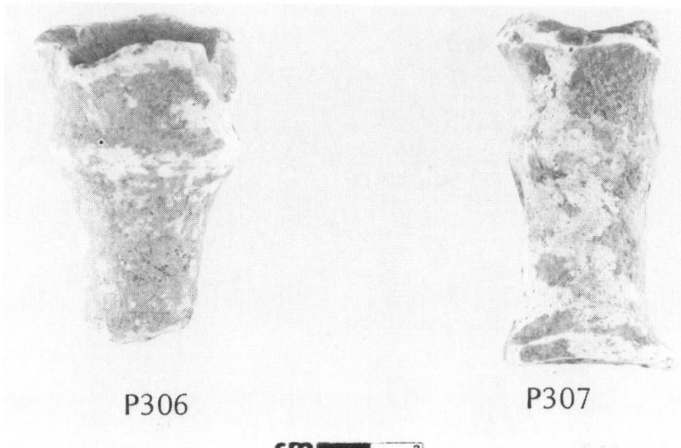

Plate 3-26. DAI, ribbed stems, Type B

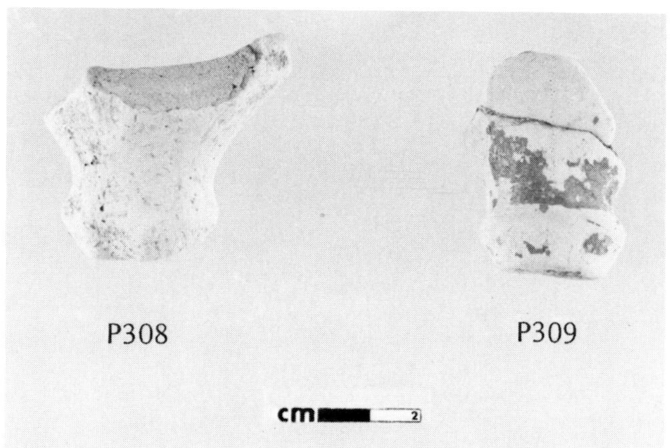

Plate 3-27. DAI, ribbed stems, Type B

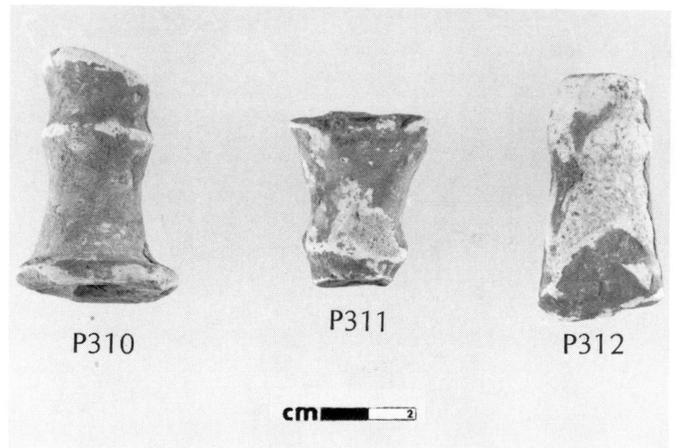

Plate 3-28. DAI, ribbed stems, Type C

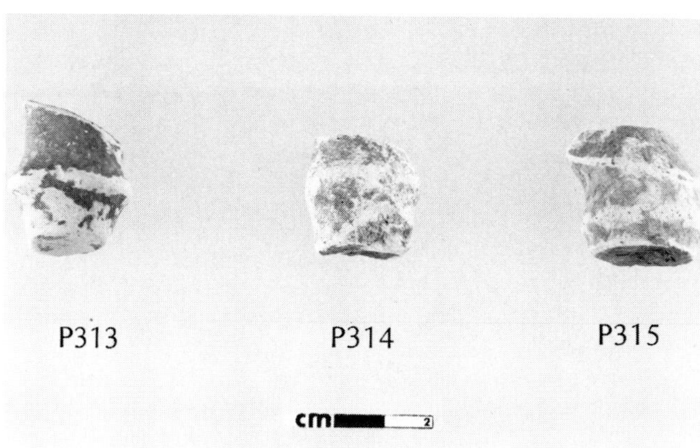

Plate 3-29. DAI, ribbed stems, Type C

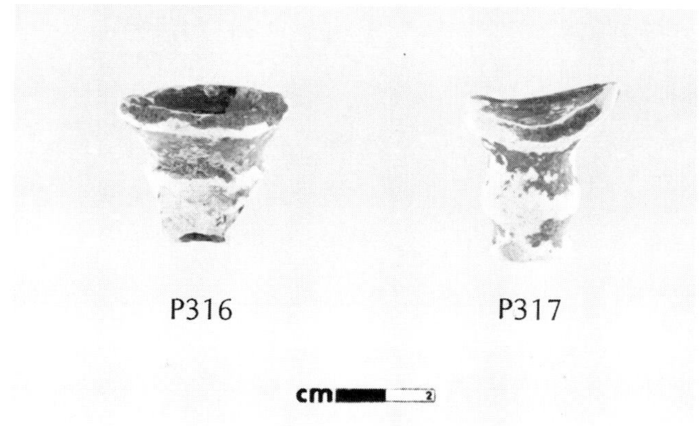

Plate 3-30. DAI ribbed stems, Type D1

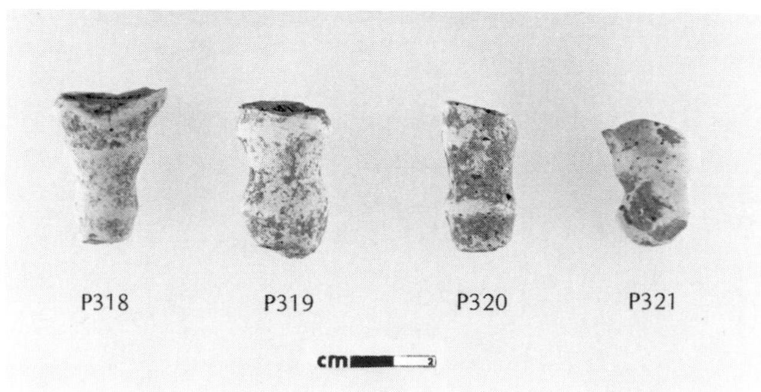

Plate 3-31. DAI, ribbed stems, Type D2

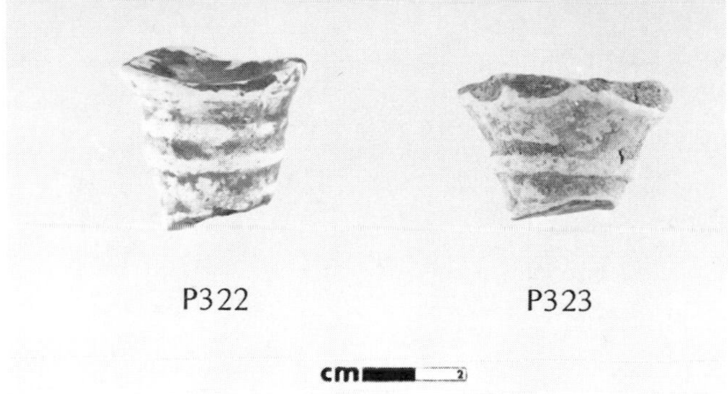

Plate 3-32. DAI, ribbed stems, Type E

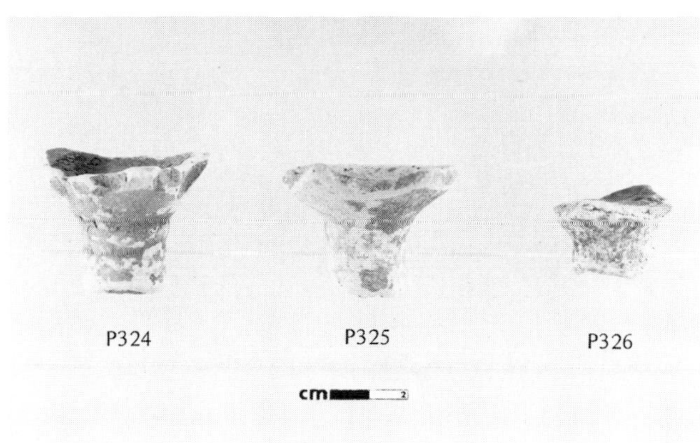

Plate 3-33. DAI, ribbed stems, Type E

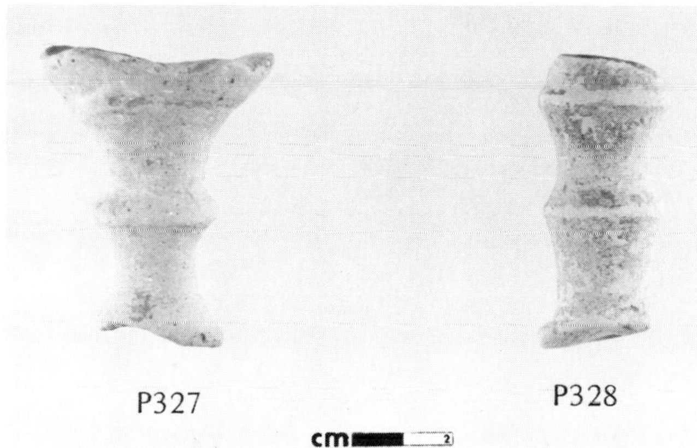

Plate 3-34. DAI, ribbed stems, Type F

Plate 3-35. DAI, ribbed stems, Type G

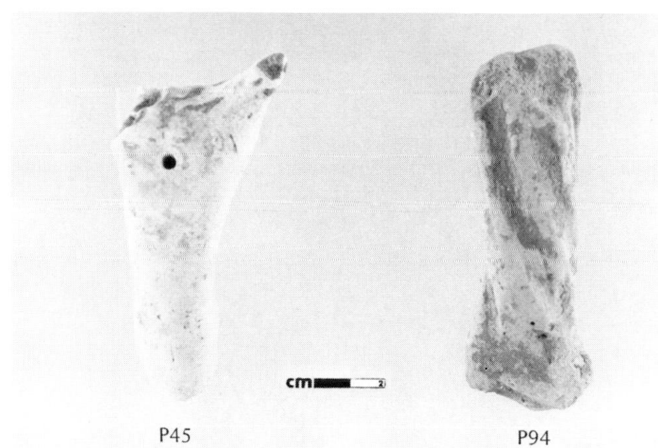

Plate 3-36. DAI, pierced amphora handle (left) and rope handle fragment (right)

Plate 3-37. DAI, decorated amphora fragment

Plate 3-38. DAI, coarse ware

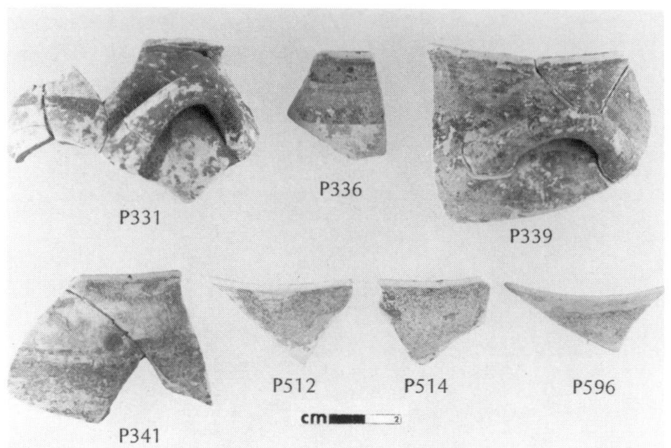

Plate 3-39. DAII rims

Plate 3-40. DAII rims

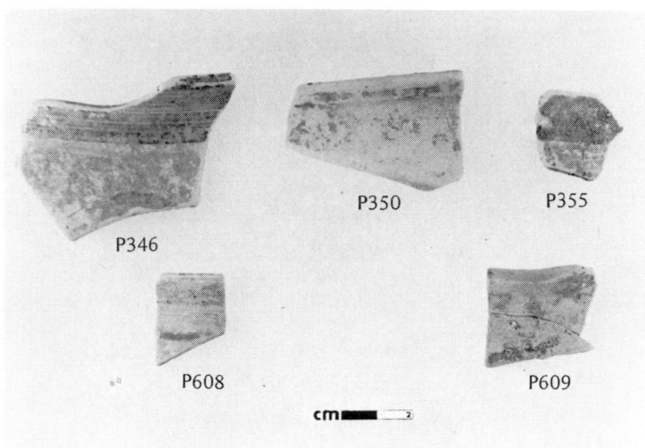

Plate 3-41. DAII rims

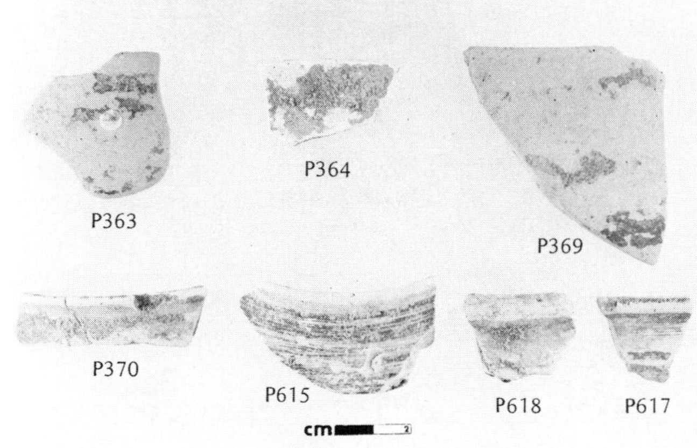

Plate 3-42. DAII rims

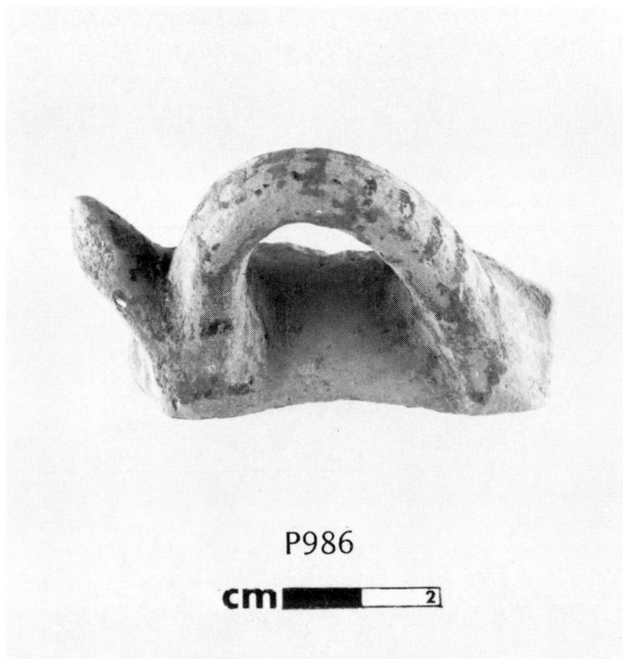

Plate 3-43. Double handle

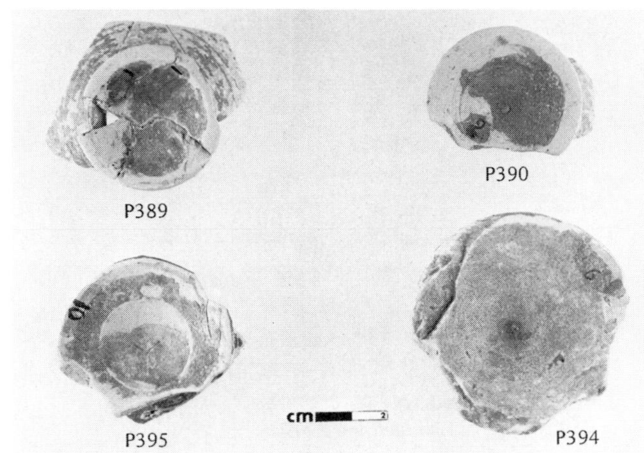

Plate 3-44. DAII bases

Plate 3-45. Flat-based skyphos, Shape 7

Plate 3-46. Flat-based skyphos, Shape 7a

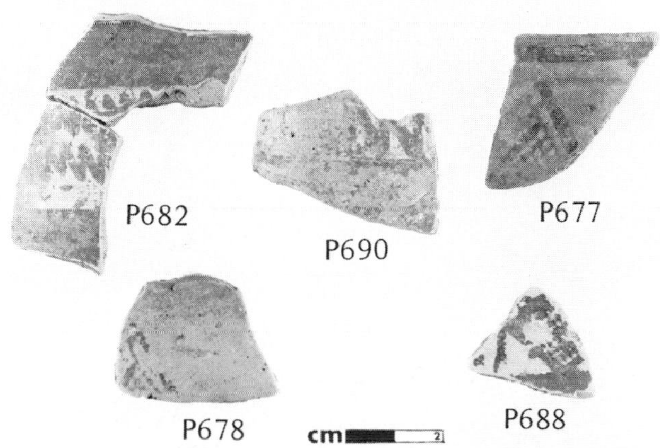

Plate 3-47. DAII decorated sherds

Plate 3-48. Motif 4a

Plate 3-49. Motif 5a

Plate 3-50. Motif 5a

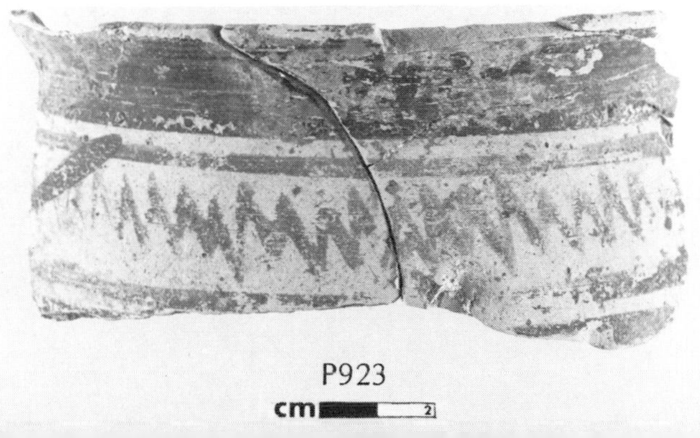

Plate 3-51. Motif 6

Plate 3-52. Motif 7a

Plate 3-52a. Motif 7a

Plate 3-53. Motif 7b

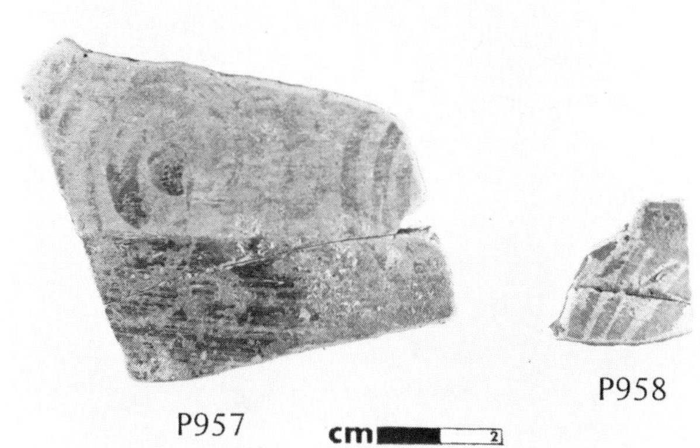

Plate 3-54. Motifs 7b (left) and 14 (right)

Plate 3-55. Motif 7b

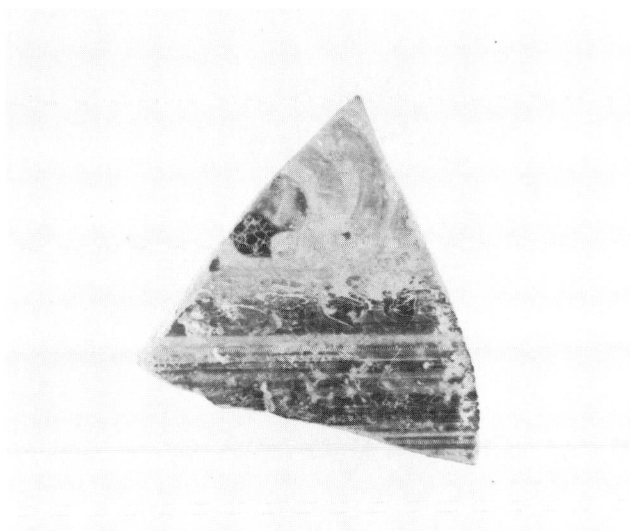

P1615

Plate 3-56. Motif 7b

Plate 3-59. Motif 10

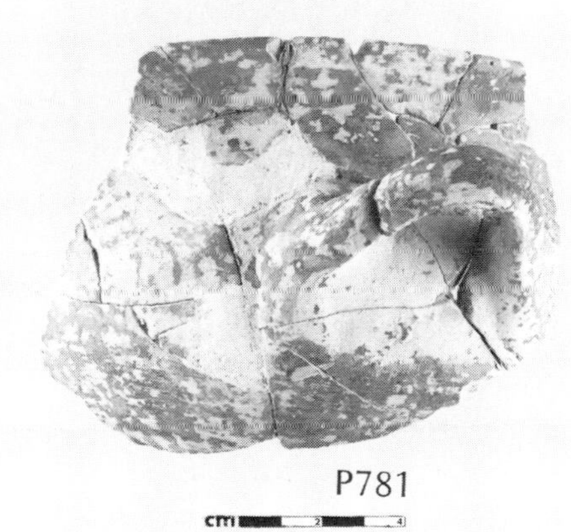

Plate 3-57. Motif 7b

Plate 3-58. Motif 9

Plate 3-60. Motif 10

Plate 3-61. Motif 10

Plate 3-62. Motif 10

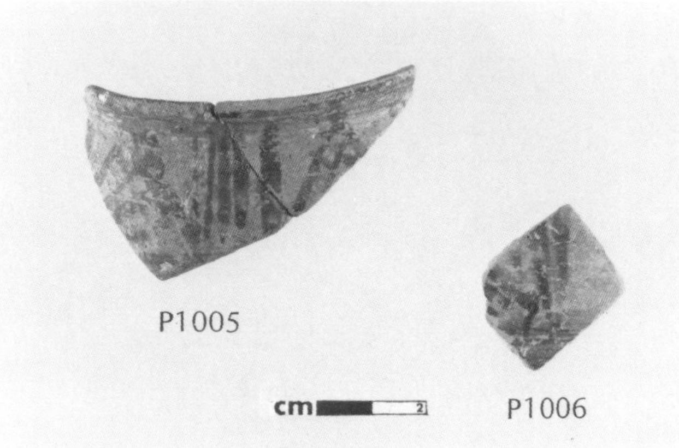

Plate 3-63. Motifs 10 (left) and 14 (right)

Plate 3-64. Motif 11

Plate 3-65. Motif 15

Plate 3-66. Motif 16

Plate 3-67. Metope-triglyph motif

Plate 3-68. Cup

Plate 3-69. Cup

Plate 3-71. Decorated underside of cup base

Plate 3-70. Cup

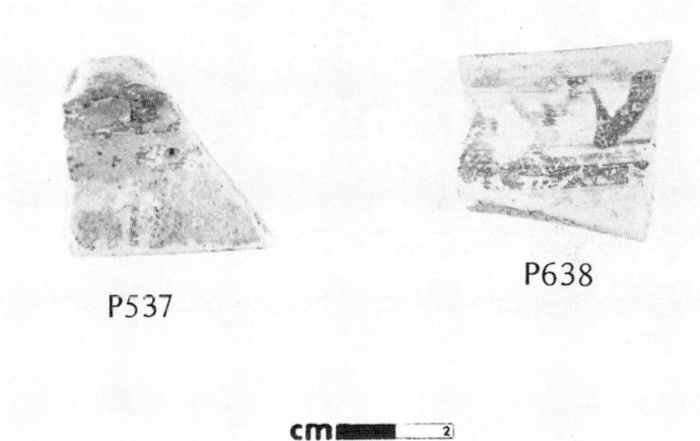

Plate 3-72. DAII krater rims

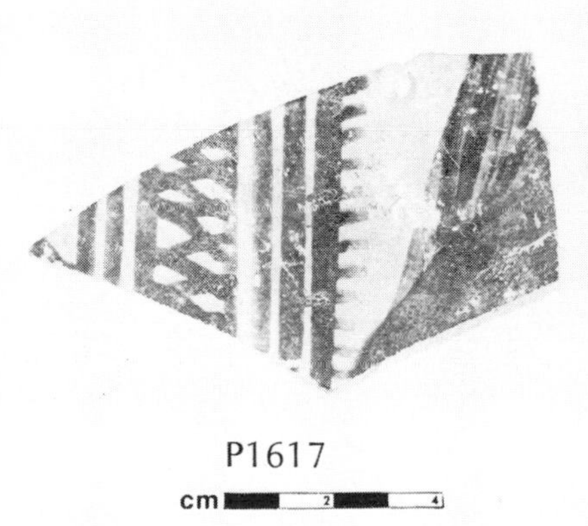

Plate 3-73. Motif 4 (krater)

Plate 3-74. Motif 6 (krater)

Plate 3-75. Motif 7 (krater)

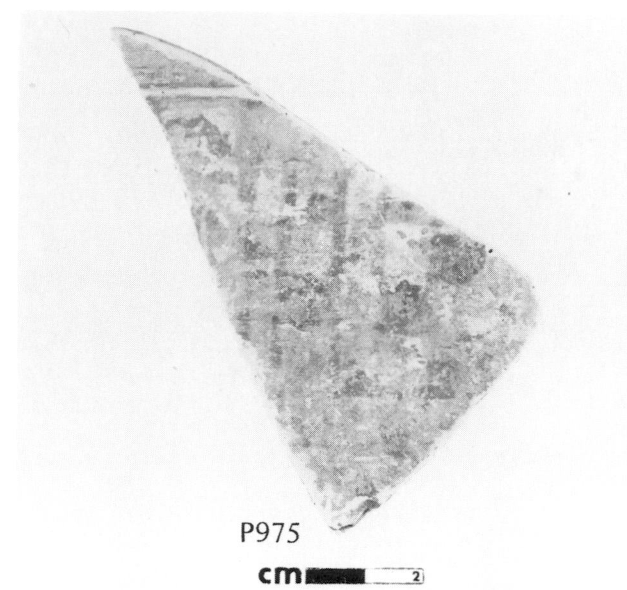

Plate 3-76. Motif 7 (krater)

Plate 3-77. Motif 9 (krater)

Plate 3-78. Strainer fragment

Plate 3-79. Strainer fragment

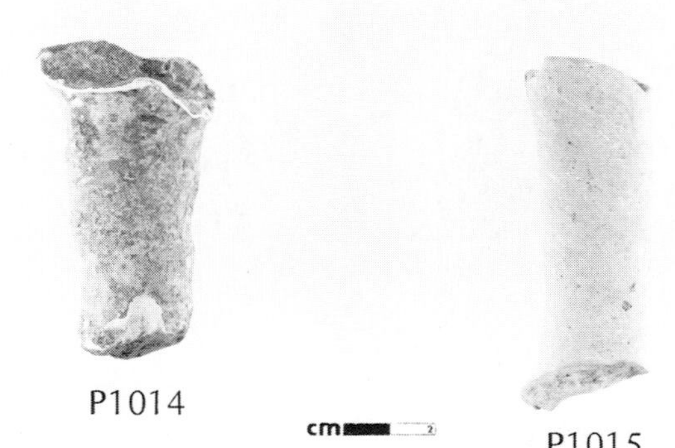

Plate 3-80. Ribbed stems, Type A(?)

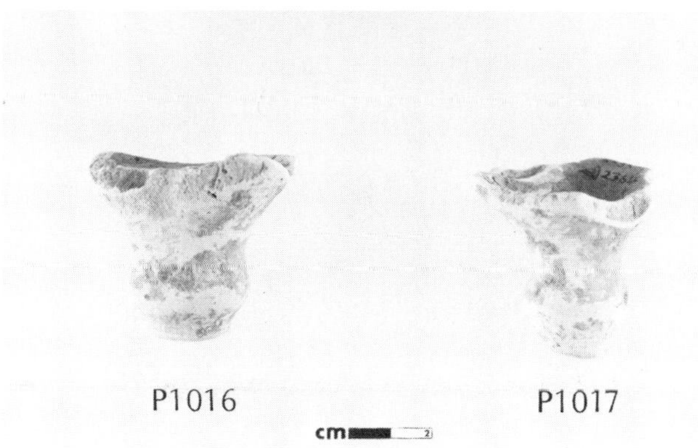

Plate 3-81. Ribbed stems, Type B

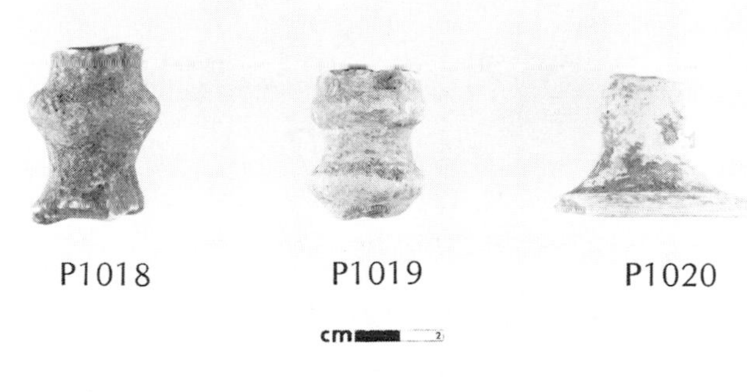

Plate 3-82. Ribbed stems, Type C

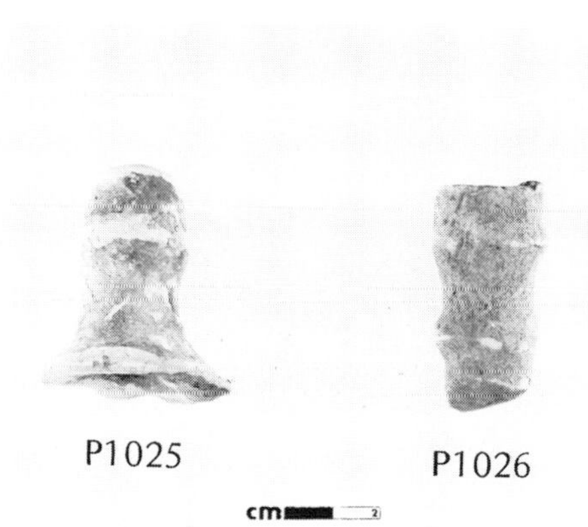

Plate 3-83. Ribbed stems, Type F

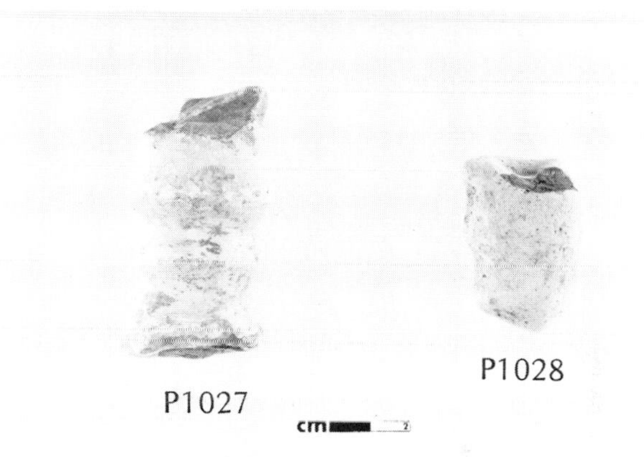

Plate 3-84. Ribbed stems, Type F

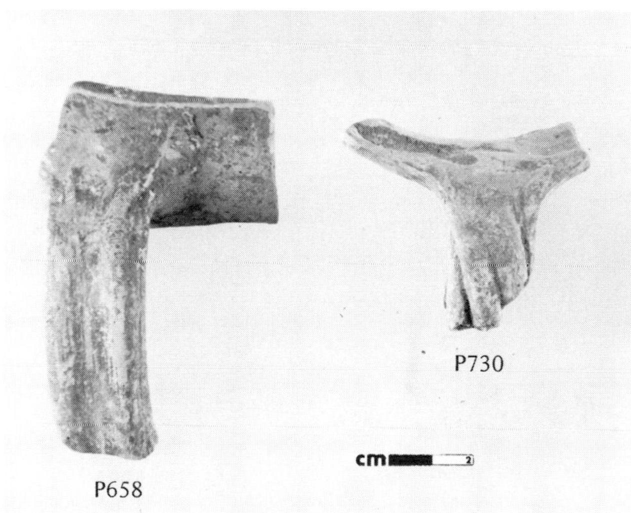

Plate 3-85. Oinochoe/jug handle

Plate 3-86. Oinochoe

Plate 3-87. Oinochoe

Plate 3-88. Motif 2 (oinochoe)

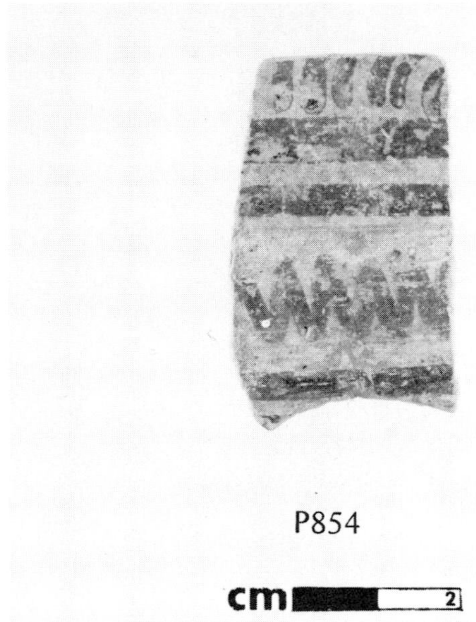

Plate 3-89. Motif 3 (oinochoe)

Plate 3-90. Motif 3 (oinochoe)

Plate 3-91. Motif 3 (oinochoe)

Plate 3-92. Motif 4 (oinochoe)

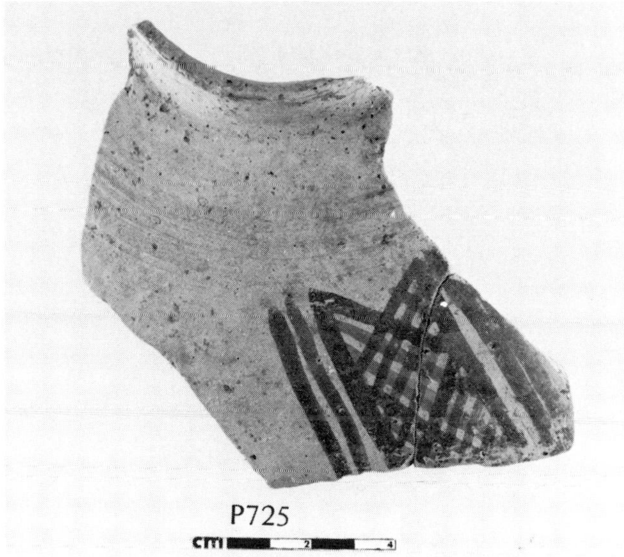

Plate 3-93. Motif 7 (oinochoe)

Plate 3-94. Motif 7 (oinochoe)

Plate 3-95. Motifs 3 and 7 (oinochoe)

Plate 3-96. Motif 8 (oinochoe)

Plate 3-97. Motif 9 (oinochoe)

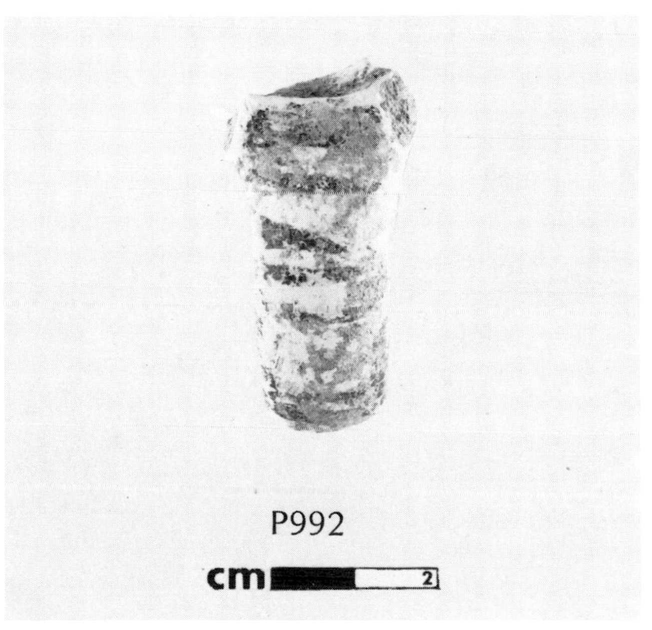

Plate 3-98. Decorated oinochoe/jug handle

Plate 3-99. Amphora rim and neck

Plate 3-100. Decorated fragment of pilgrim flask

Plate 3-101. Tripod foot

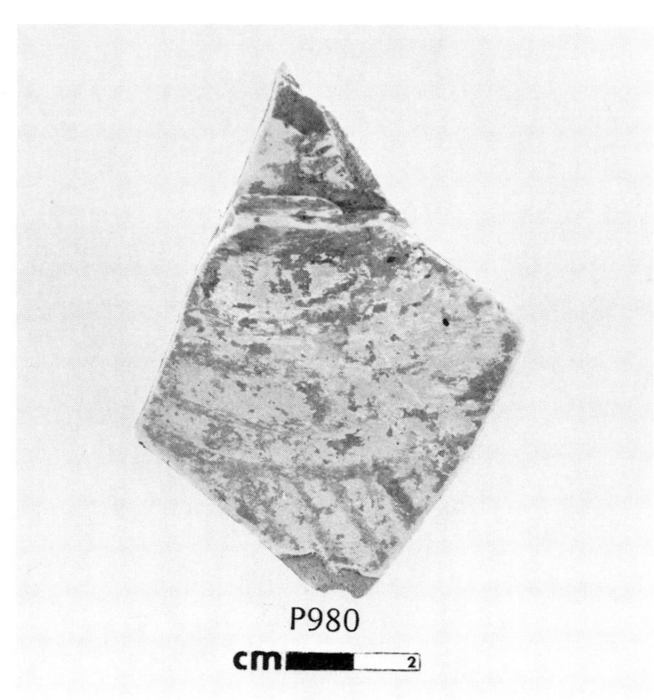

Plate 3-102. Lid fragment (?)

Plate 3-103. Lug

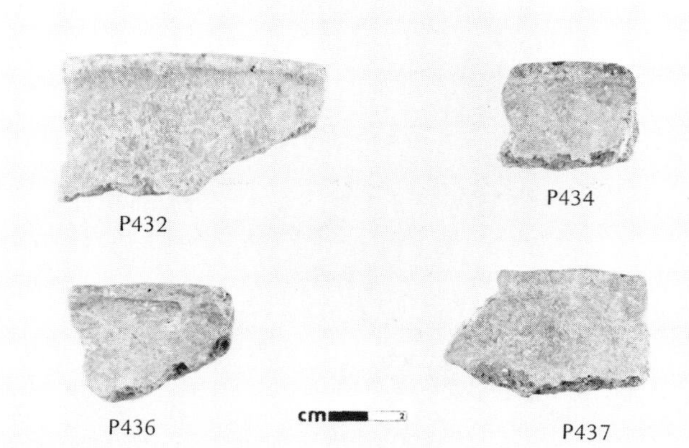

Plate 3-104. DAII, coarse rims

Plate 3-105. Coarse grooved handle

Plate 3-106. Coarse grooved handle

Plate 3-107. Coarse mug

Plate 3-108. Rim fragment with attached lug

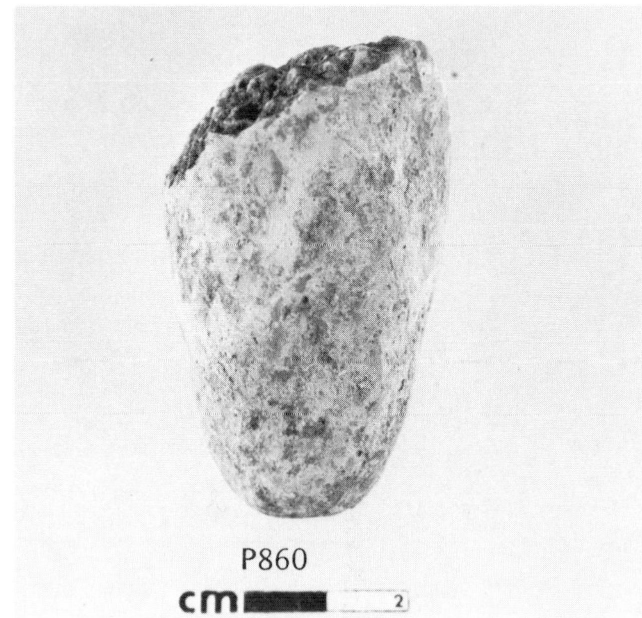

Plate 3-109. Coarse tripod leg

Plate 3-110. Coarse amphora

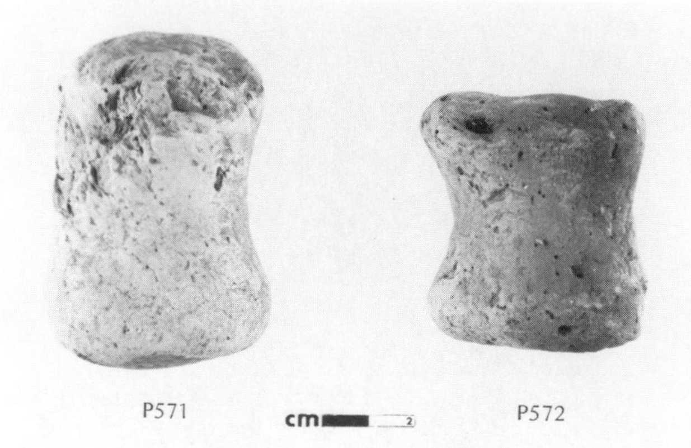

Plate 3-111. Coarse "spools"

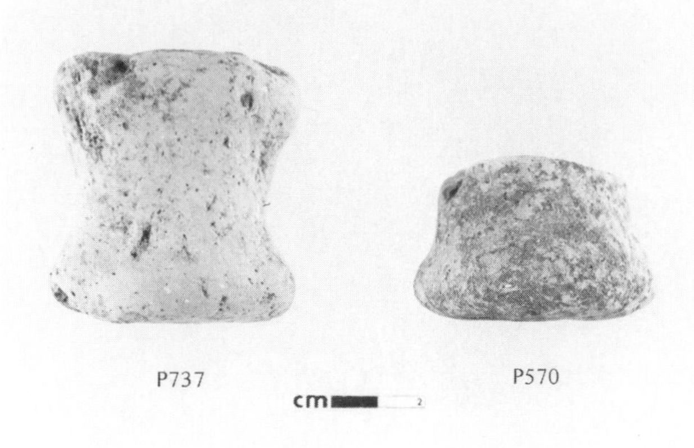

Plate 3-112. Coarse "spools"

Plate 3-113. Motif 4 (pithos)

Plate 3-114. Motif 5 (pithos)

Plate 3-115. Motif 5 (pithos)

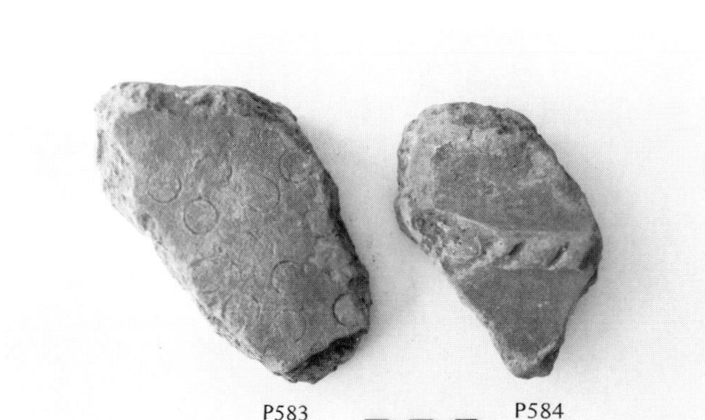

Plate 3-116. Motifs 5 and 10 (pithos)

Plate 3-117. Motif 6 (pithos)

Plate 3-118. Motif 7 (pithos)

Plate 3-119. Motif 8 (pithos)

Plate 3-120. Motif 10 (pithos)

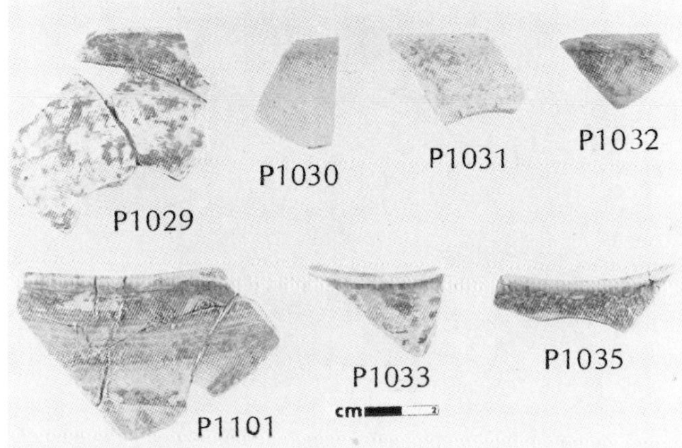

Plate 3-121. DAII/III rims

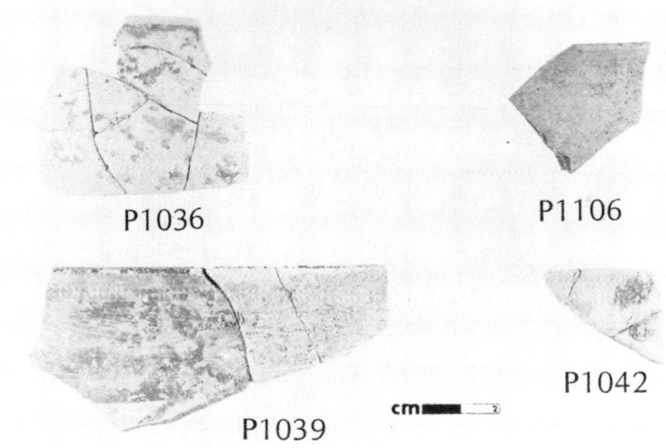

Plate 3-122. DAII/rims

Plate 3-123. Skyphos

Plate 3-124. Decorated krater fragment

Plate 3-125. Ribbed stem

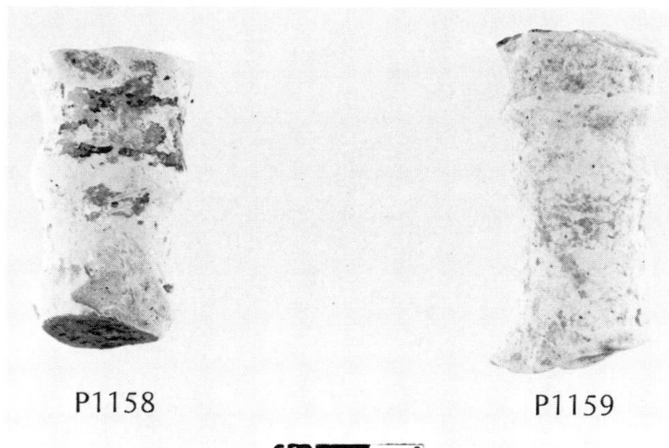

Plate 3-126. Ribbed stems

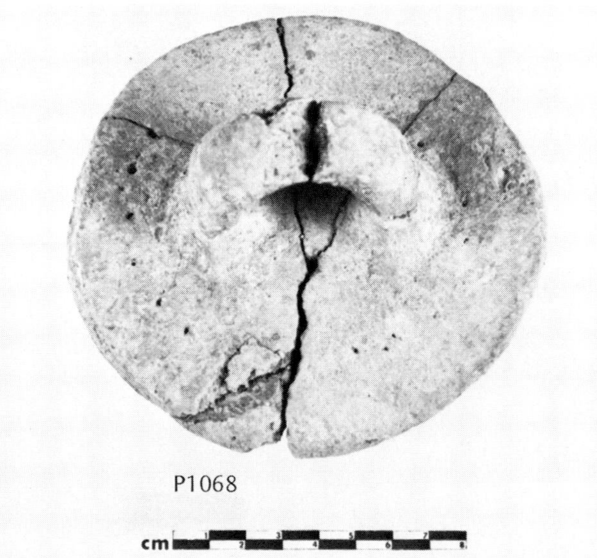

Plate 3-127. Coarse lid

Plate 3-128. Coarse lid

Plate 3-129. Coarse grill fragment (interior)

Plate 3-132. Motif 4

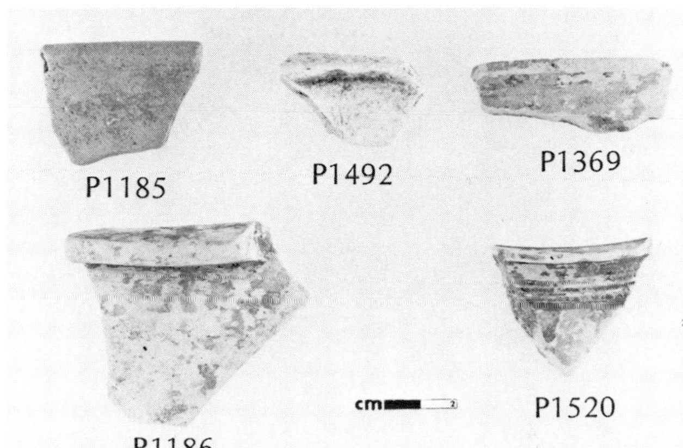

Plate 3-134. DAIII krater rims

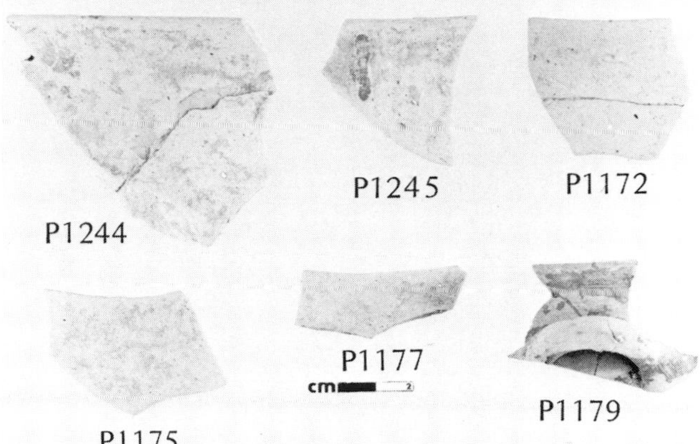

Plate 3-130. DAIII rims

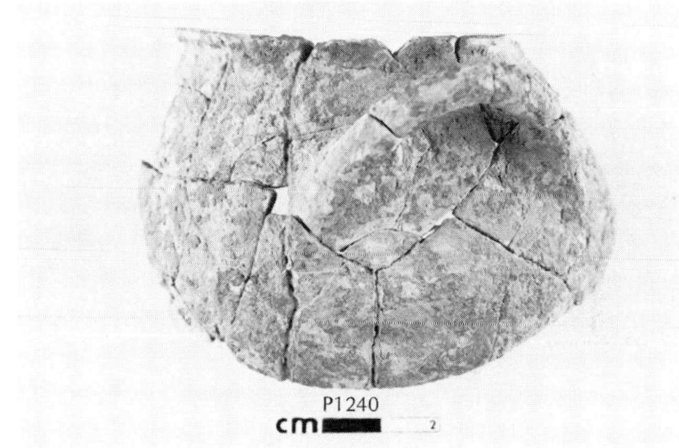

Plate 3-131. Skyphos

Plate 3-133. Cup

Plate 3-135. DAIII krater rims

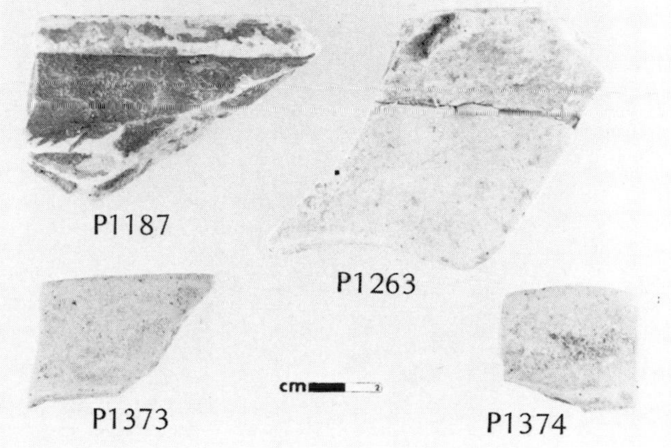

Plate 3-136. Oinochoe rim and neck

Plate 3-137. Oinochoe

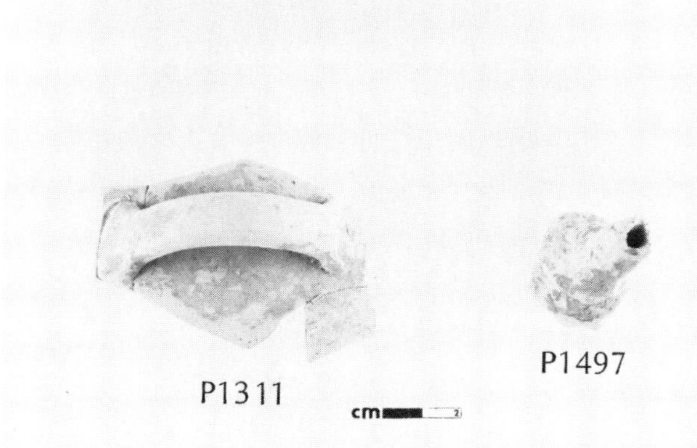

Plate 3-138. Lid (left) and spout (right)

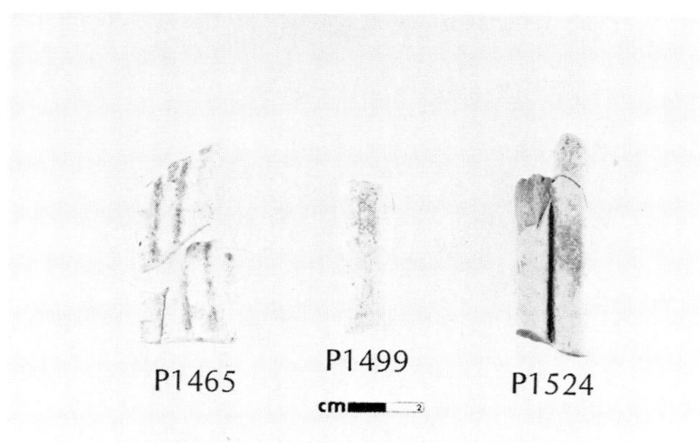

Plate 3-139. Oinochoe/jug handles

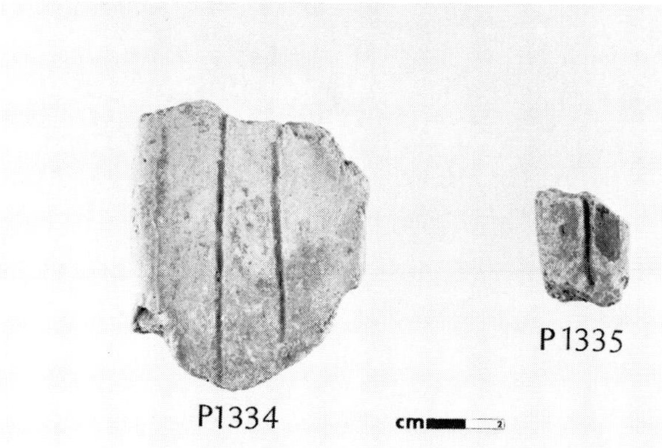

Plate 3-140. Coarse handle fragments

Plate 3-141. Incised base fragment

Plate 3-142. Dipper

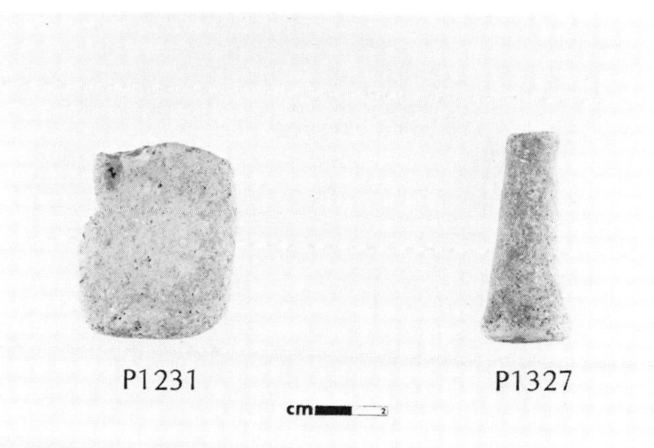

Plate 3-143. Tripod leg (left) and cooking support ("spool") (right)

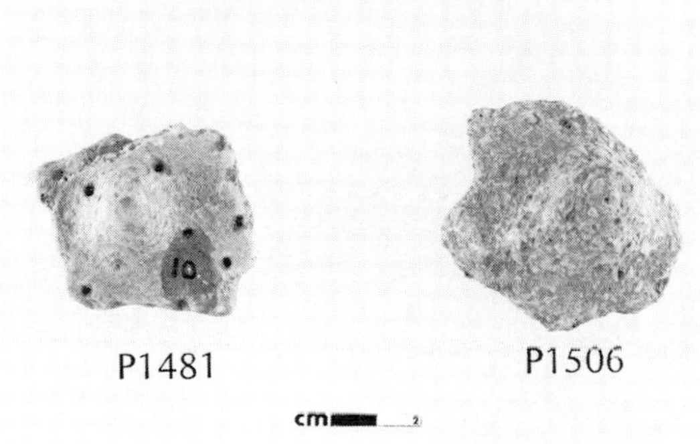

Plate 3-144. Incised body fragment (left) and strainer fragment (right)

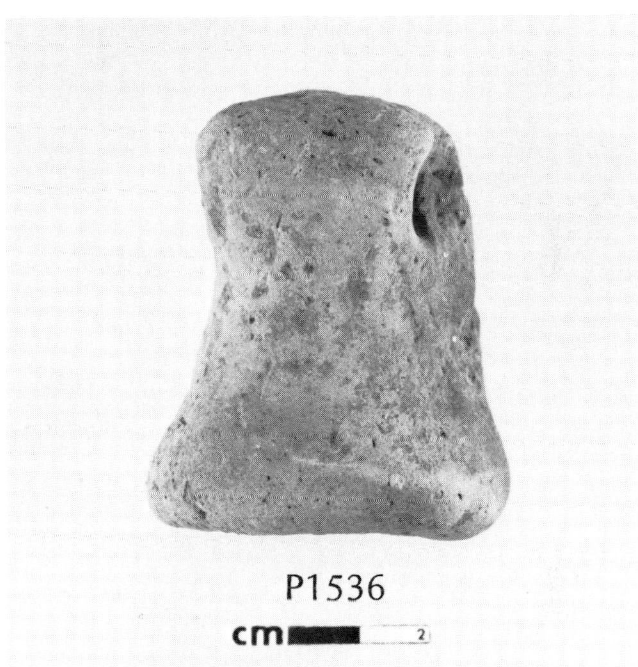

Plate 3-145. Cooking support fragment

Plate 3-146. Cooking stand fragment (exterior)

Plate 3-147. Cooking stand fragment (interior)

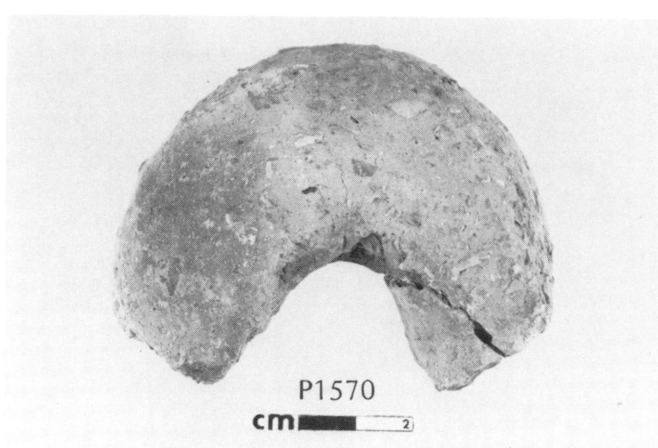

Plate 3-148. Cooking stand fragment

Plate 3-149. Grill fragment

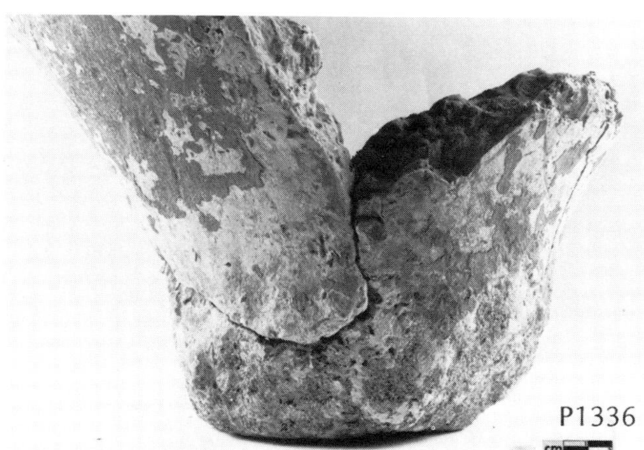

Plate 3-151. Pithos no. 1

Plate 3-150. Pithos no. 1

Plate 3-152. Pithos no. 2

Plate 3-153. Pithos no. 2

Plate 3-154. Pithos base with unbaked core

Plate 3-155. Decorated pithos fragment

Plate 3-156. Decorated pithos fragment

Plate 3-157. Kantharos

Plate 3-158. Shallow bowl

Plate 3-159. Shallow bowl

Plate 3-160. Shallow bowl

Plate 3-161. Cup

Plate 3-162. Pithos

Plate 3-163. Pyxis lid

Plate 3-164. Pyxis lid

Plate 3-165. Kotyle

Plate 3-166. Skyphos

Plate 3-167. Skyphos

Plate 3-168. Skyphos

Plate 3-169. Skyphos

Plate 3-170. Skyphos

Plate 3-171. Cup

Plate 3-172. LG sherd

Plate 4-1. View from near pithos burial, looking E

Plate 4-2. Cairn over pithos burial, from S

Plate 4-3. Stones at W edge of cairn resting on pithos, from S

Plate 4-4. Stones packed against E side of pithos, from SE

Plate 4-5. Upright stones blocking mouth of pithos, from bipod

Plate 4-6. Removing cracked upper sections of pithos

Plate 4-7. Stone over cranium inside mouth of pithos, from bipod

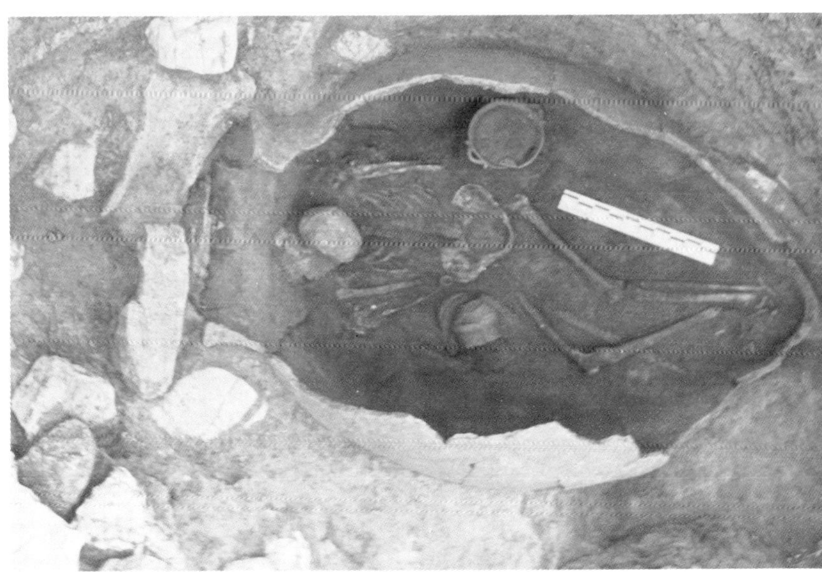

Plate 4-8. Skeleton and grave goods inside pithos, from E

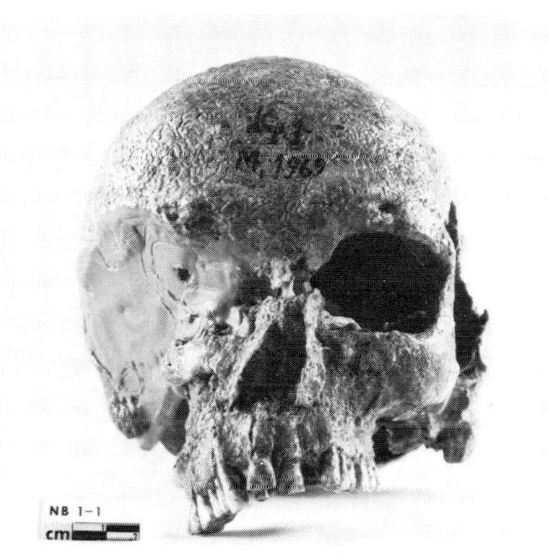

Plate 4-9. Nichoria Burial 1-1. Frontal view of reconstructed cranium

Plate 4-10. Nichoria Burial 1-1. Laterial view of reconstructed cranium

Plate 4-12. Nichoria Burial 1-1. Vertical view of reconstructed cranium

Plate 4-11. Nichoria Burial 1-1. Occipital view of reconstructed cranium

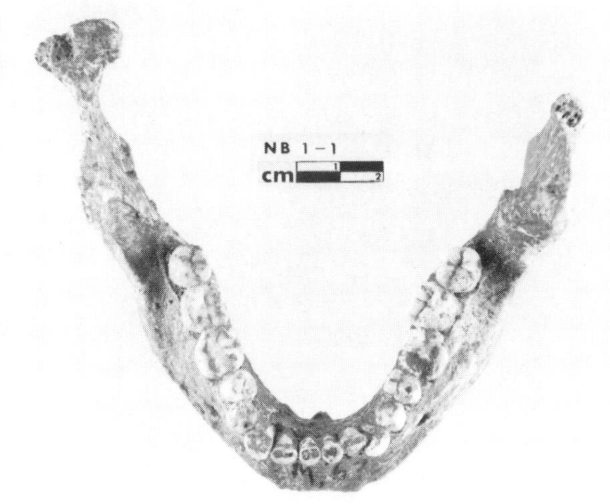

Plate 4-13. Nichoria Burial 1-1. Vertical view of mandible

Plate 4-14. Lambropoulos cist grave no. 1, from S

Plate 4-15. Lambropoulos cist grave no. 1, from NE

Plate 4-16. Lambropoulos cist grave no. 2, from E

Plate 4-17. Lambropoulos cist grave no. 2, from SW

Plate 4-18. Lambropoulos cist grave no. 3, from W

Plate 4-19. Lambropoulos cist grave no. 3, from SW

Plate 4-20. Lambropoulos cist grave no. 4, from W

Plate 4-21. Lambropoulos cist grave no. 4, from W

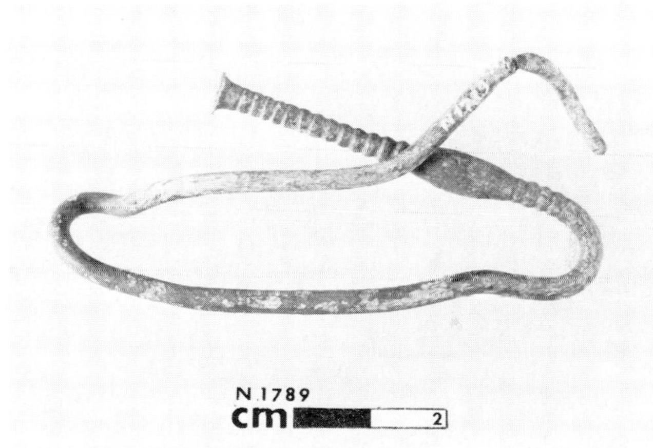

Plate 5-1. Bronze pin – bead and moldings (**5**)

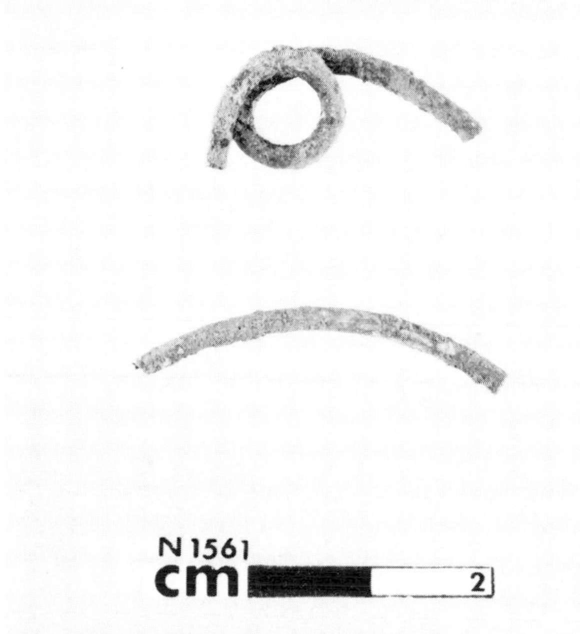

Plate 5-2. Bronze arched bow fibula (**8**)

Plate 5-3. Bronze shield boss/phalaron (**52**)

Plate 5-4. Bronze "collar," side view (**53**)

Plate 5-5. Bronze "collar," ¾ top view (**53**)

Plate 5-6. Bronze "collar," top view (**53**)

Plate 5-7. Component of large bronze object (**57**)

Plate 5-8. Bronze quadruped on stand, profile view (**58**)

Plate 5-9. Bronze quadruped on stand, bottom view (**58**)

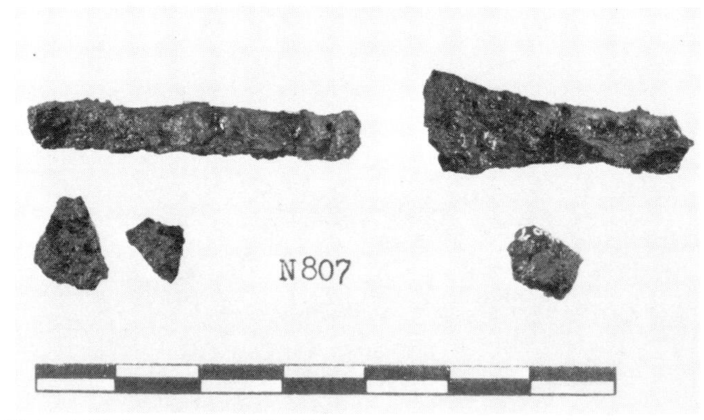

Plate 5-10. Iron tweezer(?) (**86**)

Plate 5-11. Fragment of iron ax head (**87**)

Plate 5-12. Iron weaving instrument(?) (**89**)

Plate 5-13. Bronze phiale (**122**)

Plate 5-14. Iron sword (**124**)

Plate 5-15. Terra-cotta whorl, Type A (**160**)

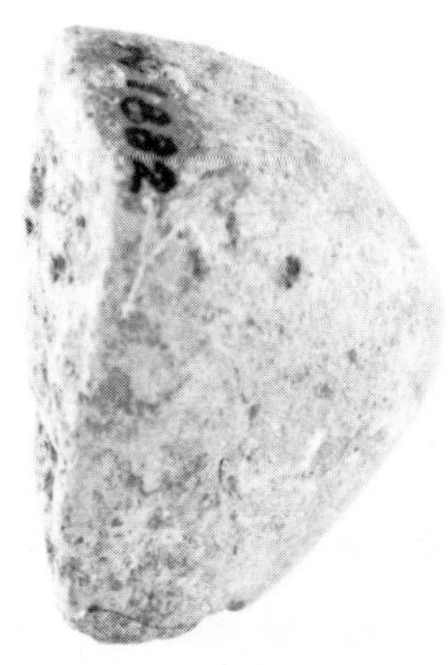

Plate 5-16. Terra-cotta whorl, Type A (**166**)

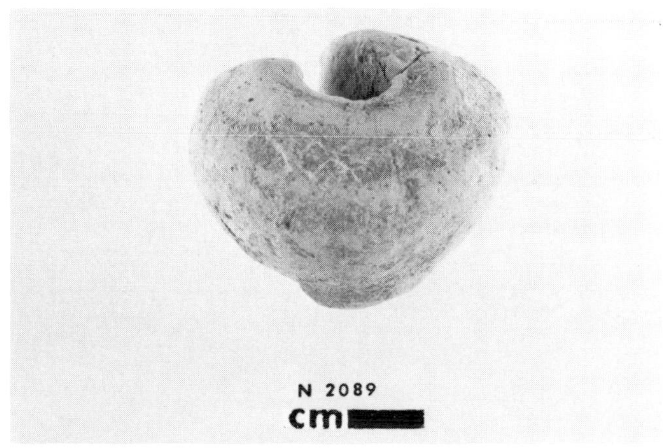

Plate 5-17. Terra-cotta whorl, Type A (**169**)

Plate 5-18. Terra-cotta whorl, Type A (**230**)

Plate 5-19. Terra-cotta whorl, Type B (**163**)

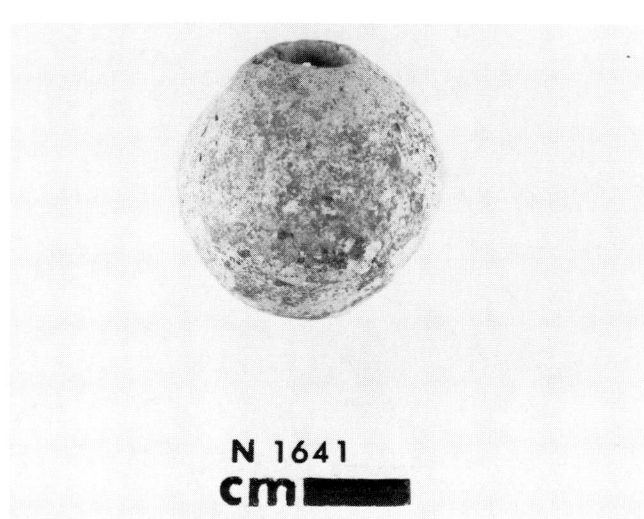

Plate 5-20. Terra-cotta whorl, Type B (**194**)

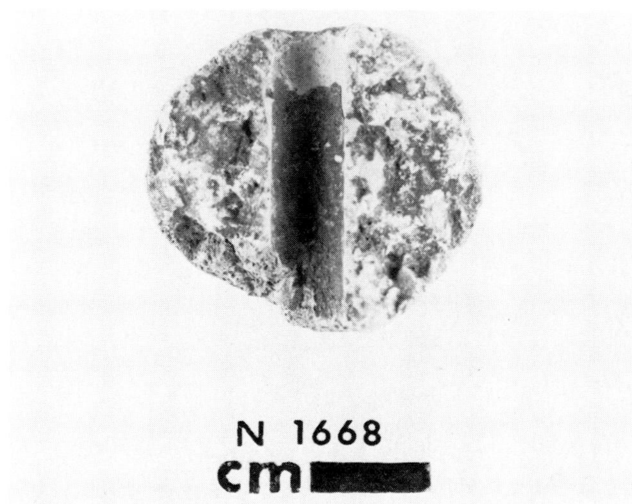

Plate 5-21. Terra-cotta whorl, Type C (**157**)

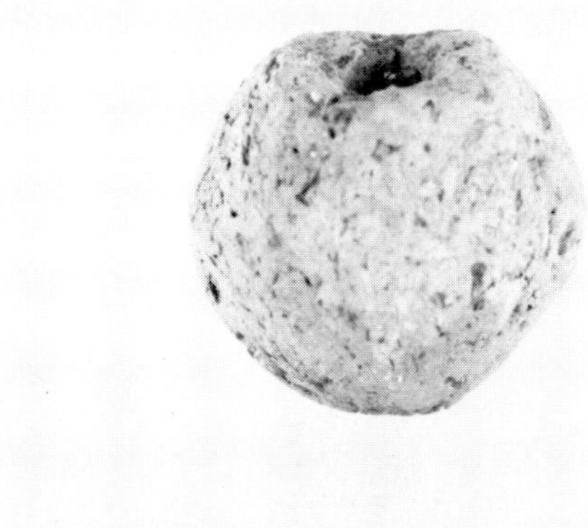

Plate 5-22. Terra-cotta whorl, Type C (**126**)

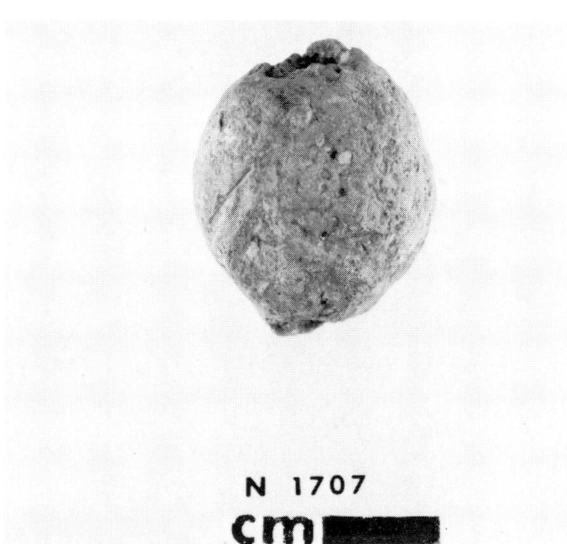

Plate 5-23. Terra-cotta whorl, Type C (**226**)

Plate 5-24. Terra-cotta whorl, Type D (**215**)

Plate 5-25. Terra-cotta whorl, Type E (**144**)

Plate 5-26. Terra-cotta whorl, Type E (**218**)

Plate 5-27. Terra-cotta whorl, Type F (**168**)

Plate 5-28. Terra-cotta whorl, Type G (**141**)

Plate 5-29. Terra-cotta whorl, Type H (**158**)

Plate 5-30. Terra-cotta whorl, Type H (**154**)

Plate 5-31. Terra-cotta whorl, Type H (**155**)

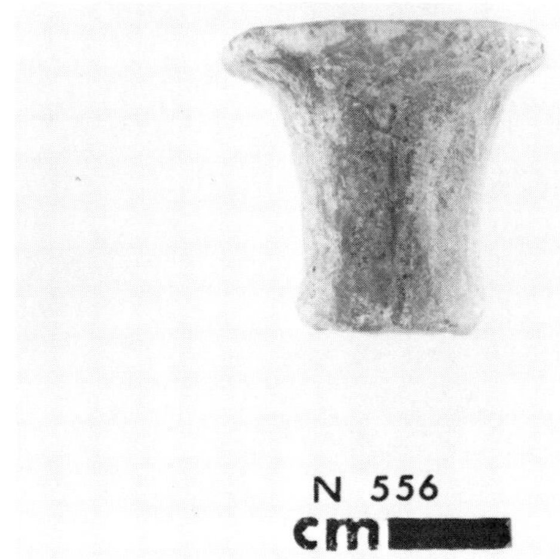

Plate 5-32. Terra-cotta whorl, Type H (**173**)

Plate 5-33. Terra-cotta whorl, Type H (**190**)

Plate 5-34. Terra-cotta whorl, Type J (**201**)

Plate 5-35. Terra-cotta whorl, Type J (**225**)

Plate 5-36. Terra-cotta whorl, Type J (**167**)

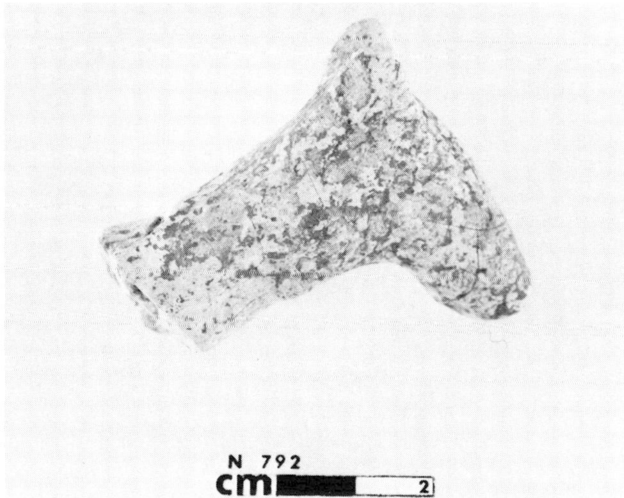

Plate 5-39. Terra-cotta animal head (**232**)

Plate 5-40. Bone bead (**233**)

Plate 5-37. Terra-cotta whorl, Type L (**217**)

Plate 5-38. Terra-cotta whorl, Type H (**159**)

Plate 5-41. Fragment of worked stone (**235**)

Plate 5-42. Stone celt (**236**)

Plate 5-44. Grinder and palette(?) (**238**)

Plate 5-45. Whetstone or pendant (**239**)

Plate 5-43. Whetstone or pendant (**237**)

Plate 5-46. Inscribed stone plaque (**240**)

Plate 7-1. Mug.

Plate 7-2. One-handled cup

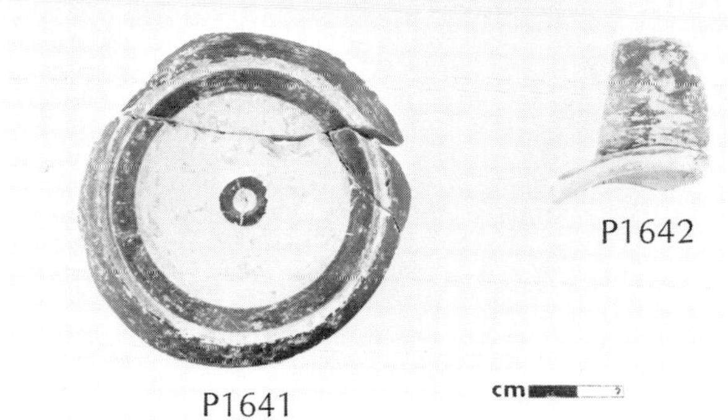

Plate 7-3. Mug bases

Plate 7-4. Lekythos

Plate 7-5. Bronze coin of Messene showing Zeus Ithomatas

Plate 7-6. Wall Q, from S

Plate 7-7. Possible temple podium, from balloon

Plate 7-8. Tear bottles, from *apothetis*, Soudhes (Feature 18)

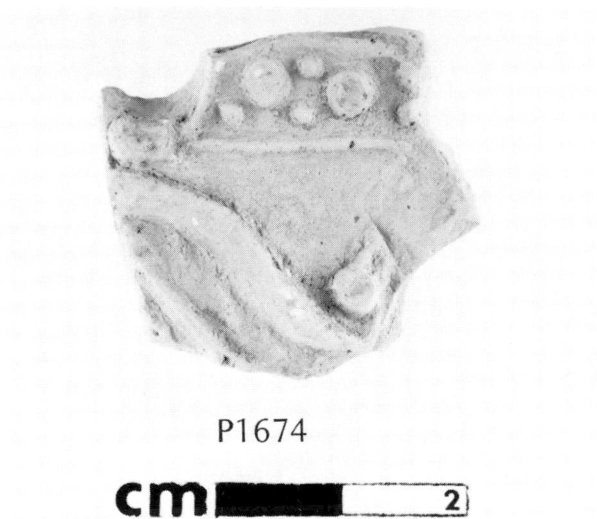

Plate 7-9. Bowl rim.

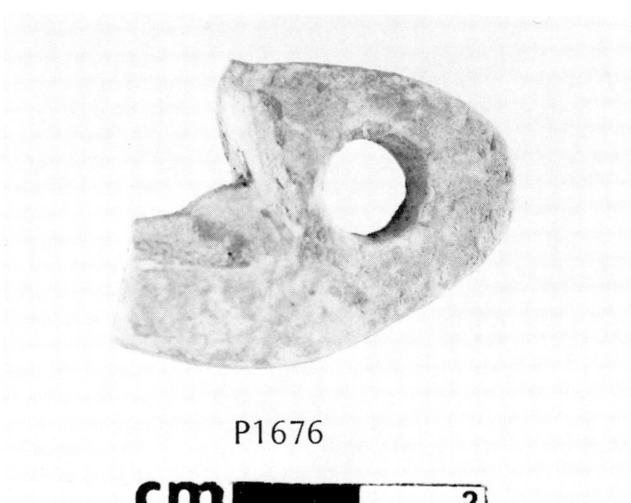

Plate 7-10. Lamp handle

Plate 8-2. Trypetorachi, rounded hill immediately SE of Nichoria ridge

Plate 8-1. Outline of kiln, Feature 45, Karia valley

Plate 8-3. Church of Ayios Vasilios, near Paniperi, from E

Plate 8-4. Church of Ayios Vasilios, Paniperi, detail of apse

Plate 8-5. Church of the Panayia, near Paniperi, from E

Plate 8-6. Late Roman(?) building, Petalidhi acropolis

Plate 8-7. Coin of Constans I (Feature 26), obverse and reverse

Plate 9-1. Area II, from balloon. N at top of picture

Plate 9-2. Earth fill in Wall A, Unit II-1

Plate 9-3. Orthostates of Wall B, Unit II-1, propped up by small stone wedges

Plate 9-4. Orthostates alternating with smaller stones laid flat, S face of Wall H, Unit II-2

Plate 9-5. Uneven lowest course of Wall C, Unit II-1 resting on Mycenaean remains, from W

Plate 9-6. Wall A, Unit II-1, set directly above Mycenaean vase, from NE

Plate 9-7. Wall D resting on fill containing Byzantine pottery, Unit II-1, from N

Plate 9-8. Depression with Mycenaean pavement and retaining walls, from bipod

Plate 9-9. Stone tumble, tile fragments, and humus N of Wall E, from N

Plate 9-10. Room 2, Unit II-2, from bipod

Plate 9-11. Stones fallen from Wall I, Unit II-2, from NE

Plate 9-12. Room 1, Unit II-2, with broken pottery on floor, from NE

Plate 9-13. Room 2 and Wall J, Unit II-2, from bipod

Plate 9-14. Room 2, Unit II-2, during excavation, from NE

Plate 9-15. Shallow depression in K25 Ia, with base of large ribbed jar, from SW

Plate 9-16. Medieval field Wall L in center foreground, overlying DA and LH levels, from S

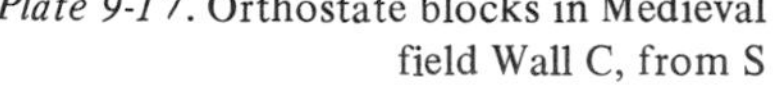

Plate 9-17. Orthostate blocks in Medieval field Wall C, from S

Plate 9-18. Unit IV-2, from balloon

Plate 9-19. Unit IV-2, mosaic of bipod photos

Plate 9-20. Unit IV-2, Phase 1, layer of stone rubble, from SW

Plate 9-21. Unit IV-2, Phase 1, layer of fallen roof tiles, mosaic of bipod photos

Plate 9-22. Unit IV-2, Phase 2, looking W at foundations of Wall R

Plate 9-23. Broken amphora in Room 3, Unit IV-2, Phase 2

Plate 9-24. Unit IV-2, early stage of clearing chapel, from W

Plate 9-25. Unit IV-2, the chapel, from E

Plate 9-26. Unit IV-2, E end of chapel, from SW

Plate 9-27. Unit IV-2, NE corner of chapel, Wall O built over Wall P

Plate 9-28. Unit IV-2, the narthex, from S

Plate 9-29. Unit IV-2, bases of glazed bowls in floor packing of narthex

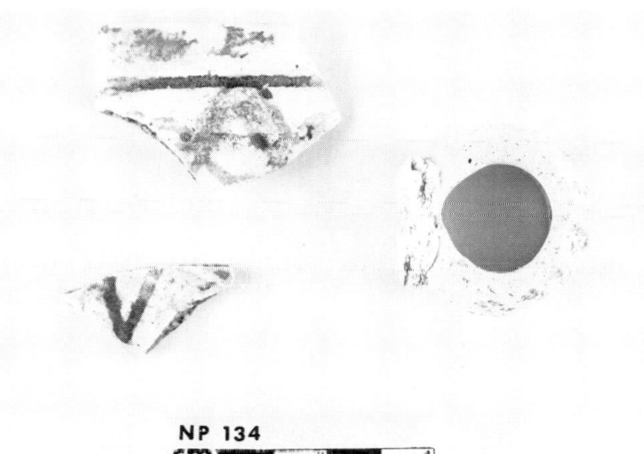

Plate 10-1. Cup (**P1667**)

NP 138
cm 2

Plate 10-3. Plate (**P1679**)

Plate 9-30. Unit L21-1, from balloon

NP 135
cm 2

Plate 10-2. Jug (**P1678**)

Plate 10-4. Spongy Ware, rim fragments (**P1683-89**)

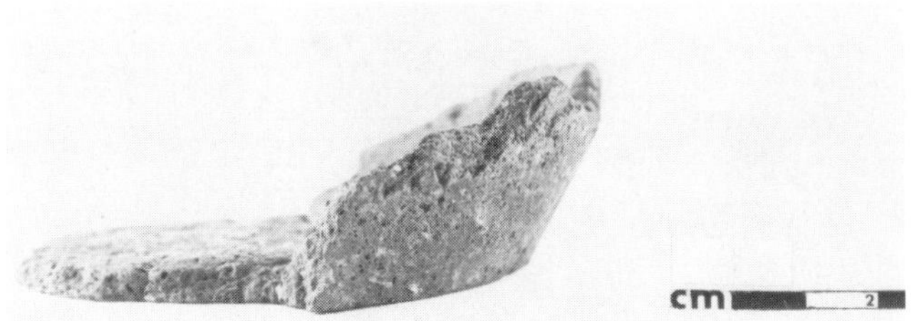

Plate 10-5. Spongy Ware jug/jar (**P1680**)

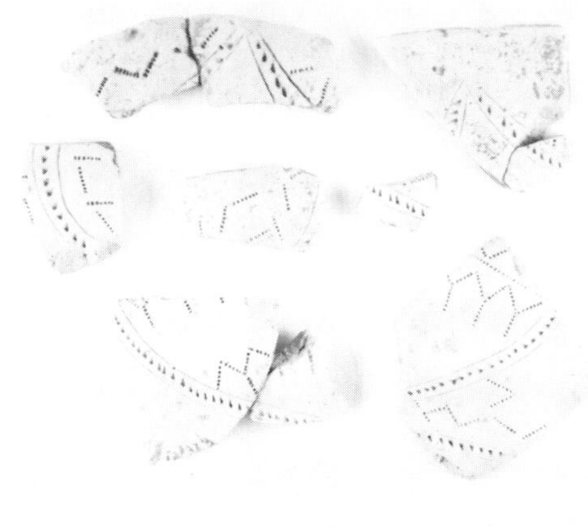

Plate 10-7. Jug(?) (**P1696**)

Plate 10-10. Amphora (**P1756**)

Plate 10-6. Jug(?) (**P1690**)

Plate 10-8. Stand(?) (**P1697**)

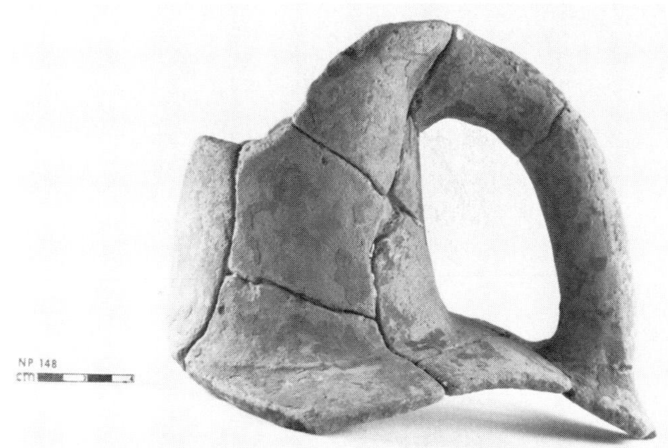

Plate 10-9. Amphora (**P1698**)

Plate 10-11. Bowl (**P1707**)

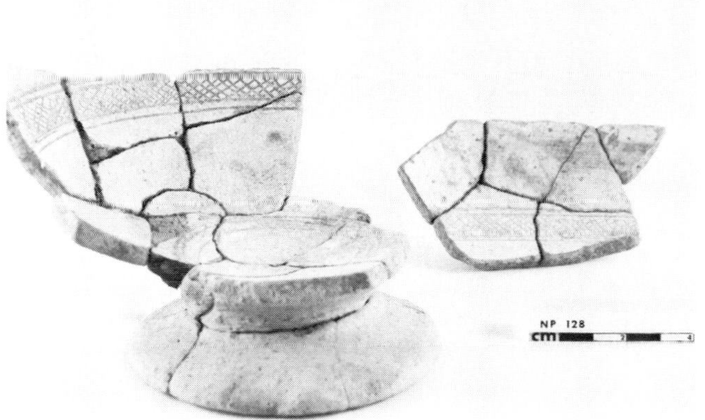

Plate 10-12. Bowl (**P1708**)

Plate 10-13. Bowl (**P1709**)

Plate 10-14. Bowl (**P1710**)

Plate 10-15. Bowl (**P1711**)

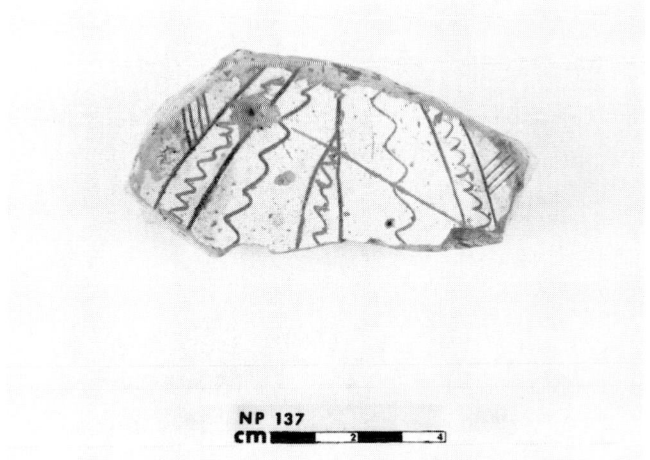

Plate 10-16. Bowl (**P1712**)

Plate 10-17. Bowl (**P1713**)

Plate 10-18. Bowl (**P1714**)

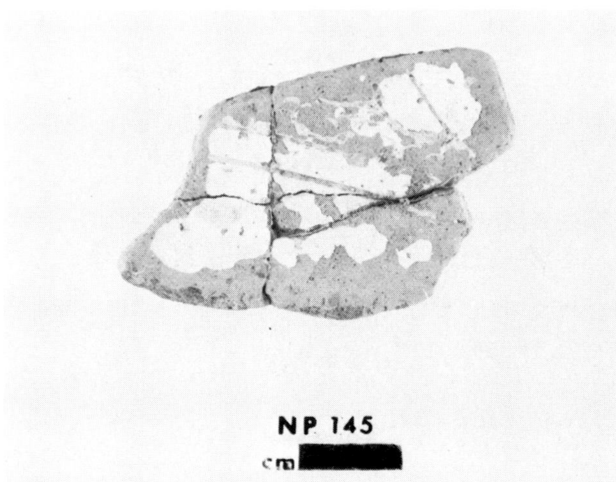

Plate 10-20. Bowl(?) (**P1716**)

Plate 10-19. Bowl (**P1715**)

Plate 10-21. Bowl (**P1717**)

Plate 10-23. Bowl (**P1719**)

Plate 10-22. Bowl(?) (**P1718**)

Plate 10-24. Bowl (**P1720**)

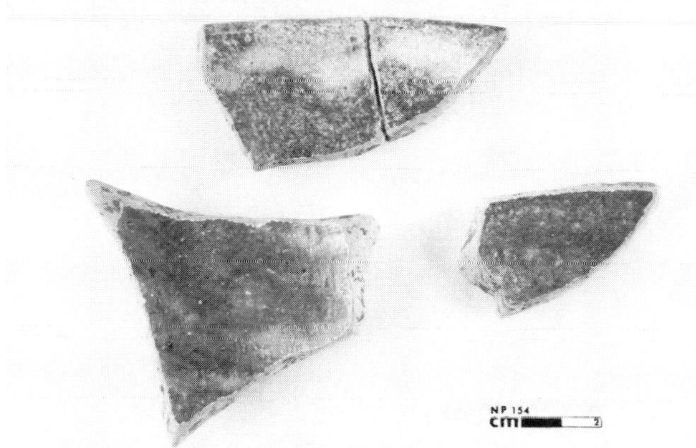

Plate 10-26. Bowl (**P1722**)

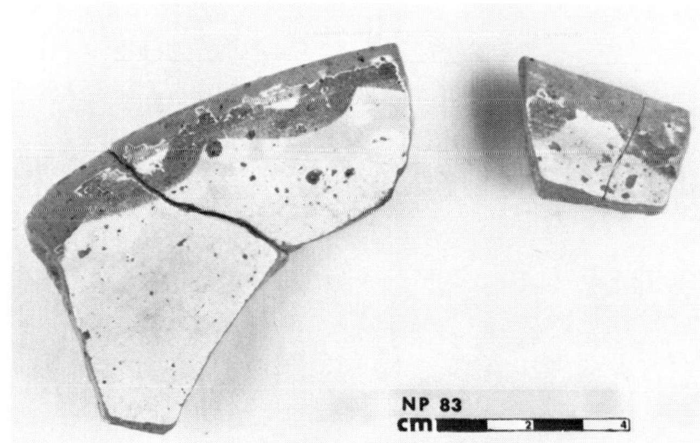

Plate 10-28. Plate (**P1724**)

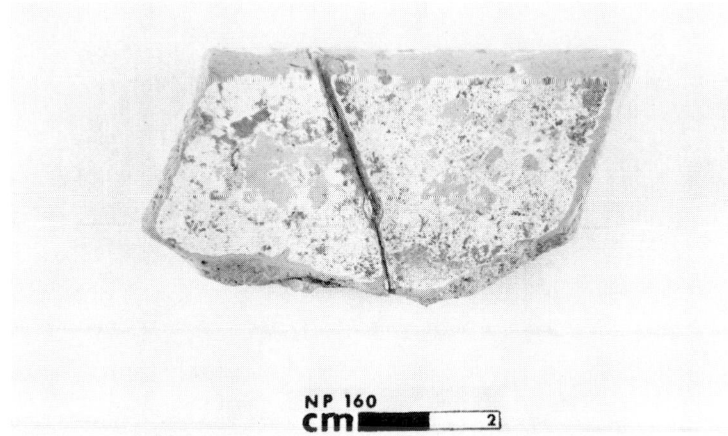

Plate 10-25. Bowl (**P1721**)

Plate 10-27. Bowl (**P1723**)

Plate 10-29. Bowl (**P1725**)

Plate 10-30. Bowl (**P1726**)

Plate 10-31. Bowl (**P1727**)

Plate 10-34. Brazier (**P1731**)

Plate 10-32. Bowl (**P1728**)

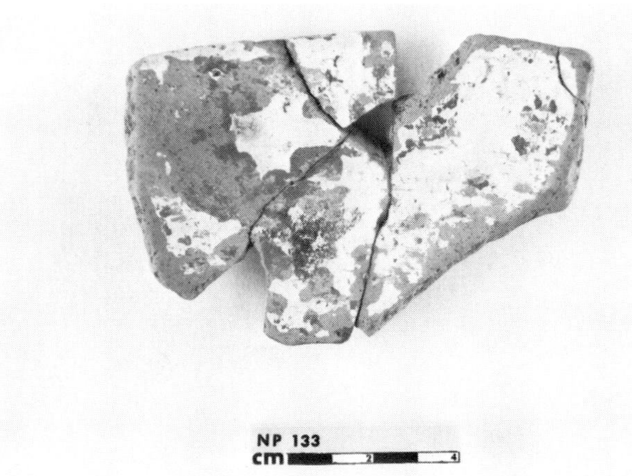

Plate 10-33. Bowl (**P1730**)

Plate 10-35. Brazier (**P1732**)

Plate 10-36. Jug (**P1733**)

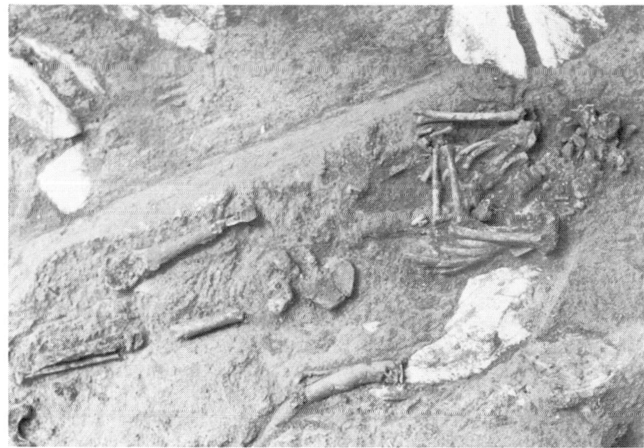

Plate 11-1. Nichoria Burial 12-1. Child Burial outside E end of chapel

Plate 11-3. Nichoria Burial 10-1. Adult female burial at SE corner of chapel, after cleaning

Plate 11-2. Nichoria Burial 10-1. Adult female burial at SE corner of chapel, before removal of cover slabs

Plate 11-5. Nichoria Burial 9-1. Vertical view of calvarium. Note open metopic suture

Plate 11-4. Nichoria Burial 9-1. Adult female burial in upper fill of tholos stomion

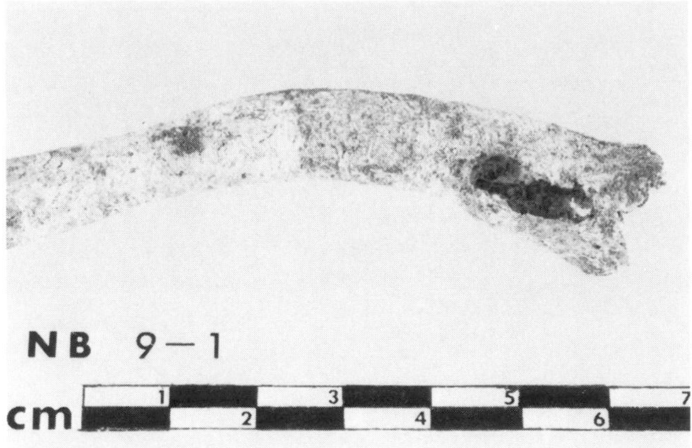

Plate 11-6. Nichoria Burial 9-1. Osteomyelitic lesion in medial end of right clavicle

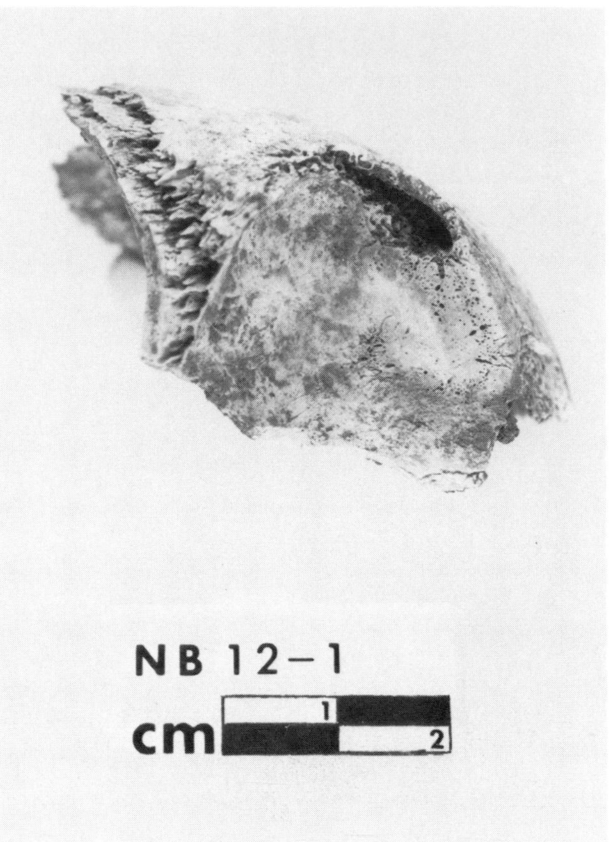

Plate 11-7. Nichoria Burial 12-1. Right orbital region

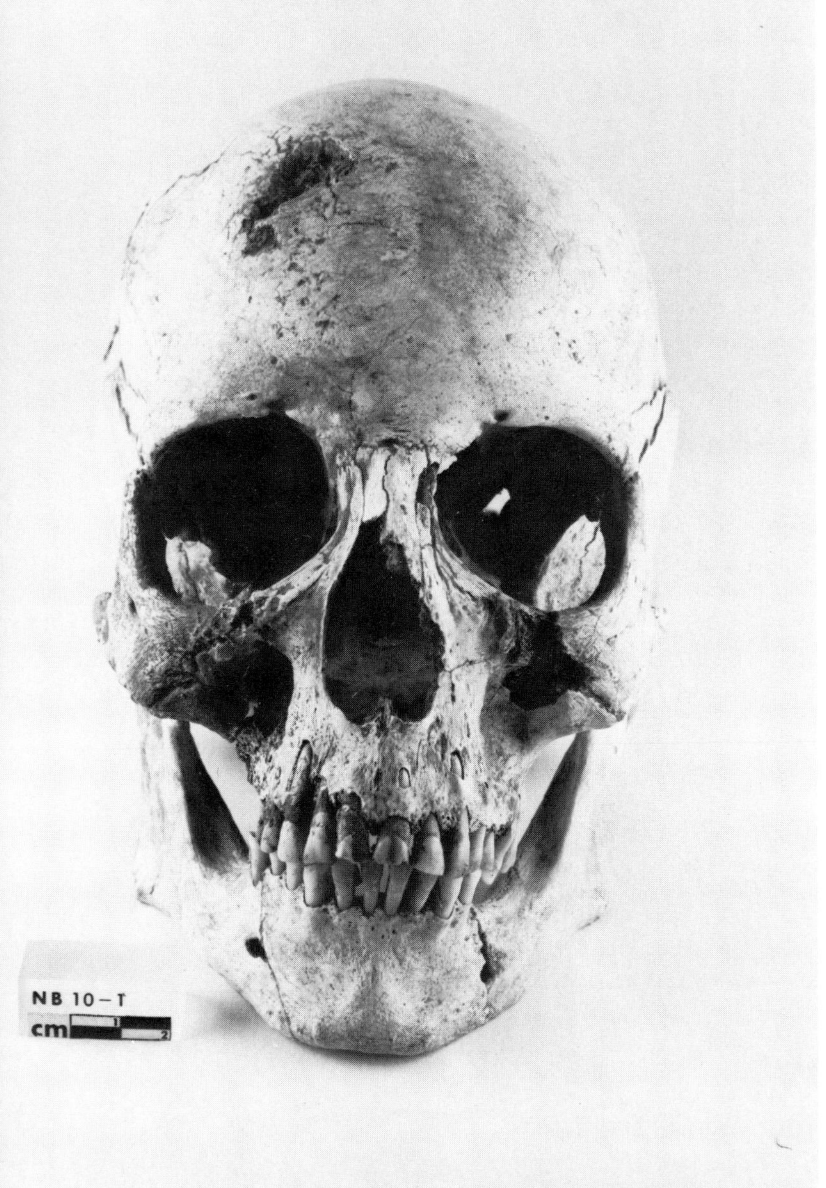

Plate 11-8. Nichoria Burial 10-1. Frontal view of cranium

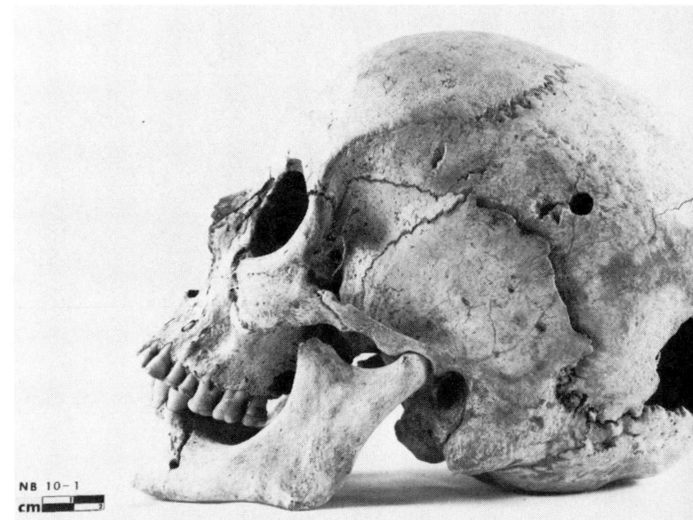

Plate 11-9. Nichoria Burial 10-1. Lateral view of cranium

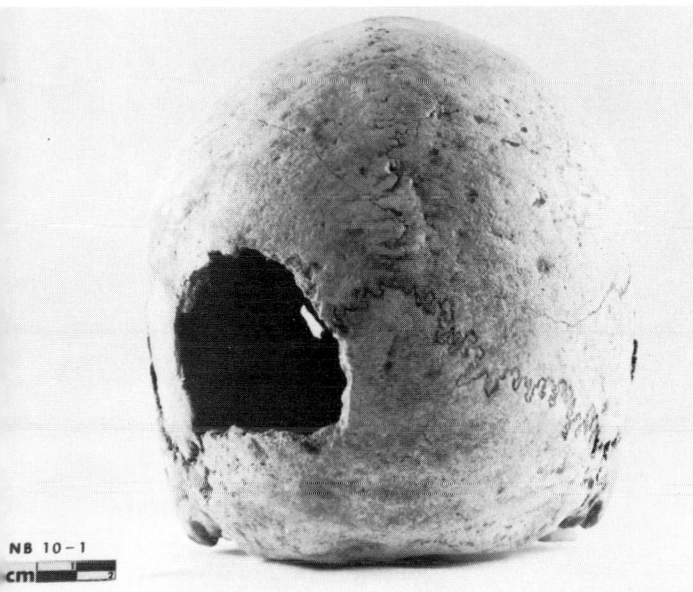

Plate 11-10. Nichoria Burial 10-1. Occipital view of cranium

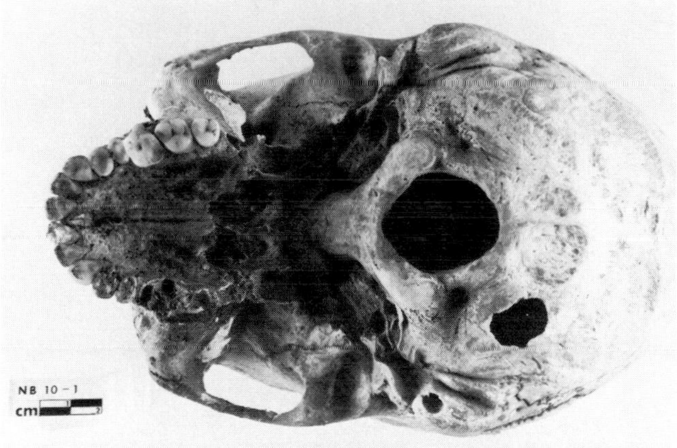

Plate 11-11. Nichoria Burial 10-1. Basal view of cranium

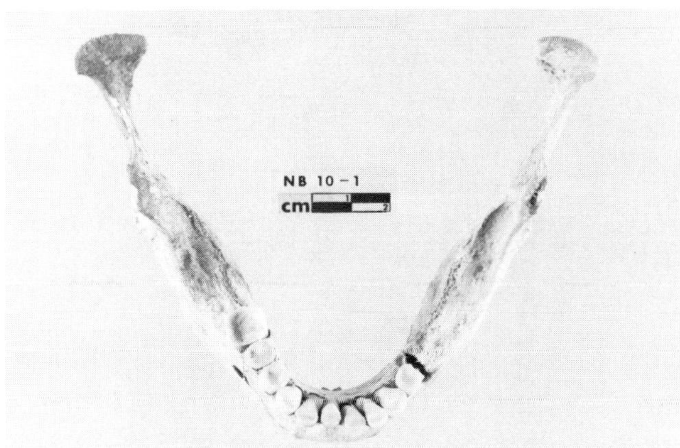

Plate 11-13. Nichoria Burial 10-1. Vertical view of mandible

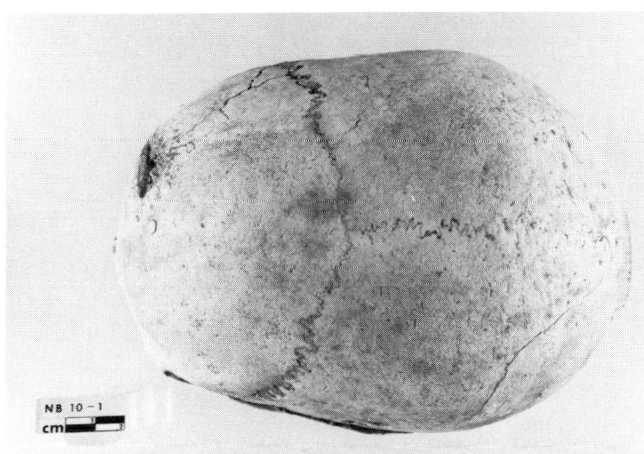

Plate 11-12. Nichoria Burial 10-1. Vertical view of cranium

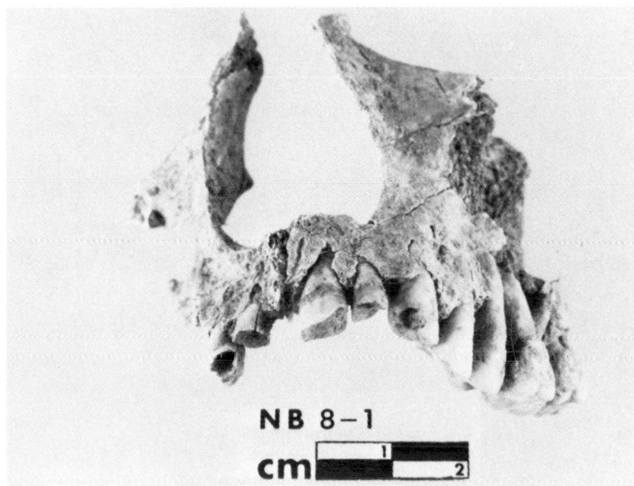

Plate 11-15. Nichoria Burial 8-1. Frontal view of maxilla

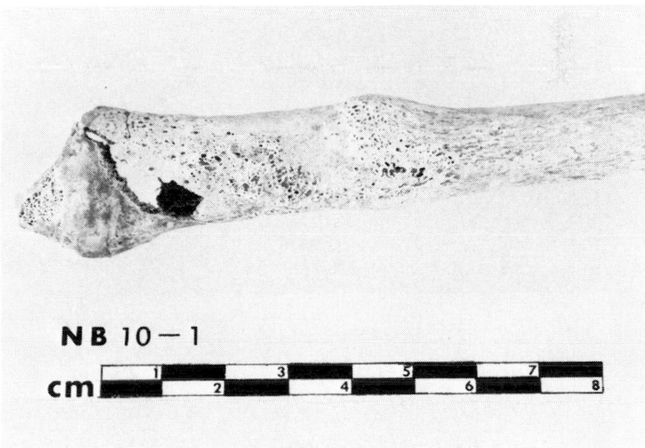

Plate 11-14. Nichoria Burial 10-1. Healed fracture in distal shaft of left fibula

Plate 12-1. Bronze coin of Basil II and Constantine VII, obverse and reverse (**501**)

Plate 12-2. Bronze coin of Manuel I comnenus, obverse and reverse (**502**)

Plate 12-3. Bronze coin of Constantine I, obverse and reverse (**503**)

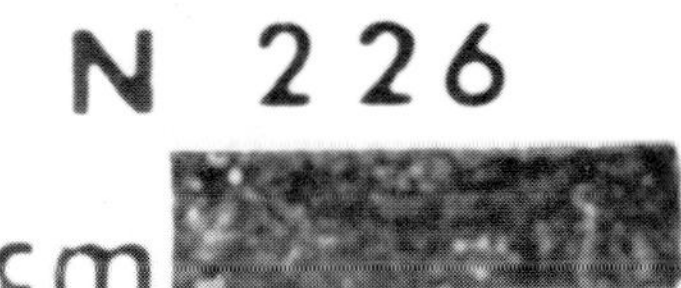

Plate 12-4. Bronze buckle (**504**)

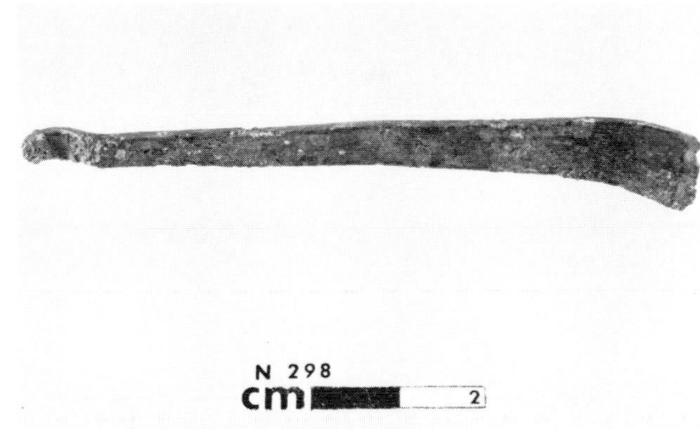

Plate 12-7. Bronze tweezers (**509**)

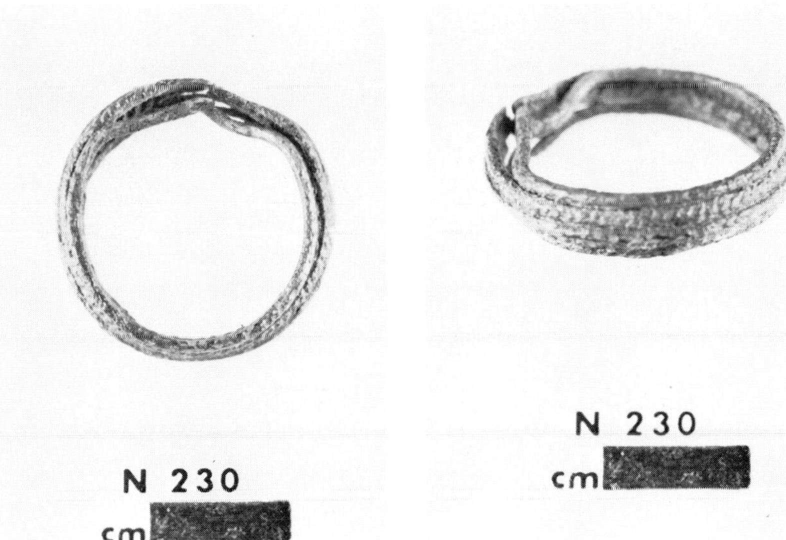

Plate 12-5. Bronze finger ring (**506**)

Plate 12-6. Bronze earring (**508**)

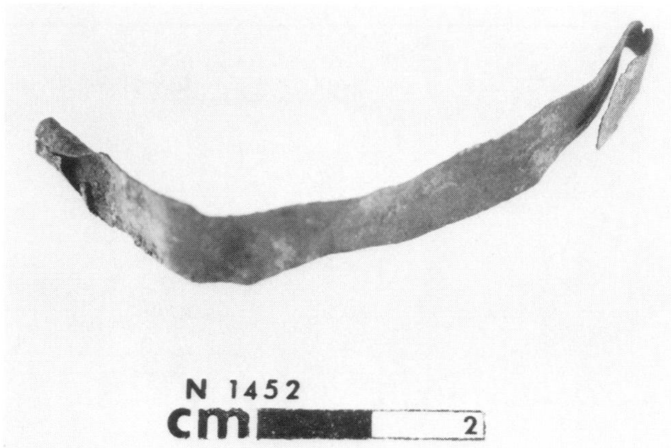

Plate 12-8. Bronze fillet (**513**)

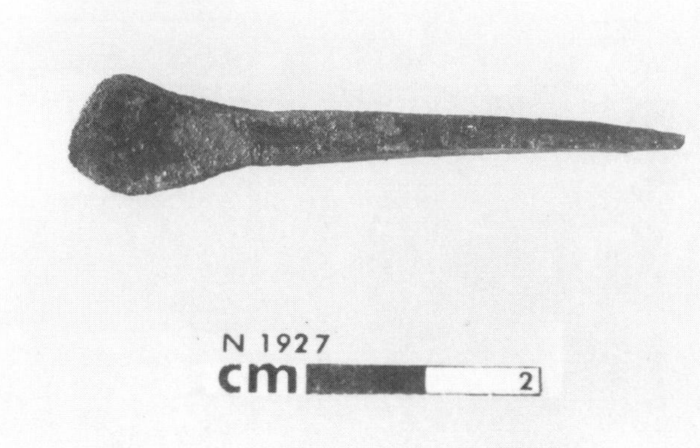

Plate 12-9. Bronze stylus(?) (**519**)

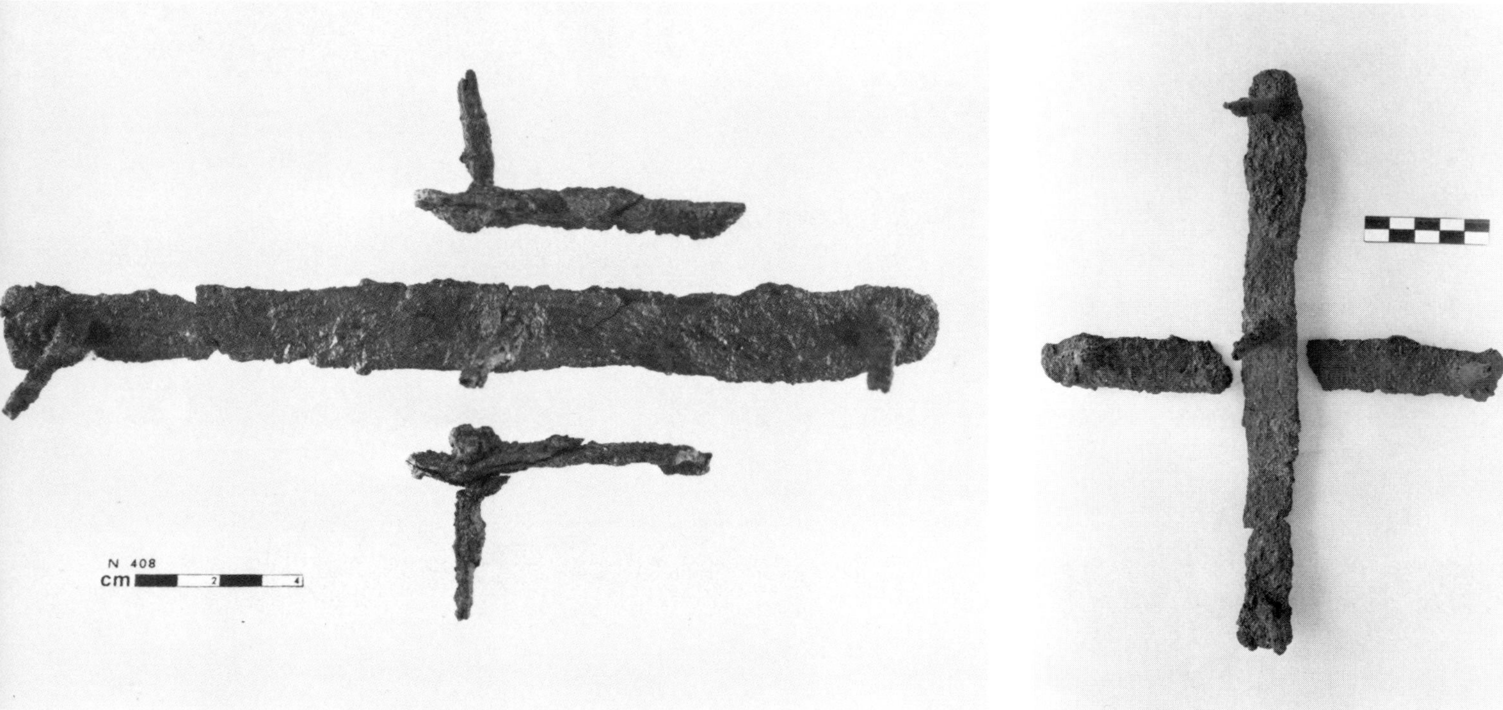

Plate 12-10. Iron attachment (cross?) (**521**)

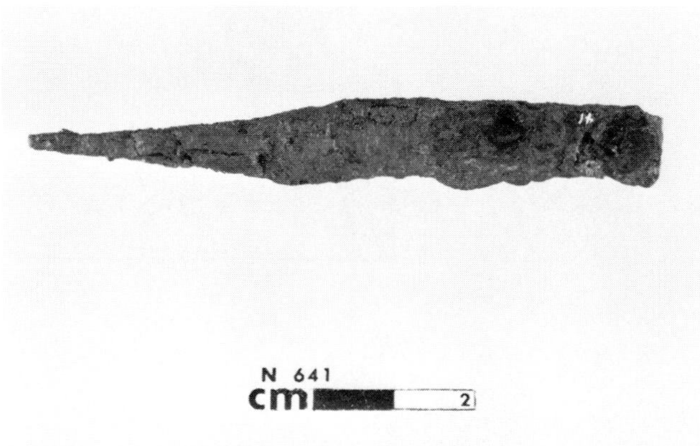

Plate 12-11. Iron blade (**522**)

Plate 12-12. Iron blade (**523**)

Plate 12-13. Iron shaft (**526**)

Plate 12-14. Iron nail (**527**)

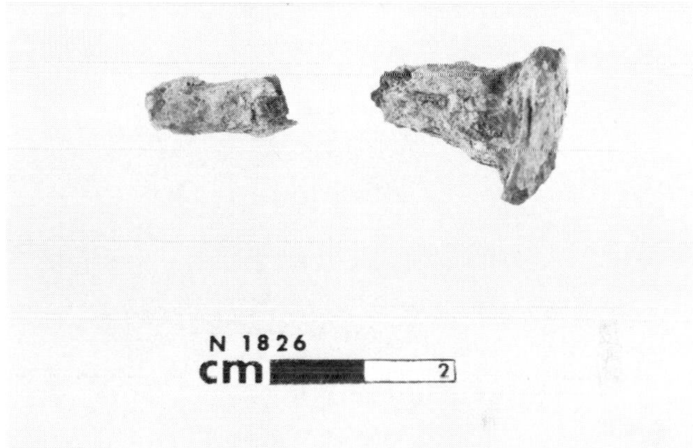

Plate 12-15. Iron nail (**533**)

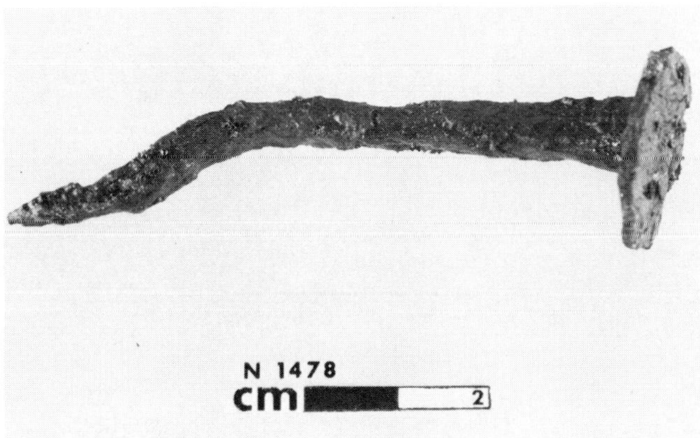

Plate 12-16. Iron nail (**534**)

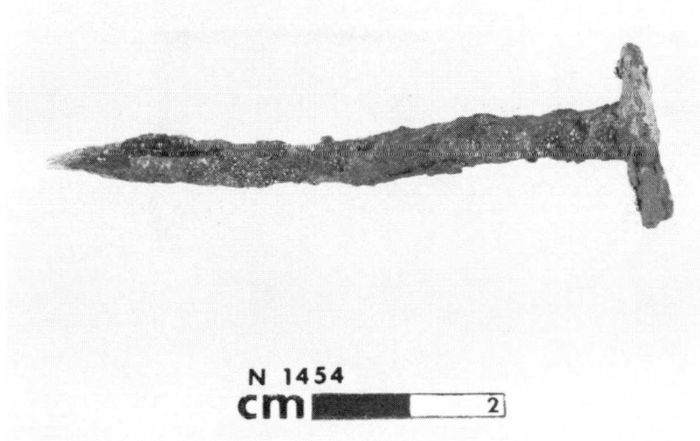

Plate 12-17. Iron nail (**535**)

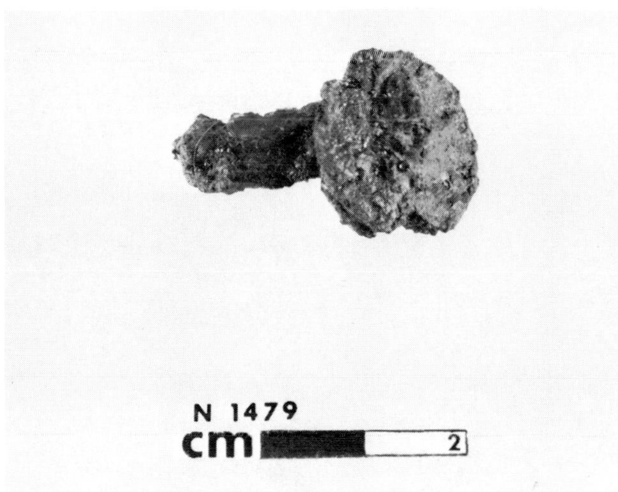

Plate 12-18. Iron nail (**536**)

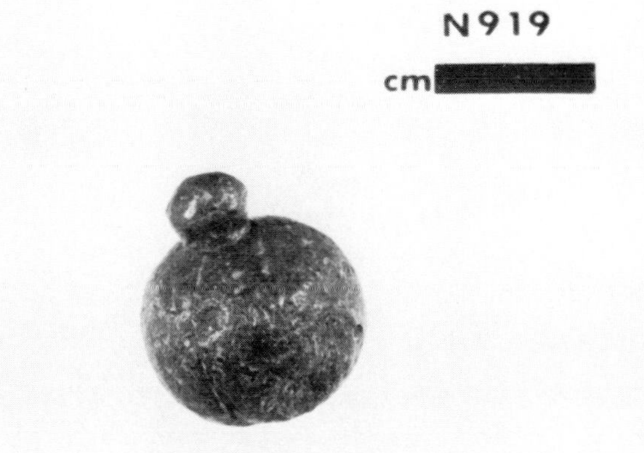

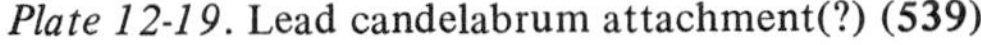

Plate 12-19. Lead candelabrum attachment(?) (**539**)

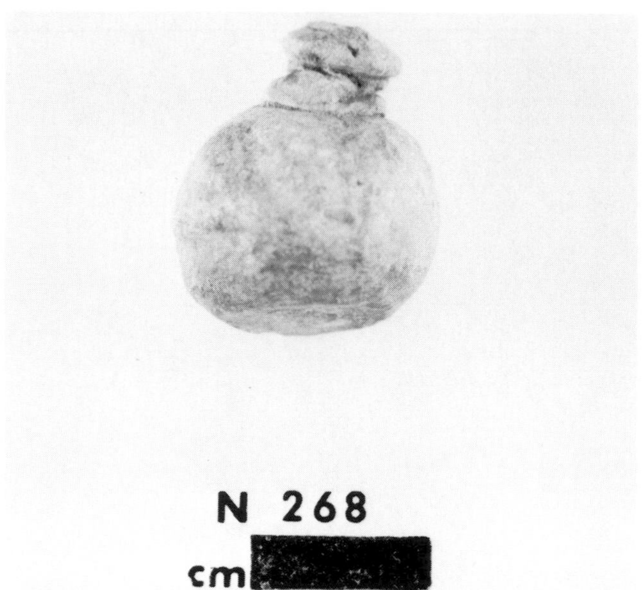

Plate 12-20. Lead candelabrum attachment(?) (**540**)

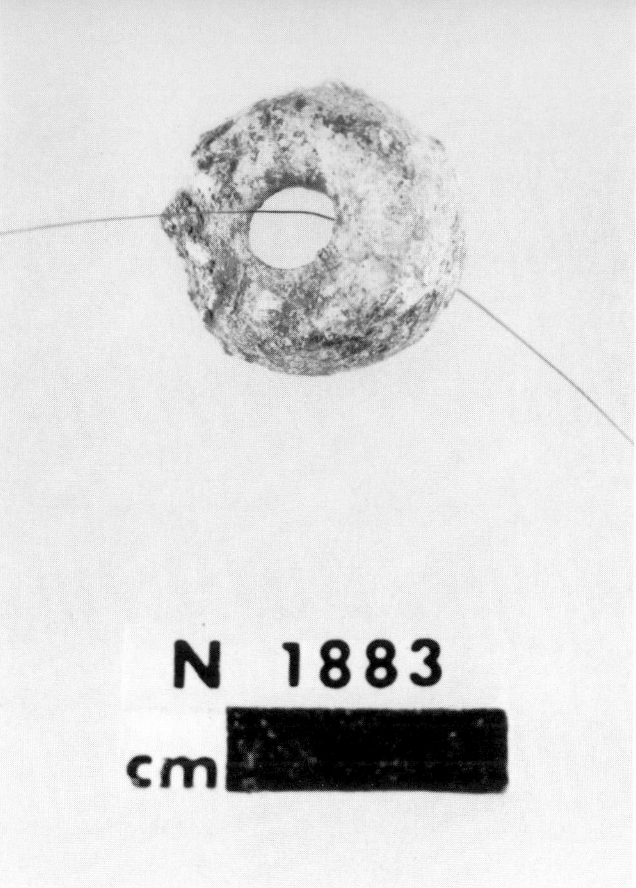

Plate 12-21. Lead bead (**542**)

Plate 12-22. Pierced stone slab (**543**)

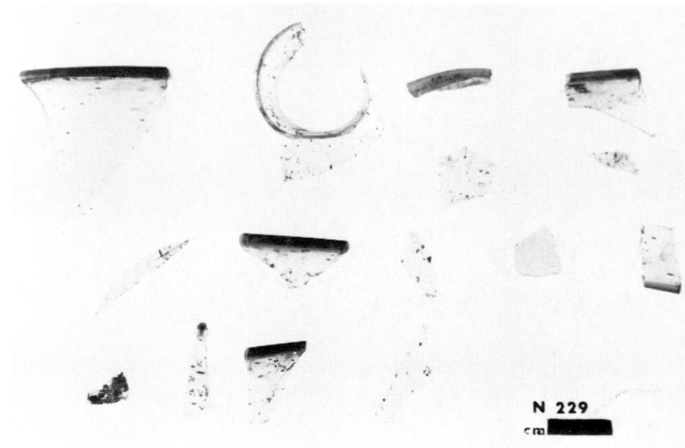

Plate 12-23. Glass lamp (**544**)

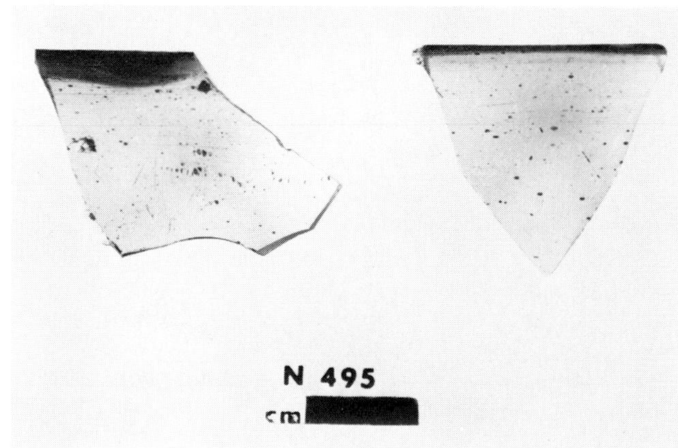

Plate 12-24. Fragments of glass bowl(?) (**551**)

Plate 12-25. Fragments of glass bottle(?) (**557**)

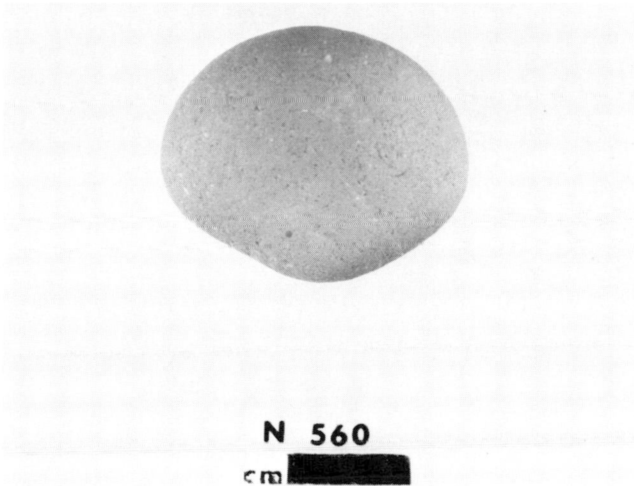

Plate 12-26. Glass pellet (**559**)

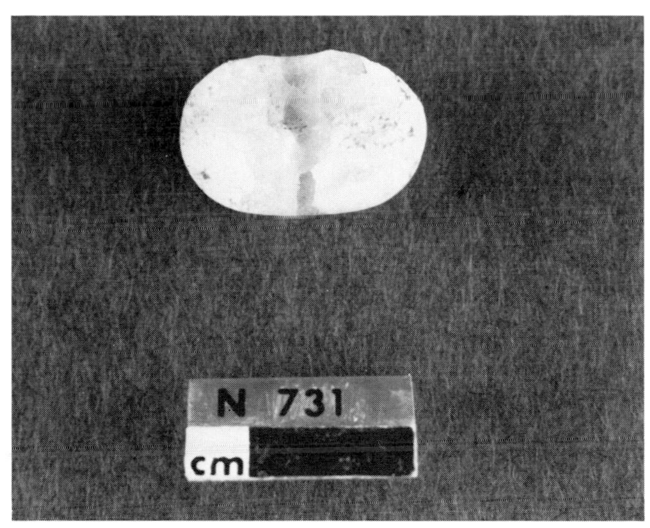

Plate 12-27. Glass bead (**560**)

Plate 12-28. Glass bead (**561**)

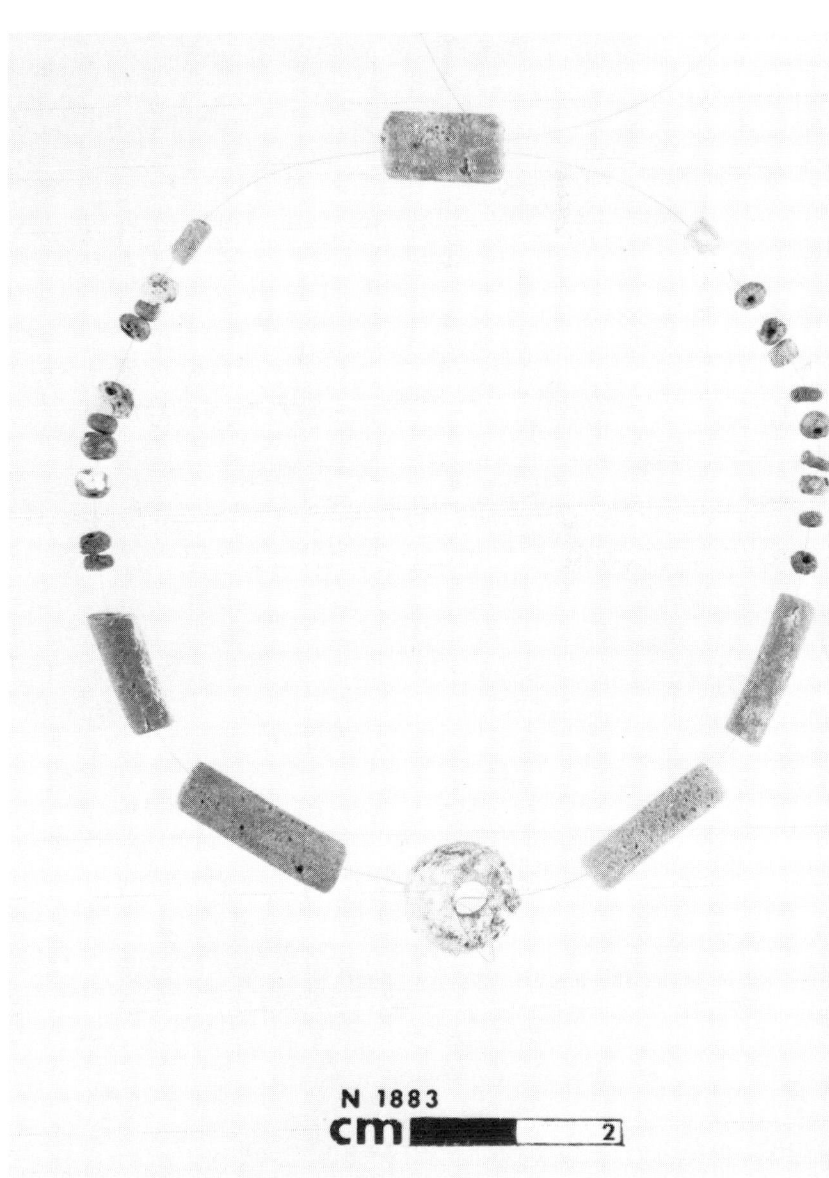

Plate 12-30. Necklace (**583**)

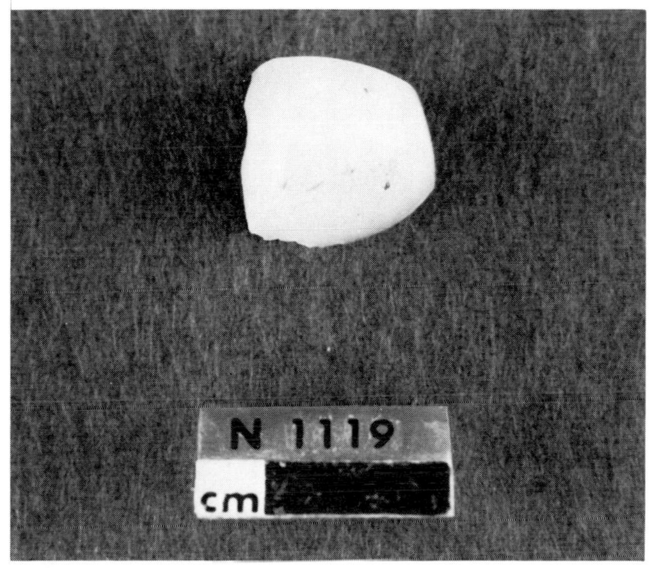

Plate 12-29. Glass bead (**562**)

Plate 12-31. Painted plaster fragments (**584**)

Plate 12-32. Painted plaster fragments (**585**)

Plate 12-33. Painted plaster fragments (**586**)

Plate 12-34. Painted plaster fragments (**587**)

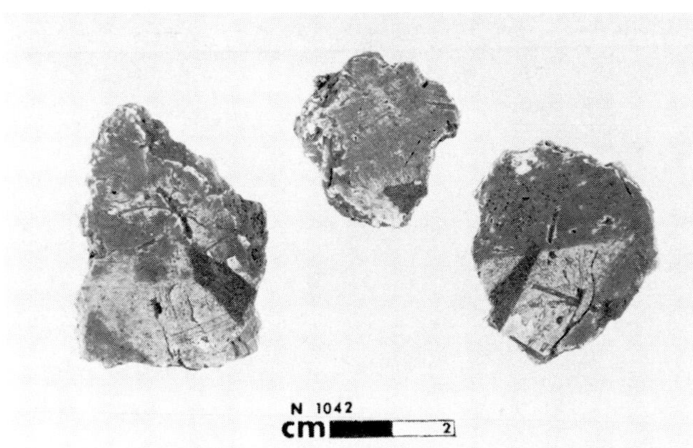

Plate 12-35. Painted plaster fragments (**588**)

Plate 12-36. Painted plaster fragments (**589**)

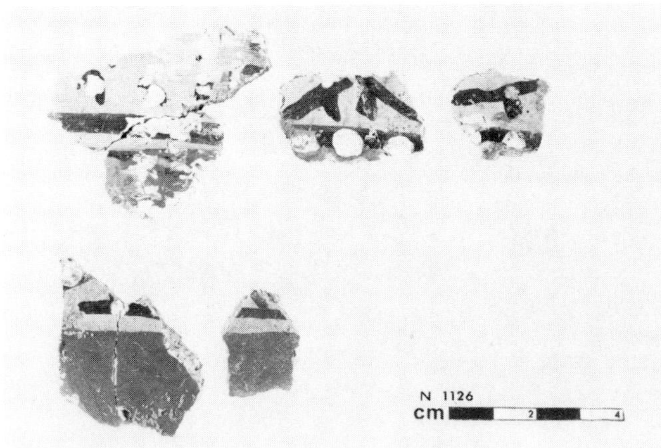

Plate 12-37. Painted plaster fragments (**590**)

Plate 14-1. Area VI and Unit VI-1, from helicopter

Plate 14-2. Unit VI-1, Room 2, Wall C and stone bench, from N

Plate 14-3. Unit VI-1, Room 2, Wall H (foreground) and recess in Wall D, from E

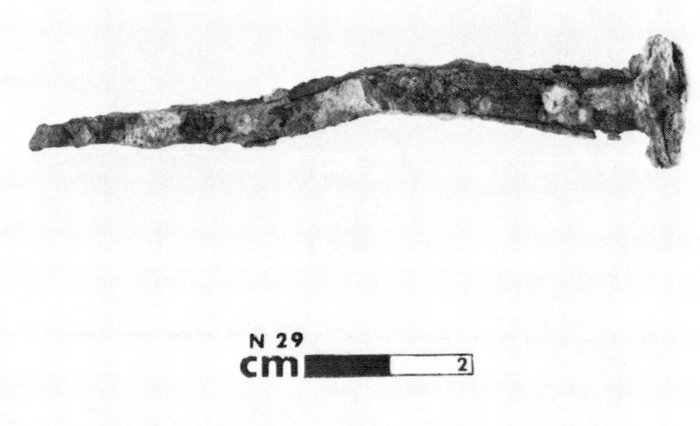

Plate 14-4. Unit VI-1, Room 2, nail (**584, 585, 586**)

Plate 14-5. Unit VI-1, Room 1, glazed sherds (**P1766**)

Plate 14-6. Unit VI-1, Room 1, roof tile (**P1765**)

Plate 14-10. Modern sherd (**P1769**)

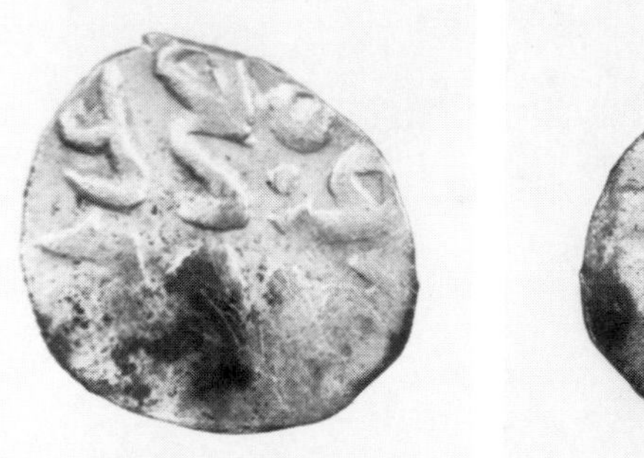

Plate 14-7. Silver coin of Mehmet III, obverse and reverse (**589**)

Plate 14-8. Venetian coin, obverse and reverse (**590**)

NP 149
cm 2

Plate 14-9. Modern sherd (**P1768**)

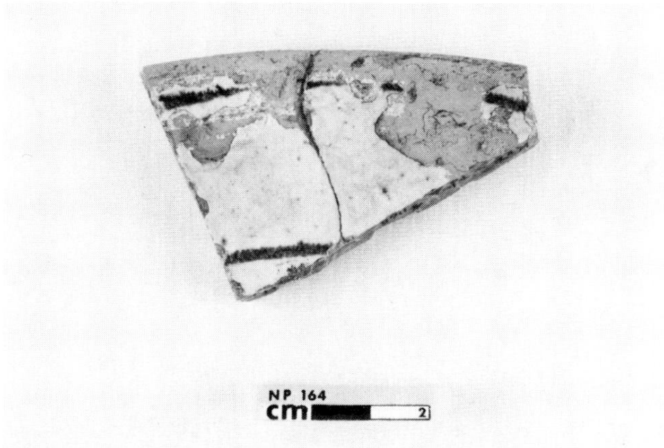

Plate 14-11. Modern sherd (**P1770**)

Concordance and Index

Concordance

Pottery
(NP = Nichoria pottery, i.e., from settlement; TP = tholos pottery)

Inventory Number	Publication Number	Museum Number	Page reference(s) in text
NP4	P1576	3106	109, 256
NP11	P1575	3113	109, 256
NP12	P1574	3114	109, 255
NP24	P766	3126	78, 216
NP46	P781	3148	76, 77, 217
NP51	P532	3153	80, 205
NP56	P972	3158	80, 227
NP61	P1240	3163	97, 240
NP72	P1531	3174	104, 253
NP73	P165	3175	66, 191
NP74	P817	3176	83, 85, 219
NP75	P830	3177	88, 219
NP76	P631	3178	80, 210
NP77	P600	3179	76, 78, 208
NP78	P602	3180	77, 208
NP79	P1312	3181	106, 243
NP80	P1213	3182	104, 239
NP81	P1629	3183	334, 348
NP83	P1724	3185	382
NP85	P1116	3187	94, 234
NP87	P1549	3189	100, 254
NP89	P1707	3191	381
NP94	P922	3196	76, 224
NP95	P1068	3197	95, 232
NP97	P1041	3199	92, 231
NP104	P1756	3206	384
NP105	P752	3207	86, 215
NP107	P1671	3209	336, 350
NP108	P844	3210	75, 220
NP111	P720	3213	83, 85, 214
NP120	P1731	3222	383
NP121	P1732	3223	383
NP122	P1709	3224	381
NP123	P1726	3225	383
NP124	P1767	3226	433
NP126	P1720	3228	382
NP127	P1711	3229	382
NP128	P1708	3230	381

Inventory Number	Publication Number	Museum Number	Page reference(s) in text
NP129	P1719	3231	382
NP130	P1723	3232	382
NP131	P1690	3233	380
NP132	P1697	3234	380
NP133	P1730	3235	383
NP134	P1677	3236	379
NP135	P1678	3237	379
NP136	P1696	3238	380
NP137	P1712	3239	382
NP138	P1679	3240	379
NP139	P1713	3241	382
NP141	P1753	3272	384
NP142	P1733	3273	383
NP143	P1718	3274	382
NP144	P1717	3275	382
NP145	P1716	3276	382
NP146	P1729	3277	383
NP147	P1714	3278	382
NP148	P1698	3279	380
NP149	P1768	3280	433
NP150	P1725	3281	382
NP151	P1710	3282	382
NP153	P1715	3284	382
NP154	P1722	3285	382, 383
NP157	P1728	3286	383
NP159	P1727	3290	383
NP160	P1721	3291	382
NP163	P1769	3294	433
NP164	P1770	3295	433, 434
NP172	P1565	3303	106, 108, 255
NP173	P1563	3304	107, 108, 255
NP174	P1560	3305	107, 255
NP175	P1564	3306	108, 255
NP195	P1097	3261	95, 233
NP196	P1069	3262	89, 95, 108, 232
NP197	P982	3263	88, 227
NP198	P1000	3264	88, 89, 229
TP1	P1627	3080	334, 348
TP2	P1628	3081	334, 348

Inventory Number	Publication Number	Museum Number	Page reference(s) in text
TP10	P1649	3089	335, 349
TP20	P1630	3099	334, 348

Small Finds

(N = Nichoria small finds, i.e., from settlement)

Inventory Number	Publication Number	Museum Number	Page reference(s) in text
N27	584	942	434
N28	585	943	434
N29	586	944	434
N31	587	946	434
N56	7	971	275, 305
N70	82, 109	985	283, 310, 311
N125	36	1040	307
N126	97	1041	310
N134	15	1049	278, 305
N135	27	1050	279, 306
N226	504	1137	406
N228	29	1139	279, 306
N229	544	1140	409
N230	506	1141	406
N232	550, 554	1143	409
N233	545	1144	409
N236	85, 528	1147	283, 310, 407
N240	523	1151	407
N242	501	1153	358, 405
N246	244	1157	336, 348
N251	524	1162	407
N252	530	1163	407
N253	556	1164	410
N254	546	1165	409
N266	505	1177	406
N268	540	1179	408
N292	105	1203	311
N294	19	1205	278, 306
N298	509	1209	406
N308	43	1218	307
N324	234	1234	293, 314
N325	557	1235	410
N328	548, 549, 555	1238	409
N345	121	1255	286, 312
N359	31	1269	279, 306
N360	126	1270	287, 312
N370	553	1280	409
N372	122	1282	286, 287, 312
N375	93	1285	284, 310
N377	76	1287	309
N382	108	1292	311
N388	107	1298	311
N399	62	1309	308
N408	521	1318	407
N427	582	1337	411
N434 }	125	1344	286, 312
N435 }		1345	
N438	100	1348	311
N443	114	1353	285, 311
N449	520	1359	407
N459	47	1369	279, 307
N464	6	1374	277, 305
N467	119	1377	285
N469	123	1379	285, 286, 312
N472	171	1382	313
N475	124	1385	286, 312
N483	71	1393	309
N487	508	1397	406
N489	88	1399	310
N495	551, 552	1405	409
N499	116	1409	311
N520	507	1430	406
N526	541	1436	408
N538	103	1448	311
N543	115	1453	311
N547	34	1457	279, 307
N556	173	1466	313
N560	559	1470	410
N566	120	1476	286, 312
N589	11	1499	278, 305
N591	525	1501	407
N594	14	1504	278, 305
N618	20	1528	278, 306
N622	99	1532	310
N627	48	1537	280, 307
N638	117	1548	311
N641	522	1551	407
N655	118	1565	311
N667	81	1576	283, 309
N681	78	1590	309
N694	72	1602	309
N699	238	1607	314
N701	243	1609	315
N705	73	1613	309
N717	527	1625	407
N718	547	1626	409
N731	560	1639	410
N734	245	1642	336, 348
N749	94	1657	284, 310
N766	233	1674	293, 314
N768	4	1676	275, 305
N775	63	1682	308
N785	558	1692	410
N788	61	1695	308
N789	106	1696	311
N792	232	1699	293, 314
N806	75	1712	309
N807	86	1713	284, 310
N808	526	1714	407
N826	242	1732	293, 315
N827	66	1733	309
N831	30	1737	279, 306
N836	503	1742	406
N844	67	1750	309
N851	77	1757	309
N853	92	1759	284, 310
N858	237	1764	314
N866	236	1772	293, 314
N867	240	1773	293, 314
N871 (A, B)	241	1777	293, 314
N888	141	1794	287, 288, 312
N910	22	1815	278, 306
N916	581	1821	411
N919	539	1824	408
N935	9	1840	278, 305
N970	144	1874	312
N999	104	1903	311
N1042	588, 589		411, 412
N1044	580	1948	411

Concordance

Inventory Number	Publication Number	Museum Number	Page reference(s) in text
N1045	538	1949	408
N1048	589	1952	434
N1060	51	1964	279, 308
N1119	562	2023	410
N1120	110	2024	311
N1123	514	2027	406
N1124	215	2028	313
N1125	584, 586		411, 412
N1126	585, 587, 590	2030	411, 412
N1206	18	2109	278, 306
N1207	45	2110	279, 307
N1208	70	2111	309
N1212	190	2115	313
N1215	69	2118	309
N1261	537	2164	408
N1282	89	2185	284, 310
N1283	57	2186	308
N1286	159A	2189	287, 313
N1287	49	2190	279, 280, 307
N1303	579	2206	411
N1304	561	2207	410
N1312	510	2215	406
N1335	53	2237	281, 283, 308
N1342 (A, B, C, D)	148-151	2244	287, 288, 312
N1401	13	2303	278, 305
N1422	96	2324	284, 310
N1426	518	2328	406
N1428	529	2330	407
N1429	91	2331	284, 310
N1444	515	2346	406
N1446	569, 570	2348	410
N1448	567, 568, 571, 572	2350	410
N1449	502	2351	406
N1451	516	2353	406
N1452	513	2354	406
N1454	535	2356	408
N1461	217	2363	313
N1462	218	2364	314
N1465	80	2367	283, 309
N1466	28	2368	279, 306
N1477	576-78	2379	410, 411
N1478	534	2380	408
N1479	536	2381	408
N1533	79	2435	309
N1538	65	2440	309
N1559	83	2461	283, 310
N1561	8	2463	278, 305
N1614	154	2514	312
N1620	10	2520	278, 305
N1623	54	2523	308
N1632	16	2532	278, 305
N1641	194	2541	313
N1656	155	2556	312
N1658	573, 574	2558	410
N1664	231	2564	293, 314
N1665	24	2565	278, 306
N1667	156	2567	312
N1668	157	2568	313
N1669	90	2569	284, 310
N1690	158	2589	287, 313
N1692	159	2591	287, 313

Inventory Number	Publication Number	Museum Number	Page reference(s) in text
N1697	225	2596	314
N1705	196	2604	313
N1706	160	2605	287, 313
N1707	226	2606	287, 288, 314
N1708	50	2607	279, 308
N1711	25	2610	278, 306
N1714	64	2613	309
N1721	161	2620	313
N1722	162	2621	313
N1723	58	2622	281, 282, 308
N1728	101, 111	2627	311
N1776	55	2674	281, 308
N1777	12	2675	278, 305
N1779	37	2677	307
N1784	59	2682	282, 308
N1787	163	2685	313
N1789	5	2687	277, 305
N1793	39	2691	307
N1802	95	2699	284, 310
N1819	239	2714	314
N1820	113	2715	285, 311
N1821	112	2716	285, 311
N1825	532	2720	407
N1826	533	2721	407
N1827	531	2722	407
N1828	84	2723	283, 310
N1829	17	2724	278, 306
N1831	102	2726	311
N1832	26	2727	279, 306
N1833	52	2728	280, 281, 308
N1834	87	2729	284, 310
N1835	235	2730	314
N1838	3	2733	275, 305
N1841	40	2736	307
N1844	38	2739	307
N1850	60	2744	282, 308
N1853	68	2747	309
N1854	98	2748	310
N1882	166	2775	313
N1883	542, 583	2776	408, 411
N1890	23	2782	278, 306
N1893	56	2785	281, 308
N1904	32	2796	279, 306
N1906	33	2798	279, 307
N1907	35	2799	279, 307
N1916	1, 46	2808	276, 277, 279, 305, 307
N1919	42	2811	279, 307
N1927	519	2819	407
N1930	566	2822	410
N1931	565, 575	2823	410
N1934	511	2826	406
N1935	512	2827	406
N1944	2	2835	305
N1945	167	2836	313
N1946	168	2837	313
N1949	41	2840	307
N1957	21	2848	278, 306
N1958	74	2849	309
N1979	230	2868	314
N1984	517	2873	406
N1987	543	2876	408
N1990	563	2879	410

Inventory Number	Publication Number	Museum Number	Page reference(s) in text
N1991	564	2880	410
N1993	44	2882	279, 307
N2089	169	2978	313
N2096	201	2985	313

Index

Index

William A. McDonald is Regents' Professor of Classical Studies, emeritus, at the University of Minnesota. He served as director of the Minnesota Messenia Expedition, the first systematic and interdisciplinary archaeological study undertaken on a regional basis in Greece, and was co-editor (with George R. Rapp, Jr.) of a comprehensive report on that study, *The Minnesota Messenia Expedition: Reconstructing a Bronze Age Regional Environment* (University of Minnesota Press, 1972). McDonald was also director of the excavation at Nichoria ridge, the subject of this volume, the third in a projected four-volume work. In 1981 the Archaeological Institute of America gave him its Gold Medal Award for Distinguished Archaeological Achievement.

William D. E. Coulson and **John Rosser** served as staff members of the Nichoria excavation. They are specialists in, respectively, the Dark Age and the Byzantine Period. Coulson is associate professor of classics and classical archaeology at the University of Minnesota, and Rosser is associate professor of history at Boston College.